$$e_{jt} = R_{jt} - \hat{R}_{jt} \tag{7A-1}$$

$$AR_t = \frac{1}{N} \sum_{j=1}^{N} e_{jt} \tag{7A-2}$$

$$CAR_T = \sum_{t=1}^{T} AR_t \tag{7A-3}$$

$$\Delta CFAT = (\Delta S - \Delta C - \Delta D)(1 - T) + \Delta D \tag{8-3}$$

$$\text{Payback period} = \frac{\text{initial investment outlay}}{\text{annual cash inflows}} \tag{8-4}$$

$$AROR = \frac{\text{annual profit}}{\text{average investment}} \tag{8-5}$$

$$PI = \frac{PV_{\text{inflows}}}{PV_{\text{outflows}}} \tag{8-8}$$

$$(1 + R) = (1 + r)(1 + p) \tag{9B-1}$$

$$S_1 = S_0 \left(\frac{1 + \dot{P}_h}{1 + \dot{P}_f} \right) \tag{9C-1}$$

$$F_1 = S_0 \left(\frac{1 + R_h}{1 + R_f} \right) \tag{9C-2}$$

$$S_n = S_0 \frac{(1 + R_h)^n}{(1 + R_f)^n} \tag{9C-3}$$

$$\beta_A = \frac{\beta_E}{1 + (D/E)(1 - T)} \tag{10-1}$$

$$V_0 = \sum_{t=1}^{N} \frac{E(\widetilde{CF}_t)}{(1 + RRR)^t} \tag{11-1}$$

$$C = \max(0, S - E) \tag{11-2}$$

$$P = \max(E - S, 0) \tag{11-3}$$

$$C - P = S - Ee^{-rT} \tag{11-4}$$

$$C = SN(d_1) - Ee^{-rT}N(d_2) \tag{11B-1}$$

$$R = P_O - P_N \tag{12A-1}$$

$$R = \frac{P_O - S}{N + 1} \tag{12A-2}$$

$$S_0 = \frac{Div_1 + S_1}{1 + k_s} \tag{13-1}$$

$$k_s = \frac{Div_1}{S_0} + \frac{S_1 - S_0}{S_0} \tag{13-2}$$

$$S_0 = \sum_{t=1}^{\infty} \frac{Div_t}{(1 + k_s)^t} \tag{13-3}$$

$$S_0 = \frac{\overline{Div}}{k_s} \tag{13-4}$$

$$S_0 = \sum_{t=1}^{\infty} \frac{Div_0(1 + g)^t}{(1 + k_s)^t} \tag{13-6}$$

$$S_0 = \frac{Div_0(1 + g)}{k_s - g} = \frac{Div_1}{k_s - g} \tag{13-7}$$

$$k_s = \frac{Div_1}{S_0} + g \tag{13-8}$$

$$g = (\text{retention ratio}) \times ROE \tag{13-9}$$

$$ROE = \frac{\text{net income}}{\text{equity}} \tag{13-10}$$

$$S_0 = \frac{EPS}{k_s} + PVGO \text{ per share} \tag{13-13}$$

$$\text{P-E ratio} = \frac{\text{price per share}}{EPS} = \frac{1}{k_s} + \frac{PVGO \text{ per share}}{EPS} \tag{13-14}$$

$$D_0 = \sum_{t=1}^{n} \frac{I_t}{(1 + k_d)^t} + \frac{M_n}{(1 + k_d)^n} \tag{14-1}$$

$$D_0 = \frac{I_t}{2}(PVFA_{k_d/2,2n}) + M_{2n}(PVF_{k_d/2,2n}) \tag{14-2}$$

$$P_0 = \frac{\overline{Div}}{k_p} \tag{14-3}$$

$$E[r_n(1)] = f_n(1) \tag{14A-5}$$

$$LP = f_n(1) - E[r_n(1)] \tag{14A-6}$$

$$E = VN(d_3) - Be^{-rT}N(d_4) \tag{14B-1}$$

$$D = VN(d_5) + Be^{-rT}N(d_4) \tag{14B-2}$$

$$ROA^* = \frac{E}{D + E}(ROE^*) + \frac{D}{D + E}(R_f) \tag{15-1}$$

$$ROE^* = ROA^* + \frac{D}{E}(ROA^* - R_f) \tag{15-2}$$

$$\beta_E = \beta_A\left(1 + \frac{D}{E}\right) \tag{15-3}$$

$$V^L = V^U + TD \tag{15-6}$$

$$ROE^* = ROA^* + \frac{D}{E}(1 - T)(ROA^* - R_f) \tag{15-7}$$

$$\beta_E = \beta_A\left[1 + \frac{D}{E}(1 - T)\right] \tag{15-8}$$

$$V^L = V^U + PV(TI) - PV(c) \tag{15-9}$$

$$LCF_{Bt} = \begin{cases} C - P(1 - T_B) & \text{for } t = 0 \\ -P(1 - T_B) - T_B D_t & \text{for } t > 0 \end{cases} \tag{18-1}$$

$$LCF_{Lt} = \begin{cases} -C + P(1 - T_B) & \text{for } t = 0 \\ P(1 - T_B) + T_B D_t & \text{for } t > 0 \end{cases} \tag{18-2}$$

$$NOI = S - TC \tag{19-1}$$

$$TVC = V \times Q \tag{19-2}$$

$$TOC = F + TVC \tag{19-3}$$

$$Q^* = \frac{F}{P - V} \tag{19-4}$$

FINANCIAL MANAGEMENT

CONCEPTS
AND APPLICATIONS

THE SOUTH-WESTERN SERIES IN FINANCE

FINANCIAL MANAGEMENT

CONCEPTS AND APPLICATIONS

3RD Edition

Ramesh K.S. Rao
University of Texas at Austin

SOUTH-WESTERN College Publishing

An International Thomson Publishing Company

Acquiring Editor: Ken King
Sponsoring Editor: Christopher Will
Production Editor: Rebecca Roby
Production House: Ruth Cottrell Books
Cover Design: Graphica
Internal Design: Seventh Street Studios
Cover Photographer: © Tatsuhiko SHIMADA
Marketing Manager: Denise Carlson

FN66CA
Copyright © 1995
by South-Western College Publishing
Cincinnati, Ohio

Library of Congress Cataloging-in-Publication Data

Rao, Ramesh K. S.
    Financial management : concepts and applications / Ramesh K. S.
  Rao. — 3rd ed.
    p.   cm.
  ISBN 0-538-84432-9
    1. Corporations—Finance.   I. Title.
  HG4026.R36   1994
  658.15—dc20   94-22216
                                                                      CIP

  2 3 4 5 6 7 8 9 0 Ki 3 2 1 0 9 8 7 6 5
Printed in the United States of America

 This book is printed on acid-free paper that meets Environmental
Protection Agency standards for recycled paper.

International Thomson Publishing

South-Western College Publishing is an ITP Company. The ITP trademark
is used under license.

PREFACE

The study of finance does not seem to require any specialized gifts of an un-usually high order. Is it not, intellectually regarded, a very easy subject compared with the higher branches of philosophy or pure science? An easy subject, at which very few excel!

—*John Maynard Keynes*

The world in general—and finance in particular—has changed greatly in the years since the 1950s. The last four decades have seen finance evolve from the rather casual discipline described by Keynes to a rigorous one based on well-developed theories of financial markets. The "art component" of finance has been gradually superseded by a "science component," and finance today is worlds away from Keynes's early view of the discipline.

This revolution in the discipline has been driven by the development of well-thought-out theories derived under the "perfect capital markets" assumption. To the extent that financial markets are perfect, the "perfect markets intuition" is a convenient heuristic and an effective pedagogical strategy. However, there is a growing awareness in the profession that the pendulum has swung too far toward the theory. Scholars recognize that for new insights into business, one must break out of the perfect markets mold to address the other important (but perhaps less formal and less quantifiable) issues confronting today's managers. This need to go beyond perfect markets becomes even more important in light of two recent developments that have permanently changed the environment facing today's business managers and educators.

First, traditional theory is no longer a sufficient guide for managers as they operate in a world of "imperfect markets." Managers are being held more and more accountable for their actions by the firm and by society as a whole. Perfect markets intuition alone does not arm managers with the skills necessary to satisfy these demands. To fulfill this need, corporate America is increasingly relying on in-house training programs to provide their personnel with programs tailor-made to address their specific institutional realities. Contemporaneously, business schools and finance educators are being pressured to teach students "relevant" and operational skills.

Second, with the increasing globalization of businesses, the "purely domestic firm" is almost a myth; even firms that do not engage in foreign businesses are affected by global markets. Thus, any meaningful education in corporate decision making will necessarily involve some consideration of international dimensions of business.

Financial Management adapts to these contemporary realities with a uniquely balanced approach. It blends the perfect markets theory with the world of market imperfections to provide managers with a useful decision-making framework. Issues of agency, control, governance, and the legal interface as well as relevant institutional details are woven in to supplement the intuition of the formal theory. The text explains the theory and practical applications and, with realistic examples and supplemental minicases, allows students to test their facility with their newly learned skills. Issues of international finance are unobtrusively woven in through-out the text to sensitize the reader to the challenges of decision making in inte-grated international markets.

THE DISTINGUISHING CHARACTERISTICS OF THIS BOOK

Financial Management has four characteristics that make it unique among cor-porate finance texts.

1. The book contains extensive new material and addresses even standard top-ics in unique ways.

Many topics and concepts important to business managers are either entirely left out or treated tangentially in many texts. In contrast, these important topics are at center stage in *Financial Management*. The text addresses fundamental is-sues such as: Why do firms exist? How do they create wealth? How does corporate wealth get transformed into investors' personal wealth? The text also provides an integrated discussion of agency theory, corporate control, corporate governance, corporate restructuring, the notion of flexibilities and negotiation in capital bud-geting, the management of "strategic risks" with derivatives, and the complexities that arise with financial distress. Even many standard issues are explained in a new way. For example, the exposition of the fundamental ideas in capital structure theory in Chapter 13 is distinctly different from that in other texts.

2. It blends the theoretical and practical aspects of corporate financial decision making.

In its approach, the book recognizes that defensible financial decisions cannot be made without meaningful theories. It also recognizes that managers confront situations that do not conform to the stylized theoretical world. Financial decision making thus involves a paradox: to make good decisions sound theories are re-quired, and yet a good theory may not be easily applicable to an actual situation. Thus, a blind application of the theory without regard to market imperfections and institutional realities would be an expression of naiveté.

Financial Management provides an introduction to financial decision making that blends the important aspects of theory and practice.

3. It employs highly effective pedagogy.

- *Motivation:* Instructors will find it relatively easy to motivate their students because the book is written from the student's perspective. The chapters open with the questions that the student will be able to answer after studying the chapter, and each chapter concludes with the answers to these questions. When-ever an idea or concept is introduced, care is taken to explain why this concept is useful to the manager. This approach, coupled with appropriate examples and illustrations, has the potential to increase the student's interest in the subject.

- *"Linearity":* The text has a "plot," or story line, much like a narrative. The or-ganization and flow of the text are summarized in the table that follows. (The supplemental end-of-part minicases are also shown.) Each chapter carefully sets the stage for the subsequent chapters, and the student will appreciate the continuity in the development of the theory. In most other books, the overall treatment of major topics is frequently disjointed because a topic is discussed in a perfect markets setting in one chapter and in an institutional framework in another. In contrast, *Financial Management* discusses issues in a unified con-text, blending the theory and practice.

*The Organization and Flow of This Book**

Part I: The Firm
1: The Firm and Its Environment
2: Maximizing Stockholders' Welfare
3: The Structure and Interpretation of Accounting Statements
The Case of Eastman Kodak: Maximizing Shareholder Wealth

Part II: Value and Risk
4: Finding the Present and Future Values of Cash Flows
5: Financial Risk: Theory and Estimation
6: Assessing Expected Rates of Return: Theory and Evidence
7: Bringing Together Risk and Expected Return: Market Values, Opportunity Costs and Market Efficiency
International Business Machines: Market Efficiency and Valuation

Part III: The Firm's Operating Decisions
8: The Basics of Capital Budgeting
9: Special Issues in Capital Budgeting Decisions
10: Adjusting for Uncertainty and Financing Effects in Capital Budgeting Decisions
11: Managing Total Risk with Derivative Securities
Mellon Oil Company: A Tale of Two Investments
Central Telephone Company: Calculating the Cost of Equity for a Nontraded Company

Part IV: Issuing and Valuing Financial Securities
12: The Capital Acquisition Process
13: Equity Financing and Stock Valuation
14: Long-Term Debt and Preferred Stock
International Business Machines: Growth Oppurtunities and Stock Price
Burlington Northern: Hundred Years of Restrictive Bond Covenants

Part V: The Firm's Financing Decisions
15: The Firm's Capital Structure
16: Resolving Financial Distress
17: The Dividend Policy Decision
18: Leasing
Chrysler Corporation: A Time for Equity?
Southland Oil Corporation: From Profitability to Financial Distress to Profitability

Part VI: Financial Planning and Working Capital Management
19: The Impact of Operating and Financial Decisions on Profits and Cash Flows
20: A Framework for Financial Planning
21: Working Capital Management
22: Managing Current Assets
23: Managing Current Liabilities
Acoustical Enclosures, Inc.: Growing Pains Pinch Profitability

Part VII: Agency Considerations and Financial Management
24: Controlling Agency Costs
25: The Market for Corporate Control
Armstrong World Industries:
The Anatomy of an Almost Merger

Part VIII: Corporate Restructuring
26: Mergers
27: Corporate Restructuring
Marriot Corporation: Restructuring Backlash from Bondholders

* Supplemental minicases are also listed

■ *Clarity:* The text's linearity is complemented by the "user-friendly" writing style and the organization. Each section within the chapter is structured carefully, linking the key ideas and bringing out their relevance to managers with examples drawn from real business situations. Where appropriate, quantitative examples are used to increase the efficiency of the learning process.

4. Its flexibility makes it usable in a variety of formats and in different courses' levels.

■ *Teaching flexibility:* There are many ways to select and sequence materials in a corporate finance course. *Financial Management* is designed to provide teachers with the maximum flexibility to choose the topics covered in their course and the style of pedagogy. As examples:
—The book can be used in a case-oriented course (with the supplemental cases) or in a lecture-oriented course. Moreover, the minicases can be assigned as homework, exams, or class discussion material. Solutions to each case are provided to the instructor.
—Agency theory is introduced early in the text as an essential part of corporate goal setting. Agency control devices and other topics not needed to support this discussion are grouped together as a later topic (Part VII).
—Some international topics, such as political risk, are interwoven in the text's chapters. Other more technical topics, such as estimating exchange rates, are provided in appendixes.
—Accounting information is included early in the text for those who will use it heavily in their courses. However, this chapter is self-contained and can be omitted without loss of continuity.
—Technical topics such as the use of the Black-Scholes option pricing model for valuing the firm's debt and equity, event study methodology, antitrust issues, and various specialized issues regarding asset and equity betas are covered in appendixes.

■ *Audience for the book: Financial Management* can be used in a variety of courses depending upon the amount of coverage required by the instructor.
—The text is ideal for an introductory MBA financial management course where most of the "core issues" are covered. It can also be used in a second graduate-level course where some of the special topics and appendixes can be covered. The text could also supplement advanced graduate courses that are often structured around selected readings and/or cases.
—Executive MBA programs are becoming increasingly popular in business schools. The text, because of its emphasis on blending theory and practice, is particularly suited for such programs.
—*Financial Management* can also be used as the main text in a more rigorous undergraduate course or as a supplemental text in such a course.

A BROAD OVERVIEW OF THE TEXT

The changes in this text from the second edition are too numerous to list. With three new chapters, nine revised chapters, and two new appendixes, the third edition is a quite different text.

PART 1: THE FIRM Chapter 1 first explains to the student why firms exist and how free enterprise can increase societal welfare. After stressing the distinction between self-interest and opportunism and the importance of ethical business practices, it identifies the firm's goals. Chapter 2 explains how wealth is determined by cash flows and not profits and illustrates how financial markets transform corporate wealth into personal wealth. The student is introduced to the notion of agency costs and how corporate governance with managers and directors can reduce these costs to some extent. This part concludes with a review of the structure of the firm's financial statements.

PART II: VALUE AND RISK The issues of magnitude, timing, and risk associated with cash flows are consolidated in this part. The student is first familiarized with the mechanics of time value calculations, and after a review of basic statistical concepts, the student learns why risk as measured by variance does not determine an asset's price. The key ideas of correlation and diversification are illustrated with data involving three major companies. The notion of systematic risk and its link to expected return are carefully developed. Practical considerations in measuring risk are addressed, as is the concept of an informationally efficient market.

PART III: THE FIRM'S OPERATING DECISIONS This part consolidates issues concerning the firm's investment decision: the basic capital budgeting process, special capital budgeting situations, and capital budgeting under uncertainty. It explains, with the aid of a numerical example, the importance of operating flexibilities and discusses how hedging affects the risk of cash flows used in capital budgeting. The complications associated with overseas investments are also addressed.

PART IV: ISSUING AND VALUING FINANCIAL SECURITIES This part simultaneously addresses the issuance and the valuation of financial securities. By integrating the institutional aspects of the financial markets and the theory of debt and equity valuation, the text provides a richer perspective on the theory and practice of corporate capital procurement. The notion of growth options and the linkage between dividends and stock prices are examined. The final chapter addresses the debt markets, and the appendixes contain both a casual and a formal discussion of the term structure of interest rates. The use of options models for valuing the firm's securities is also explained.

PART V: THE FIRM'S FINANCING DECISIONS: Building on the foundation provided in Part IV, this part provides a consolidated discussion of the firm's financing decision. How leverage affects the expected return to stockholders is explained very carefully with a numerical example. A completely new chapter (Chapter 16) examines how managers can deal with financial distress. The student is exposed to the fundamentals of the bankruptcy process and the economics of reorganization and liquidation. Part V concludes with a chapter on leasing. Instead of a "special topics" treatment as in many texts, leasing is viewed here more accurately as a means of financing investments.

PART VI: FINANCIAL PLANNING AND WORKING CAPITAL MANAGEMENT The role of technology and financing choices in determining the firm's operating and cash flow break-even points and the notion of contribution margin are first developed. The development of a cash flow budget and how managers can use projected financial statements are discussed. The management of working capital is developed over three chapters, the first discussing working capital in general, the second current assets, and the third current liabilities.

PART VII: AGENCY CONSIDERATIONS IN FINANCIAL MANAGEMENT This section is designed for instructors who choose to address agency theory in greater detail than the initial discussion in Chapter 1. An explanation of the agency problem, the sources and components of agency, and the various ways in which these costs can be controlled are discussed. A separate chapter addresses the theory and empirical evidence from the corporate control market. The procedural aspects of takeovers and a discussion of the popular antitakeover measures are also provided.

PART VIII: CORPORATE RESTRUCTURING This part examines the means by which firms can reshape themselves to meet major changes in the marketplace. Mergers and antitrust issues are addressed in Chapter 26, and the concluding chapter introduces the student to spin-offs, sell-offs, leverage buyouts, equity carveouts, and other forms of corporate restructuring. Theory, empirical evidence, and examples are provided.

A NOTE TO INSTRUCTORS

I have used my teaching experiences over the past 16 years to guide me in my decisions concerning what topics to include in this book and how to present those topics to the reader. Before closing this preface, I'd like to share some of my thoughts with you.

- Some instructors who have used textbooks that emphasize perfect markets theory may initially view *Financial Management* as not being "rigorous enough" to be effective. *Financial Management* is not a theoretical analysis of perfect markets. Rather, its aim is to make students better decision makers, and thus each possible topic is evaluated on how it contributes to this goal. For example, although topics such as the arbitrage pricing theory (APT) and Miller's personal taxes model of capital structure are dealt with in this book, they do not form the core of the relevant chapters. The coverage they receive is governed by the extent they can assist business managers. The finer nuances of these theories are not as important to a student in the course, especially when the theoretical underpinnings and the practical significance of extant asset pricing theories are being debated among both academics and practitioners.

- *Financial Management* does not use numbers for numbers' sake. Quantitative analysis is appropriate when it adds perspective and enriches the student's understanding of the issues involved in decision making. The importance of focusing on real, rather than "toy," problems is being noted more and more in finance journals such as the *Journal of Financial Economics* and the *Journal of Corporate Finance,* which emphasize the myriad legal, institutional, organizational, control, and contracting issues in business decision making—concepts that are not easily quantified for numerical analyses.

- Some instructors may not feel comfortable with the extent to which current academic challenges to the efficient markets paradigm are discussed. True, it is difficult to discuss financial management in informationally inefficient markets, but this *per se* is no justification for not discussing the academic debate on whether markets are efficient.

- Some may feel that there is too much coverage of international issues in the text. The world is becoming increasingly integrated. A text can be useful only if it recognizes the increased integration of global issues in all aspects of financial decision making. However, while it is possible to force international issues into any discussion, the text retains a focus on the major concepts involved in financial decision making. It introduces international issues only where appropriate to reinforce the student's knowledge of the topic being discussed, but the instructor should not view this also as an international finance course.

SUPPLEMENTAL MATERIALS

The text is only part of an integrated package of documents that contribute to effective teaching. This edition of *Financial Management* continues the tradition of previous editions by offering to the instructor an excellent set of supplemental documents that benefit both the teacher and the student.

- *Instructor's Manual:* A detailed manual prepared by Dr. Robert C. Duvic of the University of Texas at Austin is devoted entirely to class materials. Each chapter in the manual first summarizes the text chapter's contents and discusses its link to what has preceded it and what is to come. It then summarizes the contents and provides an outline and then a lesson plan for each section within the text chapter. Each chapter in the manual concludes with a list of the transparency overheads used to support the class discussion.

- *Supplemental Minicases:* Eleven end-of-part minicases have been developed by Dr. Susan White of the University of Texas in collaboration with me. All cases pertain to real companies, such as Marriott Corporation, IBM, Eastman Kodak, Burlington Northern, Chrysler, and Southland Oil. In two cases the company names have been disguised. These minicases are short, focused, and narrow in scope; they provide the student an opportunity to apply the knowledge gained from each part of the text. Some instructors who do not use cases may want to consider them required reading nevertheless, since the cases make interesting "stories" about contemporary business realities. These cases are available in a separate booklet and will be made available to adopters of the text.

- *Transparency Masters:* Complete transparencies that complement the lesson plans in the instructors' manual are provided on a computer disk using Microsoft's Powerpoint. This disk allows instructors to use the transparencies as provided or to modify them for their classes. Over 50 essential transparencies taken from these files will be available in hard copy format as well.

- *Solutions Manual:* A detailed manual containing detailed worked-out solutions for every problem in the text has been developed by Professor Michael Alderson of the University of Missouri—St. Louis.

- *Test Bank:* Professor Alderson has also developed a comprehensive test bank corresponding to each chapter in the book. The test bank contains 2,000 multiple-choice, true/false, and essay questions.

- *Study Workbook:* Professor Adel Turki of Purdue University has developed a study workbook. Extensive numerical examples and discussion of the important topics are provided. This workbook can be ordered in conjunction with the text, and it can be a valuable learning resource.

- *Computer Templates:* Professor Greg Dimkoff of Grand Valley State University has prepared a computer template problems set for a large variety of problems covered in the text. This template is compatible with both windows-based releases of Lotus 1-2-3 and Excel.

- *Videos:* Video snippets produced in collaboration with CNBC will be provided to instructors. These tapes contain professionally produced short (1–8 minutes each) video segments and in-depth programs (20–30 minutes). The tapes address a variety of timely business topics and current business news clips. These video segments can be used to introduce a topic, cover lecture material, or stimulate discussion in the classroom.

ACKNOWLEDGMENTS

I am grateful to several people who have played a part in the development of this text. I must first acknowledge the valuable role played by Bob Duvic in virtually every aspect of this book's production. In addition to developing the instructor's manual and transparency masters, Bob has assisted me in developing and improving the structure of the chapters, has class tested many new materials, and has participated in the book's production cycle. Thanks, Bob. Susan White deserves special thanks for the minicases. Although this was intended to be a collaborative work, Susan deserves primary credit; my role was incidental. Mike Alderson checked the manuscript for accuracy and developed the test bank. Thanks also to Adel Turki for the study workbook.

Keith Brown, Kevin Carroll, Bob Parrino, Goktekin Dincerler, Praveen Madan, Satish Peruvemba, Don Smith, Venkat Subramaniam, Ehud Ronn, and Pavan Wadhwa have helped with the book in various ways. Jill Lectka, ex-editor at Macmillan, helped me tremendously during the transition to South-Western.

Ken King of South-Western is an editor in the truest sense of the word. He has spent enormous amounts of time and effort in reading the early chapters, getting them reviewed, and providing guidance. This book's organization, design, and pedagogy have benefited greatly from his involvement. My "team" at South-Western—Chris Will, Denise Carlson Abt, Ann Sass, and Rebecca Roby—have all displayed great enthusiasm and faith in this book, and I am grateful for their support. Carol Reitz did a great job as copyeditor, and Ruth Cottrell was a pleasure to work with during the book's production stage.

The book has improved significantly from the reviews of various colleagues across the country, including:

Mukesh Bajaj, University of Southern California
Oswald Don Bowling, Texas Tech University
Wilbur John Coleman II, Duke University
Tim Dye, St. Louis University
Michael Fishman, Northwestern University
Craig Hovey, Rochester Business Institute
Michael A. Mazzeo, Michigan State University
Richard Patterson, Michigan State University
George Hettenhouse, Indiana University
Michael Ferguson, University of Arizona
Thomas George, Ohio State University
Joel Schulman, Fordham University
A. Charlene Sullivan, Purdue University
Robert Whitelaw, New York University
Bruce Horning, Vanderbilt University

I would be remiss if I did not acknowledge the help of those who reviewed in detail or provided comments on specific chapters of the previous edition. They include:

Sheldon Balbirer, University of North Carolina
William L. Beedles, University of Kansas
Robert M. Conroy, University of Virginia
William F. Hardin, University of Arkansas
James Kehr, Miami University, Ohio
Dana Johnson, Virginia Polytechnic Institute
Sam McCord, Auburn University
Theodore Moore, Indiana University

Dennis Officer, Arizona State University
Fredrick C. Scherr, West Virginia University
James Seifert, Marquette University
James Verbrugge, University of Georgia
Thomas Zorn, University of Nebraska
J. Kenton Zumwalt, University of Illinois
John Crockett, George Mason University
Wilfred L. Dellva, Iowa State University
Eugene Drzycimski, University of Wisconsin
Douglas R. Emery, University of Missouri—Columbia
Marcia H. Coornett, Southern Illinois University
Philip Fanara, Jr., Howard University
John S. Howe, Louisiana University
Ping Hsiao, San Francisco State University
Steven C. Isberg, University of Baltimore
John F. Marshall, St. John's University
Allan D. Morton, Western Connecticut State University
Cathy M. Niden, University of Notre Dame
Ralph A. Pope, California State University at Sacramento
Paula Smitz, Southwest Texas State University
Dennis P. Sheehan, Pennsylvania State University
Sidharth Sinha, University of Massachusetts, Amherst
Paul J. Speaker, West Virginia University
John G. Thatcher, Marquette University
Ashok Vora, Baruch College, City University of New York
Michael C. Walker, University of Cincinnati
Robert Kleiman, Oakland University
Gabriel Ramierez, State University of New York at Binghamton
Feng Lin, New York University
Seha M. Tinic, President, Koc University, Turkey
Marti Subrahmanyam, New York University
Stuart Gilson, Harvard University
Andrew Chen, Southern Methodist University
Stephen J. Brown, New York University
Sanjai Bhagat, Princeton University

Finally, I am grateful to my wife Anita and my son Nikhil for bearing with me during this project.

Ramesh Rao
Austin, Texas, June 1994

BRIEF CONTENTS

DETAILED CONTENTS

Dr. Ramesh K. S. Rao is Professor of Finance and a CBA Foundation Fellow at the University of Texas at Austin. He received an M.B.A. and a D.B.A. from Indiana University and has a bachelor's degree in metallurgical engineering. Dr. Rao has published in a variety of journals, including *American Economic Review, Journal of Financial and Quantitative Analysis, Journal of Macroeconomics, Journal of Financial Economics, Journal of Financial Services Research,* and *Management Science.*

Dr. Rao has extensive experience with corporate training programs with companies such as IBM, Arthur Young, Technology Futures, Texas Instruments, Motorola, Phillips Petroleum, and Halliburton Corporation, and he has participated in executive development programs in the United States, Asia, Africa, and Europe. He is currently designing and will conduct in-house corporate training programs for Chemical Bank.

He is the recipient of the Graduate Business School Outstanding Professor Award, the Joe D. Beasley Award for Teaching Excellence, the Jack G. Taylor Award for Excellence in Teaching, and the Excellence in Education Award. Most recently, he was voted the Outstanding Professor in the Executive M.B.A. Program at the University of Texas.

Dr. Rao has extensive consulting experience, and his client list includes Burlington Northern, the Federal Home Loan Banks, the Economics Crimes Division of the New Mexico Attorney General's office, and the law firm of Baker and Botts. He has testified as an expert witness in federal bankruptcy courts and has assisted various organizations in valuing businesses. He has served as director on corporate boards.

PART ONE THE FIRM

ONE   THE FIRM AND ITS ENVIRONMENT

The pursuit of gain is the only way in which men can serve the needs of others whom they do not know.

—Friedrich A. Hayek, 1978

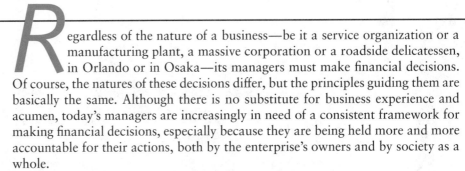

Regardless of the nature of a business—be it a service organization or a manufacturing plant, a massive corporation or a roadside delicatessen, in Orlando or in Osaka—its managers must make financial decisions. Of course, the natures of these decisions differ, but the principles guiding them are basically the same. Although there is no substitute for business experience and acumen, today's managers are increasingly in need of a consistent framework for making financial decisions, especially because they are being held more and more accountable for their actions, both by the enterprise's owners and by society as a whole.

This chapter provides an introduction to the financial decision-making framework by answering the following questions:

- What is financial management?

- How does the market economy foster the goals of our society?

- Why do business firms exist?

- Why are firms organized in different legal forms?

- Why do individuals and businesses participate in financial markets?

- What are the goals of financial management?

- Why should firms consider operating internationally?

1-1

FINANCIAL MANAGEMENT AND THE MARKET ECONOMY

Capital and Financial Management

Business organizations cannot produce goods and services without productive resources, or **capital. Nonhuman capital** includes both tangible and intangible resources, which may be converted from one form to the other. Tangible assets include **financial assets,** such as cash, and **real assets,** such as land, plant facilities, and equipment. Financial assets are used to pay salaries and to purchase raw materials, for example. Real assets may be needed to produce the goods or services that the firm wants to sell. Intangible assets include items such as "brand recognition" and reputation. **Human capital** is intangible and includes the company's productive human resources. The intellectual and entrepreneurial skills of management and the enthusiasm of employees are examples of human capital. Because it is intangible, however, the value of human capital is difficult to measure. In this book, therefore, the term *capital* is used only with reference to nonhuman capital.

A firm needs to invest in real assets in order to produce goods or services. Therefore, the firm's managers must decide what assets to own—what mix of fixed assets (plant, equipment, and land) and what mix of current assets (cash, accounts receivable, and inventories) will best facilitate the firm's production of goods and services. In other words, how much should the firm invest, and in which assets should it invest? The answer is the firm's **investment decision.**

The company needs to finance its assets by acquiring cash from financial markets. The company's managers must therefore decide what securities to issue and what mix of short-term credit, long-term debt, and equity best meets the firm's objectives. These questions are answered by the firm's **financial decision.** These two broad decisions, the investment decision and the financial decision, are the responsibility of the financial manager, and the art and science of making the right decisions for the firm are called **financial management.**

To perform these tasks, financial managers draw on the conceptual principles of economics and use information systems organized by accountants. A financial manager attempts to obtain the best long-term benefits from the allocation of the firm's scarce resources. In this sense, financial decision making deals largely with the future. Nevertheless, managers also are responsible for ensuring that their plans and policies are followed and that the proper financial objectives are pursued at all times. Financial management interacts with all functional areas in a business firm, from marketing to production. Since finance affects all areas of business, all business majors are required to take at least one course in finance.

The Driving Force in a Capitalist Economy

The American economy is based on freedom of choice, and its most important objective is the maximization of consumer satisfaction. The economic principle of free enterprise is implied by America's belief in the philosophy of **capitalism.** A capitalist society recognizes individual property rights. Individuals are allowed to own property in their own names and in almost any form. They are free to do as they please with their capital, without fear of government intervention. In contrast, under **socialism,** the government sharply limits people's right to own property. As recent events in the former Soviet Union and Eastern Europe indicate, the free-market system is gradually replacing centralized decision making.

How do people act in a capitalist society? What makes the economy tick? Is the free-enterprise system the best possible economic arrangement?

KEY CONCEPT

Because individuals can own property and because there are generally no restrictions on where and how capital should be used, people channel their capital into those activities that they expect will benefit them most. By investing their resources in what they believe to be the best alternative for them, all individuals help not only themselves but all of society. In fact, individual self-interest automatically promotes an improvement in social welfare.

The reason for this is perhaps best stated in the words of Adam Smith, who is generally regarded as the founder of modern capitalism:

Every individual endeavors to employ his capital so that its produce may be of greatest value. He generally neither intends to promote the public interest, nor knows how much he is promoting it. He intends only his own security, only his own gain. And he is in this led by an invisible hand to promote an end which was no part of his intention. By pursuing his own interest he frequently promotes that of society more effectively than when he really intends to promote it.

Adam Smith
The Wealth of Nations, 1776

Free enterprise and competition go hand in hand. To achieve its economic goals, industry must produce the right quantity of the right goods at the right time. It is the consumers, however, who decide what "right" is. If they buy the goods that industry has produced, the businesses have done the right thing. But if consumers refuse to buy the goods or services, then the firm has made an incorrect decision. Consumers are thus the most important individuals in the eyes of business, and businesses must constantly aim to please them. Consumers have the luxury of changing their values, preferences, attitudes, and habits at any time, and businesses must constantly attempt to guess these changing preferences. Thus firms are continuously struggling to attract customers by means of lower prices, better quality, more investment in research and development, and so on. As a result, the welfare of the consumer is improved.

Capitalism, Self-Interest, and Ethics in Business

Financial management decisions are based on the assumption that individuals and firms will pursue their own self-interest. This assumption is in fact required for the efficacy of a capitalist economy. Some people cringe at the thought of an entire economic system relying on such a "crass" behavioral assumption. Others equate self-interest with "immoral" behavior and frown on "big business." These reactions are based on a misunderstanding of exactly what self-interest entails.

There is nothing intrinsically wrong with the pursuit of self-interest—pursuing the course of action that one believes is best for oneself. This applies both to the speculator in the stock market and to the monk devoted to a life of prayer. Both are pursuing their self-interest; the speculator aims at becoming a millionaire, and the monk hopes for spiritual salvation. Adam Smith would agree that there is nothing fundamentally wrong with what either one is doing.

However, the functioning of the invisible hand as normally stated is too often separated from the larger ethical questions that Adam Smith also addressed. In fact, Smith, in his *Theory of Moral Sentiments,* felt that ethical considerations cannot be ignored for the smooth running of society:

> *Human society, when we contemplate it in a certain abstract and philosophical light, appears like a great, an immense machine, whose regular and harmonious movements produce a thousand agreeable effects. As in any other beautiful and noble machine that was the production of human art, whatever tended to render its movements more smooth and easy would derive a beauty from this effect, and, on the contrary, whatever tended to obstruct them would displease upon that account: so virtue, which is, as it were, the fine polish to the wheels of society, necessarily pleases, while vice, like the vile rust, which makes them jar and grate upon one another, is as necessarily offensive.*[1]

Thus, if self-interest is replaced with **opportunism,** which includes deception, unfair business practices, exploitation, expropriation, lying, deceit, stealing, and other such conduct that can be characterized as unethical, society will be worse off. In fact, Smith's concept of virtue addressed far more than pure opportunism. He recognized the possibility that self-interested factions could operate to the detriment of society as a whole and urged that the members of society, and especially their political leaders, adhere to a respect for diversity and for the common interests of society as a whole.

The capitalist philosophy, though it relies on self-interest, does not promote unethical conduct or narrow self-interest. Capitalism relies on maximizing behavior within a set of formal and informal rules, structures, or norms. To the extent

---

[1] *The Theory of Moral Sentiments* (1759), ed. D. D. Raphael and A. L. Macfie, in vol. I of *The Glasgow Edition of the Works and Correspondence of Adam Smith,* general editing by D. D. Raphael and Andrew Skinner (Oxford: Clarendon Press, 1976). Also see Jerry Evensky, "Ethics and the Invisible Hand," *Journal of Economic Perspectives* 7(1993): 197–205.

GOOD ETHICS IS GOOD BUSINESS: THE CASE OF SALOMON BROTHERS

When a business engages in illegal behavior, press coverage focuses primarily on the legal penalties imposed on the offending firm and its management. However, these legally imposed fines, civil judgments, and prison sentences are only a portion of the costs borne by the firm. As it turns out, the opportunistic firm can also be penalized in the product, service, and financial markets. We can examine how the markets discipline unethical behavior by examining the recent case of Salomon Brothers.

Salomon Brothers is a major New York investment firm which actively participates in several markets, including the buying and selling of government debt. The U.S. Treasury Department periodically issues debt through auctions. To preclude any one firm dominating this auction, the Treasury specified that no one firm could bid for more than 35% of any given Treasury debt issue. On nine occasions between December 1990 and May 1991, Paul Mozer, head of Salomon's Government bond-trading desk, used a client firm's name—without its knowledge—to bid for a larger share of specific Treasury issues. Mozer, receiving indications that regulators were suspicious, reported his illegal actions to Salomon's senior management in April 1991, but they took no action. In June 1991 the Securities and Exchange Commission and the Justice Department issued subpoenas as part of an investigation of Salomon's activities.

As a result of its investigations, the Federal Government imposed substantial penalties on Salomon Brothers in a May 1992 settlement. These included a $122 million payment to the U.S. Treasury for violating securities laws, $68 million to settle claims with the Justice Department, and $100 million to a restitution fund to pay civil judgments. In addition, Salomon agreed to create $385 million in total reserves for potential future liabilities. In addition, the Federal Reserve Bank of New York suspended for two months Salomon's authority to trade with it as a primary dealer, which cut it off from valuable information sources and cost it $4 billion in lost trading volume.

As substantial as these official penalties may appear, they were exceeded by the costs Salomon incurred in the markets. During the week in August 1991 when its actions were made public, Salomon's stock price dropped by one-third, costing it $1.5 billion in market value. This drop in Salomon's market value reflected the view of the markets that its opportunistic behavior damaged its ability to provide services to its customers.

As an investment bank, one of Salomon's major activities was underwriting new security issues (assisting firms in raising capital by issuance of new securities). In this activity, the credibility of the underwriter is crucial. The purchasers of the new securities cannot know if all material information has been disclosed, and must depend on the conscientiousness and integrity of the underwriter as assurance that

there are no "hidden surprises." Salomon's opportunistic behavior in the government debt market damaged its credibility as an underwriter, and cost Salomon a substantial amount of business. The firm fell from fifth to tenth place in underwriting business.

Its lowered credibility also damaged Salomon in its other activities. The World Bank and the State of California suspended trading with Salomon. Its trade in several other securities markets was limited because its credibility was impugned, and it was forced to cut back on its trading for its own account by one-third.

These costs were borne not just by the firm but also by several individuals. Those directly involved in the scandal, from Mozer down to the clerk who submitted the order, were removed. Resignations were requested of the chairman, president, vice-chairman, and general counsel. The outside legal counsel was replaced, an outside director appointed as interim chairman, and a new chief operating officer appointed.

These actions were not mandated by law, but were forced on Salomon by market pressures. Salomon's experiences provide a measure of how markets value integrity. Firms that pursue opportunistic behavior can see their "reputational capital" lose value and severely hamper the firm's operations and profitability.

SOURCE: Clifford W. Smith, Jr., "Economics and Ethics: The Case of Salomon Brothers," Journal of Applied Corporate Finance, September 1992.

that unethical behavior prevails, societal welfare suffers and firms that pursue opportunistic behaviors are worse off. This latter result is clearly seen in the accompanying examination of Salomon Brothers' involvement in the 1991 Treasury debt auction scandal.

1-2
THE FIRM AND ITS LEGAL FORMS

Why Do Firms Exist?

In a primitive economy, consumers' needs are basic and are satisfied by simple cooperative transactions among individuals in the community. In a dynamic, sophisticated economy, however, life is not so simple. Consumers' needs are virtually endless. Social and technological changes create new needs, and as society becomes more and more affluent, consumers demand larger and larger quantities of goods and services. To produce them, hundreds and perhaps thousands of transactions become necessary, involving large numbers of people, often dispersed over a large geographic area and with different skills and inputs. These complex transactions can no longer be organized informally because it is possible for individuals to deviate from their intended roles in the transactions. Society deals with these more complex transactions according to more formal arrangements called **contracts,** agreements that define (implicitly or explicitly) each party's obligations, with the added feature of a cost (penalty) associated with breaking the agreement.

Contracts may be explicit or implicit. For example, when The Kroger Company borrowed $200 million in 1993, the company entered into an explicit contract with its creditors whose terms were explicitly specified. Kroger agreed to repay the debt in ten years with an annual interest rate of $8\frac{1}{2}\%$. On the other hand, when you buy an IBM computer, you are also buying an implicit contract that IBM will offer facilities for servicing and repairing your computer as necessary.

Contracts apply to a firm's accounting procedures and to managers' incentive and compensation schemes. In fact, even a company's structure can be viewed as a contract: it specifies its employees' responsibilities, to whom each reports, by whom he or she is supervised, and so on. Thus a modern firm can be viewed simply as an artificial legal entity held together or connected by a set of contracts.

Why are some transactions (contracts) conducted through firms, whereas others are executed directly in the market? As Ronald Coase pointed out, firms are used whenever the cost of writing contracts and operating through a firm is lower than the cost of making individual market transactions.[2] For example, if you are building a single house, you can work through the market system and independently contract with architects, carpenters, electricians, painters, landscape specialists, and the like. But what if you are a large homebuilder constructing, say, 15 houses a month? Given the repetition of the same transactions, it is more cost efficient for you to form your own company and make several long-term contracts. As a large-scale homebuilder, you establish a firm because it is cheaper than transacting via the market mechanism.

Several economists criticize this explanation of why firms exist on the grounds that it is a tautological argument. Not all transactions are more cost effective when conducted via a firm. If such firms exist, however, it must be true that the cost of producing through them is lower, for otherwise we all would be operating through the market. Thus, they state, it is difficult to disagree with or refute Coase's explanation for the existence of a firm.

[2]R. Coase, "The Theory of the Firm," *Economica* 4(1937): 386–405.

Alchian and Demsetz suggested that a firm is a team effort, and team effort results in synergies.[3] One problem in a firm is that it is often difficult to measure the productivity of the team's various members. Alchian and Demsetz suggested that the **owner,** or **equityholder,** of a firm is a common party to all members of the team (to all contracts) and that the owner can efficiently measure the outputs and allocate the rewards. Moreover, the owner has a **residual claim** on the output— that is, the portion of the output that remains after the other team members have been adequately compensated. Because the owner's welfare depends on this residual claim, he or she has an interest in efficiently designing the contracts and monitoring the activities of the team members. This arrangement leads to greater efficiency, and hence firms are an efficient way of transacting cooperative activities.

Jensen and Meckling went a step further and contended that contractual relationships are not limited to employees but rather encompass all parties in the firm.[4] According to them, the firm is a **nexus** (or collection) **of contracts,** and alternative contractual arrangements are optimal responses to the contracting problem. In this view of the firm, the large number of participants in a modern business— managers, production workers, accountants, suppliers of capital, suppliers of raw materials, salespersons—are held together primarily through a series of contracts. Each participant in this collective endeavor has a different kind of contract, depending on the service provided.

An interesting implication of this nexus of contracts view is that the equityholders (owners) of a firm do not play a special role. Equity investors take most of the risk associated with the business because they are rewarded only if there is something left over after the firm has satisfied its obligations. Equityholders are thus the firm's **residual risk bearers.** Following this line of reasoning, Jensen and Meckling stated that ownership of capital is not the same thing as ownership of the firm. In fact, all parties to the firm—managers, suppliers, bondholders, workers, and stockholders—are owners because they all "own" different contracts with the firm. If owning a contract is "ownership," then all participants in a business are owners, although each can have a different kind of ownership arrangement. In the contract view of the firm, the ownership of the firm is an irrelevant concept; there are only owners of contracts with the firm.

Each person in a firm has an incentive to work to make the entire group (of contracts) succeed because his or her own welfare is influenced by what happens to the business. To appreciate this mutual dependence among all parties in the firm, the reader is urged to read press reports of the effects of any large company's bankruptcy, which affects not only the equityholders and creditors, but also the management, work force, subcontractors, bankers, customers, and even the local community. All participants in this collection of contracts—all who have a "stake" in the firm—benefit or are hurt by the fate of the business, and thus it is these **stakeholders** who own the firm.

The Three Basic Legal Forms of Business

The three common legal forms of business are the proprietorship, the partnership, and the corporation. As Figure 1-1 shows, in the United States proprietorships clearly dominate in terms of numbers but are typically small, whereas corporations generate the most sales dollars but are fewer in number. These legal forms of business may be seen as alternative optimal arrangements based on

[3]A. A. Alchian and H. Demsetz, "Production, Information Costs, and Economic Organization," *American Economic Review* 62(1972): 777–795.

[4]M. C. Jensen and W. H. Meckling, "Theory of the Firm: Managerial Behavior, Agency Costs and Ownership Structure," *Journal of Financial Economics* 3(1976): 305–360.

FIGURE 1-1

The Mix of Business Organizations in the United States

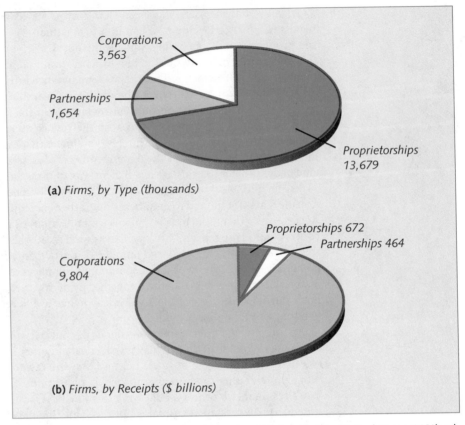

(a) *Firms, by Type (thousands)*

(b) *Firms, by Receipts ($ billions)*

SOURCE: Graphs compiled from data in *Statistical Abstracts of the United States,* 112th ed. (Washington, DC: U.S. Department of Commerce, Bureau of Census, 1992), Tables 826 and 827.

increasing size. As a firm grows, it may be necessary for it to change its legal form because its legal form affects the extent to which the firm can control its own operations and access capital. These three business arrangements can also be distinguished by their restrictions on residual claims.[5]

PROPRIETORSHIP

The oldest, simplest, and most common legal form of business is the **proprietorship,** in which a single person has the controlling interest. This person is responsible for the firm's policies, owns all its assets, and is personally liable for its debts. The firm's success or failure lies entirely in the proprietor's hands. If it prospers, the owner will receive all the benefits; if it fails, the owner will suffer all the losses. In this business arrangement, the holder of the residual claims is the decision maker, and the owner and manager of the firm are one and the same person.

The advantages of a proprietorship include its ease of formation, control, and the manner in which it is taxed. There are few legal and organizational requirements associated with setting up a proprietorship, and therefore the organizational costs are very low. One has only to "hang out a shingle" to start a business. Per-

[5]This view of the various organizational forms is discussed in E. F. Fama and M. C. Jensen, "Organizational Forms and Investment Decisions," *Journal of Financial Economics* 14(1983): 101–118; and in their other writings.

haps the most attractive feature for the owner of a proprietorship is being one's own boss—that is, having total control of the firm's management. Proprietors have complete authority unless they decide to delegate certain responsibilities to their employees. All earnings of a proprietorship are taxed at the owner's personal tax rate, which is generally different from the rate at which corporate income is taxed.

The disadvantages of a proprietorship are unlimited personal liability, limited access to funds, and a limited lifetime. Because the firm's assets and liabilities belong to the owner, the owner and the owner's business are one and the same. If creditors' claims cannot be satisfied by the firm's assets, the owner's personal assets can be attached to meet these obligations. Perhaps more important, the firm's growth is limited by the owner's personal wealth and access to short-term bank loans. Finally, the life of the business is limited to the lifetime of the proprietor. Because of these factors, a proprietorship is usually a small firm and is found most often in retail, service, and construction areas. As a proprietorship grows, it becomes increasingly attractive to the owner to take on a partner and change to the partnership form.

PARTNERSHIP

A **partnership** is similar to a proprietorship except that it has several owners. Most large partnerships are established by a written contract among the partners called the **articles of partnership**. The **Uniform Partnership Act** lays out the legal rules pertaining to partnerships. As of 1993, all states except Louisiana had adopted these rules. The act also applies to Washington, DC, the Virgin Islands, and Guam. Though not formally required (an oral understanding can suffice), a partnership agreement is important because it can eliminate future problems with regard to salaries, contributions to capital, the distribution of profits and losses, and the dissolution of the partnership. In a partnership, the residual claimants are the owners and the decision makers. However, unlike in a proprietorship, no residual claimant has complete control over the firm's operations.

The advantages and disadvantages of a partnership are similar to those of a proprietorship. The major advantages are its low cost and ease of formation. In addition, a partnership can raise a larger amount of capital (because more than one person makes contributions) and has greater creditworthiness (because the personal assets of all the partners stand behind the business). Finally, the tax features of a partnership are in many ways similar to those of proprietorships. Each partner must pay personal income taxes on his or her pro rata share of the partnership's earnings, even if the partner does not actually receive that share. This may or may not be an advantage, depending on a partner's particular tax bracket.

A partnership's main disadvantages are its unlimited liability and limited lifetime. If the business should fail, all the partners must assume its liabilities, and their personal assets may be used to meet the creditors' claims. Moreover, if one partner cannot satisfy his or her pro rata share of the partnership's obligations, the remaining partners are obligated to meet them. A partnership will be legally dissolved if one of the partners withdraws, goes bankrupt, or becomes mentally incompetent; a new partnership must be drawn up if the business is to continue.

The risks of unlimited liability can be mitigated by forming a **limited partnership,** in which one or more of the partners' liability is limited to the amount of their contributions. At least one person must be a **general** (or regular) **partner** who has unlimited liability. The **limited partners** essentially become investors and are not involved in running the business. Moreover, the partnership will not be dissolved if one of the limited partners dies, goes bankrupt, or becomes mentally incompetent. Though common in the oil and gas, leasing, and real estate industries, limited partnerships are not compatible with most other business activities.

By and large, unlimited liability and the difficulty of maintaining continuity make it hard for very large companies to operate as partnerships. With the exception of legal and accounting firms, very large partnerships are therefore rare.

CORPORATION

In terms of size rather than numbers, the public **corporation** dominates the U.S. business scene, accounting for almost 90% of total sales. The often-quoted "What's good for General Motors is good for America" is thus not entirely without truth. It is because of the immense size of corporations that their influence on the country's economic well-being is more dramatic than that of proprietorships and partnerships.

In contrast with other legal forms, a corporation is unique in that it is a legal entity created by a state charter. It is an "artificial being" and a "legal fiction" in that it is separate from its owners. Much like a person, a corporation can acquire property, issue securities, sue or be sued, and enter into contracts. Like people, it is guided by an invisible hand as it pursues a course of action that is in its own best interest. A corporation is formed through **articles of incorporation,** which state its rights and limitations.

In an **open corporation** anyone can hold a residual claim because ownership and management are separated. The residual claimant, the **stockholder,** can sever his or her relationship with the firm by simply selling the claim. A **closed corporation** is essentially a group of partners who operate under the legal status of a corporation. The investment firm of Goldman Sachs, the national accounting firm Ernst & Young, and the national law firm of Baker and Botts are examples of closed corporations. These firms' residual claims are restricted to the major internal decision makers. Stockholders in small businesses can form an **S corporation,** which is taxed not at the corporate tax rate but at the shareholders' individual tax rate. The corporate profits (losses) are distributed on a pro rata basis to the owners, who then pay personal taxes on this amount. In addition, because it is a corporation, shareholders enjoy limited liability. The main catch is that the Internal Revenue Service Code limits the number of stockholders to 35 or fewer, which largely restricts this legal form to small businesses and start-up companies.

A corporation has three major advantages: **limited liability,** unlimited life, and easy transferability of ownership. An owner's liability is limited to his or her investment; that is, the corporation can raise funds without exposing the owners to the risk of having their personal assets confiscated. This feature encourages equity investors to supply funds to companies that are working on risky projects. Because the ownership of a corporation is separate from its management, the life of a corporation is virtually perpetual. Finally, ownership is represented by shares of stock, which permits the easy divisibility and transferability of the owners' interests. In fact, a large corporation may have as many as 1 million owners, with ownership changing almost daily.

In addition to being more costly and difficult to organize, a corporation has a potential disadvantage in its tax treatment. The primary drawback is the double taxation of income. Because it is a separate entity, a corporation pays taxes on its own income. Then, if after-tax income is distributed to its stockholders as a cash dividend, the stockholders must pay a second tax on this amount.

The characteristics of each form of business organization are summarized in Table 1-1.

■

TABLE 1-1

A Comparison of Business Organizational Forms

	Ownership	Control	Personal Liability	Life of Business	Access to Capital
Proprietorship	Centralized in one person	Centralized in one person	Unlimited claim on owner's wealth	Limited to owner's lifetime	Limited to owner's capital
Partnership	Shared among partners	Shared among partners	Unlimited claim on each partner's wealth	Must be redefined upon death of any partner	Limited to partner's capital
Corporation	Shared among stockholders	Entrusted to management	Limited to investment in corporation	Unlimited	Unlimited

Because of the overbearing influence of the corporation on all business activities in the United States, the discussion in the remainder of this book will pertain to the corporation unless otherwise mentioned.

1-3
FINANCIAL SECURITIES AND FINANCIAL MARKETS

For a business to obtain the benefits of mass production, large capital outlays may be required, but such capital needs may be well beyond the wealth of one person. Individuals "tap into" the wealth-creating abilities of corporations by providing capital to the business in one form or another.

Individuals use the capital markets to reallocate their consumption across time. Some individuals find that they need more funds for their current consumption than they possess today. Capital markets allow these individuals to borrow funds today, thus increasing current consumption in return for sacrificing some of their future consumption to pay back what they borrow. Other individuals have more funds than they need for current consumption. They are willing to sacrifice some of their current consumption and lend funds to others with the expectation that they will have a higher consumption level in the future. These individuals with surplus funds are especially relevant for businesses that need capital because they are willing to "finance" the firm's operations. In return for this capital, the firm agrees to give each financier certain benefits. These benefits are not guaranteed, however, and the securityholders do take some risks. The document that spells out this transaction between the firm and the capital contributor is called a **financial security.** In this chapter, we introduce two major types of financial securities: common stocks and bonds.

Primary and Secondary Markets

When a firm issues new financial securities (i.e., raises new capital) directly to the public, the transaction is said to be a **primary market** transaction. In contrast, much of the daily activity in financial markets consists of **secondary market** transactions in which brokers and dealers buy and sell for their clients financial securities that were issued in the past. The secondary markets are extremely valuable. Individuals can get rid of their financial securities simply by selling them to someone else. Investors can thus make profits (or incur losses) in secondary market trading. Companies also benefit from secondary markets. A company may use the secondary markets to restructure its financial securities and thus reduce the amount it pays out to securityholders. It is important to remember that companies are as interested in what happens to their securities in the secondary markets as in those in primary markets. For one thing, the wealth of their stockholders is affected by the price of their stock in the secondary markets. In addition, the prices of the stocks and bonds in secondary markets influence a firm's cost of funds for future investment activity. (These issues are examined in greater detail in later chapters.)

Depending on their personal considerations, individuals provide capital to a business in two distinct forms: as equity or as debt.

Equity

When an investor provides capital to a corporation and the company agrees to give the investor a fractional ownership in the corporation, the investor becomes an equityholder or a common stockholder. A piece of paper that records this arrangement between the company and the investor is issued to the investor by the company. This document is called a **common stock certificate** or **share,** and the stockholder or shareholder is usually free to sell these certificates at any time through a financial market called a **stock market.**

REWARDS TO STOCKHOLDERS

Stockholders expect to get their rewards in one or both of two ways: via dividends and/or via capital gains. Corporations may choose to return periodically a portion of their earnings to stockholders in the form of a cash distribution, called a **cash dividend.** For example, if the Coca-Cola Company chooses to distribute 20% of its current earnings to stockholders, it declares a 20% cash dividend payout. Instead of paying a cash reward to its shareholders, a corporation may choose to issue a new share of stock for every five shares that a stockholder owns. This distribution is called a **stock dividend.** Unless it is explicitly stated otherwise, in this book the term *dividends* refers to cash dividends.

In addition to cash or stock dividends, stockholders may expect **capital gains,** in which they sell their stock in the stock market for a higher price than they paid for it. For example, if you bought a share of IBM stock for $55 on January 1 and sold it at a later date for $69, you would have a capital gain of $14.

RISKS TO STOCKHOLDERS

Although stockholders can expect dividends, there is no assurance that a firm will in fact pay dividends. The contractual agreement with common stockholders does not specify that the firm will pay dividends. Thus stockholders may not be assured of this form of reward. In addition, there is no assurance that the price of the stock will go up, resulting in capital gains when the stock is sold. The investor may be forced to accept a capital loss if he or she has to sell the stock at a particular time when the price is lower. Another risk that common stockholders face occurs when a company goes bankrupt. Then the assets of the firm are sold, and investors are repaid their contributed capital (or some fraction of it). Common stockholders can expect repayment only if there is "residue" remaining after the creditors have been paid. But stockholders cannot lose more than their contribution of capital even if the creditors cannot be paid off in full by liquidating the firm's assets; that is, stockholders have the protection of limited liability.

Debt

When investors lend capital to a company, the company agrees to repay the loan at a set interest rate (typically paid every six months). The investor is a creditor of the corporation. The document that records this arrangement between the issuing company and the investor is called a **bond.** Bondholders can sell their securities at any time in the **bond markets.** Bonds typically have a **face value,** the bond's nominal value, of $1,000 and a maturity date of several years. On the maturity date, the company agrees to pay back to the bondholder the face value of the bond.

REWARDS TO BONDHOLDERS

Like stockholders, bondholders have two sources of rewards: interest payments and capital gains. Bondholders know exactly the amount of interest they can expect periodically for lending capital to the company because the rate is stated on the bond. For example, if the Coca-Cola Company's bonds pay an interest rate of 6% per year and you own a $1,000 face-value bond, you will get annual interest of $60, payable in semiannual payments of $30. If you paid $1,000 for a bond issued by Coca-Cola on February 6 and sold it for $1,100 two years later, you would have a capital gain of $100. For both stockholders and bondholders, the capital gain expected may in fact turn out to be a capital loss, the result of selling an asset for a price less than the original purchase price.

RISKS TO BONDHOLDERS

The interest payments and the repayment of principal to the bondholders are fairly certain. The only uncertainty occurs if the firm is having serious difficulties. If the interest payments and maturity value are delayed or not paid, the firm will have defaulted on its terms, and the creditors may have to take the company to court. In addition, bondholders face a risk if they attempt to sell their bonds in the bond markets. Depending on the level of interest rates in the economy at that time, bondholders may have to sell their bonds at a price below their purchase price. Thus, bondholders must recognize the possibility of a capital loss if they wish to sell their bonds before they mature.

Other Financial Securities

In addition to common stocks and bonds, companies issue other types of securities to investors. Some of the more popular securities are preferred stock, convertible bonds, and rights. (We discuss these securities in later chapters.)

Collectively, the contributors of the different varieties of capital to the corporation are called **securityholders.** In the remainder of this chapter, we restrict our use of this term to stockholders and bondholders and, unless otherwise specified, discuss primarily debt and equity financing (i.e., bonds and stocks).

1-4

THE GOAL OF FINANCIAL MANAGEMENT

Firms, and not just individuals, are guided by the invisible hand in a capitalist economy. Because the firm is operating on behalf of the individual, it too must operate in a self-satisfying manner. The firm must make the right decisions in almost every aspect of its daily operations in order to serve the best interests of its owners.

KEY CONCEPT   The firm must attempt to maximize the welfare of its residual claimants (stockholders).

Some would argue with this business objective. In 1980 Tom Hayden wrote in *The American Future:* "What is needed is for the concept of shareholder to be broadened to that of 'stakeholder.' All those affected by corporate behavior—the general public, workers, consumers, and the surrounding community—ought to have some representation on corporate boards."[6] The stakeholder view of the firm is being espoused by more and more enterprises today. The notion of multiple stakeholders implies that in running a firm, the modern manager must be respon-

---

[6] Tom Hayden, *The American Future: New Visions Beyond Old Frontiers* (Boston: South End Press, 1980).

sive to multiple constituencies, not just the stockholders. This may result in multiple financial goals, of which maximizing the shareholders' interests is just one (and not necessarily the dominant goal). Moreover, these multiple financial goals may not be in agreement.

National Cash Register (NCR) Corporation is one of the growing list of companies that are adopting the stakeholder theory of the firm. In 1987 NCR began an advertising campaign to promote its new view of the firm. The ads proclaimed that all participants in its operations deserve as much consideration as its stockholders do. According to NCR, stakeholders include customers, employees, suppliers, the "world-wide communities in which we operate," and "our shareholders." NCR also coupled its shareholders' interests with those of "financial communities," the financial analysts or banks with which the company does business.

The "responsibilities" espoused by the stakeholder view are hard to defend because the firm's contracts with some of these parties make no implicit or explicit statement about social responsibility. Similarly, it is difficult to suggest that workers should not quit their jobs to work for a competitor on grounds of "social responsibility" or "company loyalty." Without explicit contracts, criteria for social responsibility are ambiguous, and social responsibility creates problems because it falls unequally across firms. For instance, if one mining company incurs significant costs to reduce pollution while its competitors do not, its profitability will be compromised, and its shareholders must bear the cost. They may respond by selling their shares, causing the value of the firm to fall. To society, this situation may hamper an efficient allocation of resources and ultimately retard economic growth and increase unemployment.

There is a growing belief that espousal of the objective of maximizing stakeholder welfare is a direct reaction to the negative public sentiment and congressional debate about the wave of takeovers in the 1980s, during which some firms aggressively sought to gain control of other firms. At the time, corporations, perceived as "greedy" organizations, were under increasing threat of legislation that would stifle their activities. Embracing the stakeholder view in this setting appears to have been no more than a clever attempt to mollify clamoring politicians. The courts have generally recognized that stockholders are residual risk bearers and that maximizing their welfare is the main responsibility of the firm. The courts feel that questions of corporate conscience do not apply, however, because the firm is not an individual, and that protecting other constituents is not the role of the firm because other protections are available to nonequity stakeholders.

In fact, other stakeholders frequently find it difficult to sue a corporation to enforce their rights. Although many states have passed "nonstockholder constituency statutes" to "protect" other parties to the business, these laws are typically very limited in their actual impact on corporate decisions. For example, the Minnesota statute passed in June 1987 [Minn. Stat. 302A.251 (5) (Supp. 1988)] allows a firm "in considering the best interests of the corporation, to consider the interests of the corporation's employees, customers, suppliers, and creditors, the economy of the state and the nation, community and societal considerations." However, it also states that the firm's directors may consider other stakeholders' interests *only* as long as they are in the best interests of the corporation (stockholders). Legal experts believe that this statute and many others like it really do not add anything new to the belief that the firm should be run in the best interests of the stockholders.

This does not mean that the various stakeholders of the corporation are without rights or means to enforce those rights. Examples of stakeholder protection include the courts, trade unions, local grievance committees, the Federal Trade Commis-

STRIDE RITE'S DILEMMA

Stride Rite Corporation, headquartered in Cambridge, Massachusetts, appears to have a split personality. On one hand, the company could be described as a leader in corporate responsibility and has received 14 public service awards in the last three years. Among other things, Stride Rite has:

- Created the Stride Rite Charitable Foundation, to which the company contributes 5% of its pre-tax profits.

- Provided employee day-care centers since 1971. The company has even expanded the concept into "intergenerational centers" which care for the aged as well.

- Awarded $5,000-a-year scholarships for inner-city youths to attend Harvard. These scholarship recipients then act as mentors for other inner-city youths and are eligible for $15,000 fellowships for further work in the community.

- Paid Harvard graduate students to work in a Cambodian refugee camp.

- Permitted employees to tutor disadvantaged children on company time.

However, it is also a consistently profitable company which has seen its stock price increase six-fold since 1986.

- In the past decade, the company has already closed 15 factories in the United States and moved operations to cheaper Asian areas where wages drop from a U.S. level of $1,200–$1,400 to a Taiwanese level of $100–$150.

- Faced with local unemployment rates ranging from 14% to nearly 30%, Stride Rite is currently planning to move two Massachusetts operations to a cheaper location in Kentucky.

When faced with these cuts, a local development leader stated that "the most socially responsible thing a company can do is to give a person a job." However, Stride Rite's chairman, Ervin Shames, feels that "putting jobs into places where it doesn't make economic sense is a dilution of corporate and community wealth." As Stride Rite's former chairman, Arnold Hiatt, states: "If you're pro business, you also have to be concerned about things like jobs in the inner city and the 38 million Americans living below the poverty line." However, he also recognizes that "to the extent that you can stay in the city, I think you have to," but "if it's at the expense of your business, I think you can't forget that your primary responsibility is to your stockholders." These arguments may make economic sense, but they cannot provide solace or work for the Stride Rite employees who will be turned out. As one 11-year employee asked: "Where are you supposed to go? There is no place to go."

SOURCE: "Split Personality: Social Responsibility and Need for Low Cost Clash at Stride Rite," The Wall Street Journal, May 28, 1983, p. 1. Reprinted by permission of The Wall Street Journal, © Dow Jones & Company, Inc. (1993); all rights reserved worldwide.

sion (FTC), local better business bureaus, consumer claims protection agencies, the Environmental Protection Agency, the Food and Drug Administration (FDA), and the Securities and Exchange Commission (SEC).

We seem to face a dilemma. The free-enterprise system holds that management must adopt policies that maximize the firm's market value because only then can the firm attract capital, allocate it efficiently, provide employment, and create benefits that satisfy society's needs. However, public policy, reflecting the views of society that a certain amount of government regulation is necessary for the general good, dictates that constraints be imposed on the firm's value-maximizing behavior. How do we reconcile these views? Society, through its government representatives, makes decisions regarding the relative trade-offs between desirable social goals and reduced efficiency from reallocating those scarce resources necessary to realize those goals. The firm should then be allowed to maximize the shareholders' wealth, subject to these mandatory constraints imposed by society on *all* firms. In this constrained setting, equityholders have more control over the firm's decisions than do the other stakeholders, and they are the ones who elect the managers to run the company and maximize their wealth. They still bear the risk of the firm's activities without any promised rewards.

This goal of stockholder welfare is followed even by firms that take a very serious view of their broad responsibilities to society, as shown in the preceding highlight.

1-5
INTERNATIONAL DIMENSIONS OF BUSINESS

Why Operate Internationally?

More than 85% of the world is not the United States. This suggests that in the absence of restrictive government regulations, American companies should benefit significantly from operating overseas. For example, the opening of China to U.S. firms dramatically enlarged the market for Coca-Cola, as the new market expanded by more than 1 billion people. Also, as discussed above, Stride Rite expanded its manufacturing operations overseas to take advantage of low manufacturing costs. It is this potential for added revenues and reduced costs that motivates American firms (or any nation's firms) to pursue lucrative overseas markets.

Because of the enormous resources invested by American companies overseas (especially in Europe), it is often said that the fate of some European economies is tied inextricably to the fate of American multinational corporations. The power and influence of American multinationals are immense. Every one of America's 50 largest manufacturing companies (in sales) is multinational. In fact, as Figure 1-2 shows, many companies that we think of as American derive a substantial portion of their sales from foreign markets.

The traditional justification for international trade is the **principle of comparative advantage,** which was first suggested by the economist David Ricardo in 1817. Comparative advantage arguments suggest that countries differ in attributes—what they are relatively better at doing. Countries should specialize in producing what they do best and then trade these goods among themselves. In that way, all the nations involved will benefit. This argument, however, does not explain why companies make direct investments in foreign plants and distribution centers. For instance, why doesn't Ford simply ship its American-produced cars to Europe instead of establishing manufacturing plants there? Why do American multinational companies invest billions of dollars overseas, providing employment opportunities and economic advancement to those countries?

The behavior of modern multinational corporations (MNCs) is explained by the **imperfect markets theory,** which states that firms profit by identifying and exploiting the imperfections that exist among markets. For instance, one of the most widely recognized imperfections among markets is the difference in labor costs around the world. For a labor-intensive product, American companies might find it more profitable to operate in a country such as Taiwan, where labor costs are relatively low. Products can be produced at a competitive price and then brought back to the home country for sale. The Stride Rite Corporation discussion above is an excellent example of how firms can and in fact are forced by competition to exploit labor-cost imperfections. With higher labor costs in the United States, companies with American facilities tend to be more capital intensive. Operational constraints such as transportation and insurance costs, raw material availability, and differing market characteristics are other imperfections that could induce a company to invest in plants overseas rather than at home.

FIGURE 1-2
*A Sample of U.S.
Multinationals*

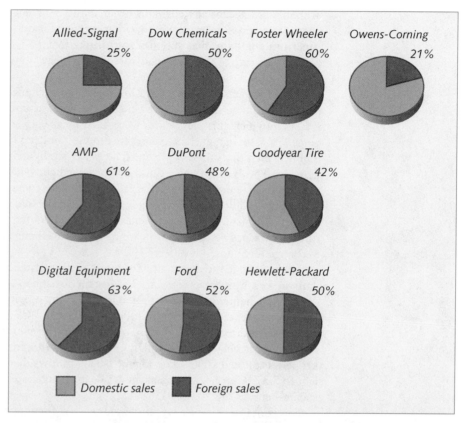

SOURCE: Graphs compiled from data in "Searching for Overseas Stock Plays? Consider U.S. Multinationals, Some Say," *The Wall Street Journal,* June 1, 1993. Reprinted by permission of *The Wall Street Journal,* © Dow Jones & Company, Inc., 1993. All rights reserved worldwide.

Prime sources of imperfections are government regulations. Companies often manufacture abroad to avoid **tariffs,** which are taxes on imported goods. To sell American-made computers in France may require a tariff payment to the French government, whereas the same computer made in France may be exempt from this fee. Because tariffs put upward pressure on the price of the final product, cost-conscious firms may be inclined to manufacture their products directly in these "host" countries. Tax laws can also make a big difference. With favorable taxation, companies have higher cash flows.

Another argument for operating on a multinational basis is diversification. Countries differ in their levels of economic activity. For example, in the early 1990s Germany and Japan were experiencing growth while the United States was in a recession. If a company receives earnings from several countries, decreased earnings from slow economies may be offset by increased earnings from growing economies. An MNC that operates in several economies can often experience a more stable pattern of earnings than a company operating in only one country.

*International Risk
Exposure*

EXCHANGE RATE RISK

Different countries have different currencies, and all the economic activity within a country uses the local currency. French people buy their wines with French francs, the English buy stout with pounds, and Japanese farmers would probably not accept any currency other than yen. Hence, a problem arises when one country does business with another. Americans may not want yen, and so an American company that supplies soft drinks to Japan will subsequently have to convert its yen to dollars. The rate of currency conversion is called the **exchange rate.**

Exchange rates are determined in the foreign exchange markets. Prior to 1973, foreign exchange markets were generally organized under a fixed exchange rate system in which currency values were fixed by the governments that issued them. Since 1973, foreign exchange markets function under a floating exchange rate system in which the values of the currencies are set by market forces of supply and demand. The exchange rate can thus be viewed conveniently as the price per unit of foreign currency. The price that an American has to pay in dollars for 1 Japanese yen (¥) is the dollar–yen exchange rate and is expressed as $/¥ (dollars per unit of foreign currency). Sometimes exchange rates are quoted as the number of units of foreign currency per dollar. For example, if the exchange rate is $0.01/¥, the same exchange rate quoted in ¥/$ is ¥100/$.

The exchange rates of major trading partners of the United States are quoted daily in *The Wall Street Journal*. Because the foreign exchange market's prices are constantly changing, the rate quoted is that of the previous day at 3:00 P.M. Eastern time. An example is shown in Figure 1-3. *The Wall Street Journal* quotes currencies both directly, as U.S. dollars per unit of foreign exchange, and indirectly, as foreign currency per U.S. dollar. On July 12, 1993, for example, the Norwegian krone was quoted at $0.1356. Figure 1-3 also shows that 1 U.S. dollar was equivalent to 7.3746 krone. Note that these two exchange rates are simply reciprocals of each other (7.3746 = 1/0.1356).

Foreign currency may be purchased or sold for immediate delivery at what is called the **spot exchange rate,** which is based on that day's market conditions. For example, a business manager who needs to convert Japanese yen to American dollars can do so immediately at the spot exchange rate (109.45 yen to the dollar on July 12, 1993). Although the price is fixed immediately, settlement, or the actual exchange of currencies, is conducted two days following the agreement. Each day the spot exchange rate changes with market conditions. Therefore, if a business-person is to receive a payment of £300,000 in 45 days, he or she must estimate what the spot exchange rate will be in 45 days in order to determine how many dollars will be received. The firm thus faces **exchange rate risk.**

Exchange rate risk is perhaps the most distinctive aspect of international management. Firms that do business overseas have the constant problem of exchange rate fluctuations. Even if foreign earnings or cash flow can be predicted accurately in terms of the foreign currency, the value in dollars will be uncertain because managers do not know the future exchange rate. Managers of international operations must take these risks into account in addition to business and financial risks.

If a firm has a receipt or payment denominated in a foreign currency, it may suffer a loss if the exchange rate changes. A short example will make this clear. Consider a Texas firm that has exported goods to a London firm and will be paid in British pounds (£) in four months. The Texas firm may be confident in the pound value of the transaction but, not knowing the exchange rate that will exist in four months, it cannot be sure of how many dollars it will ultimately receive. Let us assume that the invoice is for goods priced at £80,125. If the exchange rate drops from $1.4780/£ to $1.4420/£, instead of receiving $118,425 (£80,125 × $1.4780/£) for the merchandise, the Texas exporter will receive $115,540 (£80,125 × $1.4420/£), a loss of $2,885. If the transaction had been denominated in dollars, the Texas firm

FIGURE 1-3

*A Sample of Foreign
Exchange Rates on
July 12, 1993*

CURRENCY TRADING

EXCHANGE RATES

Monday, July 12, 1993

The New York foreign exchange selling rates below apply to trading among banks in amounts of $1 million and more, as quoted at 3 p.m. Eastern time by Bankers Trust Co., Telerate and other sources. Retail transactions provide fewer units of foreign currency per dollar.

Country	U.S. $ equiv. Mon.	U.S. $ equiv. Fri.	Currency per U.S. $ Mon.	Currency per U.S. $ Fri.
Argentina (Peso)	1.01	1.01	.99	.99
Australia (Dollar)	.6797	.6813	1.4712	1.4678
Austria (Schilling)	.08219	.08255	12.17	12.11
Bahrain (Dinar)	2.6522	2.6522	.3771	.3771
Belgium (Franc)	.02805	.02853	35.65	35.05
Brazil (Cruzeiro)	.0000176	.0000176	56742.03	56706.03
Britain (Pound)	1.4780	1.4824	.6766	.6746
Canada (Dollar)	.7825	.7822	1.2780	1.2785
Chile (Peso)	.002548	.002546	392.42	392.82
China (Renminbi)	.174856	.174856	5.7190	5.7190
Colombia (Peso)	.001486	.001488	672.97	671.99
Denmark (Krone)	.1489	.1521	6.7152	6.5761
Finland (Markka)	.17254	.17575	5.7957	5.6898
France (Franc)	.16942	.17084	5.9025	5.8535
Germany (Mark)	.5785	c.5811	1.7285	c1.7209
Greece (Drachma)	.004239	.004256	235.90	234.95
Hong Kong (Dollar)	.12882	.12895	7.7630	7.7550
Hungary (Forint)	.0106293	.0106838	94.0800	93.6000
India (Rupee)	.03211	.03211	31.14	31.14
Indonesia (Rupiah)	.0004780	.0004778	2092.01	2093.01
Ireland (Punt)	1.3957	1.4224	.7165	.7030
Israel (Shekel)	.3642	.3642	2.7455	2.7455
Italy (Lira)	.0006302	.0006390	1586.77	1564.92
Japan (Yen)	.009137	.009109	109.45	109.78
Jordan (Dinar)	1.4620	1.4661	.6840	.6821
Kuwait (Dinar)	3.3162	3.3190	.3016	.3013
Lebanon (Pound)	.000578	.000578	1730.50	1730.00
Malaysia (Ringgit)	.3885	.3884	2.5740	2.5745
Malta (Lira)	2.5641	2.5907	.3900	.3860
Mexico (Peso)	.3196420	.3205128	3.1285	3.1200
Netherland (Guilder)	.5143	.5229	1.9442	1.9124
New Zealand (Dollar)	.5495	.5490	1.8198	1.8215
Norway (Krone)	.1356	.1383	7.3746	7.2327
Pakistan (Rupee)	.0369	.0370	27.08	27.05
Peru (New Sol)	.4984	.5003	2.01	2.00
Philippines (Peso)	.03697	.03713	27.05	26.93
Poland (Zloty)	.00005785	.00005818	17285.00	17187.00
Portugal (Escudo)	.006042	.006153	165.50	162.53
Saudi Arabia (Riyal)	.26664	.26665	3.7504	3.7503
Singapore (Dollar)	.6147	.6144	1.6268	1.6275
Slovak Rep. (Koruna)	.0337382	.0340368	29.6400	29.3800
South Korea (Won)	.0012421	.0012432	805.10	804.40
Spain (Peseta)	.007528	.007672	132.84	130.35
Sweden (Krona)	.1248	.1268	8.0159	7.8884
Switzerland (Franc)	.6542	.6532	1.5285	1.5310
Taiwan (Dollar)	.038008	.038095	26.31	26.25
Thailand (Baht)	.03939	.03946	25.39	25.35
Turkey (Lira)	.0000908	.0000914	11016.00	10940.00
United Arab (Dirham)	.2723	.2723	3.6725	3.6725
Uruguay (New Peso)	.245398	.249066	4.08	4.02
Venezuela (Bolivar)	.01119	.01120	89.34	89.29
SDR	1.37825	1.38539	.72556	.72182
ECU	1.12900	1.14740	. . .	. . .

Special Drawing Rights (SDR) are based on exchange rates for the U.S., German, British, French and Japanese currencies. Source: International Monetary Fund.
European Currency Unit (ECU) is based on a basket of community currencies.
c-Corrected

SOURCE: Reprinted by permission of *The Wall Street Journal,* © Dow Jones & Company, Inc., 1993. All rights reserved worldwide.

would not face this exposure. The risk would instead be shifted to the British importer.

POLITICAL RISK

Another type of risk faced by an international company is **political risk.** Governments often affect business operations within their borders through special regulations that affect only foreign firms. The government can expropriate, or seize, foreign assets, as was done in Libya after its 1969 revolution. Even if a firm's assets are not seized, its ability to make investments or to repatriate profits back to its home country may be limited, as in India. Political risk should therefore be recognized in all foreign investment decisions.

SUMMARY

Section 1-1: Financial Management and the Market Economy

What is financial management?

■ Financial management involves decision making. Managers must decide both how the firm should invest in assets in order to produce goods and services and how the firm's asset investments should be financed.

How does the market economy foster the goals of our society?

■ Every society must set economic goals and determine how to achieve those goals. The primary goal of a free-market society is to maximize consumer satisfaction by allowing individuals, rather than governments, to freely select the goods and services they desire.

■ Individual economic decisions produce the best distribution of productive resources and the highest level of satisfaction for individual members of society, which in turn lead to the maximization of overall welfare for the society.

■ Pursuit of self-interest does not necessarily imply opportunistic behavior. Opportunistic behavior reduces the effectiveness of the free-market system.

Section 1-2: The Firm and Its Legal Forms

Why do business firms exist?

■ The market system allocates resources to those who produce the goods and services most desired by consumers. In a sophisticated economy, complex productive activities are managed within complex business organizations, which must be of sufficient size and sophistication to survive in a competitive environment.

Why are firms organized in different legal forms?

■ Business organizations, which can be viewed as collections of contracts among the parties involved in the business, take one of three legal forms: proprietorship, partnership, or corporation—each with its own advantages and disadvantages. These forms differ in terms of owners' liability, economic lifetimes, tax treatments, ease of formation, and ability to raise funds.

■ Although proprietorships are the most common form of business organization, corporations are dominant in terms of size and impact on our economy.

Section 1-3: Financial Securities and Financial Markets

Why do individuals and businesses participate in financial markets?

■ Corporations issue financial securities to investors in return for capital.

■ Financial securities are traded in two markets. Primary markets involve the creation of securities by firms and their issuance to investors. Secondary markets involve the trading of existing securities among investors. Although the firm is usually not involved in secondary markets, the price at which its securities trade is important to the firm's managers and stockholders.

- Depending on investors' needs, they can contribute capital to the firm through different forms of financial securities, each with its own risks and rewards. When buying equity securities, stockholders expect benefits from the dividends and capital gains on their stock. When buying a company's bonds, the bondholders expect interest payments and capital gains on their securities.

- Bondholders can expect a fixed interest payment, but stockholders cannot be assured of dividends.

Section 1-4: The Goal of Financial Management

What are the goals of financial management?

- For a corporation to act in the best interests of its owners, managers need a framework for making financial decisions. This framework is the focus of financial management.

- There are many potential goals for managers because there are numerous stakeholders in the firm, such as workers, managers, customers, suppliers, and government. However, the goal that benefits society most is maximizing stockholder welfare.

- The stockholder is the residual risk bearer, which means that the stockholder receives benefits only if the business firm efficiently produces goods and services desired by society's members. Maximizing the residual payment to the common stockholders fosters productive and efficient firms and advances the welfare of society.

Section 1-5: International Dimensions of Business

Why should firms consider operating internationally?

- Today, firms have the ability to seek out profitable opportunities not only in their domestic markets but also throughout the world.

- By seeking out and exploiting imperfections in various product, labor, technological, and commodity markets, the firm can better serve the interests of its owners.

- In taking advantage of these imperfections, however, firms also take on substantial exchange rate and political risks.

QUESTIONS

1. What is the driving force of a capitalistic society? How does this force guide society's production and distribution decisions?

2. How does a capitalist society encourage corporate decision makers to act in a manner that increases social welfare?

3. How does opportunism differ from self-interest? What effects does opportunistic behavior have on economic efficiency?

4. Why do firms exist?

5. How do the three organizational forms of business differ in their ability to raise capital?

6. What important functions do financial markets perform for the corporation?

7. In a meeting, a colleague states that secondary markets are unimportant to

your firm because the firm doesn't raise capital in them. How would you respond to this statement?

8. How do equity and debt securities differ?

9. Can we say that a firm's debt holders are also its residual risk bearers? Why or why not?

10. What is the goal of financial management? How does this goal conflict with or support the welfare of society as a whole?

11. What groups other than stockholders might managers seek to benefit? What effect does satisfying the goals of those other groups have on the welfare of society as a whole?

12. If ownership is not an important concept in the contract theory of the firm, then what role do stockholders play?

13. What rewards should the firm's stakeholders (other than the stockholders) expect?

14. What is the rationale for government to limit the ability of managers to maximize stockholder welfare?

15. What motivates firms to operate on an international basis?

16. What risks do firms face in the international environment?

PROBLEMS

1. Farrimore Machine Tools has sold a drill press to a French firm, Allouin S.A., and expects to be paid FFr 1,053,000 in 60 days. The current exchange rate is $0.1568/FFr. Farrimore's foreign exchange manager estimates that in 60 days the exchange rate will be between $0.16110/FFr and $0.1505/FFr.

   a. If the exchange rate remains at its current level, what will the dollar revenues from the sale of the drill press be to Farrimore?

   b. What is the range of dollar revenues that Farrimore can expect to receive given its estimates of future exchange rates?

2. Magenta Notions imports handmade art and collectibles from around the world. It has contracted to receive a shipment of decorative masks from the Hassan Trading Company, Ltd., of Amman, Jordan. Mr. Hassan, the owner of this company, has insisted that the import contract be valued in the Jordanian currency, the dinar (JD). The contract thus has a value of JD 58,000 and must be paid in 45 days. Susan Cloud, the chief financial officer of Magenta, is very concerned about the dinar payment because of possible changes in the $/JD exchange rate. At the current exchange rate of $1.4682/JD, the contract would require Magenta to pay $85,155.60 to obtain the dinar to satisfy its obligation. Ms. Cloud must choose between two conflicting estimates provided by the two banks Magenta uses in its import operations.

   a. Traviller National Bankcorp advises Ms. Cloud that the dinar should appreciate relative to the dollar to $1.4754/JD and that she should therefore not be concerned about her exposure. Is this good advice? How much would Magenta have to pay in dollars to satisfy its obligations if this estimate is correct?

b. Southwest Bankcorp estimates that the rate should change to $1.4130/JD and also says that Ms. Cloud should not be concerned about Magenta's exposure. If Southwest's estimate is accurate, how much would Magenta have to pay in dollars to satisfy its obligations?

c. Given the two conflicting estimates of the value of the dinar in 45 days, what is the range of possible dollar payments faced by Magenta?

SUGGESTED ADDITIONAL READINGS

Bear, L. A., and R. M. Bear. *Free Markets, Finance, Ethics, and Law*. Englewood Cliffs, NJ: Prentice-Hall, 1994.

Coase, R. H. *The Firm, the Market and the Law*. Chicago: University of Chicago Press, 1988.

Easterbrook, F. H., and D. R. Fischel. "Limited Liability and the Corporation." *University of Chicago Law Review* 52 (1985): 89–117.

Eiteman, David K., Arthur I. Stonehill, and Michael H. Moffett. *Multinational Business Finance*, 6th ed. New York: Addison-Wesley Publishing Company, 1992.

Friedman, Milton, and Rose Friedman. *Free to Choose*. San Diego: Harcourt Brace Jovanovich, 1980.

Kirzner, Israel M. *Discovery and the Capitalist Process*. Chicago: University of Chicago Press, 1985.

Putterman, L., ed. *The Economic Nature of the Firm: A Reader*. Cambridge: Cambridge University Press, 1986.

Shapiro, Alan C. *Multinational Financial Management*, 4th ed. Boston: Allyn & Bacon, 1992.

Williamson, O. E. *The Economic Institutions of Capitalism*. New York: Free Press, 1985.

TWO   MAXIMIZING STOCKHOLDERS' WELFARE

The truth is, being successful at marketing or product development or manufacturing isn't enough. When your primary constituents, your shareholders, make an investment in your company, they want to build appreciation in the stock price and dividend. That's their criteria for buying it. And if chief executives don't understand what creates that movement, they won't get the job done.

—William Smithburg
CEO, Quaker Oats
Enterprise, *April 1993*

In Chapter 1 we stated that managers should make decisions that maximize stockholders' welfare. The firm, in seeking the welfare of the stockholders, also benefits society through the efficient production of goods and services. In this chapter we continue this discussion by answering the following questions:

- What is the value of a firm?

- How does the firm create wealth for its owners?

- How do accounting profits and cash flows differ?

- How are cash flows and the firm's stock price related?

- What happens if the interests of the managers and the stockholders diverge?

- Why is the corporation the dominant form of business organization?

- How does the decision-making process within corporations foster stockholder welfare?

2-1

CORPORATE WEALTH-INCREASING ACTIVITIES AND OWNERS' WEALTH

Our discussion of maximizing shareholders' wealth begins with an examination of a firm's value. In particular, we distinguish between firm value determined from accounting balance sheets and firm value implied by the firm's economic balance sheet. Understanding this distinction and associated concepts of value is critical to an appreciation of the process by which a firm creates wealth for its owners.

What Is Firm Value?

In understanding what firm value is, we must carefully distinguish between two ways of examining the firm's assets and liabilities: the accounting or book-value balance sheet and the economic or market-value balance sheet.

THE ACCOUNTING BALANCE SHEET

Managers and analysts often look at a firm's accounting statements to determine its worth. The firm's assets and the claims against those assets are recorded on the **accounting balance sheet** of the company using standard accounting principles. Indeed, one of the most fundamental accounting rules is that the balance sheet must balance. The assets of the firm must equal the claims against the assets, with these claims consisting of borrowed funds (debt) and the owners' claims to the remainder (equity).

ACCOUNTING BALANCE SHEET

| ASSETS | DEBT |
| | EQUITY |

Managers and investors must realize that book values are not always the same as market values. A machine could have a book value of only $5,000, and yet the firm may be able to sell it in the marketplace for $15,000.

THE ECONOMIC BALANCE SHEET

When we consider the *market values* of the assets and claims, rather than their accounting values, the result is a market-value balance sheet, also called an **economic balance sheet.** To understand this balance sheet and how a firm can create wealth for its stockholders, we must first understand the distinction between two values that assets can have: value *in exchange* and value *in use.* The **value in exchange** is the price at which an asset can be transferred from one owner to another and is loosely known as the asset's replacement value. Assets also have a **value in use** to the firm. This is the benefit that a firm obtains from the *use* of the asset. If a firm owns this asset, the value of the asset *to the firm* includes not only the asset's value in exchange but also the extra benefits the firm gets from its use. This extra value varies with the efficiency with which the managers of the firm use the asset. The extra value is the **wealth (W)** created by the firm:

$$\text{Wealth created } (W) = \text{value in use} - \text{value in exchange} \qquad (2\text{-}1)$$

KEY CONCEPT   The value added by the firm's use of its assets represents the wealth created by the firm.

This wealth created by the use of the asset is often referred to as the firm's **economic rents** and is a part of the firm's total assets.

Consider a dump truck that has a value in exchange of $70,000. Few of us would own a dump truck because it would not be useful in our work. However, a construction company probably could use the dump truck on jobs. It would conclude that the value added by the use of the dump truck exceeds what the company would have to pay to obtain it. Someone who might inherit a dump truck would find that its value in use is less than the going value in exchange and would benefit by selling the dump truck to the construction company, where the value in use exceeds the value in exchange. Thus, in deciding to obtain or dispose of an asset, one must determine not just the asset's value in exchange—its replacement value—but also the asset's value in use based on who is using it.

The market values of the assets (including the wealth created) and the claims on those assets are listed in the economic balance sheet.

ECONOMIC BALANCE SHEET			
EXCHANGE VALUE OF ASSETS:	A	MARKET VALUE OF DEBT:	D
WEALTH CREATED:	W	MARKET VALUE OF EQUITY:	E

In a **claims definition** of firm value, the market value of a firm, V, is the market value of the claims against the assets. Thus,

$$V = D + E \qquad (2\text{-}2)$$

where D and E are the market values of the debt and equity, respectively.

In an **assets definition** of firm value, the firm's market value is the value of the firm's total assets. However, the composition of the assets in the economic balance sheet is fundamentally different from what is normally seen in an accounting balance sheet. In an economic sense, there are two types of assets. The first type are the productive assets of the firm, such as plant, equipment, patents, and other income-producing assets. The second type is the wealth created by the firm. Thus, when we define the firm's market value using the assets approach, we must consider not only the market values of the firm's productive assets but also the wealth created by the firm's use of those assets. We have

$$V = A + W \tag{2-3}$$

where A is the market value of the firm's productive assets and, as seen earlier, W is the wealth created by the firm.

Both the assets and the claims definitions should give the same firm value, so that

$$D + E = A + W = V \tag{2-4}$$

For a publicly traded firm, the market values of its debt and equity can be readily determined from published data. However, it is often difficult to determine the market value of a firm's productive assets or its wealth created. For this reason, the claims definition is more commonly used in finance and, unless it is otherwise explicitly mentioned, we will use the claims definition when determining firm value.

Wealth Created and Changes in Stockholders' Wealth

Managers, through their investment decisions, can increase the value of their firm. We now want to use an example to develop the link between changes in firm value and increases in stockholders' wealth.

Assume that Rheinhold Plastics raises $600,000 in equity to build a new plant to make plastic bags. If the entire proceeds are used to build the new plant, then the firm's book-value balance sheet looks like this:

RHEINHOLD'S ACCOUNTING BALANCE SHEET			
PRODUCTIVE ASSETS:	$600,000	EQUITY:	$600,000
TOTAL ASSETS:	$600,000	TOTAL CLAIMS:	$600,000

However, this balance sheet does not consider the wealth created by the use of the new plant. Although the plant's value in exchange is $600,000, this value does not take into account the use that Rheinhold makes of the plant. Assume that by efficiently using its assets, Rheinhold creates $100,000 in wealth. Rheinhold's economic balance sheet can then be represented as follows:

RHEINHOLD'S ECONOMIC BALANCE SHEET			
PRODUCTIVE ASSETS:	$600,000	EQUITY:	$700,000
WEALTH CREATED:	$100,000		
TOTAL ASSETS:	$700,000	TOTAL CLAIMS:	$700,000

If the total asset value for Rheinhold is $700,000, then the value of the claims must also equal $700,000. Thus Rheinhold's equity increases to $700,000, and the additional wealth created ($100,000) accrues directly to the stockholders through an increase in the market price of the stock. In well-functioning capital markets, the owners can "convert" corporate wealth into personal wealth by selling the equity. Anything that the firm does to increase its wealth increases the market value of the stock and hence stockholders' wealth. We have thus demonstrated a fundamental concept.

KEY CONCEPT   The wealth created by the firm is reflected in the market value of the equity. The equity markets convert the wealth created by the firm into increases in stockholders' personal wealth.

If Rheinhold had used some debt financing, the market value of the firm would be the value of the debt and equity. As we will see in Chapter 15, the basic results do not change.

Managers, working on behalf of the shareholders, make decisions that increase firm value. If the value of a firm's debt does not substantially change, then additional wealth accrues to the equityholders. Maximizing the firm value also increases shareholder wealth through changes in the stock price.

2-2
STOCKHOLDER WELFARE AND STOCK PRICES

For owners, their stock is typically the only connection they have with the corporation. Stockholders prosper and are willing to obtain or retain ownership of the stock only if they expect to receive adequate benefits from doing so. Managers affect this residual payment when their investment and financing decisions create additional wealth and this additional wealth is reflected in the stock price. This leads to the question, What affects the firm's stock price?

Accounting Profits   Profit maximization or earnings maximization is often offered as the firm's appropriate objective in maximizing the stock price. However, decisions based on accounting profits may not benefit the stockholders for two reasons.

First, profits or earnings are accounting measures that may or may not reflect the firm's economic realities. Different accounting conventions permit flexibility in reporting firms' activities; a different profit picture can emerge depending on which accounting methods are used. A classic example of how a few accounting adjustments can change the profits of a company is provided by USX's (formerly U.S. Steel) surprising turnaround.

In 1983 USX was the biggest money loser among the *Fortune* 500 companies, with a loss of $1.2 billion. Yet in 1984 the company showed $493 million in profits and was ranked 37 on the *Fortune* 500 list in terms of profitability. This phenomenal performance did not come about because of some miraculous recovery in the steel business. Nor were these profits made because of any changes in the oil industry, USX's biggest product line since it acquired Marathon Oil in 1982. Instead, these earnings were generated by some complicated accounting changes.

According to an analyst's calculations, only $157 million of the profits came from operations. The remaining earnings "can be attributed to a gallimaufry [hodgepodge] of nonoperating items, from asset sales to accounting adjustments."[1] According to him, USX took in $265 million before taxes by selling coal oil properties, two barge lines, and other assets. By trimming inventories and changing accounting methods, the company generated even more profits. In addition, by changing its actuarial assumptions and interest rate forecasts, it was able to change the amount it put into its pension funds. Finally, it profited by repurchasing old debt at less than its book value.

The following highlight examines accounting procedures that can be used to manipulate profits.

---

[1] Robert E. Norton, in "The Dollar Dampens the Profit Party" by Myron Magnet, *Fortune*, April 29, 1985, p. 254.

INCREASING PROFITS WITH INNOVATIVE ACCOUNTING

Profits, as we have seen, are the result of accounting conventions. The following are some entirely legal "strategies" that companies can use to boost profits independent of whether or not the company is doing well.

1. Inventory accounting. *With LIFO (last in–first out) accounting, profit is defined as sales less the cost of the most recent inventory. If inventories are reduced, profits become sales less the cost of older inventory. During periods of rising costs, inventory reductions can boost profits. For example, Texaco cut inventories by 16% when oil prices were at their peak. The LIFO "cushion" amounted to $454 million. Thus what would have been a reduction in net income turned out to be a small profit.*

2. Foreign transactions. *Recent changes in accounting rules allow a firm with foreign currency transactions to recast them retroactively. A major firm that had lagging domestic profits used its overseas reports for four years to increase its old profits per share of $6.67 to a higher $7.08 per share.*

3. Pension obligations. *Major corporations have to spend large sums of money on pension plans, the sums payable to the company's retired employees. One way to boost profits is to increase the assumed rate of return on the firm's pension fund investments. Under current accounting rules, profits increase because the firm has to set aside a smaller portion of its earnings to make the required retirement payments.*

4. Equity accounting. *Equity accounting rules allow a parent firm to include in its earnings the earnings of other firms that are more than 20% owned by it. This increases the parent's reportable earnings. Teledyne, for example, in 1983 reported $19.96 per share in profits, but a close examination revealed that $3.49 of this was from equity accounting—clearly not real earnings because there was no cash flow to the parent.*

5. Swapping debt for stock. *If the price of a corporation's bonds is far less than the bonds' face value, the company can swap the bonds for stock and, under standard accounting rules, show a profit. USX, for example, swapped $78 million in debt for 5 million shares of common stock and thus showed a profit.*

The second reason that decisions based on accounting profits may not benefit stockholders is that even if accounting profits are not distorted by accounting maneuvers, these profits cannot capture all the elements of value. Accounting rules focus at best on values in exchange and do not capture the creation of economic rents. In general, accountants, who must develop objective information to be used in controlling the firm and reporting on its performance, do not estimate the economic rents created by managerial decisions. However, these economic rents are taken into account in the stock market where the price of the stock does reflect the quality of managerial decisions.

KEY CONCEPT   The markets look at equity values in a unique way that is not captured by accounting information alone.

The Meaning of Cash Flow   The markets, when placing a value on equity, seek to develop an estimate of the wealth-creating potential of a firm. It looks not at accounting profits but at **cash flow,** which is the actual funds the firm has available for productive uses. The cash flow that the firm is expected to produce in the future determines the economic rents available to the firm's owners. We introduce this concept with a simple example.

Suppose that Graebert Company's financial manager must choose between two decisions regarding its copper-rich land. Alternative A calls for Graebert Corporation to sell the rights to copper mining on its land to Cupola, Inc., for $50 million in cash. The rights will expire in 30 years, and Graebert must repair the environmental damage caused by its strip-mining operation at an estimated cost of $51 million. Thus, rather than a profit, the loss for this alternative is $1 million. The second alternative, B, is for Graebert to buy the strip-mining equipment for $75 million today, do its own mining, and then end up with $76 million in 30 years after the cleanup costs have been paid. Because Graebert has no experience in strip mining, this alternative is very risky. The profit for this alternative is $1 million.

If the criterion for the decision is profits, alternative B is a clear winner because a profit of $1 million appears to be much better than a loss of $1 million. Yet this decision is incorrect; alternative A would benefit the stockholders more. When we focus on profits, the timing of the benefits to Graebert is not considered. Suppose that Graebert could earn 6% on its investments. Then the $50 million it would earn under alternative A (even though it does not represent a profit) could be invested at that interest rate and increase to over $287 million in 30 years. Such an investment possibility does not exist with alternative B. The significant cash flow generated under alternative A is totally disregarded by focusing on profits. Stockholders would be better off with alternative A because the cash flow from this alternative would increase their wealth. In addition, alternative B is risky, and there is no way to incorporate risk into the profit-based criterion. Thus profit-based decisions can work against the best interests of the firm's owners—the stockholders.

This discussion should not be interpreted to mean that management should not seek profits. All firms hope to make a profit. But profits can't pay bills! What determines the market value of the firm's stock is not profits per se, but cash flow. The firm's cash flow can be reinvested to increase the firm's value. Profits, on the other hand, say little about the firm's ability to take advantage of new investment opportunities.

Because of the importance of cash flow in finance, we should discuss one of the major reasons why accounting income and cash flows differ. Investment decisions create a noncash expense called **depreciation,** which is an allocation of the historical cost of an asset over its **economic life,** the period over which it is expected to provide benefits to its owner. Depreciation is best understood through an example. Assume that a firm buys a machine that will last for seven years. Initially, the firm spends a large sum of money to acquire the machine, and it will not have to spend any more on it until the end of year 7, when suddenly the machine has to be replaced. It is clearly foolish to assume that the company is making a handsome profit in years 1 through 6 and incurring a massive loss in year 7.

The truth is that the machine is not used up only in year 7; it is being used up all the time. This usage must be recognized every year, and depreciation rules stipulate the means for calculating this usage. Profits less depreciation are "true" profits, and the Internal Revenue Service (IRS) taxes the company on this amount. Thus taxable income equals profits less depreciation. What is left after the IRS has taken its cut is **net profits after taxes,** or **net income.** But if depreciation is excluded purely for tax considerations (to determine tax payable) and it is not really a dollar amount paid out, the actual cash flow to the firm can be approximated as

Cash flow = net income + depreciation (2-5)

This useful and simple definition of cash flow will be used throughout the book; however, it is an approximation because it assumes that all transactions are based on cash. In Chapter 3 we develop a cash flow statement that allows us to calculate a company's cash flow more precisely. Figure 2-1 illustrates the concepts of cash

FIGURE 2 - 1
*Roscoe's profits and
cash flow*

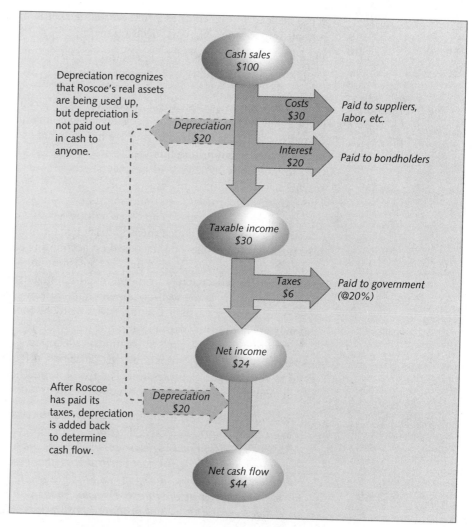

flow using the example of Roscoe Company. Out of the $100 in cash sales that Roscoe generates, it pays out $30 to the suppliers of raw materials (steel, gas, electricity, etc.). It then recognizes a depreciation of $20 because IRS rules allow firms to subtract this amount before calculating its taxes. Roscoe then pays $20 to its bondholders in the form of interest; the remaining $30 is "taxable income." If a 20% tax rate is assumed for convenience, the IRS will claim $6 in taxes, and the firm will have a net income of $24. This, plus the $20 "set aside" for depreciation, amounts to a total of $44 in cash flow—dollars actually available for the firm to do with as it pleases. Notice that the $44 in cash flow for Roscoe recognizes profits and then goes further in identifying the firm's available resources. The net cash flow is greater than the net income because depreciation acts as a **tax shield,** which reduces taxable income and thus taxes.

Managerial decisions affect the three key attributes of a firm's well-being: the magnitude and timing of the cash flows and the riskiness of those flows. A firm's success is measured by the value that investors place on the combination of the cash flow's timing and magnitude and the associated risk. Decisions viewed favorably by investors will increase demand for the company's stock. This, in turn, causes stock prices, and hence shareholder wealth, to rise. Successful management decisions lead to higher stock prices in the marketplace, and so "market values" become important to financial decision making.

KEY CONCEPT

The value of the firm's stock is determined by how managerial decisions affect the magnitude, timing, and risk of the firm's cash flow.

The Informational Content of Accounting Numbers

An important issue remains. If accounting numbers are not cash flows, of what use are they in making financial decisions or in controlling the firm? The attitudes of many individuals involved in the firm indicate that accounting numbers do matter. Managers' actions and analysts' comments often suggest that the accounting data in income statements and balance sheets provide useful information to the marketplace. Corporate managers openly acknowledge that they are concerned about the firm's earnings, and financial publications such as *The Wall Street Journal* and *Barron's* routinely report accounting earnings. Investment bankers and "takeover artists" often couch their discussion in terms of earnings, and lawmakers take positions on business policy based on accounting earnings data.

This emphasis on accounting data is consistent with the belief that accounting information, as reflected in a firm's financial statements, can reflect the firm's true economic position. Is the well-documented interest in accounting earnings an expression of investor naiveté? Can investors really be fooled by managerial actions that increase accounting earnings but not real wealth?

Accounting numbers, such as earnings, reflect past performance and thus cannot be the basis for wealth-maximizing decisions, a fact that is openly acknowledged by the accounting profession. The Accounting Principles Board (APB), in its APB Statement No. 4, dated October 1970, stated:

> *Financial accounting information is produced for certain purposes by the use of conventional principles. . . . The information they contain describes the past, while decision making is oriented towards the future. A record of past events and a knowledge of past position and changes in position, however, help users evaluate prior decisions and the information is also a starting point for users in predicting the future. Decision makers should not assume, however, that the conditions that produced past results will necessarily continue in the future.*

While recognizing that historical information is not sufficient for making economic decisions, this opinion implicitly states that accounting statements do contain useful information. Empirical evidence clearly indicates that accounting earnings are correlated with cash flows. An increase in earnings is generally associated with an increase in cash flows, whereas a decrease in earnings is generally associated with a decrease in cash flows. Thus earnings information can be a *proxy* for information about cash flows, and earnings changes do say something about changes in cash flows.

Extending this line of reasoning, we should expect earnings increases to be associated with stock price increases. Is this relationship, in fact, observed? Ball and Brown studied whether accounting earnings are empirically related to stock prices.[2] They argued that if earnings announcements have an "informational content," then they should affect stock prices and hence the returns realized by investors. Their tests indicate that the larger the increase in annual earnings is, the larger the associated stock price increase will be. This same relationship was documented

[2]R. J. Ball and P. Brown, "An Empirical Evaluation of Accounting Income Numbers," *Journal of Accounting Research* 6 (Autumn 1968): 159–178.

in subsequent studies both in the United States and abroad. Indeed, accounting numbers such as earnings do provide useful information to the market.[3]

THE AGENCY RELATIONSHIP: AN IMPEDIMENT TO STOCKHOLDER WEALTH MAXIMIZATION

In many modern corporations that have publicly traded stock, the managers and the owners are not necessarily the same parties. You can live in Newport, Rhode Island, and invest in Boeing Company stock and not be directly involved in the daily management of the company's operations. Rather, the management of Boeing in Seattle, Washington, runs the business day to day for you. Managers are paid salaries and given other benefits by the company to make decisions on behalf of the firm's owners. When viewed in this light, the manager is really an **agent** acting on behalf of the **principal** (equityholder). This relationship between the principal and the agent is called the **agency relationship.**

Shareholders expect managers to make decisions that are in the shareholders' best interest. However, managers who follow their own self-interest may seek to improve their own welfare and not that of the shareholders. Adam Smith was aware of this potential impediment to the smooth workings of the "invisible hand":

> *Like the stewards of a rich man, they [managers] are apt to consider attention to small matters as not for their master's honour, and very easily give themselves a dispensation from having it. Negligence and profusion, therefore, must always prevail, more or less, in the management of the affairs of such a company.*[4]

This **agency problem** is clearly undesirable because it leads to suboptimal decisions and inefficient allocation of resources. The resulting inefficiencies, called **agency costs,** lower the firm's value. Understanding the agency relationship is the first step in designing procedures that can lower these agency costs and thereby benefit all participants in the business organization. Agency theory can also help us better understand why the different organizational forms of business exist and help in the design of contracts best suited for specific business transactions.

Sources of Agency Costs

Agency costs have several sources. Managers clearly do not work in the shareholders' best interests out of pure altruism; they expect to be compensated. Although the **pecuniary benefits** (salary, retirement benefits, bonuses, etc.) that managers can expect are stipulated in their employment contracts, there are many **nonpecuniary benefits** (items that increase managerial prestige or lifestyle) that managers can give themselves because of the discretionary power vested in them. Because managers have some control over both their pecuniary and nonpecuniary benefits, wealth can leak from the firm to its managers. Some sources of these leaks are listed here.

- **Excessive perquisites.** Agents can give themselves extra "perks" such as working less (shirking), taking extended three-martini lunch breaks, or using the company's jet to fly to the Superbowl for "public relations" purposes.

- **Informational asymmetry.** The agent, who is "an insider," often possesses information that is not available to the principals. In fact, companies usually do

[3] For more details on this issue, the reader is referred to Chapter 3 of Ross L. Watts and Jerold L. Zimmerman, *Positive Accounting Theory* (Englewood Cliffs, NJ: Prentice-Hall, 1986).

[4] Adam Smith, *The Wealth of Nations*, 1776 (New York: Modern Library, 1937), p. 700.

not reveal all their future plans lest this information aid its competitors. For example, the entire General Motors Saturn project was shrouded in secrecy; the marketplace and even the stockholders knew little about this $2 billion project. Though often necessary, informational asymmetry can give managers a certain degree of protection by making it more difficult for the principals to monitor the agents. Managers may thus be able to "get away with" some decisions that the principals might have opposed had they known all the facts.

- **Short horizons.** Although the firm may have an indefinite life, the manager's claim on the firm is restricted to his or her tenure with the firm. Managers therefore prefer to invest in projects that will have near-term payoffs, even though they may not be as good for the firm as other projects with more distant payoffs that would not benefit the managers. This problem becomes even more serious when the firm offers managers incentives to increase short-term, say year-end, profits.

- **Human capital expropriation.** When a company decides to spend money on training and management development programs, it is in fact increasing its investment in its human capital. Clearly, firms do this in the expectation that these costs will be more than offset by increased managerial efficiency and productivity gains. But what prevents a manager from jumping ship and working with a competing firm at a higher wage? The competing firm does not have to pay for the training and so may be willing to offer a higher salary. Thus the firm that has invested in employee training has in effect trained its competitors. In recent years, this problem has been especially acute in the high-tech industry.

- **Risk aversion.** Managers with a fixed salary are hesitant to take on good but risky projects. If the project succeeds, the manager's fixed salary will not allow him to participate in the "upside." If the project is unsuccessful, the manager may lose his job. Risk-averse managers therefore do not have incentives to increase the shareholders' wealth by investing in risky projects, and this agency cost lowers the firm's value.

- **Overretention.** Managers are hesitant to increase dividends; instead, they prefer to keep these resources in the firm to increase the firm's liquidity and thereby decrease the probability of bankruptcy. The incentive to overretain earnings is the threat of job loss if the firm fails. To the extent that this excessive retention is driven by managerial self-interest, it may not be in the firm's best interests and leads to agency losses.

Who Bears the Agency Costs?

Having seen how agency costs can arise, we want to know the specific components of agency costs. However, we must first ask who bears these agency costs. The answer to this question is the key insight provided by the modern theory of agency.

If the principals can, on average, assess the impact of agency costs on their future wealth, they will take this into account in determining the benefits the agent will receive when they employ his or her services. For example, a manager who has a reputation for acting consistently in the firm's best interests can command a higher wage than does one who consumes excessive corporate perquisites. Thus managers "pay" indirectly for their tendency to act in their own interests. Even as managers climb the corporate ladder in their own firms, they must rely on past performance; each manager's reputation plays an undeniable role in shaping future rewards. Contrary to the idea that the agent can "get away with" self-serving decisions, agency theory argues that the agent pays a price for the propensity to exploit the principal. The agent, *and not the principal,* generally bears the cost of the agency relationship.

KEY CONCEPT

Agency costs are generally borne by the agent if, on average, the principal can estimate the magnitude of the agency costs.

Of course, all agency costs are not necessarily borne by the agent. Nevertheless, it is a useful concept that agents will "pay for" their self-serving behavior. Consider agency costs in the context of the value of financial securities. Because investors price securities to reflect the potential for agency costs, the existence of these costs lowers the market value. If managers are expected to act in their own interest, stockholders will pay less for equity claims. Similarly, if bondholders anticipate behavior that is not in their best interests, they too will refuse to bear the cost of the agency relationship and will pay less for the debt securities. With lower market values for the claims, firm value—previously defined as the value of the claims against the firm—is lowered. If the principal does not bear the agency costs, then they are passed back to the manager because the debt and equity securities that he or she can issue command a lower price. If the manager's rewards depend on the firm's value, he or she will suffer a loss. It is therefore in the best interests of both the agent and the principal to write contracts that minimize the total costs of the agency relationship, so that firm values are maximized and total agency costs are minimized.

The Components of Agency Costs

With an understanding of who bears the agency costs, we now ask: What are these agency costs? Exactly how are they incurred?

Shareholders attempt to minimize the incentives available to the manager to improve his or her own condition. Writing contracts that clearly stipulate what the manager can and cannot do is an obvious solution to the agency problem. In addition to the **legal and administrative costs** of writing such detailed contracts, there are **enforcement costs** related to these agreements. After all, what is the use of a contract that cannot be enforced? Enforcement costs arise from two sources. **Monitoring costs** are incurred to ensure that managers adhere to the terms of their employment contracts and not take excessive advantage of their perks. For example, managers can suggest that all travel and expenses be authorized by an in-house committee, thereby subjecting to scrutiny any potentially self-serving actions. **Bonding costs** are incurred by the manager to reassure the stockholders and bondholders that he or she will do only what is specified in the contract. Managers can spend considerable time and effort developing firm-specific skills that, though useful to the firm, are not in demand elsewhere. By doing this, such managers are implicitly bonding themselves to the firm. If the firm fails, their skills will not be as valuable elsewhere, so the managers have an incentive to worry about the survival of the firm. A final agency cost is the loss in firm value because of poor decisions induced by agency problems. This loss in firm value (as compared with the maximum value attainable in the absence of agency considerations) is called the **residual loss.**

Because managers bear most of the agency costs, any steps taken to reduce their magnitude will benefit managers directly through, say, higher salaries. The reader should now appreciate why we could not examine the components of agency costs before establishing that it is the agent who generally bears agency costs. Without recognizing this key idea, it would be difficult to understand the need for the agent to incur bonding costs.

SLOW BOATS IN CHINA: THE BENEFITS OF INCURRING BONDING COSTS

The concept that it can often be to one's advantage to incur bonding costs is illustrated in an interesting example from China.

Story has it that in mainland China, barges were towed along a small river by laborers on both banks of the river. These "barge pullers" were temporary labor, hired on a day-to-day basis. The workers (agents) found that it was easy to shirk on the job because it was difficult for their employers (principals) to monitor each puller carefully. Once the pulling began, it was virtually impossible to determine who was really expending energy in pulling the barge and who was just "resting on the rope." Because of this agency problem, the principals were forced to hire more and more laborers to pull their barges, and so they lowered the pullers' wages.

The pullers, recognizing that they were bearing the agency costs (through a lower wage) responded collectively by hiring "whippers" to monitor them carefully and to whip the pullers who were shirking. They paid for these whippers out of their own wages.

How can one explain this apparently strange behavior by the pullers? Recall that their wages fell because the principals could not control the agency problem (shirking) and also that the pullers bore the consequences of the agency problem. The bonding cost (wages to the whippers) that the pullers had to pay makes perfect economic sense. It is a way of lowering agency costs. Bonding lowered the agency costs, and by increasing efficiency it allowed the principals to hire fewer pullers and thereby revert to the higher original wage. To the extent that the bonding costs were lower than the lost wages, bonding was in the best interest of the pullers.

Of course, the ideal situation would be no shirking at all, to have no agency problem at all. If this had been the case, the bonding expenditures could have been avoided.

SOURCE: The basic idea underlying this discussion is contained in S. Cheung, "The Contractual Nature of the Firm," Journal of Law and Economics, April 1983, pp. 1–21. Our discussion has been adapted (with apologies to Professor Cheung) to fit the context of this chapter.

2-4

THE DOMINANCE OF THE CORPORATION: A PARADOX?

Figure 1-1 in Chapter 1 showed that in terms of size (receipts) rather than numbers, the corporation dominates U.S. business. Extending our view to an international scale, Figure 2-2 lists the 12 largest U.S. companies in terms of sales and compares their combined sales with the gross national products (GNP) of several countries. As Figure 2-2 shows, only a few countries' GNPs exceed the combined sales of the top 12 American companies. The immense size of the corporations makes their influence on the economic well-being of the country more dramatic than that of proprietorships and partnerships.

This is a surprising result when viewed from the agency costs' perspective. When going from the proprietorship to the corporate form of organization, the separation of ownership and management widens. But as the manager's proportionate ownership in the firm decreases, agency costs rise. Given these undesirable costs, why is it that corporations, which are most susceptible to agency problems, are the dominant organizational form?

Advantages of a Corporation

The answer is that although the agency costs of corporations are indeed larger than those of other forms of organizations, the advantages offered by corporations more than compensate for agency problems.

■ **Capital accumulation.** Proprietorships and partnerships may be incapable of raising the large amounts of capital necessary to obtain benefits of scale be-

FIGURE 2-2
*The Mighty
U.S. Corporation*

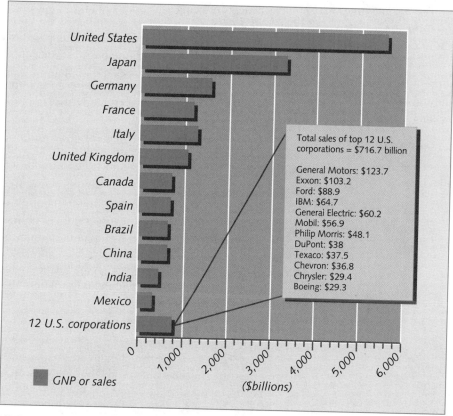

SOURCES: Corporate sales figures from *Fortune;* GNP numbers compiled from the *World Almanac* and *Facts on File World News Digest,* published by Facts on File, Inc., 1993.

cause they place all the investor's assets at risk. The limited liability feature of corporate equity makes the corporation an attractive investment and thus able to raise large amounts of capital. A corporation can raise much more capital than a proprietorship can because it has more owners with fully transferable ownership rights. Whereas partners may find it difficult to take their owner-ship interests out of the firm, owners of a publicly traded corporation can get rid of their shares at any time and, more important, incur only low transac-tions costs in doing so.

■ **Efficient risk reduction.** Even if a proprietor is very rich, he may not want to invest all of his money in one firm because of the risk. But by "putting his eggs in different baskets," he can lower the total risk. The corporate form allows investors to invest small amounts in a variety of different companies, thereby reducing their risks more efficiently. A proprietorship does not have these built-in efficiencies.

■ **Specialization.** Large businesses require many diverse skills that a single owner may not have. For example, a proprietor may be excellent in the production aspects of her firm but totally unfamiliar with finance and marketing. By hir-ing managers who specialize in these areas, a firm can increase its value. By separating ownership and management, the corporation is able to seek out managers who are knowledgeable in various functional areas and take advan-tage of their expertise.

Agency Cost-Containment Devices

The benefits of being a corporation may be substantial, but these advantages are irrelevant if the total agency costs implicit in the corporate form exceed the benefits. Each business must make this cost–benefit analysis and choose the most beneficial form of organization. Because businesses organized as corporations dominate aggregate economic activity, the advantages of the corporate structure must exceed the agency costs for them. Devices available to control agency costs may explain why the corporation continues to thrive despite the potential for severe agency problems.

Methods for containing agency costs can be classified into two categories: methods that can be instituted by and within the firm (internal control devices) and those that are outside the firm (external control devices).

- **Internal control devices** are contained within the structure of the firm. Some governance aspects, such as the formal rules under which the corporation operates, can significantly reduce the problems of owner–manager separation. Also, encouraging competition and mutual monitoring among the corporation's managers and carefully designing compensation contracts can minimize agency problems. Agency costs can be further reduced internally by the separation of the firm's management and control functions. This control device is discussed in the next section.

- **External control devices** present in the firm's environment can constrain managerial behavior. One external factor that can be highly effective in resolving agency problems is the threat of a takeover by outsiders. In addition, competitive pressures in the managerial labor market can help regulate the managers' behavior. Increasingly, firms are also responding to active institutional investors who have a substantial equity position in the firm and follow its operations carefully. Other external devices include government regulations and the threat of lawsuits (director and officer liability).

- **Corporate governance,** the administrative and legal considerations that guide and often define managers' actions, includes both internal and external control devices. Certain aspects of governance (such as the board of directors, which we examine below) are entirely firm-specific, whereas others are set by factors outside the firm—for example, state laws and legal precedents.

2-5

CORPORATE GOVERNANCE WITH MANAGERS AND DIRECTORS

The Decision-making Structure

To mitigate the effect of agency problems, the corporate decision-making structure is separated into two major functions. The **management function** consists of the development of ideas and the day-to-day running of the company. It is the responsibility of the managers hired to run the firm. When we refer to the firm's manager(s) or to management (as a noun), we usually are referring to the officers of the company, which include the chief executive officer (CEO), presidents, vice-presidents, and others. Depending on the size of the company, management can include as few as one or as many as a hundred persons. In 1991 Ford Motor Company, for example, divided its management into four groups: Office of the Chief Executive (four persons), executive vice-presidents (three), vice-presidents (27), and other officers and executives (37).[5] The **control function** consists of actions that ensure that the managers are functioning in the best interests of the stockholders. This function is the duty of the corporation's board of

[5]Ford Motor Company, *Annual Report,* 1991.

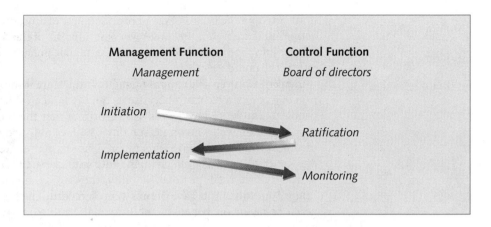

FIGURE 2-3
Management and Control Aspects of the Decision-Making Process

directors. The directors are elected by the shareholders to supervise the actions of the managers, provide advice, and veto poor management decisions. The board also has the final say in hiring and firing management personnel and in fixing the salaries and benefits packages for the senior managers. The board members are generally organized into various board committees to focus on specific issues. Ford has five board committees: Finance Committee, Executive Committee, Audit Committee, Compensation and Option Committee, and Organization Review and Nominating Committee.

SEPARATION OF MANAGEMENT AND CONTROL[6]

The two decision-making functions are carried out through the shared decision-making process of the corporation. This process consists of four sequential and interrelated activities. The interrelated nature of the decision-making process is shown in Figure 2-3.

1. **Initiation.** First, managers develop proposals for using the firm's resources and submit these proposals to the board. For example, the managers may recommend that the firm develop a new product line or expand its operations overseas.

2. **Ratification.** The board evaluates the managers' proposals and decides which proposals will actually be implemented.

3. **Implementation.** The proposals agreed upon in the ratification phase are executed by the managers.

4. **Monitoring.** The success of the company's projects is evaluated. The board makes decisions about the future direction of the firm and evaluates the managers' performance.

WHY SEPARATION OF MANAGEMENT AND CONTROL CAN LOWER AGENCY COSTS

Board members have an incentive to act in the shareholders' best interests because of their professional reputations and the threat of lawsuits from the stockholders. Moreover, board members are elected—and can be removed—by the stockholders. Because the board has to approve major decisions, the managers

[6]See also E. F. Fama and M. C. Jensen, "Agency Problems and Residual Claims," *Journal of Law and Economics,* June 1983.

must convince the board of the appropriateness of any action. The board will reject actions that are not in the long-term best interests of the residual claimants. Purely self-serving proposals brought up by the management will most likely be thrown out by the board members.

Bankers and venture capital financiers attach great importance to the composition of a company's board because its quality indicates the extent to which agency problems can be reduced. It is not surprising that the boardrooms of large companies contain well-known personalities with established reputations. Even board members who do not have direct experience in matters relating to the company's daily operations can be effective. In order to preserve their professional reputations and to reduce their personal liability, they are compelled to ask managers the "right" questions and have the answers on record. The board thus monitors managerial behavior on behalf of the principals, and to a great extent it can correct agency problems between managers and stockholders.

THE JAPANESE *KEIRETSU:* A BLENDING OF OWNERSHIP AND MANAGEMENT, OF EQUITY AND DEBT

The Japanese organizational form of keiretsu is a unique arrangement that attempts to avoid conflicts among owners, managers, and creditors. The keiretsu is a governance system that consists of several companies organized around a major bank (e.g., Sanwa, Tokai), a large trading firm (e.g., Mitsubishi, Sumitomo, Mitsui), or industrial companies (e.g., Nippon Steel, Toyota, Hitachi, and Matsushita). According to Kester, only 0.01% of Japanese companies belong to keiretsus, but these few account for approximately 25% of the total sales and paid-up capital of all Japanese corporations. Participation in a keiretsu implies extensive **reciprocal ownership** of common stock, with the members of the group owning stock in one another. For example, 20% of Mitsubishi's shares are held by others who are members of the group.† There is an implicit understanding that these reciprocally owned shares will not be sold. This understanding is strictly adhered to, thus creating a*

cadre of "stable" shareholders (or "patient" capital). On average, 33% of a Japanese company's stock is held by a financial institution (banks) and another 33% is held by other corporations.

Under the keiretsu arrangement, the stockholders' importance is diminished because the owners are stakeholders who possess a complex blend of claims against the companies in which they invest. Stakeholders may accept a below-average return on one of the claims if such acceptance can enhance the return on the overall bundle of claims. An equityholder also owns debt, and wealth transfers between the owners and the creditors lose their economic significance. In this setting, maximizing shareholder wealth may be suboptimal.

In the Japanese business concept, the firm maximizes the return on trading relationships, a concept that may be surprising to the American business manager. Japanese businesspeople believe that there is an economic value to relationships because a good relationship can lower the costs of explicit

and implicit contracting. In many situations, a manager need not worry about the possibility of opportunistic behavior on the part of a partner and, because of the implicit understanding that the shares will not be sold, a manager can make decisions based on the long-term implications of actions. Moreover, because keiretsus are organized as efficient information-sharing groups, there are fewer problems of informational asymmetry and the costs of contracting are lowered.

* Carl Kester, "Japanese Corporate Governance and the Conservation of Value in Financial Distress," Journal of Applied Corporate Finance, Summer 1991.

† It is often reported that the value of the Japanese stock markets exceeds the value of the New York Stock Exchange. This conclusion is an artifact of the reciprocal ownership of equity by Japanese companies. After one adjusts for the "double counting" that arises from cross ownership, the American equity markets are much larger than their Japanese counterparts. See K. R. French and J. M. Poterba, "Were Japanese Stock Prices Too High?" Journal of Financial Economics 29 (1991).

Some business organizations have taken other actions that affect the way the board of directors functions to control agency costs. For example, the Japanese *keiretsu* system, discussed in the preceding highlight, is a unique approach to reducing agency costs.

Responsibilities of Officers and Directors

With the decision-making structure of the firm understood, we now examine some of the specific duties of officers and directors. Knowledge of their duties allows us to better understand the role of the board in controlling agency costs.

OFFICERS' ROLES AND RESPONSIBILITIES

The officers of a corporation, along with their management staffs, are responsible for the daily management of the firm's assets. This includes, but is not limited to, managing daily operations, evaluating and selecting projects, and managing cash flow and working capital. The rights and duties of management are spelled out in the firm's **charter.**

The firm has only limited flexibility in drawing up its charter because the laws of the state in which the firm is incorporated impose specific constraints. Perhaps the most popular state for incorporation is Delaware; about 50% of all firms registered on the New York Stock Exchange (NYSE) call this state home. Delaware's legal code has well-established precedents, and the state is also home to an abundance of legal experts on corporate law. Delaware's governance system is particularly appealing to large companies because it gives management some degree of protection in the event of a hostile takeover. In addition, Delaware limits directors' personal liability from lawsuits. Charters give management broad authority in running the firm, although most major changes must be approved by the stockholders. The structure of the firm is often based on The Model Business Corporation Act, which is a document prepared by the American Bar Association. It is a working model for state legislators, law review commissions, and lawyers for revising and modernizing state corporation laws. It has been adopted in whole or in part in more than 35 states.

Most large corporations generally have at least four officers: a president, a vice-president, a secretary, and a treasurer. Most states permit one person to hold more than one office, with the exception that the president may not also serve as secretary. The separation of these two offices helps prevent collusion in falsifying records if the president is not diligently discharging the duties assigned to that office.

The number of officers, their titles, and their functions are spelled out in the **corporate bylaws,** which supplement the articles of incorporation and contain the details of corporate administration and internal operating procedures. These bylaws must be consistent with state incorporation laws and the articles of incorporation.

As agents of the shareholders, a corporation's officers owe certain fiduciary duties to the shareholders in addition to their operational duties. These **fiduciary responsibilities** are difficult to define precisely, but in general terms, the officers who accept a position as agents of the shareholders agree to perform all duties they are assigned with due diligence and with the skills that they represented themselves as possessing when they secured that position. By accepting the position, an officer also agrees to notify the principals (stockholders) of all significant matters that come to his or her attention as an acting officer, to act solely for the benefit of the stockholders and not in the interest of himself or herself or a third party, and to be loyal to the principal(s) exclusively. The duties of obedience and accountability require the officer to carry out any and all instructions received from the stockholders and to make available to the stockholders an account of all property and money received on their behalf.

Some state statutes include two additional fiduciary responsibilities that are difficult to define precisely: the duties of due care and good faith. Because there is no clear-cut definition, the burden ultimately falls on the legal process to determine, in light of the specific circumstances covering each case, whether due care and/or good faith have been exercised.

DIRECTORS' ROLES AND RESPONSIBILITIES

The board is the highest level corporate control device and thus the highest authority in the corporation. The board makes broad policy decisions and adapts the firm's strategic plan to changing economic conditions. A firm's strategic plan encompasses its purpose, scope, objectives, and strategies and therefore is its long-term course of action. In a direct sense, a firm's board injects its vision of the firm's future into daily operations by exercising its broad and powerful control rights. Although the firm's officers are free to make decisions regarding day-to-day operations and are given wide discretionary powers to carry them out, their decisions are subject to ratification by the board of directors. As a practical matter, however, the board usually reviews only major decisions that have significant strategic implications. The duties of the board of directors include monitoring the corporation's performance, setting standards for performance, reviewing the performance of the chief executive officer (CEO) and other senior managers, selecting the CEO's successor, influencing the firm's strategic directions, and managing in times of crisis. Like the officers, the directors also serve as agents of the stockholders and thus owe them the same fiduciary duties mentioned previously, with one exception. Directors are permitted to withhold certain information from stockholders if releasing it would hurt the corporation's competitive position.

SUMMARY

Section 2-1: Corporate Wealth-increasing Activities and Owners' Wealth

What is the value of a firm?

- Firm value is best defined in terms of the firm's balance sheet; however, it is important to distinguish between accounting balance sheets and economic (market-value) balance sheets.

- In an assets definition, firm value is the market value of the firm's total assets (the market value of the left-hand side of the economic balance sheet).

- In a claims definition, the firm value is the market value of the claims against the firm's assets (the market value of the right-hand side of the economic balance sheet).

How does the firm create wealth for its owners?

- In the economic balance sheet, the market value of the firm's assets can be broken down into two elements. The first is the resale value of the firm's productive assets—their value in exchange. The second is the value those assets have to the firm—their value in use.

- The difference between an asset's value in use and its value in exchange represents the wealth created by the firm. Thus the manner in which managers *use* the productive assets of the firm ultimately determines the wealth created by the firm.

- The magnitude, timing, and risk of the potential cash flows generated by the firm's investments determine the wealth created. The equity markets facilitate a conversion of this additional wealth into stockholders' personal wealth.

Section 2-2: Stockholder Welfare and Stock Prices

How do accounting profits and cash flows differ?

- Accounting profits are accounting measures that may or may not reflect the firm's economic realities, and they can be manipulated to produce different results.

- The markets look at equity value in a unique way that cannot be captured by accounting information alone.

- Cash flows are the actual funds that the firm has available for productive uses. Cash flows have earnings potential; profits may not.

How are cash flows and the firm's stock price related?

- If managers make decisions to benefit the stockholders, then the added wealth created will be reflected in the stock price; that is, the equity markets will increase the price of the stock to "capture" the increase in the firm's assets.

- Thus corporate wealth creation manifests itself in stock price appreciation and the owners become wealthier. Usually the only connection a stockholder has with the firm is through stock ownership, and thus stockholders' welfare is maximized by maximizing stock prices.

Section 2-3: The Agency Relationship: An Impediment to Stockholder Wealth Maximization

What happens if the interests of the managers and the stockholders diverge?

- In most corporations the owners hire professional managers to run the firm on a daily basis.

- Because a firm's management is often separated from its ownership, managers (agents) are likely to act in their own best interest, to the detriment of the shareholders' (principals') welfare.

- This "incentive misalignment" between managers and owners leads to agency costs—legal, administrative, monitoring, and bonding costs and residual loss—which lower the value of the securities that the firm issues.

- Although some of these costs are generally borne by the agent and not the principal, the principals' welfare is nevertheless reduced by the "agency problem." It is therefore in the firm's best interests to lower agency costs.

Section 2-4: The Dominance of the Corporation: A Paradox?

Why is the corporation the dominant form of business organization?

- Although the corporate form of organization has the most severe agency problems, it continues to dominate the economic scene.

- Presumably, the benefits of being organized as a corporation, especially its ability to raise large amounts of capital, exceed the administrative, legal, monitoring, bonding, and residual costs of the agency relationship.

- To some extent agency costs may be reduced by various internal and external control devices.

Section 2-5: Corporate Governance with Managers and Directors

How does the decision-making process within corporations foster stockholder welfare?

■ One device for reducing agency costs is the organization of the corporation's decision-making process.

■ The decision-making process allocates management and control functions between the management and the board of directors.

■ This shared decision-making structure can reduce agency costs. Managers recommend and execute courses of action. The board approves managerial recommendations and oversees the firm's operations.

QUESTIONS

1. In what sense does an asset have two values?

2. How do the accounting balance sheet and the economic balance sheet differ?

3. Why is the claims definition of firm value more commonly used?

4. Why should stockholders be concerned with the value in use of a firm's assets?

5. What factors can cause accounting profits and cash flows for a particular firm to differ?

6. Is the agency relationship confined to manager–stockholder conflicts alone? Explain.

7. What are the various sources of agency costs?

8. In a business, it is the agent and not the principal who bears the agency costs. Explain how, when, and to what extent this statement is true.

9. How do monitoring and bonding costs differ?

10. Discuss the advantages of the corporate form of organization that explain its dominance, notwithstanding the agency problems.

11. What are some of the major internal and external control devices?

12. Distinguish between management and control. How can agency problems caused by the separation of ownership and control be solved to some extent by separating management and control?

13. What is a fiduciary responsibility? Who in the firm has such a responsibility?

SUGGESTED ADDITIONAL READINGS

Fama, Eugene F., and Michael C. Jensen. "Separation of Ownership and Control." *Journal of Law and Economics* 26 (1983): 301–326.

Jensen, Michael C., and W. Meckling. "Theory of the Firm: Managerial Behavior, Agency Costs, and Capital Structure." *Journal of Financial Economics* 3 (October 1976): 305–360.

Lindenberg, E. B., and Steven A. Ross. "Tobin's q Ratio and Industrial Organization." *Journal of Business* 54 (1981): 1–32.

THREE THE STRUCTURE AND INTERPRETATION OF ACCOUNTING STATEMENTS

My problem lies in reconciling my gross habits with my net income.

—*Errol Flynn, 1946*

*I*n Chapter 1 we saw that the financial manager's primary decisions within the firm can be broadly classified as the investment decision, which assets to acquire, and the financing decision, how to finance the asset acquisitions. These decisions determine the specific asset/liability mix of the firm and also the firm's net income and cash flows. Accounting statements provide a visible picture of the firm. They are useful for examining some of the effects of managerial decisions.

This chapter is structured to address the following questions:

- What information is contained in the firm's basic financial statements?

- How do you assess the firm's cash flows?

- How can we compare a firm's financial statements with those of other firms?

- What are some of the broad features of the tax code that are relevant for financial decision making?

3-1

THE STRUCTURE OF THE FIRM'S FINANCIAL STATEMENTS

*T*he structure of the firm's financial statements allows us to examine the impact of managerial actions on the firm's accounting performance. A firm's **basic financial statements**—its balance sheet and income statement plus the statement of retained earnings—are important sources of data on its performance and condition. These statements summarize the history of various aspects of the firm's operations.

The Balance Sheet

A **balance sheet** is a summary of a firm's "financial position," its assets and the claims on those assets, at a particular time, typically the last day of the year. Table 3-1 contains two recent balance sheets for InterTech Stores, Inc., a chain of fashion clothing stores, as of December 31, 1995, and December 31, 1994.

First, the names of the assets and their respective dollar values are listed in descending order of **liquidity,** or "nearness to being cash." As seen in Table 3-1, assets are normally divided into two categories: current assets and noncurrent (long-term) assets. **Current assets** are those resources that will be converted to cash within one year or within the firm's normal operating cycle. **Prepaid expenses** are an exception in that they represent cash expenditures made in advance of the use of the goods and services and are awaiting assignment to expenses. Other examples are unexpired insurance, rent, and subscriptions. **Noncurrent** or **fixed assets** are longer-term commitments of funds (longer than one year).

The second major section of the balance sheet contains the **claims on assets,** which describe how the assets are financed by either liabilities or stockholders' equity. **Liabilities** are the firm's financial obligations to outsiders, most important its creditors. Like assets, liabilities can be either current or noncurrent. They are listed on the balance sheet roughly in order of increasing maturity; that is, current liabilities are followed on the balance sheet by long-term liabilities.

TABLE 3-1 *InterTech Stores, Inc., Balance Sheets (millions of dollars)*		*December 31, 1995*	*December 31, 1994*
Assets			
Current assets			
	Cash	$ 40	$ 37
	Marketable securities	3	3
	Net accounts receivable	96	89
	Inventories	111	92
	Prepaid expenses	7	9
	Total current assets	$257	$230
Long-term assets			
	Gross plant and equipment	85	63
	Less: Accumulated depreciation	(26)	(22)
	Net plant and equipment	59	41
	Total assets	$316	$271
Claims on assets			
Current liabilities			
	Accounts payable	$ 77	$ 63
	Notes payable: bank	31	46
	Taxes payable	3	3
	Other accruals	24	21
	Total current liabilities	$135	$133
Long-term liabilities			
	Bonds outstanding	49	33
	Deferred taxes	12	10
	Total long-term liabilities	$ 61	$ 43
	Total liabilities	$196	$176
Stockholders' equity			
	Common stock		
	(5 million shares, $5 par)	25	25
	Additional paid-in capital	22	22
	Retained earnings	73	48
	Total shareholders' equity	$120	$ 95
	Total claims on assets	$316	$271

Current liabilities are obligations that must be paid within one year or within the firm's normal operating cycle. Normally, accounts payable (credit extended by trade suppliers) is the largest item. Notes payable, however, can be sizable for firms that rely heavily on short-term credit from banks. Current liabilities and current assets are collectively referred to as **working capital.** The term **net working capital** refers to the difference between current assets and current liabilities. This figure indicates the extent to which current assets can be converted to cash to meet current obligations. The more working capital a firm has, the more liquidity it has. **Noncurrent liabilities,** such as bonds and mortgages, are long-term debt payable in more than one year. They usually have fixed periodic interest (and principal) payments associated with them.

Stockholders' equity (net worth) is simply the residual difference between assets and liabilities. It follows from the accounting identity that assets must equal (balance) liabilities plus equity:

$$\text{Total assets} - \text{total liabilities} = \text{stockholders' equity} \qquad (3\text{-}1)$$

This figure represents the firm's net worth and indicates the stockholders' wealth in book-value terms. This implies that the actual wealth of the shareholders (i.e., in market-value terms) may be higher or lower than the stockholders' equity. Book-value stockholders' equity increases when retained earnings are added to the books (i.e., when the firm retains, or "saves," part of its current earnings instead of paying them out as dividends).

The Income Statement   Whereas a balance sheet summarizes a firm's financial position at a particular time, an **income statement** reports a firm's performance by measuring the profits

A FOURTEENTH-CENTURY INCOME STATEMENT

Francesco di Marco Datini & Co. in Barcelona, Statement of Profit and Loss, July 11, 1397–January 31, 1399

	£	s.	d.
Profits on trade (*pro di mercatantie*)	689	11	5
Profits on foreign exchange (*pro di cambio*)	262	4	0
Credit balance of merchandise expense (*spese di mercatantie*)	133	13	7
Total of gross profits	1,085	9	0

	£	s.	d.	£	s.	d.
Deduct expenses						
Rent for 18 months	60	0	0			
Irrecoverable account	38	0				
Convoy expenses (*guidaggio*)	67	12	0			
Living expenses	106	1	5			
Depreciation on office equipment	16	17	0			
Reserve for unpaid taxes and other accruals (*riserbo di spese di lelde a pagare e altre spese*)	80	0	0			
Total expenses				333	18	5
Net income				751	10	7

SOURCE: *Datini Archives, Prato (Tuscany), no. 801, Barcelona,* Libro verde C. *Reprinted in "The Beginning of Double-Entry Bookkeeping in the Fourteenth Century" by Raymond De Roover and Iris Ingo,* The World of Business, *Vol. 1 (New York: Simon & Schuster 1962), pp. 81–88.*

(losses) generated over a period of time, typically a quarter or a fiscal year. The income statement shows the extent to which revenues exceed the costs of producing and marketing a product.

The need to measure performance and profitability is as old as business itself. The basic structure of the income statement has been developed over several centuries. Highlighted above is an example of an early income statement.

To facilitate a discussion of the modern income statement, Table 3-2, part a, presents InterTech's income statement in four distinct sections so that the profit (loss) after each type of expense can be analyzed. These four sections result in the determination of the gross profit, net operating income (*NOI*), net profit before taxes (*NPBT*) (also called *taxable income*), and net income (*NI*) for InterTech Stores, Inc.

PART 1: PRODUCTION ACTIVITIES

Gross profit recognizes the expense of producing (purchasing) a product by deducting the cost of goods sold from the net sales (revenues):

$$\text{Gross profit} = \text{net sales} - \text{cost of goods sold} \qquad (3\text{-}2)$$

For InterTech, the gross profit is $801 - $492 = 309.

PART 2: OPERATING ACTIVITIES

Part 2 of the income statement subtracts general and administrative, rent, and depreciation expenses from gross profits. These expenses are collectively called **operating expenses.** Thus:

$$\text{Net operating income } (NOI) = \text{gross profit} - \text{operating expenses} \qquad (3\text{-}3)$$

For InterTech, $NOI = $309 - $257 = 52.

TABLE 3-2

InterTech Stores, Inc., Income Statements and Statement of Retained Earnings (millions of dollars)

	December 31, 1995	December 31, 1994
a. Income statements		
Part 1: Production activities		
Net sales	$801	$720
Less: Cost of goods sold	492	468
Gross profit	$309	$252
Part 2: Operating activities		
Less: Operating expenses		
Selling	$ 87	$ 63
Rent	40	30
General and administrative	126	115
Depreciation	4	3
Total expenses	$257	$211
Net operating income (NOI)	$ 52	$ 41
Part 3: Financial activities		
Less: Interest expense	$ 18	$ 21
Plus: Nonoperating income	4	5
Net profit before taxes (NPBT)	$ 38	$ 25
Part 4: Taxes		
Less: Income taxes (15%)	6	4
Net income (NI)	$ 32	$ 21
b. Statement of retained earnings		
Beginning balance	$ 48	$ 32
Add: Net income (NI)	32	21
Less dividends	7	5
Ending balance	$ 73	$ 48

PART 3: FINANCIAL ACTIVITIES

Next, **financial expenses,** such as interest payments and nonoperating income (or expenses), are netted against operating income to obtain the **net profit before taxes** ($NPBT$). Nonoperating income includes income to the firm from activities not directly related to its day-to-day operations. Examples are income from royalties on patents and rental income from property. $NPBT$ is also known as *taxable income* because it is this figure that is used as income for tax purposes. Thus:

$$\begin{matrix} \text{Net profits} \\ \text{before taxes} \\ \text{(taxable income)} \end{matrix} = \begin{matrix} \text{net} \\ \text{operating} \\ \text{income} \\ (NOI) \end{matrix} - \begin{matrix} \text{interest} \\ \text{payments} \end{matrix} + \begin{matrix} \text{nonoperating} \\ \text{income} \end{matrix} \qquad (3\text{-}4)$$

For InterTech, $NPBT = \$52 - \$18 + \$4 = \$38$.

PART 4: TAXES

The U.S. Tax Code is complex and continually changing. We therefore address only the broad implications of taxes for financial decisions. A summary of the current tax code features is provided in Section 3-3.

The bottom line of the income statement gives the **net income** (NI). This amount, also called **net income after taxes,** belongs to the firm's stockholders. The firm may choose to pay out either a portion or all of the NI to stockholders as dividends. What remains goes into the firm's retained earnings account:

Retained earnings (RE) = NI − dividends   (3-5)

For InterTech, $RE = \$32 - \$7 = \$25$.

The Statement of Retained Earnings

The balance sheet and income statement contain shared information, and it is necessary to reconcile them. This is done in the **statement of retained earnings,** which is a financial statement that reconciles the changes in the book value of equity between the balance sheet dates. Table 3-2, part b contains the statement of retained earnings for InterTech.

Constructing this statement is straightforward. The retained earnings at any time are the retained earnings from last year plus any new retained earnings from the current year. For InterTech Stores, the beginning retained earnings balance for 1995 of $48 million is the ending balance for 1994. The ending balance of $73 million for 1995 is thus determined by the income earned and the dividends paid during the year.

Note two items regarding the change in retained earnings. First, this figure is a result of the interaction between the income statement and the balance sheet. Of all that happens in an income statement, interest expense and depreciation expense are perhaps the most important variables that directly affect the balance sheet. Second, earnings are retained over the entire year and are usually reinvested in assets such as plant and equipment or accounts receivable, not in cash. Cash is an asset, whereas retained earnings are claims on assets. The existence of retained earnings simply means that the past reported income has exceeded the payment of dividends from the cash account. In most cases, retained earnings have already been allocated to asset investments and may therefore not be available for distribution.

Consolidating the Financial Statements of Subsidiaries

American companies that operate subsidiaries in several countries must, at regular intervals, issue financial statements for their global operations. This entails converting each subsidiary's financial statements (stated in their own local currencies) to dollars and then combining all of the resulting dollar statements to obtain a global set of "books."

What exchange rate should be used to "translate" (convert) these statements? Some of the items, such as plant and equipment, were obtained years ago and are valued at their historical cost. Other items, such as marketable securities, are valued at their current value. Should all accounts be converted at the current exchange rate, or should the accounts be converted at the exchange rate that prevailed when the item was first added to the subsidiary's books?

For American firms, the rules for answering these questions are set by the Financial Accounting Standards Board (FASB), which in 1981 issued Statement of Financial Accounting Standards Number 52, usually called FASB 52. FASB 52 identifies which items in a firm's financial statements are to be translated at the current exchange rate and which items are to be translated at the historical exchange rate, the rate that existed when the asset was placed on the firm's books. Assets and liabilities that are translated at the current rate are "exposed" to changes in the current exchange rate. The difference between exposed assets and exposed liabilities is the firm's **net translation exposure**:

Net translation exposure (*NTE*)
$$= \text{exposed assets} - \text{exposed liabilities} \quad (3\text{-}6)$$

The change in a currency's value combined with the firm's net translation exposure determines how much the firm gains or loses from the exchange rate change.

Under FASB 52, exchange generated gains or losses for each period are generally placed in a **Cumulative Adjustment Account** in the balance sheet and do not affect the firm's net income. FASB 52, by isolating gains and losses caused by exchange rate changes, allows those interested in the firm to determine how efficiently the firm is being managed separately from how it is being affected by exchange rate changes.

These gains and losses from changing exchange rates can be significant. For instance, the 1992 annual report of Ford Motor Company stated:

Changes in foreign exchange rates increased the net loss by $73 million in 1992, decreased the net loss by $81 million in 1991, and decreased net income by $3 million in 1990. These amounts include net transaction and translation gains/(losses) before taxes of $(25) million in 1992, $662 million in 1991, and $935 million in 1990. The gains in 1991 and 1990 were offset substantially by costs of sales that reflected historical exchange rates for costs associated with inventories in countries with high inflation rates.

The consolidation of foreign subsidiary financial statements involves complexities that are far beyond the scope of this text. However, we introduce net translation exposure here because anyone who reviews the financial statements of a multinational firm should understand that changes in exchange rates can affect these statements.

3-2
DERIVATIVE FINANCIAL STATEMENTS

The basic financial statements do not give financial managers and outsiders information regarding several aspects of the firm's operations: How have the cash flows of the firm changed during the period? How were the firm's profits used? Were long-term sources of financing adequate to support major investments and sales growth? Was there an overreliance on short-term funds? What do changes in working capital imply about the firm's ability to generate funds? To answer these and similar questions, **derivative financial statements** are needed. These offer additional information for interpreting the accounting data and establishing basic financial relationships. In this section we first derive the cash flow statement. We also explain the common-size balance sheet and the common-size income statement.

The Cash Flow Statement

Corporate accounting involves determining income or profits on an accrual, or book, basis, not cash flows. The reason for this convention is that outsiders (and perhaps management) might be misled if they considered net cash flows to be the earnings (profits) for a given period.

As we saw in Chapter 2, financial management decisions should be based on cash flows rather than on profits. This is especially important when analyzing capital projects (i.e., capital budgeting), for which estimates of future incremental cash flows are used to evaluate the attractiveness of the investments. For such financial decisions, it is necessary to convert profits (as determined in the income statement) to cash flows. We did this in Chapter 2 through the simple step of adding back depreciation to net income. However, to properly make the numerous adjustments entailed in the various accounts, we must use the cash flow statement.

The basic idea in developing the cash flow statement is to start with the income statement, adjust it for changes in the balance sheet, and then use the results to explain the change in the cash balance. This new approach is more detailed but yields more information about how the flow of funds was affected by management's past decisions. To facilitate these decisions, the cash flow statement is divided into areas that examine the cash inflows and cash outflows based on management's decisions concerning operations, finance, and investment.

Table 3-3 contains InterTech Stores' cash flow statement for 1995. Cash flows from operations are generally more variable than are cash flows from financial or

■

TABLE 3-3

*InterTech Stores, Inc.,
Cash Flow Statement
(millions of dollars)*

	Net Cash Flow December 31, 1995
Operating cash flows	
Net sales	$ 801
Less: Increase in receivables	7
Cash from sales	$ 794
Cost of goods sold	$ 492
Plus: Increase in inventories	19
Less: Increase in payables	14
Cash production costs	497
Gross cash margin[a]	$ 297
Operating expenses (excluding depreciation)	$ 253
Less: Decrease in prepaid expenses	2
Less: Increase in accruals	3
Plus: Increase in other current assets	0
Cash operating expenses	$ 248
Cash from operations[b]	$ 49
Less: Income taxes paid[c]	4
Net cash flow from operations	$ 45
Financial cash flows	
Financial outflows	
Interest expenses	$ 18
Cash dividends paid	7
Decrease in notes payable	15
Total financial outflows (negative quantity)	$ −40
Financial inflows	
Nonoperating income	$ 4
Increase in long-term debt	16
Increase in new equity	0
Total financial inflows (positive quantity)	$ 20
Net financial cash flows	$ −20
Investment cash flows	
Investment outflows	
Less: Increase in marketable securities	$ 0
Less: Increase in gross plant and equipment	22
Net investment cash flows	$ −22
Net cash flow from operating, financing, and investment decisions (change in cash position)	$ 3
Plus: Beginning cash balance	$ 37
Ending cash balance[d]	$ 40

[a] Cash from sales less cash production costs.
[b] Gross cash margin less cash operating expenses.
[c] Income taxes from income statement less increase in deferred taxes.
[d] Note that this cash balance exactly matches the figure in InterTech's 1995 balance sheet (Table 3-1).

investment transactions because operational cash flows depend on sales, which may vary substantially from period to period. Operating cash flows are determined by examining changes in balance sheet accounts (Table 3-1). Depending on the account, these changes may indicate an increase or a decrease in cash. For Inter-Tech Stores, Inc., accounts receivable increased by $7 million, which means that the difference in what the firm's customers paid and what was still outstanding rose by $7 million. This amount should therefore be deducted from sales to determine the amount of cash obtained from sales. As another example, the $19 million increase in inventories must be paid for and thus represents a cash outflow. All of the operating cash inflows and outflows determine the net cash flow from operations.

The next step in determining the cash flow statement is to calculate the financial cash flows. Unlike operating cash flows, financial cash flows are determined by looking not only at the balance sheet but also at the income statement and the statement of retained earnings. From the income statement (Table 3-2, part a), interest expenses for 1995 were $18 million. From the statement of retained earnings (Table 3-2, part b), dividend payments were $7 million. For InterTech, financial inflows arose from changes in long-term debt and from nonoperating income.

The final portion of the cash flow statement concerns the firm's investment decisions. These investments may be short term, such as marketable securities, or long term, in the form of increased fixed assets. Again, the focus is on cash inflows and outflows to the firm.

The summary of operating, financial, and investment cash flows for the period is then added to the beginning cash balance to determine InterTech's ending cash balance. The $3 million figure denotes the change in InterTech's cash position, which increased from $37 million to $40 million.

Common-Size Statements

So far, we have expressed financial information in absolute dollar amounts. However, another derivative statement, the common-size statement, converts these absolute amounts to more easily understood percentages of some base amount. As a result, certain insights not evident from a review of the raw figures themselves become more apparent. In addition, the different statements can be compared both over time and across companies within the firm's industry.

A **common-size statement** is either a balance sheet or an income statement in which each item is expressed as a percentage (rather than in dollars) of some amount. Table 3-4 presents the **common-size balance sheets** for InterTech Stores (1994 and 1995), and Table 3-5 shows the **common-size income statements** for the same company, again for the same years.

■

TABLE 3-4
InterTech Stores, Inc., Common-Size Balance Sheet (millions of dollars)

	December 31, 1995		December 31, 1994		Comparative Industry Averages
Assets					
Current assets					
Cash and marketable securities	$ 43	13.6%	$ 40	14.8%	7.9%
Net accounts receivable	96	30.4	89	32.8	14.5
Inventories	111	35.1	92	33.9	52.6
Prepaid expenses	7	2.2	9	3.3	1.1
Total current assets	$257	81.3	$230	84.8	76.1
Net fixed assets	59	18.7	41	15.2	23.9
Total assets	$316	100.0	$271	100.0	100.0
Claims on assets					
Current liabilities					
Accounts payable	$ 77	24.4%	$ 63	23.3%	14.6%
Notes payable: bank	31	9.8	46	17.0	10.7
Taxes payable	3	1.0	3	1.1	3.7
Other accruals	24	7.6	21	7.7	7.4
Total current liabilities	$135	42.8	$133	49.1	36.4
Long-term liabilities					
Debenture bonds	$ 49	15.5%	$ 33	12.2%	16.3%
Deferred taxes	12	3.8	10	3.7	2.0
Total long-term liabilities	$ 61	19.3	$ 43	15.9	18.3
Total liabilities	$196	62.1%	$176	65.0%	54.7%
Stockholders' equity					
Common stock	$ 25	7.9%	$ 25	9.2%	—[a]
Additional paid-in capital	22	6.9	22	8.1	—
Retained earnings	73	23.1	48	17.7	—
Total stockholders' equity	$120	37.9%	$ 95	35.0%	45.3%
Total claims	$316	100.0	$271	100.0	100.0

[a] Not available.

■

TABLE 3-5
InterTech Stores, Inc., Common-Size Income Statement (millions of dollars)

	December 31, 1995		December 31, 1994		Comparative Industry Averages
Net sales	$801	100.0%	$720	100.0%	100.0%
Less: Cost of goods sold	492	61.4	468	65.0	64.0
Gross profit	$309	38.6%	$252	35.0%	36.0%
Less: Operating expenses					
Selling	$ 87	10.9%	$ 63	8.7%	—[a]
Rent	40	5.0	30	4.2	—
General and administrative	126	15.7	115	16.0	—
Depreciation	4	0.5	3	0.4	—
Total expenses	$257	32.1%	$211	29.3%	32.6%
Net operating income (*NOI*)	$ 52	6.5%	$ 41	5.7%	3.4%
Less: Interest expense	$ 18	2.3%	$ 21	2.9%	—
Plus: Nonoperating income	4	0.5	5	0.7	—
Net profit before taxes (*NPBT*)	$ 38	4.7%	$ 25	3.5%	2.0%
Less: Income taxes (15%)	6	0.7	4	0.6	—
Net income (*NI*)	$ 32	4.0%	$ 21	2.9%	—

[a] Not available.

COMMON-SIZE BALANCE SHEETS

In a common-size balance sheet, each item is calculated as a percentage of total assets. For InterTech in 1995 the total assets of $316 million represent 100%. Inter-Tech's $43 million in cash and marketable securities amounts to 43/316 or 13.6% of total assets. The other percentages are calculated similarly. From Table 3-4 we find that InterTech invested heavily in current assets (over 80% of total assets), especially in accounts receivable and inventories. This is typical of a retailer like InterTech; the two main sources of financing used to support assets are short-term liabilities and equity. In year-to-year comparisons, current assets declined (from 84.8% to 81.3% of total assets between 1994 and 1995), whereas investments in fixed assets increased from 15.2% to 18.7% over the same time period. This reflects InterTech's recent aggressive expansion of new store openings. InterTech also relied more on long-term liabilities—from 15.9% to 19.3%—relative to short-term liabilities, whereas its equity remained a stable source of financing. Although our discussion has focused on an arbitrary set of variables, virtually any two variables in the common-size statement can be compared in order to draw inferences.

Another useful common-size statement for analyzing such behavior over time is one that relates statement items to a base year. For example, a base year such as 1990 could be selected, and all financial statement items for that year could be designated as 100.00. Items for all subsequent years are then expressed as an index to that year.

An astute financial manager should be aware of most of these general conclusions. Although this analysis shows how InterTech has been acting over time, there is no indication of whether it has been performing well or poorly. An additional step that can answer such questions is to compare InterTech's balance sheet percentages with its industry's average percentages, which also are presented in Table 3-4.

Such an analysis leads to a number of observations. First, InterTech's current assets (as a percentage of total assets) were only slightly greater than those of the typical retailer. But the mix between accounts receivable and inventories stands out in stark contrast. In 1995 InterTech's accounts receivable and inventories amounted, respectively, to 30.4% and 35.1% of total assets. In contrast, the industry averages for these same ratios were 14.5% and 52.6%, respectively. Such pronounced deviations from the industry averages require further investigation to determine the underlying reasons. These deviations from the norm should alert the analyst to ask several questions that can identify potential weaknesses and strengths in the company. For example, does InterTech have a credit and collection policy consistent with its size? Is its management overly proficient at controlling inventory levels, or are its inventories too low, resulting in lost sales due to shortages?

InterTech also tended to rely more heavily on current liabilities than did other firms in the industry because of its much higher level of accounts payable. Is InterTech shrewdly using its trade suppliers to help carry its large investment in current assets? Or is InterTech having trouble meeting its obligations on time, which causes payables to build up? Again, this significant deviation warrants further attention.

Finally, InterTech used debt to a greater extent than normal. This conclusion follows from the observation that its equity was only 37.9% of its assets, whereas this ratio was 45.3% for the typical retailer. The financial manager needs to determine whether this mix of debt and equity is simply a temporary phenomenon or a stated policy objective.

COMMON-SIZE INCOME STATEMENTS

As Table 3-5 shows, each item in the common-size income statement is calculated as a percentage of sales (i.e., InterTech's 1994 sales of $720 million and its 1995 sales of $801 million represent 100%). The industry averages are also presented. An analysis of InterTech's common-size income statement shows that InterTech's 1995 gross and operating profit percentages improved significantly over its 1994 profit margins. This resulted mainly from an improvement in the control of its cost of goods sold even while operating expenses were increasing as a percentage of sales. The primary cause of the latter result was a sharp increase in selling expenses. Nevertheless, InterTech's overall profit picture compares quite favorably with the industry's. In fact, InterTech's 1995 net profits before taxes were more than twice the industry's average of 2.0%.

3-3

TAXES AND FINANCIAL MANAGEMENT[1]

*I*t is often said that nothing is sure except death and taxes, but there are a thousand different ways to die and at least an equal number of ways to be taxed. Financial decisions are invariably affected by tax considerations. For example, an alternative that is attractive before taxes may be unacceptable after the tax ramifications have been incorporated into the analysis.

It is impossible to include all relevant tax details in an introductory financial management textbook for three main reasons. First, the tax code applies unevenly across industries, and generalizations across firms are broad simplifications. Second, a detailed tax analysis of alternatives would take us into a discussion of tax accounting, which is outside the intended scope of this book. Finally, tax rules are subject to frequent change, and current tax rules may not apply at a later time. This substantial flux in tax laws is examined in the following highlight.

In this book we follow a more useful approach to studying financial decision making by taking a conceptual view of taxes rather than concerning ourselves with the precise technical details of the tax code. We present the general elements of the

[1]I wish to thank Professor Stephen T. Limberg for his many helpful comments on tax issues.

TAX LAWS IN A FLUX

Hewlett-Packard's tax department consists of 50 people working full time. In addition, the Internal Revenue Service has nine full-time auditors stationed at H-P's headquarters who are still reviewing the company's returns for 1984, 1985, and 1986. Larry Langdon, H-P's director of taxes and logistics who manages this massive operation, was surprised when he visited a Japanese company three times larger than H-P, and found that their tax department consisted of only five people who completed the company's taxes in a couple of weeks!

This comparison of how taxes affect American and Japanese companies demonstrates a major problem faced by American businesses. American tax laws are not only massively complex—they are also constantly changing. American firms have had to deal with several major tax laws, including

1981: Economic Recovery Act

1982: Tax Equity and Fiscal Responsibility Act

1984: Deficit Reduction Act

1986: Tax Reform Act

1988: Technical and Miscellaneous Revenue Act

1990: Omnibus Budget Reconciliation Act

1993: Omnibus Budget Reconciliation Act

The Tax Reform Act of 1986 was especially important in that it changed tax practices that had been in place for decades and was supposed to stabilize and simplify the nation's tax code. However, since that time 5,400 changes have been made in the tax code through 27 different pieces of legislation.

These changes have made it extremely difficult for companies to plan for the future. Such constant turbulence affects firms such as H-P. If certain proposed provisions of the 1993 Economic Recovery Act were actually put into effect, it could have cost H-P $100 million a year. As a controller for Hewlett-Packard said, "We talk to our tax attorneys a lot, but they're cautious about how much advice they give us because they know it's a moving target."

SOURCE: Rick Wartzman, "Whether or Not They Benefit, Companies Decry Instability in Tax Law As a Barrier to Planning," The Wall Street Journal, August 10, 1993, p. A14. Reprinted by permission of The Wall Street Journal, © 1993 Dow Jones & Company, Inc. All rights reserved worldwide.

tax system as it exists today and also discuss elements of taxation that have traditionally been a part of the U.S. tax code.

Corporate Income Taxes

ORDINARY CORPORATE TAX RATE

A corporation's taxable income is calculated by subtracting its business expenses from its revenues. As Table 3-6 indicates, current corporate income tax rates are on a graduated scale and range from 15% on the first $50,000 to 35% on taxable income above $18,333,333. A corporation with taxable income in excess of $100,000 is required to increase its tax liability by the lesser of 5% of the excess or $11,750. In addition, a corporation with taxable income in excess of $15 million is required to increase its tax liability by the lesser of 3% of the excess or $100,000. This system is called a **progressive tax system** because those firms that make greater profits pay a higher proportion of taxes. Note that the successively higher tax rates are applied only to the incremental income, or the latest income received, and are called **marginal tax rates.** In contrast, the **average tax rate** is the average tax paid per dollar of taxable income:

$$\text{Average tax rate} = \frac{\text{total taxes paid}}{\text{total taxable income}} \tag{3-7}$$

To see how to apply these tax rates, let's compute Mitus Corporation's tax liability, marginal tax rate, and average tax rate for its taxable income in 1995 of

T A B L E   3 - 6

Tax Rates Specified by the Omnibus Budget Reconciliation Act of 1993

Tax Rates on Ordinary Income for Corporations

Income	Tax Rate (%)
0–$50,000	15
$50,001–$75,000	25
$75,001–$100,000	34
$100,001–$350,000	39
$350,001–$10,000,000	34
$10,000,001–$15,000,000	35
$15,000,001–$18,333,333	38
$18,333,334 and above	35

Tax Rates on Ordinary Income for Single Individuals

Income	Tax Rate (%)
0–$22,100	15
$22,101–$53,500	28
$53,501–$115,000	31
$115,001–$250,000	36
$250,001 and above	39.6

$92,000. Using the tax rates in Table 3-6, we see that Mitus had a tax liability of $19,530:

$$
\begin{array}{rcl}
\$50,000(0.15) &=& \$\,7,500 \\
(\$75,000 - \$50,000)(0.25) &=& \$\,6,250 \\
(\$92,000 - \$75,000)(0.34) &=& \underline{\$\,5,780} \\
&& \$19,530
\end{array}
$$

Mitus's marginal tax rate, the highest rate it paid, was 34%. Its average tax rate was 21.2%:

$$
\text{Average tax rate} = \frac{\text{total taxes paid}}{\text{total taxable income}} = \frac{\$19,530}{\$92,000} = 0.212
$$

DEPRECIATION

Depreciation is an allocation of the historical cost of an asset over its economic life, the period over which it is expected to provide benefits to its owner. It makes sense to allocate this cost over the asset's estimated economic life, but it is more than just common sense. Although depreciation is an accounting expense that does not involve the payment of cash to anyone, it does affect the amount of cash paid out in the form of taxes and thus is of great importance to a firm.

Several methods are used for depreciating assets. These methods are divided into two classes, depending on the reason for developing the information: those used for financial accounting and those used for tax reporting.

Firms face numerous requirements for reporting information. Financial reports often use **straight-line depreciation**, which is the method that spreads the historical cost of an asset evenly over its economic life. The amount of depreciation taken each year—that is, the **annual depreciation**—from this method is calculated with the following formula:

$$
\text{Annual depreciation} = \frac{\text{initial cost} - \text{salvage value}}{\text{economic life}} \tag{3-8}
$$

The salvage value is the asset's value at the end of its economic life.

The book value of the asset at any time is the original cost of the asset less the total amount of depreciation taken on the asset up to that time:

$$
\text{Book value} = \text{original cost} - \text{accumulated depreciation} \tag{3-9}
$$

For example, J. T. Jacobs Instruments has purchased a new laser-guided lathe. The lathe, which cost $142,000, is expected to last for ten years and will then be sold for $10,000. Using equation (3-8), we find the depreciation to be taken each year is $13,200:

$$\frac{\$142,000 - \$10,000}{10} = \$13,200$$

From equation (3-9), the asset's value on the books of J. T. Jacobs four years into its life is

$$\$142,000 - (\$13,200)(4) = \$89,200$$

In addition to the straight-line method, other procedures are sometimes used that allow firms to claim larger annual depreciation amounts during the early part of an asset's life. The method used in the financial statements given to shareholders is decided by management. The government, however, has very strict guidelines that must be used when income is computed for tax purposes. The details of these systems may be found in various accounting texts and government tax publications. For our purposes, straight-line depreciation greatly simplifies explanations of financial concepts and so is used in our examples.

CAPITAL GAINS

Corporations purchase assets that enable them to produce goods and services. These assets may be real assets, such as trucks or complete manufacturing facilities, or financial assets, such as investments in the stock of other firms. Eventually, the firm may sell an asset. The difference between the sales price received from the asset and the original purchase price is either a gain or a loss. If the time elapsed between the sale and the purchase exceeds a specified time period, traditionally one year, the gain (loss) on the sale becomes a capital gain (loss) and is taxed at a reduced rate. A capital loss is used to offset capital gains made on other assets.

It is widely believed that investment in assets held for a substantial period of time is more likely to foster economic growth than speculative, short-term trading is. To encourage such investment, the tax laws may specify that capital gains on long-term assets be taxed at a lower rate than ordinary income. Investors then can plan their strategies to take advantage of these lower tax rates and thus produce economic growth.

Before the 1986 Tax Reform Act, special tax treatment was given to long-term capital gains, or the gains on assets held longer than six months. The long-term capital gains tax rate was the lesser of the firm's marginal income tax rate or a flat 28%. On the other hand, short-term capital gains, or the gains on assets held for six months or less, were taxed at the same marginal tax rate as was ordinary income. The Tax Reform Act of 1986 eliminated the capital gains tax, with all income taxed at the ordinary income tax rate. The 1993 tax legislation, however, reinstated the capital gains tax at 28%. As before the 1986 act, a capital loss can be used only to offset capital gains on other assets. Unused capital losses can be carried back to offset capital gains in the prior three years and then carried forward to offset capital gains for five years into the future.

OPERATING TAX LOSS CARRYBACK AND CARRYFORWARD

A corporation that incurs a net operating loss may offset this loss against taxable income in the prior three years (**loss carryback**) and as far as 15 years into the future (**loss carryforward**). The law requires any loss to be applied first to the earliest preceding year and then forward sequentially in time.

For example, the DeLaGatto Construction Company, Inc., sustained a $60,000 loss in 1995, and its accountant took the following actions to use this loss to reduce the firm's taxes. The 1995 loss was used first to offset 1992's taxable income. The firm's taxable income was $25,000 in 1992, and the firm paid $4,000 in taxes. Its 1992 taxable income was then recomputed to show zero profits, and the firm received a tax refund of $4,000. The remaining loss of $60,000 − $25,000 = $35,000 was then carried back to 1993. Any losses still remaining were carried back to 1994.

If the operating loss was greater than the operating income in all three prior years, the remaining amount would be carried forward and applied to 1996's income and sequentially to future profits thereafter.

INVESTMENT TAX CREDIT

In today's competitive world economy, governments are concerned with economic growth and employment. One strategy they follow is to identify asset investments that encourage economic growth and then grant tax credits to firms that make these investments. These **investment tax credits** (ITCs) allow a firm to deduct a portion of its new investment from its tax liability. ITCs are powerful incentives for investment because they are dollar-for-dollar reductions in the firm's taxes. The ITC was eliminated by the Tax Reform Act of 1986. It was proposed but not included in the 1993 Omnibus Budget Reconciliation Act. The ITC, which has been in and out of the tax code half a dozen times in the past 30 years, is an example of the difficulty American businesses have had in planning investments.

DIVIDEND INCOME

As explained in Chapter 1, dividends are payments made by a firm to its owners. Occasionally, a corporation may own another corporation's stock, which means that any cash dividends received from the stock of the other corporation must be reported as income. These intercompany dividends, however, are afforded special treatment; 70% of the dividends are exempt from taxes.

INTEREST EXPENSE

Interest paid on debt issued by a corporation is tax deductible. In effect, the government "pays" part of the interest expense, and so the firm's cash outflow for taxes is reduced. This gives a decided tax advantage for using debt capital rather than equity capital because dividends paid on stock are paid out of net income (after taxes) and are thus not a tax-deductible item, as shown in equation (3-10):

$$\text{After-tax cost of debt} = (\text{before-tax cost of debt})(1 - T) \qquad (3\text{-}10)$$

where T is the marginal tax rate. This relationship holds true for both dollar amounts and interest rates, and throughout the book it is used to determine the net cost of debt to the firm.

Assume that the treasurer of DeLaGatto Construction Company, Inc., must raise $100,000 and wants to determine what the after-tax cost of debt will be if the firm is in the 15% marginal tax bracket. The tax deductibility of interest payments affects the dollar amount that DeLaGatto will pay for the $100,000 it needs to raise. With a borrowing rate of 10%, the annual interest charges on the debt will be $100,000(0.10) = $10,000. But given the firm's marginal tax rate of 15%, the firm will receive a tax subsidy of 15% for every dollar of interest paid and will have the following net after-tax outflow:

$$\text{After-tax interest charge} = (\text{before-tax interest charge})(1 - T)$$
$$\$8,500 = \$10,000(1 - 0.15)$$

The tax deductibility of interest expenses reduces DeLaGatto's tax liability by $1,500! The after-tax rate of interest that DeLaGatto pays is clearly affected by the tax deductibility of the interest on its debt. Although DeLaGatto must make its full interest payments to its creditors, the net rate it pays is lower when taxes are considered:

$$\text{After-tax interest rate} = (\text{before-tax interest rate})(1 - T)$$
$$= 10\% \ (1 - 0.15)$$
$$= 8.5\%$$

Multiplying the borrowed amount by this net interest rate yields $100,000(0.085) = $8,500, which is the same answer obtained earlier for the net dollar cost of the debt.

EXECUTIVE COMPENSATION

The 1993 tax legislation limited the dollar amount of executive salaries that employers may deduct. Employers can deduct the cost of *reasonable* salaries and other compensation. The reasonableness of compensation is determined on a case-by-case basis. However, the reasonableness standard has been used primarily to limit payments by closely held companies where nondeductible dividends may be disguised as deductible compensation.

Effective generally for tax years beginning after 1993, the amount of compensation deductible by publicly traded companies is capped at $1 million for each of their top five executives. Employees covered by this provision include the chief executive officer and employees whose total compensation is required to be reported under the Securities Exchange Act of 1934 because the employee is one of the four highest compensated officers for the tax year.

The cap does not apply to performance-based compensation. Performance-based compensation includes commissions and such other incentive compensation devices as bonuses that require the attainment of certain performance goals and meet certain other disclosure and board/shareholder approval requirements. Stock options (which we discuss in subsequent chapters) are also allowed as an exception to the new rule, provided the options are disclosed and are approved by shareholders.

Personal Income Taxes   Individuals must pay taxes on wages and salaries, investment income (interest, dividends, rents, etc.), and profits from proprietorships and partnerships. In a manner similar to corporate tax rates, individual tax rates are progressive and are summarized in Table 3-6. Wages, salaries, and interest income are fully taxed at the individual's marginal tax rate.

Before the Tax Reform Act of 1986, long-term personal capital gains, the gains made on assets held by an individual, were taxed at 40% of the individual's marginal tax rate. Because long-term capital gains were taxed at lower rates than dividends were, a stockholder who did not desire current income might have preferred to receive capital gains through stock appreciation rather than to receive cash dividends. The 1986 Tax Reform Act eliminated this provision. However, the 1993 tax legislation reinstated the maximum statutory tax rate on net capital gain income (i.e., net long-term capital gain less net short-term capital loss) of individuals at 28%. Capital losses are deductible only to the extent of capital gains for the year plus $3,000 for individuals.

Although the ordinary income tax rates increased effective January 1, 1993, the maximum statutory capital gains rate remains at 28%. Since capital gains income is taxed at lower rates than ordinary income, it is more advantageous to have capital gains income where possible.

SUMMARY

Section 3-1: The Structure of the Firm's Financial Statements

What information is contained in the firm's basic financial statements?

- The basic financial statements of a company provide a view of the structure of the firm as shaped by managerial investment and financing decisions.

- The balance sheet provides a statement of the firm's assets and the claims against those assets at a particular time, typically the end of the year.

- The income statement summarizes the performance of the firm over a certain time period (e.g., quarterly or annually).

- The statement of retained earnings shows the addition to the book value of the shareholders' equity.

Section 3-2: Derivative Financial Statements

How do you assess the firm's cash flows?

- Cash flows are the total dollar amount of funds available to the firm to put to productive uses.

- The cash flow statement determines the firm's cash inflows and cash outflows based on operational, financial, and investment decisions, thus allowing analysis of how management's decisions have affected the firm's net cash flows.

How can we compare a firm's financial statements with those of other firms?

- The common-size statements convert all of the statement amounts into percentages of a base number. The common-size balance sheet states each balance sheet item as a percentage of total assets. The common-size income statement expresses each item on the statement as a percentage of net sales.

- Common-size statements allow a comparison of the firm with other firms or with an industry average.

Section 3-3: Taxes and Financial Management

What are some of the broad features of the tax code that are relevant for financial decision making?

- The system for taxing corporate income is very complex and changing and has many aspects.

- Income can be taxed as ordinary income or as a capital gain at a lower tax rate.

- Depreciation expense allows the firm to allocate its capital costs over the economic life of an asset.

- Gains and losses in a specific period can be carried back or carried forward to reduce past or future profits.

QUESTIONS

1. What kind of information is provided by each of the basic financial statements?

2. How are the basic financial statements interrelated?

3. Why do managers need a cash flow statement?

4. What is the relationship between a firm's net income and its cash flow?

5. What is the general procedure for constructing a cash flow statement?

6. If a firm pays no taxes, there is no difference between its net income and its cash flow. Is this statement true or false? Explain.

7. How are the common-size statements constructed?

8. What insights are gained by analyzing a company using common-size statements rather than basic statements?

9. Are payments to equityholders and debt holders tax deductible for a firm? What effect could the tax deductibility of such payments have on a firm's financing decisions?

10. What is the difference between the average tax rate and the marginal tax rate?

11. If you were a member of Congress and wanted to encourage employment, what provisions would you include in the nation's tax code?

12. What is the advantage of having a capital gains tax rate that is lower than the ordinary tax rate?

13. What is the principal purpose of a capital gains tax rate and an investment tax credit?

PROBLEMS

1. The long-term liabilities and stockholders' equity portion of BT&T's balance sheet on December 31, 1994, is shown here. During 1995, BT&T issued $5 million of long-term debt, issued $10 million of equity, earned $3 million, and paid $1 million in dividends. Construct a new balance sheet for December 31, 1995, that reflects these changes.

Long-term debt	$ 60 million
Preferred stock	20 million
Common stock	60 million
Retained earnings	40 million
Total long-term liabilities and stockholders' equity	$180 million

2. The balance sheet of the Oliva Manufacturing Company on June 30, 1995, is shown here. During the next quarter, Oliva has gross sales of $905,000, sells inventory valued at $600,000, and manufactures $620,000 of new inventory. It collects $780,000 of outstanding accounts receivable and extends new credit in the amount of $801,000. Net income for the period is $84,000, of which $63,000 is paid in dividends. For simplicity, assume that none of the other accounts has changed (except cash).

Cash	$ 221,000	Accounts payable	$ 417,000
Accounts receivable	385,000	Notes payable	217,000
Inventory	526,000	Current liabilities	$634,000
Current assets	$1,132,000	Long-term debt	800,000
Net fixed assets	1,613,000	Common equity	1,311,000
Total assets	$2,745,000	Total liabilities and stockholders' equity	$2,745,000

(a) Construct a balance sheet as of September 30, 1995.

(b) What was the level of net working capital on June 30, 1995?

3. The following are parts of an income statement and two balance sheets of the O'Conner Broadcasting Company. Sheila O'Conner, the station manager, has asked you to produce a statement of retained earnings. Do it.

1994 Balance Sheet		**1995 Balance Sheet**	
Long-term debt	$ 500,000	Long-term debt	$ 550,000
Common stock	600,000	Common stock	700,000
Retained earnings	750,000	Retained earnings	775,000
Total long-term liabilities and stockholders' equity	$1,850,000	Total long-term liabilities and stockholders' equity	$2,025,000

1995 Income Statement	
Net operating income	$80,000
Less: Interest expense	25,000
Plus: Nonoperating income	15,000
Net profit before taxes	$70,000
Less: Taxes	32,000
Net income	$38,000

4. Last year, the Myers Entertainment Center was formed, with current assets of $50,000, fixed assets of $150,000, and stockholders' equity of $85,000. During the past year, current assets have increased in value by $30,000, fixed assets have increased by $40,000, current liabilities have increased by $25,000, and long-term debt has increased by $37,000.

(a) What was the sum of current liabilities and long-term liabilities when the center was formed?

(b) What is the current level of stockholders' equity?

5. During 1995, Magee Auto Supply Outlets had gross sales of $900,000, cost of goods sold of $300,000, and general and selling expenses of $400,000. They also had outstanding $200,000 of 10% notes and $400,000 of 12% coupon bonds. Nonoperating income was $0, depreciation was $100,000, and dividends of $80,000 were paid.

(a) What was the *NOI*?

(b) What was the *NPBT*?

(c) What was the *NI* if the average tax rate was 40%?

(d) If retained earnings were $240,000 on December 31, 1994, what will they be on December 31, 1995?

6. Sparky's Seafood Restaurants in 1995 had a net cash flow from operations of $52,000, net financial cash outflows of $22,000, and a net investment cash outflow of $26,000.

   (a) What was Sparky's net cash flow for 1995?

   (b) If Sparky's level of cash on the balance sheet for December 31, 1994, was $42,000, what is the level of cash on the balance sheet for December 31, 1995?

7. Wilfong Brothers, Inc., reported a net cash inflow from operations of $63,000 during the fourth quarter of 1995. In addition, Wilfong had a net financial cash inflow of $12,000 and a net investment cash outflow of $52,000.

   (a) What was Wilfong's net cash flow for the fourth quarter of 1995?

   (b) If Wilfong's level of cash was $55,000 on December 31, 1995, what was it on September 30, 1995?

8. The *Athens Banner-Herald* had a cash level of $96,000 on December 31, 1995, and a cash level of $92,000 on December 31, 1994. The net financial cash outflow for the year was $47,000, and the net investment cash outflow for the year was $62,000. Cash operating expenses were $265,000.

   (a) Find the net cash income from operations.

   (b) Find the *Banner-Herald*'s gross cash margin for 1995.

   (c) Suppose that there was no change in current assets or liabilities and that the cost of goods sold (*CGS*) is always 70% of sales. Find the *CGS* and net sales.

   (d) Suppose that inventory increased by $12,000, receivables increased by $9,000, and all other current accounts stayed the same during 1995. Find the *CGS* and net sales if the *CGS* is always 70% of net sales.

9. A summary of the Alps Clothiers cash flow statement for 1995 is provided. Fill in the blanks.

Operating cash flows	
Net sales	$1,382,000
Decrease in receivables	26,000
Cash from sales	_____
Cost of goods sold	$ 857,000
Increase in inventory	12,000
Decrease in payables	16,000
Cash production costs	_____
Gross cash margin	_____
Operating expenses	357,000
Cash from operations	_____
Income taxes paid	62,000
Net cash flow from operations	_____
Financial cash flows	
Outflows	
Interest expense	$ 28,000
Dividends paid	13,000
Total outflows	_____

Inflows		
Nonoperating income	$	6,000
Increase in new equity		10,000
Total inflows		————
Net financial cash flows		————
Investment cash flows		
Decrease in marketable securities	$	8,000
Increase in gross plant and equipment		35,000
Net investment cash flows		————
Net cash flow from operating, financing, and investment decisions		
Beginning cash balance		153,000
Ending cash balance		————

10. The records of the Martin Corporation provide selected data for the period ended December 31, 1995. Using these data, prepare a cash flow statement for the period. Use cash balance 1/1/95 = $69,000 and cash balance 12/31/95 = $48,000.

Balance sheet changes	
Paid cash dividend	$ 15,000
Established with cash a scholarship fund at 8% interest	60,000
Increase in merchandise inventory	12,000
Borrowed on a long-term note	25,000
Acquired five drilling rigs (paid for in full by issuing 3,000 new shares of Martin stock, par $10, when market price was $25)	—
Increase in prepaid expenses	3,000
Increase in accounts receivable	6,000
Payment of bonds payable in full	86,000
Decrease in accounts payable	5,000
Cash from disposal of old drilling rig (sold at book value)	8,000
Income statement changes	
Sales revenue	$400,000
Cost of goods sold	(180,000)
Depreciation expense	(22,000)
Remaining expenses	(87,000)
Net income	$111,000

11. Construct a December 31, 1995, common-size balance sheet for Jet Electro and compare it with the common-size balance sheet for the industry (shown here).

(a) What accounts differ most from the industry norm?

(b) Are these deviations necessarily undesirable?

(c) Why might these deviations have occurred?

	1995 (millions)	1995 (%) Jet Electro	1995 (%) Industry
Cash	$ 10		4.5
Marketable securities	4		5.0
Net accounts receivable	11		3.2
Inventory	9		2.5
Prepaid expenses	1		0.6
Total current assets	$ 35		15.8
Net plant and equipment	183		84.2
Total assets	$218		100.0
Accounts payable	$ 8		6.2
Wages payable	2		2.0
Notes payable	15		3.3
Taxes payable	2		0.8
Other accruals	2		0.9
Total current liabilities	$ 29		13.2
Long-term debt	$ 60		27.7
Deferred taxes	3		1.3
Total long-term liabilities	$ 63		29.0
Common stock	$ 42		18.1
Additional paid-in capital	38		19.1
Retained earnings	46		20.6
Total stockholders' equity	$126		57.8
Total liabilities and stockholders' equity	$218		100.0

12. Construct a common-size income statement for Jet Electro for 1995 and compare it with the common-size income statement for the industry.

	1995 (%) Jet Electro	1995 (%) Industry	1995 Jet Electro (millions)
Net sales		100.0	$162
Cost of goods sold		73.1	118
Gross profit		26.9	$ 44
Operating expenses:			
Selling		4.1	$ 6
General and administrative		6.6	14
Depreciation		5.7	5
Total operating expenses		16.4	$ 25
Net operating income		10.5	$ 19
Interest		4.6	9
Taxable income		5.9	$ 10
Taxes		2.4	4
Net income		3.5	$ 6

13. The common-size balance sheet and income statement (in percents) for Lyon Publications as of December 31, 1995, are shown here. Lyon's level of cash on December 31, 1995, was $20,000, and interest paid during 1995 was $90,000. Determine Lyon's balance sheet and income statement (in dollars) as of December 31, 1995.

Cash	5	Accounts payable	8
Marketable securities	3	Notes payable	5
Accounts receivable	9	Wages payable	2
Inventory	12	*Current liabilities*	15
Current assets	29	Long-term debt	30
Net fixed assets	71	Common stock	30
Total assets	100	Retained earnings	25
		Total liabilities and stockholders' equity	100

Sales	100
Cost of goods sold	65
Gross profit	35
General, selling, and administrative expense	21
Net operating income	14
Interest	6
Taxes	4
Net income	4

14. The Harris Corporation has a taxable income of $128,000.

    (a) What is its total tax liability?

    (b) What is Harris's average tax rate?

    (c) What is Harris's marginal tax rate?

15. As the financial manager for a small corporation, you are faced with a loss of $42,000 for fiscal year 1995. Your incomes for the preceding three years were as follows:

1994	$12,000
1993	$32,000
1992	$34,000

    How will you use this current loss to reduce your taxes?

16. Your firm must raise $150,000 in new capital. This capital may be raised by issuing new debt, which requires interest payments of 10%. The firm's tax rate is 25%. What is the after-tax cost of acquiring the capital by issuing debt in terms of dollars? In terms of the interest rate?

17. Clifton Industries has just purchased a metal press for $120,000 and will depreciate the press using straight-line depreciation over ten years to a $5,000 salvage value.

    (a) How much is the annual depreciation claimed on the press?

    (b) What is the accumulated depreciation on the press after four years?

18. Three years ago your firm purchased a forklift for $10,000. The forklift is being depreciated straight line to a salvage value of $0 in two more years. If your firm sells the forklift today for $5,000, it will receive only $4,750 after taxes.

(a) What is the annual depreciation on the machine?

(b) What is the current book value of the machine?

(c) What is your firm's marginal tax rate?

SUGGESTED
ADDITIONAL
READINGS

Ball, J. R. "Changes in Accounting Techniques and Stock Prices." In *Empirical Research in Accounting, Selected Studies 1972*, supplement to Vol. 10 of *Journal of Accounting Research*, 1972, pp. 1–38.

Ball, J. R., and P. Brown. "An Empirical Evaluation of Accounting Income Numbers." *Journal of Accounting Research* 6 (Autumn 1968): 159–178.

Black, Fischer. "The Magic in Earnings: Economic Earnings Versus Accounting Earnings." *Financial Analysts Journal*, November–December 1980, pp. 19–24.

Foster, George. *Financial Statement Analysis*. Englewood Cliffs, NJ: Prentice-Hall, 1978.

Hawkins, D. F. "The Development of Modern Financial Reporting Practices Among American Manufacturing Corporations." *Business History Review,* Autumn 1963. Reprinted in M. Chatfiled, ed. *Contemporary Studies in the Evolution of Accounting Thought*, pp. 247–279. Belmont, CA: Dickenson, 1968.

Kaplan, R. S., and R. Roll. "Investor Evaluation of Accounting Information: Some Empirical Evidence." *Journal of Business* 45 (April 1972): 225–257.

Scholes, M. S., and Mark Wolfson. *Taxes and Business Strategy: A Planning Approach*. Englewood Cliffs, NJ: Prentice-Hall, 1992.

Watts, R. "Corporate Financial Statements: A Product of the Market and Political Processes." *Australian Journal of Management* 2 (April 1977): 253–271.

Watts, Ross L., and Jerold L. Zimmerman. *Positive Accounting Theory*. Englewood Cliffs, NJ: Prentice-Hall, 1986.

PART TWO VALUE AND RISK

FOUR

FINDING THE PRESENT AND FUTURE VALUES OF CASH FLOWS

The basic problem of time valuation which nature sets us is always that of translating the future into the present.

—Irving Fisher[1]

[1] From *The Theory of Investment* (New York: Macmillan, 1930), p. 14.

ne of the major conclusions of Part One is that the magnitude, timing, and riskiness of the firm's cash flow affect the firm's stock price. This chapter focuses on the timing dimension. We introduce techniques for recognizing the implications of cash flows that occur at different times.

After reading this chapter, you should be able to answer the following questions:

■ Why do interest rates exist?

■ What is the compounding process? What is discounting?

■ How do we deal with complex situations that involve discounting and compounding?

■ What are the financial decision-making criteria that rely on the time-value notion?

4-1

FINDING FUTURE AND PRESENT VALUES

The Time Value of Money

A fundamental principle underlying financial decision making is the **time value of money**. When we compare two cash flows that have identical magnitude and risk, the cash flow that occurs earlier in time is more valuable. For example, a dollar today is worth more than a dollar next year because a dollar invested today will earn interest and be worth more than a dollar by the end of the year. Similarly, $5,000 to be received in two years will be worth more than $5,000 in three years because even though the magnitude of the cash flows is the same, they occur at different times, and the potential to earn interest on the earlier cash flow affects its relative value.

These examples are fairly easy to understand because the magnitudes of the cash flows are the same. But what if the cash flows differ in both timing *and* magnitude, such as receiving $5,000 in two years or $5,500 in three years? Such comparisons are an integral part of financial decision making. This chapter introduces methods that make such comparisons feasible. Before discussing the mechanics of time value, however, we should examine some explanations about why interest rates exist.

Why Do Interest Rates Exist?

The time value of money exists because of interest rates. It is commonly said that the interest rate is the "price of money," but this explanation, though convenient, is not entirely correct. In fact, interest rates can exist even in a society that has no money. The **interest rate** is the difference between the values of current and future goods. Thus, as long as current goods are more valuable than future goods, interest rates will be positive.

Why are current goods considered more valuable than future goods? There are several explanations and theories, but we discuss only two of them. First, almost all people have a positive **time preference**. This is a behavioral characteristic that, for whatever reason, people prefer current consumption to future consumption. Whatever the intensity of the preference for now as opposed to later, it is almost always positive, although it may vary from one person to another and from one society to another. This time preference alone suggests why positive interest rates exist.

Second, capital can be productive, which is a technological rather than a behavioral factor. Interest rates exist because of this **productivity of capital**. Let us see why by considering Robinson Crusoe's lifestyle on his island. Crusoe barely survives by eating four clams per day, and he has to dig them out of the ground with his bare hands—an activity that consumes his energies for the entire day, leaving him little time for leisure. If he had a shovel, he could dig six clams per day and thus be better off. Yet to make a shovel would take five full days, and there is no way that he could do this without starving to death. It is clear that Robinson would be willing to borrow 20 clams now and agree to repay more than 20 clams in the future. The reason is that Robinson would not go hungry if he borrowed the clams, and with the shovel he could dig more clams daily in the future, which would allow him to not only repay the borrowed clams but also enjoy a higher standard of living. Robinson's shovel is *capital*, and because it has productive potential, he is willing to pay a premium (i.e., extra clams) to acquire it. Thus a positive interest rate exists. Note that in this example no money is involved, just capital and consumption.

K E Y   C O N C E P T   Interest rates can exist even in a society without money; all that is required is productive capital and a positive time preference.

Finding the Future Value of a Cash Flow   Consider a person who deposits $100 today into a savings account that earns 12% annual interest. How much will the account be worth at the end of the first year—that is, what will be the future value of this single sum? We have

$$FV_1 = \$100 + (\$100 \times 0.12)$$
$$= \$100 + \$12 = \$112$$

where FV_1 is the future value at the end of the first year. The future value is composed of the original principal amount, $100, plus $12 in interest. Because the original $100 is the current or present value (PV), we obtain the following expression by factoring out the common term, PV:

$$FV_1 = PV + (PV \times i) = PV(1 + i) \tag{4-1}$$

Now, what is the future value of $100 at the end of year 2?

$$FV_2 = FV_1 + (FV_1 \times i)$$
$$= \$112 + (\$112 \times 0.12) \tag{4-2}$$
$$= \$112 + \$13.44 = \$125.44$$

That is, the $112 at the end of the first year will grow by 12% to $125.44, and $100 today will be equivalent to $125.44 in two years at an interest rate of 12%. According to equation (4-1), we can substitute for FV_1 in equation (4-2), or

$$FV_2 = PV(1 + i) + [PV(1 + i) \times i]$$
$$= PV(1 + i)(1 + i) \tag{4-3}$$
$$= PV(1 + i)^2$$

which gives the same answer in one step rather than two (i.e., calculate FV_1 and then FV_2):

$$FV_2 = \$100(1.12)^2 = \$100(1.2544) = \$125.44$$

Equation (4-3) can be generalized to handle any number of years. Notice that the important change from equation (4-1) to equation (4-3) is the *exponent* on the interest factor, $1 + i$. This exponent always equals the number of periods over which interest is compounded. So for the general case, the future of a single sum in n years is determined by

$$FV_n = PV(1 + i)^n \tag{4-4}$$

Equation (4-4) is preferable to equation (4-2) because equation (4-4) does not require us to keep track of each future value. The term $(1 + i)^n$ is often replaced in calculations by the future value factor, $FVF_{i,n}$, which is the future value of $1 at interest rate i for n periods:

$$FV_n = PV(FVF_{i,n}) \tag{4-5}$$

The $FVF_{i,n}$ can also be obtained from a future value factor table (such as that at the end of this book), which contains $FVF_{i,n}$ values for selected interest rates and time periods. The present and future value tables in this book are constructed for *whole* percentages (e.g., 10%, 12%). To find the interest factor for a percentage such as 12.5% requires using the formulas in Table 4-1 (see page 87). To include the tables for all conceivable interest rates is obviously not feasible.

Using either equation (4-4) or (4-5) will give the same result. For example, the *FV* in five years of $100 deposited today is

$$FV_5 = \$100(1.12)^5 = \$100(1.7623) = \$100(FVF_{0.12,5})$$
$$= \$176.23$$

For an experienced financial decision maker, a financial calculator is indispensable for these computations. However, effectively using the concept of time value involves much more than just knowing which calculator buttons to press. The highlight on the opposite page explains why we devote time to understanding the time value of money.

Understanding the Compounding Process   Notice that in equation (4-2) the future value at the end of two years is determined by adding the first year's interest to the principal, and this total amount in turn earns interest in the second year. This process illustrates both the difference between *simple* and *compound* interest and the concept of "earning interest on interest." To understand this compounding process, let us expand equation (4-3) to

$$FV_2 = PV(1 + i)^2 = PV(1 + 2i + i^2) \tag{4-6}$$

In equation (4-6), 1 represents the original principal, $2i$ is the simple interest earned for two years, and i^2 is the interest on interest.

For our numerical example,

$$FV_2 = \$100[1 + 2(0.12) + (0.12)^2]$$
$$= \$100(1 + 0.24 + 0.0144)$$
$$= \$100 + \$24 + \$1.44 = \$125.44$$

The future value is determined by summing the original principal amount of $100, the simple interest of $24 (or $12 per year on $100 for two years), and the com-

FINANCIAL CALCULATORS: A MEANS, NOT AN END

With the easy availability of handheld calculators, why is it necessary to study the mechanics of valuation in such detail? Moreover, why use present and future value tables when a calculator can provide the answers directly?

The answer to this question lies in an examination of how a time-value problem is solved. This process has two stages. The first is the analysis and setup of the problem. This step requires understanding the principles of time value and how these principles relate to the problem at hand, being able to separate the problem into sequential steps, and knowing how each step is solved. Only when the first stage is completed can the second stage of the process, the calculation, be completed.

If finance were merely calculating numbers, then taking a finance course and reading this text would be a waste! All you would have to do is purchase a good-quality financial calculator, read its owner's manual, and start making financial decisions. As you progress through this text, you will see that the proper setup of the problem is the difficult part. Once this step is accomplished, the calculations are easy. Thus students who have good facility with calculators but only a superficial knowledge of the process of comparing cash flows may never reach the second stage if they cannot set up the problem correctly. Working out a few problems at the end of this chapter will convince the reader that this is true. Therefore, to be proficient in analyzing a time-value problem, students must understand the theory and interrelationships of the time-

value approach. Thus our emphasis on the mechanics of time value in this chapter.

Of course, once into the second stage, it makes no difference whether tables or calculators are used for computations. A good calculator can be a great asset. Given the wide choice of calculators currently available, with different features, varying methods of data entry, and different programmable functions, we cannot examine methods specific to different makes of calculators. We therefore concentrate on the first stage and explain the procedures required for solving simple and complex time-value problems. The details of calculator usage may be obtained from the calculator's user manual.

Moral: Calculators can compute, but they cannot analyze a problem.

pound interest of $1.44 (or the $12 in interest earned in the first year earns 12% in the second year).

Figure 4-1 depicts this process over five years. The medium-tone area represents the earning of simple interest, and the darker area represents the earning of compounded interest, or interest on interest. The curves in Figure 4-2 show that the future value factor increases as the number of compounding periods and the interest rate rise. From this graph the following observations can be made:

1. Because future values are greater than present values for positive interest rates, future value factors $FVF_{i,n}$ are always greater than 1.

2. The larger the interest rate i is, the larger $FVF_{i,n}$ will be for any given n and, consequently, the larger the future value FV_n will be.

3. The longer the investment (PV) earns interest (i.e., the larger n is), the larger $FVF_{i,n}$ will be and, consequently, the larger FV_n will be.

Before continuing, the reader may wish to examine a more lighthearted application of time-value concepts in the highlight on page 79.

Future Value of an Annuity

So far we have explained only how to determine the future value of a single cash flow (single sum). Most financial decisions, however, involve a series of payments or receipts. When the cash flows are equal and the time between each cash flow is

FIGURE 4-1
Simple versus compound interest

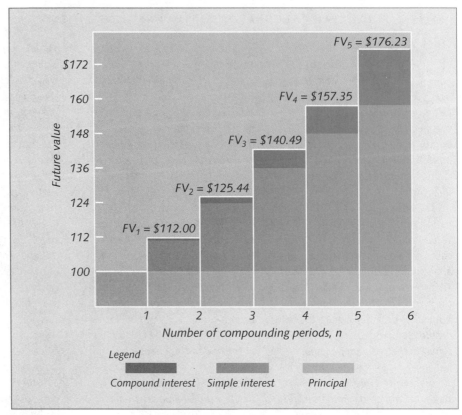

identical, we have the special case known as an annuity. An **annuity** is a sequence of uninterrupted, equal cash flows occurring at regular intervals.

An example of an **ordinary annuity** is given in Figure 4-3(a). As the time line in the figure demonstrates, determining the future value of an ordinary annuity involves calculating the future value of a series of single-sum payments, with the

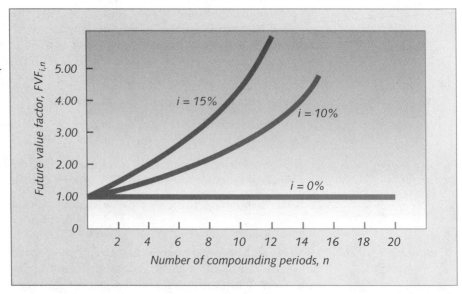

CAN TIME MACHINES EXIST? A SCIENCE FICTION APPLICATION OF THE TIME VALUE OF MONEY

Ever since H. G. Wells published The Time Machine *in 1895, numerous authors and movie makers have explored the potential consequences of time travel. Is time travel possible? Might time machines have existed in the past? What about the future?*

The answer is that as long as current economic conditions prevail, the effects of interest rates rule out the possibility of past, present, or future time machines. This implication of the time value of money is an amusing aside to the (perhaps less fascinating) discussion in the text.

One of the basic ideas underlying the theory of finance is that

people prefer more wealth to less. Consider a "time traveler" who deposits $100 in a savings account in 1994 at an annual interest rate of 10%. In seven years, equation (4-4) suggests, the value of his savings account will be $194.87. If time travel were possible, the investor could deposit the $100 in 1994, travel instantaneously to 2001, withdraw the $194.87, fly back to 1994, redeposit the $194.87, and repeat the process until he had infinite wealth. His time machine would really be a "money machine." In fact, if all citizens had access to time travel, the entire country would prosper. Everyone would have infinite wealth! Negative interest rates are also inconsistent with finite wealth in a world of

time travel because people could then travel backward through time to generate infinite wealth.

The only condition under which the time machine would not be a money machine is when the interest rate is 0%. Only then could the economy support individuals who could travel forward or backward through time without generating wealth. Because interest rates are (and have been) nonzero, this strongly suggests that time travel has never existed and, furthermore, never will.

SOURCE: Adapted from M. R. Reinganum, "Is Time Travel Impossible? A Financial Proof," Journal of Portfolio Management, *Fall 1986, pp. 10–12.*

payments occurring at the end of each period. In this example, we assume that $200 will be deposited at the end of each year for four years and that 10% interest will be earned. To find the future value of this annuity, we determine the future value of each $200 and then add these individual values.

Using a *FVF* table, we obtain

$$FVA_4 = \$200(FVF_{0.10,3}) + \$200(FVF_{0.10,2}) + \$200(FVF_{0.10,1}) + \$200(FVF_{0.10,0})$$
$$= \$200(1.3310) + \$200(1.2100) + \$200(1.1000) + \$200(1.0000)$$
$$= \$928.20$$

where *FVA* is the future value of the annuity. But because the $200 is a constant figure, we can factor it out:

$$FVA_4 = \$200(FVF_{0.10,3} + FVF_{0.10,2} + FVF_{0.10,1} + FVF_{0.10,0})$$
$$= \$200(1.3310 + 1.2100 + 1.1000 + 1.0000)$$
$$= \$200(4.6410) = \$928.20$$

Because of this special property, we can create a new interest factor called the *future value interest factor for an annuity*, $FVFA_{i,n}$, which represents the sum of a series of future value single-sum interest factors.[2] Moreover, based on this insight,

---

[2]In mathematical terms it can be shown that the future value interest factor for an annuity is just the sum of a series of future value lump-sum interest factors that reduce to the following expression, where the sigma (Σ) means to sum or add the values of n factors. This is how financial calculators or the factor tables calculate $FVFA_{i,n}$:

$$FVFA_{i,n} = \sum_{t=1}^{n} (1 + i)^{n-t} = \frac{(1 + i)^n - 1}{i}$$

FIGURE 4-3

Finding the future value of an annuity when i = 10%: (a) ordinary annuity [note that because the last deposit is made at the end of four years, it does not earn any interest; that is, $FVF_{0.10,0} = (1 + i)^0 = 1.0000$] and (b) annuity due

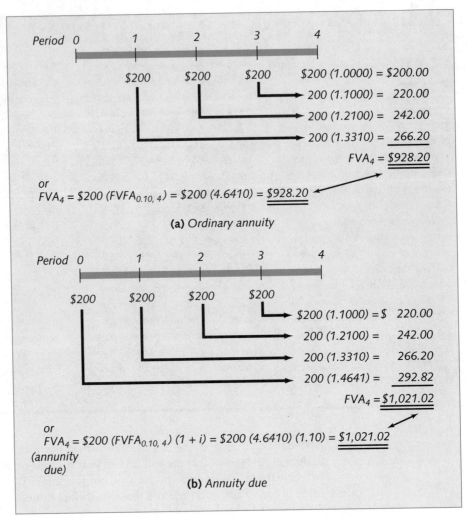

(a) Ordinary annuity

(b) Annuity due

we can create a future value factor annuity (*FVFA*) table (see the tables at the end of the book) just for $FVFA_{i,n}$. Therefore the general formula for the future value of an annuity becomes

$$FVA_n = A(FVFA_{i,n})$$ (4-7)

where *A* is the constant cash flow or annuity amount.[3]

---

[3]Proof: Consider an *n*-period annuity at an interest rate *i*. To find the future value of this annuity we compound each annuity payment to year *n*. Thus,

$$FVA_{i,n} = A(1 + i)^{n-1} + A(1 + i)^{n-2} + \cdots + A \quad \text{(a)}$$

Multiplying both sides by $(1 + i)$ gives

$$(1 + i)FVA_{i,n} = A[(1 + i)^n + (1 + i)^{n-1} + \cdots + (1 + i)^1] \quad \text{(b)}$$

Subtracting (a) from (b) and rearranging terms, we get

$$FVA_{i,n} = A\left[\frac{(1 + i)^n - 1}{i}\right]$$

which produces the $FVFA_{i,n}$.

Occasionally you may encounter another type of annuity, called an **annuity due,** which is a sequence of uninterrupted, equal cash flows with the payments (receipts) occurring at the beginning of each period. The only difference between an ordinary annuity and an annuity due is the timing of the cash flows. As the time line in Figure 4-3(b) shows, all cash flows are shifted one period closer to the current time, which means that each cash flow will receive one more period of compound interest. Therefore, the future value of an annuity due is found as

$$FVA_n = A(FVFA_{i,n})(1 + i) \tag{4-8}$$

or, using our example,

$$
\begin{aligned}
FVA_4 &= \$200(FVFA_{0.10,4})(1 + 0.10) \\
&= \$200(4.6410)(1.1000) \\
&= \$200(5.1051) = \$1{,}021.02
\end{aligned}
$$

Because ordinary annuities are the most common in finance, we use the word *annuity* to mean that the cash flows are received at the end of each period (unless indicated otherwise). We now introduce some examples of time-value problems.

FINDING THE FUTURE VALUE

SINGLE-SUM PROBLEM If you invest $10,000 today at 8% and expect to use it 20 years from now for your child's education, how much will you have at that time?

We are asked to find the future value of $10,000 at the end of 20 years if the interest rate is 8%. From our formula, $FV_{20} = PV(FVF_{0.08,20})$. Because $PV = \$10{,}000$ and $FVF_{0.08,20} = 4.6610$ according to the *FVF* table, we have

$$FV_{20} = \$10{,}000(4.6610) = \$46{,}610$$

ANNUITY PROBLEM If Ima Cooper deposits $1,000 in her savings account at the end of each year for the next 12 years, how much will she have at the end of this period if the interest rate is 6%?

From our formula, $FVA_{12} = A(FVFA_{0.06,12})$. Because $A = \$1{,}000$ and $FVFA_{0.06,12} = 16.869$ according to the *FVFA* table, we have

$$FVA_{12} = \$1{,}000(16.869) = \$16{,}869$$

Notice that in this case $\$1{,}000 \times 12 = \$12{,}000$ represents Cooper's original deposits, and the difference ($4,869) is interest earned.

SOLVING FOR THE INTEREST RATE

On occasion, the future value is known and you must solve for one of the other variables (A, i, or n). The following examples demonstrate how this is done.

SINGLE-SUM PROBLEM What interest rate must be earned on a $5,000 investment so that it will be worth $7,013 in five years?

For this question, $5,000 must equal $7,013 after compounding interest for five years. So

$$
\begin{aligned}
FV_5 &= PV(FVF_{?,5}) \\
\$7{,}013 &= \$5{,}000(FVF_{?,5})
\end{aligned}
$$

or

$$FVF_{?,5} = \frac{\$7{,}013}{\$5{,}000} = 1.4026$$

From the *FVF* table, the future value interest factor 1.4026 in the row for five years corresponds to an interest rate of 7%.

ANNUITY PROBLEM Assume that a retirement plan calls for $3,500 to be deposited at the end of every year for the next 40 years. If this plan guarantees that you will have $541,660 at the end of this time, what is the implied interest rate earned?

The problem must be consistent with equation (4-7). From this information in the problem, we obtain

$$FVA_{40} = A(FVFA_{?,40})$$
$$\$541,660 = \$3,500(FVFA_{?,40})$$

or

$$FVFA_{?,40} = \frac{\$541,660}{\$3,500} = 154.76$$

According to the *FVFA* table, the future value interest factor 154.76 in the row for 40 years corresponds to an interest rate of 6%. The number of compounding periods can also be found using a similar approach.

Present Value of a Single Sum and the Discounting Process

Finding present values (also known as **discounting**) is the reverse of what we have done so far. When we compute *future values,* we move forward through time; when we compute *present values,* we move backward through time. Until now, for instance, we wanted to know how much a single cash flow today would be worth after *n* years. Now, instead of starting with a current cash flow and finding its future value, we start with a future cash flow and find its value today. Figure 4-4 compares present and future values.

■

FIGURE 4-4
Comparison of present value and future value when i = 8%

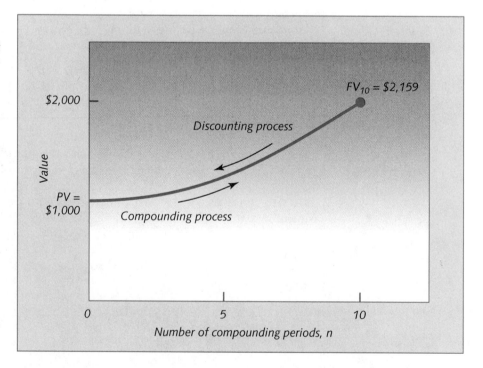

Look again at equation (4-5). If we want to find the present value of a cash flow that occurs n years from now, all we need to do is solve for PV:

$$FV_n = PV(FVF_{i,n}) \quad \text{implies} \quad PV = \frac{FV_n}{FVF_{i,n}}$$

Note that this is exactly what we did earlier. Alternatively, because $FVF_{i,n} = (1 + i)^n$,

$$PV = FV_n \left[\frac{1}{(1 + i)^n} \right] \quad \text{or} \quad PV = FV_n(PVF_{i,n}) \tag{4-9}$$

where $PVF_{i,n} = 1/[(1 + i)^n]$ is the present value interest factor for a single-sum cash flow received at the end of the nth year with interest rate i. Thus the $PVF_{i,n}$ values are just the reciprocals of the $FVF_{i,n}$ values. Selected $FVF_{i,n}$ values are listed in the tables provided at the end of the book.

Present value calculations allow one to compare cash flows at different times by valuing them all at the present time. Recall the example from the beginning of the chapter: Which is preferred, $5,000 in two years or $5,500 in three years? Unless one knows the interest rate and then compares the two dollar amounts at the same time, the answer is not clear. If $i = 12\%$, the future value in year 3 of $5,000 that can be obtained two years hence is given as

$$FV_3 = \$5,000(FVF_{0.12,1}) = \$5,000(1.12) = \$5,600$$

which is more than $5,500. Thus the $5,000 in two years is preferable because it has a higher future value.

Alternatively, we could find the present value of both cash flows by "discounting" them at 12%. Referring to the second time line in Figure 4-5 and using a present value factor (PVF) table, we have

$$PV = \$5,000(PVF_{0.12,2}) = \$5,000(0.7972) = \$3,986.00$$

FIGURE 4-5

Comparisons of two cash flows to be received at different future dates, in terms of (a) future values and (b) present values. A: $5,000 in two years and B: $5,500 in three years

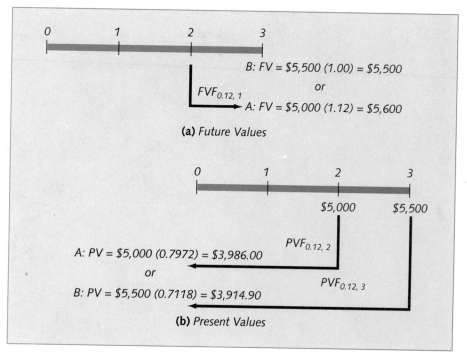

and

$$PV = \$5,500(PVF_{0.12,3}) = \$5,500(0.7118) = \$3,914.90$$

Once again, the $5,000 in two years is preferable to the other alternative because it has a *higher present value*. This is as it should be because the decision should not depend on the time that the two cash flows are compared. What is important is that both are compared at the same time, whichever time is chosen for comparison.

To help understand the relationship between present values and future values, the reader is encouraged to prove, using a *FVF* table, that the future value of $3,986 will be exactly $5,000 in two years. That is, receiving $5,000 in two years is equivalent to having $3,986 today that can be invested at 12% for two years.

Because we live in the present, which is when financial decisions are made, we rely primarily on present value comparisons from now on.

Figure 4-6 shows the relationships among present value factors, interest rates, and time. These relationships may be summarized as follows:

1. Because present values are less than future values for all positive interest rates, the present value factors $PVF_{i,n}$ are less than 1.00.

2. The larger the interest rate is, the smaller the present value factor is and, consequently, the smaller the present value is.

3. The further into the future that the cash flow occurs (i.e., the larger n is), the smaller the present value factor is and, consequently, the smaller the present value is.

We encourage you to use a *PVF* table and Figure 4-6 to confirm these observations.

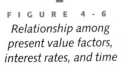

F I G U R E   4 - 6

Relationship among present value factors, interest rates, and time

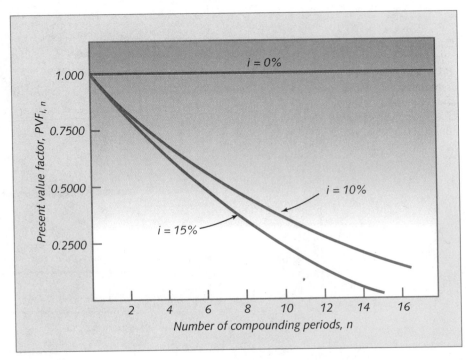

FIGURE 4-7
*Finding the present value
of an annuity when
i = 10%*

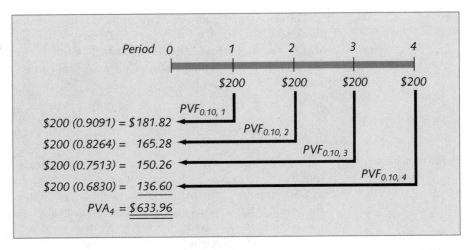

FIGURE 4-7

*Finding the present value
of an annuity when
i = 10%*

*Present Value of an
Annuity*

To find the present value of an annuity, we need to reverse the process of finding the future value of an annuity. Conceptually, each individual cash flow is discounted back to the present and then summed to obtain the present value. This means that the present value interest factor for an annuity, $PVFA_{i,n}$, is simply the sum of a series of present value interest factors for a single sum.

To see this, let us use the annuity problem described in Figure 4-3, but now we find its present value. Referring to Figure 4-7, we see that

$$PV = \$200(PVF_{0.10,1}) + \$200(PVF_{0.10,2}) + \$200(PVF_{0.10,3}) + \$200(PVF_{0.10,4})$$
$$= \$200(0.9091 + 0.8264 + 0.7513 + 0.6830)$$
$$= \$200(3.1698) = \$633.96$$

Rather than summing the individual $PVF_{i,n}$ values every time, we can use a present value factor annuity $(PVFA)$ table.[4] The general formula then becomes

$$PVA = A(PVFA_{i,n}) \tag{4-10}$$

[4]In mathematical terms, the present value interest factor for an annuity is the sum of a series of present value lump-sum factors:

$$PVFA_{i,n} = \sum_{t=1}^{n} \frac{1}{(1 + i)^t} = \frac{1 - \left[\dfrac{1}{(1 + i)^n}\right]}{i}$$

Proof: Consider the present value of an *n*-period annuity at interest rate *i*. Each annuity payment (A) is discounted to the present. Thus,

$$PVA = A\left[\frac{1}{(1 + i)^1} + \frac{1}{(1 + i)^2} + \frac{1}{(1 + i)^3} + \cdots + \frac{1}{(1 + i)^n}\right] \quad \text{(a)}$$

Multiplying both sides by $(1 + i)$ gives

$$(1 + i)PVA = A\left[1 + \frac{1}{(1 + i)^1} + \frac{1}{(1 + i)^2} + \frac{1}{(1 + i)^3} + \cdots + \frac{1}{(1 + i)^{n-1}}\right] \quad \text{(b)}$$

Subtracting (a) from (b) and rearranging terms, we get

$$PVA = A\left[\frac{1 - \left[\dfrac{1}{(1 + i)^n}\right]}{i}\right] \quad \text{(c)}$$

We can solve (c) to obtain the $PVFA_{i,n}$.

For example, if you win a sweepstakes prize that offers you either $50,000 today or $7,000 per year for the next 12 years, which alternative would you prefer if your discount rate is 12%? In this case, $50,000 is already a present value, so all we have to do is find the present value of a $7,000 annuity for 12 years. According to the *PVFA* table, we have

$$PVA = \$7,000(PVFA_{0.12,12}) = \$7,000(6.1944) = \$43,360.80$$

Therefore, the second alternative is worth less than the first one.

Present Value of a Perpetuity

A **perpetuity** is a series of equal periodic payments that continue forever (to infinity). One example of a perpetuity is the British *consol*. To finance its wars against Napoleon, the British government issued bonds, called consols, that paid the bondholders a stated money amount periodically as long as they (or their heirs) owned the consols. Sometimes preferred stock—an equity instrument that pays a fixed dividend and has no maturity—is also a perpetuity.

What is the value of a perpetuity? From earlier sections we know that the value of this asset can be obtained by discounting the perpetual income stream. But finding the present value of an annuity with $n = $ infinity is not possible with the interest tables. Fortunately, the present value of a perpetuity can easily be found with a simple formula:[5]

$$PV_P = \frac{\text{cash flow per period}}{\text{discount rate}} \qquad (4\text{-}11)$$

If the consol pays its holder £100 per year forever and if the discount rate is 10%, its value is

$$PV_P = \frac{£100}{0.10} = £1,000$$

This is a surprisingly small value for an asset that will pay millions of pounds over time. The reason for such a small value is that the more distant cash flows do not have much present value, and therefore their contribution to the perpetuity's value is very small. For example, £1 to be received in 40 years is worth only about 2 pence at a 10% discount rate.

We have now completed the discussion of the four interest factors that enter into time-value calculations. Table 4-1 summarizes these factors and their formulas and provides shorthand methods for calculating the factors when a table is unavailable or cannot be used. For example, when the interest rate is not a whole percentage point, say 4.25%, the formulas presented in Table 4-1 may be a convenient way of calculating the appropriate factor. Table 4-1 can also help the reader see how the different time-value methods are related.

Stock and Flow Variables and the Process of Capitalization

There are standard terms used in connection with time-value calculations. The cash flows we have examined can be placed into two categories. **Flow variables** consist of a stream of cash flows, such as the flow of rental income from a commercial building. A **stock variable**, on the other hand, has no time dimension; it is simply a number at a particular time. Stock variables include the wealth that a person has today, the value of his or her house, and the current market value of Exxon's ten-year bonds.

[5]For the derivation of equation (4-11) return to footnote 4. As n approaches ∞, the term $[1/(1 + i)^n]$ in (c) approaches 0 so that $PVA = A/i$.

■

TABLE 4-1

Calculation of Future Value and Present Value Interest Factors

Interest Factor	Formula	Method of Calculation
Future value of a single sum, $FVF_{i,n}$	$(1 + i)^n$	$(1 + i)^n$
Future value of an annuity, $FVFA_{i,n}{}^a$	$\sum_{t=1}^{n} (1 + i)^{n-t}$	$\dfrac{(1 + i)^n - 1}{i}$
Present value of a single sum, $PVF_{i,n}$	$\dfrac{1}{(1 + i)^n}$	$\dfrac{1}{(1 + i)^n}$
Present value of an annuity, $PVFA_{i,n}{}^b$	$\sum_{t=1}^{n} \dfrac{1}{(1 + i)^t}$	$\dfrac{1 - \left[\dfrac{1}{(1 + i)^n}\right]}{i}$

[a] Refer to footnote 2.
[b] Refer to footnote 4.

Capitalization is simply the process of converting flow variables (cash flows) into a stock variable in two steps:

1. Identifying the cash flows provided by the asset
2. Capitalizing (discounting) these cash flows at the appropriate discount rate

So, whenever you calculate the present value of a cash flow, you are capitalizing the cash flow. Capitalizing flow variables into stock variables provides equivalent information that may be easier to use in making a given financial decision.

4-2
SPECIAL TIME-VALUE CONSIDERATIONS

We now examine several special issues involved in time-value calculations: cash flows in different currencies, changing discount rates, various compounding periods, and changing cash flows in an annuity.

Comparing Cash Flows in Different Currencies

Thus far our discussion has been fairly simple because we have used only dollars. However, many business decisions involve cash flows in several currencies. Exchange rates between currencies were introduced in Chapter 1. These exchange rates can be used to determine the present values of cash flows received in different currencies.

Consider the case of Dell Computers. Dell will receive the following quarterly interest payments from its British sales subsidiary:

Pound cash flows	Jan. 1	March 31	June 30	Sept. 30	Dec. 30
		£1,132	£1,009	£1,140	£1,238

Susan Cloud, the exchange risk manager at Dell, must determine the dollar value of each payment. She obtains the following estimates of future exchange rates from Texas Commerce Bank: March 31, $1.4780/£; June 30, $1.4678/£; September 30, $1.4580/£; and December 31, $1.4290/£. These rates allow her to determine how many dollars Dell will receive each quarter. For example, Dell will receive £1,009 on June 30. If these pounds are exchanged for dollars at the estimated exchange rate, they will be worth £1,009 × ($1.4678/£) = $1,481. She finds:

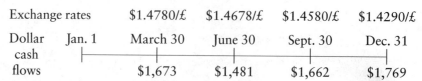

Exchange rates	$1.4780/£	$1.4678/£	$1.4580/£	$1.4290/£
Dollar cash flows	Jan. 1	March 30	June 30	Sept. 30	Dec. 31

Dollar cash flows: $1,673 (March 30), $1,481 (June 30), $1,662 (Sept. 30), $1,769 (Dec. 31)

Susan then determines the present value of these dollar cash flows at Dell's discount rate of 2% per quarter:

$$PV = \$1,673(PVF_{0.02,1}) + \$1,481(PVF_{0.02,2}) + \$1,662(PVF_{0.02,3}) + \$1,769(PVF_{0.02,4})$$
$$= \$6,264$$

Changing Discount Rates

In the examples thus far, we have assumed that the discount rate remains constant over time. This certainly need not be the case, as any casual observation of interest rates over time will show. But changing interest rates can easily be incorporated into our time-value discussion.

What is the present value of $200 to be received in three years if we expect the interest rates to be 10% in year 1, 12% in year 2, and 14% in year 3? This present value may be determined simply by applying equation (4-9) for each successive period in which the discount rate changes. This process results in equation (4-12):

$$PV = \frac{CF_n}{(1 + i_1)(1 + i_2)(1 + i_3) \cdots (1 + i_n)} \tag{4-12}$$

where *CF* represents cash flow and the subscripts refer to the appropriate years. In our example of $200, the present value may be found in this manner:

$$PV = \frac{\$200}{(1 + 0.10)(1 + 0.12)(1 + 0.14)} = \$142.40$$

Because of changing discount rates, time-value calculations for annuities are much more complex and require treating each annuity payment's present value individually. In this text we assume that most discount rates used are constant over the evaluation period.

Frequency of Compounding Periods

Thus far we have compounded interest annually, but interest can be compounded over any time period. The frequency of compounding may be handled in two ways, depending on the length of the compounding period: discrete compounding and continuous compounding.

DISCRETE COMPOUNDING

Bonds pay interest semiannually and thus have interest credited twice a year. Savings institutions typically compound interest on their accounts quarterly or even daily. These are examples of discrete compounding periods in which there is a countable number of compounding periods per year.

To reflect the frequency of compounding periods, we must make two adjustments. First, the interest rate is converted to a *per-period rate* by dividing the annual rate by the number of compounding periods in a year, *i/m*. Second, the number of years is multiplied by the number of compounding periods that occur each year, *mn*. The calculation of a future value using discrete compounding is:

$$FV_n = PV \left(1 + \frac{i}{m}\right)^{mn} \tag{4-13}$$

Using this relationship, we find that $100 deposited in an 8% savings account that pays interest quarterly will grow to $108.24 in one year:

$$FV_n = \$100\left(1 + \frac{0.08}{4}\right)^{4\times 1}$$

$$= \$100(1.02)^4 = \$100(1.0824) = \$108.24$$

Thus, although the **nominal** or **stated interest rate** of the deposit is its annual rate, the 8% in our example, the **effective interest rate** (often called the **annual percentage rate**, or *APR*) is the rate that actually determines the future value of the deposit, or 8.24%.

Problems that involve frequent compounding often use rates and time periods not contained in time-value tables. In such cases the interest factor can be computed directly using one of the methods suggested in Table 4-1 or with the aid of a financial calculator. For instance, a compound period can occur during a year rather than at the end of a year. To find the future value of a current amount in two years and six months, we use the formula

$$FV_{2.5} = PV(1 + i)^{2.5}$$

That is, the number of months is converted to a percentage of a whole year. Similarly, two years and four months are $n = 2.33$, and two years and 219 days are $n = 2 + (219/365)$ or 2.60.

CONTINUOUS COMPOUNDING

We have seen that the length of the compounding period affects the value of the deposit. What happens as the compounding period approaches 0? In this limiting case we have **continuous compounding**, and the basic calculation takes on a new form:

$$FV_n = \lim_{m \to \infty} PV\left(1 + \frac{i}{m}\right)^{mn} = PVe^{in} \tag{4-14}$$

where e is Euler's constant, which is approximately 2.7183.

From our previous example, $100 deposited at a nominal annual rate of 8% but compounded continuously will grow to:

$$FV_n = \$100e^{0.08(1)} = \$108.33$$

which gives an effective interest rate of 8.33%.

Thus, although the nominal interest rate is 8% per year, the effective rate earned on the deposit can vary from 8% with annual compounding to 8.33% with continuous compounding. The shorter the compounding period, the *larger* the future value of an amount deposited today. The reader might, as an exercise, demonstrate that the shorter the compounding period, the *smaller* the present value of a future amount.

Growing Cash Flows   The calculations for perpetuities and annuities in Section 4-1 assumed that the cash flows received in each period were constant. Through the use of geometric series, we can develop procedures for calculating the present values of payment streams that grow at a fixed rate, g.

GROWING PERPETUITIES

A growing perpetuity is one in which the cash flows increase each period by a set rate; that is, the cash flow in any period is $(1 + g)$ times larger than the previous cash flow. This gives

$$PV_{GP} = \frac{CF_1}{(1 + i)} + \frac{CF_1(1 + g)}{(1 + i)^2} + \frac{CF_1(1 + g)^2}{(1 + i)^3} + \cdots$$

where GP signifies a growing perpetuity. Provided that the growth rate, g, is less than the discount rate, i, this can be reduced to[6]

$$PV_{GP} = \frac{CF_1}{i - g} \qquad\qquad (4\text{-}15)$$

For example, consider a bond that promises to make payments indefinitely. This instrument is similar to the consol discussed in the previous section in that its discount rate is 10% and the next interest payment of £100 will be paid in one year. However, the bond has a provision that its interest payments are guaranteed to grow at the expected rate of inflation, 4%. If our discount rate is 10%, the present value of this investment is

$$PV_{GP} = \frac{£100}{(0.10 - 0.04)} = £1{,}666.67$$

which is substantially more than the £1,000 present value of the consol with fixed interest payments.

[6]The formula is based on the sum of an infinite geometric series. We start with the following geometric series:

$$\sum_{t=0}^{n} x^t = 1 + x + x^2 + x^3 + \cdots + x^n \qquad (a)$$

where x is a number whose absolute value is less than or equal to 1. Multiplying both sides by $(1 - x)$ gives

$$(1 - x) \sum_{t=0}^{n} x^t = (1 - x)(1 + x + x^2 + x^3 + \cdots + x^{n-1} + x^n)$$
$$= (1 - x) + (x - x^2) + (x^2 - x^3) + \cdots + (x^{n-1} - x^n) + (x^n - x^{n+1})$$
$$= 1 - x^{n+1}$$

Dividing both sides by $(1 - x)$ gives

$$\sum_{t=0}^{n} x^t = \frac{1}{1 - x} - \frac{x^{n+1}}{1 - x}$$

As n approaches infinity, x^{n+1} approaches 0 (since $x < 1$), giving

$$\sum_{t=0}^{\infty} x^t = \frac{1}{1 - x} \qquad (b)$$

This result can be applied to determine the present value of a growing perpetuity:

$$PV_{GP} = \frac{CF_1}{1 + i} + \frac{CF_1(1 + g)}{(1 + i)^2} + \frac{CF_1(1 + g)^2}{(1 + i)^3} + \cdots$$
$$= \frac{CF_1}{1 + g} \left[\left(\frac{1 + g}{1 + i}\right)^1 + \left(\frac{1 + g}{1 + i}\right)^2 + \left(\frac{1 + g}{1 + i}\right)^3 + \cdots \right]$$

Let $y = (1 + g)/(1 + i)$. If $g < i$, then $y < 1$. The present value of a growing perpetuity can then be stated as

$$PV_{GP} = \frac{CF_1}{1 + g} [y + y^2 + y^3 + y^4 + \cdots]$$

From (a) and (b), $y + y^2 + y^3 + \cdots = 1/(1 - y) - 1 = y/(1 - y)$. Therefore

$$PV_{GP} = \frac{CF_1}{1 + g} \left(\frac{y}{1 - y}\right) \qquad (c)$$

Substituting for y in (c) and simplifying yield equation (4-15).

GROWING ANNUITIES

A growing annuity is similar to a fixed annuity, except that its payments are not fixed but increase at a constant rate. Equation (4-16) gives the value of an n-period growing annuity, where GA signifies a growing annuity:[7]

$$PV_{GA} = \frac{CF_1}{i - g}\left[1 - \left(\frac{1 + g}{1 + i}\right)^n\right]$$

(4-16)

Assume that we have invested in a security that promises four annual payments. These payments start out at $200 but are to grow at the annual rate of 3%. What is the present value of this growing annuity if our discount rate is 10%?

$$PV_{GA} = \frac{200}{0.10 - 0.03}\left[1 - \left(\frac{1 + 0.03}{1 + 0.10}\right)^4\right] = \$660.75$$

4-3

FINANCIAL DECISION-MAKING CRITERIA

We are now ready to use time-value techniques in a more sophisticated manner. Our prime interest is how time-value calculations can assist managers in increasing the cash flows of a firm and thus stockholder wealth. We now turn to specific decision-making tools used in finance that are based on time-value principles. We introduce here the mechanics of calculating these criteria, and we elaborate on their economic meaning in succeeding chapters.

Net Present Value

The examples so far have referred to cash flows without distinguishing between cash *inflows* and cash *outflows*. In practice, cash flows are usually made up of both inflows and outflows. For example, a firm that buys a metal pressing machine initially has to pay for it (a cash outflow). Once the products made with the machine roll off the assembly line, they can be sold to generate revenues (cash inflows). When the machine has reached the point that it cannot be used, the firm will sell it, perhaps for scrap value (a cash inflow). In such situations in which both inflows and outflows occur at different times, the firm is interested in finding the net present value (NPV) of these cash flows. The economic meaning of NPV and its applications are extremely important in financial decision making and are covered in subsequent chapters. At this point, we limit ourselves to a time-value definition of NPV. The **net present value** (NPV) of a stream of cash flows is the difference between the present value of the inflows and the present value of the outflows; that is,

$$NPV = PV_{\text{inflows}} - PV_{\text{outflows}}$$

(4-17)

Calculating Net Present Value

Suppose that an initial investment of $1,000 is expected to produce the future cash inflows shown in the following time line. What is the NPV of this investment if the discount rate is 10%?

$-\$1,000$	$\$200$	$\$450$	$\$850$
0	1	2	3

[7] $PV_{GA} = PV_{GP} - (PVF_{i,n})(PV_{GP} \text{ at } t = n)$, so

$$PV_{GA} = \frac{CF_1}{i - g} - \frac{1}{(1 + i)^n}\left(\frac{CF_{n+1}}{i - g}\right)$$

But $CF_{n+1} = CF_1(1 + g)^n$. Substituting and rearranging, we get equation (4-16).

First, calculate the present value of the outflows. The only outflow is the initial investment of $1,000. As it is already at time 0, no adjustments are required:

$$PV_{\text{outflows}} = \$1,000$$

Second, calculate the present value of the inflows. Discount each cash flow amount back to time 0. Then sum these present values to get the present value of all the inflows:

$$
\begin{aligned}
PV_{\text{inflows}} &= \$200(PVF_{0.10,1}) + \$450(PVF_{0.10,2}) + \$850(PVF_{0.10,3}) \\
&= \$200(0.9091) + \$450(0.8264) + \$850(0.7513) \\
&= \$181.82 + \$371.88 + \$638.61 \\
&= \$1,192.31
\end{aligned}
$$

Finally, calculate the NPV:

$$
\begin{aligned}
NPV &= PV_{\text{inflows}} - PV_{\text{outflows}} \\
&= \$1,192.31 - \$1,000 \\
&= \$192.31
\end{aligned}
$$

Thus the investment has a positive NPV of $192.31. In succeeding chapters we explain why an investment with a positive NPV increases stockholder wealth.

Internal Rate of Return   The **internal rate of return** (IRR) is another widely used, but often misunderstood, financial management tool that measures rates of return. IRR is best understood by examining the rate of return computed using a naive approach.

As a loan officer, you have agreed to lend $10,000 to the China Inn Restaurant. The loan will be repaid over the next three years, as shown in the following time line:

What rate of return are you earning on this loan?

A naive approach that is often used is to divide the net inflows by the outflows. The general **rate of return** formula is:

$$\text{Rate of return} = \frac{\text{net inflows}}{\text{outflows}} = \frac{\text{inflows} - \text{outflows}}{\text{outflows}}$$

Net inflows are the dollar return you will receive above and beyond the original investment. From the general rate of return formula, the naive rate of return on the loan is:

$$\text{Rate of return} = \frac{\$2,000 + \$6,000 + \$8,000 - \$10,000}{\$10,000} = 60\%$$

or 20% per year.

Though adequate for computing the rate of return for a single-period investment, this formula does not work in a multiperiod setting. The bank appears to have earned a 20% annual return on the loan—a rate you would have obtained regardless of whether the largest cash inflow of $8,000 occurred in year 3, year 2, or year 1. However, you would hardly be indifferent to when you received this large cash flow. Therefore the naive approach, because it does not take into account the timing of the cash flows, is not a correct measure of return.

The *IRR* approach differs from the naive approach in that it explicitly recognizes both the amount and the timing of the inflows and outflows in determining the rate of return. It is called the *internal rate of return* because the only information needed to compute it is the magnitude and timing of the cash flows of the loan or asset. No other external information is required. In a quantitative sense, it is the discount rate that makes the *NPV* = 0, or, equivalently, the rate that makes the present value of inflows equal to the present value of outflows:

$$PV_{inflows} = PV_{outflows} \tag{4-18}$$

KEY CONCEPT   The *IRR* is the rate of return on an investment adjusted for the timing of the inflows and outflows. It is the discount rate that makes the *NPV* of an investment 0.

In our current example, the discount rate that makes the present value of the bank's cash inflows (from the loan repayment) equal to the amount it lends (the $10,000 outflow) is the true rate of interest earned on the loan. Equating the present value of the outflows and inflows produces the following equation.

$$\$2,000(PVF_{IRR,1}) + \$6,000(PVF_{IRR,2}) + \$8,000(PVF_{IRR,3}) = \$10,000$$

or

$$\$2,000(PVF_{IRR,1}) + \$6,000(PVF_{IRR,2}) + \$8,000(PVF_{IRR,3}) - \$10,000 = 0$$

Solving this equation gives an *IRR* of 22.4% per year.

Calculating Internal Rate of Return   Finding the *IRR* means solving equation (4-18) for the unknown discount rate. Depending on the cash flow pattern, the *IRR* can be found in a number of ways. We present three methods.

METHOD 1: CONSTANT ANNUAL CASH INFLOWS — AN ANNUITY PROBLEM

If the only net cash outflow occurs immediately ($t = 0$) and the future cash inflows are constant, then the *IRR* can easily be found. In this special case, the present value of cash outflows is the cash flow that occurs at $t = 0$, represented as CF_0. The cash flows in the future represent an annuity, so that in this case we can write equation (4-18) as

$$CF_t(PVFA_{IRR,n}) - CF_0 = 0 \tag{4-19}$$

where CF_t is the constant per-period future cash inflow and CF_0 is the initial cash outflow.

To illustrate, suppose that $5,000 is invested today and will generate an annual cash inflow of $1,319 for five years. Then, according to equation (4-19),

$$\$1,319(PVFA_{?,5}) - \$5,000 = 0$$

$$PVFA_{?,5} = \frac{\$5,000}{\$1,319} = 3.7908$$

From the $PVFA_{i,n}$ table, this present value interest factor for $n = 5$ indicates an implied interest rate (*IRR*) of 10%.

METHOD 2: UNEVEN ANNUAL CASH FLOWS — A TRIAL-AND-ERROR PROCEDURE

With the more common case in which the cash flows are irregular, the *IRR* cannot be determined directly, as in method 1. A trial-and-error procedure is needed because equation (4-18) becomes a polynomial of the nth degree. When n equals 2 or less, the equation can be solved directly for IRR (when $n = 2$, the quadratic formula can be used). However, most time-value calculations involve cash flows that occur over more than two years. In these cases, the IRR cannot be solved directly, and therefore the trial-and-error method becomes necessary.

We begin with a best guess of a discount rate. Then if this "guesstimate" is not reasonable, we try new discount rates repeatedly until equation (4-18) is approximately accurate.

For example, suppose that an initial investment of $1,000 is expected to produce the following future cash inflows:

$-\$1,000$	$\$200$	$\$450$	$\$850$
0	1	2	3

First, we select a discount rate. Our first approximation is 24%. This produces an imbalance between the present values of inflows and outflows of $-\$100.23$. Therefore the 24% rate is too high, and so we must try a lower value for the IRR. If we try a discount rate of 20%, we find that the imbalance is smaller ($-\$28.94$). This suggests that the discount rate is close to 20% but slightly lower. If we try a discount rate of, say, 18%, we find that the NPV equals $+\$10$. Because the NPV switched from negative to positive, the IRR must lie somewhere between 18% and 20%.

If we do not have a financial calculator available, we can get a more precise answer through interpolation. Consider the following information, which shows a project's NPV at discount rates of 18%, X%, and 20%. Note that X is the project's IRR.

Discount Rate (%)	NPV
18	$10
X (IRR)	0
20	$-\$28.94$

What is X? Notice from the data that the IRR lies between 18% and 20%. When the discount rate goes from 18% to 20%, the actual change in NPV is ($10) $- (-\$28.94) = \$38.94$. However, to find X, we must require the NPV to change by just $10 ($10 $-$ $0) from its value at 18%. With Δ used to mean "change in," X can be calculated using "interpolation" as

$$X = \text{lower discount rate} + \frac{\text{required } \Delta NPV}{\text{actual } \Delta NPV}$$

$$= 18\% + \frac{\$10}{\$10 - (-\$28.94)}$$

$$= 18\% + 0.26\%$$
$$= 18.26\%$$

(4-20)

That is, the project's IRR is approximately 18.26%. However, discount factors have a nonlinear relationship, and therefore even the interpolated answer can be imprecise. The third method, finding the IRR using a financial calculator, is the best way to proceed in this case.

METHOD 3: USING A FINANCIAL CALCULATOR OR A COMPUTER

The *IRR* can most easily be found precisely with the aid of a handheld calculator because the iterative steps in the trial-and-error procedure are preprogrammed and can thus be done more quickly and efficiently. In fact, this is the best way to gain precision in calculating the *IRR*, which for our example is 18.50%.

Uniform Annual Series

The **uniform annual series** (*UAS*) is an annuity payment that is equivalent in present value terms to an irregular cash flow pattern that occurs over the same time period. The *UAS* is helpful to restate cash flows in a manner that makes financial decision making easier. For now it is useful to see why finding the *UAS* requires converting a stock variable to a flow variable. Given the following time line, we want to find the *UAS* for the cash flows if the discount rate is 12% per year:

The *PV* of this cash flow sequence is computed as

$$PV = \$5,000(PVF_{0.12,1}) + \$2,000(PVF_{0.12,3}) + \$4,000(PVF_{0.12,4})$$
$$= \$5,000(0.8929) + \$2,000(0.7118) + \$4,000(0.6355)$$
$$= \$8,430.10$$

To find the *PV* of this cash flow stream, we have converted the flow variables to a stock variable. Now we want to know what uniform annual series for four years has the same present value of $8,430.10. The present value of the *UAS* (an annuity payment) is

$$PV_{UAS} = UAS(PVFA_{i,n})$$

or

$$UAS = \frac{PV_{UAS}}{PVFA_{i,n}} \tag{4-21}$$

Because $PV_{UAS} = \$8,430.10$ and $PVFA_{0.12,4} = 3.0373$, according to the *PVFA* table, we have

$$UAS = \frac{\$8,430.10}{3.0373} = \$2,775.52$$

Thus a uniform annual series of $2,775.52 per year for four years at 12% is equivalent to the original cash flow stream.

SUMMARY

Section 4-1: Finding Future and Present Values

Why do interest rates exist?

■ Interest rates exist because of a preference for immediate consumption and the productivity of capital. Because of interest rates, money has a time value.

■ Financial decision making often involves a comparison of cash flows that differ in both timing and magnitude. The time-value techniques of this chapter facilitate such comparisons.

What is the compounding process? What is discounting?

- The compounding process yields the future value of a cash flow given the relevant interest rate. If you know the cash value of something today and wish to know its value in the future, you compound that value.

- The discounting process yields the present value of a cash flow given the relevant interest rate. If you know the cash value of something in the future and wish to know what it is worth today, you discount the future value.

- An annuity is a series of level uninterrupted cash flows. If the first cash flow occurs today, it is an annuity due. If the first cash flow occurs next period, it is an ordinary annuity. The annuity tables provided in this book are for ordinary annuities.

- Time-value computations permit a conversion of flow variables into stock variables, and vice versa.

- Time-value calculations can be made using formulas, time-value tables, or calculators.

Section 4-2: Special Time-Value Considerations

How do we deal with complex situations that involve discounting and compounding?

- Cash flows can occur in several currencies. To determine the dollar present value of these cash flows, we convert them to dollar equivalents at the estimated exchange rate for each time period and then apply standard discounting methods.

- Although the factors provided in the present and future value tables assume that interest is paid once every period (year), the cases of semiannual, monthly, and so on compounding can be handled easily by adjusting the interest rate and the compounding period appropriately. Continuous compounding can be handled easily using a simple exponential relationship. The present value of a growing perpetuity can also be found by means of a simple formula.

Section 4-3: Financial Decision-Making Criteria

What are the financial decision-making criteria that rely on the time-value notion?

- The net present value (NPV) of an investment is the difference between the present values of cash inflows and the present values of cash outflows.

- The internal rate of return (IRR) is the rate of return earned on an investment after adjusting for the timing of the cash flows. The IRR is that discount rate that makes the $NPV = 0$.

- The uniform annual series (UAS) allows a manager to restate an uneven cash flow stream as an equivalent annuity.

QUESTIONS

1. What do higher interest rates indicate about people's preferences? What do they indicate about the productivity of capital?

2. Explain why compounding and discounting are essentially procedures for finding the value of cash flows at a future or earlier time.

3. What is the difference between simple interest and compound interest?

4. The interest rate on your investment has dropped from 12% to 8%. What will happen to the future value of your investment?

5. What is the difference between an ordinary annuity and an annuity due? Can you think of some examples? What is the significance of this difference for the computation of future values?

6. What is the difference between a perpetuity and an annuity?

7. Determine whether the following are stock variables or flow variables:

   (a) The amount of cash in your wallet

   (b) Monthly social security payments made to senior citizens

   (c) The value of your car

   (d) The monthly payments on your car

   (e) The gross national product of the United States

   (f) Rent on an apartment

8. Your friend, who was supposed to pay back an interest-free loan in one month, has now informed you that she will pay it back in three months. What has happened to the present value, to you, of that loan? Why?

9. Explain how the effective interest rate is calculated with intrayear compounding.

10. How do you find present and future value factors when the interest rate is not a whole percentage point (e.g., 14.5%), without using a programmed calculator?

11. Capitalization is the process of converting a flow variable into a stock variable. Explain.

12. For a given interest rate on your savings, would a switch from quarterly to monthly compounding be to your advantage?

13. To find the *NPV*, you need to know a discount rate. To find the *IRR*, you don't need a discount rate. True or false? Why?

14. Why is the *IRR* an "internal" rate of return?

15. What are the major differences among the *NPV, IRR,* and *UAS*?

PROBLEMS

1. If you deposit $100 in the bank today and it earns interest at a rate of 8% compounded annually, how much will be in the account 50 years from today?

2. On January 1, 1994, you received a savings account from your deceased aunt's estate. Your aunt made a deposit of $1,000 on January 1, 1944. Ten years later she made another deposit of $1,000. If the account paid 5%, compounded annually, how much have you received?

3. According to Problem 2, how much would be in the account if the interest was compounded semiannually? Quarterly? (*Hint:* $FVF_{0.025,100} = 11.814$, $FVF_{0.025,80} = 7.210$, $FVF_{0.0125,200} = 11.995$, and $FVF_{0.0125,160} = 7.298$.)

4. A loaf of bread costs $0.79 today. If the price of a loaf of bread increases by 6% per year, how much will an equivalent loaf of bread cost in 20 years?

5. The population of the earth was approximately 3.411 billion in 1970 and 4.585 billion in 1980.

   (a) At what rate (to the nearest percent) did the world's population grow during that ten-year period?

   (b) If the world's population continues to grow at this rate, what will it be in the year 2000?

   (c) The population of Harlson, Iowa, in January 1991 was 341,655. If Harlson's population grows at the same rate as that of the rest of the world, when will Harlson have a population of 500,000?

6. A friend has some interest factor tables for $PVF_{0.09,6}$ and he tells you that the number on his table is 1.677, but the heading to the table is torn off, so he does not know whether 1.677 is $PVF_{0.09,6}$ or $FVF_{0.09,6}$. Without looking at another table, can you tell which it is? Why? If this is $FVF_{0.09,6}$, what is $PVF_{0.09,6}$?

7. How much money must you deposit in a savings account today to have $20,000 20 years from today if the interest rate is 8% compounded annually?

8. A stock has paid dividends regularly for the last 20 years, starting with a $0.75 dividend in 1975 and increasing to a $4 dividend in 1995. If these dividends have been growing at a constant rate, what has that rate been for the last 20 years?

9. Your sister borrows $1,000 and promises to repay $2,000. If you want at least a 5% return on your loan, within how many years must she pay you back?

10. Which would you prefer: $1,000 now, $2,000 in five years, or $3,000 in ten years?

    (a) If your time value of money is 12%

    (b) If your time value of money is 16%

    (c) If your time value of money is 8%

11. Which would you prefer: $3,000 now, $2,000 that was placed in a savings account five years ago, or $1,000 that was placed in a savings account ten years ago?

    (a) If the interest rate on savings is 12%

    (b) If the interest rate on savings is 16%

    (c) If the interest rate on savings is 8%

12. Using a discount rate of 12%, find the present value of $100 received at the end of each of the next four years.

    (a) Use only the PVF table.

    (b) Use only the $PVFA$ table.

13. Use a discount rate of 12%, find the future value as of the end of year 4 of $100 received at the end of each of the next four years.

(a) Use only the *FVF* table.

(b) Use only the *FVFA* table.

(c) Use only your answer to Problem 12 and the fact that $FVF_{0.12,4} = 1.5735$.

14. If you save $5,000 at the end of each year for the next five years, how much will you need to save at the end of each year for years 6 through 10 to have $100,000 at the end of the tenth year, given an interest rate of 12%?

15. If the discount rate is 11%, what is the present value of $200 received at the end of each of the next ten years except for the fourth year (i.e., you get payments at the end of years 1, 2, 3, 5, 6, 7, 8, 9, and 10)? (Table 4-1 gives formulas for all instances.)

16. If the discount rate is 13%, what is the FV_{10} of $300 received at the end of each of the next ten years except for the fourth year?

17. What is the present value of a seven-year $1,000 annuity if the first $1,000 payment is made four years from today and the discount rate is 15%?

18. What is the FV_{12} of a ten-year $500 annuity for which the first $500 payment is made at the end of the third year (and the tenth payment at the end of the twelfth year) if the discount rate is 16%?

19. An annuity due (or rent annuity) is an annuity whose payments are made at the beginning of each period. What is the present value of a 20-year annuity due with $1,000 payments if the discount rate is 8%? [*Hints:* First, assume that a payment made at the end of one year (as in an ordinary annuity) has the same present value as a payment made at the beginning of the next year, as in an annuity due. That is, for purposes of finding present values, $1,000 received on December 31, 1994, is the same as $1,000 received on January 1, 1995. Second, find the *PV* of the last 19 payments and then add the *PV* of the first payment.]

20. Which of the following perpetuities represents the largest present value?

Perpetuity	Annual Amount ($)	Discount Rate (%)
A	30,000	7
B	120,000	11
C	4,000	8
D	70,000	4

21. You plan to retire in 40 years, at which time you want enough in a savings account to allow you to withdraw $20,000 at the beginning of each of the subsequent ten years (an insurance policy will support you if you live for more than ten years after you retire).

(a) If the savings account pays interest at an annual rate of 9%, how much must you have saved up by the end of the 40th year?

(b) If you deposit a fixed sum of money in the savings account at the end of each of the next 40 years to achieve the retirement goal of part (a), how much must you deposit each year?

(c) Proceed as in part (b), except that this time you save for only 20 years (at the end of each of years 21 through 40).

22. You are trying to decide whether to buy a $2,500 motorcycle on credit or to save money to buy it in 30 months. If you buy on credit, you will make 30 equal end-of-the-month payments at a finance charge of 2% per month. If you save money to buy it in 30 months, you will earn 1% per month on your savings. However, the semiannual inflation rate is 5%, and so the motorcycle will cost more in 2.5 years. (Suppose that you don't care when you take possession of the motorcycle; that is, you will make your decision solely on the basis of which plan has lower monthly requirements.)

    (a) What will your monthly payments be if you buy on credit?

    (b) What must your monthly deposits be if you choose to save money and buy the motorcycle in 30 months?

    (c) What should you do?

23. Jackne Corporation is considering two alternative bond issues. In option 1, Jackne will make interest payments indefinitely at the rate of 6%. Under option 2, Jackne will make the first interest payment in one year's time at 5.1%, but subsequent payments will increase at 4%. The discount rate is 8%. Which option should Jackne choose? Assume that Jackne borrows the same amount under each alternative.

24. Mallford, Inc., has projected that it will receive the following payments from an overseas customer in Swiss francs over a two-year period. The future exchange rates that cover this period have been estimated to be those given here.

Dates	Jan. 1, 1995	April 1, 1995	July 1, 1995	Oct. 1, 1995
Payments	SFr2,500	SFr3,800	SFr1,900	SFr3,200
Exchange rates	$0.6875/SFr	$0.6436/SFr	$0.6222/SFr	$0.5994/SFr

    What will the present value of these payments be in dollars on October 1, 1994, at a discount rate of 8.1%?

25. Compare the future value in one year of $100 to be invested today at 8% under the following scenarios.

    (a) Annual compounding

    (b) Quarterly compounding

    (c) Continuous compounding

26. Alpha, Inc., has decided to issue a bond that will pay interest indefinitely. The payment will grow 3% per year, and the initial payment is $75.

    (a) What is the value of the bond if the discount rate is 8%?

    (b) If the initial payment and the discount rate remain the same, what must happen to the growth rate if the company wants to receive $1,100 per bond?

27. Larry Bonds and Gill Clark just signed new five-year contracts with the California Giants. Larry will receive $4,000,000 at the end of this year with an annual increase in pay of 3%. Gill will receive $3,750,000 at the end of this year with an annual increase in pay of 5%.

(a) Who received the better deal if the discount rate is 10%?

(b) How much does Larry's initial salary need to change to make the present values of both deals equal?

28. Laura Jones has decided to transfer $50,000 from her money market account into one of three annuities. Annuity A will pay interest of $200 for the first month with a growth rate of 5% per month. Annuity B will pay interest of $225 for the first month with a growth rate of 4% per month. Annuity C will pay interest of $250 for the first month with a growth rate of 3% per month. The annuities are for two years and the discount rate is 10%.

(a) Which annuity is the best investment?

(b) How many contracts will she buy?

(c) Which annuity is the best investment if the growth rate for annuity A increases to 6%?

29. Calculate the present value of a growing annuity that starts off with a payment of $500 and the subsequent annual payments grow at the annual rate of 4%. The discount rate is 8%, and the security makes a total of six payments.

30. Your brother just graduated from high school and is seeking your advice as to whether he should find a job immediately or go to college for four years and then find a job. He estimates that if he gets a job immediately, he will earn $15,000 per year for the next 40 years. If he goes to college first, he estimates that he can earn $30,000 for each of the 36 years after he graduates. (Whether or not he goes to college, he plans to retire 40 years from today.) He also estimates that the four years of college will cost him $8,000 each. Assume that his time value of money is 14%. (If he goes to college first, he can borrow money at 14%, too.)

(a) What will be the present value of his cash flows if he gets a job immediately?

(b) What will be the present value of his cash flows if he goes to college first?

(c) What should he do?

31. A bond pays $80 interest every year plus $1,000 when it matures in 12 years. You can buy the bond today for $753. What is the internal rate of return of this investment?

32. A device is for sale that will save you 10% of your utility bill every year. Your time value of money is 12%, and your utility bill is $500 per year. Assuming that your utility bill remains constant and that you (and your heirs) will be around forever to enjoy the benefits of this device, how much should you be willing to pay for it?

33. You are buying a $100,000 home with a 30-year mortgage that requires payments to be made at the end of each year. The interest rate is 10% for the first 15 years of the mortgage but then increases to 15% for the last 15 years. How much will your annual payments be?

34. An automobile costs $10,000 now, requires $1,000 annually to maintain, and has a salvage value of $2,000 at the end of eight years. Your time value of money is 9%.

(a) What is the net present value of these cash flows?

(b) What is the uniform annual series of these cash flows?

35. Given the following sequence of cash inflows and assuming a 14% discount rate, compute the uniform annual series (*UAS*):

What does this *UAS* tell us?

SUGGESTED ADDITIONAL READINGS

Fama, E. F., and M. H. Miller. *The Theory of Finance*. New York: Holt, Rinehart and Winston, 1972.

Fisher, Irving. *The Theory of Interest*. New York: Augustus M. Kelley, 1965. Reprinted from the 1930 edition.

Osborn, R. *The Mathematics of Investment*. New York: Harper & Row, 1957.

FIVE FINANCIAL RISK: THEORY AND ESTIMATION

To understand uncertainty and risk is to understand the key business problem—and the key business opportunity.

—David B. Hertz, 1972

Whether we like it or not, risk and uncertainty are real. Everyone encounters uncertainty in everyday life—uncertainty about the weather, about the performance of one's investments, and about one's health. Although few people would argue with this statement, nearly all have trouble explaining the difference between risk and uncertainty. **Uncertainty** exists when a decision maker knows all the possible outcomes of a certain act but, for one reason or another, cannot assign probabilities to the various outcomes. **Risk**, on the other hand, exists when the decision maker knows not only the various outcomes but also the probability associated with each one. In other words, risk is quantifiable uncertainty. For example, if the weather forecaster says, "It may rain tomorrow," he is explaining that he is uncertain about the weather tomorrow. However, if he says, "There is a 60% chance of rain tomorrow," he has quantified the uncertainty, and so this becomes a risk situation. Despite this technical distinction between risk and uncertainty, in many practical situations the two terms are used interchangeably.

In finance, risk has a very special meaning. It refers to the uncertainty associated with the *returns* on a particular investment. A risky investment is thus one whose returns are *volatile* (vary a lot). This chapter focuses on the analysis of the risk of an investment. Although the emphasis is on the risk of a company's stock, the same ideas apply to the risk of other investments (real estate, machinery, metals, etc.). This chapter is developed over five sections and seeks to answer the following questions:

- How is uncertainty quantified into risk?

- What are probability distributions?

- How can we summarize the information contained in a probability distribution?

- How are asset returns interrelated?

- How does the relationship among asset returns affect the return and risk of a portfolio of assets?

- What practical procedures exist for measuring a security's return and risk?

5-1
BASIC RETURN AND RISK CONCEPTS

Return

As we have explained, profit-based decision making should be replaced with an analysis of cash flows. The return from any transaction should be measured in terms of the returns provided by the cash flows from the transaction. It is the uncertainty associated with these returns that introduces risk into an investment.

Most transactions can be viewed as a series of cash flows. This is true irrespective of whether the transaction is the purchase of a machine, or an investment in securities. For example, if Ms. Nessbaum purchases a security [say, Applied Science, Inc. (ASI) stock], this transaction involves a (negative) cash flow (i.e., an outflow at first) because she has to pay a seller the market price of ASI stock to acquire it. But why does she buy the stock? If her answer is "for investment purposes" or "because I expect high returns," she is really saying, "for its future cash flows (benefits)."

To understand this, remember that the purchase of a stock entitles Ms. Nessbaum to receive future dividends declared by the company. Of course, these dividends are uncertain, but they are cash inflows that Ms. Nessbaum expects to receive. In addition to dividends, when the stock is sold, she will get another cash inflow—the selling price of the stock.

MEASURES OF RETURN

To estimate the benefits from an investment such as this, the decision maker, Ms. Nessbaum in this case, must calculate the returns from this investment. Returns can be measured in absolute (dollar) terms or in relative (percentage) terms. Often, the rate of return refers to percentage returns. Unless we specify otherwise, returns in this book are in percentage or decimal terms, not dollars. The cash flow that the investor receives obviously depends on how long she owns the investment. Thus, to speak of returns in a meaningful way, it is important that we specify the period over which the return is computed. The rest of this chapter deals with *one-period* returns; that is, the assumption is that the asset will be held for one year (or one month or week) and the return will be computed over this time period.

Two different types of returns must be distinguished. An **ex ante return** is the *uncertain* return that one expects to get from an investment. If Ms. Nessbaum plans to hold her share of ASI for one year, she has to estimate the dividends to be received from ownership of the stock and the selling price in the following year. Thus the ex ante return that she computes is an *estimated* return. There is no guarantee that she will, in fact, get this rate of return. At the end of the year, she computes the actual (or realized) return from ASI based on the actual dividends received and the price she actually receives for the stock. Because a computation of the return "after the fact" contains no uncertainty, the **ex post** or **realized return** is the *certain* return that one actually obtains from an investment.[1]

The symbol $\tilde{R}_i$ is used to represent the uncertain return on an asset i. The tilde ($\sim$), more affectionately known as the "wiggle," over the $\tilde{R}_i$ denotes that it is an uncertain variable. R_i, without the tilde, represents the ex post or realized return. In the remainder of this chapter, the subscript i is omitted except where there might be confusion.

CALCULATING EX ANTE AND EX POST RETURNS

The formulas for calculating $\tilde{R}$ and R for the specific case of Ms. Nessbaum's one-period investment in ASI stock are now provided. Whether the asset in question is a lathe, a sales outlet, or a share of common stock, the analysis is similar, although the definition of returns may have to be changed slightly for different situations. This chapter focuses on common stock because it is easy to relate to this asset. In a later chapter the returns from owning a physical asset are calculated.

---

[1] As an aid to memory, note that the Latin words *ante* and *post* mean "before" and "after," respectively.

Ex ante return is calculated as

$$\tilde{R} = \frac{\left(\begin{array}{c}\text{forecasted}\\\text{dividend}\end{array}\right) + \left(\begin{array}{c}\text{forecasted end-of-period}\\\text{stock price}\end{array}\right)}{\begin{array}{c}\text{initial investment}\\\text{(i.e., beginning-of-period stock price)}\end{array}} - 1 \qquad (5\text{-}1a)$$

Equivalently, equation (5-1a) can be written as

$$\tilde{R} = \frac{\left(\begin{array}{c}\text{forecasted}\\\text{dividend}\end{array}\right) + \left(\begin{array}{c}\text{forecasted change}\\\text{in stock price}\end{array}\right)}{\begin{array}{c}\text{initial investment}\\\text{(i.e., beginning-of-period stock price)}\end{array}} \qquad (5\text{-}1b)$$

Because equations (5-1a) and (5-1b) are equivalent, either can be used to compute the ex ante return from an investment.

In contrast, the ex post or realized return is calculated using the equation

$$R = \frac{(\text{actual dividend}) + (\text{actual end-of-period stock price})}{\text{initial investment (i.e., beginning-of-period stock price)}} - 1 \qquad (5\text{-}2a)$$

or, in terms of stock price changes, as

$$R = \frac{(\text{actual dividend}) + (\text{actual change in stock price})}{\text{initial investment (i.e., beginning-of-period stock price)}} \qquad (5\text{-}2b)$$

Suppose that Ms. Nessbaum bought her stock on January 1, 1994, for $52. At the end of the year she expects to sell the stock for $68. She also expects to receive $4 in dividends over this period. Ms. Nessbaum's ex ante return from equation (5-1a) is

$$\tilde{R}_{\text{ASI}} = \frac{\$4 + \$68}{\$52} - 1 = 38.46\%$$

However, if ASI actually paid only $2 in dividends and by year end the stock was selling for only $40, her ex post or realized return from equation (5-2a) is

$$R_{\text{ASI}} = \frac{\$2 + \$40}{\$52} - 1 = -19.23\%$$

Equations (5-1b) and (5-2b) yield the same results.

Notice in this example that even though Ms. Nessbaum expected to realize a high positive return, she in fact had a negative return.

KEY CONCEPT   Whether the investment in question is a financial asset or a physical asset (capital investment), under most circumstances, ex ante returns differ from ex post returns for individual transactions.

In other words, even though investors make decisions on the benefits they expect from an investment, the actual outcomes may not correspond to their expectations. If realizations corresponded to expectations exactly, there would be no risk.

Risk and Probability Distributions   Consider an investor or a company that is planning to purchase an asset, such as Ms. Nessbaum's share of ASI stock. For simplicity, we assume that ASI pays no dividends and that the stock's current price is $50. We also assume, as before, that

Ms. Nessbaum plans to sell the stock next year at whatever price ASI commands in the market at that time.

Now, what can we say about the return from owning ASI stock for one year? Not much at this stage. If we knew, for example, that ASI stock could be sold next year for $75, then, from equation (5-1), the ex ante return could safely be computed as ($75/$50) − 1 = 50%. But this is unrealistic because no one knows the future price of ASI stock. If economic conditions improve greatly, ASI's price might rise considerably by year end. If, on the other hand, the United States goes into a recession, we expect ASI stock to fall in value.

Although such general statements are acceptable descriptions of the future, they do not help individuals predict the return from owning ASI stock. Nor does our discussion so far shed any light on whether or not ASI is a risky stock. To say anything specific about the returns from ASI stock, one has to quantify the risk of owning ASI stock, which we do by means of a probability distribution. A **probability distribution** is a collection of the different possible outcomes for an uncertain variable together with the probability of each possible outcome. A probability distribution must use all possible alternatives; that is, it must include the full probability set. This implies that the probabilities must always sum to 1.

DISCRETE PROBABILITY DISTRIBUTIONS

Assume that ASI's performance depends on how well the U.S. economy is performing. This is a reasonable assumption because, however effective a company's management is, its performance is generally better if general economic conditions are good and not so good when general economic conditions are poor. Assume that a good measure of the "state of the economy" is the Dow Jones Industrial Average (DJIA). Changes in the DJIA are often used to assess the performance of the economy as a whole. Also assume that the information in Table 5-1 represents Ms. Nessbaum's beliefs about the future.

Thus the returns on ASI stock range between +40% and −20%, depending on which state of the economy actually prevails next year. Notice that the stock can take on three values ($70, $50, or $40) with specific probabilities (0.3, 0.5, and 0.2). By specifying probabilities, Ms. Nessbaum has converted an uncertain situation to a risk situation. The probability distribution in Table 5-1 is said to be a **discrete distribution** because the variables of interest (returns or stock prices) can take on only discrete values, with a probability assigned to each value.

By plotting the probability distribution in Table 5-1, we get the distribution shown in Figure 5-1. Figure 5-1(a) represents the probability distribution for the stock *price*, and Figure 5-1(b) shows the probability distribution for *returns*.

Although such probability distributions can be drawn for either future stock prices or future returns, it is more useful to work with returns because returns recognize the total reward that an investor receives from investing. The future stock price is normally only one element in the return computation.

The DJIA, which was used in our example, is probably the best known and most widely quoted indicator of stock market performance. The highlight on page 109 provides a brief overview of the history and uses of this and other averages.

TABLE 5-1

Probability Distribution of ASI's Returns

State of the Economy	Probability	ASI Stock Price	Return[a]
DJIA > 4500 ("boom")	0.3	$70	0.40
4500 > DJIA > 3500 ("normal")	0.5	50	0.00
DJIA < 3500 ("recession")	0.2	40	−0.20

[a] Returns are computed using equation (5-1b). Assume ASI pays no dividends and its current market price is $50. Thus, in the "boom" state, for example, the return is ($70 − $50)/$50 = 40%.

■

FIGURE 5-1

Discrete probability distributions for (a) stock price and (b) stock returns

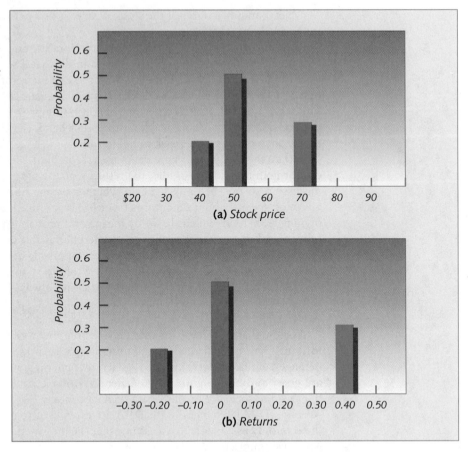

(a) Stock price

(b) Returns

CONTINUOUS PROBABILITY DISTRIBUTIONS

In Figure 5-1(b) the returns on the stock can have only three distinct values, each with a specific probability. But what if the returns on the stock can have infinitely many different values? Clearly, this is a more realistic case because the returns can fall anywhere between -100 and $+\infty$. The worst possible outcome is -100% because, with limited liability, one cannot lose more than the price of the stock. When there are infinitely many values, the uncertainty about the returns can be represented using a **continuous distribution**, in which the probability of a range of outcomes is given by the area under the curve over the appropriate range. For example, the probability of a return falling between 27% and 30% is given by the shaded area in Figure 5-2. For a continuous distribution, the probability of a return

■

FIGURE 5-2

A continuous probability distribution

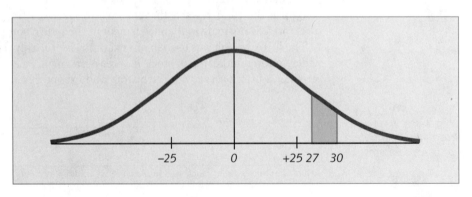

GETTING A HANDLE ON THE MARKET: STOCK EXCHANGE INDEXES

*T*he performance of a country's economy is an important variable in determining the value of an asset. How an economy is doing is frequently measured via some major equity market index. Several national equity markets have well-developed indexes.

United States: The Dow Jones Industrial Average was started in 1884, when Charles Dow added together the prices of 11 important stocks and divided the total by 11. The answer he obtained was the beginning value for his average. Changes in the values of this average are often a rough measure of the performance of the U.S. economy as a whole. In 1928 the average was broadened to include 30 stocks, and the composition has been updated occasionally over the years.

Today the DJIA consists of 30 stocks and is price weighted; that is, the component stock prices are added together and the result is divided by another figure, called the divisor. To compensate for stock splits, stock dividends, and other factors, the divisor has been changed frequently and is no longer equal to the number of stocks in the average. When this was written, the current divisor for the DJIA was 0.44731238, and the average was around 3533.

Although the industrial average is the most widely watched of the Dow Jones stock averages, there are other Dow Jones averages that cover 20 transportation-company stocks and 15 utility-company stocks, as well as a composite index of the 65 stocks in the three indexes.

Notwithstanding the historical prominence of the DJIA, several researchers and analysts today focus on Standard & Poor's 500 index (the S&P 500), which is a similar stock average that consists of 500 stocks. Like the Dow Jones averages, Standard & Poor's provides separate industrial, transportation, and utilities averages. In addition, S&P has a separate financial average.

Canada: While Canada has five stock exchanges, the Toronto Exchange dominates, with more than 75% of market turnover. The most widely used index is the TSE 300, composed of the common stock of 300 companies.

Japan: Two primary indexes measure the Japanese markets. The Tokyo Stock Price Index (TOPIX), established in 1969, is a composite index of all major securities in the Tokyo Stock Exchange. The Nikkei average is calculated by a leading business newspaper, the Nihon Keisai Shimbun, and is composed of 225 stocks from the Tokyo Stock Exchange.

France: France has seven stock exchanges, or bourses, with the Paris Bourse dominating trade with more than 95% of total turnover. The Paris Bourse publishes the Compagnie des Agents de Change (CAC) 240, composed of the largest capitalized of the 700 securities traded on the exchange, and the CAC 40, which uses a representative sampling of major securities.

Germany: The Frankfurt Stock Exchange is the largest German exchange. Of the several indexes available, one of the more popular is the Deutscher Aktienindex (DAX). This index, like the DJIA, is composed of 30 of the most heavily traded German stocks.

United Kingdom: London has a long history as a major financial market, with trading in stocks going back to the early 18th century. The London Stock Exchange has two major indexes. The Financial Times (FT) 30 measures the performance of 30 large industrial companies. The Financial Times-Stock Exchange (FTSE) 100, also known as "Footsie," is a broader-based measure.

In addition to the above national averages, there are international averages that measure economic activity in geographic regions and worldwide.

Morgan Stanley Capital International (MSCI): Morgan Stanley publishes several indexes, including the World 1500, the Europe 600, and the Europe, Australia, and the Far East (EAFE) 1000.

Dow Jones World Stock Index: This 1993 addition to the family of Dow Jones indexes measures stock performance in several areas: the Americas, Europe, Asia/Pacific, Asia/Pacific (except Japan), World (except the United States), and World.

Irrespective of the specific index under consideration, their purpose is the same: Their ups and downs provide a rough measure of the performance of the target market as a whole.

having one particular value is 0. For example, the probability of a return being exactly 28% is 0.

Although continuous distributions are more realistic descriptions of outcomes, in most practical applications one deals with discrete distributions as a simplification. Typically, probability distributions of returns are estimated using actual historical data. By studying the behavior of stock returns over the recent past, it is possible to come up with a subjective probability assessment for future returns. But in observing historical (or ex post) data, we are observing a finite number of historical returns, each with a specific frequency. Thus it is possible to determine discrete probability distributions from looking at a stock's past performance record. In this chapter we therefore deal only with discrete probability distributions in our examples.

Do Managers Use Probability Distributions?

Uncertainty is quantified into risk through a probability distribution. It is sometimes argued that managers and investors do not work with probability distributions explicitly but instead work with "likely values" based on "experience." Note that managers who do not explicitly use probabilities in their analyses are implicitly assigning a probability of 1 to their estimates—an extremely strong assumption. Furthermore, managers who arrive at most likely values based on experience are really calculating the expected value based on historical frequencies. Thus "experience" may be considered to be an informal probability distribution. While probability distributions at first may look "artificial," they do contain useful information that should be used by managers in making decisions.

5-2

SUMMARIZING AND INTERPRETING THE INFORMATION ABOUT A SINGLE ASSET

After Ms. Nessbaum has identified the probability distribution for ASI stock, she must summarize the information contained in the distribution in two simple measures in order to evaluate the stock. One measure should indicate the possible benefits from the investment, and the second measure should capture the riskiness (or variability) of these benefits. Using these two measures to summarize the information contained in the probability distribution, she can effectively throw aside the entire distribution.

The discussion of these measures revolves around returns only because that facilitates the development of the required concepts. The two measures can be calculated not only for returns but also for any random variable. For example, from a probability distribution of male life expectancy, one can calculate normal life expectancy and the variance associated with life expectancy.

Summarizing Information About Returns

Consider Figure 5-1(b). How can Ms. Nessbaum use this information? Should she assume that the return on the stock is 0%, or should she assume that it is 40%? Each of these returns is an uncertain variable that can occur with a different probability. It is therefore necessary to find an expected return that summarizes these possible outcomes by taking into consideration each possible return and its associated probability in Figure 5-1(b).

The average return from the stock should be the basis for Ms. Nessbaum's estimate of possible returns. This is provided by calculating the expected return from owning the stock. The **expected return** from an investment is the average return from the investment and is calculated as the probability-weighted sum of all possible returns:

$$E(\tilde{R}) = \sum [p(\text{return}) \times \text{return}] \tag{5-3}$$

TABLE 5-2
*Expected Return on ASI
Stock*

Return	Probability	Return × Probability
0.40	0.3	0.12
0.00	0.5	0.00
−0.20	0.2	−0.04
		0.08

$$E(\tilde{R}) = \sum [p(\text{return}) \times \text{return}] = 0.08$$

The expected return on ASI is the "probabilistic average" of the returns on ASI.

This calculation is like the calculation of an arithmetic average, except that the outcomes are uncertain. When no risk is involved, the same expected return calculation, with an assigned weighting of $1/N$ to each outcome, gives the average. Thus the expected value is a "probabilistic average." In this definition, p (return) is the probability of a particular value of return, and Σ represents the summation notation, with the summation carried over all possible outcomes. In words, equation (5-3) requires that each return be multiplied by its probability of occurrence and then all these products be added together.

Refer to the information provided in Figure 5-1(b) or Table 5-1, and calculate the expected return of the distribution. Because Figure 5-1(b) deals with ASI stock returns, the answer will yield the expected return on ASI stock. Table 5-2 illustrates the procedure for calculating this expected return, which is 8%. When evaluating ASI stock, then, Ms. Nessbaum can focus on this one return: the expected return of 8%.

*Summarizing
Information About the
Variability of Returns*

Ms. Nessbaum cannot, simply on the basis of the expected return of 8% for ASI, make any decision regarding the stock. Expected returns alone are not sufficient for a decision by any person who is averse to risk because it is really an average. A risk-averse investor who makes decisions using the expected return alone is like a nonswimmer planning to cross a river because the average depth is only 3 feet. Ignoring variability can be very costly!

How risky is the ASI stock? A popular and convenient measure of risk is the variability.

KEY CONCEPT

In finance, an investment whose returns are fairly stable is considered a relatively low-risk investment, whereas one whose returns fluctuate significantly is considered to have more risk.

For example, U.S. Treasury bills ("T-bills") are obligations of the U.S. government. Because investors' returns are guaranteed if they hold a bill over its life, T-bills are characterized as *risk-free assets*. On the other hand, stocks are risky investments because the potential return is variable. Thus, loosely defined, risk is the potential for variability in returns. Of course, it is necessary to introduce probabilities into the calculations in order to recognize the likelihood of these variable returns.

The most popular measure of risk is the variance or the standard deviation of a distribution. First we define variance, and then we calculate the variance of returns of ASI stock. Then the meaning and the calculation of the standard deviation will be clear. The **variance** (σ^2) of returns from an investment is the sum of the probability-weighted squared deviations of returns from the mean:

$$\sigma^2 = \sum \{p(\text{return}) \times [\text{return} - E(\tilde{R})]^2\} \tag{5-4}$$

All variables in this equation have been defined earlier. Variance is calculated by finding the expected return, finding the difference between each possible return

■

T A B L E   5 - 3

Calculating the Variance of ASI's Returns

Probability	Return	Deviation from Expected Return[a]	Squared Deviation	Probability × Squared Deviation
0.3	0.40	0.32	0.1024	0.0307
0.5	0.00	−0.08	0.0064	0.0032
0.2	−0.20	−0.28	0.0784	0.0157
1.0				$\sigma^2 = 0.0496$

[a] Expected return of 8% (from Table 5-2).

and the expected return, squaring this value, multiplying it by the probability of that occurrence, and summing this resulting value over all possible occurrences.

The variance of ASI stock can be calculated easily using the information in Table 5-1 and the finding from Table 5-2 that $E(\tilde{R}) = 0.08$. Table 5-3 illustrates how this is done. Although the calculations in Table 5-3 show that the variance (σ_S^2) of returns for ASI Company stock is 0.0496, Table 5-3 does not provide any meaning for the variance. To understand the practical significance of variance, it is useful to define another risk measure called standard deviation. The **standard deviation** (σ) of returns is the square root of the variance of the distribution:

$$\sigma = \sqrt{\sigma^2} \tag{5-5}$$

Whereas variance is a squared unit, squared percent or squared decimal, the standard deviation is in the same units, percent or decimal, as the mean and is thus easier to interpret. Because $\sigma^2 = 0.0496$, $\sigma = \sqrt{0.0496} = 0.2227$.

We can now summarize the information about ASI's stock returns:

Expected return from holding ASI = 8%
Variance of returns on ASI = 0.0496
Standard deviation of returns = 0.2227

Interpreting the Variability Measures

THE SIGNIFICANCE OF THE NORMAL DISTRIBUTION

Having calculated the expected return and variance of returns for ASI stock, it is now possible to draw some inferences about this investment, assuming that the returns for ASI are normally distributed. This approximation of the distribution as continuous is necessary to quantify the ranges of possible future returns and their associated probabilities.

When we say that ASI's returns are "normally distributed," we are stating that they act in a manner consistent with one of the several probability distributions used in statistical theory. A **normal distribution** is the common "bell-shaped" distribution in which the observations above and below the mean are distributed in a symmetric manner. The normal distribution occurs frequently in nature, and a variety of random variables can be characterized by this probability distribution. In fact, stock returns can be approximated with normal distributions. (Although it is beyond the scope of the book to get into details, you can obtain more information on the normal distribution from any statistics textbook.)

After the standard deviation is computed, a knowledge that the distribution is normal allows us to estimate the likelihood that an ex post observation will be within a certain range of returns. As an example, assume that a security's normal probability distribution has a mean of 16% and a standard deviation of 4%. Then, as Figure 5-3 shows, one can say that with 68.26% probability, the actual future return will fall between 16% + 1σ = 16% + 4% = 20% and 16% − 1σ =

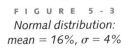

FIGURE 5-3
*Normal distribution:
mean = 16%, σ = 4%*

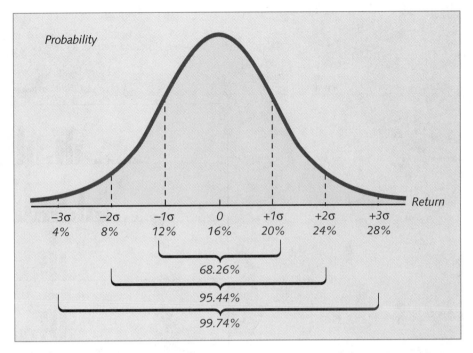

16% − 4% = 12%—that is, between 12% and 20%. Similarly, with 95.44% probability, the actual return will lie between 8% and 24%. With 99.74% certainty the actual return for the stock will be between 4% and 28%.

Thus, by using standard deviations in conjunction with the mean, it is possible to say something more specific about the actual return. Of course, the uncertainty about the future return is still not removed. But this process has helped quantify the uncertainty by saying that the actual return will lie somewhere between two values with a certain probability.

These numbers are correct for only a normal distribution of returns. For an arbitrary (nonnormal) distribution, the confidence intervals have different values. The returns on many financial assets are approximately normally distributed, and many theoretical results are based on the assumption that returns are normal. Hence the normality assumption appears reasonable, and Figure 5-3 is allowed to take on a special significance.

INTERPRETATION OF THE SUMMARY MEASURES OF ASI STOCK

For ASI stock, the average return is 8% and the standard deviation is 0.2227. If ASI stock returns are normally distributed, there is a 0.6826 probability that the actual (ex post) returns from ASI will lie between $+1\sigma$ and -1σ standard deviation from its 8% mean: between -14.27% and 30.27%. There is a 0.9544 probability that the actual returns will fall between $+2\sigma$ and -2σ standard deviations from the 8% mean: between -36.54% and 52.54%. And, finally, there is a 0.9974 probability (a virtually certain outcome) that the actual return from ASI will be between $+3\sigma$ and -3σ standard deviations from its 8% mean: between -58.81% and 74.81%.

*Historical Experience
with Asset Returns*

The actual (realized) returns and standard deviations for different financial securities between 1926 and 1992 are presented in Table 5-4. As can be verified, the larger the risk (standard deviation) is, the larger the reward (returns) will be. Com-

■

TABLE 5-4

Historical Relationship Between Risk and Return: 1926–1992

Data Series	Compound Annual Return	Standard Deviation	Distribution of Returns
Common stocks	10.3%	20.6%	
Small-company stocks	12.2%	35.0%	
Long-term corporate bonds	5.5%	8.5%	
Long-term government bonds	4.8%	8.6%	
U.S. Treasury bills	3.7%	3.3%	
Inflation	3.1%	4.7%	

−80   −60   −40   −20   0%   20   40   60   80

SOURCE: Underlying data are from the *Stocks, Bonds, Bills and Inflation 1993 Yearbook,* Ibbotson Associates, Chicago, IL (annually updates work by Roger G. Ibbotson and Rex A. Sinquefield). All rights reserved.
* The 1933 Small Company Stock Total Return was 142.9%.

mon stocks with the highest risk also enjoyed the highest return, and U.S. T-bills with the lowest risk received the lowest returns. The conclusion that one draws from this is that, in general, the marketplace appears to reward risk taking in proportion to the risk being taken.

People looking at Table 5-4 might ask, How can T-bills, described earlier as "riskless securities," have a standard deviation of 3.3%? The answer is that T-bills are riskless only for an investor who buys them and holds them until maturity; that is, they are riskless over their life. But between 1926 and 1992, the return on T-bills changed over time. This variability in returns over a 66-year period shows up as a nonzero standard deviation.

How Can We Generalize Using Ex Post Results?

Earlier in this chapter we pointed out that there is no assurance that investors' actual realizations (ex post returns) will in fact match their ex ante returns (expectations). How, then, can we justify using ex post information (Table 5-4) to conclude that the market will reward investors for bearing risk?

An investor who is investing in a particular stock for any particular period may receive low or high returns when the stock is sold.

KEY CONCEPT

On any short-term risky investment, there is no guarantee that the market will reward the investor for risk. However, if investors invest in an asset for an extended period of time, they can expect to be rewarded for their risk-taking behavior.

The reason risk is generally rewarded is that the U.S. capital markets have displayed over time the property known as *uncertainty resolution*. The longer the period of time is, the closer the ex post returns will be to the ex ante returns. Therefore, over the long run, the ex post returns will be very close to the ex ante returns. Unfortunately, it is impossible to generalize and define what *short term* and *long term* mean in this context. The longer the term is, the more likely that the results in Table 5-4 will be reproduced.

5-3

MEASURING THE RELATIONSHIPS AMONG ASSETS

Consider three securities, *A*, *B*, and *C*, and assume four "states of the world": recession, slow growth, moderate growth, and boom. If we know the probabilities associated with each state and the returns on the three stocks, we can calculate the expected returns and variances for *A, B,* and *C* using the procedures explained earlier. The information about these stocks in the four states is summarized in Table 5-5.

Although the expected returns and variances summarize the individual returns and the risk for each of the stocks, they do not convey any information about the interrelationships among the securities. To overcome this limitation we develop the ideas of covariance and correlation. Let us begin by talking about covariance.

Covariance

Covariance is similar to variance. The variance of returns for a particular asset is computed by subtracting the expected value of the return from each of the possible outcomes and then squaring that difference. The covariance between two assets is computed in a similar way except that the deviations of the possible outcomes from their expected values for two probability distributions are multiplied together and the relevant probability is a joint probability.

The **covariance** between the returns of two securities *A* and *B*, denoted σ_{AB}, is given by

$$\sigma_{AB} = \sum P_i(R_A, R_B) \times [R_{Ai} - E(\tilde{R}_A)][R_{Bi} - E(\tilde{R}_B)] \tag{5-6}$$

where, as before, Σ indicates that all possible values should be added together, and $P_i(\tilde{R}_A \tilde{R}_B)$ is the probability of the *i*th outcome.

■

TABLE 5-5

Information for Analyzing the Relationship Among Assets

a. Returns on Stocks

State of the World	Probability	Security Returns		
		A	B	C
Boom	0.2	0.25	0.23	0.05
Moderate growth	0.3	0.20	0.14	0.10
Slow growth	0.3	0.15	0.12	0.15
Recession	0.2	0.10	0.08	0.20
	1.0			

b. Expected Returns and Variances[a]

	A	B	C
Expected return	0.1750	0.14	0.1250
Variance of returns	0.0026	0.0025	0.0026

[a]The expected returns and variances are calculated using the information in this table and equations (5-3) and (5-4). The variance of returns is rounded to four decimal places.

■

P_i	R_A	$R_A - E(\tilde{R}_A)$	R_B	$R_B - E(\tilde{R}_B)$	$P_i[R_A - E(\tilde{R}_A)][R_B - E(\tilde{R}_B)]$
0.2	0.25	0.0750	0.23	0.0900	0.0014
0.3	0.20	0.0250	0.14	0.0000	0.0
0.3	0.15	−0.0250	0.12	−0.0200	0.0002
0.2	0.10	−0.0750	0.08	−0.0600	0.0009
					$\sigma_{AB} = 0.0025$

TABLE 5-6

Calculating the Covariance Between Securities A and B [a]

[a] The expected returns on securities A and B were calculated in Table 5-5(b): $E(\tilde{R}_A) = 17.5\%$; $E(\tilde{R}_B) = 14\%$.

Table 5-6 provides a sample calculation of covariance. The covariance between stocks A and B is calculated to be 0.0025.

Correlation Coefficient

The magnitude of the covariance is not very meaningful for assessing the strength of the relationship between two securities. The relationship between two assets is better explained by the **correlation** between the returns on the two assets. A standardized measure called the **correlation coefficient** is used to assess the *strength* of the relationship between two assets. The correlation coefficient between stocks A and B is often denoted by ρ_{AB} and can be calculated from the covariance:[2]

$$\rho_{AB} = \frac{\sigma_{AB}}{\sigma_A \times \sigma_B} \tag{5-7}$$

where σ_A and σ_B, as before, represent the standard deviations of the returns for securities A and B, respectively, and ρ_{AB}, being a standardized value, always lies between -1.0 and $+1.0$ (both values inclusive).

Because the covariance between stocks A and B is shown in Table 5-6 to be 0.0025 and because the variances of the returns on A and B, from Table 5-5(b), are 0.0026 and 0.0025, respectively, we can use equation (5-7) to calculate ρ_{AB}:

$$\rho_{AB} = \frac{0.0025}{(\sqrt{0.0026})(\sqrt{0.0025})} = 0.9806$$

From the same approach, the correlation coefficients ρ_{AC} and ρ_{BC} can be calculated to be -1.00 and -0.9806, respectively. These calculations are left to the interested reader as an exercise. The correlation coefficients are summarized as:

$\rho_{AB} = 0.9806$

$\rho_{AC} = -1.00$

$\rho_{BC} = -0.9806$

What the Correlation Coefficient Does and Does Not Mean

If the correlation coefficient between two securities is $+1$, the two securities are said to be **perfectly positively correlated**. This implies that the returns on these two securities move in perfect lockstep; that is, when the returns on one stock are high, so are the returns on the other. On the other hand, a correlation coefficient of -1.0 implies that the two assets are perfectly negatively correlated. In this case the returns on the two securities move in exactly the opposite directions. Thus the *sign* of the correlation coefficient (positive or negative) characterizes the nature of the interdependence between securities. The returns of positively correlated securities move in the same direction; the returns of negatively correlated securities move in opposite directions. The extent of this association is provided by the *magnitude* of the correlation coefficient.

[2] Notice that this definition suggests another way to calculate the covariance: $\sigma_{AB} = \rho_{AB} \times \sigma_A \times \sigma_B$.

The correlation coefficient is often misinterpreted; it is important to understand what this concept states and what it does not. For example, it is incorrect to conclude that if two stocks are perfectly positively correlated, a 5% rise in one stock will lead to a 5% increase in the other. To be precise, what perfect positive correlation means is that when one stock increases 5% from its long-term mean, the other will also increase 5% from its long-term mean. Also note that the correlation coefficient does not suggest that if two securities are positively correlated, then every time one security's return increases the other also increases. The returns on one stock can go down even when the other one rises. What the correlation coefficient signifies is that *on average*, both returns move in the same direction.

One way to understand correlation is to work with the squared value of the correlation coefficient (known as R^2). Since the correlation between securities A and B is 0.98, the corresponding R^2 value is $(0.98)^2 = 0.96$. R^2 measures the percentage of the variance in one security that is explained by the variability of the other. Thus 96% of A's variability can be explained by the variability of B's returns; only 4% of A's variability is due to other factors not explained by B's variability.

Correlation should not be confused with causation, which is an altogether different idea. Correlation does not imply causation. For example, if a scientific study finds that wealthier individuals have higher IQs (perhaps because of more educational opportunities), this is a statement that wealth and IQs are positively correlated. It does *not* imply that higher wealth (in and of itself) leads to or causes high IQ scores. Similarly, if two securities are perfectly positively correlated, although 100% of the variability in one is *explained* by the variability of the other, it does not mean that the variability of one stock *causes* the variability of the other.

It is useful now to discuss Figure 5-4, which illustrates the information about our three securities: A, B, and C.

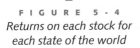

FIGURE 5-4

Returns on each stock for each state of the world

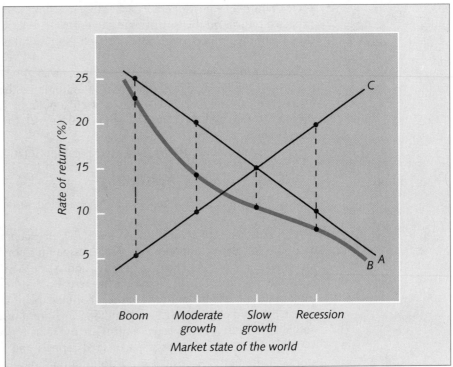

CORRELATION OF *A* AND *B*

First, notice that whenever security *A*'s returns are high, *B*'s returns are also high. When *A*'s returns are low, so are *B*'s. Thus *A* and *B* appear to behave alike, though not exactly. *A* and *B* are *positively correlated*. The *positively* simply means that when *A*'s returns change in a particular way (say, to lower returns during a recession), *B*'s returns also change in the same direction. The correlation coefficient between *A* and *B*, ρ_{AB}, in this case is greater than 0 but less than +1.

CORRELATION OF *A, B*, AND *C*

Security *C*'s returns behave in a manner opposite to those of *A* or *B*. When *A* or *B* has high returns, *C* has low returns, and vice versa. Thus *C*'s returns are *negatively correlated* with the returns of *A* and *B*. The *negatively* simply means that when *A*'s or *B*'s returns change in a particular way, *C*'s returns change in the opposite direction. However, as Figure 5-4 illustrates, the returns on *A* and *C* are perfectly negatively correlated, implying that the correlation coefficient $\rho_{AC} = -1.0$. The correlation coefficient between *B* and *C*, ρ_{BC}, though negative, is not -1.0 but lies somewhere between 0 and -1 (ρ_{BC} is -0.9806).

The Expected Return and Risk of Portfolios

In Section 5-2 we confined ourselves to analyzing the probability distribution of a single security. We could examine the expected return and the variance of a **portfolio**, which is nothing more than a group of assets, using these same equations and relationships. However, we can gain substantial additional insights into the effects of correlation on the portfolio expected returns and variance by generating these summary statistics from probability distributions of the individual assets in the portfolio.

PORTFOLIO EXPECTED RETURNS

The first step is to compute the portfolio's expected return. Calculating the expected return on a portfolio is easy because it is simply the weighted average of the expected returns on the securities in the portfolio. All that is required is information about the proportion invested in each asset and the expected return on each asset.

Let the proportion of wealth invested in security *A* be represented by X_A. Then the proportion invested in *B* must be $1 - X_A$ because the proportions invested in all assets must sum to 1. For example, if 20% of an investment is made up of *A*, then $X_A = 0.2$, and therefore $X_B = (1 - 0.2) = 0.8$ represents the proportion invested in *B*.

The expected return from a two-asset portfolio, $E(\tilde{R}_P)$, is thus given as

$$E(\tilde{R}_P) = X_A E(\tilde{R}_A) + X_B E(\tilde{R}_B) \tag{5-8}$$

where $E(\tilde{R}_A)$ and $E(\tilde{R}_B)$ represent the expected returns on assets *A* and *B*, respectively.

The expected return for a portfolio, $E(\tilde{R}_P)$, that contains stocks *A* and *B* can easily be calculated. Suppose that Ms. Nessbaum's portfolio consists of a 15% investment in stock *A*. Then $X_A = 0.15$, and $X_B = 0.85$ is the proportion of the portfolio investment in *B*. Note that the actual dollar amount invested in each is irrelevant; only the proportions matter. For example, Ms. Nessbaum might have invested a total of $100 ($15 in *A* and $85 in *B*) or a total of $5,000 ($750 in *A* and $4,250 in *B*). The expected returns are the same for both alternatives.

Table 5-5(b) summarizes the expected returns and variances of returns for stocks *A, B,* and *C*. Consider a portfolio of only two stocks: *A* and *B*. Because

$E(\tilde{R}_A) = 17.5\%$ and $E(\tilde{R}_B) = 14\%$, and using $X_A = 0.15$ and $X_B = 0.85$, we find from equation (5-8) the expected return on Ms. Nessbaum's portfolio is $E(\tilde{R}_P) = (0.15)(0.175) + (0.85)(0.14) = 0.1453$ or 14.53%.

The expected return of a portfolio that contains more than two assets is a direct extension of equation (5-8). It is still the weighted average of the expected returns of all the securities in the portfolio.[3]

THE RISK OF A PORTFOLIO

Computing the risk of a portfolio is somewhat more involved because we now require additional information. We must know not only the variance (or standard deviation) of the returns of each asset in the portfolio but also the correlation between them. In contrast to a portfolio's expected return, which can be calculated as the weighted averages of the expected returns of the securities in the portfolio, standard deviations are, in general, not weighted averages of the standard deviations of the securities in the portfolio. To understand why, we must look at the formula for computing the variance and standard deviation of a portfolio.

The variance of a two-asset portfolio is calculated as

$$\sigma_P^2 = X_A^2 \sigma_A^2 + X_B^2 \sigma_B^2 + 2 X_A X_B \rho_{AB} \sigma_A \sigma_B \tag{5-9}$$

where σ_A^2, σ_B^2, and ρ_{AB} represent the variance of security A, the variance of security B, and the correlation coefficient between A and B, respectively.

From the data in Table 5-5(b), σ_A^2 is 0.0026 and σ_B^2 is 0.0025. Earlier we found the correlation coefficient between securities A and B, ρ_{AB}, is 0.9806. Therefore the variance of a portfolio with $X_A = 0.15$ and $X_B = 0.85$ is

$$\sigma_P^2 = (0.15)^2 (0.0026) + (0.85)^2 (0.0025)$$
$$+ 2 (0.15) (0.85) (0.9806) \sqrt{0.0026} \sqrt{0.0025} = 0.0025$$

We examine the variance of a portfolio with many assets in the next chapter.

5-4
DIVERSIFICATION AND PORTFOLIO RISK

Our discussion so far has pointed out how the risk of a security can be measured. Since it is reasonable to assume that most investors like Ms. Nessbaum are risk averse, they attempt to reduce their risks. Just how can they do it? Is there some strategy that can be followed to lower the risk taken on by the investor? Indeed there is.

KEY CONCEPT **Diversification** is the process of reducing risks by forming a portfolio of imperfectly correlated securities. Investors can lower their risks by forming portfolios to get the benefits of diversification.[4]

A portfolio is simply a collection of two or more assets. The investments included in a portfolio need not be restricted to stocks only. They can consist of stocks, bonds, gold, paintings, call options, and real estate. To keep the presentation at a fairly simple level, however, we focus on stock portfolios.

To reduce risk, it is not sufficient merely to form a portfolio. Another condition must be met: The portfolio should consist of imperfectly correlated securities.

---

[3] The expected return on an n-asset portfolio is calculated as $E(\tilde{R}_P) = \Sigma_{i=1}^{n} X_i E(\tilde{R}_i)$.

[4] Harry Markowitz takes the credit for developing the ideas of diversification and mean-variance analysis. His work earned him a Nobel Prize in Economics in 1990.

This discussion is incomplete for two reasons. First, it does not explain *why* diversification reduces risk, and second, it does not bring out the significance of the term *imperfectly correlated returns*. These are the issues that we address next.

A Casual Look at Diversification

Assume that Ms. Nessbaum is evaluating two stocks: Procyc, Inc., and Countercyc, Inc. Procyc's returns are high when the economy as a whole is doing well, and they suffer badly when the economy is in a recession. Countercyc has the opposite characteristic: It performs well during bad economic times and does poorly when the economy is booming. If Ms. Nessbaum invests in Procyc alone, her returns will have a high variability between economic booms and busts. With high returns in good times and low returns in bad times, the range of outcomes (returns) is large. Because risk in finance is measured by variability, this is a high-risk investment. Similarly, an investment in Countercyc alone exposes Ms. Nessbaum to high risk.

Now assume that instead of investing in only one asset, Ms. Nessbaum forms a portfolio of both Procyc and Countercyc in equal amounts. In good times, Procyc yields high returns, but Countercyc underperforms, pulling down the total return on the portfolio. In bad times, Procyc yields very low returns, but the total return on the portfolio is not low because Countercyc pulls up the returns. Thus, by forming this portfolio, high returns are pulled down, and low returns are pulled up. In other words, the range of potential outcomes is lessened by this "dampening" effect. Figure 5-5 illustrates the dampening effect of diversification. Because the variability in returns is lowered, the risk of the portfolio also is lowered.

The two-stock portfolio reduces risk because of the nature of the relationship between Procyc and Countercyc. If they both reacted in the same way to economic conditions, the dampening effect would disappear. Diversification helped reduce risk in this example because the two stocks are "imperfectly correlated."

A More Formal Examination of Diversification

The key to understanding the risk-reduction effects of diversification is the idea that, *in general*, the risk of a portfolio measured by standard deviations is not the weighted average of the risks of the individual securities in the portfolio. To make things very clear, let us calculate the benefits of diversification as:

$$\text{Diversification gains} = \frac{\sigma_W - \sigma_P}{\sigma_W} \qquad (5\text{-}10)$$

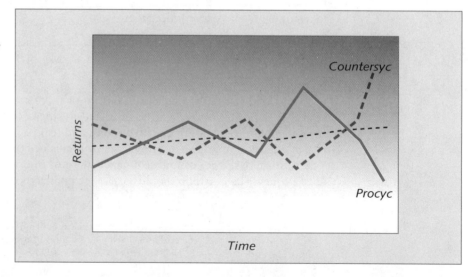

■
F I G U R E   5 - 5
Behavior of Procyc, Inc., and Countercyc, Inc.

where

σ_W is the weighted average of the standard deviations of the assets in the portfolio

σ_P is the standard deviation (risk) of the portfolio

We evaluate the risk-reduction benefits of diversification by examining two kinds of portfolios.

A SPECIAL PORTFOLIO: NO DIVERSIFICATION BENEFITS

Returning to the portfolio of securities A and B from Table 5-5, we know the standard deviations of A and B are $\sqrt{0.0026} = 0.0510$ and $\sqrt{0.0025} = 0.0500$, respectively. A weighted average of the standard deviations of A and B with 15% in A and 85% in B is $(0.15)(0.0510) + (0.85)(0.0500) = 0.05$. Earlier we calculated the correlation coefficient between A and B to be 0.9806. To illustrate a simple idea, let us approximate this to be 1.0 so that we can treat A and B as perfectly positively correlated securities. Thus the discussion here applies to a special portfolio with securities that are perfectly positively correlated. The standard deviation of this portfolio calculated from the variance in equation (5-9) yields exactly the same result, 0.05. Thus the benefits of diversification are

$$\frac{0.05 - 0.05}{0.05} = 0$$

This finding demonstrates the following key idea:

KEY CONCEPT   The standard deviation of a portfolio's returns is the weighted average of the standard deviations of the returns of the individual securities if the portfolio consists of perfectly positively correlated securities. In this situation, there are no risk-reduction benefits from diversification.

The more general case wherein the securities are not perfectly correlated is more interesting.

TYPICAL PORTFOLIOS: DIVERSIFICATION BENEFITS

Let us now calculate the variance of a two-asset portfolio with securities that are not perfectly positively correlated. Securities B and C fit the bill. Consider a portfolio distributed with $X_B = 0.15$ and $X_C = 0.85$. Earlier we found the correlation coefficient $\rho_{BC} = -0.9806$. The variance of this portfolio from equation (5-9) is

$$\sigma_P^2 = (0.15)^2(0.0025) + (0.85)^2(0.0026)$$
$$+ 2(0.15)(0.85)(-0.9806)(\sqrt{0.0025})(\sqrt{0.0026})$$
$$= 0.0013$$

so that the standard deviation is 0.0360.

Now the weighted average of the standard deviations of stocks B and C is

$$(0.15)(\sqrt{0.0025}) + (0.85)(\sqrt{0.0026}) = 0.0508$$

Thus, by forming a portfolio, we have reduced risk by

$$\frac{0.0508 - 0.0360}{0.0508} = 0.2913$$

or more than 29%.

ρ_{AB}	+1	.05	0	−0.5	−1
Portfolio variance σ_P^2	0.00255	0.00192	0.00128	0.00064	0.00001

[a] The portfolio variances are calculated using information from Table 5-5 and equation (5-9) and $X_A = X_B = 0.50$.

TABLE 5-7
Role of the Correlation Coefficient in Reducing Portfolio Risk[a]

Note that in contrast to the earlier example, stocks *B* and *C* are not perfectly positively correlated. In fact, as long as one forms a portfolio with securities that are not perfectly positively correlated, risk-reduction benefits will accrue.

This example illustrates an idea that underlies much of modern financial theory. Its importance becomes apparent in the succeeding chapters.

KEY CONCEPT
The standard deviation of a portfolio's returns is less than the weighted average of the standard deviations of the securities in the portfolio if the securities are imperfectly correlated. In this situation, diversification reduces risk.

If perfectly positively correlated securities provide no diversification benefits and imperfectly correlated securities do, the risk of the portfolio must change as the correlation coefficient changes. Indeed, as Table 5-7 illustrates, the risk of the portfolio is reduced as the correlation coefficient decreases from 1. In this table we take the variances of the individual stocks *A* and *B* as given in Table 5-5 but then vary the value of the correlation coefficient to see how the portfolio variance changes. The least risky two-asset portfolio is formed with two assets that are perfectly negatively correlated.

5-5
PRACTICAL CONSIDERATIONS IN MEASURING RISK

Our discussion of probability distributions, states of the world, and expected returns on securities thus far is intended to explain the fundamental statistical concepts that underlie the ideas in subsequent chapters. An extremely useful idea is that the nature of the relationships among assets helps us to obtain the benefits of risk reduction through diversification. Nevertheless, there are several limitations of our discussion thus far.

Ask yourself the following question: How would you actually compute the risk of, say, ASI stock? You would encounter several problems in developing an ex ante (subjective) probability distribution table like Table 5-1. First, you would have trouble defining the various states of the world and assigning probabilities to each state. Second, notice from Table 5-1 that you would need a forecast of the future price of the stock in each state. It would not be easy for you to assess these conditional forecasts. Indeed, if you could do this, it is unlikely that you would worry about projecting the next year's expected returns on ASI stock; you would instead spend your time counting the money you make from consistently picking winning stocks!

Practical Procedures for Assessing a Security's Riskiness

In practice, it is difficult to estimate (ex ante) probability distributions of returns for individual securities. The factors that can influence a security's performance are too numerous and complex for managers or investors to quantify in a realistic sense. Instead, stock analysis depends on historical information to provide *estimates* of how securities are related to each other and to the economy as a whole. These are statistical issues and our treatment here is not intended to be complete; rather, it is aimed at providing the basic ideas underlying the standard estimation procedures.

■

TABLE 5-8

Quarterly Stock Returns for Three Large U.S. Corporations, 1989–1991

Quarter	Texaco	Sears Roebuck	American Express
1–1989	0.0561	0.0802	0.1878
2–1989	0.0363	0.0135	0.0649
3–1989	0.0964	−0.0237	0.0865
4–1989	0.1820	−0.0860	−0.0226
1–1990	0.0106	0.0421	−0.2617
2–1990	−0.0239	−0.0572	0.2133
3–1990	0.0948	−0.2929	−0.3130
4–1990	0.0010	0.0191	−0.0008
1–1991	0.0703	0.4015	0.4000
2–1991	−0.0470	0.0955	−0.2056
3–1991	0.0588	0.0288	0.1500
4–1991	−0.0125	−0.0023	−0.1902

SOURCE: Quarterly returns are complied by the Center for Research in Security Prices (CRSP), University of Chicago.

As a practical matter, investors use historical information to assess the riskiness (variances) of investments and the relevant correlations and covariances. The remainder of this chapter discusses how estimates of a security's risk characteristics are developed. We defer a discussion of arriving at expected stock returns to the next chapter.

Estimating Variances, Correlations, and Covariances

Table 5-8 provides the quarterly returns for three major U.S. corporations (Texaco, Sears Roebuck, and American Express) over the period 1989–1991. We use these data to show how the risk characteristics of the stocks are estimated. In reality, this time period is too short to correctly estimate the risks of the various stocks. However, the 12 data points are adequate for our objective here—to illustrate how risks and correlations can be estimated by investors and managers by using historical (ex post) data.

From the information on quarterly returns, the expected returns for each stock in Table 5-8 are calculated as the arithmetic averages of the returns observed in each of the 12 quarters studied.[5] Variances and covariances are then calculated for these securities.[6] The results of these computations are listed in Table 5-9. You can calculate these numbers yourself.

Assume that Ms. Foster currently owns shares in Sears and, having heard about the benefits of diversification, is considering doubling her stock investment by add-

[5] $E(\tilde{R}_i) = (\Sigma_{n=1}^{12} R_{i,n})(1/12)$

[6] Variances are calculated as $\sigma^2 = \{\Sigma_{t=1}^{12} [R_{i,t} - E(\tilde{R}_{i,t})]^2\}/(N - 1)$. This definition is consistent with our variance definition [equation (5-4)] with one difference. The denominator here is $N-1$ rather than N to obtain an unbiased estimate of the variance. This is the correct definition of variance estimated from sample data. Refer to any basic statistics text for additional details.

■

TABLE 5-9

Estimating the Average Quarterly Returns, Variances, and Covariances for Three Large U.S. Corporations

(a) Average returns and variances

	Texaco	Sears Roebuck	American Express
Average return	0.04359	0.01821	0.00905
Variance of returns	0.00405	0.02481	0.04722
Standard deviation of returns	0.0636	0.1575	0.2173

(b) Covariances and Correlations

Stock Portfolio	Covariances, σ_{ij}	Correlation Coefficients, ρ_{ij}
Texaco–Sears	−0.0021	−0.21
Texaco–American Express	0.0022	0.16
Sears–American Express	0.0207	0.61

NOTE: These correlations and covariances are estimated over a very short time span. To get more reliable estimates, longer time periods would have been used.

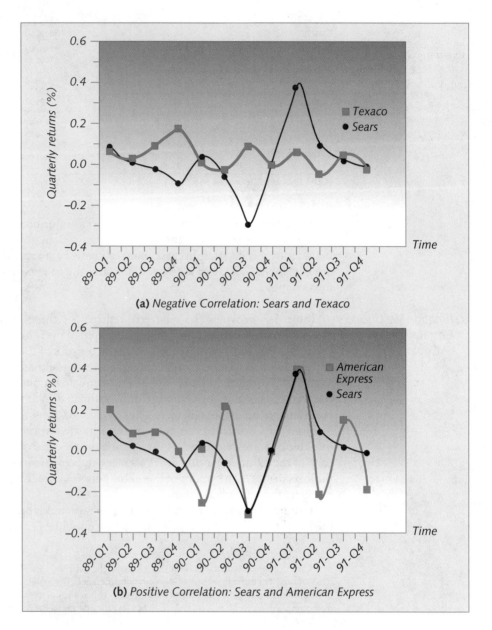

(a) *Negative Correlation: Sears and Texaco*

(b) *Positive Correlation: Sears and American Express*

ing another stock to her current holding. She wants to decide between Texaco and American Express. Her sole intent is to minimize the risk of her investment portfolio, without regard to expected returns. Which stock should she add?

Examine Figure 5-6, which shows the quarterly returns on all three stocks over time. First examine part (a). The graphs for Texaco and Sears show that Texaco is at a peak when Sears is at a trough, and vice versa. For example, when Sears appears to have reached a local low point (89-Q4 and 90-Q3), Texaco appears to have achieved a local high. Thus these two stocks appear to be negatively correlated. This should not be surprising because Table 5-9 noted that Texaco and Sears are negatively correlated. Now turn to part (b). Sears and American Express appear to be more closely following each other's performance. With exceptions (e.g., 91-Q1) this correspondence is not obvious, but all in all, there appears to be some positive correlation. Table 5-9 quantifies the correlation as 0.61. These relationships between the securities have implications for how Ms. Foster's choice will affect the risk of her portfolio.

The variance of a portfolio composed of equal portions of Texaco (T) and Sears (S) is

$$\sigma_P^2 = X_T^2\sigma_T^2 + X_S^2\sigma_S^2 + 2X_TX_S\rho_{TS}\sigma_T\sigma_S$$

$$\begin{aligned}\sigma_P^2 &= (0.5)^2(0.00405) + (0.5)^2(0.02481)\\ &\quad + 2(0.5)(0.5)(-0.21)(0.0636)(0.1575)\\ &= 0.00616\end{aligned}$$

This corresponds to a standard deviation of 0.07849. The weighted average of the standard deviations of Texaco and Sears—that is, the amount of risk the portfolio would have if there was no diversification ($\rho_{TS} = +1$)—is

$$\frac{0.0636 + 0.1575}{2} = 0.11055$$

Thus, in choosing this portfolio rather than doubling her investment in Sears stock, which would be tantamount to investing in another stock that is perfectly positively correlated with her existing investment, she has reduced the risk [using equation (5-10)] by approximately

$$\frac{0.11055 - 0.07849}{0.11055} = 0.29$$

or 29%. The negative correlation between these two stocks significantly reduces the variability of the portfolio.

The variance of a portfolio composed of equal portions of Sears and American Express (AE) is

$$\sigma_P^2 = X_S^2\sigma_S^2 + X_{AE}^2\sigma_{AE}^2 + 2X_SX_{AE}\rho_{S,AE}\sigma_S\sigma_{AE}$$

$$\begin{aligned}\sigma_P^2 &= (0.5)^2(0.02481) + (0.5)^2(0.04722)\\ &\quad + 2(0.5)(0.5)(0.61)(0.1575)(0.2173)\\ &= 0.02845\end{aligned}$$

This corresponds to a standard deviation of 0.16867. If we take the weighted average of the standard deviations of the returns of Sears and American Express, we obtain

$$\frac{0.1575 + 0.2173}{2} = 0.18740$$

Thus, if she had formed a portfolio with Sears and American Express, Ms. Foster would have reduced the variability by only

$$\frac{0.18740 - 0.16867}{0.18740} = 0.09995$$

or approximately 10%.

Since Ms. Foster is concerned solely with choosing the stock that provides the greatest diversification benefits, she will add Texaco to her portfolio.

SUMMARY

Section 5-1: Basic Return and Risk Concepts

How is uncertainty quantified into risk?

■ Investors evaluate the benefits from an investment in terms of the potential returns they can get from the investment and the risk associated with these returns.

■ Typically, the returns are one-period returns. Investments are evaluated in terms of uncertain (ex ante) returns, which are quantified by a probability distribution of returns. The actual return an investor realizes (ex post return) may be quite different from the ex ante return on any single investment.

What are probability distributions?

■ Because decision making involves uncertain ex ante returns, it is necessary to quantify the amount of uncertainty associated with these returns. Uncertainty is quantified using a probability distribution of returns. A probability distribution of returns is simply a listing of each potential return along with the probability of that return being realized. Although continuous probability distributions are perhaps more realistic, discrete distributions are often used to make an analysis more tractable.

Section 5-2: Summarizing and Interpreting the Information About a Single Asset

How can we summarize the information contained in a probability distribution?

■ The information contained in a probability distribution can be overwhelming. However, by summarizing the information into two summary measures, the expected return and the variance, we can conveniently analyze it.

■ The central tendency of the distribution is captured in its expected value. The expected return is a probability-weighted average return.

■ The variability or risk of the distribution is summarized by its variance. An equivalent risk measure is the standard deviation of the distribution, which is the square root of the variance.

■ For the special case of a normal distribution, the standard deviation takes on a special significance. It provides more precise statements about possible future returns.

■ Although risk is an ex ante concept, for most practical purposes it is estimated from an analysis of historical data.

Section 5-3: Measuring the Relationship Among Assets

How are asset returns interrelated?

■ The concepts of correlation and covariance are useful in measuring the extent and nature of the interrelationships among assets.

■ The correlation coefficient measures the strength of the association between two returns. Two assets are positively correlated if their returns, in general, move in the same direction; they are negatively correlated if, in general, their returns move in opposite directions. The correlation coefficient lies between -1 and $+1$. It is important to note that correlation does not imply causation. A closely related measure is the covariance between the returns on the assets.

■ A portfolio is a collection of two or more assets.

■ The expected return of a portfolio is the weighted average of the expected returns of the assets in the portfolio.

■ The correlation coefficients and the standard deviations of the assets in the portfolio determine the portfolio's variance.

Section 5-4:
Diversification and
Portfolio Risk

How does the relationship among asset returns affect the return and risk of a portfolio of assets?

■ Assets with correlation coefficients other than $+1$ are imperfectly correlated. Diversification is the process of reducing risk by forming a portfolio of imperfectly correlated investments. The lower the correlation among assets, the greater the diversification of risk in the portfolio.

■ The benefits of diversification arise from the fact that with imperfectly correlated assets, the standard deviation of a portfolio's returns is less than the weighted average of the standard deviations of the securities in the portfolio.

Section 5-5: Practical
Considerations in
Measuring Risk

What practical procedures exist for measuring a security's return and risk?

■ In practice, it is difficult to estimate ex ante probability distributions for individual securities. Managers use historical or ex post information to provide estimates of how securities are related to each other and to the economy as a whole.

QUESTIONS

1. What is the difference between (a) book and market measures of return and (b) ex ante and ex post returns? How can each of these returns be computed?

2. Why do ex ante and ex post returns differ?

3. What is a probability distribution? How are the two different types of probability distributions developed?

4. What are the statistics used to summarize information from a probability distribution? What is the practical significance of these measures?

5. How is risk defined in finance?

6. How does the assumption that the returns on financial assets are normally distributed give practical significance to the standard deviation measure σ?

7. If investors are rewarded for the risks they take, is it correct to state that risky investments will always provide better returns?

8. What does "imperfect correlation" mean? Why is this concept important to diversification?

9. How are the expected return and variance of a portfolio determined?

10. Explain how diversification reduces risk in two different ways: first using intuitive arguments and then using mathematical arguments.

11. Why is historical information often used to estimate expected returns and risk?

PROBLEMS

1. An investment will have a return of 30% if economic conditions improve, 20% if they stay the same, and −5% if they get worse. The probability that conditions will improve is 20%, that they will stay the same is 40%, and that they will get worse is 40%. What is the expected return from this investment?

2. TPI is considering marketing a new games cartridge for its popular TPI 3000 computer. Preliminary marketing reports suggest that the probability that the project will do very well is 30%, that it will do about average (for a new cartridge) is 30%, and that it will do poorly is 40%. You know that the project will have a 20% return if the project does about average and a −10% return if it does poorly, but a coffee stain on your report makes illegible the project's return if it does well. You do know that the expected return on the project is 12.5%. What is the illegible figure?

3. The Dow Jones Industrial Average is a number that reflects the value of a portfolio of shares of the 30 DJIA stocks. Suppose that the stocks in this portfolio have the same return as the market does and that this return is expected to be 15%. The DJIA is currently 3,050, and you expect it to be 3,392 at the end of the year. What dividend yield (dividends paid/initial value of portfolio) do you expect on this portfolio of 30 DJIA stocks?

4. Suppose that the current level of the Dow Jones Industrial Average is 3,100. You overhear two security analysts saying that for the DJIA portfolio, the expected dividend yield is 5% and the expected total return is 0.1725. You also overhear that if during the coming year the market does poorly, average, or well, they expect the DJIA to be 3,100, 3,410, or 3,875, respectively. Finally, you overhear that the probability that the market will do about average (i.e., end at 3,410) is 60%. What is the probability that the market will do well (end at 3,875) and the probability that it will do poorly (end at 3,100)? (*Hint:* Remember that all these probabilities must sum to 1.)

5. The range is a measure of risk that is simply the best possible outcome minus the worst possible outcome. Suppose that you are considering the following two investment opportunities:

	Probability	Return
Stock *A*		
Does well	0.10	0.30
Does average	0.80	0.15
Does poorly	0.10	0.0
Stock *B*		
Does well	0.30	0.25
Does average	0.40	0.15
Does poorly	0.30	0.05

(a) What is the range of stock *A*? Of stock *B*?

(b) What is the expected return on stock *A*? On stock *B*?

(c) What is the standard deviation of returns on stock *A*? On stock *B*?

(d) Would you select *A* or *B* if you were using ranges as a measure of risk? If you were using standard deviation as a measure of risk?

(e) Why is the range a poor measure of risk?

6. Assume that the returns associated with an investment in KayCee common stock are normally distributed and that $E(\tilde{R}_{KC}) = 0.204$ and its standard deviation is 0.126.

(a) Calculate the range of expected returns associated with each of the following probabilities of occurrence:
   (1) 68.26%
   (2) 95.44%
   (3) 99.74%

(b) Draw the probability distributions associated with your results in part (a).

7. Two companies respond to the economy in the following manner:

Event	Probability	Return on Vulcan Tire Recapping Co. Shares	Return on Goodwealth Tire Co. Shares
Economic upturn	0.3	0.12	0.24
No changes in the economy	0.4	0.18	0.18
Economic downturn	0.3	0.24	0.12

One of your friends argues that because both shares have the same expected return and the same risk (as measured by standard deviation of returns), investors will be indifferent to buying shares of either of the two companies. Is this true?

8. Martin Racquet Sports is considering adding two new ceramic frames to its high-performance tennis racquet line. The firm has established the following return estimates:

Market Response	Probability	Expected Returns	
		Frame A	Frame B
None	0.05	0.0120	0.0090
Poor	0.10	0.0565	0.0375
Average	0.35	0.1100	0.1325
Good	0.20	0.1450	0.1400
Excellent	0.30	0.2025	0.1860

(a) Construct a bar chart displaying each frame's $E(\tilde{R})$ under the various scenarios.

(b) Calculate the $E(\tilde{R})$ for each frame.

(c) Using the bar charts, evaluate the riskiness associated with each frame's $E(\tilde{R})$.

9. Your economic analysis has given you the following possible returns on two investments under three different scenarios:

Scenario	Probability	Return	
		X	Y
S_1	0.30	0.10	0.08
S_2	0.40	0.16	0.15
S_3	0.30	0.12	0.20

(a) Calculate the expected return on each investment.

(b) Calculate the variance and standard deviation of X and Y.

(c) Compute the covariance and correlation coefficient between X and Y.

(d) If you create a portfolio of 67% X and 33% Y, what will be the expected return, variance, and standard deviation of the portfolio?

10. Use the following possible NPVs for projects R and S under two different scenarios:

		NPV	
Scenario	Probability	R	S
S_1	0.7	$2,000	$3,500
S_2	0.3	$4,000	$3,000

(a) Calculate the expected NPV for each project.

(b) Compute the variance and standard deviation of the NPVs of R and S.

(c) Calculate the covariance and correlation coefficient between the NPVs of projects R and S.

(d) If both projects are fully funded, what will be the expected NPV, variance, and standard deviation of the undertaking?

11. You have been asked by a friend for advice in selecting a portfolio of assets based on the following data:

	Return		
Year	A	B	C
1989	0.14	0.18	0.14
1990	0.16	0.16	0.16
1991	0.18	0.14	0.18

You have been told to create portfolios by investing equal proportions (i.e., 50%) in each of two different assets. No probabilities have been supplied.

(a) What is the expected return on each of these assets over the three-year period?

(b) What is the standard deviation of each asset's return?

(c) What is the expected return on each portfolio?

(d) For each portfolio, how would you characterize the correlation between the returns on its two assets?

(e) What is the standard deviation of each portfolio?

(f) Which portfolio do you recommend? Why?

12. Use the following information for two stocks X and Y:

State of the Market	Probability	Return on X	Return on Y
Large boom	0.10	0.15	0.35
Small boom	0.20	0.15	0.27
Little or no change	0.35	0.15	0.18
Small downturn	0.20	0.13	0.08
Large downturn	0.15	0.11	0.08

(a) Find the expected returns of X and Y.

(b) Calculate the standard deviations of returns on X and Y.

(c) Calculate the standard deviation of a portfolio that has half X and half Y, given that the correlation coefficient between the returns on X and Y is 0.7549.

13. Suppose you have decided to invest all your money in some combination of Transcontinental Airlines and Axis Stores, Inc. Transcontinental Airlines has an expected return of 25% and a standard deviation of returns of 0.10. Axis Stores, Inc., has an expected return of 15% and a standard deviation of returns of 0.05. The correlation between the returns of Transcontinental and Axis is 0.2.

(a) Fill in the following chart:

Proportion Invested in Transcontinental (%)	Expected Return on Portfolio	Standard Deviation of Returns on Portfolio
100	0.25	0.10
80		
60		
40		
20		
0	0.15	0.05

(b) Which portfolios (if any) can you exclude from consideration if you are risk averse?

14. Suppose that the *Times* and the *Sun* are competing newspapers in Cleveland, Iowa, and that if one newspaper has large sales (and large cash flows), the other has small sales (and small cash flows). The pattern of return is as follows:

Event	Probability	Return on Sun's Shares (%)	Return on Times's Shares (%)
Sun has very good year	0.2	30	10
Sun has good year	0.2	24	12
Sun has mediocre year	0.2	18	14
Sun has poor year	0.2	12	16
Sun has very poor year	0.2	6	18

(a) Find the expected returns on *Sun* shares and on *Times* shares.

(b) Find the standard deviations of returns on *Sun* shares and on *Times* shares.

(c) Find the expected return and the standard deviation of returns on a portfolio composed of 75% *Times* shares and 25% *Sun* shares. Verify your answer by finding the return on your portfolio on each of the five cases that may occur (*Sun* has a very good year, etc.) The correlation coefficient is -0.9989.

15. The Hendry Corp. will have the following different returns under different economic conditions:

State of the Economy	Probability	Return on Hendry Shares
Good	0.1	0.25
Mediocre	0.6	0.10
Poor	0.3	0.05

Government T-bills will return 0.08 regardless of the state of the economy.

(a) Find the expected returns and the standard deviations on returns of Hendry shares and T-bills.

(b) Complete the following table and graph the results:

Proportion Invested in T-bills (%)	Proportion Invested in Hendry (%)	Expected Return on Portfolio	Standard Deviation of Portfolio
100	0	0.08	0.0
75	25		
50	50		
25	75		
0	100		

16. You are evaluating an investment portfolio for your client, Mr. Wilplemore. The portfolio presently contains two securities with the following characteristics:

Security	Expected Return	Variance	Correlation Coefficient
A	0.10	0.265	0.69
B	0.10	0.265	0.69

Mr. Wilplemore feels that because these securities have the same return and variance, it would be easier for him just to consolidate all of his wealth in one or the other. How can you show him that, because of their imperfect correlation with each other, he would be better off with his diversified portfolio?

17. Consider two stocks A and B with standard deviations 0.05 and 0.10, respectively. The correlation coefficient for these two stocks is 0.8.

(a) What is the diversification gain from forming a portfolio that has equal proportions of each stock?

(b) What should be the weights of the two assets in a portfolio that achieves a diversification gain of 3%?

18. Peter Goldcrest is a portfolio manager with a company on Wall Street. He invests in a certain class of stocks, each of which has the same standard deviation of 0.05. Peter wants to construct an equally weighted portfolio of any two stocks and get a diversification gain of 50%. What should the correlation between these two stocks be?

SUGGESTED ADDITIONAL READINGS

Bodie, Z., A. Kane, and A. J. Marcus. *Investments*. Homewood, IL: Richard D. Irwin, 1989.

Elton, E. J., and M. J. Gruber. *Modern Portfolio Theory and Investment Analysis*, 2nd ed. New York: John Wiley & Sons, 1984.

Haugen, R. A. *Modern Investment Theory*. Englewood Cliffs, NJ: Prentice Hall, 1986.

Hogg, Robert V., and Elliot A. Tanis. *Probability and Statistical Inference*. New York: Macmillan Publishing Company, 1977.

Ibbotson Associates, Inc. *Stocks, Bonds, Bills, and Inflation: 1992 Yearbook*. Chicago: Ibbotson Associates, 1993.

Levy, H., and M. Sarnat. *Portfolio and Investment Selection: Theory and Practice*. Englewood Cliffs, NJ: Prentice-Hall, 1984.

Markowitz, H. M. "Portfolio Selection." *Journal of Finance* 7(March 1952): 77–91.

Mendenhall, William, Richard L. Scheaffer, and Dennis D. Wackerly. *Mathematical Statistics with Applications*, 2nd ed. Boston: Duxbury Press, 1981.

SIX ASSESSING EXPECTED RATES OF RETURN: THEORY AND EVIDENCE

My ventures are not in one bottom trusted, Nor to one place; nor is my whole estate Upon the fortune of this present year. Therefore my merchandise makes me not sad.

—Shakespeare, Merchant of Venice (Antonio appearing to have captured the concept of diversification)

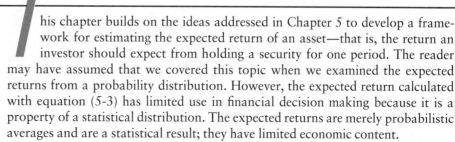

This chapter builds on the ideas addressed in Chapter 5 to develop a framework for estimating the expected return of an asset—that is, the return an investor should expect from holding a security for one period. The reader may have assumed that we covered this topic when we examined the expected returns from a probability distribution. However, the expected return calculated with equation (5-3) has limited use in financial decision making because it is a property of a statistical distribution. The expected returns are merely probabilistic averages and are a statistical result; they have limited economic content.

Any projections you make about future returns on an asset using equation (5-3) completely ignore information you may have about other economic factors that can influence the asset's future returns. After all, in projecting returns on an investment, you use your own subjective judgments based on specialized knowledge of the company, estimates of future economic conditions, or special predictive skills that you may possess.

Factoring in these details for an individual asset is an extremely difficult task. We make an attempt to do this by answering the following questions:

- How does the risk of a portfolio change as the number of assets in the portfolio increases?

- Can diversification eliminate all of the risk in a portfolio?

- What is beta risk and how is it estimated?

- What is the capital asset pricing model (CAPM)?

- What empirical evidence supports the CAPM?

- What is the arbitrage pricing theory (APT)?

Appendix 6A demonstrates how the nondiversifiable risk of an asset is calculated with a measure called beta.

6-1

THE IMPORTANCE OF COVARIANCE RISK AND THE LIMITS OF DIVERSIFICATION

Covariance Risk

Recall our example of ASI stock from the preceding chapter. How can an investor assess (estimate) the return he will get from buying a share of ASI stock and holding it for a year? The first step in the process of using equation (5-3) is to identify the distribution of returns on the stock. Even if one could assess the distribution of returns for ASI stock as in Table 5-2, it cannot be used directly to forecast the returns on ASI. We have calculated the expected return on ASI using Table 5-2 and equation (5-3) to be 8%. What does this mean? Can an investor expect the 8% return irrespective of whether the U.S. economy is booming or in recession? It would be silly to assume that just because the probabilistic average is 8%, the return on the investment next year will be 8%.

Although ex post data can yield estimates of a security's risk characteristics, the expected returns implicit in historical data for *individual* securities are not a good forecast of the securities' future performance. Estimates of the whole economy's returns are easily generated, and an understanding of the relationship between an asset's variability and that of the economy allows us to make a more meaningful assessment of the expected return. Establishing the theoretical basis for such a procedure is a major objective of this chapter.

Although our dicusssion may appear abstract at times, many practical financial decision-making procedures have little significance without this theoretical basis. Without the logical framework that is developed in this chapter, managers have little guidance on how they can maximize the wealth of shareholders.

The fundamental issue of this section is that the covariance risk of a stock is perhaps more important than its variance risk in determining price. This is seen as we examine portfolios that contain many assets.

THE VARIANCE OF A PORTFOLIO WITH MANY ASSETS

The elements involved in a portfolio's variance are given in Table 6-1, where each cell contains either a variance or a covariance term. Examine any one row at a time. Consider the third row, which is boxed. The first cell is $x_3 x_1 \sigma_{31}$. Here x_3 and x_1 are the percentages of total wealth invested in stocks 3 and 1, respectively, and σ_{31} is the covariance between the returns on stocks 3 and 1. The second cell in row 3 is $x_3 x_2 \sigma_{32}$. The third cell in row 3 is $x_3 x_3 \sigma_{33}$. But σ_{33} from the definition of covariance, equation (5-6), is σ_3^2, the variance of returns on stock 3. Thus the third cell reduces to $x_3^2 \sigma_3^2$. The Nth cell is $x_3 x_N \sigma_{3N}$. (Recall from Chapter 5 that $\sigma_{i,m} = \sigma_{m,i}$.) The cells in any other row in Table 6-1 are filled in the same way. The variance of the N-asset portfolio is the sum of all of the cells in Table 6-1.

As the reader can see, computing the variance of a portfolio with more than two assets becomes fairly complicated. As a practical matter, such computations are routinely conducted with standardized computer programs.

From Table 6-1 we can draw a few conclusions:

1. If there are N stocks in the portfolio, there is a total of $N \times N = N^2$ cells to be summed to get the portfolio variance. For example, if there are five securities, then there are 5^2 (i.e., 25) total cells in Table 6-1.

2. An N-asset portfolio has N variance terms. These are the diagonal elements in Table 6-1 ($x_1^2 \sigma_1^2, x_2^2 \sigma_2^2, \ldots, x_N^2 \sigma_N^2$).

3. An N-asset portfolio has $(N^2 - N)/2$ different covariance terms. These are the off-diagonal terms in Table 6-1. If there is a total of N^2 cells and N variance terms, then the remaining $(N^2 - N)$ terms must be the covariance terms above. With five assets, Table 6-1 contains $(5^2 - 5)/2$ or 10 different covariance terms and 20 covariance terms in all.

■
T A B L E   6 - 1
Terms That Determine the Variance of an N-Asset Portfolio

Asset	1	2	3	$\cdots$	N
1	$x_1^2 \sigma_1^2$	$x_1 x_2 \sigma_{12}$	$x_1 x_3 \sigma_{13}$		$x_1 x_N \sigma_{1N}$
2	$x_2 x_1 \sigma_{21}$	$x_2^2 \sigma_2^2$	$x_2 x_3 \sigma_{23}$		$x_2 x_N \sigma_{2N}$
3	$x_3 x_1 \sigma_{31}$	$x_3 x_2 \sigma_{32}$	$x_3^2 \sigma_3^2$		$x_3 x_N \sigma_{3N}$
.					
.					
.					
N	$x_N x_1 \sigma_{N1}$	$x_N x_2 \sigma_{N2}$	$x_N x_3 \sigma_{N3}$		$x_N^2 \sigma_N^2$

FIGURE 6-1

The relationship between the number of variance terms and the number of covariance terms as the size of the portfolio increases

Portfolio Size	Total Cells, N^2	Variance Terms, N	Covariance Terms, $N^2 - N$
2	4	2	2
8	64	8	56
15	225	15	210
50	2,500	50	2,450
100	10,000	100	9,900

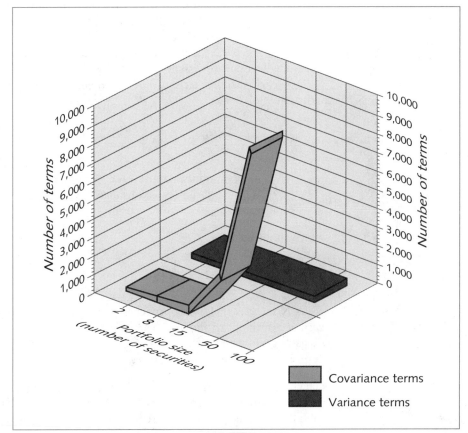

THE IMPORTANCE OF COVARIANCE IN DETERMINING PORTFOLIO RISK

Consider how the number of variance and covariance terms increases as the number of securities in a portfolio increases. The effects of increasing the portfolio size from 2 to 100 is illustrated in Figure 6-1, which also plots the numbers to dramatize the importance of the covariance terms. As N increases, the number of covariance terms increases faster than does the number of variance terms, thus "swamping" the effect of the variance terms. We conclude with a key idea:

KEY CONCEPT   As the size of a portfolio increases, the portfolio's variance is dependent more on the covariances among the securities in the portfolio than on the variances of the individual securities.

THE EFFECT OF PORTFOLIO SIZE ON PORTFOLIO RISK

When a portfolio of two imperfectly correlated securities is formed, the overall risk of the portfolio usually decreases because of diversification. As the number of securities in the portfolio increases, the risk is reduced. Why is this true?

Using the conclusions we drew from Table 6-1, we can define the variance of a portfolio as:

$$\text{Variance of a portfolio} = N \text{ variances} + (N^2 - N) \text{ covariances} \qquad (6\text{-}1)$$

Assume for simplicity that all assets have the same variance, $\bar{\sigma}^2$, and all securities are equally weighted in the portfolio. This and the subsequent simplifying assumptions that we make do not affect the generality of the results. Then $x_1 = x_2 = x_3 = \cdots = x_N = 1/N$. Each variance cell on the diagonal in Table 6-1 is $(1/N) \times (1/N)(\bar{\sigma}^2) = \bar{\sigma}^2/N^2$. If we also assume that all covariances are the same, $\bar{\sigma}_{ij}$, then each (off-diagonal) covariance cell is $(1/N)(1/N)(\bar{\sigma}_{ij}) = \bar{\sigma}_{ij}/N^2$.

Since each variance term is $\bar{\sigma}^2/N^2$ and each covariance term is $\bar{\sigma}_{ij}/N^2$, we can write equation 6-1 as:

$$\text{Variance of a portfolio} = N \times \frac{\bar{\sigma}^2}{N^2} + (N^2 - N) \times \frac{\bar{\sigma}_{ij}}{N^2}$$

number of variances   each variance term   number of covariances   each covariance term

which simplifies to

$$\sigma_P^2 = \frac{1}{N}(\bar{\sigma}^2) + \left(1 - \frac{1}{N}\right)(\bar{\sigma}_{ij}) \qquad (6\text{-}2)$$

As N increases, $(1/N)$ approaches 0 and $(1 - 1/N)$ approaches 1, so that the variance of the portfolio approaches $\bar{\sigma}_{ij}$. Therefore the variance of a portfolio is $\bar{\sigma}_{ij}$ as N gets large; that is, as the portfolio size increases, the risk of the portfolio approaches the average covariance.

KEY CONCEPTS

(1) The variance of the individual securities disappears in the portfolio variance; that is, portfolio variances can be "diversified away." (2) The variance of the portfolio becomes the average covariance as the portfolio size becomes large; portfolio covariances cannot be "diversified away."

The Limits of Diversification

Although the benefits of diversification increase as more and more securities are added to a portfolio, there is a limit to the amount of risk reduction that can be attained. Figure 6-2 illustrates the results of academic studies about the effects of portfolio size on the risk of the portfolio. It plots the total risk of a portfolio on the vertical axis and the number of securities in the portfolio on the horizontal axis. The total risk falls at a decreasing rate as the number of securities in the portfolio increases. A substantial amount of risk can be diversified away by even as few as 25 or 30 securities.[1] Notice that the total risk line gradually approaches the horizontal line that represents the minimum risk. When this happens, the portfolio is said to be fully diversified. A completely diversified portfolio has the minimum level of risk attainable; no more reduction in risk can be achieved through diversification. This minimum possible risk, as seen in the figure, approaches the average covariance risk, $\bar{\sigma}_{ij}$.

---

[1] See Meir Statman, "How Many Stocks Make a Diversified Portfolio?" *Journal of Financial and Quantitative Analysis*, September 1987.

FIGURE 6-2
Limits of diversification

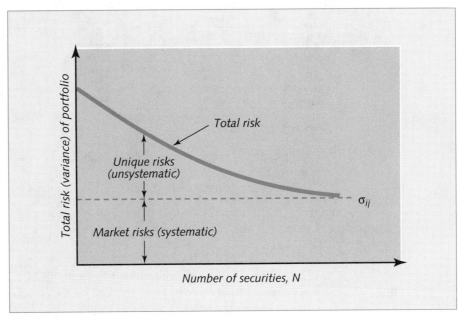

NATURE OF THE RISK COMPONENTS

It is convenient to divide total risk (variance risk) into two distinct components: **undiversifiable risks** (the covariance risk) and **diversifiable risk** (the remaining risk in the portfolio). Thus:

$$\begin{array}{ccccc} \text{Total risk} & = & \text{undiversifiable risk} & + & \text{diversifiable risk} \\ \text{(variance of returns)} & & \text{(covariance risk)} & & \text{(variance risk} - \text{covariance risk)} \end{array} \qquad (6\text{-}3)$$

To understand why some risks are diversifiable while others are not, we must examine the risk components closer to identify their determinants.

Unique risks are risks that are specific to a company. The risk of obsolescence of technology, the risk of reduced revenues caused by increasing competition, and the risks associated with patent approval, antitrust legislation, labor contracts, management styles, and geographic location all are examples of unique risks. These are risks that can be diversified away by forming a large portfolio. The contribution of each of these risks for each company included in the portfolio effectively "washes out" and is thus eliminated. Because unique risks are firm-specific risks, they are also known as unsystematic risks; they do not depend in any systematic way on general economic conditions.

Undiversifiable risks are **market risks**, also known as **systematic risks**. Market risks represent that component of total risk that is systematically dependent on the vagaries of the U.S. economy. All American firms are affected, to varying degrees, by economic conditions in the United States. If the U.S. economy thrives, most companies do well, whereas if the United States goes into a recession, even the best-managed company with the best products or services will not be able to reach its peak performance levels. In addition to the economy's overall performance, several other factors affect nearly all companies: tax changes instituted by Congress, the uncertainty associated with OPEC oil prices, the threat of war, and so on. These are factors outside the control of a corporation's management, and all corporations are subject to these uncertainties. Of course, different companies (stocks) display different sensitivities to market conditions. Companies that are very sensi-

■

TABLE 6-2
*Stock Market Correlations
Across Countries,
1971–1988*

Country	West Germany	Canada	United Kingdom	Japan	Australia	Singapore	United States
West Germany	1.00	0.31	0.41	0.40	0.28	0.24	0.34
Canada	0.31	1.00	0.53	0.27	0.57	0.39	0.70
United Kingdom	0.41	0.53	1.00	0.34	0.44	0.50	0.50
Japan	0.40	0.27	0.34	1.00	0.27	0.33	0.28
Australia	0.28	0.57	0.44	0.27	1.00	0.41	0.49
Singapore	0.24	0.39	0.50	0.33	0.41	1.00	0.45
United States	0.34	0.70	0.50	0.28	0.49	0.45	1.00

SOURCE: Monthly returns in dollars are excerpted from Bruno Solnik, *International Investments,* 2nd ed. (Reading, MA.: Addison-Wesley, 1991).

tive to changes in the economy have high market risks, and those that are less sensitive have smaller market risks.

Thus equation (6-3) can equivalently be written as

$$\underset{\text{(variance of returns)}}{\text{Total risk}} = \underset{\text{(covariance risk)}}{\text{market risks}} + \underset{\text{(variance risk} - \text{covariance risk)}}{\text{unique risks}} \tag{6-4}$$

GOING INTERNATIONAL

The limits of diversification shown in Figure 6-2 do not consider the implications of diversifying across countries. Our own domestic economy is not perfectly correlated with the other economies of the world. Table 6-2 gives the correlations of security returns among several of our trading partners, with returns measured in dollars.

Table 6-2 shows that the major world markets are not highly correlated. This means that there are risk-reduction benefits from investing overseas. In effect, each country can be thought of as a security, and investing in a global portfolio is tantamount to forming a portfolio of various imperfectly correlated securities. Thus, when the "economy" is defined as the world economy rather than a single national economy, the potential for risk diversification is vastly increased. This is demonstrated visually in Figure 6-3, which contains the total risk line for the domestic

■

FIGURE 6-3
*The limits of international
diversification*

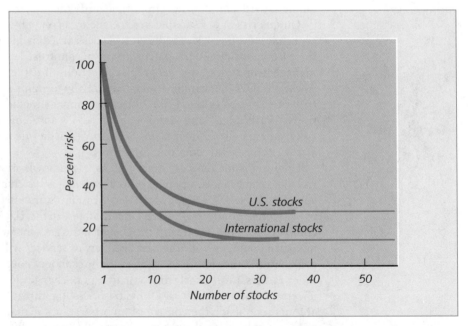

SOURCE: Adapted, with permission, from *Financial Analysts Journal,* July/August 1974. Copyright 1974, The Financial Analysts Federation, Charlottesville, VA. All rights reserved.

economy from Figure 6-1 and the total risk line that can be attained from international diversification. Systematic risk can be cut almost in half by changing from a diversified U.S. portfolio to an equivalent one that is diversified across markets.[2]

KEY CONCEPT

The benefits of diversification can be increased by including foreign investments in the portfolio. However, even in a portfolio with international investments, there are limits to the risk-reduction benefits of diversification.

Several aspects of international diversification are discussed in the highlight on page 142.

6-2

BETA: QUANTIFYING MARKET RISKS

To quantify market risks we use an economic theory in which it is optimal for investors to hold a portfolio called the **market portfolio**, which contains every asset in the economy. Financial theory makes some simplifying assumptions that ensure that all individuals invest in the market portfolio. For example, if all investors have **homogenous expectations**—that is, they all have the same assessed probability distribution of asset returns for all assets—then all individuals will hold the market portfolio because only then will the supply of stocks equal the demand and the economy is in equilibrium. It is not imporant for us to analyze the theory underlying this result further. Our intent here is to show how the notion of a market portfolio is useful for financial managers and investors alike.

If all individuals hold the market portfolio in equilibrium, the risk of a security takes on a specific interpretation. The covariance risk of a security i becomes the covariance between the return on security i and the return on the market portfolio. The covariance risk of a security i is represented as σ_{im}, where m is the market portfolio. If we further standardize this risk measure by the variance of the market returns, denoted σ_m^2, we get stock i's **beta coefficient**:

$$\beta_i = \frac{\text{covariance between the returns on stock } i \text{ and the returns on the market portfolio}}{\text{variance of returns on the market portfolio}} \tag{6-5}$$

$$= \frac{\sigma_{im}}{\sigma_m^2}$$

From the definition of covariance, $\sigma_{im} = \rho_{im}\sigma_i\sigma_m$. Substituting this into equation (6-5), we can also write beta as

$$\beta_i = \rho_{im}\frac{\sigma_i}{\sigma_m} \tag{6-6}$$

The market portfolio is a theoretical construct and thus we use a surrogate for the market portfolio in operationalizing the theory.

What Does Beta Measure?

Beta is a statistical concept that relates the sensitivity of a security's returns to changes in the returns of the market. We can see how beta relates market risk to asset risk by quantifying equation (6-4).

---

[2] See Bruno H. Solnik, "Why Not Diversify Internationally Rather Than Domestically?" *Financial Analysts Journal*, July–August 1974, pp. 48–54.

INTERNATIONAL DIVERSIFICATION: BENEFITS AND COSTS

Holding a portfolio that is well diversified across various sectors of a single economy does not provide the maximum amount of diversification available. Since various economies are imperfectly correlated, holding assets across different countries will reduce risk for investors (see Figure 6-3).

Until recently, the prospect of international diversification would have been tantalizing but unattainable for most investors. The lack of information concerning opportunities in other markets and the technical difficulties in purchasing and selling foreign securities and in handling dividends and interest payments precluded most investors from even thinking of expanding their portfolios to include German, Japanese, or Italian securities. American Depository Receipts (ADRs) have been traded in U.S. stock exchanges for years. ADRs allow Americans to hold foreign securities through a trustee who handles much of the administrative work. However, it was the rapid expansion of global mutual funds in the 1980s that has allowed investors to take advantage of not only the lower risk associated with an international portfolio but also a higher dollar rate of return on their investments.

To understand rates of return from these global mutual funds, we must include the effects of exchange rates. An internationally

diversified portfolio, while it provides diversification benefits, also exposes the investor to exchange rate variability.

Consider a U.S. investor investing abroad. His dollar return depends not only on the return earned on the foreign investment but also on the changes in the value of the foreign currency with respect to the U.S. dollar. The investor's total return from investing in a diversified foreign investment, such as a Japan fund, is:

$$R_{i,\$} = R_i + \delta_i$$

where

$R_{i,\$}$ is the rate of return earned on the foreign investment in dollars

R_i is the rate of return earned on the foreign investment in the currency in which the investment was made (yen)

δ_i is the change in the value of the foreign currency (yen) relative to the U.S. dollar

The investor may receive a larger return if the Japanese yen appreciates, or increases in value, relative to the U.S. dollar. On the other hand, the investor could see the return on his investment reduced or even eliminated by a depreciating yen, one that is losing value relative to the dollar.

Likewise, the variability of a foreign investment is affected by the variability of the currency of the investment relative to the U.S. dollar and is computed by:

$$\sigma_{R_{i,\$}}^2 = \sigma_{R_i}^2 + \sigma_{\delta_i}^2 + 2\sigma_{R_i,\delta_i}$$

where

$\sigma_{R_{i,\$}}^2$ is the variance of the dollar rate of return earned on a foreign investment

$\sigma_{R_i}^2$ is the variance of the foreign currency rate of return earned on a foreign investment

$\sigma_{\delta_i}^2$ is the variance of the exchange rate between the foreign currency and the dollar

σ_{R_i,δ_i}^2 is the covariance of the exchange rate and the foreign stock market returns

This equation shows that the risk of the foreign investment can be substantial, especially since there is usually a positive covariance between the movement of a country's equity markets and the movement of its currency. With some exchange rates changing by as much as 20% a year, this exchange rate risk adds significantly to the variability of the investment. Thus the risk-reducing diversification effects of investing globally come at the cost of increased exchange rate variability.

Do these two factors balance out, or does one dominate? Studies show that the benefits of diversification are reduced but not eliminated by exchange risk; investors are still better off with international diversification.

SOURCE: Cheol S. Eun and Bruce G. Resnick, "Exchange Rate Uncertainty, Forward Contracts and International Portfolio Selection," Journal of Finance, *March 1988, pp. 197–215.*

$$\begin{array}{ccccc} \text{Total risk} & = & \text{market risks} & + & \text{unique risks} \\ \text{(variance of returns)} & & \text{(covariance risk)} & & \text{(variance risk} - \text{covariance risk)} \end{array}$$

(6-7)

$$\sigma_i^2 = \beta_i^2 \sigma_m^2 + \sigma_{ie}^2$$

where

σ_i^2 is the total risk of asset i

σ_m^2 is the risk of the market's returns

σ_{ie}^2 is the unique risk of asset i.

KEY CONCEPT   Beta measures how responsive an asset is to market movements.

This idea is best understood through a numerical example. Consider the example of Crystal Semiconductors stock and its performance in response to general economic conditions. Assume that the market in the next period moves either up or down and that the market returns are either 15% or -10%, respectively. If market returns are good, then Crystal's returns are either 20% or 16% with equal probability. If the market returns are bad, then Crystal's returns are either -16% or -10% with equal probability. The expected return on Crystal for a given market return is then easily computed as shown in the table.

Market Returns	Crystal's Returns	Probability	Expected Return on Crystal
15%	20%	0.5	
	16%	0.5	18% [20% × 0.5 + 16% × 0.5]
−10%	−16%	0.5	
	−10%	0.5	−13% [−16% × 0.5 + −10% × 0.5]

Thus, for a *change* in the market return of 25% [15% $-$ (-10%)], the expected return on Crystal, $E(\tilde{R}_{crystal})$, *changes* by 31% [18% $-$ (-13%)]. The responsiveness of Crystal's returns to the market's returns is $\Delta E(\tilde{R}_{crystal})/\Delta R_m = 31\%/25\% = 1.24$. This "responsiveness coefficient" for Crystal is its stock beta.

Crystal's beta of 1.24 suggests that for each 1% increase in market returns, the expected return on Crystal increases by 1.24%. Similarly, for each 1% decrease in the market return, Crystal's returns will decrease, on average, by 1.24%.

Thus beta measures the volatility of an asset's returns relative to the market. The larger the beta is, the more volatile the asset. A beta of 1.0 indicates an asset of average risk. A stock with a beta greater than 1.0 is an above-average-risk stock, and so its returns are more volatile than those of the market. Similarly, a stock with a beta less than 1.0 is a below-average-risk stock. Beta can also be negative, implying that the stock moves in the opposite direction from that of the market.[3]

---

[3] Another explanation for beta: The beta of a security is the contribution of that security to the risk of the market portfolio. *Proof*: Consider security 3 in Table 6-1 . Now assume that the portfolio in Table 6-1 is the market portfolio made up of N assets. The covariance between the returns on security 3 and the market is

$$\sigma_{3m} = x_1\sigma_{31} + x_2\sigma_{32} + x_3\sigma_{33} + \cdots + x_N\sigma_{3N} = \sum_{j=1}^{N} x_j\sigma_{3j} \quad \text{(a)}$$

Now consider the variance of a portfolio σ_P^2:

$$\sigma_P^2 = \sum_{i=1}^{N} \sum_{j=1}^{N} x_i x_j \sigma_{ij} \quad \text{(b)}$$

The double summation sign ensures that we sum across all cells in any row in Table 6–1 and across all

Consider Westinghouse Electric Company's stock, with a beta of 1.25, a value that suggests that if the market returns increase by 2%, Westinghouse's return will, on average, increase by 2% × 1.25 = 2.5%. On the other hand, consider Washington Water Power Co. stock with a beta of 0.55. What happens if the market returns fall by 10%? Using the same line of reasoning, we predict Washington's stock will fall, on average, by 10% × 0.55 = 5.5%. Beta magnifies the performance of the security relative to the performance of the U.S. economy, thereby magnifying both the good and the bad.

How much riskier than Washington is Westinghouse? By comparing the magnitudes of their betas (1.25/0.55 = 2.273), Westinghouse appears to be 227% more volatile than Washington Water Power Co.

Portfolio Betas

Just as a single asset has a beta coefficient, a portfolio of several assets also has a beta coefficient. The beta coefficient for a portfolio depends not only on the betas of the assets held in the portfolio but also on the proportion of each asset in the portfolio. The equation for computing the beta for a portfolio is

$$\beta_p = \sum X_i \beta_i \qquad (6\text{-}8)$$

where β_i is the beta of asset i and X_i is the proportion of asset i in the portfolio. In effect, the beta for a portfolio is simply the weighted average of the betas of the portfolio's assets.

Consider a portfolio P that consists of equal investments in three assets: Mesa Incorporated (energy exploration, $\beta = 0.40$), Promus Company (casinos, $\beta = 2.00$), and J. P. Morgan (banking, $\beta = 1.15$). Because there are equal amounts of each asset in the portfolio, $X_i = 1/3$ ($i = 1, 2, 3$) and from equation (6-8) the portfolio beta is given by

$$\beta_p = \sum X_i \beta_i = \frac{1}{3}(0.40) + \frac{1}{3}(2.00) + \frac{1}{3}(1.15) = 1.18$$

That is, for every 1% change in the market's expected return, this portfolio's value should change by 1.18% in the same direction.

Published Sources of Betas

Betas are available from many published sources. Several investment houses periodically compute betas for various stocks. Table 6-3 provides estimates of stock betas from The Value Line Investment Survey for the securities that make up the Dow Jones Industrial Average. Published sources typically include stock (equity) betas, although any asset can have a beta—machines, bonds, real estate, and so forth. Because published sources for the betas of many assets may not be available, analysts must understand the procedures for calculating betas.

---

rows. The contribution of security 3 to the risk of the portfolio is $\partial \sigma_p^2 / \partial x_3$. Differentiating (b) with respect to x_3, we have

$$\frac{\delta \sigma_p^2}{\delta x_3} = 2 \sum_{j=1}^{N} x_j \sigma_{3j} \qquad \text{(c)}$$

Comparing (c) and (a) gives

$$\frac{\delta \sigma_p^2}{\delta x_3} = 2\sigma_{3m} \qquad \text{(d)}$$

Thus the contribution of a security to the risk of the market portfolio is proportional to the covariance of its returns with the returns on the market portfolio.

■

TABLE 6-3

Selected Stock Betas

Alcoa	1.2	DuPont	1.05	3M	1.00
Allied Signal	1.05	Eastman Kodak	1.15	J. P. Morgan	1.15
American Express	1.5	Exxon	0.95	Philip Morris	1.10
American T&T	0.95	General Electric	1.15	Proctor & Gamble	1.10
Bethlehem Steel	1.4	General Motors	1.10	Sears	1.10
Boeing	1.10	Goodyear	1.10	Texaco	0.65
Caterpillar	1.15	IBM	0.95	Union Carbide	n/a[a]
Chevron	0.85	International Paper	1.10	United Technologies	1.05
CocaCola	1.15	McDonalds	1.05	Westinghouse	1.25
Disney	1.2	Merck	1.15	Woolworth	1.25

SOURCE: Value Line Investment Survey, 1993.
[a] n/a: not available.

How Are Betas Calculated?

We now examine how the beta for a traded asset is calculated. Trading provides several estimates of market values at different times and thus enables one to calculate market returns. In addition, because the "market's" (a surrogate portfolio that represents the market) performance can be observed, it is possible to compute the covariance between the returns on the asset and the market—a necessary input in the beta calculation. When assets are not traded, more elaborate techniques, which are addressed in greater detail in later chapters, must be used.

There are two different ways in which betas can be calculated using market-based returns. We discuss each in turn.

THE CHARACTERISTIC LINE APPROACH

The characteristic line is simply a regression line that shows the average relationship between the returns on a stock and the returns on the market. Suppose it is felt that returns over the past 60 months are a good indication of the future. Then the historical (ex post) returns for each of the last 60 months are computed for both the individual stock and the market portfolio as represented by the S&P 500 index. The market index can be treated just as if it were another stock. The availability of extensive data tapes with information on stock prices, dividends, and so on makes this task easier. These historical returns are plotted on a graph to obtain a "scattergram," and a best-fit line showing the average straight-line relationship between the security and the market is drawn using regression methods that are normally available in standard computer regression packages. Figure 6-4 shows the characteristic lines for three stocks. The slopes of the characteristic lines are the betas for the respective stocks. Gensia Pharmaceuticals has a greater slope than either LA Gear or Exxon. The greater the slope of the characteristic line is, the greater the beta and, consequently, the greater the volatility of the stock. As seen in Figure 6-4, Gensia is more volatile than LA Gear, which is more volatile than Exxon. Gensia Pharmaceuticals has the highest beta, 2.20, followed by LA Gear, with a beta of 1.05, and Exxon Corp., with a beta of 0.75.

THE STATISTICAL DEFINITION OF BETA

Betas can also be calculated analytically by recognizing their statistical definition. It is not always necessary to run a regression to find an asset's beta, as in the characteristic line approach. If we use the equation for the slope of the characteristic line, we can compute the beta of an asset using historical data. A detailed example of this method using actual data is presented in Appendix 6A for Sears over the period 1989–1991.

FIGURE 6-4
Characteristic lines for three stocks

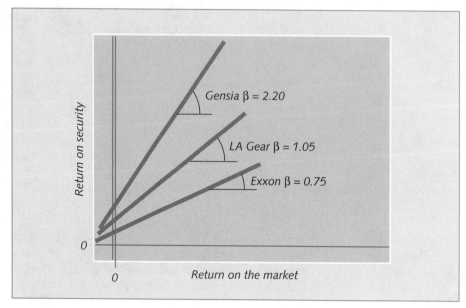

FIGURE 6-4
Characteristic lines for three stocks

6-3

THE RELATIONSHIP BETWEEN RELEVANT RISK AND THE EXPECTED RATE OF RETURN

Why Take Risks?

Because most investors are risk averse, why do they take any risk at all? Wouldn't they be better off investing in riskless investments such as U.S. T-bills? Why invest in stocks when they can possibly have negative returns?

The reason that even risk-averse investors are willing to assume some risk is that risk taking per se is not bad. As long as there are rewards from taking risk, investors are willing to do so. Of course, these rewards must be proportional to the amount of risk that one is willing to take. An investor who is willing to take more risk should expect more rewards than does an investor who insists on taking less risk. Again, the key word is *expect*; there are no guarantees in risk situations.

How do investors get these rewards, and who gives them? Rewards are distributed in the form of higher *expected* returns, and these higher returns are provided by the marketplace. The return the investor expects to obtain from a security is composed of two parts. First, the investor receives compensation for the time value of his or her funds: the risk-free interest rate. Second, the investor expects to receive a risk premium for investing in an asset that has an increased risk. The more risk the investor sees in an asset, the greater the risk premium that should be expected. We thus have the relationship:

Expected return = risk-free interest rate + risk premium   (6-9)

Financial market activity should result in market prices that yield this higher return for an asset in proportion to its risk. The major question, which we answer in the next chapter, is how to determine an appropriate risk premium.

Are the Riskiest Investments the Best?

Table 5-4 suggests that the market has historically been "fair." Investors who made riskier investments were compensated commensurate with that risk. At first glance this result may appear perplexing: If investors are guaranteed higher returns for a higher risk, as suggested by the 66-year historical record, the word *risk* appears to be inaccurate. Investors should invest in the riskiest investments because they will yield the highest rewards. This line of reasoning is incorrect because Table 5-4 deals with ex post returns over an extended period of time. All that we can conclude from Table 5-4 is that over long intervals, rewards appear to be proportional to the standard deviations of the investment.

The numbers in Table 5-4 do not apply to any one stock or bond but to all stocks and bonds. Thus one should not expect these results to pertain to any one single investment. Even between 1926 and 1992, some stocks must have earned less than 10%, and others must have earned more than this amount.

The Capital Asset Pricing Model

If investors can eliminate some of a security's risk through diversification, there is no reason why they should be compensated for the asset's diversifiable risk. The financial markets are dominated by institutional investors that have large diversified portfolios. In making their buy and sell decisions, which influence stock prices, these investors worry only about the risk that the security adds to or subtracts from their diversified portfolio. The best measure of this risk is the stock's beta. This is precisely why we call beta the "relevant risk" of the stock—the risk that influences the demand and supply of the stock and hence its price. Once an asset's beta has been estimated, the **capital asset pricing model (CAPM)** provides a simple equation that links the beta of the asset to the appropriate expected return for investing in that asset. Given the risk of an asset, the CAPM provides the "premium" that investors can expect in terms of rate of return, which induces them to purchase the asset.

KEY CONCEPT | The capital asset pricing model (CAPM) is a theory that links a security's relevant risk (beta) to the expected return on the security.[4]

Until recently, the CAPM was the predominant theory of risk and return in equilibrium and was the subject of hundreds of empirical tests. The CAPM still is extremely popular because of its intuitive appeal. The essential idea underlying the CAPM is this: Risk-averse investors will not hold risky assets unless they are adequately compensated for the risks that they bear. The greater an asset's risk, the greater its expected return should be. This gives investors an incentive to invest in high-risk securities. Without additional rewards for bearing risk, investors would invest in riskless securities such as U.S. Treasury bills (T-bills). Although the idea underlying the CAPM is fairly straightforward, the key insight is that the risk that is taken into account is the systematic risk.[5]

The CAPM makes several assumptions that have the net effect of forcing all investors to hold the same fully diversified portfolio. This fully diversified portfolio common to all investors is called a market portfolio, which we discussed earlier, which in the CAPM world contains all assets in the economy properly weighted to represent their proportionate market values. However, for most practical purposes, it is approximated by another portfolio, such as those described in the Chapter 5 highlight, "Getting a Handle on the Market: Stock Exchange Indexes." The performance of such an index is indicative of the performance of the economy as a whole. For our purposes, the variance of the market's returns, σ_m^2 in equation (6-5), represents the variance of the return on the appropriate market index.

[4]See W. F. Sharpe, "Capital Asset Prices: A Theory of Market Equilibrium under Conditions of Risk," *Journal of Finance* 19 (September 1964): 425–442; and J. Lintner, "The Valuation of Risk Assets and the Selection of Risky Investments in Stock Portfolios and Capital Budgets," *Review of Economics and Statistics* 47 (February 1965): 13–37.

[5]William F. Sharpe was a recipient of the 1990 Nobel Prize in Economics for his development of the CAPM.

In the capital asset pricing model, the expected return on an asset i is related to the risk of the asset β_i, as follows:

Expected return = risk-free rate + risk premium

= risk-free rate + (number of risk units)   (6-10)

· (premium per unit of beta risk)

$$E(\tilde{R}_i) = R_f + \beta_i[E(\tilde{R}_m) - R_f]$$

where

$E(\tilde{R}_i)$ is the expected rate of return on asset i

β_i is the beta coefficient of stock i

$E(\tilde{R}_m)$ is the expected return on the market portfolio (S&P 500)

R_f is the risk-free interest rate

The term $[E(\tilde{R}_m) - R_f]$ is the risk premium for bearing one unit of market risk.

Suppose that the risk-free interest rate (yield on U.S. T-bills) is 5%. If the market return is expected to be 9%, the expected return on Woolworth Corp. with a beta of 1.25 is

$$E(\tilde{R}_i) = 0.05 + 1.25(0.09 - 0.05) = 0.10 \quad \text{or} \quad 10\%$$

In this example, the risk premium for bearing 1 unit of market risk (the market risk premium) is 4%. If the investor buys Woolworth stock, she will be taking on 1.25 units of market risk and should therefore expect a risk premium of $1.25 \times 4\% = 5\%$. With the 5% risk-free interest rate and the risk premium of 5%, the total return that this investor should expect is 10%. Because the premium per unit of market risk increases, the total risk premium for investing in any asset therefore also increases in proportion to its market risk (beta).

The following questions and answers should clarify the CAPM further:

What is the expected return on a T-bill? Because this security has a beta of 0, its expected return from the CAPM must equal the risk-free interest rate.

What is the expected return on a stock with a variance of 25%? The variance of the stock has no direct influence on the expected return. To predict the return, one must know the stock's beta. Suppose that the asset has a beta of 0. Then the CAPM implies an expected return equal to R_f, the risk-free interest rate. This leads to the conclusion that a risk-free asset and a high-variance asset with betas of 0 have identical impacts on the expected return because the relevant risk for both is the same—0.

Is the premium per unit of risk always positive? The risk premium per unit of risk, $E(\tilde{R}_m) - R_f$, can be negative only if the expected return on the market is less than the risk-free interest rate. But this cannot happen because if the returns from a risk-free investment were greater than the expected returns from a risky investment, rational investors would cease to invest in the market, and the market would collapse. Hence $E(\tilde{R}_m)$ must be greater than the risk-free rate.

During economic downswings, isn't the return on the market less than the risk-free rate? There have, of course, been numerous instances in recent experience when the market returns have been negative at a time when the risk-free rate was positive. Although this appears to contradict the point just made, this conclusion is incorrect. The CAPM deals with expected returns, which are by definition ex ante returns. Of course, after an investment has been made (i.e., ex post), it might turn out to yield negative returns. The risk premium per unit of risk (an ex ante concept) is still positive.

What is the expected return on a negative beta asset? Because the market premium per unit of risk is positive, a negative-beta stock adds a negative risk premium, which can lower the expected return to be less than the risk-free interest rate. For example, assume that the risk premium, $E(\tilde{R}_m) - R_f$, is 10% and a stock has a beta of -0.5. If the risk-free interest rate is 6%, an investor's expected return on this investment will be $6\% - 0.5(10\%) = 1\%$. Investors require a smaller expected return from negative beta stocks because they provide "insurance" that can pay off handsomely when all other investments are doing poorly.

We discuss in the next chapter how the CAPM is useful in valuing financial assets.

Estimating CAPM Variables

The term $[E(\tilde{R}_m) - R_f]$ in the CAPM is called the market risk premium. Ibbotson and Sinquefield's data show that over the period 1926–1992 the realized average market risk premium was about 6.70%. Thus an investor who has no basis for arriving at a market risk premium for the next period may want to simply use the historical estimate of 7% in the CAPM.

However, if an investor believes that he or she has the ability to estimate future market risk premiums by interpreting current information about the economy from news reports, analysts' forecasts, government forecasts, or specialized information that he possesses, then he can directly plug this information into the CAPM.

The important point to note is that projecting the future is difficult—be it the future of individual stocks or of the economy as a whole. However, it may be easier to form estimates about the future of the overall market than for any individual stock. There are more resources devoted to forecasting overall economic performance (econometric models, government analyses, performance of various economic indicators, and so on). Knowing the sensitivity of a single asset (its beta) to general economic conditions, we are, in using the CAPM, forecasting the average response of an asset to a given forecast of future economic conditions.

6-4

CRITICISMS AND TESTS OF THE CAPM

Our discussion of the CAPM did not involve a formal derivation of the theory. There are, however, some aspects of the theory's derivation and the underlying assumptions of the CAPM that the reader should be aware of. One assumption is the absence of transactions costs and taxes. In addition, the CAPM assumes that all investors have identical expectations and assessments of an asset's risk. Although most of the restrictive assumptions can be removed to obtain modified versions of the CAPM, there are still some restrictive aspects of the CAPM. For example, the CAPM theory implies that all investors invest in a combination of riskless U.S. T-bills and the market portfolio, which is a conglomeration of all existing assets. Only then can the expected return on any asset be expressed in terms of the returns on these two assets. To ensure this result, assumptions regarding either the distribution of asset returns or the tastes of investors become necessary. But some of these assumptions are not entirely palatable.

The CAPM is not intended to be a statement of reality. Without a complete understanding of how risk and return are related, we have to work with a simplification of reality. This simplification is achieved by means of convenient assumptions made to get a tractable model. The CAPM is an intuitively appealing statement: To earn higher returns, one must bear higher risk. What is nonintuitive (at least initially) is the notion of beta being the relevant risk.

A theory is perhaps best judged not in regard to the assumptions it makes but rather by how well it conforms to empirical data. To find out whether or not the CAPM is a useful theory, the results of empirical tests conducted on the CAPM with actual data must be analyzed.

There are five testable implications for the CAPM:

1. A security's return should increase with its relevant risk (beta).

2. The relationship between return and risk should be linear.

3. Nonsystematic risk should not affect returns.

4. On average, the slope of the CAPM should equal $[E(\tilde{R}_m) - R_f]$.

5. On average, the intercept of the CAPM should equal the risk-free rate, R_f.

Historically, most academicians agree that the first three implications are supported by early empirical tests. The major problems are with the last two implications. Much of the empirical work finds a smaller slope and a larger intercept than the CAPM does. In other words, the empirically observed CAPM is "flatter" than the theoretical model. This does not mean that the CAPM is not correct; it is simply not perfect. Richard Roll criticizes the empirical tests, contending that the only meaningful test of the CAPM is whether or not the market portfolio is efficient—that is, has the highest expected return for the risk involved.

More recently, however, the CAPM has come under new attack. A recent study by Eugene Fama and Kenneth French finds no relationship between systematic risk as measured by beta and expected return.[6] Although this appears to damn the CAPM, the theory is kept alive by Richard Roll's theoretical argument that unless the market portfolio in these tests is efficient, the tests do not invalidate the CAPM and by other researchers' findings that the CAPM gives an adequate measure of the risk–return relationship.[7] Still others feel that beta may be an adequate measure of risk but that the relationship of this risk to expected return is not established. On a more general level, some business analysts feel that corporate decisions should focus on total risk, rather than systematic risk, and thus the CAPM is not appropriate for many business decisions.

We do not consider any more theoretical aspects of the CAPM. This section is intended simply to convey to the reader that the model is the subject of much debate. Beta and the CAPM have been (repeatedly) declared dead for many years, but they (also repeatedly) have risen from the dead and reappear in business decisions. The important insights provided by the CAPM—that the relevant risk of an asset is its systematic risk and that the expected return is linearly related to this risk—are still extremely useful. Because of its intuitive appeal and relative ease of application, the CAPM is seen by many to be the best framework available for

---

[6] Eugene Fama and Kenneth French, "The Cross-Section of Expected Stock Returns," *Journal of Finance* 47 (June 1992).

[7] Louis Chan and Josef Lakonishok, "Are the Reports of Beta's Death Premature?" *Journal of Portfolio Management*, Summer 1993, pp. 51–62.

facilitating financial decision making. More elaborate models, though theoretically more elegant, become increasingly more difficult to implement.

THE ARBITRAGE PRICING THEORY

Section 6-4 covered several criticisms of the CAPM. It seems appropriate, therefore, to ask whether there is an alternative to the CAPM that is "better." This section presents an alternative framework for determining expected returns, one that rests on the assumption of no arbitrage. If securities are mispriced, then there is the opportunity for **arbitrage** profits. Arbitrage is the activity of buying underpriced securities and selling overpriced ones, thereby generating a profit. If such arbitrage opportunities exist, then investors exploit them and prices adjust until eventually, there is a no-arbitrage economy in which the securities are correctly priced.

The **arbitrage pricing theory** (APT) is considered by many to overcome several objections to the CAPM. The APT, developed by Stephen Ross, assumes that the returns on a security are affected by several factors that affect the economy. The number of factors is irrelevant, except that the number of securities must be greater than the number of factors. Changes in these factors affect stock returns in several ways, depending on how sensitive the stock's return is to each of them. The sensitivity of stock i's returns to a factor, say factor 1 (whatever that factor might really be), is the **factor beta**, β_{i1}. If we assume that three principal factors affect stock returns, then there are three factor sensitivities or factor betas: β_{i1}, β_{i2}, and β_{i3}.

In addition to these systematic factors, asset returns are affected by factors unique to the firm in question. Such nonsystematic factors together are referred to as **idiosyncratic factors**. If investors form large portfolios, the returns on the portfolio, though dependent on the systematic factors, can be made independent of the idiosyncratic factors through the process of diversification. Therefore asset prices do not depend on this risk.

The reader may make several comparisons between the development of the CAPM and the APT. The CAPM assumes a world in which security returns are affected by a single factor, the market portfolio. The APT allows several factors to affect security returns. The CAPM and the APT both use diversification to eliminate unique risk and idiosyncratic risks. Because of only one factor, the CAPM world recognizes only one stock beta, the sensitivity of the asset's return to the return on the market portfolio. In the APT framework, an asset can have as many betas as there are relevant factors.

Without actually deriving the APT, we state the central result of this theory. In a no-arbitrage economy, the following relationship should hold:

$$E(\tilde{R}_i) = R_f + \beta_{i1}[E(\tilde{R}_1) - R_f] + \beta_{i2}[E(\tilde{R}_2) - R_f]$$
$$+ \beta_{i3}[E(\tilde{R}_3) - R_f] \tag{6-11}$$

where

$E(\tilde{R}_i)$ is the expected return on security i

β_{i1}, β_{i2}, and β_{i3} are the sensitivities of security i with respect to factors 1, 2, and 3

$E(\tilde{R}_1)$, $E(\tilde{R}_2)$, and $E(\tilde{R}_3)$ are the expected returns on factors 1, 2, and 3

R_f is the risk-free interest rate

According to this equation, there are only three factors that affect asset returns. If there are more factors, an extension of equation (6-11) to include all of them is straightforward.

Equation (6-11), the arbitrage pricing model, states that the expected return on stock i is the risk-free interest rate plus a risk premium. The total risk premium is the sum of the risk premiums associated with each factor. The risk premium associated with each factor k is obtained by multiplying the sensitivity of security i with the factor (β_{ik}) by the risk premium on that factor. The risk premium on a factor is the expected return on that factor less the risk-free rate.

Suppose that security i has factor sensitivities of 1.2, 0.8, and -1.0 with factors 1, 2, and 3, respectively. Then $\beta_{i1} = 1.2$, $\beta_{i2} = 0.8$, and $\beta_{i3} = -1.0$. Suppose also that the expected returns on factors 1, 2, and 3 are 12%, 9%, and 4%, respectively, so that $E(\tilde{R}_1) = 12\%$, $E(\tilde{R}_2) = 9\%$, and $E(\tilde{R}_3) = 4\%$. If the risk-free rate is 8% ($R_f = 8\%$), the expected return on security i as given by the APT is

$$
\begin{aligned}
E(\tilde{R}_i) &= 0.08 + 1.2(0.12 - 0.08) + 0.8(0.09 - 0.08) + 1.0(0.04 - 0.08) \\
&= 0.08 + 1.2(0.04) + 0.8(0.01) - 1.0(-0.04) \\
&= 0.176 \quad \text{or } 17.6\%
\end{aligned}
$$

Several aspects of this development merit a closer look. Although the APT assumes there are several factors that affect security returns, it does not explain why these are economically relevant; it merely assumes that there is a relationship between these factors and security returns. Also, it appears that the APT is a simple extension of the one-factor CAPM, in which the market portfolio is the only relevant factor. Although the CAPM is a simple case of the APT, the APT is derived from a more general theory. It is based on the simple principle that any two diversified portfolios that have identical factor sensitivities (i.e., identical relevant risk) must offer nearly the same expected returns to avoid arbitrage profits—hence, the name APT. Because the CAPM is derived from more restrictive assumptions than is the APT, the APT is a more appealing theory. Unlike the CAPM, the APT is not restricted to a single holding period. It does not make distributional assumptions regarding returns (other than that returns are a linear function of the factors) or investors' tastes. Unrestricted lending or borrowing at risk-free interest rates is not necessary to derive the APT. The net effect of these more general conditions is that, unlike the CAPM, the APT does not restrict investors to choose between risky alternatives on the basis of means and variances. It is beyond the scope of this book to examine in more detail the theoretical underpinnings of these two models.

Finally, it appears that the APT is useless unless one can say more about the factors. How many factors are relevant? What are they? Certain empirical tests have indicated that there are three relevant factors that affect security returns: unanticipated changes in inflation, industrial production, and the general cost of risk bearing. To use the APT, however, it is not necessary to identify the relevant factors. Assuming that there are four (unknown) factors, one can choose four different portfolios in such a way that they each have different sensitivities to these systematic factors. Having done this, one can use these portfolios as indexes for the factors. That is, even if one has no idea what these factors are, it is still possible to use the APT with these portfolios as indexes. This makes the APT empirically tractable.[8] An analysis of these technical issues is beyond the scope of this text.

---

[8] For estimates of the required rates of return on regulated utilities via the CAPM and the APT, see Richard W. Roll and Stephen A. Ross, "Regulation, the Capital Asset Pricing Model and the Arbitrage Pricing Theory," *Public Utilities Fortnightly*, May 26, 1983.

SUMMARY

Section 6-1: The Importance of Covariance Risk and the Limits of Diversification

How does the risk of a portfolio change as the number of assets in the portfolio increases?

- A portfolio's risk depends on the variances of the assets in the portfolio and the covariances among the assets' returns.

- As the size of a portfolio increases, the risk of the portfolio is determined more by the covariance terms than by the variance terms. In fact, in the limit, the variances of the individual securities disappear, and the variance of the portfolio becomes the average covariance.

Can diversification eliminate all of the risk in a portfolio?

- The risk of an asset is composed of two parts. The first component, called unique risk, is the risk that can be diversified away. The second part, known as systematic risk, is the risk based on the covariability of the asset with the market. This risk cannot be eliminated.

- Thus the "relevant" risk for an asset, the risk relevant for determining the asset's price, is not its variance; it is the systematic risk of the asset.

Section 6-2: Beta: Quantifying Market Risks

What is beta risk and how is it estimated?

- An asset's systematic risk depends on the beta of the asset, which measures the nondiversifiable risk of an asset, thus relating the asset's risk to the risk of the market.

- Betas exist for both individual assets and portfolios. The beta of a portfolio is the weighted average of the betas of the individual securities in the portfolio.

- Betas can be calculated using a characteristic line (regression analysis) or statistical formulas. There are also several published sources of betas.

Section 6-3: The Relationship Between Relevant Risk and the Expected Rate of Return

What is the capital asset pricing model (CAPM)?

- The capital asset pricing model is a theory that links an asset's relevant risk (beta) to the asset's expected return.

- The expected return on an asset is composed of the riskless interest rate and a risk premium that is proportional to the asset's beta. Beta multiplied by the market risk premium yields the risk premium on the asset. The market risk premium is typically estimated from the long-term historical risk premium on the market.

Section 6-4: Criticisms and Tests of the CAPM

What empirical evidence supports the CAPM?

- The CAPM has been a controversial theory and has been subjected to many empirical tests since the 1960s. These tests have sought to answer the question: To what extent have the returns on stocks conformed to the predictions of the CAPM? Traditional tests generally support the theory.

- Although some argue that the empirical tests support the CAPM, recent research suggests that they may not. A recent study by Fama and French suggests that beta is not related to the expected return. However, their conclusions have been challenged by other researchers, and some even argue that the CAPM cannot be properly tested.

Section 6-5: The Arbitrage Pricing Theory

What is the arbitrage pricing theory (APT)?

■ The arbitrage pricing theory (APT) is an alternative to the CAPM and relies on more general assumptions.

■ In contrast to the CAPM, which assumes that only one factor affects the returns on a security (the market), the APT admits several different factors for explaining the expected returns on the asset.

■ Empirical tests suggest that unanticipated changes in inflation, industrial production, and the general cost of risk bearing affect security returns.

■ Although theoretically more appealing, the APT has its own empirical limitations and is not easy to implement. Given the relative simplicity of the CAPM, it is unlikely that it will be displaced soon. Notwithstanding its limitations, the CAPM appears to be a useful framework for understanding the interdependence between risk and expected return.

QUESTIONS

1. How does the number of securities in a portfolio affect its variance?

2. What are the components of an asset's total risk? How are they different?

3. Why do we say that market risk is systematic risk?

4. When is the limit of diversification reached?

5. What does relevant risk mean? What is its practical significance?

6. How would the relevant risk of an investor's portfolio change if she moved her portfolio from domestic investments into foreign investments?

7. What does beta measure?

8. How is beta a leverage measure for market returns?

9. How is the beta of an asset calculated?

10. What are portfolio betas? How are they calculated?

11. What do the components of the CAPM's risk premium, β and $[E(\tilde{R}_m) - R_f]$, measure?

12. What are the CAPM's testable implications? What have the empirical results indicated?

13. What are some of the CAPM's weaknesses? Its strengths?

14. What is the arbitrage pricing theory?

15. How do the CAPM and the APT differ? How are they similar?

PROBLEMS

1. Consider a portfolio of four assets: *A, B, C, D*. The weights of the assets in the portfolio are 0.2, 0.3, 0.3, and 0.2, respectively. The variances of the as-

sets are 0.01, 0.02, 0.04, and 0.08, respectively. The covariance matrix is shown here. Calculate the variance of the portfolio.

	A	B	C
B	−0.01		
C	0.00	0.00	
D	0.025	0.01	0.00

2. Consider an equally weighted portfolio of 100 assets, each of which has variance equal to 0.01. Also assume that the covariance between every pair of assets is the same, 0.005. What is the variance of the portfolio? What are the portfolio variances if the number of assets is increased to 1,000 and then to 10,000?

3. You are considering an investment in Anheuser-Busch. Your statistical analysis has shown that the variance of Anheuser-Busch is 0.4928, while that of the market is 0.2982. The correlation coefficient between Anheuser-Busch's return and that of the market is +0.83. What is Anheuser-Busch's beta?

4. A security analyst is developing information on the relationship between General Mills and the economy. She has calculated General Mills' beta to be 1.15. She also has determined that the variance of the market index she is using as a proxy for the market portfolio is 0.2982. What is the covariance between the returns of General Mills and the return on the market portfolio?

5. A stock has a β_i of 1.5, and the risk-free rate is 10%. What is the expected return on the stock in the following cases?

(a) The expected return on the market is 14%.

(b) The expected return on the market is 16%.

(c) The expected return on the market is 18%.

6. A year ago you purchased some stock that had a beta of 1.5. You have not noticed how well your stock has done during the year, but you do know that the T-bill rate has remained at 10% throughout the year. As you are driving down the road, you hear on the radio that the market return was 20% during the year.

(a) Given only this information, what do you expect the return on your stock to be?

(b) If the market return was 2% instead of 20%, what would the return be?

7. A stock has a beta of 1.2 and an expected return of 15% when the market's expected return is 14%. What must the risk-free rate be?

8. Stock A has a beta of 1.2, and stock B has a beta of 1.5. You invest 40% of your money in stock A and the rest in stock B.

(a) What is the beta of your portfolio?

(b) If the expected market return is 16% and the risk-free rate is 10%, what is the expected return on your portfolio?

9. Stock X has a beta of 0.5, stock Y has a beta of 1.0, and stock Z has a beta of 1.25. The risk-free rate is 10%, and the expected market return is 18%.

(a) Find the expected return on stock X.

(b) Find the expected return on stock Y.

(c) Find the expected return on stock Z.

(d) Suppose that you construct a portfolio of 40% X, 20% Y, and 40% Z. Using your answers to parts (a), (b), and (c), find the expected return of this portfolio.

(e) What is the beta of the portfolio specified in part (d)?

(f) Using the information in the body of the problem and your answer to part (e), find the expected return on your portfolio.

10. A stock with a beta of 1.5 has an expected return of 18% if the market has an expected return of 15%. If your estimate of the expected return on the market suddenly rises to 21% (from 15%), what is the expected return on the stock?

11. Suppose that the risk-free rate is 12% and the expected market return is 20%. General Motors (GM) has a beta of 0.75, and Ford has a beta of 1.25.

(a) Find the expected return on GM Corporation.

(b) Find the expected return on Ford Corporation.

(c) Suppose that because of a sudden unanticipated increase in inflation, the risk-free rate rises to 16% and the market risk premium remains at 8%. Find the expected returns of GM and Ford.

(d) What is the expected return of a portfolio that has 20% of its value in GM and 80% in Ford?

12. Saldco shares have a beta of 1.2, are currently selling for $80 each, and pay no dividends. The risk-free rate is 10%, and the expected market return is 16%.

(a) What do you expect Saldco shares to trade for one year from today?

(b) If the expected market return is 20% (rather than 16%), what do you expect Saldco shares to trade for one year from today?

13. The Baldwin-Mills Corp. has a beta of 1.25 and pays no dividends. The expected market return is 20%, and the T-bill rate is expected to remain constant at 10%. You expect Baldwin-Mills shares to be worth $50 in one year. Using the CAPM, find the value of a share today.

14. Shares of the Mullet Corp. have a beta of 1.2 and an expected return of 22%. The T-bill rate is 10%.

(a) What is the expected return of another company that has a beta of 0.6?

(b) What is the expected return of a portfolio that has a beta of 1.0?

15. You invest $10,000 in the Jaguar Vitamin Co. (beta 1.5) and $20,000 in the Laverty Game Corp. (beta 1.2). The risk-free rate is 10%, and the expected market return is 16%.

(a) What are the beta and the expected return of your portfolio?

(b) You have decided that you want to reduce the beta of your portfolio to 1.0. What dollar investment would you have to make in Goga Transportation, Inc. (beta 0.8) to achieve this objective?

(c) If you decided to invest in T-bills to reduce the beta of your portfolio to 1.0, what dollar investment would you make in T-bills?

(d) If you decided to invest in Arab Oil, Inc. (beta -0.5) to reduce the beta of your portfolio to 1.0, what dollar investment would be necessary?

16. The Springbook Corp. has an expected return of 18% and a beta of 1.3. The Pharr Co. has an expected return of 15% and a beta of 0.8.

    (a) What is the expected return on the market?

    (b) What is the T-bill rate?

6-A
THE COMPUTATION OF BETAS

Chapter 6 explains beta but does not provide its statistical calculation. The reader who is interested in knowing the regression equation will find this appendix useful. In addition, computing beta is a necessary step in valuing physical assets that lack market prices, as we see in Chapter 7.

The beta coefficient for asset i is given by

$$\beta_i = \frac{\rho_{im}\sigma_i\sigma_m}{\sigma_m^2} \tag{6A-1}$$

where

ρ_{im} represents the correlation coefficient between the returns on stock i and the returns on the market portfolio

σ_i is the standard deviation of returns on asset i

σ_m^2 is the variance of market returns

The statistical definition of beta sheds additional light on its determinants. An asset can have betas that are positive, negative, or 0, because betas depend on the correlation coefficient. In Chapter 5 we saw that the correlation coefficient can vary between -1.0 and $+1.0$. If the correlation coefficient is 0, the asset is independent of market influences and its market risk is 0. A positive correlation coefficient implies a positive beta and consequently a positive market risk. A negative correlation coefficient suggests that the stock has a negative beta.

The sign of an asset's beta depends on the sign of the correlation coefficient between the returns on the asset and the returns on the market. Most assets in the economy have positive betas because they react sympathetically to changes in economic conditions. There are few stocks with negative betas, but they do exist (e.g., gold mining stocks) and are called countercyclical stocks because they move up when the rest of the economy is going down and they tend to produce low returns when the economy is flourishing.

In practice, the statistical equation for beta can be simplified to

$$\beta_i = \frac{\Sigma MI - n\overline{M}\,\overline{I}}{\Sigma M^2 - n\overline{M}^2} \tag{6A-2}$$

where

M is the risk premium on the market $= R_m - R_f$

I is the risk premium on asset $i = R_i - R_f$

n is the number of observations

$\overline{M}$ is the average value of M

$\overline{I}$ is the average value of I

Σ is the summation notation

R_f is the risk-free interest rate during the period

Consider Table 6A-1, in which we take the data on security variability in Chapter 5 and use it to compute the beta for Sears over 12 calendar quarters from 1989 through 1991. Column (1) provides an index of calendar time (i.e., quarters). As explained earlier, more accurate estimates would use monthly data and more than 12 data points. Column (2) provides information on the risk-free interest rate over the period. Columns (3) and (4) give the returns on the market (R_m) and the security (R_i), respectively, which are computed from historical data on the stock's market prices and dividends using the return equation developed in Chapter 5. Column (5) provides M, the "risk premium on the market," defined as the difference between the market return and the risk-free interest rate. This rate, as seen earlier, is the rate of return on risk-free U.S. Treasury bills. Column (6) calculates the risk premium on Sears, I. $\overline{M}$ and $\overline{I}$, calculated at the bottom of the table, are the arithmetic averages of M and I, respectively. Column (7) provides the squared risk premiums on the market (M^2), and column (8) lists the products of columns (5) and (6).

With the information contained in Table 6A-1, the asset's beta coefficient can readily be computed using equation (6A-2):

$$\beta_i = \frac{0.116550 \ - \ (12)(-0.0253)(-0.0507)}{(0.074021) \ - \ (12)(-0.0253)^2} = \frac{0.1012}{0.0664} = 1.524$$

Thus Sears is more sensitive to changes in general economic conditions than is the market portfolio, which has a beta of 1.0.

■

T A B L E   6 A - 1
Input for Stock i's (Sears) Beta Computation

(1) Quarter	(2) Risk-Free Rate	(3) Return on Market, R_m	(4) Return on Security, R_i	(5) Risk Premium, M (3) − (2)	(6) Risk Premium on Security, I (4) − (2)	(7) Squared Market Risk Premium, M^2	(8) $M \times I$ (5) × (6)
3/89	0.0900	0.0702	0.0802	−0.0198	−0.0098	0.000391	0.000194
6/89	0.0803	0.0853	0.0135	0.0050	−0.0668	0.000025	−0.000334
9/89	0.0784	0.1013	−0.0237	0.0229	−0.1021	0.000523	−0.002338
12/89	0.0768	0.0126	−0.0860	−0.0642	−0.1628	0.004127	0.010452
3/90	0.0785	−0.0325	0.0421	−0.1110	−0.0364	0.012328	0.004040
6/90	0.0777	0.0541	−0.0572	−0.0236	−0.1349	0.000558	0.003184
9/90	0.0729	−0.1352	−0.2929	−0.2081	−0.3658	0.043285	0.076123
12/90	0.0648	0.0846	0.0191	0.0198	−0.0457	0.000392	−0.000905
3/91	0.0582	0.1461	0.4015	0.0879	0.3433	0.007725	0.030176
6/91	0.0556	−0.0007	0.0955	−0.0563	0.0399	0.003171	−0.002246
9/91	0.0516	0.0568	0.0288	0.0052	−0.0229	0.000027	−0.000119
12/91	0.0416	0.0798	−0.0023	0.0382	−0.0439	0.001457	−0.001677

Summary information:
$\Sigma M = -0.3040$ $\Sigma I = -0.6079$ $\Sigma M^2 = 0.074021$ $\Sigma MI = 0.116550$ $\overline{M} = -0.0253$ $\overline{I} = -0.0507$

SUGGESTED ADDITIONAL READINGS

Black, F., M. Jensen, and M. Scholes. "The Capital Asset Pricing Model: Some Empirical Tests." In *Studies in Theory of Capital Markets,* edited by M. C. Jensen, pp. 79–124. New York: Praeger, 1972.

Bower, D. H., R. S. Bower, and D. E. Logue. "Arbitrage Pricing and Utility Stock Returns." *Journal of Finance,* September 1984, pp. 1041–1054.

Bower, D. H., R. S. Bower, and D. Logue. "A Primer on Arbitrage Pricing Theory." *Midland Corporate Finance Journal,* Fall 1984.

Chan, Louis, and Josef Lakonishok. "Are the Reports of Beta's Death Premature?" *Journal of Portfolio Management,* Summer 1993, pp. 51–62.

Chen, N. F., R. Roll, and S. Ross. "Economic Forces and the Stock Market: Testing the APT and Alternate Asset Pricing Theories." *Journal of Business,* July 1986, pp. 383–403.

Fama, Eugene F., and Kenneth French. "The Cross-Section of Expected Stock Returns." *Journal of Finance* 47 (June 1992).

Fama, Eugene F., and J. D. MacBeth. "Risk, Return and Equilibrium: Empirical Tests." *Journal of Political Economy* 81 (May 1973): 607–636.

Gibbons, M. R. "Multivariate Tests of Financial Models." *Journal of Financial Economics* 10 (March 1982): 3–27.

Ibbotson, R. G., and R. A. Sinquefield. *Stocks, Bonds, Bills and Inflation: The Past and the Future.* Charlottesville, VA: Financial Analysts Research Foundation, 1992.

Jensen, M. C., ed. *Studies in the Theory of Capital Markets.* New York: Frederick A. Praeger, 1972.

MacQueen, Jason. "Beta Is Dead! Long Live Beta!" In *The Revolution in Corporate Finance,* edited by Joel M. Steen and Donald H. Chew, Jr., pp. 52–57. New York: Basil Blackwell, 1986.

Modigliani, Franco, and Gerald A. Pogue. "An Introduction to Risk and Return." *Financial Analysts Journal,* March–April 1974, pp. 68–80, and May–June 1974, pp. 68–86.

Reinganum, M. R. "Misspecification of Capital Asset Pricing: Empirical Anomalies Based upon Yield and Market Values." *Journal of Financial Economics,* March 1981, pp. 19–46.

Roll, Richard. "A Critique of the Asset Pricing Theory's Tests." *Journal of Financial Economics,* March 1977, pp. 129–176.

Roll, Richard, and S. Ross. "The Arbitrage Pricing Theory Approach to Strategic Portfolio Planning." *Financial Analysts Journal,* May–June 1984.

Rosenberg, Barr, and James Guy. "Beta and Investment Fundamentals." *Financial Analysts Journal,* May–June 1976, pp. 60–72.

Ross, S. A. "The Arbitrage Theory of Capital Asset Pricing." *Journal of Economic Theory* 13 (December 1976): 341–360.

Sharpe, W. "Factors in New York Stock Exchange Security Returns, 1931–1979." *Journal of Portfolio Management,* Summer 1982, pp. 5–19.

Sharpe, William F. "Capital Asset Prices: A Theory of Market Equilibrium Under Conditions of Risk." *Journal of Finance,* September 1964, pp. 425–442.

Sharpe, William F., and G. Cooper. "Risk-Return Classes of New York Stock Exchange Common Stocks 1931–1976." *Financial Analysts Journal,* March–April 1972.

SEVEN BRINGING TOGETHER RISK AND EXPECTED RETURN: MARKET VALUES, OPPORTUNITY COSTS, AND MARKET EFFICIENCY

The real cost of any action is the value of the alternative opportunity that must be sacrificed in order to take the action.

—Paul Heyne, 1976

Chapter 1 established the basic premise underlying this book: The goal of the finance manager must be to make the shareholders wealthier by maximizing the value of the shareholders' stock. It was also argued that this is achieved not by focusing on profits but by recognizing that values are determined by cash flows. The aspects of cash flows important to us are magnitude, timing, and riskiness. Timing was addressed in Chapter 4, with risk defined in Chapter 5 and used to develop the expected return in Chapter 6.

This chapter ties together several important concepts. It introduces the notion of a required rate of return (RRR) and explains why it is the appropriate discount rate for finding the present value of future cash flows. It then explains why, when assets are properly priced in the marketplace, the RRR on an asset is equivalent to the expected return on the asset discussed in the previous chapter. These fundamental ideas are crucial for an understanding why the CAPM is a "pricing model" when all it appears to do is provide the expected return on the asset. These ideas are consolidated by answers to the following questions:

- What determines the value of an asset?

- What is an opportunity cost? How is it related to value and economic profits?

- What is the personal valuation process and how does it differ from the market valuation process?

- Why is the required rate of return (RRR) estimated by the CAPM an opportunity cost?

- How is the RRR estimated from the CAPM used in business decisions?

- What is the efficient market hypothesis (EMH) and what are its implications?

- Are markets efficient?

7-1

VALUE AND OPPORTUNITY COSTS

What is value? The question appears to be a basic one, yet most people have trouble answering it satisfactorily. The early economics literature is replete with explanations of this term, and even *Webster's New Collegiate Dictionary* gives eight different definitions of value, none of which is entirely satisfactory for financial decision making. In finance and economics, value is really economic value. Social, ethical, and moral values can affect economic values by affecting the expected cash flows that result from an economic decision. However, we do not explicitly address these broader considerations here. Instead, we assume that these important issues are subsumed in an individual's expectations about cash flows.

KEY CONCEPT

In finance, the **value** of an asset is the maximum dollar price that someone is willing to pay for it.

The Determinants of Value

For an asset to have any value, it must have two characteristics. First, the asset must have the potential for benefits. For example, a piece of paper found on the sidewalk does not normally have any economic value. But, if the same piece of paper carries an authentic signature of Abraham Lincoln, it has economic value because the owner can expect to sell the autograph for a substantial sum. Similarly, a piece of machinery has some economic value to a company because it can be used to produce goods that give the firm cash benefits. Even if the machine is incapable of operating, it can still have some economic value because the company may obtain some benefits by selling it, perhaps to a scrap dealer. It does not matter how the benefits come. As long as one can derive some benefits from a commodity or service, it can have economic value.

Second, procuring the asset must involve a cost. Consider an extreme example. A glass of water can provide benefits, yet it is (generally) not regarded as being of value. Similarly, the air around us provides benefits and yet is not regarded as having economic value. It is not enough for an asset just to offer benefits to have economic value. In addition, obtaining these benefits must involve some sacrifice. To receive the benefits from owning Lincoln's autograph (personal satisfaction and dollars) without that piece of paper would involve time and effort (to get it from somewhere else) or money (if it can be purchased from a collector). The potential benefits are associated with some sacrifice, and so the piece of paper has value. Because air and small quantities of water can generally be obtained easily without involving any sacrifice (time or money), they can be had free and thus have no economic value.

What Benefits and Costs Should Be Considered?

The benefits provided by an asset can be either tangible or intangible. Tangible benefits are those that are physical, easily quantifiable, and therefore relatively easy to identify. For example, a metal worker at Bethlehem Steel earns a salary that is a tangible benefit. Working for the White House also provides a salary. In addition to this tangible benefit, however, the worker at the White House receives intangible benefits such as prestige and influence. Other examples of tangible benefits are dividends and capital gains from owning stock and the services provided by a car in working condition. In finding the value of an asset in finance, we confine ourselves to measuring tangible benefits. The most common tangible benefit for our purposes is the *cash flow stream* (sequence) provided by an asset.

The costs considered in valuation are not accounting costs or the price paid for an asset, but rather the other alternatives that are given up, or sacrificed, to obtain the benefits being valued.

KEY CONCEPT

The true cost of anything is the most valuable alternative given up or "sacrificed." This cost is called an **opportunity cost,** and it is the relevant cost in financial decision making.

The "trick" to understanding opportunity costs is to recognize that *every act of choice involves an act of sacrifice.* Suppose that a manager must choose among three different investment proposals: *A, B,* and *C.* If he chooses *A,* this choice is equivalent to a sacrifice of *B* and *C.* Suppose that of these two, *B* and *C, B* is the better alternative. Then, by choosing *A,* the manager has incurred the cost of the next best alternative, *B.*

The principle of opportunity cost becomes clearer when we consider another example. Do you prefer studying finance on Tuesday or on Saturday? The time needed to study a chapter is the same on both days, but the cost of studying on Saturday is higher because the alternative use of your time is more valuable on

BENJAMIN FRANKLIN ON OPPORTUNITY COSTS

Remember that Time is Money. He that can earn Ten Shillings a Day by his Labour, and goes abroad, or sits idle one half of that Day, tho' he spends but Sixpence during his Diversion or Idleness,

ought not to reckon That the one Expence; he has really spent or rather thrown away Five Shillings besides.

SOURCE: Benjamin Franklin's "Advice to a Young Tradesman," in Papers, vol. 3, pp. 306–308; first

printed on July 21, 1748. Reprinted in The Political Thought of Benjamin Franklin, edited by R. L. Ketcham (Indianapolis: Bobbs-Merrill, 1965).

Saturday. There are perhaps several other more beneficial activities open to you on that day. Also, see the above highlight.

In contrast with these examples, opportunity costs in finance are quantified and usually measured as a percentage return. Suppose that a corporation has a $500,000 deposit in a bank earning 14% interest per year. All other uses of its money provide a return lower than 14%. Assume the company is considering another use for the money, a project that will improve its computer facilities. The opportunity cost for this project (alternative) is 14% because by taking the money out of the bank, the company has to forfeit a 14% rate of return. Therefore, to calculate a value for this project, the relevant cost is the opportunity cost of 14%. In fact, management will require that the new investment yield at least 14% before proceeding. For this reason, the opportunity cost associated with an investment is also called the **required rate of return** (RRR) on the investment.

KEY CONCEPT   The **required rate of return** (RRR) on an investment is the relevant opportunity cost associated with that investment.

Henceforth the terms *opportunity cost* and *required rates of return* are used interchangeably. At first glance, this definition of costs appears nonintuitive and maybe even discomforting. The reason for this discomfort is that people generally think that cost should be measured in dollars and cents rather than in percentages. "Cost" is often incorrectly equated with "price." For example, if it takes 75 cents to buy a bar of candy, the cost of that bar is generally assumed to be 75 cents. Although this use of the term is acceptable in conversational English, it is incorrect in finance and can lead to incorrect decisions. Similarly, when an accountant claims that it will "cost" $250,000 to take on a new investment, this book-value concept of cost is not the cost relevant to financial decision making. The relevant costs in finance are opportunity costs and are calculated not by looking at historical costs and prices but by evaluating the available alternatives. To ensure that you understand exactly what cost is, read the highlight on page 164.

Why Value Depends on Opportunity Costs

Let us now use an example to see how asset values depend on opportunity costs (or, equivalently, RRRs). Consider the case of Ms. Nessbaum, who is contemplating the purchase of First Regional Bank's new certificate. If Ms. Nessbaum buys First Regional's certificate today, she will receive $1,000 at the end of a year. There is no uncertainty because the certificate is insured. The question is: What is the maximum amount that Ms. Nessbaum should pay for this certificate? Ms. Nessbaum should pay at most the value of the certificate (whatever it is). If she pays

PRICE AND COST ARE NOT ALWAYS THE SAME

For most people, the terms price and cost are virtually the same. It is common to think of the cost of a book as the price one has to pay for it. Although this usage is common, these words have a very special meaning to finance people.

Price is the dollar amount that a buyer gives a seller in exchange for a good or service. Cost, on the other hand, measures the value of opportunities forgone. Surprising as it may sound, cost is a "forward-looking" concept. It is not possible to estimate costs in finance without a consideration of the future outcomes of the available alternatives. In some cases, price and cost are the same. In many other instances, however, the two concepts are not equivalent. Let us consider a few examples.

The Cost of Electricity

It is generally cheaper to generate electric power during periods of low demand and more expensive during periods of "peak" demand. Yet electricity is often priced at a fixed cost per unit. In this case, price does not equal cost because the price per kilowatt-hour does not depend on the actual generation cost.

Environmental Costs

Every year the environment is polluted by chemicals and product wastes generated by factories. Even though the companies incur no price (they do not have to pay a fee to release toxic gases into the air), the cost to society can be great. The forgone opportunities that result from environmental damage can be immense. The case of Union Carbide's disaster in Bhopal, India, is a case in point.

Monopolies

The fundamental objection to monopolies is that firms price their products far above costs. In a monopolistic economy, the prices charged for goods and services exceed the costs associated with the production of the goods.

Forgone Investments

A. H. Robins Co., the maker of the Dalkon Shield, an intrauterine birth-control device, came under legal attack after it was found that the device could cause serious illness to some users. In 1990, after almost a decade of legal battles, a settlement was reached with more than 85,000 claimants that resulted in a court-approved payment of $2.3 billion to the Dalkon Shield Claimants' Trust, the largest medical device settlement in history. When we recognize that the stockholders will earn nothing on this sum, the cost of the settlement is actually much larger.

Security Prices in a Well-Functioning Market

In a well-functioning capital market, the price of a security is said to reflect its "true" or "intrinsic" value. In this situation, prices of securities do reflect the costs involved in acquiring them. This is because an efficient market properly capitalizes a cash flow stream at the appropriate opportunity cost using all available information concerning future outcomes.

more than the value, it is an unwise investment. Of course, she will want to pay less than the value if she can.

To answer the question, we must calculate the value of the certificate. We know that value depends on the benefit of $1,000 at the end of the year and on the opportunity cost of making the investment. What is Ms. Nessbaum's opportunity cost?

Assume that Ms. Nessbaum has surveyed all the banks in the neighborhood and finds that the best interest rate she can get on a risk-free investment for one year is 10%. Then 10% is Ms. Nessbaum's opportunity cost for tying up capital in First Regional's certificate. In valuing First Regional's certificate, Ms. Nessbaum requires a minimum rate of 10%, her opportunity cost, on that investment.

Because we do not know the value of the certificate, let us assume that it is X. If Ms. Nessbaum invested X at 10% for one year, she would end up with $X + $0.10X = $X(1.10)$. This is because of the interest earned for one year. Instead, if she buys the certificates for X, she will end up with $1,000 at the end of the year.

In order that Ms. Nessbaum not lose any money from buying the certificate, we must have

$$\underbrace{\$X(1.10)}_{\left(\begin{array}{c}\text{proceeds from}\\ \text{next best opportunity}\end{array}\right)} = \underbrace{\$1,000}_{\left(\begin{array}{c}\text{proceeds from}\\ \text{investment in the certificate}\end{array}\right)}$$

$$X = \frac{\$1,000}{1.10} = \$909.09$$

The value of the certificate is $909.09 for Ms. Nessbaum. If she pays more than $909.09 for the certificate, she will "lose" money because she is paying more than the certificate is worth. If she pays $950 for the certificate, for example, Ms. Nessbaum will still end up with only $1,000. If, instead, she invested $950 in the bank at 10%, she will end up with $950(1 + 0.10) = \$1,045$. Similarly, we can verify that any price less than $909.09 for the certificate is a bargain.

Notice that if instead of a 10% opportunity cost, Ms. Nessbaum's opportunity cost was 12%, the value of the certificate would fall to $892.86 ($1,000/1.12). And if Ms. Nessbaum's opportunity cost was 6%, the value of the asset would rise to $943.40 ($1,000/1.06).

KEY CONCEPT The value of an asset bears an inverse relationship to its opportunity costs.

Relationship of Opportunity Cost to Discount Rate

To extend the discussion to multiple time periods, assume that First Regional Bank also is offering a three-year risk-free certificate. This certificate pays $1,000 at the end of the third year. How much should Ms. Nessbaum be prepared to pay for this certificate if her opportunity cost is 10%?

If $Y is the value of this certificate, we know that Y must satisfy

$$Y(1 + 0.10)(1 + 0.10)(1 + 0.10) = \$1,000$$

or

$$Y = \frac{\$1,000}{(1.10)(1.10)(1.10)} = \$751.30$$

Notice that this relationship can be written as

$$Y = \frac{\$1,000}{(1 + i)^3} \qquad \text{where } i \text{ is the opportunity cost}$$

$$= \frac{\$1,000}{(1 + 0.10)^3} = \$1,000\left[\frac{1}{(1 + 0.10)^3}\right]$$

$$= \$1,000(PVF_{0.10,3}) = \$1,000(0.7513)$$

$$= \$751.30$$

Thus Y is obtained by multiplying the cash benefit of $1,000 by the present value interest factor for three years at a discount rate of 10%. The opportunity cost (RRR) of an investment is the discount rate to be applied to that investment. The value of the certificate Y is therefore nothing other than the present value of the benefits provided by the certificate. The **discount rate** for time-value calculations is the appropriate opportunity cost. This conclusion is consistent with the Chapter 4 discussion of the mechanics of finding present values. It is tempting to conclude that this result was known even in Chapter 4. This conclusion, however,

■

TABLE 7-1

Increase in Wealth for Ms. Nessbaum[a]

Price Paid for Certificate	Wealth at the End of the Year	Increase in Wealth
$875.00	$1,000	$125.00
909.09	$1,000	90.91
950.00	$1,000	50.00

[a] Opportunity cost = 10%.

ignores a subtlety. In Chapter 4 the discount rate was not linked directly to the opportunity cost concept, as it is in this chapter. Instead, Chapter 4 linked the discount rate to some weak notion of an "interest rate."

The examples we have examined so far are very simple cases that involve only one cash benefit. In addition, we have not addressed risk considerations. In more realistic examples, benefits may occur over an extended time and in an uncertain way. When these cash benefits occur over several periods, they are often referred to as a **benefit stream, cash flow stream,** or **income stream.**

Economic Profit and Excess Returns

In the example of the $1,000 one-year First Regional Bank certificate, we calculated the value of the certificate to Ms. Nessbaum as $909.09. If she pays $909.09 for this certificate, she is paying the right amount. If she pays more than $909.09, she "loses" money; if she can buy the certificate for less than $909.09, she "makes" money.

Focus on the terms *lose* and *make money.* Table 7-1 shows three different prices that Ms. Nessbaum can pay for the certificate. In all three cases, she receives $1,000 at the end of the year. The third column shows her increase in wealth after investing in the certificate for one year. In all three cases, Ms. Nessbaum's wealth increases, which seems to imply that in all three cases Ms. Nessbaum "makes" money. But this conclusion is wrong.

It is true that Ms. Nessbaum's wealth increases in all three cases, but in only one case (in which she pays $875) does she "make" money. When she pays $950 for the certificate, she "loses" money, whereas at the price of $909.09, she neither makes nor loses money. If this appears surprising, it is perhaps because the reader is not thinking of economic profit but, instead, of accounting profit and loss.

Economic profit is the excess profit that is gained from an investment over and above the profit that could be obtained from the best alternative forgone; that is,

$$\begin{matrix} \text{Economic profit} \\ \text{from investment} \end{matrix} = \begin{matrix} \text{wealth} \\ \text{increase} \end{matrix} - \begin{matrix} \text{wealth increase from} \\ \text{best alternative forgone} \end{matrix} \qquad (7\text{-}1)$$

As we just saw, the best forgone investment for Ms. Nessbaum was yielding 10%. (That is why her *RRR* is 10%.) If Ms. Nessbaum had invested X in this investment, she would have received $1.1X$. We can now set up Table 7-2.

Instead of working with increases in wealth, we can work equivalently with rates of return. In finance, rates of return are more widely used for analysis. Table 7-2 is now restated in terms of rates of return in Table 7-3.

Notice from Tables 7-2 and 7-3 that economic profits are positive only when

■

TABLE 7-2

Economic Profits

Price Paid for Certificate	Wealth at the End of the Year for Certificate	Wealth at the End of the Year If Invested at 10%[a]	Increase in Wealth
$875.00	$1,000	$962.50	$37.50
909.09	$1,000	1,000.00	0
950.00	$1,000	1,045.00	−45.00

[a] That is, if the price paid for the certificate is invested at 10%.

TABLE 7-3 *Economic Profits in Terms of Excess Returns*	Price Paid for Certificate	Rate of Return Provided by Certificate (%)[a]	Rate of Return from Best Alternative Forgone (%)	Excess Return
	$875.00	14.29%	10.00	+4.29
	909.09	10.00	10.00	0
	950.00	5.26	10.00	−4.74

[a] Rates of return are calculated as $1,000 − price)/price.

there are excess returns. **Excess returns** result when an investment earns more than the relevant opportunity cost.

KEY CONCEPT When an asset is purchased at its "fair value," there is no economic profit or excess returns.

This is an important observation. We see later that the concept of market efficiency relates this no-excess-return situation. For now, however, it is sufficient simply to state that when an asset is purchased at its fair value, there are no excess returns. Alternatively, when there are no excess returns available in the marketplace, all assets are properly valued (i.e., "fairly priced").

Thus the age-old story of "the old man who made money in the stock market without even knowing how to spell the word *stock*" deserves closer scrutiny. Just because he bought stock at, say, $35 a share and sold it 18 years later for $145 does not necessarily mean that he made money. There is no denying, however, that he made $110 in accounting profits. Whether any economic profits were generated depends on his opportunity costs.

KEY CONCEPT An investor "makes money" only when he generates economic profits or, equivalently, excess returns.

Risk and Opportunity Costs

The example of First Regional Bank's risk-free certificate is for illustration only and is purely fictitious. To calculate risky discount rates in real life, it is necessary to identify another risk-free asset whose rate of return can qualify for the risk-free discount rate status. In practice, the rate of return offered by short-term U.S. Treasury bills, a U.S. government debt obligation, is taken to be the risk-free discount rate. The bills are risk free because the government cannot default.

Instead of being a risk-free investment, what if the First Regional certificate was risky? Risky alternatives should be evaluated at higher discount rates to calculate their values. Ms. Nessbaum evaluates a risky investment by assessing the risk of the investment and then adding a "risk premium" to the riskless rate. The appropriate opportunity cost for a risky investment is the opportunity cost of capital for a riskless investment plus a premium for bearing risk that is proportional to the risk of the investment:

$$\text{Risky discount rate } (RRR) = \text{risk-free rate} + \text{risk premium} \qquad (7\text{-}2)$$

The greater the risk is, the higher the discount rate is and therefore the smaller the value of an investment is for a given stream of benefits. Consider an example. If First Regional's certificate is risky and Ms. Nessbaum assesses a 5% risk premium for this investment, she should use a 15% discount rate. With a discount rate of 15%, the same certificate falls in value from $909.09 to $869.57, which is the present value of $1,000 due in one year at a 15% discount rate. As long as Ms. Nessbaum can buy the certificate for $869.57 or less, the risk is offset by the lower price that the asset commands. Ms. Nessbaum can expect a 15% return instead of the 10% return earlier, a premium of 5% for bearing risk.

7-2
THE VALUATION PROCESS

*T*he process of finding the values of assets is called the valuation process and consists of two steps:

1. Determining the benefits (cash flow stream) from the asset

2. Discounting this cash flow stream at the opportunity cost of capital (RRR)

Valuation is the process of capitalizing a cash flow stream at the appropriate opportunity cost.

Corporate Financial Management and Asset Values

Consider the financial manager of a corporation that is contemplating a new project—say, the opening of one more sales office. Because this project is an asset, the manager wants to know the value of this asset before he decides whether to invest in this project. This value assessment is necessary because the manager's objective is to maximize the firm's value. He clearly wants to avoid value-reducing projects.

In calculating the value of this new project (asset), the manager asks the marketing and accounting staff for help in forecasting the expected cash flows from the project. This is the first step in calculating asset values. Let us assume in this discussion that all stockholders agree with the forecasts of the project's cash flow stream.

The second step is identifying a proper discount rate to capitalize this cash flow stream. This step presents a serious problem: Whose discount rate should be used?

THE PERSONAL VALUATION PROCESS

Valuation consists of capitalizing an income or cash flow stream at an appropriate discount rate (that is, the risk-free interest rate plus a risk premium). The income stream of an asset (say, IBM common stock) is generally not known with certainty. Thus this input is subjective and varies from person to person. For example, an optimist may forecast larger cash flows from IBM than does a pessimist. The risk premium also varies with the individual. It depends on how risk is measured and on the extent to which the individual is willing to take risk. Two investors assessing IBM stock can disagree considerably on its risk. Furthermore, even if they agree on the risk, their risk premiums can be different because of their differing attitudes toward risk. The more unwilling one is to bear risk, the greater the risk premium must be for the investor. Hence these are personal inputs, and the resulting valuation of an asset is a *personal valuation*. Because of the personal nature of two inputs, two individuals can arrive at two different personal values for the same asset, yet both are correct. Value thus lies in the eyes of the beholder.

Unfortunately, personal valuations are not very useful to the financial manager for decision making. The owners of the company are the stockholders, and there could be thousands of them. Owners can calculate the value of this project by using their forecast of the cash flow stream and capitalizing it at their personal discount rates. Thus, if there are 10,000 stockholders, it is possible to have 10,000 different values for the project. Some may find the project attractive, whereas others may not. The decision of the corporate manager may not be supported by all owners.

THE MARKET VALUATION PROCESS

Suppose that the corporation hires a pollster to poll the owners and find some type of "average" discount rate. Then the manager can use this discount rate to calculate the project's value. Of course, some owners will still be unhappy, but in any event, the manager's actions reflect some consensus among the owners. Actually polling all the owners is an impractical alternative, however, for obvious reasons. Moreover, there is no guarantee that using the "average" discount rate will help the firm maximize stock prices because the financial markets do not necessarily use this "average" discount rate. This discount rate is unlikely to be the discount rate implicit in stock prices.

Financial economists overcome this problem by developing a market-based theory of asset valuation. This *market valuation theory* identifies the discount rate implicit in market prices. The theory allows us to estimate the "marginal investor's discount rate," which is the discount rate the firm should be concerned with.

To understand this concept, consider how stock prices are determined in the marketplace. The equilibrium stock price is the price at which demand and supply are exactly balanced. How does the stock reach its equilibrium price? To see this, assume that initially there is excess supply. Prices fall and "borderline" investors step in to buy stock at this lower price. Thus the demand for the stock increases and, as more and more investors step in to buy the stock, its price rises. Eventually, some investor's purchase makes the demand and supply balance. This "last" investor who equilibrates the demand and supply determines the equilibrium price of the stock. This investor is called the **marginal investor.** The market valuation theory estimates the discount rate implicit in the market price that is effectively determined by the marginal investor.

In contrast to determining the personal discount rate, where each investor estimates his or her personal risk premium, the market valuation theory assumes that all investors estimate the risk of the asset and the risk premium in the same way. Then, given the asset's risk, the market valuation theory identifies a risk premium for the marginal investor. In other words, given an estimate of the asset's risk, it is possible to go directly to the marginal discount rate that is implicit in the market value of the asset. Asset values determined using the theory's estimate of the marginal discount rate are market values, the relevant values for decision making. They are market values because they are estimated using a market valuation theory, a theory that recognizes that market prices are determined by demand and supply considerations in the marketplace. Figure 7-1 depicts the market valuation process.

Net Present Value and
Wealth Increases

Recall the definition of net present value (NPV) from Chapter 4—the difference between the present value of cash inflows and the present value of the outflows. Because present values are involved, a discount rate is needed. The NPV of an investment is a measure of the wealth created.

In Table 7-2 notice that the third column uses the 10% opportunity cost to determine the increase in wealth in the fourth column. Consider the case of a company thinking about an investment in First Regional's one-year certificate that is currently selling in the market for $909.09. The management of the company has estimated that the market discount rate is 10%. What is the NPV of this investment?

$$NPV = PV \text{ of inflows } - PV \text{ of outflows}$$
$$= \$1,000(PVF_{0.10,1}) - \$909.09$$
$$= \$1,000(0.9091) - \$909.09$$
$$= \$0$$

Looking at Tables 7-2 and 7-3, we observe from the numbers corresponding to this calculation of NPV that when the NPV of an investment is 0, the economic

FIGURE 7-1
Market valuation

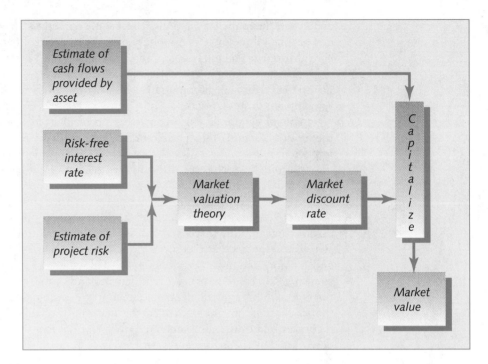

profits from that investment also are 0. Equivalently, the excess returns generated from that investment are 0. Financial managers who undertake a zero-*NPV* project are not making money for their companies because there is no net gain in market-value terms. This is not to imply that the acceptance of the project will hurt the company; a zero-*NPV* project simply recovers the firm's opportunity cost. It does not increase the value of the firm. To make money, managers should generate excess returns or economic profits, but this can happen only when the *NPV* is greater than 0. The *NPV* therefore measures, in market-value terms, the economic profits generated by the project. It represents the added wealth to the firm from taking on the investment.

The relationship between *NPV* and economic profits allows us to connect our valuation concepts to the value of the firm. Section 2-1 defined the value of the firm as the sum of the exchange value of the firm's assets plus the additional wealth created by the firm. The value is measured by computing the difference between the value in use and the value in exchange of the firm's assets. It should now be clear to the reader how this increase in wealth occurs. Managers adopt those potential projects that earn more than the opportunity costs to the firm and thus have positive *NPV*s. Their decisions result in economic profits for the firm, which are the source of the firm's additional wealth. This additional wealth accrues to the stockholders. Thus, in selecting positive-*NPV* projects, managers increase the wealth of stockholders.

KEY CONCEPT   A project's *NPV* is greater than 0 if and only if the asset's value in use exceeds its value in exchange.

This establishes the link between *NPV* and the increase in shareholders' wealth (difference between the value in use and the value in exchange) seen in Chapter 2.

7-3

ESTIMATING OPPORTUNITY COSTS: THE CAPM

Why the Expected Rate of Return Is the Required Rate of Return

To find the value of an asset we discount the expected cash flows at the relevant opportunity cost (RRR). The important question now is this: How does one estimate opportunity costs when the investment is risky?

In practice, the *expected* rate of return on an asset, estimated by a market valuation model such as the capital asset pricing model (CAPM, from Chapter 6), is used as the opportunity cost. This is an estimate of the return that investors require to justify investing in the asset.

The justification for this procedure is not obvious, and the discussion may in fact appear perplexing. Comparing equation (7-2) with the CAPM developed in Chapter 6 [equation (6-10)] , we see that our suggested procedure for estimating opportunity costs appears to be incorrect. We rewrite the CAPM as follows:

Expected return = risk-free rate + risk premium   (7-3)

Now compare equations (7-3) and (7-2). The two relationships can be equivalent only if the expected rate of return on an asset equals the required rate of return. Then the practice of equating the expected rate of return with the required rate of return makes sense.

The expected rate of return on an asset depends on the future cash flows. Similarly, as discussed, the relevant cost of an asset reflects the future implications of owning the asset. Thus there is no contradiction in the "time units" of these variables; they both reflect the future.

The Security Market Line

To understand the equivalence of the expected rate of return and the RRR, we examine the graphical representation of the CAPM. The CAPM [equation (6-10) in Chapter 6] is a relatively simple linear equation that can be represented graphically as in Figure 7-2. This straight line is called the security market line (SML),

FIGURE 7-2

Security market line. All assets in equilibrium must plot on the SML. M represents the market portfolio

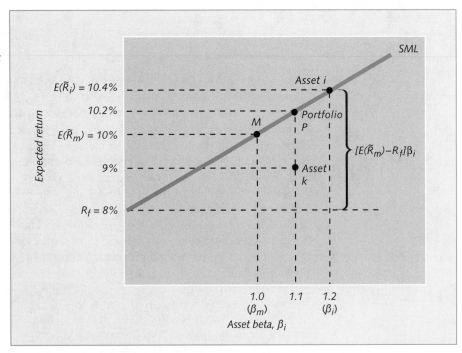

and all assets should plot exactly on this line because the CAPM and the SML are the same. The CAPM represents the relationship between relevant risk and expected return in equation form, and the SML represents the same idea graphically. This is not to suggest that temporary deviations from this line cannot occur. Such deviations from the SML, either below or above, are a temporary phenomenon; they cannot occur for an extended period of time. All assets eventually plot on the SML. When this happens, the expected rate of return on an asset equals the *RRR* on the asset.

WHY SHOULD ALL ASSETS PLOT ON THE SML?[1]

Assume that some stock, *k*, does not plot on the SML. For purposes of illustration, say that stock *k* has a beta coefficient of 1.1. According to the CAPM,

$$E(\tilde{R}_k) = R_f + \beta_k[E(\tilde{R}_m) - R_f]$$

If the risk-free rate is 8% and the expected return on the market is 10%, stock *k* should then have an expected return of

$$\begin{aligned} E(\tilde{R}_k) &= 0.08 + 1.1(0.10 - 0.08) \\ &= 0.102 \quad \text{or } 10.2\% \end{aligned}$$

But stock *k* does not plot on the SML in Figure 7-2; the expected return on *k* is in fact 9%. With a 9% expected return, stock *k* plots below the SML. The argument is that this situation cannot persist, given the assumptions underlying the CAPM (no transactions costs, taxes, etc.).

To see why, consider an investor who is forming a portfolio of equal investments in asset *i,* with an expected return of 10.4%, and the market portfolio, with an expected return of 10%. The expected return on this portfolio using equation (5-8) from Chapter 5 is

$$E(\tilde{R}_p) = \frac{1}{2}(10\%) + \frac{1}{2}(10.4\%) = 10.2\%$$

and the beta coefficient for this portfolio is, from equation (6-8) in Chapter 6,

$$\beta_p = (0.5)(1.0) + (0.5)(1.2) = 1.1$$

Thus this portfolio has a risk (beta) of 1.1, which is identical to the beta of asset *k*. Yet the stock *k* offers an expected return of only 9%. Because the portfolio offers a greater expected return for the same level of risk as stock *k*, one would be better off forming this portfolio with $\beta_p = 1.1$ instead of investing in stock *k*. Recognizing this, investors will start to sell asset *k*. Because of the greater supply, the price of asset *k* will fall. As the price of asset *k* falls, purchasing *k* becomes more and more attractive because the potential returns from owning it increase; that is, $E(\tilde{R}_k)$ rises. Similarly, because of the greater demand, the price of the portfolio *P* rises. And as the price of portfolio *P* rises, it becomes less and less attractive because the potential returns from owning the portfolio fall. These adjustments (buying the portfolio and selling asset *k*) continue until such arbitrage activity, the activity associated with seeking economic profits, by investors completely comes to an end. This happens only when both portfolio *P* and asset *k* plot exactly on the SML. Then the expected returns on asset *k* and portfolio *P* will be identical, and asset *k* will have an expected return of 10.2%. A similar set of arguments can be used to

[1] Although we explain this idea using the CAPM, the analysis is more general; all that is required is that no arbitrage opportunities exist. Thus even the APT can be used to explain this idea.

show that an asset that plots above the SML will also be forced by arbitrage activity to plot on the SML.

The fundamental driving force for this long-run phenomenon is the assumption that investors quickly "arbitrage away" any advantages. Is this a reasonable assumption? That investors do what it takes to improve their welfare is clear; it is ensured by Adam Smith's "invisible hand," an idea advanced in Chapter 1. With free access to capital markets, zero costs in buying and selling securities, and the full availability of information, the invisible hand guarantees that investors will exploit the potential advantages in the marketplace. Because these assumptions are required for the derivation of the CAPM, such arbitrage activity is a logical consequence.

KEY   CONCEPT   To preclude arbitrage opportunities, assets must be correctly priced and must plot on the security market line. When this happens, an asset's expected rate of return equals its required rate of return.

We can now see why the CAPM is called a "pricing model." Given the expected cash flows from an investment, the value of the asset is the present value of these expected cash flows, calculated at the discount rate provided by the CAPM.

OVERVALUED, UNDERVALUED, AND FAIRLY PRICED ASSETS

An asset is priced "fairly" if the market price is equal to the equilibrium price provided by the CAPM. The term *fair* suggests that the asset's current price incorporates all available information about the asset's benefits and costs. But if the price of the stock is, say, $65, it is overvalued, and if the price is $50, it is undervalued in this framework. Whenever a stock is overvalued, it falls below the SML; whenever it is undervalued, it falls above the SML. It is easy to see why these statements are true by comparing the expected benefits (the expected returns) from the stock with the economic cost (the RRR) of investing in the stock.

The linkages among market values, opportunity costs, economic profits, excess returns, and net present values are now complete.

7-4

IMPLICATIONS FOR CORPORATE FINANCIAL MANAGEMENT

Our discussion so far has developed several new concepts and ideas, and the natural question that now arises pertains to the relevance of these ideas to financial management. How does the CAPM help financial decision making? How do the concepts developed here relate to the various issues addressed in earlier chapters?

The Use of the CAPM in Financial Management

The contribution of the CAPM to financial management can be summarized in one sentence: The CAPM provides a framework for estimating the appropriate opportunity cost for evaluating an investment.

DISCOUNT RATE CALCULATIONS

In Chapter 4 we introduced the notion of money's time value. Because of this value, an opportunity cost is incurred when cash flows are delayed. To compensate, future cash flows must be discounted at the appropriate opportunity cost, or $RRR,$ to find present values. However, we explained only the mechanical procedure for finding the present and future values of cash flows; we said nothing about how the appropriate discount rate is estimated. By providing a framework for estimating the proper discount rate to be used, the CAPM thus makes the methodology suggested in Chapter 4 operational.

MARKET-VALUE CALCULATIONS

Because we stated in Chapter 2 that the goal of financial management is to maximize the market value of a firm's common stock, a financial manager must, at the very least, know what determines market values. The CAPM provides the market valuation theory that is required for calculating market values. By using the CAPM in value-maximizing decisions, corporate managers do not have to worry about the potentially different discount rates that the firm's owners may have. The market theory provides an "average discount rate" that the manager can use in an objective way.

SEPARATION OF RELEVANT AND IRRELEVANT RISKS

When making day-to-day decisions, a manager is confronted with several alternatives, each with choices that may involve different returns and risks. The CAPM theory, in a sense, simplifies the managers' decisions because it identifies those risks

HEDGING: RELEVANT OR IRRELEVANT?

The term hedging refers to activities aimed at reducing the volatility (variance) of cash flows. One such activity is buying insurance. Considering that investors and managers are risk averse, such hedging activity appears to be extremely useful and the question about its relevance seems almost frivolous.

As it turns out, hedging is valuable but not for the obvious reasons. Let us examine why. To argue that hedging is useful, one must show that such activity can increase firm value and shareholders' wealth. Consider the basic idea developed in this chapter. The value of an asset is the expected cash flows from the asset discounted at the opportunity cost (RRR). If the asset under consideration is the firm, the value of the firm is the total expected cash flows generated by the firm discounted at the RRR that is appropriate for the risk of the firm.

Why Hedging Appears Irrelevant

What is the risk of the firm's cash flows? It is the variance of the cash flows. However, this risk is not directly relevant in determining the RRR. As we have seen earlier, it is an asset's covariance risk that is relevant in determining the RRR. Thus any attempts by management to reduce the variance of the firm's cash flows through hedging activities leave unaffected the relevant risk and hence the RRR for valuing the firm. Since hedging cannot lower the relevant risk of the firm, it cannot make the risk-averse owners any happier. In this sense, hedging is irrelevant.

However, we have looked at only one side of the hedging issue. We have examined the denominator (discount rate) of the valuation equation. Now consider the numerator (expected cash flows).

Why Hedging is Relevant

Hedging can affect firm value in a different way—not by reducing risk but by altering the magnitude of the expected cash flows. The variance of a firm's cash flows affect the firm's cash flows because it affects the firm's expected tax liabil-

ity, the firm's probability of financial distress and bankruptcy, and the costs of borrowing. To the extent that hedging activities can increase the expected cash flows from the firm, they increase firm value and shareholders' wealth.* Chapter 11 addresses hedging in greater detail.

To sum up, hedging can increase firm value not because it lowers the risk borne by the owners, but because it increases their expected cash flows.

* For additional details on how hedging can benefit the firm, see, for example, "Financial Engineering: Why Hedge?" by C. W. Smith, C. W. Smithson, and D. S. Wilford, in The Handbook of Financial Engineering, *edited by C. W. Smith, Jr., and C. W. Smithson (New York: Harper Business, 1990); and "The Determinants of a Firm's Hedging Policies," by C. W. Smith and R. M. Stulz,* Journal of Financial and Quantitative Analysis, *December 1985.*

that they should recognize when making value-increasing investments and those risks that have no impact whatsoever on the market value of the project being undertaken. The only relevant risk is the systematic risk of the project as measured by its beta. Thus, if stock prices are not affected by total risk (only systematic risk), any attempts to reduce total risk through "hedging" are a waste of resources and time. Although risk reduction is not a value-enhancing activity in the CAPM framework, corporations nevertheless do spend substantial resources to reduce total risks. The preceding highlight explains why. We examine hedging in greater detail in Chapter 11.

Making Money for the Company

In Section 7-1 we defined the notion of "making money" as used in finance. To "make money" it is necessary to generate excess returns. Yet we offered no practical guidelines for calculating the excess returns on a project.

Assume that asset k in Figure 7-2 is a one-year capital budgeting project. Like stock, projects have expected returns and market risks. Should project k be accepted or rejected? Because the *NPV* should be the basis for the decision, it is necessary to calculate the project's *NPV*.

Assume, for simplicity, that this one-year project requires an initial outlay of $100. No other cash flows can be expected until the end of the year. Figure 7-2 shows that the project's beta is 1.1 and that the expected return is 9%. If there is only one cash flow at the end and this is expected to produce a 9% return, the expected cash flow at the end must be $109 (= $100 $\times$ 1.09). The *NPV* of this project is obtained by discounting this future cash flow to the present by using a market discount rate (*RRR*), which, according to Figure 7-2, is 10.2%. Therefore,

$$NPV = \text{present value of inflows} - \text{present value of outflows}$$
$$= \$109(PVF_{0.102,1}) - \$100$$
$$= \$98.91 - \$100 = \$-1.09$$

Using the *NPV* rule, managers should reject this project.

Project k, which falls below the SML, is rejected because it has a negative *NPV*. Similarly, it can be shown that any project that falls above the SML has a positive *NPV*. A project that falls on the SML has *NPV* = 0.

This suggests that the *NPV* rule developed in earlier chapters can be stated alternatively as: Accept all projects that fall above the SML and reject all projects that fall below the line.

Just as in the case of a stock, however, no project can fall above the line for an extended time. Thus "good" projects eventually lose their appeal, and "bad" projects may eventually become "good." To borrow the words of a poet,

Many shall be restored that now are fallen and many shall fall that now are in honor.

Horace, *Ars Poetica*

Regulated Companies

Regulated companies such as utilities cannot change the rates they charge their customers without the approval of the appropriate regulatory agency. The companies must justify their requests to obtain permission to raise the rates for products or services. It therefore is becoming common to use opportunity costs instead of accounting costs to calculate the appropriate rates that a company can charge its consumers. By estimating a "fair rate of return," the regulatory authority can determine the appropriate rates that consumers should pay. The CAPM can be used to calculate a company's "fair" rate of return on equity.

7-5

MARKET VALUES AND MARKET EFFICIENCY

Determining market values requires an estimate of the benefits and risks of assets. These estimates are based on expectations about the future characteristics of the asset (e.g., IBM stock). But how are these expectations formed? On the basis of available information. For example, if word got out that IBM was on the verge of a technical breakthrough, this might lead to expectations of higher future earnings. As a result, an investor's estimates of the future benefits from owning IBM stock might rise, and the market value of the stock also would rise to reflect this new information. Thus a direct link between information and market values would be established.

The concept of an efficient market pertains to the relationship between the market values of assets and the information available about that asset. An **efficient market** is a capital market in which the market value of an asset reflects all available information about the asset. Or, an efficient capital market is one in which it is not possible to generate excess returns consistently. This description is really an implication of efficient markets, but it is sometimes useful to focus on this "definition" to get a better understanding of the market efficiency hypothesis. The hypothesis that U.S. capital markets are efficient is called the **efficient market hypothesis** (EMH).

Forms of Market Efficiency

There are three forms of market efficiency, depending on how "information" is defined. The market is **weak form efficient** if the market value of an asset reflects historical price information. In a weak form efficient market, there is nothing to be gained by looking back through time to study the asset's previous price behavior. One cannot "make money" by studying the behavior of stock prices over the preceding years. The current price of the asset (security) subsumes all history of prices. Thus **technical analysis**—the name given to the study of stock price forecasting by looking at historical patterns of stock price behavior—is a useless exercise. Most researchers now agree that the U.S. stock market is at least weak form efficient. The words *at least* are used advisedly. That U.S. markets are weak form efficient does not preclude their being either semistrong form efficient or strong form efficient.

In a **semistrong efficient market,** stock prices reflect all historical and publicly available information. The stock price already incorporates any information (publicly held) that is contained in balance sheets, income statements, earnings announcements, dividend declarations, and the like. A professional analysis of these "fundamentals" (i.e., **fundamental analysis**) of the firm is useless. The general consensus today is that U.S. capital markets are semistrong efficient. In other words, it is not possible to generate consistent excess returns in U.S. financial markets today by using publicly available information.

A capital market is **strong form efficient** if the stock price already reflects both publicly available and private information. U.S. capital markets are not strong form efficient. In other words, it may be possible to generate excess returns consistently with private information. Private information refers to specialized information. For example, an oil industry analyst may know how best to evaluate the impact on oil prices of developments in the Middle East. Private information should not be confused with "insider information," the use of which is illegal. Insider information refers to the information that the corporate insiders (e.g., directors) may possess about their own company.

Having looked at the three forms of market efficiency, we naturally ask what all this means. In other words, if the statement that markets are semistrong efficient is accepted, what are the implications?

Implications of
Efficient Markets

The EMH has some staggering implications. For one thing, it implies that stock prices cannot be accurately predicted.[2] Why not? If current stock prices reflect all available information, stock prices will change only to reflect events in the future that are not anticipated today. If the events in the future cannot be anticipated, future stock prices also cannot be anticipated. If an event was anticipated, it would be "currently available information" and would already be reflected in current stock prices. An immediate consequence of these observations is that in an efficient market there is no strategy that can be followed to consistently yield excess returns.

This implication is often misunderstood. Efficient capital markets do not imply that it is impossible to "make money" (generate excess returns) in the market. The key is in the use of the word *consistently*. In efficient markets one cannot make money over an *extended* period of time and over *several* transactions. On any particular transaction one is as likely to make money as to lose money. In the long run, the excess returns will dwindle to zero. This means that investors and mutual fund managers who have generated excess returns in the past were probably just lucky; there is no guarantee that they will continue to do so in the future. Their success in the past is not necessarily a result of their superior skills at using publicly available information. Even Benjamin Graham, the father of fundamental analysis, admitted that his fundamental analysis was not a useful activity. Shortly before his death in 1976 he said that he belonged to the "efficient markets" school of thought: "I am no longer an advocate of elaborate techniques of security analysis in order to find superior value opportunities. This was a rewarding activity, say, 40 years ago, when our textbook Graham and Dodd was first published; but the situation has changed a good deal since then."[3]

If excess returns cannot be generated in the long run, then according to our earlier discussion regarding the economic significance of *NPV*s, in an efficient market all investments will in the long run have a $NPV = 0$. This is particularly true of financial securities because of the efficiency of financial markets. [The markets for real assets (e.g., machinery) are not as efficient as financial markets are.] The implication of this to the financial manager should be clear: Even if a company accepts an investment (say, software manufacturing for computer applications) because it has a positive *NPV*, in the long run this investment will turn sour because its *NPV will* become 0 and eventually negative. This happens because of competition. As more and more companies find that software manufacturing offers positive *NPV*s, they enter the market, and the resulting competition forces down prices and cash flows to the companies. And this lowers *NPV*s. Thus managers must constantly evaluate new projects to identify new positive-*NPV* investments. What is a negative-*NPV* project today may turn out to be attractive tomorrow as economic conditions change.

Another way to characterize an efficient market is to define it as one in which the market value of an asset reflects its "true" or "intrinsic" value. It is precisely for this reason that financial decisions should be made in terms of market values. A manager who announces a new investment plan for a company does so because he or she believes that this investment has a positive *NPV* of, say, $59,000. The manager believes that the company, and consequently its stockholders, will be wealthier by $59,000 if the company takes on the project. But, as we explained in

[2]There is a general "truth" recognized by many Wall Street soothsayers. To predict the market correctly, you cannot go wrong if you do either of the following: (1) If you want to predict the level of the market, don't say when. (2) If you want to discuss the market on any given day in the future, don't discuss the level for that day.

[3]"A Conversation with Benjamin Graham," *Financial Analysts Journal,* September–October 1976, pp. 20–23.

Chapter 2, stockholders will not be better off by $59,000 unless the value of their stock rises by $59,000. Only if stock prices reflect true values does this correspondence between the *NPV* and the stock price make sense. Remember that investors do not become rich because the manager has estimated that the *NPV* of the investment is $59,000. Investors make money only if this increase in *NPV is* translated into an increase in the stock price. Financial managers do not have to worry about this in efficient markets because a firm's higher value does result in an increase in the investors' stock prices.

In efficient markets, corporate financial managers can evaluate the markets' assessment of their decisions by focusing on stock prices. If a corporate decision lowers stock prices, then because it lowers the wealth of the stockholder, it is a bad decision. If a decision increases stock prices, it is a good decision. If information regarding corporate decisions is not immediately reflected in the stock prices (i.e., if markets are not efficient), decisions based on market values are meaningless. The market value of the stock does not reflect the extent of the investors' "approval" or "disapproval." In such cases, market values do not reflect true values.

Luckily, as already noted, the majority of the evidence indicates that U.S. capital markets are semistrong efficient. The implication that stock prices cannot be predicted challenges the usefulness of financial experts' recommendations. When advisory agencies come up with lists of "good buys" and "bad buys," what is the basis of these recommendations? People who believe in efficient markets often ask: If a stockbroker or an investment advisor knows how to make a "killing" in the market, does it make any sense for this person or company to sell this advice to someone else for just a few dollars?

| 7-6 |

CHALLENGES TO THE EFFICIENT MARKET HYPOTHESIS

The efficient market hypothesis has naturally been very controversial.[4] There has been a long tradition of resistance to it, and it continues to be attacked not only by practitioners but also by many academics.

The EMH rests on several assumptions that may not pertain strictly to the financial markets. For example, the EMH requires that information dissemination be costless and instantaneous. Although information is rapidly conveyed through prices, some professionals argue that there is still enough time for certain parties to act on new information before prices react completely. Others have pointed out that there may be some monopolistic elements in the markets that weaken the assumption of pure competition underlying the EMH theory.

The theory of efficient markets has been tested extensively, and the results generally support the theory. There is no strong evidence that over the long run any individual or institution (other than corporate insiders) has been able to generate excess returns consistently. Even the identification of one or more professionals who have consistently outperformed the market does not invalidate the EMH (see the next highlight, "Consistently Superior Performers: Evidence of Market Inefficiencies?"). Several anomalies have been recognized in the literature, however. For example, the "weekend effect" suggests that one should sell stocks (or short them) on Friday just before the markets close and buy them back on Monday when their prices are lower. Other anomalies include the "small-firm effect" and the "January effect." These anomalies that appear to be exceptions to the EMH may actually be

---

[4]For an interesting perspective on the debate between the academic and the practitioner viewpoints and related issues, see Adam Smith, *The Money Game* (New York: Random House, 1976).

CONSISTENTLY SUPERIOR PERFORMERS: EVIDENCE OF MARKET INEFFICIENCIES?

In almost any discussion of the EMH, it is difficult to ignore the heroes of Wall Street and those investment professionals whose performance is consistently superior. Frequently quoted examples include the performance of Value Line and J. Walter Schloss Associates. Critics of the EMH often note that Walter Schloss outperformed the market (the Standard & Poor's 500 index) in all but five years between 1954 and 1982. Doesn't this impressive 28-year track record invalidate the EMH? This is "proof" that it is possible to beat the market consistently. At least, that's how the argument goes.

Unfortunately, this argument is not convincing. There is no denying that Walter Schloss's performance speaks well of his company, but it says little about the market being inefficient.

Assume that the probability that an investor will beat the market in any one year is 50%; that is, assume that the investor's performance is decided by pure chance.

The probability of obtaining r successes in n tries is

$$\binom{n}{r} p^r (1-p)^{n-r}$$

where

p is the probability of success in any one try

$$\binom{n}{r} = \frac{n!}{r!(n-r)!}$$

n! is "n factorial" and is calculated as
$$n(n-1)(n-2)(n-3)\cdots(3)(2)(1)$$

Then the probability that this investor will beat the market in 23 out of 28 years can be calculated (using the binomial probability model) as

$$\binom{28}{23}(0.5)^{23}(0.5)^5 = 0.0003661$$

The very small probability associated with Walter Schloss's success makes that performance all the more impressive.

Now consider some additional details. The financial markets have several thousand money managers trying to beat the market. At the end of 1993, for instance, there were about 7,000 investment man-

agers registered with the Securities and Exchange Commission (SEC). It goes without saying that the actual number of investors in the market is much greater; after all, it is not just the registered managers who are active investors. Assume, for example, that there are only 10,000 investors in the market. Then the probability of finding at least one with a record as good as that of Walter Schloss is

$$1 - \binom{10,000}{0} \times$$
$$(0.0003661)^0 \times$$
$$(0.9996339)^{10,000}$$
$$= 1 - 0.0256896 = 0.9743104$$

A record like Walter Schloss's should be expected with almost certainty! Putting it another way, if we look back and analyze performances, the probability is in excess of 0.97 that we will find at least one with a record like Walter Schloss's. And this probability has little to do with the efficiency of the financial markets.

SOURCE: This example was suggested by Seha M. Tinic.

saying very little about it. Rather, they may be the result of incorrectly specifying the equilibrium risk–return relationship in the marketplace. Moreover, these anomalies are not so dramatic when transactions costs are taken into account.

Conflicting Hypotheses   More serious attacks against the validity of the EMH have been advanced in the recent academic literature. For example, the **overreaction hypothesis** (OH) essentially holds that investors in the marketplace respond irrationally by "overreacting" to new and unexpected information, both good and bad.[5] According to the OH, both economywide responses to general news and the stock price reactions to news about a specific company's stock tend to be "excessive." The prices initially tend to shoot above or below their equilibrium levels (i.e., they overreact), and only later do they slowly return (i.e., adjust) to these levels. Both the market

[5] See W. DeBondt and R. Thaler, "Does the Stock Market Overreact?" *Journal of Finance* 40 (1985): 793–805.

as a whole and individual stocks systematically exaggerate the economic consequences of major events by either responding too favorably to good news or depressing prices too much in reaction to bad news. If the overreaction hypothesis is true, the evidence poses a serious threat to the efficient market hypothesis because it provides investors with trading rules for consistently generating economic profits.

Recent empirical research, however, has questioned this notion of chronic overreaction. Although it is true that large stock price declines tend to be followed by small upward adjustments (as suggested by the OH), large daily stock price increases also are followed by small positive adjustments. That is, the evidence is inconsistent with the overreaction hypothesis in the case of good news. How do we explain this "asymmetric" response of the stock market to news events?

The **uncertain information hypothesis** (UIH) has been advanced most recently to explain this phenomenon.[6] It may be viewed as an extension of the EMH in that it relaxes the assumption that investors have immediate access to all information and that they revise security prices immediately. When a major economic event takes place, the actual implications of the event are at first not clear. The UIH maintains that because investors are risk averse, they respond to both good and bad news by setting prices below what they would if all of the information were readily available. As additional information becomes available, stock prices tend to be positive, on average, irrespective of whether the initial event conveyed good or bad news. The empirical evidence is strongly consistent with the UIH. When viewed in this light, positive price adjustments following a major news event are entirely rational, an observation that casts serious doubts on arguments based on irrational investor behavior.

The Stock Market Crash of October 1987

On October 19, 1987, the Dow Jones Industrial Average (DJIA) plunged more than 500 points, with investors unloading large amounts of equity investments in a very short time. On this day, which has subsequently earned the appellation "Black Monday," over 20% of the U.S. markets' aggregate equity value was destroyed. The common perception is that the events on Wall Street triggered a chain reaction into the global financial markets as equities all over the world saw dramatic decreases in values. This reaction was so great that it has been called the "October meltdown."

This dramatic fall in stock prices has naturally attracted intense scrutiny from many quarters—investors, investment professionals, academic researchers, officials of the stock exchanges, politicians, and journalists. Questions about what caused the crash continue to be addressed in the popular press. The search continues for the "main culprit" that caused this steep fall in stock prices in the United States and abroad.

The October meltdown immediately provided a reason for vigorous attacks against the EMH. Several apparently embarrassing questions were repeatedly raised. If the market is efficient and information is fully reflected in prices, how can one explain a loss of around $1 trillion in one day? Also, doesn't this precipitous reassessment of market values support the notion that markets are irrational and influenced by "psychological forces?" Are investors irrational? Don't market prices really reflect the available information? Are the low values the result of "overreaction" in the marketplace? and so on. In any event, it has been argued, the October meltdown is "proof" that the EMH is invalid.

[6] See K. C. Brown, V. Harlow, and S. M. Tinic, "Risk Aversion, Uncertain Information and Market Efficiency," *Journal of Financial Economics* 22 (1988): 355–386.

To answer these questions it is useful to try to explain the reasons for the stock market crash. Various explanations for Black Monday have been advanced, and we discuss some of them in very general terms. An initial explanation for the stock market crash revolved around the breakdown of extant institutional arrangements that facilitate the smooth workings of the stock market. It was argued that with a dramatic surge in trading volume, dealers simply could not cope with their buy and sell orders. These imbalances, it was suggested, distorted the smooth trading patterns in the marketplace that then led to the downward spiral. But this explanation was found inadequate by researchers who concluded that the magnitude of the crash simply could not have been the result of institutional inadequacies.

Others blamed it all on **program trading,** which, loosely speaking, uses high-speed computers to execute buy and sell transactions. The stock market is really made up of two markets: the futures market (discussed in greater detail in Chapter 11) and the stock market itself. If a stock is cheaper in the futures market than in the stock market, investors buy in the futures market and sell in the stock market and thereby make a profit. Similarly, if the futures price is higher than the stock market price, investors buy in the stock market and sell in the futures market. These arbitrage opportunities are typically identified by computer programs—hence, the name *program trading*. Again, with a dramatic surge in the volume of program trading, the continuity in the marketplace was destroyed, and the market reacted adversely. "Portfolio insurance" has also been blamed for the crash. **Portfolio insurance** is a strategy associated with managing large pools of capital. Portfolio insurance, unlike program trading, does not take advantage of pricing differences in the two markets. Rather, it is a technique for preserving capital. Suppose you have $10,000 to invest for one year but you want to ensure that the portfolio value will not fall below $9,000. You then invest most of your funds in safe assets (say, T-bills) and a small sum in equities. If the market goes up, your portfolio value will increase. If the market declines, you will simply pull out some of the equity investment and put more into the safe investments. This is the basic idea behind portfolio insurance. These explanations, based on the inefficiencies and idiosyncrasies of the U.S. markets, are also not satisfactory because, for one thing, the stock market crash phenomenon was not confined to just the United States. It was a global phenomenon. The U.S. markets were not the first to decline rapidly and, more interesting, the United States had the fifth smallest decline.[7]

Another line of reasoning holds that the stock market crash was a rational response to the unexpected arrival of important negative information. This new adverse information, according to proponents of this school of thought, came at a time when the market was already uncomfortable about the large U.S. trade deficit. The market was bracing itself for a recession immediately after the 1988 elections. Many major events with potentially profound economic ramifications all occurred contemporaneously. On October 13, the Democrats on the House Ways and Means Committee agreed to pass tax code changes that made corporate takeovers less attractive. This alone was sufficient to push down stock prices. After all, such takeover activity was credited for the dramatic stock price increases in the early 1980s. This was not all. Chemical Bank raised the prime lending rate, and then Treasury Secretary James Baker made it clear that the United States would not defend the dollar against the German mark, thereby suggesting that the higher interest rates were not a random event. To make matters worse, on October 16,

[7] See Richard Roll, "The International Crash of October 1987," in *Black Monday and the Future of Financial Markets*, edited by R. W. Khamphuis, Jr., R. L. Kormendi, and J. W. H. Watson, pp. 35–70. (Homewood, IL: Irwin, 1989).

there was the report of an Iranian attack on a U.S.-flagged oil tanker, which further increased the uncertainty in the markets. This simultaneous occurrence of major events could have resulted in the dramatic crash. As one journalist put it, "What happened on Black Monday was the utterly predictable result of the fact that information flows have become so good, so instantaneous."[8] Thus, as dramatic as the crash was, it does not invalidate the EMH.[9]

Noise in Financial Markets

Sanford Grossman points out that if all information is reflected in prices, then there is very little incentive for anyone to collect information.[10] Assume for simplicity that there are only two types of investors, informed and uninformed, and that an investor must bear some costs to become informed. If observed market prices reflect all information, then uninformed investors are better off not incurring the added expense that is required to become informed. Moreover, informed traders have good reason to be displeased because they get no advantage from becoming informed. They will stop collecting information because it offers them no advantage. However, if no one collects information, then there is an incentive for someone to do so. Thus prices can never be in equilibrium because there will always be some people who will want to change their decisions about gathering information. As Grossman and Stiglitz point out, "If markets are perfectly arbitraged all the time, there are never any profits to be made from the activity of arbitrage. But then, how do arbitrageurs make money, particularly if there are costs associated with obtaining information about whether markets are already perfectly arbitraged?"[11] They go on to suggest that one way to handle this problem is to introduce another factor that can affect prices—"noise."[12] Then prices will reflect both information and noise.

The EMH assumes that stock prices reflect available information. But a new and growing school of thought maintains that it is not information alone that influences prices; rather, **noise** can have a profound effect on them.[13] Noise is a nebulous concept based on sentiment and beliefs that do not necessarily reflect cash flows. According to this view, some people trade on information (rational or "informed" traders), and others trade on noise. "Noise traders" or "uninformed traders" trade on the advice of financial gurus, for sentimental reasons, for liquidity, or whatever. Because of the existence of noise traders, prices deviate from their fundamental values, and asset prices reflect more than just information about expected cash flows.

The existence of riskless arbitrage possibilities is basic to the validity of the EMH. Shleifer and Summers maintain not only that there are noise traders in the markets, but also that riskless arbitrage by the rational traders is often not possible.[14] They argue that there are two limits to arbitrage. The first is fundamental risk—the risk that future dividends can be better than expected. The second limit is resale risk. If stocks are mispriced today, they can be even more mispriced to-

---

[8] Susan Lee, "Efficient Market Theory Lives!" *The Wall Street Journal*, May 6, 1988, p. 20.

[9] See also Merton Miller, "Crash of 1987: Bubble or Fundamental," *Financial Innovations and Market Volatility*, chap. 6. (Cambridge: Blackwell, 1991).

[10] S. Grossman, "Further Results on the Informational Efficiency of Competitive Stock Markets," *Journal of Economic Theory* 18 (1978): 81–101.

[11] S. Grossman and J. E. Stiglitz, "Information and Competitive Price Systems," *American Economic Review* (1976): 246–253.

[12] S. J. Grossman and J. E. Stiglitz, "The Impossibility of Informationally Efficient Markets," *American Economic Review* (1980): 393–408.

[13] Fisher Black, "Noise," *Journal of Finance*, July 1986, pp. 529–541.

[14] Andrei Shleifer and Lawrence Summers, "The Noise Trader Approach to Finance," *Journal of Economic Perspectives*, September 1990, pp. 19–33.

morrow. The existence of transactions costs and investors with short horizons makes these risks relevant. Thus, according to Shleifer and Summers, a theory of asset prices must take into account both noise traders and restrictions on arbitrage.

Although the proponents of the "noise trader perspective of finance" claim to explain various anomalies in the marketplace, further research into this area is clearly warranted. The problem is that it is difficult to test theories based on noise trading; it is difficult to measure noise or distinguish information from noise. Finally, noise makes observations imperfect, which complicates matters considerably. Nevertheless, the mere acknowledgment of the noise trader appears to threaten conventional explanations of asset pricing.

SUMMARY

Section 7-1: Value and Opportunity Costs

What determines the value of an asset?

■ The two fundamental determinants of value are potential benefits and opportunity costs.

What is an opportunity cost? How is it related to value and economic profits?

■ The opportunity cost of investing in an asset is the "sacrifice" made by investing in that asset. It is the rate of return on the next best equivalent alternative forgone.

■ The relevant discount rate for discounting the cash flows from an asset is the opportunity cost, also known as the required rate of return (RRR) on the asset.

■ There is an inverse relationship between asset values and opportunity costs.

■ An economic profit is the profit earned on an investment after adjusting for the opportunity cost of that investment.

■ Economic profits are earned only when an investment earns more than its opportunity cost. In this situation, the investment generates "excess returns."

Section 7-2: The Valuation Process

What is the personal valuation process and how does it differ from the market valuation process?

■ The required rate of return or opportunity cost for an investment is the sum of a risk-free interest rate and a risk premium.

■ When personal estimates of an investment's cash flows are discounted at a rate based on a personal risk premium estimate for an individual, the resultant valuation is a personal valuation. When the expected cash flows are based on publicly available information and the relevant discount rate is derived from a market valuation theory such as the CAPM, the resulting valuation is a market valuation.

■ A financial manager should use a discount rate derived from market considerations—a market valuation process—in order to be consistent with the objective of maximizing stockholders' wealth.

■ When an investment provides excess returns, it is a positive-NPV project. This equivalence between excess returns and NPVs justifies the NPV rule for managers: Accept projects with a positive NPV to increase shareholder wealth.

Section 7-3: Estimating Opportunity Costs: The CAPM

Why is the required rate of return (RRR) estimated by the CAPM an opportunity cost?

- The CAPM provides an estimate of the expected return on an asset.

- Although there can be temporary deviations from the security market line (SML), investors who are seeking economic profits will force all assets back to the SML. When assets are correctly priced, there are no arbitrage opportunities, and all assets plot on the SML. When this happens, the discount rate implicit in the market price (the relevant opportunity cost) equals the expected rate of return on the asset. Thus the expected return estimated from the CAPM is an estimate of the relevant opportunity cost.

Section 7-4: Implications for Corporate Financial Management

How is the RRR estimated from the CAPM used in business decisions?

- Since the *RRR* implied by the CAPM is an opportunity cost, this rate can be used as the discount rate for valuing assets.

- The framework of the CAPM allows managers to focus on relevant risks.

- The CAPM helps managers identify wealth-increasing projects.

- The CAPM can be used to develop acceptable rates of return for regulated companies.

Section 7-5: Market Values and Market Efficiency

What is the efficient market hypothesis (EMH) and what are its implications?

- An efficient capital market is one in which information is quickly and efficiently reflected in asset prices. The hypothesis that the capital market is efficient is known as the efficient market hypothesis (EMH).

- There are different levels of market efficiency: In a weak form efficient market, prices reflect historical price information. Prices in semistrong efficient markets reflect all publicly available information. Prices in strong form efficient markets reflect all information, including private information.

- In efficient stock markets, it is impossible to consistently predict prices.

- In efficient markets, all assets are correctly priced; they reflect their "true" or "intrinsic" value.

- If financial markets are efficient, it is impossible to generate excess returns consistently. If asset markets are efficient, positive *NPV*s, in the long run, will disappear.

- In efficient markets, managers can look to stock prices to assess the extent of the market's approval or disapproval of their decisions.

Section 7-6: Challenges to the Efficient Market Hypothesis

Are markets efficient?

- The EMH has been tested extensively and there is a substantial body of evidence to support the theory.

- Recently, several market observers have challenged the validity of the efficient market hypothesis. Nevertheless, the EMH continues to provide a reasonable explanation for the changes in market prices and a justification for the continued use of stock prices as a guide for managerial decisions.

■ Because of the existence of noise traders, prices may deviate from their fundamental values, and asset prices may reflect more than just information about expected cash flows. The existence of noise traders weakens traditional notions of asset pricing.

QUESTIONS

1. What is the value of an asset?

2. What benefits and costs affect the value of an asset?

3. What is opportunity cost? Is it the same as the price of an asset?

4. Why does value have an inverse relationship to opportunity costs?

5. Explain the difference between accounting profit and economic profit.

6. What is (are) the essential difference(s) between the personal valuation process and the market valuation process?

7. Does $NPV = 0$ imply zero economic profit? When will economic profit be greater than 0?

8. How does the NPV relate economic profits and maximization of stockholder wealth?

9. Why is the expected return implied by the CAPM an estimate of the relevant opportunity cost?

10. Assets that lie above the SML are undervalued investments. Why?

11. Explain why an asset that plots above the SML is a positive-NPV investment.

12. Why should all assets eventually plot on the SML?

13. How can corporate financial managers use the CAPM?

14. If relevant risk is the only risk necessary to compute opportunity cost, is hedging useless?

15. What is an efficient market?

16. How can market efficiency be classified?

17. What are the implications for managers if markets are efficient?

18. Is it impossible to "make money" in an efficient market?

19. To what extent is the efficient market hypothesis valid?

20. What is "noise" in markets? How does noise affect market values?

PROBLEMS

1. A CD offered by a new bank will pay $10,000 in three years. Your current bank offers a 9% rate on three-year CDs. What is the most you should be willing to pay for the new bank's CD?

2. You have just received your MBA and your parents have offered to lend you $30,000 to buy a new car. They will require you to repay them $48,315 in five years. Your bank makes new car loans at 14%.

(a) What is your appropriate opportunity cost?

(b) Should you borrow the money for your new Porsche from the bank or from your parents?

3. Your brother has decided what model of car he wants to buy, and he is trying to choose between dealers. Dempsey Motors will sell him the car for $10,000 ($1,000 down with the rest payable on a four-year note with a monthly interest rate of 1%). Tunney Motors will sell the car for $9,500 ($1,000 down with the rest payable on a four-year note with a monthly interest rate of 1.2%). Your brother's opportunity cost is 1% per month. What should your brother do? (*Note:* You cannot use the tables for this problem. You need the formulas in Table 4-1 or a calculator.)

4. After spending $300 on advertising, Van Harlow has found a buyer for his twin-engine plane. If Van sells the plane, he can get $20,000 from the buyer, but he must then pay $500 to transport the plane to the buyer. Alternatively, Van can keep the plane for use in a new project that came up after he placed the ads to sell. What is the appropriate cost (in dollars) of keeping the plane for the project?

5. Five years ago you withdrew $2,000 from a money market fund paying 10% to place it in a mutual fund. Today your investment in the mutual fund is worth $3,000.

(a) What is your book-value profit from the investment in the mutual fund?

(b) What was the opportunity cost of your $2,000 investment? What was your economic profit from the mutual fund?

6. You are trying to choose among three one-year notes of varying risks in which to invest your money. You perceive note *A* to have virtually no risk, and you have assigned a 0% risk premium to it. Note *B* has moderate risk, and you have assigned it a 5% risk premium. Note *C* has high risk, and you have assigned it a 10% risk premium. Note *A* sells for $9,300, note *B* for $8,850, and note *C* for $8,460 (each promises to pay $10,000 in one year).

(a) What should you do if the riskless rate is 5%?

(b) What should you do if the riskless rate is 7%?

7. Your firm is considering either of two tracts of land for a new warehouse. The decision about which to buy will be based solely on cost. Hamman Realty will sell its tract for $200,000 cash, and the Wolff Investment Corp. will sell its tract for $190,000, subject to the condition that this $190,000 be borrowed from Wolff and paid off as a five-year 14% loan with equal end-of-the-year payments. If the land is purchased from Wolff, the $200,000 that your firm has allocated for the land has no better alternative use than a 10% money market fund.

(a) What would be your annual payments to Wolff?

(b) What discount rate should you use to determine the present value of these cash flows, and what is their present value?

(c) What should you do? What would your decision be if Wolff offered the land for $185,000 under otherwise similar conditions? At what price would Wolff have to offer the land for you to be indifferent?

8. You are trying to decide whether to purchase a tuxedo or simply to rent one as needed. You can purchase for $1,000 one that you estimate will last for 20 years. Alternatively, you can lease one for $60 each time you need one (you estimate that this will be twice a year). If your opportunity cost is 12%, what should you do? (For simplicity, assume that the lease expense is paid at the end of each year.)

9. Your sister has just enrolled in a business program that requires each student to purchase his or her own personal computer. Computer World will sell your sister the computer and software that she needs for $3,000 cash. Computervision will sell them for $2,750, payable at 1% per month on a 30-month note. Finally, Discount Computers will sell them for only $2,400 if your sister takes out a 48-month, 2% per month note. Your sister has determined that her opportunity cost is 0.5% per month. What should she do? (*Note:* $PVFA_{0.005,30} = 27.794$, $PVFA_{0.005,48} = 42.580$, and $PVFA_{0.02,48} = 30.673$.)

10. You are faced with a complex decision. Not only must you decide whether to accept alternative X or alternative Y, but also you must decide whether you want the payment from each project to be in a lump sum or as a series of cash flows received annually for six years. Given that you may select only one project and one method of receiving cash from that project, what choice is best? Assume an 11% opportunity cost. The following table gives the cash flow stream.

End of Year	X	Y
1	$ 850	$1,300
2	$ 850	$1,000
3	$ 850	$ 800
4	$ 850	$ 700
5	$ 850	$ 500
6	$ 850	$ 600
Lump-sum amount at time 0	$3,600	$3,620

11. You have researched a new one-year project and determined that it has a $1,000 initial outlay and a net present value of $100, given a 12% opportunity cost of funds. A coworker has argued that the $1,000 could more profitably be invested in a one-year CD yielding 11%. What is wrong with her argument? If $2,000 is available for new projects, should you adopt the project and buy the CD?

12. You have done some research on a new project and found that it requires an initial outlay of $1,000 and it has a *NPV* of $10, given the opportunity cost of 10% for new projects. A coworker argues that it is not worth going through the trouble of adopting the project for only $10. How do you respond?

13. You have narrowed your housing search to two apartments to lease for your last 12 months of school. The Cloisters will lease an apartment for $500 per month, with two months' rent required as a deposit. The Woodward Street Apartments will lease an apartment for $510 per month, with a one-month deposit. In either case, payments are made at the beginning of each month, and the deposit is returned at the end of 12 months. The Cloisters will not give you any interest on your deposit; the Woodward Street Apartments will give you interest at 1% per month. You have determined that your opportunity cost is 1% per month. What should you do?

14. Your next-door neighbor, a security analyst, has confided in you that his research (which does not involve the CAPM) causes him to think that the Johnston Glass Co. will have a return of 18%, the Theil Flooring Corp. will have a return of 20%, and Kmenta Foods, Inc., will have a return of 22%. You have found that the betas of these three firms are 0.9, 1.15, and 1.4, respectively. If your neighbor is right, which stocks are underpriced (will have a higher return than the market estimates) under each of the following conditions?

(a) The T-bill rate is 11% and the expected market return is 19%.

(b) The T-bill rate is 10% and the expected market return is 18%.

(c) The T-bill rate is 14% and the expected market return is 19%.

(d) The T-bill rate is 6% and the expected market return is 19%.

15. You are considering the purchase of 100 shares of the Mead Beverage Co. The shares pay an annual dividend of $1 (which you expect to remain constant for the next several years) and have a beta of 1.25. Although you expect the T-bill rate to remain at 10% for the next three years, you believe that the market returns will be 16%, 14%, and 12%, respectively. If you think that the share price will be $25 immediately after paying the dividend three years from today, how much are you willing to pay for a share today?

16. Assume that the following securities are priced correctly according to the security market line:

Security 1: $E(R_1) = 0.11, \beta_1 = 0.7$

Security 2: $E(R_2) = 0.22, \beta_2 = 1.8$

(a) Derive the security market line.

(b) What is the expected return on a security that has a beta of 2.4?

7A
HOW DO WE KNOW THAT STOCKHOLDER WEALTH IS BEING CREATED?

Managers' decisions are assumed to be made in the interests of the residual equity claimants, and in an efficient market, the implications of these managerial decisions should be reflected rapidly in market prices. But how do we know that a managerial action has, in fact, increased shareholder wealth?

At first glance, it appears that if the company's stock price rises in response to a managerial decision, this decision was a value-increasing one for the equityholders. The market has viewed the decision as a good move. On the other hand, if the stock price falls, this reflects the market's disapproval of the managerial decision. Although this line of thinking appears to be reasonable, it is incorrect for three reasons.

First, the stockholders' wealth from investing in the stock is determined by both dividends and stock price performance. Thus, rather than focusing on stock prices alone, it is necessary to include dividend effects. For this reason it is important to examine returns rather than prices.

Second, the market price of a stock is affected not only by company-specific events but also by economywide factors. For example, if managers announced their decision on a day when the market as a whole was dropping, it is very likely that their company's stock price would also fall. Clearly, we should be careful in concluding that the manager's decision is therefore bad. It is thus important to examine the effect of the manager's decision on equity only after adjusting (controlling) for other influences. Economywide factors must be taken into account before passing judgment.

Third, we must be careful to isolate the event. We must ensure that the returns of the stock are not being simultaneously influenced by other company-specific information—say, an anticipated lawsuit. We must make sure that no other events are confounding our interpretation of the market's reaction to this announcement.

Thus, to determine whether stockholders' wealth has increased because of managerial actions, we must compare the returns on the stock before and after the announcement of the "event" (in this case, an announcement by managers), after making the appropriate adjustments. This is essentially what has come to be known as **event study methodology.**

What Is an Event Study?

An event study is a technique or tool that enables one to draw conclusions about whether an event has increased or decreased the wealth of the equityholders. An event can be any news that is made public and that can affect a firm. Examples of an event are the announcement of increased expenditures for research and development, news of a major corporate restructuring, the announcement of a change in marketing plans, and the institution of new compensation plans for employees.

Event studies have become popular today and are the basis for drawing several general conclusions about the creation of value. For example, it is now generally accepted that the market values cash flows and not profits, that new equity issues result in negative excess returns, that the announcement of bonus contracts for managers increases a firm's value, and that an increase in research and development (R&D) expenditures boosts a firm's value. All these general conclusions are based on the results of event studies. Although it is impossible to review the results of the large body of finance literature using event studies, in all references in this text to excess returns associated with managerial actions, these return measures were derived using some variant of the statistical methodology outlined here.

How Is an Event Study Conducted?

The goal of an event study is to estimate empirically the excess returns generated around an **event date,** the date on which information first becomes available to the market. Excess returns, in the context of event studies, are returns above or below the returns that would be expected to occur in normal circumstances if no new information reached the market. They are generally related to the performance of the market as a whole on the event date. These excess returns are often referred to as **abnormal returns.** In this text, we use both terms interchangeably. We use a simple example to explain the logic of these empirical tests.

When conducting an event study, it is dangerous to make inferences from an event regarding a specific company. Event studies generally cannot answer precisely whether a single firm's management actions will increase the firm's value because the statistical procedures are not strong enough to identify the confounding effects of other influences or to handle other estimation biases. Thus event studies are typically used to investigate the impact of an event over a large sample of firms. Instead of asking whether a single managerial action is a value-increasing activity, the research rephrases the question as follows: In general, does the empirical evidence indicate that acquisitions increase value? To answer this, the research requires data from a large sample of acquisitions.

For example, a researcher wishes to conduct an event study to evaluate the effects of a new product launch on the stock price of computer companies. The researcher identifies several companies that have introduced new products and determines the event date (usually the date of an announcement) from a public source (e.g., *The Wall Street Journal*). The researcher then denotes each firm as company *j*. She then calculates the excess return for each company *j* over a particular time interval *t*—say, a month. This time *t* excess return is also called the **residual return** or abnormal return and is denoted as e_{jt}. The residual return is calculated as the difference between firm *j*'s actual return over that month and the return that would have been expected under some market valuation theory;[15] that is,

$$e_{jt} = R_{jt} - \hat{R}_{jt} \tag{7A-1}$$

where R_{jt} is the actual return on firm *j*'s stock over month *t* and $\hat{R}_{jt}$ is the return on firm *j*'s stock that would have been expected for month *t* according to some theory. The usual practice is to estimate the residual e_{jt} over an interval surrounding the economic event of interest. Differences between actual and estimated returns are then averaged across all companies for each month *t*. This information is used to calculate the **average abnormal return** for month *t*, AR_t, as

$$AR_t = \frac{1}{N} \sum_{j=1}^{N} e_{jt} \tag{7A-2}$$

where *N* is the number of companies in the study. The **cumulative abnormal return** at time *T* (CAR_T) is then calculated as the sum of the average abnormal returns over all months from the start of the data:

$$CAR_T = \sum_{t=1}^{T} AR_t \tag{7A-3}$$

where *T* is the total number of months being summed. *CAR*s are thus a measure of excess returns over the period of the event study.

Illustration of an Event Study

Table 7A-1 gives the returns for the three companies (Apco, Inc., Borvil Corporation, and Cort, Inc.) chosen by the researcher and the market returns on those days. Assume that the beta for each stock is 1. The product announcement date is denoted as 0.

[15] An excess return, as should be clear by now, is the difference between the actual return on an investment and the opportunity cost of taking on that investment. Additional issues regarding the computation of excess returns are discussed in Stephen J. Brown and J. B. Warner, "Measuring Security Price Performance," *Journal of Financial Economics* 8 (1980): 205–258; and "Using Daily Stock Returns: The Case of Event Study," *Journal of Financial Economics* 14 (1985): 3–31.

■

TABLE 7A-1

Firm Returns Relative to Event Time[a]

Event Time (days)	Apco, Inc.	Market Return	Borvil Corp.	Market Return	Cort, Inc.	Market Return
−4	0.3	0.3	−0.2	−0.4	−0.1	0.5
−3	−0.2	−0.1	0.5	−0.1	0.1	−0.1
−2	0.4	0.2	0	0.3	−0.2	0.1
−1	1.2	−0.1	0.5	0.3	0.3	0.6
0	3.5	0.5	4.2	0.6	2.1	1
1	0.4	0.5	0.8	0.4	0.1	0.5
2	0.1	0.3	−0.6	−0.2	0.5	0.3
3	−0.4	−0.7	0.4	0.4	0.2	0.2
4	0.5	0.8	0	0	−0.3	−0.2

[a]Note that we have three different market returns per day because we are in "event time," not "calendar time."

The researcher develops a *CAR* figure for these companies in three steps:

Step 1: Compute the abnormal return for each company j on each day t as the difference between the realized return and the market return (since the beta of the companies is 1.00):

Abnormal return (e_{jt}) = realized return − market return

Step 2: Calculate the average abnormal return on any given day *across* companies:

Average abnormal return $(AR_{jt}) = \sum_{j=1}^{3} \frac{1}{3} e_{jt}$

Step 3: Compute the cumulative abnormal return for day T (CAR_T) as the sum of the average abnormal returns of the preceding days.

Table 7A-2 is obtained when the above steps are carried out. Figure 7A-1 is a graph of the these results.

TABLE 7A-2

Event Study Information: New Product Announcement

Event Time (days)	Apco's Returns	Market Return	Borvil's Returns	Market Return	Cort's Returns	Market Return	Average Abnormal Return	CAR_T
−4	0.3	0.3	−0.2	−0.4	−0.1	0.5	−0.133	−0.133
−3	−0.2	−0.1	0.5	−0.1	0.1	−0.1	0.233	0.1
−2	0.4	0.2	0	0.3	−0.2	0.1	−0.133	−0.033
−1	1.2	−0.1	0.5	0.3	0.3	0.6	0.4	0.367
0	3.5	0.5	4.2	0.6	2.1	1.0	2.567	2.933
1	0.4	0.5	0.8	0.4	0.1	0.5	−0.033	2.9
2	0.1	0.3	−0.6	−0.2	0.5	0.3	−0.133	2.767
3	−0.4	−0.7	0.4	0.4	0.2	0.2	0.1	2.867
4	0.5	0.8	0	0	−0.3	−0.2	−0.133	2.733

FIGURE 7A-1

Cumulative abnormal returns over the event date

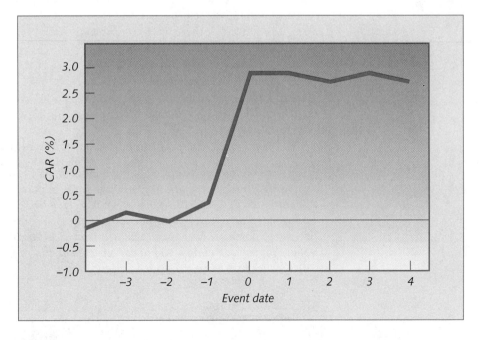

The results of the event study show that the announcement of a new product on the event day is quickly recognized by the market as good information that should increase the cash flows of the company. This information is very quickly translated into an increase in the stock prices of the firms studied that exceeds what would be expected under normal circumstances. If there were no abnormal change in the value of the firm (i.e., no excess returns) around the announcement, there should be no pattern observed in the residuals. They should fluctuate around 0 and, on average, equal 0. Then the *CAR* should also be around 0. A *CAR* that is significantly greater than 0, such as in this study, implies that excess returns were generated, whereas a negative *CAR* implies the opposite result. Thus positive abnormal returns indicate that, in general and across many firms, the evidence is consistent with the hypothesis that new products generate excess returns and hence value.

Theory in Application: The Information Effects of Marriott Corporation's Restructuring Plan

We close this chapter with an example that allows us to use a modified version of event study methodology to examine the efficient manner in which markets process information into changes in market prices. As already pointed out, event studies are properly conducted only across several companies and not just for one. Nevertheless, our discussion of Marriott has pedagogical value; it illustrates the market's reaction to news events.

On October 5, 1992, Marriott Corporation announced that it would divide its present operations into two separate companies: Marriott International, Inc. (which would include Mariott's lodging, food and facilities management, and senior living service operations), and Host Marriott (which would include Mariott's real estate properties and its airport and tollroad concessions).[16] Under the proposed restructuring, shareholders would be given a special dividend in the new company, Marriott International, Inc., in addition to each share they hold in Mariott Corporation. Marriott Corporation would then be named Host Marriott Corporation. The two companies would be run by separate management teams, and Marriott International would have very little debt.

This restructuring was conditional on several other outcomes: that Marriott's board of directors would agree to the special dividend, that a majority of shareholders would ratify the proposal, and that the IRS would provide a favorable tax ruling. Assuming that there were no problems, it was expected that the restructuring would be completed in mid-1993.

WHY THE RESTRUCTURING?

What was the motivation for the proposed restructuring? Presumably, to increase firm value and benefit the shareholders. But how did the company plan to do that?

J. W. Marriott, Jr., chairman and president of Marriott Corporation, said

> *The division into two different companies will enable us to advance our long-standing strategy of separating ownership of properties from management of operations. . . . Under this plan, we seek to enable shareholders to realize the inherent value of our management businesses more quickly while also giving them the potential over time to benefit from an upturn in real estate values. . . . Shareholders can choose to pursue investment goals in either or both companies rather than in one combined organization.*

---

[16] Marriott Corporation news release.

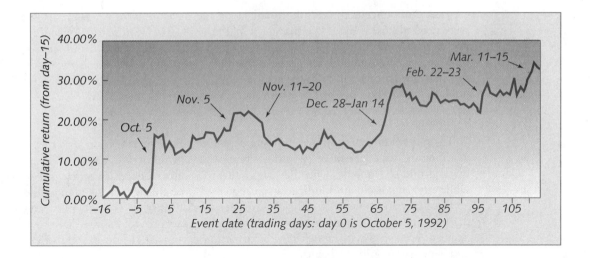

F I G U R E   7 A - 2
Marriott Corporation common stock excess returns and volume

ANALYSIS

It is not important for us to analyze here the merits of the restructuring plan or the motivations for doing so. The real question is: How did the market react to this information? And, how did the market react to subsequent developments at Marriott? The event study methodology provides a way to assess the market's interpretation of several developments (news).

Figure 7A-2 shows Marriott Corporation's common stock excess returns around the event date (October 5, 1992).[17] Remember that the cumulative abnormal returns (CARs) are plotted against the event time in an event study. As the figure shows, news of the proposed restructuring was greeted very favorably in the marketplace; the CAR jumped from about 2% to about 16%. Since excess returns represent additional wealth, the shareholders of Marriott became wealthier because of the announcement, even before the actual benefits of restructuring could accrue. In an efficient market, information is translated into an adjustment of the magnitude, timing, and risks of the future cash flows. The capitalized value of these projected cash flows increases the stock price and hence shareholders' wealth.

Many bondholders were unhappy with the restructuring because they believed it would adversely affect the value of their bonds. Several large bondholders opposed the plan and planned to block the restructuring. Not surprisingly, subsequent news announcements affected the CAR and shareholders wealth by altering the perceived probability that the plan would go through. This period of reorganization was viewed with great uncertainty prior to the change in trusteeship and, perhaps because of this, the CAR declined around November 5. On November 9, First National Bank resigned as trustee of Marriott's bonds, and on November 11, Bank One was named the new trustee.

The firm received some bad news on November 11, when Duff and Phelps downgraded Marriott's debt from BBB to B. Several bondholders brought suit against Marriott, and Merrill Lynch withdrew as advisor for the restructuring. All of this bad news resulted in the CAR declining over this period.

The period beginning December 29 saw some favorable developments. Marriott announced that it had been holding discussions with the bondholders in an effort to ease their concerns. This news was viewed as favorable, and the CAR in-

---

[17]The event study was conducted by Professor Robert Parrino.

creased. Announcements of additional favorable developments on February 22 were greeted positively in the market. On March 8, *The Wall Street Journal* reported that Marriott was offering to amend its restructuring proposal and, in fact, on March 11, the company announced that the whole transaction was being modified in accordance with an agreement between Marriott and several large bondholders. The market price of the stock increased and so did the *CAR*.

CONCLUSION

The market appears to have responded to news about Marriott's restructuring as though it was a positive (wealth-increasing) event. However, as details were worked out, the potential hurdles imposed by creditors depressed stock prices, while any new disclosures indicating an increased probability that the plan would go through were viewed favorably. The event study of Marriott not only illustrates the usefulness of the statistical methodology, but also provides some direct evidence of the speed with which new information is translated into market values and hence shareholders' wealth.

QUESTIONS

1. Why can't you just examine prices when evaluating the effect of managerial decisions on stockholder wealth?

2. What is an event study? How does it assist us in evaluating the impact of an event on stockholder wealth?

3. What is the cumulative average return?

4. What is an abnormal return?

PROBLEMS

1. The following figures present the results of a cumulative abnormal return (*CAR*) study conducted to test market efficiency when corporations announce an increase in dividend payout. Indicate in each case whether the results of the study support the weak form, the semistrong form, or the strong form of market efficiency. Why?

a) *CAR (%)*

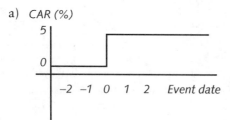

(b) *CAR (%)*

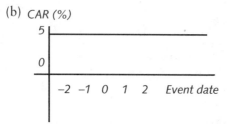

2. A *CAR* study conducted on a small set of firms that announced a *decline* in earnings came up with the following results. Do the results indicate irrational behavior on the part of investors? Why or why not?

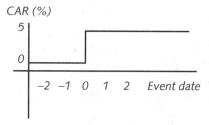

3. If the market is semistrong efficient, can abnormal returns be generated in these cases?

a) The CEO of a company gives an investor confidential information about a cure for cancer that the company has just developed. The news has not yet been announced to the public.

b) An investor buys the stock in an oil company just before it announces a major oil find in the Black Sea.

c) You buy stocks based on historical price data using sophisticated statistical methods.

How would the answers change if the market is strong form efficient?

4. You wish to conduct an event study of the effect of a new product launch on the stock price of computer companies. The following table gives the returns for three companies and the market returns on those days. The announcement date is denoted as 0. Construct a *CAR* figure for these companies assuming that the beta of each stock is 1. Why do you observe the pattern that you have constructed?

Event Time (days)	ABC's Returns	Market Return	PQR's Returns	Market Return	XYZ's Returns	Market Return
−4	0.3	0.3	−0.2	−0.4	−0.1	0.5
−3	−0.2	−0.1	0.5	−0.1	0.1	−0.1
−2	0.4	0.2	0.0	0.3	−0.2	0.1
−1	1.2	−0.1	0.5	0.3	0.3	0.6
0	3.5	0.5	4.2	0.6	2.1	1.0
1	0.4	0.5	0.8	0.4	0.1	0.5
2	0.1	0.3	−0.6	−0.2	0.5	0.3
3	−0.4	−0.7	0.4	0.4	0.2	0.2
4	0.5	0.8	0.0	0.0	−0.3	−0.2

5. The consulting firm of MacKineese and Co. recently conducted an event study to examine the implications for stock prices of firms withdrawing defective products from the market. The results of their study are depicted in the accompanying figure. Are the results consistent with market efficiency?

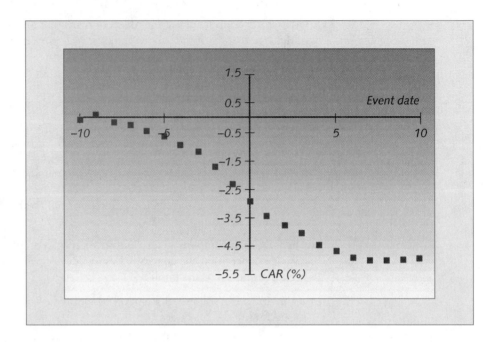

SUGGESTED
ADDITIONAL
READINGS

DeBondt, W., and R. Thaler. "Further Evidence on Investor Overreaction and Stock Market Seasonability." *Journal of Finance* 42 (1987): 557–581.

Fama, Eugene F. "The Behavior of Stock Market Prices." *Journal of Business* 38 (1965): 34–105.

Fama, Eugene F. "Efficient Capital Markets: A Review of Theory and Empirical Work." *Journal of Finance*, May 1970, pp. 383–417.

Fama, Eugene F. "Efficient Capital Markets II." *Journal of Finance* 46 (1991): 1575–1618.

Fama, Eugene F., and K. French. "Dividend Yields and Expected Stock Returns." *Journal of Financial Economics* 22 (1988): 3–25.

Fama, Eugene F., and K. French. "Permanent and Temporary Components of Stock Prices." *Journal of Political Economy* 96 (1988): 246–273.

French, K., W. Schwert, and R. Stambaugh. "Expected Stock Returns and Volatility." *Journal of Financial Economics* 19 (1987): 3–29.

Jensen, Michael. "Some Anomalous Evidence Regarding Market Efficiency." *Journal of Financial Economics* 6 (1978): 95–101.

Miller, Merton H. *Financial Innovations and Market Volatility.* Cambridge, MA: Blackwell Publishers, 1993.

Porterba, J., and L. Summers. "Mean Reversion in Stock Prices: Evidence and Implications." *Journal of Financial Economics* 22 (1988): 27–60.

Shleifer, Andrei, and Lawrence Summers. "The Noise Trader Approach to Finance." *Journal of Economic Perspectives* 4 (Spring 1990): 19–33.

PART THREE THE FIRM'S OPERATING DECISIONS

EIGHT THE BASICS OF CAPITAL BUDGETING

No gain is possible without attendant outlay, but there will be no profit if the outlay exceeds the receipts.

—Plautus, ca. 218 B.C.

Our first financial objective is to undertake projects which deliver discounted cash flows that exceed the cash required to finance the endeavor.

—William Smithburg, CEO Quaker Oats, Enterprise, April 1993

*E*ach year, American businesses invest hundreds of billions of dollars in new fixed assets. Unlike current assets, which have a short life, fixed assets require substantial cash outlays that are expected to result in benefits (cash flows) to the firm over several years. These cash outlays, called **capital expenditures**, are usually incurred to obtain **capital assets**, which the company uses in the actual production of goods and services. Capital assets can include, for example, plant facilities, computers, pollution-control devices, cars, trucks, storage facilities, and even other companies. In most cases, the volume of dollars needed to acquire these capital assets is very large, and firms must plan carefully before they commit scarce resources to these assets. The plans for capital expenditures are summarized in a **capital budget**, and the process of determining exactly which assets to invest in and how much to invest is called **capital budgeting**.

The capital budgeting decision is a complex process that includes several activities: the search for new profitable investments, marketing and production analyses to determine economic attractiveness, careful cash flow estimation, preparation of cash budgets, evaluation of proposals, and the control and monitoring of past projects. Detailed analysis is necessary to ensure that a capital investment does in fact increase wealth. Economic considerations of capital investments are the major subject of this chapter and are examined by the following questions:

- What are the various phases of the capital budgeting process?

- What are the relevant cash flows for capital budgeting?

- How do we determine whether a project increases wealth?

- Why do positive-*NPV* projects exist?

- What are operating and investment flexibilities and how do they affect a project's *NPV*?

AN OVERVIEW OF THE CAPITAL BUDGETING PROCESS

*T*he capital budgeting process involves several activities that may be conveniently grouped into six phases. In some companies the various activities are done on a companywide basis by a centralized "planning group" that conducts the capital budgeting analysis. In other firms they are done at a divisional level. In most cases, however, the capital budgeting process involves the joint efforts of various individuals at different levels in the company.

Phase 1: Identifying Long-Term Goals

The firm's ultimate objective is to maximize its stock price and, consequently, the shareholders' wealth. To accomplish this goal, firms make decisions about two types of investment: strategic investment and tactical investment.

The firm's managers must evaluate **strategic investment proposals**, which involve investments that would change the very character of the firm. Some examples of strategic investment proposals are entering a new product market, acquiring or merging with another company, establishing a major joint venture, and expanding overseas. These potential investments involve many diverse factors that often cannot be easily quantified. Managers who face such decisions are forced to think qualitatively in terms of the long-run market position of the firm. Although we obviously cannot examine all factors involved in strategic business decision making, there are two elements of the environment that we should discuss here.

First, strategic decisions must take international markets into consideration. Chapter 1 explained how firms operating internationally are able to seek out and exploit market imperfections. Increasingly, senior managers realize that they cannot ignore either foreign markets for their goods or foreign sources of production. Even smaller domestic firms are encountering foreign competition within their supposedly safe domestic markets. When major investment decisions are made in this environment, managers must consider not only business risk but also political risk and exchange rate risk. These risks are not so easily quantifiable as one might imagine and, as we see in Chapter 9, their existence modifies the basic approach taken in most traditional domestic capital budgeting situations.

Second, many proposals cannot be completely evaluated in terms of only their immediate impact on cash flows and stock price. For example, a firm's decision to spend millions of dollars on environmental improvement may lower its cash flows in the short run but be consistent with another of the company's long-term goals— acting responsibly toward other members of society. Alcoa's commitment to land restoration and beautification in areas close to its strip-mining operations is an example of this type of consideration. Thus intangible benefits that are consistent with a firm's long-term goals should be identified with each proposal, and their benefits and costs should be considered as part of the economic analysis.

Strategic considerations may be related to timing or marketing. Some *timing-related* decisions were Apple Computer's plan to develop the Macintosh computer after evaluating IBM's competing product, Vickers and General Electric's response to the British firm EMI's development of CatScan devices, and Matsushita's VHS format for videocassettes that pushed Sony's Betamax out of its leadership position. A *marketing-related* decision was Polaroid's strategy of selling cameras at giveaway prices while expecting to benefit from the sale of expensive film.

The second type of decision faced by managers concerns **tactical investment proposals**. These involve investments that would affect the firm's cash flows and economic wealth, but not necessarily change the character of the firm. Examples of tactical investments are replacing a fleet of trucks, establishing a new facility in an existing market to manufacture products that are related to the current product line, and computerizing records. These investments concern variables that are more familiar to managers and do not contain as much uncertainty concerning the firm's future cash flows as do strategic investments.

Certainly, there is no clearly defined line dividing these two types of investments. For example, international and timing considerations play a role in tactical investment decisions. And both strategic and tactical investments may involve additional considerations of, for example, proposal flexibility (perhaps to change a manufacturing process), legal ramifications (say, product liability), the ability to abandon the project later, personnel matters (the structure and organization of its labor force), and implications for the firm's other proposals. Although, *in theory,* all of these considerations can be factored into management's assessments of future cash flows, the point is that often it is very difficult to make even coarse judgments about the implications of these factors. In developing the firm's long-term goals, managers operate in an extremely ambiguous and undefined environment, and strategic decisions must often be made with incomplete information.

Our classification of strategic and tactical proposals is thus not mutually exclusive but is useful in defining the roles of quantitative versus qualitative analyses in specific capital budgeting decisions. We stress, however, that both strategic and tactical investments must further the firm's overall goal of maximizing stockholder wealth.

Once managers have determined that the proposal being considered fits with their overall goals, they collect as much information about the proposal as is economically feasible and then proceed to the screening phase, in which they determine the specific impact of the proposal on the firm.

Phase 2: Screening   With strategic goals set, the company must identify and classify specific investment proposals that will attain those goals. In the screening phase, managers identify how a capital budgeting proposal will affect the firm. Proposals can originate in a variety of ways.

One source of capital budgeting proposals is changes in the firm's environment that force the company to take action. Competitors, consumers, or governments may change the firm's product or market situation, and the firm must respond with proposals to meet this challenge.

Firms may also search out opportunities on their own initiative. Large companies have entire "project analysis divisions" that actively search for new ideas, projects, and ventures. Divisional managers and product managers usually take their proposals to a "planning committee" or even to the board of directors. Managers use the input from a variety of sources: engineers, market analysts, sales personnel, and so on. Virtually every employee of the company is a potential source of ideas, and many companies encourage their employees to develop new "concepts" for evaluation by the "investment division."

Whatever the origination of the proposal, management must first qualitatively evaluate its ability to exploit opportunities or meet challenges and gauge, in very crude terms, the potential impact of the investment on the firm's revenues and costs. If a proposal passes this initial screening, it is subjected to more detailed analysis. In this phase it is useful to categorize potential proposals as to whether they reduce the firm's costs or expand its operations. The value of the screening phase is that it forces managers to identify the source of the benefits from the investment proposal so that the project can then be evaluated in a disciplined and systematic way.

A **cost-reduction proposal** is one whose primary benefit is that it will lower the firm's operating costs. For instance, a firm may consider replacing an inefficient old lathe with a newer version that reduces waste and consumes less energy.

Proposals to expand a firm's operations generally take one of two forms. A **vertical revenue expansion proposal** is one that will increase the company's revenues if its output is increased. For example, a company that produces 5,000 barrels of formaldehyde contemplates doubling its output to 10,000 barrels. The potential for increased economies of scale is very important, especially for firms that compete on a multinational scale through more cost-effective production techniques. A **horizontal revenue expansion proposal** involves investments that are unrelated to the company's existing activities. For example, a small printing company that considers investing in a restaurant is considering a horizontal expansion that should have no effect on its printing activities.

By classifying proposals into these categories management can address and answer key questions such as: Can the existing plant be used to achieve the new production levels? Does management have the knowledge and skill to take on this new investment? Does the new proposal warrant the recruitment of new technical personnel? Having answers to these questions helps the firm screen out proposals that require a drastic change in personnel or subject the firm to new risks that management finds unacceptable. When the screening process has eliminated certain proposals based on these qualitative considerations, the capital budgeting process enters the third phase.

Phase 3: Evaluation   In the evaluation phase, an economic analysis is conducted using discounted cash flow analysis to determine whether the proposal is economically profitable. This phase consists of three distinct activities: estimating the cash flows from the various proposals, identifying projects, and applying objective criteria before accepting or rejecting the idea. To understand these activities, we must first distinguish between *proposals* and *projects*.

Any action under consideration is a **proposal**. For example, a plan to introduce a new product line, discussions about increasing the advertising budget, the idea of buying a vineyard, and a plan to cease credit sales are all capital budgeting proposals. Of the many proposals a firm may consider, several may be related to one another in terms of cash flows.

If the acceptance of a particular proposal will alter the cash flows of another proposal (or the firm's cash flows from existing activities), these proposals are said to exhibit **economic dependence**. All proposals whose cash flows are economically dependent on one another must be evaluated together as a project. A **project** is either a single proposal or a collection of dependent proposals that is economically independent of all other proposals. Appendix 8A explains in detail the process of grouping proposals into projects. For now, however, we attempt only to explain the nature of the dependencies among the cash flows of proposals.

COMPLEMENTARY PROPOSALS

Two proposals are complementary if the cash flows from adopting them together exceeds the sum of the cash flows that would be generated from them individually. For example, a soft drink manufacturer is evaluating the development of a line of snack foods. The sale of snack foods is expected to increase the sale of soft drinks. Therefore the cash flows evaluated should include not only those connected with the snack foods, but also the cash flows from the anticipated increase in soft drink sales. If the company can undertake a proposal only if another proposal is undertaken, the two proposals are called *purely* complementary proposals. This is an extreme form of complementarity.

SUBSTITUTE PROPOSALS

If the acceptance of one proposal reduces the cash flows of another proposal, these proposals are substitutes. For instance, Coors Brewing Co. decided to exploit the health-conscious attitudes of the 1980s by introducing Coors Light. However, they found that by 1987 their sales of Coors Light had severely affected their sales of Coors regular. In that year, they sold 9.7 million barrels of Coors Light and only 7.3 million barrels of Coors regular, representing an increase in Coors Light sales of 9.7% and a decrease in Coors regular of 7.6%. Thus Coors Light was a substitute for Coors regular. The managers of Coors should have considered this impact when they decided to make a light beer under the Coors name.[1]

---

[1] See Ronald Alsop, "Marketing," *The Wall Street Journal*, February 9, 1988, p. 41.

MUTUALLY EXCLUSIVE PROPOSALS

Proposals are mutually exclusive if the acceptance of one implies the rejection of another. As an example, our soft drink manufacturer is considering replacing an old warehouse. They can either build a new warehouse or lease warehouse space in a major business park. These two ways of satisfying their need for space are considered mutually exclusive.

INDEPENDENT PROPOSALS

If the acceptance of one proposal has no effect whatsoever on the cash flows of another proposal, they are independent proposals. In this situation, cash flows are additive because there is neither a gain nor a loss in cash flows from accepting both proposals. For our soft drink manufacturer, expanding into an express delivery system would have no effect on its soft drink sales.

Only proposals that are economically independent (i.e., projects) can be evaluated separately. Although identifying economic dependencies can be difficult, a proper economic evaluation of a particular proposal must consider the side effects of the proposal on all other proposals of the firm.

Once projects have been identified, economic capital budgeting criteria are applied to analyze the cash flow from each project, and the project is determined to be either acceptable or unacceptable. These quantitative procedures are the main focus of the remainder of this chapter.

Phase 4: Implementation

In the implementation phase, the company makes the required arrangements to take on the new projects. In particular, the firm must ensure that the capital required to start the projects is readily available. This initial start-up capital is often called *capital outlay*. Assuming that the firm can raise the capital outlay without serious problems, the implementation phase is fairly straightforward. The firm can proceed with the necessary changes to get the project going: training personnel, altering floor design configuration, designing new procedure manuals, and so on.

Phase 5: Control

Once the project has been implemented, the firm must constantly monitor the costs and revenues provided by the project and assess the extent to which the actual figures deviate from the forecasted values used in making the capital budgeting decision. There are advantages in doing this. For one thing, any unnecessary inefficiencies can easily be corrected. If cash flow figures deviate greatly from planned (projected) values, this could indicate a problem. The forecast may be bad, and the firm can learn from this experience and correct for potential forecast errors in future capital budgeting decisions. On the other hand, the forecast may have been good, but unpredictable events (war, tax-law changes, etc.) may have changed the situation, and the firm may have no way of controlling the new cash flows. In any event, by observing the deviation between planned cash flows and actual cash flows, the firm can gain valuable experience and can benefit in future capital investment analyses. If the deviations are too large, the firm may even decide to abandon the project.

Phase 6: Project Audit

The audit phase, often called the *postcompletion audit,* is one stage of capital budgeting that is often ignored. Strictly speaking, the post-audit deals with only completed projects. When a project is completed, the extent of success or failure should be studied carefully, and firms must attempt to identify the reasons for successes or failures. The audit phase, like the control phase, provides valuable information to the firm. Consistent errors can be rectified, overlooked areas of concern

■

TABLE 8-1

Relative Importance of Capital Expenditure Activities

Capital Expenditure Activity	Weighted Average of Time Spent on Activity
Analyzing and selecting projects (screening phase)	24.4%
Implementing projects (implementation and control phases)	22.4
Capital expenditure planning (identifying long-term goals)	20.3
Defining and estimating project cash flows (evaluation phase)	19.3
Project follow-up and review (audit phase)	13.6
	100.0%

SOURCE: Adapted from Lawrence J. Gitman and Charles E. Maxwell, "Financial Activities of Major U.S. Firms: Survey and Analysis of Fortune's 1000," *Financial Management,* Winter 1985, pp. 57–65.

can be identified, and personnel and administrative changes may be required to increase the efficacy of future project performance.

Table 8-1 summarizes the results of a survey concerning the relative importance of the various phases of capital budgeting. The importance of each activity is determined by the amount of time that managers spend on it. As the table shows, analyzing and selecting projects consume the largest amount of time, whereas project follow-up and review (the audit phase) consume the least.

8-2

CASH FLOWS RELEVANT TO CAPITAL BUDGETING

The overall attractiveness of an investment opportunity depends on the cash flows generated and on opportunity costs. In this section we focus only on analyzing the benefits. We assume the appropriate discount rate. Determining the appropriate opportunity cost or discount rate for an investment was covered in Chapter 7.

Not all cash flows are relevant to capital budgeting. First, generally **capital budgeting analysis** requires that investment and financing decisions be separated.[2] That is, management should evaluate a project without explicitly recognizing the manner in which the capital to finance the project is being raised. This implies, among other things, that the interest payments on debt should not be included in the computation of a project's cash flows. The cost of debt enters indirectly via the required rate of return (RRR) used to discount these cash flows.

Second, capital budgeting does not focus on all of the firm's operating cash flows, but only on the **incremental cash flows after taxes,** denoted as $\Delta CFATs$, which are those periodic cash outflows and inflows that occur if and only if an investment project is accepted. This concept is extremely important, so a detailed examination is warranted.

Incremental Cash Flows After Taxes

INCREMENTAL

Only those cash flows that affect a firm's existing total cash flows should be considered; only increments to existing revenues, expenses, and taxes caused by a project's acceptance are relevant. All other cash flows are irrelevant for decision-making purposes. Consider a proposal by our soft drink firm to build a new warehouse. All construction expenditures qualify as incremental because these cash outflows would not occur unless the warehouse was built. On the other hand, the

---

[2] The logic for this approach follows from the theory developed in Chapter 7. The value of an asset is equivalent to the cash flows generated by the asset discounted at the appropriate *RRR*. The cash flows generated by an asset are the operating cash flows, which do not depend on the amount of debt or interest payments being made by the company. This separation between investment and financing, which is implied by the Modigliani–Miller results discussed in Chapter 15, may break down under certain conditions (e.g., subsidized financing), which are examined in Chapter 10.

SUNK COSTS ARE IRRELEVANT

In making economically justifiable decisions, managers must focus only on incremental net cash flows: inflows and outflows that will exist only if the decision is adopted. All other costs are irrelevant.

A common mistake is to include historical or sunk costs in the analysis. Consider an example: A company spends $500,000 on research on two drugs, X and Y. Only Y is eventually approved for sale in the United States by the Food and Drug Administration (FDA). Before

Y is produced, the company wants to conduct a capital budgeting analysis of Y. How should the $500,000 already spent be factored into the capital budgeting analysis? Should it be included in the initial cash flows, or should it be spread out evenly over the assumed life of the project?

The answer is neither. The $500,000 is irrelevant to the analysis because it is a sunk cost; that is, it has already been spent and so is not incremental to project Y. Sensible economic decisions are not made by looking at the

past; only future cash flows are relevant.

The implication of sunk costs for capital budgeting decisions is often misunderstood. If the money has already been spent, it cannot be affected by the decision about the project. Managers should devote efforts to examining only those cash flows that will be affected by their decision. Determining the best course of action is based only on the incremental cash flows. The old saying "It's no use crying over spilled milk" is most appropriate to capital budgeting.

allocation of certain overhead expenses to the project, such as corporate staff salaries, is not incremental because these outlays would be incurred even if the warehouse was not built. However, occasionally overhead expenses such as indirect labor and energy costs may increase because a project is accepted. In those cases it is appropriate to include such expenses in the project's cash flow estimates.

A common error in the determination of incremental cash flows is to include **sunk costs**. Although this is now a common buzzword in business, its specific meaning is sometimes not fully appreciated. The accompanying highlight clarifies the use of sunk costs in capital budgeting problems.

CASH FLOWS

Once again, the relevant measure of dollar benefits is cash flow rather than accounting income and expenses. As noted earlier, cash flows are generally not the same as income or profits. Accountants deduct "current expenses" in order to calculate profits. But accrual accounting recognizes these expenses when they are incurred, not when they are paid. Therefore an increase in after-tax expenses does not necessarily translate into a cash outflow. Moreover, for accounting purposes, the initial cost of an asset is allocated or depreciated as a noncash capital expense over its useful life. This means that different sets of income figures for the same investment can be derived simply by changing depreciation methods. An accounting approach also ignores the fact that cash is needed initially to purchase the asset and distorts the actual cash outflows in future periods. For example, a cash flow analysis takes into account in the first year an initial $100,000 outlay for a bulldozer. An accountant, on the other hand, spreads the cost over the machine's depreciable life (e.g., deducts an annual depreciation expense of $20,000 for five years). These two approaches clearly produce different results and are equivalent only if the *RRR* is 0—a most unlikely situation.

AFTER TAXES

All cash flows must be estimated consistently on an after-tax basis for two reasons. First, the initial cash flows are normally investment outlays of after-tax dollars. Second, most investments affect a firm's tax payments. It is easier, therefore, to measure cash flows after accounting for taxes. Consider the case of a new project that will generate additional revenues and expenses. These incremental cash flows are first determined without any tax considerations. Then taxes are estimated and deducted to produce the cash flow after taxes.

A SPECIAL NOTE ON TAX LAWS AND DEPRECIATION RULES Tax laws can be incredibly complex as they apply to capital investment decisions, and as we showed in Chapter 3, they are subject to legislative changes from year to year. Moreover, these laws apply unevenly across different industries. For example, oil and gas companies are allowed depletion allowances, whereas most other industries are unable to take advantage of this preferential treatment. Such diversity forces us to treat tax effects very generally. In this book we adopt a simplified tax structure. The only detailed tax analysis in this chapter is in regard to the replacement of an old asset with a new asset.

Depreciation rules also vary with the asset in question. In this chapter we primarily consider straight-line depreciation to simplify the exposition. Occasionally other methods of depreciation are used in the problems at the end of the chapter; however, these methods are clearly specified. The depreciation per year is calculated as the asset's purchase price less salvage value divided by the useful life of the asset.

It is important to remember that the exact details of the tax code are not the subject of study here. What we are attempting to understand is the general approach to making capital budgeting decisions. The ideas developed in this chapter hold irrespective of the tax laws in effect. The various aspects of the present (or the future) tax code can easily be incorporated into the capital budgeting analysis with appropriate adjustments to the relevant cash flows.

Classification of Cash Flows After Taxes

In an analysis of cash flows, there can be many different cash flows, and it is easy to overlook some of them. A useful framework for systematically estimating all cash flows is to break up the periodic—say, annual—stream of cash expenses and benefits into three categories:

1. Initial *CFAT*

2. Operating *CFAT*

3. Terminal *CFAT*

Each category has its own type of cash flows, which we examine in greater detail.

INITIAL CASH FLOWS

Initial investments are the expenditures to acquire property, plant, and equipment when a project begins. Within this category, cash flows can conveniently be divided into the following categories:

Direct cash flows	*Indirect cash flows*
Capital expenditures	After-tax proceeds of old assets sold
Operating expenditures	Change in net working capital

A particular investment proposal may include only a few or all of these types of cash flows. A proposal to replace an existing manual spot welder with a computer-driven welder could involve all of these cash flows. A new welder could even affect net working capital if it produced fewer defects because then the number of parts in inventory might be reduced. On the other hand, a decision to buy a fleet of delivery trucks rather than use a third-party trucking service might include only direct cash flow considerations.

Whereas cash flows associated with the initial investment usually occur at the beginning of a project's life, certain nonrecurring outflows may not occur until after the first year. If this is the case, these outflows are simply lumped together with the other annual cash flows in the year they occur.

DIRECT CASH FLOWS For accounting purposes, all cash expenditures for the acquisition of an asset must be classified as either capital or operating expenditures. Most initial outlays involve capital expenditures on fixed assets such as property, plant, and equipment. Although we used this term earlier, it is useful to contrast it more completely with operating expenditures.

Capital expenditures are those cash outflows that are expected to produce future benefits that extend beyond one year. They therefore are treated as an asset on the balance sheet. Other expenditures besides purchase price may also be incurred to make an asset operational. Cash expended on freight, preparation or installation costs, removal of old assets, or building modifications is properly treated as part of the asset's cost. Together, these outlays determine the *gross* investment for depreciation purposes. (If land is purchased, its cost is included as an initial cash outflow but is not included in the project's depreciation base.)

In contrast, **operating expenditures** are those cash outlays that provide no benefits beyond those of the current period. They are expensed (charged against current revenues) rather than treated as an asset on the balance sheet. Hence they do not become a part of an investment's depreciation base. An example is the training costs required to acquaint employees with the new computerized welder's operations. Moreover, because these outlays are tax deductible, the "true" expenditure is less because the firm, in effect, receives a "rebate" from the government. In general, the after-tax or effective cost of a tax-deductible item is the before-tax cost multiplied by $(1 - T)$, where T is the firm's tax rate:

$$\text{After-tax cost} = (\text{before-tax cost}) \times (1 - \text{tax rate}) \tag{8-1}$$

If, for example, the company that purchases the welder is in the 15% tax bracket and the personnel training costs are $5,000, the net cost or the after-tax cost is $5,000 \times (1 - 0.15) = \$5,000 \times 0.85 = \$4,250$. In effect, the government picks up the other $750 in training costs.

INDIRECT CASH FLOWS If an older asset is sold, to be replaced by a new asset, tax considerations become important. Anytime an asset is sold, depending on whether there is an accounting profit or loss, the company may have to pay taxes or may be entitled to a tax credit. These tax considerations affect the cash flows from the project and must be recognized in any capital budgeting decision. Two situations may arise, depending on the relationship of the market value (MV) of the asset to its book value (BV):

Case 1: $MV < BV$. Market value (MV) is less than book value (BV)—ordinary tax loss treatment

Case 2: $MV > BV$. Market value is greater than book value—ordinary income tax treatment

To illustrate each case, assume that the asset's book value is as follows:

Original cost (OC)	$50,000
Less: Accumulated depreciation	30,000
Book value (BV)	$20,000

In Case 1, if the old asset is sold for $5,000 (MV), an ordinary profit of $5,000 − $20,000 = −$15,000 is produced. This loss represents a before-tax deduction for the asset's undepreciated cost not taken yet, which in turn helps reduce current taxes. Note that the recovered depreciation is a cash flow. It reduces taxable income and hence reduces the cash outflow for taxes paid. The tax-adjusted loss is therefore treated as if it were a cash inflow. The net effect when the firm's ordinary tax rate $T = 15\%$ is a CFAT given by

$$
\begin{aligned}
CFAT &= \text{market value of asset sold} - \text{tax liability} \\
&= MV - (MV - BV)(T) \\
&= \$5,000 - (\$5,000 - \$20,000)(0.15) \\
&= \$7,250
\end{aligned}
$$

We assume that taxes are paid as the firm becomes liable for them. If taxes are deferred, minor adjustments are needed for the CFAT calculations.

In Case 2, if the old asset is sold for $35,000 (MV), the difference between its sales proceeds and the book value is taxed at the firm's ordinary income tax rate because it represents a recapture of depreciation. The logic is that too much depreciation was taken in prior years. This results in an understatement of both taxable income and income taxes. This recapture of overdepreciation causes an increase in current taxes (cash outflow). The net effect in this case becomes:

$$
\begin{aligned}
CFAT &= \text{market value of asset sold} - \text{tax liability} \\
&= MV - (MV - BV)(T) \\
&= \$35,000 - (\$35,000 - \$20,000)(0.15) \\
&= \$32,750
\end{aligned}
$$

Another indirect cash flow that may affect an investment proposal is a change in net working capital. If a project increases a firm's revenues, for example, there is an increased need for funds to support the higher level of operations. The appropriate estimate of these additional funds should be the increase in net working capital, which is the difference between current assets and current liabilities. For example, consider a firm that is planning a new product line. It has to procure inventories (a current asset) for $35,000. If the firm has to pay for this in cash, it requires $35,000 in extra cash. Or the firm could finance these inventories through a $35,000 increase in accounts payable (a current liability) by buying on credit. This requires no cash. Thus the relevant measure of funds is not cash but, instead, net working capital. Although changes in net working capital occur throughout the life of the project, for simplicity, this book treats a project's required increase in net working capital as having occurred when the project was adopted. Thus the increased net working capital is treated as one initial cash outflow that is not affected until the end of the investment, when it is recovered.

OPERATING CASH FLOWS

In contrast with the initial investment cash flows, the operating cash flows normally represent the net benefits (incremental cash flows after taxes) received over a project's economic life. These CFATs are calculated easily after the estimates of future sales, fixed and variable costs, and depreciation have been determined. From Chapter 2 we know that the firm's cash flow is net income (NI) plus depreciation (D). On the income statement, taxable income is sales revenues (S) less costs (C) less depreciation (D). Net income is what remains after taxes have been paid. Therefore,

$$CFAT = (S - C - D)(1 - T) + D \tag{8-2}$$

or, in terms of incremental (Δ) cash flows,

$$\Delta CFAT = (\Delta S - \Delta C - \Delta D)(1 - T) + \Delta D \tag{8-3}$$

where

ΔS is incremental sales

ΔC is incremental costs

ΔD is incremental depreciation

For example, if the adoption of a project will increase a firm's revenues from $50,000 per year to $54,000 per year, ΔS = $4,000 per year. If the adoption of new manufacturing techniques will lower the operating expenses from $4,000 per year to $3,000 per year, the incremental expenditures ΔC = $-$1,000. Note the negative sign in this case because the incremental expenses are really savings. To avoid confusion it is useful to remember that all incremental values are "new value" minus "old value." Suppose also that the new project will lower the company's total depreciation from $5,000 per year to $4,500 per year. Then ΔD is the new depreciation minus the old depreciation, or $-$500 per year. For this example, if we assume that the firm is in the 15% tax bracket, the incremental cash flows after taxes are:

$$\begin{aligned}
\Delta CFAT &= (\Delta S - \Delta C - \Delta D)(1 - T) + \Delta D \\
&= [\$4,000 - (-\$1,000) - (-\$500)](1 - 0.15) + (-\$500) \\
&= \$4,175
\end{aligned}$$

Equation (8-3) is extremely convenient for calculating intermediate cash flows. Typically, the $\Delta CFAT$s are calculated for every month for project analysis. In the equation for $\Delta CFAT$, notice that if the incremental sales, costs, and depreciation are constant for every month, then the project's $\Delta CFAT$s are an annuity. If this condition is not satisfied, the $\Delta CFAT$ for each month must be calculated separately, thereby increasing the computational complexity of the analysis.

To simplify our introduction to capital budgeting analysis, the cash flows in this chapter are in U.S. dollars. Once the reader understands the basics of capital budgeting, we expand our discussion to include cash flows in other currencies and to making investments in foreign countries. The following highlight discusses one way in which operating cash flows can be affected by international considerations.

TERMINAL CASH FLOWS

The cash flows that are expected to occur at the time a project's useful life ends are the terminal cash flows. Two types of terminal cash inflows influence the capital budgeting decision: (1) salvage value of the asset(s) and (2) recovery of net working capital.

SALVAGE VALUE Often a project's fixed assets have some resale value even when their usefulness has ended (i.e., someone else may be able to use them). For instance, a firm's existing computer may be too small for its expanding operations.

INCOME SHIFTING: THE PROBLEM OF TRANSFER PRICING

An Associated Press news article contained the following quote: "In our society, a teacher or factory worker can pay more in federal income tax than a major multinational corporation with billions in annual U.S. sales," said Rep. J. J. Pickle, D-Texas, chairman of the subcommittee. "This is what is happening today, and it is terribly unfair and wrong." *

What Congressman Pickle was concerned about is **transfer pricing,** a tool used by multinational firms to increase cash flows. Transfer prices affect the firm's costs and thus its taxable profit and tax payments.

Prices between economically independent firms are generally set "at arm's length." The buyer seeks the lowest price and the seller the highest price, with the resulting price agreed to being a fair market value for the good involved. However, **transfer prices,** which are the prices charged by one affiliate of a multinational firm to another affiliate, can be set by the multinational to shift profits from one affiliate to another.

As an example, consider Texworld Manufacturing, Inc. TM manufactures and sells ventilation systems using two affiliates. TM-US assembles and markets the systems, while TM-Korea manufactures electric motors for the systems and then sells these motors to TM-US. Currently, TM-Korea manufactures and sells 10,000 electric motors annually at a price of $180 per motor. TM-US faces a U.S. tax rate of 35%, whereas TM-Korea enjoys a low 15% tax rate because its products are exported. Simplified statements for the affiliates and their parent are given below. In examining these figures, remember that the costs of TM-US are in turn the revenues for TM-Korea, and that the tax rates faced by each subsidiary differ.

	TM-US	+	TM-Korea	=	TM, Inc.
Revenues	$8,000,000		$1,800,000		$9,800,000
Costs	1,800,000		600,000		2,400,000
NOI	$6,200,000		$1,200,000		$7,400,000
Taxes	2,170,000		180,000		2,350,000
NI	$4,030,000		$1,020,000		$5,050,000

The managers of TM, Inc., plan to increase their after-tax revenues worldwide by increasing the transfer price for the motors from $180 to $220. This change would produce the result at the right:

	TM-US	+	TM-Korea	=	TM, Inc.
Revenues	$8,000,000		$2,200,000		$10,200,000
Costs	2,200,000		600,000		2,800,000
NOI	$5,800,000		$1,600,000		$7,400,000
Taxes	2,030,000		240,000		2,270,000
NI	$3,770,000		$1,360,000		$5,130,000

Changing the transfer price would not affect TM, Inc.'s overall NOI. However, the higher transfer price would lower revenues in the United States, with its higher tax rate, and increase revenues in Korea, with its lower tax rate. The net result would be a decrease in overall tax payments and thus an increase in NI of:

New NI − old NI = change in NI
$5,130,000 − $5,050,000
         = $80,000

Tax considerations play a major role in setting transfer prices. If the primary motive of TM, Inc., in changing the transfer price is to avoid U.S. taxes, the IRS may challenge the company and attempt to collect the taxes due. Their attempt might not be successful, however. In a recent study the General Accounting Office found that, for the period 1987–89, the IRS internal appeals process won on 26.6% of the $757 million it felt foreign corporations owed in taxes.[†]

There are many issues involved in setting transfer prices and many reasons in addition to taxes why a certain price might be set. In all cases, though, the multinational firm seeks to set the price for the benefit of the multinational as a whole.

* The Daily Texan, *April 10, 1992, p. 4.*
[†] The Wall Street Journal, *November 11, 1992, p. A16.*

Even though the computer is of little value to this firm, another company may find it perfectly suitable for its needs. If the computer is sold, a terminal cash inflow is generated. Even if the computer is technologically obsolete, it may still have some scrap value. To simplify the analysis of many of the problems in this text, we usually assume that the depreciated or book value of an asset is the best estimate of its salvage value.

For example, if an asset is purchased for $50,000 and is expected to have a salvage value of $10,000 at the end of five years, the straight-line depreciation per year is ($50,000 − $10,000)/5 = $8,000 per year. In five years, the asset's book value will be $10,000, which is the purchase price of $50,000 less the accumulated depreciation of $40,000. This assumption involves no tax considerations. As we saw, selling an asset for other than its book value requires adjusting the sales proceeds for its tax consequences. So if an asset is expected to have a salvage value different from its estimated book value, the *CFAT* estimate must be determined by using the tax rules discussed earlier. Similar tax adjustments may be required if this is a replacement decision. The salvage value of the old becomes important to determining the tax implication for the firm.

In replacement capital budgeting projects, salvage values may appear twice. The salvage value of the old asset is, in effect, advanced from its original date and becomes part of the indirect initial cash flows. Thus the proposed new asset's salvage value is placed on the time line at the end of its economic life, as the incremental difference between the new and old assets' salvage values.

NET WORKING CAPITAL Net working capital (*NWC*) is the difference between short-term assets and short-term liabilities. Capital budgeting, which concerns the acquisition of long-term assets, does not focus on these short-term (one year or less) items. However, because a project may involve a change in the level of *NWC* and thus affect the cash flows of the firm, we must include changes in *NWC* in our capital budgeting analysis. The management of these short-term items is an important topic in its own right and is discussed in detail in Part Six of this text.

If a project's initial investment outlays call for an increase in net working capital, this investment in *NWC* will be converted back to cash when the project terminates. Consider the earlier example regarding the introduction of a new product line. Acceptance of this project causes a net increase in inventories and accounts receivable in order to support new sales. Assume that the increase in *NWC* because of the new product is $10,000. Once the product line is dropped, the funds tied up in these noncash current items are no longer needed. The inventories can be sold and the accounts payables reduced. This can result in a net cash inflow to the firm that must be captured in the analysis.

It must be pointed out that this treatment of working capital is a simplification. In reality, working capital cannot be treated as an investment made when the project is adopted and recovered when the project ceases to exist. Working capital can change from period to period, and additional inflows or outflows may be necessary during the life of the investment. To keep the analysis manageable, however, we ignore these considerations in the examples and problems in this chapter.

The preceding discussion identified the three categories of cash flows—initial, operating, and terminal—and outlined the procedures for computing them. With this understanding it is now possible to perform an overall *CFAT* analysis that covers all these cash flows. Capital budgeting decisions require this overall *CFAT* analysis of an investment project, and the accompanying section provides exam-

CASH FLOW CLASSIFICATION AND CAPITAL BUDGETING FOR SOME SPACE SHUTTLE OPERATIONS

*T*he U.S. Air Force (USAF) and the Environmental Protection Agency (EPA) contracted with Radian Corporation to evaluate the economic feasibility of the on-site production of electricity to support space shuttle launch activities at Vandenburg Air Force Base. Radian conducted a comprehensive capital budgeting analysis of this project, and it is interesting to outline briefly the procedure it used. Observe that the cash flow classification that Radian used is illustrative of the scheme suggested in the text.

In making its final recommendation, Radian used the NPV criterion. A 22-year project life and a 11.75% discount rate were assumed, based on other analyses. All initial cash flows were divided into two categories: direct and indirect costs. The following is a summary of these initial cash flows:

1. Direct costs.

    a. Delivered equipment cost.

    b. Equipment installation. *Instruments, piping, foundations and supports, insulation, erec-*
tion and handling, painting, site development, electrical, and buildings.

2. Indirect costs.

    a. Engineering and supervision. *Construction and engineering, travel, drafting, cost engineering, purchasing, home office expenses, and accounting.*

    b. Contractor's fee.

    c. Start-up and modifications.

    d. Working capital.

In calculating the operating cash flows over the project's life, Radian identified the following incremental revenues and incremental costs (expenses):

1. Revenues. *Liquid hydrogen, liquid oxygen, liquid nitrogen, gaseous nitrogen, and electricity.*

2. Expenses.

    a. Nonfuel. *Operating materials, off-site waste disposal, operating labor, process water, supervising labor, cooling water, maintenance materials and re-*
placement parts, and plant and labor overhead.

    b. Fuel. *Electricity, natural gas, No. 2 fuel oil, No. 6 fuel oil, and coal.*

With the assumption that the terminal cash flows would be $0, the project was found to have a negative NPV. Based on this cash flow analysis, Radian recommended that the shuttle program abandon the project and, instead, buy electricity from electric utilities.

Note that this capital budgeting analysis involved no depreciation or tax considerations because the USAF does not have to pay any taxes to the federal government.

SOURCE: *Information compiled from Feasibility of Producing Commodities and Electricity for Space Shuttle Operations at Vandenburg Air Force Base,* Report EPA-600/7-84-100, *November 1984, prepared by the Radian Corporation. The assistance of P. J. Murin, one of the authors of this report, is gratefully acknowledged.*

ples of applying *CFAT* analysis to two different types of capital budgeting projects. Also see the highlight above.

Applications of CFAT *Analyses*   Earlier in this chapter, capital budgeting proposals were grouped into two categories during the screening phase: cost-reduction (savings) proposals and revenue expansion proposals. As we saw earlier, investments are also made to satisfy social, legal, or environmental requirements. Investments in new athletic facilities for employees or in safety and pollution-control devices are difficult to evaluate within this framework because they usually involve only cash outflows; that is, no (dollar) benefits can be directly measured. Such decisions are largely discretionary. For example, a decision to install scrubbers in a smelting plant may be made to forestall an even bigger cash outflow that might result from federal lawsuits. Such projects, however, fall outside the scope of this book. We give examples of projects that are most amenable to capital budgeting analysis.

COST-SAVINGS PROJECT

A replacement project is often a cost-savings project. For example, a company's decision to substitute its fuel-fired kilns with electric-arc kilns can provide both additional revenues and lower costs. The focus in this section, however, is on a *pure* cost-reduction project. A pure cost-reduction project provides no direct benefit in the form of increased sales; instead, the benefits come through higher future income because of cost reductions. The most common example of this type of investment is the replacement of existing equipment or facilities with more efficient ones. Over time, plant, equipment, and production facilities wear out or become obsolete. Older equipment eventually becomes too expensive to operate because of increased maintenance and repair (downtime) costs. Moreover, even well-functioning equipment may become obsolete because of technological advances. Decisions to increase automation in order to reduce labor costs also fall into this category. These potential cost-reduction situations may offer the company opportunities to reduce its variable operating costs by replacing employees or old, obsolete plant and equipment.

Assume that Mylanta Diversified Products wants to upgrade its current computer system by purchasing a new computer. To analyze the $\Delta CFAT$s it is necessary to identify the information relevant to the proposed situation and the existing situation.

We first discuss the *proposed situation:* The new computer costs $75,000 plus another $5,000 for installation. Its expected economic life is five years, after which it can be sold for $20,000. Its variable and fixed operating expenses are expected to be $10,000 and $5,000 per year, respectively. In addition, $2,400 needs to be spent retraining existing personnel. No change in working capital is anticipated. The company plans to depreciate the new computer over its five-year life using straight-line depreciation toward a salvage value of $20,000.

Now we consider the *existing situation:* The existing computer originally cost $48,000 (*OC*) three years ago, at which time it was assumed to have $0 salvage value after eight years. The firm now expects that its salvage value (future market value) will be $5,000 in five years. It could be sold today, however, for $28,000 (i.e., its current market value is $28,000). Its annual depreciation expense is $6,000 on a straight-line depreciation basis, and variable and fixed operating expenses are estimated to be $26,000 and $7,000 per year, respectively. The firm's marginal income tax rate is 15%.

From this information, the *CFAT*s can be calculated as in Table 8-2.

INITIAL CASH FLOWS Because our example deals with the sale of an existing computer, both direct and indirect cash flows are involved. In $\Delta CFAT$ analysis it is often convenient to label cash outflows as *O* and cash inflows as *I*. This avoids errors that can arise because of confusion about whether a cash flow increases or decreases cash to the firm.

We first consider *direct cash flows.* As can be seen in Table 8-2, the purchase of the new computer requires a cash outflow of $75,000 (*O*), and the additional installation cost of $5,000 (*O*) raises the depreciable base of the new computer to $80,000. The term *depreciable base* refers to the total amount that the IRS will recognize as being depreciable. Finally, the after-tax training costs are $2,400(1 − 0.15) = $2,040 (*O*).

■

TABLE 8-2
ΔCFAT *Analysis for Cost-Saving Project*

1. *Initial cash flows*
   Direct cash flows (new computer)

   a. Capital expenditures
      Purchase price of computer $75,000 (*O*)
      Installation costs   5,000 (*O*)

      Depreciable base $80,000

   b. Operating expenditures
      Training costs $ 2,040 (*O*)

   Total direct cash flows $82,040 (*O*)

   Total initial cash flows = $82,040 (*O*) + $28,300 (*I*) = $53,740 (*O*)

   Indirect cash flows (old computer)

   Salvage value $28,000 (*I*)
   Less book value   30,000
   Tax Loss   (2,000)

   Tax saving = $2,000 × 0.15 = $ 300 (*I*)

   Total indirect cash flows $28,300 (*I*)

2. *Operating cash flows*

$$\Delta CFAT = (\Delta S - \Delta C - \Delta D)(1 - T) + \Delta D$$
$$= [0 - (-\$18,000) - \$6,000](1 - 0.15) + \$6,000 = \$16,200 \ (I)$$

3. *Terminal cash flows*
   Salvage value of new computer $20,000 (*I*)
   Less book value   20,000

   Taxable income   0

   Total terminal *CFAT* = $20,000 (*I*)

Now we discuss *indirect cash flows:* The indirect cash flows to Mylanta include the proceeds from the sale of the old computer of $28,000 (*I*) and any other cash flows that may arise from tax considerations.

To anticipate the tax consequences of this sale, it first is necessary to calculate the book value of the old computer. The original purchase price of the computer was $48,000, and because it is being depreciated (straight line) toward a $0 salvage value over eight years, the depreciation per year is ($48,000 − $0)/8 = $6,000 per year. Thus the book value of the machine when it is sold is the original purchase price ($48,000) less the accumulated depreciation of $18,000 ($6,000 per year for three years), or $30,000. Therefore the sale yields a tax loss of $2,000. Because the market value of the computer ($28,000) is less than the book value ($30,000), the ordinary tax loss treatment applies. Because Mylanta is in the 15% tax bracket, it can expect a tax credit of $2,000 × 0.15 = $300 (*I*) as a cash inflow.

The total indirect cash flows are therefore the proceeds of $28,000 from the sale of the computer plus the tax credit of $300, yielding a total indirect cash flow to Mylanta of $28,300.

The total initial $\Delta CFAT$ is therefore the sum of the direct [$82,040 (*O*)] and indirect [$28,300 (*I*)] cash flows, for a total of $53,740 (*O*), as verified in Table 8-2.

OPERATING CASH FLOWS The operating cash flows for Mylanta can be calculated using equation (8-3), as follows:

$$\Delta CFAT = (\Delta S - \Delta C - \Delta D)(1 - T) + \Delta D$$

The procedure implicit in the use of this shortcut approach is explained in greater detail in Table 8-2.

For Mylanta, because this is a pure cost-reduction project, the incremental sales are 0, or $\Delta S = 0$.

The variable and fixed costs change, however, for this cost-reduction project. The fixed costs are expected to decrease from $7,000 to $5,000 per year, thereby changing the fixed costs by − $2,000. Similarly, the variable costs are expected to go down from $26,000 to $10,000 per year, yielding a change in variable costs of − $16,000. Thus $\Delta C = (-\$2,000) + (-\$16,000) = -\$18,000$.

The depreciation for the old machine is $6,000 per year, as calculated earlier. The new depreciation is $12,000 per year, which is calculated as follows: The depreciable base for the new computer includes the price of the computer ($75,000) plus the installation costs ($5,000) for a total of $80,000. Because it is being depreciated straight line over five years toward a salvage value of $20,000, the depreciation per year is ($80,000 − $20,000)/5 = $12,000 per year. The incremental depreciation, ΔD, is therefore the new depreciation of $12,000 per year less the old depreciation of $6,000 per year, or $\Delta D = $6,000 per year.

The operating cash flows from this project are therefore calculated using equation (8-3) as

$$\Delta CFAT = [0 - (-\$18,000) - \$6,000](1 - 0.15) + \$6,000$$
$$= (\$12,000 \times 0.85) + \$6,000$$
$$= \$16,200 \ (I)$$

Thus the effect on the operating cash flows of taking on the new computer is an increase in the *CFAT* of $16,200 per year for the next five years. In this example, the $\Delta CFAT$ is an annuity stream. In many situations, however, if the cost figures change over the life of the project, for example, the $\Delta CFAT$ has to be computed *for each year over the life* of the project using equation (8-3).

TERMINAL CASH FLOWS The final category of cash flows, the terminal cash flows, is easy to compute in this example. When the new machine is sold for $20,000 at the end of five years, Mylanta realizes a cash inflow of $20,000 (*I*). The situation is simple because there are no tax consequences. The asset is being sold for its book value, so there is neither a gain nor a loss on the sale. In cases in which there is a tax loss or gain, the tax rules discussed earlier should be applied.

THE COMPOSITE $\Delta CFAT$ PICTURE To help visualize the overall cash flow pattern and summarize the analysis of the three categories of cash flows, a "$\Delta CFAT$ time line" appears as follows:

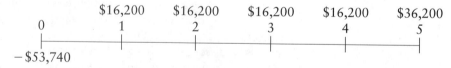

The last year's *CFAT* is a combination of the operating cash flow per year ($16,200) and the terminal cash flow ($20,000).

REVENUE EXPANSION PROJECT

The second type of capital budgeting investment is the result of either expanding current operations or introducing a new product line. The primary purpose of this type of investment is to increase revenues rather than to decrease costs. If a firm expects the future demand for its products to push plant capacity beyond its limits, it should consider projects designed to expand operations. On the other hand, competition and changing consumer tastes require a constant reassessment of existing products' market appeal. Decisions must be made about eliminating obsolete or unpopular products and introducing new ones.

When a project expands revenue through the sale of additional goods or services, it may also reduce some costs. For simplicity, however, the next example ignores cost reductions. A project that only increases revenues and has no effect on costs is a *pure* revenue expansion project. The example of this is more complicated than the last example for at least three reasons: (1) the initial investment is spread over two years, (2) net working capital considerations are required, and (3) the operating $\Delta CFAT$ sequence is not an annuity.

Suppose that a food-processing company is considering the introduction of a new line of yogurt. Based on marketing research studies, the products are expected to have a life cycle of eight years. During that time, sales are expected to increase rapidly for the first three years, level off at $80.5 million for four years, and then taper off to $35 million in the last year. An additional $9.1 million ($O$) in net working capital is needed to support these sales projections. Engineering and accounting cost studies forecast variable and fixed costs to be 40% and 18% of sales, respectively. The firm is in the 15% tax bracket. The projected incremental sales and fixed and variable costs are presented in Table 8-3, part b for years 1 through 8.

The firm's engineers estimate that a new processing plant is required, involving a capital outlay of $42.2 million over a two-year period ($38.9 million in year 1 and $3.3 million in year 2); see Table 8-3, part a. The salvage values of the assets placed in year 0 and year 1 are expected to be $3.5 million and $500,000, respectively. Because this plant does not replace an existing one, there are no cash flows

■

TABLE 8-3

Cash ΔCFAT Analysis for Revenue Expansion Project (thousands of dollars)

a. Initial Cash Flows

	Year 0	Year 1
Direct Cash Flows		
Capital expenditures		
Land	$ 7,400 (O)	0
Buildings	25,800 (O)	2,600 (O)
Equipment	5,700 (O)	700 (O)
Operating expenditures[a]		
Marketing	1,700 (O)	0
Training/relocation	2,040 (O)	0
Total direct cash flows	$42,640 (O)	$3,300 (O)
Indirect Cash Flows		
Changes in working capital		
Accounts receivable	$ 5,400 (O)	$7,100 (O)
Inventory	6,700 (O)	3,500 (O)
Accounts payable	7,200 (I)	6,400 (I)
Change in net working capital	$ 4,900 (O)	$4,200 (O)
Δ Initial *CFAT*	$47,540 (O)	$7,500 (O)

[a] These are after-tax numbers.

b. Operating Cash Flows

	Year 1	Year 2	Year 3	Year 4	Year 5	Year 6	Year 7	Year 8
Incremental sales (ΔS)	$29,500	$55,000	$80,500	$80,500	$80,500	$80,500	$80,500	$35,000
Incremental variable costs	11,800	22,000	32,200	32,200	32,200	32,200	32,200	14,000
Incremental fixed costs	5,310	9,900	14,490	14,490	14,490	14,490	14,490	6,300
Incremental costs (ΔC)	17,110	31,900	46,690	46,690	46,690	46,690	46,690	20,300
Incremental depreciation (ΔD)	3,500	3,900	3,900	3,900	3,900	3,900	3,900	3,900
$\Delta CFAT =$								
$(\Delta S - \Delta C - \Delta D)(1 - 0.15) + \Delta D$	11,056	20,220	29,324	29,324	29,324	29,324	29,324	13,080

c. Terminal Cash Flows

	Year 8
Salvage value	
Salvage value of plant and equipment	4,000 (I)
Less book value	4,000
Taxable income/loss	0
Recovery of net working capital	
Accounts receivable	12,500 (I)
Inventory	10,200 (I)
Accounts payable	13,600 (O)
Δ Terminal *CFAT*	13,100 (I)

from the disposal of old assets. Other initial costs for training and relocation and for marketing research are $2.4 million and $2.0 million, respectively. Since these costs are tax deductible, Table 8-3 shows the relevant after-tax costs, as explained below.

We examine the three categories of cash flows separately. Table 8-3 summarizes the calculations for the three cash flow categories.

INITIAL CASH FLOWS We first consider *direct cash flows:* As shown in Table 8-3, part a, the total capital expenditures amount to $38.9 million and $3.3 million for year 0 and year 1, respectively. Notice that in this example the investment in buildings is spread over two years. The firm's marketing and training expenses are $2 million and $2.4 million in year 0 and 0 in year 1. The after-tax costs are therefore $2 million × (1 − 0.15) = $1.70 million and $2.4 million × (1 − 0.15) = $2.04 million, respectively. The operating expenditures total $3.74 million in year 0.

The next topic is *indirect cash flows:* Because the sale of old machinery is not involved, there is no tax effect. Instead, this project requires additional working capital of $4.9 million and $4.2 million in year 0 and year 1, respectively. Details are presented in Table 8-3, part a. Again, it is important to stress that changes in working capital may occur over the life of the project rather than as a one-shot increase, as portrayed in this example.

OPERATING CASH FLOWS The calculations for the operating $\Delta CFAT$ are presented in Table 8-3, part b. Once the relevant estimates are generated, these cash flows can be determined using equation (8-3). Notice that in this example, the $\Delta CFAT$s are not an annuity because of varying sales, costs, and depreciation through the years. Thus equation (8-3) has to be applied to every year individually. If we assume straight-line depreciation and a salvage value of $3.5 million for items in place at the end of year 0, the depreciation for year 1 is $3.5 million {[($25.8 million + $5.7 million) − $3.5 million]/8}. Note from these computations that of the initial capital expenditures, land is not depreciable. If the salvage value for items placed in service during year 1 is $500,000, the depreciation per year is $400,000 {[($2.6 million + $700,000) − $500,000]/7}. Therefore, beginning in year 2, the total depreciation is $3.5 million + $400,000 = $3.9 million. The final values of $\Delta CFAT$ calculated using equation (8-3) are on the bottom line of Table 8-3, part b.

TERMINAL CASH FLOWS Table 8-3, part c summarizes the terminal cash flow calculations. The salvage value of the equipment and the book value of the equipment are identical, so there are no tax consequences. Thus the cash inflow of $4 million, together with the recapture of net working capital of $9.1 million, totals $13.1 million ($I$) for year 8.

THE COMPOSITE $\Delta CFAT$ PICTURE The three categories of cash flows are summarized in the following time line. The cash inflow of $26.18 million in year 8 is calculated as the sum of the terminal cash flows of $13.1 million plus the operating $\Delta CFAT$ of $13.08 million:

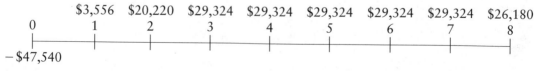

8-3

CRITERIA FOR CAPITAL BUDGETING

A criterion or rule is needed as the basis for deciding whether a particular project should be adopted.[3] The best criterion is one that is consistent with the goal of financial management—that is, one that leads to investments that increase the current shareholders' wealth. As we found earlier, the best investment is one that adequately compensates its owner for the time value of money and for risk.

Historically, practitioners have relied on two criteria for investment decisions: the payback period and the accounting rate of return methods. Even though these criteria are generally ineffective in making wealth-maximizing financial decisions, we review them here because of their widespread popularity. Then we look at three conceptually sound criteria—net present value (NPV), internal rate of return (IRR), and profitability index (PI)—in the context of capital budgeting.

Payback Period Criterion

The payback period for a project measures the number of years required to recover the initial investment. Consider a project with an initial investment of $500,000 and expected cash inflows of $100,000 per year for ten years. The payback period for this project is given by:

$$\text{Payback period} = \frac{\text{initial investment outlay}}{\text{annual cash inflows}} \tag{8-4}$$

$$= \frac{\$500,000}{\$100,000} = 5 \text{ years}$$

Thus in five years the initial investment is recovered. Even if cash flows are not uniform, the payback period can be easily calculated by summing the cash flows until the initial outlay is recovered.

Table 8-4 summarizes the cash flows from two projects, A and B. Both require a $500,000 outlay; however, their cash inflow patterns are different. As we can see, the payback period for project A is five years, and the payback period for project B is just three years. Because decisions based on the payback period involve choosing the project with the shorter payback period, project B should be chosen over project A. Firms that use the payback period method sometimes establish a minimum or required payback period to make accept/reject decisions. In this case, projects with expected payback periods longer than this standard are rejected, and those with payback periods shorter than this standard are accepted.

Although the payback criterion is quite simple, there are several problems in using it for capital budgeting.

---

[3] Some economists distinguish between the terms *criterion* and *rule*. The difference is subtle, and in this book the two terms are used interchangeably.

■

TABLE 8-4
Initial Outlays and Cash Inflows for Projects A and B

Year	Project A	Project B
Initial outlay		
0	− $500,000	− $500,000
Net cash flow		
1	$100,000	$200,000
2	100,000	200,000
3	100,000	100,000
4	100,000	5,000
5	100,000	2,000
6	100,000	0
7	100,000	0

CASH FLOWS BEYOND THE PAYBACK PERIOD

Even if project *A*'s cash flows in years 6 and 7 were $1 million each, it would not make any difference. Project *B* would still be preferred to project *A* simply because of its shorter payback period. This result of the payback criterion is clearly disturbing.

OPPORTUNITY COST CONSIDERATIONS

Suppose that project *B*'s cash flows were $0 for the first two years and $500,000 for the third year. This would leave the payback period unaltered and *B* would still be preferable to *A*. The pattern of cash flows within the payback period is totally irrelevant when this criterion is used. Sometimes, a "discounted payback rule" is used. The discounted payback period is the number of years it takes for the discounted cash flows to yield the initial investment. Although this rule is one step better than the standard payback rule, which completely ignores the time value of money, it still suffers from a serious weakness. It ignores all cash flows beyond the discounted payback period. In addition, the risks of the two projects—factors that affect the opportunity costs of investing in the projects—are completely ignored.

Despite these weaknesses, the payback period is popular, perhaps because it is easy to use. Another reason is that it emphasizes the managers' liquidity objective. The shorter the payback period is, the quicker the project will generate cash inflows. Nevertheless, the fact that stockholders want companies to take on projects with the highest market values is completely ignored.

Accounting Rate of Return Criterion

The accounting rate of return (*AROR*) criterion relates the profits provided by a project to its average investment:

$$AROR = \frac{\text{annual profit}}{\text{average investment}} \qquad (8\text{-}5)$$

Average investment can be calculated in a variety of ways. We approximate the average investment by adding the beginning and ending values of the investment and dividing this result by 2. For example, if an investment in a lathe that cost $5,000 depreciates to a value of $1,000 in four years, the average investment in the lathe is $3,000 [($5,000 + $1,000)/2]. If two projects *X* and *Y* have *AROR*s of 15% and 20%, respectively, project *Y* is better than project *X*.

The weaknesses of *AROR* should be obvious. By using profits rather than cash flows and by ignoring the time value of money, *AROR* has no relationship to market-determined return measures. Choosing the project with the highest *AROR* does not mean that the firm is choosing the project with the highest market value.

A related rate of return criterion is the average return on investment (*AROI*). This measure uses the average annual cash flow after taxes instead of the average annual profit. Although the *AROI* corrects one of the flaws inherent in the *AROR* criterion, it still ignores the time value of money.

Net Present Value Criterion

By focusing on all cash flows generated by a project and then capitalizing them at a market-determined discount rate, the net present value (*NPV*) method overcomes all the weaknesses of the payback period and the *AROR* methods. Formally,

$$NPV = PV_{\text{inflows}} - PV_{\text{outflows}} \qquad (8\text{-}6)$$

where the present values of cash inflows and outflows are determined by discounting the cash flows at a market-determined opportunity cost of capital. In calculating *NPV*s, as in equation (8-6), it is implicitly assumed that the intermediate cash flows from a project are reinvested at the opportunity cost of capital.

The required rate of return (*RRR*) for a project is the minimum expected rate of return that the project must yield to justify its acceptance. If the *NPV* is positive, it earns more than the *RRR* and produces excess returns. If the *NPV* is negative, the project earns less than the *RRR* and produces negative economic profits. The *NPV* is therefore the net or excess market value that accrues to the firm upon acceptance of the project.

This knowledge helps clarify the concept of value additivity, a property of the *NPV* criterion. If projects are valued using a market-determined discount rate, then, with two projects *A* and *B*, **value additivity** implies that

$$NPV(A + B) = NPV(A) + NPV(B)$$

or

$$MV(A + B) = MV(A) + MV(B)$$

An implication of value additivity is that a firm with market value $MV(A)$ that takes on a project with excess market value $MV(B)$ will eventually have a new market value $MV(A + B)$. Thus, as long as $MV(B)$ is positive, it makes sense to accept project *B* because it increases the firm's market value. The excess market value of *B* is no different from its *NPV*, however. Now recall from Chapter 2 that managers must pick projects that increase company wealth. Thus we have the following *NPV* rule: The *NPV* rule accepts projects with positive *NPV*s and rejects projects with negative *NPV*s.

Internal Rate of Return Criterion

Unlike the accounting rate of return method, which ignores the time value of money and is based on profits, the internal rate of return (*IRR*) is a discounted rate of return measure derived directly from knowledge of a project's cash flow pattern. The *IRR* is the discount rate that makes the excess market value (*NPV*) of a project $0.

Alternatively, as seen in Chapter 4, the *IRR* is the discount rate that makes the present value of an investment's cash inflows (PV_{inflows}) equal to the present value of its cash outflows (PV_{outflows}). Stated algebraically, *IRR* is the discount rate that causes

$$NPV = PV_{\text{inflows}} - PV_{\text{outflows}} = 0 \qquad (8\text{-}7)$$

A project is accepted or rejected by comparing its *IRR* with its required rate of return (*RRR*), which is the opportunity cost of capital. The *IRR* rule is to accept a project if *IRR* > *RRR* and to reject a project if *IRR* < *RRR*. Technically speaking, if *IRR* = *RRR*, a firm should be indifferent to (accepting or rejecting) a project. It may not make much economic sense to accept a project when the firm expects only to recover its opportunity cost.

Because the *IRR* criterion explicitly considers the timing of the *CFAT*s, it satisfies the requirement that the capital budgeting decision criteria must account for the time value of money. However, an implicit assumption in all *IRR* calculations is that the intermediate cash flows from the project are also reinvested at the *IRR*, rather than at the opportunity cost of capital. This assumption makes this a non-market-value-based criterion, which is not necessarily consistent with the goal of maximizing shareholder wealth. This and related problems with the *IRR* are addressed in greater detail in Chapter 9. Thus the *NPV* is superior to the *IRR* as a criterion for making correct capital budgeting decisions.

MANAGERS' CHOICES OF CAPITAL BUDGETING TECHNIQUES

A recent survey of the 100 largest companies in the Fortune 500 industrial firms list produced the following results:

- All of the firms responding to the survey used some form of time-value discounting, with 99% of firms using NPV or IRR as either their primary or secondary evaluative method.

- 84% of the firms used some form of the payback method,

but no firm used it as the primary evaluative method.

- Approximately 50% of the responding firms used some form of accounting rate of return.

The general finding of the survey is that managers who make capital budgeting decisions strongly prefer to use a combination of evaluative techniques rather than depend on just one. Of the firms responding, 87% used three or more methods in making capital budgeting decisions, with the re-

maining firms using two or fewer methods. The survey also found a substantial increase in managers' use of more advanced capital budgeting techniques with a strong grounding in economic principles. For example, a 1955 survey found that only 4% of managers used NPV analysis, compared with 85% in 1992.

Adapted from Harold Bierman, Jr., "Capital Budgeting in 1992: A Survey," in FM Letters, Financial Management 22, no. 3 (Autumn 1993).

Profitability Index Criterion

Another discounted cash flow criterion used to evaluate capital budgeting projects is the profitability index or benefit–cost ratio. The **profitability index** (*PI*) is simply a different way of presenting the same information that the *NPV* provides. The *NPV* is the difference between the *PV*s of the cash inflows and the cash outflows, and the *PI* is the ratio of these two values:

$$PI = \frac{PV_{\text{inflows}}}{PV_{\text{outflows}}}$$
(8-8)

The *PI* rule accepts projects if *PI* > 1 and rejects projects if *PI* < 1.[4] Because the present value of the cash outflows represents the "true" time-adjusted investment in the project, the *PI* is a *relative* measure in that it measures the benefits per dollar of investment adjusted for time value. The *NPV* criterion, on the other hand, is an *absolute* measure. This has some interesting implications.

When should the *PI* criterion be used to select capital budgeting projects? Because the *NPV* and the *PI* criteria are essentially the same, they both lead to identical accept/reject decisions. A project that is acceptable according to the *NPV* rule will also be found to be acceptable according to the *PI* rule. But the *PI* and the *NPV* can lead to conflicting decisions when one of two projects has to be chosen, a topic we examine in Chapter 9. Because this chapter is concerned with accept/reject decisions rather than ranking decisions, the *PI* and the *NPV* criteria lead to identical conclusions.

At this point, the reader may be asking to what extent managers use these methods. A recent survey's results are summarized in the highlight above.

8-4

APPLYING THE PROJECT SELECTION CRITERIA

With an understanding of the *NPV*, *PI*, and *IRR* criteria, it is now possible to decide whether the two projects (the cost-reducing computer project and the revenue-expanding yogurt project) should be accepted or rejected. Only the *NPV* and the *IRR* criteria are used here because they are perhaps conceptually the most defensible. As we found previ-

---

[4]The reader is encouraged to verify that this rule follows from the *NPV* rule.

ously, accept/reject decisions using *PI* and *NPV* are the same, and so we do not use the *PI* in the following development.

Net Present Value   Assume that both projects being evaluated have a required rate of return (i.e., opportunity cost or discount rate) of 12%. From equation (8-7), the *NPV* for each project is calculated as follows.

The composite *CFAT* time line, which gives the cash flows for the cost-reducing capital budgeting problem developed in Section 8-2, is given here:

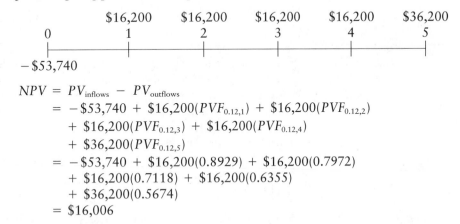

$$NPV = PV_{inflows} - PV_{outflows}$$
$$= -\$53,740 + \$16,200(PVF_{0.12,1}) + \$16,200(PVF_{0.12,2})$$
$$+ \$16,200(PVF_{0.12,3}) + \$16,200(PVF_{0.12,4})$$
$$+ \$36,200(PVF_{0.12,5})$$
$$= -\$53,740 + \$16,200(0.8929) + \$16,200(0.7972)$$
$$+ \$16,200(0.7118) + \$16,200(0.6355)$$
$$+ \$36,200(0.5674)$$
$$= \$16,006$$

Using the *NPV* rule (i.e., accept if the *NPV* is positive), management should decide to replace the computer because, in doing so, the firm's market value will increase by $16,006.

The composite *CFAT* time line for the new brand of yogurt, discussed in Section 8-2, is as follows:

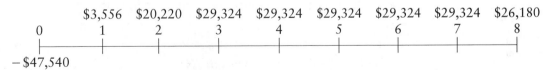

The *NPV* (in thousands) for this revenue expansion project is:

$$NPV = -\$47,540 + \$3,556(PVF_{0.12,1}) + \$20,220(PVF_{0.12,2})$$
$$+ \$29,324(PVF_{0.12,3}) + \$29,324(PVF_{0.12,4})$$
$$+ \$29,324(PVF_{0.12,5}) + \$29,324(PVF_{0.12,6})$$
$$+ \$29,324(PVF_{0.12,7}) + \$26,180(PVF_{0.12,8})$$

After substituting the appropriate present value factors, we can see that *NPV* = $66,596,460.

Expanding the yogurt line thus will be a productive endeavor because the firm's market value will go up by $66.6 million.

Internal Rate of Return   The procedure for computing *IRR*s was described in Chapter 4. With the aid of a financial calculator, the procedure is easy. But if one wants to determine the *IRR* for a project, a trial-and-error method is necessary, using the method described in Chapter 4. In the interest of brevity, the *IRR* calculations are not provided here. The reader can verify the following *IRR*s as an exercise.

The *IRR* for the computer replacement project is approximately 22%. Using the *IRR* rule, management should accept this project because the *IRR* is greater than the *RRR* of 12%.

The *IRR* for the new brand of yogurt is approximately 38%. Because the *RRR* for this project is only 12%, the *IRR* rule would lead one to accept this project.

Thus, as expected, both the *NPV* rule and the *IRR* rule agree; both suggest that the projects should be accepted. A manager who follows this recommendation is acting in the best interests of the company's owners.

In this chapter we examined only accept/reject decisions. In other words, the framework developed here can help determine only whether a project should be accepted or rejected. There are several other complications in capital budgeting decisions that we examine in Chapter 9.

8-5
COMPETITIVE ADVANTAGE AND OPERATING FLEXIBILITIES

The principle underlying the capital budgeting process should be fairly clear by now: Accept only those projects that can increase the firm's wealth. Or accept only those projects that can earn a return higher than the opportunity cost of taking on that investment.

The capital budgeting process as presented here makes two implicit assumptions: First, firms can indeed find positive-*NPV* investments if they examine enough alternatives and, second, issues of operating flexibility and strategy are not important. We examine these assumptions in order to better understand the limitations of capital budgeting.

NPVs in the Long Run

Projects with positive *NPV*s earn excess returns. However, if the markets are efficient in the long run, these positive-*NPV* projects eventually disappear because any attractive investment invites competition, which causes a firm to respond by cutting prices until the project is no longer attractive. This series of events seems to argue against the usefulness of seeking out long-run positive-*NPV* projects. To understand why companies do find and enjoy such projects, we must understand the limits of market efficiency and how firms seek out and create market inefficiencies.

THE ORIGINS OF POSITIVE-*NPV* PROJECTS

The "trick" to preserving a positive *NPV* is to ensure that the firm never reaches this "long-run" situation by finding and exploiting imperfections in the various markets in which it operates. These imperfections can arise from several sources.

Major imperfections are created by the very nature of the financial markets and the markets for physical goods and services. As we saw in Chapter 6, the major stock markets in various countries are not highly positively correlated. Moreover, these financial markets differ substantially in their legal and institutional characteristics, and also in the availability of information and the ability of investors to act on this information. American investors are generally much more knowledgeable about the economic conditions in the United States than they are about corresponding issues in France. Therefore firms that are large enough and knowledgeable enough can potentially exploit these imperfections. So-called Euromarkets for short-term and long-term capital are available only to large, well-known firms. Obtaining capital at reduced rates is itself a market imperfection that can be wealth enhancing.

The markets for physical goods and services are even more imperfect than financial markets. Many factors of production, such as labor and raw materials, are not mobile. Firms that can seek out low-wage labor can exploit this advantage and enjoy positive excess returns. Knowledge and technology are in some areas worldwide and easily movable. In other instances, however (such as computer software technology in the United States and manufacturing technology in Japan), knowledge is specialized to certain countries. Companies in these areas that can tap into this knowledge base can gain a competitive advantage over their global competition.

Some market imperfections are not inherent in the market but are rather created by firms that operate in that market. An important source of economic value (positive *NPV*) is **product differentiation**. Firms devote substantial wealth to advertising and other activities to create a brand name or other means of differentiating their product from those of their competitors. By packaging or marketing its product or service as unique, a company can effectively create a "new product" that appeals to consumers. Consider a mundane household product, bleach. Even in this market there is a high degree of competition, and firms go to great lengths to differentiate their product as "unique." The product differentiation comes from subtle changes in the product's texture, form (powder or liquid), fragrance, packaging, and claimed benefits. To the extent that the differentiation convinces the market that the product is new and desirable, the firm enjoys a monopoly in that specialized market.

A firm can also structure its operations to obtain wealth-enhancing advantages over its competition. **Economies of scale** can reduce the threat of competition. Because there are cost advantages to being large and because such large firms require enormous amounts of capital, it is not easy for a new entrant to compete in this market. The ability to get the product to the marketplace through good **distribution networks** can help a firm increase its sales and beat a competitor without such access to the consumer. In addition, a firm may possess other **quasi rents**: short-term advantages that arise from factors such as specialization, favorable locations, and excess capacity. A firm may also have a more efficient structure of contracts. A company's assets, its organizational structure, and other contracting relationships may be such that its agency costs are lower than those of the others in the same business.

Still another source of market imperfections is government actions. If a firm has government-awarded **patents** on a certain product, then competition is limited for at least the life of the patent. Alternatively, government policy can afford a degree of protection from competition. This is particularly true of the pharmaceutical and trucking industries in which **government regulations** can deter, if not preclude, new entrants. Government regulations that impose trade quotas and restrict the activities of foreign companies can also help companies protect their positive-*NPV* projects from being expropriated by other firms.

In efficient markets, arbitrage profits are rapidly eliminated. However, most of the physical asset markets in which firms operate are not efficient, especially when evaluated on a global level, and they can provide positive-*NPV* opportunities. Certainly, as companies seek out and exploit these advantages, such advantages are reduced. However, firms, governments, or the markets themselves change continually, and this change can create new imperfections and new opportunities.

Positive *NPV*s can also originate from the specific characteristics of an investment and from the decision of when to make the investment. These increases in wealth arise from operating flexibilities and investment flexibilities inherent in the project. These are examined next.

THE VALUE OF OPERATING FLEXIBILITY

In capital budgeting analyses, it is important to consider **operating flexibilities** that can increase a project's *NPV*. Operating flexibility refers to the ability of managers to use the capital assets in different ways to respond to changing economic conditions.

The capital budgeting procedures outlined in the preceding sections are straight-forward applications of the discounted cash flow idea. However, they do not accommodate the notion of operating flexibility. The process of evaluating a project, as discussed thus far, is virtually identical to the process of valuing a bond that has a fairly simple stream of fixed interest payments. Although it is true that in a project analysis we are concerned with depreciation, salvage values, and tax effects, all this information merely helps us identify the cash flows from the project. Once they have been identified, the project valuation using standard capital budgeting techniques and bond valuation are equivalent.

In effect, traditional capital budgeting analysis evaluates a project as if considerations of strategy and flexibility are unimportant. The analysis implicitly assumes that after a project is adopted, it will be run according to plan until its useful life is over. It is as if the project is a toy top that will be allowed to spin on its own until it ultimately loses its momentum. In reality, though, several other possibilities are inherent in a flexible project, and so management has several operating options.

To understand at a very intuitive level why the flexibility offered by a project has value, compare these two alternatives. Project A is a 15-year venture for the continuous manufacturing of sulfuric acid. Once production begins, the "wet process" cannot be stopped or the chemicals will "dry up" in the pipes and vats. This project offers few operating flexibilities (managerial options), and it has an NPV of $675,000. Project B uses a "dry process" for making sulfuric acid. It has a 15-year life, and its NPV is also $675,000. Unlike project A, however, project B can be stopped at any time, the production levels can be varied, and even other chemicals can be produced in lieu of sulfuric acid if management so desires. Which project should a manager pick? Choosing B is implicitly stating that operating flexibilities have value.

KEY CONCEPT   Operating flexibility offers managerial options and hence has economic value.

It is difficult to incorporate operating flexibilities in an analysis. First, it is not easy to identify the various flexibilities available to management over time. Second, even if we can identify these future flexibilities, how can we value them? Preliminary research is under way to devise techniques for determining the values of such managerial options, but the methods developed so far are stylized and difficult to implement. We have to await further developments that can provide guidelines on exactly how we should value options.

Some interesting practical guidelines have emerged from our discussion nevertheless. Managerial options cannot have a negative value because they offer only greater possibilities and never curtail existing alternatives. If option values are not negative, then it may make sense to adopt even projects that are determined to have a negative NPV by conventional capital budgeting methods. For example, if a project has a NPV (ignoring the value of any built-in options) of − $2,000, it may still be attractive if the present value of the options that come with the project is, say, $8,000. In this case, the project's "option-adjusted NPV" is $6,000, and so the project is desirable. Again, whether the market value of these options is actually $8,000 or only $1,000 is difficult to determine, and so management must weigh each case separately.

THE VALUE OF INVESTMENT FLEXIBILITY

Investment flexibility in capital budgeting situations refers to the ability to delay an irreversible investment until additional information becomes available. Very often, large sums of money may have to be invested today in anticipation of future benefits that are extremely uncertain (e.g., research and development of new technology). However, if after the technology is developed, tests reveal that the project should be abandoned, the company may be unable to recover its large initial investment. In such situations, negotiating for investment flexibility can be valuable.

KEY CONCEPT   Delaying a major and irreversible investment until more information becomes available may itself be wealth enhancing.

AN EXAMPLE We now examine an example that illustrates how negotiating for investment flexibility can have economic value. Applied Research Technologies (ART), a mechanical engineering firm based outside of Gaithersburg, Maryland, has obtained patents and is developing prototypes for new transmissions that have the potential to dramatically reduce the cost of automobiles. The firm has invested substantial sums of money in developing the product, and so the owners have begun to market the technology even as the testing progresses.

You are the CEO of the Advanced Motors Group (AMG), based in Detroit. You are impressed with the technology, and you want to buy an exclusive license to use the technology in your cars because you believe that it will give you a significant edge over the competition. Your negotiation team meets with the principals of ART for negotiation.

CASE 1. TAKE IT OR LEAVE IT (NO FLEXIBILITY) During the meeting, John Banner, CEO of ART, offers you an exclusive license for $130 million and says "take it or leave it." Your investment group adjourns to the next room for private discussions and reasons as follows: Since the final prototypes have not been built and the final test results will not be known until the end of year 1, the potential benefits to AMG are uncertain. Your associates suggest that with 50% probability the test results will be as expected, and in that case AMG can generate incremental cash flows of $18 million into perpetuity starting at the end of year 1 (when the test results are known). If the results are disappointing, the cash flows will be only $6 million into perpetuity. The annual expected cash flows are thus $0.5 \times \$18$ million $+ 0.5 \times \$6$ million $= \$12$ million. At a discount rate of 10%, the *NPV* of the license for AMG is

$$NPV \text{ (without flexibility)} = -\$130 \text{ million} + \frac{\$12 \text{ million}}{0.1} = -\$10 \text{ million}$$

Since the *NPV* is negative, you decide to call off the negotiation and return to Detroit. However, just as it appears that the deal is falling through, John Banner softens his hard line and exhibits a willingness to negotiate. He asks you for alternative ideas to make the discussion a "win-win situation for both of us."

CASE 2. PROJECT WITH INVESTMENT FLEXIBILITY Mr. Banner now proposes that if AMG will show some "genuine commitment" today, he will let the company make its final decision about purchasing the license at the same price a year later when the test results will be known. Specifically, in return for a cash payment today of $12 million, he is willing to offer AMG the flexibility to decide on whether or not to invest in this project one year from now.

Is this a good deal for AMG? How much should Mr. Banner be willing to pay for this flexibility? That is, what is the economic value of this option that is being offered to AMG?

You return to the next room to caucus with your team. You reason that this flexibility option makes the whole situation different. AMG would now have the luxury of waiting for a year and then buying the license if and only if the test results are good. The probability that AMG will buy the license next year is 0.5, and the *NPV* one year hence is

$$NPV \text{ (next year)} = 0.5\left(-\$130 \text{ million} + \$18 \text{ million} + \frac{\$18 \text{ million}}{0.1}\right) = \$34 \text{ million}$$

The first term in parentheses is the cost of the license, the second term represents the first cash inflow of $18 million, and the third term is the present value of an $18 million perpetuity. The net present value *today* is the present value of $34 million, discounted at the opportunity cost of 10%. Thus:

$$NPV \text{ (with flexibility)} = \$34 \text{ million}(PVF_{0.1,1})$$
$$= \$34 \text{ million} \times 0.9091 = \$30,909,400$$

You now find this an economically viable investment. Flexibility has "converted" the negative-*NPV* project to a positive-*NPV* project. What is the value of this flexibility if it is defined as the change in *NPV* that arises from the flexibility?

$$Value \text{ of flexibility} = NPV \text{ (flexibility)} - NPV \text{ (no flexibility)}$$
$$= \$30,909,400 - (-\$10,000,000)$$
$$= \$40,909,400$$

Flexibility is thus a managerial option that increases the *NPV* of an investment. If forced to invest today (case 1), AMG "kills" the value of the option, and this is an opportunity cost of taking on the investment.

KEY CONCEPT   In evaluating a project with built-in investment flexibility, the true cost of the investment is not only the initial investment but also the value of the flexibility option.

The "**modified NPV**," which includes the cost of the option, must be positive to justify project acceptance. Since the option costs AMG $12 million (as proposed by Mr. Banner), the modified *NPV* of the deal to AMG is:

$$Modified \text{ } NPV = NPV \text{ (flexibility)} - \text{cost of option}$$
$$= \$30,909,400 - \$12,000,000$$
$$= \$18,909,400$$

You return to the negotiation room, shake hands with John Banner, write out a check for $12 million, and celebrate the deal. Both you and John Banner feel that this is a "win-win" deal.

On the way back to Detroit, your colleague Pete Marshall asks you whether the deal would have been dead if Mr. Banner had insisted on $20 million as the option price. You point out to your friend that as long as the option price was less than $30,909,400, the modified *NPV* would have been positive and the deal would have gone through.

A Final Note   Just as management must not be in a hurry to dismiss projects that have a negative *NPV* before considering the value of flexibility, it should also be careful about accepting projects that have a positive *NPV*. Blind reliance on such numbers can lead a company to make incorrect decisions, not because there is anything intrinsically wrong with *NPV* analysis, but because management may have made some inconsistent or unreasonable assumptions that imply a positive *NPV*. In a competitive, efficient marketplace, existing positive *NPV*s eventually disappear as companies vie with one another and compete for that project. Thus a company with a positive *NPV* must ask how and why it is able to generate a positive *NPV*. If it cannot find an answer, it must carefully reevaluate its capital budgeting decision to see whether it made any inconsistent or unrealistic assumptions.

Whatever the advantage(s), it behooves the company to be aware of these factors as the fundamental source of positive *NPV*s. Armed with a knowledge of the prime source of value, it can go ahead and plan defensive and offensive strategies to preserve and enhance this advantage. Managers must identify the factors that generate positive *NPV*s and then protect and enhance them.

SUMMARY

Section 8-1: An Overview of the Capital Budgeting Process

What are the various phases of the capital budgeting process?

- In making capital budgeting decisions, managers must use both strategic qualitative evaluation and quantitative analysis to determine whether the project is wealth increasing.

- The capital budgeting process consists of six different phases—identification of the project's impact on long-term goals, the screening phase, the evaluation phase, the implementation phase, and the control and audit phases.

- For proper capital budgeting analysis, all economic dependencies must be examined and proposals grouped into projects.

Section 8-2: Cash Flows Relevant to Capital Budgeting

What are the relevant cash flows for capital budgeting?

- The relevant benefits for capital budgeting analysis are the incremental cash flows after taxes ($\Delta CFAT$) produced by the project. These are not the total cash flows of the firm, but rather the cash flows that would occur only if the project is undertaken. Sunk costs are irrelevant.

- Capital budgeting analyses often separate investment and financing decisions. Thus the desirability of an investment in a capital asset is evaluated separately from how that investment is to be financed.

- The incremental cash flows after taxes are categorized into three types: the initial cash flows necessary to begin the project, the operating cash flows produced by the project, and the terminal cash flows related to the termination of the project. The initial cash flows can be further classified into direct and indirect cash flows.

- Capital budgeting projects often fall into one of two categories: cost-savings projects and revenue expansion projects.

Section 8-3: Criteria for Capital Budgeting

How do we determine whether a project increases wealth?

- After cash flows have been estimated, procedures must be developed for evaluating these cash flows and determining whether or not stockholder wealth will be increased if a project is accepted.

- The payback criterion measures how long it takes to recover the initial investment. In emphasizing the project's liquidity, it ignores the time value of money during the payback period and the cash flows after the payback period.

- The accounting rate of return criterion focuses on accounting profitability and ignores the time value of money and opportunity costs. It is thus inadequate for capital budgeting analyses.

- Net present value measures the economic profit created by accepting the project. It considers opportunity costs and cash flows. Because of value additivity, accepting a project with a positive *NPV* increases the company's market value by that amount.

- The internal rate of return (*IRR*) on a project is the time-value adjusted rate of return on the investment. If the *IRR* exceeds the opportunity cost of taking on an investment, the project should be accepted.

- The profitability index (*PI*) is a measure of the relative economic profitability of a project. It compares the present value of the inflows and the present value of the outflows. A *PI* in excess of 1 warrants project acceptance.

- Of all these methods, the *NPV* criterion is the most useful in evaluating the effect of a project on stockholder wealth.

Section 8-4: Applying the Project Selection Criteria

- Both cost-saving proposals and revenue-expanding proposals are evaluated in essentially the same way. The incremental cash flows after taxes are first estimated and then the standard capital budgeting criteria are applied to determine whether or not the project should be accepted.

Section 8-5: Competitive Advantage and Operating Flexibilities

Why do positive-NPV projects exist?

- In efficient markets, arbitrage profits are quickly eliminated. Many markets in which a firm operates—product markets, labor markets, raw materials markets—are not efficient and thus allow positive-*NPV* projects to exist. One of the firm's major objectives is to seek out and take advantage of these market imperfections.

- Positive *NPV*s can arise from product differentiation, economies of scale, the existence of distribution networks, quasirents, patents, government regulations, and operating and investment flexibilities.

What are operating and investment flexibilities and how do they affect a project's NPV?

- Operating flexibility refers to the ability of managers to use the capital assets in different ways to respond to changing economic conditions. Investment flexibility refers to the ability to delay an irreversible investment until additional information becomes available.

- Flexibility offers managerial options and hence has economic value. These options can transform an uneconomic investment into an attractive one.

- The ability to delay an investment until additional information becomes available can itself be wealth increasing. In this situation, negotiating for additional time by paying an up-front fee can be in the firm's best interest.

- For a project with investment flexibility, the true cost of the investment includes the value of the flexibility option.

QUESTIONS

1. What are the important features of each stage of the capital budgeting process?

2. Why is it sometimes difficult to quantify strategic issues involved in the capital budgeting process? How do managers proceed when faced with such difficulties?

3. A proper capital budgeting analysis requires grouping proposals into projects. Explain the rationale for this statement.

4. What are the different kinds of economic dependencies among projects?

5. What is the meaning of the term *incremental* in "incremental *CFAT*"?

6. Explain the three categories of *CFAT*s in a capital budgeting analysis.

7. What is the difference between direct and indirect cash flows?

8. What are the possible tax consequences of selling an asset?

9. How do capital and operating expenditures differ?

10. Because depreciation is not a cash flow, it is irrelevant in a capital budgeting analysis. Why is this statement false?

11. What are the weaknesses of the payback period and the accounting rate of return criteria?

12. What is the significance of value additivity?

13. Will *NPV* and *PI* lead to the same accept/reject decision? Why?

14. Given a project's *CFAT*s and the discount rate, finding the *NPV* simply means using the procedures developed in Chapter 4. True or false?

15. How do market imperfections create wealth-increasing possibilities that could produce positive-*NPV* capital budgeting investments?

16. How does the potential for operating flexibility in future investments affect the value of a capital budgeting project?

17. How much would you pay for the flexibility to defer an irreversible investment?

PROBLEMS

1. Five years ago, the Van de Graaf Electric Company purchased a generator for $180,000. At that time, the generator was estimated to have a salvage value of $30,000 in 15 years (i.e., ten years from today). Van de Graaf has an ordinary tax rate of 25% and uses straight-line depreciation.

    (a) What is the book value of the generator today?

    (b) What will Van de Graaf's cash flow after taxes (*CFAT*) be if it sells the generator today for $100,000?

    (c) What will Van de Graaf's *CFAT* be if it sells the generator today for $150,000?

2. The Maxey Printing Company purchased a wet press for $120,000 two years ago and has been depreciating it (using the MACRS method) to a salvage value of $30,000 three years from today. The manager, Glen Maxey, is considering selling the old press today and buying a more modern one. The com-

pany's marginal ordinary tax rate is 25%. *Note:* In the MACRS method, the depreciation in any year is calculated as $(K + 1)/[N(N + 1)/2] \times$ (depreciable base), where N is the life of the asset, K is the remaining life, and the depreciable base is calculated as purchase price less salvage value.

(a) What is the book value of the old press today?

(b) What will be the net cash flow from selling the press if it is sold for $50,000?

(c) What will be the net cash flow from selling the press if it is sold for $90,000?

3. Gamma Rayco is planning to replace an old cathode ray tube (CRT) (book value: $15,000) with a newer model that costs $30,000. The old CRT can be sold for $10,000. Furthermore, the new CRT has installation costs of $1,000 and an anticipated salvage value of $5,000 in ten years. Gamma Rayco has a marginal ordinary income tax rate of 25%. What net cash outflow is associated with the purchase of the new CRT (and the sale of the old one)?

4. The Lloyd Paint Company currently manufactures paint with a machine that cost $1.1 million five years ago and that is being depreciated (straight line) to a salvage value of $200,000 ten years from today. The raw materials for a gallon of paint cost $2.00, and the sales price is $3.50 per gallon. Lloyd sells 25,000 gallons per year. Beverly Reeves, Lloyd's new manager, estimates that Lloyd can sell 20% more paint if she replaces the current machine with a new one that produces a higher-quality paint at the same cost. The new machine will cost $1.5 million and be depreciated (straight line) to a value of $500,000 ten years from today. Lloyd's marginal tax rate is 25%.

(a) What is Lloyd's annual operating cash flow from operations with the current machine?

(b) What will Lloyd's annual operating cash flow from operations be with the new machine?

(c) Find the incremental change in the annual cash flow from operations if the old machine is replaced. Is there a way to answer this without doing parts (a) and (b)?

5. The Godfrey Vending Company plans to replace ten of its vending machines with newer models. The current machines were purchased three years ago for $8,000 each and are being depreciated (straight line) to a salvage value of $2,000 five years from now. The machines collectively generate annual revenues of $30,000 and annual expenses of $12,000. New machines can be purchased for $12,000 each and can be depreciated (straight line) to a salvage value of $7,000 five years from now. The new machines will generate annual sales of $40,000 (because of less downtime than with the old machines) and annual expenses of $8,000 (smaller repair bills than the old machines). If Godfrey's marginal tax rate is 25%, what will be the incremental change in its annual cash flow if the old machines are replaced?

6. The Hart Medical Supplies Company is thinking of replacing a machine that currently produces the pacemakers it sells. The existing machine cost $150,000 three years ago and is being depreciated (straight line) to a salvage value of $40,000 seven years from now. It can be sold today for $100,000. The new

machine will cost $200,000 and be depreciated (straight line) to a salvage value of $60,000 ten years from now. The cost of training employees to use the new machine will be $5,000, and installation costs for the new machine will be $3,000. Finally, the new machine will necessitate an increase in working capital of $10,000. Hart's marginal tax rate is 25%. Find the net initial outlay associated with replacing the old machine.

7. Barbarian's Pizza is analyzing the prospect of purchasing an additional fire-brick oven. The oven will cost $200,000 and be depreciated (straight line) to a salvage value of $120,000 in ten years. The extra oven will increase annual revenues by $120,000 and annual operating expenses by $90,000. Barbarian's marginal tax rate is 25%.

   (a) What annual cash flow will be generated by the new oven?

   (b) What is the payback period for the additional oven?

   (c) What is the accounting rate of return for the additional oven?

   (d) Barbarian's Pizza's required rate of return is 12%. What is the net present value of the additional oven?

   (e) What is the profitability index for the additional oven?

   (f) What is the internal rate of return for the additional oven?

8. Chin Jen Lie is considering the expansion of his chain of Chinese restaurants by opening a new restaurant in Duluth, Minnesota. If he does, he estimates that the restaurant will require a net initial outlay of $500,000. Furthermore, he estimates that the restaurant will generate annual cash flows of $20,000 and that he can sell the restaurant for $1,000,000 in ten years.

   (a) If Mr. Lie's required rate of return is 10%, what will be the net present value of opening the restaurant? Should he open it?

   (b) If Mr. Lie's required rate of return is 14%, what will be the net present value of opening the restaurant? Should he open it?

9. Victoria Korchnoi is thinking of importing caviar to sell to restaurants and specialty stores. She estimates that this venture will require an initial outlay of $300,000 to buy a refrigerated storage unit that can be depreciated (straight line) to a salvage value of $50,000 in eight years. In addition, Ms. Korchnoi estimates that she will need $40,000 in working capital during the eight years of the project. Annual sales are estimated to be $110,000 and annual expenses, $20,000. Ms. Korchnoi estimates that the marginal tax rate will be 25% during the project's lifetime.

   (a) What is the initial outlay associated with opening up the importing business?

   (b) What is the annual cash flow from operations?

   (c) What will be the terminal cash flow in year 8?

   (d) What is the payback period for this project?

   (e) What is the accounting rate of return of this project?

   (f) If Ms. Korchnoi requires a 16% rate of return to make this investment, what is the project's net present value? What is the profitability index?

   (g) What is the project's internal rate of return?

10. Universal Farm Supply's management has observed that it can sell as much fertilizer as it can stock, and it is considering the possibility of purchasing a forklift and expanding warehouse space in order to handle and stock more fertilizer (both are necessary to expand sales). The forklift will cost $42,000 and be depreciated straight line to a salvage value of $0 in seven years, even though it is expected to last for ten years. The warehouse expansion will cost $100,000 and be depreciated straight line to a salvage value of $60,000 in ten years. The expansion will allow Universal to sell 1,000,000 more pounds per year at $0.20 per pound (the fertilizer actually costs Universal $0.17 per pound to manufacture). Universal's marginal tax rate is 34%, and its required rate of return is 12%.

(a) Find the net initial outlay associated with the expansion.

(b) Find the annual cash flow from operations during years 1 to 7.

(c) Find the annual cash flow from operations during years 8 to 10.

(d) Find the net present value of the expansion project. Should Universal expand to sell the extra fertilizer?

(e) Find the net present value of the expansion project if Universal's discount rate is 20%. What is the profitability index?

(f) Based solely on your answers to parts (d) and (e), what can you say about the expansion project's internal rate of return?

11. Joley's Department Store has recently received the results of a study that suggest that potential sales are being lost because many customers dislike having to use the elevator in Joley's and prefer to go across the street to Foske's Department Store, which has an escalator. Consequently, Joley's is considering replacing the elevator with a new escalator. The elevator was purchased ten years ago for $140,000 and is being depreciated (straight line) to a salvage value of $40,000 ten years from now. It can be sold today for $80,000. The escalator can be purchased for $300,000 and be depreciated (straight line) to a salvage value of $100,000 in ten years. In addition, Joley's anticipates that having an escalator rather than an elevator will increase sales by $25,000 annually and decrease operating expenses by $5,000 annually. Variable costs are 60% of sales prices. Joley's has a marginal tax rate of 25%.

(a) What is the present book value of the elevator?

(b) What is the initial cash outflow associated with replacing the elevator?

(c) What will be Joley's incremental change in annual cash flow if it replaces the elevator?

(d) What is the payback period for the replacement decision?

(e) If Joley's uses a 12% discount rate to value projects, what is the net present value of the replacement decision? What is the *PI* at 12%?

(f) If Joley's uses a 16% discount rate to value projects, what is the net present value of the replacement decision? What is the *PI* at 16%?

(g) What is the internal rate of return of the replacement decision?

12. Catherine Mauzy cannot decide between two machines that manufacture umbrellas. Each machine costs $100,000 and can produce 10,000 umbrellas an-

nually (the umbrellas can be sold for $4 each). Machine *A* can be depreciated straight line to a salvage value of $0 in ten years, and the annual expense of producing 10,000 umbrellas is $13,350. Machine *B* can be depreciated to a salvage value of $90,000 in ten years, and the annual expense of producing 10,000 umbrellas is $15,650. Ms. Mauzy's corporation has a marginal tax rate of 25%.

(a) Find the net present value of each machine if the relevant discount rate is 10%. If Ms. Mauzy uses the net present value method to rank the machines, which will she choose?

(b) Find the internal rate of return of each machine. If Ms. Mauzy uses the internal rate of return to rank the machines, which will she choose?

13. The Ronn Airline Co. is considering the replacement of its fleet of ten twin-prop planes with five new jets. One jet can replace two of Ronn's current planes. The company has prepared an analysis indicating that each new plane will cost $347,000 and will generate net cash after taxes of $100,000 per year for five years. Assume that after five years the salvage value will be $0 for both old and new planes. The planes currently in use earn net cash after taxes of only $10,000 per year per plane and have a $0 salvage value. Ronn's cost of capital is 10%.

(a) Should Ronn purchase the new jets? Why?

(b) What would you recommend if the salvage value of the old planes was $40,000 each?

14. The Redwood Corp. has a project that requires an initial investment of $8,000 and has a three-year life. The tax rate is 34%. The project will earn $10,000 in year 1, $9,000 in year 2, and $8,000 in year 3. Operating costs during the three years of the project will be $1,000, $1,600, and $0, respectively. Redwood's discount rate is 10%, and the firm uses MACRS as its depreciation method (see Problem 2). What are the project's *NPV* and *IRR*? Is the project acceptable?

15. Dinesh Vaswami of the Dutch League Importing Company is considering a project that will require an initial outlay of $1.25 million for a freighter plus $500,000 for working capital. The freighter will be depreciated (straight line) to a salvage value of $250,000 in ten years. This project is expected to produce sales of $850,000 and require expenses of $425,000 annually for the next ten years. Dutch League Importing has a marginal tax rate of 25%.

(a) Calculate the annual cash flow from operations for this project.

(b) Calculate the net present value of this project for the following discount rates: 6%, 8%, 10%, 12%, 14%, and 16%. Draw a graph of the *NPV* on the vertical axis and the discount rate on the horizontal axis. Where does the *NPV* curve cross the horizontal axis? Does this point have any special significance?

16. Jenkins Trucking Co. has bid on a major contract to haul industrial chemicals. The contract award decision will be announced 12 months from now, and Jenkins estimates that it has a 60% probability of being awarded the contract. In anticipation of this potential project, Jenkins must commit to the truck manufacturer now to purchase the trucks next year at a cost of $696,000. If

Jenkins gets the contract, the vehicles will produce expected cash flows of $182,000 per year for eight years, with a *RRR* of 12%. The vehicles will not be needed if Jenkins does not receive the contract. What is the maximum that Jenkins should be willing to pay to the manufacturer today for an option to purchase the vehicles only if it gets the contract?

8A

GROUPING PROPOSALS INTO PROJECTS

For a proper capital budgeting analysis, all proposals being considered by a firm must first be grouped into projects because, as we have pointed out, a project is either a single independent proposal or a collection of all economically dependent proposals. A project is therefore economically independent of all other projects being analyzed by the firm.

This appendix has the following purposes:

1. Outline the procedure for grouping proposals into projects.

2. Outline the procedure for choosing *the best* project.

3. Establish a framework for deciding on the scale of the investment. That is, how many projects should the firm adopt?

This is an important aspect of capital budgeting because the process becomes very detailed when a firm is considering several proposals. A systematic approach not only makes the decision process easier but also ensures that projects are chosen correctly.

Step 1: Identify All Proposals Being Considered

Several proposals being considered by the "investment group" of Elchem Enterprises are listed in Table 8A-1. Notice that the proposals are diverse and range from peach farming to computer software. Each of these proposals is a "feasible proposal"; that is, it is within the scope of Elchem's strategic goals and policies, expertise, and interest. But it is not clear at this point whether these proposals will increase the firm's market value, and it is not even known how many of the proposals should be adopted.

Step 2: Identify Economic Dependencies Among Proposals

There are economic dependencies possible among the cash flows of the various proposals. Management must, in this stage, identify these dependencies. This task may be difficult. It requires experience and an understanding of the various businesses, from computer software to peach farming.

Table 8A-2 lists the dependencies that management has identified. For example, proposals 1 and 2 are mutually exclusive because if Elchem grows peaches on its farmland, it cannot grow oranges there. Proposals 3 and 4 are complementary

■

TABLE 8A-1
Proposals Under Consideration by Elchem Enterprises

Proposal	Description
1	Start peach farming on company land.
2	Start orange growing on company land.
3	Introduce a new line of designer jeans.
4	Establish a fashion boutique.
5	Open a dry-cleaning operation at location *x*.
6	Buy a cosmetics franchise.
7	Open a liquor store at location *x*.
8	Market peach preserves or orange marmalade.
9	Open a photo service at the local mall.
10	Expand into computer peripherals.
11	Develop computer software.
12	Invest in rental property.

TABLE 8A-2
Identification of Dependencies

Proposals 1 and 2	are mutually exclusive
Proposals 1 and 8	are complements.
Proposals 2 and 8	are complements.
Proposals 3 and 4	are complements.
Proposals 4 and 6	are complements.
Proposals 5 and 7	are mutually exclusive.
Proposals 10 and 11	are complements.
Proposals 9 and 12	are completely independent of all other proposals.

because management believes that a fashion boutique will increase the cash flows from the designer jeans venture.

Step 3: Group Proposals into Projects

The 12 proposals may be grouped into 18 different projects. First, each proposal can be adopted by itself in isolation. Thus there must be at least as many projects as there are proposals. In addition, all proposals with economic dependencies may be grouped together to create new projects. For example, proposal 1 can be adopted in isolation or with proposal 8 because they are complements. Notice that although proposals 1 and 2 are economically dependent, they also are mutually exclusive and therefore cannot be grouped together into one project. The other projects identified are $(2 + 8)$, $(3 + 4)$, $(3 + 4 + 6)$, $(4 + 6)$, and $(10 + 11)$, resulting in a total of 18 projects.

Step 4: Calculate the NPV for Each Project

Eighteen capital budgeting analyses are required to find the *NPV* of each of these projects. This requires identifying the three categories of Δ*CFAT*s. The project with the highest *NPV* is the best one.

Step 5: Choose the Scale of the Investment

Although Step 4 identified the best project, it does not address the question of scale. It may not always be optimal for the firm to pick the highest-*NPV* project if it has capital constraints. For example, assume that the combination $(3 + 4)$ turns out to be the best project with an *NPV* of $1.5 million. If these projects are also the ones that require the largest initial outlays (say, $6 million in total), Elchem may not be able to accept the best project if its capital budget (or the amount it has for investments) is only $5 million. Of course, if Elchem has no trouble obtaining additional funds, this is not a problem. In fact, without such constraints, Elchem could adopt all projects that have positive *NPV*s. If funds are limited, however, it should choose that combination of projects that maximizes the *NPV* without exceeding its capital constraint.

SUGGESTED ADDITIONAL READINGS

Alchian, A. A. "The Rate of Interest, Fisher's Rate of Return over Cost and Keynes' Internal Rate of Return." *American Economic Review,* December 1955, pp. 938–942.

Bierman, Harold, Jr., and Seymour Smidt. *The Capital Budgeting Decision.* New York: Macmillan, 1984.

Bower, J. L. *Managing the Resource Allocation Process.* Cambridge, MA: Harvard University, Division of Research, Graduate School of Business Administration, 1970.

Grant, Eugene L., William G. Ireson, and Richard S. Leavenworth. *Principles of Engineering Economy.* New York: Ronald Press, 1976.

Hayes, R. H., and D. A. Garvin. "Managing As If Tomorrow Mattered." *Harvard Business Review* 60 (May–June 1982): 70–79.

Kemna, Angelien G. Z. "Case Studies on Real Options." *Financial Management* 22, no. 3 (Autumn 1993): 259–270.

Klammer, T. "Empirical Evidence of the Adoption of Sophisticated Capital Budgeting Techniques." *Journal of Business,* July 1972, pp. 387–397.

Levy, Haim, and Marshall Sarnat. *Capital Investment and Financial Decisions.* Englewood Cliffs, NJ: Prentice-Hall, 1982.

Majd, S., and Robert S. Pindyck. "Time to Build, Option Value and Investment Decisions." *Journal of Financial Economics,* 1987, pp. 7–28.

Myers, S. C. "Finance Theory and Financial Strategy." *Interfaces* 14 (January–February 1984): 126–137.

Pindyck, Robert S. "Irreversible Investment, Capacity Choice, and the Value of the Firm." *The American Economic Review* 78, no. 5 (December 1988).

Reinhardt, U. E. "Break-even Analysis for Lockheed's Tri Star: An Application of Financial Theory." *Journal of Finance,* September 1973, pp. 821–838.

Schall, L. D. G., L. Sundem, and W. R. Geijsbeek. "Survey and Analysis of Capital Budgeting Methods." *Journal of Finance,* March 1978, pp. 281–287.

Schwab, B., and P. Lusztig. "A Comparative Analysis of the Net Present Value and the Benefit–Cost Ratios As Measures of the Economic Desirability of Investment." *Journal of Finance,* June 1969, pp. 507–516.

Shapiro, A. E. "Corporate Strategy and the Capital Budgeting Decision." *Midland Corporate Finance Journal,* Spring 1985, pp. 22–36.

Trigeorgis, Lenos. "Real Options and Interactions with Financial Flexibility." *Financial Management* 22, no. 3 (Autumn 1993): 202–224.

NINE SPECIAL ISSUES IN CAPITAL BUDGETING DECISIONS

If you have read this far, there is no dignified way of escape left to you. You have paid your fare, and climbed to the highest peak of the rollercoaster. . . . It is no use trying to back out. . . . The going will be rough but I will promise you excitement aplenty.

—B. Hoffman[1]

[1] From *The Strange Story of the Quantum, an Account for the General Reader of the Growth of the Ideas Underlying Our Present Atomic Knowledge*, 2nd ed. (New York: Dover Publications, 1959).

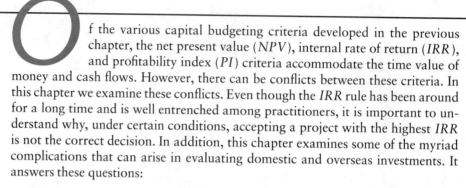

Of the various capital budgeting criteria developed in the previous chapter, the net present value (*NPV*), internal rate of return (*IRR*), and profitability index (*PI*) criteria accommodate the time value of money and cash flows. However, there can be conflicts between these criteria. In this chapter we examine these conflicts. Even though the *IRR* rule has been around for a long time and is well entrenched among practitioners, it is important to understand why, under certain conditions, accepting a project with the highest *IRR* is not the correct decision. In addition, this chapter examines some of the myriad complications that can arise in evaluating domestic and overseas investments. It answers these questions:

- What are the limitations of internal rate of return and profitability index as capital budgeting criteria?

- How are projects with different lives evaluated?

- How do we choose among projects when the amount of capital available is limited?

- What is the optimal time to replace an asset?

- What factors must be considered when evaluating foreign projects?

Appendix 9A discusses those conditions in which conflicts in project ranking may occur. Appendix 9B shows how capital budgeting decisions are made in an inflationary environment. Some of the important determinants of exchange rates and hence future cash flows from overseas investments are examined in Appendix 9C.

9-1

PROBLEMS WITH THE *IRR* AND THE *PI* AS DECISION CRITERIA

The NPV *Profile*

Three methods for finding a project's *IRR* were presented in Chapter 4. We now discuss a fourth method, the *NPV* profile. The *NPV* profile is especially useful for achieving some of the objectives of this chapter—cataloging the weaknesses of the *IRR* criterion and highlighting the potential for conflict between the *NPV* and the *IRR* when projects are ranked. An *NPV* profile is a graphical representation of a project's *NPV*s corresponding to different discount rates.

Because the *IRR* is defined to be the discount rate at which *NPV* = 0, the *NPV* profile is a graphical approach to determining the *IRR* for a project. This method identifies a project's *NPV*s for different discount rates and then fits a curve through these points. Figure 9-1 shows the *NPV* profile for Mylanta's computer replacement project (see Chapter 8). Using the cash flows after taxes ($\Delta CFATs$) for this example, we first calculate the *NPV* of the project using a 0% discount rate. For this example, the *NPV* turns out to be $47,260 because when the discount rate is 0%, the cash flows can simply be summed after carefully distinguishing between inflows and outflows. Next, a low and a very high discount rate are arbitrarily

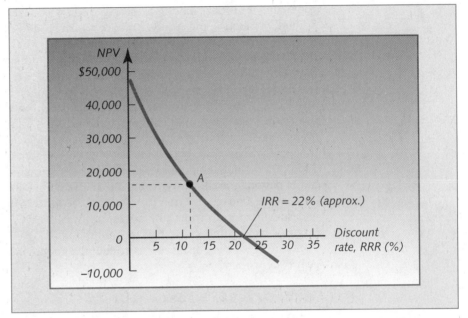

FIGÜRE 9-1

Using the NPV *profile to find the* IRR *for Mylanta's computer replacement project*

	RRR	NPV
	0%	$47,260
	5	32,068
	10	20,089
	15	10,508
	20	2,745
IRR →		
	25	(3,620)
	30	(8,897)

selected, say 5% and 30%, and their implied *NPV*s are calculated and plotted. Figure 9-1 shows the calculation of the *NPV*s for the different discount rates. With this information a curve can be fitted through these points, and in this case the curve intersects the horizontal axis. Of course, the more rates that are selected, the more precise the profile is.

Notice in Figure 9-1 that the intercept on the horizontal axis corresponds to the discount rate at which the *NPV* is $0. According to the definition, because this discount rate has to be the project's *IRR*, the *IRR* for this project can be read from the *NPV* profile as approximately 22%.

The *NPV* profile also illustrates the correspondence between the *NPV* and the *IRR* criteria. If the required rate of return, *RRR*, is 12%, the computer project should be accepted, using both criteria, because the *NPV* is positive and because the project's 22% *IRR* is greater than the required rate of return of 12%. In fact, when the required rate of return is less than the *IRR* (i.e., all points to the left of the *IRR*), the *NPV* is always positive. Thus both the *NPV* and the *IRR* criteria accept this project when the required rate of return is less than the *IRR*. Similarly, both criteria reject this project if the required rate of return is greater than the *IRR*.

For projects such as Mylanta's computer replacement decision, a manager using either the *NPV* or the *IRR* criterion will arrive at the same accept/reject decision. If the project is acceptable according to the *NPV*, it is also acceptable according to the *IRR*. Similarly, if it is rejected according to the *NPV*, it is also rejected according to the *IRR* rule. Thus, in this case, there is no conflict between the recommendations of either criterion, but this result cannot be generalized to all projects or to situations in which a project ranking is required.

Problems with the IRR   Given that one of the objectives of this chapter is to show the superiority of the *NPV* criterion over the *IRR* criterion, the reader may wonder why a detailed discussion of the *IRR* is even necessary. If the *NPV* is better than the *IRR*, why not just disregard the *IRR* altogether?

One cannot ignore the *IRR* criterion for a variety of reasons. First, in theory, the *IRR* rule often leads to the selection of the same projects as the *NPV* rule does, at least for independent projects. But, under certain conditions, these two rules give conflicting decisions, and it is these exceptions that warrant a closer examination. Second, in practice, the required rate of return used to perform a *NPV* analysis is not generally known at lower levels of management in large corporations (e.g., at the divisional or production level). In these cases, projects are initially ranked by their *IRR*s, and then the better projects are forwarded to upper-level management. It is at this level that a formal *NPV* analysis is conducted. Also, corporations have historically viewed investments in terms of their profitability, and the *IRR* does just this by measuring the return per dollar invested. Many managers have trouble evaluating the attractiveness of an investment using the *NPV*. For example, although a rate of return of 68% makes a project appear very attractive, an *NPV* of $45,000 does not communicate the level of "performance." The real estate industry, in particular, relies heavily on *IRR* analyses of investments and uses the *NPV* only as a secondary criterion for assessing the investment's merits. Because of the widespread appeal of this rate of return measure, it is useful to understand the extent of its usefulness as well as its limitations.

Before proceeding further we introduce the notion of *conventional* and *nonconventional* projects.

MULTIPLE *IRR*s FOR A PROJECT

CONVENTIONAL AND NONCONVENTIONAL CASH FLOWS If net cash outflows are characterized by a minus sign and net cash inflows are identified with a plus sign, Mylanta's computer replacement project (see Chapter 8) can be represented as follows:

That is, Mylanta's proposed project has the net annual cash flow pattern (−, +, +, +, +). In this example notice that the sign changes only once, from − to + in year 1. A project with the $\Delta CFAT$ pattern (−, +, +, . . .) is known as a **conventional project**; a project with any other cash flow pattern is called a **nonconventional project**.

In many situations large capital outlays are required initially just as a new project is implemented, and after the project becomes operational, the $\Delta CFAT$s are positive over the life of the project. Unlike these conventional projects, in many other situations, a project may periodically require a large cash outlay (e.g., for maintenance and repairs) over its life, and thus some future net cash flows may be negative. As an example, consider a strip-mining operation. Strip mining typically needs very large cash outflows at both the beginning and the end of the project. Initially, capital and revenue expenditures cause large outflows, whereas at the end, when the project is terminated, land restoration costs cause large net cash outflows. The operating $\Delta CFAT$s, however, are net inflows as revenues are generated from the sale of the ore.

NONCONVENTIONAL CASH FLOWS AND MULTIPLE *IRRS* Nonconventional projects can pose special problems for the financial manager who uses the *IRR* criterion. A conventional project has only one real (positive or negative) *IRR*. In contrast, a nonconventional project may have as many real *IRR*s as there are sign changes in its cash flow pattern. Because finding an *IRR* is equivalent mathematically to solving a polynomial of the *n*th degree, there are *n* possible solutions. In the case of a conventional project, there is only one (unique) *IRR*. The other $n - 1$ solutions are imaginary and therefore make no economic sense. With a nonconventional project, however, more than one possible real solution (*IRR*) may result, one for each change in signs. For example, if a project's cash flow pattern is $(-, +, -, +, +)$, there are three sign changes and possibly three real *IRR*s.

To illustrate, suppose that Walker Plastics is considering a two-year project that has the following cash flow pattern:

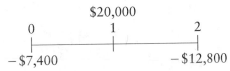

This project's cash flow pattern $(-, +, -)$ indicates two possible *IRR* solutions. Solving for the *IRR* yields

$$NPV = -\$7,400 + \$20,000(PVF_{IRR,1}) - \$12,800(PVF_{IRR,2}) = 0$$

Walker finds that the *IRR* for its project equals 4.08% *and* 66.19%.

If Walker's required rate of return (*RRR*) for this project is 15%, should it accept or reject the project? The answer is not obvious. To see why, examine Figure 9-2, which shows the *NPV* profile for this project. First notice that the *NPV* is positive over the range 4.08% to 66.19% and is negative otherwise. If the required rate of return is 15% and the *IRR* is "really" 4.08%, the project should be rejected because *IRR* < *RRR*. If the *IRR* is "really" 66.19%, the project should be accepted because *IRR* > *RRR*.

Next, notice that this dilemma is highlighted by the "nonconventional" *NPV* profile of this project. The *NPV* profile in Figure 9-2 begins with a negative *NPV*, which increases slowly, then becomes positive for a range of discount rates, and finally returns to a negative value. Of course, nonconventional projects' *NPV* profiles may take any number of forms depending on the number as well as the magnitude and timing of the future net cash outflows.

When multiple *IRR*s exist, which one is correct? The answer is that all are correct. Each *IRR* causes *NPV* = 0, and according to the definition of *IRR*, any discount rate that satisfies this condition is an *IRR*. Although multiple *IRR*s may be the mathematically correct rates of return for a set of cash flows, managers, understandably, have difficulty interpreting the economic significance of such a result. They must then turn to the *NPV* criterion.

Fortunately, cash flow patterns that have multiple *IRR*s are uncommon because they result from extreme cases such as many sign reversals or unusually large cash outflows. Nevertheless, they do occur. Three interesting cases in which multiple *IRR*s occur more commonly are oil and gas development projects, mineral recovery projects, and leveraged leases. In the first two cases, additional funds may be invested in order to speed up the recovery of a wasting asset. For example, an oil company may spend money on a fracture job or a chemical injection to accelerate the recovery of an oil reserve. (Some analysts might argue that this should be viewed as a separate project rather than a negative cash flow within an existing

FIGURE 9-2

NPV *profile for a nonconventional cash flow with multiple* IRRs

Assumed Discount Rate	NPV
0%	−$200
4.08	0
5	38
10	203
15	313
20	378
25	408
30	411
35	392
40	355
45	305
50	244
55	175
60	100
65	20
66.19	0
70	−64

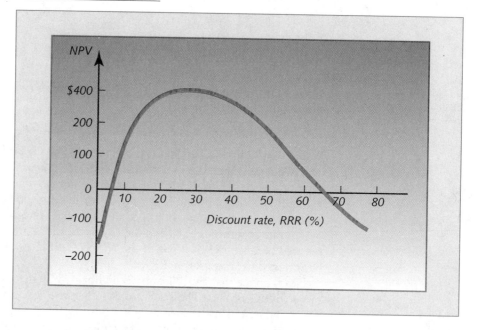

project.) In a leveraged lease, a leasing company may borrow funds from a bank, use these funds to buy a computer, and then lease it to another company. This investment produces net cash inflows (lease payments less the interest on the bank loan) for a number of years. However, several large cash outflows occur when the loan is repaid, which is then followed by a large cash inflow when the computer is sold at the lease's expiration. In such situations, it is best to avoid the multiple-*IRR* problem and base the decision on a project's *NPV*.

NO *IRR* MAY EXIST FOR A PROJECT

For certain nonconventional projects, it may be impossible to find a discount rate that makes the project's *NPV* = 0 (i.e., some projects may have no *IRR*). The reason is that the *NPV* for these projects does not decline smoothly with higher discount rates. Consider the following example:

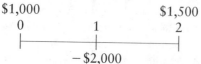

F I G U R E   9 - 3

NPV *profile for a nonconventional cash flow with no* IRR

Discount Rate	NPV	Discount Rate	NPV
0%	$500	40%	$337
5	456	45	334
10	421	50	333
15	395	55	334
20	375	60	336
25	360	65	339
30	349	70	343
35	342		

The *NPV* profile shows that there is no point where the *IRR* is determined.

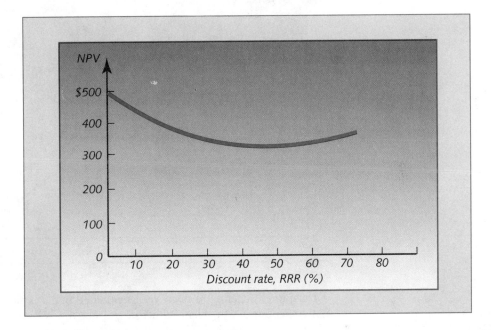

Figure 9-3 shows the *NPV* profile for such a project. As this graph indicates, there is no discount rate for which *NPV* = 0, even though there are two sign changes. In fact, at discount rates greater than 50%, the *NPV* actually rises. This situation may occur in cases in which the initial cash flow is positive—for example, when a firm initially borrows funds but does not invest the money until later, or a firm receives a substantial government subsidy to entice it to take on an investment. This is especially true for companies that are considering investments in developing countries.

CONFLICTS IN USING THE *IRR* AND *NPV* CRITERIA

There are two different issues that a decision maker usually confronts. A capital budgeting decision can involve either a project selection or a project ranking. **Project selection** simply refers to the analysis of whether or not a project is acceptable. **Project ranking**, on the other hand, attempts to identify (rank) various projects in order of decreasing attractiveness. Project ranking is especially important when a company has limited funds and must select, say, only the three best projects that can be adopted with the limited funds. In addition, when projects are mutually exclusive, ranking is important because the acceptance of any one project rules out the others. Obviously, in this situation, the firm should choose the best (highest-ranked) project. To avoid any confusion, readers may want to ask themselves throughout this chapter whether a particular discussion pertains to a ranking situation or simply to a selection situation.

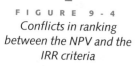

FIGURE 9-4
Conflicts in ranking between the NPV and the IRR criteria

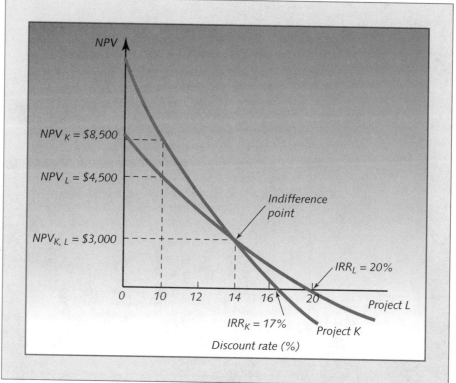

If capital budgeting projects were evaluated one at a time, one would not normally encounter a problem with using either the *NPV* or the *IRR*. The accept/ reject decisions would be identical according to both criteria. (Of course, this observation does not apply to cases with multiple *IRR*s or in which an *IRR* cannot be determined.) But when two or more projects must be ranked because they are mutually exclusive, the rankings based on their *IRR*s may differ from the rankings based on the *NPV*s.

To clarify these points, consider Figure 9-4, which shows the *NPV* profiles for two mutually exclusive projects, *K* and *L*. The *NPV*s of these projects intersect at a discount rate of 14%. At this required rate of return (*RRR*), they have identical *NPV*s and thus are equally attractive to the firm that is considering them. Moreover, from the profiles of *K* and *L*, their respective *IRR*s are $IRR_K = 17\%$ and $IRR_L = 20\%$. We now consider two separate problems.

INDEPENDENT PROJECTS: AN ACCEPT/REJECT DECISION Assume that a manager is interested in evaluating *K* and *L* independently (i.e., each one separately) by using the *NPV* and the *IRR* criteria and that the *RRR* is 10% for both projects. At this discount rate, $NPV_K = \$8,500$ and $NPV_L = \$4,500$. Because both have positive *NPV*s, both are acceptable projects using the *NPV* criterion.

Now use the *IRR* criterion to evaluate acceptability. Because $IRR_K = 17\%$ and $IRR_L = 20\%$, both projects have *IRR*s greater than the *RRR* of 10%. Hence both *K* and *L* are acceptable projects. For independent projects both the *NPV* and the *IRR* lead to identical accept/reject decisions. If a project is acceptable according to the *NPV* criterion, it is acceptable according to the *IRR* criterion. Similarly, if a project is rejected by the *NPV* criterion, it is rejected by the *IRR* criterion.

MUTUALLY EXCLUSIVE PROJECTS: A RANKING DECISION The ranking of projects is important when management is choosing among a number of alternative or competing investments. If only one is to be chosen, the projects need to be ranked in descending order according to their *NPV* and *IRR* values, and the project with the highest (best) value chosen. Using the *NPV* criterion in Figure 9-4, we get the following ranking of *K* and *L* for a *RRR* of 10%:

Project	Criterion: NPV	Rank
K	$8,500	1
L	4,500	2

On the other hand, with the *IRR* criterion, project *L*'s *IRR* = 20% is clearly superior to *K*'s *IRR* = 17%. In this case, the ranking of *K* and *L* is reversed for an *RRR* of 10%:

Project	Criterion: IRR	Rank
K	17%	2
L	20	1

Thus, with *RRR* = 10%, there is a conflict in the project ranking. The *NPV* ranks project *K* over *L*, and the *IRR* ranks project *L* over *K*. Because the *NPV* rule is the preferred method, selecting the investment with the highest *IRR* leads to accepting the less lucrative project. Notice, however, that this ranking conflict disappears to the right of the indifference (crossover) point, which was earlier determined to be 14%. That is, if *RRR* = 16%, both the *NPV* and the *IRR* criteria rank project *L* over *K*. It can therefore be concluded that when one is ranking mutually exclusive projects, the *NPV* and the *IRR* can lead to conflicting decisions. Whether or not a conflict occurs depends on the *RRR* being used.

KEY CONCEPT   For making accept/reject decisions, both the *NPV* and *IRR* criteria lead to identical recommendations. Conflicts can arise, however, when projects must be ranked.

Conflicts Between the NPV and the PI in Project Ranking   Just as the *IRR* and the *NPV* can lead to ranking conflicts, the *NPV* and the *PI* can lead to different project selections. Because the *PI* is a relative measure of profitability, it ignores the size of the initial investment. For example, which of the following projects should be chosen if only one can be accepted?

Project	NPV	Initial Investment	PI
A	$400	$ 800	1.50
B	600	1,400	1.43

Both the *NPV* and the *PI* indicate that both *A* and *B* are acceptable. But to pick only one project, these projects must be ranked. The *NPV* criterion would choose project *B* over project *A*, and the *PI* criterion would prefer project *A* to project *B*. However, project *B* would lead to a greater increase in firm value because it has the higher *NPV*, and so it should be the one selected.

A Final Word   When capital budgeting projects are evaluated, both the *NPV* and the *IRR* criteria are preferable to criteria that ignore the time value of money. Yet because

CAPITAL BUDGETING DECISIONS: DO THEY REALLY INCREASE FIRM VALUE?

*T*he entire justification for using the NPV *criterion is that the* NPV *of an investment measures the increase in wealth to the firm that adopts the investment. This concept was explored in Chapter 7, and this chapter relies on the NPV rule when making capital budgeting decisions.*

How does the theory carry over to practice? Is there any evidence that capital budgeting decisions actually affect the value of the firm or the wealth of the stockholders?

That is, when managers announce their capital budgeting decisions, does the market respond by revaluing the companies' stock? According to the theory, we know that it should.

Two researchers examined precisely this issue.* They analyzed what happened to the stock prices of 658 corporations when managers announced unexpected increases in capital expenditures. Between 1975 and 1981, the evidence indicated that increases in planned corporate capital expenditures resulted in increases in stock

prices (increases in excess returns, to be precise). The data also showed the opposite effect when firms reduced their capital expenditures.

This is strong evidence that stockholder wealth does indeed increase for those firms whose capital expenditure decisions are motivated by maximizing firm value.

* See John J. McConnell and Chris J. Muscarella, "Corporate Capital Expenditure Decisions and the Market Value of the Firm," Journal of Financial Economics, September 1985, pp. 399–422.

there can be ranking conflicts between the *NPV* and the *IRR* and because there can be more than one *IRR* for some projects, it is advisable to use the *NPV* criterion. The *NPV* criterion is always consistent with the goal of maximizing shareholder wealth. A properly determined discount rate for *NPV* calculations allows the financial manager to make decisions that increase the company's market value and, consequently, its stock price. See the highlight above.

9-2

SPECIAL CAPITAL BUDGETING SITUATIONS

*I*n this section we present various special capital budgeting situations, but the reader is urged to examine Figure 9-5 before proceeding. Figure 9-5 is, in effect, a summary of this entire section.

FIGURE 9-5
Capital budgeting decisions under special conditions

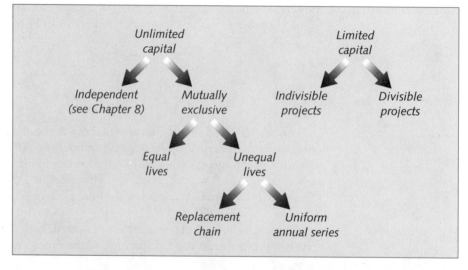

Evaluating Mutually Exclusive Projects with Different Lives

In the capital budgeting ranking situations we have presented so far, we implicitly assumed that the mutually exclusive projects had the same economic life. This may not be the case in reality. For example, two machines may do exactly the same job, but one may last longer. If they are independent projects, the unequal lives are not a problem. As long as their *NPV*s are positive, they should be accepted. If they are mutually exclusive (competing) investments, however, the use of the *NPV* criterion may have to be modified. This occurs when the task or activity lasts longer than the assets that perform it; that is, the assets must be replaced at a future date in order to continue the activity.

Take the case of a firm that is evaluating two mutually exclusive machines, *X* and *Y*. If machine *X* has a three-year life and machine *Y* has a two-year life, a simple *NPV* comparison will fail. Why? Because one must properly account for any cash flows (or alternative investment opportunities) that exist at the end of the shorter-lived investment. If the shorter-lived machine is chosen and if the job it performs is an ongoing operation, a decision to replace this machine in two years with a (similar) machine must be considered.[2]

One solution to the problem of different economic lives is to evaluate both projects over the longer (three-year) horizon by arbitrarily assuming that machine *Y* will produce $0 cash flow in the third year. This is clearly unreasonable. Another approach is to evaluate both projects over the shorter (two-year) horizon. This means estimating the remaining value of the longer-lived machine and treating it as a cash inflow in the second year. This approach is also somewhat arbitrary: Why assume that machine *X* has a shorter useful life than it really has? The key observation, though, is that the projects must be analyzed over a common economic life. We now introduce two evaluation methods that incorporate this feature into the analysis: the replacement chain method and the uniform annual series method.

THE REPLACEMENT CHAIN METHOD

Consider a decision to purchase either a "deluxe" or an "economy" model machine. Machine *D* has a useful life of four years, costs $24,000, and will provide net benefits of $8,000 per year. Machine *E* costs only half as much but has a useful life of just two years. Its annual benefits are estimated to be $7,400. The question becomes: Is it better to purchase the more expensive machine with its larger benefits (larger cost savings and depreciation) or the less expensive machine with smaller benefits over a shorter period?

First, let us evaluate these projects incorrectly by means of the standard *NPV* method, which ignores their unequal lives. For an *RRR* equal to 10%, these calculations are summarized as follows:

Project	Initial Investment $CFAT_0$	CFAT *in Year*				NPV (RRR = 10%)
		1	*2*	*3*	*4*	
Machine *D*	−$24,000	$8,000	$8,000	$8,000	$8,000	$1,359
Machine *E*	−$12,000	7,400	7,400	—	—	843

[2] Although mutually exclusive projects with different lives usually cannot be compared, such projects may be comparable if they require only a one-time investment. An example is a firm that has developed a microcomputer software program. The firm could (1) sell the rights to this software to another firm or (2) retain the rights and proceed with manufacturing and marketing the software. The two proposals should be evaluated according to the *NPV* criterion. If selling the software rights will produce an immediate cash inflow (*NPV*) of $500,000 (the software's development costs are *sunk* costs and are the same for both projects; hence they do not affect the decision) and if manufacturing the software will generate cash flows that have *NPV* = $800,000 over five years, manufacturing the product is more attractive.

It appears that D is better than E on the basis of their NPVs, but such a conclusion is premature. Because the difference in their lives has not been explicitly recognized, this method is best described as comparing apples with oranges.

To recognize differences in project lives, it is necessary to modify the NPV comparison. Assume that after two years, machine E will be replaced by an identical machine. This creates a **replacement chain** that makes machines D and E comparable because they now have the same useful lives. The cash flows and NPV associated with machine E are now as follows:

Project	Initial Investment $CFAT_0$	CFAT in Year				NPV (RRR = 10%)
		1	2	3	4	
Machine E plus replacement	− $12,000	$7,400	$7,400 −12,000	— $7,400	— $7,400	
$CFAT$ and NPV for the replacement chain	− $12,000	7,400	−4,600	7,400	7,400	$1,540

Notice that the replacement chain requires another $12,000 investment for a new machine at the end of year 2, followed by two more years of $7,400 in benefits. That is, the replacement chain method assumes replacement with an identical machine that has the same operating costs and benefits. Moreover, the NPV for the replacement chain now results in a reversal of the previous decision: machine E is more desirable than D. Therefore, when mutually exclusive projects have different lives, the opportunity to reinvest in similar projects must be considered.

One aspect of this method is to find the common useful life. The lowest common multiple of the lives of the two projects should be determined. For example, if machine D will last three years and E will last two years, the lowest common life is six years. Often, this results in a time period longer than the life of the longer-lived project. Therefore, a replacement chain for machine D must also be determined, with one replacement occurring at the end of year 3. In contrast, machine E will be replaced twice—once at the end of year 2 and again at the end of year 4.

The logic behind the replacement chain method is straightforward. Nevertheless, consider the case in which machines D and E have 17- and 7-year lives, respectively. This implies that the two projects must be compared over a common useful life of $17 \times 7 = 119$ years, with D being replaced 7 times and E 17 times. Not only are the calculations cumbersome, but one also is implicitly assuming that the projects can be repeated under similar circumstances over the next 119 years. This is highly unlikely because a single activity will not remain unchanged for that long. In addition, the costs and benefits of the projects will certainly change over time. Thus there is no easy solution.

In practice, differences in useful lives are often ignored under the following conditions:

1. The difference in the useful lives is very small (e.g., 5 versus 6 years).

2. The shorter-lived project expires after a considerable length of time (e.g., 15 years).

The reason is that the present value of the projects' differential cash flows caused by their unequal lives becomes less important. Although there are no more satisfying solutions, a computationally simpler method does exist.

THE UNIFORM ANNUAL SERIES METHOD

An alternative method for choosing among mutually exclusive projects with different lives is the uniform annual series (*UAS*) criterion. As seen in Chapter 4, the *UAS* converts project *NPV*s into uniform annual equivalent cash flows that then can be compared. The *UAS* is especially useful when the lowest common multiple of the projects' lives is a large number.

To illustrate, suppose that a firm wants to replace a machine and is considering two alternatives:

Project A: Buy a machine that requires an initial investment of $22,500 and will generate net cash flows of $6,500 per year for five years.

Project B: Buy a machine that requires an initial investment of $28,000 and will generate net cash flows of $5,800 per year for eight years.

In this case, the lowest common multiple is 40 years, which leads to very tedious calculations with the replacement chain method. Let us see how the *UAS* method handles this situation if the required rate of return (*RRR*) is 10%:

Step 1: Calculate the *NPV* of each project over its own useful life. Because both projects' future cash flows are annuities, we have

$$NPV = CFAT_0 + \sum_{t=1}^{n} CFAT_t(PVF_{k,t})$$

or

$$NPV_A = -\$22,500 + \$6,500(PVFA_{0.10,5})$$
$$= -\$22,500 + \$6,500(3.7908) = \$2,140$$

$$NPV_B = -\$28,000 + \$5,800(PVFA_{0.10,8})$$
$$= -\$28,000 + \$5,800(5.3349) = \$2,942$$

If replacement of project *A* at the end of five years is not considered, the *NPV* of project *B* indicates that *B* is preferable. Recall, however, that the standard *NPV* comparison may give an erroneous decision when unequal lives are involved.

Step 2: Determine the *UAS* for each project by using the equation for the present value of an annuity; that is, divide their respective *NPV*s by their *PVFA* factor found in Step 1:

$$NPV = UAS(PVFA_{k,n})$$

or

$$UAS_A = \frac{NPV_A}{PVFA_{0.10,5}} = \frac{\$2,140}{3.7908} = \$565$$

$$UAS_B = \frac{NPV_B}{PVFA_{0.10,8}} = \frac{\$2,942}{5.3349} = \$551$$

Given this new information, project *A* becomes more desirable because it has a higher *UAS*. This is the same decision the replacement chain method would have yielded. The calculations in implementing the *UAS* criterion are much simpler, however. Many practitioners also may feel more comfortable using the *UAS* rather than the replacement chain method because the *UAS* does not appear to require the rather unrealistic assumption of identical replacement. But this rationale is incorrect. The *UAS* criterion is just a special case of the replacement chain method because the assumptions implicit in the *UAS* method are identical to the assumptions for the replacement chain analysis: (1) the longevity of the activity equals the lowest common multiple of the projects' lives and (2) the shorter-lived project (or both projects) will be replaced with an identical project at the same cost.

In many instances, firms need to compare and choose between mutually exclusive projects with different lives that provide identical annual benefits. In such cases, one can make a decision based solely on costs. These cases are solved using modified versions of the replacement chain and the *UAS* methods, with the objective being to choose the alternative that has the lowest present value of cost, or the lowest uniform annual cost.

Capital Rationing: Another Situation Involving a Ranking Decision

The development of the capital budgeting procedures so far has centered on maximizing the stockholders' wealth. By applying the required rate of return to each project's expected cash flows and then accepting every project that has a positive *NPV,* the firm determines the amount of funds needed for investments (the size of the capital budget).

For one reason or another, firms often reverse this process, in effect by imposing a limitation on capital expenditures during a particular year and then deciding which projects to accept, a process called **capital rationing**. It is important to note that this approach is inconsistent with the goal of value maximization. Rather than accepting all attractive investment opportunities, the firm attempts to select the combination of projects that will provide the greatest increment to firm value, subject to the budget constraints.

REASONS FOR SEEMINGLY IRRATIONAL FUNDING

TO CONSTRAIN ORGANIZATIONAL UNITS' GROWTH A company that feels its divisional managers are overenthusiastic in their budget requests might choose to impose a capital expenditure limit on a particular division. Moreover, divisions may have few acceptable projects but undertake undesirable projects simply to allocate all their funds.

TO CONSTRAIN A FIRM'S OVERALL GROWTH Management may think that it will be difficult to keep control of operations if it accepts projects beyond a certain level. This may be true especially when the size of a project's investment is large relative to the firm's present size. A good example of this is the 1983 acquisition of Qualicare by Universal Health Services, a rapidly growing hospital management company. This investment effectively doubled Universal's size but heavily penalized its earnings growth and stock price (which traded at less than half its 1983 high) for several years before this major investment was assimilated into its existing operations. More recently, Data General in 1991 introduced a work station "Avion" and budgeted its new investments to keep operations "in check."

Lack of sufficient managerial skills and other dislocation costs are also given as reasons for this limitation of growth. It can be argued that this is not a valid reason for imposing capital constraints. Rather, it is a problem of not correctly specifying the costs associated with a project. Although firms may face growing pains associated with large capital budgets, such costs should properly be estimated and included in a project's cash flows. With the same *RRR,* fewer projects will be accepted because the project's *NPV* was initially overestimated—not because of less capital.

TO CONSTRAIN FINANCING TO INTERNALLY GENERATED FUNDS
Management (especially in closely held firms) may prefer in some cases to avoid using long-term debt or new equity issues to fund projects. This attitude usually stems from an aversion to the risks of debt or the fear of losing ownership control if new common shares are sold to outsiders. In such cases, the size of the capital budget becomes restricted to the availability of "excess" cash inflows from operations (cash, marketable securities, and retained earnings). Management must weigh the loss of incremental wealth from rejecting acceptable projects because of any capital constraint against the "benefits" from being debt free or retaining control.

In these situations in which capital expenditures are subject to a constraint, the firm is described as facing capital rationing. In perfect capital markets, even capital rationing due to external (market) constraints makes no sense. Regardless of how high the opportunity cost of capital may be, the firm should accept projects only if their *NPV*s are positive when evaluated at this discount rate. Thus it makes no sense to say that capital rationing exists because financing becomes very expensive after a certain level of investment. Capital rationing introduces a market imperfection, and the *NPV* rule loses its power. In many instances, capital rationing does not invalidate the *NPV* rule so long as the firm's stockholders have free access to capital markets.

PROJECT SELECTION UNDER CAPITAL RATIONING

Before examining the process of selecting investment projects under capital rationing, it is necessary to see that some projects are indivisible and that others are divisible. Projects that must be accepted or rejected in their entirety are **indivisible**. For example, if a project includes the purchase of a corporate jet, we either accept the project (i.e., buy the jet) or reject it. It makes no sense to think about accepting half the project. On the other hand, projects may be **divisible**. For instance, if a rental car company is considering the replacement of all the tires on its fleet of cars, we can think of one-half or one-third of the project. The company can replace the tires on just part of its fleet.

INDIVISIBLE PROJECTS Consider Thibbadeaux Co., which has decided to invest a maximum of $30,000 in new projects this year. Thibbadeaux's required rate of return is 15%, and it has identified four potential (independent) investments with the following information:

Project	Initial Investment	NPV (RRR = 15%)
A	$15,000	$1,970
B	8,000	1,130
C	12,000	6,840
D	30,000	6,900

Which projects should be accepted if all the projects are indivisible and we cannot take multiples of each project?

At first glance it is tempting to conclude that project *D* is the best investment because it has the highest *NPV* and because its initial investment just satisfies the capital budget. But this conclusion is incorrect. Why? Because it may be possible to identify a combination of other, smaller projects that can lead to higher *NPV*s. To choose the projects correctly in this case, the following rule should be used:

■

TABLE 9-1

Selecting Capital Budgeting Projects Under Capital Rationing Where Projects Are Indivisible

Feasible Project Combination[a]	Size of Capital Budget	NPV (RRR = 15%)
A	$15,000	$1,970
B	8,000	1,130
C	12,000	6,840
D	30,000	6,900
A + B	23,000	3,100
A + C	27,000	8,810
B + C	20,000	7,970

[a] All other combinations exceed the $30,000 capital budget constraint.

Choose that combination of projects that maximizes the sum of their *NPV*s without exceeding the capital constraint.

To see how we can use this rule, consider the information in Table 9-1. First, identify all the feasible project combinations and the associated *NPV* for each combination. By feasible, we mean a combination that does not exceed the capital constraint. According to Table 9-1, the combination (*A* + *C*) is the best because Thibbadeaux will receive a *NPV* of $8,810 with a $27,000 investment. All other projects must be rejected, including project *D*, which initially appeared to be the best.

Note that under capital rationing, the firm attempts to maximize shareholder wealth subject to the constraint that the allocated funds are not exceeded. Clearly, this constrained *NPV* maximization behavior will lead to less incremental wealth ($8,810) than will the more desirous unconstrained *NPV* maximization (*A* + *B* + *C* + *D* = $16,840).

Moreover, although this method is straightforward, it is tedious and can become complicated when the number of combinations is large. For instance, if there are *n* different projects with positive *NPV*s, then 2^n different combinations are possible, including the alternative of accepting no project. With just 10 projects, there are $2^{10} = 1,024$ different combinations to be considered. From this, the infeasible projects must be culled. A more efficient procedure requires using a computer and mathematical programming techniques to simplify the problem. This text does not delve into mathematical programming.[3]

DIVISIBLE PROJECTS What if Thibbadeaux's four projects were divisible? The method suggested earlier no longer leads to the correct decision. When projects are divisible, the profitability index criterion can be used to make the right decision. Recall from Chapter 8 that

$$PI = \frac{PV_{\text{inflows}}}{PV_{\text{outflows}}}$$

With *PI*, the problem of choosing the right divisible projects under capital rationing is resolved in the following way: If projects are divisible and there is a capital constraint, we rank projects by their *PI* values from highest to lowest, and then select all the highest-ranked projects that do not exceed the imposed capital budget. The simplicity of the *PI* method for a one-year analysis is somewhat deceptive

---

[3] Extensive research and applications using mathematical programming models in business are currently being done. For example, integer programming can be used to select indivisible projects, and linear programming can be used to choose divisible projects. For an introduction to their application to capital budgeting, refer to M. Weingartner, *Mathematical Programming and the Analysis of Capital Budgeting Problems* (Englewood Cliffs, NJ: Prentice-Hall, 1963); and J. C. T. Mao, *Quantitative Analysis of Financial Decisions* (New York: Macmillan, 1969).

TABLE 9-2
Selecting Capital Budgeting Projects Under Capital Rationing When Projects Are Divisible

Project	Initial Investment	NPV (RRR = 15%)	Profitability Index (PI)	Rank
A	$15,000	$1,970	1.13	4
B	8,000	1,130	1.14	3
C	12,000	6,840	1.57	1
D	30,000	6,900	1.23	2

Step 1: Accept project C first, with $PI_C = 1.57$. Because $C = \$12,000 < \$30,000$, all funds have not been allocated, so proceed to Step 2.

Step 2: Accept project D next, with $PI_D = 1.23$. However, $C + D = \$12,000 + \$30,000 > \$30,000$. Therefore solve the following equation to determine what portion of D (X_D) to accept:

$$\$12,000 + \$30,000 X_D = \$30,000$$

$$X_D = \frac{\$30,000 - \$12,000}{\$30,000} = 0.60$$

because it fails whenever more than one year's capital budget is rationed. Moreover, difficulties arise whenever there are other constraints on projection selection. For example, the *PI* method cannot handle cases in which the projects are mutually exclusive.

Table 9-2 summarizes the relevant information required for this analysis. Based on their *PI*s, the projects are ranked in descending order as *C, D, B,* and *A.* As the table indicates, *C* should be accepted first, requiring a $12,000 investment. That leaves $18,000 for further investing. Project *D* should be chosen next; however, this requires $30,000 when only $18,000 remains. Therefore, only 60% of project *D* can be undertaken. Because fractional projects are allowed, Thibbadeaux's capital budget would be composed of project *C* and 60% of project *D.* Notice that this budget is completely different from that found in the first case, in which the projects were indivisible.

WHY THE *PI* CRITERION APPLIES WHEN CAPITAL IS RATIONED

When we examined the *PI* criterion in Section 9-1, we warned that ranking projects by their *PI*s could be misleading because the *PI* ignores the scale of the investment. Yet, as we have just shown, the *PI* can be useful in capital-rationing situations when the projects are divisible.

Why does the *PI* criterion apply in this case? Without capital rationing, decisions are based on *NPV* because the objective is to choose all projects that increase wealth ($NPV > 0$). With capital rationing, however, funds are not available to finance all projects that increase wealth. Our objective now is to maximize the increment in wealth per dollar invested. That is, a financial manager faced with capital rationing must select projects such that the present value of benefits for every dollar invested is as high as possible. This is exactly what the *PI* criterion does.

Optimal Replacement Decisions for Existing Assets

Assume that a firm has already bought a lathe that will produce a cash flow of $5,000 per year for three years. Although the lathe has a three-year life, this does not mean that it is optimal for the firm to use it for the entire period. The machine could be replaced by another machine next year.

It is often useful to ask how long an existing asset or project should be used before it is abandoned. To answer this question, it is necessary to know the appropriate discount rate and the asset's market (salvage) value at the end of each year. We assume the following relevant information for the lathe:

$$RRR = 10\%$$

$$CFAT_0 = -\$15,000$$

$$CFAT_t = \$5,000 \text{ for each year } t$$

Year	Market Value
0	$15,000
1	10,000
2	9,000
3	4,000

To determine how long an asset should be used, we compute the *UAS* for each possible life of the asset(s) and choose the highest *UAS* to find the optimal life of the asset(s). Recall, however, that to calculate the *UAS*, it is first necessary to calculate the *NPV* for each possible life. If the lathe is replaced at the end of year 1, we have

$$NPV_1 = -\$15,000 + \underbrace{\$5,000(PVF_{0.10,1})}_{PV \text{ of } CFAT_1} + \underbrace{\$10,000(PVF_{0.10,1})}_{PV \text{ of salvage value}} = -\$1,364$$

Similarly, if the machine is replaced at the end of year 2 or year 3,

$$NPV_2 = -\$15,000 + \$5,000(PVFA_{0.10,2}) + \$9,000(PVF_{0.10,2}) = \$1,115$$

$$NPV_3 = -\$15,000 + \$5,000(PVFA_{0.10,3}) + \$4,000(PVF_{0.10,3}) = \$440$$

From this information, the three *UAS*s can be easily calculated.

Replace-ment Year	(1) NPV	(2) $PVFA_{0.10,n}$	(3) UAS (1)/(2)
1	−$1,364	0.9091	−$1,500
2	1,115	1.7355	642
3	440	2.4869	177

A replacement policy of two years has the highest *UAS*. Thus the lathe should be replaced at the end of two years.

9-3

CAPITAL BUDGETING IN AN INTERNATIONAL ENVIRONMENT

Participation in the Global Economy

Business firms maximize stockholder wealth by identifying the comparative advantages they have that allow them to exploit specific imperfections in product, factor, or financial markets. Firms that operate globally may identify many more wealth-enhancing projects than those firms that are limited to their own domestic markets.

There are several ways to exploit comparative advantages. Some firms are exporters. They manufacture their products in their home country and then export them to foreign markets. Exporters enjoy international markets for their goods, while keeping their productive operations in a known domestic market. Some firms, such as Marriott International, Inc., have a comparative advantage in managing a specific activity (hotel management), and they exploit this advantage by offering management services to investors. This allows the company to apply its skills internationally, while avoiding the requirement of making a substantial investment in foreign properties.

However, there are some comparative advantages that are not embodied in a product or identified with a particular skill. This type of comparative advantage consists of the very process of continually identifying and exploiting imperfections in various markets. Firms that pursue this type of comparative advantage make **direct foreign investment (DFI)**. Capital budgeting for DFI is, in theory, identical to domestic investment analysis: Identify the cash flows generated by an investment and find their net present value using the appropriate opportunity cost. If the *NPV* is positive, the project is a worthwhile endeavor.

Unfortunately, in practice, the analysis is more difficult to implement in the case of direct foreign investment because several additional factors must be considered. As mentioned in Chapter 1, firms face political risk and exchange rate risk. Because of these risks, estimates of cash flows have a wider margin of error. Rather than try to develop a quantitative framework for making capital budgeting decisions in this environment, we identify several special considerations that must be borne in mind when making the *NPV* analysis. Careful attention to these factors can help the financial manager make a better decision using the *NPV* criterion.

Political Risk: Conflicts Between Government and Business Goals

One important aspect of international capital budgeting analysis is political risk. Political risk can affect the expected cash flows of both overseas and domestic investments and should be recognized in capital budgeting decisions.

A CONFLICT OF GOALS

Political risks arise out of a conflict between the goals of businesses that operate with a given country and the goals of that country's government. National governments have sovereignty, or complete control, within their borders, including determining the trade-offs between socially beneficial goals and economic efficiency. The goals of a government are affected by the country's economic, political, and social conditions and, unfortunately, occasionally corruption and dictatorship. Respect for property rights and private enterprise differs throughout the world, and corporations that operate in a given country must operate within the framework specified by that country's government.

In operating a foreign investment, a firm faces two dimensions of risks: the nature of the risk and the manner in which the risk affects the firm.[4] The first dimension involves two sources of risk: country-specific risks, which affect all firms operating within a country, and firm-specific risks, which affect only specific firms within the country. An example of country-specific risks is certain business practices, such as bribes, that may be expected of all businesses operating in a country, both local and foreign-owned. The foreign company is, in this situation, faced with the same difficulties as its local competitors. More problematic to a foreign firm are firm-specific risks, such as extra taxes placed on foreign-owned firms, restrictions placed on foreign firms that extract natural resources like minerals or oil, or even limits that might be imposed on future foreign ownership of businesses. In facing firm-specific risks, the foreign firm is at a disadvantage to its domestic competitors and must ensure that its investment will produce sufficient cash flows with these extra costs included.

After the sources of risk are identified, managers must understand how these risks will affect the firm's cash flows. These risks affect both the firm's ownership of its assets and the cash flows received from its assets. The primary risk to a firm's ownership of its assets is **expropriation**, which is the seizure of a company by the local government. In the past, Chile expropriated American copper operations and Libya nationalized American oil interests. Expropriation does not have to be sudden or dramatic. A government can "gradually nationalize" a business, demanding greater and greater influence in the management and ownership of the firm until there is a de facto expropriation. Unanticipated actions by local authorities sub-

[4]This classification scheme is suggested in Stephen J. Kobrin, *Managing Political Risk Assessment: Strategic Response to Environmental Change* (Berkeley: University of California Press, 1982), p. 35.

stantially affect the cash flows from the investment and, consequently, the value of the parent company.

Even if a firm does not face expropriation, its cash flows can still be reduced by government interference with repatriation of earnings, or blocked funds, which means that profits are prevented from being sent back to the parent company. Companies that do business overseas are at the mercy of the local government, which may completely prohibit the withdrawal of funds from that country. The U.S. government's blockage of Iraqi funds during the recent Gulf War is an example of blocked funds. As another example, in 1972 Uganda's Idi Amin prohibited the withdrawal of cash by Kenyans of Indian origin who had invested heavily in Uganda. The possibility of blocked funds can severely affect the profitability of a company's operations in that country, even if it is eventually allowed to repatriate the funds to the parent. In a capital budgeting context, a blockage of funds, or even a delay in funds, can lower dramatically the *NPV* of overseas investments.

MANAGING POLITICAL RISK

At least to some extent, firms can cope with political risk in a variety of direct and indirect ways. As an example, a large U.S. company (company *X*) had a subsidiary in Colombia that had a large amount of blocked pesos. Another U.S. company (company *Y*) also had a subsidiary in Colombia at that time. The subsidiary of company *X* "lent" these blocked pesos to the subsidiary of company *Y* at a very favorable rate. The parent company *Y* reciprocated by "lending" company *X* in the United States a similar amount, also at a very attractive rate. Another means of reducing political risk is by involving more of the local population in both ownership and management. With the local population becoming stakeholders in the firm, the political risks can be reduced.

Alternatively, the multinational firm can obtain political risk insurance from a variety of agencies. The Overseas Private Investment Corporation (OPIC), for example, insures multinational companies from the risk of funds freezing, expropriations, and changes in foreign laws. Other potential insurance sources are the Foreign Credit Insurance Association (FCIA) and Eximbank. In addition, the Agency for International Development (AID) may provide companies with some protection of their direct foreign investments in certain countries.

The Forward Exchange Rate

As defined in Chapter 1, the exchange rate is the price of one currency in terms of another. If an American firm makes a capital investment in its subsidiary in a foreign country, it expects to receive cash flows from that investment over several years. However, these cash flows are likely earned in the local currency, not dollars, and must be translated into dollars.

While managers know the value of currencies today in the spot exchange market, this does not help them with cash flows that are received in the future. However, there is another market for currencies that allows managers to fix the price at which they will buy or sell currencies at a future date. This is the **forward market**, in which currencies are traded today for delivery at a future date at an exchange rate called the **forward exchange rate**. For example, if a manager expects to get a yen payment in 90 days, he may wish to avoid the uncertainty of the exchange rate at that time. The manager can lock in a future exchange rate by agreeing today to sell yen in the 90-day forward market at the forward exchange rate, which we assume to be 109.44 yen per dollar. The manager is entering into a contract today in which he or she promises to sell yen for $1/109.44 each in 90 days. Thus he has eliminated exchange rate risk. The manager has locked in a price of 0.00914 dollar per yen.

Both spot and forward market transactions occur in the **interbank market**. This market is an informal one composed of electronic linkages among banks that deal with foreign exchange and their corporate and government customers. Firms that need currencies often call around to several banks to get the best exchange rate.

Whereas developed currency forward markets exist for shorter time periods, forward contracts generally do not extend for more than two years. The firm must thus estimate not only the foreign cash flows of the project but also the future exchange rate at which those cash flows will be translated into dollars. The possible means of estimating exchange rates in capital budgeting are addressed in Appendix 9-C.

Factors in International Capital Budgeting

CASH FLOW CONSIDERATIONS

The important issue to remember when foreign investments are made is that the manager's ultimate objective should be to enrich the shareholders of the parent company. Thus the value of foreign investments to stockholders rests crucially on the cash flows that can be repatriated either immediately or at a later date. Thus the possibility of funds blockages or expropriation must be recognized when estimating potential cash flows. Of course, as we have seen, firms can minimize this risk through insurance. Insurance is not free, however, and this expense must be treated as a cash outflow in capital budgeting decisions.

Opening a new overseas operation can sometimes result in an indirect cost to the firm. For example, if an American car manufacturer sets up a new plant in Brazil, it is with the expectation that the new sales of cars to Brazilians will increase the company's revenues. For example, this investment may increase the car maker's revenues by 12%. Yet this estimate of the new revenue is not the relevant incremental revenue to the car maker. Because the cars are being made in Brazil, the parent company will lose some of its original exports to Brazil, which is an indirect cost. The incremental revenues for this proposed investment should therefore recognize this potential reduction in the revenues of the domestic company. Put it another way, if the firm can generate some of the revenues from the proposed project independent of that project, the indirect costs of taking on that project should be taken into account when calculating the incremental cash flows. These indirect costs are the same as the economic dependencies that we discussed in a domestic setting in Chapter 8. However, these economic dependencies may be more difficult to recognize in an international environment.

A unique aspect of international financial cash flows is **supervisory fees** and **royalties**. These are contractually arranged periodic remissions of funds by the subsidiary to the parent company and represent a "fee" for, say, the supervision of patent use. These fees are simply devices that multinational companies have used to protect themselves in repatriating funds back home. Because they are fees (rather than profits), local governments are less likely to prevent this cash drain from the subsidiary in the host country into the coffers of the multinational. These periodic cash inflows to the parent firm should therefore be part of the capital budgeting decision. In many cases, however, this fee is set at an artificially high level. In cases in which this cash flow is not really tied to the merits of the project but instead represents an accounting adjustment by management, the fee and royalty amounts should be adjusted downward in the *NPV* analysis of the project.

Along the same lines, a **tie-in sale** is a fairly common arrangement that parent firms have with their subsidiaries. A tie-in sale may require the subsidiary to buy certain materials from the parent. Tie-in sales can be useful to the parent because they may enable it to supply the product at the lowest possible cost; in other instances, tie-in sales arrangements ensure that quality components are supplied to the subsidiary. For example, a capital investment in Mexico to manufacture hand-held calculators may require the Mexican subsidiary to buy the electronic chips from the parent in the United States. Presumably, the parent feels that the quality of its product is superior. In situations such as this, again, care must be taken when calculating the incremental cash flows from the proposed project. The benefits to the parent are the net flows from the overseas project.

Sometimes the parent company may choose to transfer its used equipment to the new foreign subsidiary. Equipment transfers can be advantageous to the parent because the parent may be able to realize higher salvage values in the foreign country. How does one cite the cost of this transferred machinery in the capital budgeting analysis? The relevant cost that must be charged to the project is not the depreciated book value of the machinery; instead, the opportunity cost of acquiring a similar piece of equipment in the foreign country is the appropriate cost.

The tax laws of the local country are obviously a major determinant of the profits and cash flows generated by a project. The level of complexity in making tax adjustments to profits is heightened by the fact that tax adjustments must be made at two levels: at the level of the host country and again when the profits are repatriated to the United States. Tax laws relating to international investments are extremely complicated and are not presented in this book.[5] It is important to remember, again, that the tax adjustments must be viewed in light of their effect on the cash flows to the parent.

DISCOUNT RATE CONSIDERATIONS

As we know so well, capital budgeting analyses are not meaningful without a properly specified discount rate (opportunity cost) used to find the present values of the cash flows generated by an investment. The proper discount rate includes a riskless interest rate plus a premium for bearing risk. In the case of domestic capital budgeting, the discount rate can be estimated by, say, the CAPM. How does one find the proper discount rate to be applied to a multinational company's investment overseas? The relevant risk of the investment should first be estimated, and then an appropriate risk premium must be identified. In a strict sense, one needs to develop an international capital asset pricing model (ICAPM) to do this correctly. Indeed, such models do exist, but their use is severely limited. For a variety of reasons, this approach of risk adjustment—adjusting the discount rate upward for risk—is not recommended. The risks in international finance are much more difficult to estimate, and the world markets are not subject to as high a level of integration as that of the various domestic financial asset markets. Therefore it may be better to adjust the cash flows downward for risk in making the *NPV* calculations. These cash flow adjustments must reflect the political risks, tax implications on cash flows, and the other factors specific to multinationals.

In summary, cash flow adjustments are preferred purely on the grounds of pragmatism. There is more information available than can meaningfully be used to make cash flow adjustments. And risk adjustments to the discount rate are severely hampered by the problems of using the information available to quantify the relevant risks of the investment.

---

[5] U.S. tax laws regarding profits and losses on translation gains and forward contracts require the definition of a "functional currency." FASB 52 is the accounting standard adopted in these matters.

SUMMARY

What are the limitations of internal rate of return and profitability index as capital budgeting criteria?

■ The *NPV* profile is a graph of the *NPV* of a project on the vertical axis and the various discount rates on the horizontal axis. The *IRR* is that discount rate at which the *NPV* profile crosses the horizontal axis.

■ Using the *IRR* for capital budgeting can be problematic because projects can sometimes have several *IRR*s, all of them correct, or a project may have no *IRR* at all. To avoid these situations, the financial manager is better off using the *NPV* criterion.

■ The multiple *IRR* situation does not arise for conventional projects. For non-conventional projects, the maximum number of real *IRR*s is equal to the maximum number of sign changes in the project's cash flow sequence.

■ For accept/reject decisions, both *NPV* and *IRR* criteria yield identical recommendations. However, in a ranking decision involving mutually exclusive projects, *NPV* and *IRR* can lead to conflicting results.

■ Whether a conflict between *NPV* and *IRR* will occur depends on the *RRR*. To resolve the conflict, the manager is well advised to follow the *NPV* criterion, simply because the *NPV* is consistent with the manager's objective of maximizing stockholder wealth. The *IRR* may not be consistent with this objective because it is a relative measure that ignores the net addition in wealth for a company that takes on a project.

■ The profitability index criterion can conflict with the *NPV* in ranking decisions because the *PI* measures relative economic profitability but, unlike the *NPV*, does not take the scale of the investment into account. Again, this problem can be overcome by using the *NPV* in such situations.

How are projects with different lives evaluated?

■ In the evaluation of mutually exclusive projects, care must be exercised to ensure that their economic lives are the same. When projects with different lives have to be compared, the manager must use the replacement chain method or the uniform annual series (*UAS*) method. Although both methods use the same principles, the *UAS* method is preferable because it is computationally simpler.

How do we choose among projects when the amount of capital available is limited?

■ Many firms have capital constraints imposed on them by either choice or circumstance. In any event, capital budgeting with capital expenditure limits can be handled in one of two ways, depending on the nature of the projects. If the projects are divisible, the *PI* criterion can be used as follows: Rank projects from the highest *PI* to the lowest *PI,* and then choose all the highest-ranked projects that do not exceed the capital budget. If projects are indivisible, however, the *PI* rule fails. In this case, management must find the combination of projects that yields the highest *NPV* without exceeding the amount of capital available.

What is the optimal time to replace an asset?

■ It may sometimes be to the stockholders' advantage for the firm to abandon a project and replace it with a new one. In particular, machinery may sometimes be replaced before its anticipated economic life ends. The *UAS* method can be used to evaluate these optimal replacement decisions: Compute the *UAS* for each assumed life of the asset, and then choose the highest *UAS* to find the optimal life of the asset.

Section 9-3: Capital Budgeting in an International Environment

What factors must be considered when evaluating foreign projects?

■ Capital budgeting decisions increasingly involve foreign investments, which add exchange rate risk to capital budgeting considerations. Managers must thus factor exchange rate changes into their cash flow calculations. The forward exchange market can enable the manager to avoid some of the exchange rate risk.

■ Firms must recognize that their goals may differ from the goals of host governments. This goal divergence creates political risk, which managers must be able to recognize and manage.

■ Considering the complexities associated with overseas investments, it is more practical to adjust the expected cash flows from a foreign investment downward instead of making risk adjustments in the discount rate.

QUESTIONS

1. What information is required to generate a *NPV* profile for a project?

2. How can the correspondence between the *NPV* and the *IRR* criteria be illustrated using an *NPV* profile?

3. What is the difference between a conventional and a nonconventional project? What is the practical significance of this distinction?

4. When a project has more than one *IRR,* which is the correct one?

5. What might cause a project to have no *IRR*?

6. Explain the distinction between a ranking decision and an accept/reject decision. In what type of decision can the *NPV* and the *IRR* criteria conflict?

7. Because *NPV* and *PI* use the same basic elements in their determination, there can be no conflicts between their rankings of mutually exclusive projects. Is this statement correct? Why or why not?

8. What difficulties are encountered when mutually exclusive projects with unequal lives are evaluated?

9. What is the advantage of the *UAS* method over the replacement chain method when projects with different lives are compared?

10. What are some commonly cited reasons for capital rationing within a company?

11. How can a manager optimize *NPV* when faced with indivisible projects?

12. Explain why the *PI* criterion is suitable for choosing among divisible projects under capital constraints.

13. Why might you want to dispose of an asset before the end of its planned economic life?

14. How can the *UAS* for a project be used to decide the optimal time to replace an asset?

15. What information is required to make an optimal replacement decision? Which of these items of information may be difficult to obtain?

16. Why would firms want to participate in a global rather than a domestic market?

17. How does political risk arise? How can managers reduce its impact on the firm?

18. What is the difference between a spot exchange rate and a forward exchange rate?

19. How do international considerations affect a firm's cash flows and discount rate?

PROBLEMS [6]

1. The Anthracide Coal Company is considering a strip-mining project that requires a $230,000 initial outlay and will generate cash inflows from operations of $100,000 at the end of each of the next ten years. At the end of the tenth year, a $1,000,000 expenditure will be necessary to restore the land environmentally.

   (a) Find the net present value of the strip-mining project if the discount rate is 0%, 5%, 10%, 15%, 20%, 25%, 30%, and 35%.

   (b) What can be said about the uniqueness of the *IRR* of this project?

   (c) Would you accept this project if the required rate of return was 5%? 20%? 40%?

2. A project requires an initial outlay of $3,000 and has a cash inflow at the end of year 1 of $5,000 and a cash outflow at the end of year 2 of $3,000.

   (a) Find the net present value of this project if the discount rate is 5%, 10%, 15%, 20%, 30%, and 35%.

   (b) Assuming that the trend from a 20% to a 35% discount rate continues, what can you say about the *IRR* of this project?

   (c) Is there any required rate of return under which you would accept this project?

3. Plot an *NPV* profile for Barbarian's Pizza in Problem 7 of Chapter 8. Use discount rates of 0%, 5%, 10%, 15%, 20%, and 25% when drawing the graph. What is the approximate *IRR* for the additional oven?

4. Your first task as financial manager of the Reginald Corporation is to choose between two alternative plans for producing and marketing videocassettes. Plan *A* requires an initial outlay of $100,000 and will generate annual cash

---

[6]Some problems require the use of present value factors not found in the time value tables in Chapter 4. Consult more complete tables or use a financial calculator.

flows of $16,000 during its 12-year life. At that time, its salvage value will be $48,000. Plan B also requires an initial outlay of $100,000 but will generate annual cash flows of $17,500 during its 12-year life. Its salvage value at the end of year 12 is estimated to be $10,000. Your firm uses a 12% discount rate to value either project.

(a) Find the NPV of project A.

(b) Find the IRR of project A to the nearest tenth of a percent (using a calculator).

(c) Find the NPV of project B.

(d) Find the IRR of project B to the nearest tenth of a percent (using a calculator).

(e) Which project should you choose, and why?

(f) A cohort of yours argues that because project B has the higher IRR, it should be adopted. Show that comparing the two projects using the NPV method correctly implies that project A should be chosen.

5. As part of a package deal with another corporation, your firm will acquire the use of a huge tract of land near Texas Christian University in Fort Worth, Texas, for the next 20 years. You have narrowed the possibilities for use of the land to two: a large parking lot with a shuttle bus service to TCU or a large apartment complex. The parking lot and shuttle bus service would require an initial outlay of $300,000 and would generate cash inflows of $70,000 each year. The apartment complex would require an initial outlay of $12 million and would generate cash inflows of $1.4 million each year. At the end of 20 years, the other corporation (from which you acquired use of the land) would pay you $20 million in exchange for the apartment complex that you built on their land. Your firm's required return on either investment is 12%.

(a) Find the net present value of the parking lot project.

(b) Find the net present value of the apartment project.

(c) Find to the nearest tenth of a percent the IRR of the parking lot project.

(d) Find to the nearest tenth of a percent the IRR of the apartment project.

(e) Which project should you adopt? Why?

6. Mike Bukala of the Charmin Shoe Corporation is trying to choose between two machines to manufacture a new line of shoes. Machine X requires a net initial outlay of $20,000, has a salvage value of $4,000 in eight years, and has annual materials expenses of $3,200 and annual revenues of $12,000. Machine Y requires an initial outlay of $14,000, has a salvage value of $2,000 in four years, and has annual materials expenses of $2,800 and annual revenues of $11,500. Charmin uses straight-line depreciation and has a marginal tax rate of 25%. Mike has determined that although the firm uses a 14% discount rate on projects of average risk, these projects are of above-average risk, and he is using a 16% discount rate to value them.

(a) What is the annual cash flow of projects X and Y?

(b) What is the IRR of each of projects X and Y?

(c) What is the net present value of each of projects X and Y?

(d) Using the replacement chain method, determine which project should be adopted.

(e) Using the uniform annual series method, determine which project should be adopted.

(f) Suppose that Mike has determined that project Y is more risky than project X and has decided to use an 18% discount rate for project Y. Recalculate the net present value of Y.

(g) Using the replacement chain method (and an 18% discount rate for Y), determine which project should be adopted.

(h) Using the uniform annual series method (and an 18% discount rate for Y), determine which project should be adopted.

7. Eileen Reinauer is trying to choose between a square egg maker (project A) and an egg scrambler (project B) as a promotional gimmick for her new coffee shop. If she chooses one, she will not choose the other (i.e., she considers them mutually exclusive projects). The square egg maker would require a net initial outlay of $21,000 and have no salvage value in six years. It would generate sales of $11,000 and have raw material expenses of $3,500 annually. The egg scrambler would cost $21,500 today and have a salvage value of $14,000 in eight years. It would generate sales of $10,000 and have raw material expenses of $4,000 annually. Eileen uses straight-line depreciation and her tax rate is 25%.

(a) Find the annual cash flows from operations of each of projects A and B.

(b) Find the internal rate of return of each of projects A and B.

(c) If the discount rate is 10%, find the net present value of each of projects A and B.

(d) Using the replacement chain method, determine whether you should adopt project A or B if your discount rate is 10%.

(e) Using the uniform annual series method, determine whether you should adopt project A or B if your discount rate is 10%.

(f) If the discount rate is 16%, find the net present value of each of projects A and B.

(g) Using the replacement chain method, determine whether you should adopt project A or B if your discount rate is 16%.

(h) Using the uniform annual series method, determine whether you should adopt project A or B if your discount rate is 16%.

8. You have discovered oil under the land that you have previously used for growing peanuts. You have decided to extract the oil and then sell the land and retire. Either you can lease the necessary equipment and extract and sell the oil yourself, or you can lease the land to an oil-drilling company. If you choose the former, your net annual cash flow from the drilling operations will be $300,000 at the end of each year for the next six years, and you can sell the land for a net cash flow of $1 million in six years when the oil is depleted. If you choose the latter, the drilling company can extract all the oil in only three years, and you can sell the land for a net cash flow of $800,000 in three years. Your net cash flow from the lease payments from the drilling company will be

$400,000 at the beginning of each of the next three years. Your discount rate is 14%.

(a) What is the net present value of the plan to drill the oil yourself and sell the land in six years?

(b) What is the net present value of the plan to lease the land and then sell it in three years?

(c) What is the uniform annual series of the plan to drill the oil yourself and then sell the land in six years?

(d) What is the uniform annual series of the plan to lease the land and then sell it in three years?

(e) Which should you do? Why?

9. The city of St. Louis has hired you to conduct a study to determine the cheapest method of cutting grass in the city's numerous parks. You have eliminated all but two plans. One plan calls for the city to buy several automatic mowers at an initial expense of $1,800,000. These mowers will last eight years and will require labor and maintenance expenses of $200,000 annually. The other plan is to enter into a four-year contract with a local lawn care service. The contract calls for annual payments of $500,000, payable at the end of each year. The discount rate you are using in making this decision is 8%.

(a) Using the replacement chain method, determine which plan to adopt.

(b) Using the uniform annual series method, determine which plan to adopt.

10. The Morgan Corporation has decided to open a new computer facility to serve customers in the Birmingham, Alabama, area. Your task is to determine which of two air-conditioning units to buy for the new building. The Contex Corporation has a unit available that costs $500,000 and would require annual electricity and maintenance expenses of $50,000 during its ten-year life. It would have a salvage value of $100,000 in ten years. The Pure-Air Corporation sells a similar but slightly less efficient unit for $300,000. It would require annual electricity and maintenance expenses of $60,000 during its eight-year life. It would have a salvage value of $0 in eight years. Morgan Corporation uses straight-line depreciation and has a marginal tax rate of 33%. It is using a 12% discount rate in determining which machine to use.

(a) What is the net annual cash outflow from depreciation and operating expenses of the Contex machine?

(b) What is the net annual cash outflow from depreciation and operating expenses of the Pure-Air machine?

(c) What is the net present value of buying and operating the Contex machine?

(d) What is the net present value of buying and operating the Pure-Air machine?

(e) What is the uniform annual series of the Contex machine?

(f) What is the uniform annual series of the Pure-Air machine?

(g) What should Morgan Corporation do? How did you reach that decision?

11. Anne Schwarz, owner of an apartment complex, recently discovered that the insulation for the complex contains asbestos and must be replaced. She is considering two types of nonasbestos replacements, both of which will last forever. The first, Airtite, will require an initial net cash outflow of $400,000 and annual cash outflows of $100,000 at the end of each of the next four years. The other, Insul-out, will require an initial net cash outflow of $300,000 and annual cash outflows of $150,000 at the end of each of the next three years. Anne's discount rate is 14%.

   (a) What is the net present value of the Airtite insulation?

   (b) What is the net present value of the Insul-out insulation?

   (c) What is the uniform annual series of the Airtite insulation?

   (d) What is the uniform annual series of the Insul-out insulation?

   (e) Which should Anne choose? How did you reach that decision?

12. Lloyd Dugger of Dugger Importing purchased some French wine at a total expense of $200,000. The wine will become more valuable as it ages, with the following anticipated future values:

Year	Value	Year	Value	Year	Value
1	$220,000	5	$383,000	9	$706,000
2	246,000	6	460,000	10	804,000
3	280,000	7	534,000	11	885,000
4	325,000	8	619,000	12	973,000

   The wine will increase in value by 10% annually after year 12. When should Lloyd sell the wine if he has a 14% discount rate? (*Hint:* Use the decision rule for optimal replacement of existing assets.)

13. Merlin Pet Stores, Inc., is planning to open stores in shopping malls in each of several cities. It has estimated the following required initial outlay, net present value, internal rate of return, and profitability index for each of the stores:

City	Net Initial Outlay	NPV	IRR	PI
San Francisco	$300,000	$40,000	18%	1.133
Phoenix	250,000	30,000	16	1.12
Austin	250,000	35,000	17	1.14
Baton Rouge	150,000	22,000	19	1.146
Atlanta	100,000	15,000	18	1.15
Richmond	50,000	10,000	16	1.2

   Merlin is subject to capital rationing and has decided to spend no more than $600,000. In which cities should Merlin open new stores?

14. The Bruce Construction Company specializes in building hospitals and has requests from a number of companies in various cities to do so. The cities making the requests, together with the initial outlay required, the number of labor hours required for construction, and the net present value of the projects are as follows:

City	Initial Outlay	Labor Hours (thousands)	NPV
Los Angeles	$200,000	80	$30,000
San Diego	150,000	70	26,000
Santa Fe	150,000	60	25,000
El Paso	100,000	60	23,000
Kansas City	100,000	50	20,000
Pittsburgh	50,000	50	12,000
Miami	50,000	40	10,000

The financial manager of Bruce Construction is subject not only to capital rationing (he is not allowed to have initial outlays exceeding $400,000) but also to rationing labor hours (only 200,000 hours of labor are available). Which contract offers should be accepted? (*Hint:* Find all the feasible combinations that satisfy the capital rationing. Then exclude from this list those that exceed the 200,000 labor hours available, and proceed from there.)

15. Webster's Discount Store has recently experienced a great number of stock-outs, and to alleviate this problem, management has decided to increase the storage areas in their regional warehouses. This will cost $4 per square foot of warehouse area. The maximum area by which each regional warehouse might be expanded, together with the net present value of future benefits from this maximum expansion, is shown in the following table:

City	Maximum Addition Possible (square feet)	NPV of Maximum addition
Los Angeles	100,000	$50,000
Dallas	80,000	45,000
Atlanta	75,000	40,000
St. Louis	60,000	35,000
Chicago	50,000	30,000
Philadelphia	40,000	20,000
Baltimore	30,000	18,000
New York	25,000	15,000

These projects are divisible, and the *NPV* of an addition smaller than the maximum is proportional to the *NPV* of the maximum addition. For example, if the Los Angeles facility is increased by 75,000 square feet, the *NPV* of this addition will be $37,500.

(a) Find the initial outlay and the profitability index for the expansion projects in each of the eight cities.

(b) If Webster's can allocate only $1.5 million to the expansion project this year, how should this money be spent?

16. The Douglass-McDowell Company has a contract with the federal government to provide 100 X-17 aircraft during the next five years. The timing of delivery of the aircraft to the government within the five-year period is up to Douglass-McDowell, but it will not be paid for the aircraft until they are delivered. The net cash flow to the firm per aircraft produced and delivered is $1.2 million each. Douglass-McDowell is considering two delivery programs: The first calls for a net initial outlay of $82 million and the production and sale of 20 planes for each of the next five years; the second calls for a net ini-

tial outlay of $87 million and the production and sale of 25 planes for each of the next four years. Douglass-McDowell's discount rate for either of these projects is 10%.

(a) What is the *NPV* of the five-year plan? Of the four-year plan?

(b) What is the uniform annual series of the five-year plan? Of the four-year plan?

17. Tex Pub. Co. is considering the construction of a new power plant. The firm has estimated that a coal plant will require $88 million in initial investment and $26 million per year for operating costs. A nuclear plant will require $112 million in initial investment; the operating cost in the first year will be $30 million, but thereafter it will decrease by $3 million per year until it levels off at $15 million. Both plants have expected useful lives of 30 years. Tex Pub. Co.'s required rate of return is 8%.

	Coal Plant	Nuclear Plant
Initial investment	$88 million	$112 million
Annual operating costs	26 million[a]	30 million[b]

[a] Fixed over life of project.
[b] This is the estimated cost for the first year.

(a) Which plant should be built?

(b) Assume that if the nuclear plant is not built, the needed power can be purchased elsewhere for $27 million per year. Should it be built?

9A
CONDITIONS WHEN THERE MAY BE CONFLICTS IN PROJECT RANKING

Why is the choice of a project (its ranking) sensitive to the discount rate used? How is any conflict resolved? The first question is best answered by describing two conditions in which ranking conflicts may arise.

Differences in the Size of Projects' Initial Investments

The *IRR* criterion ignores the scale of the investment. An exaggerated example demonstrates this point. Assume that Tetron, Inc., has a five-acre plot of land and is considering two competing projects. Project *S* is to build a silicon wafer manufacturing plant. This project calls for an initial investment of $2.5 million and has *IRR* = 20%. An alternative use for the land is to grow tulips. Management believes that tulips can be sold at $10 per dozen. They estimate that with only a $25,000 initial outlay, this investment (project *T*) will yield *IRR* = 48%. Given that the required rate of return is 12%, both projects are very attractive. Nevertheless, if management uses the *IRR* to choose between (rank) *S* and *T*, project *T* is preferred to project *S*.

Now intuition alone suggests that this is the wrong decision; a 20% return on $2.5 million is really not worse than a 48% return on $25,000. The reason the *IRR* might provide an erroneous decision is that it ignores the criterion of maximizing the value of the firm. That is, decisions based on the *IRR* do not always maximize the stockholders' wealth because the *IRR* criterion does not evaluate the net addition to the firm's value from accepting a project. The *IRR* fails to recognize the importance of the differential cash flows between the projects. The market value of the differential cash flows is never considered. The project with the larger early cash flows offers an opportunity for a larger immediate reinvestment. Because

■

TABLE 9A-1

Analysis of Differential Cash Flows for Two Mutually Exclusive Projects When the Scale of Investment Differs

Project	Initial Investment	CFAT at the End of Year 1	NPV (RRR = 10%)	IRR
S	−$2,500,000	$3,000,000	$227,300	20%
T	−25,000	37,000	8,637	48
New project (S − T)	−$2,475,000	$2,963,000	$218,663	19.7

$$NPV_{S-T} = \$2,963,000(PVF_{0.10,1}) - \$2,475,000$$
$$= \$2,963,000(0.9091) - \$2,475,000 = \$218,663$$

Decision: The new project is acceptable, which implies that project S should be accepted.

the NPV assumes that all cash flows from the investment are reinvested at the opportunity cost (RRR), it is consistent with the market-value framework. With the reinvestment assumption, the NPV automatically recognizes the value of the differential cash flows caused by the projects' size differences.[7]

To see why this is true, examine Table 9A-1, which summarizes the details regarding projects S and T. The differential (or incremental) cash flows can be viewed as a new project. That is, the difference in the initial outlay of $2.475 million is treated as if it were invested in a new project. If this new project ($S - T$) is evaluated at an RRR of 10%, its $NPV = \$218,663$ and its $IRR = 19.7\%$. Thus this new project should be accepted using either criterion because when the differential cash flows are analyzed, the potential conflict between the NPV and the IRR criteria has been eliminated. Moreover, note that accepting this new project is equivalent to accepting project S, even though project S has a lower IRR than project T does.[8]

Differences in the Timing of Projects' Cash Flows

Conflicts between the NPV and the IRR criteria also occur when there are differences in the timing of projects' cash flows, even if their initial investments are the same or similar. Some projects generate large cash flows earlier and smaller cash flows later in their useful lives. Other projects reverse this pattern by producing larger cash flows later in life, after the project "matures." The rates at which the initial investment is recovered can vary widely. When two mutually exclusive projects have a ranking conflict because of different recovery rates, a correct decision must once again include an analysis of the differential cash flows.

Consider Table 9A-2, which presents information on two projects, X and Y. Assume for simplicity that both require a $9,000 initial investment and have a four-year life. But the pattern of cash inflows is quite different. The result is that at an RRR of 10%, the NPV criterion would select project X, whereas the IRR criterion would select project Y. Nevertheless, when the two projects are correctly evaluated in terms of their differential cash flows, the conflict disappears. Because the new project ($X - Y$) has both $NPV > 0$ and $IRR > RRR$, project X should be accepted.

[7] Some people prefer the NPV rule to the IRR because of the "conservative reinvestment assumption." NPV assumes that cash flows are reinvested at the opportunity cost of capital, and IRR assumes that they are invested at the usually higher IRR. Although these investment assumptions are true, the argument is fallacious. By worrying about the reinvestment rate on another project in the future, the decision maker is ignoring the principle of opportunity costs developed in Chapter 7. The potential return on another independent decision should never affect the current investment decision. The value of a project today should depend on the returns on the other available opportunities today. (See A. A. Alchian, "The Rate of Interest, Fisher's Rate of Return over Cost and Keynes' Internal Rate of Return," *American Economic Review*, December 1955, pp. 938–942, for a discussion of this in greater detail.)

[8] Another way of viewing this differential or incremental cash flow approach is to think of it as if it were a replacement decision like that studied in Chapter 9. That is, project S can be viewed as a "replacement" for project T. If accepting S ("substituting" S's $CFAT$ pattern for T's $CFAT$ pattern) leads to a $CFAT$ pattern that has an IRR greater than the required rate of return ($NPV > 0$), we "replace" T with S; otherwise, we "keep" (accept) T.

■

TABLE 9 A - 2

Analysis of Differential Cash Flows for Two Mutually Exclusive Projects When the Timing of Cash Flows Differs

Project	Initial Investment	Annual CFAT				NPV (RRR = 10%)	IRR
		1	2	3	4		
X	−$9,000	$ 480	$3,700	$6,550	$3,780	$1,997	18%
Y	−9,000	5,800	3,250	2,000	1,561	1,527	20
New project (X − Y)	$ 0	−$5,320	$ 450	$4,550	$2,219	$ 470	14.6

$$NPV_{X-Y} = -\$5,320(PVF_{0.10,1}) + \$450(PVF_{0.10,2}) + \$4,550(PVF_{0.10,3}) + \$2,219(PVF_{0.10,4}) - \$0$$
$$= -\$5,320(0.9091) + \$450(0.8264) + \$4,550(0.7513) + \$2,219(0.6830) - \$0$$
$$= \$470$$

Conclusion: The new project is acceptable, which implies that project X should be accepted.

In conclusion, to use the *IRR* criterion correctly for ranking purposes, the differential or incremental cash flows must be evaluated as if they represented a separate project (the larger-scale project's cash flows minus the smaller-scale project's cash flows). If this new project is acceptable according to the *IRR* criterion, the larger project should be accepted; otherwise, the smaller project (if its *IRR* > *RRR*) should be accepted. Alternatively, this problem can be avoided by using the *NPV* criterion.

Using NPV *Profiles to Illustrate the* NPV *and* IRR *Conflict*

To help visualize the *NPV* versus *IRR* conflict, it is useful to construct *NPV* profiles for projects *X* and *Y* as in Figure 9A-1. In part (a), the conflict arises when the required rate of return is less than 14.6%, the indifference point between the

■

FIGURE 9 A - 1

NPV *profiles of mutually exclusive projects X and Y and the incremental project (X − Y)*

Assumed Discount Rate	(1) NPV_X	−	(2) NPV_Y	=	(3) NPV_{X-Y} (1) − (2)
0%	$5,510		$3,611		$1,899
10	1,997		1,527		470
14.6	774		774		0
20	−418		0		−418
30	−2,138		−1,160		−978

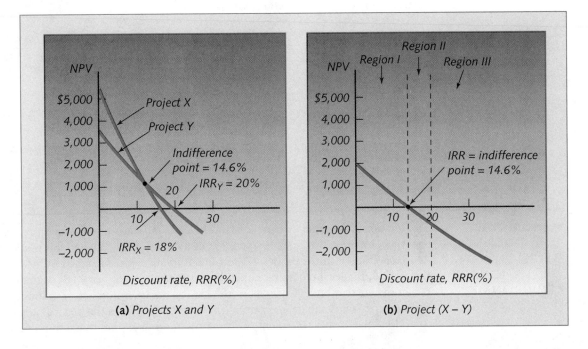

(a) *Projects X and Y*

(b) *Project (X − Y)*

two projects. If the required rate of return is between 14.6% and 20%, no conflict arises. Beyond 20%, both projects are rejected because both projects' NPVs are negative.

Next, some additional insights can be derived from constructing an NPV profile for the new (incremental) project, $X - Y$. First, by focusing on the differential point cash flows, a single NPV profile that results from subtracting Y's profile from X's profile can be created, as in Figure 9A-1(b). Second, notice that the indifference point (14.6%) in part (a) is just the IRR for the new project, part (b). Three decision regions emerge:

Region I: If $RRR < 14.6\%$, accept project X.

Region II: If $14.6\% < RRR < 20\%$, accept project Y.

Region III: If $RRR > 20\%$, reject both projects.

Therefore, when the differential cash flows are evaluated as if they represented an individual project, any ambiguities are removed. Moreover, although only the two mutually exclusive projects that had significant differences in the timing of their cash flows have been discussed here, the reader may want to prove that this approach can also be used to explain the potential conflict that can arise when the scale of investment also differs.

PROBLEM

1. Harris Paint Products is considering two projects that have the same economic lives but quite different cash flows. Hercules Paint Lifter is a chemical agent that removes old paint. It is not flashy, but it is expected to develop a larger market share as painters become familiar with it. Diablo Paint Gun is a heat gun that looks somewhat like a hair dryer. It melts paint and makes it easy to scrape away. The product looks quite impressive in initial use, but its market share is expected to decrease once it becomes known that it may have the unfortunate side effect of setting wood on fire. The cash flows for the two projects are given below. The discount rate is 10%.

	0	1	2	3	4	5	6
Hercules	−$110,000	$6,000	$16,000	$28,000	$32,000	$66,000	$32,000
Diablo	−$150,000	$120,000	$19,000	$10,000	$6,000	$4,000	$32,000

(a) Compute the NPV and IRR for Hercules Paint Lifter.

(b) Compute the NPV and IRR for Diablo Paint Gun.

(c) Evaluate the differential cash flows between the two projects. Which project should Harris Paint Products adopt? Why?

9B

CAPITAL BUDGETING DECISIONS IN AN INFLATIONARY ENVIRONMENT

Inflation is the reduction in money's ability to purchase goods and services over time. Inflation was not considered to be a major problem when this book went to press, but in the early 1970s, annual inflation rates reached 14%. During this period, the level of capital expenditures made by U.S. firms fell dramatically. Given the current budget deficits in the United States, a number of managers anticipate a revival of inflationary trends in the near future. In this regard, it is useful to address the proper treatment of future inflation in capital budgeting decisions.

The Impact of Inflation   Because any capital budgeting decision requires a forecast of future cash flows, the impact of inflation on these cash flows needs to be examined. Revenues, wages, and other costs increase over time during inflationary periods. Depreciation, however, does not change with changes in inflation because the U.S. tax code allows depreciation based on an asset's original purchase price, rather than on its (increasing) market or replacement value. Moreover, the discount rate, or *RRR*, that should be applied to these cash flows to find their present value does change with inflation. The *RRR* is a market-determined rate that takes into account inflationary expectations. The greater the expected rates of inflation are, the higher the *RRR* needs to be because the *RRR* is a nominal rate that reflects the real rate of return and inflation. A famous economist, Irving Fisher, developed the following relationship among nominal interest rates, real interest rates, and inflation:[9]

$$(1 + R) = (1 + r)(1 + p) \tag{9B-1}$$

where

R is the nominal rate of interest

r is the real rate of interest

p is the expected rate of inflation [10]

For example, if the real rate of interest is expected to be 4% and the expected rate of inflation is 6%, then the nominal rate of return will be 10.24%; that is,

$$1 + R = (1 + 0.04)(1 + 0.06) = 1.1024$$

or

$$R = 1.1024 - 1.00 = 0.1024$$

Thus both future cash flows and the discount rate are sensitive to inflation expectations.

Fortunately, in a conceptual sense, the proper treatment of inflation in capital budgeting decisions is straightforward. The financial manager can use one of two ways to evaluate capital budgeting projects:[11]

1. Discount *nominal* cash flows with the *nominal* required rate of return.

2. Discount *real* cash flows with the *real* required rate of return.

When the financial manager consistently follows one of these rules, identical results should be obtained.

Why Faster Payback Projects May Be Preferred During Inflationary Periods   When we discussed the payback period criterion, we had little to say that was good. In the presence of inflation, however, management tends to choose projects with shorter payback periods. Because large investments tend to have longer payback periods, the level of capital expenditures usually falls in an inflationary

---

[9] See Irving Fisher, *The Theory of Interest* (New York: Augustus M. Kelley, 1965).

[10] Often in practice $R = r + p$ is used as an approximation of this fundamental relationship. The logic is as follows:

$$1 + R = (1 + r)(1 + p) = (1 + r + p + rp)$$

and because rp is a very small number for low levels of inflation (e.g., $0.04 \times 0.03 = 0.0012$), we have

$$R = 1 + r + p - 1 = r + p$$

[11] Term structure issues and nonneutral inflation issues are ignored. "Neutral" inflation implies that all components of the cash flow stream (revenues and costs) inflate at the same rate.

TABLE 9B-1

Effect of Inflation on a Project's Real ΔCFAT[a]

a. Nominal and real ΔCFAT with 0% inflation

	Year			
	1	2	3	4
Δ Revenues − Δ costs =	$40,000	$40,000	$40,000	$40,000
Δ Depreciation	25,000	25,000	25,000	25,000
Δ Taxable income	15,000	15,000	15,000	15,000
Δ Income taxes (50%)	7,500	7,500	7,500	7,500
Δ After-tax income	7,500	7,500	7,500	7,500
Add back depreciation	25,000	25,000	25,000	25,000
Nominal ΔCFAT	$32,500	$32,500	$32,500	$32,500
Real ΔCFAT	$32,500	$32,500	$32,500	$32,500

b. Nominal and real ΔCFAT with 10% inflation[b]

	Year							
	1		2		3		4	
Δ Revenues[c] − Δ costs =	$44,000	(100)	$48,400	(100)	$53,240	(100)	$58,564	(100)
Δ Depreciation	25,000	(57)	25,000	(52)	25,000	(47)	25,000	(43)
Δ Taxable income	19,000	(43)	23,400	(48)	28,240	(53)	33,564	(57)
Δ Income taxes (50%)	9,500	(22)	11,700	(24)	14,120	(27)	16,782	(29)
Δ After-tax income	9,500		11,700		14,120		16,782	
Add back depreciation	25,000		25,000		25,000		25,000	
Nominal ΔCFAT	$34,500	(78)	$36,700	(76)	$39,120	(73)	$41,782	(71)
Real ΔCFAT	$31,364	(71)	$30,331	(63)	$29,391	(55)	$28,538	(49)

[a] The real ΔCFAT is found as follows:

$$\text{Real } \Delta CFAT = \frac{\text{nominal } \Delta CFAT_t}{(1 + 0.10)^t} \quad t = 1, 2, 3, 4$$

[b] The parenthetical expressions represent the relevant accounting item as a percentage of revenues minus costs.
[c] Assumes "neutral" inflation whereby all revenues and costs increase at a 10% inflation rate.

environment. The reason is that the U.S. tax code requires firms to calculate depreciation (and thereby cash flows) on the basis of original costs. Consequently, a project's real *CFAT* declines over time. An example illustrates this phenomenon more clearly.

Suppose that a firm in the 50% tax bracket is considering a proposal that calls for an investment of $100,000. Assume that the entire investment is depreciable over a four-year period to a $0 salvage value using straight-line depreciation. Table 9B-1 contains the relevant cash flow analyses with 0% and 10% inflation rates.

In Table 9B-1, part a, nominal and real *CFAT*s are equal because inflation is 0%. According to Table 9B-1, part b, if inflation is expected to be 10% per annum for the next four years, a completely different picture emerges. Because revenues and costs are assumed to increase at a 10% rate, this seems to imply that the nominal *CFAT* should also increase at the same rate. To complicate matters, inflation usually offsets different cash flow items in different ways. Revenues may be affected differently from material, labor, and utility costs, and so they should be adjusted separately. Therefore adjusting revenues and costs by a general price index, such as the Consumer Price Index, often does not suffice. It does increase, but only at a rate of 6% to 7%. The reason is that depreciation expenses inadequately reflect the changing market (replacement) value of the project's assets. Only if depreciation also grew at a 10% rate would the firm be indifferent to the effect of inflation because only then would the nominal *CFAT* be adequately accounting for inflation. Moreover, this "inflation penalty" actually benefits Uncle Sam. To see these points, note that while depreciation steadily declines from 57% to 43% of revenues less costs, taxes increase from 22% to 29%. Together, these explain the decrease in the nominal *CFAT* from 78% to 71% of revenues less costs.

More important, the firm's real *CFAT* decreases in both a relative and an absolute sense. The conclusion is that the net effect of inflation makes the government's share of the real returns rise and the shareholders' share fall. To illustrate further, notice the following effect of inflation on the project's *IRR:*

	With 0% Inflation	With 10% Inflation
Nominal	11.4%	18.5%
Real *IRR*	11.4	7.7

As we learned earlier, the potential loss in purchasing power is offset by adding an inflation premium to returns. Notice, however, that with 10% inflation, the nominal *IRR* should be 22.5% but is in fact only 18.5%.

An inflation premium is intended to provide an "extra payment" to maintain real returns. Although it is not "income," U.S. tax laws treat it as if it were. Moreover, because of fixed depreciation charges and the resulting disproportionately higher income taxes, the real *IRR* drops from 11.4% to 7.7%. Given this scenario, firms have a disincentive to invest heavily during inflationary periods and tend to select projects with faster paybacks. As a result, investments in longer-term assets for the economy as a whole usually fall. (Notice that when the payback period is calculated using the real *CFAT,* the project has a faster payback with 0% inflation.)

One way to remedy this situation is to use a faster depreciation schedule for tax purposes. But even accelerated depreciation methods such as double-declining balance *may* not provide an adequate increase in projects' real returns.

QUESTIONS

1. How would an increase in the inflation rate affect the firm's *RRR* ?

2. Does an increasing rate of inflation affect the firm's cash flows? How?

3. How does the existence of the "inflation penalty" affect capital budgeting decisions?

PROBLEM

1. The following is a routine analysis of a capital budgeting project for the Payne Co.:

	0	1	2	3	4	5
Investment	2 million					
Working capital (*WC*)	160,000					
Increase in operating income		700,000	700,000	700,000	700,000	700,000
Straight-line depreciation		400,000	400,000	400,000	400,000	400,000
Taxable income		300,000	300,000	300,000	300,000	300,000
Income tax @ 40%		120,000	120,000	120,000	120,000	120,000
Net income		180,000	180,000	180,000	180,000	180,000
Add: Depreciation		400,000	400,000	400,000	400,000	400,000
Add: Reclaimed *WC*						160,000
Cash flow	(2.16 million)	580,000	580,000	580,000	580,000	740,000

NPV at 12% *RRR* = $21,558
IRR = 12.39%

Payne's president, Bill Bigbucks, observes: "This project meets our requirement of a 12% return for its risk class. However, our economist is projecting a prolonged period of 6% annual inflation. All of our revenues and expenses will be affected. Moreover, the purchasing power of our working capital must be maintained at a level reflecting the increased inflation. Therefore, I want you to reanalyze this project, incorporating the effects of 6% annual inflation into your analysis."

(a) Prepare the analysis as requested by Mr. Bigbucks.

(b) Should Payne change its 12% required return? If so, to what?

9C

ESTIMATING EXCHANGE RATES

In making capital budgeting decisions for direct foreign investments, managers must estimate unknown exchange rates. The accuracy of their estimates has a significant effect on the validity of their entire capital budgeting process. Firms can obtain estimates of future exchange rates from banks, economic consulting firms, their own in-house planning groups, or other experts knowledgeable about the currencies involved. It is beyond the scope of this text to examine in detail the factors considered in developing long-run estimates of exchange rates. Instead, we introduce and explain some of the factors that can influence these estimates. In this appendix we discuss two of these influences: relative inflation rates and relative interest rates.

Inflation Rates

Inflation is measured as the rate of change in prices. For instance, if a basket of consumer goods costs $120 in 1994 but rises in cost to $126 in 1995, then prices have risen by

$$\frac{\$126 - \$120}{\$120} = 0.05 \quad \text{or } 5\%$$

If the price levels in one country change at a different rate from those in another country, then the exchange rate changes in response. **Purchasing power parity (PPP)** theory seeks to explain this movement in exchange rates. PPP is based on an economic relationship called the law of one price, which implies that goods of equal value in differing countries may be equated by an exchange rate. For instance, if a loaf of bread costs $1 in the United States and 110 yen in Japan, the exchange rate should be 110 yen/$. Though logical, this relationship looks at the prices of individual goods and does not help us evaluate changes in a country's overall price level. The relative version of PPP is more useful because it states that *changes* in the exchange rate should be related to the *relative changes* in the purchasing power of the currencies involved over a given period. Relative PPP theory in equation form is

$$S_1 = S_0 \left(\frac{1 + \dot{P}_b}{1 + \dot{P}_f} \right) \tag{9C-1}$$

which states that the future spot exchange rate, S_1, depends on the current spot rate, S_0, and the relative inflation rates between the two countries. $\dot{P}_b$ and $\dot{P}_f$ are the inflation rates in the home and foreign countries, respectively.

Given forecasts of inflation, relative purchasing power parity theory can be used as an estimator of future exchange rates. Assume the current exchange rate in Mexico is $0.31964/peso and Mexico's expected inflation rate is 15% annually. If the

United States expects an inflation rate of 3%, the PPP theory indicates an exchange rate of approximately $0.28629/peso in one year:

$$S_1 = \$0.31964/\text{peso} \left(\frac{1.03}{1.15} \right) = \$0.28629/\text{peso}$$

The interpretation of these numbers is fairly simple. The peso is losing value, or depreciating, and will buy fewer goods in Mexico in the future than it does today. The peso is a **depreciating currency**, losing value at a faster rate than the U.S. dollar. Therefore the peso should in one period be worth less than the dollar and therefore buy fewer American goods also. We could also explain this relationship by saying that the dollar is an **appreciating currency**, gaining value relative to the peso.

If we were interested in the exchange rate between the peso and the dollar in five years and we assumed that relative inflation would remain fairly stable over this period, the peso would be worth

$$S_5 = \$0.31964/\text{peso} \frac{(1.03)^5}{(1.15)^5} = \$0.18423/\text{peso}$$

Although there are some technical difficulties with PPP, it does reflect a major factor in the movement of exchange rates over time. A country that experiences relatively higher rates of inflation generally sees the value of its currency fall relative to other currencies. Therefore companies with **direct foreign investments** (DFI) in countries that are experiencing relatively high inflation rates should take PPP into account when estimating the dollar value of the cash flows to be received from the investment.

Interest Rates

A second major factor in determining exchange rates is relative interest rates. For example, if yields (interest rates) on one-year investments are relatively higher in Germany than in the United States, American short-term funds are attracted to Germany as American businesses attempt to earn higher returns on their cash holdings. As a result, there is increased demand for the mark by dollar holders, and the spot value of the mark will go up. However, investors will use the forward markets, defined in Section 9-3, to lock in their yields by selling marks in the forward market to regain their dollars at the end of the investment period. This selling pressure reduces the value of the mark in the forward market. Because of market supply and demand conditions, interest rate differentials between the two countries cause changes in the exchange rate. More specifically, forward and spot rates adjust to reflect parity between similar risk investments in different countries.

Interest rate parity (IRP) theory is expressed as

$$F_1 = S_0 \left(\frac{1 + R_h}{1 + R_f} \right) \tag{9C-2}$$

which states that the forward exchange rate F_1 depends on the current spot exchange rate, S_0, and the differences in the nominal interest rates in the two countries involved over the corresponding period, with R_h and R_f representing the interest rates in the home and foreign country, respectively. This designation is important because these exchange rates are stated as the home currency price of one unit of foreign currency, $S_0(H/F)$.

To illustrate IRP, suppose you are considering investing $100,000 for one year in either U.S. Treasury bills at 4.58% or the German money market at 8.6%. The current spot exchange rate is $0.5785/DM. Using the preceding equation yields

$$F_1 = \$0.5785/DM \times \frac{1.0458}{1.0860} = \$0.5571/DM$$

Interest rate parity means that, even if nominal rates are higher in Germany, American investors cannot profit from the differential because trading activity between the German and American interest-bearing investments reduces the forward value of the mark. While Americans would indeed receive 8.60% on their German investment, they would also experience a loss of

$$\frac{\$0.5571/DM \;-\; \$0.5785/DM}{\$0.5571/DM} = 0.03841 \quad \text{or } 3.84\%$$

in the value of the currency in which the investment was made. This depreciation of the mark means that American investors receive a net yield (rate earned on the foreign investment plus change in the value of the foreign currency) approximately equal to what they would earn on the American investment. If the forward rate deviates significantly from the above value, then traders in the market can make arbitrage profits. Foreign exchange dealers, however, are always looking for these types of discrepancies and, by acting on them quickly, tend to force the market into equilibrium.

The above American investment in Germany is defined as an application of **covered IRP**, in that the investor uses the forward rate to guarantee, or cover, the conversion of cash flows at the end of the period back into dollars. Although these forward rates are not normally available beyond two years, a modified version of IRP, called **uncovered IRP**, is useful in estimating future exchange rates for longer-term cash flows such as those used in capital budgeting decisions. Uncovered IRP uses the interest rates in two countries as obtained through their yield curves to estimate exchange rates into the future with the following equation:

$$S_n = S_0 \frac{(1 + R_h)^n}{(1 + R_f)^n} \tag{9C-3}$$

As an example, as part of a capital budgeting analysis, we estimate that we will receive a dividend payment from a Thai subsidiary, in bhats, of B185,000 in four years. Examining the respective yield curves of the United States and Thailand, we see that annual rates for four-year instruments are estimated to be 4.5% and 19.8%, respectively. If the current exchange rate is $S_0 = \$0.03932/B$, then the exchange rate used to convert bhats into dollars in our calculations is

$$S_4 = \$0.03931/B \times \frac{(1 + 0.045)^4}{(1 + 0.198)^4} = \$0.02276/B$$

We would thus expect to receive B185,000 × $0.02276 = $4,210.60 in four years.

Our brief discussion of how relative inflation rates and interest rates affect exchange rates shows how different economies are interrelated. The reader is encouraged to consult any good international finance text for a more detailed analysis of how exchange rates are forecasted.

QUESTIONS

1. How does inflation affect a currency's value?

2. How do interest rate differentials affect a currency's value?

PROBLEMS

1. Eurocars, Inc., can purchase a luxury German auto for a wholesale price of $62,400. This dollar price is obtained by taking the German price, DM 120,000, and converting it into dollars at the current exchange rate, $S_0 = \$0.5200/DM$. This price, however, is subject to change with changes in the price levels of the United States and Germany. The dealer's bank has forecasted that inflation in the United States and Germany will be 3% and 4.5%, respectively, over the next year.

   (a) What will the wholesale price of the auto be in Germany in one year?

   (b) What is the exchange rate expected to be in one year?

   (c) What will the dealer's dollar price for the auto be in one year?

2. A banker notices that the annual interest rates in the United States and Japan are 3% and 2%, respectively, and that the current exchange rate is $S_0 = \yen103/\$$.

   (a) The banker has received a call from a good business customer who needs to arrange for the purchase of Japanese yen in one year. What should the banker quote as the forward rate?

   (b) Using this forward rate, could the banker make a profit by investing $1,000,000 in yen rather than investing that same amount in dollars?

SUGGESTED ADDITIONAL READINGS

Bacon, P. W. "The Evaluation of Mutually Exclusive Investments." *Financial Management,* Summer 1977, pp. 55–58.

Baumol, W., and R. Quandt. "Investment and Discount Rates Under Capital Rationing—A Programming Approach." *Economic Journal,* June 1965, pp. 317–329.

Bernhard, Richard H. "Mathematical Programming Models for Capital Budgeting—A Survey, Generalization, and Critique." *Journal of Financial and Quantitative Analysis,* 6th ed., June 1969, pp. 111–158.

Eiteman, David K., Arthur I. Stonehill, and Michael H. Moffett. *Multinational Business Finance,* 6th ed. Reading, MA: Addison-Wesley Publishing Company, 1992.

Forsyth, J. D., and D. C. Owen. "Capital Rationing Methods." In *Capital Budgeting Under Conditions of Uncertainty,* edited by R. L. Crum and F. G. J. Derkinderen, pp. 213–235. Hingham, MA: Nijhoff, 1981.

Hawawini, Gabriel A., and A. Vora. "Yield Approximations: A Historical Perspective." *Journal of Finance,* March 1982, pp. 145–156.

Hirshleifer, J. "On the Theory of Optimal Investment." *Journal of Political Economy,* August 1958, pp. 329–352.

Lorie, J. H., and L. J. Savage. "Three Problems in Rationing Capital." *Journal of Business,* October 1955, pp. 229–239.

Myers, Stewart C., and Gerald A. Pogue. "A Programming Approach to Corporate Financial Management." *Journal of Finance,* May 1974, pp. 579–599.

Shapiro, Alan C. *Multinational Financial Management.* Boston: Allyn and Bacon, 1992.

TEN ADJUSTING FOR UNCERTAINTY AND FINANCING EFFECTS IN CAPITAL BUDGETING DECISIONS

*Take calculated risks.
That is quite different
from being rash.*

—George S. Patton,
1944

*I*n Chapters 8 and 9 we discussed several of the qualitative and quantitative considerations involved in capital budgeting. The general rule from both of these chapters is: Evaluate the project's net present value (*NPV*) and adopt the project if it is positive. By following this rule, the firm can increase the wealth of its stockholders.

Unfortunately, this rule appears to reduce the entire capital budgeting problem to a simple mechanical procedure. In principle, following this rule would be relatively easy for a manager if he could assign some members of the staff to provide the expected cash flows, assign another team to compute the appropriate discount rate, and delegate still others to calculate the *NPV*s. The problem is not so simple in practice because there is no clear-cut procedure for forming expectations of the project's future cash flows.

Managers make decisions in a very uncertain and changing environment in which cash flows and their volatility are not easily analyzed. Thus it is very important to make allowances for the risk associated with future cash flows. This is particularly true when it is virtually impossible to form realistic expectations of future cash flows before the project details are fully implemented. In this regard, a good manager asks several "what if" questions to understand how sensitive the *NPV* analysis is to changes in the various assumptions. This is the first issue addressed in this chapter.

Another problem in implementing the *NPV* rule is that there is no simple scheme for identifying the appropriate discount rate for valuing these flows. Most managers would agree that an investment's expected benefits should provide some minimum required rate of return (*RRR*). But agreeing with this basic concept and implementing it are two different things. The discount rate question is the second issue that we address here.

We begin by examining a traditional procedure known as the weighted average cost of capital (*WACC*) method. We then discuss how some of the weaknesses of this approach are overcome by the adjusted present value (*APV*) approach, which can also accommodate the effects of subsidized financing. To implement the *APV* approach, one must estimate the risk (beta) of an unlevered firm. If historical information is available, this is relatively easy; if not, we have to use a technique known as the "pure-play" method.

This chapter answers the following questions:

■ What are some practical procedures for dealing with the uncertainty associated with a project's cash flows?

■ What is the weighted average cost of capital (*WACC*) method and how is it used?

■ What is adjusted present value (*APV*) and how can this concept be used?

■ How is the unlevered equity beta calculated?

■ What is the pure-play method and how is it implemented?

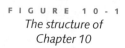

FIGURE 10-1
The structure of Chapter 10

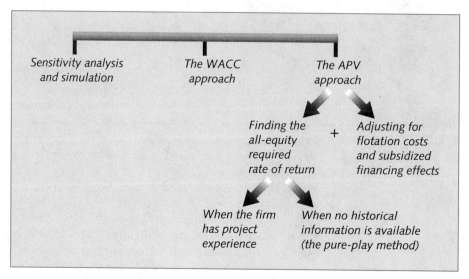

Figure 10-1 lays out the structure of the chapter. It may be useful for the reader as we progress through the chapter. Appendix 10A explains the procedure for calculating betas when historical information is available.

10-1

ASSESSING THE IMPACT OF UNCERTAIN CASH FLOWS

In most situations, the future cash flows from an investment are not known precisely. Managers must rely on estimates, which should be based on the most realistic possible case. Nonetheless decision makers should recognize that forecasts of future cash flows are uncertain, and they should adjust their analyses of projects accordingly.

Consider the operating cash flows for Baxter, Inc.'s proposed new drug project. The relevant information is presented in Table 10-1. Baxter estimates that an initial investment of $150,000 is required to launch the project. The cash flow picture, however, looks promising. A positive $\Delta CFAT$ of $61,500 per year is expected over the life of the project (which Baxter expects to be five years). The cash flow number assumes that the entire $150,000 investment is depreciated straight line over the five years to a $0 salvage value. Thus the annual depreciation amounts to $30,000. In addition, Baxter's calculations assume that it is in the 30% tax bracket over the life of the project. As we can see, if Baxter's opportunity cost is 10%, the *NPV* of the project is $83,134, and Baxter is justified in accepting this project.

Nonetheless, Baxter's management feels uneasy about this project because there are too many uncertain elements that it has not considered in its analysis. Baxter's cash flows in Table 10-1 are expected cash flows; there is no guarantee that they will indeed materialize. For one thing, the company is not confident about its revenue forecasts. Management believes that if competing firms enter the market, Baxter will lose a substantial portion of its projected revenues, that it simply does not have the established marketing network that many of its larger competitors have. Second, the production manager is unwilling to commit to the cost figures; he is not certain about the variable and fixed costs. Recognizing these uncertainties, management wants to assess the various potential future outcomes and then make an "executive decision" about whether or not to accept this project.

What are the various ways in which Baxter can approach this problem of un-

<table>
<tr><td>**TABLE 10-1**
Baxter, Inc.'s
Drug Project</td><td colspan="2">Initial outlay
Life of project
Opportunity cost (required rate of return)
$\Delta CFAT$</td><td>$150,000
5 years
10%
$61,500/year</td></tr>
</table>

$$NPV \text{ at } 10\% = -\$150,000 + \$61,500(PVFA_{0.10,5})$$
$$= -\$150,000 + \$61,500(3.7908)$$
$$= \$83,134$$

certainty regarding future cash flows? Two methods can be used: sensitivity analysis and computer simulation.[1] Each has advantages and disadvantages.

Sensitivity Analysis

What if sales fall below expected values because the drug does not gain market acceptance? What would happen to the *NPV* if the drug becomes an instant success and revenues exceed the expected values? What if labor and distribution costs (variable costs) increase after the product is introduced? Would the project's *NPV* become negative? Or would it still be positive? How much of an increase in fixed costs can Baxter take before the project becomes unattractive (i.e., becomes a negative-*NPV* project)? A lengthy list of such questions arises. One way to answer them is by means of sensitivity analysis (sometimes casually referred to as "what if" analysis).

Sensitivity analysis, as the name implies, means examining the sensitivity of some variable to changes in another variable. In the Baxter, Inc., case, management is interested in understanding the impact on the *NPV* of changes in sales revenues, fixed costs, and variable costs. Thus it is useful to get an idea of how sensitive the *NPV* is to changes in each of these variables.

Based on information from the company's marketing and production departments, Baxter has assembled data on the expected, pessimistic, and optimistic estimates of the variables that affect the cash flows from this project. As Table 10-2,

---

[1] Another approach to dealing with cash flow uncertainty uses *decision trees*. When a particular decision today depends on the outcome of some variable in the future, this eventually must be recognized. Decision trees are extremely tedious to use, and this approach is not examined in this book.

TABLE 10-2
Sensitivity Analysis for Baxter's Drug Project

a. Estimates

	Year 0	Years 1–5		
		Pessimistic	*Expected*	*Optimistic*
1. Initial investment	$150,000			
2. Revenue (Q × P)		$160,000	$200,000	$240,000
3. Variable costs		120,000	100,000	90,000
4. Fixed costs		30,000	25,000	21,000
5. Depreciation		30,000	30,000	30,000
6. Net operating income (2 − 3 − 4 − 5)		−20,000	45,000	99,000
7. Taxes at 30%		0	13,500	29,700
8. Net income (6 − 7)		−20,000	31,500	69,300
9. Operating cash flow (8 + 5)		10,000	61,500	99,300

b. Results of NPV Analysis[a] (opportunity cost = 10%)

	Pessimistic	*Expected*	*Optimistic*
Revenues	−$23,008	$83,134	$189,277
Variable costs	+30,063	83,134	109,670
Fixed costs	+69,866	83,134	93,748

[a] Interpretation: For example, consider the *NPV* of $69,866. This *NPV* is calculated assuming a pessimistic outcome for fixed costs ($30,000 from part a), and all other cash flows are the expected cash flows from part a. In other words, the *NPV* of $69,866 will result if all cash flows except fixed costs are as expected and fixed costs are $30,000.

part a shows, the marketing staff believes that in a pessimistic "worst-case scenario," the revenues from the drug will fall to $160,000 per year, and in an optimistic "best-case scenario," the revenues from the drug will be $240,000 per year. Along the same lines, the production department has provided its optimistic and pessimistic estimates for fixed and variable costs.

Table 10-2, part b gives the results of Baxter's sensitivity analysis. Consider the *NPV* of $189,277. What is the significance of this number, and how was it determined? The *NPV* is calculated by assuming that the optimistic revenue figure of $240,000 per year is the actual revenue figure and that all other cash flows are the expected cash flows; that is, the variable costs are $100,000, fixed costs are $25,000, and so on. In other words, the project will have an *NPV* of $189,277 if the optimistic sales figures materialize and all other numbers remain unchanged. To consider another case, if the drug sales are not encouraging, the project will have an *NPV* of − $23,008, which would clearly be a bad situation for Baxter. Notice from the analysis that the uncertainty in the fixed or variable costs is not as crucial as is the uncertainty associated with the sales revenues. Even with the pessimistic fixed and variable cost numbers, Baxter's project will have positive *NPV*s.

So what is Baxter's management to conclude? All in all, the project appears to be a good one. Except for one case, all the *NPV*s are positive. Baxter need not worry too much about its production manager's uncertainty, but it should examine its sales revenue forecasts more carefully. What can the company do to increase sales? After all, this is the main factor in determining the project's attractiveness for Baxter. Perhaps a lower selling price can decrease the probability of the worst-case scenario, or perhaps management should hire an aggressive marketing agency to target the pharmaceutical market audience.

If management is reasonably confident that it can avoid this pessimistic sales forecast by, say, a change in pricing policies or advertising, it may choose to proceed with the project. Any proposed changes should be reexamined in a "what if" analysis. It is virtually impossible to anticipate all the questions that management can ask and to catalog the myriad possibilities for corrective action. Each situation must be considered on a case-by-case basis, which requires a detailed knowledge of the business, the company, and the firm's management philosophy.

WEAKNESSES OF SENSITIVITY ANALYSIS

Although sensitivity analysis can be a useful tool for alerting management to its potential for error, it is at best an aid in the decision process and, like other tools, should not be used in isolation. Some aspects of sensitivity analysis should be explained further.

First, what do *optimistic* and *pessimistic* mean here? Different decision makers may define these words differently. In fact, even within the same company, there may be disagreement. For example, the marketing department of Baxter, Inc., may consider $160,000 in sales to be pessimistic, whereas its production department may define this as a reasonable measure of success.

Unfortunately, this problem cannot be resolved simply by management's telling all departments how *optimistic* and *pessimistic* are to be defined. The number and type of variables that affect the sales of the product are different from the number and type of factors that production departments consider. For example, rising costs can be a favorable signal to a marketing manager concerned with sales revenues but may be an unfavorable outcome for a cost-conscious production manager.

Second, what happens if the variables under consideration are related to one another? An optimistic variable cost estimate can arise, for example, because most of the costs become fixed. Such relationships between the variables cannot be handled easily in a sensitivity analysis.

Finally, wouldn't it be more helpful to assess the various "what if" scenarios by evaluating the impact of changes in a few variables simultaneously? Sensitivity analysis allowed Baxter, Inc., to evaluate the effects on *NPV* of changes in certain variables taken one at a time. What if Baxter wanted to evaluate simultaneously the joint effects of, say, pessimistic sales and optimistic cost figures?

Computer Simulation   Unlike sensitivity analysis, computer simulation allows one to evaluate the impact of changes in several variables simultaneously. The **Monte Carlo simulation method,** in fact, permits one to examine the impact of changes in all possible combinations of variables. Some elaborate computer programs even conduct the analysis that provides the entire distribution of potential outcomes.

The following is Baxter's procedure for a Monte Carlo simulation of its capital budgeting project:

Step 1: Model the problem. Baxter first must define the problem for the computer. It must enter the equation for determining cash flows, the equation to calculate the *NPV,* and, of course, the appropriate opportunity cost that the computer must use to discount the cash flows.

Step 2: Characterize the uncertainty. In this stage the computer is given information about the uncertainty associated with each variable. This uncertainty is characterized as a probability distribution of forecasting errors for each variable. A sample probability distribution (a triangular distribution) is shown in Figure 10-2, which suggests that the mean forecast error is 0%, but the error could be as large as +15% or −15% for sales and +10% or −10% for variable costs. Management must come up with these numbers based on the confidence it attaches to its forecasted expected values.

Step 3: Provide data. The expected cash flow information (Table 10-2) is then entered.

Step 4: Run the simulation. This is a computational stage performed entirely by the computer. The computer takes samples from the distributions of forecast errors, forecasts each variable, and then calculates the cash flows. This sequence of calculations is known as an *iteration.* After several iterations, the computer can provide the probability distribution of cash flows. Hypothetical computer outputs for Baxter's cash flow simulation for the first two years are presented in Figure 10-3.

Step 5: Analyze the results. With the distribution of cash flows in hand, Baxter can evaluate the cash flows. The output of the simulation provides the mean cash flow, the range of potential outcomes, and the probability that the actual cash flows will fall within a particular range (say, between $16,000 and $23,000) for each year. In addition, management can ask such questions as: What is the probability that the cash flows will exceed $17,000 per year? By obtaining answers to these questions, management is in a better position to assess the impact of cash flow changes on the project's *NPV.*

DISADVANTAGES OF SIMULATION

The major disadvantage of simulation is that it may be too expensive and time consuming for small projects. Thus, although oil companies and aircraft manufac-

FIGURE 10-2
Expressing the uncertainty associated with (a) sales and (b) variable costs for Baxter's drug project in a simulation. There is triangular distribution of forecast errors with a mean forecast error of 0%. Management has more confidence in its ability to forecast variable costs than in its ability to forecast sales.

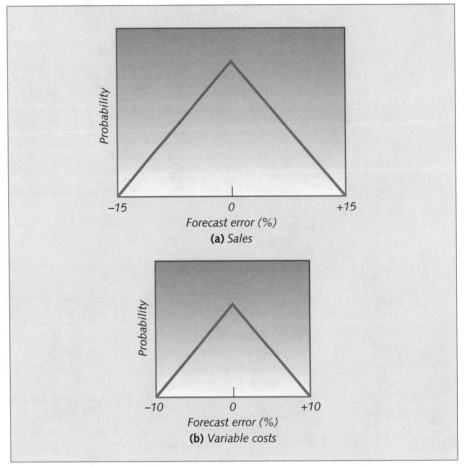

(a) Sales

(b) Variable costs

■

FIGURE 10-3
Hypothetical output for Baxter's simulation. The shaded area is the probability that the cash flows will be between $16,000 and $23,000 in (a) year 1 and (b) year 2.

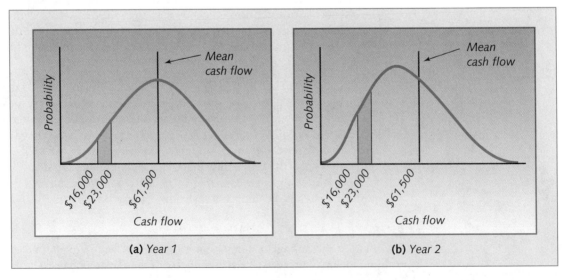

(a) Year 1   **(b)** Year 2

MISUSING SIMULATION

*T*he procedure for incorporating uncertainty into capital budgeting decisions is not simple. Several different approaches have been advocated in the literature. In this search for better risk-adjustment techniques, many have been unjustifiably impressed with simulation in its various forms.

Consider the following early approach to simulation: Instead of obtaining a probability distribution of cash flows, as in the example in the text, managers obtain a probability distribution of NPVs. That is, they let the computer calculate several potential values of the NPV and give a distribution of NPVs directly. To avoid double counting the risk, the cash flows are discounted using the risk-free interest rate. The simulation output provides the expected NPV and the variance of NPVs. This distribution of NPVs should be the basis for decision making. Unfortunately, this approach cannot be defended because it is inconsistent with the NPV concept. Why?

1. Opportunity costs are ignored. Notice that in this procedure of finding the NPVs, the risk-free interest rate is used. What does NPV mean then? From Chapter 7 we know that for an NPV to be helpful, the discount rate used should be the opportunity cost.

2. Relevant risk is ignored. Even if the company uses a higher discount rate, how should management assess the project's risk? Recall that only the undiversifiable risk of a project affects the discount rate.

3. Market values are ignored.

Because the relevant risk of the project cannot be determined in this procedure and because the discount rate used has no relationship to opportunity costs, it is extremely unlikely that a project's NPV computed in this manner will have any relationship to market values.

Why is management conducting the complicated analysis in the first place? Presumably to see whether the project in question will increase stockholder wealth. However, it may not be achieving its objectives by using this analysis. Suppose that the expected NPV from a simulation is $40,000. Management simply has no basis for expecting the wealth of its stockholders to increase by $40,000 if it accepts this project. In fact, when using this procedure, one has no way of determining whether the project is good.

turing companies have been known to use simulation extensively, most smaller companies find it either too tedious or too expensive. Even though computing-time cost considerations are not as important in these days of efficient high-speed computers, a proper simulation model is difficult to build and requires specialized technical skills. In addition to these problems, the output of computer simulations is often misinterpreted (see the highlight above). If the management of a company does not have experience in interpreting the output, the laborious analysis may simply not be worthwhile.

10-2

THE WEIGHTED AVERAGE COST OF CAPITAL APPROACH

*T*he net present value of a project is the expected cash flows from the project discounted at the required rate of return (RRR). The **weighted average cost of capital** ($WACC$) approach is a traditional method for determining the RRR for capital budgeting projects. We first examine how this risky discount rate is calculated and define the situations in which the $WACC$ is properly used. We then examine the weaknesses of the $WACC$ approach.

The Weighted Average Cost of Capital

Perhaps the most basic intuition underlying all business decisions is that the return from an investment must exceed the cost of the capital used to finance the investment. Since the capital raised by a firm comes from various sources, financial managers have historically relied on what is known as the weighted average cost of capital (*WACC*) approach to estimating a firm's cost of capital. This cost of capital is used as an estimate of the discount rate for evaluating potential projects. The *WACC* is computed in two simple steps:

1. Compute the cost of individual sources of capital—that is, debt and equity.

2. Compute the weighted average of these individual costs, with the weights depending on the proportion of each component (in terms of market value) in the firm's capital structure.

In the *WACC* approach, if a firm's cost of capital calculated in this manner is 11%, then a project whose *NPV* is positive at a discount rate of 11% is a good project because this can happen only if the project's *IRR* is greater than 11%. (This was seen in Chapter 8.) Thus this procedure seems reasonable because it ensures that only projects with *IRR*s greater than the cost of the investment will be undertaken.

Consider a simple example. Suppose that Fleener Corporation is financed with two capital components: $400,000 in debt and $600,000 in equity.[2] Because the company incurs a cost in using this capital, it is necessary to estimate the "component costs of capital." Assume that the costs of debt and equity are 8% and 16%, respectively. From this, Fleener's *WACC* is computed as follows:

Capital Component	(1) Dollar Amount	(2) Weight	(3) Component Cost	(4) Weighted Component Cost (2) × (3)
Debt	$400,000	0.40	0.08	0.032
Equity	600,000	0.60	0.16	0.096
	$1,000,000	1.00		
				WACC = 0.128

Thus the company's average cost for every dollar of capital raised is 12.8%.

Now, how can Fleener use the *WACC* to determine which projects are acceptable? It should accept any project that offers a rate of return greater than its 12.8% cost of capital. Conversely, Fleener should reject any project whose return is less than 12.8%; otherwise, it will be raising capital with a 12.8% cost and investing this capital in projects with lower returns. Figure 10-4 shows graphically Fleener's accept/reject criterion. First note that the *WACC* is a single-point estimate (i.e., it is constant regardless of how risky a project is). Projects *B, D,* and *E* are acceptable, whereas *A* is clearly undesirable. Fleener is indifferent to project *C.*

Calculating the Cost of Capital

What are these costs of capital incurred by firms? Recall from Chapter 1 that all investors, regardless of whether they are stockholders or bondholders, invest with the expectation of receiving rewards. Stockholders expect dividend payments and capital appreciation; bondholders expect interest payments and potential capital gains. If the firm does not, in fact, provide these expected benefits, investors sell their securities, thereby depressing their market prices. Thus, even if a firm is not paying out dividends, there is an *implicit cost* associated with retaining funds; they are not free in an opportunity cost sense. The expected return on a stock has two components: dividends and capital gains. It is easy to see how dividends can be a

[2] A company can have other components in its capital structure (say, preferred stock). The procedure for calculating the *WACC* is the same, the only difference being that there are more components and more component costs.

FIGURE 10-4

Using the WACC to estimate the risk-adjusted discount rate for risky projects

Project	IRR (%)	Decision
A	10	Reject
B	15	Accept
C	12	Indifferent
D	18	Accept
E	16	Accept

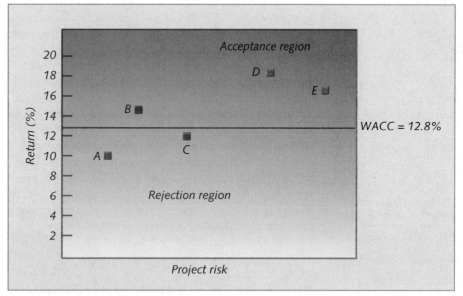

cost to the firm, but the logic for capital gains being a cost to the firm may not be obvious. True, the firm does not incur any direct cash flows when the price of the stock goes up or down, but that is irrelevant. The capital gains are part of the investors' *opportunity* cost.

We now examine the methods for calculating the costs of equity and debt.

COST OF EQUITY

The cost of equity is mathematically equal to the return expected by the stockholders. This is because an outflow from the firm to the owners (cost) is an inflow (return) for the stockholders. The cost of equity can thus be determined by calculating the return expected by the stockholders, which can be computed using the capital asset pricing model (CAPM) or the arbitrage pricing theory (APT). According to the CAPM, the expected return on the stock is

$$E(\tilde{R}) = R_f + \beta[E(\tilde{R}_m) - R_f]$$

where

$E(\tilde{R}_m)$ is the expected market return

R_f is the risk-free rate

β measures the volatility of the stock's returns relative to the market's returns

Suppose that Fleener Corporation has an equity beta of 1.25. Let us also assume that the expected market return is 14% and the risk-free rate is 6%. The cost of equity can be calculated by using the above equation:

$$E(\tilde{R}) = 0.06 + 1.25(0.14 - 0.06) = 0.16$$

So the cost of equity for Fleener is 16% because this is the return expected by the stockholders for Fleener's stock.

COST OF DEBT

When a company issues bonds, the financial intermediary is an investment bank. The investment bank charges fees, called **flotation costs**, at the time the bonds are issued. To find the net proceeds to a company from issuing bonds, we subtract the flotation costs from the price of the bonds. To calculate the firm's pretax cost of debt, we substitute the net proceeds from the bond issue for the price and calculate the bond's internal rate of return (IRR). The IRR on the bond is the investors' pretax required rate of return (RRR) on the bond.[3]

CALCULATING THE COST OF DEBT Suppose that the Fleener Corporation issues a new series of coupon bonds with a face value of $1,000, a coupon rate of 10% annually (to be paid in equal semiannual installments), and 20 years to maturity. The investment bank that underwrites (sells) the issue guarantees to sell the bonds at face value and charges a 5% underwriting fee. The underwriting fee amounts to $50 per bond, so that the net proceeds to Fleener are $950 per bond. Fleener is subsequently obligated to pay $50 every six months for each bond outstanding, plus $1,000 per outstanding bond to be paid on the maturity date.

If the IRR on the bond is X%, then X is the solution to the equation

$$\$950 = \$50(PVFA_{X\%,40}) + \$1,000(PVF_{X\%,40})$$

After this equation is solved, the yield of Fleener's bonds, its IRR, is seen to be 10.60% compounded semiannually. This is Fleener's *pretax* cost of debt.

However, since interest payments on corporate debt are tax deductible, debt provides a tax shield. All we need to do to find Fleener's after-tax cost of debt is multiply the pretax cost by 1 minus the tax rate. Suppose that Fleener is in the 24.5% marginal income tax bracket. Because the pretax cost of the bonds to Fleener is 10.60%, the after-tax cost of capital for the bonds is 10.6% × (1 − 0.245) = 8.00%.

Although this method for the calculation of the cost of debt seems simple enough, some complications need to be addressed. Let us briefly consider one of these—bankruptcy risk.

ADJUSTING FOR BANKRUPTCY RISK In the example presented above, we saw that the pretax cost of debt to the firm is the bondholders' IRR. Let us now consider what happens if there is some risk that the firm will default on its obligation. Assume that there is a 5% chance that at the end of 20 years Fleener Corporation will default. Also assume that in this case the bondholders will get only 50% of their investment back (i.e., 50% of $1,000). The expected cash flow to the bondholders at the end of 20 years is

$$(0.95 \times \$1,000) + (0.05 \times \$500) = \$975$$

Thus the expected cash flows are lower, and the bondholders expect a higher rate of return to compensate them for the risk of default. To adjust for the risk of default, bondholders "bid up" the interest rate and thus the firm's interest costs rise. In other words, the firm's cost of debt increases because of the risk of default.

In principle, then, calculating the cost of debt requires that we identify the "bid up" interest rate on the bonds. The problem with implementing this procedure is that estimating the probability of default is not easy. Nor is the expected payoff to

---

[3] Review the computation of IRR from Chapter 4 if necessary.

bondholders in the event of default obvious. In fact, as we see in a later chapter, the payoffs to debt holders in bankruptcy cannot be assessed without a consideration of the firm's options for a private renegotiation with the creditors and the possibility of going to the courts to resolve the bankruptcy. Further complications exist because bankruptcy brings with it not only the risk of default but also bankruptcy costs that have to be paid out to lawyers and others. From the stockholders' perspective, these costs are to be treated just like a payment to the bondholders and thus become a part of the *IRR* equation. However, the difficulty again lies in estimating the bankruptcy costs in advance.

In light of these difficulties associated with risky debt, we can at best *approximate* the firm's cost of debt capital as $r(1 - T)$, where r is the promised (coupon) rate on the bond and T is the firm's marginal tax rate. The justification for this approximation is that bondholders, in anticipation of default and bankruptcy costs, have "bid up" the promised interest rate. We assume that the effects of default are already reflected in the promised interest rate.

KEY CONCEPT   In the interest of practicality, the after-tax coupon rate on the bond is used as an *approximation* for the cost of debt financing.

Advantages of the WACC *Approach*

At first glance, the *WACC* approach seems extremely appealing. Consider the following line of reasoning: A firm relies on different sources of capital to finance its asset investments. Each dollar invested can be viewed as being a mix of debt and equity. The firm pays the different owners of the capital their required rates of return. Accordingly, the firm's average cost of capital (as a percentage) is simply a weighted average of all these costs. Finally, as logic would seem to conclude, any attractive investment opportunity should return at least the average cost of the financing required for the investment. The simplicity of the underlying concept is one of the reasons for the appeal of the *WACC* approach.

Yet despite its apparently straightforward logic, the *WACC* method cannot always be used to estimate a project's discount rate. It is necessary to look at the *WACC* more closely to see why this approach may not always be appropriate.

Disadvantages of the WACC *Approach*

In most instances, a firm does not necessarily take on only projects that are carbon copies of itself. When a firm takes on a project with cash flows that do not have the same characteristics as the firm's existing assets, the *WACC* approach fails.

The *WACC* approach assumes that the cash flows from the project under consideration will be as risky as the cash flows from the existing operations of the firm. Only then will the *WACC*, which reflects the firm's risk, also reflect the risk of the project being considered. This means that the *WACC* is company-specific and not project-specific. Therefore the *WACC* procedure is strictly correct only in cases where the project's cash flows are perfectly correlated with the firm's existing cash flows. Such projects are called **scale-enhancing** projects.

Reconsider the Fleener Corporation. According to our calculation, the *WACC* for this company is 12.8%. The *WACC* approach implies that all projects should meet the same test to be acceptable, but this is unrealistic when applied to non-scale-enhancing projects. A very low risk (or risk-free) investment can never be expected to earn the 12.8% rate if interest rates are much lower. Even more important, the *WACC* criterion is biased in favor of accepting high-risk projects. The reason, of course, is that high-risk investments tend to have expected returns higher than those of lower-risk projects. Moreover, a low-risk division within a firm may be unable to get capital even if it can find projects that offer returns higher than those required for the risk involved. These implications will lead to a lower stock price if the *WACC* is used.

Thus the *WACC* approach can lead to erroneous decisions because it is often inconsistent with the opportunity cost principle. Recall from Chapter 7 that the *RRR* is the opportunity cost of an investment. Assume that Boeing Corporation is considering a $50 million investment in a medical electronics business. How can this capital budgeting decision be made? The principles developed in Chapters 6 and 7 require that Boeing assess the risk of this new investment and then estimate the appropriate market-determined discount rate to calculate the project's *NPV*. Notice that this procedure does not consider the components of Boeing's capital structure or the individual costs of each type of capital. The *WACC* simply does not enter the picture. The appropriate market-determined *RRR* for this investment should be the same regardless of whether the project is being analyzed by Boeing, Lockheed, Kodak, or Southland Oil. Projects should be evaluated on the basis of a market-determined opportunity cost because only then will the accepted projects lead to an increase in the firm's value.

KEY CONCEPT
The *RRR* for an investment should be project specific and not company specific.

The opportunity cost for a particular project depends on the project's (not the company's) risk and is determined by the market (not by the company's management).

A PRACTICAL RECOMMENDATION

We have seen that the *WACC* approach is intuitively appealing but it is strictly correct for only scale-enhancing projects. Thus, when a firm is evaluating projects that have the same risk as current operations, the *WACC* approach is theoretically defensible. Unfortunately, as mentioned earlier, firms seldom restrict themselves to investing in pure scale-enhancing projects. As an approximation, the *WACC* can be used for projects that are "close" to being non-scale enhancing. That is, the *WACC* may be a reasonable procedure even when applied to projects that have "somewhat different risk" than the firm's existing operations. Unfortunately, it is not easy to specify exactly what "close" and "somewhat different risk" are.

The justification (rationalization) for the *WACC* approach is as follows. First, it is very difficult to estimate precisely the risk of a proposed project. Second, as explained earlier, the relevant cost of debt used in practice is approximated as the after-tax coupon rate. Third, the *WACC* approach does not fully recognize the effects of debt financing.[4] Fourth, agency costs implicit in the firm's operations may also change. It is virtually impossible to evaluate the net impact of all of these factors. In the interest of practice, using the *WACC* for projects that are not scale enhancing may be acceptable.

KEY CONCEPT
The *WACC* approach is strictly valid for scale-enhancing projects and is an approximation for some non-scale-enhancing projects.

10-3

THE ADJUSTED
PRESENT VALUE
APPROACH

*T*here are three main effects of debt financing:

1. Flotation costs

2. Tax benefits from debt

3. Effects of subsidized financing

[4] These effects of debt financing are discussed in the following section.

We saw in the last section that the *WACC* approach handles the first two but does not address the last effect. The adjusted present value (*APV*) approach addresses this and other deficiencies of the *WACC* approach.

Steps in the APV *Approach*

In the *APV* approach, we first calculate the *NPV* of the project under hypothetical all-equity financing; that is, we calculate the project's *NPV* assuming that only equity is used to finance the project. Then, this "**all-equity *NPV***" is adjusted for each effect of debt financing. This explains why we call it the adjusted present value approach.

In general, the application of the *APV* technique involves these three steps:

1. Calculate the *NPV* under all-equity financing.

2. Adjust the *NPV* for the effect of flotation costs of debt.

3. Adjust the *NPV* for tax shield and subsidized financing effects of debt.[5]

An Illustration of the APV *Approach*

An example illustrates the three-step *APV* approach. Classic Enterprises is considering a $50 million project that will last ten years. The assets are depreciated to a $0 salvage value using the straight-line method to yield a depreciation expense of $5 million per year. The incremental cash revenues less the cash expenses are $11 million per year. Classic can obtain a ten-year loan for $30 million at a subsidized interest rate (a below-market interest rate through government programs) of 8%. The flotation costs will be 0.25% of the gross proceeds of the loan. The company is in the 25% tax bracket, the current Treasury bill rate is 10%, and the cost of unlevered equity (the equity of a zero-debt firm) is 16%.

An unlevered firm is one that has no debt. The unlevered cost of equity is thus the cost of equity for a zero-debt firm. (The relationship between the costs of levered and unlevered equity is the subject of a later chapter.)

STEP 1: THE ALL-EQUITY *NPV*

The incremental annual after-tax cash inflow under all-equity financing is:

$$\Delta CFAT = (\Delta S - \Delta C - \Delta D)(1 - T) + \Delta D$$
$$= (\Delta S - \Delta C)(1 - T) + \Delta DT$$

The first term in the rearranged equation is the after-tax cash flow without the depreciation effect; the second one is the depreciation tax shield. We separate the two because their risk characteristics are different, and thus we need to discount them at different rates. For the sake of simplicity, we discount the first term using the cost of unlevered equity and the second depreciation tax shield at the risk-free rate.

	Time 0	End of Years 1 to 10
Initial outflow	− $50,000,000	
Depreciation tax shield: 0.25 × $5,000,000		$1,250,000
Revenue less cash expenses after taxes: (1 − 0.25) × $11,000,000		$8,250,000

The *NPV* under the all-equity financing is:

$$NPV = -\$50,000,000 + \$1,250,000(PVFA_{10\%,10}) + \$8,250,000(PVFA_{16\%,10})$$
$$= -\$2,445,350$$

[5]The implication of leasing an asset can also be included in the *APV* approach. However, we defer this discussion to a later chapter that addresses leasing issues in greater detail.

Clearly, this project is not acceptable under all-equity financing because it has a negative *NPV*. Can debt financing make a difference? To answer this, we must assess the effects of the flotation costs associated with the borrowing and the benefits of the subsidized financing.

STEP 2: THE EFFECT OF FLOTATION COSTS

The flotation costs associated with raising debt amount to $75,000 (0.25% of the gross proceeds of $30,000,000). Although the flotation costs are paid immediately, they must be deducted from taxes by amortizing them over 10 years on a straight-line basis. The following cash flows are related to the flotation costs:

	Time 0	End of Years 1 to 10
Flotation costs	− $75,000	
Tax shield from flotation costs: $0.25\left(\dfrac{\$75,000}{10}\right)$		$1,875

The net present value of the tax shields associated with the flotation costs is

$$\$1,875 \ (PVFA_{10\%,10}) = \$11,521$$

Thus the net costs of flotation are

$$-\$75,000 + \$11,521 = -\$63,479$$

and the net present value of the project after adjusting for the flotation costs is

$$-\$2,445,350 - \$63,479 = -\$2,508,829$$

The project is still (not surprisingly) unattractive. It was unattractive in Step 1 and all we did was recognize the flotation costs without factoring in the benefits of debt financing. Let us now adjust the *NPV* in Step 2 for the benefits of debt.

STEP 3: THE EFFECTS OF SUBSIDIZED FINANCING AND TAX SHIELD

The loan of $30 million is received at the beginning of year 1 and the ten interest payments are made at the end of every year from year 1 onward. The cost of interest is lessened because of the tax deductibility of interest expense. The relevant cash flows are as follows:

	Time 0	End of Years 1 to 9	End of Year 10
Loan received minus flotation costs	$30,000,000		
Interest cost after taxes: $-(1 - 0.25) \times 8\% \times \$30,000,000$		− $1,800,000	− $1,800,000
Repayment of debt			− $30,000,000

The *NPV* of the loan is

$$\$30,000,000 - \$1,800,000(PVFA_{10\%,10})$$
$$- \$30,000,000(PVF_{10\%,10}) = \$7,374,720$$

The adjusted present value of the project with this financing is:

$$
\begin{aligned}
APV &= \text{all-equity value} - \text{flotation cost of debt} + NPV \ (\text{loan}) \\
&= -\$2,445,350 - \$63,479 + \$7,374,720 \\
&= \$4,865,891
\end{aligned}
$$

Thus, Classic Enterprise's project, which could not be justified under all-equity financing, becomes viable if the firm adjusts for debt.

This example illustrates the use of the *APV* approach. As we can see, this approach is better at handling the effects of subsidized financing. In Step 3, the interest payments are calculated at the subsidized rate of 8%, but they are discounted at the market rate of 10%.

10-4
PRACTICAL ISSUES IN IMPLEMENTING THE *APV* APPROACH

In Step 1 of the *APV* approach, we used "the cost of unlevered equity" to calculate the *NPV* under the all-equity scenario. How do we get this? The cost of unlevered equity has to be estimated. Since most firms have certain levels of debt, estimating the cost of unlevered equity is not easy. We now examine how to estimate the cost of unlevered equity by first calculating the unlevered beta or project beta (β_{proj}).[6]

What Does β_{proj} Really Mean?

It is necessary to determine the beta of the capital budgeting project under consideration to find the appropriate *RRR*. But what does project beta (β_{proj}) mean? What factors determine β_{proj}? How can they be estimated?

Just as a stock's relevant risk (β_e) is measured in terms of the relationships between the returns from the stock and the returns on the market portfolio, a project's relevant risk is measured in terms of the relationship between the returns generated by the project and the returns on the market portfolio. A **project beta** (β_{proj}) measures the sensitivity of changes in a project's returns to changes in the market's returns.

Estimating Project Betas

To estimate a project beta, it is necessary to use the procedures outlined in Chapter 6. Recall how this problem was approached when the systematic risk of a stock was being determined. The historical information about stock prices and dividends was used to determine the historical returns per period for the stock. These returns were then regressed against the historical returns on the market to estimate the stock's beta coefficient.

Unfortunately, this procedure cannot generally be replicated to find a project's beta, β_{proj}. Although historical information about stock prices and dividends is readily available, historical information about asset values is not. Asset prices are determined in product markets rather than in financial markets, and data bases for asset prices are not extensive. Because most nonfinancial assets, unlike stocks, do not have active secondary markets, finding the β_{proj} from historical information may not be feasible.

There are a few exceptions, however. Certain assets have active secondary markets, and the prices for these assets are well established, depending on how old they are. For example, machine tool prices can be estimated fairly easily, given the age of the machine. An expert on machine tools can estimate the price of, say, a two-year-old Drillomatic center-drill lathe. Similarly, the used-car market has a "blue book" that can be used to assess the wholesale market value of a particular model of car. In addition, there is a growing market for "residual value insurance," a service that guarantees the owners of an asset a prespecified future price.

---

[6] The terms "unlevered equity beta," "all-equity beta," and "asset beta" are equivalent, and they are all used as estimates of the "project beta." The reader should not be confused by the terminology.

In these special cases it may be possible to estimate project betas using historical information. When historical information about asset values is not available, however, a "proxy" beta for a project must be inferred from an equity beta.

CASE 1: ESTIMATING A PROJECT'S BETA WHEN HISTORICAL INFORMATION IS AVAILABLE

The first case is the simpler situation when project betas can be estimated using historical information. The following steps are used in this approach:

1. Collect the historical information about the project's market values over the recent past—say, ten years.

2. Calculate the actual cash flows after taxes (*CFAT*) produced by the project each period over the last ten years.

3. Compute the return on the project for each period.

After the returns on the project and the returns on the market are obtained, the project's beta can be calculated using either of the procedures outlined in Chapter 6 for calculating stock betas. Once the project's beta (β_{proj}) is known, this value can be substituted directly into the CAPM equation to find its *RRR*. When the *CFAT* for a proposed investment in a project is discounted at this *RRR*, a positive *NPV* signifies a good project that should be accepted.

Of course, as in all other techniques that rely on historical information, it is implicitly assumed that past experience with such a project is a good indication of things to come. By using statistically justifiable procedures, the historical occurrences are weighted by the likelihood of each occurrence. In this sense it is not a naive extrapolation of historical experience. Moreover, we are assuming that economic conditions in the future (the risk-free rate and market returns) are approximately the same, on average, as they were in the past. In many instances, these assumptions are reasonable. Care should be exercised, nevertheless, in using this approach to evaluate the relative risk of projects exposed to rapid technological obsolescence (e.g., computers, calculators). The future in these cases may be nothing like the past.

CASE 2: ESTIMATING PROJECT BETAS WHEN HISTORICAL INFORMATION IS NOT AVAILABLE

Consider the case of General Motors planning an "across-the-board expansion" that increases the scale of all aspects of its operations. In this situation it is reasonable to assume that this expansion project is an exact replica of GM and that in this specific situation GM is justified in using the *WACC* approach to determine the *NPV* of the project. On the other hand, if GM's project is an individual asset and if historical information on its market values and *CFAT*s is available, then the β_{proj} for this asset can be calculated as it was in Case 1.

A more complicated situation occurs when GM considers investing in a totally different project (in terms of risk) and historical information about the investment is not readily available. For example, if GM plans to enter the pharmaceutical drug business, another method must be used to estimate the project beta using a proxy (or surrogate) for the pharmaceutical drug project. The "pure-play" method is a possibility.

The Pure-Play Method   The basic idea underlying the pure-play method is that if a proposed project is similar to the projects undertaken by another publicly held firm, then the other firm's equity beta can be used to derive the project's *RRR*. It is useful to first list the four essential steps involved in the pure-play technique. The entire process becomes clearer in the discussion that follows.

Step 1: Find a publicly traded firm whose business is as similar as possible to your project's business. The company thus identified is called a **pure-play company.**

Step 2: Determine the equity beta, β_E, for the pure-play firm's stock.

Step 3: Calculate the pure play's asset beta (unlevered equity beta), β_A, from its β_E by explicitly adjusting the β_E for the pure play's financial leverage.

Step 4: Find the *RRR* for your project, using the estimated pure play's β_A from Step 3 as a surrogate for your project's beta, and then decide on the project using the *NPV* criterion.

KEY CONCEPT   In the pure-play method, the risk of the project is approximated as the risk of the pure play's unlevered equity beta.

Steps in the Pure-Play Technique

STEP 1: FIND THE PURE-PLAY COMPANY

If GM is considering a project that involves the production of pharmaceuticals, the relevant risk to be considered is the market risk of the project, β_{proj}. To estimate β_{proj}, GM could examine another publicly traded company that is solely in the business of manufacturing medicinal drugs. Assume that GM has identified Marion Laboratories as a pure-play firm.

As a practical matter, instead of identifying only one firm to represent the pure play and finding its equity beta, it is better to work with industry betas. Instead of using just Marion Labs as a pure play for its pharmaceutical drug project, GM would be wiser to focus on the beta for the pharmaceutical industry as a whole because estimates of individual stock betas are susceptible to serious measurement errors. When betas for single stocks are estimated from sample data, the estimates usually have very large standard errors; however, the standard errors associated with beta estimates of portfolios are much smaller. As the theory of statistics has shown, an estimate of the average beta for a sample of N stocks has a standard error of about $1/N$ of the average standard error of the N individual betas. Because an industry beta is just the beta of a portfolio of stocks in that particular industry, it is better to work with industry betas. Therefore the pure play becomes the industry as a whole rather than a single company. Nevertheless, for the purpose of this discussion, we continue to treat Marion as the pure-play company.

STEP 2: DETERMINE THE EQUITY BETA FOR THE PURE-PLAY COMPANY

Although the betas of individual stocks (and industries) can be estimated by regression analysis, they can also be obtained directly from published services. Several investment advisory services, including the Value Line Investment Survey, Merrill Lynch, and William O'Neil & Co., publish stock betas. From these individual betas, industry betas can be calculated. Alternatively, published sources of industry betas may be available for direct use. For example, Table 10-3 contains average industry betas.

Since the pure-play company under consideration by GM is publicly traded, an estimate of Marion Laboratories equity beta, β_E, is easily obtained from published sources. Assume that Marion's equity beta is 1.45.

■

TABLE 10-3

Sample of Average Industry Betas

Industry	Beta	Industry	Beta
Nonferrous metals	0.99	Motor vehicles	1.27
Energy raw materials	1.22	Aerospace	1.30
Construction	1.27	Electronics	1.60
Agriculture, food	0.99	Photographic, optical	1.24
Liquor	0.89	Nondurables, entertainment	1.47
Tobacco	0.80	Trucking, freight	1.31
Apparel	1.27	Railroads, shipping	1.19
Forest products, paper	1.16	Air transport	1.80
Containers	1.01	Telephone	0.75
Media	1.39	Energy, utilities	0.60
Chemicals	1.22	Retail, general	1.43
Drugs, medicine	1.14	Banks	0.81
Soaps, cosmetics	1.09	Miscellaneous finance	1.60
Domestic oil	1.12	Insurance	1.34
International oil	0.85	Real property	1.70
Tires, rubber goods	1.21	Business services	1.28
Steel	1.02	Travel, outdoor recreation	1.66
Producer goods	1.30	Gold	0.36
Business machines	1.41	Miscellaneous, conglomerate	1.14
Consumer durables	1.44		

Source: B. Rosenberg and J. Guy, "Predictions of Beta from Investment Fundamentals," *Financial Analysts Journal,* July–August 1976, p. 66.

STEP 3: ESTIMATE THE PURE PLAY'S ASSET BETA

CASE A (PURE PLAY IS ALL EQUITY) If a firm is completely financed by equity, its β_E should equal the β_A for the company:

MARKET VALUE
BALANCE SHEET OF UNLEVERED (NO DEBT) FIRM

ASSETS (A)	EQUITY (E)

Therefore,

$$\beta_A = \beta_E$$

The logic underlying this is as follows: Because the value of a company can be viewed as the combined value of all the projects held by the firm, the beta of the assets reflects an average project risk if all projects have about the same risk. For example, the asset beta for Marion can be viewed as the average beta of all projects adopted by Marion. With this approximation in mind, we can use β_E (which, for an unlevered firm, equals β_A) as a proxy or surrogate for β_{proj}. The assumption in this case is that the project's risk is similar to the company's equity risk of β_E. Thus, if Marion is an all-equity firm, Marion's asset beta, β_A, equals its stock beta, and thus Marion's β_E of 1.45 can be used directly as a surrogate for GM's project beta, β_{proj}.

Note, however, that this line of reasoning applies only when the firm in question has no debt in its capital structure. If the firm is financed with both debt and equity, an adjustment for financial leverage is necessary in order to find β_{proj} because the asset beta is not the same as the equity beta. This adjustment is discussed next.

CASE B (PURE PLAY IS LEVERED) The β_E of the pure play, discussed in Case a, cannot be used as an estimate for project risk if Marion has debt in its capital structure. The risk of a firm's equity and therefore its equity beta depend on both business and financial risk. Figure 10-5 depicts this relationship. Although the risk premium for business risk remains the same regardless of how an asset is financed, the equity beta (and thus the *RRR*) increases linearly as the debt–equity

FIGURE 10-5
Relationship between required rates of return and leverage. RRR$_U$ is the required rate of return for an unlevered firm or project, and RRR$_L$ is the required rate of return for a levered firm or project.

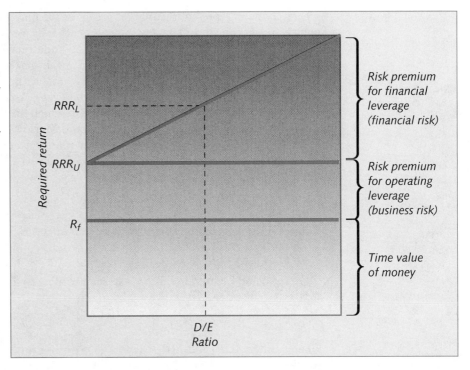

ratio, D/E, increases. Therefore Marion's β_E reflects the manner in which Marion has financed its assets.

The major implication, of course, is that if the pure-play company or industry uses more financial leverage than does the firm performing the analysis, using the pure play's β_E as a surrogate risk measure will yield a higher RRR_L (see Figure 10-5) than is required. For example, if the proxy company uses a mix of debt and equity and the company calculating the β_{proj} uses no debt, according to Figure 10-5, the firm would be incorrect in using a levered required return RRR_L if it did not adjust for financial risk. Instead, the appropriate required return would be RRR_U for an unlevered situation. Naturally, the opposite situation occurs if the pure-play firm has less debt than does the company performing the analysis.

Because β_{proj} should not incorporate any effects of Marion's financing mix, it is necessary to "undo" or purge the β_E of the financial risk found in the pure-play firm.[7] To do this, it is necessary to establish an intermediate step that derives the beta of the proxy firm's assets, β_A, from its equity beta, β_E. Only then does the beta truly measure the riskiness associated with just the firm's assets.

This adjustment procedure is facilitated by the following relationship between a firm's unlevered or asset beta and the beta of its equity:[8]

$$\beta_A = \frac{\beta_E}{1 + (D/E)(1 - T)} \tag{10-1}$$

[7]Remember that the appropriate risk of an investment should not depend on the company that is making the investment. Financial structure considerations (which are firm specific) should therefore be removed from the risk assessment.

[8]This result is derived in Chapter 15 [equation (15-3)]. A derivation is not offered in this chapter because it requires understanding "the value of tax shields," an idea that has not yet been fully presented to the reader.

where D and E represent the market values of the pure-play company's debt and equity, and T is the pure play's tax rate. Notice that in every case (except the no-debt case), β_A is less than β_E because β_E reflects an additional (financial) risk borne by stockholders as residual owners. Moreover, recall that a project's risk should be evaluated only in regard to its operating characteristics (i.e., financial considerations should not be taken into account). This is what using β_A does—it identifies the risk of the project without regard to the manner in which the project is financed.

We return now to our discussion of GM and Marion Laboratories, whose β_E is 1.45. If Marion's debt–equity ratio is 0.30 in market-value terms and the firm is in the 30% tax bracket, then according to equation (10-1), Marion's asset beta is

$$\beta_A = \frac{1.45}{1 + 0.3(1 - 0.3)} = \frac{1.45}{1.21} = 1.20$$

Thus GM can approximate the risk of the pharmaceutical project (β_{proj}) as 1.20.

STEP 4: DETERMINE THE PROJECT'S *RRR* AND *NPV*

There is nothing new in this final step. According to the CAPM, an asset's *RRR* with a systematic risk level proxied by β_{proj} is

$$E(\tilde{R}_{\text{proj}}) = R_f + \beta_{\text{proj}}[E(\tilde{R}_m) - R_f]$$

where, as before, R_f and $E(\tilde{R}_m)$ denote the risk-free interest rate and the expected required return on the market, respectively, and β_{proj} is assumed to be equal to the pure play's asset beta. The project's expected cash flows should then be discounted at the *RRR*. If the project's *NPV* is positive, it should be accepted. Since β_{proj} has been estimated to be 1.2,

$$
\begin{aligned}
E(\tilde{R}_{\text{proj}}) &= R_f + \beta_{\text{proj}}[E(\tilde{R}_m) - R_f] \\
&= 0.10 + (1.2)[0.15 - 0.10] \\
&= 16\%
\end{aligned}
$$

Now if the project under consideration by GM has a five-year life and is expected to generate annual cash flows of $2,000,000, should GM accept the project if the initial investment required is $6,000,000? To answer this we find the project's *NPV* using 16% as the *RRR*:

$$
\begin{aligned}
NPV &= -\$6,000,000 + \$2,000,000(PVFA_{RRR,5}) \\
&= -\$6,000,000 + \$2,000,000(PVFA_{0.16,5}) \\
&= -\$6,000,000 + \$2,000,000(3.2743) \\
&= \$548,600
\end{aligned}
$$

Thus GM should accept this project because it can be expected to increase the firm's market value by $548,600.

In summary, to infer an estimate of β_{proj} for a proposed investment when historical data are lacking, we must first find a pure-play firm's (or industry's) equity beta, β_E. If the pure play uses any debt in its capital structure, we need to adjust downward or "deflate" the β_E for leverage using the pure play's debt–equity ratio. The resulting value is the β_A, which then serves as an estimate of β_{proj}. With this estimate of project risk, the CAPM yields the *RRR* to be used in computing the project's *NPV*.

An example of how the pure-play method has been used in practical financial decision making is given in the following highlight.

THE PURE-PLAY ARGUMENT AND VALUATION: THE BANKRUPTCY OF JARTRAN, INC.

Jartran, Inc., had a nationwide network of almost 2,000 independent dealer agents. With growing competition from such firms as U-Haul, RSI, and Hertz, Jartran was forced in 1982 to file for bankruptcy and seek protection under Chapter 11 bankruptcy.

The bankruptcy court decided that it needed to assess Jartran's value as a going concern; that is, the court wanted to estimate the value of Jartran's debt plus equity. Dr. Robert Hamada of the University of Chicago was asked to provide this estimate.

Dr. Hamada's testimony explained how the pure-play technique was used to arrive at these estimates, using 11 firms as pure plays: Interway Corporation, Transport Pool Corporation, Ryder Systems, Bermec Corporation, Luby Corporation, Hudson General, RLC Corporation, CLC of America, Inc., Avis, Xtra Corporation, and Trans Union Corporation. With additional information about these firms' debt and equity values, Dr. Hamada estimated the asset beta for Jartran with a variant of equation (10-1). His estimate of Jartran's asset beta (unlevered beta or project beta) was 0.6506. He then used the CAPM to estimate the required rate of return on Jartran's assets as 7.4%. This information was used to derive Jartran's estimated values.*

Given the uncertainties associated with the various inputs to his analysis, Dr. Hamada did not give the court a single estimate of Jartran's value. Instead, he offered a sensitivity analysis of values, which allowed the court to decide on the final value based on various assumptions implicit in the valuation estimates. The sensitivity analysis revealed that Jartran's value varied between $69 million and $175 million, depending on which assumptions the court chose to accept. The most likely value was $130 million.

* For details, the reader is referred to the original case: Jartran, Inc., Bankruptcy, No. 81 B 16118, U.S. Bankruptcy Court, Illinois, September 29, 1984.

SUMMARY

Section 10-1: Assessing the Impact of Uncertain Cash Flows

What are some practical procedures for dealing with the uncertainty associated with a project's cash flows?

- There is no clear-cut theory for forming expectations of a project's cash flows.

- The uncertainty associated with future cash flows can be handled by either sensitivity analysis or more complicated simulation methods. Explicitly focusing on the uncertainty of cash flows can give the analyst useful information for management strategy.

- Sensitivity analysis shows managers how sensitive the project's *NPV* is to their assumption about any one variable. With a framework for identifying those variables that are crucial for generating a positive *NPV*, the decision maker can take action to reduce the uncertainty about this variable.

- Computer simulation allows managers to examine the impact on the *NPV* of simultaneous changes in several variables.

Section 10-2: The Weighted Average Cost of Capital Approach

What is the weighted average cost of capital (WACC) method and how is it used?

- The basic idea underlying the *WACC* approach is that a project must return more than the cost of the funds raised to support it.

- Since the firm raises capital from different sources, the market-value weighted average of the costs of each component represents the firm's *WACC*.

- The *WACC* approach is strictly correct for scale-enhancing projects and may be a reasonable approximation for projects with risks that are "not too different" from that of the firm's existing assets.

Section 10-3: The Adjusted Present Value Approach

What is adjusted present value (APV) and how can this concept be used?

- The adjusted present value (*APV*) method is a three-step procedure that is better suited than the *WACC* for incorporating the effects of financing costs, tax shields, and subsidized financing.

- The *APV* method begins by calculating *NPV* assuming all-equity financing. It then adds to this the effects of flotation costs, tax shields, and subsidized financing.

Section 10-4: Practical Issues in Implementing the APV Approach

How is the unlevered equity beta calculated?

- The first step in the *APV* method requires that we find a project's *NPV* assuming that the project is all-equity financed. This requires an estimate of the appropriate discount rate that would apply if the project were all equity. To get this discount rate, it is necessary to estimate the risk of the unlevered project.

- If the firm has experience with this project, historical information may be available to estimate the project's beta. If historical information is unavailable, the project's beta must be estimated using a proxy firm with the pure-play method.

What is the pure-play method and how is it implemented?

- The pure-play method is a procedure for estimating a project's beta, which is required for calculating the investment's "all-equity" *NPV*.

- In the pure-play method, the risk of the project is approximated as the risk of the pure play's unlevered equity beta (asset beta).

- The pure play's unlevered equity beta is inferred from its equity beta by "purging" the effects of financial leverage.

- With an estimate of the project's beta, the relevant discount rate for determining the all-equity *NPV* can be obtained directly from the CAPM.

QUESTIONS

1. How does sensitivity analysis aid managers in evaluating capital budgeting projects?

2. What are the advantages and disadvantages of sensitivity analysis?

3. What is the Monte Carlo simulation method? How does it overcome certain weaknesses of sensitivity analysis?

4. What are the weaknesses of simulation?

5. What is the logic underlying the *WACC* approach?

6. What are some of the difficulties associated with calculating the cost of debt?

7. Why is the *WACC* a company-specific rather than a project-specific discount rate?

8. The *WACC* is often inconsistent with the opportunity cost principle. Explain.

9. When would it be appropriate to use the *WACC* approach to evaluate capital budgeting projects?

10. What is the adjusted present value approach? What aspects of debt financing does it take into account?

11. What is the major practical difficulty with implementing the *APV* approach?

12. How are project betas measured when historical information is available?

13. Under what circumstances would the pure-play method be used?

14. What is the logic underlying the pure-play method?

15. Explain the adjustments required to find a project's beta by means of a pure play's equity beta.

PROBLEMS

1. The Yorkshire Shrubbery Co. uses the weighted average cost of capital (*WACC*) approach to determine the required rate of return for new projects. Yorkshire's financial manager, Steve Smith, has determined that the relevant cost of equity is 18% and the relevant cost of debt is 12%. He wishes to maintain Yorkshire's current mix of 70% equity, 30% debt.

   (a) What is Yorkshire's *WACC* for the coming year?

   (b) Suppose that next year Yorkshire's relevant cost of equity is 19% and its *WACC* is 17.5%. If Steve has maintained the same capital structure (70% equity, 30% debt), what must the relevant cost of debt be?

2. The Swamp Kasle Ice Cream Co. is considering expanding to a new area. This expansion would cost $192,000. Swamp Kasle knows that demand for its product can change as can other factors such as its operating costs. Its managers have therefore estimated annual cash flows for the eight years of the investment's life for various scenarios as given below. They want to see how sensitive the investment is to changes in these factors. Swamp Kasle's discount rate is 10%.

	Pessimistic	Expected	Optimistic
Revenues	$120,000	$160,000	$190,000
Operating costs	85,000	110,000	123,000
Depreciation	24,000	24,000	24,000
NOI	$11,000	$26,000	$43,000
Taxes (@ 20%)	2,200	5,200	8,600
NI	$8,800	$20,800	$34,400
Net cash flow (NI + depreciation)	$32,800	$44,800	$58,400

   (a) If all factors are as expected except for operating costs, which are at the pessimistic level, should the project be undertaken?

   (b) If all factors are as expected, should the project be undertaken?

(c) If revenues reach the optimistic level and all other variables are as expected, would the project have a positive *NPV*?

3. Uncle Charlie's (UC's), a chain of fast food restaurants, is considering expanding into new business lines. The company is planning to invest $5 million to open a store that sells environment-friendly clothes, clothes made from "organic cotton" and only vegetable dyes. The project is to be depreciated using the straight-line method over its life (assumed to be ten years). The expected earnings before depreciation, interest, and taxes are $800,000 per year. UC's can obtain a ten-year, 12% loan from a local bank to finance the project. The bank will charge UC's flotation fees of 0.5% of the gross proceeds of the loan. UC's is in the 25% corporate tax bracket, and the current Treasury bill rate is 6%. If the project is financed with 100% equity, the cost of capital would be 15%.

(a) Which method, *WACC* or *APV*, is better suited to calculate the viability of the project? Why?

(b) Using *APV*, determine whether UC's should undertake the project or not.

(c) On hearing about the project, an environmental organization offers to lend UC's the initial investment at a subsidized interest rate of 8%. UC's will not have to pay any flotation costs either. Should UC's accept this loan and undertake the project?

4. Trilogy Software, Inc., is embarking on an ambitious project to develop a new software package. The software can be developed over one year and only on a mainframe computer that costs $10 million. Assume that the firm uses straight-line depreciation. The operating income in the second year is expected to be $2 million, after which it will grow at the rate of 40% per year. After the fifth year, a complete new version of the software will replace the older one. Thus the project will have a life of five years. Trilogy can obtain a five-year, 18% loan for $6 million to partly finance the project. The bank will charge flotation fees of 1% of the gross proceeds of the loan. The corporate tax bracket is 25%, and the current Treasury bill rate is 6%. If Trilogy financed the project with 100% equity, the cost of capital would be 22%.

(a) Using the *APV* method, determine whether Trilogy should undertake the project or not.

(b) What is the highest possible rate of interest for the loan at which the project would be viable? (*Note:* It would be easier to answer this question using a spreadsheet.)

5. Phoenix Cement Company is considering a proposal for setting up a steel plant. The capital-intensive project requires a $500 million investment that will be spread equally over two years. The project will be depreciated using the straight-line method over its 15-year life. The annual operating income is expected to be $70 million. Phoenix can obtain a ten-year, 10% loan for $300 million to partly finance the project. The bank's flotation fees amount to 0.2% of the gross proceeds of the loan. Phoenix is in the 25% tax bracket, and the current Treasury bill rate is 6%. Phoenix has identified Hercules Steel Corporation as a pure-play company. Hercules has a β_E of 1.3 and a debt–equity ratio of 2.0. Its corporate tax rate is 25%. The expected return on the market portfolio is 22%.

(a) Calculate β_A and the cost of unlevered equity for the project.

(b) Using the *APV* method, determine whether Phoenix should undertake the project.

6. The board of directors of Allen's Haberdashery, located in Dallas, is considering opening up a new branch in Houston. They have decided to use the rates of return on the Dallas store and on the S&P 500 during the last six years to estimate the store's beta. Accordingly, they have accumulated the following information:

Year	Risk Premium on Dallas Store (%)	Risk Premium on the Market (%)
1	8	8
2	5	17
3	3	−8
4	−9	−16
5	10	17
6	16	27

(a) Based on this information, estimate the Dallas store's beta.

(b) Suppose that the risk-free rate is expected to remain at 12% and the market return is estimated to be 18% for the indefinite future. What discount rate should the board of directors use in deciding whether to open the new store?

7. Your rich uncle is considering the acquisition of a privately owned chain of auto parts stores. He has estimated the cash flows from the stores, but he has asked you to help him determine what discount rate to use. You do not trust the firm's financial statements, and so you have decided to use the pure-play technique. You have calculated that the average capital structure of other auto parts stores is 70% equity and 30% debt and that the average beta of the auto parts stores' equity is 0.8 and that of their debt is 0. Assume no taxes.

(a) If the auto parts store your uncle is considering purchasing is 100% equity, what beta should he use to find the discount rate (RRR) for valuing the cash flows to equity?

(b) If the T-bill rate is expected to remain at 10% and the market return is expected to be 18% for the foreseeable future, what discount rate should he use for valuing the cash flows to equity?

(c) If the auto parts store your uncle is considering purchasing is 60% equity and 40% debt, what beta should he use for valuing the firm's equity?

8. Petapetroleum Corporation, an independent oil company, plans to enter the apparel business. Assume that Petapetroleum has determined the equity beta for a pure-play firm is 1.2. If the pure play's market-value debt–equity ratio is 0.5 and it has a 25% tax rate, what is an appropriate project beta for Petapetroleum's new venture?

9. BBM, a computer manufacturer, is considering an investment in the small appliance industry. The pure-play company identified by BBM has the following characteristics:

Equity beta = 0.8

Market value of debt = $50 million

Market value of equity = $150 million

Tax rate = 33%

If the risk-free rate is 10% and the expected return on the market is 15%, what rate of return should BBM expect on its new investment?

10. Weed Out, Inc., a weed trimmer manufacturer, has decided to become a player in the bicycle/skateboard industry. Weed Out has identified a pure-play company, Weenie Wimp Wheels, with the following characteristics:

$\beta_E = 1.1$

Debt = $50 million of $1,000 bonds maturing in two years with an 8.5% coupon (interest paid semiannually) and a present yield to maturity of 10%

Equity = 3 million common shares outstanding; yesterday's close was $35\frac{5}{8}$

Tax rate = 34%

If $R_f = 9\%$ and $E(\tilde{R}_m) = 17\%$, what discount rate should Weed Out use to value its investment in the bicycle/skateboard industry?

11. Multiple Interests Company (MIC) has a number of investments under consideration. Using data from Table 10-3, estimate the return that each project needs for acceptance. Assume that the risk-free rate is 7% and the expected market return is 16%.

(a) An insurance company

(b) A tobacco plantation

(c) An airline (transportation)

(d) A gold mine

(e) A coal mine

12. Felicia Elmore is a financial adviser for Martek. Martek can begin producing a new 35-mm camera on which it holds the patent. The initial (year 0) outlay is $2.5 million. The cash flows for the next ten years are as follows:

Year	Cash Flow
1	$50,000
2	120,000
3–5	200,000
6–8	350,000
9–10	600,000

Elmore anticipates the value of the project in ten years to be $6 million. Assuming a T-bill rate of 8% and an expected market return of 13.65%, find the *NPV* of the project. Should Elmore support the camera production? (*Hint:* Use Table 10-3 to get a pure-play project beta.)

13. Ralph Person works for a large firm that is concerned about the impact of future tax rate changes. Ralph knows that the company's debt–equity ratio is

0.60. He also knows that management would like to maintain this ratio in the future. Given that the asset beta is 1.2, what will the equity beta be with the following tax rates?

(a) 0%

(b) 10%

(c) 20%

(d) 35%

(e) 50%

14. You have been hired by the investment banking firm of Velimirovic, Sansing, and Tal, and one of your first assignments is to help determine the discount rate for use in pricing the shares of Unsmog, a new manufacturer of antipollution devices required by law in some states. Unsmog intends to pay a $1 dividend at the end of the year, and dividends are expected to grow at an annual rate of 6%. There are three other major firms in the industry, with firm market values (debt plus equity), debt–equity ratios, and equity betas as follows (each firm's debt beta is 0; taxes are 0):

Firm	Market Value	Debt–Equity Ratio	Equity Beta
Oxidation Equipment	$12,000,000	1.0	1.8
Pollutionbusters	8,000,000	0.50	1.2
Klenair Korp.	10,000,000	0.25	0.9

(a) Find the beta of the assets of each of the three firms.

(b) What is the total market value of all three existing firms? What proportion is each firm's value of the total?

(c) What is the average value of all three firms' assets' betas (sum of proportion of total value multiplied by the firm's asset beta)?

(d) Suppose that the T-bill rate is expected to remain at 13% and the market return is expected to be 18% for the foreseeable future. If Unsmog has no debt, what discount rate should be used in determining the value of a share? What is the value of a share? (*Hint:* Use the growing perpetuity formula from Chapter 4.)

(e) Suppose that the T-bill rate is expected to remain at 13% and the market return is expected to be 18% for the foreseeable future. If Unsmog's assets are to be financed with 75% equity and 25% debt, what is the value of a share?

15. Maggie Martin is considering starting a radio station that broadcasts only financial news. She has determined that her initial investment will be $800,000 and that $\beta_A = 0.85$. What should her D/E ratio be in order to achieve the following β_E's? (Ignore taxes.)

(a) 0.85

(b) 1.0

(c) 1.9

(d) 2.6

16. Using the information from Problem 15, determine the proper D/E ratio to achieve the desired β_E's if Maggie's tax rate is 34%. Compare the results with those from Problem 15. What is the general effect on the D/E ratio of introducing taxes?

17. Amy Sevice is considering forming a corporation that will sell medical equipment to hospitals. She has determined that the necessary initial investment will be $200,000 and that the beta of assets is 0.8. How much of the $200,000 should be equity and how much should be debt (ignore taxes) if she wants the beta of equity given here?

    (a) 0.8

    (b) 1.0

    (c) 1.25

    (d) 1.5

    (e) 3.0

18. Randy Speiguts has recently purchased Uncle Charlie's, a bar between a university campus and a state legislature. Randy is considering altering Uncle Charlie's capital structure, which currently is $240,000 equity and $80,000 debt (both market values). Also, Uncle Charlie's equity beta is now 1.2. Ignore taxes.

    (a) What is Uncle Charlie's beta of assets?

    (b) Suppose Randy figures that he can add up to $400,000 in new assets without changing the beta of assets. If he wishes to borrow money to finance this expansion and wants an equity beta of 1.5 when he finishes, what will the dollar amount of the expansion be?

    (c) Suppose Randy wants to undertake a $120,000 expansion that will leave the beta of assets unchanged. What proportion of this expansion will be financed with debt and what proportion with equity if he wants Uncle Charlie's equity beta to remain at 1.2?

    (d) Suppose Randy wants to undertake a $120,000 expansion that will leave the beta of assets unchanged. What proportion of this expansion will be financed with debt and what proportion with equity if he wants Uncle Charlie's equity beta to rise to 1.35?

10A

ESTIMATING PROJECT BETAS WHEN HISTORICAL INFORMATION IS AVAILABLE

This appendix outlines the procedure for estimating project betas using historical information. As stated earlier, this method can be used only in those special situations in which there is an active secondary market for assets. The required methodology is no different from that used in finding equity betas, as in Chapter 6.

Consider Table 10A-1, which is used to find the beta of a center-drill lathe. In Table 10A-1, part a, historical information is provided about the lathe's original purchase price, cash flows from the lathe for each year over its eight-year useful life, and the lathe's market value at the end of each year. Notice that the market value in year 8 is the lathe's salvage value. From this information the annual returns generated by the lathe can be calculated. Table 10A-1, part b offers the nec-

TABLE 10A-1

Historical Information on a Center-Drill Lathe, the Market Portfolio, and the Risk-free Rate

a. Center-Drill Lathe Information

Time	Market Value at Time t, A_t	Realized Cash Flows at t, CF_t	Annual Realized Return at t, $R_{proj,t}$: $\dfrac{CF_t + (A_t - A_{t-1})}{A_{t-1}}$
0	$100,000[a]	$ 0	
1	85,000	25,000	10.0%
2	65,000	19,000	−1.2
3	50,000	16,000	1.5
4	40,000	22,000	24.0
5	28,000	20,000	20.0
6	15,000	18,000	17.9
7	8,000	9,000	13.3
8	2,000[b]	6,000	0.0

b. Market Information

Time	Realized Market Return, R_{mt}	Risk-free Rate, R_{ft}
1	15%	5%
2	−5	6
3	−8	4
4	20	6
5	14	7
6	12	7
7	10	8
8	−3	5

[a] Purchase price.
[b] Salvage value.

essary market information. The second column gives the realized return on the market at time t, R_{mt}, and the third column lists the risk-free rate over the same period.

Table 10A-2 combines the information from Table 10A-1 and performs the necessary computations to calculate the project's beta. Recall from Chapter 6 that the beta is the slope of a linear regression line. The slope can be determined using the formula

$$\beta = \frac{\Sigma MI - n\overline{MI}}{\Sigma M^2 - n\overline{M}^2} \tag{10A-1}$$

where

$$M = R_{mt} - R_{ft} \text{ is the risk premium on the market at time } t$$

$$I = R_{it} - R_{ft} \text{ is the risk premium on asset } i \text{ at time } t$$

TABLE 10A-2

Calculating β_{proj} for a Center-Drill Lathe

(1) Time	(2) Market Return, R_{mt}	(3) Risk-free Rate, R_{ft}	(4) Excess Return on Market $R_{mt} - R_{ft}$ (2) − (3)	(5) $(R_{mt} - R_{ft})^2$ (4)²	(6) Project Return, $R_{proj,t}$	(7) Excess Return on Project, $R_{proj,t} - R_{ft}$ (6) − (3)	(8) (4) × (7)
1	0.15	0.05	0.10	0.0100	0.100	0.050	0.0050
2	−0.05	0.06	−0.11	0.0121	−0.012	−0.072	0.0079
3	−0.08	0.04	−0.12	0.0144	0.015	−0.025	0.0030
4	0.20	0.06	0.14	0.0196	0.240	0.180	0.0252
5	0.14	0.07	0.07	0.0049	0.200	0.130	0.0091
6	0.12	0.07	0.05	0.0025	0.179	0.109	0.0055
7	0.10	0.08	0.02	0.0004	0.133	0.053	0.0011
8	−0.03	0.05	−0.08	0.0064	0.000	−0.050	0.0040
Total	0.55	0.48	0.07	$\Sigma M^2 = 0.0703$	0.8550	0.375	$\Sigma MI = 0.0608$
Average	0.07	0.06	$\overline{M} = 0.01$		0.107	$\overline{I} = 0.047$	

n is the number of observations

$\overline{M}$ is the average value of M

$\overline{I}$ is the average value of I

To estimate the lathe's beta, this equation can be used directly. If β_{proj} is used to denote this project's beta, then from the information in Table 10A-2, we have

$$\beta_{proj} = \frac{0.0608 - 8(0.01)(0.047)}{0.0703 - 8(0.01)^2} = 0.82$$

Thus the project's beta of 0.82 indicates that it has less market risk than does the typical or average security found in the market portfolio. It is a "defensive" investment because its beta is less than 1.00.

PROBLEM

1. Henry Construction Co. is considering investing in a fleet of dump trucks. It has gathered information on the market values of dump trucks and also on the historical performance of certain market variables given below. What is the appropriate beta to use in determining the RRR of this project?

Time	Market Value at Time t, A_t	Realized Cash Flows at t, CF_t	Realized Market Return, R_{mt}	Risk-free Rate, R_{ft}
0	$128,500	$ 0		
1	108,000	32,000	12%	6%
2	92,000	32,000	11	5
3	84,500	22,000	14	6
4	63,000	22,000	9	4
5	50,100	18,000	6	3
6	28,000	18,000	5	2

SUGGESTED ADDITIONAL READINGS

Ang, James S., and Wilbur G. Lewellen. "Risk Adjustment in Capital Investment Project Evaluations." *Financial Management,* Summer 1982, pp. 5–14.

Arditti, Fred D., and Haim Levy. "The Weighted Average Cost of Capital As a Cutoff Rate: A Critical Examination of the Classical Textbook Weighted Average." *Financial Management,* Fall 1977, pp. 24–34.

Beranek, William. "The Weighted Average Cost of Capital and Shareholder Wealth Maximization." *Journal of Financial and Quantitative Analysis,* March 1977, pp. 17–32.

Bower, Richard S., and Jeffrey M. Jenks. "Divisional Screening Rates." *Financial Management,* Autumn 1975, pp. 42–49.

Brennan, M. J. "A New Look at the Weighted-Average Cost of Capital." *Journal of Business Finance,* May 1973, pp. 24–30.

Chen, Andrew. "Recent Developments in the Cost of Debt Capital." *Journal of Finance,* June 1978, pp. 863–883.

Harlow, Van, and Ramesh K. S. Rao. "Asset Pricing in a Generalized Mean–Lower Partial Moment Framework: Theory and Evidence." *Journal of Financial and Quantitative Analysis,* September 1989, pp. 285–311.

Hertz, D. B. "Investment Policies That Pay Off." *Harvard Business Review,* January–February 1968, pp. 96–108.

Hertz, D. B. "Risk Analysis in Capital Investment." *Harvard Business Review,* January–February 1964, pp. 96–106.

Lessard, Donald R., and Richard S. Bower. "An Operational Approach to Risk Screening." *Journal of Finance,* May 1973, pp. 321–338.

Lorie, J. H., and R. A. Brealey, eds. *Modern Developments in Investment Management,* 2nd ed. New York: Praeger, 1978.

Merton, R. C. "On Estimating the Expected Return on the Market: An Exploratory Investigation." *Journal of Financial Economics,* December 1980, pp. 323–361.

Miles, J., and R. Ezzell. "The Weighted Average Cost of Capital, Perfect Capital Markets and Project Life: A Clarification." *Journal of Financial and Quantitative Analysis,* September 1980, pp. 719–730.

Myers, Stewart C. "Procedures for Capital Budgeting Under Uncertainty." *Industrial Management Review,* Spring 1968, pp. 1–20.

Myers, Stewart C., and Stuart M. Turnbull. "Capital Budgeting and the Capital Asset Pricing Model: Good News and Bad News." *Journal of Finance,* May 1977, pp. 321–333.

Nantell, Timothy J., and C. Robert Carlson. "The Cost of Capital As a Weighted Average." *Journal of Finance,* December 1975, pp. 1343–1355.

Reilly, Raymond R., and William E. Wacker. "On the Weighted Average Cost of Capital." *Journal of Financial and Quantitative Analysis,* January 1973, pp. 123–126.

Sharpe, W. F. "Capital Asset Prices: A Theory of Market Equilibrium Under Conditions of Risk." *Journal of Finance,* September 1964, pp. 425–442.

Stapleton, R. C. "Portfolio Analysis, Stock Valuation and Capital Budgeting Decision Rules for Risky Projects." *Journal of Finance,* March 1971, pp. 95–117.

Wagner, W. H., and S. C. Lau. "The Effect of Diversification on Risk." *Financial Analysts Journal,* November–December 1971, pp. 48–53.

ELEVEN   MANAGING TOTAL RISK WITH DERIVATIVE SECURITIES

I have never tried to make money forecasting the market. I have noticed that my competitors that have done this continuously have, as a rule, failed in business. We have always kept our stocks of wheat either sold in the shape of flour, or in sales of options for future delivery. . . .[1]

—W. H. Dunwoody

[1]This is an excerpt from a 1903 letter quoted in "The Selected Writings of Holbrook Working" (Chicago: Chicago Board of Trade, 1977), p. 124. Mr. Dunwoody's firm grew to become General Mills Inc., a company that continues to actively hedge risks.

*T*his chapter discusses some of the different ways in which a firm can cope with volatility in commodity prices, interest rates, and exchange rates. These "strategic risk factors" affect the firm's cash flows and hence its value. By using derivative instruments to reduce the risk of the firm's cash flows, managers can increase firm value and hence shareholders' wealth. We examine how the firm can use derivative securities—in particular, futures contracts, forwards, options, and swaps—to reduce some risks.[2]

In recent years, the use of derivative securities has grown by leaps and bounds. In addition to corporations using derivatives to reduce risks, even state and federal government agencies have recognized the value of using derivatives to reduce the risks associated with their day-to-day business. The state of Texas, for example, uses derivative instruments to reduce the risk of its oil revenues, and the U.S. Postal Service is considering the use of derivatives such as futures, options, and swaps to protect itself from adverse fuel cost fluctuations, currency swings, and interest rate changes. With revenues of $46.7 billion, the U.S. Postal Service qualifies as one of the nation's ten largest businesses. Its fuel costs in 1991 were $865 million, it faces exchange rate risk from reimbursing foreign authorities for the local delivery of U.S. mail, and with $10 billion in debt, it faces considerable interest rate risk. A detailed 74-page proposal for using derivatives to reduce these risks is expected to be presented to the board of governors for approval.[3]

This chapter is designed to answer the following questions:

- What is "strategic risk"? Why should a firm manage such risks?

- What are long and short positions in an asset? What are the payoffs from these positions?

- What are futures and forward contracts? How can they be used for speculating and hedging?

- What are put and call options? How can they be used by the firm?

- How can swaps be used to manage interest rate risks?

Appendix 11A presents the derivation of the put-call parity relationship and lists several properties of call options that place upper and lower bounds on the call option price. Appendix 11B shows how to use the Black-Scholes options pricing model to value options.

---

[2] The options sections can be read on their own. If necessary, the reader can omit the discussions of futures and swaps without loss of continuity.

[3] "Derivatives May Deliver Postal Savings," *The Wall Street Journal*, November 11, 1993, p. C1.

11-1

STRATEGIC RISKS AND FIRM VALUE [4]

Another Look at Risk

n Chapter 7 we defined the value of any asset as the present value of its expected cash flows discounted at the opportunity cost (the required rate of return, *RRR*). This definition of value can be represented by the following simple equation:

$$V_0 = \sum_{t=1}^{N} \frac{E(\widetilde{CF_t})}{(1 + RRR)^t}$$

(11-1)

where $E(\widetilde{CF_t})$ represents the expected cash flows from the asset.

When this definition is applied to the value of the firm, firm value is the expected cash flows of the firm discounted at the *RRR*. If managers want to increase firm value, their decisions must either increase the firm's cash flows or decrease the *RRR*.

Part Two of this text showed that the *RRR* is determined by the firm's non-diversifiable (beta) risk. Since factors unique to the firm (unique risk) can be diversified away, the risk that remains is related to how the firm's cash flows are correlated with the economy. This systematic risk cannot be diversified away and is factored into the firm's *RRR*. Thus, for a firm whose owners hold diversified portfolios, the total risk of the firm has no effect on the firm's *RRR* and thus has no effect on firm value. Only beta risk affects the *RRR*.

Total risk can still affect firm value through its impact on expected cash flows, however. We see this by first defining strategic risk.

THE NATURE OF STRATEGIC RISK

The cash flow variability produced by changes in the firm's economic environment is known as **strategic risk.** The first element of strategic risk is *exchange rate volatility*. The firm's value depends on its dollar cash flows. However, the firm's foreign operations produce cash flows in other currencies, which must be transferred into dollars. The exchange rates in our current flexible exchange rate system can cause considerable variability in the firm's dollar cash flows. Revenue and cost estimates are affected by exchange rate volatility.

The second element of strategic risk is *interest rate volatility*. The cost of short-term borrowings to the firm and the returns to the firm on marketable securities or other investment instruments are affected by changes in interest rates. These rate changes can affect the firm's cash flows.

Finally, the firm's cash flows can be affected by *commodity price volatility*. The firm's inputs and products can fluctuate in price. For example, a breakfast cereal producer must obtain large quantities of corn, wheat, oats, and other grains. The prices of these commodities vary tremendously with the size of the harvest, weather conditions, foreign supplies, and other factors. As these prices fluctuate, the cash flows of the firm fluctuate, thus affecting the value of the firm.

WHY MANAGE STRATEGIC RISKS? [5]

Managers should be concerned with reducing the volatility of expected cash flows in order to reduce "market imperfections" such as financial distress costs,

---

[4] The reasons for hedging were introduced in a highlight in Chapter 7 as part of our discussion of the differences between total and systematic risk.

[5] These and related reasons for corporate risk-reducing activities are discussed in R. Stulz and C. W. Smith, "The Determinants of the Firm's Hedging Policies," *Journal of Financial and Quantitative Analysis,* December 1985, pp. 391–405, and in A. C. Shapiro, "Currency Risk and Relative Price Risk," *Journal of Financial and Quantitative Analysis,* December 1984, pp. 365–373.

taxes, and agency costs. With these costs lowered, the firm's expected cash flows are higher for at least three reasons.

First, reducing strategic risks can reduce the firm's operating costs. Firms are concerned with avoiding financial distress, a situation in which they are not able to cover their obligations to creditors. (Financial distress is covered in detail in Chapter 16.) A firm that is perceived as being unable to satisfy these obligations may incur substantial operating costs. Suppliers and customers, seeing a potential disruption in their relationship with the distressed firm, may withhold their business, thus causing the firm to pay a higher price for its inputs and lose revenues. How financial distress affects the firm depends on the magnitude of these costs and their probability of occurring. If managers can reduce the volatility of the firm's cash flows, then the probability of bearing these costs of financial distress can be lessened and the value of the firm increased.

Second, reducing the volatility of cash flows can help a company reduce its tax burden. With volatile cash flows and a progressive tax rate, a firm (especially a smaller firm) may have low taxable income and a low tax payment in some periods and then high taxable income and a high payment in other periods. With less variability in its taxable income, a firm faces a lower average effective tax rate and hence higher expected cash flows after taxes.

Finally, a more stable cash flow pattern can lower the firm's agency costs and allow the firm to take on more investments. Reduced cash flow volatility mitigates the fundamental conflict between the interests of the stockholders and the bondholders—that is, the agency problem between stockholders and bondholders. The bondholders bear a "downside" risk because if the cash flows of the firm decrease, the firm may not be capable of meeting its debt obligations. On the other hand, the stockholders face a limited loss on their investment but also substantial potential gains if the firm does well. Thus volatile cash flows threaten the bondholders and benefit the stockholders. This potential for "**wealth transfers**" away from the bondholders and toward the owners results in the bondholders paying less for the debt of a firm with volatile cash flows than for the debt of a firm with stable cash flows. Moreover, bondholders are likely to impose more restrictions on the investment and financing choices that face the firm, and these **restrictive covenants** can decrease the firm's operating and financing flexibility. If managers can reduce cash flow volatility—that is, reduce total risk—they can lower the probability of default, reduce the agency costs of debt, borrow with less restrictive covenants, and increase firm value.

KEY CONCEPT   By managing strategic risks, a firm can increase the magnitude of the expected cash flows and hence increase firm value.

Basic Payoff Patterns   The first step in managing strategic risk is to understand how the risk associated with commodity prices, interest rates, and exchange rates affects the firm's cash flows. These effects are generally classified as being either *directly* or *inversely* related to changes in firm value.

A ''LONG'' POSITION IN AN ASSET

A firm is said to take a **long position** in an asset when it currently holds the asset or will receive the asset in the future. Under a long position, there is a *direct* relationship between changes in the value of the asset and changes in the firm's value.

Consider the example of a firm that faces exchange rate risk. National Energy Support, Inc. (NES), has sold a shipment of oil pipe to an English drilling firm for use in the North Sea oil field. It expects to be paid £1,250,000 in 60 days. NES

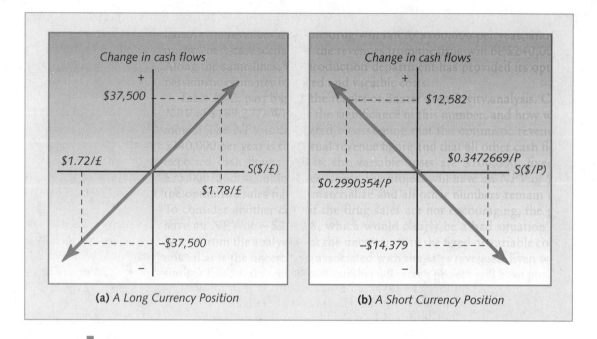

(a) *A Long Currency Position*   **(b)** *A Short Currency Position*

■
F I G U R E   1 1 - 1

Long and short currency exposure payoff patterns for NES (S is the spot exchange rate.)

is said to have a **long exposure** (or simply long position) in pounds. If the value of the pound increases, the dollar amount of the payment received will also increase. At the current exchange rate of $1.75/£, NES will receive $1.75/£ × £1,250,000 = $2,187,500 in 60 days. If the pound increases in value to $1.78, NES will receive $1.78/£ × £1,250,000 = $2,225,000, a gain of $37,500. On the other hand, if the pound decreases to $1.72, the company will receive only $1.72/£ × £1,250,000 = $2,150,000, a loss of $37,500.

These gains and losses are not caused by NES's products or competitors, but by changes in the exchange rate. These numbers are graphically represented in Figure 11-1(a), where the horizontal axis shows the exchange rate. The vertical axis represents changes in the firm's cash flows, with positive numbers signifying an increase in the cash flows of the firm.

A "SHORT" POSITION IN AN ASSET

A firm assumes a **short position** in an asset when it is obligated to give up the asset in the future or must obtain the asset in the future at an unknown price. In a short position, there is an *inverse* relationship between the value of the firm and the value of the asset held short.

Let us assume NES has obtained packaging components from a Mexican firm and must pay for them in pesos. In this case, NES has a short position, or a **short exposure** in pesos. If the peso increases in value, the dollar amount of the payment NES makes will be larger, meaning that its cash flow and thus the firm value are reduced. If NES must pay P559,000 in 30 days, how will its dollar cash flows be affected by exchange rate changes? The current exchange rate is $0.3215434/P. At this exchange rate, NES expects to pay P559,000 × $0.3215434 = $179,743. If, however, the peso increases to $0.3472669/P or decreases to $0.2990354/P, the expense to NES could be $194,122 or $167,161, respectively. Thus NES's cost could increase by $14,379 (reducing the firm's cash flows by $14,379) or decrease by $12,582 (increasing the firm's cash flows by $12,582), based solely on changes in the value of the peso relative to the U.S. dollar. This relationship, in which the value of the firm increases if the value of the peso decreases, is shown in Figure 11-1(b), with the horizontal axis showing the exchange rate, $S(\$/P)$ and the vertical axis showing the change in cash flows.

This discussion is summarized in the following key concept.

KEY CONCEPT A long position in an asset creates a *direct* relationship between changes in the firm value and the value of the asset held long. A short position creates an *inverse* relationship between the firm value and the value of the asset held short.

Derivative Assets
Most assets (be it stocks, bonds, metals, or foreign exchange) are **primary assets.** These assets are bought and sold in the corresponding **primary markets.** The net increase in wealth to the buyer or seller is affected by changes in the values of the assets as they trade in the primary markets. The owner of a primary asset has a *direct* claim on the benefits provided by the asset.

Derivative assets are assets whose values depend on (or is derived from) some primary assets. Derivative assets thus represent an *indirect* claim on an underlying asset, with the value of the derivative asset derived from the value of the underlying asset. As the value of the underlying asset changes, so does the value of the derivative asset. Derivative assets (or **derivative securities**) are based on a variety of underlying assets, including common stock, currencies, interest rates, and commodities. Just as with other assets, derivative securities produce both long and short payoff patterns. The specific nature of these payoff patterns varies with the type of derivative security.

Before examining individual types of derivatives, we must understand the two basic ways firms manage risk: through speculation and hedging.

Managing Risk
Firms involved with productive activities cannot avoid strategic risk. However, firms can decide how to deal with strategic risk by either choosing to accept its effect on the firm's cash flows or shifting the risk to other parties.

SPECULATION: ACCEPTING RISK

Speculation is taking above-average risks with the expectation of receiving substantial returns. **Investing,** on the other hand, involves accepting reasonable risks in the expectation of gaining a reasonable return on the investment. Just as there is no easy way to define "above average" or "reasonable," there is no easy way to separate these functions. The classification of a given party as a speculator or an investor depends to an extent on the views of the individual who is making the classification. Loosely speaking, however, we would say that an investor, though wanting a return on his or her investment, is also concerned about the safety of capital. A **speculator,** on the other hand, more willingly places his or her capital at risk in the hope of receiving a larger return.

A speculator takes a position in an asset with the expectation of making a profit from that position. For instance, if a speculator feels that the price of copper in three months will be higher than is generally expected, then the speculator purchases copper today, creating a long position in copper. If the price of copper does, in fact, rise, he profits. However, if the price of copper drops, he loses.

If, on the other hand, the speculator expects the price of copper to decrease over time more than is generally expected, he creates a short position in copper by, say, borrowing copper from another party and then selling it today, with the expectation of replacing the borrowed copper at a lower price sometime in the future. If the price of copper decreases, the speculator makes a profit on this transaction.

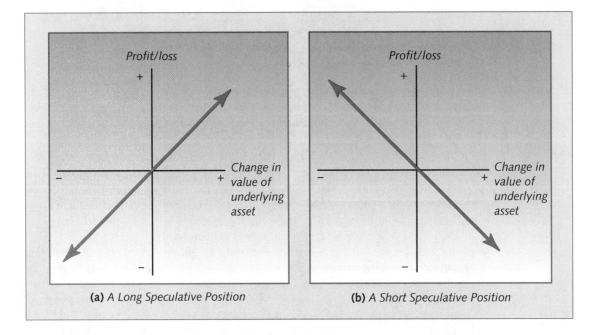

(a) *A Long Speculative Position*   (b) *A Short Speculative Position*

■

FIGURE 11-2
*Payoff patterns from long
and short speculations*

The payoffs from long and short speculative positions in an asset are shown in Figure 11-2.

HEDGING: REDUCING RISK

In contrast to speculation, risk reduction is the motivation for hedging. In **hedging,** a firm examines a strategic risk element and determines whether it has a short or long exposure. It then takes an offsetting position in another asset (either primary or derivative) to reduce the risk. The resulting payoff pattern for the combined positions in the two assets is much less variable than before the hedge transaction. Hedging, in principle, is like buying insurance against unwanted price swings. To see how hedging works in practice, we discuss specific derivative securities. We examine how the firm can hedge specific strategic risks with futures, options, and swaps.

11-2

**FUTURES
CONTRACTS**

Contracts to buy or sell a good—such as wheat or French francs—in the **cash markets** require the immediate delivery of the asset. But there are also contracts to buy or sell certain assets in the future at a price that is set today in the marketplace. These are called **futures contracts,** and they have become an important force in financial markets since their introduction in the mid-1970s.

A futures contract obliges its purchaser to buy a given amount of a specified asset at some stated time in the future (known as the **delivery date**) at the **futures price.** Similarly, the seller of the contract is obliged to deliver the asset at the futures price. In the futures market, though, less than 3% of the contracts traded involve the actual delivery of the underlying asset that has been contracted for purchase or sale. Rather, the buyers of futures contracts usually sell their contracts before the delivery date, thus offsetting ("unwinding") their position. Similarly, investors who have sold futures usually "cover" their short position sometime between the sale and the contract's delivery date by buying the futures contract. Although there is an actual buyer and seller in every transaction, the subsequent sale or purchase need not be made with the same buyer and seller, thereby facilitating a much more orderly and efficient market.

The principles underlying futures trading date as far back as the heyday of the Greeks and Romans. The organization of centralized futures markets in medieval England was significant to the country's successful commerce. In America, commodities futures trading of livestock and meats, grains, metals, and other goods was established in the mid-19th century. Currently, futures contracts are created and traded on organized **futures exchanges.**

Types of Futures Contracts and the Futures Exchanges

There are four broad types of futures: *futures on commodities* (such as grains and oilseeds, livestock and meat, food and fiber, metals, and petroleum), *futures on currencies* (such as the Japanese yen, German mark, Canadian dollar, British pound, Swiss franc, and Australian dollar), *futures on interest-bearing instruments* (such as U.S. Treasury bonds, notes, and bills), and *futures on stock indexes* (such as the Standard & Poor's 500, the Tokyo Exchange Nikkei average, and the NYSE composite index). Table 11-1 is a listing of exchanges and the types of futures traded on them.

Because of futures markets, many commodities, currencies, and interest-bearing instruments can have two prices: a **spot price,** its price in the cash market, and a futures price, its price in the futures markets. Both spot and futures prices are determined by the demand and supply for the asset in the cash and futures markets, respectively. Under normal supply and demand conditions, futures prices tend to rise and fall with cash prices in a fairly predictable manner. On the date that the futures contract expires, the futures price approaches the spot price.

Like most assets, the profit or loss on a futures contract is determined by the difference between the buying and selling prices of the contract. However, unlike cash markets, in which the profit/loss is recognized only when the asset is sold, profits/losses on futures contracts are realized daily. To understand this unique feature of the futures markets, we now examine how futures trading is conducted on the exchanges.

THE IMPORTANCE OF STANDARDIZATION

The ability to trade on organized exchanges is a major reason for the popularity of futures. One of the primary advantages of exchange-traded futures is standard-

■
TABLE 11-1
U.S. Futures Exchanges

Exchange and Year Founded	Commodities	Currencies	Interest Rates	Indexes
		Types of Contract		
Chicago Board of Trade (CBT), 1948	X		X	X
Chicago Mercantile Exchange (CME), 1919	X	X	X	X
Coffee, Sugar, and Cocoa Exchange (New York), 1882	X			X
Commodity Exchange, Inc. (COMEX) (New York), 1933	X			
Kansas City Board of Trade (KCBT), 1856	X			X
Mid-America Commodity Exchange (Chicago), 1880	X	X	X	
Minneapolis Grain Exchange, 1881	X			
New York Cotton Exchange, Inc., 1870	X	X		X
Citrus Associates of the New York Cotton Exchange, 1966	X			
Petroleum Associates of the New York Cotton Exchange, 1971	X			
New York Futures Exchange (NYFE), 1979				X
New York Mercantile Exchange, 1872	X			
Chicago Rice and Cotton Exchange, 1976	X			

ization of the contracts traded. For instance, the CBT's wheat futures contract requires the delivery of a standard type of wheat: No. 2 Soft Red, No. 2 Hard Red Winter, No. 2 Dark Northern Spring, or No. 1 Northern Spring. The contract also specifies that the amount of a single contract is 5,000 pounds of wheat and that the contract expires on a given day in the months of March, May, July, September, and December. Finally, the contract specifies how the wheat is to be delivered. This standardization facilitates the smooth operation of the secondary market in futures contracts on wheat. This standardization is seen in all assets traded in the organized futures markets.

Standardization allows futures contracts to be sold to another party before they become due. For instance, an investor purchases a long futures contract on wheat on the Chicago Board of Trade (CBT). The investor has an obligation to purchase the wheat through this contract. However, with the secondary market provided by the CBT, the investor can sell the futures contract in the marketplace at the prevailing contract price. Thus an investor can get into and out of a futures contract before it matures and so have greater liquidity. Furthermore, this flexibility can be obtained at a low transaction cost (commissions). Buying and selling futures through the CBT are relatively inexpensive. Indeed, all the advantages of exchange-traded futures have resulted in a dramatic increase in the volume of this kind of trading.

MANAGING CREDIT RISK

A second major advantage of organized exchanges is their ability to manage credit risk. **Credit risk** is the risk that a holder of an unprofitable futures contract will default on his or her obligations under the contract. To preclude this possibility, some checks are built into the futures markets system.

First, holders of futures contracts are required to post a **margin,** a portion of the full purchase price of the commodity or security. Margin connected with futures is not the same as margin as used with broker accounts, which is equity against which the investor may borrow (e.g., "buying on margin"). Rather, margin in a futures account is a guarantee that the holder of the contract is able to absorb losses on the contract.

The **performance period** on a contract is the period between the time a contract is agreed upon and the time it is exercised and the profits or losses recognized. In futures markets, the performance period is set at one day through the process of **marking-to-market.** In marking-to-market, the contract is in effect revalued at the end of each day's trading, and gains or losses are computed. These gains or losses are then used to adjust the contract holder's margin account. Gains increase the value of the margin account and may be withdrawn by the margin holder. Losses, on the other hand, reduce the value of the margin account. If the margin account drops below a certain level, called the **maintenance margin,** the holder of the futures contract gets a **margin call** from a broker and must deposit additional funds into the account to bring the margin account back to its initial level. If the holder fails to do so, the contract is closed by the broker, usually before any substantial losses are experienced. This ability to recognize losses rather than let them accumulate is a major factor in protecting the futures markets from credit risk.

Finally, the exchanges themselves provide assurances that contracts will be honored through clearinghouses. A **clearinghouse** is a corporation established by an exchange to facilitate the trades made on the exchange. One of the primary roles of the clearinghouse is to be the opposite party to all trades. Buyers and sellers of futures contracts do not deal directly with each other but with the clearinghouse.

FIGURE 11-3
*Growth in currency
futures trading on
the IMM*

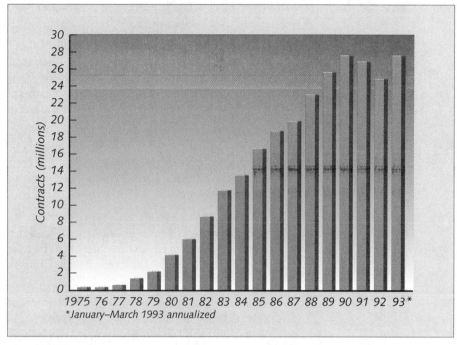

SOURCE: Chicago Mercantile Exchange. Trading figures are for the International Monetary Market (IMM), a division of the Chicago Mercantile Exchange.

If sellers of a futures contract in copper default on a losing position, the default is handled by the clearinghouse, which settles with the buyers of the copper contract. Because clearinghouses guarantee the futures contracts, buyers and sellers can trade them without fear of default.

The efficiency offered by organized futures exchanges has resulted in explosive growth in these instruments. Figure 11-3 shows the growth in the volume of currency futures trading on the International Mercantile Exchange.

Understanding the Use of Futures Contracts: The Case of Pacific Exporters, Inc.

Pacific Exporters, Inc., a firm based in Belmont, California, manufactures heating elements and sells them primarily in the western United States. We now examine how Pacific Exporters can use futures contracts to both speculate and hedge in the commodities markets for copper.

PACIFIC EXPORTERS SPECULATES IN COPPER

Pacific's management believes that it has an in-depth knowledge of global copper markets, and they would like to exploit this comparative advantage by speculating with copper futures contracts. They therefore purchase a single copper futures contract, which controls the delivery of 25,000 pounds of copper at a price of $0.78/lb. The value of the futures contract, calculated as the number of units of the underlying asset multiplied by the futures price per unit, is 25,000 × $0.78 = $19,500. This purchase requires Pacific to post an initial margin of $2,000 and to keep a maintenance margin of $1,500 (margins are part of the contract specification). Although futures have high commissions (about 5% of the value of the contract), we ignore this detail in our example.

What happens each day to Pacific Exporters' margin account—and thus its profits or losses—as the price of copper in the futures markets changes?

Day 0: When the contract is purchased, its value is $19,500 and the margin account has a balance of $2,000.

Day 1: The copper futures price falls to $0.76/lb at the end of the day. This loss of 2 cents per pound reduces the value of the contract by $500 (25,000 lb × $0.02). At the end of day 1, this loss reduces Pacific Exporters' margin account by $500. Note that the loss in the futures position is recognized immediately because the margin account now has only $1,500.

Day 2: The copper futures price declines further to $0.75/lb, causing an additional loss of 25,000 lb × $0.01 = $250. At the end of day 2, this loss is subtracted from Pacific's margin account, reducing it to $1,250. Since this is below the maintenance margin of $1,500, Pacific gets a margin call, requiring it to contribute an additional $750 to bring the account back to the initial margin.

Day 3: The copper price reverses its falling trend and rises to $0.78/lb. The 3 cent per pound profit increases the value of the futures contract by $750, which is credited at the end of the day to Pacific's margin account, which now stands at $2,750.

Day 4: The copper price rises further to $0.82, and Pacific decides to unwind its position by selling the contract. The profit of $1,000 is credited to the margin account, and the account is closed when Pacific withdraws $3,750.

For Pacific Exporters, the net profit on the copper futures contract is the ending margin account value ($3,750) less the margin contributions ($2,000 + $750), or $1,000. The transactions that produced this profit are summarized in Table 11-2.

Speculators such as Pacific Exporters can use a relatively small margin account to control a large position in an asset to take advantage of a change in its price. The speculator takes on risk with the expectation of receiving a substantial profit if the forecast is correct. However, it is important to recognize that this profit is not realized entirely at the sale of the futures contract.

KEY CONCEPT | Profits and losses from a futures contract accrue on a daily basis because of the mark-to-market feature inherent in futures trading.

PAYOFF PATTERNS ON PACIFIC'S FUTURES CONTRACT

We saw that Pacific's futures contract produced a $1,000 profit because the copper futures price increased to $0.82/lb. But what if the price had gone up to only $0.80/lb? To $0.88/lb? To $0.74/lb? What if, instead of a long futures position, Pacific had assumed a short futures contract (i.e., had sold a futures contract)? Answers to these questions are given by a futures contract's payoff pattern.

Futures contracts have two different payoff patterns, depending on whether the position is a long or a short one. A futures contract to *purchase* an asset produces a long position, with the value of the futures contract increasing as the value of the underlying asset increases.

■

T A B L E   1 1 - 2
Pacific Exporters' Margin Account Transactions

Day	Beginning Copper Price ($/lb)	Ending Copper Price ($/lb)	Change in Copper Price ($/lb)	Value of Contract	Ending Amount in Margin Account
0	n/a	$0.78	n/a	$19,500	$2,000
1	$0.78	0.76	−$0.02	19,000	1,500
2	0.76	0.75	−0.01	18,750	2,000[a]
3	0.75	0.78	0.03	19,500	2,750
4	0.78	0.82	0.04	20,500	3,750

[a] $1,250 plus additional margin contribution of $750.

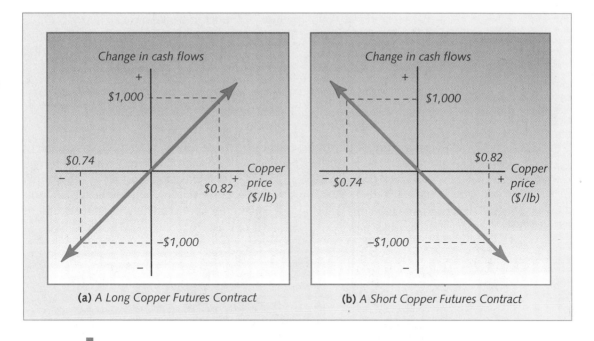

(a) *A Long Copper Futures Contract*   **(b)** *A Short Copper Futures Contract*

FIGURE 11-4

Long and short copper futures positions

Figure 11-4(a) contains the payoff diagram for Pacific Exporters' long copper futures position. The horizontal axis represents the copper futures price and the vertical axis the profit/loss on the contract position. When the futures price is $0.82/lb, as seen earlier, Pacific has a $1,000 profit. If the futures price was $0.74/lb instead, Pacific would have a loss of $1,000. (The reader may find it instructive to verify this.)

A futures contract to *sell* an asset produces a short position, which means that the value of the contract increases as the value of the underlying asset decreases. This short payoff pattern is shown in Figure 11-4(b).

Note from Figure 11-4 that with a futures contract, the investor has unlimited "upside potential" and potentially large "downside risk."

HOW PACIFIC EXPORTERS HEDGES COMMODITY PRICE RISK WITH FUTURES

Most business firms are not interested in speculation; rather, they are concerned with reducing the strategic risk they face in their production of goods and services. Pacific Exporters uses copper in the manufacture of its equipment, and although the price of copper is currently $0.78 per pound, this price can change on a daily basis. Pacific Exporters can hedge the strategic risk involved in this transaction in three steps.

Step 1: Identify the nature of the exposure faced by the firm. In three months Pacific Exporters must purchase 100,000 pounds of copper to replenish its inventory. Pacific Exporters thus has a short position in copper, and it must obtain the materials in the future. If the price of copper increases in the cash market, Pacific's costs will increase, thus reducing its cash flows.

Step 2: Identify the hedging instrument. Pacific Exporters can fix the price of copper by entering into futures contracts to buy copper at a contract price of $0.78/lb. Since Pacific needs 100,000 pounds of copper and each contract is for 25,000 pounds, four contracts must be purchased. Note that if

Pacific needed 105,000 pounds of copper, it would have an **imperfect hedge** because it cannot buy a fraction of a futures contract.

Step 3: Combine the two exposures to determine the net exposure (payoff pattern) of the firm. By combining its future purchase of copper in the cash market with the futures contracts, Pacific Exporters can fix the effective price it will pay for the copper regardless of how the cash market price of copper changes.

We can see the result of these actions by first assuming that the cash price of copper increases to $0.80/lb. This means that Pacific Exporters will have to pay $0.02 more per pound ($0.80 − $0.78) than expected, costing an additional $2,000 (100,000 lb × $0.02/lb = $2,000). However, the value of the futures contract to purchase copper has also increased by approximately the same amount.

■

FIGURE 11-5

Pacific Exporters' payoff patterns for a hedged copper position

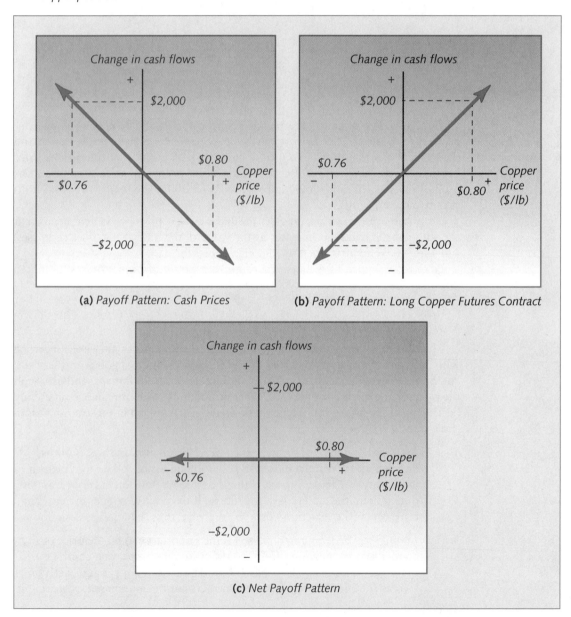

(a) *Payoff Pattern: Cash Prices*

(b) *Payoff Pattern: Long Copper Futures Contract*

(c) *Net Payoff Pattern*

We say "approximately" because the spot and futures prices are highly, but not perfectly, correlated. Thus the losses in the cash market transactions are offset by the gains in the futures contract. This process works in a similar manner if the price of copper decreases to $0.76 in the cash market. Pacific Exporters is assured of obtaining its materials at a known price, thus reducing the variability of its cash flows. The payoff patterns involved with this hedging strategy are given in Figure 11-5.

THE COST OF HEDGING WITH FUTURES CONTRACTS

Figure 11-5(c) shows how Pacific Exporters can generally eliminate the uncertainty associated with the price of copper by using futures contracts. Thus futures contracts can be used as a form of insurance against adverse price changes. However, insurance is not free, and there must be a cost to hedging with futures contracts. Pacific's cost of hedging does not involve any explicit payment (other than commissions); rather, the **cost of hedging** is an opportunity cost. By hedging with futures Pacific does not have any losses from adverse price changes in copper. However, by hedging, it forfeits the potential for profits if copper prices move in its favor. Thus hedging is not free, and Pacific's management must decide whether this opportunity cost is justified or not.

Forward Contracts

A **forward contract** may be viewed as a simpler version of the futures contract. A buyer of a three-month forward contract on, say, copper agrees today to purchase a specified amount of copper at the end of three months at a price agreed upon today, called the **forward price**. Unlike futures contracts, forward contracts are not traded on exchanges (they are **over-the-counter** or OTC contracts) and are not as widely used except in foreign exchange markets where they are very popular. Forwards are privately negotiated between two parties and, not surprisingly, they are not liquid. Both buyer and seller are obligated to perform. The profit or loss from a forward contract depends on the difference between the spot price of the asset and the forward price on the day the forward contract matures. This is because forward contracts are settled only at maturity. Unlike futures, there is no mark-to-market feature on forwards, and so the entire profit or loss is realized on the day the forward contract matures. The payoff diagrams for long and short positions in forwards are identical to the payoff diagrams for futures. There are no margin requirements for trading in forwards, and for that reason, a forward contract is often considered to be a credit instrument (like a loan). Because of this, they are viewed as having high risk. Secondary market trading is very limited and hence forwards are illiquid. The cost of hedging with forwards, as with futures, is the opportunity cost of giving up favorable movements in asset prices.

Some of the differences between futures and forwards are listed in Table 11-3.

■

TABLE 11-3

Differences Between Forward Contracts and Futures Contracts[a]

Futures Contract: *Standardized Sizes and expiration periods*	Forward Contract: *Customized Sizes and Time Periods*
(+) It enhances liquidity and flexibility. Hedge position can be entered and exited as needed.	(−) Custom-made product may be difficult to exit.
(−) Hedge position may not provide an exact dollar-for-dollar offset to underlying exposure.	(+) It creates a "perfect" hedge that exactly matches underlying exposure.
Futures Exchanges	**Forward (OTC) Markets**
(+) Pricing is extremely efficient.	(−) Participants must shop for best rates and prices.
(+) Prices are the same for all.	(−) Prices are based on credit and relationship.
(+) There is virtually no credit risk.	(−) Credit of counterparty is of crucial importance.
(−) Margin system requires administrative expenses.	(+) There is no margin system, and thus they are easier to administer.

[a](+) for advantages; (−) for disadvantages.

THE BASICS OF CALL AND PUT OPTIONS

*M*anagers may be concerned with an adverse movement in the underlying strategic risk element such as commodity prices, interest rates, or currency values and hedge these risks. However, managers may also desire to take advantage of favorable movements in these variables. Managers thus look for a derivative security that can protect them from events that would decrease their cash flows, but allow them to benefit from events that would increase their cash flows. An option is such a derivative security. If Pacific Exporters' management decides that the (opportunity) cost of forwards and futures is "too high," it may find hedging with options attractive.

An **option** is a derivative security that gives the holder the right, but not the obligation, to buy or sell a specified quantity of a specified asset within a specified time period. An option is fundamentally different from a futures contract. A futures contract defines a future *commitment* to buy or sell an asset. The holder of the futures contract has no discretion concerning its execution, regardless of how prices in the cash market move. An option, on the other hand, offers *flexibility* by providing protection from an adverse movement in the cash market while allowing the holder to benefit from a favorable change in the cash market prices of the asset on which the option is based.

Options were originally developed to assist trade in commodities, and options on commodities remain popular. Options on common stock are also widely used now, as are options based on interest-bearing assets and currencies.

Options Markets

OVER-THE-COUNTER MARKET

One way of creating options is through single contracts that are individually negotiated between parties, usually firms and their banks. These contracts allow firms to hedge against uncertain risks associated with their operations or investments. These OTC options are tailor-made agreements between two parties and are less liquid and more expensive than exchange-traded options.

ORGANIZED EXCHANGES

There are several options exchanges, with each exchange specializing in certain types of contracts. For instance, the Chicago Board Options Exchange (CBOE) is the primary trading center for stock options, and the Chicago Board of Trade (CBOT) is important in the trading of options for interest-rate-based assets such as Treasury bonds, notes, and bills, as well as municipal bonds and foreign interest rates. The Chicago Mercantile Exchange (CME) offers options on commodities and indexes based on stock market averages. The Philadelphia Exchange is widely used for trading currency options. Table 11-4 lists options exchanges and identifies the assets underlying the options.

Like the futures markets, organized options exchanges provide the advantages of liquidity, low transactions costs, and safety through the standardization of the assets on which the contracts are based and of the contract sizes and maturity dates. For instance, the CBOE provides an active secondary market in stock options. An investor has not only the ability to exercise or let the option expire, but also the ability to sell the option in the marketplace at the prevailing option price. Thus an investor can get into and out of options before they mature and thus have greater liquidity.

Credit risk in options exchanges is different than in the futures markets. The buyer of an option has the right to obtain the asset through the option contract. However, the buyer of an option also has the implicit right *not* to complete an

■

TABLE 11-4

U.S. Options Exchanges

	Types of Contract				
Exchange and Year Founded	Commodities	Currencies	Interest Rates	Indexes (Primarily Stock)	Stocks
American Stock Exchange, 1921				X	X
Chicago Board of Trade (CBT),[a] 1948	X		X	X	
Chicago Board Options Exchange (CBOE), 1973			X	X	X
Chicago Mercantile Exchange (CME),[a] 1919	X	X	X	X	
Coffee, Sugar, and Cocoa Exchange (New York), 1882	X				
Commodity Exchange, Inc. (COMEX)[a] (New York), 1933	X				
Kansas City Board of Trade (KCBT),[a] 1856	X				
Mid-America Commodity Exchange[a] (Chicago), 1880	X				
Minneapolis Grain Exchange,[a] 1881	X				
New York Cotton Exchange, Inc., 1870	X	X	X		
New York Futures Exchange (NYFE), 1979				X	
New York Mercantile Exchange, 1872	X				
New York Stock Exchange, 1792				X	X
Pacific Stock Exchange, 1957				X	X
Philadelphia Stock Exchange		X		X	X

[a] These exchanges offer options on futures contracts, a specialized type of derivative security that we do not discuss in this text.

unprofitable contract. This means that there is no risk of default on the buyer of an option. However, there is a default risk on the party issuing the option. Therefore clearinghouses and margin accounts are still necessary in the options exchanges, but the risk of default is primarily on one side of the option contract.

Options on various assets have increased dramatically in popularity as managers, investors, and speculators have gained knowledge about them and as the exchange markets that offer them have become more liquid and offered more contracts. Figure 11-6 shows the increased popularity of options in the growth of the volume of currency options traded on the Philadelphia Exchange.

FIGURE 11-6

Growth in currency option trading on the Philadelphia Stock Exchange

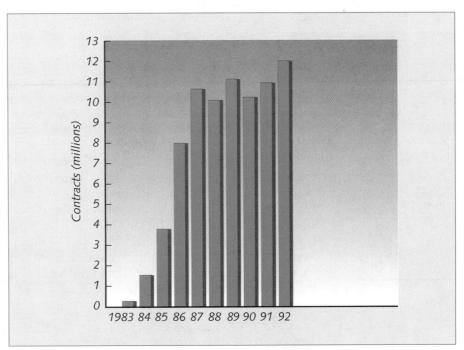

SOURCE: Philadelphia Stock Exchange, 1992.

Characteristics of Option Contracts

There are several important characteristics of options.

■ Options are not free. An option gives its buyer the right to buy or sell an asset at a specified price. The seller of the option is obligated to take the other side of the transaction. That is, if an option gives the holder the right to buy an asset, the seller must surrender the asset upon demand. This commitment on the seller's part has economic value to the holder, who must compensate the seller by paying an **option premium** at the time the option is purchased. This option premium is the compensation to the option seller for taking on the risk involved with the option and it is nonrefundable. (The option premium is the option's price.)

■ Options have a fixed maturity; they expire on a certain date. If the holder of the option does not exercise it before this maturity date, the option expires and can no longer be exercised. Then the option has no economic or market value.

■ Options can be exercised at a specified price called the **exercise price** or **striking price.** Guaranteeing a future price today is a major benefit of purchasing an option. An **American option** is one that can be exercised at any time before its maturity. This contrasts with a **European option** that can be exercised only at maturity.

■ Options may or may not be exercised. The holder of an option decides to exercise it only if it is to his or her advantage to do so. The decision is based on a comparison of the exercise price of the option with the current cash market price of the asset on which the option is based.

■ Options themselves do not affect the market value of the underlying asset. Options derive their value from the underlying asset on which they are based.

Types of Options

There are two basic types of options: calls and puts. Given the popularity of stock options, we describe these option types with options on shares of Hewlett-Packard stock as examples.

CALL OPTIONS

A **call option** on an asset allows the holder of the option to buy (to "call") a fixed quantity of the underlying asset at a specified price within a specified time period. Table 11-5 presents the prices and other relevant details for Hewlett-Packard call options on a day when Hewlett-Packard stock closed at a price of $67\frac{7}{8}$.

Assume that an investor purchases a three-month call option on Hewlett-Packard stock at an exercise price of $65 when the stock price is $60. The option holder then has the right to purchase one share of Hewlett-Packard for $65 at any time during the option's life, regardless of the actual price of Hewlett-Packard stock during that time. Clearly, the option buyer will not buy this option if he does not expect the stock price to rise above $65. If the stock price rises to $70, for example, by exercising the option the option holder effectively "buys" this stock for the lower ($65) exercise price. Thus a **call buyer** expects the price of the underlying stock to rise over the exercise price. A **call seller** expects the opposite.

■
T A B L E   1 1 - 5
Hewlett-Packard Call Options

Stock Price	Exercise Price (striking price)	Price of Call for Different Expiration Dates		
		September	October	November
$67\frac{7}{8}$	$65	3	4	$5\frac{1}{4}$
$67\frac{7}{8}$	70	$\frac{1}{16}$	$1\frac{5}{16}$	$\cdots$
$67\frac{7}{8}$	75	$\cdots$	$\frac{5}{16}$	—

A call option for which the exercise price exceeds the current stock price is said to be "**out of money**" because the holder of the option will not benefit if the option is exercised immediately. On the other hand, if the stock price exceeds the exercise price, then it is possible to make a profit by exercising the option immediately, and thus the option is "**in the money.**" An option for which the current stock price and the exercise price are the same is said to be "**at the money.**"

Consider the example in which the current stock price is $70 and the exercise price on the call option is $65 (an "in the money" option). The minimum value of this call option must be $5. Why? Assume that the option price is $3. Then an investor could buy the option for $3, exercise it for $65, and sell the stock for its market price of $70, thereby earning a profit of $2. To avoid a guaranteed loss to the option seller, the option must sell for at least $5. For an "in the money" option, the minimum value must be the difference between the stock price and the exercise price. The minimum value for an "**out of the money**" option is $0.

As it turns out, options sell for more than their minimum value (i.e., they are worth more than the difference between the stock price and the exercise price) if there is any time remaining before the option expires.

Table 11-5 shows nine different call options (three different expiration dates for each of three different exercise prices) on the stock. Notice that the options sell for more than their minimum values because there is always some probability that the stock price will rise before the option expires. The following are additional properties of call options:

1. *The longer the remaining life of the call option is, the larger the option premium is.* For example, consider the Hewlett-Packard call options in Table 11-5 with an exercise price of $65. The September option sells for $3, the October option sells for $4, and the November option is the most expensive at $5\frac{1}{4}$.

2. *The higher the exercise price is, the smaller the price of the option is.* Consider the October options on Hewlett-Packard. The $65 exercise price option costs $4, the option with the $70 exercise price costs $1\frac{5}{16}$, and the cheapest option ($\frac{5}{16}$) is the one with the highest exercise price, $75.

3. *A call option's price increases as the market value of the stock increases.* This property follows from our discussion above about the minimum value of an option.

4. *A call option's price increases as the volatility of the underlying stock increases.* The intuition for this result is that a more volatile stock is more likely to be in the money at expiration. An out of the money call option on a fairly stable stock is less likely to be in the money at expiration.

5. *The price of the call option increases as the risk-free interest rate increases.*

PUT OPTIONS

A **put option** on a common stock allows the holder of the option to sell (to "put") a share of the underlying stock at a specified price within a specified time period. In contrast with a call option, a put buyer expects the price of the underlying stock to fall below the exercise price. A put seller bets on the opposite.

A put option for which the exercise price exceeds the current stock price is said to be "in the money" because the holder of the option will benefit by exercising the option immediately. On the other hand, if the stock price exceeds the exercise price, the put holder will lose by exercising the option immediately, and so the option is "out of the money."

■

T A B L E   1 1 - 6

Hewlett-Packard Put Options

Stock Price	Exercise Price (striking price)	Price of Put for Different Expiration Dates		
		September	October	November
$67\frac{7}{8}$	$65	$\frac{1}{16}$	$1\frac{3}{16}$	$2\frac{1}{8}$
$67\frac{7}{8}$	70	$2\frac{1}{4}$	$3\frac{3}{8}$	...
$67\frac{7}{8}$	75	$7\frac{1}{4}$	$7\frac{3}{8}$	...

Table 11-6 shows the put option prices for Hewlett-Packard stock as of September 17, 1993.

In contrast with a call option, the minimum price for an "in the money" put option is the difference between the exercise price and the price of the underlying stock.

Option Payoffs

To understand how corporations use options, we must first examine the payoffs from basic put and call options and the relationship between put and call option prices. In discussing these payoff patterns, we continue to use our example of Hewlett-Packard stock.

CALL OPTIONS PAYOFFS

Consider the owner of an American call option. Under what conditions will she exercise her option? Only if exercising the option is to her advantage.

1. If the stock price at expiration (S) is greater than the exercise price (E) of the option, she should exercise the option and make a profit of $\$(S - E)$. Therefore, at expiration, the value of the option (C) must equal this amount; that is, at expiration, $C = S - E$.

2. If S is equal to or less than the exercise price, there is no advantage to exercising the option, and so the option is worthless; that is, $C = 0$.

Combining these two possibilities, we can represent the value of the call option at expiration as

$$C = \max(0, S - E) \tag{11-2}$$

That is, the call option is worth either $0 or the potential profit, whichever is larger.

The payoffs from the call option at expiration are charted in Figure 11-7. It is clear that unless the stock price exceeds the exercise price, the call option will expire worthless. The "downside risk" protection feature of options also is evident. Although the investor's upside potential is unlimited as the stock price increases beyond E, the maximum loss is limited (at expiration) to $0.

PUT OPTIONS PAYOFFS

In contrast with a call option, the put owner will exercise the option *only* if the stock price (S) on the expiration date is less than the exercise price (E) of the put option.

1. If the stock price at expiration (S) is less than the exercise price (E), then by exercising the option, the put owner can realize a profit of $\$(E - S)$. Therefore, in this case, the put option price at expiration (P) must equal ($E - S$).

2. If the stock price exceeds the exercise price of the put at expiration, the put owner has no reason to exercise the option; therefore, the put option must be worthless.

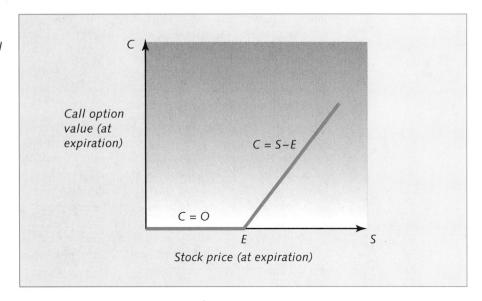

When these two possibilities are combined, the value of the put at expiration is

$$P = \max(E - S, 0) \tag{11-3}$$

Figure 11-8 summarizes this discussion.

The reader will note from this figure that when the stock price is low, the put option pays off handsomely, but when the stock is doing well, the put option offers no advantage. Thus put options may be viewed as a form of "insurance" because they pay up when the underlying ("insured") asset performs poorly.

THE RELATIONSHIP BETWEEN PUT AND CALL PRICES

The payoffs from the call and put options suggest a relationship between put and call option prices. This relationship, called **put-call parity,** is derived in Appendix 11A and is also shown as equation (11-4). This is an extremely useful equation because it allows us to infer the value of a call option from the price of a similar

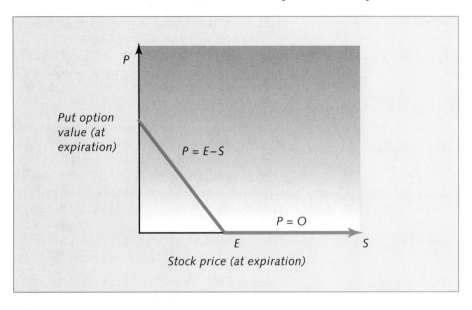

put option, and vice versa. Thus, if we know how to value call options, the put-call parity result makes it unnecessary to develop a theory for the value of a similar put. We have

Call price − put price = stock price − present value of exercise price

or, in algebraic terms,

$$C - P = S - Ee^{-rT} \tag{11-4}$$

where Ee^{-rT} represents the present value of E with continuous compounding. The letter e is the number used as the base in the system of natural logarithms.

The put-call parity theory, therefore, is the relationship of the call price, the put price, the underlying stock price, the common exercise price of the options, the life of the options (T), and the riskless interest rate r. If the relationship did not hold, it would be possible to make an infinite profit by arbitraging the pricing discrepancy.

For example, if a six-month call option (exercise price $42) on a stock that currently sells at $45 is worth $5, what is the price of a similar put option on the stock if the risk-free interest rate is 7%? Using the put-call relationship in equation (11-4), we have

$$\$5 - \$P = \$45 - \$42e^{-(0.07)(0.5)}$$

which implies that the value of the put (P) must be $0.56.

The prices of options in our examples so far are given; the question of how these prices are determined in the marketplace has not been addressed. The price of options can be estimated using the **Black-Scholes option pricing model,** which is examined in Appendix 11B.

How Pacific Exporters Can Hedge Foreign Exchange Risk with Options

We used common stock options to give a general understanding of options. Using option theory in corporate decision making involves managing strategic risk, which we do now with the same three steps we used to examine hedging with futures contracts.

Consider another situation faced by Pacific Exporters. Pacific Exporters has imported a turning machine from a manufacturer in Dusseldorf, Germany. It must pay for the machine in German deutsche marks and is thus exposed to foreign exchange risk. Pacific Exporters can deal with this exposure in three steps.

Step 1: Identify the nature of the exposure faced by the firm. Pacific must pay DM 375,000 in 90 days for the machine. It thus has a short position. The current exchange rate is $0.6140/DM, which means a payment of DM 375,000 × $0.6140/DM = $230,250. However, if the DM increases in value, the firm will have to pay more dollars. Pacific Exporters is thus concerned about a strengthening of the DM. Its short exposure is shown in Figure 11-9(a).

Step 2: Identify the appropriate hedging instrument. Pacific Exporters can obtain three 90-day call options on the mark, with each contract worth DM 125,000, with an exercise price of $0.6140. (Because its exposure is DM 375,000, Pacific needs DM 375,000/DM 125,000 = 3 contracts.) These call options create a long position in DM that balances off the short position the DM obligation creates. If the DM increases in value relative to the dollar, the firm can exercise the option at the exercise price of $0.6140 and eliminate the downside risk it faces. This payoff pattern is shown in Figure 11-9(b).

Step 3: Evaluate the company's net position. If the DM increases in value to $0.6200/DM, Pacific Exporters has to pay an additional $0.6200 −

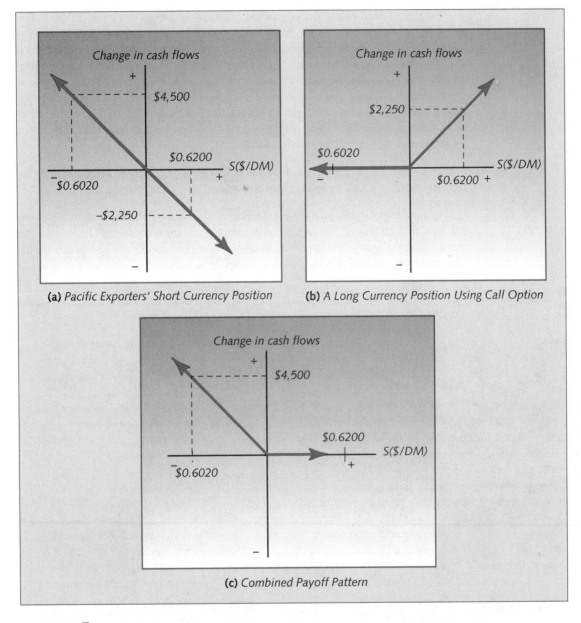

(a) Pacific Exporters' Short Currency Position

(b) A Long Currency Position Using Call Option

(c) Combined Payoff Pattern

■
FIGURE 1 1 - 9
*Hedging currency
exposure with options*

$0.6140 = $0.006 per mark or $0.006 × DM 375,000 = $2,250 to satisfy its obligation. However, the value of the call option increases by this same amount. That is, the call option gives Pacific Exporters the ability to purchase its currency at the $0.6140 strike price and then sell the currency for the $0.6200 spot price, gaining $0.006 per mark covered by the option. Thus, holding the option produces a gain of $2,250, exactly offsetting the loss generated by the obligation to pay for the turning machine.

Now, what happens if the mark depreciates in value to, say, $0.6020? This is a good deal for Pacific Exporters because the price of each mark drops by $0.6140 − $0.6020 = $0.012, which means that the dollar price of the turning machine drops by $0.012 × DM 375,000 = $4,500. But what about the option? Well, the option is no longer profitable, so Pacific Exporters lets it expire and pockets the $4,500 savings.

The payoff pattern for the combined position is shown in Figure 11-9(c). The flexibility of the option allows Pacific Exporters to benefit from a downward movement in the DM, but at the same time protect itself from appreciation in the DM.

As with futures, we have not included several variables, such as the option premium, that are normally part of the hedging decision. Hedging risks with options is not free; the option price is the cost associated with hedging, and this cost should also be reflected in Figure 11-9. Including these details in the figure would have complicated the exposition and perhaps obscured the fundamental reason for hedging with options: they provide flexibility.

KEY CONCEPT   Options offer a firm protection from adverse changes in prices while at the same time allowing the firm to profit from advantageous price movements.

The benefits of managing strategic risks with derivative financial securities seem self-evident. However, several large international companies still lack even the most elemental protections against strategic risk. The losses of the Korean multinationals are examined in the following highlight.

HEDGING: A TALE OF WON

*D*erivative securities are basic tools for strategic risk management. American firms are experienced users of forward contracts and exchange-traded futures and options. European firms faced with the disruption of the European monetary system have been active newcomers to American futures and options exchanges and have driven trading on European derivative markets up by 66% in 1992.

In contrast, major South Korean firms have not used these derivatives and are heavily exposed to exchange rate risk. Ninety percent of South Korean trade is invoiced in dollars, with most of the remainder invoiced in yen. However, most Korean firms take little action to manage this exposure. For instance, Hyundai, the large auto manufacturer, has had no foreign exchange forward contracts since 1988. Samsung hedges only half of its total exports of $77 billion (which make up 10% of South Korea's total ex-

ports). Samsung Electronics has 50% of its exports in DM and 80% of its imports in yen, but has done nothing to manage its DM or yen exposure.

Why haven't the managers of these firms, who are intelligent enough to develop their firms into world-class competitors, taken advantage of the basic risk-reduction techniques covered in this chapter? First, the foreign exchange markets in South Korea are not well developed. South Korean foreign exchange markets account for less than 0.1% of daily worldwide foreign exchange turnover. Thus Korean managers do not have ready access to local derivative markets capable of handling their hedging needs. Second, and not surprisingly, the managers of Korean firms are not familiar with foreign exchange derivative instruments and how these markets can be used to manage risk. Finally, the government has played a substantial role in limiting the use of hedging instruments. In 1988, in an attempt

to reduce foreign exchange speculation, the government placed stringent antispeculation regulations on using futures and options, which resulted in depriving Korean firms of these instruments.

The lack of foreign exchange hedging has been devastating for Korean firms. Samsung, Yukong, KEPCO, Samsung Electronics, Hyundai Motors, and POSCO each experienced foreign exchange losses of over 20% of their profits during the first half of 1993. The South Korean government, responding to this crisis, is reducing its limits on using financial derivatives. Managers in Korea are also waking up to the tremendous impact foreign exchange volatility has on their profitability. It is hoped that they will take advantage of the financial markets with which their European and American competitors are quite familiar.

SOURCE: "South Korean Corporate Finance: Unhedged," The Economist, October 2, 1993.

Options and Corporate Finance

Before beginning our next topic, we digress from our basic theme of hedging risk and discuss other applications of options theory in corporate finance. Options on a firm's equity do not play a direct role in the company's day-to-day operations. Thus the existence of Hewlett-Packard call and put options has no direct effect on Hewlett-Packard's required rate of return or cash flows. Also, options are not a source of financing to the firm. The presence of options on a company's stock may stabilize the price of the stock in the marketplace,[6] but the financial manager has no direct control over this. Nevertheless, corporate financial managers can use the option framework to give a different perspective on several financial management problems and to provide both qualitative and quantitative guidelines for the manager.[7] Note the following examples.

- The debt and equity of a company can be viewed as options. This perspective offers certain insights into the valuation of these liabilities in the marketplace and is explored further in Appendix 14B.

- Chapter 8 emphasized the importance of the flexibility provided by operating options in capital budgeting. Although it is difficult to define or quantify the value of *flexibility* precisely, most managers agree that flexibility is valuable. In Chapter 8 we saw that a project's "modified *NPV*" is the *NPV* of the project less the value of the flexibility option. However, we did not discuss how the flexibility option should be correctly priced. To know whether a firm has paid too much or too little for investment flexibility (as in the AMG example in Chapter 8), it is important to know how options are priced. Options pricing theory is increasingly used to address these aspects of investment decisions.[8]

- The value of other contingent claims (assets whose value depends on the value of some other asset) can be determined in an options framework. For example, convertibles and warrants can be valued in an options framework.

11-4

INTEREST RATE SWAPS [9]

Consider a corporation's choice between short-term and long-term financing sources. Factors such as the flexibility, cost, and risk of each type of debt should be taken into account before any funding decision is made. What happens, however, if after choosing to finance its current assets with a short-term scheme (such as a revolving credit agreement), the corporation decides to change its strategy and use long-term debt instead? Conversely, what problems arise if the firm wants to convert an existing long-term funding source to one with a shorter maturity?

---

[6] Recent research has documented evidence for this view. See J. Conrad, "The Price Effect of Option Introduction," *Journal of Finance*, June 1989, pp. 487–498.

[7] The use of options for reducing the risk of financial decisions is a problem well treated in the investments literature, and the reader is referred to any good investments text for details on this aspect of options.

[8] See the references provided in Chapter 8.

[9] This section was written by Professors Keith C. Brown, University of Texas, and Donald J. Smith, Boston University. Portions of this section have been adapted from their article "Plain Vanilla Swaps: Market Structures, Applications, and Credit Risk," which appeared in C. Beidleman, ed., *Interest Rate Swaps* (Homewood, IL: Business One–Irwin, 1990). This same volume contains other articles on the interpretation and applications of swaps that the reader may find interesting.

The most straightforward approach to making either of these changes is for the corporation to pay off (i.e., refund) early its present liability position by creating a new liability that has more desirable characteristics. For instance, if the company had originally negotiated with its bank a ten-year loan requiring quarterly interest payments based on a fixed rate of interest, it could refinance this position by directly issuing 90-day commercial paper to investors in the capital market. Of course, if the company actually needed these funds for the entire ten-year period, it would have to refund its new position in three months when the commercial paper matured, possibly with another 90-day commercial paper issue. As an extension of this reasoning, one strategy for securing financing for the full decade would be for the company to reissue commercial paper every 90 days for the next ten years. An immediate consequence of this choice would be that the firm's funding cost would no longer be fixed; it would vary on a quarterly basis as interest rates in the commercial paper market change over time. This could be beneficial if the company expected that future commercial paper rates would generally stay below the fixed rate on its original bank loan. On the other hand, the company would face myriad transaction costs that it would not have if it had maintained its initial position. These new costs include any prepayment penalties on the original bank loan as well as 40 separate placement fees for the commercial paper program (i.e., quarterly issues for ten years).

What Is an Interest Rate Swap?

Swaps are considered to be *interest rate risk management tools* because they give a corporation an efficient means of adjusting the exposure of its asset and liability positions in accordance with changing market conditions. A swap is not a funding transaction; there is no principal payment at origination, no amount borrowed or lent.

An **interest rate swap** is an agreement between two parties—usually a corporation and a financial institution such as a commercial bank—to exchange cash flows on a periodic basis for a specified length of time. The distinguishing trait of this arrangement is the manner in which the cash flows are calculated. In its simplest form, the so-called **plain vanilla swap** requires one of the participants (more commonly referred to as a *counterparty*) to make its payments based on a fixed rate of interest that does not change throughout the life of the agreement. The level of the other counterparty's required payments is then structured to vary with the movements of an interest rate index that changes over time. In practice, several different indexes are used, including the **London Interbank Offered Rate (LIBOR)**, commercial paper rates, Treasury bill rates, certificate of deposit rates, and the prime rate. As the swap market has evolved, the LIBOR is by far the most common variable-rate index used.

To get a better idea of how the swap works, let us consider a hypothetical transaction between two firms that we call Counterparty *A* and Counterparty *B*. The terms of their agreement, which is usually confirmed by a telex between the two companies, are as follows:

Initiation date:	June 10, 1991
Maturity date:	June 10, 1996
Notional principal:	U.S. $20 million
Fixed-rate payer:	Counterparty *A*
Fixed rate:	9.26%

Fixed-rate receiver:	Counterparty B
Floating rate:	Six-month LIBOR
Settlement dates:	June 10 and December 10 of each year
LIBOR determination:	Determined in advance, paid in arrears

The first thing to notice is that this arrangement is scheduled to last for five years and calls for a semiannual exchange of cash flows. In this swap, the floating-rate (i.e., variable) cash flows are based on the LIBOR associated with a six-month borrowing. It is important to recognize that the fixed and floating rates in this deal are not directly comparable. Specifically, the fixed rate of 9.26% assumes a 365-day year, as do U.S. Treasury notes and bonds. On the other hand, the U.S. dollar LIBOR is a money market yield based on a 360-day year. Furthermore, because these rates are annualized, they need to be prorated to the actual number of days that have elapsed between settlement dates in order to calculate the payments. The equations for determining the fixed-rate and floating-rate settlement cash flows are as follows:

Fixed-rate settlement payment

$$= (0.0926)\left(\frac{\text{number of days}}{365}\right)(\$20\text{ million}) \quad (11\text{-}5)$$

Floating-rate settlement payment

$$= (\text{LIBOR})\left(\frac{\text{number of days}}{360}\right)(\$20\text{ million}) \quad (11\text{-}6)$$

Note that both of these equations specify the **notional principal** amount ($20 million). This is simply the dollar amount used to determine the scale of the transaction. It is not actually exchanged between the two counterparties. The notional principal is needed only to translate interest rates into exact settlement cash flows. Once this notional principal and the number of days between settlement dates (number of days) are determined, the complete fixed-rate payment schedule can be calculated. The floating-rate schedule, though, depends on the LIBOR's future levels and therefore cannot be established at the time of the initial agreement.

The usual convention in the swap market is to fix the floating-rate index one settlement date ahead of the payment date. Therefore the floating rate that corresponds to the first settlement date on December 10, 1991, is the six-month LIBOR that prevailed on June 10, 1991. This implies that the next net settlement payment, both the amount and the owing counterparty, is always known six months in advance. Although the swap agreement nominally requires each counterparty to make a payment on every settlement date, the usual practice is to make net settlement payments. On each settlement date, the counterparty with the larger obligation to the other writes one check that covers the difference between the two amounts.

Table 11-7 illustrates this settlement process from Counterparty A's perspective for a hypothetical LIBOR series. The rightmost column of the display indicates the net swap payment or receipt. As the fixed-rate payer, Counterparty A makes (receives) the net settlement payment whenever the bond basis-adjusted level of LIBOR is less than (exceeds) 9.26%. Finally, notice once again that no exchange of the $20 million principal amount takes place at either the inception or the maturity of the swap.

TABLE 11-7

Swap cash flows from Counterparty A's perspective

Settlement Date	Number of Days	LIBOR	Fixed-Rate Payment[a]	Floating-Rate Payment[b]	Counterparty A Net Payment[c]
6/10/91	—	8.25%	—	—	—
12/10/91	183	8.50	$928,537	$838,750	$89,787
6/10/92	183	8.75	928,537	864,167	64,370
12/10/92	183	9.00	928,537	889,583	38,954
6/10/93	182	9.25	923,463	910,000	13,463
12/10/93	183	9.50	928,537	940,417	−11,880
6/10/94	182	9.75	923,463	960,556	−37,093
12/10/94	183	9.50	928,537	991,250	−62,713
6/10/95	182	9.25	923,463	960,556	−37,093
12/10/95	183	9.00	928,537	940,417	−11,880
6/10/96	183	—	928,537	915,000	13,537

[a] Calculated using equation (11-5).
[b] Calculated using equation (11-6). Note that the floating-rate index is one settlement date ahead of the payment date.
[c] Calculated as the difference between the previous two columns.

Swap Market Pricing Conventions

Swap market terminology is an often confusing blend of banking, capital market, and futures market trading vocabulary. Figure 11-10 provides a "box and arrow" picture of a plain vanilla swap agreement, assuming as before that the floating-rate index is a six-month LIBOR and that settlement payments are made semiannually. By convention, the floating-rate side of the exchange is quoted flat, or without any credit adjustment. The two parties to the agreement are designated as the *pay-fixed* (Counterparty A) and the *receive-fixed* (Counterparty B) sides of the swap. It is also common, though not so widely done, to refer to the fixed-rate payer as having "bought" the swap or, equivalently, to have taken the *long* position in the swap. Conversely, the fixed-rate receiver is sometimes said to have "sold," or to be *short*, the swap.

At first glance, it may seem strange to characterize an arrangement in which either counterparty could be responsible for making a net settlement cash flow payment with terms such as *buying* and *selling*. Perhaps the best way to understand this terminology is to recognize that Counterparty A in Figure 11-10 has agreed that on each settlement date in the future, it will receive a LIBOR-based cash flow in exchange for a set amount that depends chiefly on the given fixed rate and the notional principal. Counterparty A can be thought of as having a contract to "buy" LIBOR at each settlement date for the single fixed rate agreed upon at the outset. Similarly, Counterparty B, the fixed-rate receiver, can be viewed as having contracted to "sell" LIBOR on each settlement date for a specified price. In this sense, LIBOR is the traded "commodity" and the fixed rate is its "price."

Another swap market convention evident in Figure 11-10 is that the fixed-rate side of a plain vanilla swap is quoted in the form of two separate components: (1) the Treasury bond yield and (2) a credit spread. The rationale behind this is that, like any other credit-related instrument, the value of the swap is affected if

FIGURE 11-10

Swap market pricing mechanics

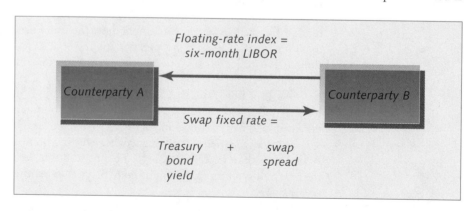

either of the two counterparties defaults on its obligation. Thus, because the Treasury bond yield serves as a proxy for the return on a riskless security, the real issue in setting the fixed rate on a swap is not determining the absolute level but rather the increment over the risk-free yield. This default risk premium is typically called the **swap spread.** The particular Treasury bond yield selected as the base depends on the maturity of the swap agreement. For instance, the fixed rate on the five-year swap agreement we are considering is the yield to maturity of the most recently issued five-year Treasury bond plus the credit spread for swaps with maturities of five years.

One of the most convenient facets of the market conventions just described is that they reduce the quotation of the entire swap transaction to the specification of just the swap spread. In fact, so pervasive is this convention that those financial institutions that serve their corporate clients as swap market makers, or *dealers,* usually quote two different swap spreads: one for deals in which they will pay the fixed rate and one in which they will receive the fixed rate. For example, a dealer might quote five-year swaps at "70–76," meaning that it will "buy a swap at 70 basis points over Treasuries" and "sell a swap at 76 basis points over Treasuries." (Recall that a market maker who enters a swap in which it will be the fixed payer is said to be buying the swap. Thus the *bid* quote is applicable because the bid–ask spread is always interpreted from the point of view of the market maker. On the other hand, the *ask* swap spread is quoted in situations in which the market maker receives the fixed rate.)

Part a of Table 11-8 lists representative quotes for swaps of various maturities. Notice that as the maturity of the swap lengthens, the absolute level of the swap spread increases. Thus it is apparent that at any particular time there exists a term structure of swap spreads in addition to the term structure of Treasury yields. Furthermore, across all maturities the bid–ask differential never exceeds seven basis points. (A basis point is $\frac{1}{100}$ of 1%). Because this spread serves as the market maker's profit margin, it is apparent that the swap market has become quite competitive as it has grown in size and importance since the first swaps were transacted in the early 1980s. Part b of Table 11-8 shows the five-year swap assuming that Counterparty B plays the role of the swap dealer. Barring default by either Counterparty

TABLE 11-8
Swap Market Pricing Conventions

(a) Representative Swap Market Quotes

Swap Maturity (years)	Treasury Yield	Bid Swap Spread	Ask Swap Spread	Effective Fixed Swap Rate
2	7.98%	67	74	8.65–8.72%
3	8.17	72	76	8.89–8.93
4	8.38	69	74	9.07–9.12
5	8.50	70	76	9.20–9.26
7	8.75	71	77	9.46–9.52
10	8.94	73	79	9.67–9.73

NOTE: All swap spreads are quoted in basis points, based on a six-month LIBOR.

(b) The Five-Year Swap Illustrated

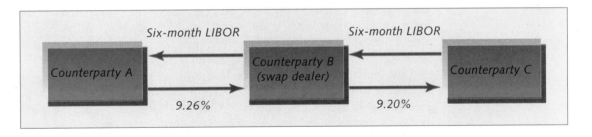

A or Counterparty *C,* the go-between in this transaction is not affected by fluctuations in the six-month LIBOR because these cash flows are simply passed through on each settlement date. The annual compensation for the dealer amounts to the difference between the fixed rate it receives and the fixed rate it pays (i.e., 9.26% − 9.20%, or six basis points) times the notional principal common to the two transactions.

A Basic Swap Application

Although the preceding discussion outlined the mechanics of how the plain vanilla swap market works, it did not explain how these agreements are used. Generally speaking, swaps are considered to be interest rate risk management tools because they give a corporation an efficient means of adjusting the exposure of its asset and liability positions to changing market conditions. All such swap-related adjustments can be put into one of three categories: hedging, speculation, or arbitrage. Although the latter two applications are certainly important in their own right, the usefulness of the swap transaction is best illustrated by focusing on its flexibility for a company that is hedging against the financial consequences of future interest rate movements. The following example demonstrates this point.

Suppose that in order to finance its current asset position, two years ago Company *X* negotiated a five-year bank loan that requires semiannual payments based on a floating-rate index of the six-month LIBOR + 1%. Assume also that when the firm incurred this obligation, its net revenues were closely tied to fluctuations in short-term interest rates. Therefore the bank loan gave the firm a natural hedge against adverse interest rate movements because the characteristics of its liabilities matched those of its assets. Because both revenue and loan payment cash flows would respond quickly to shifts in interest rates, the market values of the assets and liabilities—hence the value of the firm—were not very sensitive to interest rates. Now suppose that there has been a fundamental change in the nature of the firm's assets such that net revenues are expected to be roughly constant in nominal terms over the next few years. This creates a risk mismatch because there is now a different degree of interest rate sensitivity on the asset side of the balance sheet than on the liability side. Clearly, in this case the company is now exposed to the risk that interest rates will increase, thereby raising the interest expense of the bank loan with no compensating increase in revenues.

Company *X* can protect itself from rising interest rates in two ways: (1) issuing a new three-year fixed-rate debt obligation (such as a corporate bond or medium-term note) in an amount sufficient to pay off the remaining portion of the existing loan or (2) combining the bank loan with a three-year, pay-fixed interest rate swap that has semiannual settlement dates timed to match the loan's interest payment dates. There are three reasons that the second solution is preferable from the firm's perspective. First, refinancing the existing loan with a new bond issue requires an additional capital market transaction, which invariably leads to additional underwriting or transaction fees. The interest rate swap, on the other hand, can be made with virtually no transaction costs. Second, without an explicit prepayment agreement with the original lender, there may also be penalties associated with refinancing the loan. Finally, interest rate swaps can be reversed almost as easily as they can be implemented, and consequently they are a more flexible solution to a risk management problem that may be temporary.

The combination of the existing loan and the pay-fixed interest rate swap is equivalent to a synthetic three-year fixed-rate bond with semiannual coupon payments. To see this, assume that the pricing information in Table 11-8 is still valid, and so the market maker's asking quote on a three-year swap against a six-month LIBOR is 76 basis points over the current Treasury yield of 8.17%. Once Com-

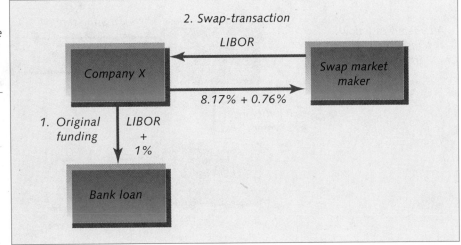

FIGURE 11-11

Transforming floating-rate liability cash flows with a swap

Effective Annual Financing Cost (on a 365-day bond basis)

1. Bond coupon payment:
(LIBOR + 1%)(365/360) =
(LIBOR)(365/360) + 1.014%

2. Swap transaction:
(a) Payment = 8.93%
(b) Receipt = (LIBOR)(365/360)

Net cost of funds = 8.93% + 1.014% = 9.944%

pany X agrees to these terms, two things will happen on each of its remaining coupon payment dates. First, because the original loan is still in place, the firm is responsible for making an interest payment based on the prevailing LIBOR plus 100 basis points. Thus the swap agreement supplements rather than replaces Company X's obligation to its existing creditor. Second, by the design of the swap, the firm receives from its counterparty payments based on the same six-month LIBOR that it must pay out on the loan, whereas its obligations under the swap agreements are payments based on the fixed rate of 8.93%.

These two steps are shown in Figure 11-11. After adjusting for differences in rate-quotation methods, the effective cost of the fixed-rate financing for Company X is 9.944%. An important caveat in interpreting this synthetic fixed rate is that it is not directly comparable with the fixed rate that Company X would have obtained via the direct loan-refunding scheme because it involves credit exposure to the swap counterparty. Barring default on the part of the counterparty, however, the combination of the bank loan and the pay-fixed swap allows the firm to hedge its exposure to rising interest rates.

Alternative Swap Applications and Structures

The example just considered showed how a swap can be used to transform a variable-rate debt obligation into the equivalent of a fixed-coupon bond. Is it also possible to reverse this process—that is, to use a swap to convert a fixed-rate bond to a variable-rate issue? Figure 11-12(a) shows that it is. Suppose that Company Y has the opposite problem of that faced by Company X; namely, it has issued a fixed-rate bond to finance its current asset position but would now like to transform the cash flows it is obliged to pay into ones that vary directly with changes in interest rates. In lieu of repurchasing its outstanding debt issue with new variable-rate debt, the firm can supplement its existing position with a receive-fixed swap that has a maturity and notional principal to match. Notice in Figure 11-12 that Company Y essentially acquires the fixed-rate payment it needs to satisfy its bondholders by agreeing to pay the financial intermediary serving as the swap counterparty payments based on a floating-rate index. In this regard, it is important to keep in mind that the terms of an interest rate swap are fully negotiable between the two counterparties, so that Company Y can end up with payments linked to its choice of any of several different rates, including the commercial paper rate, prime rate, or Treasury bill rate, in addition to the usual convention of the LIBOR.

■
F I G U R E   1 1 - 1 2
*Alternative cash flow
transformations
using swaps*

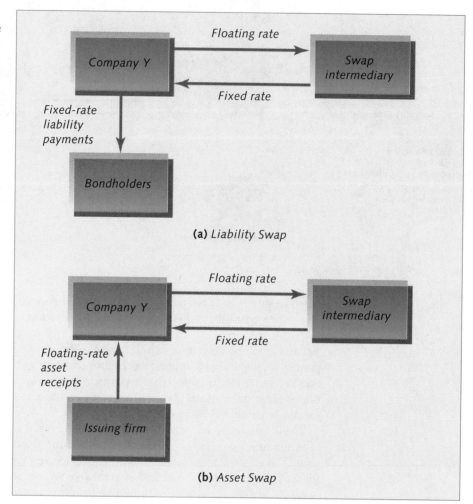

(a) *Liability Swap*

(b) *Asset Swap*

A common feature of the last two examples is that a swap agreement is used to alter the interest rate sensitivity of a firm's liability structure. An alternative use of the plain vanilla swap is to transform the cash flows generated by a financial asset. To see how this is done, suppose that Company Y has traditionally invested its temporary excess cash balances in short-term instruments such as certificates of deposits and Treasury bills. It now wants to convert this revolving, variable-rate asset portfolio into the equivalent of a fixed-coupon bondholding. Figure 11-12(b) demonstrates how this sort of *asset swap* can be accomplished. In essence, the receive-fixed swap allows the firm to collect floating-rate cash flows from its underlying security holdings and pass them through to the swap counterparty in exchange for a predictable set of fixed cash flows. Notice further that this receive-fixed swap was also the solution to Company Y's problem of how to convert its fixed-rate debt to a floating-rate issue. Said differently, the same swap can be attached to either a current asset or a current liability in order to solve a hedging problem.

These examples are indicative of the flexibility inherent in the most basic form of an interest rate swap. However, the fact that these agreements are described as plain vanilla suggests that there are also other more elaborate swap structures. This is indeed the case. There are several well-established departures from the simplest format, including a **basis swap,** in which both rates are floating (e.g., LIBOR versus a commercial paper index rate); a **currency swap,** in which the rates are denominated in different currencies (e.g., a fixed rate in Japanese yen versus U.S. dollar LIBOR); an **amortizing swap** that has a notional principal that declines over the lifetime of the agreement; an **off-market** or **non-par-value swap,** in which one party makes an initial payment to the other; and a **forward swap** that moves the start date of the agreement into the future. Although there are valuable hedging applications associated with these more advanced transactions, a complete description of each is beyond the scope of our discussion.

Credit Risk on a Plain Vanilla Swap

Throughout our analysis of the plain vanilla swap transaction we have referred to the fact that these transactions are subject to default risk. The credit risk on a swap agreement is not at all like that of a capital market instrument of a similar amount and maturity. A swap is not a funding transaction; there is no principal payment at origination—no amount borrowed or lent—and so the initial credit risk must also be zero. Of course, the credit exposure on a traditional debt security is the amount of principal, and this exposure can only decline in the future as principal payments are made. On the other hand, the potential credit risk on a swap is bilateral because the risk exposure starts out at zero but can become a positive amount for either counterparty. At any one time, however, only one counterparty bears the credit risk of the other; that is, the actual credit risk is unilateral.

An example helps to clarify the difference between the potential and actual credit risks of a swap. Consider a five-year, semiannual settlement, $20 million notional principal, 10%-versus-LIBOR interest rate swap between Counterparty *A* (the fixed payer) and Counterparty *B* (the fixed receiver). Suppose that two years and four settlement payments pass without event. Then just after the fourth payment is made, Counterparty *A* falls into serious financial distress. How much will Counterparty *B* lose if the other company defaults on the remainder of the swap agreement? The answer depends on the new price for a replacement swap—a three-year, semiannual settlement, $20 million, fixed-versus-LIBOR swap.

Suppose that under current market conditions, the replacement swap calls for a fixed rate of 9.5% against the LIBOR flat. Note that the replacement fixed rate can be less than the original rate for any number of reasons: a downward shift in the Treasury yield curve, a downward shift in the swap spread curve, or simply movement along the same Treasury yield and swap spread curves (i.e., lower rates for three-year maturities than for five-year maturities). Default on the part of Counterparty *A* means that Counterparty *B* will suffer a loss of $50,000 per period for the remaining six periods (three years). The old swap specified fixed receipts of approximately (depending on the actual number of days in each semiannual settlement period) $1 million, and the new swap, only $950,000. With a 9.5% discount factor, the present value of that annuity is $255,826. Given a replacement fixed swap rate of 9.5%, the actual credit risk exposure to Counterparty *B* is $255,826. That amount also represents the economic value of the swap—a positive value to Counterparty *B* because it has an existing agreement to receive what is currently an "above-market" fixed rate. A swap, though, is a zero-sum game in that the positive value (and therefore the risk) to Counterparty *B* is fully offset by the negative value to Counterparty *A* because the latter is now paying the above-market fixed rate.

Now suppose that the replacement swap fixed rate is 10.5% instead of 9.5%. Notice that the swap under these market conditions has positive economic value to Counterparty A because it has, under contract, an agreement to pay the other firm a "below-market" fixed rate in receipt of the LIBOR flat. The value of the swap is $251,768, slightly less than above, because the same $50,000 annuity now is discounted by 10.5%. The increase in market rates has made the swap an asset rather than a liability to Counterparty A. In this case, Counterparty A (or its bankruptcy trustee) would not want to default on the swap, despite the firm's financial distress, regardless of the LIBOR's current level. Presumably the swap could be assigned to a third party or be closed out by negotiation with Counterparty B to capture some or all of this economic value.

These examples demonstrate that two events are necessary for default loss on a swap: the actual event of default on the agreement and an adverse change in the swap's fixed rate. But those two factors are not mutually exclusive. Some firms, like utilities and thrift institutions, have balance sheets that are notoriously sensitive to interest rates. Therefore the role of a swap in a firm's financial structure can and does matter greatly. A swap used as a hedge can reduce credit risk, whereas a speculative swap can increase it. In any case, both counterparties initially must assess the likelihood of default by the other. This is the sense in which potential credit risk is bilateral.

Concluding Remarks

The simplicity of a plain vanilla swap should not belie its importance as an innovative tool for interest rate risk management, perhaps the most creative innovation of the 1980s, at least in terms of market impact. The extraordinary growth and depth of the swap market can be attributed to the range of its applications—from defensive hedging strategies to aggressive speculative views of future interest rates, to arbitrage transactions that create links between markets. Interest rate swaps over the last few years have passed through the classic stages of market development, from occasional customized brokered deals to standardized plain vanilla intermediated deals. Investment and commercial banks have become active market makers to meet their clients' risk management needs and have developed the analytic techniques necessary to offer a wide range of swap products and variations.

In this section we have shown how interest rate swaps can be used to transform the nature of a firm's current asset and liability positions. A major advantage of using swaps in this manner is that the company is able to affect the desired pattern of cash flows without disrupting its existing balance sheet. It should be noted that other financial instruments, such as exchange-traded interest rate futures and option contracts, are capable of achieving the same results. It is also important to keep in mind that the firm's flexibility in setting the terms of the swap agreement makes it a sufficiently unusual form of contracting to prevent it from being easily duplicated in practice. Consequently, because plain vanilla swaps are likely to be at the forefront of financial innovation for years to come, a thorough understanding of both the instrument and its attendant market conventions seems to be essential knowledge.

A Comparison of the Derivative Instruments

We conclude the chapter with Table 11-9, which summarizes some of the important characteristics of the derivative securities we have discussed in this chapter.

TABLE 11-9
Comparison of Basic Derivative Features

	Typical Settlement (Term)	Type of Contract	Principal	Premiums and Margins	Traded on Exchange?	Obligations to Perform	Benefits/Risks
FORWARDS	Settled at maturity	Custom-tailored contracts	At risk	—No premiums	No	Both buyer and seller obligated to perform	—No secondary markets —Exposed to high credit risk —Downside risk unlimited —Upside potential unlimited —No leverage
FUTURES	Marked to market daily	Standardized contracts	At risk but rarely delivered	—No premiums —Margin accounts maintained —Relatively inexpensive —Round turn commissions	Yes	Both buyer and seller obligated to perform	—Nominal credit risk due to clearinghouse and margin accounts and marked to market —Less than 3% settled —Downside risk unlimited —Upside potential unlimited —No leverage —High commissions (5%–15% of the value of the contract)
OPTIONS	Four three-month trading cycles	Standardized contracts	At risk	—Large premiums —Buyer no margin —Seller margin	Yes and no	Buyer has right but not obligation to perform Seller has obligation to perform	—Downside risk limited to premium —Upside potential unlimited —Very high leverage
SWAPS	One to ten years typical	Custom-tailored contracts	Not at risk	—No premiums —No margins	No	Both buyer and seller obligated to perform	—Imposes some credit risk of other party, however no principal at risk —Replacement cost of missing interest rate stream —Very small secondary market

SUMMARY

Section 11-1: Strategic Risks and Firm Value

What is "strategic risk"? Why should a firm manage such risks?

- Strategic risk arises from the possibility that changes in the firm's economic environment can affect its cash flows. Examples of strategic risks are exchange rate volatility, interest rate volatility, and commodity price volatility.

- Firm value is increased by managerial action that either lowers the discount rate for valuing the cash flows or increases the firm's expected cash flows. The former does not depend on total risk, and hence managers cannot affect the relevant discount rate through strategic risk management.

- Because of market imperfections such as financial distress costs, taxes, and agency costs, strategic risk management can increase the firm's expected cash flows and hence firm value.

What are long and short positions in an asset? What are the payoffs from these positions?

- A firm with a long position in an asset either already holds the asset or is obligated to own the asset in the future. In a long position, there is a direct relationship between firm value and the value of the asset held long.

- A firm holds a short position in an asset when it is obligated to give up the asset in the future. In a short position, there is an inverse relationship between the value of the firm and the value of the asset held short.

Section 11-2: Futures Contracts

What are futures and forward contracts? How can they be used for speculating and hedging?

- Futures contracts are exchange-traded derivative instruments on physical assets, interest-bearing instruments, stock indexes, or currencies.

- By posting a margin, a firm can take a long (short) position in a futures contract to hedge the risk associated with an asset held short (long). As the futures price changes, the firm incurs a profit or loss that is reflected in the value of the margin account, which is changed because of the daily mark-to-market feature.

- Futures contracts result in unlimited upside potential and unlimited downside risk. The cost of a futures contract is the opportunity cost of not being able to take advantage of favorable price movements.

- Forward contracts are generally over-the-counter derivative instruments that, unlike futures, are settled only at maturity. Forwards are less liquid and more expensive than futures contracts. The payoffs from forwards are similar to the payoffs from futures. With the exception of forwards on currencies, they are not as widely used as futures. The cost of a forward contract, as with futures, is an opportunity cost.

Section 11-3: The Basics of Call and Put Options

What are put and call options? How can they be used by the firm?

- Unlike futures and forwards, options provide the holder the right, but not the obligation, to either buy (for a call option) or sell (for a put option) the underlying asset at the exercise price on (for a European option) or before (for an American option) a certain date.

- Options are exchange traded and liquid. Because the buyer pays for the option via the option premium, no margins are involved.

- The relationship between the prices of a call option and a put option is identified by the put-call parity theory. If we know the price of a call option, the theory allows us to infer the price of an equivalent put option on the same stock.

- Hedging and speculating with options allow the firm to protect itself against adverse changes in prices while retaining the potential to profit from favorable price movements.

Section 11-4: Interest Rate Swaps

How can swaps be used to manage interest rate risks?

- An interest rate swap is an agreement between two parties to exchange cash flows on a periodic basis for a specified length of time.

- In a basic swap, one party makes payments calculated on the basis of a fixed interest rate on a notional principal. The other party makes payments on a variable interest rate based on an index.

- A major advantage of using swaps is that a firm can affect the desired pattern of cash flows without altering its balance sheet.

QUESTIONS

1. What are strategic risks and why should managers worry about them?

2. What are some of the factors that justify the practice of corporate hedging?

3. What is the difference between the following pairs?

   (a) Speculation and hedging

   (b) Primary assets and derivative assets

   (c) Long and short positions in an asset

   (d) A spot and a futures price

   (e) A put and a call option

   (f) A European and an American option

   (g) A futures and a forward contract

4. The profits and losses on forwards and futures are identical; the only difference is the manner in which they are realized. True or false?

5. What is the cost of hedging with forwards and futures? What is the cost of hedging with options?

6. It is the standardization of futures contracts in organized exchanges that makes them liquid. True or false?

7. What are the fundamental properties of options? How does the existence of put and call options on IBM stock affect the company itself?

8. What kind of investor buys a call option? A put option? Identify the payoffs to the holder of a call option at expiration. How would the payoffs change if she held a put option instead? Draw the payoff diagrams (at expiration) from holding call and put options.

9. If a manager knew the riskless interest rate, the exercise price of a call option, and its life, what additional information would be needed to determine the price of a put option (on the same stock)?

10. Is a call option worth more than a long position in the same stock? Why? Is a put worth more than a short position in the same stock? Why?

11. Why would a firm want to use interest rate swaps?

12. Do swap transactions involve credit risk? Why?

13. Compare and contrast forwards, futures, options, and swaps on the basis of their settlement terms, whether standard or customized, risk of principal, premiums and margins, the nature of the contracts' obligations, and finally their risks.

PROBLEMS

1. The purchasing agent for Mayfair Bakery, a mail-order specialty confectioner, is arranging for future supplies of wheat. It is now February, and she is making plans for the busy Christmas season. Although wheat currently sells for $3.98 per bushel, Mayfair's major purchases, 60,000 bushels, will be made in September. Rather than waiting and taking whatever the cash market offers, the agent can obtain futures contracts on wheat on the Minneapolis Grain Exchange (MPLS). Each contract is for 5,000 bushels, and the current price on the exchange for September delivery is $4.50. Based on an analysis of market

conditions, the agent thinks this is a good estimate of what the cash price of wheat will be when she makes her September purchases.

(a) Draw three payoff diagrams for the unhedged position, the futures contract, and the hedged position for the following September spot prices: $3.90, $4.25, $4.50, $4.95, $5.25, $5.50. Calculate the profit or loss on the hedge (futures position).

(b) If she does not hedge, what is the expected cost of the wheat purchases in September?

(c) If she purchases wheat futures on the MPLS, what is the cost of the September purchases (including any gains or losses on the hedge) if the cash price of wheat at that time is $4.25? Has hedging helped or hurt Mayfair given this realized September spot price?

2. Tri-Mark Financial Services receives a $1,200,000 payment from a major contract on December 18. These funds are not needed for six days and, rather than putting them into short-term marketable securities, Tri-Mark's Chief Financial Officer (CFO) wants to use these funds to speculate in pork bellies. He purchases 55 contracts. Traded on the Chicago Mercantile Exchange (CME), each pork belly futures contract is for 40,000 pounds and requires a $2,150 initial margin and a $1,800 maintenance margin. The current futures price for February delivery is $0.5380 per pound. The contracts are purchased at this price.

(a) What is the initial value of Tri-Mark's margin account?

(b) Immediately after the CFO purchases the contracts, the government issues a major report on dietary fat that is expected to reduce the public's bacon consumption. On succeeding days after the purchase of the contracts, pork belly futures trade at $0.5312, $0.5300, $0.5120, $0.4998, $0.4887, and $0.4880. Compute the changes in the margin account on each of these days. Assuming that Tri-Mark closes its position at the end of the sixth day, what is its profit/loss on its speculation?

3. Jackne Concrete Co. of New Mexico has purchased 100,000 tons of limestone at 1 peso per pound from a Mexican aggregate dealer. Delivery will be in one month, and Jackne is to pay for the materials within three months after delivery. Exchange rate information obtained by Jackne's financial officer from its bank is given below:

Current spot exchange rate:	$0.31538/P
30-day forward rate:	$0.31987/P
60-day forward rate:	$0.32477/P
90-day forward rate:	$0.32964/P
120-day forward rate:	$0.33185/P

(a) What risk does Jackne face in this transaction? Draw the payoff diagram for the following exchange rates: $0.28000/P, $0.29000/P, $0.30000/P, $0.31000/P, $0.32000/P, $0.33000/P.

(b) Jackne has decided not to hedge its exposure and must decide whether to pay for the limestone immediately upon delivery or wait until three months after delivery to pay. If Jackne expects future spot rates to correspond to the forward rates given above, which payment plan should it adopt? Why is this plan better? What is the dollar difference between these two payment plans?

4. Mid-States Refinery (MSR) produces No. 2 heating oil from Light Sweet Crude Oil. MSR's comptroller is concerned about its gross profits over the next six months. Futures prices on heating oil No. 2 contracts (42,000 gallons per contract) and on Light Sweet Crude Oil (1,000 barrels per contract) on the New York Mercantile Exchange (NYM) for the next six months are as follows:

| | | Future Contracts on NYM | |
| | | --- | --- |
Month	Expected Output (Gallons)	Price per Gallon Heating Oil No. 2	Price per Barrel[a] Light Sweet Crude Oil
January	2,100,000	$0.4380	$14.58
February	2,016,000	$0.4490	$14.77
March	1,806,000	$0.4630	$15.30
April	1,680,000	$0.4625	$15.46
May	1,344,000	$0.4605	$15.84
June	840,000	$0.4610	$16.05

[a] 42 gallons per barrel

(a) If MSR hedges its output, what monthly gross profits (revenues − cost of inputs) are expected in each of the next six months? Given MSR's *RRR* of 12%, what is the present value of its gross profits?

(b) MSR's controller expects energy prices to be 10% higher than is generally expected by the markets. He therefore hedges his purchases of Light Sweet Crude Oil but does not hedge his sales of heating oil. If he is correct, and both heating oil and light crude spot prices are 10% higher than those given in the table, what is MSR's gross profit per month? What is the present value of those gross profits?

(c) Unfortunately, MSR's old controller was wrong in his expectations concerning energy prices, which actually decreased by 15% over the period. As the replacement for the old controller, determine MSR's monthly gross profits and the present value of those gross profits.

5. A distributor has just purchased DM 375,000 worth of fine German beer for the central Ohio market and must pay for the beer in 90 days. The distributor is concerned about changes in the value of the German mark during that period. It has accumulated the following information:

Today's spot exchange rate: $S_0(\$/DM) = 0.5019$

Exchange rate available on three-month futures contract: $F_{1/4}(\$/DM) = 0.5028$

Distributor's estimate of the spot exchange rate in three months: $S_{1/4}(\$/DM) = 0.5050$

Option Information	Call Option	Put Option
Contract size	DM 62,500	DM 62,500
Exercise price	$0.5050/DM	$0.5090/DM
Premium	$0.0010/DM	$0.0012/DM

(a) If the distributor remains unhedged, how much will he expect to pay in dollars for the beer? Draw the payoff pattern.

(b) If currency futures contracts are used to hedge (each contract is for DM 125,000), how much will the distributor pay in dollars for the beer? Draw the payoff pattern for the futures contract and for the hedged position.

(c) If the distributor hedges this exposure with an option, which type of option should he use? Assuming that the distributor's estimate of the future spot rate is accurate, should the distributor exercise this option? If the distributor exercises the option, how many dollars will he pay for the beer? Draw the payoff pattern for the option contract and for the hedged position.

(d) Given your answers to the above questions, which is the better way to hedge the distributor's currency risk?

6. A firm is thinking of purchasing a put option on the DM. The option has an exercise price of $0.5000 and a premium of $0.05. The current spot rate is $0.5300.

(a) Draw the payoff diagram for the option, labeling all of its parts.

(b) Is the option in or out of the money? By how much?

(c) What is the intrinsic value of the option?

(d) What is the time value of the option?

7. A person interested in speculating in the DM has gathered the following information:

Today's spot exchange rate: $S_0(\$/DM) = \$0.5019/DM$

Estimate of the spot exchange rate in six months: $S^*_{1/2}(\$/DM) = \$0.5045/DM$

Option Information	Call Option	Put Option
Contract size	DM 62,500	DM 62,500
Exercise price	$0.5050/DM	$0.5060/DM
Premium	$0.0010/DM	$0.0012/DM

Should he buy a call option or a put option? What will the profits in dollars be from this strategy if one DM option contract is purchased?

8. Gettman Inc., a manufacturer of sports footwear, recently negotiated a ten-year, $5 million bank loan with Texas Commerce Bank (TCB). The loan requires semiannual payments based on a floating-rate index of six-month LIBOR + 1%. Furthermore, the loan contains a covenant stipulating that Gettman should hedge within the next 60 days, to the degree possible, the interest rate risk in the loan. The CFO of Gettman decides to achieve this objective by entering into an interest rate swap, where the firm will receive floating and pay fixed. The swap dealer quotes ten-year swaps at "80–87." The current ten-year Treasury bond yield is 7%.

(a) What is the percentage coupon rate (as a function of LIBOR, on a 365-day basis) received by TCB on this loan?

(b) What is the fixed rate paid by Gettman Inc. to the dealer?

(c) What is the floating rate paid by the dealer to the firm?

(d) What is the net interest cost for Gettman on its borrowed funds?

(e) Can you offer a plausible reason why TCB may want the firm to hedge the interest rate risk when presumably the bank itself could have provided a fixed-rate loan to the firm?

9. Consider a five-year, semiannual settlement, $100 million notional principal, 8%-versus-LIBOR interest rate swap between Firm X (the fixed payer) and Firm Y (the fixed receiver). Also suppose that just after the sixth payment (i.e., after three years), Firm X falls into financial trouble and files for Chapter 7.

   (a) What is the loss per period to Firm Y if the market today offers swaps for a fixed rate of 7.2% against LIBOR flat?

   (b) What is the economic value of the swap?

   (c) If instead the market today offers swaps for a fixed rate of 8.4% against the LIBOR, what is the loss to Firm Y? What is the economic value of the swap in this case?

11A

TECHNICAL ASPECTS OF OPTIONS

Derivation of the Put-Call Parity Relationship

Consider the following two investment strategies:

Strategy 1: Buy a call option (with value C) and sell a put option (with value P). Both options are written on the same stock and have the same exercise price (E) and time to expiration (T). This investment position is worth $C - P$.

Strategy 2: Buy the underlying stock (S) and, in addition, borrow the present value of the exercise price at the riskless interest rate (r). This investment position is worth $S - Ee^{-rT}$.

We now calculate the payoffs from the two strategies when the options expire. In strategy 1, if the stock price exceeds the exercise price, the call option is worth $S - E$ and the put is worthless. Therefore the investment is worth $(S - E) - 0 = S - E$. On the other hand, if the stock price is less than the exercise price, the call is worthless, the put is worth $(E - S)$, and the investment position is worth $0 - (E - S) = S - E$. Thus in both cases, the investment in strategy 1 is worth $S - E$ when the options mature.

In strategy 2, when the debt matures, the total payment due on it is E, and therefore investment strategy 2 is worth $S - E$. Because both strategies have identical payoffs of $S - E$ when the option expires, they must be worth the same amount today; that is, $C - P$ must equal $S - Ee^{-rT}$. This result is the put-call parity relationship.

Bounds on Call Option Prices

A number of basic properties describe option price behavior. Although these properties do not dictate exact option prices, they place important bounds on the possible option price. All of the properties described next are based on the assumption of dominance. For securities of equal risk, if security A gives a return at least as great as that from security B in all circumstances and in at least one situation gives a greater return, then A has at least as high a price as B. If A is priced lower than B, no rational investor will be interested in buying B.

Property 1: The value of a call option (C) is greater than or equal to 0:

$$C \geq 0 \qquad (11A\text{-}1)$$

Because an option is a limited liability instrument, its value can never be less than 0.

Property 2: At expiration, an option's value is the greater of $0 or $S - E$ dollars:

$$C = \max(0, S - E) \tag{11A-2}$$

At expiration, the call holder has the right to purchase the security for the exercise price (E). If the security price (S) is greater than E, the option should be exercised. If S is lower than E, the option should be allowed to expire unexercised.

Property 3: An option's price is always at least as great as its intrinsic value:

$$C \geq \max(0, S - E) \tag{11A-3}$$

If an option sells for less than $S - E$, there is an unlimited arbitrage opportunity in which an investor can buy the option, exercise it, and then sell the underlying securities for an immediate profit.

Property 4: All other variables being identical, an option with a longer time to expiration (T_1) is worth at least as much as one with a shorter time to expiration (T_2):

$$C_{T1} \geq C_{T2} \quad \text{for } T_1 > T_2 \tag{11A-4}$$

Because the longer-term option has all the same characteristics of the shorter-term one, it must be worth at least as much as the shorter-term option is. The longer-term option, however, can still be exercised after the shorter-term one has expired. Therefore it has some desirable characteristics that its shorter-term counterpart does not possess. Consequently, it must be worth at least as much as the shorter-term option.

Property 5: A call option with a lower exercise price is worth at least as much as an option with a higher exercise price, *ceteris paribus:*

$$C_{E1} \geq C_{E2} \quad \text{for } E_1 < E_2 \tag{11A-5}$$

If $S < E_1$ and $S < E_2$, both options are worthless. If $E_1 < S < E_2$, then the option with E_1 has a value of $S - E_1$, and the option with E_2 remains worthless. If $E_1 < E_2 < S$, the option with E_1 is worth more than the option with E_2. Because the option with E_1 is always worth at least as much as the option with E_2, and possibly more, its price must be at least as great.

Property 6: A call option can never be worth more than its underlying asset if the call has a limited time to expiration (T) and an exercise price (E) greater than 0:

$$S \geq C \tag{11A-6}$$

A security can be thought of as an option with $E = 0$ and $T = \infty$. From Properties 4 and 5, we know that both a lower E and a greater T increase an option's value. Options put restrictions on the holder's right to purchase the underlying security by placing a time limit on the option and an exercise price that must be paid. These restrictions ensure that the option can never be more valuable than owning the security outright.

Property 7: In percentage terms, option price changes are at least as great as security price changes. This is true because the investment in the option is less than the price of the security, yet the investor can benefit from the complete movement in the security price.

The preceding seven basic option properties allow us to illustrate graphically the bounds of call option values, as shown in Figure 11A-1.

FIGURE 11A-1

Bounds on call option values

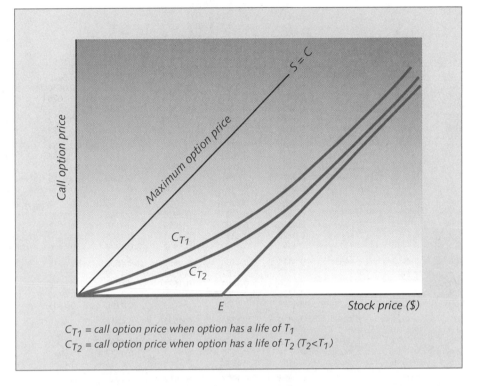

C_{T_1} = call option price when option has a life of T_1
C_{T_2} = call option price when option has a life of T_2 ($T_2 < T_1$)

11B

VALUING OPTIONS USING THE BLACK-SCHOLES MODEL

As we stated in Section 11-3, the value of a call option (i.e., the call premium) on a stock depends not only on the value of the stock on which it is written (S) but also on the life of the option (T), the option's exercise price (E), the risk-free interest rate (r), and the variance of the underlying stock's returns (σ_S^2). Although we discussed these factors earlier to provide some qualitative insight into the value of options, we offered no simple technique for calculating the value of a call option in terms of these variables. To calculate the price of an option in dollars and cents, it is necessary to use the Black-Scholes model, which was developed by Fischer Black and Myron Scholes in 1973.[10] Their contributions, both quantitative and qualitative, have revolutionized finance by giving researchers a new perspective for analysis. The work of Professor Robert Merton has also enabled corporate finance issues to be viewed in a contingent claims perspective. According to the Black-Scholes model, the value of a call option is given as

$$C = SN(d_1) - Ee^{-rT}N(d_2) \qquad (11B\text{-}1)$$

where

$$d_1 = \frac{\ln(S/E) + (r + \sigma_S^2/2)T}{\sigma_S\sqrt{T}}$$

and

$$d_2 = d_1 - \sigma_S\sqrt{T}$$

[10] See F. Black and M. Scholes, "The Pricing of Options and Corporate Liabilities," *Journal of Political Economy*, May–June 1973, pp. 637–654.

■

TABLE 11B-1

N(x) Table

x	0.00	0.01	0.02	0.03	0.04	0.05	0.06	0.07	0.08	0.09
0.0	0.0000	0.0040	0.0080	0.0120	0.0160	0.0199	0.0239	0.0279	0.0319	0.0039
0.1	0.0398	0.0438	0.0478	0.0517	0.0557	0.0596	0.0636	0.0675	0.0714	0.0753
0.2	0.0793	0.0832	0.0871	0.0910	0.0948	0.0987	0.1026	0.1064	0.1103	0.1141
0.3	0.1179	0.1217	0.1255	0.1293	0.1331	0.1368	0.1406	0.1443	0.1480	0.1517
0.4	0.1554	0.1591	0.1628	0.1664	0.1700	0.1736	0.1772	0.1808	0.1844	0.1879
0.5	0.1915	0.1950	0.1985	0.2019	0.2054	0.2088	0.2123	0.2157	0.2190	0.2224
0.6	0.2257	0.2291	0.2324	0.2357	0.2389	0.2422	0.2454	0.2486	0.2517	0.2549
0.7	0.2580	0.2611	0.2642	0.2673	0.2704	0.2734	0.2764	0.2794	0.2823	0.2852
0.8	0.2881	0.2910	0.2939	0.2967	0.2995	0.3023	0.3051	0.3078	0.3106	0.3133
0.9	0.3159	0.3186	0.3212	0.3238	0.3264	0.3289	0.3315	0.3340	0.3365	0.3389
1.0	0.3413	0.3438	0.3461	0.3485	0.3508	0.3531	0.3554	0.3577	0.3599	0.3621
1.1	0.3643	0.3665	0.3686	0.3708	0.3729	0.3749	0.3770	0.3790	0.3810	0.3830
1.2	0.3849	0.3869	0.3888	0.3907	0.3925	0.3944	0.3962	0.3980	0.3997	0.4015
1.3	0.4032	0.4049	0.4066	0.4082	0.4099	0.4115	0.4131	0.4147	0.4162	0.4177
1.4	0.4192	0.4207	0.4222	0.4236	0.4251	0.4265	0.4279	0.4292	0.4306	0.4319
1.5	0.4332	0.4345	0.4357	0.4370	0.4382	0.4394	0.4406	0.4418	0.4429	0.4441
1.6	0.4452	0.4463	0.4474	0.4484	0.4495	0.4505	0.4515	0.4525	0.4535	0.4545
1.7	0.4554	0.4564	0.4573	0.4582	0.4591	0.4599	0.4608	0.4616	0.4625	0.4633
1.8	0.4641	0.4649	0.4656	0.4664	0.4671	0.4678	0.4686	0.4693	0.4699	0.4706
1.9	0.4713	0.4719	0.4726	0.4732	0.4738	0.4744	0.4750	0.4756	0.4761	0.4767
2.0	0.4772	0.4778	0.4783	0.4788	0.4793	0.4798	0.4803	0.4808	0.4812	0.4817
2.1	0.4821	0.4826	0.4830	0.4834	0.4838	0.4842	0.4846	0.4850	0.4854	0.4857
2.2	0.4861	0.4864	0.4868	0.4871	0.4875	0.4878	0.4881	0.4884	0.4887	0.4890
2.3	0.4893	0.4896	0.4898	0.4901	0.4904	0.4906	0.4909	0.4911	0.4913	0.4916
2.4	0.4918	0.4920	0.4922	0.4925	0.4927	0.4929	0.4931	0.4932	0.4934	0.4936
2.5	0.4938	0.4940	0.4941	0.4943	0.4945	0.4946	0.4948	0.4949	0.4951	0.4952
2.6	0.4953	0.4955	0.4956	0.4957	0.4959	0.4960	0.4961	0.4962	0.4963	0.4964
2.7	0.4965	0.4966	0.4967	0.4968	0.4969	0.4970	0.4971	0.4972	0.4973	0.4974
2.8	0.4974	0.4975	0.4976	0.4977	0.4977	0.4978	0.4979	0.4979	0.4980	0.4981
2.9	0.4981	0.4982	0.4982	0.4982	0.4984	0.4984	0.4985	0.4985	0.4986	0.4986
3.0	0.4987	0.4987	0.4987	0.4988	0.4988	0.4989	0.4989	0.4989	0.4990	0.4990

$N(x)$ is the cumulative probability for a unit normal variable calculated at a value of x. $N(x)$ can be easily calculated using standard tables like Table 11B-1, which shows the $N(x)$ values for selected values of x. The following highlight clarifies the use of the table.

The properties of option prices discussed earlier in the context of Hewlett-Packard options are retained by the Black-Scholes model. The value of the call option increases with the stock price, the volatility of the stock, and the life of the option. It decreases as the interest rate decreases and also as the exercise price increases.

As an example of using the Black-Scholes model to find call option values, consider a three-month call option (i.e., $T = \frac{1}{4}$ year) on Teradyne stock, with an exercise price of \$45. If Teradyne is currently selling at \$50 and the risk-free interest rate is 5%, what will be the price of the option? The standard deviation of the rate of return of Teradyne stock (σ_S) is 0.4. We first calculate $N(d_1)$ and $N(d_2)$ and then substitute the appropriate values into the Black-Scholes equation (11B-1):

$$d_1 = \frac{\ln \dfrac{50}{45} + \left[0.05 + \dfrac{(0.4)^2}{2} \right](0.25)}{0.4\sqrt{0.25}} = 0.6893 \cong 0.69$$

From Table 11B-1,

$$N(d_1) = 0.5 + 0.2549 = 0.7549$$

A standard normal probability density function is a normal density function with a mean of 0 and a standard deviation of 1. The bell-shaped curve in Figure 11B-1 is a standard normal density function.

N(x) is the cumulative probability from −∞ to x standard deviations above the mean. The probability contained in the shaded area thus represents the value of N(x). For example, if x = 1.52, then N(1.52) is the shaded area in Figure 11B-2.

Using Table 11B-1, we calculate N(1.52) in two steps. First, look for the value of x closest to 1.52 in the first column of the table. This is 1.5. Then move along that row to the column headed with the value of the second decimal place (0.02).

This yields a value of 0.4357. This is the area from 0 to 1.52 in Figure 11B-2. Second, add to this the area from −∞ to 0, which is 0.5 for a symmetric distribution such as the normal. Thus N(1.52) = 0.5 + 0.4357 = 0.9357.

Calculating N(−1.52) is easy because N(−x) = 1 − N(x). Thus N(−1.52) = 1 − 0.9357 = 0.0643.

■
FIGURE 11B-1
Standard normal probability density function

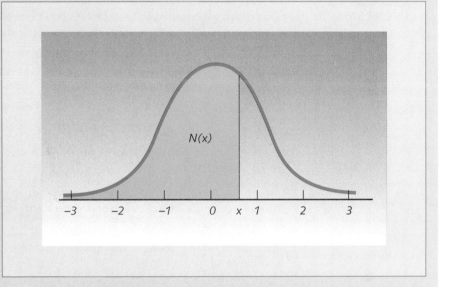

■
FIGURE 11B-2
Calculating N(1.52)

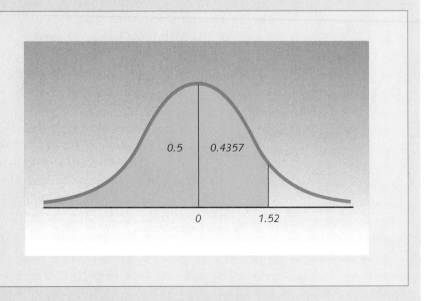

Similarly,

$$d_2 = 0.6893 - (0.4)\sqrt{0.25} = 0.4893 \cong 0.49$$

and

$$N(d_2) = 0.5 + 0.1879 = 0.6879$$

With the appropriate values substituted into the Black-Scholes equation, the call option price is determined to be

$$C = (50)(0.7549) - (45)e^{-(0.05)(0.25)}(0.6879)$$
$$= \$7.18$$

PROBLEMS

1. Consider a call option on the stock of Arkla Natural Gas. The stock currently trades for $22.75 per share. The option has one month to expiration and an exercise price of $20. The riskless interest rate is 5% (annually), and the variance of Arkla's stock is 0.45.

    (a) What is the value of the call option?

    (b) The price exceeds $2.75. Why?

    (c) Suppose the risk-free interest rate was 7% instead of 5%. Find the option's value. Is the result consistent with your expectation, given the discussion in the chapter?

2. Consider a call option on Union Carbide Company's stock. Currently the stock is selling for $28.75. The stock's standard deviation is equal to 0.35 and the risk-free interest rate is 7.5%.

    (a) Find the value of a call option with six months to maturity and an exercise price of $30.

    (b) Redo part (a) for an exercise price of $35.

    (c) The answers to both parts (a) and (b) are greater than 0 even though the option has no intrinsic value today; that is, it is "out of the money." Why does that make sense?

    (d) Repeat parts (a) and (b), but assume that the option has nine months to expiration. What will be found, and why?

3. Consider a put option on the stock of AMR.

    (a) What inputs are needed to value this put option using the put-call parity relationship?

    (b) Given that the one-year risk-free interest rate is 8% and AMR's stock has a standard deviation of 0.31, find the value of a put option with six months to maturity and an exercise price of $70. AMR's stock is currently trading for $68.50 per share.

    (c) Repeat the calculations for part (b) with the following modifications:

    (i) The stock price is currently $67.50 per share.

    (ii) The stock price is currently $67.00 per share.

    (iii) The stock price is currently $65.00 per share.

4. Consider a six-month call option on IBM stock. The following data are provided:

Exercise price: $110

Current market price: $120

Risk-free interest rate: 6%

Variance of rate of return on stock: 0.3

(a) Use the Black-Scholes valuation model to price the call option.

(b) What is the value of the corresponding put option?

SUGGESTED ADDITIONAL READINGS

Black, F. "Fact and Fantasy in the Use of Options." *Financial Analysts Journal,* July–August 1975, pp. 36–41, 61–72.

Black, F., and M. Scholes. "The Pricing of Options and Corporate Liabilities." *Journal of Political Economy,* May–June 1973, pp. 637–654.

Cox, J. C., and M. Rubinstein. *Options Markets.* Englewood Cliffs, NJ: Prentice-Hall, 1985.

Galai, D., and R. W. Masulis. "The Option Pricing Model and the Risk Factor of Stock." *Journal of Financial Economics,* January–March 1976, pp. 53–81.

Hull, J. *Options, Futures and Other Derivative Securities.* Englewood Cliffs, NJ: Prentice-Hall, 1989.

Kolb, Robert W. *Understanding Futures Markets.* Miami, FL: Kolb Publishing Company, 1985.

Mason, S. C., and R. C. Merton. "The Role of Contingent Claims Analysis in Corporate Finance." In *Recent Developments in Corporate Finance,* edited by E. Altman and M. Subrahmanyam. Homewood, IL: Irwin, 1985.

Miller, Merton H. *Financial Innovations and Market Volatility.* Cambridge, MA: Blackwell Publishers, 1993.

Putnam, B. "Managing Interest Rate Risk: An Introduction to Financial Futures and Options." In *The Revolution in Corporate Finance,* edited by J. M. Stern and D. H. Chew. New York: Basil Blackwell, 1986.

Ritchken, Peter. *Options, Theory, Strategy and Applications.* Glenview, IL: Scott, Foresman, 1987.

PART FOUR ISSUING AND VALUING FINANCIAL SECURITIES

TWELVE THE CAPITAL ACQUISITION PROCESS

The Exchange business is comparable to a game. Some of the players behave like princes and combine strength with tenderness and amiability with intelligence, but there are some participants who lose their reputation and others who lack devotion to their business even before the play begins.

—Joseph De La Vega, 1688[1]

[1] From *Confusion de Confusiones* (the first book on exchanges), reprinted in Publication No. 13, Kress Library of Business and Economics, copyright 1957.

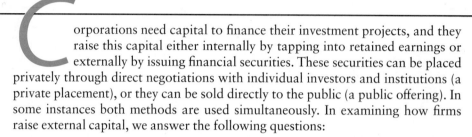

Corporations need capital to finance their investment projects, and they raise this capital either internally by tapping into retained earnings or externally by issuing financial securities. These securities can be placed privately through direct negotiations with individual investors and institutions (a private placement), or they can be sold directly to the public (a public offering). In some instances both methods are used simultaneously. In examining how firms raise external capital, we answer the following questions:

- What decisions must a firm make when it decides to raise external capital?

- What is an investment banker?

- How does the investment banker assist the firm in raising capital?

- How are corporate securities marketed?

- Should the firm raise capital at home or abroad?

- How do markets react when firms issue new securities?

- What is an initial public offering (IPO)? How are IPOs priced?

Appendix 12A contains a quantitative analysis of **rights offerings,** a procedure in which new shares are offered to existing shareholders rather than to the general public.

12-1
THE SECURITY SELECTION DECISION

An Overview of How Firms Acquire Capital

Although this chapter deals primarily with equity financing, the same principles and procedures generally hold true for raising debt. When the applications to the debt and equity markets diverge, the differences are noted and explained. Figure 12-1 gives an overview of how firms may acquire external capital. We examine the various elements of Figure 12-1 as we progress through the chapter.

A firm that needs capital can raise it either as venture capital, through a **public issue** of securites, or through a **private placement.** Venture capital is discussed in Chapter 13, and here we discuss the public and private placement of securities. A public issue can be either a **general cash offer** to investors or a **rights offering.** In a general cash offer, the firm typically employs the services of an **investment banker** to sell its securities to the public for cash. The investment banker is often referred to as an **underwriter.** In a rights offering, the firm offers its securities on a pro rata basis to existing shareholders.

If the firm employs an underwriter, it can either negotiate the offering terms with the underwriter or structure the deal internally and place the offering for **competitive bid.** The resulting underwriting contract can be based on either a firm commitment or a best-efforts agreement. Finally, the issue can be registered with the SEC under traditional registration procedures, or if the firm qualifies, it can file

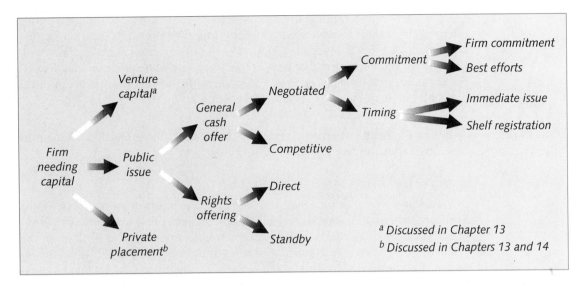

Firm needing capital → *Venture capital[a]*

Firm needing capital → *Public issue*

Firm needing capital → *Private placement[b]*

Public issue → *General cash offer*

Public issue → *Rights offering*

General cash offer → *Negotiated*

General cash offer → *Competitive*

Negotiated → *Commitment*

Negotiated → *Timing*

Commitment → *Firm commitment*

Commitment → *Best efforts*

Timing → *Immediate issue*

Timing → *Shelf registration*

Rights offering → *Direct*

Rights offering → *Standby*

a Discussed in Chapter 13
b Discussed in Chapters 13 and 14

■
FIGURE 12-1
Sources of External Capital

Choosing an Investment Banker

a **shelf registration,** in which the firm preregisters all of the securities it intends to sell during the following two years. We examine these aspects of investment banking in the remainder of this section.

Investment bankers are mediators between the users and suppliers of capital. As such, they are an integral part of the supply-and-demand matching process that drives the capital markets. In addition to possessing valuable knowledge about the "tone" or mood of the markets, investment bankers offer the highly specialized skills needed to "float," effectively and efficiently, a firm's security offering.

After a firm has ascertained its future financing needs, it must decide which type of security to offer. This is a complicated decision and must take into consideration such things as the current market prices of similar offerings, the expected market reactions to the announcement of the new issue, and the flotation costs associated with launching the offering. Flotation costs are investment banking fees, offering registration fees, and other expenses in completing or "floating" the issue. In addition, the firm must decide whether the issue will be sold privately or to the general public. The firm must thus weigh the trade-offs and make the choice deemed most favorable at that time. An investment banker can help the firm in making some of these decisions.

Firms often choose their investment bankers based on their skill in a particular area. When seeking an investment banker, firms consider several factors, including the banker's reputation for successfully marketing similar offerings. Most major investment banking houses engage in a broad range of underwriting activities, although some of them have distinctive competencies within certain industry niches. Firms in those industries are attracted to and courted by those specialized bankers. Like the choice of security type, the choice of investment banker is critical because an association with a highly regarded banker who has industry-specific expertise can greatly enhance the credibility of the company's issue in the marketplace.

After an investment banker has been selected for the offering, the method of distribution must be chosen. Several alternatives are available to the firm, each with its own advantages and disadvantages. In addition to the cost differentials among the various distribution methods, the type of security offered and the likely receptivity of the markets to the issue must be considered.

Firms that are entering the capital markets for the first time with **initial public offerings** (IPOs) face a very different environment than do regular market participants with "seasoned" offerings. Many new issues are from start-up firms with risky, unpredictable futures that have no track record and no past earnings history. For them, making the right decisions concerning the various alternatives outlined in the preceding discussion is vital to their continued existence.

The Role of the Investment Banker

Investment bankers perform important functions in the capital acquisition process: origination, underwriting, and distribution.

ORIGINATION

Once chosen by a firm to float its offering, the investment banker reviews the firm's preliminary decisions, evaluating their appropriateness against the backdrop of current market conditions. The banker's role as adviser and consultant in the origination of the issue is important to its eventual sale. Also at this time, the investment house begins a routine *due diligence* investigation, in which it fully investigates all aspects of the firm seeking to raise capital. Due diligence is important to the investment banker, particularly in regard to new issues, because the investment house is associating its reputation with the issuing firm.

The banker's critical role at this point is to approve or modify the firm's choice of security type to issue and to suggest the issue's initial timing, pricing, and characteristics. For example, given current market conditions, a firm may be advised to offer less equity and more debt or even to substitute debt with special features for a straight debt issue.

The investment house also prepares other marketing and informational material. Because many of the potential buyers are customers of the firm (particularly institutional investors), it is relatively easy for the investment house to "test market" the proposed offering before completing all the required documents and filings.

UNDERWRITING

In an underwritten offering, the initial negotiations between the firm and its investment banker focus on the amount of capital to be raised, the type of security to be issued, and the terms of the offering. If an agreement is reached, the underwriter then begins examining the capital markets to determine the firm's prospects for capital acquisition. The investment banker also procures an audit and a legal opinion from its accounting and legal firms. Typically, the issuing firm, the underwriter, the accounting firm, and the legal firm all participate in filing the SEC registration documents. (SEC requirements are discussed later in this section.)

Investment bankers often assume the risk of the issue, thereby guaranteeing the offering. This guarantee means that if investors fail to buy the entire offering—that is, if it is not fully subscribed—then the underwriter (i.e., the investment house) buys the remaining unsold lots at a previously specified price. This is known as a **firm commitment offering.** Thus, once an underwriter has guaranteed the issue, the issuing company is assured of receiving a specified amount of capital. The risk of the issue's salability is borne by the investment house. As compensation for that additional risk, however, the underwriter receives a larger fee than if there is no guarantee.

When there is no guarantee, the issue is underwritten with only a promise of **best efforts.** This is often done with new, more speculative issues such as initial

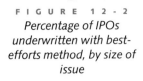

FIGURE 12-2
Percentage of IPOs underwritten with best-efforts method, by size of issue

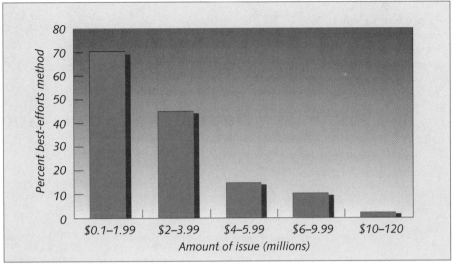

Compiled from J. B. Ritter, "The Costs of Going Public," *Journal of Financial Economics* 19(1987): 269–282.

public offerings (IPOs). If the issue fails to sell out, the issuing company bears the risk of failing to raise enough capital, despite the expenses it has already incurred. Offerings are made on a best-efforts basis either when the investment house deems the issue too risky to guarantee or when the issuer is confident of the issue's salability and chooses to save the higher charge for the guarantee. Between 1977 and 1982, more than 35% of all IPOs were underwritten on a best-efforts basis. As shown in Figure 12-2, the best-efforts method was used almost exclusively for smaller issues. During this period, 1977 to 1982, 72% of all issues less than $2 million were underwritten with the best-efforts method, whereas only 3% of all issues greater than $10 million used this method.

Investment bankers often form underwriting **syndicates** and selling syndicates with other underwriters in order to reduce the risk and increase marketing outlets. These syndicates may be as small as two or three people or, for a very large offering, as large as a few hundred. The hierarchy in an underwriting syndicate is clear from the so-called tombstone announcements of offerings in the business press. According to Figure 12-3, the new issue of 4.6 million shares of Herman's Sporting Goods, Inc., was handled by 80 brokers/dealers. The lead underwriters were Merrill Lynch Capital Markets and Bear, Stearns & Co. The size of the letters indicates these underwriters' greater importance compared with that of the other 78 members of their syndicate. Table 12-1 shows the underwriters of the most issues in 1993. Although the ranking may differ from year to year, these same firms usually make up the top ten underwriters.

The period following the initial offering of a security to the public is known as the **aftermarket,** during which underwriting syndicate members are required by the National Association of Security Dealers (NASD) to sell the shares for the offering price contained in the prospectus or less. Underwriting contracts between the issuer and the syndicate, however, typically stipulate that the new securities cannot be sold for less than the offering price until the syndicate has been terminated.

In order to support the market for and stabilize the price of the new issue, the principal underwriter is permitted to buy securities in the market if the market price falls below the offering price. In addition, if the issue remains unsold after a

■
FIGURE 12-3
Example of tombstone announcement for common stock offering.

NEW ISSUE

4,600,000 Shares

Herman's Sporting Goods, Inc.

Common Stock

Price $16.50 Per Share
The New York Stock Exchange Symbol is HER

Copies of the Prospectus may be obtained in any State in which this announcement is circulated from only such of the undersigned or other dealers or brokers as may legally offer these securities in such State.

Merrill Lynch Capital Markets   **Bear, Stearns & Co.**

Alex. Brown & Sons   The First Boston Corporation   Dillon, Read & Co., Inc.   Donaldson, Lufkin & Jenrette
Incorporated   Securities Corporation

Drexel Burnham Lambert   Goldman, Sachs & Co.   Hambrecht & Quist   E.F. Hutton & Company, Inc.
Incorporated   Incorporated

Kidder, Peabody & Co.   Lazard Freres & Co.   Montgomery Securities   Morgan Stanley & Co.
Incorporated   Incorporated

PaineWebber   Prudential–Bache   Robertson, Colman & Stephens
Incorporated   Securities

L.F. Rothschild, Unterberg, Towbin   Salomon Brothers Inc.   Shearson Lehman Brothers Inc.

Smith Barney, Harris Upham & Co.   Wertheim & Co., Inc.   Dean Witter Reynolds Inc.
Incorporated

F. Eberstadt & Co., Inc.   A.G. Edwards & Sons, Inc.   Oppenheimer & Co., Inc.   Thomson McKinnon Securities Inc.

ABD Securities Corporation   Advest, Inc.   Allen & Company   Bacon Stifel Nicolaus
Incorporated   Stifel Nicolaus & Company, Incorporated

Robert W. Baird & Co.   Bateman Eichler, Hill Richards   Sanford C. Bernstein & Co., Inc.
Incorporated   Incorporated

William Blair & Company   Blunt Ellis & Loewi   J.C. Bradford & Co.   Butcher & Singer Inc.
Incorporated   Incorporated

Cowen & Co.   Dain Bosworth   Daiwa Securities America Inc.   Deutsche Bank Capital
Incorporated   Corporation

Dominion Securities Pitfield, Inc.   Eppler, Guerin & Turner, Inc.   EuroPartners Securities Corporation

First of Michigan Corporation   Robert Fleming   Janney Montgomery Scott Inc.   Kleinwort, Benson
Incorporated   Incorporated

Ladenburg, Thalmann & Co., Inc   Cyrus J. Lawrence   McDonald & Company   McLeod Young Weir Incorporated
Incorporated   Securities

Moseley, Hallgarten, Estabrook & Weeden Inc.   Neuberger & Berman   The Nikko Securities Co.
International, Inc.

Nomura Securities International, Inc.   Piper, Jaffray & Hopwood   Prescott, Ball & Turbep, Inc.
Incorporated

The Robinson-Humphreys Company, Inc.   Rotan Mosle Inc.   Rothschild Inc.

Swiss Bank Corporation International   Tucker, Anthony & R.I. Day, Inc.   Underwood, Neuhaus & Co.
Securities, Inc.   Incorporated

Wheat, First Securities,Inc.   Wood Gundy Corp.   Yamaichi International (America) Inc.

Algemene Bank Nederland N.V.   Banque Bruxelles Lambert S.A.   Banque National de Paris

Banque de Paris et des Pays–Bas   Bayerische Landesbank Girozentrale   Bayerische Vereinsbank
Aktiengesellschaft

European Banking Company Limited   Handelsbank N.W. (Overseas) Limited   Morgan Grenfell & Co. Limited

Orion Royal Bank Limited   J. Henry Schroder Wagg & Co. Limited   Vereins–und Westbank
Aktiengesellschaft

■
TABLE 12-1
Top Ten Underwriters (billions), January–June 1993

1.	Merrill Lynch & Co.	$100.2
2.	Goldman Sachs	68.3
3.	Lehman Brothers	61.2
4.	First Boston	51.2
5.	Kidder Peabody	43.5
6.	Salomon Brothers	42.4
7.	Morgan Stanley	32.8
8.	Bear, Stearns	25.1
9.	Donaldson, Lufkin & Jenrette	17.7
10.	Prudential Securities	13.3

SOURCE: Compiled from data in *Institutional Investor,* September 1993.

certain period of time (usually 30 days), members can leave the syndicate and sell shares at any price they are able to obtain from buyers.

A **green shoe** is a provision in many underwriting contracts that grants to the syndicate the option to purchase a predetermined number of additional shares at the offering price within a certain time period. This option also allows underwriters to cover excess demand for the issue, and so a green shoe represents a benefit to the syndicate and a cost to the issuer. For example, if the market price of the issue exceeds the offering price within the stated time period, then the green shoe provision permits underwriters to buy shares from the issuer and sell them to the public, thereby reaping an immediate, risk-free profit.

DISTRIBUTION AND SEC PROCEDURES

The investment banker has several distribution functions, including fulfilling legal requirements; determining the issue's final size, timing, and pricing characteristics; and selling the issue through the banker's distribution channels.

Most public interstate offerings valued for more than $1.5 million must be registered with the Securities and Exchange Commission (SEC).[2] The SEC requires that a **registration statement,** consisting of the **offering circular,** or the **prospectus,** and other legal documents, be filed before the actual sale. The circular or the prospectus gives investors the company's financial statements, management, history, projections, and intended use of the proceeds.

An offering cannot proceed until the registration statement becomes effective. Oral sales efforts are permitted during the waiting period, but any customer's indication of interest in the offering is not legally binding. No written sales efforts are permitted other than the "**red herring**" prospectus and "**tombstone advertisements.**" The registration statement is typically amended to include the offer price and the date after the SEC has examined the rest of the statement. This allows the firm and underwriter to postpone the effective date of the statement and the price of the issue until they agree that the offering should proceed. Once the underwriter files the offer price with the SEC, the "rules of fair practice" of the National Association of Security Dealers prohibit the sale of securities above this price, although they can be sold at a lower price.

The SEC can withhold approval of the offering until its staff is satisfied that the disclosure in the prospectus is adequate and accurate. The agency does not pass judgment on the merits of the investment, only on the accuracy and adequacy of the information provided. SEC documents require that all risks be made clear to the investor. Thus the typical prospectus is filled with warnings about any riskiness of the investment. The SEC may write a **deficiency memorandum** to the company for anything it wishes changed in the prospectus. The company files an amended statement in response and then must wait at least 20 days before actually making the offer.

During the 20-day **waiting period,** the issuer is permitted to distribute the prospectus without undue publicity, as long as the prospectus carries a warning in red ink that it is not an offer to sell at that time. These preliminary prospectuses are known as red herrings and contain substantially the same information as does the offering prospectus except the price of the offering.

---

[2]The SEC does not require registration for certain categories, including issues sold entirely intrastate; issues that are short term, usually 270 days or less; and issues already controlled by another agency, such as a public utility.

The actual prospectus must be given to all buyers. Most investors seek the counsel of lawyers or accountants in analyzing it. A registrar is usually appointed by the company to record the issue of stock to investors, and transfer agents are named to take care of transferring the new securities.

SHELF REGISTRATION

Because of the time-consuming preparation required for raising public funds, the SEC decided in 1982 that companies may, after the preparation process, wait for up to two years before actually bringing an issue to sale. This concept became known as **shelf registration** because it permitted corporations to leave the offering documents for raising funds "on the shelf" until they were needed.

Shelf registration is extremely popular because of the timing and flexibility it permits. The corporation may respond to a change in the market more quickly when it already has filed all the required documents and obtained approval. This allows the company to meet market needs not only when it believes the market will be most receptive but also in amounts that the market may wish to buy.

Established companies that make issues fairly often are eligible for shelf registration. They file a master registration statement and then follow that with a short-form statement when they actually offer the securities. Shelf registration does not require the corporation to issue the registered securities all at once but, rather, in any partial amounts and at any time it wishes within that two-year period. Firms may also modify their debt instruments and sell them without first filing an amendment to the registration statement. This gives the firms flexibility in both structuring debt issues and timing all security issues.

Shelf registration is used more frequently with debt than with equity issues because if managers and potential shareholders have different information, managers have more opportunities to exploit their information. Stockholders usually anticipate this problem and lower the price they are willing to pay for the stock. Therefore common stock price reactions to announcements of shelf-registered equity offerings are generally more negative than if they are registered according to traditional procedures.

Shelf registration also usually affects the cost of issuing the securities. The fixed costs of public debt issues, for example, should be lower with shelf registration. Studies by Kidwell, Marr, and Thompson and by Rogowski and Sorensen showed, in fact, that shelf registration does lower interest rates on public debt issues by 20 to 40 basis points.[3] One reason for the lower cost according to Kidwell, Marr, and Thompson is that shelf registration increases underwriter competition, thereby lowering the firm's issue costs.

STATE LAWS

Investment bankers also must be sure that their clients are complying with the laws in the states in which they are operating. Many states, such as Ohio, have laws protecting stockholders that are stricter than those set by the SEC. Companies that are issuing stock in relatively new, more speculative issues must be cognizant of the **blue-sky laws** of some states, which are intended to protect state residents from being misled by untrustworthy securities marketers.

---

[3]D. S. Kidwell, M. W. Marr, and G. R. Thompson, "SEC Rule 415: The Ultimate Competitive Bid," *Journal of Financial and Quantitative Analysis* 19 (1984): 183–195; and R. J. Rogowski and E. H. Sorensen, "Deregulation in Investment Banking: Shelf Registrations, Structure, and Performance," *Financial Management* 14 (1985): 5–15.

SETTING THE PRICE

The ease in setting the price of an issue depends on the type of issue. For bonds or other fixed-rate debt, it is fairly straightforward. The bond coupon rate, the stated rate of interest on the bond, is usually set so that the bond price is close to its $1,000 par value. Bond interest rates, in turn, are sensitive to current market interest rates, a relationship examined in Chapter 14.

The pricing of cash offerings of **new equity issues,** or **initial public offerings (IPOs),** however, has no market basis, by definition. The costs of miscalculations can be substantial. If the price is set too low, the company gives up funds it could have received from the offering. But if the price is set too high, the company may have trouble selling its offering and fail to obtain enough capital. Generally, underwriters prefer to err with a price too low rather than with a price too high.

The pricing of **seasoned issues,** which are new issues of stock in a firm that already has publicly traded stock, is based on market prices. Investment bankers must balance the size of the offering against the potentially dilutive effects on ownership and earnings. When there is a dilutive effect, it lowers the price of all the company's stock, not just that of the new issue. Financial theorists have debated the extent of this effect. The prospect of an influx of capital into a company, which could have promising intended uses, could alter perceptions of the company and, as a result, affect its stock price. In general, however, new issues are generally sold at below-market prices.

Flotation Costs   The costs of raising capital consist of the underwriters' spread and administrative costs. Underwriters typically earn their fee, expressed as a percentage of the whole deal, by buying the offering at a discount from the actual offering price. The "spread" between those two costs is their income. Administrative costs consist of legal and accounting fees, printing costs, and other expenses.

Fees vary according to the size of the offering, the underwriter, and the type of offering. The larger the offering is, the smaller the underwriters' fees are as a percentage of the gross proceeds. Administrative fees drop sharply as a percentage of transactions as they grow larger, reflecting economies of scale. Many of the administrative costs, such as attorneys' fees for due diligence, require a minimum number of hours of work, regardless of the size of the transaction. Printing costs, which require high front-end expenses, increase at small increments with the volume after reaching a certain amount. For rights offerings, investment bankers receive the **standby commitment fee,** which is based on the total number of shares to be distributed, and other fees as appropriate.

Investment house pricing policies differ. Morgan Stanley, for example, is known on Wall Street for charging higher fees than do many of its counterparts. Its rationale is that its transaction–employee ratio is lower. Thus customers pay for more personalized attention. Also, on new issues, some investment bankers receive additional compensation in the form of options for stock in the company at a future date. For example, suppose that an investment banker holds a three-year option to buy a new company's stock for its $20 initial public offering price. If the company's stock price rises to $30 a share in the intervening three years, the investment banker may choose to exercise the option at $20 and thus make an instant $10 profit (on paper anyway because the banker has not sold the stock yet) and thus reap an additional profit from underwriting the issue.

Studies show that the flotation costs associated with underwritten equity issues are 3 to 30 times higher than the costs of nonunderwritten rights issues. Despite this tremendous cost differential, over 80% of the firms that issue equity employ investment bankers to handle their offerings. This is often referred to as the *equity underwriting paradox.*[4] A popular explanation for this paradox is that investment bankers are good at monitoring a firm's activities, and this monitoring can be valuable because of the different values of information to managers and to outside stockholders. Although monitoring is expensive, it is deemed justifiable because the periodic surveillance of a firm's managers raises the price that external stockholders are willing to pay for the firm's security.

Equity cash issues are the most expensive offerings. Offerings of less than $2 million can cost the issuer between 7% and 13% of gross proceeds for the underwriting cost and another 4% to 9% in administrative charges. Offerings larger than $10 million, however, are much less expensive, with underwriter compensation of less than 5% and administrative costs falling to less than 1% of the total proceeds.

Rights issues are somewhat less expensive than general cash offerings for issues up to $20 million. Beyond $20 million, the cost advantage largely disintegrates, and the fees are about the same as those for general cash offers.

Except for the smallest offerings, bond issues are significantly less expensive than equity offerings, with underwriting costs falling to less than 2% of the gross proceeds for issues over $5 million. Administrative expenses are similar to those of general cash offerings.

Private offerings are substantially cheaper than public ones because of savings in SEC filings and other requirements. As a rule of thumb, private offerings cost about one-fourth to one-half of the cost of public offerings.

Negotiated Versus Competitive Bid Contracts

Public utility holding companies are required to sell securities through competitive bid unless exempted by the SEC. Exemptions are granted only if the firm cannot secure competitive bids or if market conditions are deemed "unsettled." The empirical evidence suggests that total flotation costs are higher for firms that use negotiated offerings, by 1.2% of the proceeds.[5] In addition, in negotiated offerings, each component of the total cost is higher.

Although the evidence indicates that competitive bid offerings are much cheaper to float than underwritten offerings are, the major users of competitive bids are firms that are required to do so by regulation. Firms that are not required to use competitive bids almost exclusively select negotiated offers; 97% of equity and 85% of debt and preferred stock public offerings are issued through negotiated underwriting contracts.

There are two explanations for this preference for negotiated underwriting contracts. First, Bhagat and Frost suggest that this behavior is because of differences in managers' and shareholders' incentives and the costs of controlling managers.[6] They believe managers may benefit from (1) under-the-table payments from investment bankers, (2) increased compensation if tied to accounting profits, and (3) less variation in cost (if managers are risk averse).

Alternatively, Smith found an information asymmetry between managers and shareholders that produces a need for monitoring.[7] In a competitive bid offering,

---

[4] See C. W. Smith, Jr., "Investment Banking and the Capital Acquisition Process," *Journal of Financial Economics* 15 (1986): 3–29; and Robert S. Hansen, "The Demise of the Rights Issue," *Review of Financial Studies* 1 (1989): 289–309.

[5] See Dennis E. Logue and Robert A. Jarrow, "Negotiation vs. Competitive Bidding in the Sale of Securities by Public Utilities," *Financial Management* 7 (1978): 31–39.

[6] Sanjai Bhagat and Peter A. Frost, "Issuing Costs to Existing Shareholders in Competitive and Negotiated Underwritten Public Utility Equity Offerings," *Journal of Financial Economics* 15 (1986): 233–260.

[7] C. W. Smith, Jr., "Investment Banking and the Capital Acquisition Process," *Journal of Financial Economics* 15 (1986): 3–29.

the firm specifies the details of the offering, which enables managers to use their privileged information to set the terms without negotiating with investment bankers. Potential shareholders usually recognize this control factor and accordingly reduce the price they are willing to pay for the issue. Because the monitoring provided by investment bankers through the negotiated contract is valued by outside shareholders, firms have a greater incentive to use negotiated offerings, despite the higher flotation costs.

Rights Offerings   In rights offerings, the new shares are offered to existing shareholders rather than to the general public. Some firms stipulate their preemptive rights in their corporate bylaws. The purpose of these rights is to protect the interests of existing holders by requiring that any equity distributions, such as a new stock offering, be offered first to the owners of the outstanding shares. The procedure for such a distribution through a rights offering differs from that of a cash offering only slightly in preparation but substantially in the selling process.

Typically, each shareholder receives options to buy the newly issued securities in the form of a "right" issued for each share held. The contract that supports the offering states the number of rights required to purchase a unit of the newly issued security, the exercise price, and the expiration date. Rights offerings must also be registered with the SEC, and the rights themselves can be traded, usually on the same exchange as the underlying security.

Rights offerings can be underwritten or nonunderwritten. In a nonunderwritten rights offering, firms avoid paying underwriting fees by directly marketing the new shares to current shareholders, but the gross proceeds of the offering are not guaranteed. In an underwritten rights offering, or a standby offering, the underwriter guarantees the gross proceeds by agreeing to purchase and resell all shares not sold through the rights offering. This protects the firm from undersubscription, which can result from the shareholders failing to exercise their rights. Although both types of rights offerings incur very low flotation costs, stock prices usually fall by approximately 4% at the time of the announcement and rise approximately 2% soon thereafter.[8] Thus shareholders incur extra flotation costs through the decline in the value of their stock, which make rights offerings even more expensive than underwritten public issues. (In Appendix 12A we examine the rights offering process in greater detail.)

12-2

CHOOSING A CAPITAL MARKET

After a firm has chosen its investment banker, it must determine the capital markets in which it will market the security.

For a corporation, one of the major objectives in issuing a financial security is to obtain the best price. For equity, this means issuing the security at the highest price possible, thus gaining the most capital for the amount of control surrendered and the dilution of earnings to existing shareholders. For debt, the firm wants to pay the lowest amount of interest on the capital borrowed. Increasingly, the pursuit of the best price involves an examination of which capital markets throughout the world offer the best deal for the corporation. (Examples of several equity markets were given in the highlight in Chapter 5.) In making this decision, the firm and its investment banker must first determine the degree to which these capital markets are integrated—that is, the degree to which the prices of securities issued in these different markets are the same.

---

[8] See Hansen, "The Demise of the Rights Issue."

If capital markets are integrated, they offer similar risk–return relationships, similar average price–earnings ratios, and similar real interest rates. This integration would have implications for the corporation and its investment banker. They would find the same real price for their newly issued securities in all capital markets throughout the world and would therefore be indifferent about which market issues their securities. However, research has shown that world capital markets are not integrated. Instead they are to a significant degree **segmented,** meaning that they offer different risk–return trade-offs and thus different prices for newly issued securities. Differences in capital markets were discussed in Chapter 6, with the low correlations among major markets shown in Table 6-2. These low correlations show that the markets are different in their price movements and thus offer different opportunities to both investors and corporations. Managers must therefore understand the causes of market segmentation and how these causes affect their choice of a capital market.

Reasons for Market Segmentation

Most markets exist within national economies and are affected by the legal, cultural, and economic environments of their home countries.

The United States has a well-developed system of laws and regulations that govern the issuance and trading of financial securities. These laws require a substantial amount of disclosure about firms wishing to issue securities that can be traded publicly, and they also limit behaviors such as collusion among groups of investors and trading by managers using insider information. Many other nations do not have such severe laws, and thus foreign companies are often reluctant to list their securities in the United States in order to avoid these laws.

Systems of accounting also differ from one country to another. For example, German companies are permitted to hold "hidden" reserves, which are reserves not disclosed in their financial statements that can be drawn upon to smooth out earnings over time. These are not acceptable under American accounting procedures for public corporations. Accounting statements issued by German firms could be misleading if read by an American investor unfamiliar with German conventions for handling depreciation, inventory, and retained earnings.

Capital markets may have different conventions and procedures for conducting trades. For instance, the New York Stock Exchange allows continuous trading on all securities. The Paris Bourse previously used a "call" system, which meant that a stock could be traded only twice a day when its name was called. The London exchange, which used to have a trading floor, now uses computer trading entirely. These differences in the trading and functioning of markets discourage investors from moving freely between markets, and thus create different market conditions for financial securities. To these technical difficulties can be added the substantial differences in the size and liquidity of markets.

A corporation's desire and ability to issue financial securities are also affected by legal, cultural, and structural differences among countries. In several European countries, unlike in the United States where it is illegal, it is common practice for banks to hold substantial equity positions in corporations and to develop long-term relationships with these corporations. This has led to much greater use of debt in these European companies, which affects the functioning of their capital markets in general.

Finally, both investors and corporations that wish to operate in foreign markets must deal with foreign exchange risk. As discussed in our treatment of capital budgeting, the home-currency value of cash flows is significantly affected by changes in exchange rates.

*Trends in Market
Integration*

Market segmentation, which is a type of imperfection we talked about in Chapter 1, presents opportunities for exploitation. However, as with all market imperfections, cumulative acts of exploitation lead to a reduction in the imperfection. As multinational corporations seek out differences in capital markets, we should see a tendency for capital markets to become less segmented in the future. An example of a type of corporate action that will lead to more integrated capital markets is given in the highlight.

FOREIGN COMPANIES LISTING ON THE NYSE: THE CASE OF DAIMLER-BENZ

On October 5, 1993, the shares of Daimler-Benz AG began trading on the New York Stock Exchange. This event marked a change in European attitudes toward American markets and shows the benefits and costs of firms raising funds in segmented markets.

Benefits

Daimler-Benz was driven to list on the NYSE because of its urgent demand for capital. It had to go where the money was. Interest rates in the United States were low because of low inflation and slow economic growth. These low rates sent American investors searching for higher returns in the bond and stock markets, raising the price they are willing to pay for these instruments, thus benefiting the firms issuing these securities. Besides the cheap capital, the U.S. market is also very large and liquid, with large numbers of sophisticated investors with funds to invest.

Given these conditions, Daimler-Benz found that it could gain capital to raise its profits, expand its stockholder base, and thus raise its stock price. After its listing announcement, Daimler-Benz stock rose 30%, much more than the rise in the Dow Equity Market Index for Germany, which rose only 11% over the same period.

That other foreign firms are joining Daimler-Benz in U.S. markets can be seen in Figure 12-4, which shows the growth in foreign offerings of financial securities over the past 14 years.

Costs

Foreign participation in U.S. capital markets is not without costs. One of the major costs to a foreign firm is the conversion of its accounting system to provide the substantial amount of information required by U.S. security laws. According to Daimler-Benz's chief financial officer, "There's a big gap between German accounting standards and U.S. principles. U.S. accounting discloses so much more and tells you what's really happening in a company." Prior to its NYSE listing, Daimler-Benz could use "hidden" reserves, reserves that had been accumulated from previous earnings but not recorded as earnings, to smooth out its reported earnings. Its switch to more stringent American accounting methods caused it to report a first-half loss of $592 million, its first loss since the end of World War II.

Changing accounting methods may be so costly as to discourage foreign firms from following Daimler-Benz. For instance, Germany's largest bank, Deutsche Bank, has a 28% ownership stake in Daimler-Benz and similar large holdings in

other German companies. For Deutsche Bank to list in the United States, it would have to issue financial statements consolidating these holdings.

The Future of Market Segmentation

The participation of foreign companies in foreign capital markets will continue to grow. One major factor in this growth is the accelerating pace of privatization of formerly state owned or controlled industries. These industries must seek out markets large enough to provide the capital needed to accomplish privatization. For instance, YPF, the Argentine Oil Company, was privatized in 1993 in the world's largest initial public offering. Of the $3.04 billion of stock issued, 75% was placed outside Argentina. While, as with Deutsche Bank, the costs of issuing in foreign markets may prevent some firms from taking advantage of the benefits offered, many corporations will increasingly "shop around" for the capital they need.

SOURCE: Anita Raghavan and Michael R. Sesit, "Financing Boom: Foreign Firms Raise More and More Money in the U.S. Market," The Wall Street Journal, Tuesday, October 5, 1993. Reprinted by permission of The Wall Street Journal, © Dow Jones & Company, 1993. All rights reserved, Worldwide.

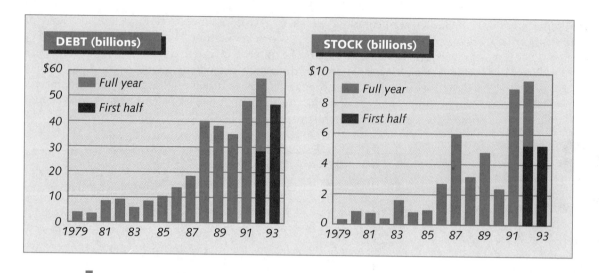

■
FIGURE 12-4
*Public and Private Foreign
Security Offerings in
U.S. Markets*

12-3

RECENT TRENDS IN PUBLIC OFFERINGS

Between 1984 and 1988, $1.137 trillion of capital was raised in the United States through 16,824 transactions involving issues of common stock, preferred stock, IPOs, straight debt, and convertible debt. Figure 12-5 shows the percentage of the total amount of capital raised during this period for each of these different types of securities. As the chart reveals, straight debt issues completely dominated all other security issue types during this period, accounting for over 72%, or $826.6 billion, of the total capital raised between 1984 and 1988.

Because capital market prices provide critical signals for corporate investment decisions, it is important that a corporation correctly gauge the market reaction to the announcement that it is entering the markets to raise capital. Common sense suggests that firms enter the capital markets to obtain long-term financing for positive-*NPV* projects. As a result, one would expect that the announcement of external financing would cause a firm's market value to rise.

■
FIGURE 12-5
*Percentage of capital
raised by security type,
1984–1988*

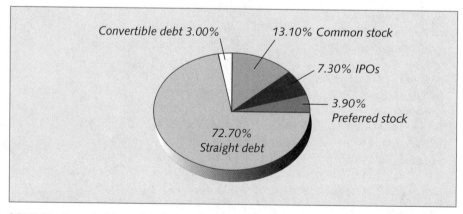

SOURCE: Compiled from data in *Investment Dealers' Digest*, January 9, 1989, pp. 27–31.

	Type of Issuer	
Type of Security Offering	Industrial	Utility
Common stock	−3.14	−0.75
Preferred stock	−0.19	+0.08
Convertible preferred stock	−1.44	−1.38
Straight bonds	−0.26	−0.13
Convertible bonds	−2.07	n.a.

TABLE 12-2
Average Two-Day Abnormal Stock Returns from Studies of Announcements of Security Offerings

SOURCE: Compiled from C. W. Smith, Jr., "Investment Banking and the Capital Acquisition Process," *Journal of Financial Economics* 15 (1986): 3–29.

The Market's Reaction to Security Issues

One study (see Table 12-2) of two-day common stock price reactions to the announcement of public issues of common stock, preferred stock, convertible preferred stock, straight debt, and convertible debt by industrial and utility firms observed the following four generalizations:

1. Average abnormal returns were negative.

2. Abnormal returns associated with common stock sales were negative and were larger than those associated with preferred stock or debt.

3. Abnormal returns associated with convertible bonds were negative and were larger than those observed for straight securities.

4. Abnormal returns associated with industrials were negative and were larger than those for utilities.

Explaining the Market's Reaction to Security Issues

There are several hypotheses to explain this pattern of stock price effects.

The **optimal capital structure hypothesis** holds that there is an optimal capital structure—a mix of debt and equity—that maximizes the value of the firm [9] and that market reactions to the announcement of new security issues reflect the change in the firm's value associated with the change in the firm's capital structure. Reductions in firm value associated with voluntary security sales are puzzling, however. Security offerings may be an optimal response to an adverse change in a firm's prospects, with the negative price reaction reflecting the adverse change. But it is difficult to test optimal capital structure hypotheses by observing stock price reactions to announcements of security issues. Therefore the study of security sales produces very weak tests of the optimal capital structure hypothesis.

The **implied cash flow change hypothesis** postulates that stock price reactions offer information about a firm's future net operating cash flows. Because a firm's sources must equal its uses of funds, a cash inflow from a security sale must be matched by a cash outflow from a new investment, a liability reduction, a dividend increase, or a reduction in net operating cash flow.

In general, the empirical evidence is consistent with the hypothesis that participants in capital markets make inferences about changes in operating cash flows from announcements that do not explicitly match the sources and uses of funds. Therefore unexpected security sales are generally associated with smaller than expected operating cash flows and thus are bad news for investors. This expected bad news is subsequently reflected in negative stock price reactions to announcements of security sales.

The **unanticipated announcement hypothesis** states that stock price changes reflect only the unanticipated part of the announcement. Therefore the more predictable the event is, the smaller the associated stock price change will be. Studies have found that new debt issues are more likely to be predictable than new equity

[9] We examine this topic in detail in Chapter 15.

issues are because principal repayments are more predictable than earnings. Studies have also found that utilities are likely to tap external capital sources more frequently than industrials are, and thus their security sales are more predictable than industrials' sales are.

The **information asymmetry hypothesis** indicates that corporate managers have more information than securities purchasers do and so are more likely to issue new securities when they are overpriced in the market.

Because debt and preferred stock are more senior claims, their values are less susceptible to changes in firm value than is the value of common stock. Similarly, convertible issues are more susceptible to changes in firm value than are nonconvertible issues but are less susceptible than is common stock. Also, because utilities are required to petition their regulatory agencies for permission to issue new securities, the price reaction to utilities' announcements, versus industrials' announcements, should be smaller. The empirical evidence is consistent across classes of securities with the information asymmetry hypothesis, although some data within security classes are not consistent.

The **ownership changes hypothesis** states that transactions that affect the distribution of control rights in a firm affect its share prices. Part of the observed price reaction in some transactions reflects important changes in ownership and control. On average, studies indicate that organizational restructuring benefits a firm's stockholders. Indeed, the evidence suggests that announcements of transactions that increase ownership concentration result in higher share prices, whereas the reverse is true of dilutive transactions.

Note that these hypotheses are not mutually exclusive. Thus elements of more than one hypothesis may explain the price reactions of common stock to various security issue announcements. Selecting the appropriate security to issue depends on the firm's optimal capital structure, its projections of future financing needs, and current market signals. Because the type of security selected is likely to have a significant impact on the firm's current common stock price, it is a decision that must be made with great care and only after much study.

12-4

INITIAL PUBLIC OFFERINGS (IPOS)

Private firms have two major alternatives: to remain private or to go public. Private firms that elect to go public usually obtain the services of an investment banker to launch an initial public offering (IPO) of equity.

Unique Traits of IPOs

IPOs differ from previously discussed security offerings in two ways:

1. The uncertainty of the market price for IPOs is significantly greater than it is for corporations with currently traded shares. This uncertainty is because most IPOs are floated by firms that have little or no earnings history and also uncertain futures. Often these firms are start-up companies with no product or with only one product that has an unknown demand. Floating an issue for a firm like this is extremely risky.

2. Because the firm issuing the IPO has no currently traded shares, it is impossible to examine stock price reactions to new issue announcements. This, of course, makes pricing new issues very difficult and leads to the widely held conclusion that IPOs are purposely underpriced by investment bankers so that they will be sold quickly.

Reasons for Underpricing

Several empirical studies indicate that the average IPO is offered at a 15% or greater discount from the price expected in the aftermarket, with aftermarket returns appearing to be normal. Several hypotheses have been developed to explain this phenomenon.

The **risk-averse underwriter hypothesis** states that investment bankers purposely underprice IPOs in order to reduce the risks of being stuck with an unsuccessful offering and its associated losses. The empirical evidence, however, fails to support this theory. If the principal reason for underpricing is the desire to reduce risk, one would expect only firm-commitment IPOs to be underpriced. Likewise, best-efforts IPOs should be higher priced because the investment banker's risks are minimal in such an agreement. However, a study by Ritter indicates that best-efforts IPOs are priced even lower than are firm-commitment offerings.[10]

The **monopsony power hypothesis** states that the gross underpricing of IPOs may be the result of the monopsony power of the investment bankers that underwrite the common stocks of small, speculative firms. This conclusion is based on the observation that large, well-known investment bankers seldom choose to underwrite the offerings of equally large, well-known firms. According to this hypothesis, the IPO market is segmented, and the IPOs of small firms are underwritten by investment bankers who exert great bargaining power over the issuers. These bankers intentionally underprice new issues and keep them for their own large, regular customers.

There are three apparent flaws in this theory. First, the hypothesis fails to explain why reputable investment bankers seldom underwrite IPOs for small, speculative firms. Second, market segmentation does not automatically guarantee monopsony power. Third, the hypothesis implies that issuers are unable to learn from past experience and seek investment bankers who price their new issues higher.

According to the **speculative bubble hypothesis,** excess returns are deemed to result from the speculative demand of investors who are unable to obtain shares of oversubscribed IPOs at the offering prices from their underwriters. That is, upon issuance, the prices of securities are consistent with their true economic value, but then they are pushed well above this intrinsic value by speculation in the aftermarket. The speculative bubble hypothesis predicts that the initial positive excess returns generated by IPOs will be followed by negative excess returns at a later date when the "bubble" bursts. There is, however, no empirical evidence to support this hypothesis. All studies thus far have indicated that the returns of IPOs in the aftermarket are virtually indistinguishable from those of more seasoned equities.

The **asymmetric information hypotheses** are based on two competing viewpoints: the Baron model and the Rock model.[11] The Baron model assumes that investment bankers possess more knowledge about investors' demand for securities than do issuers. In addition, the model indicates that an investment banker's reputation helps certify the quality of an issue and generate a demand that otherwise may not exist. Also included in this model is the assumption that the issuer lets the underwriter set the offering price because of its superior knowledge of the capital markets. In return for the use of this superior information, the issuer must compensate the investment banker by allowing it to offer the issue at a discount from its expected aftermarket price. The model describes the discount as increasing

[10] See J. B. Ritter, "The 'Hot Issue' Market of 1980," *Journal of Business* 57 (1984): 215–240.

[11] See D. P. Baron, "A Model of the Demand for Investment Banking Advising and Distribution Services for New Issues," *Journal of Finance*, September 1982, pp. 955–976; and K. Rock, "Why New Issues Are Underpriced," *Journal of Financial Economics*, January–February 1986, pp. 187–217.

with the issuer's uncertainty about the market demand for its offering and predicts greater average underpricing as this uncertainty increases. Empirical evidence does not support the Baron model.

The Rock model is also based on an asymmetric information assumption but focuses on the disparity in the quality of information among investor groups instead of between issuers and their investment bankers. The model assumes that there are two groups of potential investors: informed and uninformed. Informed investors buy IPOs only when they expect the aftermarket price to exceed the offering price. Conversely, uninformed investors indiscriminately subscribe to every IPO. Because there is always uncertainty concerning aftermarket prices, an attempt to issue all IPOs at expected market-clearing prices would result in uninformed investors' regularly purchasing disproportionately larger amounts of overpriced issues when compared with the purchases of informed investors. Thus, according to the Rock model, investment bankers must offer IPOs at discounts from their expected aftermarket prices in order to keep the uninformed investors in the IPO market. Rock's model, like Baron's, also showed that underpricing increases with market uncertainty. Also, as was the case with Baron's model, the empirical evidence fails to support the hypothesis purported by Rock's model.

The **insurance hypothesis** states that underpricing serves as a type of insurance that insulates issuers and their investment bankers from any legal liability and/or damage to reputation that may result from floating an IPO.[12] Potential legal liabilities pose serious threats to investment bankers. Because due diligence investigations for start-up firms are difficult and uncertain, the costs of legal liabilities associated with IPOs can be high. The lack of information about start-up firms makes it difficult to meet the standards imposed by law for diligence investigations, which results in a considerable risk of legal liability to firms and their investment bankers.

An obvious means of protection would be for the issuer and its investment banker jointly to purchase an insurance policy protecting them from any claims that result from the IPO. But owing to the subjectivity of due diligence investigations, it is unlikely that the investment banker and the insurance company could arrive at a mutually agreeable definition of due diligence. Therefore it seems unlikely that an explicit insurance policy could be procured. According to the insurance hypothesis, the issuer and the underwriter may more efficiently use underpricing as an implicit form of insurance to protect themselves against potential legal liabilities and the associated damage to their reputations.

SUMMARY

Section 12-1: The Security Selection Decision

What decisions must a firm make when it decides to raise external capital?

■ Firms that need capital must either obtain it from retained earnings or raise it from external sources by borrowing or by issuing equity securities. Raising funds externally has become the preferred method since the end of World War II.

■ Firms raise external capital primarily through debt and equity, with debt being predominant.

[12] See Seha Tinic, "Anatomy of Initial Public Offerings of Common Stock," *Journal of Finance* 43 (1988): 789–822.

What is an investment banker?

■ Investment bankers are the intermediaries between firms that need capital and the capital markets. Firms depend on the expertise and advice of the investment banker to assist them in raising capital in the most efficient manner.

How does the investment banker assist the firm in raising capital?

■ The investment banker assists the firm in planning the origination of the financial securities. The investment banker conducts a full examination of the firm that is seeking to raise capital, and advises the firm on the timing, pricing, and other characteristics of the securities offered.

■ The investment banker may underwrite the security as a firm commitment offering. As underwriter, the investment banker guarantees that the issue will be fully sold, even if the investment banker has to buy that part of the offering not desired by the markets.

■ Investment banks often form syndicates with other investment banks in underwriting issues, thus reducing the risk of the offering and increasing the number of investment bankers selling the securities.

■ Instead of underwriting the issue, the investment banker may not be willing to assume the risk of the offering. Then it guarantees only that it will contribute its best efforts to the offering.

■ The investment banker is also involved with the securities distribution. The investment banker must ensure that all regulatory provisions concerned with issuing securities to the public have been satisfied.

How are corporate securities marketed?

■ Firms must decide whether to offer their securities to existing securityholders through a rights offering or to issue the securities via a public or a private offering.

■ If dealing with an investment banker, the firm must decide whether to negotiate the underwriting relationship or have investment banks bid for the ability to underwrite the security issue.

■ Finally, firms must decide whether to issue the securities immediately or take advantage of recent changes in the security laws that permit them to prepare the issue, but delay the actual sale of the securities for as long as two years.

Section 12-2: Choosing a Capital Market

Should the firm raise capital at home or abroad?

■ Firms must choose not only the type of security to issue but also the market to issue the security. Differing characteristics of national capital markets produce market segmentation, in which firms may receive different prices for their securities in different markets. The firm must consider the possibility of raising capital in foreign markets that offer higher prices for its securities.

■ Any potential price advantages that arise from raising capital in foreign markets must be balanced against the added complexities that accompany foreign capital acquisitions. Differences in trading conventions, accounting rules, and disclosure requirements can reduce the potential advantages of foreign capital market security issues.

Section 12-3: Recent Trends in Public Offerings

How do markets react when firms issue new securities?

- The announcement of an issue of financial securities—both debt and equity—generally creates a negative abnormal return in the firm's common stock value. Various hypotheses attempt to explain the market's negative reaction.

Section 12-4: Initial Public Offerings (IPOs)

What is an initial public offering (IPO)? How are IPOs priced?

- An IPO is the first equity issue a firm makes when it goes public.

- Pricing IPOs is more difficult than pricing the equity of a publicly traded firm. The firms that issue IPOs are often new firms with only a limited earnings history and no equity price record.

- Various theories have been proposed for the IPO underpricing phenomenon.

QUESTIONS

1. What elements should a corporate CEO consider when deciding on the type of security to offer?

2. Describe the role of the investment banker in the capital acquisition process.

3. Describe each of the main functions of the investment banker.

4. Describe the mechanics of an underwriting syndicate.

5. Why are IPOs considered more risky than seasoned offerings?

6. Briefly discuss the various hypotheses offered to explain IPO underpricing. Which is the most plausible? Why?

12A

RIGHTS OFFERINGS

As defined in the chapter, a rights offering consists of new shares that are offered to existing shareholders rather than to the general public. When a company announces a rights offering, it sets a **record date.** Investors may already own shares in the company or may choose to buy shares in the company before the record date, which allows them to buy shares with rights, or **rights-on shares.** Shares bought after the record date are sold without the rights and are thus called **ex-rights shares.** Rights-on and ex-rights shares sell at different prices.

Rights-on stockholders are informed by the company of the number of rights they own and the number of rights that are required to purchase each new share of stock at the **subscription price.** For example, a company may stipulate that four rights are needed to purchase one new share of stock at the subscription price of $45.

Rights-on stockholders may exercise their rights (i.e., exchange their rights and the required cash for new shares), sell them, or simply ignore them. Stockholders who choose to exercise their rights send the proper materials to the **subscription agent,** who handles the paperwork for the rights sale. If stockholders wish to sell their rights, they may also do so through the subscription agent, for a fee. Investors who simply ignore these rights are ignoring an instrument of value because the right to buy stock at a reduced rate has some value as long as the market price does not fall below the discount price.

Between the time a company announces its rights offering and when it is closed, the market price of the stock can change. When the market price falls below the subscription price, rational stockholders do not act on the rights offering because shares clearly are cheaper in the market than the company's offer. The company is then unable to obtain any of the capital it wishes to raise through the offering. Recognizing this possibility, most companies pay for an underwriter's **standby commitment** that the underwriter will buy the shares at a specified price below the subscription if the company cannot sell them on the market.

Setting Specific Terms   A company that is raising new capital through a rights offering must address several issues: How many new shares should be issued? What should the subscription price be? And so on. To illustrate how these questions can be answered and how the value of a right can be determined, consider the case of Valerion Corporation.

Valerion Corporation, an all-equity firm, wishes to raise $20 million. Valerion has 2 million common shares outstanding, and the market price of its shares is $55.

1. What is the market value of Valerion Corporation?

Let P and Q denote the price per share and the number of shares outstanding, respectively. Before any offering, the company's total value is:

Total value $= PQ = \$55 \times 2{,}000{,}000 = \$110$ million

2. What should the subscription price be?

The subscription price (S) must be set lower than the market price of $55 because more shares outstanding will dilute the value, all else remaining the same. The extent of such dilution is debated, but it is generally believed that this does not matter because the market equilibrates on its own. Assume that Valerion sets the subscription price at $50.[13]

3. How many new shares should Valerion issue?

The subscription price (S) of $50 multiplied by the number of new shares sold (Q_N) should equal $20 million:

$SQ_N = \$20$ million

or

$Q_N = 400{,}000$ shares

4. How many rights (Q_R) are required for each new share?

Recall that in the rights offering, the cost of each new share is the subscription price plus a certain number of rights. Because there are 2 million shares outstanding originally, there are 2 million rights for the 400,000 new shares, or five rights per share:

$$Q_R = \frac{\text{number of old shares}}{\text{number of new shares}} = \frac{2{,}000{,}000}{400{,}000} = 5$$

where Q_R is the number of rights per share. Therefore the company will sell each new share for $50 plus five rights.

---

[13] In efficient markets, the subscription price is not very important.

5. What is the new market price of Valerion stock?

Before the offering,

$$\frac{\text{Per-share}}{\text{old market value}} = \frac{\text{old market value of firm}}{\text{old shares outstanding}}$$

$$= \frac{\$110,000,000}{2,000,000} = \$55 \text{ per share}$$

After the offering,

$$\frac{\text{Per-share}}{\text{new market value}} = \frac{\begin{array}{c}\text{old market value of firm}\\ + \text{ value of new equity}\end{array}}{\text{total number of shares outstanding}}$$

$$= \frac{\$110,000,000 + \$20,000,000}{2,000,000 + 400,000}$$

$$= \frac{\$130,000,000}{2,400,000} = \$54.17 \text{ per share}$$

6. What is the market value of each right?

Suppose that instead of exercising his rights for new shares, a stockholder decides to sell the rights in the marketplace. How much will each right be worth? The value of each right can easily be calculated as the difference between the prices of the rights-on shares (old shares) and the rights-off shares (new shares). The value of each right is therefore $55 − $54.17 = $0.83, or

$$R = P_O - P_N \tag{12A-1}$$

where

P_O is the market price of the old, or rights-on, shares

P_N is the market price of the new, no rights, or ex-rights shares

R is the value of each right

The value of a right is also given as

$$R = \frac{P_O - S}{N + 1} \tag{12A-2}$$

In the case of Valerion,

$$R = \frac{\$55 - \$50}{5 + 1} = \$0.83$$

confirming the result obtained earlier.

Equation (12A-2) is derived as follows. Consider an investor who owns N shares before the rights offering. When the offering is made, he exercises his N rights by paying $$S$, the subscription price. The total amount he has invested in the company is therefore $$NP_O + S$. After the rights issue, each share sells for $$P_N$, but he now has $(N + 1)$ shares. The total amount he has invested is therefore $$(N + 1) \times P_N$. If the investor is not to lose wealth because of the rights offering, the following equality must hold:

$$\$(NP_O + S) = \$(N + 1) \times P_N \tag{12A-3}$$

Substituting the result $P_N = P_O - R$ from equation (12A-1) into equation (12A-3) and solving for R yield the result in equation (12A-2).

These derivations should make it clear that theoretically, the subscription price has no effect on the future stock price because, as equation (12A-1) shows, P_N depends on the initial stock price and the value of the right. Regardless of the subscription price, the market prices the rights such that P_N is given by equation (12A-1).

PROBLEMS

1. Masonic Inc. wishes to raise $15 million by selling new shares through a rights offering. There are currently 1.2 million shares outstanding, with a market price of $60 per share. The subscription price for the new shares will be $50.

    (a) How many rights will be issued?

    (b) How many rights will be required to buy one share?

    (c) What is the value of one right?

    (d) What will the share price be after all the rights have been exercised?

2. The O. F. Bill Co. is making a rights offering. The stock price was $40 per share when the rights offering was announced, and eight rights are required to buy one new share for $32.

    (a) What is the value of one right?

    (b) What will shares trade for after all the rights have been exercised?

    (c) Ken Landreaux has $4,000 in the bank and 80 shares, for a total wealth of $4,000 + (80)($40) = $7,200. If he exercises all his rights, what will his wealth be?

    (d) What will Ken's wealth be if he sells all his rights?

    (e) What will Ken's wealth be if he lets his rights expire without exercising or selling them?

3. The National Micronics Corporation is thinking of issuing new shares through a rights offering. National Micronics currently has outstanding 400,000 shares and wants to raise $2 million by selling new shares for $25 each. The share price is currently $30 per share.

    (a) How many rights will be issued?

    (b) How many rights will be required to buy one share?

    (c) What is the value of one right?

    (d) William Day owns 100 shares of National Micronics and has $2,000 in the bank, for a total of 100($30) + $2,000 = $5,000. If he exercises his rights, what will be the value of all his shares? His new bank balance? His total wealth?

    (e) If Day sells his rights, what will be the value of all his shares? His new bank balance? His total wealth?

    (f) If Day lets his rights expire, what will be the value of all his shares? His new bank balance? His total wealth?

4. National Environmental Controls just had a rights offering with six rights required to buy one new share. The subscription price was $30, and the share price is now $60 per share. National now has 700,000 shares outstanding.

   (a) What was the value of a right?

   (b) What was the value of a share before the rights offering?

   (c) How many shares were outstanding before the rights offering?

   (d) How much money did National Environmental Controls raise through the rights offering?

5. The Hunt Mining Corp. recently had a rights offering. The price per share before the offering was $55, and the current price is $50. Before the offering, Hunt had 400,000 shares outstanding, and today it has 500,000 shares outstanding.

   (a) How many rights were required to buy one new share?

   (b) What was the value of a right?

   (c) What was the subscription price?

   (d) How much money did Hunt raise through the rights offering?

SUGGESTED ADDITIONAL READINGS

Baron, D. P. "A Model of the Demand for Investment Banking Advising and Distribution Services for New Issues." *Journal of Finance,* September 1982, pp. 955–976.

Beatty, Randolph P., and Jay R. Ritter. "Investment Banking, Reputation, and the Underpricing of Initial Public Offerings." *Journal of Financial Economics* 15 (1986): 213–232.

Bhagat, Sanjai, and Peter A. Frost. "Issuing Costs to Existing Shareholders in Competitive and Negotiated Underwritten Public Utility Equity Offerings." *Journal of Financial Economics* 15 (1986): 233–260.

Bower, Nancy L. "Firm Value and the Choice of Offering Method in Initial Public Offerings." *Journal of Finance* 44 (1989): 647–662.

Hansen, Robert S. "The Demise of the Rights Issue." *Review of Financial Studies* 1 (1989): 289–309.

Logue, Dennis E., and Robert A. Jarrow. "Negotiation vs. Competitive Bidding in the Sale of Securities by Public Utilities." *Financial Management* 7 (1978): 31–39.

Rock, K. "Why New Issues Are Underpriced." *Journal of Financial Economics,* January–February 1986, pp. 187–217.

Smith, C. W., Jr. "Alternative Methods for Raising Capital: Rights Versus Underwritten Offerings." *Journal of Financial Economics* 5 (1977): 273–307.

Smith, C. W., Jr. "Investment Banking and the Capital Acquisition Process." *Journal of Financial Economics* 15 (1986): 3–29.

Smith, Richard L. "The Choice of Issuance Procedure and the Cost of Competitive and Negotiated Underwriting: An Examination of the Impact of Rule 50." *Journal of Finance* 42 (1987): 703–720.

Tinic, Seha M. "Anatomy of Initial Public Offerings of Common Stock." *Journal of Finance* 43 (1988): 789–822.

THIRTEEN   EQUITY FINANCING AND STOCK VALUATION

Don't gamble; take all your savings and buy some good stock, and hold it till it goes up, then sell it. If it don't go up, don't buy it.

—Will Rogers on equity investments

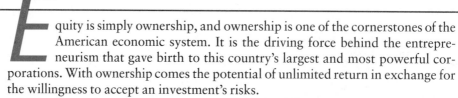

*E*quity is simply ownership, and ownership is one of the cornerstones of the American economic system. It is the driving force behind the entrepreneurism that gave birth to this country's largest and most powerful corporations. With ownership comes the potential of unlimited return in exchange for the willingness to accept an investment's risks.

This chapter has two purposes: to explain the different aspects of equity securities and the various sources of equity capital available, and to examine the valuation of common stock. These objectives allow you to answer the following questions:

- What rights do equityholders possess?

- How can stockholders exercise control over the firm?

- How can businesses raise equity capital?

- What are the benefits and costs in becoming a publicly traded firm?

- How do dividends affect stock prices?

- How do cash flows from future growth opportunities affect stock prices?

13-1
EQUITY OWNERSHIP [1]

*E*quity is ownership. The legal document of ownership in a corporation is the stock certificate, and for this reason, stocks are called **equities.** A distinguishing feature of corporate equity is that it offers the investor limited liability; that is, the investor does not risk any more than the amount invested. Strictly speaking, limited liability is not absolute. The courts have, in some instances usually involving fraud, allowed creditors to "pierce the corporate veil" and go after the shareholders' personal assets. However, this is extremely rare, and when it does happen, the company is usually a closely held corporation. Shareholders in publicly traded corporations need almost never worry about this threat.

Equity is a residual claim on the firm, and limited liability offers some benefits for residual claimants. First, the limited liability of the residual claim reduces potential losses to equityholders. The investors' welfare is ultimately determined by management's actions made on their behalf. If investors had all of their wealth at risk based on managers' decisions, careful monitoring would become extremely important. But a diversity of equity claims across many firms, each with limited liability, lowers the equityholders' need to monitor management. Passive ownership makes sense in this context, and managers can devote their attention to running the firm. This in turn lowers the overall cost of its operation.

Limited liability also reduces the cost of monitoring other shareholders. Without limited liability, each shareholder's wealth would become important to the

[1] For a detailed examination of these issues, see F. H. Easterbrook and D. R. Fischel, "Limited Liability and the Corporation," *University of Chicago Law Review* 52 (Winter 1985): 89–117.

other shareholders. If there is a claim on personal assets, the wealthier the other shareholders are, the smaller is the probability that any one equityholder's assets must pay the judgment. Moreover, in the event of a claim on personal assets, stockholders have an incentive to transfer their assets to, say, their children and thus avoid any liability. To prevent such behavior, stockholders would have to monitor one another's activities. Limited liability eliminates the need for this because the identity and personal wealth of the other shareholders are not as important.

This, in turn, implies that residual claims can be bought and sold easily and that managers have incentives to act efficiently. If the firm has too many agency problems, the shares can be acquired by an outsider who can take over the firm and displace the management. Put another way, limited liability facilitates the workings of the takeover market in disciplining managerial behavior. Limited liability also enables shares to reflect fair market values. All shares are the same, and there is only one price. Without limited liability, the shares held by different investors could not be compared (their personal wealth would matter), and corporate managers could not look to stock prices for guidance. In sum, limited liability underlies the entire theory of corporate financial management.

Accounting Terms

To understand equity ownership, we need to also understand the stockholders' equity portion of the corporate balance sheet. Table 13-1 gives the equity portion of Robert Jones & Co.'s balance sheet as of December 31, 1995. Under common stock, the balance sheet shows that the company is authorized by its stockholders to issue up to 200 million shares, which means that management must seek the shareholders' approval if it wants to issue more than 200 million shares. As of the end of 1995, only 65,163,882 of those shares had been issued or were outstanding.

Companies very rarely have trouble obtaining the stockholders' approval to increase the number of authorized shares. Typically, when seeking approval, companies try to get a large number of shares authorized "for general corporate purposes," to avoid the time and expense involved in getting the shareholders' authorization when they do actually plan to issue the shares. The proposal for an increase in the number of authorized shares usually shows up as an item to be decided at the annual meeting of stockholders, unless it is related to a merger, in which case special meetings are usually called.

The **par value** of the shares is a technical value placed on the shares to comply with state law and has little to do with the stock's market value. It is usually set very low because some states require that if there is a bankruptcy, any shareholder who bought the stock for less than par value must contribute the difference between the price paid and the par value. That problem is easily avoided by never selling the stock below par. Another common way to avoid that problem is simply to set no par value, which is also permitted.

In the Robert Jones example, the par value is set at $1 a share, so that for bookkeeping purposes only, the stock is valued at about $65,164,000. The additional funds received beyond the $1 per share when those shares were issued are entered as the additional **paid-in capital,** which is $9,027,000.

TABLE   13-1

Stockholders' Equity: Robert Jones & Co. Balance Sheet

Year ended December 31, 1995 (thousands of dollars):

Common stock: Authorized 200,000,000 shares, par value $1 per share; issued 65,163,882 shares	$ 65,164
Additional paid-in capital	9,027
Retained earnings	438,587
Less: Treasury stock at cost, 861,207 shares	7,177
Total stockholders' equity	$505,601

For a company with no par value for its shares, some states require that the company set a stated value, which has much the same effect as par value does. If no stated value is required, the common stock and additional paid-in capital accounts are combined into one contributed capital or common stock account and include all the capital raised from the sale of the no-par-value shares.

The company's net income after payment of dividends is added to the **retained earnings** account, making it $438,587,000. This account includes all the net income since the corporation's inception that has been reinvested in the company rather than distributed to stockholders as dividends. **Treasury stock** consists of shares that were sold to investors but repurchased by the company and is recorded at cost. Treasury stock pays no dividends and has no voting rights. It may be retained in the account indefinitely, retired, or resold.

Book value can be determined by dividing the total amount of common stockholders' equity by the shares outstanding. Book value generally is of little consequence to the market value of most companies. One notable exception is the utilities industry: Regulators calculate earnings per share as a percentage of book value when determining whether to allow a rate increase. To illustrate the computation, the book value of Robert Jones stock on December 31, 1995, is:

$$\text{Book value} = \frac{\text{stockholders' equity}}{\text{shares outstanding}} = \frac{505,601,000}{65,163,882} = \$7.76 \text{ per share}$$

Rights and Privileges Stock ownership entitles the holders to certain rights and privileges. Such rights and privileges are relatively innocuous when owners and managers are the same. But when owners include outsiders, management must consider the best interests of the company apart from its own best interests. Outside shareholders generally remain quite passive unless they become disenchanted with the company's performance. Particularly when the stock price is depressed as a result of poor performance, shareholders can and sometimes do challenge current management. Table 13-2 summarizes the rights and privileges of stockholders, the most important of which we cover in detail.

Evidencing ownership is the stock certificate, shown in Figure 13-1 for Hickok Electrical Instrument Co. Note the type of information on the stock certificate:

1. The 35 common shares owned

2. The $1 par value

3. The serial number on the left

4. The date of transfer of ownership

5. The state in which the company is incorporated

6. The registrar and transfer agents used by the company in issuing the shares

■
TABLE 13-2
Rights of Stockholders

Holders of common stock have certain fundamental rights or privileges that cannot be revoked, including
1. *Limited liability.* Stockholders cannot lose more than they have invested.
2. *Proportionate ownership.* Stockholders have ownership in the company in the same proportion as their shares to the total of all shares outstanding.
3. *Transfer rights.* Stockholders may give away or sell shares to anyone they choose.
4. *Dividends.* Stockholders share in the profits if dividends are declared. There is no guarantee, however.
5. *Inspection of corporate books.* Stockholders have the right to see annual reports and the like, but this does not include detailed books of accounts, minutes from internal meetings, and other such items.
6. *Preemptive right.* Stockholders have the right to subscribe proportionately to any new issue of stock.
7. *Votes at shareholders' meetings.*
8. *Residual claims to assets at dissolution.* If the corporation ceases to exist, stockholders have the right to corporate assets only after all debt claims and other securityholders' claims are satisfied.

FIGURE 13-1
Stock certificate

The highlight on page 390 explains how to obtain information concerning stock prices and trades from the newspaper.

CONTROL

The shareholders have the right to choose and replace the company's management. The management is chosen by the firm's board of directors, who in turn are elected by the stockholders. In small companies, the process is almost redundant because the biggest shareholders are the directors and hold most of the top management positions. In large companies, however, the directors are usually a minority of internal managers and a majority of outside directors. Often the outside directors are managers of other companies, and some sit on several boards.

Corporations must hold annual meetings for their stockholders, at which directors are elected, auditors are chosen, and other business is addressed. Management often gives a summary of the past year's performance and the outlook for the coming year. Usually these statements are found in the annual report, which the company must prepare for stockholders, or in the first-quarter statement. The ability of stockholders to vote gives them some measure of control over the firm's operations, and this control feature of stock ownership has economic value. It has been estimated that voting stock bears a 5%–6% premium over no-voting stock, which suggests that investors are willing to pay more for the control feature.[2] Evidence also suggests that in addition to investors, managers value these voting rights.[3]

KEY CONCEPT   The voting privilege associated with stock ownership, and hence control, has economic value.

[2] R. Lease, J. J. McConnell, and W. H. Mikkelson, "The Market Value of Differential Voting Rights in Closely Held Corporations," *Journal of Business* 57 (1984). Also see the article by the same authors, "The Market Value of Control in Publicly Traded Corporations," *Journal of Financial Economics* 14 (1985): 33–69.

[3] H. DeAngelo and L. DeAngelo, "Managerial Ownership of Voting Rights: A Study of Public Corporations with Dual Classes of Common Stock," *Journal of Financial Economics* 20 (1985).

DECIPHERING THE STOCK PAGES

Suppose that a neophyte investor wants to follow certain stocks in the daily newspaper. The investor can look up major stocks in the business pages of the local daily newspaper. He is more likely to find more information and more obscure stocks in financial publications, such as The Wall Street Journal (see Figure 13-2).

First, to find a particular stock, one must know where it is traded: on the New York Stock Exchange, the American Stock Exchange, or the NASDAQ Over-the-Counter (OTC) Market. The OTC stocks are further categorized by the amount of investors' interest, with the most heavily traded listed in the National Markets Issues, followed by the NASDAQ Bid and Asked Quotations and additional OTC Quotes.

Suppose that an investor owns some shares in Texas Instruments, which is traded on the New York Stock Exchange, as are most major public companies. Looking in the pages of The Wall Street Journal, where stock quotations read from the back of the newspaper forward, he finds it listed as TexInstr. Because it is easy to confuse the list-

ing with, say, TexInd, which refers to Texas Industries, he might want to consult a broker if he is unsure.

The newspaper consists of 12 columns of information for each stock listed on the New York Stock Exchange. The first seven columns give some history and perspective on the stock, and the last five columns indicate the results of the previous trading day's activities.

In the Monday, August 16, 1993, issue of The Wall Street Journal, the listing is for trading that occurred the last business day before—Friday, August 13. The first two columns show $78\frac{3}{8}$ and $36\frac{3}{4}$ as the highest and the lowest levels, respectively, at which Texas Instruments stock was traded within the last 52 weeks.

The third column simply lists the abbreviated name of the stock. To distinguish trading of the company's common stock from its preferred stock, the letters pf follow the preferred stock name listing. The fourth column gives the stock's ticker symbol—here, TXN. The fifth column indicates the company's dividend payout at an annual rate, based on the company's last declared quarterly or semiannual dividend rate. A variety of footnotes, denoting stock splits, extra

dividends, ex-rights, and the like, may also appear here, with the explanatory notes found at the end of the exchange table. In Texas Instruments' case, its annual dividend payout rate is $0.72 and there are no footnotes.

The sixth column shows the dividend payout rate of $0.72 as a percentage of the company's current price, or 0.9% of $76\frac{1}{4}$, where it closed. The next column gives the company's price–earnings ratio (P/E) of 22, meaning that its selling price of $76\frac{1}{4}$ is about 22 times its annual per-share earnings level.

The eighth column gives the trading volume, in hundreds of shares, for Friday, August 13. The figure 5500 means that 550,000 shares of Texas Instruments were traded that day.

The next three columns give the high, low, and closing prices for Friday, indicating that Texas Instruments traded as high as $76\frac{1}{2}$ and as low as $75\frac{3}{4}$, and closed at the end of the day at $76\frac{1}{4}$.

The final column shows the change in the stock's closing price from the day before. Therefore the price of Texas Instruments stock has decreased by $\frac{3}{8}$ point from the day before, meaning that the previous day's closing price was $75\frac{7}{8}$.

Stockholders may vote in person or by **proxy,** which is a document that transfers the right to vote to another party, which under normal circumstances is the current management. In large companies, very few stockholders actually attend the meeting; most stockholders vote by proxy.

CLASSES OF STOCK

On rare occasions, with the shareholders' approval, a company may wish to segregate stock to allow a variance in the rights and privileges available to all stockholders. In these instances, companies may create new classes of stock to facilitate those needs, such as "class A common" or "class B common." Such designations carry no standard meaning across companies.

Quotations as of 5 p.m. Eastern Time
Friday, August 13, 1993

52 Weeks Hi	Lo	Stock	Sym	Div	Yld %	PE	Vol 100s	Hi	Lo	Close	Net Chg
54¹/₄	41	TemplInland	TIN	1.00	2.4	20	1433	41¹/₂	41¹/₄	41³/₈	+ ¹/₄
▲ 23³/₄	14¹/₂	TemplMktFd	EMF	6.02e	26.2	...	2851	23³/₄	22¹/₂	23³/₄	+1¹/₈
10¹/₄	8¹/₄	TemplGlbGvt	TGG	.72	8.2	...	267	8¹/₈	8¹/₄	8¹/₈	+ ¹/₈
9¹/₄	7³/₄	TemplGlob	GIM	.60	7.5	...	2295	8¹/₈	8	8¹/₈	...
52¹/₄	32³/₄	Tenneco	TGT	1.60	3.1	dd	3106	50³/₄	50	50¹/₄	− ¹/₈
41¹/₄	34³/₄	Tenneco pf		2.80	6.8	...	446	41³/₄	41¹/₄	41¹/₄	− ¹/₈
27¹/₂	19³/₄	TeppcoPtnrs	TPP	2.20	8.2	12	178	26¹/₄	26¹/₄	26¹/₄	...
27¹/₂	11³/₄	Teradyne	TER	...	...	39	2836	27¹/₄	26¹/₄	26³/₄	+ ¹/₈
12¹/₄	6³/₄	TerexCp	TEX	...	...	dd	315	7¹/₄	7	7	− ¹/₄
5¹/₂	3¹/₄	TerraInd	TRA	...	...	19	413	4¹/₄	4¹/₄	4¹/₄	...
6¹/₄	2¹/₂	Tesoro	TSO	...	...	dd	268	6¹/₄	6¹/₄	6¹/₄	...
▲ 21³/₄	7³/₈	Tesoro pf		...	...	...	33	22³/₄	21³/₄	21³/₄	+ ¹/₈
65³/₄	57³/₄	Texaco	TX	3.20	5.1	15	8977	63³/₈	62³/₄	62⁵/₈	− ¹/₄
54¹/₂	51¹/₂	Texaco pfC		3.38e	6.4	...	64	53	52³/₄	52³/₄	− ¹/₄
28³/₄	19³/₄	TexInd	TXI	.20	.9	cc	47	23³/₄	23	23	− ¹/₄
78³/₈	36¹/₄	TexInstr	TXN	.72	.9	22	5500	76¹/₂	75¹/₄	76¹/₄	− ⁵/₈
39	32³/₄	TexInstr pf		2.26	5.8	...	1015	38⁵/₈	38¹/₄	38⁵/₈	...
19¹/₂	16¹/₄	TexPacTr	TPL	.40	2.1	25	32	19³/₈	19¹/₄	19¹/₄	− ¹/₈
▲ 48³/₄	40³/₄	TexUtil	TXU	3.08	6.4	15	4190	48⁵/₈	48	48³/₄	− ¹/₈
n 25¹/₂	25³/₄	TxUtEl pfA		...	...	...	442	25¹/₄	25¹/₄	25¹/₄	+ ¹/₈
n 26¹/₄	24¹/₄	TxUtEl pf		2.05	7.7	...	78	26¹/₄	26¹/₄	26¹/₄	...
9	4¹/₄	TexfiInd	TXF	...	...	6	176	5¹/₈	5	5	...
▲ 56³/₈	34³/₄	Textron	TXT	1.24	2.1	15	1218	57¹/₂	56³/₈	56³/₄	+ ³/₈
13¹/₂	8¹/₄	ThaiCapFd	TC	.30e	2.2	...	115	13³/₈	13¹/₄	13¹/₄	− ¹/₈
22¹/₄	14¹/₄	ThaiFd	TTF	.87e	3.9	...	200	21¹/₄	21¹/₄	21³/₄	+ ¹/₈
61³/₈	37³/₄	ThermoElec	TMO	...	...	24	1324	59³/₄	58	59³/₄	+1
24³/₄	14³/₄	Thiokol	TKC	.68f	3.0	7	294	22⁵/₈	22¹/₄	22¹/₄	...

EXPLANATORY NOTES

The following explanations apply to New York and American exchange listed issues and the National Association of Securities Dealers Automated Quotations system's over-the-counter securities. Exchange prices are composite quotations that include trades on the Chicago, Pacific, Philadelphia, Boston and Cinncinnati exchanges and reported by the NASD.

Boldfaced quotations highlight those issues whose price changed by 5% or more if their previous closing price was $2 or higher.

Underlined quotations are those stocks with large changes in volume, per exchange, compared with the issue's average trading volume. The calculation includes common stocks of $5 a share or more with an average volume over 65 trading days of at least 5,000 shares. The underlined quotations are for the 40 largest volume percentage leaders on the NYSE and the NASD's National Market System. It includes the 20 largest volume percentage gainers on the Amex.

The 52-week high and low columns show the highest and lowest price of the issue during the preceding 52 weeks plus the current week, but not the latest trading day. These ranges are adjusted to reflect stock payouts of 1% or more, and cash dividends of 10% or more.

Dividend rates, unless noted, are annual disbursements based on the last quarterly, semiannual, or annual declaration. Special or extra dividends, special situations or payments not designated as regular are identified by footnotes.

Yield is defined as the dividends paid by a company on its securities, expressed as a percentage of price.

The P/E ratio is determined by dividing the closing market price by the company's primary per-share earnings for the most recent four quarters. Charges and other adjustments usually are excluded when they qualify as extraordinary items under generally accepted accounting rules.

Sales figures are the unofficial daily total of shares traded, quoted in hundreds (two zeros omitted).

Exchange ticker symbols are shown for all New York and American exchange common stocks, and Dow Jones News/Retrieval symbols are listed for Class A and Class B shares listed on both markets. Nasdaq symbols are listed for all Nasdaq NMS issues. A more detailed explanation of Nasdaq ticker symbols appears with the NMS listings.

FOOTNOTES: ▲—New 52-week high. **▼**—New 52-week low. **a**—Extra dividend or extras in addition to the regular dividend. **b**—Indicates annual rate of the cash dividend and that a stock dividend was paid. **c**—Liquidating dividend. **cc**—P/E ratio is 100 or more. **dd**—Loss in the most recent four quarters. **e**—Indicates a dividend was declared or paid in the preceding 12 months, but that there isn't a regular dividend rate. **f**—Annual rate, increased in latest declaration. **g**—Indicates the dividend and earnings are expressed in Canadian money. The stock trades in U.S. dollars. No yield or P/E ratio is shown. **gg**—Special sales condition; no regular way trading. **i**—Indicates amount declared or paid after a stock dividend or split. **j**—Indicates dividend was paid this year, and that at the last dividend meeting a dividend was omitted or deferred. **k**—Indicates dividend declared or paid this year on cumulative issues with dividends in arrears. **m**—Annual rate, reduced on latest declaration. **n**—Newly issued inthe past 52 weeks. The high-low range begins with the start of trading and doesn't cover the entire period. **p**—Initial dividend. **pf**—Preferred. **pp**—Holder owes installment(s) of purchase price. **pr**—Preference. **r**—Indicates a cash dividend declared or paid in the preceding 12 months, plus a stock dividend. **rt**—Rights. **s**—Stock split or stock dividend amounting to 10% or more in the past 52 weeks. The high-low price is adjusted from the old stock. Dividend calculations begin with the date the split was paid or the stock dividend occurred. **t**—Paid in stock in the preceding 12 months, estimated cash value on ex-dividend or ex-distribution date, except some Nasdaq listings where payments are in stock. **un**—Units. **v**—Trading halted on primary market. **vi**—In bankruptcy or receivership or being reorganized under the Bankruptcy Code, or securities assumed by such companies. **wd**—When distributed. **wi**—When issued. **wt**—Warrants. **ww**—With Warrants. **x**—Ex-dividend, ex-rights or without warrants. **z**—Sales in full, not in hundreds.

Sometimes classes are established when the company's founding owners go public. This permits the founders to have, for example, the only voting power or twice as much voting power as new stockholders have, for a certain period. In exchange for the additional voting power, the founders may be prohibited from selling their stock for a certain number of years.

The case of Waldbaum, Inc., a regional supermarket chain, is illustrative of this. The company's founders owned 49% of the stock and wanted to keep control of the company even if some shares of the family block were sold. The Waldbaums created two classes of stock so that the family could retain as little as 10% of the outstanding stock and still retain control.

Here is how it worked: Waldbaum shareholders were asked to approve two new classes of stock. They then were to choose the type of share they desired. Approval of the proposal was essentially a foregone conclusion because the Waldbaum family was to vote its 49% block in favor of its own proposal.

The two classes, approved in July 1985, were:

1. Class A shares, whose holders would receive a 5-cent annual dividend and one vote per share

2. Class B shares, whose holders would receive no dividend but be given ten votes per share

The essence of the two-class plan was that most shareholders would choose the shares that pay a 5-cent dividend, whereas the Waldbaums said in proxy material accompanying the sale that they intended to convert at least 44% of their stock to the class B shares. By the family's calculations as expressed in the proxy material, less than a 10% ownership would still permit the family to retain control of the company.

Separate classes of stock may be designated for other managerial purposes as well. For example, General Motors issued about 13.6 million shares of class E stock in October 1984 when it acquired Electronic Data Systems (EDS) in a transaction valued at $2.5 billion. The purpose was to give holders of this "GME stock," as it was called on Wall Street, a continuing stake in EDS's earnings by tying GME dividends to the income of EDS and its subsidiaries. Creation of the class E stock was also intended to help prevent key EDS people from leaving.

TYPES OF VOTING

Corporate directors may be elected in two ways: by **majority voting** and by **cumulative voting.** In both methods, each share entitles its owner to one vote for each of the directorship seats. Thus, if a shareholder has 100 shares and is to vote on 8 directorship seats, the shareholder has 100 votes × 8 directorships = 800 votes in total. The difference between the two methods lies in the way these votes can be distributed. Under majority voting, the shareholder votes on each director independently, thus casting 100 votes in each of the eight elections in the preceding example. With cumulative voting, however, the stockholder may cast any or all of her votes for a single director. The stockholder in the earlier example may distribute her total of 800 votes in any way that she chooses. If she wants to elect one particular nominee, she can cast all 800 votes for that one nominee. Cumulative voting therefore gives dissidents a better chance of gaining a seat or two on a large company's board. However, complications associated with cumulative voting may account for its declining use in recent years. In a study of firms listed on one of the national stock exchanges between 1962 and 1980, Bhagat and Brickley found that 52 firms eliminated cumulative voting as an option, while only 18 authorized it.[4]

The existence of more than one class of shares has led to **class voting,** or **series voting.** In class (series) voting, each class of shares votes as a separate unit. The company's articles of incorporation and/or bylaws may stipulate multiple classes of directors, with each class of director elected by a separate class of shares. In addition, these documents can specify that each class can cast votes only in certain matters (e.g., mergers). **Contingent voting** is another variation designed to handle multiple voting classes. With contingent voting, certain classes of stock earn the right to vote upon the occurrence of certain contingencies. For example, many state laws require that otherwise nonvoting preferred stockholders be given contingent voting powers when the firm defaults on certain dividend terms. When the contingency is over, this special privilege expires and the class reverts to its normal status.

Disproportionate voting benefits are sometimes afforded to certain classes of shares. For example, whereas common stock has one vote per share, preferred stock can have 1.1 votes per share. However, some states, such as Illinois, do not allow for departures from the one vote–one share arrangement. The question of whether disproportionate voting is beneficial or detrimental to the firm continues to be debated. Harris and Raviv argue that disproportionate voting can enable the firm to raise capital at the lowest possible cost and thus increase shareholders' wealth.[5] In fact, there is some empirical evidence to support this view. Partch examined 44 recapitalizations between 1962 and 1984 and found that stock prices reacted favorably to the announcement of the creation of lower-voting stock.[6] Grossman and Hart suggest that a determining factor is whether or not shareholders expect that management will maintain voting control. If so, they argue, a change to disproportionate voting can be beneficial to the shareholders, but if not, shareholders may be harmed.[7]

Finally, **nonvoting shares** may be issued in some jurisdictions. In general, there are severe restrictions on their issuance. For example, the New York Stock Exchange prohibits the listing of a company that has nonvoting common stock in public hands.

PROXY FIGHTS

When dissident shareholders wish to solicit the votes of other stockholders in their efforts to challenge management, they typically wage a **proxy fight.** These battles are usually over the dissidents' efforts to elect their own nominee(s) to the board of directors. Proxy fights typically take place by mail, telephone, and advertising in business periodicals. Thus they can be very expensive. The company generally has the advantage in such fights because its defense campaign can be financed by corporate funds and the company has control of corporate information. For example, although dissidents are entitled to the roster of the corporation's stockholders, companies have been known to delay producing it in an attempt to

[4] S. Bhagat and J. A. Brickley, "Cumulative Voting: The Value of Minority Shareholder Voting Rights," *Journal of Law and Economics* 27 (1984).

[5] M. Harris and A. Raviv, "Corporate Governance: Voting Rights and Majority Rules," *Journal of Financial Economics* 20 (1988).

[6] M. M. Partch, "The Creation of a Class of Limited Voting Stock and Sharehholder Wealth," *Journal of Financial Economics* 18 (1988).

[7] S. Grossman and O. Hart, "One Share–One Vote and the Market for Corporate Control," *Journal of Financial Economics* 20 (1988).

THREE PROXY FIGHTS OF 1992

JEFFERSON-PILOT

Jefferson-Pilot is an insurance and communications firm based in North Carolina. At its May 4, 1992, meeting, seven dissidents challenged management's slate of directors on the grounds that the company was not doing enough to maximize shareholders' wealth. The dissidents were headed by Louise Price Parsons, granddaughter of the company's founder and an owner of 1% of the outstanding shares. Her group's primary target was W. Roger Soles, who as chairman, president, and CEO, had run the company for 25 years. The dissidents complained that Soles was grossly overpaid, that he had unduly benefited from unrestricted grants of stock to him (disclosed in the company's proxy), and that the company was not aggressive enough in "growing" the firm.

The company claimed that the stock grant to Soles was a mistake, but Parsons claimed fraud. A federal court agreed with Ms. Parsons, and the grants were rescinded. However, the company was in a strong financial position and was one of the most conservative and successful insurers in the business. Management defeated the dissi-

dents' slate of directors by a margin of 3 to 1. Jefferson-Pilot was supported by institutional investors by a 14-to-1 margin. The firm spent more than $2.5 million defending itself in the proxy fight. The dissident group spent between $3 million and $4 million.

UJB FINANCIAL

UJB Financial is a bank holding company that had suffered from a declining real estate market and a general downturn in the economy. In January 1992, Chilmark Capital (UJB's largest shareholder with 9.9% ownership) and a group of investors planned to seek control over UJB's board and requested a shareholder list from the company to solicit proxies. UJB filed suit against Chilmark, charging that Chilmark had misled the public and the government in acquiring its stake in the firm. During this period, the firm's performance improved and shareholders supported management. At the April 20 meeting, management received more than 72% of all votes cast. However, the large number of votes garnered by the dissidents suggests that shareholders did not support management wholeheartedly in this proxy fight.

VAN DORN

In February 1992, Crown-Cork and Seal made a $20 per share purchase offer for Van Dorn. It was rejected. Shareholders and institutional investors disagreed with the reasons given by William Pryor, Van Dorn's CEO, for rejecting the offer, and the displeased shareholders attempted to replace the three Van Dorn directors up for election. William Frazier, an attorney with 5% of Van Dorn's shares, nominated himself and two other candidates to the board. Two of the incumbent directors announced at the time of the meeting that they had opposed the rejection of the Crown offer. It turned out that 62% of the votes cast were for management and 38% for the dissidents. The dissidents, using cumulative voting, managed to elect one director (Frazier) to the board in this proxy fight.

This discussion is adapted from information contained in "Voting by Institutional Investors on Corporate Governance Issues" by Sharon Pamepinto Light (Washington, DC: Investor Responsibility Research Center, December 1992).

shorten the dissidents' time to solicit proxies before the scheduled annual meeting. Proxy fights are waged by individual investors alone or in collaboration with institutional investors. The highlight above illustrates the proxy fight process.

PREEMPTIVE RIGHTS

To protect current stockholders, corporations may, in their bylaws, give them **preemptive rights** that allow them to buy any additional shares offered by the company. Preemptive rights generally are in effect for voting shares and thus include common stock, voting preferred stock, and convertible securities, but not debt or

Treasury stock. They do not apply to employee stock plans or shares issued specifically for a merger transaction. For example, if a firm has $50 million of equity outstanding and wishes to raise an additional $25 million in equity capital from the current owners, it must go through a **rights offering,** which is also called a **privileged subscription.** Each share is entitled to one right. The firm announces that shareholders as of a certain future date, usually within several weeks of the announcement, may purchase additional shares in the company for a certain number of rights plus a certain amount of cash. That cash price is set below the market price of the stock.

The purpose of preemptive rights is to protect stockholders from **dilution** of the value of their shares. Recall that earnings per share are determined by net income divided by the number of shares outstanding. If the number of shares outstanding is increased without a corresponding increase in net income, the earnings per share are reduced, thus diluting them. Assuming that the same price–earnings ratio remains in effect, the stock price falls because the earnings per share are less.

The potential dilutive effect on earnings per share and on the stock price (everything else remaining equal, *ceteris paribus*) is shown next. Suppose that earnings are $50 million, shares outstanding are 20 million, and the stock's price–earnings ratio is 8. Then

$$EPS = \frac{\text{net income}}{\text{shares outstanding}}$$

$$= \frac{\$50 \text{ million}}{20 \text{ million}}$$

$$= \$2.50$$

$$\text{Price–earnings ratio} \times EPS = \text{stock price}$$
$$8 \times \$2.50 = \$20$$

When an additional 1 million common shares are sold, the potential dilutive effect, *ceteris paribus,* is

$$EPS = \frac{\$50 \text{ million}}{21 \text{ million}} = \$2.38$$

$$8 \times \$2.38 = \$19.05$$

Thus the dilutive effect is the $0.95 per share difference between, before, and after the offering. Preemptive rights, provided that the holders wish to exercise them, preserve the owner's share of the total pie by giving him or her more shares, or more pieces of the pie.

Preemptive rights also protect stockholders from any attempt by management itself or through friendly third parties to control a larger percentage of the company's outstanding shares by issuing a large number of new shares to themselves or to friendly groups. This block may be large enough to give management greater control of the company by, for example, electing more of its own directors using cumulative voting.

RETURNS

As we pointed out in earlier chapters, stockholders' rights to income from the company are based on the company's performance. They receive a return on their capital only after creditors and preferred stockholders have been paid. Income may be received in cash dividends or stock dividends or from the sale of the equity owners' shares. Although dividends are treated as ordinary income by the Internal Revenue Service, the sale of stock held at least six months and a day is a return of capital and is given capital gains or loss treatment, which effectively lowers the marginal tax bracket applicable to that income.

13-2
SOURCES OF EQUITY CAPITAL

Most major corporations begin as start-up organizations and then turn to a widening variety of financing sources as they mature. In this section we cover the genesis of new businesses and how they raise equity capital to finance their growth.

Seed Capital

The start-up funds for a new business are called **seed capital.** These funds may be obtained from such sources as an entrepreneur's savings, the sale of personal or business assets, or an inheritance. If the money is solely from the entrepreneur's family, it is probable that the company began as a proprietorship or partnership.

Seed capital might also be raised from family and friends who are willing to risk their capital in exchange for a "piece of the action." This is often the easiest way to raise start-up funds, the only way, or both. When a start-up company is established with less casual contributors, its owners often incorporate the company, which costs about $200. These arrangements still form the most informal of ownership agreements. As long as a corporation is involved, however, these holders are entitled to the rights outlined previously.

Venture Capitalists

Another means of raising capital for the entrepreneur or small businessperson is to approach **venture capitalists.** Venture-capital firms are owned by individuals or corporations that have raised funds to invest in portfolios of promising, young companies. Some invest in start-up operations, and others prefer one- to three-year-old businesses. Some even seek out ailing, young businesses and try to turn them around. Venture-capital firms may also prefer certain industries or certain types of companies as well as certain geographic locales. For example, U.S. Venture Partners of Menlo Park, California, prefers to invest in companies less than three years old, in high technology or specialty retailing, that are located in the northeastern or far western United States.

Venture-capital firms generally exchange their funds for substantial positions in the companies. If possible, they try to take a majority ownership position. The venture capitalists often anticipate that they will receive their return by taking the companies public some years later. This avenue permits them to sell all or most of their ownership and receive capital gains tax treatment on their shares.

One reason that new companies find venture-capital firms attractive is that venture capitalists typically view their investment as long term and are willing to wait several years before reaping their returns. Another reason is that many venture capitalists provide the connections, management, and marketing know-how that new companies often need very badly. On the other hand, because many new ventures must give up control to venture-capitalist firms, management sometimes must accept big changes dictated by the venture-capital firm, including the forced departures of some members of the management itself, perhaps even the founder.

Most venture-capital firms are not much older than the companies they finance. Although organized venture capitalists date back to the 1950s, most of today's firms were started in the early 1980s. Some venture-capital firms are subsidiaries

Firm Name and Location
Warburg, Pincus Ventures, Inc., New York
First Chicago Venture Capital/First Capital Corp. of Chicago (SBIC),[a] Chicago
Aeneas Venture Corp./Harvard Management Co., Inc.,[b] Boston
Schroder Venture, New York
BancBoston Capital Inc./BancBoston Venture, Inc. (SBIC),[a] Boston
Security Pacific Capital Corp./ First SBIC of California,[a] SBIC of California,[a] Costa Mesa, California
Morgan Capital Corp./Morgan Investment Corp. (SBIC),[a] Wilmington, Delaware
Clinton Capital Corp. (SBIC)/Columbia Capital Corp. (MESBIC), New York
Chemical Venture Partners/Chemical Venture Capital Associates LP (SBIC),[a] New York
Boston Venture Management Inc./Boston Venture LP, Boston

TABLE 13-3
*Some large venture–
capital firms*

[a] Bank-affiliated.
[b] Subsidiary of Harvard University.

of large manufacturing or banking companies. Others are privately managed funds that raise the money to invest in the new companies from pension funds, individuals, foreign investors, and corporations. Table 13-3 lists some of the large venture-capital firms in the United States.

Private Placements

As a firm becomes more established and has built a track record, it can remain private and still raise capital from new, more conservative sources. One means of reaching a limited number of investors is through private placement: The company finds a small group of large, usually institutional, investors to provide the entire amount of new capital sought. The stock sold by the private company in return for the capital is called **letter stock** because the buyer must give the Securities and Exchange Commission (SEC), the securities regulatory agency, a letter stating that it did not buy the stock for resale. The SEC requires the letter to ensure that the buyers are aware of the illiquidity of the investment.

Private placements have largely been the domain of small- to medium-sized firms that are seeking equity capital of $500,000 to $5 million. In recent years, however, large, established public firms have used the private placement method to raise hundreds of millions of dollars.

The advantages and disadvantages of private placements of equity are similar to those of private placements of long-term debt, covered in Chapter 14. Typically, the private placement is faster and less costly than a public offering because filings with the SEC, marketing, and other activities can be avoided. The fees levied in private placement reflect the risk assumed by the investors, including illiquidity and more intensive due diligence on the part of the investors.

Public Offerings

As a company continues to mature, it must eventually decide whether it should become a public company. If it chooses to go public, the procedures and alternatives for raising equity funds differ significantly from those used by a privately held company, or a **closely held company,** which is controlled by a small group. Most firms opt to go public, although there are many large private companies, such as the Bechtel Group, United Parcel Service, Hughes Aircraft, and Hallmark Cards.

ADVANTAGES OF GOING PUBLIC

There are two major considerations underlying a company's decision to go public. First, the current owners often want to take their capital investment out of the company and/or diversify their holdings into other companies. Selling their stock is a means by which to obtain capital gains treatment on the returns they are receiving for their stockholdings.

The second consideration is that it is easier for a public corporation to raise external funds. Investors find publicly held companies' shares more attractive than stock in private companies because it is liquid and may be resold at any time in the marketplace. In addition, publicly held stock automatically carries a market valuation, whereas the valuation of privately held companies is determined by independent appraisals or other subjective valuation methods.

Furthermore, a company that has been publicly traded is familiar to analysts and investors and thus is more likely to attract their attention. Ultimately, the stock price is expected to rise because of the greater demand for it and the greater interest in it. That attention level rises rapidly when the company chooses to increase its stature by trying to get its stock traded on the major stock exchanges.

DISADVANTAGES OF GOING PUBLIC

The major disadvantages of going public are, first, management's reduced flexibility in running the company and, second, the large increase in disclosure requirements and filings to the stockholders and the SEC.

In going public, firms experience an increased separation of management and control. This separation introduces, as we saw in Chapter 2, agency problems. Managers' flexibility is reduced because they must overtly demonstrate that they are exercising their **fiduciary responsibility** to the shareholders. This means that they are acting in the shareholders' best interests, not necessarily in management's best interest. These responsibilities become particularly important when the company's performance is lagging, thus exposing the managers to criticism. Management must be able to justify to stockholders its salaries and benefits as well as expenditures made on behalf of the company. In addition, the SEC prohibits management from engaging in any **insider dealings,** which include trading of the company's stock based on **insider information,** which is company information that has not yet been made public. In private companies, however, managers need only justify to their investor group or to themselves how they have spent corporate funds or arranged favorable deals for themselves with the company. The Internal Revenue Service does limit such dealings, but any penalization is associated with tax liability, not with corporate bylaws. If the IRS views a salary as excessive, for example, it might treat the excess amount as a dividend, which, unlike a salary, the corporation cannot deduct.

The disclosure requirements of public companies can also be burdensome. Public companies are required by the SEC to disclose fully any material information relating to the company and to make sure that this information is fully disseminated. The intent of the requirements is to disallow any unfair information advantage over other people. The SEC also requires the company to make regular and timely filings of its activities to the agency.

The Goldman Sachs highlight examines the pressures faced by Goldman Sachs that may impel it to issue publicly traded stock.

LISTING ON AN EXCHANGE

If the corporation decides to go public, its first offering is called, not surprisingly, an initial public offering (IPO). It is usually first traded in the **over-the-counter (OTC) market.** The OTC market is not physically located in a specific place. Instead, trades are made by communications, usually by telephone or computers, among brokers across the country. Dealers act as either principals or brokers for customers. The computerized system, National Association of Security Dealers Automated Quotations, known as the NASDAQ, displays many OTC stock bid and asked prices. Although most over-the-counter companies are relatively young, OTCs also include such well-established companies as Hoover Co.

WHY GO PUBLIC? THE CASE OF GOLDMAN SACHS

A privately controlled firm is able to pursue its business without interference from outsider owners who have an investment in the firm but do not participate in its management. Privately held firms are also exempted from requirements to make public large amounts of information on their situation and plans and are thus free to conduct their affairs as they see fit. However, in deciding to remain private, such firms also give up access to the equity markets, a decision which may hinder them in attaining their major business goals.

Goldman Sachs is a well-respected, profitable Wall Street firm which during its long history has never issued publicly traded stock. In fact, it is the last major securities firm to refrain from going public. While its partners zealously guard their ability to manage their firm, they are also evaluating how their private status limits their ability to grow.

The control exercised by its partners allows Goldman Sachs to pursue its long-term goals without outside criticism. However, its partners are finding their firm limited in its ability to raise capital. Goldman Sachs wants to expand its operations into foreign trading and derivative securities. It also wants to give some of its general partners the ability to "cash out" or convert some of their equity in the firm to other forms of wealth. It has obtained capital by borrowing and by bringing in foreign partners; however, further use of these avenues could jeopardize its credit rating.

Thus the partners of Goldman Sachs will either continue to enjoy control of a smaller firm or will sacrifice some control over a larger firm.

ALSO SEE: "The Street's Big Holdout May Have To Go Public," Business Week, November 25, 1991.

Certain new issues that are purposely priced very low are sometimes called **penny stocks.** According to the *PennyStock News,* a penny stock is any issue whose shares are offered for less than $5 a share. Some stocks actually sell for a penny a share. These issues are highly speculative for two reasons. First, the companies are young, many of them start-ups. Second, the due diligence requirements of the underwriters are considered more lax than those for issues that are not marketed as penny stocks. **Due diligence** refers to the verification that facts, projections, and other information regarding the company are not false or misleading. Denver, Colorado, is called the "Penny Stock Capital of the World" because so many speculative issues, particularly mining issues, have originated there.

As opposed to the penny stocks, those companies traded on the most prestigious exchange, the New York Stock Exchange (NYSE), or the "Big Board," command the most respect among investors. Of all the exchanges, the NYSE has the most stringent requirements for listing, as illustrated in Table 13-4.

In addition to the exchange requirements listed in the table, the NYSE requires some measures that are even more protective of shareholders than some corporate bylaws are. If a firm fails to meet such requirements, it faces the possibility of being delisted by the exchange. For example, the NYSE began delisting proceedings against Allis-Chalmers Corporation for converting $65 million of debt to equity without prior shareholder approval. Although the Big Board later finished a review of its own shareholder approval policies, its then-current policy required the share-

TABLE 13-4

New York Stock Exchange sample of original listing requirements

- National interest in the company.
- At least 1 million shares publicly held among at least 2,000 stockholders who own at least 100 shares each.
- Pretax earnings of at least $2.5 million in the preceding year and at least $2 million in each of the preceding two years.
- At least $16 million in net tangible assets.
- Publicly held common shares with a market value of at least $16 million.

SOURCE: New York Stock Exchange.

■
T A B L E   1 3 - 5
Stock Exchanges

United States	
American Stock Exchange	New York
Boston Stock Exchange	Boston
Cincinnati Stock Exchange	Cincinnati
Intermountain Stock Exchange	Salt Lake City, Utah
Midwest Stock Exchange	Chicago
New York Stock Exchange	New York
Pacific Stock Exchange	San Francisco and Los Angeles
Philadelphia Stock Exchange	Philadelphia
Spokane Stock Exchange	Spokane, Washington
Canada	
Alberta Stock Exchange	Calgary, Alberta
Montreal Stock Exchange	Montreal, Quebec
Toronto Stock Exchange	Toronto, Ontario
Vancouver Stock Exchange	Vancouver, British Columbia
Winnipeg Stock Exchange	Winnipeg, Manitoba

holders' approval for increases of more than 18.5% in common shares outstanding. Allis-Chalmers's debt–equity conversion had the potential of increasing the number of outstanding common shares by 79%.

Traditionally, companies have tried to move up from listing on a regional exchange to the American Stock Exchange (AMEX) and then to the New York Stock Exchange. More recently, however, many companies, such as Apple Computer and MCI Communications, have opted to remain with the NASDAQ. Such developments have resulted in increasingly aggressive efforts by the exchanges and the NASDAQ to attract members.

The various stock exchanges located in the United States and Canada are listed in Table 13-5. Note that the regional exchanges trade stocks listed on the NYSE and American Stock Exchange as well as the stocks of local companies.

13-3

DIVIDENDS AND STOCK PRICES

*I*n general, valuing an asset requires estimating both the future cash flows from the asset and the appropriate discount rate (*RRR*). But often, one of two approaches is taken to simplify the exposition. In some instances, the question of estimating the *RRR* is set aside. With an estimate of the cash flows from the asset, the value of the asset is found using an assumed *RRR*. In other instances, the estimated cash flows are taken as a given, and so estimating the discount rate is the major hurdle to be crossed before valuing the asset.

The first approach is the subject of the remainder of this chapter. Given the discount rate, we see how the values of common stock are determined. The cash flow discussions of this chapter can easily be integrated with the in-depth examination of the appropriate discount rate in Part Two of the text. In an actual valuation situation, both cash flows and the discount rate must be determined. Neither factor is a given.

In applying the time-value techniques introduced in Chapter 4 to the case of common stocks, we experience two problems:

1. The future stream of cash flows is more uncertain compared with those of other financial assets, such as bonds. Whereas interest payments on bonds must be paid, dividends and potential capital gains to stockholders are uncertain.

2. These cash benefits to owners occur in perpetuity because the firm is viewed as an ongoing concern. Even though a firm may not exist forever, the stock valuation models developed in this chapter are derived as if they are expected to exist forever. An understanding of the stock valuation models that follow

makes clear how a company's stock can be valued if it is expected to live forever.

What cash flows are relevant to common stock investors? In Chapter 1 we identified the two cash flows: cash dividends and potential capital gains. It is the receipt of dividends and the price expected when the stock is sold at a future date that induce investors to buy stocks. To discount these cash flows, then, it is necessary to make assumptions regarding the time at which the stock will be sold. In addition, it is necessary to forecast the future cash flows.

In the remainder of this section we address two different situations. In the first segment we examine different assumptions about the holding period of the stock. In the second segment several cases are taken up under various assumptions regarding the growth of future dividends.

Stock Valuation Under Different Holding Period Assumptions

CASE 1: SINGLE-PERIOD VALUATION

Consider the simplest case, that of Bev Carlson, an investor who anticipates that she will hold Bering Company stock for one year before she sells it. Bering is expected to pay a dividend at the end of the year. The stock's current price, S_0, is given by

$$S_0 = \frac{Div_1 + S_1}{1 + k_s} \tag{13-1}$$

where

Div_1 is the dividend *expected* in one year

S_1 is the *expected* stock price at the end of one year

k_s is her discount rate

If Ms. Carlson expects a $1.20 dividend and an ending stock price of $38 and requires a 12% return, the stock's value is

$$S_0 = \frac{\$1.20 + \$38}{1.12} = \$35$$

It is instructive to view this situation from a different perspective and verify why a stock price of $35 leads to a 12% return. We can rewrite equation (13-1) in terms of the discount rate as

$$k_s = \frac{Div_1 + S_1}{S_0} - 1$$

or

$$k_s = \frac{Div_1}{S_0} + \frac{S_1 - S_0}{S_0} \tag{13-2}$$

Equation (13-2) demonstrates that Ms. Carlson's total percentage return is composed of two parts: an expected **dividend yield**, Div_1/S_0, and an expected **capital gains yield**, $(S_1 - S_0)/S_0$:

$$k_s = \frac{\$1.20}{\$35} + \frac{\$38 - \$35}{\$35}$$

$$= 0.034 + 0.086$$
$$= 12\%$$

KEY CONCEPT The expected return on a stock is composed of two elements: expected dividend yield and expected capital gains yield.

Equation (13-2) can also be used to calculate the dollar return from owning the stock. Multiplying the initial stock price by the rate of return gives the dollar return; that is, from equation (13-2),

$$k_s S_0 = Div_1 + (S_1 - S_0)$$

and therefore, for the preceding example,

$$k_s S_0 = \$1.20 + \$3 = \$4.20$$

Ms. Carlson therefore expects to receive her return in the form of a \$1.20 dividend and \$3 in stock appreciation. The financial manager of Bering Company thus affects Bev Carlson's returns through the dividend decision (how much of its earnings to pay out) and the investment financing decision (which determines the change in stock price).

CASE 2: MULTIPLE-PERIOD VALUATION

Using the time valuation concepts of Chapter 4, we can easily extend the valuation to multiple holding periods, where the stock is held for several periods and then sold. With multiple holding periods, one takes the present value of each dividend and the present value of the terminal value of the security and discounts them at the required rate of return. However, as we stated above, the stock is generally valued as an infinite-lived asset. The most general formulation of common stock valuation treats the firm and its stock as if they will exist forever. In this case, the stock's value represents a stream of expected dividends in perpetuity. The stock valuation equation thus becomes

$$S_0 = \frac{Div_1}{1 + k_s} + \frac{Div_2}{(1 + k_s)^2} + \cdots + \frac{Div_\infty}{(1 + k_s)^\infty}$$

or

$$S_0 = \sum_{t=1}^{\infty} \frac{Div_t}{(1 + k_s)^t} \tag{13-3}$$

or the sum of dividends from now to infinity. For obvious reasons this formulation is referred to as the **discounted dividend valuation model.**

Notice a very interesting aspect of this formulation: The assumption of an infinite life provides a valuation equation that does not require estimating a future stock price. Thus it can be used irrespective of the investor's holding period, be it one month or three years. However, there is a stumbling block we must overcome before the infinite-period model can be transformed into a usable market valuation equation. We must estimate an infinite stream of dividends, and so we examine how the discounted dividend model can be used under different assumptions concerning the growth pattern of dividends.

Stock Valuation Under Different Assumptions About the Growth Rate

CASE 1: ZERO DIVIDEND GROWTH

Sometimes a firm is expected to pay a stable dividend and there is little chance for growth in the foreseeable future. In this situation, a zero growth dividend pattern is implied, in which

$$Div_1 = Div_2 = \cdots = Div = \overline{Div}$$

As pointed out in Chapter 4, a constant cash flow to infinity can be valued as a perpetuity. Algebraically, this reduces the general stock valuation model in equation (13-3) to

$$S_0 = Div(PVFA_{k_s,\infty})$$

or

$$S_0 = \frac{\overline{Div}}{k_s} \qquad\qquad (13\text{-}4)$$

With zero growth, the value of a share of stock is equal to the value of a perpetual dividend dollar amount divided by the discount rate. If all investors agree on the dividend and the discount rate used is a market-determined *RRR*, then the resulting stock valuation is a market valuation.

Suppose that Senneco Corporation is expected to pay indefinitely a constant $3 dividend. If an investor requires a 15% return on his stock, the price per share of Senneco from equation (13-4) is

$$S_0 = \frac{\$3}{0.15} = \$20$$

Even though few firms can be expected to pay a constant dividend forever, this valuation model can be a useful approximation when the current level of dividends continues indefinitely. Equation (13-4) is used shortly to value a preferred stock.

CASE 2: CONSTANT DIVIDEND GROWTH

Perhaps a more realistic assumption about dividends for many firms is that they increase steadily at a constant growth rate forever. According to equation (13-3), the current stock price is found as

$$S_0 = \frac{Div_1}{1 + k_s} + \frac{Div_1(1 + g)}{(1 + k_s)^2} + \cdots + \frac{Div_1(1 + g)^\infty}{(1 + k_s)^\infty} \qquad (13\text{-}5)$$

where *g* is the constant rate of growth in dividends. Notice, however, that with a constant dividend growth assumption, Div_1 can be estimated using the current dividend—that is, $Div_1 = Div_0(1 + g)$. Substituting the latter expression into equation (13-5) simplifies the model to

$$S_0 = \sum_{t=1}^{\infty} \frac{Div_0(1 + g)^t}{(1 + k_s)^t} \qquad\qquad (13\text{-}6)$$

Comparing this result with the general model in equation (13-3), we can see that the only difference is in the numerator.

Notice yet another simplification provided by this approach. The constant growth assumption has eliminated the problem of estimating each period's dividend individually. When simplified, equation (13-6) becomes[8]

$$S_0 = \frac{Div_0(1 + g)}{k_s - g} = \frac{Div_1}{k_s - g} \qquad\qquad (13\text{-}7)$$

Equation (13-7) is called the **Gordon valuation model** and is probably the most

[8] The dividends in equation (13-7) are a growing perpetuity. This equation is thus an application of equation (4-15), which was derived in Chapter 4.

widely cited dividend valuation model, mainly because its application is so straightforward.[9]

If all investors use the same estimate of future dividends and if the *RRR* used is the appropriate market-determined discount rate, then this valuation is a market valuation.

To illustrate, consider the no-growth example discussed earlier (Senneco Corporation), but now assume that future dividends will grow at a 5% rate. Because the current dividend is $3, the next dividend can be calculated as $Div_0(1 + g)$. Equation (13-7) therefore implies that Senneco's stock price should be

$$S_0 = \frac{\$3(1 + 0.05)}{0.15 - 0.05} = \frac{\$3.15}{0.10} = \$31.50$$

Small changes in dividend growth can have a dramatic impact on stock prices. In the example, the current stock price increased from $20 to $31.50.

This valuation model can also be used to reveal the components of the investor's total return. By rewriting equation (13-7) in terms of the discount rate, we obtain

$$k_s = \frac{Div_1}{S_0} + g \tag{13-8}$$

This states that the total expected return is composed of an expected dividend yield and the future growth in dividends, which represents the expected capital gains yield.[10] Therefore, for this example, the individual contribution to total return from these two components is

$$k_s = \frac{\$3.15}{\$31.50} + 0.05$$

$$= 0.10 + 0.05 = 0.15$$

Estimating the Growth Rate

To use the Gordon valuation formula, three inputs are necessary: the next period's expected dividend (Div_1); the discount rate (k_s), which is assumed to be known (at least for this chapter); and the growth rate (g). How does one estimate g?

Consider the dividend payment process. Out of its earnings, a company decides to pay a certain proportion as dividends. This proportion (or ratio) of earnings paid out as dividends is called the **dividend payout ratio** and is merely the dividends divided by the earnings. For example, if a company decides to distribute as dividends 20 cents on every dollar of earnings, then the payout ratio is 20/100, or 20%. The **retention ratio** is given by (1 − payout ratio), which in this case is 80%.

What does the firm do with the dollars it retains in the business? Presumably, it reinvests all the money to earn more for the company next year. Because the re-

---

[9] An equivalent model was actually derived earlier by J. B. Williams in *The Theory of Investment Value* (Cambridge, MA: Harvard University Press, 1938).

[10] Notice that this valuation model implies that the stock price increases at the same rate that dividends are growing. The next period's price is given by

$$S_1 = \frac{Div_2}{k_s - g}$$

But $Div_2 = Div_1(1 + g)$, or

$$S_1 = \frac{Div_1(1 + g)}{k_s - g}$$

Finally, because we know that $S_0 = (Div_1)/(k_s - g)$, we can substitute this to verify that $S_1 = S_0(1 + g)$.

tained earnings represent equity capital, and if we assume that the dividend payout ratio is fixed, the dividend growth rate can be readily calculated as [11]

$$g = (\text{retention ratio}) \times ROE \qquad (13\text{-}9)$$

where ROE is the book return on equity. ROE is often calculated as

$$ROE = \frac{\text{net income}}{\text{equity}} \qquad (13\text{-}10)$$

The reader may be wondering why the book ROE is being used here after the extensive discussion in Chapter 7 about market values. Notice that g is the growth in dividends, which depends on earnings and the payout ratio (book-value concepts).

To demonstrate, assume that Clarion Records has had a fixed dividend payout ratio of 25% for the last 15 years and management sees no reason to change its policy. The book return on equity has been a stable 20%. If its last dividend was $2 per share and Laurence Booth requires a 20% rate of return, what is the maximum price that he should pay for Clarion Records stock?

Step 1: Calculate g, the growth in dividends:

$$\begin{aligned}
g &= (\text{retention ratio}) \times \text{book } ROE \\
&= (1 - \text{payout ratio}) \times \text{book } ROE \\
&= 75\% \times 20\% = 0.15 \quad \text{or } 15\%
\end{aligned}$$

Step 2: Calculate Div_1:

$$Div_1 = Div_0(1 + g) = \$2(1 + 0.15) = \$2.30$$

Step 3: We use the Gordon formula to find the stock price. According to equation (13-7),

$$S_0 = \frac{Div_1}{k_s - g} = \frac{\$2.30}{0.20 - 0.15} = \$46$$

Thus $46 is the maximum price that Mr. Booth should pay for Clarion stock.

Weaknesses and Extensions of the Constant Growth Models

A few aspects of equation (13-7) require special consideration. First, for the stock to have a meaningful price from equation (13-7), the discount rate (k_s) must be greater than the growth rate (g). If k_s equals g, the stock price is indefinite, and if k_s is less than g, the stock has a negative price. A negative price implies that a company will pay someone to take its stock. This situation is therefore ruled out. Second, it is important to restate the critical assumptions underlying equation (13-7). It has been derived under the assumption that the growth rate in dividends not only is constant but also continues to grow at this rate forever.

This is clearly unrealistic. The first difficulty is in determining the future growth rate, which itself is not an easy task. Then it must be assumed that this rate is sustained forever. No company can maintain a constant growth rate forever, especially if its current growth rate is high. For example, consider Pyrotech, Inc., a new company with a current dividend of $1 and a growth rate of 20%. Even if we believe that this growth will continue somewhat longer, it cannot last forever. After three years (say) the growth rate may come down to a stable 5% per year. How do we value this company's stock? The use of the Gordon valuation model appears to be clearly ruled out because the growth rate changes after three years.

---

[11] Several publications (e.g., Value Line) provide estimates of g.

■

FIGURE 13-3
Calculating Pyrotech's stock price

Given: Current dividend (Div_0) = $1.00
Required rate of return (k_s) = 10%
Growth rate = 20%/year for three years; 5%/year thereafter

Year	Dividend, Div_t	Expected Stock Price
1	$1.20[a]	
2	1.44[a]	
3	1.73[a]	$S_3 = \dfrac{Div_4}{k_s - g} = \dfrac{\$1.82}{0.10 - 0.05} = \$36.40$
4	1.82[b]	

[a] Dividend 20% more than previous dividend.
[b] Dividend 5% more than previous dividend.

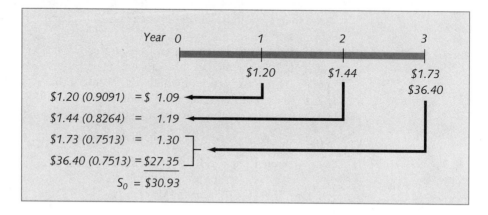

CASE 1: CHANGES IN GROWTH RATES

In a situation such as this, we can still use the Gordon model, but certain other steps are necessary in our calculation. The trick is to recognize that the Gordon model applies from year 3 onward, because after year 3, the growth rate is a constant 5%.

Let us consider the proposed example of Pyrotech, Inc. Figure 13-3 shows how Pyrotech's stock price can be calculated, assuming a discount rate of 10%. Consider an investor who plans to hold the stock for three years. What are the cash flows? Clearly, the investor receives the dividends of $1.20, $1.44, and $1.73 for the three years in addition to S_3, the price of the stock in year 3. Figure 13-3 shows how these dividends are calculated. If S_3 can be estimated, the current stock price (S_0) is simply the sum of the present values of the dividends and S_3, discounted at the investor's discount rate of 10%. To find S_3, we can use the Gordon valuation model because from that year, the constant growth rate of 5% per year is assumed to be sustained forever. As Figure 13-3 illustrates, S_3 equals $36.40, and so the current stock price for Pyrotech is $30.93.

Two questions now arise:

1. What if the investor does not sell the stock in year 3?

The assumption that the stock is sold in year 3 is not critical. It was made purely to demonstrate the use of the Gordon valuation model for the example in Figure 13-3. In fact, even if it is assumed that the stock is sold in year 4, year 5, or year 6, the current price calculated is not different. For example, if the stock was sold in five years, an extra dividend would be earned: Div_5 = $1.91. The sixth dividend, $2.00, would be used to determine the stock price at the end of the fifth year:

$$S_5 = \frac{\$2.00}{0.10 - 0.05} = \$40$$

The present value of the fourth and fifth dividends, plus the present value of the stock price in year 5, would, taking rounding errors into account, give us the same price of the stock today.

2. Having argued that a constant perpetual growth rate is unrealistic, aren't we guilty of the same lack of realism in this adjusted approach?

The reason for adjusting the Gordon valuation model to recognize high current growth rates is that no firm can maintain a constant growth rate forever. Yet in calculating Pyrotech's stock price, we again used the Gordon valuation model, assuming a constant growth rate of 5% after year 3. How, then, can we defend the logic of this approach?

It is true that assuming a constant perpetual growth rate of 5% from year 3 onward is unrealistic. The growth rate is expected to change over time, and thus the use of the Gordon valuation model is expected to introduce some errors. Yet such errors would pertain to the future, and so when present values are calculated, the present values of these errors are not large. Thus estimates of growth rates for the immediate future are more important than estimates of growth rates in the distant future. This observation is true in almost all other aspects of finance. The impact on current decisions of errors made in the distant future is less than that of errors made in the immediate future.

CASE 2: VARIABLE DIVIDEND GROWTH

Our two common stock valuation models (zero and constant growth) are simple to use, but they do not allow for variability in expected growth rates. Finding the current stock price when dividend growth rates are variable is complex. Nevertheless, the process of valuation remains relatively straightforward because we can use the multiperiod valuation model mentioned earlier.

To illustrate, Figure 13-4 contains information on Howser Corporation's future

FIGURE 13-4

Howser Corporation: information on future dividends and ending price

Year	Dividend Div_t	Implied Variable Growth Rate	Ending Stock Price
1	$1.00	0%	
2	1.00	20	
3	1.20	15	
4	1.38		$50

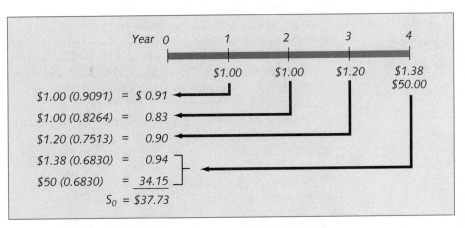

dividends for the next four years as well as the expected ending price. If an investor's discount rate is 10%, this implies a current stock price of

$$S_0 = \$1(PVF_{0.10,1}) + \$1(PVF_{0.10,2}) + \$1.20(PVF_{0.10,3})$$
$$+ \$1.38(PVF_{0.10,4}) + \$50(PVF_{0.10,4})$$

$$= \$37.73$$

Value Can Lie in the Eye of the Beholder

The dividend valuation models of stock prices assume that the price of a stock today is the present value of all cash flows investors *expect* to receive from that stock. How do investors form these expectations about the future cash benefits from owning the stock? Presumably from information about the company, the economy, and so on.

It is important at this time to review the notion of efficiency in financial markets as discussed in Chapter 7. An **efficient market** is one in which an asset's (here, stock) price reflects all of the available information. If we assume that investors form their expectations from, say, publicly available information in newspapers, company statements, and so on, it is unlikely that any one investor has information that is not reflected in the market price. If investors form their expectations with common information, it is difficult to talk about "overvalued" and "undervalued" investments because the market price reflects an investment's "true" value.

KEY CONCEPT The notion of "overvalued" and "undervalued" investments in an efficient market can be rationalized only if an investor has information that the market does not.

We have examined several different methods for calculating stock prices when the discount rate is given. How should these calculations help us?

For one thing, the formulas explain qualitatively the impact of various changes on stock prices. If the discount rate goes up, equation (13-7), for example, clearly suggests that stock prices should fall. In fact, we can draw several other qualitative conclusions from equation (13-7) when we look at the factors that determine k_s, the discount rate.

For example, if an investor calculates the stock price to be $40 and her broker tells her that the stock is selling for $45, the stock is *overvalued*. Conversely, a market price of $36 suggests that the stock is *undervalued* by the market. When we recall that the calculated stock price is based on an individual's personal estimates of k_s and g, it becomes clear why the labels *overvalued* and *undervalued* make sense only to the person who is making the calculations. Another person could take the opposite viewpoint, and both would be right. After all, both people define under- or overvalued stock according to their personal calculations of formula values. It makes no sense for a broker to call a client's attention to an "undervalued" stock. Depending on the discount rate used and the forecasted dividends, any "undervalued" stock can be "converted" into an "overvalued" stock, and vice versa. Thus value lies in the eyes of the beholder, a concept that is illustrated in the following highlight. It is precisely because two people disagree about values that they have an incentive to trade.

For these valuation models to be market valuations, not only must all investors agree on the future cash flows, but in addition, the RRR used in the valuation must be a market-determined rate. Unfortunately, it is not possible to say when these conditions are satisfied in this framework.

A TALE OF TWO RATS

Advice on overvalued and undervalued stocks has always been available to investors. Of course, the usefulness of acting on such advice in an efficient market is questionable. Taking a jab at "knowledgeable" stockbrokers, G. E. Hanson wrote the following amusing story in Life *magazine (May 26, 1887):*

An old rat, whose long resi-dence in the city had given him great knowledge of the wiles of civilized life, observed one eve-ning a tempting bit of cheese close by his favorite hole in the wall.

Instead of greedily rushing at it, he called a young friend, say-ing, "Whiskerando, some kind person has prepared a feast for us. Help yourself."

The guileless innocent rushed on the cheese, which he devoured voraciously: but, alas! in a few minutes he rolled over on his back, stone dead. The dainty was poisoned.

"My experience in Wall Street has stood me well," mused the old rat as he turned into his hole: "It is safer to give other folks pointers, and pocket your commission, than to risk your all on a wildcat investment."

Dividends and Stock Prices

At first glance it appears from equation (13-7) that dividends are a crucial determinant of stock prices. In fact, if a firm is not expected to pay any dividends, then $Div_1 = 0$ and the implied stock price appears to be \$0. This conclusion is incorrect, however. Table 13-6 presents a partial list of stocks that have never paid a dividend in years, and all of them have nonzero prices. Thus actual economic experience indicates that it is not mandatory for a firm to pay dividends. How can one explain this apparent paradox? On the one hand, equation (13-7) gives a value of $S_0 = 0$ if no dividends are paid, yet Table 13-6 lists several non-dividend-paying stocks, all of which have a nonzero market price.

In the derivation of stock valuation equations, like equation (13-6) or (13-7), the price of the stock is calculated as the present value of an infinite series of dividends. The focus on an infinite dividend series means that the selling price of the stock at a future date does not enter the calculations. But even if a company pays no dividends at all, there is still an **implicit dividend** built in: Someday the firm will liquidate and pay a **liquidating dividend.** Thus the stock that pays no cash dividends can be treated as a property right that is expected to yield the investor a fractional ownership in the firm when it liquidates. The present value of this liquidating dividend contributes to the value of the stock. Even if investors cannot wait until the day of liquidation to get their "reward," they may be willing to pay a price for the stock because this property right (stock) is readily tradable. That is, when investors need cash, they can expect to sell the stock at a positive price to someone else. Others may be willing to buy the stock from these investors again for a similar reason. There is a value in holding property rights in the economy. As long as property rights are recognized and not threatened by major socioeconomic or political changes, an active secondary market exists for stocks that pay no dividends. Property rights are a fundamental characteristic of the U.S. capitalist sys-

TABLE 13-6
Some Corporations That Pay No Dividends

Bio-Rad Labs	Photo Controls
Crown-Cork & Seal	Quotron Systems
Data General	SCI Systems
Digital Equipment	Teradyne, Inc.
Federal Express	Timesharing
Kevex Corporation	U.S. Surgical
LaQuinta Inns	Whitehall Corporation
May Petroleum	Xidex

tem. Hence dividend payments are not necessary as long as investors can expect to be able to sell their property rights in the marketplace.

13-4

GROWTH OPTIONS AND STOCK PRICES

Increasing Dividends Can Lower Stock Prices

Stock valuation models based on dividend growth rates imply that (all else held constant) the stock price increases with an increase in dividends. This may appear reasonable at first, but a little reflection exposes some troublesome aspects of this result. Stock prices can go down even when the firm's dividends are increasing. Dividends can increase for a firm that is in a declining industry with few good investment opportunities.

The key to understanding this idea is to recognize that a firm can increase its dividends even if its managers follow a policy of "empire building"—that is, increasing the size of the company by investing in new projects that are not in the shareholders' best interests. There is some evidence that managers do engage in empire building just to increase the size of the company. Managers' total compensation is often related to firm size,[12] and management may want the firm to grow even if this growth comes at the expense of shareholders (the agency problem). The firm can keep increasing dividends if it is "wasting" its earnings by investing in negative-NPV projects. It can keep increasing dividends, but stock prices may decline. These ideas are best seen through a simple example.

Consider Mirrimar Inc., a company that produces computerized medical testing devices. The company currently follows a 100% dividend payout policy, but it wants to increase its size by going to a 40% dividend payout policy and investing the resulting extra funds in a new model of a testing device. Introducing this new device would produce a 5% rate of return. If this plan is implemented, the firm would have annual earnings of $75,000. For simplicity, we assume that these earnings go into perpetuity. We also assume that the stockholders' required rate of return is 10%.

If the returns from the investment in the new model of the device are 5% per year (ROE), what are the firm's dividends over the next three years? From equation (13-9), the growth rate in dividends g = (retention ratio) $\times$ ROE = 0.60 $\times$ 0.05 = 3%. Therefore:

Year 1 dividends: $75,000 $\times$ (1 − retention ratio) = $75,000 $\times$ (1 − 0.60)
= $30,000

Year 2 dividends: $30,000(1 + g) = $30,000(1.03) = $30,900

Year 3 dividends: = $30,000(1 + g)^2 = $30,000(1.03)^2 = $31,827

Notice that Mirrimar's dividends are growing by the investment in the next generation of testing equipment. So, from our preceding discussions, it appears that the stock price should increase.

What will actually happen to Mirrimar's stock price? The answer to this is easy. The stock price must go down. If investors' required rate of return is 10% and Mirrimar's new project is earning 5%, the new investment is actually a negative-NPV investment. Since stockholders' wealth decreases when the firm takes on a negative-NPV investment, the stock price will trend downward.

The example of Mirrimar illustrates an important idea:

---

[12] See M. C. Jensen, G. P. Baker, and K. J. Murphy, "Compensation and Incentives: Practice vs. Theory," *Journal of Finance* 43 (1988): 593–616.

KEY CONCEPT

A firm cannot increase its stock price simply by increasing dividends. Increasing dividends can increase stock prices only if the dividend increases are not associated with negative-*NPV* investments.

Growth Options

Now suppose that Mirrimar has good investment opportunities (positive-*NPV* investments). Assume that next year (time 1) the firm can invest $60,000 in new equipment to make leather briefcases. The new investment will earn the firm $35,000 per year into perpetuity. The following time line summarizes this information.

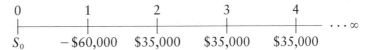

This briefcase-making opportunity (growth option) available to Mirrimar *next year* is reflected in the stock price today (time 0). How?

First consider the value of Mirrimar stock if it chooses to pay out 100% of its earnings as dividends, thereby forgoing its growth options. If there are 10,000 shares outstanding, then dividends/earnings per share (*EPS*) = total earnings/number of shares = $75,000/10,000 = $7.50. Thus

$$S_n = \frac{EPS}{k_s} = \frac{\$7.50}{0.10} = \$75 \tag{13-11}$$

where S_n is the value of the stock without growth options.

Now, the market knows that Mirrimar has a growth option with a time 1 *NPV* of:

$$NPV_1 = PV(\text{cash inflows}) \text{ at time } 1 - PV(\text{cash outflows at time } 1)$$

$$= \frac{\$35,000}{0.10} - \$60,000$$

$$= \$290,000$$

We define the *present value* of this growth option as *PVGO*:

$$PVGO = PV \text{ of } NPV_1 = \frac{\$290,000}{1.10} = \$263,636$$

Since the firm has 10,000 shares outstanding,

$$PVGO \text{ (per share)} = \frac{\$263,636}{10,000} = \$26.36$$

To the extent that the market knows that the firm has this growth option available, Mirrimar's current stock price with the growth option (S_0) is:

$$S_0 = S_n + PVGO \text{ (per share)}$$
$$= \$75 + \$26.36 \tag{13-12}$$
$$= \$101.36$$

Stock Prices and Earnings per Share

From equations (13-11) and (13-12) the current stock price of a company is related to its earnings per share and the growth options as:

$$S_0 = \frac{EPS}{k_s} + PVGO \text{ per share} \tag{13-13}$$

Since S_0 is the price per share, we can divide both sides of equation (13-13) by *EPS* and write the price–earnings ratio (P-E ratio) as

$$\text{P-E ratio} = \frac{\text{price per share}}{EPS} = \frac{1}{k_s} + \frac{PVGO \text{ per share}}{EPS} \tag{13-14}$$

P-E ratios have a long history in the investment community. The P-E ratio is often viewed as the dollar price one has to pay for each dollar of the firm's earnings. Not surprisingly, it is often thought that buying stocks with "low P-E's" and selling stocks with "high P-E's" are sound investment strategies.[13] However, it is difficult to justify this view because two firms with identical P-E ratios may differ in terms of risks and investment opportunities and accounting methods. The linkages described next are evident from an inspection of equation (13-14).

P-E RATIOS AND GROWTH OPTIONS

Firms with growth options have higher P-E ratios. A firm with a low *EPS* but with spectacular growth opportunities can have a high P-E ratio. This implication is consistent with the data. Several growth-oriented firms in the high-tech industry have very little (or no) earnings, but because of the value of their growth options (i.e., positive-*NPV* investment opportunities) they have high P-E ratios. For example, Genentech stock had a price of $47.50 on November 11, 1993. However, Genentech pays no divided and has a P-E ratio of over 100. Avoiding these firms solely because of their high P-E's is unwise.

P-E RATIOS AND FIRM RISK

There is an inverse relationship between the P-E ratio and the firm's discount rate (k). Since the discount rate increases with the risk of the firm, P-E ratios decrease as the firm's risk increases. This appears to be consistent with the intuition that risk-averse investors will pay more per dollar of earnings if the risk associated with the earnings is lower.

P-E RATIOS AND ACCOUNTING METHODS

We saw in Chapter 2 that a firm's earnings are sensitive to the accounting methods used. Thus a firm that follows conservative accounting methods likely generates lower earnings and *EPS* and hence has a higher P-E ratio. Aggressive accounting methods that magnify earnings have the effect of lowering the P-E ratio.[14]

SUMMARY

Section 13-1: Equity Ownership

What rights do equityholders possess?

- Equity is simply ownership and carries certain rights with it, including limited liability, which protects their wealth not invested in the firm, proportionate ownership and preemptive rights, the right to inspect the firm's books, the ability to freely sell ownership shares, and the right to dividends and any residual upon dissolution of the corporation.

[13] See E. F. Fama and K. French, "The Cross-section of Expected Stock Returns," *Journal of Finance* 47 (1992): 427–466.

[14] Also see the discussion in Chapter 2 on fooling the marketplace by accounting manipulations.

■ Limited liability protects owners' wealth that is not invested in the firm, lowers equityholders' need to monitor management, and makes the wealth of the other shareholders unimportant. By making it easy to buy and sell shares, it facilitates the working of the takeover market, thus reducing agency costs and increasing firm value.

How can stockholders exercise control over the firm?

■ Shareholders elect the board of directors, and through the board, they can choose and replace management. Directors are elected by majority voting or cumulative voting.

■ Voting stock bears a premium over nonvoting stock. This implies that control has economic value.

■ Stockholders can vote in person or by proxy. In large companies, most of the voting is by proxy. A proxy fight ensues when a dissident group solicits votes of other stockholders to elect its own board.

■ Occasionally, companies create multiple classes of stock, each with different rights and privileges. Multiple stock classes give rise to class or series voting, contingent voting, and disproportionate voting arrangements.

Section 13-2: Sources of Equity Capital

How can businesses raise equity capital?

■ Ownership in a corporation can begin as informally as trading a piece of the company to a relative for seed capital. Capital may be acquired from venture capitalists, who provide capital for a firm to grow and often expertise not possessed by the entrepreneur who began the firm.

■ As a firm grows, it may seek to place its equity with investors through a private placement, which is quick and private but is more expensive for the firm because of the illiquidity and risk of the stock. Such stock is called letter stock.

■ Private placements have historically been used by small to medium-size firms; however, recently, large firms have also used this method.

What are the benefits and costs in becoming a publicly traded firm?

■ By going public the owners can "cash out" some or all of their wealth in the firm and/or diversify their holdings into other firms. Public corporations can also raise external funds more easily.

■ There are disadvantages to going public. Managerial flexibility is reduced, and disclosure and filing requirements can become burdensome.

Section 13-3: Dividends and Stock Prices

How do dividends affect stock prices?

■ The price of a stock is the present value of the expected benefits to the stock, discounted at the investors' required rate of return (or opportunity cost), which is the sum of the expected dividend yield and the expected capital gains yield.

■ If we assume that the dividends grow at a constant rate forever, the stock price can be calculated using the Gordon valuation model. The growth rate is estimated as the product of the firm's retention ratio and the return on equity.

Section 13-4: Growth Options and Stock Prices

How do cash flows from future growth opportunities affect stock prices?

■ Managers who pursue goals of "empire building" can increase dividends by investing the firm's earnings in negative-*NPV* projects. In this case, the firm's stock price falls because investors cannot recover their opportunity cost. Increasing dividends can increase stock prices only if the firm's investments have positive *NPVs*.

■ The price of a stock is the sum of two factors: the stock price that would exist if the firm had no growth options and the present value of the firm's growth options per share.

■ Firms with high growth options see high P-E ratios. Increasing risk and aggressive accounting procedures lead to lower P-E ratios.

QUESTIONS

1. List the customary rights of common stockholders.

2. What is the difference between majority voting and cumulative voting?

3. How is the number of votes needed (under cumulative voting) to ensure a director's election calculated?

4. What are preemptive rights? Why are they issued? What is the "dilution effect" caused by these rights?

5. What are the advantages and disadvantages of a private placement of equity?

6. Explain why "going public" can reduce management's flexibility.

7. Explain why raising additional equity capital can "dilute" the value of current stockholders' shares.

8. What are the advantages of a company going public?

9. What are some of the considerations in the decision of whether to be listed on an exchange?

10. What are the crucial assumptions underlying the Gordon valuation model? How is the growth rate *g* estimated?

11. How do the growth opportunities in a firm affect its stock price?

12. How are a firm's earnings per share (*EPS*) and price–earnings ratio (P-E) interrelated with the firm's growth opportunities?

PROBLEMS

1. Bulls-eye Stores, Inc., has 2 million common shares outstanding. The share price is currently $20, and the annual dividend paid at the end of the year will be $0.75 per share. What is the expected rate of return on a share under these conditions?

   (a) The share price will be $21 at the end of the year.

   (b) The share price will be $22.50 at the end of the year.

2. One year ago an investor purchased 100 shares of Pacific Oil for $25 each. The annual dividend per share was $1, and the share price today is $27. On

the same day she purchased the shares, her brother purchased 100 shares of Georgia Edison for $15 per share. The annual dividend per share was $2.30, and the share price today is $14.50. Who earned a greater rate of return?

3. A broker expects Trans-Earth Airlines common shares to earn a 20% return during the coming year. The share price is currently $15, and the dividend is expected to be $0.50 per share. What does the broker expect the share price to be at the end of the year?

4. Sergeant Motors' common shares are trading for $30 each. Annual dividends (paid at the end of the year) are expected to be constant at $1 for the next four years. If an investor wants a 15% return on the investment, what is the share price expected to be in four years?

5. The Centurion Corporation's common shares are trading for $23 each. Annual dividends are expected to be $0.75 for each of the next five years. If the share price is expected to be $40 at the end of five years, what annual rate of return is anticipated during this five-year period?

6. TLL Corp. has announced that it will keep its annual dividend at $1.50 forever. If a share costs $10, what rate of return is earned?

7. The Midwest Grain Co. pays an annual dividend of $1.80 and is expected to do so permanently. If an investor requires a 15% return on his investment, how much is he willing to pay for a share?

8. The Libre Noir Referral Service is about to issue stock. The end-of-the-year dividend is expected to be $1.20, and an investor requires an 18% return to buy the shares. How much is she willing to pay for a share if she expects dividends to grow indefinitely at the following annual rates?

    (a) -5% (b) 0%   (c) 5%   (d) 10%

9. Shares of Telstar, Inc., just paid a $1.60 dividend, and the dividend was $0.89 12 years ago. What has been the annual growth rate in dividends during this time? If the growth rate remains the same, how much should an investor be willing to pay for a share if the following returns are required?

    (a) 10%   (b) 12%   (c) 14%   (d) 16%

10. C-Paul Restaurant has common shares outstanding that are currently trading for $12 each. The end-of-year dividend is expected to be $0.80, and dividends will grow indefinitely at a rate of 6%. What rate of return is anticipated on the stock?

11. Richard Smith currently leases a phone and will pay a $2.50 charge at the end of this month. He expects this rate to increase by 0.5% per month. He is considering the purchase of a phone (which he anticipates will last forever).

    (a) If Richard requires a return of 2% per month to "invest" in a phone, how much is he willing to pay for one?

    (b) If the phones are currently selling for $50 each, what will be the monthly rate of return from investing in a phone? With monthly compounding, to what annual rate of return does this correspond?

12. A friend is incorporating her business, the Office Box. She has promised to pay a $1 annual dividend at the end of each of the next three years, with divi-

dends to grow at an annual rate of 8% after that. How much should an investor be willing to pay for a share with these rates of return?

(a) 10%

(b) 14%

(c) 18%

13. Compuchat, Inc., paid a dividend of $0.68 five years ago and has just paid an annual dividend of $1. Ms. Becker expects dividends to grow at the same annual rate for the next four years. After that, she expects dividends to grow at an annual rate of 12%. How much is she willing to pay for a share if she requires a 16% rate of return?

14. The Martin Management Company has paid the following dividends over the past six years:

Year	Dividend per Share
1994	$2.87
1993	2.73
1992	2.60
1991	2.48
1990	2.36
1989	2.25

The firm's 1995 dividend is expected to be $3.02.

(a) If 11.5% can be earned on similar-risk investments, what is the most an investor will pay per share for Martin's common stock?

(b) If 14% can be earned on similar-risk investments, what is the most an investor will pay per share?

(c) Compare and contrast the findings in parts (a) and (b), discussing the impact of changing risk on share value.

15. Baltimore Gas & Electric recently paid an annual dividend of $2.50. An analyst for Gensen Harris Investments believes that the dividend will grow at an average rate of 4% in perpetuity.

(a) What is the value of the stock if the discount rate is 10%?

(b) If tomorrow the discount rate falls to 8%, what is the effect on the stock price?

16. New Age Electronics expects to earn $100,000 this year. Earnings will grow 3% if the firm makes no new investments. The company has the opportunity to add a line of computer accessories to the business. The immediate outlay for this opportunity is $75,000, and the earnings from the line will begin one year from now. The computer accessories business will generate $25,000 in additional earnings. These earnings will also grow at 3%. The firm's discount rate is 10%, and 250,000 shares are outstanding.

(a) What is the price per share of stock without the new line, assuming that all of the earnings are paid out as dividends?

(b) What is the value of the growth opportunities that the new line offers?

(c) If the computer accessories line is added, what is the value of the firm's stock?

(d) With this new line, what is the P-E ratio of the firm?

(e) Does a high P-E ratio always imply that a firm has high growth potential?

17. General Auto Corporation is looking to produce a line of electric cars. Its earnings over the next 12 months will be $700,000. Earnings from the electric car line will be $300,000 per year, starting in 12 months, and will continue at this level indefinitely. Outstanding shares total 300,000, and the discount rate is 7%.

(a) What is the P-E of the firm without the new line, assuming that all of the earnings are paid out as dividends?

(b) What is the maximum initial investment that the firm will make to create the electric car line?

(c) If the initial investment is $4,000,000, what is the P-E ratio of the firm?

SUGGESTED ADDITIONAL READINGS

Bierman, H., Jr., and J. Hass. "Normative Stock Price Models." *Journal of Financial and Quantitative Analysis,* September 1971, pp. 1135–1144.

Bodie, Z., A. Kane, and A. Marcus. *Investments.* Homewood, IL: Richard D. Irwin, 1989.

Fabozzi, Frank J. *Fixed Income Mathematics.* Chicago: Probus, 1988.

Francis, J. C. *Investments: Analysis and Management,* 4th ed. New York: McGraw-Hill Book Co., 1986.

Gladstone, David. *Venture Capital Investing.* Englewood Cliffs, NJ: Prentice-Hall, 1988.

Hansen, R. S., and J. M. Pinkerton. "Direct Equity Financing: A Resolution of a Paradox." *Journal of Finance,* June 1982, pp. 651–666.

Haugen, R. A. *Modern Investment Theory.* Englewood Cliffs, NJ: Prentice-Hall, 1986.

Henderson, James W. *Obtaining Venture Financing: Principles and Practices.* Lexington, MA: Heath, 1988.

Pessin, Allan H. *Fundamentals of the Security Industry.* New York: New York Institute of Finance, 1985.

Radcliffe, Robert C. *Investment: Concepts, Analysis, and Strategy.* Glenview, IL: Scott, Foresman, 1982.

Shapiro, E., and C. R. Wolf. *The Role of Private Placements in Corporate Finance.* Boston: Harvard University Graduate School of Business Administration, 1972.

Soldofsky, Robert M. "The History of Bond Tables and Stock Valuation Models." *Journal of Finance,* March 1966, pp. 103–111.

Williams, John B. *The Theory of Investment Value.* Cambridge, MA: Harvard University Press, 1938.

FOURTEEN LONG-TERM DEBT AND PREFERRED STOCK

The human species, according to the best theory I can form of it, is composed of two distinct races, the men who borrow and the men who lend.

—Charles Lamb, 1818

O f all the methods used to raise long-term capital, long-term debt is the most popular and its significance to American corporations cannot be overemphasized. Long-term debt financing accounted for more than 80% of all new financing raised by corporations between 1989 and 1991, as shown in Table 14-1. Life insurance companies' investments and pension funds dominate these corporate debt purchases. There are three major reasons for the widespread use of long-term debt. First, compared with equity, it is less costly because of the tax deductibility of the interest costs. In effect, the cost of the debt is offset partially by the tax savings provided by the debt. Second, debt provides financial leverage (discussed in detail in later chapters), which allows for a magnification of profits (and losses). Third, compared with short-term debt, long-term debt offers greater flexibility to the borrower in that it allows much longer periods for repayment.

Although widely used, long-term debt is not necessarily attractive for all companies. Firms that experience big swings in income might find it difficult to meet the regular interest payments on the debt. For some firms, the possibility that financial leverage can magnify losses instead of profits may be too great a risk. In addition, firms that have had losses or low income may have little income from which to deduct the interest, and thus the tax advantages of interest deductibility may be nonexistent. Nonetheless, although all these considerations are valid, most corporations view long-term debt as an indispensable financing tool in maximizing their shareholders' wealth.

In this chapter we examine some of the considerations important to firms that use debt. Since preferred stock has several of the characteristics of debt, we also examine preferred stock. This chapter answers the following questions:

- What are some of the characteristics of a debt issue?

- How are debt securities issued?

- How are bond values determined?

- How are bond prices and interest rates related?

- How do the various types of bonds differ?

- What is preferred stock? How is its value determined?

Appendix 14A examines the **term structure of interest rates**. Appendix 14B shows how option pricing theory can be used to value debt and equity.

14-1

BASIC DEBT CHARACTERISTICS

 e first introduce some basic terminology associated with debt and then examine some common characteristics of debt securities.

■

SOURCES: IDD Information Services Inc. and the Board of Governors of the Federal Reserve System.

Type of Issue	1989	1990	1991
Bonds	$318,300	$299,884	$390,018
Stocks	57,870	40,165	75,467
All issues	$376,170	$340,049	$465,485

TABLE 14-1
New Security Issues Offered by U.S. Corporations (millions)

Terminology

Technically, a **bond** is a security evidencing long-term debt that matures in a year or more. Usually the term *bond* refers to long-term debt that is secured by assets. **Debentures,** often called "debs," are unsecured bonds, not secured by assets. The **par value,** also known as the **face value** or **maturity value,** of a bond or debenture is $1,000 unless otherwise specified. This is the amount of principal to be repaid at maturity. The **coupon interest rate** is the stated annual rate of interest on the bond. This rate gets its name from the coupons that are literally attached to bonds. Bondholders tear off the dated coupons and redeem them at a local bank or the bond issuer's agent. The coupon interest rate on the bond is printed on the coupon before the bond is issued. The coupon interest rate is also known as the **promised interest rate.** Issuers typically seek to sell bonds at as close to the par value as possible, so that the coupon rate on the bond is determined by current market interest rates, allowing the bond price to be set near $1,000. We have much more to say on this subject later.

When the annual interest of a bond or debenture is stated in dollar terms, it is called the **coupon amount.** Figure 14-1 shows the August 1993 public announcement of Aetna Life and Casualty Company's offering of $400 million of ten-year notes and 30-year debentures. The coupon interest rate on the 30-year debenture offering is $7\frac{1}{4}$%, and so the coupon amount is $72.50 a year. The coupon amount is found simply by multiplying the annual interest rate by the face value (0.0725 × $1,000). Although the semiannual payments can be calculated easily, we assume annual payments for ease of discussion.

For the Aetna *debenture* issue in Figure 14-1, the price is set at "99.974% plus accrued interest." The use of a percentage figure is standard in the industry and reflects the percentage of the $1,000 face value. **Accrued interest** refers to the practice by issuers of charging buyers the interest accrued on the bond or debenture from the date on which the interest rate was set. For example, if an investor buys a debenture today on which interest has been accruing for two weeks, she pays accrued interest of ($72.50/365 × 14 days) = $2.78. The interest plus $999.74, the price of the bond, amounts to a total cost of $1,002.52.

Bonds issued for the first time are called new or **unseasoned issues,** whereas those that have been on the market for more than a couple of weeks are called **seasoned** or **outstanding issues.** Unseasoned issues are generally considered more risky than seasoned ones.

Long-term debt may be sold publicly through an underwriter, who is usually an investment banker, or through private placement directly with institutions, which may number as few as two or as many as 20.

Debt Characteristics

Long-term debt comes in many varieties, shapes, and sizes. But all these debt instruments, despite some seemingly complex elements, possess five characteristics: maturity, security, repayment provisions, interest rates, and denomination.

Debt that is considered conventional simply consists of packages of characteristics that are commonly used. Small changes in the conventional elements can produce significantly different debt instruments. As a result, with a little creativity, the capital markets have developed new debt entities.

■

FIGURE 14-1
Debenture offering announcement

$400,000,000

Aetna Life and Casualty Company

$200,000,000
6⅜% Notes due August 15, 2003
Price 99.308%
Plus accrued interest from August 15, 1993

$200,000,000
7¼% Debentures due August 15, 2023
Price 99.974%
Plus accrued interest from August 15, 1993

Upon request, a copy of the Prospectus Supplement and the related Prospectus describing these securities and the business of the Company may be obtained within any State from any Underwriter who may legally distribute it within such State. The securities are offered only by means of the Prospectus Supplement and the related Prospectus, and this announcement is neither an offer to sell nor a solicitation of an offer to buy.

Goldman, Sachs & Co.

Merrill Lynch & Co.

J.P. Morgan Securities Inc.

August 17, 1993

MATURITY

Short-term debt is generally considered to be debt that matures in a year or less. Debt that matures after a year or more is often called **funded debt.** The word *funded* has no meaning except to indicate that the time to maturity is a year or longer. Funded debt is sometimes divided into medium-term and long-term debt. Medium-term or intermediate-term debt refers to one- to ten-year periods. In this usage, long-term debt encompasses anything longer, with most debt maturing in less than 30 years.

Term loans are borrowings on which fixed amounts of principal and interest are regularly paid over the life of the loan. Term loans typically run from three to seven years, although their maturities vary widely. Usually term loans are borrowed from a bank or a group of banks, but insurance companies often participate as well. Term loans are typically used by smaller companies.

Bonds mature in seven to 30 years from issue. Traditionally bonds were issued for 20 to 30 years, but more recently, in periods of high interest rates, seven- to ten-year maturities have become more popular.

SECURITY

Security refers to the recourse of the debt holder in the event of default. Term loans are usually unsecured. When they are secured, it is usually by equipment, to finance equipment purchases. They may also be used for other purposes, such as interim financing.

Bonds may also be secured by plant, equipment, and other securities. When they are secured by a mortgage, they are called, not surprisingly, **mortgage bonds.** When a company's stocks, notes, or bonds are pledged as security, or collateral, for a bond issue, they are called **collateral trust bonds.** There are first-mortgage and second-mortgage bonds, indicating the priority of claims.

Debentures are riskier than even second-mortgage bonds because debentures are unsecured, giving debenture holders only a general claim on a company's un-mortgaged assets. Debenture holders are second to bondholders in making claims on a company's mortgaged assets. Debentures thus pay a higher return to investors for the greater risk. Debentures are usually sold only by well-established companies that have high credit ratings. Debentures may also be classified as **senior** or **subordinated**—another reference to the claims status in case of default. Subordinated debenture holders are paid after senior debenture holders. Unless specifically stated otherwise, all issues are senior issues.

REPAYMENT PROVISIONS

For term loans, these provisions vary widely, depending on the company's history, cash flows, age, profitability, management, and other factors. Repayment may be in the form of equal monthly or quarterly payments of interest and principal, or it may be minimal in the first few years, with a balloon upon maturity. Term loans are often tailored to a company's expected needs; for example, the repayment schedule may be tied to projected cash flows.

Interest payments on American bonds are usually semiannual, whereas bonds issued in other countries may have annual interest payments. Principal repayments are contingent on the stipulations set forth in a legal document known as an **indenture,** which specifies all the requirements and conditions that must be met by bondholders and the corporation in order to protect both parties. To make sure that the company abides by the indenture, a **trustee,** usually a bank official, is named to act on behalf of the bondholders who have the fiduciary responsibility. If the company fails to adhere to the indenture's requirements, the indenture gives the trustee or some of the bondholders the right to declare the entire issue due and payable immediately.

These requirements are important, not only because of the consequences for the company if they are not met, but also because they greatly influence the risk and return of the bond and thus its value. The following discussion explains the basic provisions of an indenture.

SINKING FUND Bonds that are publicly traded are usually repaid through the use of a **sinking fund.** The sinking fund provision usually requires the company to retire, regularly, a specified amount of outstanding bonds. Some sinking funds tie bond redemptions to profits, but these are unusual. The firm may either buy back bonds in the marketplace or retire them by serial number, determined by a lottery, as set forth in the indenture. In any case, the effect is to require the company to make regular cash payments on its debt, not unlike regular payments on a term loan.

The term *sinking fund* originally referred to an actual money fund that was set aside, invested, and then used to retire bonds at maturity. But problems with this practice (the fund often was found to be insufficient to retire all the bonds) led to the current practice of actually retiring bonds before their maturity. The original method of funding is rarely used anymore.

Although a bond's maturity date may be 20 years from the date of issue, very few of the bonds may actually be outstanding on that maturity date. For example, in October 1992, May Department Stores made an offering of $200 million in $8\frac{3}{8}$% debentures due in 2022. The sinking fund of these 30-year debentures is to begin on October 1, 2003, ten years after the issue date. The company is required to redeem $10 million of its bonds annually. Thus the sinking fund is designed to retire 95% of the debentures before maturity. At maturity in October 2022, May Department Stores Company should have no more than 5%, or $10 million, of the debentures outstanding.

The $10 million represents the maximum principal amount of bonds left outstanding. It is not necessarily the actual amount expected to be outstanding. The sinking fund is a mandatory means of reducing the outstanding bonds, but there are other ways for the issue to be retired that are optional for both bondholders and the company. Bonds in this May Department Stores issue may be callable by the firm under certain conditions.

CALL PROVISIONS When a company redeems bonds before their maturity, it is said to *call* them. The company may call any or all of the bond issue as long as the indenture allows it under the sinking fund provision or its **call provision,** which usually specifies the **call price** at a particular time. In the May Department Stores offering, May Department Stores has the option to call, in part or as a whole, the offering according to the schedule shown in Figure 14-2. The call price includes a **call premium,** an amount related to the coupon interest rate added to the par value.

When a company replaces an entire old issue with a new one, the company is said to engage in a **refunding operation.** A refunding operation is attractive when interest rates have fallen since the date of the first issue. To carry out a refunding operation, the company must first be permitted to do so by the call provision, and then the company must consider the flotation costs and call premium involved to determine whether refunding is justified.

When a call is prohibited for a certain initial period, say ten years, the issue is said to carry a **deferred call provision.** Issues may also be **freely callable** or **noncallable,** terms that are self-explanatory. Call provisions give the issuer more flexibility but restrict a bondholder's potential earnings from the issue because, as we noted, the issuer is likely to carry out a refunding operation when it is paying a higher rate than that found in the current market. As a result, investors usually do not pay more than the call price for an issue because they know that companies will call their bonds if they become worth substantially more than the call price. Thus a callable bond has a ceiling on its price, whereas a noncallable bond does not.

For the May Department Stores example, notice the callability condition in Figure 14-2. The firm has a deferred call provision (noncallable until October 1, 2002), and the premiums are specified on the schedule. In practice, many 25- to

■

FIGURE 14-2
*May Department Stores
debenture issue with call
provisions*

MAY DEPARTMENT STORES CO. (THE)
Debentures 8-2/16s, due 2022: May Department Stores Co. debentures 8-3/8s, due 2022:

Moody's Rating—A2

AUTH—$200,000,000.

OUTSTG—Oct. 1, 1992, $200,000,000.

DATED—Oct. 1, 1992. DUE—Oct. 1, 2022.

INTEREST—8-1/8% per annum payable each A&O 1, to holders registered M&S 15.

TRUSTEE—The First National Bank of Chicago; and Citibank, N.A., N.Y.C.

DENOMINATION—Fully registered, $1,000 or any multiple thereof. Transferable and exchangeable without service charge.

CALLABLE—As a whole or in part, at option of Co., on or after Oct. 1, 2002, on at least 30 but not more than 60 days' notice to each Sept. 30 as follows:

2003	....	104.044	2004	....	103.640	2005	....	103.235
2006	....	102.831	2007	....	102.426	2008	....	102.022
2009	....	101.618	2010	....	101.213	2011	....	100.809
2012	....	100.404						

and thereafter at 100 plus accrued interest. Also callable for sinking fund.

SINKING FUND—Subject to mandatory annual sinking fund payments sufficient to retire $10,000,000 aggregate principal amount of the debentures on each Oct. 1 commencing Oct. 1, 2003. Such mandatory sinking fund payments are calculated to retire 95% of the aggregate principal amount of the debentures prior to maturity.

SECURITY—Not secured. Ranks on a parity with Co.'s other unsecured indebtedness. Unless the aggregate principal amount of all outstanding secured indebtedness of Co. and its restricted subsidiaries, the unsecured funded debt of the restricted subsidiaries, and the indebtedness to be secured does not exceed 15% of consolidated net tangible assets, Co. may not, and may not permit any restricted subsidiary to mortgage, pledge or create any lien, security interest, conditional sale or other title retention agreement or other similar encumbrance on any of the assets of Co. or any of its restricted subsidiaries, without making effective provision to secure the debentures at least equally and ratably with such indebtedness, so long as such indebtedness is so secured.

INDENTURE MODIFICATION—Indenture may be modified, except as provided, with consent of a majority of debs. outstg.

RIGHTS ON DEFAULT—Trustee, or 25% of debs. outstg., may declare principal due and payable (30 days grace for payment of interest).

PURPOSE—Proceeds will be used for general corporate purposes, including capital expenditures and working capital needs.

OFFERED—($200,000,000) at 99.713 (proceeds to Co., 98.838) on Oct. 1, 1992 thru Morgan Stanley & Co. and Merrill Lynch & Co.

SOURCE: *Moody's Industrial News Reports,* December 15, 1992, p. 3452.

30-year industrial bonds are nonrefundable for ten years. Medium-term bonds, maturing in seven to ten years, generally restrict the call option to the last two years, if one is permitted at all.

Most bonds issued today are callable. Various explanations have been advanced to explain their popularity. When the information possessed by management is not the same as the information available to the marketplace (informational asymmetry), managers can signal the firm's prospects to outsiders by their choice of the financing instrument. According to the **signaling explanation,** managers can signal the firm's better prospects through a call provision on the debt.[1] The issuance of callable debt, which involves a call premium, tells outsiders that the firm expects to pay off the debt at some point because the cash flows from its projects are good. Conversely, the issuance of noncallable debt (or equity) signals bad news.

At least two agency hypotheses try to explain the popularity of callable debt. The **underinvestment problem explanation** is that the call feature can lower agency costs by reducing the firm's incentive to pass up certain wealth-increasing projects.

---

[1] See E. H. Robbins and J. D. Schatzberg, "Callable Bonds: A Risk-Reducing Signalling Mechanism," *Journal of Finance,* September 1986, pp. 935–949.

As we know, stockholders may refuse to invest in low-risk projects that primarily benefit bondholders. The existence of a call feature on the bond thus allows stockholders to "get rid of" the debt when they have good, low-risk projects.[2] By calling in the debt, they can capture the project's benefits without having to share them with the creditors. This objective cannot be fully realized with a call provision, however. When the bonds are called, the bondholders are paid a call premium, and hence the gain to the bondholders when the firm invests in low-risk projects is not entirely eliminated; it is limited to the call premium. The **wealth transfer explanation** holds that bondholders favor call provisions because they can transfer wealth away from the stockholders in certain situations.[3] If the call price of the bond exceeds the market value of the bond when the firm calls in the bond, bondholders benefit and stockholders lose. Why would a firm call in a bond in this circumstance? There may be other offsetting benefits to the stockholders, some of which we examine next.

The **bond-refunding explanation** maintains that the only reason for a call feature is to reduce future interest costs. If interest rates decline in the future, the firm can call in the debt and reissue new debt at lower rates. If the present value of the interest saved exceeds the cash outlays required in calling in the debt, this can be a wealth-increasing decision for the firm. The **leverage-change explanation** states that firms use callable debt to change their capital structures. A closely related argument is that this change in capital structure can communicate valuable information to the market about the firm's future performance and thus affect stock prices. Some economists have suggested that the main reason for calling in the debt is to eliminate some restrictive covenant in the bond's indenture. If the restrictive covenant is too constraining and thereby undesirable, the **restrictive covenant explanation** says that calls can go around it.

It is difficult to separate out these various motives, and the empirical evidence has been unable to determine why call features exist. Vu's empirical test, for example, found that no one of these hypotheses alone can explain observed call behavior.[4] The data suggest that there are many motives for calling in the debt and therefore no single dominant one.

RESTRICTIVE COVENANTS The indenture also specifies restrictive covenants, which are the conditions under which a company must operate to ensure the bond's value over time. If these covenants are broken, the issue can become due immediately. Restrictive provisions include production investment, financing, and dividend covenants.

Generally, **production and investment covenants** can prohibit certain actions by a company, such as limiting the company's stake in other enterprises. They can also require certain actions, such as investing in particular projects, holding specified assets, requiring maintenance of the firm's properties, and requiring a level of the firm's working capital above a certain minimum level. Although enforcement may not be easy, violation of the covenants is usually regarded as a signal that there are problems in the company. The violation of, say, the working capital require-

[2]Z. Bodie and R. A. Taggart, "Future Investment Opportunities and the Value of a Call Provision on a Bond," *Journal of Finance*, September 1978, pp. 1187–1200.

[3]A. Barnea, R. A. Haugen, and L. W. Senbet, "A Rationale for Debt Maturity Structure and Call Provisions in the Agency Theoretic Framework," *Journal of Finance*, December 1980, pp. 1223–1234.

[4]Joseph D. Vu, "An Empirical Investigation of Calls on Non-convertible Bonds," *Journal of Financial Economics* 16 (1986): 235–265.

ment is a warning to bondholders, lenders, and equityholders to investigate a probable cash flow problem.

Financing and dividend covenants are aimed at restricting the company from engaging in activities that can hurt the safety of the bondholders' position, or that can benefit stockholders at the expense of the bondholders. Covenants may be written so that, for example, after closing a large bond issue, the company may not borrow a large amount of additional funds that might hurt the safety of the bonds just sold.

A typical financing covenant requires an industrial company's net tangible assets to be at least 2.5 times its long-term debt before it may incur additional debt. For example, the dividend restrictions that accompany Toll Brothers Inc.'s March 1993 offering of 9.5% subordinated notes specify that the company "may not pay cash dividends on, or acquire capital stock in excess of consolidated earnings subsequent to October 31, 1991, plus net proceeds after such date, from sale of stock and indebtedness converted into stock plus $20,000,000."[5]

Companies that break the covenants are considered to be in technical default, meaning that their entire debt becomes due immediately. As with defaults on payments, though, lenders and trustees typically work closely with companies and allow grace periods or renegotiation of debt agreements. The creditor may, for instance, grant waivers of the broken covenants, meaning that the violation is ignored for a certain period of time to give the company a chance to cure the default.

In addition to the restrictive covenants connected with debt, there are other ways in which managerial decisions are affected by the presence of debt. The manner in which debt affects the conflict of interests between owners and stockholders is examined in the Hidden Benefit highlight.

INTEREST RATES

The interest on term loans may be either fixed or floating, but it is usually floating. Floating rates are often tied to the prime lending rate, which is considered to be the rate that banks charge their most creditworthy customers. Actually a number of large, healthy companies pay a percentage point or two less than the prime rate. By contrast, small businesses usually are charged at least 1.5% to 2% above the prime. Interest may also be tied to rates for commercial paper, T-bills, or the London Interbank Offered Rate (LIBOR).

Bond rates are simply the interest rate on the coupon, regardless of changes in market interest rates. However, bond prices do reflect swings in the market interest rates, which we see later.

Swings in the market interest rate expose corporate issuers to interest rate risk. Corporate managers have found that one means by which to protect corporate issues from exposure to that risk is the financial futures market. In the futures market, contracts are made to buy or sell a particular good or service in the future at a price set today (as opposed to the cash market, in which most securities are sold, which requires delivery immediately or within a few days). This market allows the corporate manager to take a position in the futures market opposite to his or her position in the cash market, thereby insulating the manager from unwanted price swings in the cash market. Interest rate exposure can also be managed through interest rate swaps, which were discussed in Chapter 11.

---

[5] *Moody's Industrial News Reports,* April 13, 1993, p. 2934.

The most common reason given for a company's preference for borrowing rather than issuing new equity is that debt is cheaper because interest payments on the debt are tax deductible. However, there may be other benefits from a firm's use of debt, benefits related to the reduction of the agency costs that arise from conflicts between the managers and owners over the control and use of the firm's resources.

Problems that Arise from "Free Cash Flow"

Michael Jensen defines a firm's "**free cash flow**" as the cash flow in excess of that required to finance all positive-NPV projects.* According to Jensen, large firms have substantial free cash flows, which managers can use at their discretion. Managers have strong incentives to use these free cash flows to make the firm grow beyond its optimal size by investing in negative-NPV projects.

A firm with free cash flows should return them to the shareholders, but firms are reluctant to do so. Instead, managers prefer to retain the cash within the firm and see the firm expand. In 1989, for example, when there was overcapacity in the automobile industry, Ford Motor Company had nearly $15 billion in cash and marketable securities. Similarly, the development of the steel-belted tire increased tire life three times and led to overcapacity in the tire industry. At that time, Goodyear Tire Company made several unproductive investments that were not in the owners' best interests. As another example, in the late 1970s oil companies had overcapacity, and a number of firms in the industry had large free cash flows. These oil firms embarked on massive investment programs into areas of business they were not familiar with. Mobil purchased Marcor (retailing), Exxon purchased Reliance Electric (manufacturing) and Vydec (office equipment), and Sohio purchased Kennecott Copper (mining). However, according to Jensen, these acquisitions turned out to be among the least successful investments over the last decade.

Why Free Cash Flows Lead to Agency Problems

One reason managers may make poor investment decisions is that managerial compensation is often positively correlated with growth in sales rather than with increases in shareholder wealth. Managers may also want to increase firm size to enhance their own power and prestige, often at the expense of the owners. Moreover, the promotion-based reward system in many companies fosters excess growth. Instead of rewarding managers with, say, year-to-year bonuses, there are strong biases to create new positions to which managers can be promoted. This too can hurt the shareholders. These factors, individually or collectively, provide incentives for managers to keep growing the firm as much as possible even when this may not be in the owners' best interest, thus leading to the "agency problem" (discussed in Chapter 2).

How Debt Can Reduce the Agency Cost of Free Cash Flows

Jensen suggests that "the struggle over free cash flow is at the heart of the role of debt in the public corporation,"† and that debt can reduce some of the agency problems arising from cash flow. He argues that some important aspects of debt are often overlooked. He suggests that debt creation, without retention of the proceeds of the issue, limits the wasting of free cash flow and hence reduces agency costs. Since the firm must pay interest on the debt to stay afloat, debt forces managers to disgorge cash rather than invest the funds in negative-NPV projects. By raising debt, a firm in effect bonds its managers' promise to pay out future cash flows in a way that dividends cannot. Thus debt, by acting as a "bonding device," can lower agency costs and increase firm value. In addition, debt may be a powerful agency for change. A company with a large amount of debt that is having trouble meeting its interest obligations is forced to rethink its entire strategy. By creating a "crisis atmosphere" within the firm, debt forces managers to cut back on all but the best investments and hence curtail needless growth. Moreover, a firm in violation of debt covenants can create a board-level crisis to force quick and dramatic changes that can make the firm a more efficient organization.

If debt can lower agency costs, then a large publicly traded company with diffuse owners may find it advantageous to "go private" by paying off the shareholders with borrowed money. These transactions, known as **leveraged buyouts** (LBOs), are discussed in greater detail in Chapter 27. Such highly debt-financed organizational restructurings in the late 1980s may well have been motivated by the potential advantages of debt for lowering agency costs.

*M. C. Jensen, "Agency Costs of Free Cash Flow, Corporate Finance and Takeovers," American Economic Review, 1986.

†M. C. Jensen, "Eclipse of the Public Corporation," Harvard Business Review, September/October 1989.

DENOMINATIONS

EUROBONDS A bond offering made in a country but denominated in a foreign currency is called a **Eurobond offering.** International bond markets and development banks provide intermediate- to long-term sources of funds for the multinationals. An international bond is any bond sold outside the country of the borrower. There are two types of international bonds: the foreign bond and the Eurobond. The **foreign bond** is a bond issued in the currency of the country in which the bond is sold or traded. These bonds are traded in the secondary market in the country of issue. The main difference between these and domestic bonds is that the issuer is a foreign government or corporation, and it is subject to the security regulations of the country in which it is issued.

The **Eurobond** is denominated in a currency different from that of the country or countries in which it is issued. Typically, it is internationally syndicated, and a secondary market exists among the banks that deal in Eurobonds. Like Eurocurrency, Eurobonds have fewer regulatory requirements and therefore lower transaction costs.

EURODOLLARS Unsecured debt offerings for dollars in Europe are called **Eurodollars.** Similarly, other countries issue debt in U.S. dollars. The Eurocurrency markets provide for borrowing Eurodollars, usually through lines of credit or revolving credit arrangements in which the bank charges a commitment fee as well as interest on the principal borrowed. The Eurodollar is defined as a dollar-denominated deposit held in a bank outside the United States. Some people include even the deutsche mark deposits in Europe under the term **Eurodollar.**

There is an active market for these deposits, especially in Europe. The rate paid on Eurodollars is quoted in terms of the London Interbank Offer Rate (LIBOR), the rate that large London banks charge one another for Eurocurrency loans. Loans to large multinational companies are usually quoted in terms of the LIBOR plus a percentage for the risk premium based on the borrower's creditworthiness.

The principal advantage of Eurodollar deposits is that they are not under the scrutiny of U.S. regulatory agencies and therefore have no reserve requirements or FDIC insurance premiums required against them. With the associated lower costs, banks may offer a higher rate for these deposits, making them attractive to holders of excess dollar liquidity. Processing and overhead costs for loans are also lower because only large corporations with high credit standings may participate; thus borrowing may be at an attractive rate as well.

Table 14-2 summarizes each of the five characteristics of long-term debt financing, listing the conventions that are typically used within each category.

■

TABLE 14-2

Summary of Conventions in Term Loans and Bonds

	Term Loans	Bonds
Maturity	Three to seven years	Seven to 30 years *Medium-term bonds:* 7–10 years *Long-term bonds:* 10–30 years
Security	Unsecured or secured by equipment	*Most bonds:* secured by plant and equipment *Mortgage bonds:* mortgages *Debentures:* unsecured
Repayment provisions	Varies, ranges from equal monthly payments to custom designed for company's needs	Usually semiannual interest payments; principal repaid based on sinking fund, call, and refunding provisions
Interest rate	Usually floating, tied to prime rate or other accepted rate; sometimes fixed	Fixed
Denomination	Usually U.S. dollars	Usually U.S. dollars; Eurobonds are next most common denomination

14-2

DEBT OFFERINGS

Public debt offerings constitute the majority of corporate debt. Publicly offered bonds are so voluminous that they have helped establish not only the investment banking industry (discussed in Chapter 12) but also a ratings system for easier evaluation. The ratings procedures are discussed later in this section, but first we consider privately placed debt. Although small relative to public debt, this group is important to small companies and is gaining in use by large companies.

Private Placements

Term loans are privately arranged, but longer-term debt may be negotiated with a small group as well. Traditionally, private placements have been attractive to small and medium-sized companies that need to raise capital of less than $5 million. Now larger companies' placements reaching the $100 million level have gained in popularity. Private placements account for roughly one-fourth of all long-term corporate debt securities.

The debt may be placed with just two or three institutional investors or with as many as two dozen. For example, in June 1985, ICN Pharmaceuticals, Inc., signed an underwriting agreement with 22 Swiss banks, covering the placement of the equivalent of $19.2 million in Swiss currency of 5.75% convertible bonds, due in 1995. In 1993, IMC Fertilizer Group raised $260 million in a private placement with two institutional buyers, Lehman Brothers and Citicorp Securities Markets Inc.

ADVANTAGES OF PRIVATE PLACEMENTS

Companies find private placements desirable because they are far less costly than public placements. They need not be registered with the Securities and Exchange Commission (SEC), and companies avoid large underwriting fees and other flotation costs. Companies generally pay just a finder's fee to the investment bank, if there is one, that helps arrange the private placement. Speed and confidentiality are important advantages of private placements.

Private placements typically are custom made for a firm's needs, whereas offerings need to be more uniform to sell publicly. The investors are more willing to allow nonstandard terms because they perform intensive due diligence—a legal term that describes their investigation of all aspects of the firm's business, finances, management, projections, and so on. Thus they are more familiar and more comfortable with the company.

Such special treatment, however, is not free. The savings over public placements are partially or wholly offset by increased interest costs owing to the illiquidity of the private placement, the costs of research into the company, and the inherent risks of the debt.

RULE 144a

Traditionally, companies were free to sell their securities directly to large private investors, but these investors were required by the **Securities and Exchange Commission (SEC)** to hold on to the securities for at least two years before selling them. Because of this rule, many large institutional investors shied away from the private markets and companies were forced to pay higher interest rates on the debt to compensate investors for this illiquidity.

The SEC modified this rule, known as Rule 144a, in 1990 by removing the two-year waiting period for "large" investors, those with portfolios in excess of $100 million. The modified rule includes debt of both domestic and foreign companies.

This relaxation of Rule 144a may have far-reaching implications. First, because of the increased liquidity in the markets, the cost of borrowing to firms may go down. Transactions costs may decrease, making the debt cheaper to issue. Additionally, foreign companies may be more willing to invest in this market because of the increased flexibility and privacy. Moreover, corporate managers can persuade investment companies to commit to large sums of debt as soon as there is a possibility of a takeover. This increased flexibility in financing takeovers can only encourage greater activity in the takeover market. It has been pointed out that U.S. capital markets will see more foreign investment and American companies will find it easier to raise new capital.

The critics, however, contend that the new rule makes the financial system riskier. They suggest that the rule will set a trend toward less disclosure and that large investors who do not carefully examine the creditworthiness of the companies in which they invest can face serious financial problems.

Public Placements   The procedures for bringing a debt issue to the public market were examined in detail in Chapter 12, which covered both bonds and stocks. What is peculiar to bonds and not stocks, however, is the system of rating the bond issues. Investors rely on this system, which is intended to measure creditworthiness, so heavily that a ratings reduction generally results in a lower bond price, at least temporarily. In fact, the market often anticipates rating changes and depresses the value of the bond in question.

RATINGS FIRMS

Three major ratings firms in the United States, Standard & Poor's Corporation (or S&P), Moody's Investors Service, and Fitch Investor Services, "grade" bonds on their default risk. These debt ratings provide an easily recognizable yet simple measure that links a possibly unknown issuer of debt with a symbol of credit quality. Each debt rating becomes an indication of the firm's creditworthiness with respect to a specific debt issue.

Ratings range from triple A to C or D, depending on the rating service. Moody's definitions are shown in Table 14-3. For example, debts rated Aaa are judged to be of the "best quality" (i.e., to have the least degree of investment risk), whereas debts rated C are those with the lowest rating (i.e., "having extremely poor prospects of ever attaining any real investment standing").

Junk bonds are rated BB (double B) and below. Junk bond dealers argue that the appellation *junk bonds* is undeserved. In support of their argument, they point to the changing nature of the non-investment-grade debt markets since the nadir of junk bonds in 1990. The type of firm entering this market has changed. More creditworthy firms are entering the market seeking to refinance debt as compared with the 1980s, when firms used junk bonds to facilitate leveraged buyouts. Also, investors learned valuable lessons in the 1980s and are more demanding in the disclosure of information and more discriminating in accepting risks. Junk bond yields waned in use in the late 1980s, but they have recently become very attractive. For the one-year period ending November 1993, junk bond mutual funds earned an annualized rate of return of 21.03%, almost twice the return on high-quality corporate bond mutual funds (11.21%).[6]

The ratings, as measures of risk, are critical to the cost of the debt. The lower the rating is, the higher the cost is. Dating back to the turn of the century, the

---

[6]Information from Morningstar Mutual Funds, November 12, 1993.

TABLE 14-3
Moody's Bond Ratings[a]

Aaa: Bonds that are rated Aaa are judged to be of the best quality. They carry the smallest degree of investment risk and are generally referred to as "gilt edge." Interest payments are protected by a large or an exceptionally stable margin, and the principal is secure. Although the various protective elements are likely to change, such changes as can be visualized are most unlikely to impair the fundamentally strong position of such issues.

Aa: Bonds that are rated Aa are judged to be of high quality by all standards. Together with the Aaa group, they comprise what are generally known as high-grade bonds. They are rated lower than the best bonds because the margins of protection may not be as large as in Aaa securities, the fluctuation of protective elements may be of greater amplitude, or there may be other elements present that make the long-term risks appear somewhat larger than in Aaa securities.

A: Bonds that are rated A possess many favorable investment attributes and are to be considered upper-medium-grade obligations. Factors giving security to principal and interest are considered adequate, but elements may be present that suggest a susceptibility to impairment sometime in the future.

Baa: Bonds that are rated Baa are considered medium-grade obligations; that is, they are neither highly protected nor poorly secured. Interest payments and principal security appear adequate for the present, but certain protective elements may be lacking or may be characteristically unreliable over any great length of time. Such bonds lack outstanding investment characteristics and in fact have speculative characteristics as well.

Ba: Bonds that are rated Ba are judged to have speculative elements; their future cannot be considered as well assured. Often the protection of interest and principal payments may be very moderate and thereby not well safeguarded during both good and bad times over the future. Uncertainty of position characterizes bonds in this class.

B: Bonds that are rated B generally lack the characteristics of a desirable investment. Assurance of interest and principal payments or maintenance of other terms of the contract over any long period of time may be small.

Caa: Bonds that are rated Caa have a poor standing. Such issues may be in default or may have elements of danger with respect to principal or interest.

Ca: Bonds that are rated Ca represent obligations that are highly speculative. Such issues are often in default or have other marked shortcomings.

C: Bonds that are rated C are the lowest-rated class of bonds, and issues so rated can be regarded as having extremely poor prospects of ever attaining any real investment standing.

[a]Moody's applies numerical modifiers, 1, 2, and 3, to each generic rating classification from Aa through B in its corporate bond rating system. The modifier 1 indicates that the security ranks in the higher end of its generic rating category, the modifier 2 indicates a mid-range ranking, and the modifier 3 indicates that the issue ranks in the lower end of its generic rating category.

SOURCE: *Moody's Bond Record.*

ratings have become so well established that the bylaws of most pension funds prohibit investment in bonds below investment-grade level, or below triple B, thus restricting purchasers. Figure 14-3 shows the relative costs of debt at different rating levels—that is, the increasing costs over time to companies for each lower grade received from Moody's. It is clear that as interest rates fluctuated, the spread among the various grades also fluctuated, though not by very much.

RATINGS CRITERIA

The procedure for assigning a debt rating begins with a firm's formal request for such a service. After the request, the main tool that a rating agency uses to determine a firm's ability to make timely payments of principal and interest is a financial statement analysis, especially a ratio analysis, such as discussed in Appendix 20A. Special emphasis is placed on ratios that relate income and cash flows available to service the firm's debt obligations. Rating agencies also examine such ratios as operating profit margins, return on capital, and return on total assets.

As for asset protection, the ratio most commonly used is long-term debt to assets. This figure helps assess how much book value in assets is available to pay off debt if the need arises. Another balance sheet measure of relative debt burden is the ratio of long-term debt to total capital.

Many other factors also come into play: industry risk and the issuer's market position in the industry, operating efficiency, management, and accounting quality. The rating factors used by Standard & Poor's for industrial companies are reproduced in Figure 14-4. The categories cover virtually every conceivable aspect of a business, although it is clear that some factors are much more important than

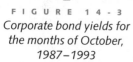

FIGURE 14-3
Corporate bond yields for the months of October, 1987–1993

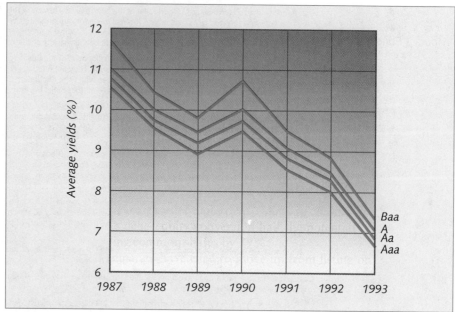

SOURCE: Graph compiled from *Moody's Bond Record,* showing Moody's corporate bond yield averages.

others. For example, the ratings agency may pay special attention to energy costs in evaluating the "issuer's operating efficiency" if the company is an airline, but it is less inclined to do so if the company makes shoes.

The rating services say that they do not use any formulas, and statistical surveys bear out this contention. In any case, it is difficult to quantify many of these qualitative judgments. For instance, S & P lowered its rating of Union Carbide Corporation's debt on January 8, 1985, following the December 3, 1984, gas leak disaster at its Bhopal, India, plant, which killed more than 2,000 people. The downgradings, which included reduction to BBB from A− of the company's subordinated long-term debt, was not because of liability but because of the accident's "potential negative spillover" onto suppliers and customers, the diversion of management's attention to defending itself against lawsuits, and the company's "constrained access to capital markets during a period of great uncertainty." Union Carbide's response was that the extent of the downgrading was "an overreaction."

Salomon Inc. had its debt downgraded following revelations about the Treasury rule violations (see the discussion in Chapter 1). Figure 14-5 reproduces Standard & Poor's downgrading announcement in the September 9 *CreditWatch* publication.

DEBT INSURANCE AND BOND RATINGS

The importance of ratings in setting the cost of debt has prompted some companies to find new ways to keep costs down. One method is by purchasing what amounts to debt insurance. The firm purchases a surety bond from an insurance company for its entire debt issue. With such insurance, the investors look to the rating of the insurance company rather than the issuing company. In one transaction, Samuel Montagu & Co. and Morgan Guaranty Ltd. in 1984 sold a $100 million, seven-year Eurobond insured by Aetna Casualty and Surety Co., in which the issuer's identity was never revealed.

FIGURE 14-4
Standard & Poor's rating criteria

Rating Profile Outlines

Industrial company rating methodology profile

I. **Industry risk:** Defined as the strength of the industry within the economy and relative to economic trends. This also includes the ease or difficulty of entering this industry, the importance of any diversity of the earnings base and the role of regulation and legislation.
   A. Importance in the economic cycle.
   B. Business cyclicality; earnings volatility, lead-lag and duration, diversity of earnings base, predictability and stability of revenues and earnings.
   C. Economic forces impacts; high inflation, energy costs and availability, international competitive position, social-political forces.
   D. Demand factors; real growth projections relative to GNP and basis for projections, maturity of markets.
   E. Basic financial characteristics of the business: fixed or working capital intensive; importance of credit as a sales tool.
   F. Supply factors: raw materials, labor, over/under utilized plant capacity.
   G. Federal, state, foreign regulation.
   H. Potential legislation.
   I. Fragmented or concentrated business.
   J. Barriers to entry/ease of entry.

II. **Issuer's industry position—market position:** The company's sales position in its major fields and its historical protection of its position and projected ability for the future.
   A. Ability to generate sales.
   B. Dominant and stable market shares.
   C. Marketing/distributing requirements of business—strengths, weaknesses, national, international, regional.
   D. R&D—degree of importance—degree of obsolescence—short or long product life.
   E. Support/service organization.
   F. Dependence on major customers/diversity of major customers.
   G. Long-term sales contracts/visibility of revenues/backlogs/prepayments (*e.g.*, subscriptions).
   H. Product diversity.

III. **Issuer's industry position—operating efficiency:** This covers the issuer's historical operating margins and assesses its ability to maintain or improve them based upon pricing or cost advantages.
   A. Ability to maintain or improve margins.
   B. Pricing leadership.
   C. Integration of manufacturing operations.
   D. Plant and equipment: modern and efficient or old and obsolete. Low or high cost producer.
   E. Supply of raw material.
   F. Level of capital and employee productivity.
   G. Labor: availability, cost, union relations.
   H. Pollution control requirements and impact on operating costs.
   I. Energy costs.

IV. **Management evaluation:**
   A. The record of achievement in operations and financial results.
   B. Planning—extent, integration and relationship to accomplishments. Both strategic and financial. Plan for growth—both internal and external.
   C. Controls—management, financial and internal auditing.
   D. Financing policies and practices.
   E. Commitment, consistency and credibility.
   F. Overall quality of management; line of succession—strength of middle management.
   G. Merger and acquisition considerations.
   H. Performance vs. peers.

V. **Accounting quality:** Overall accounting evaluation of the methods employed and the extent to which they overstate or understate financial performance and position.
   A. Auditor's qualifications.
   B. LIFO vs. FIFO inventory method.
   C. Goodwill and intangible assets.
   D. Recording of revenues.
   E. Depreciation policies.
   F. Nonconsolidated subsidiaries.
   G. Method of accounting and funding for pension liabilities. Basic posture of the pension plan assumptions.
   H. Undervalued assets such as LIFO reserve.

VI. **Earnings protection:** Key measurements indicating the basic long-term earnings power of the company including:
   A. Returns on capital.
   B. Pretax coverage ratios.
   C. Profit margins.
   D. Earnings on asset/business segments.
   E. Sources of future earnings growth.
   F. Pension service coverage.
   G. Ability to finance growth internally.
   H. Inflation-adjusted earning capacity.

VII. **Financial leverage and asset protection:** Relative usage of debt, with due allowance for differences in debt usage appropriate to different types of businesses.
   A. Long-term debt and total debt to capital.
   B. Total liabilities to net tangible stockholders' equity.
   C. Preferred stock/capitalization.
   D. Leverage implicit in off-balance sheet financing arrangements, production payments, operating rentals of property, plant and equipment, nonconsolidated subsidiaries, unfunded pension liabilities, etc.
   E. Nature of assets.
   F. Working capital management—accounts receivable, inventory, and accounts payable turnover.

(*continued*)

■

F I G U R E   1 4 - 4
continued

G. Level, nature and value of intangible assets.
H. Off-balance sheet assets such as undervalued natural resources or LIFO reserve.

VIII. **Cash flow adequacy:** Relationship of cash flow to leverage and ability to internally meet all business cash needs.
   A. Evaluation of size and scope of total capital requirements and capital spending flexibility.
   B. Evaluation of variability of future cash flow.
   C. Cash flow to fixed and working capital requirements.
   D. Cash flow to debt.
   E. Free cash flow to short-term debt and total debt.

IX. **Financial flexibility:** Evaluation of the company's financing needs, plans, and alternatives and its flexibility to accomplish its financing program under stress without damaging creditworthiness.
   A. Relative financing needs.
   B. Projected financing plan.

C. Financing alternatives under stress—ability to attract capital.
D. Capital spending flexibility.
E. Asset redeployment potentials—nature of assets and undervalued liabilities.
F. Nature and level of off-balance sheet assets or liabilities. This would include unfunded vested pension benefits and LIFO reserves.
G. High level of short-term debt/high level of floating rate debt.
H. Heavy or unwieldy debt service schedule (bullet maturities in future)—either of debt or sinking fund preferred stock.
I. Heavy percentage of preferred stock as a percentage of total capital.
J. Overall assessment of near-term sources of funds as compared to requirements for funds/internal financial self-sufficiency/need for external financing.
K. Ownership/affiliation.

SOURCE: *Standard & Poor's Credit Overview*, pp. 90, 91. Reprinted with permission.

That aspect is particularly attractive to private companies that wish to keep such information private. The secretive Rockefeller Group in 1984 sold a $100-million Eurobond issue at nine points above Treasury rates, much less than conventional financing, and its balance sheet remained a private matter. The catch is that insur-

■

F I G U R E   1 4 - 5
Standard & Poor's announcement concerning Salomon Inc.

SALOMON INC.

UPDATE: NEGATIVE DOWNGRADED

	TO	FROM
Sr. debt	A	A+
Sub. debt	A–	A
Pfd. stock	BBB+	A–

UPDATE: NEGATIVE

Comm. pap.	A-1

Rated debt: $4 bil.

Salomon Inc.'s ratings are lowered but remain on CreditWatch with negative implications. The commercial paper rating is not lowered and remains under surveillance. The original CreditWatch listing occurred on Aug. 26. The downgrades reflect Salomon's reduced financial flexibility following revelations about Treasury rule violations in its government securities operation. The commercial paper rating is not being lowered at this time because S&P believes that the firm has sufficient liquidity to meet maturing debt obligations until confidence in the firm is restored and normal short-term funding operations are resumed. The firm uses commercial paper to fund liquid security inventories.

However, all ratings remain on CreditWatch because of the risk that confidence in Salomon Brothers—on the part of lenders and trading counterparties—could erode further in the present environment. This risk is aggravated by the ongoing government scrutiny of both Salomon Brothers and the government securities market, and the attendant publicity. It is S&P's opinion at this time that Salomon's fundamental operations remain sound and thus far have not been irreparably damaged by the present circumstances. Furthermore, new management is acting aggressively to reinforce internal controls and distance the firm as quickly as possible from the conditions that led to the present turmoil. Nevertheless, the reduction in the long-term rating reflects some probable lingering impact on the reputation of the firm, as well as direct monetary cost of litigation and government fines that may be incurred and the amount of which is unknown at the present time. The rating anticipates that these costs, while likely to be material, will not be large enough to seriously damage the firm's financial strength.

SOURCE: Standard & Poor's *CreditWatch*, September 9, 1991, p. 12.

ers are reluctant to insure the debt of companies whose ratings are less than investment grade. In addition, some insurers require collateral to back the surety bond.

<table>
<tr><td>**14-3**</td></tr>
<tr><td>VALUING BONDS</td></tr>
</table>

We examine bond valuation through the eyes of Jack Farmer, a recent university graduate now working for a major pension fund. Jack must make long-term bond purchase recommendations to the fund's investment committee. In particular, the committee has instructed Jack to include value and rate of return calculations in his recommendations. A portion of the fund's portfolio is invested in riskless debt, with risk here defined by the likelihood that the bond issuer will default on its obligations. Therefore riskless debt is government debt that has no default risk or highly rated corporate debt that has an extremely small probability of default. Risky debt, on the other hand, is debt for which default probabilities are nonnegligible.

Valuing Riskless Bonds   Because the cash flows of a bond are a *contractual* payment of a fixed amount of interest over a certain number of years, plus the face value at redemption, Jack can determine the bond's current market value using equation (14-1):

$$D_0 = \sum_{t=1}^{n} \frac{I_t}{(1 + k_d)^t} + \frac{M_n}{(1 + k_d)^n} \tag{14-1}$$

or

$$D_0 = \underset{\substack{\text{present value of an} \\ \text{annuity stream of} \\ \text{cash flows}}}{I_t(PVFA_{k_d,n})} + \underset{\substack{\text{present value of} \\ \text{a future lump-} \\ \text{sum payment}}}{M_n(PVF_{k_d,n})}$$

where

D_0 is the current market price of the bond

I_t is the periodic coupon interest paid at the end of period t (I_t = coupon rate $\times M_n$)

k_d is the required rate of return (RRR) on the bond

n is the number of periods that remain before the bond is redeemed

M_n is the principal (or face amount) of the bond

Suppose that Jack must value a 20-year, $1,000 par value U.S. Treasury bond that has an annual coupon rate of 10% (i.e., $0.10 \times \$1,000 = \$100$ in interest is paid every year). If Jack determines that the appropriate RRR for this bond is 12%, what is its current price (market value)? According to equation (14-1),

$$D_0 = \sum_{t=1}^{20} \frac{\$100}{(1 + 0.12)^t} + \frac{\$1,000}{(1 + 0.12)^{20}}$$

$$= \$100(PVFA_{0.12,20}) + \$1,000(PVF_{0.12,20})$$

$$= \$100(7.4694) + \$1,000(0.1037) = \$850.64$$

The bond is selling for less than par value. The reason is that the discount rate on the bond (12%) is greater than the coupon rate offered by the bond (10%). If

If:[a]	Then
k_d > coupon rate	Bond sells at a discount.
k_d = coupon rate	Bond sells at par.
k_d < coupon rate	Bond sells at a premium.

[a] k_d = RRR on the bond.

TABLE 14-4
Relationship Among Required Rates of Return, Coupon Rates, and Bond Prices for Riskless Debt

investors require a 12% return and the bond pays a 10% rate, how can investors get their required rate? Clearly, by paying less than $1,000 for the bond. Bonds that sell at less than par value are said to be *selling at a discount*. This is not to be confused with *discount bonds,* which are bonds that pay no coupon interest. They are also known as *zero-coupon bonds,* or *zeros*. Investors buy these bonds at a discount from the par value—hence the name.

What happens to this bond's value if Jack's *RRR* on the bond changes from 12% to 8%? In this case, only k_d changes, so that

$$D_0 = \sum_{t=1}^{20} \frac{\$100}{(1 + 0.08)^t} + \frac{\$1,000}{(1 + 0.08)^{20}}$$

$$= \$100(PVFA_{0.08,20}) + \$1,000(PVF_{0.08,20})$$
$$= \$100(9.8181) + \$1,000(0.2145) = \$1,196.31$$

The bond's market value is greater than its par value. In this case, market interest rates are lower than they were when the bond was issued. Bonds that sell for more than par value are said to be *selling at a premium*. A bond's market value equals its par value whenever the coupon rate and the discount rate are the same.

Table 14-4 summarizes the relationship among coupon rates, required rates of return, and the par value of bonds. This table applies only to riskless debt.

DETERMINING A BOND'S YIELD TO MATURITY

In calculating the bond price, Jack's discount rate (k_d) was a given. At a required rate of return of 8%, Jack's calculated bond price is $1,196.31. Suppose that the market price of the bond was in fact only $1,150. Then, for Jack, the bond would be a "good buy." Whether Jack finds the bond a good buy or a bad buy depends on the cash flows provided by the asset and Jack's discount rate.

Now consider a slightly different problem. Jack has to evaluate the purchase of a ten-year U.S. Treasury bond. Instead of calculating the price of the bond, he wants to calculate the rate of return the fund will get if he buys the bond at the existing market price (irrespective of whether it is over- or underpriced) and holds it until it matures. The rate of return that an investor can expect by purchasing a bond at its current market price and holding it until it matures is the **yield to maturity** (**YTM**). The yield to maturity of a bond is the discount rate that equates the present value of the bond's cash flows to the current market price. It is the same as the bond's internal rate of return (*IRR*).

If the ten-year, $1,000 par value bond has an annual coupon rate of 8% and its current price is $935.80, what is the yield to maturity? Jack can enter the variables given into the basic bond valuation model, equation (14-1):

$$\$935.80 = \$80(PVFA_{?,10}) + \$1,000(PVF_{?,10})$$

Because the price is less than par value, the yield to maturity must be more than 8%. By means of trial and error, we find the yield to maturity to be 9%.

YIELD TO MATURITY VALUES

Yield to maturity equals the coupon interest rate if, and only if, the bond is purchased at its par value or, put differently, the "going rate of interest" is equal to the coupon rate. For example, if the price is known to be greater than the par value, it is clear that the yield to maturity must be lower than the coupon rate. This is the starting point.

Analyses that use yield to maturity are helpful as a starting point but can be dangerous if used blindly. Just like the *IRR,* the *YTM* is an overall rate that implicitly discounts all payments to the investor at the same rate. This may be fallacious if, say, the bondholder's required rate changes over time, as is more realistic. Those payments are also assumed to be reinvested at the same rate, which is likely to be misleading. Several other weaknesses of the *IRR,* discussed in Chapter 9, also apply to the *YTM.*

In addition, it is important to note that bond prices are not determined by the yield to maturity; rather, yield to maturity can be determined only after the market value of the bond is known. That market value, in turn, is determined by the discount rate.

SEMIANNUAL COUPON PAYMENTS

How should Jack modify his calculations if, instead of annual interest payments, the bond pays interest semiannually? The procedure used to value bonds in this situation is similar to that studied in Chapter 4. The process has three steps:

Step 1: Convert the annual interest, I_t, to semiannual interest, by dividing it by 2.

Step 2: Convert the remaining number of years to maturity, n, to the number of six-month periods to maturity, by multiplying n by 2.

Step 3: Convert the required return from an annual rate, k_d, to a semiannual rate, by dividing it by 2.

Applying these changes to equation (14-1) yields

$$D_0 = \sum_{t=1}^{2n} \frac{\dfrac{I_t}{2}}{\left(1 + \dfrac{k_d}{2}\right)^t} + \frac{M_{2n}}{\left(1 + \dfrac{k_d}{2}\right)^{2n}}$$

or

$$D_0 = \frac{I_t}{2}(PVFA_{k_d/2,2n}) + M_{2n}(PVF_{k_d/2,2n}) \qquad (14\text{-}2)$$

Consider the earlier example of a 20-year, $1,000 par value bond with an annual coupon rate of 10% and a 12% required rate of return. If this bond is now assumed to pay interest semiannually, Jack will find using equation (14-1) that the current bond price is:

$$D_0 = \frac{\$100}{2}(PVFA_{0.12/2,2\times20}) + \$1,000(PVF_{0.12/2,2\times20})$$

$$= \$50(PVFA_{0.06,40}) + \$1,000(PVF_{0.06,40})$$
$$= \$50(15.0463) + \$1,000(0.0972) = \$849.52$$

This price is slightly lower than the $850.64 value found using annual compounding.

The Basics of Risky Debt Valuation

Thus far Jack has valued riskless debt on which the issuer will not default on its obligations. However, his fund also invests in low-rated corporate debt, which is considered risky because default is almost certainly a possibility. If the firm that is issuing the debt is unable to generate enough cash flows from operations and is unable to raise additional capital through new security issues, it will be unable to meet its fixed obligations to the creditors and the firm will default on its debt.

Jack's specific valuation task concerns the debt issued by Omega Manufacturing, Inc., for which the total face value and the total market value are $100,000. This is known as **par debt** because the debt's market value equals its par or face value. Omega's debt has a 8% coupon (or promised) interest rate and matures next year. Thus the promised cash flows to the creditors are $108,000 ($100,000 in principal plus $8,000 in interest).

Can Omega deliver on its promise to its creditors? That depends on Omega's cash flows next year. Assume, for simplicity, that there are two potential outcomes next year. Omega's cash flows are either $115,000 (in "state 1") or $96,000 (in "state 2"), depending on the condition ("state") of the U.S. economy. Assume that the probabilities of states 1 and 2 are 0.8 and 0.2, respectively. In state 1, Omega is solvent and the bondholders are fully paid off. Thus their cash flows in state 1 are $108,000. However, in state 2, Omega does not have enough money to pay off the creditors. Because the stockholders have limited liability, creditors cannot expect them to make up the difference. So creditors simply take whatever is available; they take all of the $96,000 in the firm's cash flows. Thus, even though the *promised* cash flows to the bondholders are $108,000, the *expected* cash flows to the creditors are:

$$E\left(\begin{array}{c}\text{cash flows}\\\text{to debt}\end{array}\right) = \left(\begin{array}{c}\text{probability}\\\text{of state 1}\end{array}\right) \times \left(\begin{array}{c}\text{cash flows}\\\text{in state 1}\end{array}\right) + \left(\begin{array}{c}\text{probability}\\\text{of state 2}\end{array}\right) \times \left(\begin{array}{c}\text{cash flows}\\\text{in state 2}\end{array}\right)$$

$$= 0.8 \times \$108,000 + 0.2 \times \$96,000$$
$$= \$105,600$$

Because the firm can default on the debt, the expected cash flows to creditors are less than the promised cash flows.

Now, how much is this bond worth? The current bond price must be the present value of the expected cash flows of $105,600 next year. Since the bond is selling at par, we have $100,000 = \$105,600/(1 + k_d)$, so that the required rate of return on the bond $k_d = 5.6\%$. If we approach this problem from a slightly different angle, what rate of return can Jack expect if he buys this bond at the existing market price of $1,000? Jack's expected rate is 5.6%.

KEY CONCEPT
With risky debt, creditors' expected cash flows are less than the promised cash flows, and the expected return on the debt is lower than the promised interest rate.

This result for risky debt contrasts with that for riskless debt summarized in Table 14-4. For example, the result that for a bond selling at par the coupon rate and the expected rate are equivalent no longer applies when the firm can default on its debt.

14-4

BOND PRICE BEHAVIOR

I n the previous section we developed means of calculating a bond's market value and showed how the value of the bond is inversely related to the discount rate of the bond. In this section we examine this relationship in more detail.

*Price–Interest Rate
Relationships*

A bond's coupon interest rate never changes. The Aetna offering is set at $7\frac{1}{4}\%$, and so it always pays $7\frac{1}{4}\%$ of the par value, regardless of changes in the market interest rates. Once issued, however, bonds trade in the market, and the bond's price strongly reflects changes in the market. This relationship is shown quantitatively below.

The fundamental principle in bond price behavior is that when market interest rates rise, bond prices fall. Conversely, when market interest rates fall, bond prices rise. Intuitively, this makes sense: Suppose that the market interest rate jumps to 10%. A buyer is not going to pay par value for Aetna's $7\frac{1}{4}\%$ bond when she can get a 10% return elsewhere—unless she can get the bond at a discount, which is a price less than the $1,000 par value. By paying less for the bond, the buyer is raising the effective rate of return to herself because the actual interest payment to her never changes.

Similarly, if market rates fall to 5%, the seller is not willing to part with the bond unless she could obtain a premium price for the bond, a price greater than the par value. Put differently, if buyers have a choice between paying $1,000 for this $7\frac{1}{4}\%$ bond and $1,000 for a 5% bond, the buyers naturally seek the $7\frac{1}{4}\%$ bond. They bid up the price of the $7\frac{1}{4}\%$ bond to the level at which they are indifferent between the $7\frac{1}{4}\%$ bond and the 5% bond.

What is the bond's market value? It is simply the present value of the bond's future cash flows, or the interest payments, plus its principal repayment upon maturity. The appropriate discount rate at the time of purchase is the rate of return that the investor is forgoing in order to lock in the bond's $7\frac{1}{4}\%$ rate, assuming equal levels of risk. This rate is the investor's discount rate.

For discussion purposes, assume that this rate is 8%. That means that the investor is forgoing a return of 8% in the market in order to buy the $7\frac{1}{4}\%$ bond. Therefore she is willing to buy the bond only at a discount, thereby raising her effective rate of return.

For Aetna's 30-year, $7\frac{1}{4}\%$ debenture, at a discount rate of 8%, the amount the investor is willing to pay today is

$$
\begin{aligned}
PV &= [\text{annual coupon interest (\$)}](PVFA_{0.08,30}) \\
&\quad + (\$1,000 \text{ par value})(PVF_{0.08,30}) \\
&= (\$72.50 \times 11.2578) + (\$1,000 \times 0.0994) \\
&= \$915.59
\end{aligned}
$$

Thus the debenture is worth only $915.59 when the alternative market rate is 8%. Because bond prices are quoted as a percentage of their par value, the bond in the example is priced at 91.559%. Clearly, if the market rate was higher, the applicable discount rate would be higher, and the bond's value would fall further. On the other hand, if interest rates fell, the bond's value would be higher.

The 8% discount rate illustrates the point well but is unrealistic for most investors. As stated earlier, the coupon rate on an offering typically is established so that the bonds sell initially at or close to their $1,000 par value. Thus the coupon rate is intended to reflect the investors' discount rate; for most investors, the rate is about $7\frac{1}{4}\%$.

*Bond Values
Over Time*

As bonds approach their maturity date, their values come nearer to their par value. Why does this happen? The answer lies in how bond values are calculated.

This phenomenon is best illustrated by looking at a 30-year, 8% bond due in 2000. Suppose that immediately after this bond was issued in 1970, the market interest rate changed to 6%. Using the preceding *PV* equation, an investor in

■

TABLE 14-5

*Present Values on an 8%
Bond, 6% Discount Rate,
Approaching Maturity*

Year (for 1970 Bond Issue)	Years Until Maturity	Present Values				
		Annuity	+	Principal	=	Total
1970	30	$1,101.18	+	$ 174.10	=	$1,275.28
1980	20	917.59	+	311.80	=	1,229.39
1990	10	588.81	+	558.40	=	1,147.21
1999	1	75.47	+	943.40	=	1,018.87
2000	0	0	+	1,000	=	1,000

1970 would have been willing to pay ($80 × 13.7648) + ($1,000 × 0.1741) = $1,275.28.

In 1980, ten years later, with the same market rate of 6%, how much would the investor have been willing to pay? Using the 20-year period remaining in the life of the bond, we find the amount is $1,229.39. Table 14-5 shows that as the years until maturity grow fewer, the bond's value approaches the par value. With just one year before the bond matures, the investor is willing to pay only about $19 over the par value.

Figure 14-6 depicts this movement graphically, not only for a premium bond (a bond for which the market value exceeds the face value), which was used in the Table 14-5 example, but also for a par value bond (a bond for which the market value is the same as the face value), for which interest rates are assumed constant at 8%, and for a discount bond, for which interest rates are assumed constant at 10%. Clearly, if rates are expected to change, the bond values fluctuate as well.

That fluctuation is much greater for long-term debt than for short-term debt. To understand why this is so, look again at Table 14-5. Think of the calculations given in the table as showing several bonds of different maturities rather than one bond at different stages in its life. Indeed, the table gives precisely the same calculations as if there were a 30-year bond, a 20-year bond, a ten-year bond, and a one-year bond.

Now suppose that interest rates change from 8% (which is the coupon interest rate and for which investors are willing to pay $1,000 for the bond) to 6%, the rate assumed in the calculations. It should be clear that the long-term bonds are much more responsive to the interest rate change than is the short-term debt. For example, the 20-year bond's price moves $229 from the $1,000 level, whereas the one-year debt, which is called a note, moves only about $19.

■

FIGURE 14-6

*Bond values approaching
maturity: 30-year bonds,
8% coupon interest rate,
and $1,000 par value*

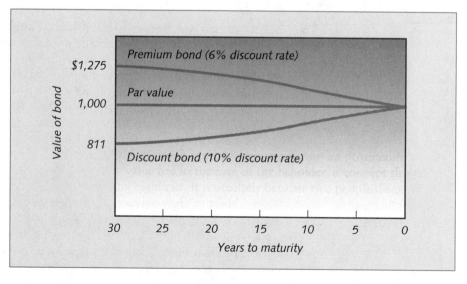

For the investor who intends to hold a bond until maturity, these fluctuations in interest rates are irrelevant as long as he chooses to ignore discount rates. No matter what happens, he will still receive the interest payments and $1,000 upon maturity. He would be foolish, though, to ignore alternative investments if they could bring a higher return.

14-5
DEBT INNOVATIONS

*T*he debt characteristics described in Section 14-1 pertain to corporate issues, although special treatment by law or a change in any one of the five factors creates a new type of debt that behaves differently. Drastic changes in the economy, such as fluctuating interest rates and inflation, have spurred innovative thinking in the bond community. Variations on conventional bond financing abound and probably will continue to proliferate in response to changes in the economic environment. Some have yet to prove themselves more than fads; nonetheless, the innovations are worthy of examination.

Our first type of bond was created by statute to encourage development and pollution control as beneficial to the public interest. Other bonds were created in the marketplace in response to the economic environment and specific market needs.

Government-Related Bonds

Federal law provides for special financing treatment of corporate investments deemed to be in the public interest. These are development bonds, sometimes called industrial development bonds, and pollution-control bonds. Their big advantage is their tax-exempt status. Bondholders' net interest is not taxable, thus giving the company a financing mechanism that costs about one third less than conventional bond financing.

Here is how government-related bonds work: The company qualifies for the use of proceeds from the bonds if its planned investment meets federal criteria. An example of this is the building of a plant in an economically depressed area or the installation of federally mandated pollution-control devices. The company guarantees the bonds and agrees to meet their retirement provisions and other requirements. The bonds are then issued through state or local industrial development or pollution-control agencies.

Convertible Bonds

These bonds permit bondholders to change (at their option) their debt to equity at certain prespecified prices. *Converts,* as they are called, carry dates that require conversion before maturity and, like conventional bonds, are subject to sinking fund and call provisions. At the time of issue, their **conversion price** is set at a premium over the stock price, usually ranging from 15% to 30%. The $1,000 par value of a bond divided by this price gives the **conversion ratio,** or the number of shares the bond is worth. Suppose that the conversion price is $25. The conversion ratio is $1,000/$25 = 40, meaning that each bond may be converted to 40 shares.

The attractiveness of convertible bonds to buyers lies in the prospect of receiving income while waiting to convert to stock. Of course, the flexibility of choosing to keep the bond rather than converting it is a big advantage, although the benefit of flexibility reduces the risk and thus the return to the buyer.

This lower cost of debt capital, in turn, is one of the prime benefits of converts for issuers. Savings in interest rate costs over a conventional nonconvertible bond may range from 300 to 600 basis points (1/100 of a percent), equivalent to 3% to 6%, a significant difference in large offerings. Converts also give issuers, in effect, an equity offering for the future, assuming that the bonds are converted, and the chance to sell equity at prices higher than the current level.

For example, in August 1981, MCI Communications Corporation sold $100 million of B-rated, 10.25% convertible debentures in less than an hour, and its shares were selling at a premium a month later. MCI would have had to pay 18% if it had offered straight debentures. The convertible gave the holders the right to trade their bonds for common stock at an 18% premium over the MCI share price of $21.75 on the day of issue. Conversion of all the shares would mean an issue of 3.9 million additional common shares. (MCI common shares were selling at between $6 and $11.375 in 1985; likewise, its debentures were selling at a discount.)

Bonds with warrants operate in a similar fashion, giving the bondholder the option to buy common stock at a given price. The warrant is an inducement for investors to pay a lower interest rate on the bonds.

Income Bonds

Interest on income bonds is paid only out of income. This variation in the repayment characteristic means a higher risk to the bondholder, which in turn results in a higher coupon rate. If the company has no income, the bondholder does not receive any interest. But when the company again is profitable, income bondholders generally receive the accrued interest owed to them before the company pays preferred or common stock dividends. The advantage to the issuer, of course, is protection from default if earnings should fall.

Zero-Coupon Bonds

Zero-coupon bonds are another example of how a change in the repayment provision changes the character of the bond. Zero-coupon bonds pay no interest (i.e., have no coupon rate). They made their debut in the early 1980s in response to high interest rates and were sold primarily to pension funds and other tax-exempt organizations. Essentially, they were bonds sold at deep, or very big, discounts that paid nothing until maturity.

The advantage to the corporate issuer is that because this instrument pays no interest until maturity, it need not worry about meeting regular payments. Yet at the same time, it can take a tax deduction each year of an amount equal to the amortization of the discount (the difference between the $1,000 principal and the price paid for the bond). The disadvantages are the noncallability of the issue and the large payment at maturity.

The advantages to the buyer are the bond's noncallability and the guarantee of the yield on the bond. The holder need not be concerned about interest rate risk because there are no coupons to be reinvested.

Two developments affected the appeal of "zeros." First, in 1983 the Internal Revenue Service effectively eliminated the bonds' tax advantages to the issuer by specifying less favorable tax treatment in the early years and an after-tax cost equal to that of a conventional bond. Second, brokerage houses introduced zero-coupon bonds that were default free, and pension funds found these more attractive. These variations were a new type of security backed by Treasury securities. Merrill Lynch's first version of these securities was called Treasury investment growth receipts, known as TIGRs (pronounced "tigers").

Here is how they work: A pension fund manager buys from Merrill Lynch a series of TIGRs that mature at different times, say, in 1997, 1998, and 1999, to match his expected cash outflows in pension annuities. He buys the TIGRs today at a deep discount and receives nothing until 1997, 1998, and 1999, when he will receive the face amount of each of the TIGRs. The net effect is no different from that of zero-coupon bonds.

The difference, however, is that the TIGRs are default free. To establish the program, Merrill Lynch bought $500 million of 30-year Treasury bonds and literally stripped off the coupons from the bonds. The brokerage firm then offered TIGRs with maturities set every six months over the 30 years, corresponding to the interest coupon dates. These coupons pay the face amount of the bonds as they come due.

Put Bonds

The volatility in interest rates prompted the invention of **put bonds**—conventional bonds that the holder may redeem at par value at a specified time before maturity. This added feature has proved attractive to investors. Put bond issues soared to more than $10 billion in 1984 from $346 million in 1978, when they were first offered. Their use has dwindled, however, over the last few years.

The big advantage to the bondholder is that the investor can "put" the bond back to the issuer if interest rates go up. For example, suppose that interest rates have risen sharply since the bonds were issued. Without the put feature, the bond would sell for, say, $800 as a result. With the put, the investor can at that time receive the $1,000 par value of the bond from the issuer instead of receiving just $800 from selling the bond in the market. As might be expected, this safety feature results in a lower yield to the investor; this is the issuer's advantage. In the case of Chrysler Financial Corporation's ten-year put bond offering in October 1984 with a put option exercisable in the fifth year, it cost Chrysler a 0.7% annual return, or $48 per $1,000 bond compounded.

As another example, U.S. Home Corporation agreed in June 1993 that "in the event that for two consecutive fiscal quarters company's consolidated tangible net worth is less than $115 million, company will be required to purchase 10% of the then principal amount of the notes at 100 plus accrued and unpaid interest."[7]

Project Financing

Project financing is a form of lending that has arisen in recent years, usually for large, complicated mineral extractive or processing operations. Examples of such projects are offshore oil exploration, refineries, and nuclear power plants. Typically, a large bank or banks lend to an entity specifically created for the project that is a joint venture or other affiliate of a large company. Because the lending is intended for only one project, so is the timing of its repayment.

Security varies considerably. It may be tied to the sale of the assets (e.g., flow of oil), or it may be a *comfort letter*—assurances from the parent company that are not legally binding. Usually surrounding the comfort letter are contractual obligations between purchasers of the project's product and the project operator and other arrangements. In addition, the lenders have claims against the project operators' equity in the project.

One advantage of project financing is said to be the segregation of high-risk projects from the rest of a company's balance sheet, although the true nature of such segregation is debated. The projects are segregated because the lending is backed by the project and is project specific. Some proponents believe that investment in politically unstable countries is better off financed by project because those governments have more to lose in, say, expropriating a foreign subsidiary tied to several large banks than one financed solely by its parent company.

Project financing is only one method of raising long-term debt privately; there also are other ways to raise debt privately.

[7] *Moody's Industrials*, August 6, 1993, p. 3971.

PREFERRED STOCK

Preferred stock is often seen as a hybrid of two securities: bonds and common stock. In terms of riskiness, preferred stock is always subordinate to bondholder claims, but it has a claims status superior to that of common stock. Thus, if a firm is faring poorly, it first pays its bondholders their required interest and then pays dividends to its preferred stockholders. Anything left over goes to the common stockholders.

Preferred stock is usually sold at par values of $25 or $100 with a given dividend rate. For example, the 1982 issue of Crown Zellerbach Corporation $3.05 cumulative preferred stock was issued at $20 a share, thus yielding a 15.25% annual rate. As in the case of bonds, the $3.05 rate is fixed, with the preferred stock's price on the market fluctuating to reflect current interest rates. Unlike bonds, however, the company is permitted to omit dividend payments to preferred stockholders. Although such an action has a detrimental effect on the company in the credit markets, it does not carry the dire consequences that default on bond payments does.

The **cumulative provision** of preferred stock stipulates that the company must pay all the preferred dividends that it has skipped, called **arrearages,** before it can pay common stock dividends. In any case, a company can never pay a common stock dividend without paying a preferred one first. The preferred stockholders earn no interest on the arrearages. For example, Storage Technology Corporation in March 1993 issued $50 per share convertible preferred stock with a par value of one cent. The preferred stock is callable and convertible and is entitled to a cumulative $3.50 annual dividend payable quarterly beginning June 15, 1993.

The regular dividends paid to holders give preferred stock its fixed income financing status in the credit markets. Also, since the late 1970s, preferred stock has usually carried with it a sinking fund or some type of retirement requirement, similar to that for bonds. For example, Figure 14-7 shows a Quaker Oats Co. retirement provision for its $9.56 preferred stock for which serial numbers are drawn by lottery. As another example of a sinking fund provision, Texas Utilities Electric Company's 1993 issue of $100 million in preferred stock requires the company to annually retire 50,000 shares at $100 per share beginning October 1, 2003.

Another bondlike aspect of preferred stock is that its holders usually do not have voting privileges, except under certain circumstances. Any matters that affect the seniority of their claim usually require a two-thirds approval of preferred stockholders. Also, after a preferred stock payout is omitted, most preferred stock covenants provide that holders of preferred stock obtain a minority position on the board so as to protect their interests.

Tax issues play a large role in the attractiveness of preferred stock. Until 1985, corporations were permitted to deduct 85% of the dividends received from ownership in other corporations. Individuals, on the other hand, were entitled to exempt only the first $100 of dividends received each year ($200 for married taxpayers). As a result, preferred stock is mainly a corporate investment.

Table 14-6 summarizes the characteristics of preferred stock together with those of debt and common equity. The hybrid nature of preferred stock can be seen clearly from the table. For example, preferred stock shares may have no specified maturity date, like common stock shares, but they may have a sinking fund that provides for effective retirement, like bonds.

Roughly half of preferred stock issues in recent years have been convertible into common stock. Like convertible bonds, convertible preferred stocks are more attractive to investors than are comparable securities without the convertibility. But the price also reflects that added flexibility for the investor. Thus individual own-

FIGURE 14-7

*Quaker Oats Company
preferred stock call notice*

QUAKER OATS CO.: $9.56 preference stock: $40,000 (see below) at $100 per sh. plus ac-crued dividends on July 20, 1985 at Harris Trust & Savings Bank, Chicago, or Harris Trust

Certificate Number	Number of Shares	Certificate Number	Number of Shares
CPB1481	200	CP5160	100
CPO1749	30	CPO887	10
CPB1525	150	CPO1707	50
CP5129	100	CPO1724	50
CPO754	20	CPO1634	40
CPO1530	20	CPB1526	150
CPO1757	5	CPO1678	1
CPB1533	110	CPB1462	1,500
CPO744	20	CP5151	100
CPO1759	15	CP1258	100
CPO683	30	CPO1713	20
CPO1548	50	CPO862	10
CP1008	100	CP1013	100
CP1253	100	CP832	100
CP1363	100	CP1269	100
CPB1446	500	CPB1452	1,000
CPB1453	1,000	CP1292	100
CPB1293	500	CPB1347	1,000
CPB1348	1,000	CPB1497	15,000
CPB623	500	CP998	100
CP5118	100	CPB996	5,000
CPB1482	1,000	CPB1538	1,000
CP5143	100	CP5176	100
CP5181	100	CP1389	100
CPO1770	70	CP5221	100
CP5197	100	CPB1261	200
CP1250	100	CPO748	10
CPO1551	10	CPO749	50
CPO1583	50	CPB842	200
CPO1525	2	CPO856	30
CPO819	20	CPO654	10
CPO1538	50	CPO770	10
CPO1647	20	CPB1393	700
CPB703	170	CP1392	100
CPO1521	10	CP1228	100
CPO1611	20	CPO1592	20
CPO715	25	CPB748	1,000
CP5167	100	CPB511	290
CPO890	20	CPO587	10
CPO830	10	CPO732	50
CP1230	100	CPO685	10
CPO806	50	CPO1504	50
CP854	100	CPO1793	20
CPO721	10	CP5124	100
CPO533	25	CPO1718	10
CP5165	100	CPO1679	10
CP5192	100	CPO723	50
CPO665	30	CP5184	100
CPO1644	15	CPO1554	10
CP5189	100	CP5208	100
CPB975	150	CPO1787	80
CP857	100	CP5126	100
CPB846	300	CPO1596	12
CPO868	10		
CPO829	30		
CP1387	100		
CPO1732	60		
CPB1487	2,630		

SOURCE: *Moody's Industrial News Reports,* July 2, 1985, p. 3789.

ership is much higher among convertible than among nonconvertible preferreds. Some preferred stocks are also issued with call provisions, which allow the firm to redeem the stock after a predetermined time and price.

*Preferred Stock
Valuation*

Preferred stock is a *hybrid* security in that some of its characteristics are similar to those of both common stocks and bonds. Legally, it represents a part of equity or ownership in a firm. On the other hand, it has only a limited claim on a firm's earnings and assets, compared with bonds.

In contrast with common stocks, preferred stocks are much easier to value because their cash benefits are regular, fixed dividends. Moreover, because they usually do not have a maturity date, a preferred's constant dividends can be treated as a *perpetual annuity stream of cash flows*. According to the stock valuation model [equation (13-3) in Chapter 13], a share of preferred stock, P_0, is valued the same as a common stock with a zero dividend growth rate:

$$P_0 = \frac{\overline{Div}}{k_p} \tag{14-3}$$

where $\overline{Div}$ is the constant dividend per period and k_p is the investor's discount rate. Note that k_p usually is not the dividend yield stated when the preferred stock is originally issued. This is because preferred stocks are *fixed-income securities*. As investors' discount rates change, k_p also changes.

■

TABLE 14-6
Comparison of Preferred Stock with Bonds and Common Stock

	Bonds	Preferred Stock	Common Stock
Relative risk–return ratio	Lowest	Medium	Highest
Maturity	Set, but may be shortened by call and sinking fund provisions; may also have convertibility limits	Usually none, but may be affected by call and sinking fund provisions; may also have convertibility limits	None
Security	Usually secured by plant, equipment, or property. Debentures are unsecured	None, senior in claims only to owners of common stock	None
Repayment provisions	Regular interest payments required or security is in default; principal payments usually set by sinking fund provision; restrictive covenants in effect	Irregular dividend payouts acceptable, but any arrearages must be paid before dividends are paid to holders of common stock; restrictive covenants	No obligation to pay dividend; no restrictive covenants
Interest rate (dividend payout rate)	Fixed, stated coupon rate	Relatively fixed at stated rate; changes are at directors' discretion	Variable; may be omitted entirely[a]
Tax-deductible aspects			
To issuer	Interest, fully deductible	Dividends are not deductible	Dividends are not deductible
To holder	No tax advantage	To corporate holders, dividends are 70% deductible; to individuals, limit is $100/person	To corporate holders, 70% deductible; $100 limit/person
Participation voting	None	None, although omission of dividend may trigger participation, such as a seat on board of directors	Usually full participation except for limitations on classes of stock
Price appreciation	Indirectly, reflected in bond rating and therefore bond price	Yes	Yes

[a]Corporate managers, however, are very concerned about projecting images of progression, not regression, and thus carefully avoid being forced to reduce or omit dividend payouts unless they absolutely must.

As an example, assume that Greyhound Corporation's $4.75 cumulative preferred is issued with a $100 par value. This implies a stated dividend yield of $4.75/$100 = 4.75%. Yet if investors later require a 9% return, this stock's value will be only

$$P_0 = \frac{\$4.75}{0.09} = \$52.78$$

SUMMARY

Section 14-1: Basic Debt Characteristics

What are some of the characteristics of a debt issue?

■ A bond is a security evidencing long-term (more than one year) debt. Debentures are unsecured debt. A bond has a par value (or face value), a coupon rate (also known as the promised interest rate), and a specified maturity. Interest payments on American bonds are generally semiannual. Publicly traded bonds are typically repaid through a sinking fund plan.

- Different debt instruments can be compared based on the five attributes that define the debt's cash flows and risk: maturity, security, repayment provisions, interest rates, and denomination.

- Term loans, typically used by smaller firms, run from three to seven years and represent borrowings on which fixed principal and interest payments are made over the life of the loan. Bonds mature in 7 to 30 years from issue.

- Bonds secured by a mortgage are called mortgage bonds, and bonds secured by the company's stocks or bonds are collateral trust bonds.

- The indenture is a legal document that specifies the restrictive covenants (the different conditions that must be met by the firm). A trustee oversees this compliance. Restrictive covenants include production and investment covenants and financing and dividend covenants.

- A bond offering denominated in a foreign currency is a Eurobond, and unsecured debt offerings for dollars in Europe are called Eurodollars. The interest paid on Eurodollars is tied to the LIBOR rate.

- Most bonds today are callable. Callable bonds may be freely callable at the call price, or they may have a deferred call provision. Various hypotheses have been proposed to explain call features. Callability can be used to signal the firm's prospects to outsiders, to lower agency costs that arise from underinvestment, to preclude wealth transfers from bondholders to stockholders, to reduce future interest costs, to change capital structures, and to eliminate restrictive covenants.

Section 14-2: Debt Offerings

How are debt securities issued?

- Long-term debt may be placed privately or sold publicly.

- Private placement with institutional investors may be beneficial to both these investors and the firm. Private placement usually costs less and provides financing custom tailored to the firm's needs. However, privately placed debt is not readily sellable and thus has a higher rate of return.

- If sold publicly, bonds are graded for their creditworthiness, which translates into relatively higher or lower interest costs. Rating firms consider a variety of factors, both financial and nonfinancial, in their gradings.

Section 14-3: Valuing Bonds

How are bond values determined?

- Riskless debt is government debt or highly rated debt. The value of a riskless bond is simply the present value of the promised interest and principal payments, discounted at the appropriate required rate of return (RRR).

- Investors adjust the price they are willing to pay for a bond to ensure that they get their RRR. Whenever a riskless bond's RRR is greater than the coupon rate, it sells at a discount. When the coupon rate exceeds the RRR, it sells at a premium.

- With semiannual interest payments, the bond valuation model must be properly adjusted.

- The yield to maturity of a bond is the internal rate of return on the bond. It is the rate of return earned by an investor if the bond is purchased at the market price and held until maturity.

■ Risky debt, which has a nontrivial possibility of default, must be valued by taking into account the likelihood that in some states the firm will not be able to satisfy its debt obligations. With default a possibility, creditors' expected cash flows are less than the promised cash flows, and the expected return on the debt is less than the promised interest rate.

Section 14-4: Bond Price Behavior

How are bond prices and interest rates related?

■ As bonds approach their maturity date, their prices come nearer to their par values.

■ Bond prices reflect changes in market interest rates as well as the riskiness of the bond issue, as measured by bond rating services. Yield to maturity is useful as a rough measure of a bond's returns, but it can be dangerous to rely on this measure alone.

■ Long-term bonds are more responsive to interest rate changes than are short-term bonds.

Section 14-5: Debt Innovations

How do the various types of bonds differ?

■ Changing economic conditions have fostered numerous variations in fixed-income securities.

■ Government-related bonds allow government agencies to raise funds and to encourage social goals such as development and pollution control.

■ Different types of bonds are innovative responses to changing conditions in the financial markets. Convertible bonds allow bondholders to convert the bonds into equity, thus sharing in the growth of the firm; income bonds, zero-coupon bonds, and put bonds have different bases for computing interest or redemption; and project-financing bonds allow financing for risky projects separate from the balance sheets of firms involved in the project.

Section 14-6: Preferred Stock

What is preferred stock? How is its value determined?

■ Preferred stock is a hybrid version of bonds and common equity and, for tax reasons, is attractive mainly to corporate purchasers.

■ Preferred dividends are subordinate to interest payments to bondholders but are superior to common equity dividends in that they have a cumulative provision. Preferred stockholders generally do not have voting privileges, except in matters that directly affect their interests or in situations where the preferred dividend is omitted.

■ Because of the fixed nature of their cash flows, preferred stocks are valued as perpetuities. Their values are determined as perpetuities in a manner similar to common stock with a zero dividend growth rate.

QUESTIONS

1. Why is debt important to a corporation?

2. What are the five characteristics of long-term debt?

3. Why do bond issues often carry sinking fund requirements, call provisions, and restrictive covenants?

4. What are the advantages and disadvantages of callable bonds to the issuing company? To the bondholder?

5. What are the advantages of a private debt placement?

6. Explain the rating criteria for publicly placed debt. Who rates the debt?

7. What are the advantages to a firm in taking out debt insurance?

8. The coupon rate on a bond determines only the interest payments on the bond, not the investor's effective yield on the bond. True or false? Why?

9. How can an approximate yield to maturity (YTM) be calculated? What are the weaknesses of the YTM?

10. How does the valuation of risky debt differ from that of riskless debt?

11. Explain in intuitive terms when a bond sells at a discount, at par, and at a premium.

12. Why do bond values approach their par values at maturity? Is this true for both premium and discount bonds?

13. What are some of the recent innovations in the debt markets? Outline their essential characteristics.

14. How do income bonds and convertible bonds provide special benefits to the issuing corporation?

15. Compare preferred stock with bonds and common stock.

16. Explain why preferred stock has hybrid characteristics.

17. What would happen to the price of a bond if its Moody's rating changed from Ba to Baa? What if it changed from A to Caa?

18. Put bonds give investors a lower yield compared with that of bonds (nonputtable) that have similar characteristics. Why?

PROBLEMS

1. For some unforeseeable reason, the issuance of a 12-year, 12% bond of Morris Enterprises has been delayed for one month. What is the price of the bond if there is no accrued interest?

2. Is a bond selling at a discount or a premium if the annual coupon interest rate is 14% and the market requires a return of 12%? How much is an investor willing to pay for this bond if it matures in 15 years?

3. A bond with six years left to maturity has a coupon rate of 9% and a par value of $1,000. How much is an investor willing to pay for the bond if he requires the following annual rates of return?

    (a) 7%   (b) 10%   (c) 12%

4. A corporation just issued a five-year and a ten-year bond, each with a coupon rate of 10%. Both bonds have a par value of $1,000, and both are issued at par (consequently, each has a promised yield of 10%).

    (a) What is each bond worth if interest rates drop to 6%?

    (b) What is each bond worth if rates rise to 14%?

5. Sam Malone, vice-president of AMI, Inc., wishes to find the yield to maturity (YTM) on his company's ten-year, 10% bond that sells for 106.38% of the par value of $1,000.

   (a) Calculate the YTM by trial and error.

   (b) Find the YTM using the approximation equation.

6. An investor wants to know the YTM on an eight-year, 7% bond selling for 88.95% of its par value before he invests in it.

   (a) Find the bond's YTM using the trial-and-error procedure.

   (b) Find the YTM with the approximation equation.

7. A bond is currently selling for $700 and has eight years left to maturity and a par value of $1,000. The bond has a 7% coupon (payable annually). What is its promised yield to maturity (IRR) to the nearest tenth of a percent?

8. What is the effective promised yield to maturity of the 7% coupon bond described in Problem 7 if the payments are semiannual?

9. A bond pays interest annually and sells for $835. It has six years left to maturity and a par value of $1,000. What is its coupon if its promised yield to maturity is 12%?

10. Crandall Ceramics Enterprises issues par debt with a face value of $150,000 and a coupon rate of 6%. Assume that Crandall's cash flows next year are either $200,000 (probability 0.7) or $140,000 (probability 0.3).

    (a) What are the promised cash flows to bondholders?

    (b) What are Crandall's expected cash flows next year?

    (c) What are bondholders' expected cash flows next year?

    (d) What is the expected return to bondholders if they buy the debt at par?

    (e) Would bondholders buy the debt under these conditions if their required rate of return is 2%?

    (f) Assume that bondholders' required rate of return is 12%. Does this mean that Crandall cannot sell debt in the marketplace? At what price can Crandall sell the debt?

11. Magsy, Inc., has an outstanding bond issue that will mature in 11 years at its $1,000 par value. The bond carries a 12% annual coupon.

    (a) What is the value of the bond if the required return (k_d) is 12%? 15%? 8%?

    (b) Plot your findings in part (a) on a set of required return (x-axis) versus market value (y-axis) axes.

    (c) Use your findings in parts (a) and (b) to summarize the relationships among coupon rate, required return, market value, and par value.

12. A 20-year, 10% coupon interest rate bond has a $1,000 par value. The market rate of interest is 8%.

    (a) Compute the market price of this bond if it has 20 years to maturity, 15 years to maturity, 10 years to maturity, 5 years to maturity, and 0 years to maturity. Assume that the interest is paid annually.

(b) Draw on a graph the relationship between the value of the bond and the remaining life of the bond.

13. A share of preferred stock has an annual dividend of $5. If an investor requires a 12% return, how much is she willing to pay for a share?

14. The Nate Foll Production Co. wishes to estimate the value of its outstanding preferred stock. The issue has a $90 par value and pays an annual dividend of 9.5%. Similar-risk preferreds are currently yielding a 10.7% annual rate of return.

(a) What is the market value of Foll's outstanding preferred?

(b) If an investor purchases the preferred at the price calculated in part (a), how much will his gain (loss) per share be if the discount rate on similar-risk preferreds falls to 9.8%?

14A

THE TERM STRUCTURE OF INTEREST RATES

The relationship between a bond's yield to maturity and its maturity is called the **term structure of interest rates.** We examine this term structure in two steps. First we give an intuitive explanation of the term structure and theories concerning how the yield curve is formed. We then take a more quantitative look at interest rates and develop some relationships among these rates over time.

Theories that explain the term structure have been the subject of considerable debate for years among economists, financial theorists, and practitioners. One reason for the ongoing debate is that each theory has some appeal but no single theory covers everything satisfactorily. Term structure is important to both the corporate manager as a borrower and the investor as a lender because understanding term structure helps these decision makers choose between long- and short-term forms of debt.

Yield curves are graphical representations of the term structure and help us visualize the relationships among interest rates over time. This relationship between yield and maturity has generally been upward sloping (i.e., the longer the maturity of the investment is, the higher the yield is). Figure 14A-1 contains this historical relationship and shows the yields for debts of varying maturities on particular days in 1983 and 1993. The diagram shows that on these particular days, rates on long-term debt were higher than rates for short-term debt. However, this need not al-

FIGURE 14A-1
Historical yield curve

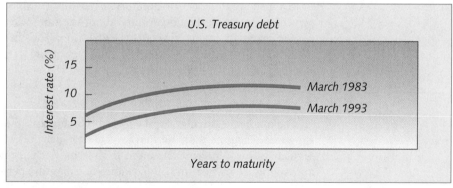

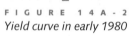

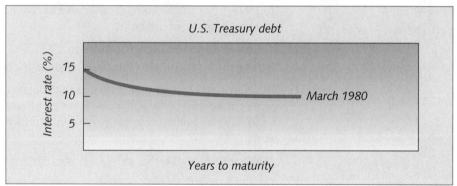

ways be the case. Short-term rates can rise above long-term rates, thereby inverting the slope of the line, as seen in Figure 14A-2.

Note that the rates of the yield curve are the rates paid for new issues of varying maturities and are not the rates expected in the future. The curve shows the current rate earned on a bond with a given maturity.

An Informal Discussion of Theories of the Term Structure

THE EXPECTATIONS THEORY

The **expectations theory** postulates that current interest rates reflect expectations about future interest rates. According to this theory, if interest rates are expected to rise, the yield curve should be upward sloping; if they are expected to go down, it should be downward sloping; and if they are expected to remain flat, the curve is flat.

Expectations about future interest rates are dominated by expectations about inflation. Therefore, if inflation is expected to rise, interest rates will rise as well, and vice versa. The expected interest rate, according to proponents of this theory, can be obtained by adding the real, or inflation-free, rate to the expected rate of inflation. Forecasts of the expected level of inflation are published in the financial press.

THE LIQUIDITY PREFERENCE THEORY

As the name suggests, the **liquidity preference theory** states that investors prefer to make investment decisions for the short term and therefore must be offered an inducement to invest for a longer term. The theory implies that long-term rates are higher than short-term rates because of investors' preference for having the funds on hand, or being liquid.

Investors' preference for liquidity arises out of (among other things) reinvestment risk, which is the uncertainty about the rate of return that an investor can receive on funds from subsequent reinvesting. The theory asserts that investors prefer to lend short and borrowers prefer to borrow long. Therefore, the upward-sloping yield curve is the end result.

THE MARKET SEGMENTATION THEORY

The **market segmentation theory,** to which many practitioners on Wall Street subscribe, suggests that the marketplace for debt offerings is divided into three segments: short, intermediate, and long term. Each segment has its own demand and supply characteristics. For example, generally, pension funds dominate the long-term market, corporations dominate the intermediate market, and individuals' and nonprofit institutions' funds dominate the short-term market.

The theory thus suggests that each segment is a function of its own characteristics and that rates among the three groups are less interactive than assumed by the other two theories. There is little empirical support for this theory, however; the bulk of the evidence points toward the expectations and liquidity preference theories.

The market segmentation theory is based on the self-imposed limitation of acting within a particular segment. If even one individual or institution is willing to cross segments, this theory loses its relevance. For example, one could borrow at the lower-cost interest rate in one segment and lend at a higher interest rate in another segment, thereby earning excess returns. If this were possible, demand and supply considerations would affect bond prices and, consequently, the interest rates until such "arbitrage incentives" disappeared.

THE SLOPE OF THE YIELD CURVE

Interest rates can change at any time, and they do. Figure 14A-2 shows the downward-sloping relationship between yield and years to maturity in early 1980. This inversion of the historical relationship between yield and years to maturity marked the first time in history that rates for short-term debt were higher than rates for long-term debt. Although it did not last long, the inversion created a furor in investment circles. The slope of the yield curve, then, simply reflects the relationship between long-term and short-term rates. Changes in that relationship alter the slope of the curve.

In addition to slope changes, it is important to understand the implications of shifts in the yield curve, upward or downward. Suppose that normal conditions—meaning an upward-sloping relationship—exist as in Figure 14A-1 and that a bond investor expects overall interest rates to fall. The investor, then, is expecting a shift of the entire curve downward, as shown in Figure 14A-3. Understanding that this is the case, the investor wants to invest long term today to lock in the higher rate before the curve shifts downward, thereby yielding a lower return.

Suppose that instead of an investor, a corporate borrower has the same expectations of lower interest rates. Assume that the same normal upward-sloping term structure exists. This borrower takes the opposite tack. Because he expects rates to fall, he chooses to wait, hoping to lock in the lower long-term rate that he is ex-

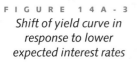

FIGURE 14A-3

Shift of yield curve in response to lower expected interest rates

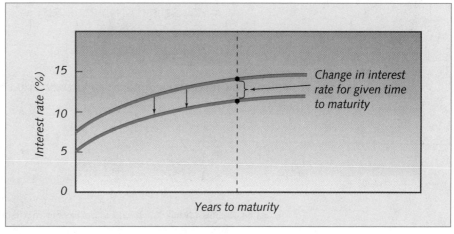

pecting rather than the higher long-term rate currently available. In the meantime, then, he borrows short, raising enough funds for the short-term period while he waits for the rates to fall.

A More Formal Examination of Two Term Structure Theories[8]

We can discuss the expectations and liquidity preference theories of the term structure in more quantitative terms with the use of some new terminology. Although we routinely refer to "the interest rate" in casual conversation, there are several interest rates, depending on the risk and longevity of the investment. In this appendix we explore the effect of longevity, assuming that the bond will not default. Defining $r_t(n)$ as the interest rate at time t on an n-period investment, we can state that $r_0(1)$ is the interest rate today for a one-period investment, $r_2(2)$ is the interest rate at time 2 for a two-period investment, and $r_3(1)$ is the one-period interest rate at time 3. These rates and maturities are shown in the following time line:

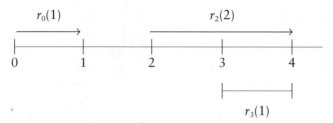

The **spot interest rate** is the rate quoted for a financial contract or security for immediate purchase or sale. That is, the spot rate is the rate you can obtain on a financial instrument issued at time t. The spot interest rates at time t are interest rates $r_t(1), r_t(2), \ldots, r_t(n)$. Thus the spot interest rates today are $r_0(1), r_0(2), \ldots, r_0(n)$ and are observable. For example, if spot rates today are $r_0(1) = 4\%$ and $r_0(2) = 4.25\%$, an investor can purchase a debt instrument that will earn 4% over the next year or 4.25% over the next two years, with both instruments beginning today.

In addition to spot interest rates, there are future interest rates that can be computed from information contained in the yield curve. Consider two alternative investments strategies of \$1 for two periods. In strategy 1, the investor invests \$1 in a one-period bond at $r_0(1)$ and, when it matures, reinvests the proceeds from her first investment, $\$1[1 + r_0(1)]$, for another period at $\tilde{r}_1(1)$. In period 2, she expects to receive $\$1[1 + r_0(1)][1 + \tilde{r}_1(1)]$:

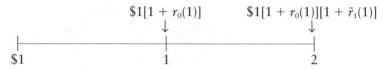

In strategy 2, the investor invests her \$1 in a two-period bond at an interest rate of $r_0(2)$ to get $\$1[1 + r_0(2)]^2$:

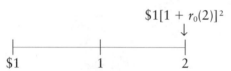

[8] This section contains advanced material and can be omitted without loss of continuity.

To preclude arbitrage (riskless profits) the payoffs from both strategies must be the same, or

$$[1 + r_0(1)][1 + \tilde{r}_1(1)] = [1 + r_0(2)]^2 \qquad (14A\text{-}1)$$

In this result, $r_0(1)$ and $r_0(2)$ are observable because they are spot rates, whereas $\tilde{r}_1(1)$, an unobservable at time 0, is the implied **forward rate.** We must solve this equation for $\tilde{r}_1(1)$ to find the implied forward rate.

We can use $f_1(1)$ to denote the forward rate. Thus the "no-arbitrage result" becomes $[1 + r_0(1)][1 + f_1(1)] = [1 + r_0(2)]^2$. We can generalize this two-period result to n periods as:

$$[1 + r_0(n)]^n[1 + f_n(1)] = [1 + r_0(n + 1)]^{n+1} \qquad (14A\text{-}2)$$

For instance, if $r_0(1) = 4\%$ and $r_0(2) = 4.25\%$, then the implied forward rate for the second year, $f_1(1)$, must be

$$[1 + r_0(1)][1 + f_1(1)] = [1 + r_0(2)]^2$$
$$[1 + 0.04][1 + f_1(1)] = [1 + 0.0425]^2$$
$$[1 + f_1(1)] = \frac{1.0868}{1.04} = 1.045$$

which implies that, given the current yield curve, an investor who is planning to purchase a debt instrument in one year for a one-year period can expect to receive a return of $f_1(1) = 4.5\%$.

Implied forward rates carry a lot of information. The relative magnitudes of forward rates in two adjacent time periods determine the shape of the yield curve. We examine two theories of the term structure to see this.

THE EXPECTATIONS HYPOTHESIS

Under the expectations hypothesis (EH), investors are concerned solely with the expected payoffs from alternative investments (risks don't matter). In our earlier example of a two-period investment, we showed that

$$E[1 + r_0(1)][1 + \tilde{r}_1(1)] = E[1 + r_0(2)]^2 \qquad (14A\text{-}3)$$

where E is the expectation at time 0. The $\sim$ on $\tilde{r}_1(1)$ denotes that at time 0, $\tilde{r}_1(1)$ is unknown. We can therefore write equation (14A-3) as

$$[1 + r_0(1)][1 + E\{\tilde{r}_1(1)\}] = [1 + r_0(2)]^2 \qquad (14A\text{-}4)$$

Set $n = 1$ in equation (14A-2) and compare it with equation (14A-4). We note that $E[r_1(1)] = f_1(1)$. In general, under the expectations hypothesis,

$$E[r_n(1)] = f_n(1) \qquad (14A\text{-}5)$$

for all n.

We have an important idea:

KEY CONCEPT   The implied forward rate is the market's expectation of the future spot rate.

This concept suggests that under the EH, one-period forward rates are unbiased predictors of future spot rates. Under the EH, the yield curve is upward sloping if, and only if, the expected future spot rate is greater than the current spot rate for an n-period investment.

Consider Figure 14A-4 to demonstrate this idea. When would you observe this? If the curve is upward sloping, $r_0(n + 1) > r_0(n)$, which implies that $[1 + r_0(n +$

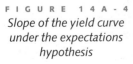

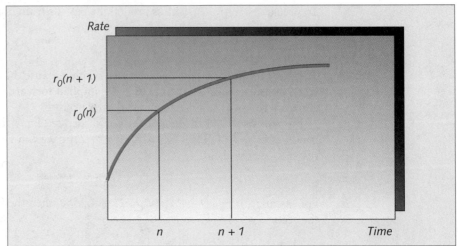

1)] > [1 + r_0(n)]$ or that $[1 + r_0(n + 1)]^{n+1} > [1 + r_0(n)]^{n+1}$. Substituting for $[1 + r_0(n + 1)]^{n+1}$ from equation (14A-2) implies that $[1 + r_0(n)]^n[1 + f_n(1)] > [1 + r_0(n)]^{n+1}$. This can be true only if $f_n(1) > r_0(n)$. But by equation (14A-5), $f_n(1) = E[\tilde{r}_n(1)]$. Thus $E[\tilde{r}_n(1)] > r_0(n)$.

THE LIQUIDITY PREFERENCE HYPOTHESIS

What if investors are concerned with risk? The EH, which assumes that only the expected payoffs matter, no longer applies. The liquidity preference hypothesis (LPH) accommodates risk aversion.

Consider a world in which investors care about the longevity of their investments. Let us assume that they prefer (for whatever reason) shorter-lived investments to longer-lived investments. Such investors are said to have a **liquidity preference**.

Consider two strategies A and B:

Strategy A: The expected payoff at time 2 is $E[1 + r_0(1)][1 + \tilde{r}_1(1)]$.

Strategy B: The expected payoff at time 2 is $E[1 + r_0(2)]^2$.

Strategy A is a shorter (two-period) investment, whereas strategy B is a long-term investment. If investors have a liquidity preference, they require additional compensation (called the **liquidity premium**) to invest in the longer-term investment. Thus, even over two periods, the expected payoff from strategy B must exceed that from A. This gives us

$$E[1 + r_0(2)]^2 > E[1 + r_0(1)][1 + \tilde{r}_1(1)]$$

which implies that $f_1(1) > E[\tilde{r}_1(1)]$.[9]

The liquidity premium (LP) is defined as

$$LP = f_n(1) - E[r_n(1)] \qquad \text{(14A-6)}$$

Under the liquidity preference hypothesis, the LP is nonnegative.

[9]**Proof:** If $E(\text{payoff}_B) > E(\text{payoff}_A)$, $E[1 + r_0(2)]^2 > E[1 + r_0(1)][1 + \tilde{r}_1(1)]$. This implies that $[1 + r_0(2)]^2 > [1 + r_0(1)][1 + E[\tilde{r}_1(1)]]$ or, since $E[\tilde{r}_1(1)] = f_1(1)$ from equation (14A-5), we can write this result as $[1 + r_0(2)]^2 > [1 + r_0(1)][1 + f_1(1)]$. Comparing this result with equation (14A-4), we find that $1 + f_1(1) > 1 + E[\tilde{r}_1(1)]$ or $f_1(1) > E[\tilde{r}_1(1)]$, which is the required result. In more general terms, $f_n(1) > E[\tilde{r}_n(1)]$.

1. What is the yield curve? Explain intuitively the three theories that explain the shape of the yield curve.

2. What is a forward interest rate? Is it observable? How does one estimate the forward rate from a given yield curve?

3. What does it mean to say that under the expectations hypothesis, forward rates are unbiased predictors of future spot rates?

4. The magnitudes of the forward rates in two adjacent time periods determine the shape of the yield curve. True or false? Why?

5. The implied forward rate is the expectation of the future forward rate in an economy with risk-averse investors. True or false? If true, why? If false, what leads to a divergence between the implied forward rate and the expected future spot rate?

1. The following table gives the current prices of pure discount bonds with different maturities. Calculate the current spot rates for each maturity.

Time to Maturity	Price
1	$925.93
2	849.46
3	773.25
4	645.48

2. Given the current yield curve from the following annual interest rates, determine the implied forward rates for a one-year investment at the beginning of each year.

Investment Period (Years)	Interest Rate
1	5.00%
2	7.00
3	7.83
4	8.37

3. On the basis of information given in Problem 2, calculate the implied forward rates for a two-year and a three-year investment to be made at the beginning of year 2.

4. According to the expectations hypothesis and based on the data in Problem 2, what are the market's expectations of the future spot rates of interest?

5. Assume that the liquidity preference hypothesis holds and that the annual spot rates are expected to stay constant at 10%. The liquidity premium is 1% per year. Calculate the implied forward rates for years 2 and 3. Also, calculate the yields for pure discount bonds with maturities of 1 year, 2 years, and 3 years.

[10] These problems assume that the reader has studied the latter (more formal) part of this appendix.

14B

VALUING DEBT AND EQUITY USING THE BLACK-SCHOLES MODEL

Firm Equity Value Implied by the Black-Scholes Model

We established the fundamental features and properties of options in Chapter 11. In this appendix we show how corporate debt and equity can be priced with the Black-Scholes option pricing model.

It was Black and Scholes who first suggested that a firm's equityholders have, in effect, a call option on the firm's value, with an exercise price equal to the face value of the debt and the maturity of the debt being the life of the option. If equity is valued using the Black-Scholes model, the firm value V replaces the stock price S and the face value of the debt (B) replaces the exercise price of the option. The value of the firm's equity is therefore

$$E = VN(d_3) - Be^{-rT}N(d_4) \qquad\qquad (14B\text{-}1)$$

where

$$d_3 = \frac{\ln\dfrac{V}{B} + \left[r + \dfrac{\sigma_V^2}{2}\right]T}{\sigma_V\sqrt{T}}$$

$$d_4 = d_3 - \sigma_V\sqrt{T}$$

As an example, Bridgeport Precision Plastics has a firm value (V) of \$60,000. Its debt matures in three months $(T = 0.25$ year) and has a face value (B) of \$20,000. If the standard deviation of the rate of return on the firm's assets (σ_V) is 0.8 and the annualized risk-free interest rate is 5%, what is the market value of the firm's equity (E)?

Using the relevant information, we have $d_3 = 2.98$ and $d_4 = 2.58$. Referring to a table like Table 11B-1, we find that $N(d_3) = 0.9986$ and $N(d_4) = 0.9951$. When we substitute the appropriate values for the different variables in equation (14B-1), the value of Bridgeport's equity is calculated to be \$40,261.23.

We summarize our discussion of valuing a firm's equity by using option pricing theory:

1. The higher the value of the firm is, the higher the value of the firm's equity is.

2. The longer the maturity of the debt is, the greater the value of the equity is.

3. The higher the face value of the debt is, the lower the value of the equity is.

4. The greater the variance of returns for the firm is, the greater the value of the equity is.

5. The higher the riskless interest rate in the economy is, the higher the value of the equity is.

The standard call option properties therefore suggest that the value of a firm's equity increases with the firm's value, the volatility of the firm's value, and the time until the debt's maturity date. Equity value decreases with increases in interest rates and the face value of the firm's debt.

The reader should verify that these properties of equity follow directly from the properties of call options on stock discussed earlier, except that the underlying asset is now the value of the firm.

The Value of Risky Debt Implied by the Black-Scholes Model

The value of the firm's risky debt implied by the Black-Scholes model can easily be calculated using the results developed thus far. The value of the debt must be the value of the firm as a whole, less the value of the firm's equity, $D = V - E$. The value of equity implied by the Black-Scholes model has already been calculated. When simplified, this value of equity, then subtracted from the firm value V, yields the market value of debt as:

$$D = VN(d_5) + Be^{-rT}N(d_4) \tag{14B-2}$$

where

$$d_5 = -d_3 = \frac{\ln\dfrac{B}{V} + \left[r - \dfrac{\sigma_V^2}{2} \right]T}{\sigma_V\sqrt{T}}$$

with d_3 and d_4 as previously defined.

What, then, is the value of Bridgeport Precision Plastics' debt? We can find the market value of the firm's debt in two ways. First, because $D = V - E$ and because $V = \$60,000$ and $E = \$40,261.23$ from the previous example, the market value of Bridgeport's debt must be $19,738.77. The second method of finding the value of the firm's debt uses equation (14B-2). For obvious reasons, the same value of debt should result.

1. The higher the value of the firm is, the higher the value of its debt is.

2. The longer the maturity of the debt is, the lower its market value is.

3. The higher the face value of the debt is, the higher the value of the debt is.

4. The more volatile the value of the firm is, the lower the value of the risky debt is.

5. The higher the risk-free interest rate is, the lower the value of the risky debt is.

PROBLEMS

1. Consider a firm that has issued zero-coupon bonds with a face value of $45 million. The firm has an asset value of $65 million, and the asset returns have a standard deviation of 0.35. If the debt matures in one year and the riskless interest rate is 10%, find the value of the firm's equity. Suppose the firm's asset structure can be altered so that the standard deviation of the assets increases to 0.65. Calculate the equity value in this scenario. Provide an intuitive explanation for the differences in equity values.

2. Consider a firm that has two claims outstanding: common equity and an issue of zero-coupon bonds with a face value of $105 million. The firm's value is $175 million. The bonds mature in one year, and the riskless interest rate is 9%. If the firm's assets have a variance of 0.23, find the market value of the firm's outstanding bonds. Solve this problem in two ways: (a) Find the equity value and invoke the equation $V = D + E$, and (b) use equation (14B-2).

3. Reconsider the firm in Problem 2. Now assume that the firm's assets have a variance of 0.33 and the riskless interest rate equals 8%.

   (a) If an investment project will increase the assets' variance to 0.38 and the maturity of the bonds will be reduced to ten months, will the bondholders accept the proposal? (*Note:* This is a comparison with the variance of 0.33 and one-year maturity on the bonds.)

(b) What if the payoff to the bondholders will rise to $106 million? To $109 million?

(c) Why must the parameters be altered in the manner implied in parts (a) and (b) in order to win the bondholders' approval? (Identify the expected changes associated with each input alteration.)

4. Consider a firm, XYZ, Ltd., that has only two claims: equity (E) and an issue of noncallable convertible debt (D). Let the face value of debt be B. Assume that the debt matures T periods hence. Also assume that the value of the firm is $V = D + E$. No dividends are paid until the debt matures. Use the options framework to value convertible debt. The conversion fraction is:

$$F = \frac{n}{n + N}$$

where

n is the number of shares arising out of exercise of full conversion

N is the original number of shares of common stock

(a) Express the condition for conversion at maturity in terms of the given parameters.

(b) For the following conditions, explain the period effects on D, the value of noncallable, convertible debt. The answer should be one of these: increases the value of D, decreases the value of D, or has an ambiguous effect on D. For each part, consider all other parameters of the problem to be fixed (i.e., evaluate the partial effects).

(i) An increase in the value of the firm, V

(ii) An increase in the riskless rate of interest, r

(iii) An increase in the face value of debt, B

(iv) An increase in the conversion fraction, F

(v) An increase in the time to maturity, T

SUGGESTED ADDITIONAL READINGS

Barnea, A., R. Haugen, and L. W. Senbet. "A Rationale for Debt Maturity Structure and Call Provisions in the Agency Theoretic Framework." *Journal of Finance,* December 1980, pp. 1223–1234.

Bierman, H., Jr. "The Bond Refunding Decision." *Financial Management,* Summer 1972, pp. 27–29.

Carleton, W., and I. Cooper. "Estimation and Uses of the Term Structure of Interest Rates." *Journal of Finance,* September 1976, pp. 1067–1084.

Donaldson, Gordon. "In Defense of Preferred Stock." *Harvard Business Review,* July–August 1962, pp. 123–136.

Fabozzi, Frank J. *Fixed Income Mathematics.* Chicago: Probus, 1988.

Fisher, L. "Determinants of Risk Premiums on Corporate Bonds." *Journal of Political Economy,* June 1959, pp. 212–237.

McCulloch, J. "Measuring the Term Structure of Interest Rates." *Journal of Business,* January 1971, pp. 19–31.

Soldofsky, Robert M. "The History of Bond Tables and Stock Valuation Models." *Journal of Finance,* March 1966, pp. 103–111.

Taggart, Robert A. "Corporate Financing: Too Much Debt?" *Financial Analysts Journal,* May–June 1986, pp. 35–42.

Taggart, Robert A., Jr. *Secular Patterns in the Financing of U.S. Corporations.* Cambridge, MA: National Bureau of Economic Research, 1985.

Weinstein, Mark I. "The Seasoning Process of New Corporate Bond Issues." *Journal of Finance,* December 1978, pp. 1343–1354.

Williams, John B. *The Theory of Investment Value.* Cambridge, MA: Harvard University Press, 1938.

PART FIVE THE FIRM'S FINANCING DECISIONS

FIFTEEN   THE FIRM'S CAPITAL STRUCTURE

The two greatest stimulants in the world are youth and debt.

—Benjamin Disraeli, 1837

All businesses need capital to keep their operations alive. Capital is required to finance investments in such things as inventory, accounts receivable, and plant and equipment. Most firms rely on both debt and equity capital, and the proportion of each component of capital used by a firm constitutes the firm's **capital structure.** For example, if a company has $2 million in debt (market value) and $4 million in equity (market value), this company's capital structure is its debt–equity ratio of 0.5 ($2 million/$4 million). A firm that has no debt in its capital structure is an **unlevered firm;** a firm that has debt in its capital structure is a **levered firm.**

An important decision that a company must make is the relative amounts of debt and equity in its capital structure. In what proportions should the debt and equity be raised? Or, asked in another way, how levered should the firm be? Should a firm raise $0.40 in debt for every $1 in equity? Or is a debt–equity ratio of 30% better? Is there any rule that the financial manager can follow to determine the "optimal" debt–equity ratio? Addressing such questions is the main purpose of this chapter. By the theory of capital structure we mean the study of the relationship between the firm's capital structure and its market value. Such an analysis can give the manager guidelines for maximizing the owners' wealth.

This chapter answers the following questions:

- What is the firm's capital structure and why is it of interest?

- What are the rates of return on unlevered and levered equity and how are they related?

- How does the risk of the equity change with financial leverage?

- Is firm value higher or lower with leverage?

- How do corporate taxes affect firm value?

- How does the probability of default affect the value of the firm?

- How do agency considerations affect the capital structure decision?

The three appendixes to this chapter address special issues in capital structure theory. Appendix 15A examines default and bankruptcy costs, Appendix 15B shows how a firm's leverage choices can signal information about its economic health, and Appendix 15C discusses share repurchases and exchange offers.

15-1

CAPITAL STRUCTURE AND FIRM VALUE

This chapter examines the implications of a firm's financial policies for its market value. Our particular interest is to identify the firm's optimal capital structure: the debt–equity ratio that maximizes the firm's value, which, as we know from Chapter 2, is based on the market value of the firm's debt and equity.

We have two immediate objectives: first, we examine the meaning of the terms "return on the unlevered firm" and "return on levered equity." Second, we examine why we are defining optimality in terms of firm value when we have already established that "best" should be evaluated from the stockholders' perspective.

We return to the example of Rheinhold Plastics, which we began in Chapter 2, to see how capital structure choices can affect firm value. It may be useful to reproduce here the essential details of the example from that chapter. Initially, assume that there are no taxes.

The Value of an Unlevered Firm

Assume that Rheinhold is initially all equity (unlevered) and that the firm's net present value (NPV) is $100,000. Then Rheinhold's unlevered balance sheet is as follows:

RHEINHOLD'S (UNLEVERED) MARKET-VALUE BALANCE SHEET

PHYSICAL ASSETS: $600,000	EQUITY: $700,000
NPV: $100,000	

The right-hand side of the economic balance sheet gives the value of the firm. Since Rheinhold is presently unlevered, the value of the unlevered firm (V^U) is also the value of the unlevered equity ($700,000), and these two terms can be used interchangeably.

The Expected Return for an Unlevered Firm

The unlevered equityholders have a $700,000 investment in the firm. The fact that the stockholders have invested only $600,000 in physical assets is irrelevant in calculating the expected returns. The expected returns should be calculated on the basis of the current market value of the equity because that is the amount of the stockholders' wealth "tied up" in the firm. They can readily sell their equity for this amount in the marketplace. We assume that the investment will generate an expected operating cash flow of $798,000 in the next period and define the expected rate of return on the unlevered firm's assets as ROA^*. ROA^* is the expected future operating cash flows from the investment less the initial investment divided by the initial investment:

$$ROA^* = \frac{\$798,000 - \$700,000}{\$700,000} = 14\%$$

To simplify the exposition we henceforth ignore the term *expected* and simply talk in terms of the return on the unlevered firm or unlevered equity.

The Value of a Levered Firm

Now assume that Rheinhold changes its financial policy to include some debt financing. All details remain the same except that the equityholders now contribute only $300,000 to the firm and finance the remaining $300,000 required to buy the assets by issuing riskless (default-free) debt that carries an 8% interest rate. The riskless case is considered for simplicity. The following results can also be derived with risky debt if some additional assumptions are made. If the firm's investment plan remains the same, the firm's cash flows and the risk are the same and thus the NPV is fixed and equal to $100,000. This goes to the equityholders. Rheinhold's market-value balance sheet is given here:

RHEINHOLD'S (LEVERED) MARKET-VALUE BALANCE SHEET

PHYSICAL ASSETS: $600,000	DEBT: 300,000 (D)
NPV: $100,000	EQUITY: $400,000 ($E$)
	($300,000 contributed plus $100,000 NPV)

Note that the debt (D) and equity (E) values are market values. The value of the levered firm, V^L, is thus $700,000 and is identical to the value of the unlevered firm, V^U. The method of financing has no impact on firm value. The firm can use any debt–equity ratio to finance its investments. This irrelevance argument, which holds in the absence of tax effects, was first advanced by Modigliani and Miller and is known as the **M & M hypothesis.**[1]

The crucial assumption underlying the discussion about the irrelevance of capital structure is that the NPV of the project is unaffected by the firm's capital structure choices. When is this assumption reasonable? If the magnitude and risk of the firm's expected operating cash flows are not affected by the debt–equity decision, then the discount rate for capitalizing these cash flows is also unaffected, and hence the firm value is unchanged. This concept becomes clear as we progress through this chapter.

KEY CONCEPT   As long as the ROA^* is not affected, the firm's value is independent of its capital structure. With riskless debt and the absence of taxes, capital structure is irrelevant.

The Return on Levered Equity

As before, the equityholders can sell their interests at market value, and thus their investment in the levered firm is effectively $400,000. Their investment generates operating cash flows of $798,000 in the next period, out of which the creditors must be repaid the principal of $300,000 and the interest of $24,000 (8% of $300,000). Thus the cash flow to the equityholders is $798,000 − $324,000 = $474,000. The rate of return on the levered equity, ROE^*, is therefore:

$$ROE^* = \frac{\$474,000 - \$400,000}{\$400,000} = 18.5\%$$

A comparison of this $ROE^* = 18.5\%$ with the earlier $ROA^* = 14\%$ demonstrates an important idea:

KEY CONCEPT   Debt increases the expected rate of return on the equity, and so the equityholders of a levered firm can expect a higher rate of return than can their counterparts in a similar but unlevered firm.

The Relationship Between the Returns on Levered and Unlevered Equity

We derive the relationship between the expected return on the levered equity (ROE^*) and the expected return on the unlevered equity (ROA^*). Again, at least initially, we ignore taxes, and for simplicity we assume that the debt is riskless.

Because the values of the levered and unlevered firms are the same, we can write the firm's assets $A = E + D$. The value of the firm can thus be viewed as a "portfolio" whose value equals the value of its debt plus the value of its equity. As seen in Chapter 5, the expected return on a portfolio is the weighted average of the expected returns on the components of the portfolio or, in this case,

Expected return on assets = (proportion of equity) × (expected return on equity)
+ (proportion of debt) × (expected return on debt)

Algebraically,

$$ROA^* = \frac{E}{D+E}(ROE^*) + \frac{D}{D+E}(R_f) \qquad (15\text{-}1)$$

---

[1] See F. Modigliani and M. H. Miller, "The Cost of Capital, Corporation Finance and the Theory of Investment," *American Economic Review*, June 1958, pp. 261–297.

where R_f, the risk-free interest rate, is the expected return on the debt. This must be true because debt is assumed to have zero market risk. Rearranging this relationship yields the result

$$ROE^* = ROA^* + \frac{D}{E}(ROA^* - R_f) \tag{15-2}$$

We can go back to Rheinhold Plastics to verify that equation (15-2) holds. Since Rheinhold's ROA^* is 14%, its debt is $300,000, equity is $400,000, and the interest rate on the debt is 8%, the expected return on Rheinhold levered equity is:

$$ROE^* = 14\% + \frac{\$300,000}{\$400,000}(14\% - 8\%) = 18.5\%$$

thus confirming our earlier calculations.

In equation (15-2) we have set the expected return on debt to equal the risk-free rate. If the debt is risky, then the expected return on the debt is higher. When default is a possibility, R_f should be replaced by the appropriate expected return on the debt.

When Maximizing Firm Value Is in the Best Interests of the Shareholders   We defined the firm's optimal capital structure as the debt–equity ratio that maximizes firm value. We now examine when firm value maximization and stockholders' wealth maximization are equal objectives for the financial manager.

Return to the market-value balance sheet for Rheinhold when it is levered. The value of Rheinhold when levered is: $V^L = D + E$, so the value of Rheinhold's equity is

$$
\begin{array}{ccccc}
E & = & V^L & - & D \\
\text{value} & & \text{value} & & \text{value} \\
\text{of equity} & & \text{of firm} & & \text{of debt}
\end{array}
$$

Now assume Rheinhold changes its capital structure by issuing $50,000 in new debt and then using the proceeds to purchase $50,000 of its own shares. If the new debt does not increase the riskiness to the old bondholders, the total value of the debt is now $350,000 ($300,000 + $50,000). But what is the value of equity now? That depends on the new value of Rheinhold. If the value of the debt remains constant, then the market value of Rheinhold's equity varies directly with the market value of Rheinhold.

For example, if Rheinhold's market value is $650,000, then the value of the equity is $650,000 − $350,000 = $300,000. If Rheinhold's market value changes to $700,000, the equity value changes to $700,000 − $350,000 = $350,000. Notice that because the value of debt remains constant, any change in firm value affects the shareholders directly. Thus the greater the value of the firm is, the better off stockholders are.

In this example, the risk of debt has not changed, which is why the value of the total debt is $300,000 + $50,000 = $350,000. But if the new debt increases the risk of the old bonds, the value of the old bonds falls. If the value of the old bonds falls to $250,000, the total debt for Rheinhold is worth $250,000 + $50,000 = $300,000, and the value of equity is now higher for any given value of the assets. By altering its capital structure, Rheinhold can provide gains to the stockholders at the expense of the bondholders. To prevent such adverse effects, bondholders typically insist that certain conditions (called *restrictive covenants*) be agreed upon before the debt is raised. Similarly, if the firm makes any decision that lowers the risk of the bonds, the value of the bonds rises and so does the value of the firm. In this case, stockholders do not benefit from an increase in the firm's value.

The point here is that maximizing firm value is, in general, beneficial to stockholders as long as not all of the increase in firm value accrues to the bondholders. In that case, stockholders do not benefit. It is not that bondholders' wealth should not increase; all that is required is that stockholders have some benefit. Only then can financial managers, working in the shareholders' best interests, justify their decision to the owners. Assuming that management, working in the interests of the owners, avoids decisions that increase firm value while lowering stockholders' wealth, we can justify talk of an optimal capital structure in terms of firm value instead of stock values. Thus the optimal capital structure can be defined as the debt–equity ratio that maximizes the market value of the firm under the assumption that managers make decisions with shareholders' interests in mind.

To avoid confusion, recognize that we are not being inconsistent with our earlier goal of maximizing equity value. We are simply adding to that objective. To the extent that managers make decisions that increase stockholders' wealth, equity value maximization and firm value maximization are equivalent objectives.

15-2

CAPITAL STRUCTURE, EXPECTED RETURNS, AND RISK

We have seen that equityholders' expected return increases with leverage. However, this does not necessarily mean that stockholders are better off when the firm borrows because we must also see what happens to the risk of the equity. Because the market value of an asset depends on its expected return and its market risk (beta), an analysis of the market values of stock, debt, and the firm as a whole can be conducted in the risk–return framework used in earlier chapters. In addition, it is possible in this framework to see explicitly how changes in the risk and expected returns of a firm's assets affect the expected return and risk of its equity.

The Relationship Between the Risk of the Firm and the Risk of Levered Equity

Since $A = D + E$, the firm's assets can again be viewed as a portfolio that contains debt and equity. Because the beta of a portfolio is simply the weighted average of the betas of the components of the portfolio, we have

$$\beta_A = (\text{proportion of debt})(\beta_D) + (\text{proportion of equity})(\beta_E)$$

$$= \frac{D}{D + E}(0) + \frac{E}{D + E}(\beta_E)$$

Rearranging this equation yields the relationship between the market risk of equity and the market risk of assets:

$$\beta_E = \beta_A\left(1 + \frac{D}{E}\right) \tag{15-3}$$

Thus, as illustrated by equation (15-3), the equity risk does, in fact, increase as the debt–equity ratio increases.

Again, remember that β_E is the risk of levered equity, and β_A, the risk of the firm's assets, is the same as the risk of unlevered equity. Assume that the expected return on the market $E(\tilde{R}_m)$ is 15% and that the riskless interest rate is 8%. Since the unlevered equity's expected return is still 14%, we can use the capital asset pricing model (CAPM) to calculate the risk (beta) of the unlevered firm. The *required* rate of return on Rheinhold's unlevered equity is given by the CAPM as

$$ROA^* = R_f + \beta_A[E(\tilde{R}_m) - R_f]$$
$$14\% = 0.08 + \beta_A(0.15 - 0.08)$$

which implies that $\beta_A = 0.8571$.

Now consider Rheinhold when its capital structure consists of $300,000 debt and $400,000 equity (i.e., a debt–equity ratio of 0.75). What happens to the risk of the equity? Rheinhold's levered equity risk from equation (15-3) is

$$\beta_E = 0.8571(1 + 0.75) = 1.50$$

Thus, although the expected return to equity has gone up, the risk has also increased. According to the CAPM, equity with a beta of 1.50 should have an expected return of

$$\begin{aligned} ROE^* &= R_f + \beta_E[E(\tilde{R}_m) - R_f] \\ &= 0.08 + 1.50(0.15 - 0.08) \\ &= 0.185 \quad \text{or} \quad 18.5\% \end{aligned}$$

again consistent with our earlier result about Rheinhold's ROE^*.

Is Firm Value Higher or Lower with Leverage?

Because expected equity returns increase with debt, *if* the market risk of equity decreases or even remains constant, we have to conclude that increasing debt raises the equity value. However, since both the expected returns and the risk increase, the net impact on the equity value is unclear.

To examine the impact on Rheinhold's firm value, we examine what happens to Rheinhold's ROA^* as it takes on leverage. Using equation (15-1) for Rheinhold, we have

$$ROA^* = \frac{\$400,000}{\$300,000 + \$400,000}(0.185) + \frac{\$300,000}{\$300,000 + \$400,000}(0.08) = 14\%$$

Notice that the expected return on Rheinhold's assets has not been changed by introducing debt. It follows from our discussion earlier that since the operating cash flows have not changed and the ROA^* is not affected, firm value is also unaffected. Capital structure is thus irrelevant.

An Intuitive Explanation for Capital Structure Irrelevance

One way to understand the irrelevance of capital structure is to recognize that individuals and businesses invest in companies only because the companies can provide risk–return possibilities that they cannot find elsewhere. By altering its capital structure, the firm does not do anything for investors that they could not have done themselves. An investor who borrows money and buys the stock of an unlevered firm can, in effect, replicate the leverage of the firm. If an investor owns $100 worth of Rheinhold's stock and he buys the stock with $43 in borrowed funds (8% interest), he has an equity investment of $57 and has, in effect, created a "personal debt–equity ratio" of $43/$57 = 0.75. This **"homemade leverage"** replicates corporate leverage. What is the investor's ROE^*? In other words, what is the return on his $57 of equity in this investment? We can arrive at the answer in two equivalent ways.

First, his payoff from the stock next period is $14 ($100 × 0.14). Out of this, he must pay $3.44 as interest on his borrowings ($43 × 0.08). Thus his net payoff is $10.56, and the return on his equity in the investment is therefore $10.56/$57 = 18.5%.

Second, note that equation (15-2) should hold regardless of whether the returns are measured for companies or individuals. Thus

$$ROE^* = ROA^* + \frac{D}{E}(ROA^* - R_f)$$

$$= 14\% + (0.75)(14\% - 8\%) = 18.5\%$$

which is identical to what the firm yielded, provided that the investor can borrow under the same conditions as the firm can. As long as this requirement is met, homemade leverage is a perfect substitute for firm leverage, and the firm has created nothing new for the investor by borrowing. Therefore the market attaches no additional value to leverage.

A Closer Look at the Irrelevance Argument

THE PERFECT CAPITAL MARKETS ASSUMPTION

The most important assumptions for this irrelevance result is that capital markets have no imperfections such as taxes, brokerage fees, and bankruptcy costs. Most of these assumptions are also required for the CAPM. However, the irrelevance proposition does not require the CAPM arguments; they are used only to provide an example. Is an assumption of no transactions costs reasonable? Although transactions costs are definitely not zero, they can be relatively small for certain market participants. For example, despite their large dollar volume of transactions, institutions have surprisingly small transactions costs, and the assumption appears to be a reasonable approximation. But taxes and bankruptcy costs cannot be overlooked. These "imperfections" are dealt with later in the chapter.

HOMEMADE LEVERAGE

In the M&M analysis, homemade leverage and corporate leverage are perfect substitutes. It is assumed that the investor can borrow on his own account as the corporation can, and at the same terms. The first question that arises is whether in fact an individual can borrow at the same terms as a corporation can. Shouldn't corporations be able to borrow money at a lower rate than individuals can? The evidence is not clear, but it appears that corporate borrowing is not very different from individual borrowing. High-grade corporate debt carries interest rates very close to those on individuals' home mortgages. Also, the rates banks pay on term loans (short-term bank debt) are very close to the rates individuals pay on margin debt (the debt investors incur when they borrow from stockholders with securities as collateral). In addition, institutional investors may be able to borrow at the same rate as can the corporation in question.

One difference between homemade leverage and corporate leverage relates to *limited liability*. When a corporation borrows money, it borrows with limited liability. If the borrowing corporation goes broke, the investors' losses are limited to the value of their stock. On the other hand, when an individual takes out a loan and defaults, his or her personal assets can be seized to pay off the loan. In addition, an individual who is borrowing on margin is subject to margin calls. Thus it appears that homemade leverage is much riskier than corporate leverage is and that borrowing by corporations has some special value. This argument seems to invalidate the M&M proposition. However, why should we restrict homemade leverage to individuals? Other corporations and financial institutions with limited liability can engage in the arbitrage process, and the capital structure irrelevance result should hold. There is nothing sacrosanct in the example provided earlier about individuals engaging in homemade leverage. The individual could just as well be another company, and the M & M result would then survive this criticism.

INSTITUTIONAL RESTRICTIONS

Another factor that can challenge the M & M argument is institutional restrictions. We have argued that institutions and not necessarily individuals can engage in homemade leverage. But what if institutional restrictions forbid institutions from engaging in such transactions? Life insurance companies and many pension funds, for example, are not allowed to enter into certain transactions. This does not really affect the M & M result. As long as some individuals or institutions can engage in homemade leverage, the M & M theory cannot be dismissed altogether, at least on this count. Capital structure does not affect firm value.

Thus the M & M irrelevance proposition appears to be far more robust than at first glance. It is extremely general and contends that both the *composition* (the proportion of debt, equity, and other instruments) and the *structure* (long-term or short-term debt, common stock or preferred stock, class A stock or class B stock, etc.) of the right-hand side of the balance sheet are immaterial. What matters is the value of the firm's assets. That is the only truly productive component of a firm's possessions. The financial instruments it issues do not affect their productivity and thereby their value.

When Do Capital Structure Decisions Affect Firm Value?

The M & M proposition implies that managers really do not need to worry about capital structure in perfect markets and, in many instances, even when the perfect market assumptions do not strictly hold. The more severe the imperfections (the more restrictive the "real-world" considerations) are, the stronger the case is for the relevance of the financing decision. Generalizations, though, can be extremely difficult. Only a case-by-case analysis can determine the role of capital structure under nonmarket (institutional) considerations.

An important idea bears repeating, however. As long as capital structure decisions intended to benefit securityholders can be replicated by investors, these decisions provide nothing new and thus offer no new value. If, however, a financing decision can offer something new or valuable that is not available to investors elsewhere, capital structure is relevant. For example, if a financial manager can identify the need of a particular type of investor (e.g., those in high tax brackets) and offer a new security that he or she desires but cannot find elsewhere, this security, when added to the firm's capital structure, affects a firm's value if it is issued. Nevertheless, given the myriad securities available in the marketplace, the creation and issuance of a new type of security, though not impossible, may not be easy. As we will see, when corporate taxes are recognized, the firm can provide a risk–return possibility that investors cannot find on their own.

15-3

TAXES AND CAPITAL STRUCTURE

What happens to the argument of capital structure irrelevance if an imperfection—corporate taxes—is introduced? Is capital structure still irrelevant? The recognition of corporate taxes implies that a firm should be totally debt-financed. This is because debt provides valuable tax shields.

Tax Shields from Debt

To understand what these tax shields are, consider two firms that have identical operating incomes but different capital structures. According to Table 15-1, the

■

TABLE 15-1

Income Available to Stockholders and Bondholders with Different Capital Structures

	Firm U (Unlevered)	Firm L (Levered)
Capital Structure (market values)		
Debt (8%)	$ 0	$25,000
Equity	65,000	40,000
Total	$65,000	$65,000
Income Statement		
Net operating income	$ 8,000	$ 8,000
Less: Interest (8%)		2,000
Taxable income	$ 8,000	$ 6,000
Less: Taxes (50%)	4,000	3,000
Net income	$ 4,000	$ 3,000
Income to Securityholders		
Income to		
Bondholders (interest)	$ 0	$ 2,000
Stockholders (net income)	4,000	3,000
Total income to bondholders and stockholders	$ 4,000	$ 5,000

NOTE: The increased income to Firm L's securityholders (of $1,000) is supported by the $1,000 reduction in taxes to Firm L.

unlevered firm has $65,000 in equity, and the levered firm's capital structure is composed of $40,000 in equity and $25,000 in debt with a coupon interest rate of 8%. If we assume (for simplicity) a 50% marginal tax rate, the total income available to securityholders in firm L is greater than that for the unlevered firm, by $1,000. The reason is that interest expenses are tax deductible, which lowers the levered firm's taxable income and, consequently, its taxes (by $1,000). Debt-financed firms are, in effect, "subsidized" by the federal government because the levered firm pays less in taxes than does the unlevered firm. In effect, the government is picking up $1,000 of interest payments. It is as if the levered firm has received a "bonus" of $1,000. This bonus is called a **tax shield** and is computed as:

$$\text{Tax shield} = T \times I$$

where T is the corporation's tax rate and I is the dollar amount in interest paid by the firm. For Firm L,

$$\text{Tax shield} = 0.50 \times \$2{,}000 = \$1{,}000$$

Notice in Table 15-1 that the difference in total income to bondholders and stockholders is greater for the levered firm by an amount exactly equal to the tax shield. Thus, because of taxes, it is as if every time an investment is financed with debt, the government is "throwing in" another project with a cash savings equal to the tax shield. Because this "project" generates savings, it is valuable. Tax shields should therefore increase a firm's value, and this increase in value should eventually accrue to the stockholders. If a levered firm can generate tax shields into the future, the value of these tax shields is given simply by the discounted values (present values) of these future tax shields.

Consider the balance sheets (market values) of the levered and unlevered companies:

UNLEVERED FIRM

ASSETS: $65,000	DEBT: $0
	EQUITY: $65,000

LEVERED FIRM WITHOUT TAXES

ASSETS: $65,000	DEBT: $25,000
	EQUITY: $40,000

LEVERED FIRM WITH CORPORATE TAXES	
ASSETS: $65,000 + *PV* of tax shields	DEBT: $25,000
	EQUITY: $40,000 + *PV* of tax shields

Based on these balance sheets, because of corporate taxes, the value of a levered firm is greater than the value of an unlevered firm by the present value of the tax shields:[2]

$$\text{Value of levered firm} = \begin{array}{c}\text{value of}\\ \text{unlevered firm}\end{array} + \begin{array}{c}\text{present value}\\ \text{of tax shields}\end{array} \qquad (15\text{-}4)$$

To calculate the increase in firm value, one must calculate the present value of these tax shields. The firm's interest payments are fairly predictable. It is also reasonable to assume that the tax rate does not change much from year to year. Thus the magnitude of the tax shields becomes fairly predictable.[3] To find their present value, these tax shields must be discounted at the appropriate discount rate. What is the appropriate market-determined discount rate that must be applied? The answer depends on the riskiness of these projected tax shields. Although this may not be easy to determine precisely, as a practical matter, tax shields are about as risky as is the debt that the firm has issued, and so the appropriate discount rate is the required rate of return on debt.

Assume that Goodfly Corporation has $500,000 in debt with a 10% coupon rate. If the debt matures in four years and the debt holders' required rate of return on debt is 12%, what is the present value of the tax shields if the company is in the 40% tax bracket? We have

$$\begin{aligned}PV(\text{tax shields}) &= PV(T \times I)\\ &= (0.40 \times 0.10 \times \$500,000)(PVFA_{0.12,4})\\ &= (0.40 \times 0.10 \times \$500,000)(3.0373)\\ &= \$60,746\end{aligned}$$

Goodfly's value is $60,746 higher than that of a comparable unlevered firm.

Permanent Debt:
A Special Case

The calculation of the present value of tax shields is easier when permanent debt is assumed. When the debt matures, if the firm refinances it and continues to "roll over" the debt on the same terms, the tax shields become a perpetual benefit. According to Chapter 4, the value of this perpetuity can be calculated as

$$PV = \frac{T \times I}{\text{required rate on debt}}$$

or

$$\text{Value of perpetual tax shield} = T \times D \qquad (15\text{-}5)$$

where $D = I/(\text{required rate on debt})$ is the market value of the debt. Thus, with permanent debt, corporate taxes imply that

$$\text{Value of levered firm} = \begin{array}{c}\text{value of}\\ \text{unlevered firm}\end{array} + \text{value of tax shield}$$
$$D + E \qquad = \qquad A \qquad + \qquad TD$$

[2] As seen earlier in the balance sheets, assets include the physical assets plus the *NPV*s.
[3] This magnitude may change greatly if the tax *law* changes; the law is the basis of prediction.

FIGURE 15-1
Value of a firm as its debt–equity ratio changes.

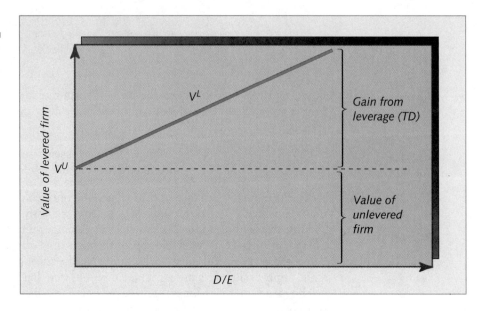

where A, the market value of the unlevered firm's assets, equals the market value of the unlevered firm. That is,

$$V^L = V^U + TD \qquad (15\text{-}6)$$

Equation (15-6) is M & M's original proposition adjusted for corporate taxes. It states that a firm with debt is more valuable than is a similar firm with no debt. Figure 15-1 shows that a levered firm and an unlevered firm have equal values only when $D = 0$ or the corporate tax rate is 0%.

The Relationship Between Expected Returns and Risk with Taxes

Because the value of a levered firm is greater than the value of an unlevered firm when corporate taxes are taken into account, what happens to the risks and expected returns of assets and equity? In other words, what is the relationship between ROA^* and ROE^*? What is the relationship between β_A and β_E when corporate tax effects are explicitly recognized?

Using our earlier approach, we have

Expected return on assets = (proportion of equity) × (expected return on equity)
+ (proportion of debt) × (expected return on debt after taxes)

This time, however, there is a difference. With corporate taxes, the assets of the levered firm are the sum of A (the unlevered firm's assets) and TD (the tax shields). In calculating the debt and equity as a proportion of the unlevered firm's assets, we must subtract the value of the tax shields:[4]

$$ROA^* = \frac{E}{D + E - TD}(ROE^*) + \frac{D}{D + E - TD}(R_f)(1 - T)$$

which, when simplified, yields the tax version of equation (15-2):

[4]Why is the proportion of equity equal to $[E/(D + E - TD)]$? Because corporate taxes imply that $A + TD = D + E$, the value of the *unlevered* firm's assets (which does not include the tax shields) is $A = D + E - TD$. Hence equity as a proportion of the unlevered firm's assets (E/A) is given as $[E/(D + E - TD)]$. A similar line of reasoning applies to the case of debt.

$$ROE^* = ROA^* + \frac{D}{E}(1 - T)(ROA^* - R_f) \qquad (15\text{-}7)$$

The difference between this result and the no-tax result derived in equation (15-2) is the presence of the tax adjustment term.

It is important to note that ROA^* is the return on the firm's "old assets"—all assets other than the tax shield. ROA^* does not change with taxes because it is determined only by the firm's investments.

The Relationship Between the Risk of the Firm and the Risk of Equity

Using the same procedure as before, but this time recognizing that the proportions of debt and equity in the capital structure are different because of the tax shields, we can calculate the beta of the assets of the firm as

$$\beta_A = (\text{proportion of debt})(\beta_D) + (\text{proportion of equity})(\beta_E)$$

$$= \frac{D}{D + E - TD}(0) + \frac{E}{D + E - TD}(\beta_E)$$

which, when rearranged, yields the relationship between the risk of a firm's assets and the risk of equity:[5]

$$\beta_E = \beta_A\left[1 + \frac{D}{E}(1 - T)\right] \qquad (15\text{-}8)$$

In the case of Rheinhold Corporation used earlier without tax considerations, how is Rheinhold's ROE^* affected if the company is in the 30% tax bracket? There are two ways to find Rheinhold's ROE^*. The first uses equation (15-7) directly:

$$ROE^* = 0.14 + (0.75)(1 - 0.3)(0.14 - 0.08) = 17.15\%$$

The second approach calculates Rheinhold's equity beta using equation (15-8) and then the CAPM. Because Rheinhold's asset beta is 0.8571, its equity beta from equation (15-8) is

$$\beta_E = 0.8571[1 + (0.75)(1 - 0.3)] = 1.3071$$

Its expected return on equity from the CAPM is

$$ROE^* = R_f + \beta_E[E(\tilde{R}_m) - R_f]$$
$$= 0.08 + 1.3071(0.15 - 0.08)$$
$$= 17.15\%$$

The (expected) ROE^* in both cases is the same.

The Optimal Capital Structure with Corporate Taxes

Figure 15-1 depicts the relationship between the value of a firm and its debt–equity ratio. This figure is troubling because it implies that a firm can increase its value simply by increasing its debt–equity ratio. The value of the firm is the highest when the firm is entirely debt-financed; that is, with corporate taxes, the optimal capital structure consists of 100% debt. But this is a meaningless conclusion. What is the practical significance of 100% debt financing? When all capital is raised through debt, the debt holders become the owners of the firm, and the situation reverts to 100% equity! Thus this is not possible, even in theory.

The capital structures of U.S. corporations show that all corporations have some amount of equity. Because the M & M result is logically consistent, the only

---

[5] The reader should recognize this result from Chapter 10, in which this result was used to calculate the beta of an asset from the beta of a firm's equity.

explanation for this bizarre implication that 100% debt is optimal must be that some other factors, not yet considered, restrain firms from moving toward a 100% debt structure. For example, we have ignored what happens to a firm that engages in such heavy borrowing. Perhaps its default risk increases and the firm becomes vulnerable to bankruptcy and its associated costs. If this is true, the expected bankruptcy costs offset the benefits from increased tax shields.

Personal Taxes

Our analysis so far has considered only corporate taxes. It is clear that the use of debt can lower the firm's tax liability and thereby increase the total cash flow to stockholders and bondholders. However, the stockholders and bondholders also pay personal taxes on these cash flows, and therefore they are concerned with the cash flows that accrue to them after they have paid their personal taxes. As it turns out, personal taxes offset, to some extent, the tax savings at the corporate level. The important question is to what extent? The answer is not clear at this point.

One school of thought maintains that the tax advantages of debt at the corporate level are completely offset by the disadvantages from personal taxes.[6] If one accepts this argument, the implication is that the value of a firm should be independent of its capital structure. Any advantages to debt from corporate taxes are removed by the offsetting disadvantages of personal taxes. Several simplifying assumptions are implicit in the development of this theory, and the issue is far from settled. Nevertheless, it is perhaps safe to say that the majority view today is that there is, on balance, a net advantage to using debt even when personal tax considerations are recognized. It also appears safe to conclude that the net tax advantages of debt financing are somewhat lower than those suggested by equation (15-6).

15-4
FINANCIAL DISTRESS AND DEFAULT CONSIDERATIONS

As the amount of debt increases, the probability that a firm will be unable to meet its financial obligations also increases. If this situation worsens, financial distress may result. For instance, the firm may be unable to pay preferred dividends, or suppliers or banks may stop extending credit.[7] Such restrictions ultimately may or may not have any effect on the firm. If this state of affairs continues over an extended period, the firm may be forced to forgo attractive investment opportunities, thereby damaging its profitability. At an extreme, financial distress may lead to bankruptcy. We examine financial distress and two different types of bankruptcy in the next chapter. For now, we simply examine the implications of default, which happens when the firm is unable to meet its debt obligations.

---

[6] Merton Miller argued that with personal taxes, the market value of the tax shields can be written as

$$T_c D \left[1 - \frac{(1 - T_c)(1 - T_e)}{1 - T_d} \right]$$

where T_c, T_e, and T_d are the tax rate for the firm, the personal tax rate on equity income, and the tax rate on debt income, respectively. Miller argues that in equilibrium, $[(1 - T_c)(1 - T_e)/(1 - T_d)]$ equals 1, so that the value of the tax shields is $T_c D(1 - 1) = 0$. Thus, for any individual firm, capital structure again becomes irrelevant. But this result assumes that the corporate tax rate is less than the tax rate on debt income. With the passage of the 1993 Omnibus Budget Reconcilation Act, the highest corporate tax rate now is 39%, the highest marginal tax rate is 39.6%, and the optimal capital structure again has reverted to one with all debt. It is for this reason that we do not proceed further in a discussion of Miller's personal taxes model. See M. Miller, "Debt and Taxes," *Journal of Finance* 32 (1977): 261–275.

[7] In some instances, *financial distress* is defined as only the situation in which a firm fails to meet its contractual obligations.

Even before actual default occurs, the costs of financial distress may begin to mount. Nevertheless, the tax advantages of corporate borrowings' tax shields may outweigh these costs, making debt still an attractive source of funds. When the firm defaults, however, the picture changes drastically.

In default, the stockholders elect, in effect, to surrender the firm's assets to its creditors. The stockholders can simply walk away, letting the creditors fight over the remains, but they do this only if the value of the firm's assets is less than the value of the bondholders' claims. With default a possibility, bondholders always bear the risk of getting back less than what is due them. To make matters worse, default costs, such as lawyers' and accountants' fees or reorganization costs, can further jeopardize the bondholders' position. Three interesting questions arise:

1. Can the threat of default affect the firm's value if default is costless?

2. Can the threat of default affect the firm's value if default is not costless?

3. Are default costs significant, or can they safely be ignored?

Does the Threat of Costless Default Affect Firm Value?

When focusing only on the influence of default, we assume initially that corporate and personal tax rates are again 0%. If creditors face the possibility of not recovering their total claims as the debt–equity ratio rises, it appears that the firm's value should depend on the probability of default. For example, consider two firms, A and B, identical in every respect except that A has a higher debt–equity ratio than B does. If A has a 30% chance of defaulting, whereas B has only a 5% chance of defaulting, it would seem that firm A's value should be less than that of firm B. As it turns out, the threat of costless default alters the relative values of a firm's debt and equity, but the value of the firm as a whole is unchanged. The possibility of costless default has no effect on a firm's value, and capital structure is irrelevant. Appendix 15-A provides an example to illustrate this result.

Does the Threat of Costly Default Affect Firm Value?

The costs associated with default are often referred to as **bankruptcy costs.** As a practical matter, there are two types of bankruptcy costs: direct and indirect. *Direct costs* are legal and accounting fees, reorganization costs, and other administrative expenses. *Indirect costs* are less tangible. These are the net costs associated with financial distress. For instance, when managers are dealing with default (even imminent default), their efforts and resources are diverted from maximizing the firm's value to halting a deteriorating situation. Chrysler Corporation's near bankruptcy caused management to devote a great deal of time and expense to rebuilding the public's confidence in its ability to continue operations. Other examples of indirect but difficult-to-measure costs are lost sales, lost profits, higher costs of credit, and the inability to invest in profitable opportunities because external financing sources are not available. How much these indirect costs affect a firm's value is not clear, but both direct and indirect bankruptcy costs affect the returns to security-holders if a firm is in default. In Appendix 15A we discuss in greater detail, with the aid of a numerical example, the impact of bankruptcy costs on firm value.

In the case of *costly* default, a levered firm's value is lower by the present value of expected bankruptcy costs. Equation (15-4) becomes

Market value of levered firm	=	market value of unlevered firm	+	present value of tax shields	−	present value of bankruptcy costs	(15-9)
V^L	=	V^U	+	$PV(TI)$	−	$PV(c)$	

where c is the expected bankruptcy costs.

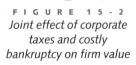

FIGURE 15-2
Joint effect of corporate taxes and costly bankruptcy on firm value

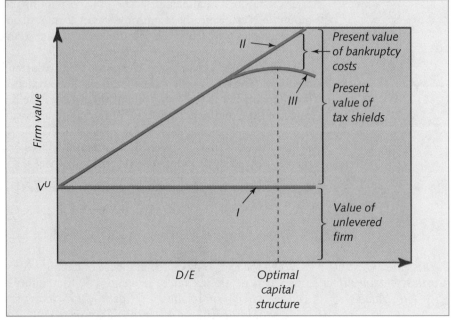

We now modify Figure 15-1 to account for bankruptcy costs in order to demonstrate the joint effect of corporate taxes and costly default on firm value. In Figure 15-2, line I is the original case, in which the levered and unlevered firms' values are equal under a perfect market setting. Line II represents the case of M&M with corporate taxes, in which firm value increases with the D/E ratio until a maximum is reached at 100% debt. In contrast, line III indicates that with costly default, firm value increases initially, reaches a maximum, and then decreases with leverage. In other words, at low levels of debt, the probability of default is very low. Then the firm's value increases with leverage because its debt's tax advantages predominate. After a "reasonable amount" of debt, though, the probability of default and hence the present value of expected bankruptcy costs become significant. Even though the tax shield benefits continue to increase with relatively more debt, bankruptcy costs begin to damage the firm's value. This trade-off between the potential benefits and the associated disadvantages of increased debt results in an optimal debt–equity ratio. At this point, firm value is maximized (i.e., there is an optimal capital structure), and we have made, for an individual firm, the first clear-cut case for capital structure *relevancy*.

Are Bankruptcy Costs Significant?

What if bankruptcy costs are so small or insignificant that they can be ignored? Our exercise in search of an optimal capital structure will have been in vain. If the present value of expected bankruptcy costs is 0 (or immaterial), then equation (15-9) reverts to the M&M proposition with corporate taxes and 100% debt is optimal.

In a study of 11 railroad bankruptcies, Jerold Warner attempted to measure the magnitude of bankruptcy costs. He found that the direct costs were small, ranging from about 1% to 5% of the firms' market values up to seven years before and just before bankruptcy.[8] Moreover, there were "economies of scale" in going bankrupt.

[8]See Jerold B. Warner, "Bankruptcy Costs: Some Evidence," *Journal of Finance,* May 1977, pp. 337–348. Because railroad bankruptcies are invariably reorganizations, one must expect a downward bias in these estimates of bankruptcy costs.

As a percentage of firm value, bankruptcy costs were smaller for larger firms than for smaller firms, thus implying that capital structure decisions for smaller firms should be more influenced by bankruptcy considerations.

Warner's study indicated that bankruptcy costs were trivial, but he did not include indirect costs.[9] Using a measure of both direct and indirect bankruptcy costs, Edward Altman found that for 19 bankrupt industrial firms, the present value of bankruptcy costs was not trivial. It ranged from 11% to 17% of firm value up to three years before bankruptcy.[10] In fact, he found that the present value of bankruptcy costs often exceeded the present value of the tax benefits from leverage, which implies that firms were overleveraged.

Some researchers have advanced very persuasive theoretical arguments to suggest that bankruptcy cost considerations should be entirely irrelevant to determining firm value.[11] According to this reasoning, the presence of bankruptcy costs affects only the relative values of equity and debt, not the firm as a whole. Complicating matters even further, there are several factors that can limit the costs of financial distress, factors that effectively lower the net bankruptcy costs. These are discussed in the highlight on page 482.

So what is the final word on the magnitude of bankruptcy costs? We must wait for the results of more studies before we can provide a definitive answer.

15-5

AGENCY COST CONSIDERATIONS

Agency cost considerations, introduced in Chapter 2, can also have a significant impact on a firm's capital structure. It is generally believed that as a firm increases its debt, its total agency costs rise and, as a result, the benefits of the tax shields are reduced. (Other viewpoints, which we explore later, suggest that agency costs can decrease with debt.) Agency cost increases arise from, for example, the bondholders' need to monitor the firm's actions more closely. Such costs lower the value of the debt and hence the value of the firm. Figure 15-3 shows the effect on a firm's value of both taxes and debt-related agency costs. Notice that the addition of agency costs causes the optimal capital structure to occur at a debt–equity ratio somewhat lower than that with corporate taxes and bankruptcy costs only.

How Agency Costs Can Influence Capital Structure

What exactly are these agency costs? Where do they fit into capital structure considerations?

The agency costs that arise from the separation of ownership and control were introduced in Chapter 2. Here we concentrate on those agency problems that can have an impact on the capital structure decision. **Compensation contracts** (such as options) that are used to reduce agency costs can have the undesirable effect of inducing managers to adopt low debt levels. With increasing debt, there is an increase in both the probability of default and the probability that the stock and hence the option will become worthless. Therefore managers generally prefer higher equity levels and lower debt–equity ratios.

[9] Warner also followed up his investigation of bankruptcy costs in another study that examined the returns on defaulted railroad bonds. His evidence showed that bondholders realized significant negative abnormal returns on the bankruptcy petition filing date. This indicates that the marketplace did not ignore bankruptcy costs (i.e., they were not trivial). See J. B. Warner, "Bankruptcy, Absolute Priority, and the Pricing of Risky Debt Claims," *Journal of Financial Economics*, May 1977, pp. 239–276.

[10] Edward I. Altman, "A Further Empirical Investigation of the Bankruptcy Cost Question," *Journal of Finance*, September 1984, pp. 1067–1089.

[11] See R. A. Haugen and L. W. Senbet, "The Insignificance of Bankruptcy Costs to the Theory of Optimal Capital Structure," *Journal of Finance*, May 1978.

FACTORS THAT LIMIT THE COSTS OF FINANCIAL DISTRESS

MANAGERIAL TURNOVER A firm that is in financial distress sees significant changes in its management. To the extent that the existing management has led the firm to the present condition, its removal opens up the possibility of new blood running the company. This can lead to a significant reassessment of the firm's existing operating and financial policies and thus benefit the firm.

Gilson examined 381 publicly traded corporations that experienced serious financial distress (as measured by stock price declines) over the period 1979–1984.* He found that 52% of all firms had changes in senior level management (CEO, president, and chairman of the board) during the period of distress. (The corresponding turnover rate for nondistressed firms was only 19%.) What is particularly interesting is that direct intervention by bank lenders accounted for 21% of all management changes in financially distressed firms. Moreover, even though the average departing manager's age was only 52, none of them held a senior management position at another exchange-listed firm during the next three years. Thus it appears that managers bear real costs if their firm becomes distressed.

A more recent study by Gilson and Vetsuypens provides additional evidence that managers of financially distressed firms incur real costs.† In examining 77 publicly traded firms that either filed for bankruptcy or privately restructured their debt during 1981–

1987, they find that almost one-third of the CEOs are replaced in a given year around default and those that remain experience substantial pay cuts and reduced bonuses. Moreover, management compensation is tied to the successful resolution of the bankruptcy or debt restructuring or based on the value of the payoffs to creditors. Their evidence, taken collectively, suggests that compensation policy is often an important aspect of the firm's plans to deal with financial distress.

CHANGES IN ORGANIZATIONAL STRUCTURE AND STRATEGY

Wruck argues that financial distress forces a change in the firm's economic activities and the way these activities are organized.‡ These restructurings often create value for the shareholders. In rethinking their recovery strategies, firms are forced to confront their operating procedures and business strategies and depart from the status quo. Often unprofitable assets are sold and others are reorganized and restaffed. Many firms in the U.S. steel industry were forced into financial distress during the 1980s because of fierce international competition. Some (e.g., Wheeling Pittsburgh) filed bankruptcy, whereas others (e.g., Inland Steel) restructured privately. In general, these financially distressed firms reduced the scope of their operations to produce primarily specialty steel products.

Organizational changes to improve efficiency are not confined to the steel industry alone. Consider the case of Halliburton Corporation, one of the world's largest diversified energy services, engi-

neering, maintenance, and construction companies. In response to declining performance and cash flow constraints, Halliburton announced on June 16, 1993, a massive reorganization plan effective July 1, 1993. In addition to a major rearrangement of the company's operating units, there were several changes in top management: the CEO was replaced and a new president appointed. In justifying the need for the reorganization, the chairman of the board, Thomas H. Cruikshank, said:§

> The purpose of the reorganization is to improve responsiveness to the needs of customers while reducing operating costs. . . . The new organization will also permit the provision of all services and products by a single company operating under a single, simplified management. This will facilitate the sales of multiple lines of services and products, as well as the provision of a full range of integrated services and products for a single well or a multiple well program. The new Halliburton Energy Services organization is designed to meet existing as well as emerging opportunities in the most efficient manner and to enhance future earnings.

* S. C. Gilson, "Management Turnover and Financial Distress," Journal of Financial Economics 25 (1989).
† S. C. Gilson and M. Vetsuypens, "CEO Compensation in Financially Distressed Firms," Journal of Finance, June 1993.
‡ K. H. Wruck, "Financial Distress and Organizational Efficiency," Journal of Financial Economics 27 (1990).
§ Press release, June 16, 1993, Halliburton Company.

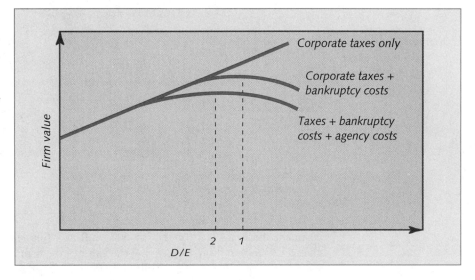

Managers also invest in **firm-specific human capital.** For example, they may invest considerable time and effort in "learning the organization." This firm-specific knowledge is of great use to those firms that choose to reward such knowledge. Firms may decide to pay their managers even more than their opportunity costs. But if such managers lose their jobs upon bankruptcy, the next firm that employs them may not value this knowledge because it may not be relevant to the new firm's well-being. For example, in many organizations the "head secretary" is often alleged to know more about the organization than the CEO does, and it is not uncommon to refer to this secretary as the "real power" in the organization. But although this secretary has skills that are useful and valuable to the present organization, they may not be of great value in another job setting. Risk-averse managers usually avoid very highly leveraged capital structures. The growing popularity of "golden parachutes" is one device that encourages managers to take on financial leverage.

*Stockholder–
Bondholder Agency
Problems*

Managers make decisions in the interests of the shareholders. In this regard, two problems are important: expropriation and underinvestment. Both affect bondholders, but rational bondholders, of course, take them into consideration when pricing bonds.

As an illustration of the expropriation problem consider the Hartem Company, which has the current market-value balance sheet shown in Table 15-2, part a. Management is considering a new, risky one-year project that calls for an initial investment of $10 million. The expected returns are a $30 million gain with a probability of 0.60 and a $15 million loss with a probability of 0.40. The expected return is therefore ($30 × 0.60) + (− $15 × 0.40) = $12 million.

Assume that the project's *NPV* is − $1 million. Normally this project should be rejected. But suppose that stockholders are willing to take the risk of accepting this project because the odds favor an extremely attractive return if they are lucky. If they are unlucky, however, they will lose, but the bondholders may also share in the loss. In a sense, the bondholders will subsidize the stockholders' losses.

If the project is accepted, assume that the immediate effect on Hartem's balance sheet is as given in Table 15-2, part b. If the $10 million for the new investment is financed with cash, the current assets decrease by $10 million while the new in-

TABLE 15-2

Hartem Company's Market-Value Balance Sheets (in millions)

a. Before accepting risky project

Assets		Claims on Assets	
Fixed and current assets	$60	Debt	$35
NPV of investments	0	Equity	25
	$60		$60

b. After accepting risky project (expropriation of bondholder wealth example)

Assets		Claims on Assets	
Fixed and current assets	$60	Debt	$30
NPV of investments	−1	Equity	29
	$59		$59

c. After accepting risky project (underinvestment example)

Assets		Claims on Assets	
Fixed and current assets	$60	Debt	$36
NPV of investments	+1	Equity	25
	$61		$61

vestment increases fixed assets by $10 million, thus leaving the total assets unchanged at $60 million. Notice that the value of the firm falls by $1 million because a project with $NPV = -\$1$ million has been accepted. Also, the value of bonds has fallen by $5 million because of the increased risk of the debt, but the value of equity has risen by $4 million. In other words, the stockholders have gained at the expense of the bondholders. Because the firm has taken on a very risky project, bond values have suffered.

How can this happen? Bondholders are forced to share the risk of failure but are denied the benefits if the project is successful (they are entitled to only a fixed return). In other words, because of the proportionately higher risk of bankruptcy, bond values decline by an amount greater than the amount by which the firm's value decreases, and hence the value of equity must increase. If the project fails, it will result in a total loss of $25 million—that is, the $10 million initial investment and the $15 million expected cash outflow (loss) at the end of one year. Therefore, at most, the firm will be worth only $60 - \$25 = \$35$ million, which leaves very little asset coverage for the bondholders' claims if the firm should go bankrupt.

Now consider what would happen if the same project had a $+\$1$ million NPV. Assume that the new project has lowered the risk of the firm so that the bondholders' risks decrease and the bond values increase from $35 million to $36 million. In this case, the value of the equity is the value of the firm's assets ($61 million) less the value of the debt ($36 million). Then, as Table 15-2, part c shows, the equity value remains unchanged at $25 million. Because the stockholders will not benefit from the $+\$1$ million NPV, they (or the manager) will not invest in this project. This is the **underinvestment problem.**

Financial managers can accept very risky projects or make other decisions that hurt bondholders. To protect themselves, therefore, bondholders usually include certain *restrictions* or *covenants* in their lending agreements.

In general, there are four broad categories of covenants. Table 15-3 lists these categories together with the relative frequency with which they are used. Covenants that restrict new debt are necessary to ensure that any new debt is subordinated to the existing debt's protection. Sometimes these restrictions also include rules regarding leases, rentals, and sinking fund requirements. Restricting the dividends prevents shareholders from granting themselves a liquidating dividend and thereby preempting the bondholders' asset claims. A merger can also hurt bondholders. For example, if a company with little debt acquires another firm that has excessive amounts of debt, the acquiring firm's bondholders are subjected to higher risk because they must assume the acquired firm's debt obligations. Finally, bond covenants occasionally restrict the use of a firm's assets. For example, these restric-

	Type of Covenant	Percentage of Time Used
	1. Restrictions on use of new debt	90.8%
	2. Restrictions on cash dividends	23.0
	3. Restrictions on potential mergers	39.1
	4. Restrictions on disposition of assets	35.6

TABLE 15-3
Four Common Types of Bond Covenants Found in Lending

SOURCE: Clifford W. Smith, Jr., and Jerold B. Warner, "On Financial Contracting: An Analysis of Bond Covenants," *Journal of Financial Economics,* June 1979, pp. 117–161.

tions may require a firm to maintain all existing assets. Some restrictions pertain to the sale of certain assets and the use of these assets as collateral or other loans.

Although bond covenants help protect bondholders, they cannot cover every condition or eventuality. Sometimes there are problems with ensuring a firm's compliance with a covenant. For instance, it is difficult to monitor and influence the operational or investment decisions that management makes. Bondholders must therefore still take on some risk despite well-intended safeguards.

More important, do these "monitoring costs" affect the capital structure? As a firm increases the relative amount of debt, it is easier for managers to exploit the bondholders. Bondholders should realize that their loan arrangements and other safeguards are not complete insurance. To protect themselves, therefore, they demand higher and higher interest rates on the debt they supply, to compensate themselves for the higher risk they bear.

Other Stakeholder-Related Agency Costs

Our discussion so far has considered only three stakeholders in the firm: the managers, the stockholders, and the bondholders. It should come as no surprise that many other stakeholders also are affected by a firm's capital structure decisions. As the firm's financial leverage increases, the probability of bankruptcy rises as well, and stakeholders such as customers, workers, and suppliers accordingly bear greater risks. Bondholders protect themselves by demanding higher interest rates. Similarly, suppliers of raw materials and customers become more concerned about doing business with the firm as its leverage increases.

This is particularly true of a firm that is in financial distress. Using the threat of liquidation, a firm can force suppliers to yield concessions that they otherwise would not.[12] If the firm is liquidated, the claims of suppliers and customers can be put aside, and as a result, stockholders and bondholders can benefit. That is, the explicit and implicit contracts that the firm has with these stakeholders no longer hold. This implies that some claims against the firm have been removed, and so equity and debt can increase in value. For example, in 1982 International Harvester sought relief from suppliers and employees to the extent of $50 million, on the grounds that such steps were necessary to avoid bankruptcy.[13] Financially weak firms suffer large reductions in revenue even before their actual bankruptcy. For example, the customers of a computer manufacturer, doubtful about the company's ability to service its product in the future, may avoid purchasing the product in the first place. Similarly, suppliers may be hesitant to sell to the company on favorable terms.

Other stakeholders may also be adversely affected by excessive debt levels. With a greater probability of bankruptcy, an entire community can be hurt. For example, Austin, Texas, relies heavily on IBM Corporation. The company not only

---

[12] A firm liquidates when it dismantles operations, distributes the proceeds, and then ceases to exist. See Sheridan Titman, "The Effects of Capital Structure on a Firm's Liquidation Decision," *Journal of Financial Economics* 13 (1984): 137–151.

[13] *The Wall Street Journal,* September 17, 1982, p. 1.

is a source of employment but also generates property taxes, sales taxes, and utility charges billed on the "industrial user" scale (which allows individuals to pay lower rates). If this company used debt sufficient to result in bankruptcy, the impact on the community would be tremendous. In addition, the claims of the state and federal governments would be affected. It is clear, therefore, that a firm's leverage decisions can affect all stakeholders.

It should be clear to the reader that the optimal capital structure issue is far from resolved. The relationship between the debt–equity ratio and the value of a firm is still not completely clear. One rule for decision makers, however, is certain: When making capital structure decisions, management must focus on firm value considerations instead of other criteria, such as earnings maximization. This observation, coupled with a knowledge of the potential for agency costs, can help management take a more educated approach when making capital structure decisions. As we have seen, despite the tax advantages of debt financing, it may not be in the firm's best interest to borrow excessively. Of course, at this level of generality, it is impossible to define *excessive*. The manager of a company must make this decision based on a good understanding of the company itself and the theoretical arguments advanced in this chapter.

SUMMARY

Section 15-1: Capital Structure and Firm Value

What is the firm's capital structure and why is it of interest?

- A firm's capital structure is the mix of financial securities used to finance its operations. An unlevered firm has only equity and no debt; a levered firm has both debt and equity.

- The optimal capital structure of a firm is that mix of debt and equity that maximizes the value of the firm.

- The firm's managers, making decisions that maximize shareholders' wealth, must choose the debt–equity ratio that maximizes firm value.

What are the rates of return on unlevered and levered equity and how are they related?

- The expected return on unlevered equity (ROA^*) is the expected return to the stockholders of an unlevered firm. It is determined by the unlevered firm's investments.

- The expected return on levered equity (ROE^*) is the expected return to the equityholders of a levered firm. It represents the return on their equity investment in the firm.

- ROE^* increases linearly with the debt–equity ratio only as long as ROA^* exceeds the cost of borrowing. For an unlevered firm, there is no difference between ROA^* and ROE^*.

Section 15-2: Capital Structure, Expected Returns, and Risk

How does the risk of the equity change with financial leverage?

- Although the expected return on equity increases with leverage, this does not mean that the firm's owners are always better off with leverage. The risk of the equity also increases with debt.

- The beta of the equity is the beta of the unlevered firm multiplied by 1 plus the debt–equity ratio.

Is firm value higher or lower with leverage?

- The market value of a firm can be calculated in two ways. It is the value of the firm's assets, by which we mean the firm's physical assets and the *NPV*s of its investments. The value of the firm can also be calculated as the sum of the market values of its debt and equity, which are the claims against the assets.

- A change in a firm's capital structure affects firm value only if it affects the magnitude, timing, or risk of the firm's cash flows and thus its *ROA**. As long as a firm's operating cash flows are unaffected by leverage, capital structure has no influence on firm value, and the optimal capital structure issue is irrelevant.

- In perfect markets, the firm's *ROA** is unaffected by the level of debt, and the capital structure decision is irrelevant. Changes in capital structure do affect the firm's *ROE**, but the risk of the *ROE** also increases, leaving unaffected the stock price.

- With market imperfections, firm value is affected by leverage.

Section 15-3: Taxes and Capital Structure

How do corporate taxes affect firm value?

- When corporate taxes are taken into account, investors cannot replicate what firms can do for them, and so the amount of debt held by the firm does affect market value.

- Interest payments are tax deductible, and thus borrowing reduces the firm's tax liability. The ability of the firm to lower its taxes by "shielding" some income is an asset, so tax shields increase firm value.

- The value of a levered firm is the value of a similar but unlevered firm plus the value of the debt tax shields.

- With corporate taxes, the optimal amount of debt is 100%. In reality, however, firms are not (and cannot be) 100% debt-financed, so we must look for other factors to explain the capital structures of American companies. Personal taxes somewhat offset the advantages of debt financing.

Section 15-4: Financial Distress and Default Considerations

How does the probability of default affect the value of the firm?

- The potential for costless default has no effect on firm value. The fact that the firm may file for bankruptcy is in itself of no special significance.

- Costly default has a negative effect on firm values. As debt increases, the rise in the firm's value because of more tax shields must be weighed against the increasing present value of expected default costs. In this framework an internal (less than 100% debt) optimal capital structure can exist, although it is not easy to characterize the optimal debt–equity ratio. Several factors that limit the costs of financial distress must be factored in.

- Several studies seem to indicate that the magnitude of default costs is very small, thereby limiting the significance of an optimal debt–equity ratio.

Section 15-5: Agency Cost Considerations

How do agency considerations affect the capital structure decision?

- Agency costs are incurred by managers who, guided by their own interests, make decisions that are not necessarily in the best interests of the stockholders.

Risk-averse managers are likely to prefer lower levels of leverage especially if their compensation is tied to the survival of the company.

■ Another source of agency costs is the conflicts that can arise between bondholders and stockholders. Bondholders and stockholders thus insist on restrictive covenants in their lending agreements.

■ Because convenants cannot protect bondholders in every possible management decision, bondholders must monitor the firm, and these agency costs are reflected in the higher required rates of return to bondholders as the firm increases its debt. These monitoring costs also lower the firm's tax advantages of debt and may lead to an optimal debt–equity ratio.

■ There are other stakeholder-related agency costs. Since it is extremely difficult to quantify these costs, it is unclear to what extent they influence the manager's capital structure decision.

QUESTIONS

1. Under what conditions is firm-value maximization equivalent to stock-price maximization?

2. If ROA^* and ROE^* are the required rates of return on a firm's assets and equity, respectively, how are ROA^* and ROE^* related to the CAPM?

3. Capital structure is irrelevant when a firm's operating cash flows are not affected by changes in the firm's debt level. Why? What does *irrelevant* mean in this context?

4. What are the assumptions underlying the M & M hypothesis? Why is it not easy to dismiss them as being "unrealistic"?

5. With corporate taxes, the market value of a levered firm exceeds the market value of a similar but unlevered firm. Why?

6. How is the value of tax shields measured?

7. How does the beta of a firm's equity vary with the firm's debt–equity ratio?

8. What is the optimal capital structure implied by corporate tax considerations? How do personal taxes affect this result?

9. Why is costless bankruptcy irrelevant to determining a firm's value? What happens if bankruptcy becomes costly? Why?

10. What are the direct and indirect costs of bankruptcy? Are they significant?

11. Explain the notion of agency costs as it pertains to the capital structure issue. What impact do they have on the optimal capital structure?

12. What are the most often cited determinants of capital structure?

PROBLEMS [14]

1. Suppose you buy $100,000 in Celeron Corporation Stock with $40,000 in borrowed money at a 10% interest rate. If you expect a return of 20% on your investment, what rate of return could you have earned if you had used no leverage? (Ignore taxes.)

---

[14] In these problems assume that the debt is risk free unless stated otherwise.

2. Grant Engelhardt, financial manager of the Milledge Corp., is trying to determine the ROA^* of his firm. He knows that the debt–equity ratio (in market-value terms) is 0.5 and that the required rates of return on debt and equity are 10% and 16%, respectively. Suppose there are no taxes.

   (a) What is the ROA^*?

   (b) If Grant subsequently discovers that the return on equity is really 19%, what then is the ROA^*?

3. Connie Cousins of Lumpkin Fitness Centers, Inc., knows that the return on the unlevered firm (ROA^*) is 15% and that the cost of debt is a constant 12% for any capital structure. If there are no taxes, what is the required return on equity (ROE^*) for the following values of the firm's debt–equity ratio?

   (a) 0

   (b) 0.25

   (c) 0.5

   (d) 1

   (e) 2

   (f) 5

   (g) 25

4. Cindy Jorgensen knows that her firm has a cost of debt of 10%, a return on assets of 12%, and a required return on equity of 15%, all measured in market value terms.

   (a) What is Cindy's firm's debt–equity ratio (expressed in market-value terms)?

   (b) What is Cindy's firm's debt–total assets ratio (expressed in market-value terms)?

5. The relationship between the beta of the levered and unlevered equity in equation (15-3) was derived assuming that the debt is risk free (i.e., $\beta_D = 0$.). Derive the corresponding result when β_D cannot be set equal to 0.

6. Tim Worley knows that the beta of the Bulldog Leasing Co's. debt is 0.3 and the beta of its equity is 1.5. What must be the beta of the unlevered firm with the following debt–equity ratios (in market-value terms)? Assume zero taxes.

   (a) 0.50

   (b) 0.75

   (c) 1.00

   (d) 1.25

7. The Soomy Electronic Co. has an equity beta of 1.2 and a debt beta of 0.2. The risk-free rate of return is 8%, and the expected market return is 18%. If the required return on the firm's assets is 16%, what must its capital structure be?

8. Jack Tuggle is doing a financial analysis of the consequences of various capital structures for the Dahlonega Mint Coin Stores. He knows that the beta of

their debt is 0 and the beta of their unlevered assets is 0.8. Calculate the beta of equity under the following conditions.

(a) The market value of debt is $200,000 and the market value of equity is $400,000.

(b) The market value of debt is $400,000 and the market value of equity is $800,000.

(c) The market value of debt is $300,000 and the market value of equity is $300,000.

(d) The market value of debt is $400,000 and the market value of equity is $200,000.

9. Elizabeth Webb is going to enter the catering business. She figures that her initial investment will be $85,000, and she expects her tax rate to be 28%. Liz estimates that her annual net operating income will be $17,000 for the next five years, and her required rate of return will be 10%. She is considering three different capital structures for her business: 100% equity, 75% equity–25% debt, and 50% equity–50% debt. The debt, if issued, will mature in five years and carry a 7% annual coupon. (Assume that the $85,000 initial investment also represents the firm's market value.)

(a) Which capital structure will result in the greatest total income to security-holders? (Ignore bankruptcy and agency costs.)

(b) Determine the firm's market-value balance sheet under each different capital structure.

(c) Which capital structure should Liz choose? Why?

10. Fairmont Publishing has an equity beta of 1.5 and is in the 40% tax bracket. The company is evaluating a new project that requires a $50,000 up-front investment. The project is assumed to generate net incremental sales (i.e., incremental sales less incremental variable costs) of $10,000 per year and an annual depreciation of $5,000. Assume that these flows extend into perpetuity. If Fairmont estimates the project's *NPV* to be $30,000, what is Fairmont's debt–equity ratio if the riskless rate is 5% and the expected return on the market is 10%?

11. Joshua Corp. is in the 28% tax bracket and uses a discount rate of 14% when making investment decisions. Joshua's current market value is $30 million. Assume bankruptcy is costless.

(a) What will Joshua's annual tax savings from interest deductions be if it issues $4 million of seven-year bonds with an 11% coupon? What will be the value of the firm?

(b) What will Joshua's annual tax savings from interest deductions be if it issues $4 million of perpetual bonds with an 11% coupon? What will be the value of the firm?

12. The Dooley Co. is in the 34% tax bracket, and its current market value is $10 million. Assume there are no default-related costs.

(a) What will Dooley's annual tax savings from interest deductions be if it issues $2 million of five-year bonds at a 12% interest rate and uses the proceeds to retire equity? What will be the value of the firm?

(b) What will Dooley's annual tax savings from interest deductions be if it issues $2 million of perpetual bonds at a 12% interest rate and uses the proceeds to retire equity? What will be the value of the firm?

13. Linda Dubberly is trying to determine whether or not there is an optimal capital structure for her new firm. She needs to raise a total of $2 million, and she expects her tax rate to be 34%. Any debt financing will be with perpetuities. She has estimated the present value of the costs of bankruptcy to be $500,000, and she has estimated the probabilities of bankruptcy under the following possible capital structures:

Debt–equity (%)	0	10	20	30	40	50	60
Probability of bankruptcy (%)	1	3	8	15	25	40	60

(a) What is the value of Linda's firm under each of the capital structures if bankruptcy costs are ignored?

(b) What is the value of Linda's firm under each of the capital structures if the expected value of bankruptcy costs is included?

15A

DEFAULT AND BANKRUPTCY COSTS

Why Costless Default Has No Effect on Firm Value

Consider two firms that have different probabilities of defaulting (because of different cash flows) but are otherwise identical. Bedrock, Inc., is a very safe company. It has a zero probability of default only because its stockholders agree to be personally liable to the bondholders if the firm has financial difficulties.[15] On the other hand, Quicksand Corporation has a chance of default and does not have the unlimited liability feature. Both companies have $500,000 in bonds with a 10% coupon interest rate.

If the firms are liquidated at the end of the year, the total returns to bondholders and stockholders depend on the market value of the firms' assets. Table 15A-1 contains the potential returns for different ending values. Notice that the expected total returns to both firms' securityholders are identical in all cases—column (6). Therefore the sum of the values of debt and equity must be the same for both Bedrock and Quicksand. Moreover, because the value of a firm is just the sum of the values of its securities, both firms' current values must also be the same.

But what are the individual values of debt and equity for each company? Column (5) in Table 15A-1 indicates that Bedrock's stockholders are worse off than Quicksand's stockholders are because of their unlimited liability. The value of Bedrock's equity therefore is lower than the value of Quicksand's equity. Because the values of both firms are the same, this implies that the value of Bedrock's debt is larger than Quicksand's debt. Thus, although the threat of costless default alters the value of a firm's capital components, it does not affect the value of the firm itself.

Evaluating the Impact of Bankruptcy Costs on Firm Value

In this chapter we saw that bankruptcy costs can reduce a firm's value. Who bears these bankruptcy costs? Why do these costs affect firm value? To answer these questions, we return to the case of Quicksand Corporation.

If we assume that bankruptcy costs are $25,000, Table 15A-2 shows the returns to Quicksand's securityholders when the ending asset values are the same as those

---

[15] We consider the zero default case only for illustration. In the real world, stockholders seldom give up the limited liability feature.

■

TABLE 15A-1

Potential Returns to Bondholders and Stockholders at the End of One Year Under the Threat of Costless Default

	(1)	(2)	(3)	(4) Total	(5)	(6)
	Market Value of Assets	*Returns to Bondholders*	*Stockholders' Personal Liability to Bondholders*	*Returns to Bondholders[a] (2) + (3)*	*Returns to Stockholders (1) − (4)*	*Sum of All Returns (4) + (5)*
	Bedrock, Inc.: no default because of unlimited liability					
	$400,000	$400,000	$150,000	$550,000	− $150,000	$400,000
	500,000	500,000	50,000	550,000	− 50,000	500,000
	600,000	550,000	0	550,000	50,000	600,000
	700,000	550,000	0.	550,000	150,000	700,000
	Quicksand Corp.: default possible; limited liability					
	$400,000	$400,000	0	$400,000	$ 0	$400,000
	500,000	500,000	0	500,000	0	500,000
	600,000	600,000	0	550,000	50,000	600,000
	700,000	700,000	0	550,000	150,000	700,000

[a] Total liability to bondholders is $500,000 in principal plus 0.10 × $500,000 = $50,000 in interest.

■

TABLE 15A-2

Potential Returns to Quicksand's Bondholders and Stockholders at the End of One Year Under the Threat of Costly Default

	(1)	(2)	(3)	(4)	(5)
	Market Value of Assets	*Bankruptcy Costs*	*Returns to Bondholders*	*Returns to Stockholders*	*Sum of All Returns (3) + (4)*
	$400,000	$25,000	$375,000	$ 0	$375,000
	500,000	25,000	475,000	0	475,000
	600,000	0	550,000	50,000	600,000
	700,000	0	550,000	150,000	700,000

found in Table 15A-1. Compare column (5) in Table 15A-2 with column (6) in Table 15A-1. Note that when $25,000 in bankruptcy costs are expected, the total dollar return to all securityholders is lower by this amount. For example, if Quicksand's assets are worth $400,000 at the end of a year, the total return to bondholders and stockholders is lower ($375,000 instead of $400,000) by an amount equal to the bankruptcy costs. Thus, with costly bankruptcy, a levered firm's value is lower by the present value of the expected bankruptcy costs.

QUESTIONS

1. Costless default has absolutely no impact on the market values of the debt and equity. True or false? Why?

2. As long as default is costless, the optimal capital structure issue is irrelevant. True or false? Why?

15B

THE INFORMATIONAL CONTENT OF LEVERAGE CHOICES AND CAPITAL STRUCTURE CHANGES

The popular argument that debt increases agency costs seems, on the face of it, to be plausible. It can also be argued, however, that debt can lower agency costs because the firm's leverage ratio can contain information about the managers' confidence in the firm. High leverage can be used by good managers as a **bonding mechanism** to signal to the marketplace their superior skills.[16] Because we know that risk-averse managers shy away from very high levels of debt, managers who choose very high levels of debt for their firm may, in fact, be signaling to the world that they have confidence in their own (and the firm's) abilities to avoid bankruptcy.

[16] Sanford Grossman and Oliver Hart, "Corporate Financial Structure and Managerial Incentives," in *The Economics of Information and Uncertainty,* edited by J. McCall, pp. 107–140 (Chicago: University of Chicago Press, 1982).

The Informational Content of a Firm's Leverage Ratio

When viewed in this light, increased debt levels can lower the expected bankruptcy costs because the probability of default is perceived to be lower. The firm's value, accordingly, may rise. What is interesting about this view is that not only do compensation contracts limit agency problems, but also managerial actions can signal managerial quality. By adopting high debt levels, confident managers are telling the market that this may be optimal given their compensation contracts. That is, they believe that the firm is unlikely to go bankrupt.[17] High leverage ratios can reveal that the firm's investment opportunities are of high quality.

It has long been recognized that managers have strong incentives to increase the size of their firm and its sales. Their salaries and prestige often go hand in hand with size, and therefore managers may make certain investments (i.e., let the scale of operations "grow") even if they are not in the firm's best interests (the growth is with negative-*NPV* investments). Thus the firm may have **free cash flows,** those in excess of what is required to finance all positive-*NPV* projects, and these free cash flows can increase agency costs and lower firm value. Debt can also be used to lower the agency costs of free cash flows. This **control hypothesis for debt** maintains that the use of debt, without managers' retention of the proceeds, can lower agency costs.[18] By increasing the firm's debt, managers are, in effect, bonding themselves to the stockholders because the firm cannot reduce its debt obligations without risking bankruptcy. In this scenario, the greater use of debt should increase rather than decrease the firm's value. The recent popularity of LBO (leveraged buyout) transactions, in which the firm bears large amounts of debt, demonstrates the bonding feature of debt.

The empirical evidence regarding the use of debt as a bonding mechanism is limited. Jensen uses the free cash flow hypothesis to explain the takeover activity in the oil industry, and the empirical evidence of positive excess returns for LBO transactions, stock repurchases, and other leverage-increasing activities is consistent with this theory.

The principal conclusion that emerges from our discussion of manager–stockholder agency problems is that debt increases agency costs in some situations, but in others, where it can be an effective bonding device, it lowers agency costs. It is difficult to pinpoint exactly how and in what situations debt has a positive or a negative impact on the firm's value.

The Informational Content of Capital Structure Changes

Whatever a firm's optimal capital structure is, we must assume that management's decisions about capital structure are aimed at reaching an optimal mix of debt and equity. Thus both debt and equity issues and, similarly, debt and equity reductions (debt retirement, share repurchases) must be viewed as attempts to reach an optimal "target" capital structure. In fact, dividend payments can also be viewed as capital structure changes because dividends represent equity. If this line of reasoning is correct, then we can expect any capital structure change to be greeted favorably by the market because this puts the firm in a more desirable situation. Similarly, we should expect any dividend changes to be viewed favorably.

The empirical evidence is far from being supportive of this conjecture, however. Most security sales and dividend decreases result in negative abnormal returns, and security repurchases and dividend increases lead to positive abnormal returns.

---

[17] Stephen A. Ross, "The Determination of Financial Structure: The Incentive-Signalling Approach," *Bell Journal of Economics* 8 (1977): 23–40.

[18] Michael C. Jensen, "Agency Costs of Free Cash Flow, Corporate Finance and Takeovers," *American Economic Review,* May 1986, pp. 323–329.

How can this be explained? Although the answer is not yet entirely clear, some possible explanations can be offered by examining the content of capital structure changes.

CAPITAL STRUCTURE CHANGES AS SIGNALS OF A FIRM'S EARNINGS

Changes in a firm's capital structure can communicate information to the market about a firm's cash flows. Because the firm's sources of funds must equal its uses, any increases in security offerings to raise external funds or any cuts in dividends can be interpreted to imply a concomitant decrease in other sources of funds to the firm. For example, this may indicate an anticipated decrease in the firm's current earnings. Similarly, a firm that reduces the amount of its securities outstanding (security repurchases) or that raises its dividends can be pointing to higher earnings. If the firm's investment opportunities are relatively fixed, the market can "learn" from a firm's need for external capital. Thus this theory suggests that the market regards any external financing (whether debt or equity) as a bad omen of the firm's earnings.[19]

CAPITAL STRUCTURE CHANGES AS SIGNALS OF MANAGERS' SUPERIOR INFORMATION

Managers can be expected to have better information about the firm's prospects than outsiders have. But this superior information cannot be easily transmitted to the marketplace, and so the markets' and managers' estimates of the market value of the securities can differ.[20] This wedge in estimated security prices is caused by **informational asymmetry,** which is a situation that managers can exploit. Whenever managers believe that their stock is undervalued by the market, they buy back the stock, and similarly, when the stock appears to be overvalued, they sell. Thus any sale of new equity may reveal that the equity is overpriced in the market, and the market reacts to announcements of new security offerings by lowering the stock price. Indeed, the empirical evidence is consistent with this view because new stock issues in the marketplace lead to negative excess returns.

Because it is a company's stock that is most affected by informational asymmetry, this theory predicts that the negative reactions to other security issues will not be so dramatic. It also follows that managers would rather use retained earnings as much as possible because relying on internal funds communicates nothing to the market about the managers' personal evaluation of the "correct" value of the securities offered in external financing. Capital structure changes thus can be viewed as managers' attempts to signal their firm's investment prospects.

QUESTIONS

1. How can a firm's debt level signal its investment opportunities?

2. The sale of an equity security can imply that managers believe that the equity is overpriced in the market. What is the basis for this statement?

---

[19] Merton Miller and Kevin Rock, "Dividend Policy Under Asymmetric Information," *Journal of Finance* 40 (1985): 1031–1051; and Kose John and Joseph Williams, "Dividends, Dilution and Taxes: A Signalling Equilibrium," *Journal of Finance* 40 (1985): 1053–1070.

[20] Stewart Myers and Nicholas Majluf, "Corporate Financing and Investment Decisions When Firms Have Information Investors Do Not Have," *Journal of Financial Economics* 13 (1984): 187–221.

15C

SHARE REPURCHASES AND EXCHANGE OFFERS

Appendix 15B concluded that capital structure changes may be attempts by management to signal the firm's prospects. In this appendix we examine two popular capital structure changes: share repurchases and exchange offers. At some time, many firms consider one of these financial restructuring transactions.

The two transactions are related. **Share repurchases** are cash offers made for outstanding shares. Although this might not affect a firm's debt, a share repurchase does reduce the amount of outstanding equity, thereby increasing the firm's debt–equity ratio. **Exchange offers,** on the other hand, give one or more classes of securities the right or option to exchange part or all of their holdings for a different class of the firm's securities.

Share Repurchases

A corporation may choose to conduct a share repurchase through **open-market purchases,** through a **tender offer,** or through **private negotiation.** In an open-market transaction, the firm buys back its stock directly from the stock markets. In a tender offer, the firm makes a public announcement to buy back the stock at a particular price. In a privately negotiated purchase, the firm buys the stock from one or more parties through a private transaction.

Purchases are most frequently made on the open market. In November 1989, for instance, General Electric Co. announced a five-year $10 billion stock buyback on the open market, the largest in 1989, in an attempt to boost its share price. The market viewed this as a favorable move, although some investors had expected a special dividend instead of a buyback. Once a firm announces that its directors have authorized the repurchase of a certain amount of its common stock, the firm is free to commence the repurchase, which may extend over several months or even years. Although disclosures of intent to repurchase are not required by law, not announcing this may violate the antimanipulation and antifraud provisions of the Securities and Exchange Act of 1934.

Some firms (e.g., PepsiCo) often repurchase shares, whereas others repurchase shares only occasionally. Table 15C-1 lists some of the largest repurchases announced in 1993.

Repurchases through tender offers are less common than open-market purchases, but tender offers usually offer to repurchase a larger percentage of the outstanding shares than open-market purchases do. The aim is not to transfer control from one entity to another but to consolidate the firm's outstanding capital structure.[21] Negotiated repurchases therefore are used more often, and their use in this market is growing.

In a cash tender offer, a firm decides on the amount of shares it plans to repurchase, the price at which the repurchase will be made, and the time during which the offer will be open. The tender offer price is generally higher than the market price at the time of the offer. If the number of shares offered for repurchase exceeds the limit set in the original repurchase agreement, the firm may choose to purchase

---

[21] Tender offers aimed at acquiring control of the corporation are discussed in Chapter 25.

TABLE 15C-1 *Largest Share Repurchases Announced in 1993*	*Company*	*Common Shares (millions)*	*Value (millions)*
	Pepsico	50	$1,900
	Archer Daniels Midland	20	462
	Sherwin-Williams	6	187
	Sunbeam-Oster	12.4	174
	Calgon Carbon	2	24
	Wachovia	2	68

all or a fraction of those shares above the limit, or on a pro rata basis if it purchases less than the limit. Usually a firm's officers and directors cannot tender their holdings in a repurchase.

The empirical evidence regarding cash tender offers to repurchase is more extensive than that regarding open-market purchases because the market for tender offer repurchases is larger and the time period is better defined. The two key issues here are the premium offered to shareholders over the present market price and, more important because this has implications for shareholder value, the abnormal return up to the period after the tender offer is closed.

The evidence indicates that most issues have a cumulative abnormal return of 13% from five days before the announcement to 60 days afterward.[22] Oversubscribed issues offered a 24% premium, compared with 20.5% for undersubscribed issues. The target fraction is 13% for oversubscribed issues, and it is more than 18% for those that were subsequently undersubscribed. Similar results were found in other studies, independent of the type of repurchase examined.[23]

Another issue pertains to the division of the wealth—that is, what portion goes to tendering shareholders and what portion goes to nontendering shareholders. Weston, Chung, and Hoag, using Vermaelen's data, found that tendering shareholders receive a much smaller share of the wealth effects than do nontendering shareholders, by a ratio of 1 to 2.5.[24]

Several hypotheses have been developed to account for what appears to be a permanent 13% to 15% increase in a firm's common stock market price after tender offers. The **bondholder expropriation hypothesis** suggests that a firm repurchases its shares in order to increase its value at the expense of its bondholders. Studies linking the movements in common stock prices to those in the price of the debt at the time of a repurchase have, however, shown a positive correlation between share prices and straight or convertible debt. This is inconsistent with the hypothesis because one would expect debt prices to fall if it was believed that the repurchase would hurt bondholders. The **wealth transfer hypothesis** maintains that wealth is transferred between those shareholders who offer to repurchase and those who choose not to do so. If wealth transfers were the motive behind repurchases, one would expect to see insiders tendering because presumably they would undertake the repurchase only if they felt that as shareholders they would gain more by selling their holdings. But this implication is inconsistent with the data because most of the wealth appears to go to nontendering shareholders, thereby indicating that wealth transfers do not motivate firms to initiate share repurchases.

This theory leads to yet another hypothesis, the **information** or **signaling hypothesis**, according to which the announcement of a repurchase is a signal to investors. A decision to buy back its shares may tell a firm's investors that management thinks the stock is undervalued, a view supported by Vermaelen's research. A firm that makes a repurchase later will report financial results above those that would have been expected using a time series, indicating that management is using the

[22] Theo Vermaelen, "Common Stock Repurchases and Market Signalling: An Empirical Study," *Journal of Financial Economics* 9 (1981): 139–183.

[23] Michael Bradley and Lee M. Wakeman, "The Wealth Effects of Targeted Share Repurchases," *Journal of Financial Economics* 11 (1983): 301–328; James Brickley, "Shareholder Wealth, Information Signalling, and the Specially Designated Dividend: An Empirical Study," *Journal of Financial Economics* 12 (1983): 103–114; and Ronald W. Masulis, "Stock Repurchase by Tender Offer: An Analysis of the Causes of Common Stock Price Changes," *Journal of Finance* 35 (1983): 305–319.

[24] J. Fred Weston, Kwang S. Chung, and Susan E. Hoag, "Share Repurchase and Exchanges," in *Mergers, Restructuring and Corporate Control*, pp. 440–456 (Englewood Cliffs, NJ: Prentice-Hall, 1990).

repurchase to demonstrate its belief in the firm's better performance in the future. The signaling hypothesis is also consistent with the empirical data because the new information released is valuable, which results in a permanent rise of 13% to 15% in the stock price.

According to the **dividend hypothesis,** share repurchases are substitutes for dividends. When some shares are bought back, the price of the remaining shares increases and the owners have effectively been paid a dividend. Although a share repurchase is associated with transactions costs, these costs are lower than they would be if the firm issued a dividend. The evidence, however, is not very clear. If this is a reason for the gains seen in repurchases, it is still not possible to explain a permanent gain of 13% to 15% using this hypothesis.

Another possible explanation for the gains is the **leverage hypothesis.** When a firm makes a repurchase, its debt–equity ratio increases, owing to the lower equity level and, often, additional debt, on which the interest is tax deductible. If the added tax-deductible interest can be seen as a subsidy and if this is passed on to the shareholders, this theory suggests that the stock price should rise to reflect the potentially higher earnings. Although Masulis claims to show support for this hypothesis, Vermaelen argues that the idea, although it might play a role, is not as important as the information explanation.

The **takeover defense hypothesis** states that repurchases set up a defense against takeovers. The argument is that if a firm offers to repurchase shares at a premium of, say, 23%, it is thereby establishing a minimum level for any future takeover because this indicates that the firm's management believes that any such move must carry at least a 23% premium. This, in turn, conveys information to outsiders regarding the firm's value, which causes a permanent jump in share prices.

Although these explanations all have some appeal, the strongest support for the wealth effect seen in share repurchases comes from the information hypothesis, followed by the takeover defense, leverage, and dividend explanations.

Exchange Offers

Exchange offers, like share repurchases, give securityholders the option to exchange part or all of their holdings in return for some consideration. But then they part ways. Whereas share repurchases pertain to only common stock, exchange offers can be initiated for any of the firm's securities. Furthermore, whereas share repurchases pay the securityholders in cash, exchange offers exchange one class of securities for another. In 1988, for example, Savin Corporation attempted to avoid bankruptcy by exchanging its debt for convertible preferred stock because its existing debt was becoming increasingly difficult to service.

The empirical evidence concerning exchange offers is mixed. Table 15C-2 summarizes the results of several studies of exchange offers. As can be seen, the market

■

TABLE 15C-2

Types of Exchange Offers and the Returns Associated with Each

Exchange offers associated with positive returns	
Debt for common stock[c]	+14.0%
Preferred for common stock[a,c]	+8.2
Debt for preferred stock[a]	+2.2
Exchange offers associated with negative returns	
Common stock for debt[a]	−9.9%
Preferred stock for debt[a]	−7.7
Common stock for preferred[a,b]	−2.6
Conversion of debt through call provisions[c]	−2.1

[a] Ronald W. Masulis, "The Impact of Capital Structure Change on Firm Value: Some Estimates," *Journal of Finance,* March 1983, pp. 107–126.
[b] J. Michael Pinegar and Ronald C. Lease, "The Impact of Preferred-for-Common Exchange Offers on Firm Value," *Journal of Finance,* September 1986, pp. 795–814.
[c] W. H. Mikkelson, "Convertible Security Calls and Security Returns," *Journal of Financial Economics* 9 (1981): 237–264.

regards exchanges that move away from debt as adding value, and it sees any move to convert a security to another that is closer to straight debt than the original issue as being negative. For example, although Masulis found positive abnormal returns for exchanges of debt for preferred and preferred for common stock, he found negative abnormal returns for exchanges of common stock for preferred or preferred for debt.

Various explanations for these results have been advanced. One is that exchange offers that generally increase leverage, that indicate higher cash flows in the future, and that reflect an undervalued stock tend to have positive returns. Of the four transaction types with positive returns, two are seen as increasing management's share ownership, and in three of the four, management's control over the use of cash is reduced. These factors seem to imply that the higher leverage is perceived as motivating management, as are the reduced agency costs that arise out of the last two factors. On the other hand, when an exchange offer is announced, the implied increase in cash flows and the undervalued stock cause the stock price to rise for accounting reasons. The transactions that were regarded as having negative abnormal returns are also seen as having opposite explanations: They increase agency costs, reduce future profits, and do not motivate management further.

Share repurchases and exchange offers have similar motivations and similar effects on shareholder wealth. Whereas the most tenable explanation of the permanent increase of 13% to 15% seen in firms' stock prices after a tender offer is announced is that the announcement releases valuable information, exchange offers do not always enhance the securityholders' wealth. This conclusion is in addition to the dividend, leverage, and takeover defense hypotheses, all of which appear, in different cases, to explain some of the gains. Exchange offers appear to generate positive abnormal returns if they are perceived as reducing agency costs (implying higher future cash flows), indicating undervalued stock, or increasing the firm's leverage.

QUESTIONS

1. What is (are) the difference(s) between share repurchases and exchange offers?

2. What are some explanations for the observed increases in stock prices following repurchases?

SUGGESTED ADDITIONAL READINGS

Auerbach, A. "Real Determinants of Corporate Leverage." In *Corporate Capital Structures in the United States*, edited by B. Friedman, pp. 301–322. Chicago: University of Chicago Press, 1985.

Brennan, M. J. "Corporate Income Taxes, Valuation, and the Problem of Optimal Capital Structure." *Journal of Business*, January 1978, pp. 103–114.

DeAngelo, H., and R. Masulis. "Optimal Capital Structure Under Corporate and Personal Taxation." *Journal of Financial Economics*, March 1980, pp. 3–30.

Hamada, R. S., and M. Scholes. "Taxes and Corporate Financial Management." In *Recent Advances in Corporate Finance*, edited by M. G. Subramanyam and E. J. Altman, pp. 187–276. Homewood, IL: Irwin, 1985.

Harris, John M., Jr., Rodney L. Roenfeldt, and Philip L. Cooley. "Evidence of Financial Leverage Clienteles." *Journal of Finance*, September 1983, pp. 1125–1132.

Haugen, R. A., and L. W. Senbet. "Corporate Finance and Taxes: A Review." *Financial Management,* Autumn 1986, pp. 5–21.

Kim, H. "A Mean-Variance Theory of Optimal Capital Structure and Corporate Debt Capacity." *Journal of Finance,* March 1978, pp. 45–64.

Long, M. S., and E. B. Malitz. "Investment Patterns and Financial Leverage." In *Corporate Capital Structures in the United States,* edited by B. Friedman, pp. 325–348. Chicago: University of Chicago Press, 1985.

Masulis, R. W. *The Debt/Equity Choice,* Institutional Investor Series in Finance. Cambridge, MA: Ballinger, 1988.

Miller, Merton H. "Debt and Taxes." *Journal of Finance,* May 1977, pp. 261–275.

Modigliani, Franco, and Merton H. Miller. "The Cost of Capital, Corporation Finance and the Theory of Investment." *American Economic Review,* June 1958, pp. 261–297.

Modigliani, Franco, and Merton H. Miller. "The Cost of Capital, Corporation Finance and the Theory of Investment: Reply." *American Economic Review,* September 1958, pp. 655–669.

Modigliani, Franco, and Merton H. Miller. "Taxes and the Cost of Capital: A Correction." *American Economic Review,* June 1963, pp. 433–443.

Modigliani, Franco, and Merton H. Miller. "Reply." *American Economic Review,* June 1965, pp. 524–527.

Myers, S. C. "Determinants of Corporate Borrowing." *Journal of Financial Economics,* November 1977, pp. 147–176.

Myers, S. C. "The Capital Structure Puzzle." *Journal of Finance,* March 1984, pp. 575–592.

Rubinstein, M. E. "A Mean-Variance Synthesis of Corporate Financial Theory." *Journal of Finance,* March 1973, pp. 167–181.

Titman, S. "The Effects of Capital Structure on a Firm's Liquidation Decision." *Journal of Financial Economics* 13 (1984): 137–151.

Titman, S., and R. Wessels. "The Determinants of Capital Structure Choice." *Journal of Finance,* March 1988, pp. 1–20.

Warner, Jerold B. "Bankruptcy Costs: Some Evidence." *Journal of Finance,* May 1977, pp. 337–348.

SIXTEEN RESOLVING FINANCIAL DISTRESS

---

*Everybody in Vanity Fair
must have remarked
how well those who live
in debt are comfortable
and thoroughly in debt;
how they deny
themselves nothing;
how full and easy they
are in their minds.*

*—W. M. Thackery,
Vanity Fair, 1874,
chap. 22*

The concept of financial distress is as old as business itself. The word *bankruptcy* comes from the French words *banque* ("bench") and *ruptus* ("break"). The word picked up its meaning in the 16th century, when anyone who was no longer able to satisfy his creditors was seized and the workbench where he did business broken before his eyes. The unfortunate was then taken to debtors prison.

Although the concept of financial distress is an old one, it is still widely misunderstood. To some it means the death of the firm, whereas to others it means that the firm is experiencing temporary hardships. Under either definition, it connotes some type of unsatisfactory performance. The terms *failure, insolvency, default, liquidation,* and *bankruptcy* are widely used to describe an unsuccessful business enterprise, and it is important that these terms be distinguished.

This chapter examines the economic issues and the private and legal avenues for resolving financial distress. It is organized into five sections to answer the following questions:

- What is financial distress and how is it different from bankruptcy and insolvency?

- What are the different types of bankruptcies?

- When does a firm resort to private financial distress-resolution procedures and when is it likely to pursue legal avenues?

- What is the difference between Chapter 7 liquidation and a Chapter 11 bankruptcy?

- When does a firm liquidate and when does it reorganize?

- What are some similarities and differences between Chapter 7 and Chapter 11 bankruptcy procedures?

- What is the absolute priority rule?

- What are some implications of courts' deviations from the absolute priority rule?

- What does it mean to say that firms can use bankruptcy "as a strategic device"?

16.1 THE TERMINOLOGY OF FINANCIAL DISTRESS AND BANKRUPTCY

Basic Terminology

A business is said to be experiencing **failure** when the realized rate of return on that business is consistently less than investors' opportunity costs. That is, the return provided by the firm is not adequate to offset the risk of the firm.[1] Note that this definition says nothing about whether the firm can continue operations or will cease to exist. Corporate **financial distress,** however, threatens the viability of the firm. The firm's alternatives for resolving financial distress have become major issues in recent years.

[1] Dun & Bradstreet, a firm that specializes in providing business statistics, uses the term *business failure* to denote "unsatisfactory business conditions."

FIGURE 16-1
*Different avenues for
resolving financial
distress*

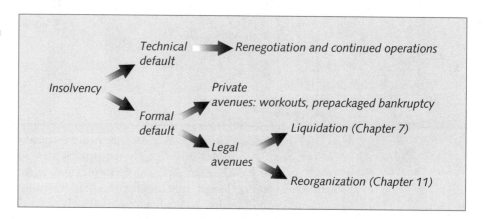

FIGURE 16-1
*Different avenues for
resolving financial
distress*

A firm is said to be experiencing financial distress if it faces **insolvency.** Insolvency implies that the firm is in default, and there are two variants. A financially distressed firm may be in **technical default** or in a more serious situation of **formal default.** Technical default arises when the firm violates a legally binding agreement with a creditor. For example, there is a technical default if the restrictive covenants on the debt require a current ratio of 2.3 and the firm's current ratio is 2.0. Typically, the firm renegotiates with the creditors and operations continue. It continues to operate as it works with the creditors to solve the problem.

*An Overview of
Financial Distress
Resolution Procedures*

The more serious formal default arises when the firm is unable to meet its interest obligations to the creditors. The firm is usually given about a month to remedy this situation. As Figure 16-1 illustrates, the firm may pursue either private or public (legal) alternatives to resolving distress. A private negotiation with the creditors is called a **workout.** In a workout, the firm that has already violated or is about to violate its debt covenants renegotiates with its creditors to have these covenants relaxed. These informal, out-of-court negotiations between the firm's representatives, lawyers, investment bankers, and other lenders may be less expensive than going to the courts. In a workout, creditors agree to effectively exchange their existing claims for new ones. The term **bankruptcy** generally refers to a situation where the firm pursues the legal avenue to resolve its problems. If the workout fails, the firm can work with just a few of the creditors and file for a **prepackaged bankruptcy,** in which the bankruptcy petition and the reorganization plan are filed together. If the firm is unable to get the cooperation of all or even some of its creditors, it follows the formal (legal) route of a **bankruptcy filing** in the Federal District Court. Here, there are two potential outcomes: **liquidation** (under **Chapter 7** of the bankruptcy code) and **reorganization** (under **Chapter 11** of the code). Figure 16-1 shows these different procedures for resolving financial distress.

Bankruptcies have proliferated rapidly in recent years. During the period 1989–1992, 34 firms with liabilities greater than $1 billion filed for protection under Chapter 11 of the Bankruptcy Code. In 1992, corporate bankruptcies totaled 70,643.[2] Both large and small firms have filed for bankruptcy. Table 16-1 lists some of the major recent bankruptcies. It has been suggested that managerial incompetence is the overwhelming cause of firm failure.[3] Altman points out that in a 1991 survey of over 1,300 turnaround managers conducted by Buccino & Asso-

[2] Kenneth Bacon, "Losses in Bankruptcies Spur Lenders to Strive to Protect Themselves," *The Wall Street Journal,* June 17, 1993.

[3] E. I. Altman, *Corporate Financial Distress and Bankruptcy,* 2nd ed. (New York: John Wiley & Sons, 1993).

■
TABLE 16-1
Largest U.S. Bankruptcies,[a]
September 30, 1992

Company	Liabilities (millions)	Bankruptcy Date
Texaco (incl. subsidiaries)	$21,603	April 1987
Olympia & York[b,c]	19,800	May 1992
Executive Life Insurance	14,577	April 1991
Mutual Benefit Life	13,500	July 1991
Campeau (Allied & Federated)	9,947	January 1990
First Capital Holdings	9,291	May 1991
Baldwin United	9,000	September 1983
Continental Airlines (11)	6,200	December 1990
Lomas Financial	6,127	September 1989
Macy's[c]	5,300	January 1992
Columbia Gas	4,998	July 1991
LTV (incl. LTV Int'l NV)	4,700	July 1986
Maxwell Communication	4,100	December 1991
TWA	3,470	January 1992
Southland	3,380	October 1990
Penn Central Transportation	3,300	June 1970
Eastern Airlines	3,196	March 1989
Drexel Burnham Lambert	3,000	February 1990
Pan Am World Airlines	3,000	January 1991
Westpoint Acquisition	2,300	June 1992
Interco	2,213	May 1990
Laventhol & Horvath	2,000	November 1990
Wickes	2,000	April 1982
Cardinal Industries	1,800	August 1992
Global Marine	1,800	January 1986
ITEL	1,700	January 1981
Public Service, New Hampshire	1,700	January 1988
Continental Information Systems	1,669	January 1989
Integrated Resources	1,600	February 1990
REVCO	1,500	July 1988
Placid Oil[c]	1,488	April 1985
Ames Department Stores	1,440	April 1990
Southmark	1,395	July 1989
Carter Hawley Hale Stores	1,385	February 1991
Best Products	1,367	January 1991
National Gypsum (AANCOR)	1,345	October 1990

SOURCE: Edward I. Altman, *Corporate Financial Distress and Bankruptcy,* 2nd ed. (New York: John Wiley & Sons, 1993).
[a]Does not include commercial banking entities.
[b]Bankruptcy filing in United States and Canada; not all liabilities in bankruptcy.
[c]Privately held firm.

ciates of Chicago, 88% of the respondents cited quality of management as the difference between success and failure.

Because of the increase in the number of bankruptcies in recent years, much has been written about predicting bankruptcy. A study by Gilson reveals some of the characteristics of financially distressed firms.[4] They are typically large, highly levered, less profitable, less likely to pay a dividend, more likely to have negative accounting earnings, and more likely to have reduced dividends in response to binding debt covenants than most firms. Can this information be used to actually predict bankruptcy?

Altman developed the original financial distress prediction model in 1968 and has over time refined his model.[5] His model uses information on the firm's balance sheet and income statement and the stock price (for a publicly traded firm) to calculate a "Z-score" that can be used to assess the probability of bankruptcy.[6] Some authors have argued, however, that it is not possible to predict bankruptcy on the

[4]S. C. Gilson, "Management Turnover and Financial Distress," *Journal of Financial Economics* 25 (1989).
[5]E. Altman, "Financial Ratios, Discriminant Analysis and Corporate Bankruptcy," *Journal of Finance,* September 1968.
[6]For details on the Z-score model and a comprehensive bibliography of failure classification models in the United States, the reader is referred to E. Altman, *Corporate Financial Distress and Bankruptcy,* 2nd ed. (New York: John Wiley & Sons, 1993).

basis of financial ratios because the decision to file is based as much on strategic considerations as on financial ratios and on several other factors such as managerial incentives and voluntary and involuntary restructuring.[7] Financial ratios are likely to be one but certainly not the only determinant of the firm's bankruptcy decision, as this chapter illustrates.

<table>
<tr><td>

16.2

PRIVATE OR LEGAL RESOLUTION OF FINANCIAL DISTRESS?

</td><td>

Whether the firm will follow private avenues or take the legal route depends on at least four factors: cost and holdout considerations and legal and tax impediments.

</td></tr>
</table>

Cost Considerations

The first question in choosing an avenue to resolve financial distress is which avenue leaves the firm's claimants better off? This depends on the costs associated with the private and legal routes. It is generally recognized that the private route is cheaper. By settling privately, the firm can avoid the usually high costs associated with filing in the courts, paying lawyers and accountants, and so on. Moreover, private renegotiation can be faster than bankruptcy litigation because formal legal documents must be filed and argued before the judge throughout the bankruptcy process.

There are two advantages to the legal route, however. In Chapter 11 bankruptcy, the court imposes a clear queuing order on creditors so that considerable confusion is avoided and new lenders to the firm have **superpriority status;** that is, their debt is made senior to that of the existing creditors. This can infuse new funds into the distressed firm, and this financing, known as **debtor in possession (DIP) financing** (explained shortly), can help the firm increase value by permitting new investments.

Holdout Considerations

A second determining factor is whether or not the creditors and equityholders can agree on how to share the cost savings from pursuing the private route.[8] Sometimes individual claimants refuse to cooperate because they may expect more from a court-ordered restructuring plan. This is the **"holdout problem."** In this case, either a prepackaged (with a few creditors agreeing) or regular bankruptcy ensues.

If a firm has to restructure debt outside Chapter 11, all creditors must unanimously agree to the new terms. The more creditors are associated with a restructuring plan, the more severe the holdout problem is likely to be. The complexity of the restructuring is another factor to consider. If the firm's debt claims involve creditors with different security (collateral), seniority rights, and so on, it is harder to get a consensus than if the debt claims are homogeneous. The type of debt (bank loans or publicly traded debt) can make a difference. Under the Trust Indenture Act of 1939, firms are severely restricted from changing certain terms of a debt issue unless every creditor's consent is obtained. Thus publicly traded debt is typically restructured via an **exchange offer** whereby the firm does not alter the terms of the debt. Instead, creditors voluntarily tender their bonds to the firm and receive a new package of securities (new bonds and often some equity). To reduce the holdout problem, these new bonds have greater seniority and earlier maturity dates

---

[7]G. L. Menon and K. Schwartz, "Predicting Bankruptcy for Firms in Financial Distress," *Journal of Business Finance and Accounting,* Spring 1990.

[8]S. C. Gilson, K. John, and L. H. P. Lang, "Troubled Debt Restructurings," *Journal of Financial Economics* 26 (1990).

than the old bonds. It is often suggested that if the firm's debt is primarily trade credit, then the holdout problem is severe because there are usually numerous trade creditors and they are "more difficult to deal with." The extent to which there is informational asymmetry between creditors and stockholders can affect the holdout problem. Creditors know that the firm's owners are likely to distort the firm's future prospects to make it more rosy, and this can reduce their incentives to negotiate privately.

Gilson, John, and Lang studied a sample of 169 financially distressed firms and found that about half successfully restructure their debts outside Chapter 11. Their analysis of the stock prices of these firms suggests that stockholders are better off when the firm is restructured privately.

Legal Impediments

There are legal obstacles to private restructuring. The **"LTV ruling"** makes it difficult to have an out-of-court settlement. In the LTV bankruptcy case, some bondholders participated in a private exchange offer. The judge ruled that the bondholders who agreed to the exchange offer *before* the Chapter 11 filing were not entitled to a claim equal to the face value of their new bonds; instead, he limited their claims to the market value of the new bonds. Since this decision, only one major private workout has been successful and it was structured to overcome this potential adverse ruling.[9]

The laws of **fraudulent conveyance** can hinder private restructuring of debt. Consider a leveraged buyout (LBO). A firm borrows money and buys back its stock. Subsequently, the firm's cash flows are insufficient to service the debt. The firm fails in its efforts to get the debt restructured and files for bankruptcy. The courts can rule this a fraudulent conveyance of assets on the grounds that in paying stockholders the cash, the firm transferred assets out of the firm before the creditors were paid off. In effect, the firm has defrauded the creditors by doing an LBO and then filing for bankruptcy. The fact that the firm may not have known that it would be bankrupt is not crucial; even though this may not be *intentional fraud,* there is *constructive fraud.* Under fraudulent conveyance laws, the courts can go back and undo the LBO by ordering all shareholders who sold the stock to return the proceeds to the bankruptcy estate. Similarly, the LBO lenders' claims can be subordinated, and even fees paid to professionals who arranged the LBO can be recovered.

If the law allows for a recovery of cash from shareholders, advisors, and financiers in a private restructuring of debt, it is more and more difficult to get the parties to agree to a private restructuring.[10] The incentives to formally file for bankruptcy increase. Thus, even when economic considerations provide incentives to stay out of court, legal practices can force the claimants into court.

Tax Impediments

Tax considerations may favor the filing of Chapter 11 bankruptcy over a private restructuring.[11] The reason for this is that under the extant tax code, the act of restructuring gives rise to a positive corporate income tax liability. If, for example, a firm's creditors agree to a writedown of $50 million in debt to $20 million, the tax code views that firm as having earned $30 million, which becomes taxable.

[9] See "U.S. Bankruptcy Judge Rules in Favor of LTV," Reuters Newswire, January 30, 1990. (As this book goes to press, it appears that the courts have overturned the LTV ruling; details, however, are unclear.)

[10] Also see A. Michel and I. Shaked, "The LBO Nightmare: Fraudulent Conveyance Risk," *Financial Analysts Journal* 46 (March–April 1990): 41–50.

[11] Merton H. Miller, "Tax Obstacles to Voluntary Corporate Restructuring," *Journal of Applied Corporate Finance* 4, no. 3 (1991): 20–23.

Thus the tax treatment of the cancellation of debt (COD) associated with restructuring creates disincentives for private restructuring. On the other hand, if the firm files for Chapter 11 bankruptcy, all COD income associated with the reorganization can be exempt from taxable gross income.

16.3

THE ECONOMICS OF LIQUIDATION VERSUS REORGANIZATION

In a Chapter 7 liquidation, the firm's assets are sold off piecemeal and the proceeds distributed to the creditors; the firm ceases to exist. In a Chapter 11 reorganization, the firm is restructured with new debt provisions and it operates with the expectation of being able to honor this restructured debt. In addition to this legal distinction between liquidation and bankruptcy, it is important to understand the economics of liquidation and bankruptcy.[12]

A firm is **distressed on a flow basis** when it does not have enough cash to honor its obligations. It is **distressed on a stock basis** when it has no positive *NPVs*. A firm that is distressed on a flow basis can, if it is *not* distressed on a stock basis, raise new capital to meet its obligations; its *NPVs* will "support" the raising of new capital.

The basic idea underlying the liquidate/reorganize decision is this: If a firm is "worth more dead than alive," it should be liquidated. However, if its **going-concern value,** the value of the firm after a reorganization, exceeds the liquidation value, it should be reorganized. A firm is liquidated when it is distressed on both flow and stock criteria; a firm is reorganized when it is distressed on a flow basis only. After the reorganization, the firm can be solvent on a stock basis; that is, the assets will exceed the liabilities and the firm will have a nonzero equity value.

KEY CONCEPT

If the firm's going-concern value exceeds its liquidation value, then the company will be reorganized; otherwise, it will be liquidated.

Freemont Tires and ITI: Should They Be Liquidated or Reorganized?

Consider two companies that are currently in financial distress, Freemont Tires and International Technologies Inc. (ITI). Because of poor sales, neither has been able to honor its debt obligations. Both have $1,000 in debt obligations (principal and interest) due today, but they do not have sufficient cash flows to honor their obligations. The relevant question is this: should these firms be liquidated or reorganized? To understand the different outcomes of this financial distress situation, assume that all investors are risk neutral and all assets are valued at a discount rate of 10%.

Both firms are identical in all respects save one—their future cash flow potential. Freemont's cash flows next period are either $1,300 or $400, each outcome with a probability of 0.5. On the other hand, ITI's cash flows next period are either $1,998 or $400, each with probability 0.5. This is represented pictorially in Figure 16-2.[13]

BONDHOLDERS' OPTIONS IN FINANCIAL DISTRESS

Let us analyze the question from the bondholders' perspective. Bondholders have three options in this situation. We analyze each separately for both firms.

---

[12] An early analysis of this issue was provided by Merton H. Miller in "The Wealth Transfers of Bankruptcy: Some Illustrative Examples," *Law and Contemporary Problems* 41 (1977).

[13] Cash flows in the example include the liquidation value of the assets.

FIGURE 16-2
Freemont Tires and ITI

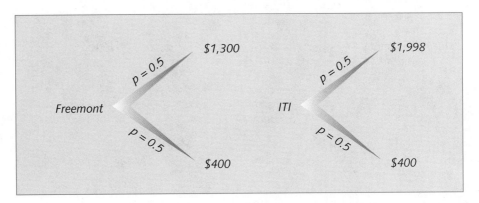

FIGURE 16-2
Freemont Tires and ITI

OPTION 1 (LIQUIDATE THROUGH CHAPTER 7) Since the firm is in default, the bondholders can take over the firm and become the owners. They can then liquidate the firm if they choose to do so. Assume that both firms' liquidation value today is $900. Thus bondholders' cash flows today under the liquidation option are $900. Under this option, the value of both Freemont and ITI is $900.

OPTION 2 (TAKE OVER AND RUN THE FIRM) Instead of liquidating the firm, bondholders may take over and run the firm themselves. Since they are then the owners, they are entitled to all of the future cash flows. To avoid confusion, we continue to call them bondholders (although they are technically the owners of the firm). This action produces the following results (see Figure 16-3).

For Freemont:

- Expected cash flows to Freemont's bondholders = $1,300 × 0.5 + $400 × 0.5 = $850

- Value of Freemont's debt = $850 × $PVF_{10\%,1}$ = $850 × 0.9091 = $773

For ITI:

- Expected cash flows to ITI's bondholders = 0.5 × $1,998 + 0.5 × $400 = $1,199

- Value of ITI's debt = $1,199 × $PVF_{10\%,1}$ = $1,199 × 0.9091 = $1,090

Thus, under this option, Freemont and ITI are worth $773 and $1,090, respectively.

FIGURE 16-3
Freemont Tires and ITI: Bondholders take over and run the firm

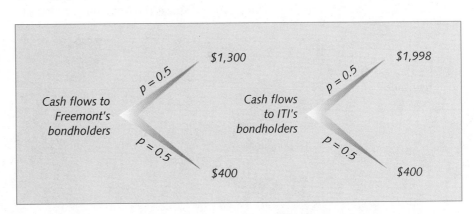

FIGURE 16-4

Freemont: Chapter 11 reorganization

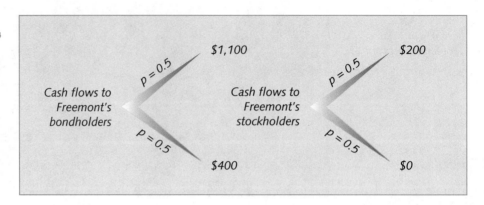

OPTION 3 (REORGANIZE THROUGH CHAPTER 11) If the bondholders agree to wait an extra period to get their obligations honored, then each firm must promise to pay the bondholders $1,100 next period—the $1,000 due today plus the interest for the next period. The debt is thus restructured and the existing management runs the company.

When Freemont's cash flows are $1,300, bondholders can be fully paid off. They get $1,100 and the stockholders get the remaining $200. When Freemont's cash flows are $400, the bondholders' claims cannot be satisfied; they claim all of the firm's cash flows and the stockholders get nothing. This is summarized in Figure 16-4. The action produces the following results for Freemont.

For Freemont debt:

- Expected cash flows to Freemont's bondholders = $1,100 × 0.5 + $400 × 0.5 = $750

- Value of Freemont's debt today = $750 × $PVF_{10\%,1}$ = $750 × 0.9091 = $682

For Freemont equity:

- Expected cash flows to Freemont's equityholders = $200 × 0.5 = $100

- Value of Freemont's equity today = $100 × $PVF_{10\%,1}$ = $100 × 0.9091 = $91

The value of Freemont as a reorganized company is $682 + $91 = $773.

When ITI's cash flows are $1,998, the bondholders are fully paid at $1,100 and the stockholders receive $898. When ITI's cash flows are $400, all of it goes to the bondholders. The relevant cash flows to debt and equity are shown in Figure 16-5. This action produces the following results.

FIGURE 16-5

ITI: Chapter 11 reorganization

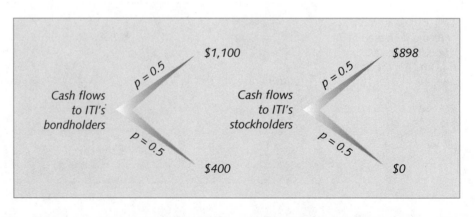

TABLE 16-2

Values for Stockholders and Bondholders of Freemont and ITI

	Freemont			ITI		
Option	Debt	Equity	Firm	Debt	Equity	Firm
1. Liquidate firm	$900	$0	$900	$900	$0	$ 900
2. Take over and run firm	773	0	773	1,090	0	1,090
3. Reorganize	682	91	773	682	408	1,090

For ITI debt:

- Expected cash flows to ITI's bondholders = $1,100 \times 0.5 + $400 \times 0.5 = $750

- Value of ITI's debt = $750 \times PVF_{10\%,1} = $750 \times 0.9091 = $682

For ITI equity:

- Expected cash flows to ITI's equityholders = $898 \times 0.5 = $449

- Value of ITI's equity = $449 \times PVF_{10\%,1} = $449 \times 0.9091 = $408

Thus the value of ITI is $682 + 408 = $1,090

SUMMARY OF OPTIONS

The values of the debt, the equity, and the firm under the three outcomes are listed in Table 16-2.

Conclusions

We can draw some conclusions from Table 16-2. Freemont's highest value ($900) is under the liquidation option. Thus Freemont is worth more dead than alive, and bondholders are best off by liquidating the firm under Chapter 7. Bondholders should push for liquidation. However, stockholders will resist because liquidation provides them with nothing. If they try to reorganize through the courts, they can increase the value of their equity to $91. Thus there is an incentive misalignment between the stockholders and the bondholders.

Liquidation does not make sense for ITI because its highest value ($1,090) arises from the other two options. However, bondholders will want to take over the firm because the debt is worth $1,090 under this option. Under reorganization they get only $682. Shareholders will want to reorganize because then their wealth goes up to $408.

In both situations, stockholders and bondholders have conflicting interests. Can they privately negotiate to avoid the costs of going to court?

Freemont's bondholders could agree to make a side payment of $91 to the stockholders to stay out of court. If bondholders liquidate the firm and make this side payment, they would then have $900 − $91 = $809, which exceeds the value of the debt under reorganization ($682). Thus both bondholders and stockholders benefit from a private negotiation.

The same solution does not work in the case of ITI. It is optimal for ITI's bondholders to take over the firm and run it (they get $1,090). However, stockholders would oppose this (they get nothing) and take the matter to court. They would accept no side payment from bondholders that is less than $408 to settle privately. But bondholders could not afford to give them $408 because this private arrangement would reduce their wealth to $682 ($1,090 − $408)—exactly what they would get if they went to court. Creditors thus have little incentive to make this side payment. Private resolution is unlikely and a bankruptcy filing appears inevitable.

These examples also illustrate the importance of capital structure decisions. For example, many of the agency problems could have been ameliorated by making the debt convertible or by having call features on the debt.

	Chapter 7	Chapter 11	Total
Business filings	37,047	18,333	55,380
Nonbusiness filings[a]	619,578	3,118	622,696
Total	656,625	21,451	678,076

■

TABLE 16-3
Bankruptcy Filings Under Chapters 7 and 11, for the First Quarter of 1993

SOURCE: Administrative Office of the U.S. Courts, Table F-2 (business and nonbusiness bankruptcy cases commenced, by chapter of the bankruptcy code), March 31, 1993.
[a]Nonbusiness filings include individuals filing bankruptcies for their proprietorships.

16.4

CHAPTER 7 AND CHAPTER 11 BANKRUPTCY PROCEDURES

The original Bankruptcy Act enacted in 1898 was amended in 1938 by the Chandler Act. The bankruptcy laws were overhauled with the passage of the Bankruptcy Reform Act of 1978. This act was amended in 1984 to clear up many of the deficiencies created by the overhaul in 1978, and it was amended again in 1986. The new Bankruptcy Code contains nine chapters (1, 3, 5, 7, 9, 11, 12, 13, and 15). In this book we are concerned with only Chapters 7 (liquidation) and 11 (reorganization). Table 16-3 summarizes information on the numbers of business and nonbusiness bankruptcy filings for the first quarter of 1993 (as of March 31).

Figure 16-6 summarizes the fundamental differences between Chapters 7 and 11. It may be useful for the reader to refer to this figure while reading the subsequent discussion. Note that the first three steps in Figure 16-6 are common to both types of bankruptcy.

Chapter 7 Bankruptcy

Chapter 7 bankruptcy, often referred to as "straight" or ordinary bankruptcy, provides for the liquidation of the firm's assets for cash, which is then distributed equitably among creditors. Chapter 7 bankruptcy begins with the filing of a petition. If the debtor files the petition, it is a "voluntary" bankruptcy, whereas if creditors file the petition, it is an "involuntary" bankruptcy.

■

FIGURE 16-6
Bankruptcy Procedures in Chapters 7 and 11

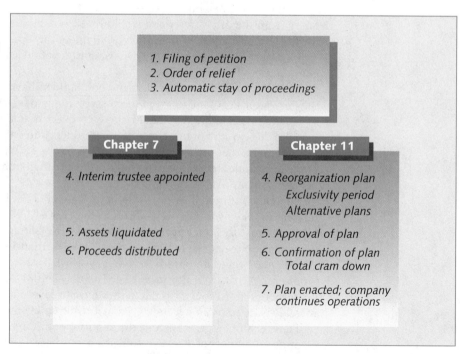

1. Filing of petition
2. Order of relief
3. Automatic stay of proceedings

Chapter 7

4. Interim trustee appointed

5. Assets liquidated
6. Proceeds distributed

Chapter 11

4. Reorganization plan
   Exclusivity period
   Alternative plans

5. Approval of plan
6. Confirmation of plan
   Total cram down

7. Plan enacted; company continues operations

For a voluntary filing, an **order for relief** is entered if the petition is found to be proper. If it is an involuntary petition and the debtor challenges it, a hearing is held. If the court grants an order for relief, there is an **automatic stay.** An order for relief is granted if the court finds either of the following: (1) the debtor is generally not paying debts as they become due or (2) a general receiver, assignee, or custodian took possession of or was appointed to take charge of substantially all of the debtor's property within 120 days before the filing of the petition. An automatic stay suspends virtually all litigation and other actions by creditors against the debtor. Creditors cannot commence or continue most legal actions such as foreclosure on liens or repossession of property.

An order for relief triggers the bankruptcy process, and an interim **trustee** is appointed until the first meeting of creditors. For example, when Eastern Airlines filed for bankruptcy in 1989, the U.S. bankruptcy judge named airline industry veteran Martin Shugrue to serve as trustee. Although Texas Air continued to own Eastern, its CEO, Frank Lorenzo, had little say in the bankruptcy proceedings. At the first meeting of creditors, either a permanent trustee is elected or the interim trustee becomes the permanent trustee. The trustee's main duty is presiding over the debtor's property, determining the bankruptcy estate, liquidating this estate, and distributing the proceeds to the appropriate creditors. The bankruptcy estate includes all legal and equitable interests of the debtor and all tax benefits to which the debtor is entitled—for example, tax loss carryforwards, claims for a tax refund, and investment credit carryovers. After the administration of the estate, the trustee is discharged and the case is closed.

Chapter 11 Bankruptcy

Chapter 11 bankruptcy is available to individuals, partnerships, and corporations. It is the most common type of bankruptcy proceeding used by corporations. Chapter 11's aim, according to the bankruptcy code, is to rehabilitate a business so that it "may continue to operate, provide its employees with jobs, pay its creditors, and produce a return for its stockholders." As in liquidation, when a Chapter 11 petition is filed, all creditor actions against the debtor are stayed. This stay allows the debtor and creditors to come together for discussion, explanation of the firm's financial problems, and negotiation. The stay also prevents creditors from acting unilaterally to gain an advantage over other creditors or to pressure the debtor into action.

An initial question is who should operate the firm? Unless it can be shown that there is gross mismanagement or criminal fraud, the debtor continues to operate the business. The **debtor in possession** (DIP) has the duty to preserve the assets, continue operations, and pursue the rehabilitation of the business. The DIP is expected to operate the business without depleting the firm's assets through waste or loss.

Typically, the debtor formulates the **plan of reorganization,** which includes the debtor's commitment to pay creditors and the proposed modification of the firm's operations. The plan must be fair and equitable and must conserve and administer the debtor's assets in the hope of an eventual return to successful operation and solvency. The debtor has an **exclusivity period;** only the debtor may file a plan within the first 120 days after the date of the order for relief. If the debtor does not submit a plan or fails to obtain the required creditor consent within 180 days, any party may propose a plan. The plan must do three things. First, it must designate classes of claims and interests. Second, it must specify the treatment to be afforded the classes. (The plan must provide the same treatment for each claim in a particular class.) Finally, the plan must provide an adequate means for execution.

Once the plan has been formulated, it is submitted to each class of creditors for acceptance.

The bankruptcy judge can extend the 120-day exclusivity period, and it is common for companies to delay plan submissions. For example, the judge in the LTV bankruptcy extended the exclusivity period to five years.

The classes of creditors and securityholders are represented by committees designed to negotiate and consult with the trustee or DIP. These committees investigate the financial standing of the debtor, the desirability of continued operations, and any other matters relating to the plan. Each class of creditors must accept the plan unless the class is not adversely affected. A class has accepted the plan when a majority of the creditors, representing two-thirds of the amount of the total claim, and at least 50% of creditors in each class vote to approve it.

A plan is **confirmed** only if it is "in the best interest of the creditors." The plan is not confirmed if it is likely to be followed by liquidation even if it is accepted by all classes. In addition, at least half of the creditors must accept the plan. A plan may be confirmed even if an impaired class fails to accept by the requisite majority vote. The plan may be "**crammed down**" without the acceptance of that impaired class. Cram down simply requires that the plan meet the standards of fairness to dissenting creditors or equityholders. This general principle, according to the bankruptcy code, permits "confirmation notwithstanding nonacceptance by an impaired class, if that class and all below it in priority are treated according to the absolute priority rule" (defined later).

The reorganization plan is binding upon confirmation. The plan states the rights of the debtor and creditors and creates a new relationship between the two. Thus the debtor is reorganized with the purpose of carrying out the plan and satisfying the obligations set out in the plan or reorganization.

The bankruptcy code allows managers to make certain trade-offs between firm value and their own self-interest at the expense of the creditors. Managers are unlikely to recommend that the firm be liquidated even if it is the best decision (they would lose their jobs). A reorganization plan must be voted on by all shareholders and the impaired creditors.

The right to vote for a reorganization allows shareholders to extract wealth from the creditors. This is easily seen by returning to the liquidation versus reorganization cases of Freemont Tires and ITI. Notice from Table 16-2 that a court-sponsored Chapter 11 restructuring gives stockholders an option worth $91 and $408 for shareholders of Freemont and ITI, respectively.

Morse and Shaw studied 162 firms that filed for Chapter 11 bankruptcy during the period 1973–1982.[14] They found that 60% of the firms emerge with a reorganized plan, 7% of these firms merge with other companies, and 15% subsequently liquidate under Chapter 7 (information is not available on the remaining 18%). In a study of 37 firms that filed for Chapter 11, Weiss found that 95% reemerge under a new plan and 5% liquidate.[15] The data thus indicate that reorganized firms, to a large extent, appear to avoid subsequent liquidation. Thus Chapter 11 appears to have some success in rehabilitating distressed firms.

The bankruptcy procedures followed in other countries are outlined in the highlight.

[14] D. Morse and W. Shaw, "Investing in Bankrupt Firms," *Journal of Finance* 43 (1988): 1193–1206.
[15] Lawrence A. Weiss, "Bankruptcy Resolution, Direct Costs, and Violation of Priority of Claims," *Journal of Financial Economics* 27 (1990): 285–314.

CORPORATE BANKRUPTCIES IN OTHER COUNTRIES

JAPAN: Workers and equityholders have the highest priority. Legal bankruptcy proceedings are an exception rather than the rule. Japanese businesses tend to see more informal "rescues," typically by the bank or a partner with interests in the firm. In Japan, the equityholders and the workers are accorded the highest priority in these rescues, and the rescuer typically has to make large financial commitments to propose a plan consistent with these priorities. When legal proceedings become inevitable, there are three legal options. Under bankruptcy law (the most popular redress), the firm is simply liquidated and creditors paid off with the proceeds. Rarer options involve composition law and company rearrangement law, under which firms are restructured.

GREAT BRITAIN: Creditors are of paramount importance. In addition to a "voluntary arrangement"

with a creditor, British firms have four formal options. Large firms typically "go into administration" and keep the company alive as an ongoing concern. However, a lawyer or accountant typically runs the firm. Alternatively the firm can go into "administrative receivership," in which case the secured creditors appoint a "receiver" to manage the firm. The receiver's main goal is to raise enough funds to meet the secured creditor's claims. The firm can be liquidated under a "voluntary liquidation" or an "involuntary liquidation." In the former, shareholders appoint a liquidator to sell assets and pay off creditors. In the latter, the liquidator enters the picture only after the court authorizes it upon a request by the creditors.

FRANCE: Creditors are treated harshly. A firm goes into redressement judiciaire when the firm declares bankruptcy and goes to court. This must happen within two weeks of defaulting on creditors' claims. A court official then helps

managers (who retain their jobs) draw up a plan that usually takes one of three forms: continuation, raising new capital and selling assets, and liquidation. Under French law, creditors have no say whatsoever in the plan that the court ultimately adopts.

GERMANY: The German system emphasizes the retention of equity value. A financially distressed firm is usually helped along by its supervisory board or a coalition of bankers. If they do not succeed, the firm must file for bankruptcy. Creditors can liquidate or reschedule the debt. The court decides whether the firm can be saved in such a way that at least 35% of creditors' claims are satisfied. However, unlike their neighbors in France, creditors can veto any court-drafted plan. Shareholders play little part in this process. However, in Germany, many of the shareholders are banks that lend money to the firm, and the shareholder–bondholder distinction is not so sharp.

The Absolute Priority Rule

In distributing the firm's assets, courts have historically been expected to follow the **absolute priority rule,** which requires that the claims be paid in order of **priority.** Each class of claims has a priority, and furthermore, all claims of a given class must be satisfied before distributions are made to a lesser class. If the assets are insufficient to satisfy the claims of a given class, the proceeds are distributed proportionally within that class. The priority of claims and the order of distribution are listed in Table 16-4.

Weiss found that absolute priority is more likely to be violated for relatively larger firms. Moreover, deviations appear more common for firms that file in the Southern District of New York.

■

T A B L E   1 6 - 4

Priority of Claims in Chapter 11 Bankruptcies

1. Debtor in possession (DIP) loans (defined later)
2. Obligations incurred in procuring supplies and services after filing for Chapter 11
3. Unsecured claims for salaries, wages, and commissions
4. Unsecured claims arising from contributions to employee benefit plans
5. Secured creditors
6. Senior creditors
7. Unsecured creditors (other than senior creditors)
8. Subordinated debt claims
9. Equityholders

Franks and Torous studied 27 firms that emerged from bankruptcy between 1971 and 1986.[16] They found that 21 of these firms (78%) show deviations from absolute priority and that in 18 firms (67%), equityholders receive some cash flows even though the senior claims have not been fully satisfied.

WHY ARE THERE DEVIATIONS FROM ABSOLUTE PRIORITY?

It is difficult to justify courts' deviations from absolute priority. This is a violation of the contractually agreed-upon priority of claims. Yet there are two economic explanations for these deviations.

First, the United States is one of the few countries that allows existing management to run the company (see the preceding highlight). Incumbent management has 120 days to propose its plan and that too is subject to court-allowed extensions. In situations where bondholders propose their own plan, the court procedures become very time consuming and expensive. The creditors have to bring in witnesses and experts to convince the judge that their proposal uses reasonable economic values. In contrast, when the debtor proposes a plan, all that is required by law is that the judge feel that the plan is "fair and equitable." Thus creditors have incentives to agree to departures from absolute priority. Their expected proceeds after the deviations can exceed the net benefits of their insistence that the courts enforce strict priority.

Second, bankruptcy judges may choose to depart from the priority scheme to satisfy other claims. For example, Judge Lifland, in the Southern District of New York, decided to keep Eastern Airlines afloat "for the benefit of consumers." As we see subsequently, such arbitrary deviations from established procedures can have major negative ramifications.

For absolute priority to be followed, senior claimants must be paid before junior claimants (including stockholders) receive any payments whatsoever. Although the courts are expected to adhere to the absolute priority rule, they have routinely violated it. Weiss, for example, studied 37 companies that filed for bankruptcy during the period 1979–1986 and found that strict priority was violated in 29 (80%) cases. Shareholders received nothing in only seven cases (20%). In three cases, stockholders received all-cash settlements ranging from $233,000 to $1,500,000. In 15 cases (41%), shareholders received 25% or less of the reorganized company. In 12 cases (32%), they ended up with equity in excess of 25%. Weiss's findings are reproduced in Table 16-5.

IMPLICATIONS OF DEVIATIONS FROM ABSOLUTE PRIORITY

There is considerable debate as to whether deviations from absolute priority are good or bad. Since this issue is unresolved, we discuss both sides of the debate here.

The practice of deviating from absolute priority can have adverse implications not only for the financially distressed firm but also for the economy as a whole. To the extent that junior creditors know that the courts can deviate from absolute priority, they can put more pressure on the senior claimants with a view to expropriate wealth from them. This increases the negotiation time, stretches the period of bankruptcy reorganization, and further lowers the value of the distressed firms. If such deviations from absolute priority become commonplace, it can raise the cost of debt capital and lower the value of all companies (the Modigliani–Miller results are unlikely to hold with costly default). Creditors, when they loan money

---

[16] J. R. Franks and W. N. Torous, "An Empirical Investigation of U.S. Firms in Reorganization," *Journal of Finance* 44 (1989): 747–779.

■

TABLE 16-5

Weiss's Study on Deviations from Absolute Priority

Firm Name	Percentage of Claims Received in Bankruptcy		
	Secured Creditors	Unsecured Creditors	Equityholders
Priority Held[a]			
Bobbie Brooks	100%	100%	100%
Branch Inds	100	100	100
Brody (B) St	100	51	0
Flanigan's	100	100	0
Garland Corp	100	100	> 0
Ronco Telepd	100	Balance	0
Tenna Corp	74	0	0
U.N.A. Corp	100	1 CS[b] per $1 claim	0
Priority violated for unsecured creditors only			
AM Intl	100	94%	47%
Anglo Energy	100	58%	25%
Beker Inds	100	<20%	38%
Berry Inds	100	Cash and PS[c]	60%
Combustion	100	From 49% to 82%	$316,000
Cook United	100	93% of CS	7%
Goldblatt	100	24%	53%
HRT Inds	100	75%	25%
Imperial Inds	100	37%	100%
KDT Inds	100	36%	$1,500,000
Lionel Corp	100	Up to 100%	100%
Manville	100	Up to 100%	5%
McLouth Stl	100	90% of CS	10%
Morton Cos	100	33%	$233,000
Penn-Dixie	100	45% of claim + 50% of CS	50%
Revere Copper	100	65%	77%
Richton Intl	100	60%	100%
Salant Corp	100	97%	99%
Saxon Inds	100	From 33% to 49%	PS
Seatrain Ln	100	CS	Warrants
Shelter Res	100	5% of CS	5%
Spencer Cos	100	30% of claim + 60% of CS	17%
Tacoma Boat	100	96% of CS	4%
Towle Mfg	100	60%	7%
White Motor	100	51%	10%
Wickes Cos	100	From 59% to 92%	19%
Priority violated for secured creditors			
Crompton Co	85%	20%	0
Evans Pds	76%	87%	0
Stevcoknit	From 37% to 77%	33%	12%

SOURCE: Lawrence A. Weiss, "Bankruptcy Resolution. Direct Costs and Violation of Priority of Claims," *Journal of Financial Economics* 27 (1990): 285–314.

[a] Priority of claims holds when secured creditors are satisfied first, then holders of various grades of subordinated debt and equityholders last.

[b] CS = Common stock.

[c] PS = Preferred stock.

to the firm, expect to recover their opportunity costs. If they believe that their risk is increasing because of courts' deviations from absolute priority, they demand higher required rates of return, thus raising the firm's cost of capital. Moreover, senior claimants, anticipating potential court-sanctioned cash flows to junior claimants in default, can refuse to allow junior claimants into the firm's capital structure. When carried to the extreme, such restrictions may reduce all claimants to one class and distort the risk-sharing function in the financial markets. With the absence of risk capital and increases in the cost of debt, firms may take on fewer projects. Reduced economic growth and unemployment would thus be a result of courts' systematic deviations from absolute priority.

In his decision to let Eastern Airlines stay afloat, as seen earlier, the judge effectively supported the weak airline. Because Eastern was offering extremely low fares, other airlines were forced to cut their fares to compete. However, many of these competing airlines were also in financial distress, and the unfair competition caused by the court's subsidization of Eastern forced other airline companies into bankruptcy. One could make a case that the court's objective of deviating from contracted provisions to "serve the consumer" did, in fact, hurt the consumer.

Some researchers have argued that deviations from absolute priority are rational responses by bondholders and the courts to the management–debtor bargaining power in reorganization.[17] There may actually be advantages to departing from the strict priority rule if the reorganization can be effected sooner, thus preserving more value in the firm. Other authors have suggested that deviations from absolute priority can actually be good because they can mitigate some stockholder–bondholder agency problems. For example, Eberhart and Senbet suggest that deviations from absolute priority can reduce the incentives for stockholders to "go for broke" when the firm is doing poorly.[18] With strict enforcement of priority as the firm slides toward bankruptcy, shareholders have an incentive to shift to risky projects because they have everything to gain and little to lose. However, if because of courts' deviations from absolute priority, they can get some cash flows in bankruptcy, they are less likely to indulge in this form of opportunistic behavior. In this sense, the deviations can be part of an optimal bankruptcy plan.

16.5
BANKRUPTCY AS A STRATEGIC DEVICE

Since firms today can voluntarily file for bankruptcy and since the U.S. courts emphasize the equityholders' claims, bankruptcies can be used as a strategic business decision. Bankruptcy today does not have the stigma it had even a few years ago. Contrast Braniff's bankruptcy of the early 1980s with that of Continental Airlines. Whereas Braniff grounded all its planes and sent its customers to other airlines, Continental's bankruptcy actually increased its market share from 9.1% to 9.3%. It has been observed that "what was designed as a shield has become a weapon."[19] What are the advantages of choosing to file for bankruptcy? We examine a few recent instances where firms used bankruptcies to their strategic advantage.

Bankruptcies Aimed at Increasing the Firm's Borrowing

As perverse at it sounds, a firm can actually increase its borrowing capacity by filing for bankruptcy. Consider some examples. Midway Airlines spent months trying to arrange for credit to help its cash flow crisis. Unable to obtain any relief, Midway filed for bankruptcy in March 1991. Immediately, Continental Bank offered Midway a $40 million line of credit. Similarly, Interco, a St. Louis-based conglomerate (whose core businesses include Florsheim and Converse shoes, Lane and Broyhill furniture), filed for bankruptcy to avoid paying the interest on its debt; yet 14 banks rushed in to offer the bankrupt firm $185 million in new loans.[20]

Banks obtain advantages by lending money to bankrupt companies. This lending, known as **debtor in possession (DIP) financing,** places the banks in a **super-priority status.** Their claims become senior to those of all other creditors, making DIP loans perhaps the safest form of lending. Thus lending money to bankrupt

---

[17] See, for example, R. Giamarrino, "The Resolution of Financial Distress," *Review of Financial Studies,* Spring 1989, pp. 25–47; and Y. Bergman and J. Callen, "Opportunistic Underinvestment in Debt Renegotiations and Capital Structure," *Journal of Financial Economics,* March 1991, pp. 131–171.

[18] A. Eberhart and L. W. Senbet, "Absolute Priority Rule Violations and Risk Incentives for Financially Distressed Firms," *Financial Management* 22, no. 3 (1993): 101–116.

[19] "American Bankruptcy: The Uses and Abuses of Chapter 11," *The Economist,* March 18, 1989.

[20] D. L. Boroughs, "It Pays to Go Broke," *U.S. News & World Report,* April 8, 1991.

TABLE 16-6
DIP Financing: Examples and Typical Revenues to Lenders

Examples of DIP financing
Chemical Bank (Macy's, Zale Corporation, Allied Stores, and Allegheny International)
Continental Bank (Tracer Inc.)
Wells Fargo (Revco, Insilco Corp.)
Bankers Trust (Macy's, Pan Am, Southland Corp., Federated Department Stores)
Toronto–Dominion (Greyhound)
General Electric Credit Corporation (U.S. Home, Seamen's Furniture, Rexene Chemical, and National Gypsum)

Typical DIP financing revenues:[a] Up-front fee: 2%–4% of amount borrowed, 1%–3% interest rate above prime, an unused line fee of 0.5%, administrative fees (monitoring costs) of $12,000 to $20,000 per month, and letter of credit fee (where applicable) of 2%–3% of loan amount

[a] From Edward I. Altman, *Corporate Financial Distress and Bankruptcy,* 2nd. ed. (New York: John Wiley & Sons, 1993).

firms is becoming a major trend. Table 16-6 provides some examples of DIP financing and the associated revenues to the lending firms.

Bankruptcies to Get Around Uncooperative Creditors

In recent years, prepackaged bankruptcies have become increasingly common. This method of resolving financial distress is a "hybrid" between an organized Chapter 11 filing and a private workout. The firm effectively works out a relaxation of any binding covenants outside the courtroom and, with the full cooperation of *most* of its creditors, files a plan of reorganization in the courts. The first major prepackaged bankruptcy was that of Crystal Oil in 1986 (see the highlight).

EXAMPLES OF PREPACKAGED BANKRUPTCIES: CRYSTAL OIL COMPANY AND LIVE ENTERTAINMENT, INC.

CRYSTAL OIL COMPANY

The first major corporation to file for a prepackaged bankruptcy was Crystal Oil Company, headquartered in Louisiana. On October 1, 1986, the company filed for bankruptcy, and it was reorganized in three months with a completely different capital structure. The firm's total indebtedness was reduced from $277 million to $129 million. The firm offered creditors a package of common stock, convertible preferred stock, convertible notes, and warrants in exchange for their old debt.

Three months before filing for Chapter 11, the firm had presented a reorganization plan to its creditors. All classes of public debt holders accepted the plan. However, Crystal's most senior creditors, Halliburton Corporation and Bankers Trust, refused to accept the plan. Although Bankers Trust accepted a revised plan, Halliburton refused to go along. Eventually the court "crammed down" the revised plan on Halliburton.

After the reorganization, Crystal Oil Company scaled down its operations, reduced its debt burden, and increased its profitability.

LIVE ENTERTAINMENT, INC.

LIVE Entertainment, Inc., filed a prepackaged Chapter 11 plan on February 2, 1993, in the Central District of California. Six weeks later, on March 17, the plan was confirmed, and on March 23 the plan closed.

In 1987, LIVE Entertainment purchased Lieberman, a company that provides specialized merchandise services to merchandisers and retailers. LIVE sold that company because of its poor performance at a loss of almost $100 million, causing the debtor to become unable to service its $100 million public debt. As a result the debtor filed for Chapter 11 protection. The prepackaged plan met with overwhelming approval from the creditors, which helped the debtor emerge from bankruptcy in just seven weeks.

The debtor offered to exchange $8 million in cash, 6 million shares of preferred stock, and $40 million in exchange notes for $110 million in principal amount of outstanding notes and 1,050,000 shares of outstanding preferred stock.

SOURCES: Crystal Oil: John McConnell and Henri Servaes, "The Economics of Pre-Packaged Bankruptcy," Midland Journal of Corporate Finance, *Summer 1991.* Live Entertainment, Inc.: Abridged from "Special Report, Player's Piece: Who's Who in LIVE Entertainment Inc.," Turnarounds and Workouts (Washington, DC: Beard Group, May 1, 1993). Reproduced with permission of Nadine Granoff, editor.

Since then, there have been several more. In 1989, Republic Health Corp. filed a prepackaged bankruptcy plan after it failed to appease all of its creditors in a private workout. However, the prepackaged plan was supported by 86% of its creditors. The firm entered bankruptcy with debts of $645 million and emerged from Chapter 11 with only $379 million in debt. Other recent successful prepackaged bankruptcies are Memorex-Telex (1992), Edgell Communications (1991), Taj Mahal Hotel (1991), TIE Communications (1991), and JPS Textiles (1991).

A prepackaged bankruptcy can have benefits. First, it can reduce the magnitude of the "holdout problem" addressed earlier. The firm has effectively obtained the agreement of most creditors before it files for bankruptcy. For a Chapter 11 bankruptcy, a plan of reorganization becomes effective if it is approved by 50% of its creditors in each class and 67% by dollar amount. The plan can thus be forced upon some uncooperative and perhaps intransigent creditors. This can speed up the bankruptcy reorganization process and preserve value in the company. Second, a prepackaged bankruptcy can avoid the possibility that creditors' claims can be invalidated by the courts (because of the LTV case). Third, potential tax benefits can be obtained through a prepackaged plan that are not available in an informal reorganization.

Bankruptcies to Reject Collective Bargaining Agreements

Several firms have filed for bankruptcy to reject collective bargaining agreements and thereby reduce wages to nonunion levels. Continental Airlines is considered the first instance of a firm that filed for bankruptcy to break existing contracts with machinists and flight attendant unions. The company argued in court that these parties had no claim because there must be damages for a party to make a claim. Continental then argued that there were no damages in rejecting the contracts because the high labor costs would have forced the company into bankruptcy anyway. Appletree Stores filed for bankruptcy in January 1992 to lower its labor costs. Its reorganization proposal contained new labor rates for all members of the United Food and Commercial Workers Union. Appletree's bankruptcy reduced its total labor costs by 16%. A landmark case, *National Labor Relations Board (NLRB)* vs. *Bildisco* (1984) made it easier for companies to reject labor contracts. It set the appropriate standards by which labor contracts can be rejected, and Congress approved Section 1113, which outlines a method by which trustees can either reject or renegotiate collective bargaining agreements. Northwest Airlines in July 1993 threatened to file for Chapter 11 unless its workers agreed to a sizable reduction in the benefits due to them from earlier contract negotiations.

Bankruptcies to Reject Obligations to Suppliers

A failing firm can sever ties with its suppliers and customers by rejecting, as **executory contracts,** all obligations to these parties. An executory contract (in contrast to an executed contract) is one in which the contract has not yet been fully performed on both sides. All contracts with suppliers can be rejected because they are not yet performed. Southland Corporation, for example, sold off its assets (e.g., Citgo), rejected its contracts with suppliers as executory contracts, and thus forced a renegotiation of lease contracts. Jim Walter Corporation, Appletree Stores, and R. H. Macys Company are other examples of firms that renegotiated their contracts along these lines.

Chapter 11 may offer special advantages to retailers. Retailers typically have numerous trade creditors, and it can be extremely difficult for a firm to negotiate with this group because they often have claims with different characteristics and because they are unlikely to work together as a group. Rather than deal with each trade creditor individually, the firm that files for Chapter 11 deals with all of them simultaneously (since their claims are lumped together and dealt with as one class), and protracted negotiations can be avoided. Wruck suggests that this is one of the factors that prompted Revco to file for Chapter 11.[21]

Bankruptcies To Avoid Litigation

In August 1992, Johns-Manville Corporation, a major asbestos producer, filed for bankruptcy even though it was solvent. This voluntary bankruptcy filing was triggered by the fact that the company had around 16,000 lawsuits pending for injuries caused by asbestos exposure. The firm intended the bankruptcy to give the company a "fresh start." Manville's creditors and the people hurt by asbestos exposure argued that the filing was not in good faith, but the court sided with Manville, saying, "It is no longer necessary for a petitioner for reorganization to allege or show insolvency to pay debts as they mature."

Other examples are A. H. Robins and Texaco. In response to the extensive litigation over its contraceptive Dalkon Shield, A. H. Robins filed for bankruptcy (August 1985) even though its cash flow position was not weak. Texaco filed for Chapter 11 when it lost a multibillion dollar suit filed by Pennzoil in connection with Texaco's takeover of Getty Oil.

SUMMARY

Section 16.1: The Terminology of Financial Distress and Bankruptcy

What is financial distress and how is it different from bankruptcy and insolvency?

■ Financial distress occurs when a firm faces insolvency. Insolvency may be technical, in which the firm violates a legally binding agreement with its creditors, or formal, when the firm is unable to meet its obligations to its creditors.

■ Bankruptcy occurs when the firm and/or its creditors pursue formal legal proceedings in bankruptcy court to resolve its problems.

What are the different types of bankruptcies?

■ The two types of bankruptcy are liquidation, in which the assets of the firm are sold off to repay the firm's creditors, and reorganization, in which the obligations of the firm are restructured in order to allow it to continue as a going concern.

Section 16.2: Private or Legal Resolution of Financial Distress?

When does a firm resort to private financial distress-resolution procedures and when is it likely to pursue legal avenues?

■ The costs of private and legal alternatives, the possibility of "holdout," potential legal impediments, and tax issues ultimately determine the firm's optimal course of action.

■ Private procedures are generally considered to be cheaper than legal avenues; however, Chapter 11 has two important benefits. It imposes a queuing order that can reduce considerable confusion, and debtor in possession (DIP) financing can provide new funds for investment.

■ When the "holdout problem" is severe, the firm is likely to file either a prepackaged or a regular bankruptcy.

[21] Karen H. Wruck, "What Really Went Wrong at Revco," *Journal of Applied Corporate Finance,* Summer 1991.

- The laws of fraudulent conveyance may hinder a private restructuring of the debt.

- The cancellation of debt (COD) in a private restructuring creates a positive tax liability and this creates incentives for firms to file for Chapter 11.

Section 16.3: The Economics of Liquidation Versus Reorganization

What is the difference between Chapter 7 liquidation and a Chapter 11 bankruptcy?

- In Chapter 7 liquidation, the firm's assets are sold off and the proceeds distributed to the creditors; the firm ceases to exist.

- In a Chapter 11 bankruptcy, the firm is restructured with new debt and the reorganized firm continues to operate.

When does a firm liquidate and when does it reorganize?

- When a firm's "going-concern value" exceeds its liquidation value, it will be reorganized; otherwise, it will be liquidated.

Section 16.4: Chapter 7 and Chapter 11 Bankruptcy Procedures

What are some similarities and differences between Chapter 7 and Chapter 11 bankruptcy procedures?

- Both types of bankruptcy begin with the filing of a petition. This is followed by an order of relief from the court, and all proceedings are stayed.

- In Chapter 7, an interim trustee is appointed to liquidate the firm's assets and distribute the proceeds.

- In Chapter 11, the debtor typically files a plan of reorganization within a 120-day exclusivity period. The debtor in possession (DIP) runs the firm if the plan is confirmed by the courts. In some instances, the plan may be "crammed down."

What is the absolute priority rule?

- The absolute priority rule requires that the claims be paid in order of priority. All claims of a given class must be satisfied before distributions can be made to a lesser class.

- Creditors may find it cost efficient to agree to departures from absolute priority.

- Bankruptcy judges have been known to deviate from absolute priority to satisfy other claims.

What are some implications of courts' deviations from the absolute priority rule?

- The potential for deviations from absolute priority can increase negotiation time, stretch the period of bankruptcy reorganization, and further lower the value of the distressed firm.

- Deviations from absolute priority can raise the cost of debt capital and perhaps distort the risk-sharing function in the capital markets.

- The potential for deviations from absolute priority may also have advantages. It can encourage faster reorganizations that can preserve more of the distressed firm's value. Moreover, the potential for deviations from priority can mitigate some of the stockholder–bondholder agency problems. Stockholders have less incentive to invest in extremely risky projects.

Section 16.5:
Bankruptcy As a
Strategic Device

What does it mean to say that firms can use bankruptcy "as a strategic device"?

■ Bankruptcy can be filed for "strategic considerations"—to increase borrowing capacity, to get around uncooperative creditors, to reject collective bargaining agreements, to reject obligations to suppliers, and to avoid litigation.

QUESTIONS

1. Distinguish among the terms *business failure, financial distress, insolvency,* and *default.*

2. When does a firm have incentives to restructure its debt privately and when does it seek legal avenues?

3. Explain the nature of the "holdout problem."

4. Distinguish between "liquidation" and "reorganization." Explain the procedures employed by the courts under either arrangement.

5. Filing for bankruptcy is a choice faced by management. Do you agree with this statement?

6. What is the empirical evidence on the advantages of restructuring privately?

7. Explain the notion of "constructive fraud" in a fraudulent conveyance context.

8. It may make economic sense for bondholders to make "side payments" to the stockholders to keep them out of court. Explain the factors that can justify this statement.

9. What is the priority scheme underlying the absolute priority rule?

10. To what extent is the the absolute priority rule violated? What are the potential advantages and disadvantages of deviations from absolute priority?

11. List and discuss some of the "strategic uses" of bankruptcy.

PROBLEMS

1. National Marketing, Inc., is currently in financial distress. Because of poor sales it has been unable to repay a $2,000 debt obligation due today. According to one estimate, National Marketing's next period cash flows are either $3,000 with a probability of 0.6 or $1,500 with a probability of 0.4. The current market value of National Marketing's assets is $1,650. Assume that the market discount rate for valuing all assets and financial instruments is 10%.

   (a) Should the company be liquidated or reorganized?

   (b) What is the market value of the debt if the company is reorganized?

   (c) If the debt holders have the option to take over and then run the company, will they choose to do so?

   (d) Do you expect that the equityholders will allow the company to be taken over by the debt holders?

2. Creative Products, Inc., is currently in financial distress because of its failure to

repay $1,000 in debt obligation. The current market value of its assets is $875. The estimated next period cash flows are as follows:

Cash Flows	Probability
$900	0.5
$1,200	0.5

Compute the market discount rate at which the debt holders will be indifferent between the two alternatives: of taking over and running the firm or reorganizing the firm. What will be the market value of the payoff to equityholders under these two alternatives? If the market interest rates are greater than the discount rate you have computed, then what must the debt holders do?

3. Western Disposal Services Corporation has filed for bankruptcy under Chapter 11. Western Disposal's current debt obligation is $1,000, and its market value of assets is $975. The equityholders unanimously agree with the following estimates of next period cash flows:

Cash Flows	Probability
$1,350	0.7
$750	0.3

However, the debt holders feel that these cash flows are grossly overestimated and that the firm must therefore be liquidated. What is the minimum side payment that the debt holders must make to the equityholders in order to force a liquidation? Assume that the market discount rate is 12%.

SUGGESTED ADDITIONAL READINGS

Baldwin, Carliss Y., and Scott P. Mason. "The Resolution of Claims in Financial Distress: The Case of Massey Ferguson." *Journal of Finance* 38 (1983): 505–523.

DeAngelo, Harry, and Linda DeAngelo. "Dividend Policy and Financial Distress: An Empirical Investigation of Troubled NYSE Firms." *The Journal of Finance* 45, no. 5 (1990): 1415–1430.

Easterbrook, Frank H. "Is Corporate Bankruptcy Efficient?" *Journal of Financial Economics* 27 (1990): 411–417.

Gilson, Stuart C., Kose John, and Larry H. P. Lang. "Troubled Debt Restructurings." *Journal of Financial Economics* 26 (1990): 1–37.

John, Kose. "Managing Financial Distress and Valuing Distressed Securities: A Survey and a Research Agenda." *Financial Management* 22, no. 3 (1993): 60–78.

Kaen, Fred R., and Hassan Tehranian. "Information Effects in Financial Distress. The Case of Seabrook Station." *Journal of Financial Economics* 26 (1990): 143–171.

Titman, Sheridan. "The Effect of Capital Structure on Firm's Liquidation Decision." *Journal of Financial Economics* 13 (1984): 137–151.

Warner, Jerold. "Bankruptcy Costs: Some Evidence." *The Journal of Finance* 32, no. 2 (1977): 337–348.

Weiss, Lawrence A. "Bankruptcy Resolution. Direct Costs and Violation of Priority of Claims." *Journal of Financial Economics* 27 (1990): 285–314.

Wruck, Karen Hooper. "Financial Distress, Reorganization, and Organizational Efficiency." *Journal of Financial Economics* 27 (1990): 419–444.

SEVENTEEN THE DIVIDEND POLICY DECISION

Do you know the only thing that gives me pleasure? It's to see my dividends coming in.

—John D. Rockefeller, 1901

The issue of how much a company should pay its stockholders as dividends has concerned managers for a long time. All firms operate in order to generate earnings. Stockholders supply equity capital, expecting to share in these earnings either directly or indirectly. When a company pays out a portion of its earnings to stockholders in the form of a dividend, the stockholders benefit directly. If, instead of paying dividends, the firm retains the funds to exploit other growth opportunities, the stockholders can expect to benefit indirectly through future increases in the price of their stock. Thus shareholder wealth can be increased through either dividends or capital gains. Because the amount of dividends paid to stockholders is a decision made by management, managers need guidance on how to evaluate the effect of their dividend policy decision on shareholder wealth.

In simplest terms, a firm's dividend decision involves two issues. First, should a dividend be paid at all and, if so, how much it should be? Second, what is the optimal dividend policy? That is, what dividend payout ratio (the ratio of dividends paid to net income) is in the best interest of the shareholders? This chapter answers the following questions:

- What are some standard corporate dividend payment policies and procedures?

- What are stock dividends and stock splits? Why do firms split stocks and pay stock dividends?

- Why do firms repurchase shares?

- What is the link between dividend payments and firm value in perfect markets?

- What is the empirical evidence in regard to dividends?

- What are some of the factors that can influence dividend policy?

- How can agency costs and psychological factors affect dividend policies?

It is interesting to explore the legal definitions of dividends, earnings, and profit. These definitions are important to assessing whether a firm's dividend policy has resulted in "improperly accumulated earnings," which are penalized by the tax authority. It is commonly believed that publicly held corporations need not worry about the penalty levied on improper accumulations, but this is not strictly correct. Many public companies (including Coca Cola) have been challenged by the Internal Revenue Service and forced to pay a fine.

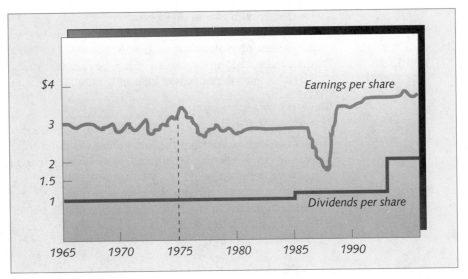

FIGURE 17-1

Bates, Inc., dividends and earnings per share

17-1

DIVIDEND PAYMENT POLICIES AND PROCEDURES

Dividend Payment Policies

[handwritten: CONSTANT Dividend Policy →]

[handwritten: "GRADUALLY INCREASING D PAYMENT Policy"]

A lthough each corporation has its own dividend payment procedure, most companies follow one of three broad dividend payment policies.[1] These policies are discussed next.

CONSTANT DIVIDEND PER SHARE *[handwritten: Corporations decide on a fixed $ amount]*

Many corporations decide on a fixed dollar amount of annual dividends per share and pay out this dividend regularly. Companies that follow this procedure do not increase dividends when earnings increase temporarily. Management is unlikely to raise dividends unless it expects a permanent increase in the firm's future earnings stream. Similarly, these companies are hesitant to cut dividends solely because of a temporary dip in the firm's earnings. Figure 17-1 shows this dividend payment procedure for a hypothetical furniture company, Bates, Inc.

Notice that Bates's dividend in 1965 was $1 out of an earnings per share of $3. The 1965 dividend payout ratio was therefore $1/$3 = 0.33, or 33%. Bates continued to pay out $1 until 1985, even though its earnings did jump earlier (1975). Management did not alter its dividends in 1975 because it did not expect the sudden increase in earnings to be permanent. Similarly, management did not cut dividends in 1987 despite a drastic decrease in earnings. Apparently, the company believed that the decrease was only temporary. In fact, in 1985, management actually raised the dividends per share to $1.20 because a sustained higher level of earnings was anticipated and management's dividend payments were influenced primarily by long-term permanent earnings trends.

If it is reasonable to assume that a company's earnings will increase through time, the constant dividend payout procedure can be more accurately characterized as a "gradually increasing dividend payment policy."

Another variant of this approach to dividend payments is the so-called stable growth policy. Companies that espouse this practice have decided to maintain a

---

[1] In the 1950s Lintner conducted several interviews with corporate managers and found that managers tend to follow certain general policies, which we discuss in this chapter. See J. L. Lintner, "Distribution of Incomes Among Dividends, Retained Earnings, and Taxes," *American Economic Review* 46 (1956): 97–113.

constant growth rate in dividends. For example, a firm may plan to pay out dividends so that the growth rate in dividends over an extended period is, say, 5%. For this procedure to work, earnings must increase at a fairly reasonable rate. In inflationary periods, this requirement can be met more easily, which is perhaps why this stable growth policy was especially popular in the mid-1970s.

CONSTANT PAYOUT RATIO

A firm that decides on a certain dividend payout ratio and sticks to it is following a constant payout policy. For example, if Bates follows a 20% payout policy, it would pay out $0.20, $0.80, and $0.40 in annual dividends per share if its earnings were, respectively, $1.00, $4.00, and $2.00 per share over the next three years. Because earnings invariably fluctuate over time, a constant payout ratio procedure yields an uneven stream of dividend payments. Managers generally prefer to hold the dollar amount of dividends stable, so the constant payout ratio policy is not pervasive in business.

REGULAR PLUS EXTRA DIVIDENDS

Certain corporations like a policy of a low regular dividend plus an annual "extra" dividend plan. Clearly, management has more flexibility with this approach than with the constant dividend procedure. A company with fluctuating earnings may find this policy especially attractive. If earnings are high, the company can issue an extra annual dividend. If earnings are below expectations, the extra dividend can be reduced or even eliminated. In either case, this policy attempts to maintain some stability in dividend payments.

WHY STABILITY?

It is generally accepted that managers like to follow a stable dividend payment procedure. The three procedures just outlined all maintain some stability. Why focus on stability? If managers can argue successfully that stable dividend payments increase the stock price, their insistence on stability is justified. But if the stability of dividends is irrelevant to the stock price, this preference for stability is beside the point. Although formal valuation models have not been able to demonstrate satisfactorily the link between dividend stability and value, it is generally agreed that a stable dividend policy may have a positive impact on stock prices.

LEGAL HISTORY Several fiduciary institutions are restricted in their equity investments, in that they can buy the stock of only companies on their "legal list." Legal listings are of potential investment candidates. Firms like to be on such a list because it increases the demand for their stock. Although different institutions use different criteria in deciding whether a company should be included on this list, a common requirement is that the company's record reflect a stable, nondecreasing dividend policy. For this reason, the stability of dividends is deemed important. Because the purchase of their stock by these large institutional investors can put upward pressure on the stock price, managers seek to offer stability in dividends.

THE INFORMATIONAL CONTENT OF DIVIDENDS It has often been pointed out that a company that raises its dividends often experiences an increase in its stock price and that a company that lowers its dividends has a falling stock price.[2] This seems to suggest that dividends do matter; they do affect stock prices.

[2]Empirical evidence to support this statement can be found in several dividend studies. See, for example, G. Charest, "Dividend Information, Stock Returns and Market Efficiency," *Journal of Finan-*

But this causal relationship has been refuted by several researchers on the grounds that dividends per se do not affect stock prices. Rather, it is the informational content of dividends that affects stock prices.

Recall that managers have a propensity to follow a stable dividend policy. In light of this, it is argued that any change in dividends is a signal from managers to stockholders about the future prospects of the firm. A dividend increase, for example, might convey that management expects future earnings prospects to improve. For temporary earnings increases, managers would not raise dividends. Similarly, given the reluctance of management to cut dividends, any dividend decreases tell stockholders that future earnings levels are expected to be lower.[3] Of course, a company may succeed in "fooling" stockholders in the short run by not reducing dividends even if a permanent decline in earnings is expected. Sooner or later, however, stockholders are able to see through this ploy.

M. H. Miller and F. Modigliani, proponents of this theory of the informational content of dividends, also contend that stockholders' reactions are only temporary. Although stockholders may view a dividend increase as a harbinger of good news, they can soon verify whether their interpretation of the dividend increase is justified. Even if dividends have no informational content, the stock price rises when the public sees the firm's higher earnings. Thus there should be no direct link between dividends and stock prices. There may be a short-term link because of the dividends' informational content. Indeed, in an empirical study of firms listed on the New York Stock Exchange, DeAngelo, DeAngelo, and Skinner conclude that dividend policy does indeed have informational content because knowledge that a firm has reduced dividends improves the ability of current earnings to predict future earnings.[4]

The effect of a stable dividend policy on stock prices is not fully understood. What is lacking is a detailed study of this issue using a large number of stocks. Until we have this, the general belief that a stable dividend policy helps a company's stock price cannot easily be verified.

Dividend policy is normally set by managers based on criteria such as we have discussed thus far. However, it is possible for other factors to enter into the firm's dividend decisions, as shown in the Ford highlight.

Dividend Payment Procedures

Most American corporations pay dividends quarterly. In addition, about 10% of U.S. companies declare an extra annual dividend. All dividend payments must be declared by the board of directors. The date on which the board declares the dividend for the next quarter is appropriately known as the **declaration date.** The board also specifies a **date of record.** All stockholders on the date of record are eligible to receive the cash dividend. It is therefore on this date that the registrar of the company "closes" the books to mail out the dividend checks to the shareholders "on record."

Another date that has special significance is the **ex-dividend date,** which is the fourth business day preceding the date of record. If a weekend falls between the ex-

cial Economics 6 (1978): 297–330; and J. Aharony and I. Swary, "Quarterly Earnings and Dividend Announcements and Stockholders' Returns: An Empirical Analysis," *Journal of Finance* 35 (1980): 1–12.

[3] Evidence that managers are extremely reluctant to omit dividends is contained in H. DeAngelo and L. DeAngelo, "Dividend Policy and Financial Distress: An Empirical Investigation of Troubled NYSE Firms," *Journal of Finance*, December 1990, pp. 1415–1431.

[4] H. DeAngelo, L. DeAngelo, and D. J. Skinner, "Dividends and Losses," *Journal of Finance* 47 (1992): 1837–1864.

HENRY FORD'S DIVIDEND POLICY

Although dividend payments are not a legal requirement for corporations in all states, this was not always true. The story of Henry Ford's dividend policies is an interesting aside to the dividend policy discussion in the text.

In 1916, stockholders John and Horace Dodge sued the Ford Motor Company for not paying a "reasonable" dividend. After an adverse decision in a lower court, the case was appealed to the Michigan Supreme Court, and early in 1919, Ford was ordered to pay a delayed dividend of $19 million with interest at 5% from the date of the first decision. The supreme court's decision stated that nonpayment of dividends to the stockholders was, considering the remarkable profits, "illegal and arbitrary."

Angered by this ruling, Henry Ford vowed to eliminate all other shareholders in his company by repurchasing shares, regardless of

cost. On his original investment of less than $2,500, Couzens received $29 million from Ford. His sister, Mrs. Haus, who had put in $100 in 1903, received $200,000. Anderson and Racklam each made $12.5 million on their original $5,000 investment, and the Dodges took in $25 million on their $10,000 investment. All this money was in addition to $30 million paid to them as shareholders over 16 years.

How did Ford pay for this expensive repurchase? Even the incredible Ford Motor Company could not come up immediately with $75 million in cash. To finance this repurchase, Ford embarked on a brilliant idea involving his Model T car.

Henry Ford first borrowed his $75 million from Old Colony in Boston and Chase Securities in New York, agreeing to repay the loan in April 1921. To avoid defaulting on the bank loans, Henry Ford ordered his company to produce 90,000 Model T cars at in-

credible speed. These cars were to be shipped off to the dealers, even though the dealers had not asked for them. The cars were to be transported at the receivers' expense, and cash was expected upon delivery.

The dealers, anticipating a deluge of cars they had not ordered, threw up their hands in despair and challenged Ford's demands. Ford responded with a warning: If they did not take the cars and pay for them in cash, they would lose their franchises. In complete helplessness, the dealers raised the cash through local banks. Thus Henry Ford received the cash to finance his repurchase from local banks all over the country.

SOURCE: Compiled from information in Roger Burlingame, Henry Ford: A Great Life in Brief *(New York: Knopf, 1955). From the Harry Ransom Collection, University of Texas at Austin. The assistance of Van Harlow is acknowledged.*

dividend date and the record date, the ex-dividend date is six days before the record date. Whereas the company that pays the dividend decides on the date of record, the securities industry establishes the ex-dividend date. Consider a typical NYSE corporation with thousands of shares traded every day. They are traded even on the record date, and it takes some time before the company's books reflect these ownership changes. The ex-dividend date is set merely to ensure that the "right" owners receive the dividend check.

All investors who own shares before the ex-dividend date are entitled to receive a cash dividend. If Mr. X buys the stock from Ms. Y on or after the ex-dividend date, Mr. X is not entitled to the dividend because the company's books list Ms. Y as the owner of the shares. When the share goes ex-dividend, the price of the stock falls by an amount approximately equal to the dividend payment, net of taxes.[5] The **payment date** is the date on which the firm actually mails out the dividend checks.

---

[5]In the absence of taxes, the stock price is expected to fall by exactly the amount of the declared dividend.

TABLE 17-1

Some Companies That Frequently Split Their Stock or Pay Stock Dividends

Alaska Airlines	General Tire and Rubber	Mesa Petroleum
Boeing	Heinz	Parker Pen Company
Church's Fried Chicken	Hewlett-Packard	Southwest Airlines
Federal Express	Luby Cafeterias	Wendy's International

AUTOMATIC DIVIDEND REINVESTMENT PLANS

Many corporations allow shareholders to reinvest their cash dividends in additional shares of the firm's stock. These are **automatic dividend reinvestment plans,** or DRIPs. There currently are two standard DRIP plans.

The first arrangement has a trustee (usually a bank) collect the dividends from all stockholders who opt for automatic reinvestment and buy the company's shares in the open market. Because the volume of transactions is usually large, the brokerage fees are relatively small.

The second arrangement calls for the purchase of newly issued stock. To encourage the purchase of new shares, the company typically offers a 5% to 10% discount from the current market price of the stock. American Express, First Union Corp., Kemper Corp., Piccadilly Cafeterias, and Universal Foods are examples of companies that offer a 2% or greater discount. Using this plan, a company can raise new equity capital without incurring additional flotation costs. Approximately one-fourth of all new common stock issued by corporations is sold through DRIPs. One factor that detracts from the broad appeal of DRIPs is that shareholders must pay ordinary income taxes on the dividends, even though they do not actually receive them when they participate in a DRIP plan.

STOCK DIVIDENDS AND STOCK SPLITS

Companies sometimes "pay" investors dividends with financial securities instead of cash. These payments may take two similar forms: stock dividends or stock splits.

STOCK DIVIDENDS A **stock dividend** is a dividend payment to owners of additional shares of stock instead of cash. Table 17-1 is a partial list of companies that have had stock dividends or stock splits extensively over the last decade.

We can understand the procedures involved in a stock dividend through the example of Gamma Ray Co. Table 17-2 lists the net worth accounts for Gamma Ray Co. before and after a stock dividend is paid. Gamma currently has 500,000 shares outstanding ($10 par), and the stock's current market price is $30. Gamma's net income is $750,000. Assume that Gamma declares a 10% stock dividend. Table 17-2, part b shows what happens.

With a 10% stock dividend, 50,000 new shares are created, and shareholders receive one new share for every ten shares they own. Because the stock price is $30 in the marketplace, Gamma has effectively "created" $30 $\times$ 50,000 = $1.5 million that must be accounted for somehow. A stock dividend does not really in-

TABLE 17-2

Stock Dividends, Gamma Ray Co.[a]

a. Before stock dividend		b. After stock dividend	
Common stock		Common stock	
($10 par, 500,000 shares)	$5,000,000	($10 par, 550,000 shares)	$ 5,500,000
Paid-in capital	2,000,000	Paid-in capital	3,000,000
Retained earnings	8,000,000	Retained earnings	6,500,000
Net worth	$15,000,000	Net worth	$15,000,000

$$EPS = \frac{750,000}{500,000} = \$1.50 \qquad\qquad EPS = \frac{750,000}{550,000} = \$1.36$$

[a] Stock dividends = 10% or 50,000 shares; net income = $750,000; current stock price = $30.

crease the firm's net worth. Instead, the total value of the firm's equity is now spread over a larger number of shares. For this reason, a few accounting changes are made to reflect the effects of the stock dividend. The $1.5 million is removed from the retained earnings account and transferred to the common stock and paid-in capital accounts. Gamma's par value is unchanged, but the common stock account increases by $10 × 50,000 shares, or $500,000. The remaining $1 million from retained earnings goes into the paid-in capital account.

Notice that the net worth for Gamma Ray Co. and the par value of Gamma's stock do not change. It is only the number of shares and the various components of net worth that are different. Because the number of shares increases while the net profits after taxes stay the same, the earnings per share fall from $1.50 to $1.36. However, the total earnings to the stockholders remain unaffected. To see this, note that a stockholder with ten shares before the stock dividend has $1.50 × 10 = $15 in earnings. After the stock dividend, his earnings are $1.36 × 11 = $15. The stockholder now has more shares, but each share earns proportionately less. Thus the stock dividend does not increase the wealth of the shareholder; it is purely an accounting change. In fact, stock dividends are not taxable because the IRS itself does not recognize them as objects of value.

Then why do companies issue stock dividends? There must be some benefit to either the company or the stockholders. Most of the explanations focus on a psychological impact on investors who receive stock dividends. For example, it has been argued that an investor who wishes to liquidate some stock may be more comfortable with liquidating the stock dividend because she does not view this as "dipping into principal." Another argument for stock dividends is that they (like cash dividends) convey some information. If a company in a growth phase wishes to pay dividends but at the same time needs to conserve cash, the stock dividends convey the same signal as cash dividends would have done. Perhaps this is why most growth companies issue stock dividends. Although these explanations are far from entirely satisfactory, there is one situation in which stock dividends do result in an actual dividend increase. This happens when management chooses to maintain the same cash dividends per share even after the stock dividends. Stockholders receive the same dollar amount in cash dividends for each share they own, but they now own more shares.[6] Finally, firms may use stock dividends to keep their stock's market price below a prespecified limit. Some believe that there are advantages to having the stock price sufficiently low because it can increase the demand for the firm's stock. Others have argued that this can actually hurt investors because the commissions on lower-priced stocks tend to be proportionately higher. With a stock dividend, the *EPS* falls, but if the price–earnings (P-E) ratio is the same, the stock price falls.

The disadvantage of stock dividends is that they are much more expensive to administer than cash dividends are. Thus, when used instead of cash dividends, stock dividends can work against the firm's best interests.

STOCK SPLITS A **stock split** is similar to a stock dividend. In fact, a stock split is sometimes considered a large stock dividend. The New York Stock Exchange defines a stock dividend greater than 25% as a stock split. The fundamental difference between a stock dividend and a stock split is that a stock split lowers the stock's par value, whereas a stock dividend has no effect on par value.

---

[6] This is in reality just an increase in the cash dividend, and it may be cheaper for the firm to directly increase the cash dividend. Perhaps the firm is faced with restrictive covenants that prevent dividend increases.

TABLE 17-3
*Two-for-One Stock Split:
Beta Scan Corporation*

a. Before stock split		b. After stock split	
Common stock		Common stock	
($10 par, 200,000 shares)	$2,000,000	($5 par, 400,000 shares)	$2,000,000
Paid-in capital	1,000,000	Paid-in capital	1,000,000
Retained earnings	4,000,000	Retained earnings	4,000,000
Net worth	$7,000,000	Net worth	$7,000,000

Table 17-3 shows the net worth accounts for Beta Scan Corporation before and after a two-for-one stock split. In a two-for-one stock split, every share held by stockholders before the split becomes two shares after the split. Note in Table 17-3 that, just like the stock dividend, the company's net worth is unaffected by the stock split. In a two-for-one stock split, the par value is halved and the number of shares is doubled, but the common stock account, the paid-in capital account, and the retained earnings account are otherwise unaffected.

Stock splits, like stock dividends, do not transmit any extra value to the stockholder. They are accounting rearrangements. Companies announce stock splits primarily to lower the price of their stock so that it is in an "optimal trading range." Consider a stock that was selling at $160 before a split. Management might feel that the stock is "too expensive" for most investors and so lowers it to $80 with a two-for-one split or to $40 with a four-for-one split. Presumably, because the stock is now "more affordable," the increased demand for the stock puts upward pressure on the stock price.

Companies may also split their stock simply to increase the number of shares outstanding. A company that is contemplating being listed on the NYSE may find this appealing. To be listed on the NYSE, a company must have a minimum number of shares outstanding, and a stock split is one way of increasing the number of shares in a short period.

Reverse splits are another form of stock splits, except that the objective is to reduce the number of shares outstanding and increase the price per share. For example, if Beta Scan Corporation (Table 17-3) announces a one-for-two reverse split, every two shares that stockholders own are replaced by one new share. Beta Scan's par value per share now doubles to $20, and the total number of shares outstanding falls to 100,000. Again, the net worth is unaffected.

Some companies announce stock reverse splits to avoid the "penny stock" label. Stocks that sell on, say, the OTC markets for less than $10 are often labeled penny stocks and are generally considered to be very speculative. Many institutional investors are not allowed to invest in these stocks. With a reverse split, a company can appeal to these potential investors. Nonetheless, most participants in the marketplace regard a reverse split as a desperate attempt by a company to prop up its sagging stock price. Whether or not this is true depends on the company's record of past earnings and its potential for future earnings growth.

CORPORATE SHARE REPURCHASE

A corporate share repurchase is often viewed as an alternative to paying dividends. If a firm has some surplus cash (or if it can borrow), it may choose to buy back some of its own stock. Stock can be repurchased in one of two ways: by means of a tender offer or by direct operation in the stock market. In any event, repurchased stock becomes "treasury stock" and plays no real part in the firm's day-to-day affairs. Treasury stock carries with it no voting rights and is not eligible for dividend payments.

It is instructive to see why share repurchases may be viewed as an alternative to paying dividends. One reason a company may repurchase stock is to reduce the number of its shares outstanding. If the P-E ratio does not change after the repurchase, the stock price must rise. In effect, shareholders can realize capital gains with share repurchase, instead of ordinary income with cash dividends. Of course, if the investor is in a high tax bracket, he or she might prefer share repurchases to cash dividends because the present value of the tax liability is lower when the tax is deferred. Thus one of the motives for a share repurchase may be avoiding taxes, although the IRS may, under certain conditions, impose a penalty if it deems this to be the only reason for repurchase.

A second reason for share repurchase also pertains to avoiding taxes. A company may use repurchases to establish a tax-free exchange in a merger. Here is how this works: If Gordy's, Inc., plans to acquire Brittaini Co., Gordy's can simply buy the stock of Brittaini with cash. But exchanging cash for stock forces the current owners of Brittaini to pay taxes on their capital gains. One way to avoid this is for Gordy's to use the cash to repurchase some of its own stock and then use this repurchased stock to acquire Brittaini in a tax-free exchange. Such nontaxable mergers are scrutinized by the IRS, however, and in many instances, the IRS has considered any stock repurchase within two years of a merger as simply a tax-avoidance scheme.

The **good-buy argument** is a third reason advanced for stock repurchase. If it feels that current stock prices are depressed, management may invest in this good buy through a repurchase. For example, Tandy Corporation has, on several occasions, repurchased its own stock:

> *What is the rationale behind the decision to repurchase shares? Tandy management and directors believe the shares represent an attractive investment for the Company and its stockholders. At prices prevailing in recent years, which have been quite modest multiples of current earnings relative to historical norms, the purchase of shares with borrowed funds will enhance the future return on equity and earnings per share growth because the profit margins of the Company are in excess of the interest costs of the funds borrowed.*
>
> *A Statement of Financial Policy,*
> *Tandy Corporation Annual Report, June 30, 1977*

This rationale for repurchase has serious problems. For one thing, when shares are repurchased, there is upward pressure on stock prices. At the same time, if the firm is forgoing better investments to make this repurchase, there is downward pressure on the stock price. Which effect dominates?

Several ethical questions also arise. If management feels that its stock is undervalued, then clearly it has some information that the marketplace does not have. Because it is reasonable to assume that the management of a company has access to information about the company that outsiders do not, does this make repurchases "insider trading"? Insider trading is unfair to certain investors. In the case of a stock repurchase, if management buys "undervalued" stock, then those shareholders who did not sell realize a capital gain. All that has happened is a transfer of wealth from selling shareholders to nonselling shareholders. No value has been created.

Sometimes stock repurchases are justified on the grounds that the company needs the stock for instituting employees' stock option plans. This reason is questionable. Why not issue new shares, instead, to employees who exercise their options?

Finally, stock repurchases, it is sometimes argued, are a way of altering the firm's debt–equity ratio. For a firm that wishes to increase its financial leverage, one al-

MOTIVES FOR STOCK REPURCHASE

*T*here is no agreement on why firms repurchase their shares. The ten most popular explanations for share repurchases provided by managers who did repurchase their shares are the following, in order of frequency of response:

1. Management feels that the stock is undervalued.

2. Repurchase is a signal to investors of management's confidence in the company's future earnings and prices.

3. Repurchases are a means of increasing the firm's leverage.

4. The company has excess cash.

5. The company does not have other investment opportunities for its available cash. (This is similar to #4.)

6. This was a way of providing shares for employee retirement/bonus plans.

7. The firm's stock price has recently lagged in the market. (This is similar to #1.)

8. The general level of market prices is low.

9. It is part of a defensive strategy to avoid a takeover.

10. It provides shares for dividend reinvestment plans.

SOURCE: Information adapted from James Wansley, William Lane, and Salil Sarkar, "Management's View on Share Repurchase and Tender Offer Premiums," Financial Management 18 (Autumn 1989): 97–110.

ternative is to issue new debt and use the proceeds to buy back some common stock. But this is seldom done. The most popular reasons for share repurchases are given in the highlight above.

17-2
DIVIDENDS AND FIRM VALUE

Dividends in Perfect Capital Markets

*P*erfect markets are an idealized version of the capital markets where there are no transactions costs or taxes, all investors have identical beliefs, and so on. The dividend policy implications in this simplified scenario provide some powerful insights into the basic conditions under which dividends can affect stock prices.

Dividend policy can be viewed as one of a firm's investment decisions. Consider a firm that is planning to pay out dividends from its current earnings. Management's choice of the dollar amount of the dividend is determined by the dollar amount of investment in acceptable projects. If the amount required to accept all available projects is less than the total earnings and other internally available funds, the residual or surplus sums are paid out to stockholders in the form of dividends. If, on the other hand, the firm's earnings are insufficient to accept all of the good investments available, the firm does not pay dividends. In fact, management must raise additional capital to finance all the investments. The firm in question is thus treating dividend policy as strictly a financing decision. In this framework, dividend policy is a residual decision.

THE RESIDUAL THEORY OF DIVIDENDS

According to the **residual theory of dividends,** dividend policy is a residual of investment policy. Whether or not a company pays dividends depends on its investment policy.

How does the residual theory work? After examining all the investment alternatives, the firm first estimates its dollar investment requirement and then its funds available from internal sources (earnings and depreciation). Next the firm decides on a long-run target debt–equity ratio and whether any residual funds are available for dividend payments. If there is a residual, the ratio of these residual funds to total earnings becomes the firm's long-run **target payout ratio.** If no residual funds are expected, the firm adopts a **zero payout ratio** (i.e., it pays no dividends).

In perfect markets, the dividends themselves are not relevant to the stockholder. The seminal article on dividend irrelevance in perfect capital markets is by Merton H. Miller and Franco Modigliani (M & M).[7] If the firm can use the funds to earn a return greater than the investor's required rate of return, the investor will not object to the firm's retention of earnings. But if the return from the firm's investment opportunities is less than his or her required rate of return, the investor will want the firm to pay dividends. Thus there is no need for management to waste time analyzing the effect of dividends on value; the company merely needs to analyze its investment opportunities carefully. Dividend policy is thus a policy for disbursing surplus funds.

Although the residual theory of dividends appears to make any further analysis of dividend policy unnecessary, it is actually not clear that dividends are solely a means of disbursing excess funds. It is therefore imprudent to conclude that there are no other implications of dividend policy, and so we take a closer look at the relationship between dividends and value.

THE DIVIDEND IRRELEVANCE ARGUMENT

We assume that the firm's dividend policy decision is made after its investment decisions are made and that the firm borrows no more money. By holding these variables constant, we can examine whether dividends are relevant by investigating the effect of a change in cash dividends on the shareholders' wealth. Notice that if the firm does not wish to borrow any more, then plans to increase dividend payments must be financed by issuing new stock.

In the simplified world of perfect markets, it can be argued that dividends have no impact on stock prices. To understand this, consider Jennifer Camden, a stockholder in Greenwich Diecast Company. Her stock currently has a market value of $3 per share. Since Greenwich Diecast has 1,000,000 shares outstanding, this translates into an equity market value of $3,000,000 ($3 × 1,000,000). Greenwich Diecast also has debt with a market value of $2,000,000, giving it the following market-value balance sheet:

GREENWICH DIECAST BALANCE SHEET BEFORE DIVIDENDS

ASSETS: $5,000,000	DEBT:	$2,000,000
	EQUITY:	3,000,000
		$5,000,000

Since the market value of the firm is the sum of the market values of the claims on the firm, Greenwich Diecast has a market value of $5,000,000. Jennifer wants to receive some extra cash from her investment. How can she do this? She has two alternative ways of getting this cash:

Alternative 1: Greenwich pays an extra cash dividend.

Alternative 2: She sells all or some of her stock in the marketplace.

Through simple analysis, Jennifer can see that, in perfect capital markets, the alternatives are equivalent.

[7]"Dividend Policy, Growth, and the Valuation of Shares," *Journal of Business,* October 1961, pp. 411–433.

ALTERNATIVE 1 If Greenwich Diecast pays a cash dividend of $0.50 per share, it must raise new capital if it still wants to make its investments. Because it cannot borrow money, the firm sells new stock after paying the extra dividend to its existing stockholders such as Jennifer. The value of the firm does not change because it depends on the return offered by the firm's assets, the investments have already been chosen, and there is no more borrowing. This follows from our finding in earlier chapters that the value of the firm is determined by the firm's operating cash flows.

If Greenwich Diecast's value is not changing and new stockholders buy newly issued stock, the old stockholders must suffer a loss of wealth because the firm's value has to be shared with the new stockholders. What is the value of this capital loss? It is equal to that part of the firm's value that belongs to the new stockholders. If the new stockholders pay a fair price for their stock, however, the value of the new stockholders' equity must equal the extra dividends paid to the old owners. Thus the old stockholders suffer a capital loss exactly equal to the dividends they receive, and their total wealth has not changed. After the extra dividends, old stockholders own the same number of shares, but each is worth less than before.

Since there are 1,000,000 shares, the firm must issue $500,000 in new equity to finance the dividend payments to old equityholders. The value of the old shares must equal $2,500,000 [$5,000,000 (assets) less $2,000,000 (debt) less $500,000 (new equity)]. Since there are 1,000,000 shares, each share is therefore worth $2.50. Thus the number of new shares issued is $500,000/$2.50 = 200,000.

Greenwich Diecast's balance sheet now looks like this:

GREENWICH DIECAST BALANCE SHEET AFTER IT PAYS A $0.50/SHARE DIVIDEND

ASSETS: $5,000,000	DEBT:	$2,000,000	
	NEW EQUITY:	500,000	(200,000 SHARES @ $2.50)
	OLD EQUITY:	2,500,000	(1,000,000 SHARES @ $2.50)
		$5,000,000	

In this situation, the wealth of the old shareholders is $2,500,000 + $500,000 (dividends) = $3,000,000.

ALTERNATIVE 2 Now consider the second alternative. If Jennifer sells some of her stock to someone else, she has fewer shares of stock and each share is worth exactly the same amount as before the sale because no new shares are issued. Clearly, Jennifer's realized cash (effectively, a dividend) equals the loss in her equity ownership of the firm.

Old shareholders such as Jennifer can liquidate some of their shares to create **homemade dividends.** Since there are no new shares issued in this situation, the number of shares remains 1,000,000, each worth $3. To create $500,000 in homemade dividends, the shareholders liquidate $500,000/$3 = 166,666.67 shares. The value of the old shares must now equal $5,000,000 − $2,000,000 − $500,000 = $2,500,000. The new balance sheet looks like this:

GREENWICH DIECAST BALANCE SHEET AFTER CREATION OF "HOMEMADE DIVIDENDS"

ASSETS: $5,000,000	DEBT:	$2,000,000	
	NEW SHAREHOLDERS:	500,000	(166,666.67 SHARES @ $3
	OLD SHAREHOLDERS:	2,500,000	(833,333.33 SHARES @ $3)
		$5,000,000	

Irrelevance of dividends in perfect markets. The old stockholders can achieve the same effect (cash) without any action by the firm. Thus no dividend policy decision has an impact on the stockholders' wealth.

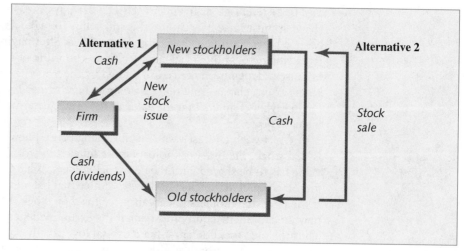

The wealth of the old shareholders is $2,500,000 + $500,000 (liquidated shares) = $3,000,000.

These two alternatives are equivalent. If the firm pays a dividend, it is doing what Jennifer can do by herself. To be more specific, there is no difference between alternative 1, in which the firm pays a dividend and lowers the stockholder's equity position, and alternative 2, in which the stockholder sells off some of her equity by herself. Stockholders can, in effect, create homemade dividends, and the act of paying dividends by the firm should have no effect on their value. In other words, dividend policy is irrelevant. Figure 17-2 depicts this discussion. Note that the benefits from a dividend payment can be replicated by stockholders without any action by the firm. Why, then, should dividends increase stock values? In perfect capital markets, dividends have no impact on stock price. These arguments for dividend irrelevance in perfect markets were first put forth by Miller and Modigliani.

WHAT HAPPENS WHEN A COMPANY CUTS ITS DIVIDENDS?

Our discussion so far has considered the case of a firm increasing its dividend. But what if the firm plans to cut its dividends? Because investment and borrowing policies are assumed to be fixed, the reduction in dividends must be matched by a reduction in the number of shares of stock to be issued or by a repurchase of already existing stock. This is the exact opposite of the previous situation, in which a firm issues stock. By repurchasing stock, the firm decreases the number of shares outstanding, and because the firm's value is unchanged, each share is worth more. As far as the stockholder is concerned, the reduction in dividends is matched by an increase in the value of his shares, and so repurchase has no net impact on his wealth.

A CLOSER LOOK AT THE IRRELEVANCE ARGUMENT

Having examined the basic insights provided by Miller and Modigliani (M & M) with regard to dividend irrelevance in perfect markets, we now look more closely at some issues crucial to this result.

The most important requirement for dividend irrelevance is that markets be efficient. When a company issues new stock to finance its increased dividend, dividend policy is irrelevant if the new stock is sold at a fair price. Because efficient markets ensure that all assets are fairly priced, the dividend irrelevance arguments really require that markets be efficient. This is crucial to the validity of the M & M results.

A common criticism of the dividend irrelevance argument is the "bird-in-the-hand" argument. An investor's return from owning stock comes from yields in dividends and capital gains. It is generally accepted that stocks with high dividend yields provide smaller capital gains. Even if an increase in dividend yields is exactly offset by a decrease in capital gains, one cannot choose between the two without looking explicitly at risk. Managers like to follow a stable dividend policy and, because they cannot control the vagaries of the stock market, the "bird-in-the-handers" contend that dividend payments are less risky and therefore risk-averse investors should prefer them.[8] This argument is fallacious, however, because the value of the firm is determined by the overall cash flows generated by the assets—and this does not depend on dividend policy. We are really saying that net operating income is not affected by a firm's dividend payout. (Also remember that borrowing and investment decisions have already been made.)

KEY CONCEPT   In perfect markets, it is investment policy, not dividend policy, that determines firm value.

Dividends with Market Imperfections and Taxes

As we have seen, the irrelevance of dividend policy rests on the assumption of perfect and efficient markets. But the real world has several imperfections, and it is interesting to look at the impact of some of them on dividend policy.

FLOTATION COSTS

The dividend irrelevance discussion assumes that if a company chooses to pay an extra dividend, it can easily finance this by issuing new equity. Because the costs of selling the new equity are not recognized, new equity, in effect, becomes a perfect substitute for the extra dividend. As a practical matter, however, flotation costs—the costs associated with issuing a new security (e.g., brokers' commissions)—make retained earnings more attractive to the firm than a new stock issue. With transactions costs, dividends and new equity are no longer essentially the same, and it does not make economic sense to pay out dividends and then to replace the lost funds with more costly new equity. Thus flotation costs tend to favor lower dividend payouts.

TRANSACTIONS COSTS

Whenever investors sell or buy a financial asset, they incur transactions costs in the form of brokerage commissions. Consider the case of a stockholder who desires a higher dividend. This could be achieved by selling some of his own stock (alternative 2). However, because of transactions costs, this investor prefers higher dividends on his current stock. With higher dividends, the sale of the stock may become unnecessary, and the investor may avoid the transactions costs entirely. This shareholder should therefore prefer that the company pay higher dividends (ignoring tax considerations).

This preference does not necessarily mean that the firm should favor higher dividend payouts because other investors may not need the dividend to increase their current consumption; instead, they may want to increase their capital gains. For such investors, a firm's dividend payment may not be an attractive feature because the dividends must be reinvested in another financial asset. Because of brokerage

---

[8] Recall from Chapter 13 that a firm can increase dividends and lower stock prices by investing in economically unattractive projects.

commissions, these investors are forced to incur additional expenses. On the other hand, if the firm retains the dividend and invests it on behalf of the stockholder, the investor receives an eventual capital gain without incurring any transactions costs in the meantime.

Thus, given investors' different preferences for dividends and capital gains, there is no clear implication for a firm's dividend policy. Firms that have high dividend payout ratios attract investors who prefer current income, and low-payout firms attract stockholders who prefer capital gains. This is the **clientele effect**—a firm attracts the clientele that approves of its dividend policies. As a result, companies have an incentive to publicize their dividend policies by maintaining a stable, predictable dividend. Potential shareholders can then know beforehand whether a particular firm's dividend policy is in their best interest. A sudden change in dividend policy will cause some rearrangement in the firm's ownership. Disapproving stockholders may sell out, thereby putting downward pressure on stock prices. Because of this, managers favor a "sticky" (stable) dividend policy. Table 17-4 is a partial list of companies that have consistently paid dividends.

INSTITUTIONAL CONSTRAINTS

CONTRACTUAL CONSTRAINTS When a firm borrows money (debt capital), the contract between the firm and the creditors may include some constraints to protect the bondholders. Similarly, a firm that issues preferred stock may be constrained in some ways to protect the preferred stockholders. For example, firms are sometimes allowed to declare dividends only out of earnings generated after the debt contract goes into effect. Additional restrictions on the firm's working capital are common. Preferred stock contracts usually stipulate that common stockholders cannot be paid any new dividends unless all preferred dividends in arrears have been paid.

LEGAL CONSTRAINTS Many institutions are not allowed by law to invest in securities that have not had a long record of high dividends. Perhaps these legal requirements are the result of historical beliefs that dividends reveal a firm's health. Such restrictions force these institutions to prefer firms with liberal dividend payouts. At the minimum, many institutional investors require a "token" dividend as an "entrance requirement," particularly since the Employee Retirement Act of 1974.

Several universities and trusts are forbidden by law to use capital gains from their investments. Instead, they rely on the cash "throw-off" from their stock (i.e., dividends) to fund scholarships, endowments, and so on. These institutions, too, have a logical preference for stocks with high dividend payouts. The dividend income is used to service other fixed obligations. Dividends become all the more attractive because most universities do not pay taxes.

TABLE 17-4
Some Consistent Dividend-Paying Companies[a]

American Express	Heinz (H.J.)	Pfizer, Inc.
Anheuser-Busch	Johnson & Johnson	Quaker Oats
Beneficial Corp.	Mercantile Stores	SAFECO Corp.
duPont (EI) deNemours	Minnesota Min'g. & Mfg.	Thomas & Betts
Dun & Bradstreet	Monsanto Co.	Transamerica Corp.
First of America Bank	Norfolk Southern	UST Inc.
First Tennessee National	Ohio Casualty	U.S. Trust
First Union Corp.	Old Kent Financial	Washington Gas Light
Florida Progress.	PPG Industries	Wilmington Trust Corp.
GATX Corp.	Peoples Energy	

SOURCE: *The Outlook*, August 25, 1993.
[a] These are some well-known corporations that have been paying at least one annual dividend consistently for more than 50 years.

State laws can also affect dividend policy, at least to the extent that insolvent firms are not allowed to pay dividends. A firm is declared insolvent when the value of its liabilities exceeds the value of its assets. Zero payout is a legal requirement for insolvent firms.

CORPORATE TAXES Corporate taxes have no impact on the dividend decision because dividends are paid only out of net income (NI).[9] Corporate taxes enter the picture before the dividend issue needs to be addressed by management. Thus corporate tax effects should not influence a firm's optimal dividend policy. There is, however, an exception. If a company retains an excessive amount of earnings without paying dividends, the IRS may penalize it for "improper accumulation." The IRS interprets this to be a tax dodge unless the firm is able to justify its need for internally generated funds. By retaining "too much" within the firm, investors can benefit from lower taxes. Retention increases the price of the stock, and taxes on capital gains can be deferred. Justifying their need for internally generated funds is not, however, a difficult task for most (large) companies.

PERSONAL TAXES Unlike corporate taxes, investors' personal taxes should influence dividend policy. Except for the period between the 1986 Tax Reform Act and the Omnibus Budget Reconciliation Act of 1993, the tax law has clearly favored low payouts by firms because shareholders have to pay higher marginal tax rates on dividend income than on long-term capital gains. In addition, with capital gains, the investor has the option of deferring taxes until the stock is actually sold. Depending on their particular tax liabilities, investors who are in a low tax bracket lean toward high dividend payout firms, investors who are in a high tax bracket prefer low-payout firms, and investors who are exempt from paying taxes are indifferent, all else being the same. It is this clientele effect that can be used to argue that dividend policy is irrelevant even when investors' marginal tax rates are taken into account.

This argument is as follows: Given that different investors have different tax rates and consequently different preferences for dividends, companies should recognize the demand for different payout policies and adjust their dividend policies to satisfy the demands of these different clienteles. For example, assume that there are only two classes of investors: those in the 10% tax bracket (preferring dividends) and those in the 30% tax bracket (preferring capital gains). If all firms in the economy were high-payout firms, it would be in the best interests of a company to switch to a low-payout policy to attract investors in the 30% tax bracket. By increasing the demand for its stock, the company is increasing its stock price. Thus it appears that dividends do affect value, although this is only a short-run phenomenon. As firms switch to low-payout policies, the demand for low-payout stocks is eventually filled, and when this happens, changing the dividend policy will not affect stock price. In this equilibrium setting, dividend policy is irrelevant.

But if dividends are irrelevant, why do so many companies pay them? And why are some dividends so large? A partial explanation is that the market imperfections examined earlier may encourage dividends. Shouldn't the tax law bias that favors lower dividends be the dominant factor affecting dividend policy? That is, shouldn't the taxation of dividends encourage firms to pay lower dividends? How can we explain the empirical evidence, which seemingly makes no sense? There must be

---

[9] One can argue that if the alternative to paying dividends is retention of funds within the firm, then the value of the retained funds will be based on capitalization of after-tax earnings on those funds. In this sense, the dividend question may not be entirely independent of corporate taxes.

AVOIDING TAXES ON DIVIDENDS

*I*f the current tax law favors low dividends, the reason for the high payouts of corporations is perhaps that investors can avoid paying taxes on dividends. In fact, Miller and Scholes argue that there is ample opportunity to avoid personal taxes on dividends.* Let us see how.

Consider the case of Mr. Rostow, who currently owns $25,000 worth of Ziebolt, Inc. stock. Zieboldt has a current dividend yield of 6% and an expected capital gain of 4%. At the end of the year Mr. Rostow will therefore have to declare $1,500 (6% of $25,000) in dividends and $1,000 (4% of $25,000) in capital gains in his tax return. Mr. Rostow can neutralize the tax on dividend income by borrowing, say, $25,000 at an interest rate of 12% and investing this sum in Ziebolt stock. Mr. Rostow's tax situation is summarized below:

Dividends from stock: 6% of ($25,000 + $25,000)	$3,000
Interest on borrowing: 12% of $25,000	−3,000
Net income	0
Expected capital gain: 4% of $50,000	$2,000

Because dividends are ordinary income for tax purposes and interest payments are deductible from ordinary income, the personal tax on dividends is $0 for Mr. Rostow. However, he has picked up an expected $2,000 in capital gains. One could argue that the benefit of avoiding taxes on dividends has been offset by the increased risk that Mr. Rostow is taking (borrowing and investing in risky stock). If Mr. Rostow wanted to avoid this risk, he could do so by using an insurance annuity or by increasing his contributions to a pension fund.

Instead of borrowing $25,000, Mr. Rostow could borrow only $12,500 at 12% interest and invest these proceeds in a single-premium insurance annuity. If Mr. Rostow does this, the insurance company has to invest the funds in a risk-free asset and repay Mr. Rostow $12,500 with compounded interest at a later (prespecified) date. Mr. Rostow's risk has therefore not increased, and he has avoided taxes on dividends:

Dividends from stock: 6% of $25,000	$1,500
Interest on borrowing: 12% of $12,500	−1,500
Net income	$0

In addition, recognize that the insurance company does not pay taxes, so some day in the future, Mr. Rostow will incur a capital gain. However, the benefits of tax-deferred income can be substantial before then.

*See Fischer Black and Myron Scholes, "The Effects of Dividend Yield and Dividend Policy on Common Stock Prices and Returns," Journal of Financial Economics, May 1974, pp. 1–22.

some other reason involving taxes that reveals this apparent discrepancy between theory and evidence. How do we reconcile the tax-induced bias toward low dividends and the liberal payout policies of several major corporations?

As it turns out, it may be possible to avoid personal taxes on dividends by investing in life insurance companies and pension funds. Thus personal tax considerations may be irrelevant from the dividend policy standpoint (see the highlight). It is not easy to avoid taxes on dividends, though, because the procedures for doing so can be used only in special circumstances. Also, the tax code does not allow many "tax-neutralizing schemes."

THE EMPIRICAL EVIDENCE REGARDING DIVIDENDS AND TAXES

If dividends are taxed at higher rates than capital gains are, as they were before the 1986 Tax Reform Act and now under the Omnibus Budget Reconciliation Act of 1993, then we expect that stocks that pay high dividends will sell for lower prices (and so have higher yields) than stocks that pay low dividends. There is a large body of empirical evidence about the effect of dividend yields on stock returns.[10] Most of the studies support the argument that high-dividend stocks do in

[10] For example, F. Black and M. Scholes, "The Effects of Dividend Yield and Dividend Policy on Common Stock Prices and Returns," *Journal of Financial Economics* 1 (1974): 1–22; R. H. Litzenber-

fact have lower prices and thus higher returns. Despite the substantial evidence supporting this view, however, the issue has not yet been resolved, and the debate is continuing. Some economists contend that there are serious technical problems inherent in all these tests because they cannot satisfactorily establish the link between dividend yield and expected return. Moreover, considering that a firm pays dividends only a few times a year, how can a high- or low-dividend stock be identified? Should a high-yield stock on the day of the dividend payment be considered a high-dividend stock two months later when its dividend yield is lower?

Because of these and other technical problems pertaining to these empirical tests, we do not explore them further. In any case, the tax implications of dividend policy are still not clear.

Market Reaction to Dividend Initiations, Stock Splits, and Stock Repurchases

FIRST-TIME DIVIDENDS

Although most companies pay dividends, some companies never do. How does the market respond to the first dividend payment made by one of these firms? In May 1987, Apple Computer declared its first dividend—a cash dividend of 4 cents per share on its common stock, for a total of $5 million. On the day this announcement was made, the market value of the company's equity rose by $219 million. Is this a typical reaction? How can we explain this increase in stockholder wealth after having argued that dividends do not matter?

Remember that it is not the dividends per se but the information contained in the change of financial policy that is significant. Does the decision to pay dividends indicate a permanent increase in future earnings? In this case, the increase in equity values can be explained as the market's reaction to a more optimistic forecast of a firm's operations.

Using 131 stocks on the New York and American Stock Exchanges, Healey and Palepu examined the earnings growth pattern after dividends were first paid, between 1970 and 1979.[11] They found that these firms exhibited flat earnings until the year before they announced their first dividend payment. Then their earnings rose at impressive rates over the next three years. This is strong evidence that initiating dividends can communicate to market managers the expectation of the firm's future earnings.

STOCK SPLITS

When General Motors announced a two-for-one stock split in February 1989, the market value of the firm's equity increased by $1.3 billion. Most managers claim that General Motors split its stock in order to lower the stock price so that it would be within the optimal trading range. Firms with permanent earnings increases tend to split their stock to put pressure on the price to rise above this range. On the other hand, firms with only temporary earnings increases do not split their stock because that will not put pressure on the stock price. Thus, if managers have better information than the market does, a stock split may signal a permanent increase in earnings.

---

ger and K. Ramaswamy, "The Effect of Personal Taxes and Dividends on Capital Asset Prices: Theory and Empirical Evidence," *Journal of Financial Economics* 7 (1979): 163–195; "The Effects of Dividends on Common Stock Prices: Tax Effects or Information Effects," *Journal of Finance* 37 (1982): 429–443; and M. H. Miller and M. Scholes, "Dividends and Taxes: Some Empirical Evidence," *Journal of Political Economy* 90 (1982): 1118–1141.

[11] P. Healey and K. Palepu, "Earnings Information Conveyed by Dividend Initiations and Omissions," *Journal of Financial Economics* 21 (1988): 149–176.

Asquith, Healey, and Palepu followed 121 stock distributions between 1970 and 1980 to determine whether firms that split their stock did have permanent increases in earnings.[12] Their results indicate not only that such companies had large earnings increases for several years before the split, but that they also had larger earnings in the year of the split. Moreover, these earnings did not drop over the next five years, which suggests that stock splits do appear to signal permanent increases in earnings. The higher stock prices thus seem to be a result of the market's revised estimate of a firm's equity value after the new information implicit in the stock split.

STOCK REPURCHASES

Several studies have investigated the market's response to stock repurchases.[13] The market seems to look with favor on stock repurchases through the open market or tender offers. In these cases, the firm's managers seem to have better information about future prospects, and so they buy back the stock because it is undervalued. This signal to the marketplace pressures the stock price to go up. Thus signaling through repurchases is an alternative to signaling through dividends. Indeed, in many corporate repurchases between 1971 and 1974, dividend increases were under a voluntary freeze.

Single-block repurchases, especially those that end a takeover threat, are injurious to stockholders' returns.[14] If management can keep control of the firm in these cases, the market appears to "give back" the value gains that it had expected from the new management's greater efficiency.

17-3

OTHER FACTORS THAT AFFECT THE FIRM'S DIVIDEND POLICY

In addition to the market imperfections that can affect a firm's dividend policy—transactions costs, flotation costs, institutional restrictions—other firm-specific factors must be considered when dividend decisions are made.

THE FIRM'S FINANCIAL RESERVES

Managerial Considerations

The dollar amount of dividends that a company pays is influenced to a great extent by its financial reserves. Cash, other liquid assets, and unused borrowing capacity are examples of financial reserves. Consider a company that has an unexpected but temporary reduction in earnings. Rather than lower the amount of dividends it pays, the company could draw on its financial reserves to keep the dividends at their originally planned level. In another situation, if the firm's financial reserves are deemed to be excessive, management can reduce this excess by temporarily increasing its dividends.

FLEXIBILITY

If a firm can postpone some new investments, this flexibility may help management maintain a stable dividend policy. Temporary decreases in earnings thus need

[12] P. Asquith, P. Healey, and K. Palepu, "Earnings and Stock Splits," *Accounting Review*, July 1989, pp. 387–403.

[13] For example, R. M. Masulis, "Stock Returns by Tender Offer: An Analysis of the Causes of Common Stock Price Changes," *Journal of Finance* 35 (1980): 305–319; L. Y. Dann, "Common Stock Repurchases: An Analysis of Returns to Bondholders and Stockholders," *Journal of Financial Economics* 9 (1981): 113–138; and T. Vermaelen, "Common Stock Repurchases and Market Signalling: An Empirical Study," *Journal of Financial Economics* 9 (1981): 139–183.

[14] For example, M. Bradley and L. M. Wakeman, "The Wealth Effects of Targeted Share Repurchases," *Journal of Financial Economics* 11 (1983): 301–328.

not lead to dividend decreases. Funds earmarked for specific investments can instead be used to pay dividends.

ACCESS TO EQUITY CAPITAL

Access to new equity capital plays a major role in influencing a management's decision to pursue a residual or a nonresidual dividend policy. Recall that a residual policy implies that the firm first uses its earnings to accept new investments and then pays out the surpluses, if any, as dividends. Following a residual policy may spare a firm the problem of fresh equity financing. But if equity capital is easily available at a reasonable cost, the company may find it advantageous to deviate from its residual policy. If its stockholders want a larger dividend, the company can go ahead and issue new stock to finance the extra disbursement. All firms may not be able to do this, however. Larger, more established firms have more ready access to new equity capital than do smaller, developing companies. This is one reason that most of the new high-tech companies pay very low dividends. Maintaining a stable dividend policy is easier when there is ready access to new equity. Even with temporarily depressed earnings, dividends may not have to be cut if new, inexpensive equity capital is readily available.

CONTROL CONSIDERATIONS

With a liberal dividend policy, a company increases its chances of raising fresh capital at some future date. If the current shareholders cannot subscribe (or do not subscribe) to the new shares, new stockholders dilute their controlling interest in the firm. Thus stockholders who are very sensitive to a potential loss of control prefer a low dividend payout policy.

ABILITY TO BORROW

There is no reason that a company should finance future needs with equity only. It need not rule out debt, the other obvious alternative. Short-term borrowing capacity through established lines of credit with a bank can increase the firm's flexibility and, consequently, its dividend payouts. In addition, the ability to float a new bond issue increases the company's ability to pay dividends. But management may often be unwilling to increase its debt for one reason or another. For example, the firm might already have excessive financial leverage, or the debt may be too expensive. In such cases the company may not be able to be very generous with its dividend payments.

INFLATION

During periods of inflation, funds generated from depreciation may be insufficient to replace outdated or unusable plant and machinery. Replacement costs may be so high that companies may have to acquire new equipment with a fresh influx of capital. In situations such as this, a company may want to reduce its payout ratio to ensure that it has sufficient amount of internally generated funds to finance necessary replacements or even a new expansion.

DIVIDEND CUTS AS A STRATEGIC DEVICE

DeAngelo and DeAngelo find evidence that managers may cut or reduce dividends to increase their bargaining position with organized labor or other stakeholders.[15] Bethlehem Steel, for example, reduced its dividends and indicated that

---

[15] H. DeAngelo and L. DeAngelo, "Dividend Policy and Financial Distress: An Empirical Investigation of Troubled NYSE Firms," *Journal of Finance* 45 (December 1990): 1415–1431.

"it would seek to restructure its labor agreement with the United Steelworkers union 'well before' the contract expires." Thus management may use dividend cuts to communicate credibly to organized labor that the firm is, in fact, experiencing serious trouble.

Agency Explanations of Dividends

Some economists believe that management decides to pay dividends in order to reduce agency costs.[16] By issuing dividends, management is forced to go to the capital markets for additional financing. Each time it attempts to raise fresh capital, its operations are intensely scrutinized by investment bankers, accountants, and other market professionals. Because these parties have a comparative advantage over the bondholders in monitoring the firm's activities, dividend payments accompanied by subsequent new financing may lower monitoring costs and thereby increase firm value.

Dividend payments accompanied by new security issues can lower another agency cost that arises from managers' risk aversion. Given that stockholders have limited liability, they want managers to invest in risky projects. Bondholders, on the other hand, want the opposite. Managers whose livelihoods depend on the firm's success and survival tend to avoid risky projects because they increase the chance of bankruptcy. Thus, even when it is in the best interests of the shareholders, managers' risk aversion can force them to make suboptimal decisions (i.e., safe projects). This agency cost can be reduced by a firm that repeatedly visits the capital markets. New investors carefully evaluate management's behavior before buying stock, and they bid down the price of the stock if they see managers making self-serving investment decisions. Thus managers of firms that repeatedly raise capital are under pressure to lower these agency costs by behaving in the best interests of the stockholders. In this manner, dividends and repeated capital acquisition can increase a firm's value.

Psychological Aspects of Dividends

Many investors favor dividends, and so companies continue to pay them. Standard explanations of this preference for dividends are unsatisfactory. It is unlikely that investors who think rationally about every other aspect of the market are inexplicably irrational about their desire for dividends. But this apparently irrational preference has been explained on behavioral grounds using the theory of self-control and the theory of choice under uncertainty.[17]

In the theory of self-control of investor behavior, all individuals have two conflicting aspects: that of a farsighted "planner" who is concerned with the future and that of a selfish "doer" who wants to consume now. A planner may establish rules to control the doer, who favors dividends. For example, the planner may institute a rule of "never spending capital." A young investor with a strong desire to save may invest in stocks that do not pay dividends. His savings will steadily increase as long as he maintains his personal rule against spending capital. An older investor, on the other hand, may invest heavily in stocks that do pay divi-

[16] See F. H. Easterbrook, "Two Agency Cost Explanations of Dividends," *American Economic Review* 74 (1984): 650–659. Also see M. S. Rozeff, "Growth, Beta and Agency Costs As Determinants of Dividend Payout Ratios," *Journal of Financial Research* 5 (1982): 249–259.

[17] D. Kahneman and A. Tversky, "Prospect Theory: An Analysis of Decision Under Risk," *Econometrica,* March 1979, pp. 263–291; H. M. Shefrin and M. Statman, "Explaining Investor Preference for Cash Dividends," *Journal of Financial Economics,* February 1984, pp. 253–282; and R. Thaler and H. M. Shefrin, "An Economic Theory of Self-Control," *Journal of Political Economy* 89 (1981): 392–406.

dends because he can spend his dividend checks without violating the rule against spending capital.

Dividends also are attractive because they assure investors of receiving at least a minimum return on their investment. Any capital gains are viewed as an added bonus. According to the theory of choice under uncertainty, losses seem worse than gains. That is, the unhappiness caused by a $100 loss is proportionately greater than the happiness created by a $100 gain. This is consistent with the observation that the decreases in stock prices that accompany dividend cuts are larger than the stock price gains that accompany dividend increases.[18] Companies can get around this psychological barrier by declaring a special or "extra" dividend when they have a temporary increase in earnings, instead of raising the regular dividend. If they later have to cut one of them, it will be more palatable to cut the extra dividend rather than the regular dividend. The loss of the extra dividend is perceived as a failure to receive a bonus, whereas a cut in the regular dividend is viewed as a damaging loss in income.

Because of investors' feelings of loss, dividends and proceeds from the sale of stock are not perfect substitutes, and thus consumption from dividends is preferred to consumption from capital for investors who may have such feelings.

A Concluding Comment

The previous paragraphs have highlighted some of the factors that must be taken into account when managers set dividend policy. Unfortunately, there is no clear-cut formula or decision-theoretic methodology for setting dividend policy. Part of the problem is that the link between dividends and firm value is not altogether clear. This problem is compounded by the effects of several other factors—liquidity, control considerations, access to equity markets. Even if dividends do affect a firm's value, unless management knows exactly *how* they affect value, there is not much they can do to increase the stockholders' wealth. The following sentiments of a corporate executive defending his company's decision not to pay dividends illustrates the general problem:

> *The whole issue of financial structure, cash needs of a corporation, and maximizing return on investment in an inflationary business environment is a complex and multifaceted issue in an ever-changing environment. There may be a time when the capital requirements of the Company, dividend tax policy, and money market patterns will point to the adoption of a dividend program for the common stock. Until then, however, it appears the most effective service to shareholders will be the continued effort to provide capital appreciation through continued growth of our Company.*
>
> *Gerald P. Asher,*
> *Director of Financial Planning, Tandy Corporation*

Incorporating all these factors into a valuation framework, even if possible, would be unlikely to provide simple operational guidelines for management. It is somewhat ironic that after so much research into the dividend policy of a firm, we still have no recommendations. To conclude, we quote Fisher Black: "What should corporations do about dividend policy? We don't know."[19]

---

[18] Another explanation for this might be that since dividend decreases are less common (than increases), they are more unexpected.

[19] See Fischer Black, "The Dividend Puzzle," *Journal of Portfolio Management*, Winter 1976, pp. 5–8; reprinted in C. W. Smith, Jr., ed., *The Modern Theory of Corporate Finance*, pp. 215–220 (New York: McGraw-Hill, 1990).

SUMMARY

Section 17-1: Dividend Payment Policies and Procedures

What are some standard corporate dividend payment policies and procedures?

- Managers tend to follow stable dividend policies characterized by constant dividends per share, constant payout ratios, or regular dividends accompanied with "extras." Legal listing is one reason for the stability.

- Dividends have informational content and signal the firm's prospects to the marketplace.

- On the ex-dividend date, the stock price falls by approximately the amount of the declared dividend.

- Many firms offer automatic dividend reinvestment plans.

What are stock dividends and stock splits? Why do firms split stocks and pay stock dividends?

- A stock dividend is a dividend payment to owners with additional stock. A stock dividend leaves the stock's par value unaffected.

- After a stock split, the owner of the stock has more shares of the firm's stock, but each share is worth proportionally less. In a stock split, the stock's par value is lowered. A reverse split reduces the number of shares outstanding.

- There is no clear agreement on why firms issue stock dividends or split stocks.

- Most explanations of stock dividends focus on either the positive informational impact or the psychological impact it can have in the marketplace. Another explanation is that there is an advantage to keeping the stock price "sufficiently low," and stock dividends, because they lower stock prices, benefit the firm. Some argue that this actually hurts the investors by increasing their transactions costs.

- Some managers believe that by splitting a stock, they can lower its price to be within the "optimal trading range" so that the demand for the stock increases. A firm that plans to be listed on a major stock exchange may split stock simply to meet exchange requirements about the number of outstanding shares.

Why do firms repurchase shares?

- A share repurchase is an alternative to paying a cash dividend. One argument for repurchases is that they allow the owners to benefit from lower taxes or to avoid taxes altogether in a tax-free exchange.

- With informational asymmetry between managers and the marketplace, managers may know that the stock is undervalued relative to the information that they possess, and buying back the stock can benefit stockholders.

- Some argue that firms repurchase shares to place them in employees' stock option plans. Others suggest that share repurchases are used to alter the firm's debt–equity ratio. Neither explanation is entirely satisfactory.

Section 17-2: Dividends and Firm Value

What is the link between dividend payments and firm value in perfect markets?

- In perfect markets, the firm's dividend policy has no impact on wealth. It is the firm's investment policy that determines stockholders' wealth.

■ Any cash dividend payment by the firm can be replicated by investors who can liquidate some shares to create "homemade dividends." Thus dividends are irrelevant in perfect markets.

What is the empirical evidence in regard to dividends?

■ Although the issue is unresolved, there is extensive evidence to indicate that high-dividend stocks have lower prices and higher returns.

■ Firms that initiate a dividend experience earnings increases in subsequent years.

■ Stock splits are accompanied by stock price increases.

■ Stock repurchases generally have a positive impact on the price of a firm's stock.

Section 17-3: Other Factors That Affect the Firm's Dividend Policy

What are some of the factors that can influence dividend policy?

■ Taxes, transactions costs, flotation costs, and legal and contractual constraints can influence the firm's dividend payouts.

■ Managerial considerations that can influence the firm's dividend policy include the level of the firm's financial reserves, flexibility, the firm's access to capital, control issues, the firm's borrowing capacity, inflation, and its negotiations with organized labor.

How can agency costs and psychological factors affect dividend policies?

■ A firm that pays out dividends must enter the capital markets to raise new capital. Each trip to the markets exposes the firm to extensive monitoring. Since the market has a comparative advantage in monitoring the firm, paying dividends and raising capital can lower the monitoring costs and increase firm value.

■ Some researchers suggest that investors who do not like to "spend their capital" prefer dividends and that if losses are viewed as being worse than gains, a dividend cut can be greeted unfavorably in the market.

QUESTIONS

1. Describe the three dividend payment procedures that corporations use.

2. Why do managers like to follow a stable dividend policy?

3. What does it mean to say that dividends have an "informational content"?

4. To what do the ex-dividend date, the declaration date, and the date of record refer?

5. What is the residual theory of dividends? What are the implications of this theory?

6. Explain why dividends are irrelevant to perfect capital markets. What does *irrelevant* mean here?

7. Because stockholders can create "homemade dividends," corporate dividends should not affect firm value. Explain this argument.

8. All else remaining constant, how should an increase in the corporate tax rate affect a firm's optimal dividend policy?

9. Stock dividends and stock splits increase the stockholders' wealth. True or false? Why?

10. What are some of the common reasons for repurchasing shares? Do these arguments have merit? Explain.

11. What are the implications for a firm's dividend policy of the various "imperfections" in the marketplace?

12. What is the "clientele effect"? How can management cope with the diversity in the firm's owners?

13. Explain the significance of various management considerations that affect dividend policy.

14. List the factors that managers must take into account when deciding whether to pay dividends.

PROBLEMS

1. A company declares a dividend on May 10, 1990, to all stockholders on record on May 14, 1990. If Howard Smith buys the stock from Ralph Biggy on May 16, 1990, who is entitled to the dividend?

2. Zetamax Corporation has expected earnings of $4.5 million. It plans a total investment outlay of $3 million this year. Historically, Zetamax has had a dividend payout ratio of 25%. Calculate the amount of dividends that the company will distribute.

3. Newelson Company's 1990 annual report showed that the company had originally issued 300,000 shares ($4 par) at $16 per share. Over time, the company's accumulated earnings amounted to $3 million. If the board of directors now declares a four-for-one stock split, how would the stockholders' equity section of the balance sheet for Newelson look before and after the split?

4. Cathode Ray Company has issued 100,000 shares ($2 par value) for $15 per share. The company's retained earnings amount to $5 million, and its current stock price is $50 per share. If the company declares a 15% stock dividend, how will the stockholders' equity section of the company's balance sheet appear before and after the stock dividends?

5. Conrad Doenges owns 200 shares of GDC stock. If GDC declares a dividend of $5 per share (current price of GDC is $65), what is the price of the stock on the ex-dividend date? (Assume that the stock price is constant until then.) Has Conrad lost money because his stock is worth less?

SUGGESTED
ADDITIONAL
READINGS

Black, Fischer. "The Dividend Puzzle." *Journal of Portfolio Management* 2 (Winter 1976): 5–8.

Black, Fisher, and Myron Scholes. "The Effects of Dividend Yield and Dividend Policy on Common Stock Prices and Returns." *Journal of Financial Economics*, May 1974, pp. 1–22.

Easterbrook, Frank H. "Two Agency-Cost Explanations of Dividends." *American Economic Review*, September 1984, pp. 650–659.

Miller, M. H., and K. Rock. "Dividends Policy Under Asymmetric Information." *Journal of Finance*, September 1985, pp. 1031–1051.

EIGHTEEN LEASING

*The house . . . of Bàl, . . .
which is the property of
AplÉ, . . . he gave for
house rent to Bàl-nÉdin-
shumu . . . from the
fourth day of Shebat . . .
for one and a half mine
of refined silver. . . .
AplÉ . . . bears the
responsibility for not
repossessing the house.
If the house . . . is
demanded, the money,
namely one and a half
mine, AplÉ shall return
to Bàl-nÉdin-shumu, and
there shall be no claim
on his part against Bàl-
nÉdin-shumu concerning
the rent of the house.*

*—Early Babylonian
lease agreement*[1]

---

[1] From an early Babylonian lease agreement recorded on a clay tablet, No. 14, Darius II, year of accession, Shebat 4th, from "Murashû Sons of Nippur—Records of an Early Babylonian Family of Businessmen," in *The World of Business*, Vol. I (New York: Simon and Schuster, 1962).

One of the principal concerns of a growing company is the acquisition of physical and capital assets. These assets are presumably employed in an efficient manner in some productive activity that maximizes shareholder wealth or total firm value. The decision to acquire assets is generally accompanied by and intertwined with the problem of optimally financing this acquisition. Chapter 9 dealt with this problem in terms of the conventional forms of debt and equity. Leasing represents yet another financing alternative by which firms raise a substantial amount of capital. Approximately 20% of new equipment acquired by companies is lease-financed. Leasing can be viewed as a type of debt through which the firm is able to obtain the use of a physical asset, though not its legal ownership. It is this use, however, and not the actual ownership, that is of interest to the firm in pursuing its wealth-maximizing objectives.

This chapter presents the different types of leasing arrangements in use today, the advantages of leasing, and the approaches to deciding whether an asset should be leased or purchased. When the proper framework is established for evaluating leases, the firm can better achieve its prescribed objectives.

This chapter answers the following questions:

- What is a lease and how is it different from borrowing?

- Why are assets leased?

- What are some of the different types of leasing arrangements?

- How do managers decide whether an asset should be leased or purchased?

- How is a lease evaluated from the lessor's perspective?

- What are some other nontax reasons for leasing?

18-1

THE FUNDAMENTALS OF LEASING

What Is a Lease?

A lease is a rental agreement that typically requires a series of fixed payments that extend over several periods. A lease represents a contract under which one party (the **lessee**) is entitled to use an asset for a specified period. In consideration of this use, the user is required to make periodic payments to the owner of the asset (the **lessor**).

Figure 18-1 compares leasing with purchasing and illustrates the general relationship between the lessor and lessee and the use of an asset. Notice the similarities in the leasing and buying alternatives to the acquisition of an asset. If a company chooses to buy an asset, it must raise the required capital through transactions in the capital markets. With the funds raised in this manner, it purchases (i.e., obtains the use, value, and title to) the asset from, say, an equipment dealer. This relationship contrasts with that of a lease purchase. If the firm decides to be the lessee in a lease contract, it simply enters into a lease contract with a leasing firm (lessor) and obtains the use of the asset. The lessor, in this case, enters the capital market to raise capital to purchase the asset from the equipment dealer.

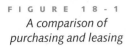

FIGURE 18-1

A comparison of purchasing and leasing

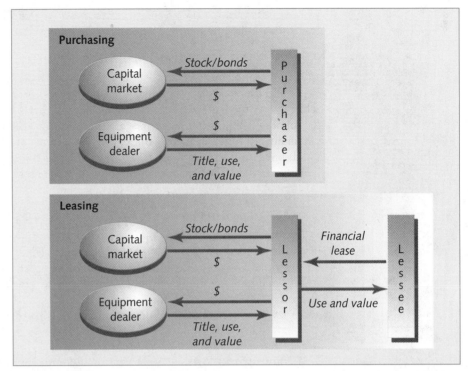

Consider the example of Classic Enterprises, whose situation we discussed in Chapter 10. Classic must use some expensive excavating equipment for the next two years. One obvious alternative is to purchase the equipment directly. However, if the company does not have the cash, it can perhaps raise new money in the capital markets by issuing stock or bonds. With the new funds, Classic can buy the excavating machines. As an alternative, Classic can approach Associated Leasing, Inc., and lease the equipment from this company by agreeing to specific terms spelled out in the lease contract or leasing agreement. Associated, in turn, acquires the asset from the manufacturer in one of several possible ways. In this case, Classic is the lessee and Associated Leasing is the lessor.

Leasing Versus Borrowing

From a conceptual viewpoint, leasing represents an alternative to borrowing. The cash flows for lease payments are very similar to those for an amortizing loan, with part of the payments applied toward principal and part toward interest. Leases frequently contain restrictive covenants like the requirement to maintain minimum debt–equity ratios or minimum levels of liquid assets. Thus lease agreements are similar to loan agreements, although the former are generally less restrictive.

Leasing is fundamentally different from debt in one respect—the legal ownership of the asset. When an asset is purchased with borrowed money, the company using the asset holds the title to it. When an asset is acquired through a lease, however, the lessor holds the title instead of the lessee.

Why Lease?

Why do companies lease assets? How does one explain the phenomenal growth of the leasing industry in recent years? In addition to the potential economic advantages of leasing described later in this chapter, several qualitative considerations can make leasing attractive to a company.

Even before examining the benefits of leasing, we should note that leasing can be important because it can make an otherwise nonviable project worthwhile. In

Chapter 10 we saw how an unattractive (negative *NPV*) project can become attractive with debt financing. Leasing has the potential to do the same.

INCREASED FLEXIBILITY

A short-term lease is a cancelable lease that offers flexibility to a firm. If Classic expects to use the excavating machines for only a short time, it may not be worthwhile to buy the machines and later sell them. With a cancelable lease, Classic can return the machines to the lessor when it no longer needs them. This flexibility is especially attractive in the case of computer systems and other products that are undergoing rapid technological advances. If a technologically superior product comes to market, the firm can cancel the lease and enter into a new one for the new machine. Many managers cite flexibility as an important reason for leasing.

CERTAIN MAINTENANCE AT A KNOWN COST

Leased equipment may include maintenance arrangements by the lessor, or alternatively a maintenance contract can be purchased at a known cost. This upper limit on maintenance expenditures makes future cash flows less uncertain.[2] Of course, maintenance contracts are also available for assets purchased by the firm. However, for leased assets, maintenance contracts are often offered by the lessor and are typically cheaper than the contracts available through a third party.

LOWER ADMINISTRATIVE COSTS

A company can lower its organizational complexity and administrative costs through leasing. In very large operations, a company may find it more attractive to let some other party take care of the assets instead of having to create a new department within the firm to take care of the acquisition, maintenance, and eventual sale of the assets. Specialized leasing companies can usually do this job at a lower cost.

HIGHER TAX RATE OR LOWER BORROWING RATE FOR LESSOR

A lessor firm may be in a higher tax bracket than the lessee firm. Then the lessor can benefit more from the tax advantages of owning an asset than the lessee firm can. The depreciation tax shields to the lessor are higher than they are for the lessee firm. The lessor can pass on the tax advantages to the lessee in the form of lower lease payments. Similarly, if the lessor firm can borrow money at a lower rate than the lessee firm can, the lessee is better off with the lessor borrowing to purchase the asset, which it then leases.

LOWER COSTS TO THE LESSOR

There are several advantages available to the lessor that may not be available to the lessee. For example, because of the typically large volume of cars purchased by an automobile leasing company, automobile manufacturers usually offer their cars to these companies at "fleet rates." These rates may be much lower than the price that a company has to pay for purchasing a car. In addition, because of the large volume, insurance rates, maintenance expenditures, ease of eventual sale of the equipment, and so on are more favorable to the lessor. These advantages can be passed on to the lessee in the form of lower lease payments.

MISCONCEPTIONS ABOUT LEASING

There are an incredible number of incorrect justifications for leasing. For example, "leasing defers capital expenditures," "leasing reduces property taxes," and

---

[2] As seen in Chapter 11, reducing total risk can increase firm value.

"operating leases increase short-term incomes" are reasons commonly cited for leasing. Leasing does not defer capital expenditures, although it does defer the expenditure of cash. But the same effect can be achieved by borrowing. Although the lessee may avoid property taxes, the lessor does pay the property taxes, and this cost should be reflected in the lease payments. Thus this apparent cost-avoidance argument does not hold. The fact that leasing can affect book income should have no impact on the firm's value. In efficient markets, investors can see through this fallacy. The net operating income of the firm determines the value of the company.

Until recently, leasing was viewed as a form of debt financing that does not show up on the balance sheet. It was considered a form of hidden debt. In this sense, leasing was considered to offer the advantage of off-balance-sheet financing. With the FASB 13 rule, however, capital leases are recognized as liabilities incurred by the firm and show up on the balance sheet.[3] FASB stands for Financial Accounting Standards Board, an organization that prescribes the correct accounting conventions in use today. When leases are properly accounted for, analysts should treat them as another factor that contributes to increased financial leverage. Yet many managers believe that leases are not properly accounted for as debt in financial analyses. Whether this argument is valid is open to question. It is unlikely that a company can fool analysts by using this strategy.

Types of Leases

Several types of leases are utilized in financial markets. In general, they may be classified as operating (or service) leases and financial (or capital) leases. Special types of financial leases are the sale-leaseback, the direct lease, and the leveraged lease, to name but a few.

OPERATING LEASES

The principal characteristic of **operating leases** is that the maintenance and service of the leased equipment are provided by the lessor, with the cost of the maintenance and service incorporated into the lease agreement or stated in a separate service contract. Typically, operating leases are for terms shorter than the usable life of the equipment. Because the lease payments do not ordinarily amortize the lessor's cost for the equipment (that is, the lease payments are not set to fully recover the lessor's cost), the returns to the lessor in addition to the lease payments are in the form of subsequent lease renewals or proceeds from the disposal of the equipment upon expiration of the lease.

Another common feature of operating leases is a cancellation clause that gives the lessee the right to cancel the lease agreement before expiration of the lease term. This has the effect of shifting the risks associated with technological obsolescence from the lessee to the lessor. This feature has important implications for both parties to the lease when the usefulness of the equipment is particularly exposed to technological advances, such as those commonly seen in the computer industry.

FINANCIAL LEASES

A **financial** or **capital lease** differs from an operating lease. It is a noncancelable, longer-term lease that fully amortizes the lessor's cost for equipment (that is, the lease payments are set to fully recover the lessor's costs). Under this form of lease, service and maintenance are usually provided by the lessee. Furthermore, the lessee may have to provide insurance and pay property taxes. In contrast with operating leases, financial leases usually have a term that corresponds more closely to the

[3]Information about operating leases is also supposed to be disclosed in footnotes to the company's annual report.

productive life of the asset. Automobile leases are an example of such financial leases.

Some financial leases provide for certain renewal or purchase options at the end of the lease term, although these options are subject to certain IRS restrictions.

SALE-LEASEBACK ARRANGEMENTS A special type of financial lease often used by firms is the **sale-leaseback arrangement.** Under this arrangement, assets that are already owned by a firm are purchased by a lessor and leased back to the firm. The firm, as lessee, executes a lease agreement with the lessor, which ordinarily is a financial institution such as a commercial bank, insurance company, or leasing company.

The structure of this arrangement is analogous to that of a mortgage on the asset taken out by the lessee. Rather than making a series of payments to amortize a loan, however, the lessee makes a series of payments that amortize the lessor's acquisition costs and give the lessor the required return. By entering into this type of arrangement, the lessee firm (Classic) can free the capital originally invested in the equipment. Presumably, some market imperfections, such as taxes, make this a more attractive (cheaper) alternative to the lessee firm.

DIRECT LEASES A **direct lease** is identical to the sale-leaseback arrangement except that the lessee does not necessarily own the leased asset. The lessor already owns or acquires the asset, which is then provided to the lessee. Often the lessor is a manufacturer or a leasing company that is providing the asset and its financing to the lessee.

As an example, if Classic learned that its competitor, Rockstar, Inc., had advertised the excavating equipment for sale, Classic could ask Associated Leasing to purchase the asset from Rockstar and then lease it to Classic.

LEVERAGED LEASES A **leveraged lease** is a special lease arrangement under which the lessor borrows a substantial portion of the acquisition cost of the leased asset from a third party. The *leverage* refers to the financial leverage used by the lessor in structuring the lease, and the risk associated with default by the lessee is partially borne by the third-party lender. Leveraged leases usually involve only large assets because of the complexity and expense of structuring the lease arrangement. The third party that finances the asset is usually an institution such as an insurance company or pension fund. Often this lender takes assignment of the lessor's interest in the lease and receives the lease payments directly.

We return to our example. If Associated Leasing is unable to enter into the direct lease arrangement proposed by Classic because it (Associated) is unable to come up with the capital to buy the equipment from Rockstar, Associated can finance its purchase of the excavating equipment with a loan from the Prudent Insurance Company. It can then enter into a direct lease with Classic. This set of transactions constitutes a leveraged lease.

Tax Considerations in Leasing

Taxes play a very important role in the structure of leases and in the value of leases to both the lessor and the lessee. It is essential, therefore, to discuss certain IRS requirements imposed on lease agreements if one is to understand how and when the various tax benefits associated with leasing can be captured and to whom these benefits apply. We keep this discussion of the tax aspects of leasing to a minimum. The IRS guidelines have changed in recent years and are, of course, subject to future change. Because the actual details may vary in different lease situations,

CROSS-BORDER LEASING

An interesting innovation in leasing is the practice of cross-border leasing. Cross-border leasing can give companies a cheap way to finance capital assets by exploiting differences in tax systems between countries—especially, different methods for claiming deductions. In a cross-border lease, the lessor is in one country and the lessee is in another. A company may want to lease from a foreign entity for a number of reasons. These include making use of lower financing costs available abroad, facilitating the acquisition of an asset from a foreign manufacturer, and getting more favorable tax treatment elsewhere.

Cross-border leases can be classified as single or double dip, depending on how many agencies claim the depreciation benefits. Triple-dip leases also exist but are relatively rare. Although the process becomes complicated as the number of parties increases, the benefits also rise dramatically. In a famous triple-dip transaction done by Bankers Trust in the mid-1980s, a U.S. manufacturer leased aircraft to a Japanese firm, which leased it to a Belgian firm, which leased it to a South African company. Firms in Japan, Belgium, and South Africa all reduced their taxable income by taking the depreciation expense.

Countries suitable for cross-border lease transactions are those that have either a large base of big investors seeking to reduce their taxable income or a tax and legal environment suited to cross-border leases. In 1989, the biggest markets for cross-border leases were Japan, the United States, Hong Kong, France, and Sweden. Tax-driven cross-border leasing is generally seen in deals involving high-cost items where leasing offers a clear advantage over purchasing. The largest sector for cross-border leasing is aircraft leasing. Other commonly leased items are rail cars, power plants, ships, and containers.

These transactions are unpopular with many governments because of the loss of tax revenues for them. Therefore governments constantly try to devise new rules to deny these tax advantages. However, clever intermediaries like banks, leasing companies, and financial institutions stay one step ahead of governments by devising new lease structures.

we outline only the general framework for recognizing these tax aspects. The tax adjustments used are very general, but they capture the substance of the current tax code.

In general, a lease can be categorized as either a true lease or a conditional sale lease, depending on the nature of the lease agreement. The difference between these two types of leases is important to the IRS.

TRUE LEASE

Under a **true lease,** the lessee is able to deduct the lease payments fully for tax purposes. The lease payments are included as an operating expense in the lessee's income statement. Furthermore, the lessor may retain the tax depreciation deductions. By offering tax shields to the lessor, therefore, the true lease can, in certain cases, reduce the effective lease costs to the lessee. (These costs and the benefits of leasing are discussed in the next section.) A lease can qualify as a true lease if various IRS guidelines are met. These guidelines are intended to distinguish a lease from a sale. The IRS is concerned with the possibility that sales may otherwise be labeled leases to avoid taxation.

The five IRS requirements for a true lease are as follows:

1. The estimated fair market value of the leased asset at the expiration of the lease must equal or exceed 20% of the asset's original cost (excluding the effects of inflation or deflation).

2. The estimated remaining useful life of the leased asset beyond the term of the lease must equal or exceed 20% of the original estimated useful life of the asset and must be at least one year.

3. The lessee must not have the right to purchase the asset from the lessor at a price less than the fair market value.

4. The lessor must have a minimum "at risk" investment equal to at least 20% of the cost of the leased asset. This "at risk" investment represents the lessor's equity interest in the leased asset.

5. The lease must provide a reasonable return to the lessor, relative to the return on loans.

CONDITIONAL SALE LEASE

If any of the conditions just listed are violated in a lease arrangement, the lease becomes a **conditional sale lease.** A conditional sale lease is not particularly interesting in terms of the analysis of this chapter. It is viewed simply as an installment loan by the IRS. In other words, the lessee is viewed as having, in fact, purchased the asset rather than having leased it, and the lessor is viewed as having financed this purchase with a loan. The IRS assumes that this is a regular purchase being labeled a lease simply for certain tax benefits.

For tax purposes, the lessee treats the property as owned and claims the depreciation. The lease payments are treated as loan payments, and the lessee may deduct only the portion that is equivalent to "interest" on the "loan." Therefore, for all intents and purposes, a conditional sale lease is a sale, and such a transaction can be analyzed using the concepts discussed earlier in this book.

18-2

LEASE ANALYSIS FROM THE LESSEE'S PERSPECTIVE

A manager must answer two fundamental questions in regard to the acquisition of physical assets. First, should the asset under consideration be acquired? Second, if the firm decides to acquire the asset for other than a cash payment, should it be purchased with borrowed funds or leased? Putting this another way, because leasing is an alternative to borrowing, should the asset be lease-financed or debt-financed?

A manager must pursue the alternative that is in the best interests of the stockholders. Thus the manager should select the alternative that will have the more favorable impact on firm value. To assess the impact of either alternative on firm value, a net present value (*NPV*) analysis for leasing is required.

To develop a framework for determining when leasing is financially attractive, we begin by considering financial leases. Operating leases are more complex to value because they often can be canceled; therefore they are not discussed in this chapter. As alluded to earlier, financial leases are substitutes for debt because they provide for the use of an asset and commit the firm to a predetermined payment obligation. This fixed obligation forms the basis for our analysis of leases. Based on the concepts developed earlier in this text, any procedure for determining the value of leasing must include an examination of the cash flows that result from the leasing decision.

In this context, we refer again to Chapter 10. There we used the adjusted present value (*APV*) method for evaluating the net present value (*NPV*) of projects involving debt. This same procedure can be modified easily for use in projects that involve leasing. In such cases, we calculate the all-equity value of the project and then add the effect of the lease. Thus $NPV = NPV$ with all-equity financing + NPV of the lease. In practice, however, a conceptually simpler method exists and is discussed below.

Why APV Computations Are Unnecessary in the Lease/Borrow Decision

At this point, one could proceed by defining the total cash flows to the firm provided by leasing and by determining the appropriate required rate of return (RRR) for use in discounting. The adjusted present value (APV) method can then be used to calculate the NPV of the project with either borrowing or leasing. A comparison of the two APVs determines whether the firm should lease or borrow. Alternatively, lease and debt financing can be compared by examining the incremental (or decremental) cash flows incurred through leasing as compared with borrowing. This is sufficient because the cash flows from the project itself are the same, regardless of the type of financing.

This can be explained as follows. The project's APV using debt is

$$APV_D = NPV \text{ (all-equity)} + NPV \text{ (flotation costs)} + NPV \text{ (subsidized financing)}$$

The project's APV under leasing is

$$APV_L = NPV \text{ (all-equity)} + NPV \text{ (lease)}$$

To compare APV_L and APV_D, it is not necessary to compute NPV (all-equity) because this is the same under both alternatives. Leasing is preferred to debt financing when $APV_L > APV_D$. This can happen only when NPV (lease) > NPV (flotation costs) + NPV (subsidized financing). Because of its simplicity we do not work with APV to make the lease or borrow decision. We simply examine the incremental (decremental) cash flows associated with either alternative. We are also assuming that NPV (flotation costs) and NPV (subsidized financing) are 0. This makes the analysis much simpler because we need to find out only whether or not NPV (lease) is greater than 0.

Classic Enterprises: The Lease/Borrow Decision

Let us revisit the example of Classic Enterprises from Chapter 10. Assume that Classic is considering a project that will last ten years. Classic requires the use of some property for this project that costs $30 million. It has previously determined the project to be acceptable regardless of the way in which it is financed; that is, management has already determined that the project has a positive NPV even with all-equity financing. The question now facing Classic is whether to finance the property with conventional debt (i.e., a term loan) or to lease it. The firm does not wish to use any equity to purchase the property. Classic can borrow money at 8%. In addition, if Classic buys the property, it can depreciate it straight line over the ten years toward a $0 salvage value. (In this chapter and in the end-of-chapter problems, it is assumed that the entire asset value is depreciable, unless otherwise mentioned.[4]) Classic is in the 25% tax bracket. Associated Leasing has agreed to a lease arrangement with Classic with the following terms: life of lease, 11 years; annual lease payment, $4 million, with the first payment due upon the signing of the lease agreement. (The lessor's decision to provide such a lease under these terms is considered later as a separate issue.) We now examine the required analysis for this lease/buy decision.

---

[4]If the asset is *sold* at the end of the project period, we would need to show a corresponding cash flow. If the asset is sold at *more than its book value*, we also need to show a cash flow corresponding to the tax treatment of the gain recorded on the asset's sale.

■
T A B L E 1 8 - 1

*Lease Cash Flows
to the Lessee*

	Year Ending	
	0	*1–10*
Property cost	$30,000,000	
Lease payment	−4,000,000	−$4,000,000
Tax shield on lease payments[a]	1,000,000	1,000,000
Lost tax shield on depreciation[b]	0	−750,000
Net cash flow	$27,000,000	−$3,750,000

[a] $4,000,000 × 0.25.
[b] $3,000,000 × 0.25.

Because leasing is a substitute for debt, the leasing decision can be approached by considering the opportunity costs of financing with a lease. If Classic chooses to lease the property, it will lose the tax shield provided by depreciation—a benefit that would have accrued to Classic if it had bought the property. Also, there is the loss of the interest tax shield available through debt financing. But the lease payments can be treated as an expense for tax purposes.

Let LCF_{Bt} represent the lease cash flows in period t, where the subscript B denotes the lessee as a borrower. Also note that B distinguishes the lessee (borrower) from the lessor (lender). Then LCF_{Bt} can be calculated as:[5]

$$LCF_{Bt} = \begin{cases} C - P(1 - T_B) & \text{for } t = 0 \\ -P(1 - T_B) - T_B D_t & \text{for } t > 0 \end{cases}$$ (18-1)

where

C is the cost of the equipment/property leased

P is the lease payment

D_t is the forgone (lost) depreciation in period t

T_B is the firm's (lessee's) marginal tax rate

LCF_{B0}, the initial (period 0) cash flow from the lease arrangement, is positive because the firm obtains the asset (effectively a cash inflow) without a net cash outlay.

For Classic,

$$LCF_{B0} = \$30,000,000 - \$4,000,000(1 - 0.25)$$
$$= \$27,000,000$$

$$LCF_{Bt} = -\$4,000,000(1 - 0.25) - (0.25)(\$3,000,000)$$
$$= -\$3,750,000$$

Table 18-1 shows the details of the calculations implicit in the use of these equations for determining the lease cash flows.

Note that the cash flow components of LCF_{Bt} may not contain the same risk. For example, the lease payment tax shield may be riskier than the lease payment if the firm will not have enough taxable income in future years to use the deduction. If that is the case, there will be separate discount rates for each of the respective cash flow items. For our purposes, we assume that all cash flows have the same risk. The question now is how to use the aforementioned lease cash flows in a

[5] Because the first lease payment is due at the *beginning* of year 0 and the first depreciation expense is recognized at the *end* of year 0, there is a difference of one year between the two incremental cash flows. Therefore we start the lease payments from year 0, but we capture depreciation effects only in year 1 and thereafter.

decision framework such that the lease and debt financing alternatives can be properly evaluated.

Evaluating a
Lease/Buy Decision

APPROACH 1: THE EQUIVALENT LOAN APPROACH

Because financing an asset with leasing is a substitute for debt financing, the leasing and borrowing alternatives can be compared by constructing an equivalent loan. An **equivalent loan** is a loan with net after-tax cash commitments imposed on the firm that are identical to those imposed by leasing.

The idea underlying this approach to deciding between leasing and buying is simple. In the Classic example, an annual cash outflow of $3.75 million for ten years generates a time 0 cash inflow of $27 million for the company. The relevant question now is: What loan (i.e., what cash inflow) can Classic get from its bank that will result in ten annual cash payments of $3.75 million? The answer yields the equivalent annual loan. If the equivalent annual loan is greater than $27 million, Classic should borrow from the bank and buy the property. If the equivalent annual loan is less than $27 million, Classic should sign the lease agreement with Associated Leasing.

Calculating an equivalent loan is fairly straightforward. It is similar to the calculation of a uniform annual series, which we studied in Chapter 4. Because Classic can borrow at 8% and because its tax bracket is 25%, the after-tax cost of the loan is $8\%(1 - 0.25) = 6\%$. Let the equivalent annual loan be $\$X$. Then

$$\$X = \$3,750,000(PVFA_{0.06,10})$$

That is,

$$\begin{aligned}\$X &= \$3,750,000(7.3601) \\ &= \$27,600,375\end{aligned}$$

The equivalent annual loan is therefore $27,600,375. A loan of $27,600,375 from Classic's bank will impose on Classic a series of annual cash outflows identical to the lease.

Because the lease and the equivalent loan represent identical cash flow liabilities to the firm, one merely has to compare the net financing provided by the two alternatives, as shown in Table 18-2. Clearly, the leasing option available to the firm generates $600,375 less financing in this example. Thus the leasing alternative should be rejected, and Classic should fund the project with debt.

APPROACH 2: THE DISCOUNTING APPROACH

Another approach to evaluating financial leases is to discount the lease cash flows with the appropriate discount rate. This approach is essentially the same as the previous approach, but it makes the decision using the *NPV* rather than the equivalent loan.

Let us begin by considering the lessee's before-tax cost of debt. Given that lease cash flows are debt-equivalent cash flows, it is appropriate to discount the after-tax lease cash flows with an after-tax discount rate. In this case, the after-tax cost

■

T A B L E   1 8 - 2
Comparison of Lease and
Equivalent Loan
Cash Flows

	Year Ending	
	0	*1–10*
Lease cash flows	$27,000,000	− $3,750,000
Equivalent loan cash flows	27,600,375	− 3,750,000
Difference	$ 600,375	$ 0

of debt to the firm is $(1 - T_B)k_d$ because the payments on debt are tax deductible. As seen earlier, this works out to 6.0%.

Now we determine the NPV of the lease. This is simply the net amount of financing provided by leasing less the present value of the lease cash flows. Because the lease alternative generates $27 million in financing (Table 18-1) and requires net annual payments of $3.75 million, the NPV of this transaction is:

$$NPV_B = \$27,000,000 - \$3,750,000(PVFA_{0.06,10})$$
$$= \$27,000,000 - \$3,750,000(7.3601)$$
$$= -\$600,375$$

Because the NPV is negative, Classic should not accept the lease financing and, instead, should borrow.

18-3

LEASE ANALYSIS FROM THE LESSOR'S PERSPECTIVE

What about the lessor's perspective on leasing? It is clear that the lessor is willing to enter into a lease agreement if the project earns, at a minimum, the company's weighted average cost of capital, $WACC_L$ (the subscript L denotes the lessor as a lender). Thus the lease is structured so that the implicit interest rate paid by the lessee is at least as much as the lessor's $WACC_L$. $WACC$ is used instead of RRR only to simplify the exposition. The implicit assumption here is that the lease project has the same risk level as does the leasing company itself.

The lessor's cash flows are analogous to those of the lessee, but with a reversal of sign. In addition, the lessor is exposed to his own marginal tax rate, T_L. The cash flows to the lessor can therefore be denoted as:

$$LCF_{Lt} = \begin{cases} -C + P(1 - T_B) & \text{for } t = 0 \\ P(1 - T_B) + T_B D_t & \text{for } t > 0 \end{cases} \qquad (18\text{-}2)$$

Table 18-3 depicts these cash flows to the lessor under the assumption that the lessor has the same tax rate as the lessee (i.e., $T_L = T_B = 0.25$).

The value of the lease to the lessor in this example can be determined by discounting the lessor's cash flows, LCF_{Lt}, by the lessor's opportunity cost, $WACC_L$. Let us assume that $k_d = 0.08$, so that $WACC_L = (1 - T_L)k_d = 0.06$. Because the net cash outflow to the lessor at time 0 is $27 million and the cash inflows amount to $3.75 million per year for ten years, the NPV of this project to the lessor is:

$$NPV_L = -\$27,000,000 + \$3,750,000(PVFA_{0.06,10}) = \$600,375$$

Notice that NPV_L is exactly the same as NPV_B except for the opposite sign. Thus, with $T_L = T_B$ and $WACC_L = (1 - T_L)k_d$, the gains to the lessor from leasing are exactly offset by the losses to the lessee (and vice versa). Of course, with differ-

TABLE 18-3

Cash Flows to the Lessor

	Year Ending	
	0	1–10
Property cost	− $30,000,000	
Lease revenue[a]	4,000,000	$4,000,000
Tax on lease payments[b]	− 1,000,000	− 1,000,000
Tax shield on depreciation[c]	0	750,000
Net cash flow to lessor	− $27,000,000	$3,750,000

[a] Lease payment required by lessor.
[b] $4,000,000 × 0.25 = $1,000,000
[c] Depreciation × 0.25 = ($3,000,000)(0.25) = $750,000

ent tax rates to the lessor and lessee, both can benefit. In fact, differential tax rates, differential borrowing rates, and differential agency costs and agency considerations can make the leasing arrangement a positive-*NPV* investment for both lessor and lessee. Indeed, it is market imperfections that drive leasing decisions and it is market imperfections that rationalize the leasing business. We examine some of these later in the chapter.

18-4

NONTAX CONSIDERATIONS IN THE LEASE/BUY DECISION

When explaining the lease/buy decision in the previous sections, we emphasized tax considerations. Although taxes are extremely important in a manager's decision to lease an asset, there are several other nontax implications of leasing an asset as opposed to buying it.[6] For example, even though taxes can explain when a firm will lease to another firm (i.e., be a lessor) and when a company will lease from another company (i.e., be a lessee), tax calculations cannot tell us why certain kinds of assets are routinely leased and others are almost always purchased. To address this and similar issues, we expand our analysis of leasing to recognize the implications of agency costs. In this more general framework, the characteristics of the lessor and the lessee become important variables, and the nature of the asset in question also becomes important.

Agency Considerations in the Lease/Buy Decision

Certain characteristics of the user of the asset can have a significant impact on the lease/buy decision. We begin by examining the agency problem of asset substitution. As we saw in an earlier chapter, once an asset has been purchased for a specific use, managers may want to switch from a low-risk to a high-risk project. A long-term noncancelable lease can prevent this from happening. The lease contract commits the firm to using the asset for an extended time period, and moreover, the lease contract can restrict the use of the asset. Thus, to the extent that the lease contract restricts management's behavior, leasing can be a bonding device that reduces agency costs.[7] This advantage is somewhat dampened by a counterbalancing factor. Because leases have priority over debt in bankruptcy, leasing reduces the coverage on the debt issues and thereby increases the bondholders' risk. This negative effect of leasing can, however, be reduced by limiting leasing activities through provisions in the bond covenants.

To some extent, a long-term lease can even mitigate the underinvestment problem. Positive-*NPV* projects that management might forgo could be undertaken if they are financed with a lease contract. To see why, recognize that the underinvestment problem arises in the first place because if a debt-financed project is very successful, the bondholders' risk will be lower and their wealth will be greater. But if the project is lease-financed, any windfall gain will go directly to the stockholders, thereby removing the managerial incentive to forgo positive-*NPV* projects.[8]

Managerial compensation contracts often contain bonus schemes. Consider a manager whose bonus depends on the return on the firm's invested capital. This manager will want to lease rather than to buy an asset because an outright pur-

---

[6] A detailed examination of the nontax incentives for leasing is contained in C. W. Smith and L. M. Wakeman, "Determinants of Corporate Leasing Policy," *Journal of Finance,* July 1985, pp. 895–908.

[7] C. W. Smith and J. B. Warner, "On Financial Contracting: An Analysis of Bond Covenants," *Journal of Financial Economics,* June 1979, pp. 117–162.

[8] R. M. Stulz and H. Johnson, "An Analysis of Secured Debt," *Journal of Financial Economics* 14 (1985): 501–522.

chase increases the invested capital and lowers the project's return, whereas a lease can leave the computation of invested capital unaffected. This problem can be avoided by explicitly requiring that the "invested capital" reflect the capitalized value of the lease.

Leasing may also be beneficial to undiversified sole proprietors. For certain kinds of activities, there may be no net gain from converting from a proprietorship to a corporate form. For example, for a small family-owned grocery store, the advantages of risk diversification from incorporating may be outweighed by the disadvantages that arise from potential agency problems. For such businesses, the manager/owner cannot obtain the benefits of diversification. To the extent that leasing an asset (say, a refrigeration plant) lowers his investment in the firm, a proprietor risks a smaller portion of his wealth by not purchasing the asset. Leasing may thus be the preferred alternative. Of course, the proprietor can borrow, but as seen in an earlier chapter, proprietorships have less access to the capital markets and borrowing may not be feasible.

Another important factor pertains to the lessee's incentives not to maintain and service the asset. If the firm owns the asset, then it clearly has a good reason to make the optimal amount of maintenance expenditures. Moreover, managers ensure that the asset is not being abused by workers because the residual value of the asset (salvage value) accrues to the firm. This is not the case with a leased asset, however. The firm does not have these incentives to keep the asset in good repair. Thus the extent to which the value of the asset depends on the maintenance and use by the lessee influences the leasing decision. If the lessor is at the mercy of the lessee, the required lease payments will be much higher, and the lessee may be better off buying the asset. Assets that are less sensitive to abuse and neglect by the lessee tend to be leased.

Asset specificity is another factor that can determine which assets are leased and which are purchased.[9] When an asset loses value in alternative uses, it is said to have a high degree of asset specificity because the value that it creates is specific to the firm using it. For example, consider a firm that has a rotary jig that can make the ball bearings for a very specialized product for which the firm has patents. The jig is obviously extremely valuable to this firm. But if this jig has to be sold, its value falls because the new firm cannot use the jig to create the same value. The jig's use is thus highly specialized, and so such an asset is most likely owned by the firm. A lessor would be reluctant to lease this asset to the firm because upon default, the repossessed asset may have a very small value in the marketplace. The only way that a lessor can justify this risk is by demanding very high lease payments, and this would make it cheaper for the lessee to buy the asset. In general, highly specialized assets are bought rather than leased, which avoids the problems of **bilateral monopoly.** Although the lessor and lessee enter into an agreement in a competitive market, the situation changes dramatically once the lease contract is signed. Competitive forces are replaced by a situation in which each party is held hostage by the other. If the lease contract is broken, both parties can lose. To prevent this there are additional costs of negotiation and administration before the contract is signed. This can make the leasing of organization-specific assets more expensive.

The period over which the firm intends to use an asset is also an important variable. For short-term use, it may be more economical for the firm to lease rather than to buy because the costs of gathering information about the asset and hiring

[9] See O. E. Williamson, *The Economic Institutions of Capitalism* (New York: Free Press, 1985).

personnel or entering into maintenance contracts can be very high. For example, if a company anticipates the need for expensive earth-moving equipment for six months, it may be better off leasing. The cost of any suboptimal decisions associated with leasing are likely to be smaller than the cost of investigating the quality, reliability, after-purchase servicing by the company, and so on.

Lessor Characteristics That Influence the Lease/Buy Decision

A few important lessor characteristics can influence corporate leasing policy— not only the decision to lease but also the type of asset that is leased.

If the manufacturer of an asset has some **market power** to extract higher prices for its product, the manufacturer may want to become a lessor rather than a seller of the asset. The reason is that the manufacturer may be able to charge two different prices for the same asset, depending on whether the asset is leased or purchased. Even when a firm leases an asset, there is an implicit purchase price—that is, the amount a firm could have paid for the asset and financed it to incur an obligation equivalent to the lease payments. If a manufacturer can make a larger profit by price discriminating through the implicit purchase price in a lease contract, then becoming a lessor of the asset makes economic sense.

Leasing by a manufacturer can also be interpreted as a bonding device. To the extent that a manufacturer bears the cost of poor workmanship and quality in a lease, the agency costs associated with the transaction decrease when the asset is leased. Thus consumers who have serious doubts about a company's commitment to a product may have fewer fears if the manufacturer is willing to lease the asset to the customer.

Finally, if the lessor has a comparative advantage in disposing of the asset, this encourages leasing it. For example, if the lessor can easily find a buyer for a sophisticated used computer, then a firm may be better off letting the lessor dispose of the asset. Therefore it leases the asset.

SUMMARY

Section 18-1: The Fundamentals of Leasing

What is a lease and how is it different from borrowing?

- A lease is an agreement between a lessor and a lessee in which the lessor who owns the asset allows the lessee to use the asset for a prespecified period in return for a series of (typically) fixed lease payments.

- Conceptually, leasing is an alternative to borrowing. Leases, like loans, require fixed payments and both involve restrictive covenants. However, unlike with borrowing, when an asset is acquired through a lease, the lessor owns the title to the asset.

Why are assets leased?

- In most general terms, market imperfections explain leasing.

- Leasing can offer increased flexibility to the lessee. It can make the firm's cash flows more predictable and lower the firm's administrative costs.

- The lessor firm can have lower maintenance costs. The lessor firm can be in a higher tax bracket than the lessee firm and benefit more from the tax shields. Similarly, the lessor may be able to borrow at a lower rate. All of these benefits to the lessor can be passed on to the lessee in the form of lower lease payments.

What are some of the different types of leasing arrangements?

- In an operating lease, the maintenance and service of the leased asset are provided by the lessor, and the lease term is typically shorter than the usable life of the asset. Leases often include cancellation clauses to benefit the lessee. Lease payments for operating leases generally do not amortize the lessor's costs.

- A financial or capital lease is a noncancelable, longer-term lease that fully amortizes the lessor's cost of the equipment. Service and maintenance are provided by the lessee. The terms for these leases generally correspond to the useful life of the leased asset.

- Sale-leasebacks, direct leases, and leveraged leases are special types of financial leases.

Section 18-2: Lease Analysis from the Lessee's Perspective

How do managers decide whether an asset should be leased or purchased?

- Managers can calculate the *NPV* under the leasing arrangement. If *NPV* (lease) is positive, they lease the asset; otherwise, they purchase the asset.

- One way to compare the relative costs of leasing and borrowing is by constructing an "equivalent loan." The cheaper alternative is obviously preferred.

- In the "discounting approach," the lease cash flows are discounted at the appropriate discount rate and the decision to lease is based on the *NPV*. This approach is essentially the same as the equivalent loan approach.

Section 18-3: Lease Analysis from the Lessor's Perspective

How is a lease evaluated from the lessor's perspective?

- To justify leasing the asset to the lessee, the lessor must recover the relevant opportunity cost.

- Market imperfections such as differential taxes, differential agency costs, or costs of capital can make a lease a positive-*NPV* transaction for both lessor and lessee.

Section 18-4: Nontax Considerations in the Lease/Buy Decision

What are some other nontax reasons for leasing?

- Agency considerations can rationalize leasing.

- A long-term noncancelable lease can solve the "asset substitution problem."

- Long-term leases may mitigate the "underinvestment problem" by removing managers' incentives to forgo positive-*NPV* projects.

- Leasing may reduce the risk to proprietorships that have limited borrowing potential.

- To avoid the problem of bilateral monopoly, highly specialized assets are generally not leased.

- Many characteristics of the lessor (e.g., market power and lessor's comparative advantage in asset disposal) can influence the leasing decision.

QUESTIONS

1. What are the advantages of leasing?

2. What is the difference between operating and financial leases? What are some of the special forms of these leases?

3. What are true and conditional sale leases?

4. How would a manager calculate the lease cash flows to a firm that is leasing an asset? Why?

5. Explain the equivalent loan approach to making a lease/buy decision.

6. What is the standard *NPV* approach to making a lease/buy decision?

7. How are the cash flows to a lessor calculated? Why?

PROBLEMS [10]

1. Sally Wheeler needs a crane for her construction business and cannot decide whether to buy or lease it. The crane costs $50,000 and can be depreciated straight line to a $0 salvage value in five years. Sally has a marginal tax rate of 34%. Lease payments are $11,000 annually.

   (a) What will be the net initial outlay and the tax shield on depreciation for each of the next five years if the crane is purchased?

   (b) Suppose that the lease expense is payable at the beginning of each of the next five years and that the tax savings that result from the lease deduction are recognized as the payment is made. Find the cash flow after taxes from the leasing alternative for each of the next five years.

   (c) What amount of financing does the lease provide? What is the decremental cash flow for each of the next five years?

   (d) What should Sally do if her firm's before-tax cost of debt is 10%? What if it is 15%?

2. Linda Gillum has been assigned the task of acquiring laser equipment to be used for printing and binding by her employer, the Gambit Publishing Company. Linda can purchase the equipment for $120,000 and will depreciate it straight line to a salvage value of $0 in five years. Alternatively, the equipment can be leased for $30,000 annually, payable and deductible at the beginning of each of the next five years. Gambit's marginal tax rate is 25%.

   (a) What will be the net initial outlay and the tax shield generated by depreciation each year if the equipment is purchased?

   (b) Find the cash flow after taxes associated with the leasing alternative for each of the next five years.

   (c) What amount of financing does the lease provide?

   (d) What should Linda do if the before-tax cost of debt is 16%?

   (e) What should Linda do if the before-tax cost of debt is 20%?

3. William Juraschek, co-owner of Topologico's Bar and Grille, intends to acquire the use of a margarita machine for each of his three restaurants. The machines cost $30,000 each. If purchased, they will be depreciated straight line to a salvage value of $0 in five years. They are actually expected to last for eight years and to have a salvage value of $0 at that time. The machines can be leased for $5,000 each per year, payable and deductible at the begin-

---

[10] Some of the problems in this chapter require the use of a financial calculator.

ning of each year. Topologico's marginal tax rate is 34%, and the before-tax cost of debt is 16%.

(a) What net initial outlay is associated with the purchase of the machines? What tax shield is generated by depreciation for each of the next eight years?

(b) What is the annual after-tax lease expense?

(c) What immediate savings are incurred (financing provided) by the lease? What is the decremental cash flow for each of the next eight years?

(d) What should William do?

(e) What should William do if the machines are actually expected to last ten years rather than eight years?

4. Larry Moss, financial manager of Goring Industries, is trying to determine whether Goring should lease or buy five new trucks that are necessary for a six-year project that is being undertaken. The trucks cost $18,000 each. The trucks, if purchased, will be depreciated straight line to a salvage value of $5,000 each at the end of six years. The lease payments for the five trucks will be $14,000 annually, payable at the beginning of each year. The tax savings from the lease deduction are recognized as the payment is made. Goring's marginal tax rate is 25%, and the before-tax cost of debt is 15%.

(a) What will be the initial outlay and the subsequent after-tax cash flows at the end of each of the next five years if the trucks are purchased?

(b) Find the annual after-tax cash flow for the leasing alternative.

(c) Find the financing provided by the lease and the decremental cash flow for each of the next six years.

(d) What should Larry do?

5. Richard Wood, owner of the Victoria Child Care Center, Inc., is considering the acquisition of 20 personal computers for a class he is developing. The computers can be purchased for $2,000 each and would be depreciated straight line over five years. Their anticipated value at the end of five years is $0. Alternatively, the 20 computers can be leased for $10,150 annually, payable at the end of each year. The tax deduction is recognized as the payments are made. Richard's before-tax cost of debt is 15%.

(a) What initial outlay is associated with purchase? What are the annual tax savings from depreciation if the center's tax rate is 34%?

(b) What annual after-tax cash flow is associated with leasing if the tax rate is 34%?

(c) What net financing is provided by the lease? What is the decremental cash flow from the lease?

(d) Should Richard lease or buy the computers?

(e) What are the annual tax savings from depreciation if the center's tax rate is 25%?

(f) What annual after-tax cash flow is associated with leasing if the tax rate is 25%?

(g) What is the net financing provided by the lease? What is the decremental cash flow from the lease? What should Richard do? The tax rate is 25%.

6. The Ajax Leasing Company has just received an order from a client who wishes to lease four cement mixers for five years. Ajax can buy the cement mixers for $25,000 each. Ajax will depreciate them straight line to a salvage value of $0 in five years. Ajax will finance this project with debt; it can secure a five-year note at the prime rate of 16%. Lease payments will be received at the beginning of each year and are subject to taxation immediately upon receipt.

   (a) What must Ajax's annual rental be if it is in the 34% tax bracket and the cement mixers have a salvage value of $0 in five years?

   (b) What must Ajax's annual rental be if it is in the 15% tax bracket and the cement mixers have a salvage value of $0 in five years?

   (c) What must Ajax's annual rental be if it is in the 34% tax bracket and the cement mixers have a salvage value of $4,000 each in five years?

   (d) What must Ajax's annual rental be if it is in the 15% tax bracket and the cement mixers have a salvage value of $4,000 each in five years?

7. John Feo, financial manager of the National Delivery Service, needs to acquire the use of 200 Jeeps for the next six years. The Jeeps can be purchased for $12,000 each and can be sold for $3,000 each in six years. They will be depreciated straight line to a salvage value of $0 in three years. Alternatively, the Jeeps can be leased for $2,320 each annually, due at the beginning of each year. National's before-tax cost of debt is 16%, and its tax rate is 34%.

   (a) Suppose that the tax deduction for the lease payments is recognized as the payment is made. What is the after-tax lease expense each year? What amount of financing is provided by the lease, and what is the decremental cash flow for each year? What should John do?

   (b) Suppose that the tax deduction for the lease payments is not recognized until the next tax bill is due, one year after the payment is made (e.g., the payment made now is deducted one year from today, the payment made one year from today is deducted two years from today, and so on). What is the after-tax payment made today? What is the after-tax cash flow for each of years 1 to 5? What is the after-tax cash flow for year 6? What should John do?

8. Fill in the blanks for the following calculations of an equivalent loan. The tax rates remain the same for all five years. (*Hint:* Start with the last column and work backward.)

			Year			
	0	*1*	*2*	*3*	*4*	*5*
Principal balance (end of year)			$16,346.38	$9,327.16	$1,886.79	$0
Interest (10%)	$0				932.72	188.68
Tax shield on interest	0					
Effective after-tax interest expense	0					113.21
Payment of principal	0			$7,019.22	7,440.37	1,886.79
Net cash flow		− $8,000	− $8,000	− $8,000	− $8,000	− $2,000

9. Don Morrison of the Morrison Construction Company needs to acquire the use of a tractor for the next three years. Don has found a used tractor that he can purchase for $18,000. The tractor will be depreciated straight line to a salvage value of $0 in three years. Alternatively, Don can lease the tractor for $5,000 annually, due at the beginning of each year. The tax deduction for the lease payments is realized as soon as the payments are made. Don can take out a bank loan at a 15% interest rate. The company's marginal tax rate is 25%.

(a) What is the net financing provided by the lease?

(b) What is the after-tax lease payment at the end of each of years 1, 2, and 3? What is the tax shield generated from depreciation?

(c) Find the equivalent loan of the lease. Should Don lease or buy the tractor?

10. Virginia Pierson is trying to decide whether to lease or buy a smelting oven for the construction of an electric plant. The oven costs $60,000 and will be depreciated straight line to a salvage value of $0 in five years. Virginia's firm's tax rate is 34%, and the before-tax cost of debt is 15%.

(a) What initial outlay is required to purchase the oven?

(b) What cash flow will be generated from depreciation at the end of each of the next five years?

(c) Using the after-tax cost of debt, find the *PV* of all cash flows associated with the purchase of the oven.

(d) Suppose that Virginia can lease the oven for $15,000 annually, payable at the beginning of each year, and the resulting tax deduction is recognized immediately. What is the after-tax lease payment? What is the *PV* of the after-tax lease payment? Should Virginia lease or buy?

(e) Suppose that Virginia can lease the oven for $13,000 annually, payable at the beginning of each year, and the resulting tax deduction is recognized immediately. What is the after-tax lease payment? Should Virginia lease or buy?

(f) What would the annual lease payment have to be in order for Virginia to be indifferent between leasing and buying?

SUGGESTED ADDITIONAL READINGS

Bower, R. S. "Issue in Lease Financing." *Financial Management*, Winter 1973, pp. 25–34.

Brealey, R. A., and C. M. Young. "Debt, Taxes, and Leasing—A Note." *Journal of Finance*, December 1980, pp. 1245–1250.

Crawford, P. J., C. Harper, and J. J. McConnell. "Further Evidence on the Terms of Financial Leases." *Financial Management*, Winter 1981, pp. 7–14.

Fabozzi, F. J. *Equipment Leasing: A Comprehensive Guide for Executives.* Homewood, IL: Dow Jones-Irwin, 1982.

Flath, D. "The Economics of Short-Term Leasing." *Economic Inquiry*, April 1980, pp. 247–259.

Levy, Haim, and Marshall Sarnat. "Leasing, Borrowing, and Financial Risk." *Financial Management*, Winter 1979, pp. 47–54.

Lewellen, Wilbur G., Michael S. Long, and John J. McConnell. "Asset Leasing in Competitive Capital Markets." *Journal of Finance*, June 1976, pp. 787–798.

Miller, Merton H., and Charles W. Upton. "Leasing, Buying, and the Cost of Capital Services." *Journal of Finance*, June 1976, pp. 761–786.

O'Brien, Thomas J., and Bennie H. Nunnally, Jr. "A 1982 Survey of Corporate Leasing Analysis." *Financial Management*, Summer 1983, pp. 30–36.

Schall, L. D. "The Lease-or-Buy and Asset Acquisition Decisions." *Journal of Finance*, September 1974, pp. 1203–1214.

Schallhein, J. S., R. E. Johnson, R. C. Lease, and J. J. McConnell. "The Determinants of Yields on Financial Leasing Contracts." *Journal of Financial Economics*, September 1987, pp. 45–67.

Smith, C. W., and L. M. Wakeman. "Determinants of Corporate Leasing Policy." *Journal of Finance*, July 1985, pp. 895–908.

Sorenson, I., and R. E. Johnson. "Equipment Financial Leasing Practices and Costs: An Empirical Study." *Financial Management*, Spring 1977, pp. 33–40.

PART SIX   FINANCIAL PLANNING AND WORKING CAPITAL MANAGEMENT

NINETEEN   THE IMPACT OF OPERATING AND FINANCIAL DECISIONS ON PROFITS AND CASH FLOWS

Early tomorrow, Jan. 2, 1496, I shall make the leather belt and proceed to a trial. . . . One hundred times in each hour 400 needles will be finished, making 40,000 in an hour and 480,000 in 12 hours. Suppose we say 4,000 thousands (implying ten machines) which at 5 solidi per thousand gives 20,000 solidi; 1,000 lira per working day, and if one works twenty days in the month 60,000 ducats the year.

—Theodor Beck, from
Leonardo da Vinci[1]

[1] Quoted in Abbott Usher, *A History of Mechanical Inventions* (New York: McGraw-Hill, 1929).

W e have defined the two major decisions managers face. They must first decide what projects to invest in, and then they must decide how to finance those investments. The investment decision is made with information about a project's cash flows, which are determined, among other things, by the costs associated with the project. These costs, in turn, depend on the managers' choice of technology. For example, a firm can make its products using a completely automated production process, in which case the fixed costs of production are relatively high. Alternatively, it can produce the same product using a labor-intensive process that has relatively high variable costs. The choice of technology thus determines the firm's cost structure (proportions of fixed and variable costs), and this can affect the variability in the firm's income and accounting measures of return.

In this chapter we develop an understanding of how managerial decisions affect the operating and net performance of the firm by examining some of the basic linkages among sales revenues, fixed and variable costs (technological/investment choices), the financing choice, and accounting profits and cash flows. We examine the break-even point and contribution margin concepts. The analysis of this chapter not only exposes how operating and financing decisions can affect the firm's cash flow volatility but also reveals (in Appendix 19B) how the firm's accounting variables are linked to the firm's beta, the systematic risk measure described in earlier chapters.

The chapter is structured to address the following questions:

- How do managers plan for the firm's survival?

- How do managers' investment decisions affect the firm's profitability?

- How do managers' financing decisions affect the firm's profitability?

- How is the combined leverage effect on the firm measured?

- How does leverage affect the firm's book *ROA* and book *ROE*?

- How do managers' investment and financing decisions affect the firm's cash flows?

Appendix 19A describes the derivations of several formulas used in this chapter. Appendix 19B explains how the firm's operating and financing decisions determine its beta.

19-1

BREAK-EVEN ANALYSIS AND CONTRIBUTION MARGIN

A s we saw in Chapter 1, one characteristic of a business firm is its drive for survival. Managers must ensure that their firm sells enough of its output (goods and/or services) to cover the costs of producing those outputs. If the firm fails in this task, it does not survive. Managers therefore need a way of relating inflows and outflows to determine whether or not the firm is covering its costs. A useful tool for accomplishing this is **break-even analysis.** Although break-even analysis is, by itself, no substitute for a comprehensive capital budgeting analysis, it is still used. More elaborate "feasibility studies," "project plans," and "cost-volume-profit studies" developed by corporate managers to justify and defend their proposed projects inevitably include some break-even analysis.

To illustrate the relationship of cost, volume, and profits, we consider the start-up of a new manufacturing operation. Initially, the production volume is low, sales revenues are insufficient to cover all costs, and because of this, operating losses result. As the production and sales volumes begin to pick up, losses decrease. So the immediate objective of the financial manager is to reach, as quickly as possible, the "break-even point" at which revenues exactly offset all operating costs. Break-even analysis helps identify this break-even point. The **break-even point** or **break-even quantity** is that level of production and sales at which total revenues (or dollar sales) are exactly equal to total operating costs (TC). That is, the break-even point occurs at the production level at which the net operating income (NOI) is $0. The NOI, sometimes called operating profits, deals with only revenues and production costs. Nonoperating costs such as taxes and financial costs (e.g., interest expenses) are not included at this stage, but we address them later in this chapter.

Equation (19-1) is a representation of NOI. We focus on the revenues and operating costs.

$$\begin{aligned} \text{Net operating income} &= \text{dollar sales} - \text{total operating costs} \\ NOI &= S - TC \end{aligned} \tag{19-1}$$

Revenues

Revenues are the total dollar amount that a firm derives from selling its goods and services. It is the selling price per unit (P) multiplied by the quantity of units sold (Q); that is, $S = P \times Q$. For example, if Lumen Light Company wants to manufacture and sell the "eternal light bulb" for $10 per bulb, Figure 19-1 shows that the more Lumen sells, the larger its revenues are.

Operating Costs

Operating costs are divided into three categories: fixed, variable, and semifixed or semivariable.

FIGURE 19-1

Lumen Light Company's revenue (sales) line for different levels of quantity sold. It is assumed here, as in the text, that the firm sells everything it produces.

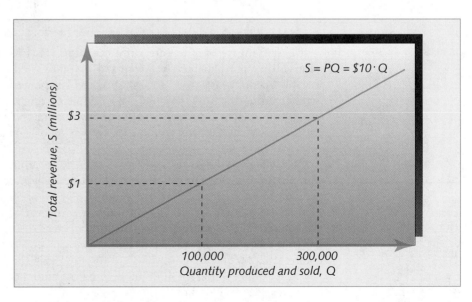

FIXED OPERATING COSTS

Fixed operating costs—such as depreciation and insurance—do not vary with the level of production (i.e., they are fixed). They are incurred whether the firm produces 100 units or 100,000 units. If, for example, Lumen Light Company purchases a machine that can produce 300,000 bulbs per year and costs $200,000, this cost must be borne at any level of production up to 300,000 bulbs. It is thus a fixed cost.

But what if the company wants to make 400,000 light bulbs a year? Then another machine must be bought to increase plant capacity, which results in higher fixed costs. Because even fixed costs change when a firm expands its plant capacity, a more precise definition is that fixed operating costs (F) are those costs that do not depend on the number of units produced *within a given range of production.* This definition reveals that in the long run, fixed costs typically do not remain fixed because most companies keep growing, thereby increasing their fixed costs.

Because break-even analysis deals with fixed operating costs and because these costs are fixed for only a given plant capacity (or range of production), break-even analysis is valid only over the short run.

VARIABLE OPERATING COSTS

Variable operating costs are those expenses that vary directly with the level of production and sales. Items such as direct labor wages and the cost of raw materials fall into this category. The **variable cost per unit** (V) is constant, whereas **total variable operating costs** (TVC) increase or decrease as the quantity produced increases or decreases. Thus,

$$\text{Total variable costs} = \text{variable cost per unit} \times \text{quantity produced}$$
$$TVC = V \times Q \qquad (19\text{-}2)$$

Equation (19-2) illustrates the significance of the phrase "varies directly with production." If production increases by 5%, total variable costs also increase by 5%. **Total operating costs** can now be defined as

$$\text{Total operating costs} = \frac{\text{fixed}}{\text{operating costs}} + \frac{\text{total variable}}{\text{operating costs}}$$
$$TOC = F + TVC \qquad (19\text{-}3)$$

SEMIFIXED OR SEMIVARIABLE OPERATING COSTS

It is not always easy to categorize operating costs as either fixed or variable because they may, in fact, be **semifixed** or **semivariable**. A semifixed or semivariable operating cost is a "hybrid" because one portion of this cost is fixed and another portion of it is variable. An example of this is a marketing executive's compensation, which consists of a fixed base amount and a commission that varies with sales. When a cost is semifixed, one portion of it must be allocated to fixed costs and another to variable costs.

Once all operating costs have been classified, "cost lines" can be constructed in a graph. Assume that Lumen's fixed costs are $1 million, and its variable cost is $5 per unit. From Figure 19-2(a), at a production level of 300,000 bulbs, the vertical distance from point A to point C is Lumen's total variable costs of $1.5 million. But equation (19-3) indicates that the total operating cost is the sum of the fixed and variable operating expenses, and so we can add the two cost lines to get Figure 19-2(b). This diagram indicates more clearly that the total operating expenses are $2.5 million for 300,000 light bulbs (point A to point D). This greatly facilitates determination of the break-even point.

FIGURE 19-2

Lumen Light Company's cost lines for fixed and variable costs: (a) individual cost lines and (b) combined cost lines

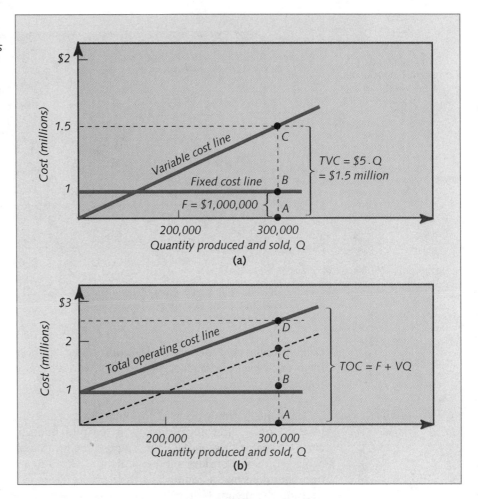

(a)

(b)

The Break-even Point

If we superimpose Figure 19-1 on Figure 19-2(b), we get Figure 19-3, which shows that the break-even point, Q^*, is the intersection of the total operating cost and total revenue lines. For Lumen, this occurs at a production and sales level of 200,000 units. At levels of production to the *right* of Q^* (say, $Q_2 = 300,000$), the firm realizes a profit, and to the *left* of Q^* (say, $Q_1 = 10,000$), the firm suffers a loss.

If Figure 19-3 was drawn to scale on graph paper, the break-even point could be found easily. But there is an easier way. The following equation yields the answer directly:[2]

$$Q^* = \frac{F}{P - V} \qquad\qquad (19\text{-}4)$$

where Q^* is the break-even quantity or "break-even point." The information on fixed costs, sales price per unit, and variable cost per unit yields

$$Q^* = \frac{\$1 \text{ million}}{\$10 - \$5} = 200{,}000 \text{ light bulbs}$$

the same result that was obtained with the graphical approach. $P - V$ in the denominator of equation (19-4), called the **contribution margin per unit**, denotes the

[2] All derivations are given in Appendix 19A.

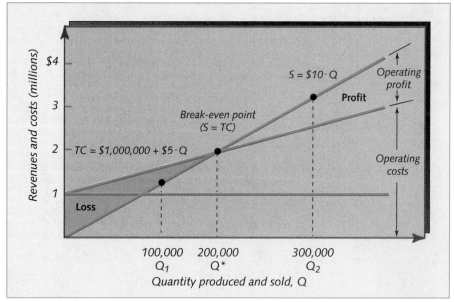

dollar amount that each unit sold "contributes" to meeting the fixed costs. Once the break-even point is reached, $P - V$ measures the amount that each unit "contributes" to profits.

Contribution Margin Analysis

The contribution margin is a useful concept for evaluating operating (in contrast to capital budgeting) decisions. In a capital budgeting analysis, the project is evaluated before it is undertaken. Ex-post, the firm's cash flows can be lower than projected. Now consider another situation. Often managers have to "live with" unprofitable projects adopted by their predecessors in the firm. The investment decision has already been made and the money already invested.

The manager's logical decision would be to shut down the project immediately. However, quite often, the project involves future commitments such as lease payments or service contracts that may have to be honored even if operations cease. In this case, managers must decide whether to continue operations until the project can be terminated or to cease operations immediately.

Because this is an operating rather than a capital budgeting decision, managers can use contribution margin analysis. A common rule of thumb is to continue an unprofitable project in the short run as long as its contribution margin is positive (that is, revenues exceed variable costs). If its variable costs are covered, the firm benefits from running the project (say, producing one more unit of output). True, the firm is not covering all costs (fixed and variable) and thus cannot generate profits. However, as long as the contribution margin is positive, the firm is covering all of its variable costs and some of its fixed costs, thus reducing its losses.

KEY CONCEPT

Even if a project is unprofitable, it can still make sense to continue operations just a little longer. If the contribution margin is positive, the firm's short-term losses are reduced.

Eventually, when the commitments expire, the project should be shut down. We give an example of how contribution margin is used in the accompanying highlight.

CONTRIBUTION MARGIN IN ACTION: AIRLINES' "OUT-OF-POCKET" COSTS

One measure of an airline's productivity, and hence its potential profits, is its "load factor," which may be defined as the average percentage of its available passenger seats filled per flight. The national average is about 60% to 65% during normal economic periods. If an airline's management finds that only 50% of its available seats are being filled, it would appear that by eliminating a few of its less popular flights (e.g., its 3:11 A.M. flight out of Steamboat Springs, Colorado), it should be able to increase its average load and thereby its profits. However, it does not work that way. The improved load factor actually means reduced profits. This conclusion is explained by the concept of contribution margin.

Consider the case of Avian Airlines, Inc., to see how Avian's economic planners translated contribution margin analysis into hard, dollar-and-cents decisions and why the old business adage "Nobody ever made a profit without meeting all costs" is misleading.

Put simply, contribution margin analysis suggests that a company should undertake any new activity that adds more to revenues than it does to "costs." It should not limit itself to those activities whose revenues equal "fully allocated costs" (or variable plus allocated fixed operating costs). It is important to recognize that in this context, the word costs refers to what

we have been calling variable operating expenses. Also, whereas we have discussed contribution margin on a "per unit" basis ($P - V$), here we are referring to this margin on a "total dollar" basis (i.e., revenues minus variable costs).

Now we get to Avian's approach. It first requires that the entire schedule of flights return at least their fully allocated costs. Fixed costs such as overhead, depreciation, and insurance are real expenses and must be covered. The out-of-pocket costs come into play only after the basic schedule has been set. The airline then sees whether adding more flights will contribute to the corporate net income. If it is thinking of dropping a flight that has a disappointing record, it puts it under the contribution margin microscope. If the revenues will be more than its out-of-pocket costs, Avian will keep the flight.

By "out-of-pocket costs" Avian means just that: the actual dollars that Avian has to pay out to run a flight (i.e., the variable operating expenses). It gets this figure not by applying any hypothetical equations but by circulating a proposed schedule to every operating department concerned and finding out just what extra expenses each flight will entail. If a ground crew already on duty can service the plane, the flight will not be charged a penny of their salary expense. There may even be some costs eliminated in running the flight. Avian will not need workers to roll an incoming

plane to a hangar, for instance, or to rent an overnight hangar if the plane flies to another stop. The following problem shows how Avian's thinking might run with regard to a proposal for an additional flight to Mineral Wells, Texas.

Contribution Margin Analysis in a Nutshell

Should Avian Airlines add an extra daily flight from Houston to Mineral Wells? Here are the facts: (1) fully allocated (total operating) costs of this flight: $4,500; (2) out-of-pocket (variable) costs of this flight: $2,000; and (3) revenues generated by this flight: $3,100.

The decision is to run the flight. It will add $1,100 (contribution margin in total dollars) to net profit (and to covering fixed costs) because it will add $3,100 to revenues and only $2,000 to costs. Overhead and other fixed costs totaling $2,500 ($4,500 − $2,000) are incurred whether or not the flight is run. Therefore the fully allocated costs of $4,500 are not relevant to this business decision. It is the out-of-pocket (variable) costs that count.

No firm can survive long term by covering only its variable costs. It should cover all costs and then some. However, consider what we are analyzing here. This is an operating decision involving an investment that has already been made. Sure, the firm is losing money by running some flights, but contribution margin analysis tells how to lower the losses.

With the rapid development of computer-based financial planning systems, break-even analysis has been extended to a variety of complex considerations. In addition to the standard use of break-even analysis studied so far, break-even analysis is helpful in deciding whether to expand a company's operations, introduce new products, or adopt new production technology. In each of these situations, managers must determine whether the firm can produce revenues in excess of its costs. Though useful in many decision-making situations, break-even analysis also has several limitations. For example, the relevant cost and revenue lines may actually be curved lines (and not straight lines), requiring more complex mathematics. The firm could also have multiple products, rather than a single one, and thus be required to calculate break-even points for each product, or focus on break-even revenues rather than break-even quantities. The reader may consult an accounting text to learn more about the uses and limitations of break-even analysis.

Fixed Versus Variable Costs

We discussed break-even analysis to introduce the types of costs that the firm faces. We now examine whether or not a firm should have high fixed costs relative to its variable costs.

The mix of fixed and variable costs depends on the firm's choice of technology. For example, if a firm decides to automate its plant and reduce direct labor costs, then fixed costs will necessarily be high and variable costs will generally decrease. It is already clear that a firm that has high fixed costs must produce and sell more units to break even than must a firm with low fixed costs. Therefore more capital-intensive companies must produce and sell more just to survive.

Ever since Henry Ford introduced the assembly line process, auto companies have been moving toward more mechanization (higher fixed costs). According to the break-even equation, firms with high fixed costs should generate more revenues in order to break even. This means that the Big Three—General Motors, Ford, and Chrysler—depend heavily on vigorous sales. If the economy weakens and car sales fall, these companies can easily move from the profit region to the loss region depicted in Figure 19-3. In fact, this was exactly what happened in the late 1970s when fierce Japanese competition began to cut into domestic auto demand, followed by a recession in 1981–1982. The Big Three suffered tremendous losses. For example, Chrysler ran up nearly *$3.5 billion* in operating losses during this period and had to resort to a $1 billion bailout through federal loan guarantees. As Chrysler's chairman, Lee Iacocca, stated, most of his energy had to be spent on getting Chrysler's break-even point down from 2.4 million vehicles to less than 1 million through a massive cost-reduction program that included increasing automation and slashing labor costs.

How, then, can a large investment in fixed assets be rationalized? Isn't a company better off staying with low fixed costs and minimizing its exposure to heavy losses? These issues are examined in greater detail in the following section.

19-2

MANAGERIAL
INVESTMENT
DECISIONS AND
OPERATING
LEVERAGE

We have seen how financial managers can estimate the break-even point. In the case of a new firm, reaching this level of production is a major milestone in its growth toward becoming a fully established firm. Once the firm's revenues cover its total costs, the next logical step is to continue to increase production and sales because, given linear costs and revenues, any production level greater than the break-even quantity puts the firm in the profit region. As the quantity produced and sold increases, profits also increase. Any business that operates to the right of the break-even point knows that it will make a profit.

This raises an interesting question. If a firm is to make a profit, it should produce at least the break-even quantity. According to equation (19-4), the lower the fixed costs are for a firm, the lower the break-even quantity is. Then why not minimize fixed costs? In that way, the firm can enter the profit zone very quickly.

Something is wrong with this argument, though, because we know that Ford and Exxon have very high fixed costs. Obviously, these highly capital-intensive firms have high fixed costs for some reason that must be to their advantage. Indeed, as we see shortly, fixed costs provide operating leverage for the firm. Businesses with high fixed costs hope to "lever up" or magnify their earnings from small increases in sales by using operating leverage.

KEY CONCEPT

Operating leverage is the extent to which a firm's fixed production costs contribute to its total operating costs at different levels of sales. In a firm that has operating leverage, a given change in sales results in a larger change in the net operating income (NOI).

We introduce a means of measuring this leverage effect and then show how this magnification occurs. The presence of operating leverage in a firm is measured by the **degree of operating leverage** for a fixed production level Q, DOL_Q. This measure permits the financial manager to compute and evaluate more easily the effects of operating leverage. If firm B has a lower degree of operating leverage than does firm A at a certain production level, we can conclude that firm B has less operating leverage at that production level than firm A does. To simplify the notation, the subscript Q is henceforth omitted from DOL_Q. The degree of operating leverage (DOL) at a particular production level Q measures the percentage change in NOI ($\%\Delta NOI$) for a given percentage change in sales ($\%\Delta S$):

$$DOL = \frac{\text{percentage change in } NOI}{\text{percentage change in sales}}$$

This can be written as (see Appendix 19A for a derivation)

$$DOL = \frac{Q(P - V)}{Q(P - V) - F} \tag{19-5}$$

In equation (19-5), note that $Q(P - V)$ is not the percentage change in NOI and that $Q(P - V) - F$ is not the percentage change in sales. Equation (19-5) is just the result of substituting and simplifying the correct expressions for $\%\Delta NOI$ and $\%\Delta S$.

A sampling of DOL estimates by industry is given in Table 19-1. Although all DOL numbers should theoretically be equal to or greater than 1, the DOL numbers in this table are estimated from an empirical sample and thus in some cases are less than 1.

The situation faced by the managers of Lumen Light Company shows how a firm's investment decision affects its profitability. Lumen makes eternal light bulbs and has $F = \$1$ million, $V = \$5$, and $P = \$10$ at $Q = 250{,}000$ units. Its degree of operating leverage at a production level of 250,000 bulbs is given by equation (19-5) as:

$$DOL = \frac{250{,}000(10 - 5)}{250{,}000(10 - 5) - 1{,}000{,}000} = 5.0$$

■

T A B L E   1 9 - 1

DOL *Estimates by*
Industry

Industry	Estimated DOL[a]
Food	0.42
Tobacco	0.73
Waste	0.96
Chemicals	1.01
Broadcasting	1.14
Petroleum	1.34
Packaging (containers)	1.49
Trucking	1.66
Plumbing and valves	1.80
Distillers	1.87
Metals (minor)	1.96
Herbicides	1.97
Steel	2.21
Fiberglass	2.43
Building materials	3.03
Paper and lumber	3.21

SOURCE: This information was compiled from T. J. O'Brien and P. A. Vanderheiden, "Empirical Measurement of Operating Leverage for Growing Firms," *Financial Management,* Summer 1987, pp. 45–53.
[a]Estimated *DOLs* are averages for various firms in each industry. Because these numbers are estimates from empirical data, some of the *DOL* numbers are less than 1.

From the definition of the degree of operating leverage, this means that if Lumen's sales go up by 5%, its *NOI* will go up by 25% because

$$DOL = \frac{\%\Delta NOI}{\%\Delta S} \quad \text{or} \quad \%\Delta NOI = DOL \times \%\Delta S$$
$$= 5.0 \times 5\%$$
$$= 25\%$$

Notice from the example that the degree of operating leverage is a "magnification factor." A 5% sales increase is magnified to a 25% *NOI* increase. This magnification is achieved by using fixed costs. To see why, assume that a firm has zero fixed costs. Then equation (19-5) suggests that the magnification factor for this firm is 1.0. In other words, there is no real magnification when there are no fixed costs.

Operating leverage exists because of fixed costs, and fixed costs amplify changes in the *NOI* for small changes in sales. So it appears that in order to have maximum magnification in its *NOI*, a firm must have the maximum degree of operating leverage. Equation (19-5) must be interpreted carefully. At first glance it appears to suggest that increasing fixed costs increases the *DOL*. However, this conclusion is strictly accurate only if variable costs do not change. In general, variable costs do decline with increasing fixed costs, and *DOL* increases with *F* only if the increase in $Q(P - V)$ in percentage terms is less than the percentage increase in *F*.[3]

Let us now see, by means of a more comprehensive example, that it may be imprudent to increase operating leverage indiscriminately. We return to the case of

[3]Assume that a firm raises its fixed costs *F* to *lF*, with $l > 1$. Assume also that the corresponding decrease in variable costs changes $Q(P - V)$ to $kQ(P - V)$. Then the new *DOL* is

$$\frac{kQ(P - V)}{kQ(P - V) - lF}$$

which can be rewritten as

$$\frac{Q(P - V)}{Q(P - V) - (l/k)F}$$

The new *DOL* is larger than the old *DOL* only if $(l/k) > 1$ or $l > k$.

Lumen and its light bulbs and assume that management is evaluating a proposal to close its current manufacturing facility and double its capacity by constructing a $1.2 million plant at Shallowater, Texas. This new facility would use robotics and CAM (computer-assisted manufacturing) technology that allows the light bulbs to be assembled, tested, and packaged—untouched by human hands. This new technology would drastically alter Lumen's cost structure. Fixed costs would rise from the current $1 million to $1.54 million per year, but the variable cost per bulb would drop to $3 and the break-even point would increase from 200,000 bulbs to

$$Q^* = \frac{\$1,540,000}{\$10 - \$3} = 220,000 \text{ bulbs}$$

Because Lumen is currently producing 250,000 bulbs per year, management needs to evaluate what its operating incomes (NOI) would be under the existing and the proposed technology. What if as few as 150,000 or as many as 350,000 bulbs are produced and sold? Table 19-2 demonstrates the sensitivity of Lumen's profits under these scenarios. Three observations are evident. First, the break-even level is higher under the new technology. Second, the existing level of production currently yields a profit of $250,000 but gives a profit of $210,000 under the proposed technology. Third, the variation in losses and profits is greater under the new technology.

If the break-even point would rise and the profits at a sales level of 250,000 bulbs would decrease, why is Lumen even considering an increase in its fixed costs? The answer is easy. Lumen expects that the demand for its bulbs will increase. This expected increase in sales (if it is correct) can produce a magnification in the NOI if the firm had greater operating leverage (i.e., new technology). But if sales fall, the higher operating leverage under the proposed technology would also magnify losses!

Table 19-2 shows that with the existing technology, if sales rise from 250,000 to 350,000 bulbs (%ΔS = 40%), the NOI will increase from $250,000 to $750,000 (%$\Delta NOI$ = 200%). On the other hand, if Lumen adopts the new technology that will increase its DOL, then for the same 40% increase in sales, the NOI will increase by 333%—from $210,000 to $910,000. This illustrates the impact of operating leverage.

■

TABLE 19-2

The Effect of Choice of Technology on Lumen Light Company's Profitability[a]

	Production and Sales Level Q		
	150,000	250,000	350,000
	Plan A: Existing technology (DOL = 5.0)		
Revenues ($S = \$10 \times Q$)	$1,500,000	$2,500,000	$3,500,000
Less: Variable operating costs ($V = \$5 \times Q$)	−750,000 [43%]	−1,250,000 [56%]	−1,750,000 [64%]
Less: Fixed operating costs (F)	−1,000,000 [57%]	−1,000,000 [44%]	−1,000,000 [36%]
Net operating income (NOI)	−$ 250,000	$ 250,000	$ 750,000
	Plan B: Proposed technology (DOL = 8.33)		
Revenues ($S = \$10 \times Q$)	$1,500,000	$2,500,000	$3,500,000
Less: Variable operating costs ($V = \$3 \times Q$)	−450,000 [23%]	−750,000 [33%]	−1,050,000 [41%]
Less: Fixed operating costs (F)	−1,540,000 [77%]	−1,540,000 [67%]	−1,540,000 [59%]
Net operating income (NOI)	−$ 490,000	$ 210,000	$ 910,000

[a] Numbers in brackets are variable or fixed costs as a percentage of total operating costs.

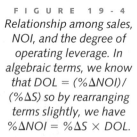

TABLE 19-3

The Concept of Operating Leverage: Measuring the Sensitivity of Lumen Light Company's Operating Profits to Changes in Sales Levels

	Plan A Existing Technology	Plan B Proposed Technology
	Sales drop to 150,000 bulbs	
Percentage change in sales	$\dfrac{1{,}500{,}000 - 2{,}500{,}000}{2{,}500{,}000} = -40\%$	$\dfrac{1{,}500{,}000 - 2{,}500{,}000}{2{,}500{,}000} = -40\%$
Percentage change in *NOI*	$\dfrac{-250{,}000 - 250{,}000}{250{,}000} = -200\%$	$\dfrac{-490{,}000 - 210{,}000}{210{,}000} = -333\%$
	Sales rise to 350,000 bulbs	
Percentage change in sales	$\dfrac{3{,}500{,}000 - 2{,}500{,}000}{2{,}500{,}000} = 40\%$	$\dfrac{3{,}500{,}000 - 2{,}500{,}000}{2{,}500{,}000} = 40\%$
Percentage change in *NOI*	$\dfrac{750{,}000 - 250{,}000}{250{,}000} = 200\%$	$\dfrac{910{,}000 - 210{,}000}{210{,}000} = 333\%$

Now examine Table 19-3. Under plan *A*, if sales fall by 40%, the *NOI* will fall by 200%; under plan *B*, if sales fall by 40%, profits will also fall by 333%. Thus operating leverage does not discriminate. It is a magnifying influence—it magnifies both profits and losses. If things go well for the firm, operating leverage helps, but if sales are not far enough to the right of the break-even point, the firm can get wiped out. Operating leverage helps a firm magnify its operating profits as long as it sells more than the break-even quantity. But if a firm has losses, operating leverage magnifies them also.

Because the variability of the *NOI* under plan *B* is greater than in plan *A*, the degree of operating leverage is said to measure the firm's "business risk." For Lumen, plan *B* thus has more business risk than plan *A* does.

Figure 19-4 is a useful diagram to remember because it illustrates that the percentage change in the *NOI* is found by just multiplying the percentage change in sales by the degree of operating leverage. For Lumen Light Company:

$$\%\Delta NOI_A = \%\Delta S \times DOL = 0.40 \times 5.0 = 2.00 \quad \text{or } 200\%$$
$$\%\Delta NOI_B = \%\Delta S \times DOL = 0.40 \times 8.33 = 3.33 \quad \text{or } 333\%$$

if production and sales are increased to 350,000 bulbs from their current levels. As can be seen, these results are identical to those obtained from Tables 19-2 and 19-3.

Consider two more examples to better understand operating leverage. A small fur company in Mashpee, Massachusetts, has a current *NOI* of $200,000. Next

FIGURE 19-4

Relationship among sales, NOI, and the degree of operating leverage. In algebraic terms, we know that DOL = (%ΔNOI)/ (%ΔS) so by rearranging terms slightly, we have %ΔNOI = %ΔS × DOL.

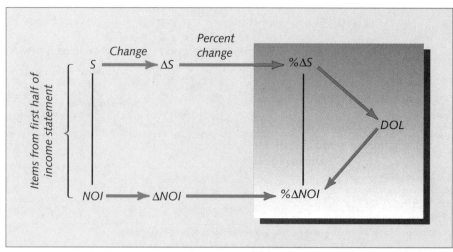

year's *NOI* is expected to be $300,000 because sales are expected to go up by 25%. What does this imply about the company's *DOL*? We have:

$$\%\Delta S = 25\% \quad \text{and} \quad \%\Delta NOI = \frac{\$300,000 - \$200,000}{\$200,000} = 50\%$$

According to Figure 19-4, $\%\Delta S \times DOL = \%\Delta NOI$, or

$$DOL = \frac{\%\Delta NOI}{\%\Delta S} = \frac{50\%}{25\%} = 2.0$$

By examining how the firm's *NOI* reacts to changes in sales, we have inferred the firm's *DOL*. Now consider another example.

Zee-Zee Tops, Inc., manufactures plaid vinyl and chenille car tops for convertibles. These roofs sell for $200 each and have a variable cost per unit of $120. Management fully expects next year's sales and its *NOI* to drop sharply, by 20% and 50%, respectively, owing to a lack of demand (i.e., "consumer resistance"). If Zee-Zee's current level of production and sales is 112 car tops, what is its level of fixed costs? We have:

$$\%\Delta S = -20\% \quad \text{and} \quad \%\Delta NOI = -50\%$$

According to Figure 19-4,

$$DOL = \frac{\%\Delta NOI}{\%\Delta S} = \frac{-50\%}{-20\%} = 2.5$$

and according to equation (19-5),

$$DOL = \frac{Q(P - V)}{Q(P - V) - F}$$

$$2.5 = \frac{112(\$200 - \$120)}{112(\$200 - \$120) - F}$$

or

$$F = \$5,376$$

When we know how sensitive Zee-Zee Tops' *NOI* is to sales, the formula for *DOL* allows us to infer Zee-Zee's fixed costs.

We summarize this discussion about operating leverage as a key concept.

KEY CONCEPT The degree of operating leverage, *DOL*, measures the sensitivity of *NOI* to changes in the firm's revenues.

19-3

MANAGERIAL FINANCING DECISIONS AND FINANCIAL LEVERAGE

The next logical question is: If a financial manager can use fixed operating costs to magnify the sensitivity of changes in *NOI* to changes in sales in the first half of the income statement, can she also do something to magnify the sensitivity of net income (*NI*) to changes in *NOI* in the second half of the income statement? (Recall from Chapter 3 that the progression from *NOI* to *NI* occurs in the second half of the income statement.)

This can, in fact, be done by financing a firm's assets with debt. Because this type of financing carries a fixed obligation or cost in the form of interest and because this fixed obligation arises from a financial rather than an operating decision, it is called **financial leverage.**

KEY CONCEPT

Financial leverage measures the sensitivity of the firm's net income (NI) to changes in its net operating income (NOI). In contrast to operating leverage, which is determined by the firm's choice of technology (fixed and variable costs), financial leverage is determined by the firm's financing choices (the mix of debt and equity).

As the proportion of debt to equity increases, financial leverage also increases, resulting in greater fluctuations in NI for changes in NOI. Keep in mind that we are not saying that NI goes up with financial leverage, only that the *changes* in NI are greater for a given change in sales or NOI.

Investors and creditors often view financial leverage and financial risk as being one and the same. Financial risk, however, is defined in *market-value* terms, whereas the equation for the degree of financial leverage is calculated using *book-value* information (book values of debt and equity). Because we have not discussed market-value measures, financial leverage temporarily serves as a measure of variability. The **degree of financial leverage** (DFL) measures the percentage change in net income ($\%\Delta NI$) for a given percentage change in NOI ($\%\Delta NOI$).

DFL is expressed as $(\%\Delta NI)/(\%\Delta NOI)$ and can be shown to equal:

$$DFL = \frac{NOI}{NOI - I} \tag{19-6a}$$

or, substituting $Q(P - V) - F$ for NOI, we obtain

$$DFL = \frac{Q(P - V) - F}{Q(P - V) - F - I} \tag{19-6b}$$

where I is the dollar amount of interest expenses. Taxes do not enter into the equation because taxes affect both the numerator and the denominator and cancel out. From these equations it is easy to see why financial leverage exists because of debt financing. For a firm that uses no debt, I is 0 and DFL equals 1.0. This means there is no magnification effect in the second half of the income statement.

Now we reexamine Lumen Light Company's proposed technology change (plan B) in light of this new leverage concept. In addition to the financial projections for plan B in Table 19-4, we assume that Lumen has two alternative schemes for financing the $1.2 million production facility:

■

TABLE 19-4

The Effect of the Two Alternative Financing Plans on Lumen Light Company's NI[a]

	Plan B-1: All Equity	Plan B-2: 40% Debt, 60% Equity
	Profitability	
Revenues	$2,500,000	$2,500,000
Less: Variable operating costs	−750,000	−750,000
Less: Fixed operating costs	−1,540,000	−1,540,000
Net operating income (*NOI*)	$ 210,000	$ 210,000
Less: Interest expenses	0	−100,800[b]
Net profits before taxes	$ 210,000	$ 109,200
Less: Taxes (40%)	−84,000	−43,680
Net income (*NI*)	$ 126,000	$ 65,520
	Degree of financial leverage[c]	
	$\dfrac{NOI}{NOI - I}$	$\dfrac{NOI}{NOI - I}$
	$\dfrac{\$210,000}{\$210,000 - \$0}$	$\dfrac{\$210,000}{\$210,000 - \$100,800}$
	1.00	1.92

[a]Production level = 250,000 light bulbs.
[b]Interest expenses are $720,000 × 0.14 = $100,800.
[c]This table uses equation (19-6a), but equation (19-6b) is equivalent and gives the same answer.

1. Plan *B*-1 finances the entire expenditure from internal funds (i.e., equity).

2. Plan *B*-2 uses 40% equity ($480,000) and 60% debt ($720,000) with a stated interest rate of 14%.

Management wishes to analyze the effects of these two financing plans on reported earnings available to common stockholders (i.e., net income). According to Table 19-4, the *NOI* is the same for both plans because it is not affected by the mode of financing. However, the *NI* under plan *B*-1 is almost twice that under plan *B*-2. This seems to argue that the equity plan is superior (i.e., why not always use equity and avoid fixed financial charges?). But the debt–equity financing plan has a *DFL* of 1.92, and the all-equity plan has a *DFL* of only 1.0 (i.e., no magnification effect). This means that if management can expect a production and sales level greater than the current 250,000 units, the percentage change in *NI* under plan *B*-2 will be nearly twice that of plan *B*-1. As long as fixed financial charges are covered, stockholders will receive a magnification of their earnings.

As with *DOL*, this outcome can be portrayed graphically, as in Figure 19-5. According to this diagram, the exact percentage change in *NI* can be determined by multiplying the percentage change in *NOI* by the degree of financial leverage. So if management thinks that a 40% increase in production to 350,000 light bulbs is a more reasonable projection, all other things constant, *NOI* will increase by 333% (refer to Table 19-3). Hence the percentage change in *NI* will be:

$$\%\Delta NI_{B\text{-}1} = 3.33 \times 1.00 = 3.33 \quad \text{or } 333\%$$

$$\%\Delta NI_{B\text{-}2} = 3.33 \times 1.92 = 6.39 \quad \text{or } 639\%$$

Don't forget, however, that financial leverage is a two-way street. If production had, instead, fallen 40% to 150,000 light bulbs, these appealing results would switch signs and produce a disastrous outcome for Lumen.

Before concluding our discussion of financial leverage, consider two more examples. The first example focuses on financial leverage only; the second deals with both operating and financial leverage.

Mercedes Company expects that next year its *NOI* will fall by 10%, and because of this its *NI* will fall by 33%. If these estimates are correct, what degree of financial leverage will Mercedes have? According to Figure 19-5,

■
FIGURE 19-5
Relationship among NOI, NI, and the degree of financial leverage. In algebraic terms, we know that DFL = (%ΔNI)/(%ΔNOI), and so rearranging terms yields %ΔNI = %ΔNOI × DFL.

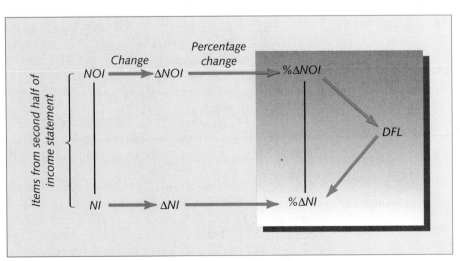

$$\%\Delta NOI \times DFL = \%\Delta NI$$
$$10\% \times DFL = 33\%$$

Therefore $DFL = 33\%/10\% = 3.3$.

Now we assume that Mercedes has a DOL of 2.0 at the current level of production. If sales are expected to go up by 12%, by how much will NOI and NI increase? According to Figure 19-4,

$$\%\Delta NOI = \%\Delta S \times DOL$$
$$= 12\% \times 2.0$$
$$= 24\%$$

Then

$$\%\Delta NI = \%\Delta NOI \times DFL$$
$$= 24\% \times 3.3$$
$$= 79.2\%$$

19-4
COMBINING INVESTMENT AND FINANCING LEVERAGE EFFECTS

What is the combined effect of managers' investment and financing decisions on the firm? Two distinct concepts of leverage have been developed so far: DOL (which works in the first half of the income statement) is first-stage leverage, and DFL (which works in the second half of the income statement) is second-stage leverage. These two leverage effects can be combined into an overall measure of leverage called *combined* or *total leverage*.

KEY CONCEPT   **Combined leverage** measures the overall sensitivity of net income (NI) to a change in sales. The degree of combined leverage (DCL) is defined as the percentage change in net income for a given percentage change in sales.

It can be shown that (see Appendix 19A for details)

$$DCL = \frac{Q(P - V)}{Q(P - V) - F - I} \tag{19-7}$$

To calculate the DCL, we can use equation (19-7) or compute it indirectly by multiplying the DOL by the DFL; that is,

$$DCL = DOL \times DFL \tag{19-8}$$

For a given change in sales, the DCL measures the combined magnification of the NI induced by fixed operating costs and interest payments. If sales change, the operating leverage magnifies the NOI, and this change in NOI is translated into a magnification of net income by financial leverage. Instead of this two-step magnification procedure, combined leverage directly magnifies sales changes into changes in net income.

Consider two examples. If Ajax Appliance Corporation has a DOL of 2.0 at a production level of 10,000 refrigerators and its DFL is 1.5, its $DCL = DOL \times DFL = 2.0 \times 1.5 = 3.0$. If Ajax's sales increase by 10%, its NI will increase by $\%\Delta S \times DCL = 10\% \times 3.0 = 30\%$.

Meditech Products is a small electronics firm that makes digital thermometers. Management feels that if sales go up by 10%, its NI will increase by 40%. Meditech has a DFL of 2.0. What is the level of fixed costs (F) for Meditech at a production level of 1,000 thermometers if the contribution margin per unit is $5?

We have:

%Δ*S* × *DCL* = %Δ*NI*
10% × *DCL* = 40%

Therefore *DCL* = 4.0. Because it is also true that

DCL = *DFL* × *DOL*
4.0 = 2.0 × *DOL*
DOL = 2.0

According to equation (19-5) for *DOL*,

$$DOL = \frac{Q(P - V)}{Q(P - V) - F}$$

Recognizing that *Q* = 1,000, *P* − *V* = \$5, and *DOL* = 2.0, we have

$$2.0 = \frac{1,000 \times 5}{(1,000 \times 5) - F} \quad \text{or} \quad F = \$2,500$$

19-5

LEVERAGE, BOOK ROA, AND BOOK ROE

I t should be clear by now that operating and financial leverages affect the bottom line of the income statement (net income). Leverage can thus affect rates of return. In this section we define two important rates of return, and then show how they are affected by operating and financial leverage.

Accounting Rates of Return

People who analyze financial statements typically think in terms of rates of return (or percentage returns) as well as in terms of dollar returns when evaluating a company's profitability. It is precisely because of this that two return measures were developed: return on assets (*ROA*) and return on equity (*ROE*). These terms have been defined and used in various ways, but in this book we define them as follows:

$$\text{Book } ROA = \frac{\text{after-tax } NOI}{\text{total assets}} = \frac{NOI(1 - T)}{A} \tag{19-9}$$

$$\text{Book } ROE = \frac{NI}{\text{stockholders' equity}} = \frac{NI}{E} \tag{19-10}$$

It is useful to understand exactly why two measures of return were developed. Consider a firm that manufactures silicon photovoltaic cells. If we calculate this firm's *ROA*, we are assessing the profitability of producing these cells, and this depends on the price at which these cells can be sold, the firm's fixed and variable costs, and the firm's tax rate. Notice that only these items are required in the numerator of the *ROA* formula. The question of how this firm is to finance this project (i.e., via debt or equity) is immaterial and does not enter the *ROA* calculation. Thus the *ROA* measures the profitability of a firm (or investment) without regard to the manner in which the firm is financed.

For the analyst of a firm's financial statements, the relevant measure of return is the return on equity (*ROE*). When calculating their returns, stockholders are concerned with their investment in the company (equity) rather than in total assets. In addition, they are concerned with the net income to the company, which reflects the firm's financing characteristics, because the interest payments are subtracted from the operating income before the net income is determined. Obviously, if the firm uses no debt, its interest payments are $0 and its net income does not differ from its operating income. Thus the *ROE* depends not only on the profitability of an investment but also on the manner in which it is financed.

KEY CONCEPT   The return on assets (*ROA*) measures the accounting performance of the investment without regard to the manner in which the asset is financed. The return on equity (*ROE*) measures the net effects of both the investment and financing decisions.

RELATIONSHIP BETWEEN BOOK *ROA* AND BOOK *ROE*

The relationship between *ROA* and *ROE* is shown in equation (19-11):[4]

$$ROE = ROA + \frac{D}{E}(ROA - i_{at})$$ (19-11)

$$\underbrace{\hspace{3cm}}$$
premium from using
borrowed funds

where

D is the value of the firm's debt

E is the value of the firm's equity

i_{at} is the after-tax cost of debt

How is i_{at} determined? If a firm is paying interest rate *i* on its debt and has a tax rate of *T*, its net cost or after-tax cost $i_{at} = i(1 - T)$. For example, if a firm is

---

[4]By definition, $ROA = NOI(1 - T)/A$. Because net income $NI = (NOI - I)(1 - T)$, it follows that

$$ROA = \frac{NI + I(1 - T)}{A}$$

Multiplying both sides of this equation by A/E yields

$$ROA\left(\frac{A}{E}\right) = \frac{NI + I(1 - T)}{E} = \frac{NI}{E} + \frac{I}{E}(1 - T)$$

or

$$ROA\left(\frac{A}{E}\right) = ROE + \frac{I}{E}(1 - T)$$

Because $A = D + E$ (where *D* is the total book value of debt—current liabilities plus long-term debt—used by a firm; note that *D* here has a meaning different from that in the rest of the chapter, where *D* represents depreciation),

$$ROA\left(\frac{D + E}{E}\right) = ROE + \frac{I}{E}(1 - T)$$

that is,

$$ROA\left(1 + \frac{D}{E}\right) = ROE + \frac{I}{D}(1 - T) \times \frac{D}{E}$$

$$ROA + \frac{D}{E}ROA = ROE + i_{at} \times \frac{D}{E}$$

where $i_{at} = (I/D)(1 - T)$. Rearranging, we obtain equation (19-11).

paying 10% on its debt and it is in the 30% tax bracket, then $i_{at} = 10\%(1 - 0.30) = 7\%$. Alternatively, if the firm is paying $\$I$ of interest on $\$D$ of debt, its before-tax interest rate in percentage terms is I/D, so that the after-tax cost of debt i_{at} is $I(1 - T)/D$. As an example, a firm that pays $\$12,000$ in annual interest payments on a debt of $\$100,000$ is paying $\$12,000/\$100,000 = 12\%$ on its debt. Thus the after-tax interest cost $i_{at} = (0.12)(1 - 0.3) = 8.4\%$ if the firm is assumed to be in the 30% tax bracket.

THE IMPLICATIONS OF EQUATION (19-11)

Equation (19-11) indicates the following points:

1. If a firm uses no debt, $D = 0$ in equation 19-11 and $ROA = ROE$. That is, without debt, the return to stockholders is exactly that return provided by the investment. Hence, for the ROE to be greater than the ROA, it appears that a firm should use debt.

2. For the ROE to be greater than the ROA with debt, one additional condition must be satisfied: ROA must be greater than i_{at}. The project should generate a return greater than the after-tax cost of borrowing. This makes sense. If we borrow money at 10% after taxes, the investment must make more than 10% for this borrowing to be justified. In equation (19-11), if ROA is less than i_{at}, then the term in parentheses is negative, and ROE is less than ROA. The stockholders' returns decrease. It is only when ROA is greater than the after-tax cost of funds that debt financing makes sense. This is because it is only under this condition that ROE is greater than ROA.

The following highlight is a casual example that brings out the linkages between rates of return and leverage.

Leverage and Rates of Return

With the basic rates of return defined, we can now see how they are affected by operating and financial leverage. Return to the example of the company that makes voltaic cells. If the company has $DOL = 1.5$ and $DFL = 2.0$, then $DCL = 1.5 \times 2.0 = 3.0$. If sales are expected to rise by 10%, then $\%\Delta ROA$ is $\%\Delta S \times DOL = 10\% \times 1.5 = 15\%$. Similarly, $\%\Delta ROE$ is $\%\Delta ROA \times DFL = 15\% \times 2.0 = 30\%$. Of course, the $\%\Delta ROE$ figure could have been derived directly by recognizing that

$$\%\Delta ROE = \%\Delta S \times DCL = 10\% \times 3.0 = 30\%$$

Thus changes in ROA and ROE are also related to DOL and DFL.

| 19.6 |

BREAK-EVEN ANALYSIS, LEVERAGE, AND CASH FLOWS

The view of the firm provided by accounting statements allows us to see how managerial decisions affect firm profitability. However, as we stressed in Chapter 2, cash flow, and not accounting profit, affects stockholder wealth. In this last section we make the transition from accounting values to cash flows. It is essential that a financial manager be able to examine the impact of operating and financing decisions on cash flows. Accountants may conclude that a firm's NOI is expected to increase by 10%. But the manager often wants to know how this will affect the firm's cash flows. Recall again that a firm's profit (NOI) does not pay the bills; it is cash flows that do this job. Adapting the development so far to a cash flow context is the objective of this section.

AN APPLICATION OF *ROA – ROE* ANALYSIS: HOUSING AS AN INVESTMENT

During the late 1970s and early 1980s, it was extremely profitable to invest in housing, especially in California. The values of houses were appreciating at impressive rates of nearly 15% annually, and almost everyone in the cocktail party circuit was "into" real estate investing. Yet by the early 1980s the situation had changed considerably. Housing had lost its luster and a variety of other investments, from jojoba beans to active yogurt culture farms, were being touted as the most lucrative ventures.

The ROA–ROE framework can be used to explain what may have happened. For purposes of illustration, we use some convenient numbers and ignore complex tax considerations. It is important to realize that the example is purely for motivating ROA–ROE analysis and is not intended to be the sole criterion for real estate investment decisions.

Consider Mr. Joe Investor, who is in the 20% tax bracket. Assume that Joe is able to obtain a FHA loan on an $100,000 home at a 10% interest rate. Furthermore, all he has to put down is 20%, or $20,000. Assume also that the inflation rate at this time is 15%. What is Joe's ROE?

Because the house will appreciate at 15%, the return on this asset (ROA) is 15%. There are no taxes on this appreciation until the house is sold. Notice that this return measure does not take into account any financing details. Joe's after-tax interest cost i_{at} is 10%(1 − T) or 10%(1 − 0.20) = 8%. However, Joe's equity in this investment is only 20%. Hence he is using financial leverage to increase his returns. Joe's ROE can be calculated as follows:

$$ROE = ROA + \frac{D}{E}$$
$$\times (ROA - i_{at})$$
$$= 15\%$$
$$+ \frac{\$80,000}{\$20,000}(15\% - 8\%)$$
$$= 15\% + 4(7\%)$$
$$= 43\%$$

Thus, although the value of the property itself is appreciating at only 15%, Joe is getting a premium for borrowing funds of 28% (43% − 15%) because the return on the asset is greater than Joe's after-tax cost of the borrowed funds. This is indeed a very attractive rate of return and perhaps explains the excessive interest in housing as an investment at that time.

In the early 1980s interest rates shot up to record highs—up to almost 17% in some cases—and inflation came down to around 5%. What is the ROE for an investor in a situation similar to Joe's who now has to borrow at, say, 12%? The after-tax interest cost is 12%(1 − 0.2) = 9.6% and

$$ROE = 5\% + \frac{\$80,000}{\$20,000}$$
$$\times (5\% - 9.6\%)$$
$$= 5\% + 4(-4.6\%)$$
$$= -13.4\%$$

Leverage thus works both ways, and this example clearly indicates that it is not always good to borrow.

Cash flows can be viewed in two different ways: as operating cash flows (*OCF*) and as net cash flows (*NCF*). Operating cash flows are generated from the firm's operations in the first half of the income statement. Net cash flows, on the other hand, are the "bottom-line cash flows." With the operating cash flows the firm still has to pay interest to its creditors. Thus net cash flows are operating cash flows less the after-tax cost of interest.

Because our focus has changed from accounting costs to cash outflows, we must modify our definition of fixed costs. The total fixed costs, *F,* are composed of two parts: cash fixed costs and accounting expenses (such as depreciation), which are not cash outflows. Although we are not directly concerned with depreciation in a cash flow context, it has cash flow implications because it is tax deductible. We therefore introduce a new measure of **cash fixed costs,** *F′,* which is defined as:

$$F' = F - D$$

(19-12)

The firm's operating and net cash flows can now be calculated as:

$$OCF = [Q(P - V) - F' - D](1 - T) + D \qquad (19\text{-}13)$$

$$NCF = [Q(P - V) - F' - D - I](1 - T) + D \qquad (19\text{-}14)$$

where T is the tax rate and D is the amount of depreciation taken by the firm.

A Cash Flow Break-even Point

Instead of finding the profit break-even point, a manager may find it more useful to calculate the operating cash flow break-even point. The **cash flow break-even point** is the level of production at which the operating cash flows equal 0. A net cash flow break-even point can also be developed along the same lines and is left as an exercise for the interested reader. At this level of production, a firm has sufficient cash flows to cover its operations. The cash flow break-even point is calculated as

$$BE(CF) = \frac{F' - Adj}{P - V} \qquad (19\text{-}15)$$

where $Adj = TD/(1 - T)$ is an *adjustment factor* to convert accounting-based (profits) analysis to cash flow-based analysis.

Cash Flow Leverage Measures

The **degree of operating cash flow leverage**, $DOL(CF)$, is the sensitivity of operating cash flows (OCF) to changes in sales. That is, $DOL(CF) = (\%\Delta OCF)/(\%\Delta S)$ and can be calculated as

$$DOL(CF) = \frac{Q(P - V)}{Q(P - V) - F' + Adj} \qquad (19\text{-}16)$$

Similarly, the **degree of financial cash flow leverage**, $DFL(CF)$, measures the sensitivity of net cash flows (NCF) to changes in operating cash flows (OCF). In other words, $DFL(CF) = (\%\Delta NCF)/(\%\Delta OCF)$ and can be calculated using the following equation:

$$DFL(CF) = \frac{Q(P - V) - F' + Adj}{Q(P - V) - F' - I + Adj} \qquad (19\text{-}17)$$

where the adjustment factor is defined as before.

As the reader might have guessed, these two cash flow leverage measures can be combined to give a combined cash flow leverage factor. The **combined cash flow leverage factor**, $DCL(CF)$, measures the sensitivity of net cash flows to changes in sales and is measured as

$$DCL(CF) = \frac{\%\Delta NCF}{\%\Delta S}$$

It can be calculated as

$$DCL(CF) = \frac{Q(P - V)}{Q(P - V) - F' - I + Adj} \qquad (19\text{-}18)$$

Note that in all these equations, if taxes are $0 or if depreciation is $0, the adjustment factor becomes 0. In this case, all the equations degenerate to those developed earlier for profits, with the proper adjustments.

As an example of these cash flow leverages, suppose that Brezner Radionics makes ultrasonic testing devices for nondestructive testing. Its cash fixed costs are $80,000. In addition, the firm takes a $14,000 depreciation charge (a noncash item) on its plant. Brezner's variable cost per unit is $400, it sells the devices at $1,400 each, and it is in the 30% tax bracket. Calculate Brezner's cash flow break-even point.

First, the adjustment factor for Brezner is

$$Adj = \frac{TD}{1 - T} = \frac{0.30 \times \$14,000}{1 - 0.30} = \$6,000$$

Equation (19-15) gives us

$$BE(CF) = \frac{F' - Adj}{P - V} = \frac{\$80,000 - \$6,000}{\$1,400 - \$400} = 74 \text{ units}$$

Thus, at a level of production of 74 units, the firm's operating cash flow equals $0. Now we calculate Brezner's break-even quantity. Equation (19-4) yields

$$BE = \frac{F}{P - V} = \frac{\$80,000 + \$14,000}{\$1,400 - \$400} = 94 \text{ units}$$

Thus Brezner will have a 0 *NOI* at a production level of 94 units. Finally, we calculate the impact of a sales increase of 10% on the operating cash flow and the *NOI* when $Q = 120$:

$$DOL(CF) = \frac{Q(P - V)}{Q(P - V) - F' + Adj} = \frac{120(\$1,400 - \$400)}{120(\$1,400 - \$400) - \$80,000 + \$6,000} = 2.61$$

$$DOL = \frac{Q(P - V)}{Q(P - V) - F} = \frac{120(\$1,400 - \$400)}{120(\$1,400 - \$400) - \$94,000} = 4.62$$

From the definition of the respective leverage measures:

$$\%\Delta OCF = \%\Delta S \times DOL(CF) = +10\% \times 2.61 = +26.1\%$$
$$\%\Delta NOI = \%\Delta S \times DOL = +10\% \times 4.62 = +46.2\%$$

Suppose that Brezner's net cash flows are expected to go up 28.71% because of the 26.10% increase in operating cash flows. How much will Brezner pay in interest (dollars)? From the definition of *DFL(CF)*,

$$DFL(CF) = \frac{\%\Delta NCF}{\%\Delta OCF} = \frac{28.71}{26.10} = 1.10$$

Note from the data already provided that $Q = 120$, $P = \$1,400$, $V = \$400$, $F' = \$80,000$, $T = 0.30$, $D = \$14,000$, and $Adj = \$6,000$. Substituting the appropriate values into equation (19-17), we have

$$DFL(CF) = 1.10 = \frac{120(\$1,400 - \$400) - \$80,000 + \$6,000}{120(\$1,400 - \$400) - \$80,000 - I + \$6,000}$$

Solving this expression for I, the interest payments, we find that $I = \$4,181.82$.

Figure 19-6 depicts the relationship between leverage and performance measures. Figure 19-6(a) shows the leverage effect on accounting profitability mea-

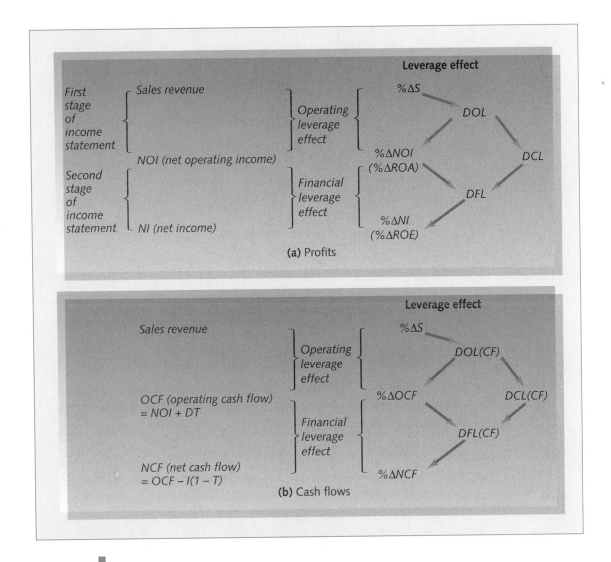

FIGURE   19-6

The concepts of leverage—a composite picture: (a) profits and (b) cash flows

sures, both dollars and rates of return. Figure 19-6(b) shows a similar leverage effect on cash flows.

SUMMARY

Section 19-1: Break-even Analysis and Contribution Margin

How do managers plan for the firm's survival?

■ All firms must strive to survive in a competitive economic environment. To survive, managers must ensure that their firms exceed the break-even point—that level of production at which revenues are equal to total operating costs.

■ Total operating costs are composed of fixed operating costs, which do not vary with the level of production, and variable operating costs, which vary with the level of output. The mix of fixed and variable costs is usually a function of the technology the firm uses in its production process.

■ For an operating decision, a positive contribution margin can justify the continuance of operations even if the firm is unable to cover its total costs.

Section 19-2: Managerial Investment Decisions and Operating Leverage

How do managers' investment decisions affect the firm's profitability?

■ Managers must focus not only on survival but also on profitability. Knowing that the firm will be able to break even, the manager typically makes operating and financial decisions that will magnify profits.

■ Operating leverage, also called first-stage leverage, works in the first half of the income statement and exists because of fixed operating costs. Technological considerations are the prime determinant of operating leverage.

■ Operating leverage is measured by the degree of operating leverage (DOL), a number that translates a given percentage change in sales into a greater percentage change in net operating income.

Section 19-3: Managerial Financing Decisions and Financial Leverage

How do managers' financing decisions affect the firm's profitability?

■ Managerial financing decisions also involve a fixed cost: interest expense. Fixed interest expense produces the financial leverage effect.

■ Financial leverage is measured by the degree of financial leverage (DFL), which translates a given percentage change in net operating income into a greater percentage change in net income.

Section 19-4: Combining Investment and Financing Leverage Effects

How is the combined leverage effect on the firm measured?

■ Managerial decisions that affect fixed operating costs and fixed financing costs create a leverage effect that magnifies a given change in sales into a larger change in net income.

■ The combined effect of managerial investment and financing decisions is measured by the degree of combined leverage, which is the product of the DOL and the DFL.

■ Because leverage magnifies both profits and losses, it can be considered a measure of business risk. Managers must weigh carefully the risks of increasing leverage.

Section 19-5: Leverage, Book ROA, and Book ROE

How does leverage affect the firm's book ROA *and book* ROE*?*

■ The firm's profitability can be measured not only in dollars but also in rates of return. The firm's book return on assets, *ROA*, measures the rate of return earned by the firm without regard to the manner in which the assets are financed. The firm's book return on equity, *ROE*, measures the return to the equityholders on their investment in the firm.

■ *ROE* increases linearly with the debt–equity ratio as long as the *ROA* exceeds the after-tax borrowing cost.

■ The sensitivity of the book return measures to changes in sales can be related to the firm's *DOL* and *DFL*. *DOL* relates a percentage change in sales to a greater percentage change in *ROA*. *DFL* relates a percentage change in *ROA* to a greater percentage change in *ROE*.

<table>
<tr><td>

Section 19.6:
Break-even Analysis,
Leverage, and
Cash Flows

</td><td>

How do managers' investment and financing decisions affect the firm's cash flows?

- Although accounting profits are useful to develop the concept of leverage, managers are ultimately interested in how their decisions affect the magnitude of the firm's cash flows.

- Cash flow leverage measures are easily developed by modifying accounting leverage measures. These relationships show the impact on cash flows of changes in managerial investment and financing decisions.

- By understanding leverage, managers are in a better position to decide on the appropriate choice of technology and financing in light of their projections about the firm's future sales performance.

</td></tr>
</table>

QUESTIONS

1. What are the uses of break-even analysis?

2. What are the limitations of break-even analysis?

3. What is the significance of the contribution margin?

4. What are the determinants of operating leverage?

5. What are the advantages and disadvantages of operating leverage?

6. Technological considerations determine a firm's *DOL*. Explain.

7. What are the determinants of financial leverage?

8. What are the advantages and disadvantages of financial leverage?

9. Financial policies determine a firm's *DFL*. Explain.

10. How are *DOL* and *DFL* integrated with the notion of *DCL*?

11. Is it correct to say that a firm's *DCL* is determined by both its operating and its financial policies? If yes, by what aspects of its operating and financial policies?

12. How are book *ROA* and book *ROE* different?

13. Normally, is *ROA* expected to be greater than *ROE*?

14. Why should one distinguish between the quantity break-even point and the cash flow break-even point?

15. What is the adjustment factor (*Adj*) in the formulas for *BE*(*CF*), *DOL*(*CF*), and *DFL*(*CF*)? When does *Adj* equal 0?

PROBLEMS

1. David Willis is considering opening a new copy center store near a large university. If he does, he will rent six machines for $1,200 per month for each machine. Rent, utilities, and wages will total $2,000 per month. David's cost of paper and ink will be $0.01 per copy, and he plans to charge $0.05 per copy.

(a) What will be his break-even point?

(b) Suppose that David thinks he can get by with only four machines. What will his break-even point be?

(c) Suppose that David rents four machines and sells 200,000 copies in one month. What will be his *NOI* for that month?

(d) David is considering placing in the student newspaper a $200 ad with a coupon for $0.04 per copy for orders of 50 copies or more. He estimates that if he places the ad, he will sell 250,000 copies and that about 50% of his customers will use the coupon. If he places the ad and rents four machines, what will be his break-even point and his *NOI*?

2. Denise Smith is considering translating instruction manuals from French into English and then printing and selling them in the United States. For each manual, she must pay the author a fixed sum plus some percentage of the manual's gross sales revenues. The printing expense includes a setup cost plus a cost per book. Finally, her hours of labor to translate, the sales price, and the anticipated sales volume are as follows:

Manual	Printing and Printing Setup Cost	Royalty Cost per Book	Royalty Fixed Sum	Percent of Gross	Hours to Translate	Sales Price	Sales Volume
A	$4,000	$4.50	$3,000	10%	65	$12.00	700
B	2,000	5.50	2,000	15	80	15.00	1,000
C	4,000	5.00	3,500	5	70	15.00	1,000
D	5,000	2.00	1,000	20	40	9.00	1,350
E	2,500	3.50	2,000	15	50	10.00	1,300

(a) Suppose that Denise decides she will translate a manual only if she earns $30 (or more) per hour of translation. Using break-even analysis, decide which manuals she should translate and which ones she should not.

(b) What if Denise decides that she will translate a manual if she earns $25 (or more) per hour of translation?

3. The Acme Hardware Co. has a markup policy of 20% (whatever its variable costs for an item are, its sales price is 20% more) and total fixed costs of $8,000 per month. What is its break-even point in total sales volume?

4. The Mobile Shoe Co.'s weekly fixed costs (rent, utilities, etc.) have just increased to $42,000. Its variable costs for producing shoes include $5 per pair for raw materials and one-sixth labor hour. Mobile has a labor force of 100 employees, who are paid $24 per hour of labor and $27 per hour for overtime (more than 40 hours per week).

(a) Suppose that Mobile sells shoes for $12.00 per pair. What is its break-even point?

(b) Suppose that Mobile sells shoes for $10.00 per pair. What is its break-even point?

(c) What is the break-even point if overtime labor costs $30 per hour instead of $27 per hour?

5. Jim Korp designs game cartridges for home computers. His total fixed cost for designing a game package is $4,000. The cartridges the game is programmed

into cost $4 each, and he sells them for $20 each. He currently sells 300 cartridges for each game he designs.

(a) What are his break-even point, *NOI,* and *DOL* now?

(b) If the cost of a cartridge rises to $6 and Korp keeps the sales price constant at $20, what will be the new break-even point, *NOI,* and *DOL?*

(c) If the price of a cartridge rises to $6 and Korp simultaneously raises the sales price to $22, what will be the new break-even point, *NOI,* and *DOL?*

(d) Redo part (c), assuming that fixed costs also increase to $4,500.

6. The C & D TV store currently has fixed costs of $6,000 per month and $400 in variable costs per TV set. Its sales price for each TV set is $700, and its current volume is 25 sets per month.

(a) Find C & D's break-even point and its *NOI* and *DOL* at the current level of sales.

(b) Find C & D's break-even point and its *NOI* and *DOL* if fixed costs decrease to $4,750 and at the same time the cost of the TV sets rises to $450.

7. The Newcastle Utility Company has fixed costs of $20,000 per month and sells electricity for $0.015 per kilowatt-hour. It costs $0.005 per kilowatt-hour to produce the electricity.

(a) What is Newcastle's break-even point?

(b) What is Newcastle's degree of operating leverage at a sales level of 2.75 million kilowatt-hours?

8. The W. V. Scott Co. has sales this year of $600,000, *NOI* of $20,000, and a degree of operating leverage of 4. Assume that fixed costs do not change.

(a) Suppose that next year's sales are $630,000. What will next year's *NOI* be?

(b) Suppose that next year's sales are $550,000. What will next year's *NOI* be?

(c) Suppose that next year's *NOI* is $25,000. What must sales have been during the year?

(d) What will be Scott's break-even level of sales?

(e) What will be Scott's fixed costs? (*Hint:* In general, what does the *NOI* equal when sales are 0?)

9. Last month Grant Airlines had sales of $1.2 million, *NOI* of − $60,000, and a degree of operating leverage of − 12.

(a) Suppose that sales fall to $1.1 million. What will the *NOI* be?

(b) Suppose that sales rise to $1.4 million. What will the *NOI* be?

(c) What is Grant's break-even point in sales?

(d) What are Grant's fixed costs?

10. The Magee Publishing Co. last year had sales of $800,000, *NOI* of $20,000, and a degree of operating leverage of 6.

(a) What will the *NOI* be if sales increase to $900,000?

(b) What will the *DOL* be at a sales level of $900,000?

11. The Lankford Battery Company last year had total sales of $60,000, fixed costs of $30,000, variable costs of $20,000, interest expenses of $5,000, and a tax rate of 28%.

    (a) Find the *NOI* and earnings.

    (b) Find the *DOL*.

    (c) Find the *DFL*.

    (d) Find the *DCL*.

    (e) If sales next year fall to $57,000, use the answers to parts (a), (b), and (d) to find next year's *NOI* and earnings.

12. Swinehart Rentals last year had sales of $200,000, *NOI* of $40,000, and earnings of $20,000. Its *DOL* was 3.5, and its *DFL* was 1.333. This year earnings are $21,000. Assume that fixed costs, interest, price per unit, and cost per unit are constant from one year to the next. Calculate the following for Swinehart:

    (a) *NOI* this year

    (b) Sales this year

    (c) Fixed costs

    (d) Interest (*Hint:* Using information from previous parts, find earnings in terms of *NOI* for this year and last year, and then divide.)

13. Klinger's Clothiers is considering expanding the production of a new line of women's clothing, and it is examining two different financing plans to raise the required $4 million. The first plan (all equity) would involve the sale of 200,000 new shares at $20 each. The second plan (50% equity, 50% debt) would involve the sale of 100,000 new shares at $20 each and 2,000 12% coupon, 20-year bonds at par. In either case, annual fixed costs will be $2 million, the average cost per unit produced will be $15, and the average price per unit produced will be $50. Klinger currently has 400,000 shares outstanding and a 25% tax rate.

    (a) For each plan, find net profit after taxes, earnings per share, and the *DFL* if the expected sales level is 70,000 units.

    (b) At what level of sales (in units) will earnings per share be equal under either plan?

14. Boyle's Flaws, a company that sells irregular lab equipment, had sales last month of $20,000, *NOI* of $2,000, earnings of $900, an interest expense of $500, and earnings per share (*EPS*) of $0.90. In addition, the *DOL* was 8.5. Sales for the coming month are expected to be $22,000.

    (a) What are the *DFL* and *DCL* for Boyle's Flaws?

    (b) What was the profit before taxes last month?

    (c) What is the *NOI* expected to be for the coming month?

    (d) What is the profit before taxes expected to be for the coming month?

    (e) What are earnings expected to be for the coming month?

    (f) What is the *EPS* expected to be for the coming month?

Problems 15–20 use the following information for Ranger, Inc. The corporation has total assets of $200,000 and a debt of $100,000. It is in the 20% tax bracket. All the following numbers for Ranger are in thousands.

Revenues: $100

Variable costs: $40

Fixed costs: $20

Interest expense: $10

15. (a) What is the after-tax *NOI* for Ranger, Inc.?

    (b) What is the taxable income?

    (c) What is the tax liability for Ranger, Inc.?

    (d) What is Ranger's net income?

16. (a) What is the book *ROA*?

    (b) What is the book *ROE*?

    (c) What is the *DOL* for Ranger, Inc.?

    (d) What is the *DFL*?

    (e) What is the *DCL*?

17. (a) What is the before-tax cost of debt?

    (b) What is the after-tax cost of debt?

    (c) Use equation (19-11) to calculate the *ROE*.

    (d) Compare your answer in part (c) with your answer in Problem 16, part (b). Are they the same?

18. Assume that revenues increase by 10%.

    (a) What is the change in the *ROA*?

    (b) What is the change in the *ROE*?

19. Assume that the revenue for Ranger, Inc., decreased to $72,000 (everything else kept constant). Use equation (19-11) to calculate the new *ROE*.

20. (a) With respect to Problem 19, is the *ROE* greater than the *ROA*? Why?

    (b) How does the original *ROE* (in Problem 17) compare with the *ROA*?

    (c) What conclusion can you draw from this with respect to financing leverage?

21. The Oconee Manufacturing Co. produces aluminum alloy wheels for the sports car aftermarket. The wheels sell for $40 each and have direct costs of $30 each. Oconee has annual cash fixed costs of $3 million, annual depreciation of $1.8 million, and a tax rate of 28%. Last year Oconee sold 600,000 wheels.

    (a) Find Oconee's break-even point for profits and its break-even point for cash flows.

    (b) What was Oconee's *NOI* last year? Its operating cash flow?

(c) What is Oconee's *DOL*? Its *DOL(CF)*?

(d) Using your answers to parts (b) and (c), find Oconee's *NOI* and operating cash flows for the coming year if sales increase to 750,000 wheels.

22. The Harrington Bicycle Co. manufactures bicycles for $60 each and sells them for $150. Harrington's annual cash fixed costs are $9 million, and its annual depreciation is $7 million. Harrington's tax rate is 30%. Last year 120,000 bicycles were sold.

    (a) Find the break-even point for accounting profits and the break-even point for cash flows. Which is greater? Will this always be the case?

    (b) Find the *DOL* and the *DOL(CF)*. Which is greater? Will this always be the case? Under what conditions will this be the case?

23. The McGovern Freight Corp. has a break-even point for cash flow of 160,000 units and a break-even point of 200,000 units. Annual depreciation is $120,000, and annual fixed costs are $300,000. Find McGovern's tax rate.

24. The Farenthold Plumbing Co. has a *DOL* of 2.0 and a *DOL(CF)* of 1.6. Annual fixed costs are $480,000, and Farenthold's tax rate is 30%. What is Farenthold's annual depreciation?

25. Peter Guerrero of Lasorda Motors has been accumulating information in an effort to determine the sensitivity of cash flow, *NOI*, and earnings to sales. Fixed costs for the previous quarter were $30,000, depreciation was $20,000, and Lasorda's average tax rate was 28%. Sales totaled 25 vehicles, with an average price of $12,000 and an average dealer invoice price of $10,000. Interest paid during the period totaled $10,000. Lasorda Motors is a family-owned business and has only 50 shares outstanding.

    (a) What was the *NOI* for the preceding quarter? Earnings per share (*EPS*)? Total cash flow from operations? Cash flow per share?

    (b) What were the *DOL*, *DFL*, and *DCL* for the preceding quarter?

    (c) What were the *DOL(CF)*, *DFL(CF)*, and *DCL(CF)* for the preceding quarter?

    (d) Suppose that fixed costs, depreciation, interest expense, and the average tax rate are the same in the next period as in this period. Using only your answers to parts (a), (b), and (c), calculate the operating cash flow, *NOI*, *EPS*, and cash flow per share next quarter if sales total 20 vehicles and 35 vehicles, respectively. Check your answers by calculating these values using the information given in the problem.

26. Sax Outlets, a clothing store that specializes in factory seconds, has a *DOL(CF)* of 1.625 and a *DFL(CF)* of 1.5. Last year total sales were $64 million, operating cash flow was $16 million, and net cash flow per share was $1.28.

    (a) What is the *DCL(CF)*?

    (b) If sales rise to $72 million, what will the operating cash flow be? What will the net cash flow per share be?

    (c) To what value must sales fall for the operating cash flow to be $10 million? For the operating cash flow to be $0?

(d) To what value must sales fall for the cash flow per share to be $1.00? For the cash flow per share to be $0?

27. The Russell Sign Co. has a $DOL(CF)$ of 1.6 and a $DFL(CF)$ of 1.5625. The operating cash flow is $293,750, and the net cash flow per share is $2.625. There are 10,000 shares outstanding, and sales are 20,000 signs.

(a) If sales rise to 30,000 signs, what will be the new level of operating cash flow? The new level of net cash flow per share?

(b) If sales fall to 15,000 signs, what will be the new level of operating cash flow? The new level of net cash flow per share?

(c) Russell has a new project opportunity that will increase sales to 27,500 signs. What will the net cash flow per share be if the project is adopted? How many new shares can Russell issue if it wants the net cash flow per share to be at least $2.50?

19A

DERIVATION OF LEVERAGE EQUATIONS

*T*he derivation of the cash flow leverage equations and the profit leverage equations are similar in spirit. In the interest of space, we derive the cash flow break-even point and the cash flow leverage measures. The profit leverage measures can then be derived easily as special cases.

The Cash Flow Break-even Point, Equation (19-15)

The cash flow from operations is given by

$$OCF = [Q(P - V) - F' - D](1 - T) + D$$

where F' are cash operating costs. At the break-even point,

$$OCF = 0 \quad \text{or} \quad [Q(P - V) - F' - D](1 - T) + D = 0$$

Solving for Q, we get

$$Q = \frac{F' + D - \dfrac{D}{(1 - T)}}{P - V} = \frac{F' - Adj}{P - V}$$

where $Adj = -D + [D/(1 - T)]$. Adj can be simplified as follows:

$$-D\frac{(1 - T)}{(1 - T)} + \frac{D}{(1 - T)} = \frac{-D(1 - T) + D}{(1 - T)} = \frac{TD}{(1 - T)}$$

The Degree of Operating Cash Flow Leverage, Equation (19-16)

$$DOL(CF) = \frac{\%\Delta OCF}{\%\Delta S}$$

where OCF is the operating cash flows and ΔS is the change in sales. Because $OCF = [Q(P - V) - F' - D](1 - T) + D$ and F' and D do not change with a change in sales,

$$\Delta OCF = \Delta Q(P - V)(1 - T)$$

and

$$\%\Delta OCF = \frac{\Delta OCF}{OCF} = \frac{\Delta Q(P - V)(1 - T)}{[Q(P - V) - F' - D](1 - T) + D} \tag{19A-1}$$

Because $S = Q \times P$, we have $\Delta S = \Delta Q \times P$ and

$$\%\Delta S = \frac{\Delta S}{S} = \frac{\Delta Q}{Q} \tag{19A-2}$$

According to equations (19A-1) and (19A-2),

$$
\begin{aligned}
DOL(CF) = \frac{\%\Delta OCF}{\%\Delta S} &= \frac{\Delta Q(P - V)(1 - T)}{[Q(P - V) - F' - D](1 - T) + D} \times \frac{Q}{\Delta Q} \\
&= \frac{Q(P - V)(1 - T)}{[Q(P - V) - F' - D](1 - T) + D} \\
&= \frac{Q(P - V)}{[Q(P - V) - F'] + \left(\dfrac{TD}{1 - T}\right)} = \frac{Q(P - V)}{Q(P - V) - F' + Adj}
\end{aligned}
$$

where $Adj = TD/(1 - T)$.

The Degree of Financial Cash Flow Leverage, Equation (19-17)

$$DFL(CF) = \frac{\%\Delta NCF}{\%\Delta OCF}$$

where NCF = net cash flow = $OCF - I(1 - T)$. Because $\Delta NCF = \Delta OCF$ (when interest expenses and tax rates remain the same), we have

$$\%\Delta NCF = \frac{\Delta OCF}{OCF - I(1 - T)} \tag{19A-3}$$

and

$$\%\Delta OCF = \frac{\Delta OCF}{OCF} \tag{19A-4}$$

Equations (19A-3) and (19A-4) yield

$$DFL(CF) = \frac{\%\Delta NCF}{\%\Delta OCF} = \frac{\Delta OCF}{OCF - I(1 - T)} \times \frac{OCF}{\Delta OCF}$$

Substituting $OCF = [Q(P - V) - F' - D](1 - T) + D$ and rearranging give us

$$
\begin{aligned}
DFL(CF) &= \frac{Q(P - V) - F' + \left(\dfrac{TD}{1 - T}\right)}{Q(P - V) - F' - I + \left(\dfrac{TD}{1 - T}\right)} \\
&= \frac{Q(P - V) - F' + Adj}{Q(P - V) - F' - I + Adj}
\end{aligned}
$$

The Degree of Combined Cash Flow Leverage, Equation (19-18)

$$
\begin{aligned}
DCL(CF) &= \frac{\%\Delta NCF}{\%\Delta S} = \frac{\%\Delta OCF}{\%\Delta S} \times \frac{\%\Delta NCF}{\%\Delta OCF} \\
&= DOL(CF) \times DFL(CF)
\end{aligned}
$$

which from equations (19-16) and (19-17) imply by inspection

$$DCL(CF) = \frac{Q(P - V)}{Q(P - V) - F' - I + Adj}$$

HOW THE FIRM'S OPERATING AND FINANCING POLICIES DETERMINE BETA

What determines a stock's beta? If you examine the definition of beta in equation (6-5) in Chapter 6, it is "the covariance between the returns on the stock and the market portfolio divided by the variance of market returns." That is right, but this answer does not explain what within the firm determines the beta.

As it turns out, the equity betas we examined in earlier chapters are determined by the firm's operating and financing decisions. To be specific, the ratio of the present value of the fixed costs to firm value determines the firm's beta, and the present value of the fixed costs and the relative amounts of debt and equity together determine the levered firm's equity beta.

To see this consider the cash flows (CF) to the equityholders of a firm. These are the firm's revenues (R) less the fixed costs (F) incurred from operations, less the total variable costs (TVC) and less the interest payments on the debt (I).[5] Thus

$$CF = R - F - TVC - I \tag{19B-1}$$

Since these are cash flows, we can take the present value of each term in equation (19B-1) and write

$$PV_{CF} = PV_R - PV_F - PV_{TVC} - PV_I \tag{19B-2}$$

But the present value of the cash flows to the owners PV_{CF} is the market value of the equity (E). The present value of the interest payments to the bondholders PV_I is the market value of the debt (D). Thus equation (19B-2) becomes

$$E = PV_R - PV_F - PV_{TVC} - D \tag{19B-3}$$

Since the value of the firm under the claims definition is $V = D + E$, equation (19B-3) becomes

$$V = PV_R - PV_F - PV_{TVC} \tag{19B-4}$$

Think of V on the left-hand side of equation (19B-4) as a "portfolio" consisting of three "securities": PV_R, PV_F, and PV_{TVC}. Since the beta of a portfolio is the weighted average of the betas of the individual securities in the portfolio as seen in Chapter 6, we have

$$\beta_V = \left(\frac{PV_R}{V}\right)\beta_R - \left(\frac{PV_R}{V}\right)\beta_F - \left(\frac{PV_{TVC}}{V}\right)\beta_{TVC} \tag{19B-5}$$

Assume that $\beta_F = 0$ and $\beta_R \approx \beta_{TVC}$, so equation (19B-5) simplifies to

$$\beta_V = \beta_R\left[\frac{PV_R - PV_{TVC}}{V}\right] \tag{19B-6}$$

But $PV_R - PV_{TVC}$ from equation (19B-4) is $V + PV_F$. Substituting this into equation (19B-6) yields

$$\beta_V = \beta_R\left[1 + \frac{PV_F}{V}\right] \tag{19B-7}$$

Thus the beta of the firm (debt plus equity) is independent of the amount of debt and depends on the ratio of the present value of fixed costs to firm value.

---

[5] We assume for simplicity that the debt is perpetual and riskless. We also ignore taxes. These simplifications do not affect the intuition we are developing here.

However, the beta of the equity depends on the firm's financial policy. To see this, begin with equation (19B-3) and replicate the procedure just used. The equity beta is seen to be

$$\beta_E = \beta_R \left[1 + \frac{PV_F + D}{E} \right] \tag{19B-8}$$

In other words, the total risk of the firm is independent of its debt policy, but the beta risk for the equity depends on the amount of borrowing.

SUGGESTED ADDITIONAL READINGS

Jaedicke, Robert K., and Alexander A. Robichek. "Cost-Volume-Profit Analysis Under Conditions of Uncertainty." *Accounting Review*, October 1964, pp. 917–926.

Morrison, Thomas A., and E. Kaczka. "A New Application of Calculus and Risk Analysis to Cost-Volume-Profit Changes." *Accounting Review*, April 1969, pp. 330–343.

O'Brien, T. J., and P. A. Vanderheiden. "Empirical Measurement of Operating Leverage for Growing Firms." *Financial Management*, Summer 1982, pp. 45–53.

Raun, D. L. "The Limitations of Profit Graphs, Break-even Analysis, and Budgets." *Accounting Review*, October 1964, pp. 927–945.

Reinhardt, V. E. "Break-even Analysis for Lockheed's Tri Star: An Application of Financial Theory." *Journal of Finance*, September 1973, pp. 821–838.

Shalit, Sol S. "On the Mathematics of Financial Leverage." *Financial Management*, Spring 1975, pp. 57–66.

Usher, Abbot. *A History of Mechanical Inventions.* New York: McGraw-Hill, 1929.

TWENTY A FRAMEWORK FOR FINANCIAL PLANNING

Annual income twenty pounds, annual expenditure nineteen six, result happiness. Annual income twenty pounds, annual expenditure twenty pounds ought and six, result misery.

—Charles Dickens, David Copperfield

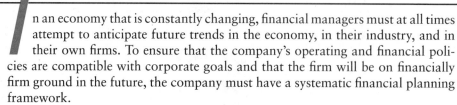

*I*n an economy that is constantly changing, financial managers must at all times attempt to anticipate future trends in the economy, in their industry, and in their own firms. To ensure that the company's operating and financial policies are compatible with corporate goals and that the firm will be on financially firm ground in the future, the company must have a systematic financial planning framework.

The term **financial planning** means different things to different managers, depending on the nature of the business, the firm's size and organizational structure, and other factors. However, in the most general terms, financial planning primarily involves anticipating the impact of operating and financial policies on the firm's future financial position and instituting remedial measures as needed. *Short-term financial planning* refers to the planning function as it applies to, say, a one-year period, and *long-term financial planning* in this context usually refers to three, four, or even five years.

The basic and derivative financial statements introduced in Chapter 3 are used to analyze past performance and to provide some indication of the firm's future financial position. These financial statements are not, however, financial forecasts. To develop forecasted financial statements, much more information is necessary—information that the various functional and divisional managers must give to the planner.

Developing financial planning statements is complex and cannot be completely covered in a basic financial text. We therefore limit our analysis to short-term financial planning and address the following questions:

- How do managers estimate the firm's future cash needs?

- What are pro forma statements?

- How do managers forecast the firm's income using the pro forma income statement?

- How do managers forecast the firm's future levels of assets and liabilities using the pro forma balance sheet?

- How are the short-term planning statements interrelated?

20-1
THE CASH FLOW BUDGET

*T*able 20-1 illustrates the short-term financial planning process. As the reader can see, short-term financial planning requires the development of three pro forma (projected) statements. The interdependence of the decisions made in the various divisions in the firm is also shown in Table 20-1. Note that forecasted cash flows originate from sales, operational activities, and financial activities. Typically, each of these forecasts is prepared separately by different persons, although certain estimates require an interdivision cooperative effort. The financial manager uses this basic information to prepare an overall cash flow budget and

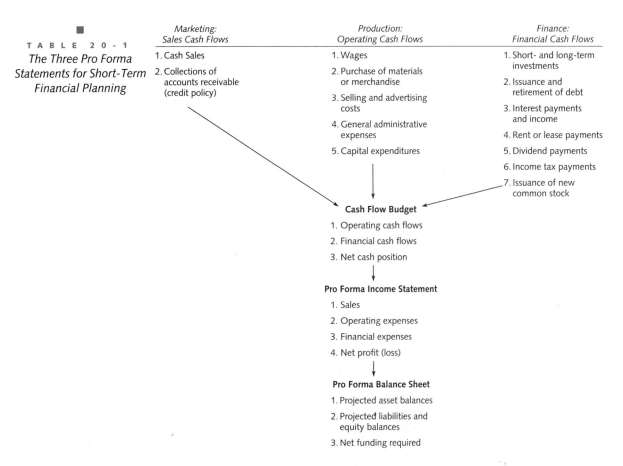

T A B L E   2 0 - 1

The Three Pro Forma Statements for Short-Term Financial Planning

Marketing: Sales Cash Flows	Production: Operating Cash Flows	Finance: Financial Cash Flows
1. Cash Sales	1. Wages	1. Short- and long-term investments
2. Collections of accounts receivable (credit policy)	2. Purchase of materials or merchandise	2. Issuance and retirement of debt
	3. Selling and advertising costs	3. Interest payments and income
	4. General administrative expenses	4. Rent or lease payments
	5. Capital expenditures	5. Dividend payments
		6. Income tax payments
		7. Issuance of new common stock

Cash Flow Budget

1. Operating cash flows
2. Financial cash flows
3. Net cash position

Pro Forma Income Statement

1. Sales
2. Operating expenses
3. Financial expenses
4. Net profit (loss)

Pro Forma Balance Sheet

1. Projected asset balances
2. Projected liabilities and equity balances
3. Net funding required

forecast of the firm's ending cash position at different points during the planning period. Finally, the financial manager combines these data with other financial information to determine how the income statement and balance sheet appear at the end of the planning period. Despite their close interrelationship, each report provides a different perspective and different information to the financial decision maker. These various reports can also be compared with one another as a check on the forecasts' internal accuracy and consistency. In fact, one way to increase internal accuracy and consistency is to prepare the pro forma income statement and the balance sheet independent of the cash flow budget information.

Most firms can be divided into three different activities along functional area lines: marketing, production (or purchasing), and finance. Because the word *production* often does not properly describe the activities of certain types of firms, such as airlines or retailers, it is also used to mean *purchase, merchandise,* or *cost of goods.* Carrying out the marketing and production decisions requires substantial outlays of cash. As a result, an extremely important job for the financial manager is to anticipate the cash flow implications of these two activities and to gauge the timing and magnitude of future cash flows in order to aid the firm's internal planning and to maintain control over the firm's cash position. This task is accomplished by preparing a cash flow budget (or just cash budget).

A **cash flow budget** is a detailed estimated schedule of future cash inflows (receipts), outflows (expenditures), and balances at different times over a specific interval. It shows how a firm's cash will be spent on wages, merchandise, overhead, and other items and how much funding and investment will be required. Normally, the time interval covered by a cash flow budget is less than one year, with the forecasts being made weekly or monthly. Many large firms use computerized financial models that do most of the forecasting work for short- and long-term planning. Most firms, regardless of their size, now have microcomputers. Larger firms also prepare daily cash forecasts for the upcoming week or two so as to plan for any problems that may affect their liquidity position. Failure to anticipate cash flows properly can lead to idle cash balances, lower profits, cash shortages, and possibly even a liquidity crisis.

Besides facilitating the short-term planning function, a cash budget is useful for control purposes. Forecasted cash flows can be used as a standard with which actual cash flows may be compared. This helps in monitoring planned receipts and disbursements. Any significant deviations between planned and actual cash flows require further investigation by management to find out their causes.

Constructing a Cash Flow Budget

A cash flow budget is the result of a rather complicated and time-consuming process because it represents a number of individual budgets prepared by the entire management team. Management requires different departments (and divisions) to prepare their own cash budgets. Some of these budgets are sales, production or purchasing, advertising, administrative expenses, and capital expenditures. The starting point is a forecast by the marketing manager of expected sales. Given this sales forecast, the production department works up a budget that estimates the costs for meeting the projected sales figures and for providing an adequate level of inventory. Next, the financial manager is responsible for combining the sales, production, and other expense information into a summary of the operating cash inflows and outflows. Finally, this summary is combined with the projected financial cash flows, such as interest expenses, dividends, and repayment of long-term debt (which are usually known in advance). The end result is the cash flow budget.

Before we examine the cash flow budget in detail, certain preliminary calculations are necessary. To discuss these calculations and to prepare for a discussion of the financial planning implications of a cash budget, we develop a three-stage approach to cash budgeting. Stages 1, 2, and 3, when combined into a single statement, yield the desired cash budget.

STAGE 1: ESTIMATING THE OPERATING CASH FLOWS

The first stage of the cash budget for InterTech Stores, Inc., is presented in Table 20-2. The major sources of operating cash inflows are cash sales and collections of accounts receivable. "Cash sales" is self-explanatory, but "collections of accounts receivable" deserves some discussion. Most corporations extend credit to their customers and carry them as accounts receivable. Credit sales become cash only after a lapse of time as customers pay off their accounts. An assumption must therefore be made about the payment pattern or rate at which credit sales become cash. This assumed rate is usually based on an analysis of the firm's past sales and collection experience. One reason for this intermediate step (Table 20-2) in developing the cash budget is to recognize that actual cash collections are not the same as sales. In effect, stage 1 of the cash budget (i.e., Table 20-2) adjusts for the fact that the cash collections in any particular month depend on the firm's sales performance in previous months and on its collection policy.

To be specific, for the fourth quarter, InterTech's monthly operating cash flow budget in Table 20-2 indicates that 30% of sales are assumed to be for cash and 68% of sales are on credit. The remaining 2% are assumed to be uncollectible and are charged against sales as a bad-debt expense. Furthermore, 60% of sales will be realized as cash one month later (i.e., after the customers are billed and have paid

	Aug.	Sept.	Oct.	Nov.	Dec.
Operating cash inflows:					
Total sales	($51)	$66	$ 59	$158	$208)
Cash sales (30%)			18	47	62
Collections of accounts receivable[b] (68%)					
One month later (60%)			40	35	95
Two months later (8%)			4	5	5
Total operating cash inflows			$ 62	$ 87	$162
Operating cash outflows:					
Purchases on account	($90	$ 72	$ 62	$ 39)	
Payment of payables[c]			90	72	62
Wages and salaries			12	19	24
Selling and advertising			9	14	21
General and administrative			5	7	7
Capital expenditures			9	3	4
Total operating cash outflows			$125	$115	$118
Net operating cash flows			–$ 63	–$ 28	$ 44

TABLE 20-2

*InterTech Stores, Inc.,
Summary of Projected
Operating Cash Flows,
Fourth Quarter, 1996 (in
millions)[a]*

[a]All numbers are rounded to the nearest whole number. Circled numbers do not directly enter into the calculations of the totals.

[b]Two percent of total sales are assumed to be uncollectible and are charged against sales as a bad-debt expense.

[c]All merchandise is assumed to be purchased on crdeit and is then paid off one manth later. For example, the October payment figure is $90 million, which represents purchases made in September.

for their purchases). Another 8% will become cash only after a two-month lag. For example, October collections will be $(0.60 \times \$66) + (0.08 \times \$51) = \$44$ million. The $51 million and $66 million figures are the total sales figures for August and September, respectively.

In the estimations of operating cash outflows, the list of cash uses could be a long one—cash purchases, payments of payables, wages, utilities, capital expenditures, and so on. Table 20-2 summarizes InterTech's major operating expenses. The most important item is the payment of payables, which represents prior purchases made by InterTech. Most firms have well-defined credit arrangements with their suppliers, and the items bought on credit are reflected as accounts payable (*payables*). Note that the payment of payables may also be treated like credit sales in that just like their customers, firms pay back their suppliers slowly. Most purchases made in a particular month are paid for in a later month. As in accounts receivable, this does not imply that the level of accounts payable is reduced to 0 at some point. Purchases (receivable) occur continually, so that a certain amount of existing payables (receivables) is paid off each month. Current purchases (sales) build the account back up. To simplify the situation, InterTech's purchases are assumed to be paid for after a one-month delay.

STAGE 2: ESTIMATING THE FINANCIAL CASH FLOWS[1]

The financial manager is responsible for forecasting the expected cash inflows and outflows associated with a firm's financial activities. Table 20-3 contains these forecasts for InterTech's fourth quarter. In contrast with operating cash flows, financial flows are scheduled well ahead of time and generally occur at known points in time. In fact, interest and dividend payments are made at around the same time every year. The significant cash flows expected for InterTech are a scheduled new issue of long-term debt of $30 million to finance new store openings and a repayment of short-term debt totaling $28 million.

[1]To keep matters simple, the discussion of the second stage does not include delayed collections or disbursements of cash, as in stage 1. Thus Table 20-3 is identical to stage 2 for the completed cash budget presented in Table 20-4. It is entirely conceivable that financial cash flows may also require adjustments, as in Table 20-2.

■

TABLE 20-3
*InterTech Stores, Inc.,
Summary of Projected
Financial Cash Flows,
Fourth Quarter, 1996
(in millions)*

	Oct.	Nov.	Dec.
Financial cash inflows:			
Maturing marketable securities	$ 2	$ 1	0
Issuance of long-term debt	0	30	0
Other financial receipts (nonoperating income)	0	2	1
Total financial cash inflows	$ 2	$33	$ 1
Financial cash outflows:			
Rent[a]	$ 2	$ 2	$ 3
Interest payments	0	5	0
Income taxes	0	0	4
Dividends	0	0	6
Repayment of short-term debt	8	8	12
Total financial cash outflows	$ 10	$15	$ 25
Net financial cash flows	−$ 8	$18	−$24

[a]Rental or lease payments normally appear as an operating expense in the income statement. In finance, these expenses are viewed as *financial* expenses because long-term leases serve to reduce outlays on fixed assets.

STAGE 3: CALCULATING THE BOTTOM LINE

We now examine Table 20-4, which shows the final statement, the cash flow budget. Notice that stages 1 and 2 are the same as Tables 20-2 and 20-3, respectively. Stage 3 of the cash flow budget, however, is new.

Line 20 in the cash flow budget is the net cash flow from all activities—operating and financial. Now look at line 21 in October. The starting cash balance for InterTech for this month, $48 million, is based on information that is obtained from outside the table. The starting cash balance in any month is the ending cash balance for the previous month. Thus September must have ended with a cash

■

TABLE 20-4
*InterTech Stores, Inc.,
Cash Flow Budget, Fourth
Quarter, 1996 (in
millions)*

	Oct.	Nov.	Dec.
Stage 1			
Operating cash inflows			
1. Cash sales	$ 18	$ 47	$ 62
2. Collection of accounts receivable	44	40	100
3. Total operating cash inflows	$ 62	$ 87	$162
Operating cash outflows			
4. Payment of payables	$ 90	$ 72	$ 62
5. Wages and salaries	12	19	24
6. Selling and advertising	9	14	21
7. General and administrative	5	7	7
8. Capital expenditures	9	3	4
9. Total operating cash outflows	$125	$115	$118
Stage 2			
Financial cash inflows			
10. Maturing marketable securities	$ 2	$ 1	$ 0
11. Issuance of long-term debt	0	30	0
12. Other financial receipts	0	2	1
13. Total financial cash inflows	$ 2	$ 33	$ 1
Financial cash outflows			
14. Rent	$ 2	$ 2	$ 3
15. Interest payments	0	5	0
16. Income taxes	0	0	4
17. Dividends	0	0	6
18. Repayment of short-term debt	8	8	12
19. Total financial cash outflows	$ 10	$ 15	$ 25
Stage 3			
20. Net cash from all activities (lines 3 less 9 plus 13 less 19)[a]	($ 71)	($ 10)	$ 20
21. Plus: Cash at the beginning of the month	$ 48	($ 23)	($ 33)
22. Cash at the end of the month	(23)	(33)	(13)
23. Less: Minimum cash balance	14	14	14
24. Cumulative cash position (surplus/deficit)	($ 37)	($ 47)	($ 27)

[a]All numbers in parentheses are negative numbers.

balance of $48 million. The cash at the beginning of the month plus the cash actually generated in that month yield the cash at the end of the month (line 22). From line 22 is subtracted a "minimum cash balance" figure of $14 million. This minimum cash balance is the result of a management decision. It is the amount of cash that the company wishes to hold as a safety margin. Remember that nearly all items in the cash flow budget are estimates, and this safety or buffer of cash can compensate for some errors in estimation. Subtracting the $14 million minimum cash balance from the − $23 million cash position at the end of October yields the cumulative cash position in line 24. In October, InterTech has a cash shortage of $37 million. With the same procedure, the November and December cumulative cash positions are deficits of $47 million and $27 million, respectively. For obvious reasons, line 24 in the cash budget is often called the *bottom line,* a line that takes on a special significance in financial planning.

Using the Cash Flow Budget in Financial Planning

Having drawn up the cash flow budget, the financial manager can use this pro forma statement in a variety of ways.

MONITORING AND CONTROLLING OPERATIONS

The cash flow budget can shed light on several aspects of the firm's operations for perhaps a closer scrutiny by management. Then any undesirable patterns or trends observed can be remedied, if necessary. An examination of the cash budget clearly indicates the seasonal nature of InterTech's cash flow pattern. Most retailers realize the majority of their sales in the fourth quarter because of the holiday season. Note that InterTech experiences a sharp increase in sales and operating cash inflows during December. Operating outflows, on the other hand, remain fairly stable from month to month because the decrease in purchases is offset by the increases in wages and selling expenses as the holidays approach. The net result is a net cash outflow in October–November and a sizable net inflow in December. In contrast, the expected financial flows have a more erratic pattern, but this is because of the large debt offering in November. If this issuance were not planned, the financial cash flows would have been negative throughout the quarter. This implication of the proposed debt issuance, for example, would not have been obvious without a cash budget.

SOLVENCY CONSIDERATIONS

InterTech's cash budget indicates that it will have serious liquidity problems in the last quarter of 1996 if it does not take remedial action to cover the cash deficits. The bottom line thus alerts management to both the timing and the magnitude of the firm's cash surplus or deficit. If a company has a surplus, it should plan to invest it in short-term interest-bearing securities (marketable securities), and to use this surplus, it must make additional investment plans. A firm cannot pursue its objective of maximizing the shareholders' wealth if its cash flow cannot sustain its operations. If the cash flows from operations (i.e., internally generated cash flows) are not adequate, management must arrange to generate cash flows from outside. However, a firm cannot continue indefinitely without positive operating cash flows. Negative operating cash flows for an extended period of time can spell disaster (see the following highlight).

The simplest way for InterTech to cope with its deficits would be to establish a line of credit with a bank for the maximum deficit shown on the bottom line—$47 million in Table 20-4. A line of credit for $47 million is an arrangement that allows the company to borrow up to $47 million over the specified period of the agree-

CASH FLOWS FROM OPERATIONS: W. T. GRANT COMPANY'S BANKRUPTCY

The importance of monitoring cash flows has been stressed repeatedly. Although a firm can generate cash in a variety of ways from external sources, it is important that it be able to generate cash flows from its day-to-day operations (i.e., operating cash flows). Operating cash flows should be monitored carefully because they can convey information not indicated by net income.

Consider the following extreme example. Assume that a company has only credit sales and that total sales exceed total expenses. This firm will show profits, but there may be a significant time lag before it actually receives any cash. Because profits cannot pay the bills, these cash flows cannot be delayed forever without endangering the company's survival. If a company cannot generate cash flows from operations for an extended period,

the probability of its bankruptcy increases.

The case of W. T. Grant Company provides a good illustration of this possibility. W. T. Grant was the biggest retailer in the United States before its bankruptcy in 1975. Figures 20-1 and 20-2 are an intrafirm analysis of W. T. Grant and show the firm's liquidity ratios and profitability ratios, respectively. Figure 20-3 traces the company's net income and operating cash flows.

Between 1966 and 1975 the intrafirm analysis shows that Grant's book ROA and ROE were steadily declining. Yet although they are a cause for concern, they are not alarming; the returns are still positive in 1975. Similarly, the liquidity ratios show a gradual decline without cause for alarm. In fact, the quick ratio is fairly stable over the entire nine-year period.

Figure 20-3, which focuses on the cash flows from operations, tells an entirely different story. No-

tice that except over approximately two years (1968–1970), W. T. Grant was unable to generate positive cash flows from operations. Yet an investor looking at net income would not have recognized the firm's gradually worsening health. After 1972 the cash flows become extremely poor, and in 1975 the net income was negative. In 1975 W. T. Grant was bankrupt; it could not sustain its operations.

It is not unusual for a firm to report losses in any particular year, and one bad year does not usually spell disaster. W. T. Grant became bankrupt not because it had losses in 1974 but because it was suffering from severe cash flow problems—a hidden "cancer" that could not have been detected with basic financial statement analysis.

Moral: Even if net income is heading north, if operating cash flows head south for an extended period—watch out!

FIGURE 20-1

Liquidity ratios

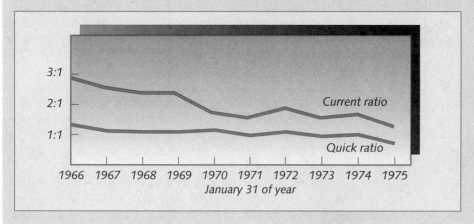

3:1

2:1

1:1

Current ratio

Quick ratio

1966 1967 1968 1969 1970 1971 1972 1973 1974 1975
January 31 of year

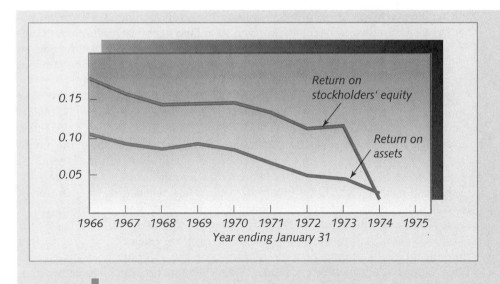

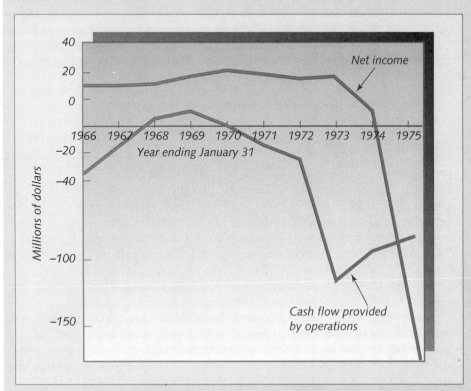

FIGURE 20-2
Profitability ratios.

FIGURE 20-3
Net income and cash flow.

SOURCE: Figures 20-1, 20-2, and 20-3 adapted, with permission, from *Financial Analysts Journal,* July/August 1980. Copyright 1980, The Institute of Chartered Financial Analysts, Charlottesville, VA. All rights reserved.

ment. InterTech would borrow $37 million in October, another $10 million in November, and then in December repay $20 million of the $47 million loan outstanding. These amounts follow from the bottom line. Remember that the bottom line is a cumulative statement and reflects the borrowing decisions of the previous months.

A monthly cash budget does not describe the timing of the cash flows within the month. Daily cash flows are often quite variable, and therefore a monthly budget may mask a mismatch in cash flows. For example, Table 20-4 indicates a net inflow from all activities in December. If the outflows occur at the beginning of the month and the inflows toward the end, InterTech may be "cash short" during December. A daily or weekly cash budget helps to predict such an occurrence and may provide a different picture of the firm's financing needs. Thus, whereas the preparation of a cash budget is straightforward, the management of cash is quite complicated.

It would be prudent for InterTech to arrange for additional financing in case the cash budget understates its actual needs. Forecasts are estimates, and the further into the future the forecast period is, the greater is the uncertainty associated with these estimates. One way that a prudent financial manager could handle this situation is to prepare three forecasts for each estimate: a pessimistic, an optimistic, and a most likely. (Table 20-4 would be considered the most likely case.) This procedure produces a range of ending cash balances and allows an examination of the impact of alternative assumptions on sales, expenses, and financial inflows.

A more sophisticated approach to assessing cash flow uncertainty is to simulate the cash flows with the use of a computer, such as discussed in Chapter 10. This technique considers more information and allows a probability assessment to be made about the ending cash flows. In turn, this provides a better measure of the cash flow estimates by quantifying the degree to which deviations may occur. With the recent proliferation of spreadsheet software, such detailed financial analyses of pro forma statements are becoming more and more feasible.

DEBT POLICY AND DIVIDEND POLICY PLANNING

Other ways to balance the cash budget are to postpone the projected repayment of short-term debt and to delay the payment on accounts payable. In addition, management can look at the cash budget and draw inferences about the feasibility of planned dividend payments. Such analyses require further scrutiny. Because these debt- and dividend-related decisions alter the firm's cash flow pattern, a revised budget is necessary. For example, if a seasonal bank loan is taken out, this loan generates an additional cash inflow, and its interest expenses produce an outflow. New cash budgets may be required to try out several "what if" scenarios because the feasibility of such alternatives cannot even be explored without a cash budget.

ESTABLISHING CREDIT

The cash budget not only helps the manager identify the company's cash needs but may also be required by the bank in deciding whether to grant a loan. No bank lends money to a company without expecting to be repaid. To assess a company's ability to repay the debt, banks often examine its cash budget to be sure that they are not subsidizing a lost cause. If the bottom line of the cash budget has no hope of showing a surplus, this information jeopardizes the approval of the company's loan request. Of course, companies realize that banks are influenced by their cash budget, and banks, in turn, are aware of companies' propensity to present the rosiest cash budget possible. For this reason, banks often prepare their own pro forma cash budget for the firm, using more stringent assumptions. Alternatively, a bank may ask the company to prepare several revised cash flow budgets with certain specific assumptions imposed by the bank. The purpose of these exercises is to provide a conservative picture of the firm's cash flow pattern.

RAISING EQUITY CAPITAL

When firms raise equity capital, the suppliers of the equity capital (even more than the firm's creditors) base their decisions on the company's future prospects. Although this is true of all companies, it is especially important in the case of young start-up or developmental-stage companies—new companies that typically have severe shortages of capital. As we saw in Chapter 13, many of these firms raise equity capital through venture capitalists. Venture capitalists supply capital to a company in return for a percentage of the firm's ownership. Often these capital suppliers make their decisions on whether to take an equity position in the firm by evaluating the projected financial statements prepared by the company in a proposal called the **business plan.** Although venture capitalists also construct their own versions of the firm's future financial statements, most rely heavily on the firm's cash budget and the projected balance sheets. Cash budgets usually provide information for a "go–no go" decision. The projected balance sheets and income statements over, say, the next four years form the basis of the negotiation regarding the percentage of the firm's ownership that must be given up for the equity capital being provided.

20-2

FINANCIAL PLANNING USING THE PRO FORMA INCOME STATEMENT

Cash forecasts are limited to cash flows and thus provide no information about expected profits or performance. One way to learn this information is to prepare a **pro forma income statement,** which is simply a forecast of the expected revenues, expenses, and profits over some planning period. Because this statement represents a summary of all projected transactions over a particular planning period, the information in the cash budget is a vital input into its construction. Projected financial relationships such as ratios are also often used.

Constructing a Pro Forma Income Statement

Table 20-5 is InterTech's pro forma income statement. As in the cash budget, the sales forecast is the key variable in a pro forma income statement. In Table 20-5, the $425 million sales figure was obtained by summing the three monthly sales estimates in the operating cash flow budget (Table 20-2): $59 + $158 + $208 = $425 million. The descriptions in the "Information Source" column reveal that all items except the cost of goods sold, income taxes, provisions for bad debts, and depreciation are derived from the cash budget. The cost of goods sold figure is based on a historical percentage of sales average (from the common-size statements) because a portion of the merchandise expected to be sold was instead purchased earlier in the year. If the payment of payables figure had been used instead, the cost of goods sold and hence profits would be misstated. Similarly, the quarterly income tax estimate of $4 million (Table 20-3) understates InterTech's estimated tax liability of $9 million. The $4 million figure is used instead of the $9 million figure because accelerated depreciation is used for taxes in this example. Only $4 million is actually paid in cash this quarter; the remainder is deferred to a subsequent quarter. These two items once again reveal the differences between accrual and cash accounting. Finally, depreciation is a noncash expense and therefore does

	(millions)	Information Source	Table
Net sales	$425	Operating cash budget	20-2
Less: Cost of goods sold	268	63% of expected sales	
Gross profit	$157		
Less: Operating expenses[a]			
Wages and salaries	$ 55		
Selling and advertising	44	Operating cash budget	20-2
Provision for bad debts	9	2% of total sales	
Rent	7	Financial cash budget	20-3
General and administrative	19	Operating cash budget	20-2
Depreciation	2	Depreciation schedule	
Total	$136		
Net operating income (*NOI*)	$ 21		
Less: Interest expense	5	Financial cash budget	20-3
Plus: Nonoperating income	3	Other receipts from	
		financial cash budget	20-3
Taxable income	$ 19		
Less: Income taxes (45%)	9	Historical average (%)	
Net income (*NI*)	$ 10		

TABLE 20-5
InterTech Stores, Inc., Pro Forma Income Statement, Fourth Quarter, 1996

[a] Operating expenses, with the exception of the provision for bad debts and depreciation, are expected to be paid as incurred rather than carried over as accruals into the first quarter of 1997.

not appear in the cash budget. This figure is derived from the existing depreciation schedule, with adjustments for new investments in fixed assets included.

Using the Pro Forma Income Statement in Financial Planning

MONITORING AND CONTROL

Like the cash budget, the pro forma income statement can be used to coordinate and control policy decisions. If the cash budgets have been accurately predicted, the actual income statement should be similar to the pro forma income statement. If not, significant deviations warrant an investigation to determine their cause. The pro forma income statement provides the financial manager with a basis for assessing the company's expected profitability and performance. In addition, because this statement depends heavily on operating cash forecasts, the financial manager has the responsibility of coordinating and advising other officers on the development and implications of their forecasts. In fact, the financial manager in most large corporations heads a planning staff that coordinates and consults when the operating cash forecasts are developed. For example, if the gross profit margin is too low, the marketing and purchasing decisions need to be reexamined to eliminate this potential problem. If the operating profit margin is unacceptable, operating expenses may be too high. In this case, the operations manager should be consulted, and cost-cutting actions should be taken if needed.

NEWS RELEASES

It is common business practice, at least for large companies, to provide, say, quarterly news releases to the business press, investment bankers, and industry specialists. These announcements emphasize projections of the company's realized earnings. But the announcements are often based on projections of the company's future performance, and companies generally recognize that large deviations from these projections can adversely affect the stock price. Quarterly pro forma income statements are the basis for these announcements.

Another common practice in large corporations is an annual stockholders' meeting, at which the chairman of the board usually predicts the firm's expected profits for that year. These estimates are typically based on the projected income statements.

WAGE NEGOTIATIONS

In 1985 the United Auto Workers met with the management of General Motors to renegotiate salaries, benefits, and job security considerations. In such negotiations between labor and management, both parties typically use their own versions of pro forma statements to make their cases. Clearly, the more profitable the company is expected to be, the stronger is labor's negotiating power. Another example involves Chrysler's labor force, which in 1985 demanded compensation for wage concessions it had granted during the company's less profitable years. Their new demands stemmed from the large profits projected by auto industry experts.

TAX PLANNING

Managers must carefully consider the tax consequences of their decisions. In particular, managers must know the company's cash flow situation and projected income statement in order to assess the magnitude and nature of the impact of taxes. Accountants use the projected income statement in conjunction with other financial statements to suggest policy changes to management that can lower the firm's tax liability.

Another use of projected income statements is for estimation of the firm's marginal tax rate. Whereas the example in Table 20-5 used a historical average tax rate, management may require more precise estimates for certain decisions. Capital budgeting decisions depend on estimates of the after-tax cash flow from an investment, and the precision of these estimates depends on the accuracy of the tax rate estimation. Pro forma income statements generated with computer programs can address several "what if" questions in estimating the tax rate more accurately.

20-3
FINANCIAL PLANNING USING THE PRO FORMA BALANCE SHEET

Unlike a cash flow budget, a **pro forma balance sheet** gives the cumulative funds required over a period of time rather than at the precise time (within the period) that the funds are needed. In addition, cash budgets are directly related to only a few balance sheet items, such as cash, whereas a pro forma balance sheet forecasts all assets and claims on assets. Based on this projected statement, additional information on the company's future financial condition and performance can be obtained by performing a ratio analysis of the pro forma statements and by constructing pro forma derivative statements such as a common-size statement.

A pro forma balance sheet thus is a direct estimate of the expected ending values for all asset, liability, and equity accounts for a future planning period. Because a cash flow forecast is normally prepared first and because most approaches to constructing a pro forma balance sheet depend on cash flow estimates, this statement is not only a supplementary source of information but also a check on the consistency of the two forecasts. Besides cash flow estimates, the construction of a pro forma balance sheet relies on the current period's ending balance sheet and the pro forma income statement.

Constructing the Pro Forma Balance Sheet

The starting point for creating the pro forma balance sheet is the latest period's ending (actual) balance sheet. The following general rule is then applied to each balance sheet item:

Beginning (actual) balance

$+$ Inflows

$-$ Outflows $\Big\}$ net change in the balance

Ending (forecasted) balance

To illustrate this rule, we use the major sections of InterTech Stores' pro forma balance sheet in Table 20-6 to describe how the forecasted changes and ending balances were derived. We also make use of the supporting worksheet information in Table 20-7. The reader is urged to examine Tables 20-6 and 20-7 as we work through our discussion.

ASSETS

CASH AND MARKETABLE SECURITIES The projected cumulative cash position for InterTech is a deficit of $27 million (see Table 20-4). This implies that cash declines by $61 million [$48 − (−$13) = $61] during the fourth quarter. The implications of a negative cash balance are discussed shortly.

All of InterTech's marketable securities are projected to mature during the fourth quarter. Thus the ending balance in this account is $0.

ACCOUNTS RECEIVABLE According to Table 20-2, credit sales amount to $298 million because they are expected to be 70% of total sales, or 0.70 × $425 million = $298 million. But management expects that 2%, or $9 million, of

■

TABLE 20-6
InterTech Stores, Inc., Pro Forma Balance Sheet, December 31, 1996 (in millions)

	Starting Balance Sheet: Actual Value Sept. 30, 1996	Net Change, +/(−)[a]	Pro Forma Balance Sheet: Ending Value Dec. 31, 1996
Assets			
1. Current assets			
Cash	$ 48	($ 61)	($ 13)
Marketable securities	3	(3)	0
Net accounts receivable[b]	46	105	151
Inventories	191	(95)	96
Prepaid expenses	6	0	6
Total current assets	$294	($ 54)	$240
2. Net fixed assets	72	14	86
Total assets	$366	($ 40)	$326
Claims on Assets			
3. Current liabilities			
Accounts payable	$ 90	($ 51)	$ 39
Notes payable—bank	73	(28)	45
Accrued taxes	5	5	10
Other accruals	20	0	20
Total current liabilities	$188	($ 74)	$114
4. Long-term liabilities			
Debenture bonds	$ 49	$ 30	$ 79
Deferred taxes	14	0	14
Total long-term liabilities	$ 63	$ 30	$ 93
5. Stockholders' equity			
Common stock	$ 25	$ 0	$ 25
Paid-in capital	22	0	22
Retained earnings	68	4	72
Total stockholders' equity	$115	$ 4	$119
Total claims	$366	($ 40)	$326

[a] Detailed calculations of net change (+ / −) are provided in Table 20-7.
[b] Includes bad-debt allowances.

		Change	Source
TABLE 20-7 *Worksheet for Pro Forma Balance Sheet (in millions)*	**Cash**	($61)	
	Beginning cash $ 48		Table 20-4
	Ending cash (13)		Table 20-4
	Marketable securities	($3)	
	Beginning balance $ 3		
	+ Additions 0		
	− Maturing 3		
	Ending balance $ 0		
	Accounts receivable	$105	
	Beginning accounts receivable $ 46		
	+ Net credit sales 298		Table 20-2
	− Provisions for bad debts 9		Table 20-5
	− Accounts receivable collected 184		Table 20-4
	Ending accounts receivable $151		
	Inventory	($95)	
	Beginning inventory $191		
	+ Purchases 173		Table 20-2
	− Cost of goods sold 268		Table 20-5
	Ending inventory $ 96		
	Net fixed assets	$14	
	Beginning net fixed assets $ 72		
	+ Capital expenditures 16		Table 20-2
	− Depreciation expense 2		Table 20-5
	Ending net fixed assets $ 86		
	Accounts payable	($51)	
	Beginning accounts payable $ 90		
	+ Purchases 173		Table 20-2
	− Payment of payables 224		Table 20-2
	Ending accounts payable $ 39		
	Notes payable	($28)	
	Beginning notes payable $ 73		
	+ New borrowing 0		
	− Repayment of bank debt 28		Table 20-3
	Ending notes payable $ 45		
	Accrued taxes	$5	
	Beginning accrued taxes $ 5		
	+ Income tax liability 9		Table 20-5
	− Income taxes paid 4		Table 20-3
	Ending accrued taxes $ 10		
	Debenture bonds	$30	
	Beginning debenture bonds $ 49		
	+ Issuance of new bonds 30		
	− Retirement of existing bonds 0		
	Ending debenture bonds $ 79		
	Stockholders' equity	$4	
	Beginning retained earnings $ 68		
	+Net income 10		Table 20-5
	− Dividend payments 6		
	Ending retained earnings $ 72		

total sales will prove to be uncollectible and will be charged against sales as a bad-debt expense (see Table 20-5). Net credit sales are therefore $289 million (0.68 × $425 million = $289 million). However, the actual collection of accounts receivable is $184 million. This produces an ending level of receivables of $151 million. The change in receivables is therefore the ending value of $151 million less the beginning value of $46 million, or an increase of $105 million. This is shown in the worksheet in Table 20-7.

INVENTORY The ending inventory balance requires that the difference between purchases and the cost of goods sold be added to the beginning inventory figure. Purchases represent the sum of the monthly purchase in Table 20-2. Although purchases increase inventories, the costs of goods sold from the pro forma income statement represent how much inventories are expected to decrease. The result is a net decrease of $95 million to an ending balance of $96 million.

NET FIXED ASSETS The change in net fixed assets depends on the budgeted expenditures on plant and equipment less the expected depreciation expense. Capital expenditures are found by summing the monthly estimates in the cash flow budget, and the $2 million depreciation expense comes from the pro forma income statement. The net effect is an increase of $14 million to $86 million.

LIABILITIES

CURRENT AND LONG-TERM LIABILITIES The net decrease of $51 million in accounts payable is derived by subtracting the summed monthly estimates for the payment of payables (Table 20-2) from planned purchases. This reduces accounts payable to an ending balance of $39 million. A scheduled $28 million repayment of bank debt (Table 20-3) produces an ending notes payable balance of $45 million. Ending accrued taxes are obtained by subtracting the estimated cash tax payments in December (Table 20-3) from the tax liability incurred (but not paid) on fourth-quarter profits (Table 20-5) and adding this figure to the beginning balance. Finally, InterTech Stores has arranged to issue new bonds in November (Table 20-3). No retirement (repayment) of existing bonds is scheduled, and therefore this account increases by $30 million to $79 million.

STOCKHOLDERS' EQUITY Common stock and paid-in capital are normally assumed to remain unchanged because any changes are made at the discretion of management. The only change in equity thus occurs with regard to the retention of earnings. From the pro forma income statement (Table 20-5), net income after taxes is expected to be $10 million. But InterTech will pay a $6 million dividend in December (Table 20-3). The difference between these two figures results in retained earnings increasing to $72 million.

Using the Pro Forma Balance Sheet for Planning

FUNDS PLANNING

InterTech's pro forma balance sheet provides certain details for funds planning. First, InterTech will experience a $27 million (−$13 million − $14 million = −$27 million) cash shortfall if the total asset projection of $326 million holds true. This result is consistent with the negative cash flow forecasted in the cash budget and reinforces the fact that additional financing needs to be arranged to meet the projected shortfall in assets. The financial manager must decide what mix of short- and long-term financing is best, as well as the type of financing.[2]

PERFORMANCE EVALUATION

The financial manager could analyze InterTech's projected financial condition and performance using common-size statements and financial ratios. These results can be compared with the firm's past performance and with industry averages. If any weaknesses or serious deviations are discovered, management will be forewarned to take corrective measures. For example, accounts receivable are expected to balloon to approximately 46% of assets ($151/$326) from about 13%

---

[2] Of course, this assumes that the Modigliani–Miller assumptions are unlikely to hold. The financing mix decision may be relevant.

($46/$366) ending September 30, 1996 (refer to Table 20-6). InterTech's credit and collection policy should probably be examined to determine the reason for this situation.

ENSURING COMPLIANCE WITH INDENTURE AGREEMENTS

When firms raise debt capital, they are often required to agree to certain conditions spelled out in a document called the *indenture agreement*. For example, management might agree not to allow the long-term debt–equity ratio to fall below a certain value. Similarly, banks may require a company to maintain, say, a current ratio of at least 0.6 until the loan is paid off. Because a variety of financial decisions affect these ratios, the manager needs to try out several plans in order to make sure that the proposed policies do not violate any of these agreements.

BOND RATING CONSIDERATIONS

The debt levels raised by companies have different risks. Bond rating agencies assign a letter grade to each bond based on a variety of criteria, which rely to a great extent on the company's financial statements. Managers generally regard major deviations in certain key ratios as having an adverse impact on their debt rating, and therefore they carefully examine the effects of several decisions on future balance sheet ratios. Pro forma balance sheets and income statements offer a convenient vehicle for such analyses.

Interrelationship Among the Various Pro Forma Statements

The pro forma balance sheet and the pro forma income statement are linked in that the balance sheet cannot be prepared without the income statement. This is because the level of retained earnings projected in the balance sheet depends on the net income projected in the income statement. InterTech's projected net income is $10 million, and with the planned dividend of $6 million, the increase in retained earnings in the projected balance sheet is therefore $4 million. The pro forma balance sheet provides information about the required total borrowings, and the interest on these borrowings affects the pro forma income statement. This complication can be overcome by using a computer to prepare the two statements simultaneously, recognizing this interrelationship.

Financial managers often learn more by looking at more than one pro forma statement at a time.[3] For example, note that the cash flow estimate in Table 20-4 indicates a substantial negative cash position. Yet the pro forma income statement indicates a profit. If financial managers relied only on this pro forma statement, they would see a rosy picture of InterTech's financial performance. The cash budget tells them, on the other hand, that substantial short-term financing must be arranged to meet InterTech's obligations. Remember that profits do not pay bills.

Finally, note that both the pro forma income statement and the balance sheet were based on the most likely cash flow estimates. Financial managers may want to develop additional statements by using the most pessimistic and most optimistic cash forecasts or by varying the different assumptions underlying the various forecasts. This additional information would provide a range of estimates and thus a range of financial conditions and performances that would better help them gauge the seriousness of any financing requirements or deviations from the desired results. This procedure can be done with an interactive computer spreadsheet recognizing the interrelationships among the various statements. See the following highlight.

---

[3] We examine pro forma statements over just a few months to keep the exposition simple; in reality, these statements are analyzed for a longer period—say, a whole year.

MICROCOMPUTERS AND FINANCIAL PLANNING

Microcomputers offer ways to improve the efficiency of planning processes. Application software for micros falls into four main areas: word processing, spreadsheet/graphics, database management, and telecommunications. Integrated software packages combine all these features in one program.

Spreadsheet software is particularly useful for financial planning. A spreadsheet program displays a row–column screen on the terminal. Each cell represents a variable. Text, numbers, or formulas (which refer to different cells in the spreadsheet) may be entered into the cells. The screen always displays text or numbers (which may be a result of an equation entered into that cell).

Every time the contents of a cell are changed, the entire spreadsheet is recalculated. This provides a powerful tool to perform "what if" analyses for any set of financial statements. For example, one may set up pro forma financial statements (income statement, balance sheet, etc.), with appropriate relationships among them to compute successive statements, by using figures from the preceding statements. It then is possible to change any one (or more) number in one statement and see the effects ripple into the other pro forma statements, thereby improving the financial manager's productivity.

What makes the micros and spreadsheet programs more useful

are their capabilities to transfer data from one user to another user. First, data from one spreadsheet may be incorporated into another spreadsheet at the press of a button. The numbers transferred may be simply copied, or they may be added to (or subtracted from) the numbers in another spreadsheet. This operation allows for the consolidation of divisional budgets/forecasts/statements into one statement at the touch of a button. Second, the data may be sent over telephone lines using a telecommunication program. This allows fast communication among physically distant units of the organization.

Implications for Financial Planning

The interactive nature of the financial statements allows a company to set up what may be called a distributed planning system among its various functional areas. Marketing managers and the production department, for example, can directly provide information for the financial manager's pro forma statements. To set up such a distributed planning system, the firm must first develop models of divisional cash flow statements and then tie them into a consolidated model for the financial manager. Then managers must be trained (or provided with staff) to work with the micros. The following advantages result for the planning process:

1. Plans are made with a smaller set of assumptions. Financial managers need not make assumptions about how marketing or operations

managers plan for their functions. Financial managers need only be concerned with the results of their plans.

2. The numbers have greater validity. Not only are there fewer assumptions underlying the plans, but they also are based on the intimate knowledge that functional managers have of their own departments, thus making the planning process more intelligent.

3. It is possible to run through the planning process a number of times within a short interval. Managerial time is a valuable resource for the firm. Planning sessions among department managers are often difficult to schedule, and physical distances compound the situation. These problems are overcome by having managers perform planning in their departments and then telecommunicate the results to be consolidated by the financial manager.

4. Increased iterations enable better problem solving by allowing functional experts to examine more alternatives. Microcomputers and distributed planning systems do not by themselves guarantee better problem solving, but they increase the likelihood of producing better financial plans. To the extent that financial planning is facilitated, it will cease to be a rote exercise. Instead, it will prepare the firm to deal with future operational and financial obstacles.

In Chapter 8 we developed rules for analyzing investments that increase the company's value. Managers want to invest only in projects that increase the firm's value. It is important to keep in mind that maximizing firm value is not guaranteed solely by choosing the best projects. Management must constantly make financial planning analyses to ensure that they do not overlook operational details and institutional realities. Even the best investment in the world is of little value to a firm if it has not been well planned. And if the company's basic financial stability is threatened, the full benefits provided by even the best project may never be realized.

SUMMARY

Section 20-1: The Cash Flow Budget

How do managers estimate the firm's future cash needs?

- Managers forecast the firm's future cash needs by means of the cash flow budget, which is a detailed estimated schedule of future cash inflows, cash outflows, and cash balances at different times over a specific interval. These cash flows occur from sales, operating, and financial activities.

- The cash flow budget enables managers to predict both the magnitude and timing of cash deficits and surpluses in the future. This information can provide ample time for them to arrange for lines of credit or to plan for the investment of future cash surpluses.

- Cash flow budgets also facilitate monitoring and control. If actual receipts or expenditures are significantly different from projected values, management is alerted to a potential problem and is able to take immediate corrective action.

- In addition to internal planning, cash flow budgets are often required by outside parties such as banks and other lenders of funds. For start-up companies, even suppliers of equity capital may require cash budgets.

Section 20-2: Financial Planning Using the Pro Forma Income Statement

What are pro forma statements?

- Pro forma statements are projected financial statements that enable managers to estimate the firm's future financial status and thus assist them in accomplishing their stated goals.

How do managers forecast the firm's income using the pro forma income statement?

- The pro forma income statement is a forecast of the expected revenues, expenses, and profits of the firm over some specific planning period.

- Pro forma income statements can be used to coordinate and control policy decisions. They can also provide estimated earnings for the public and can be used in wage negotiations and tax planning.

Section 20-3: Financial Planning Using the Pro Forma Balance Sheet

How do managers forecast the firm's future levels of assets and liabilities using the pro forma balance sheet?

- The pro forma balance sheet is an estimate of the expected ending values for all asset, liability, and equity accounts for a specific planning period.

- To forecast future levels of assets and liabilities, managers begin with the latest balance in each item. To this they add all inflows and subtract all outflows.

- The pro forma balance sheet allows managers to plan future financing needs. It can also be used in performance evaluation, to ensure that the firm adheres to its bond indenture agreements, and to evaluate how managerial actions may affect the firm's bond rating.

How are the short-term planning statements interrelated?

- The cash flow budget provides input data for the pro forma income statement.

- The pro forma income statement provides the estimate of retained earnings for the pro forma balance sheet.

- The pro forma balance sheet contains details of the firm's borrowing, information that is necessary to compute projected interest expenses in the pro forma income statement.

- Because of their interrelatedness, the cash flow budget and the pro forma statements are usually developed simultaneously and analyzed together to provide managers with information concerning the future profitability and financial health of the firm.

QUESTIONS

1. What is financial planning?

2. What is a cash flow budget? Why is it important to a firm?

3. What are the different stages or steps in developing a cash budget?

4. What is the bottom line of the cash flow budget? What does it tell the financial manager?

5. What are the differences between the cash flow budget discussed in this chapter and the cash flow statement discussed in Chapter 3?

6. How is the cash flow budget used in financial planning?

7. Who would be interested in the information in the pro forma income statement? How would they use this information?

8. How is the pro forma balance sheet used in financial planning?

9. How are the cash flow budget, the pro forma balance sheet, and the pro forma income statement interrelated?

PROBLEMS

1. Nater, Inc., expects sales of $4,000 in March, $6,000 in April, $5,000 in May, $4,000 in June, and $5,500 in July. On average, it collects 35% of its monthly sales in cash, 45% in one month, and 19% in two months (the remaining 1% is a bad-debt expense and is never collected). Find Nater's expected cash inflows during May, June, and July.

2. Bilch's Fried Chicken is a fast-food chain. Although its expenses depend mainly on sales, these expenses are not necessarily paid in cash in the month of the sale. For example, wage expense amounts to 25% of a month's sales but is paid on the first day of the next month (the wage expense incurred in January is not actually paid until February). Chicken is purchased for the current month (its cost represents 20% of the sales volume) and is paid for in cash. Frozen

french fries, oil, and other supplies cost 30% of a given month's sales. They are purchased with cash one month before the sale. Finally, Bilch has rent expenses totaling $220,000 per month. Its expected sales are as follows:

Month	Aug.	Sept.	Oct.	Nov.	Dec.	Jan.
Expected sales	$1,000,000	$1,200,000	$1,100,000	$850,000	$700,000	$950,000

(a) Find Bilch's expected cash outflows for September, October, November, and December.

(b) Bilch's is currently experiencing cash flow problems and is considering an offer by the chicken supplier to take 60 days' credit with a credit charge of 2.5% for this two-month period. Find Bilch's expected outflows for September, October, November, and December if it takes advantage of this offer.

3. Koufand's Jewelers has expected cash inflows, variable cash outflows (outflows that depend on sales), and fixed cash outflows as follows:

	Jan.	Feb.	Mar.	Apr.
Inflows	$600,000	$700,000	$620,000	$500,000
Variable outflows	290,000	330,000	270,000	235,000
Fixed outflows	320,000	320,000	320,000	320,000

Koufand's has a cash balance of $50,000 as of January 1 and a minimum desired balance of $40,000. Find Koufand's expected net cash flow for each of the four months listed, and construct a monthly cash budget for the four months.

4. The following table lists the cash flow budget (in thousands) for the Baxter Corporation, a retailing firm, for the last quarter of 1996.

	Aug.	Sept.	Oct.	Nov.	Dec.
Total sales	$720	$760	$840	$920	$900
Cash sales (35%)			294	322	315
Collections from previous month (35%)			266	294	322
Collections from second previous month (30%)			216	228	252
Total operating cash inflows			$776	$844	$889
Cash outflows					
Payment of accounts payable			$172	$197	$225
Wages and salaries			152	165	182
Selling			145	151	154
General and administrative			153	159	157
Capital expenditures			18	9	18
Rent			120	120	120
Taxes			0	0	45.9
Interest			17	17	17
Total cash outflows			$777	$818	$918.9
Net cash flow			−$1	$26	−$29.9
Beginning cash balance			300	299	325
Ending cash balance			$299	$325	$295.1
Minimum desired			250	250	250
Surplus (deficit)			$49	$75	$45.1

Depreciation for the quarter is $164,000, and the cost of goods sold generally averages about 20% of sales. Baxter's tax rate is 34%. Baxter pays its accounts payable one month after its purchase of inventory; December purchases will be 30% of sales. Construct a pro forma income statement for the last quarter of 1996.

5. The following balance sheet is for the Baxter Corporation as of September 30, 1991. Construct a pro forma balance sheet for December 31, 1996. (Refer to the data in Problem 4 if necessary.)

Cash	$300
Accounts receivable	512
Marketable securities	36
Inventory	421
Current assets	$1,269
Net fixed assets	5,208
Total assets	$6,477
Accounts payable	$169
Notes payable	142
Taxes payable	44
Total current liabilities	$355
Long-term debt	2,900
Common stock	1,700
Paid-in capital	721
Retained earnings	801
Total claims on assets	$6,477

6. Which of the following balance sheet items would ordinarily be expected to increase spontaneously with sales?

Cash	Accounts payable
Marketable securities	Wages payable
Accounts receivable	Notes payable
Inventory	Long-term debt

20A

FINANCIAL RATIO ANALYSIS

*M*anagement must constantly evaluate its financial statements to ensure that it is using its resources efficiently. For example, are its assets being used in the most profitable way? Is the company sufficiently liquid to meet its current obligations? Is the firm profitable enough to guarantee the interest and principal payments on its long-term debt? The financial statements alone may not be able to provide the answers, and so a common approach to answering such questions is to perform a financial ratio analysis. **Financial ratio analysis** is the systematic use of ratios to interpret financial statements and thereby determine a firm's existing strengths and weaknesses, as well as its historical performance and current financial condition. The information in financial statements is reduced to a small set of indexes or percentage values that then form the basis for measuring different aspects of a firm's activities.

Out of the possibly hundreds of ratios that could be developed from the financial statements, only a few are commonly used. These ratios can conveniently be examined in four categories: short-term liquidity, long-term liquidity, asset utilization, and profitability. In this appendix on ratio analysis we first define the various ratios and then compute each one for InterTech Stores for 1994 and 1995.

Short-Term Solvency Ratios

Short-term solvency or **liquidity ratios** measure a firm's ability to meet its short-term obligations. They focus on whether a firm has enough cash or assets readily convertible into cash to pay its current liabilities. If a firm has adequate cash, it should have no problem paying its bills on time (i.e., it is solvent). If it has insufficient cash, a short-term crisis called **insolvency** occurs. Insolvency can be disastrous for a firm. Banks become reluctant to lend money, suppliers balk at selling goods on credit, and the firm's overall creditworthiness drops.

Two ratios are calculated to measure liquidity: current and quick ratios.

CURRENT RATIOS

The **current ratio** is defined as current assets divided by current liabilities:

$$\text{Current ratio} = \frac{\text{current assets}}{\text{current liabilities}} \qquad (20\text{A-1})$$

For InterTech:

$$1995: \frac{\$257}{\$135} = 1.90 \qquad 1994: \frac{\$230}{\$133} = 1.73$$

The current ratio measures the extent to which those assets closest to being cash cover those liabilities closest to being payable. Normally, larger values of this ratio are desirable.

QUICK (ACID TEST) RATIOS

The current ratio assumes that all current assets are equally liquid. Inventories, however, are often quite illiquid compared with marketable securities or accounts receivable. The **quick ratio** considers only assets that can be most readily converted to cash and is therefore a stricter test for liquidity:

$$\text{Quick ratio} = \frac{\text{current assets} - \text{inventories} - \text{prepaid expenses}}{\text{current liabilities}} \qquad (20\text{A-2})$$

$$1995: \frac{\$257 - \$111 - \$7}{\$135} = 1.03 \qquad 1994: \frac{\$230 - \$92 - \$9}{\$133} = 0.97$$

Long-Term Solvency Ratios   **Long-term solvency ratios** emphasize the longer-term commitments to creditors. Claims by creditors on a firm's income arise from contractual agreements that must be honored before any income can become available to stockholders. Furthermore, the greater the amount of these claims, the greater are the chances that a firm will fail to satisfy these claims. Failure to meet these claims may result in legal action to force their fulfillment, which might force the company to liquidate (sell) part or all of its assets to satisfy these obligations. These ratios fall into two groups: debt utilization and coverage ratios.

DEBT UTILIZATION RATIOS

Debt utilization ratios measure a firm's degree of indebtedness. The term *degree of indebtedness* refers to the proportion of the firm's assets that are financed by debt relative to the proportion financed by equity. The information needed to compute this ratio is found in the balance sheet.

The **debt–equity ratio** is the value of total debt divided by the book value of equity:[4]

---

[4] In those cases in which the firm also has preferred stock, there are two versions of this debt–equity ratio. One version treats preferred stock as equity and adds it to the denominator in equation (20A-3). The other version treats preferred stock as debt and adds it to the numerator.

$$\text{Debt–equity ratio} = \frac{\text{current liabilities} + \text{long-term liabilities}}{\text{stockholders' equity}} \quad \text{(20A-3)}$$

$$1995: \frac{\$135 + \$61}{\$120} = 1.63 \qquad 1994: \frac{\$133 + \$43}{\$95} = 1.85$$

Two variants of the debt–equity ratio may be used, depending on how debt and equity are defined. For example, only long-term debt may be included in the numerator of equation (20A-3). This is because only long-term debt involves a fixed obligation extending beyond one year, and hence it is more suitable for assessing long-term insolvency. This obligation is usually in the form of interest payments, and occasionally the periodic repayment of principal, and is called a *sinking fund payment.*[5] Another type of debt ratio uses the book value of assets (debt + equity) in the denominator and is called the **debt-to-assets ratio.** It is used to focus on the percentage of total funds contributed by debt.

COVERAGE RATIOS

Coverage ratios measure the degree to which fixed payments are "covered" by operating profits. The emphasis here is on assessing a firm's ability to service its financial (nonoperating) expenses. Information for these ratios comes from the income statement. This type of solvency ratio looks at the servicing of fixed obligations rather than the extent to which the debt is utilized.

The **times interest earned** (or **interest coverage**) **ratio** is the most common coverage ratio and measures how many times interest expenses are "earned" or "covered" by profits:

$$\text{Times interest earned} = \frac{\text{net profits before taxes} + \text{interest expenses}}{\text{interest expenses}} \quad \text{(20A-4)}$$

$$1995: \frac{\$38 + \$18}{\$18} = 3.11 \text{ times} \qquad 1994: \frac{\$25 + \$21}{\$21} = 2.19 \text{ times}$$

The **fixed-charge coverage ratio** is a more meaningful ratio because it considers the extent to which all fixed financial charges (long-term leases, rental expenses, etc.) are covered:

$$\text{Fixed-charge coverage} = \frac{\begin{array}{c}\text{net profits} \\ \text{before taxes}\end{array} + \begin{array}{c}\text{interest} \\ \text{expenses}\end{array} + \begin{array}{c}\text{lease and rental} \\ \text{payments}\end{array}}{\text{interest expenses} + \text{lease and rental payments}} \quad \text{(20A-5)}$$

$$1995: \frac{\$38 + \$18 + \$40}{\$18 + \$40} = 1.66 \qquad 1994: \frac{\$25 + \$21 + \$30}{\$21 + \$30} = 1.49$$

This ratio is especially relevant today because leasing is gaining popularity as an alternative to debt financing.

Asset Utilization Ratios   **Asset utilization** (or **turnover**) **ratios** relate sales to different types of assets to indicate how efficiently management is using assets to generate revenues. The purpose is to obtain an idea of the speed with which assets generate sales. The more rapidly assets are "turned over," the more efficient the use of assets is.

An implicit assumption of any turnover ratio is that there is some optimal mix between sales and asset investments. By analyzing these ratios, one can determine

---

[5] Sometimes firms have mortgage payments on property. Then the periodic payments include both interest and principal.

whether too many or too few resources are invested in a particular asset. It is possible, for example, that too much is invested in accounts receivable. This discovery might suggest that the firm's credit policy is too lax and that the inflated receivables hide an excessive amount of delinquent debts. All three of the most widely used asset utilization ratios relate sales to accounts receivable, inventories, and fixed assets.

ACCOUNTS RECEIVABLE

The **average collection period ratio** is a measure of the efficiency of a firm's credit policy. It estimates the number of days it takes for the firm to collect a dollar in sales:

$$\text{Average collection period} = \frac{\text{accounts receivable}}{\text{net sales per day}}$$
$$= \frac{\text{accounts receivable}}{\text{sales/365 days}}$$

(20A-6)

$$1995: \frac{\$96}{\$801/365} = 43.7 \text{ days} \qquad 1994: \frac{\$89}{\$720/365} = 45.2 \text{ days}$$

Often the level of sales and the investment in assets fluctuate throughout the year, especially if the sales demand is seasonal in nature. Therefore asset utilization ratios should be computed throughout the fiscal year if they are to have any real meaning. Unfortunately, information about these asset accounts may not be available that often. An approximation using the average level of the current asset account is therefore often used. The average can be computed by adding the beginning and ending account values and dividing by 2. If, on the other hand, quarterly information is used, the average is computed by summing the four values and dividing by 4.

Accounts receivable reflect only *credit* sales, and so the denominator should contain only credit sales. But often *total* sales are used because accurate information about the breakdown of revenues into cash and credit sales is not readily available. Sometimes this calculation is based on a 360-day calendar year, a practice that grew out of the banking industry's simplifying practice of assuming a convenient 30 days in a month.

INVENTORY

The **inventory turnover ratio** is used to determine whether there is too much or too little invested in inventories. Too much inventory may mean that resources are being used unproductively. Too little inventory may mean that sales, and hence profits, are being lost because of "stockouts" (shortages).

$$\text{Inventory turnover} = \frac{\text{cost of goods sold}}{\text{inventories}}$$

(20A-7)

$$1995: \frac{\$492}{\$111} = 4.43 \qquad 1994: \frac{\$468}{\$92} = 5.09$$

A 5.09 ratio suggests that given the rate of sales in 1994 and given the amount of inventory on hand, the firm had to restock inventory more than five times. Note that "cost of goods sold" rather than "sales" is used in the numerator. Accounts receivable are carried at the prices at which the products are sold. The appropriate way to measure how efficiently the investment in this asset is used is to relate it to sales. Inventories, however, are carried at what it cost to produce or acquire them. To be consistent, then, inventory utilization should be measured in terms of the "cost of goods sold." Nevertheless, total sales are often used in practice because either the sales figure is easier to obtain or the firm "produces" a service, in which case, the cost of goods sold has no meaning. Also, "average" inventories are often used in the denominator of this ratio to account for fluctuations in inventory levels.

FIXED ASSETS

The **fixed-asset turnover ratio** indicates how well the investment in long-term (fixed) assets is being managed. Normally, the higher this turnover ratio is, the more efficiently assets are being used to generate sales:

$$\text{Fixed-asset turnover ratio} = \frac{\text{net sales}}{\text{net fixed assets}} \qquad \text{(20A-8)}$$

$$1995: \frac{\$801}{\$59} = 13.6 \qquad 1994: \frac{\$720}{\$41} = 17.6$$

A **total asset turnover ratio** (sales divided by total assets) may also be calculated. This ratio signifies how efficiently total resources are being used. It is like a "summary" turnover ratio because all of the other turnover ratios are included in, and hence affect, its value.

Profitability Ratios

Profitability financial ratios measure management's overall record of producing profits. If a firm does not earn an adequate profit, its long-term survival is threatened. If profits are too low, for example, investors are reluctant to provide new capital, which, in turn, stifles or even halts its growth.

How do we determine when profits are low or high? The level of profits alone does not answer this question. Profits must be converted to a measure of profitability, which then reveals how successful past decisions and policies have been in earning a return for its investors. We next examine four profitability ratios. Like all ratios, it is important to note that profitability ratios can measure only past performance. Too often, it is assumed that these figures will persist into the future. Little evidence can be found to show that past performance is repeated consistently in the future. For example, Dorchester Gas Corporation received considerable publicity in 1981 for being ranked number one (in the *Fortune* 500 list) in total return to investors over the preceding ten years—a respectable 43% per year. Because of a sharp drop in natural gas prices and demand, however, Dorchester's 1982 return plummeted to 13%.

OPERATING PROFIT MARGIN

The operating profit margin determines the percentage of each sales dollar that is represented by operating profits. It indicates how good a job management has done in controlling its costs and how effective its pricing policy has been:

$$\text{Operating profit margin} = \frac{\text{net operating income}}{\text{net sales}}$$

$$= \frac{\text{net sales} - \text{cost of goods sold} - \text{operating expenses}}{\text{net sales}} \qquad \text{(20A-9)}$$

$$1995: \frac{\$801 - \$492 - \$257}{\$801} = 6.5\% \qquad 1994: \frac{\$720 - \$468 - \$211}{\$720} = 5.7\%$$

NET PROFIT MARGIN

The net profit margin goes one step further and considers income after all costs (operating + financial + taxes) have been deducted. It is found by dividing net income after taxes by net sales:[6]

$$\text{Net profit margin} = \frac{\text{net income}}{\text{net sales}} \qquad (20A\text{-}10)$$

$$1995: \frac{\$32}{\$801} = 4.0\% \qquad 1994: \frac{\$21}{\$720} = 2.9\%$$

BOOK RETURN ON ASSETS

The book return on assets (ROA) is a guide to a firm's overall profitability and measures the after-tax returns without regard to the manner in which the assets were financed:[7]

$$\text{Book return on assets }(ROA) = \frac{\text{net operating income}(1 - T)}{\text{total assets}} \qquad (20A\text{-}11)$$

where T is the firm's tax rate.

$$1995: \frac{\$52(1 - 0.15)}{\$316} = 13.99\% \qquad 1994: \frac{\$41(1 - 0.15)}{\$271} = 12.86\%$$

BOOK RETURN ON EQUITY

Unlike book ROA, which measures a firm's profitability without regard to the manner in which the assets are financed, book return on equity (ROE) recognizes both—the profitability of the underlying assets and the manner in which the assets are financed:

$$\text{Book return on equity }(ROE) = \frac{\text{net income}}{\text{stockholders' equity}} \qquad (20A\text{-}12)$$

$$1995: \frac{\$32}{\$120} = 26.67\% \qquad 1994: \frac{\$21}{\$95} = 22.11\%$$

Stockholders are usually interested in the total return, net of all other considerations, on their equity investment. Book ROE is useful for this purpose.

Using Ratio Analysis   As with the percentage values in the common-size statements, a ratio by itself normally has little meaning. For example, a firm with a current ratio of 1.0 may be cash rich, whereas another firm that has lots of inventory and a 4.0 current ratio may be struggling to pay its bills. In addition, higher values for some ratios are preferred to lower values; for others, the opposite is true. To illustrate this and other aspects of ratio analysis, two types of analyses can be done: an interfirm (industry) analysis and an intrafirm (trend) analysis.

[6]For firms that deal in merchandise—retailers, for example—another profitability ratio, called the *gross profit margin*, is often calculated. This ratio measures the percentage of each sales dollar that remains after the cost of goods sold has been deducted. The higher the margin is, the more efficient management's control of the cost of its merchandise has been. The ratio is defined as:

$$\text{Gross profit margin} = \frac{\text{net sales} - \text{cost of goods sold}}{\text{net sales}}$$

[7]Note that this differs from the standard accounting treatment of this ratio calculated as net income divided by total assets. ROA is the book return on the unlevered firm's assets as seen in Chapter 19.

■

TABLE 20A-1

Major Sources of Industry and Other Comparative Ratios

Dun & Bradstreet: Dun & Bradstreet, Inc., annually publishes a survey of 125 different types of retailing, wholesaling, manufacturing, and construction companies. From their financial statements, statistics on the median, upper-quartile, and lower-quartile values for 14 key ratios are reported.

Robert Morris Associates: This national association of bank loan and credit officers compiles statistics on the median, upper-quartile, and lower-quartile values for 16 key ratios for over 300 lines of businesses, by firm size, and publishes them in its *Annual Statement Studies.*

Financial and investor services: The *Standard & Poor's Industry Survey and Analyst's Handbook, Moody's Manuals and Handbook of Common Stocks,* and the *Value Line Investment Survey,* to name a few of the more popular services, provide comparative ratios on the companies and industries they follow.

Government agencies: The Federal Trade Commission and the Securities and Exchange Commission (SEC) have a joint publication called the *Quarterly Financial Report for U.S. Manufacturing Corporations.* It contains quarterly financial data such as common-size and other financial statements, by firm size and industry. The Small Business Administration and the U.S. Department of Commerce also issue periodic financial statement studies.

Trade associations: Various trade associations, such as the American Paper Institute and the National Retail Merchants Association, have staffs that collect financial data and compute standards for their respective industry members. This information is usually available upon request.

Business periodicals: Business Week, Forbes, and *Fortune* magazines regularly provide summary data on a limited number of financial ratios.

Corporations' annual and quarterly reports: Many corporations now present different financial ratios in summary statements in their published stockholders' reports and SEC 10-K reports.

Miscellaneous sources: Major commercial banks and public accounting firms also compile financial ratio statistics on their clients and customers. For example, the Accounting Corporation of America publishes its semiannual *Barometer for Small Business,* which supplies financial data for firms by sales and geographical location. Computerized financial data bases, such as the Compustat Investor Service (a subsidiary of Standard & Poor Corporation), contain a wealth of financial data that can be used to form industry ratios by means of relatively simple "canned programs." In addition, a publishing house, Prentice-Hall, makes available annually its *Almanac of Business and Industrial Financial Ratios,* which includes ten financial ratios grouped by asset size. This service is also one of the few sources in which ratios on industries in finance insurance and real estate can be found.

An **interfirm analysis** interprets ratio values by comparing a firm's financial ratios with related firms' financial ratios at one point in time. Interfirm analysis involves no time dimension and can thus be considered a "static" ratio analysis. An **intrafirm analysis** interprets ratio values by examining the behavior of a firm's individual ratios over time. Because of the time dimension, intrafirm analysis may be considered a "dynamic" ratio analysis.

INTERPRETING RATIOS WITH AN INTERFIRM ANALYSIS

An interfirm analysis uses industry-based ratio averages as standards of comparisons, or norms. These ratio standards represent the appropriate ratio values for a typical firm in the industry. The implication is that the ratios of companies in the same industry should be very close to one another. Industry ratios are available from a number of sources. The more important ones are listed in Table 20A-1, and Table 20A-2 provides an example from Dun & Bradstreet.[8]

To interpret an individual ratio value, it is compared with the industry average and then classified as "good," "satisfactory," or "poor," depending on the direction and extent to which it deviates from the average. A "poor" rating is given to a current ratio that is too low. Poor ratios normally indicate weaknesses or potential trouble spots that require further investigation. This investigation should reveal whether any serious problems exist and suggest what action might be taken to improve the situation. "Good" ratios, of course, indicate areas of major strength. The difficult part is assigning a rating to a particular ratio value. There are no hard and fast rules to follow. Judgment and experience end up being the final criteria.

A ratio analysis of InterTech Stores' most recent financial statements is presented next. Table 20A-3 contains a summary of its ratios by categories and industry averages.

[8] To estimate an industry average, Dun & Bradstreet draws the year-end financial statements for 400,000 firms from its computerized financial statement file and categorizes each firm into one of the 125 industries it follows. Then 14 ratios are calculated for each company. Next, the individual ratio values are arranged by size from the best ratio to the weakest. The value that falls exactly in the middle of this series becomes the *median* or "average" for that ratio in that line of business.

TABLE 20A-2
Examples of Dun & Bradstreet's 14 Ratios for Ten Manufacturing Industries[a]

Ratios[b]	SIC 01 Agric. Prdctn Crops (No Breakdown) 1990 (1749 Estab.)			SIC 01 Agric. Prdctn Crops Northeast 1990 (193 Estab.)			SIC 01 Agric. Prdctn Crops Central 1990 (582 Estab.)			SIC 01 Agric. Prdctn Crops South 1990 (461 Estab.)		
	UQ	MED	LQ	UQ	MED	LQ	UQ	MED	LQ	UQ	MED	LQ
Solvency												
Quick ratio (times)	2.7	0.9	0.4	2.5	0.9	0.4	2.3	0.7	0.3	3.2	1.0	0.3
Current ratio (times)	5.8	2.1	1.1	5.3	1.7	0.9	4.9	1.9	1.1	8.7	2.5	1.1
Curr liab. to NW (%)	7.4	26.1	73.4	7.5	31.3	97.5	8.1	26.5	64.8	6.0	20.2	65.6
Curr liab. to inv. (%)	36.3	94.2	191.6	52.9	131.1	233.2	41.4	94.2	176.3	21.8	77.2	170.8
Total liab. to NW (%)	20.0	65.0	150.5	15.8	67.2	189.7	23.7	65.4	140.8	16.3	46.9	126.5
Fixed assets to NW (%)	42.4	82.7	130.5	46.9	87.1	145.6	50.1	90.5	133.7	41.3	78.3	118.3
Efficiency												
Coll. period (days)	11.5	27.4	52.8	14.0	37.8	54.1	7.7	20.4	35.2	10.1	23.9	45.6
Sales to inv. (times)	21.5	7.1	3.2	19.1	9.8	5.3	22.1	7.1	3.3	14.9	5.2	2.6
Assets to sales (%)	42.0	76.4	140.1	37.5	62.8	125.1	42.2	81.7	158.0	41.8	81.1	156.8
Sales to NWC (times)	12.2	5.4	2.6	13.8	6.8	3.3	11.9	5.4	2.6	13.0	4.8	2.2
Acct. pay. to sales (%)	1.3	3.8	8.3	1.1	4.0	9.1	1.3	3.6	7.4	1.2	3.7	7.2
Profitability												
Return on sales (%)	14.5	5.4	0.9	8.0	2.8	0.3	13.5	4.4	0.7	15.4	5.8	1.1
Return on assets (%)	12.7	5.4	0.7	8.5	2.6	0.2	11.0	4.8	0.7	14.3	5.8	0.9
Return on NW (%)	24.3	10.4	1.9	16.9	6.1	0.4	25.7	9.1	1.9	23.8	10.5	2.3

[a] The *median* represents the ratio value that falls exactly in the middle of the series. The *upper quartile* represents the ratio value lying halfway between the median and the top of the series. The *lower quartile* is the ratio value lying halfway between the median and the bottom of the series.
[b] NWC = net working capital; NW = net worth (book value of equity)
SOURCE: Dun & Bradstreet, Inc., *Selected Key Business Ratios in 125 Lines of Business,* 1991. Copyright 1991. Dun & Bradstreet, Inc. All rights reserved. Reprinted with permission.

TABLE 20A-3
InterTech Stores, Inc., Summary of Financial Ratios and Industry Averages, 1995

Ratio	Formula	InterTech 1995	Industry Average	Evaluation
Short-term solvency				
Current ratio	$\dfrac{\text{Current assets}}{\text{Current liabilities}}$	1.90	2.4	Poor
Quick ratio	$\dfrac{\text{Current assets} - \text{inventory} - \text{prepaid expenses}}{\text{Current liabilities}}$	1.03	1.05	Satisfactory
Long-term solvency				
Debt–equity ratio	$\dfrac{\text{Total liabilities}}{\text{Stockholders' equity}}$	1.63	1.2	Poor
Times interest earned	$\dfrac{\text{Net profits before taxes} + \text{interest expenses}}{\text{Interest expenses}}$	3.11	2.6	Good
Fixed-charge coverage	$\dfrac{\text{Net profits before taxes} + \text{interest expenses} + \text{lease and rental payments}}{\text{Interest expenses} + \text{lease and rental payments}}$	1.66	1.5	Good
Asset Utilization				
Average collection period	$\dfrac{\text{Accounts receivable}}{\text{Sales per day}}$	43.7 days	20.9 days	Poor
Inventory turnover	$\dfrac{\text{Cost of goods sold}}{\text{Inventories}}$	4.43	3.3	Good
Fixed-asset turnover	$\dfrac{\text{Sales}}{\text{Net fixed assets}}$	13.6	14.1	Satisfactory
Profitability				
Operating profit margin	$\dfrac{\text{Net operating income}}{\text{Net sales}}$	6.5%	3.5%	Good
Net profit margin	$\dfrac{\text{Net income}}{\text{Net sales}}$	4.0%	1.6%	Good
Book return on assets	$\dfrac{\text{Net operating income}(1 - T)}{\text{Total assets}}$	13.99%	5.1%	Good
Book return on equity	$\dfrac{\text{Net income}}{\text{Stockholders' equity}}$	26.67%	10.0%	Good

SHORT-TERM SOLVENCY Normally, the higher the liquidity ratios are, the better. This generalization should be viewed cautiously, however, because these ratios can be too high. A high current ratio, for example, may mask an excessive and nonproductive investment in current assets.

This is not the case with InterTech. Its current ratio is rated "poor" in Table 20A-3, and the quick ratio receives a "satisfactory" rating. The low *current ratio* would normally imply that InterTech is having problems meeting its current obligations. But the satisfactory quick ratio, which reflects only very liquid assets, indicates that this is not the situation.

The common-size balance sheet in Table 3-4 in Chapter 3 shows that for its size, InterTech has a below-average holding of inventories and an above-average amount of accounts receivable and current liabilities. According to the definitions of the two short-term liquidity ratios in Table 20A-3, note first that if current liabilities are larger than average and current assets are average, the current ratio will be less than the industry's. Second, because InterTech has less inventory than usual and because inventories are excluded from the numerator in the *quick ratio,* the quick ratio tends to be higher than it would be if InterTech had an average amount of inventory.

Three additional comments on liquidity ratios are in order. A better measure of the ability to pay bills on time is an analysis of a firm's cash flow pattern because bills are paid with cash rather than with other assets (this is the subject of a later chapter). Low liquidity ratios may also mean that a firm is very efficient in managing its cash position and does not need to maintain as liquid a position as do other firms. This is a case in which "poor" may actually be good. Finally, low liquidity ratios may be only temporary. An intrafirm analysis will help determine whether this is indeed so.

LONG-TERM SOLVENCY InterTech's long-term solvency ratios also reveal a mixed picture. Its *debt–equity ratio* of 1.63 is considerably higher than the industry norm of 1.2. A ratio value greater than 1.0 simply says that a higher proportion of debt than equity is being used to finance assets. Although there are advantages to borrowing funds, the financial manager should be concerned about the reaction of its current (and future) creditors and stockholders to this relatively high level of debt. A high debt burden makes creditors less certain of receiving all their payments, and they therefore become reluctant to lend more money to InterTech. Additional funds then must carry a higher rate of interest to entice creditors into lending more money.

Stockholders, however, should be concerned because a higher debt ratio and the resulting higher interest expenses imply that less income may be available to them. On the other hand, higher levels of debt carry the potential advantage of "financial leverage"—a topic examined closely in Chapter 19. Thus increasing debt may or may not be to the advantage of the stockholders. The financial manager needs to establish whether the firm's debt ratio is consistent with its financial policy, taking these trade-offs into consideration.

The *times interest earned ratio* receives a "good" rating, thereby reducing somewhat the concern about InterTech's high debt ratio because this coverage ratio focuses on the ability to service periodic interest payments out of current income. The level of debt may be low or high, but it is the ability to meet debt obligations that really matters. For example, InterTech's ratio of 3.11 suggests that future profits before taxes could drop to zero before its ability to pay interest became impaired. To see this, note from the definition of this ratio that when net profits before taxes equal 0, interest expenses are just met, and the ratio value is 1.0. Thus we may tentatively conclude that InterTech has a relatively small chance of defaulting on its debt interest. Of course, before we could decide this definitely, the financial manager would need to check the extent to which other fixed charges must come out of profits. The fixed-charge coverage ratio is useful for this. InterTech's 1995 *fixed-charge coverage ratio* is 1.66, much better than the average for the industry. Thus the conclusion that the company's chances of default are not too high appears to be reasonable.

ASSET UTILIZATION InterTech's *average collection period* of 43.7 days is over twice the industry average of 20.9 days and is clearly a potential trouble spot. The most obvious reason, as seen earlier, is the disproportionate investment in accounts receivable for a retailer of InterTech's size. Management must determine whether this is consistent with a good credit policy. InterTech's policy may be too lenient, or its customers may be slow in making payments or may even be defaulting on their payments.

InterTech's *inventory turnover* brings a "good" rating (i.e., it is turning over its inventory at a faster rate than does the average retailer). On the surface this implies InterTech does a good job of keeping inventories at a low level (the common-size statement also indicated that InterTech had a below-average holding of inventory). But this may be a case of "good but too high." The reason is that good inventory management attempts to optimize—not minimize—inventory. Too low a level of inventories may reflect "lost sales" owing to shortages. Only a closer inspection of InterTech's inventory controls can tell.

InterTech's *fixed-asset utilization ratio* is neither too low nor too high. The financial manager does need to consider two things before drawing any conclusions, however. First, the book value of fixed assets changes little from year to year. There is normally a continuous process of depreciation and replacement of fixed assets. Moreover, as sales increase, fixed assets tend to increase, so that the fixed-asset turnover ratio does not change much from year to year. For this reason it is better to examine this ratio over time rather than at one point in time. What the analyst must look for is any significant deviation from a relatively constant ratio level. Second, the use of book values may disguise important information. Because book values depend on original cost, age, and the rate of depreciation, it is possible for two firms to have similar assets and sales and yet have very different turnover ratios. The major implication of this is that a high or rising ("improving") turnover ratio may be deceptive. It may just mean that a firm is operating with old plant and equipment. A failure to make new investments in fixed assets may prove disastrous if this continues because the firm will begin to lag in its industry and lose market share (i.e., lose sales and thereby reduce profits).

PROFITABILITY The profitability ratios provide a yardstick to measure the overall effectiveness of prior managerial decisions, and the higher the better. InterTech's management clearly distinguishes itself in this area. Returns on sales and investments all are well above average and deserve a "good" rating.

Nevertheless, two additional observations are necessary. First, profitability on sales refers to an ability to generate revenues in excess of expenses. Because operating profits are determined by the difference between sales and operating expenses, InterTech's good *operating profit margin* says that its pricing policy and/or its cost controls are very effective. The *net profit margin* supports this and indicates further that interest expenses are not too high. (This supports the earlier conclusion about the interest coverage ratio.)

The second observation is that InterTech's good profitability picture applies to only one point in time. Perhaps it just got lucky that year, or perhaps 1995 was an exceptionally good year for the economy as a whole. The true test is to look at profitability over time. This will indicate whether 1995's results were a fluke. This comment applies equally to returns on investment. The intrafirm (trend) analysis discussed in the next section is designed for this very purpose—to examine the patterns in a firm's ratios through time.

INTERPRETING RATIOS WITH AN INTRAFIRM ANALYSIS

Although interfirm analysis is helpful in assessing InterTech's current condition, a number of questions regarding the interpretation of certain ratios' values have not yet been answered. Specifically, should the financial manager be concerned about InterTech's low liquidity and high average collection period and whether its high profitability was only happenstance? Were these situations just temporary or, for example, did the poor ratios reflect a deterioration in those areas of InterTech's operations?

These questions arise because the analysis dealt with data for one year only. Moreover, reliance on a single set of ratio values can often be misleading. An intrafirm or trend analysis is important because it examines the historical pattern of each ratio and identifies those ratios that are deteriorating or improving over time. For example, a ratio rated poor may actually have been improving steadily for the last few years. In such a case, no remedial action may be necessary.

By taking an additional step and combining this information with the historical performance of the industry averages, a more complete picture of a firm's overall condition and performance emerges. Furthermore, knowledge of developing trends is useful in monitoring management's past decisions and policies and in deciding whether any future changes are required.

Figure 20A-1 contains a graphical representation of a trend analysis of Inter-Tech's "questionable" financial ratios for the last five years. The behavior of InterTech's *liquidity ratios* confirms some of the earlier suspicions. The ratios have been below average for the last three years and have been in a downward trend until recently. It is now evident that management needs to investigate the cause of this deterioration. On a positive note, the liquidity ratios recorded a slight improvement, so perhaps this situation has been turned around.

The trend analysis also shows that InterTech's use of debt exceeded the industry average over the entire time period, with 1993 witnessing a sharp increase in the debt–equity ratio, to above 2.0. Although a small decrease in debt utilization is noticeable, InterTech apparently overrelied on debt to finance its investments. A reduction in debt would seem advisable because any slowdown in sales could shrink InterTech's excellent net profit margin and book return on equity.

The trend in InterTech's average collection period is above the industry average ratio. InterTech's excellent profitability picture is no fluke, as the trends in the profit margin and return on assets indicate. InterTech consistently turned in an above-average performance in this area. The deterioration in 1993 in the net profit margin and *ROA* was because of a sharp increase in debt, but even these two ratios appear to have been improving more recently.

In conclusion, management has several issues to investigate regarding information not given in the financial statements. The interfirm and intrafirm analyses identified those areas where performance deviated from the industry norm. InterTech's

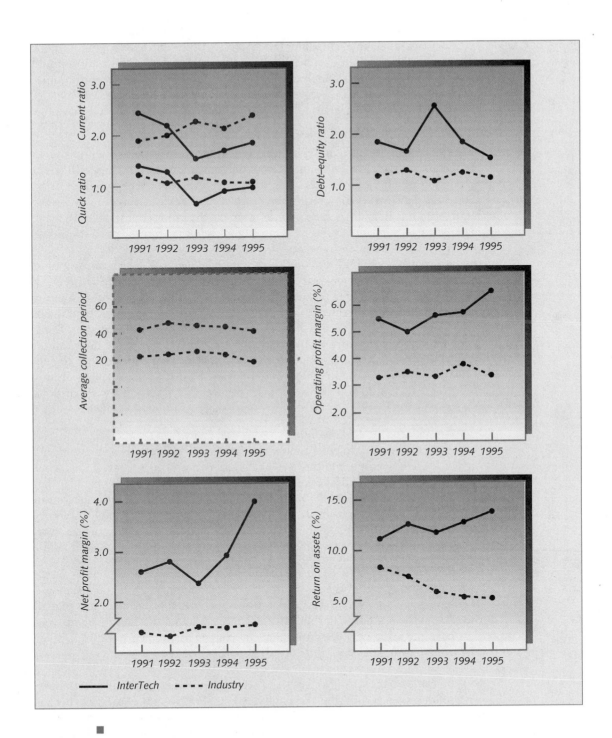

FIGURE 20A-1

Trend analysis of InterTech Stores' financial ratios, 1991–1995

weaknesses appear to be a poor liquidity position and high debt utilization. The long average collection period does not appear to be as serious a problem as was first thought. Nevertheless, management should keep an eye on its accounts receivable in case there is any further deviation from the norm. Finally, InterTech's profitability is clearly its greatest strength. Management has apparently promoted good pricing and cost control policies. Moreover, this strength has helped offset an otherwise high debt burden.

Limitations of Ratio Analysis

As we saw while analyzing InterTech Stores, ratios indicate only good or poor performance; they do not explain this performance. Because of this, ratios should be viewed only as a tool of analysis, not an end in itself. Unfortunately, some analysts lose sight of this and become too enamored with the mechanics of "number crunching." There also are several limitations inherent in any ratio study.

DIFFERENT ACCOUNTING PRACTICES

Ratios depend on accounting information and therefore are only as reliable as the accounting data are. Different firms in the same industry may follow different accounting practices for depreciation, inventory valuation, recognition of sales, and so on. This makes an interfirm analysis more difficult because the data must be adjusted for these differences in order to make the ratios comparable. To make matters worse, some managers are tempted to "smooth earnings" or to show continued growth in earnings by taking liberties with accounting practices.

For example, in 1982, Datapoint Corporation, a one-time favorite among computer companies, saw its ten-year growth rate of 40% per year come to a screeching halt. Up to that point, management apparently took advantage of the accounting practice of recording revenues as soon as products were shipped in order to maintain its enviable growth record. This meant that at the end of the quarter, Datapoint employees were working overtime to get shipments out of the door to beef up quarterly results at the last minute. Eventually, Datapoint ended up choking on a glut of unwanted computers that were returned by distributors. The result was that profits dropped, and the stock market rewarded Datapoint with an 80% plunge in its stock price, from around $60 per share to a low of $12 per share.

WHAT IS A ''GOOD'' OR A ''BAD'' RATIO?

It is not always easy to determine what a good or a bad ratio is. For example, a high quick ratio seems to indicate a strong liquidity position, which is "good," but in fact this may be "bad" because excessive cash is a nonproductive asset that contributes little to profits. On the other hand, a "poor" quick ratio may mean that management is very efficient in managing its cash flow. A high inventory turnover is often rated "good" but in fact may be "bad" if the high turnover stems from the firm's having inadequate inventory with a result of lost sales and profits.

USING INDUSTRY AVERAGE RATIOS

An interfirm analysis of ratios resorts to averages of industry ratios as a standard of comparison in interpreting a firm's ratio levels. This approach assumes that all the companies in a particular industry produce the same product or service and thus have the same operating and financial characteristics. This is true in some cases, but in general it is not the rule.

MULTIPRODUCT SUBSIDIARIES Many companies, especially large ones, have products or services that cross industry lines. For example, Sears, Roebuck is classified as a "retailer–general merchandiser," yet Sears also has subsidiaries in insurance (Allstate), real estate (Coldwell Banker), and financial services (Dean Witter). Firms like this usually defy a clear-cut industry identification. So comparing this type of firm with a single industry's average ratios may be comparing apples with oranges. In these cases, a company's activities must be broken up by lines of business (i.e., by industry), and separate sets of ratios must be calculated for each operation.

INDUSTRY PERFORMANCE Just like individual companies, an industry may be growing or facing a decline in demand for its products. Using industry average ratios implicitly assumes the former (i.e., performance is satisfactory on average). If, on the other hand, an industry has failing health, then comparing a firm's ratios with an industry average just says that a firm is an average *sick* firm. A better alternative is to compare a firm's ratios with the ratios of the industry's leaders.

SAME PRODUCT The use of industry ratios assumes that firms make or sell the same product and therefore have the same business characteristics. This is not always valid. For example, The Limited is a retailer that specializes in the sale of medium-priced fashion apparel to younger women. Pic'n'Save, on the other hand, specializes in the sale of close-out or discontinued lines of merchandise at 40% to 70% off the original retail price. Although these two firms are grouped in the same industry, they have *very* different operating characteristics. The Limited tends to have a high profit margin but low turnover ratios; Pic'n'Save tends to have a lower profit margin but high turnover ratios. Therefore industry averages do not represent the target or norm that a firm must achieve in order to receive a satisfactory rating. Rather, industry averages provide only a general guideline as to what is good, satisfactory, or poor. Any ratio that departs from the "norm" should be interpreted to mean only that further investigation and analysis are necessary.

QUESTIONS

1. What are the different categories of financial ratios? What is the primary purpose of computing ratios in each of these categories?

2. What is the difference between interfirm and intrafirm ratio analysis?

3. What are the weaknesses inherent in ratio analysis?

PROBLEMS

1. The December 31, 1995, balance sheet and income statement for Mayberry Cafeterias, Inc. are given here.

Balance Sheet

Cash	$ 17		Accounts payable	$ 7
Marketable securities	5		Notes payable	3
Accounts receivable	3		Taxes payable	2
Inventory	16		Other accruals	3
Prepaid expenses	6		Current liabilities	$ 15
Current assets	$ 47		Long-term debt	$ 35
Gross plant and equipment	$126		Preferred stock	10
Less: Accumulated depreciation	(57)		Common stock	20
			Capital contributed in excess of par	10
Net plant and equipment	$ 69		Retained earnings	26
Total assets	$116		Total liabilities and stockholders' equity	$116

Income Statement

Net sales	$1,072
Cost of goods sold	921
Gross profit	$ 151
Selling expenses	86
General and administrative expenses	26
Depreciation	6
Net operating income	$ 33
Interest expense	4
Profit before taxes	$ 29
Taxes	12
Net income	$ 17

(a) Compute the specified ratios and compare them with the industry averages (better or worse).

(b) If you were appointed financial manager of the company, what decisions would you make based on your findings?

Ratios	1995 Mayberry	Better or Worse	1995 Industry Average
Current			2.86
Quick			2.31
Debt–equity			0.51
Times interest earned			12.36
Average collection period			1.06
Inventory turnover			95.71
Fixed-asset turnover			16.15
Operating profit margin			0.036
Net profit margin			0.019
Book return on assets			0.192
Book return on equity			0.271

2. On January 1, 1993, Tanya Dawkins was appointed financial planner and manager for a family-owned local chain of seafood restaurants. Using the company's balance sheets for the last three years, evaluate her performance in each of the following areas: improvement of the firm's short-term solvency, asset utilization, and profitability.

Balance Sheets	Dec. 31, 1993 (millions)		Dec. 31, 1994 (millions)		Dec. 31, 1995 (millions)
Cash		$ 27		$ 28	$ 32
Marketable securities		16		18	13
Accounts receivable		21		18	13
Inventory		13		17	18
Current assets		$ 77		$ 81	$ 76
Gross plant and equipment	$192		$198		$219
Less: Accumulated depreciation	(61)		(66)		(74)
Net plant and equipment		131		132	145
Total assets		$208		$213	$221
Accounts payable		$ 29		$ 26	$ 20
Wages payable		3		3	4
Notes payable		52		56	60
Total current liabilities		$ 84		$ 85	$ 84
Long-term debt		60		60	60
Common stock		20		20	20
Additional paid-in capital		20		20	20
Retained earnings		24		28	37
Total liabilities and stockholders' equity		$208		$213	$221

Income Statements	Dec. 31, 1993 (thousands)	Dec. 31, 1994 (thousands)	Dec. 31, 1995 (thousands)
Sales	$912	$921	$942
Cost of goods sold	827	833	851
Gross profit	$ 85	$ 88	$ 91
Selling expenses	37	41	46
General and administrative expenses	27	24	10
Depreciation	4	5	7
Net operating income	$ 17	$ 18	$ 28
Interest	12	11	10
Taxable income	$ 5	$ 7	$ 18
Taxes	2	3	7
Net income	$ 3	$ 4	$ 11

Ratios	1993	1994	1995	1995 Industry Average
Current				1.36
Quick				1.21
Debt–equity				1.03
Times interest earned				4.51
Average collection period				4.96
Inventory turnover				117.80
Fixed-asset turnover				7.61
Operating profit margin				0.036
Net profit margin				0.012
Book return on assets				0.098
Book return on equity				0.113

3. Fill in the blanks:

Cash	$ 100,000	Accounts payable	$150,000
Marketable securities	50,000	Notes payable	50,000
Accounts receivable	_____	Long-term debt	_____
Inventory	_____	Common stock	_____
Net plant and equipment	_____	Retained earnings	200,000
Total assets	$1,000,000	Total liabilities and stockholders' equity	$ _____
Sales	$1,200,000	*Ratios:*	
Cost of goods sold	_____	Current	2.0
Gross profit	_____	Quick	1.5
Fixed costs	_____	Times interest earned	6
Net operating income	_____	Debt–equity	1
Interest	_____	Gross profit margin	0.30
Taxes	40,000	Book return on equity	0.02
Net income	$ _____		

4. The balance sheet and income statement for Genco Olive Oil Co. as of December 31, 1995, are as follows (in millions):

Cash	$ 26	Accounts payable	$ 42
Marketable securities	3	Notes payable	31
Accounts receivable	13	Current liabilities	$ 73
Inventory	28	Long-term debt	43
Current assets	$ 70	Common stock	38
Net fixed assets	114	Retained earnings	30
Total assets	$184	Total liabilities and stockholders' equity	$184
Sales	$835		
Cost of goods sold	631		
Gross profit	$204		
Fixed costs	187		
Net operating income	$ 17		
Interest	11		
Earnings before taxes	$ 6		
Taxes	3		
Net income	$ 3		

Genco is considering the purchase of some oil processors on credit from your firm. Mr. Jenkins of the collections department reports that another firm, Barzini Oil, is considered a marginal client because of its high credit risk. He recommends that your firm not extend credit to any firm riskier than Barzini. Barzini's current ratio is 0.98, its quick ratio is 0.81, and its inventory turnover is 36.1. Compute these ratios for Genco and on that basis decide whether or not credit should be extended.

5. At the same time as in Problem 4, Genco applies to a bank for a three-year loan. The bank has also decided not to lend money to any firm riskier than

Barzini. However, the bank uses different ratios for making the decision—the debt–equity ratio and the times interest earned ratio. If these two ratios for Barzini are 1.32 and 2.56, respectively, will the bank lend money to Genco?

6. The common-size balance sheet and income statement (in percent) for Lyon Publications as of December 31, 1995, are given here. Lyon's level of cash on December 31, 1995, was $20,000, and interest paid during 1995 was $90,000.

Cash	5%		Accounts payable	8%
Marketable securities	3		Notes payable	5
Accounts receivable	9		Wages payable	2
Inventory	12		Current liabilities	15
Current assets	29		Long-term debt	30
Net fixed assets	71		Common stock	30
Total assets	100%		Retained earnings	25
Sales	100%		Total liabilities and stockholders' equity	100%
Cost of goods sold	65			
Gross profit	35			
General, selling, and administrative expenses	21			
Net operating income	14			
Interest	6			
Taxes	4			
Net income	4%			

(a) Determine Lyon's balance sheet and income statement (in dollars) as of December 31, 1995.

(b) Calculate the following ratios for Lyon as of December 31, 1995:

Current ratio	Fixed-asset turnover
Quick ratio	Operating profit margin
Debt–equity ratio	Net profit margin
Times interest earned	Book return on assets
Average collection period	Book return on equity
Inventory turnover	

7. John Easterwood recently inherited a large sum of money and is considering the purchase of one of two family-owned companies that are for sale in his hometown of Eastaboga, Alabama. The two firms are the Ancel Grocery Store and Starks Furniture Store. The balance sheets and income statements for these firms are given here (in thousands).

	Ancel Grocery	Starks Furniture
Income Statements		
Sales	$1,200	$200
Cost of goods sold	960	100
Gross profit	$ 240	$100
General, selling, and administrative expenses	210	32
Net operating income	$ 30	$ 68
Interest	6	20
Taxes	12	24
Net income	$ 12	$ 24

Balance Sheets

Cash	$ 30	$ 15
Marketable securities	10	5
Accounts receivable	30	40
Inventory	20	60
Current assets	$ 90	$120
Net fixed assets	110	120
Total assets	$200	$240
Accounts payable	$ 15	$ 20
Notes payable	15	40
Current liabilities	$ 30	$ 60
Long-term debt	25	30
Common stock	85	70
Retained earnings	60	80
Total liabilities and stockholders' equity	$200	$240

(a) Calculate the operating profit margin ratio, the net profit margin ratio, the book return on assets, and the book return on equity for each firm.

(b) What advice would you give Mr. Easterwood? What are the weaknesses of a recommendation to purchase either company using these data?

SUGGESTED ADDITIONAL READINGS

Anthony, R. N. *Planning and Control Systems: A Framework for Analysis.* Cambridge, MA: Harvard University, Division of Research, Graduate School of Business, 1965.

Carleton, W. T., C. L. Dick, Jr., and D. H. Downes. "Financial Policy Models: Theory and Practice." *Journal of Financial and Quantitative Analysis,* December 1973, pp. 691–709.

Drucker, P. "Long-Range Planning: Challenge to Management Science." *Management Science,* April 1959, pp. 238–249.

Foster, George. *Financial Statement Analysis.* Englewood Cliffs, NJ: Prentice-Hall, 1978.

Francis, Jack Clark, and Dexter R. Rowell. "A Simultaneous Equation Model of the Firm for Financial Analysis and Planning." *Financial Management,* Spring 1978, pp. 29–44.

Grinyer, P. H., and J. Wooller. *Corporate Models Today—A New Tool for Financial Management.* London: Institute of Chartered Accountants, 1978.

Helfert, Erich A. *Techniques of Financial Analysis.* Homewood, IL: Irwin, 1977.

Myers, S. C. "Finance Theory and Financial Strategy." *Interfaces,* January–February 1984, pp. 126–137.

Pan, Judy, Donald R. Nichols, and O. Maurice Joy. "Sales Forecasting Practices of Large U.S. Industrial Firms." *Financial Management,* Fall 1977, pp. 72–77.

TWENTY-ONE WORKING CAPITAL MANAGEMENT

Sufficient working capital must be provided in order to take care of the normal process of purchasing raw materials and supplies, turning out finished products, selling the products and waiting for payments to be made. If the original estimates of working capital are insufficient, some emergency measures must be resorted to or the business will come to a dead stop.

—W. H. Lough[1]

[1] In *Business Finance* (New York: Ronald Press, 1917), p. 355.

n Chapter 3 we examined the firm's balance sheet and saw that its assets and liabilities are conveniently grouped as being either short term or long term. The capital budgeting chapter (Chapter 8) was concerned with long-term asset investments, and the chapter on capital structure (Chapter 15) dealt with long-term liabilities. In this chapter we examine the importance of decisions that involve short-term assets and liabilities, commonly called **working capital management.**

To some the term *working capital* refers to only current assets. However, in more common usage, working capital refers to both current assets and current liabilities. The term **net working capital** refers to the difference between a firm's current assets and current liabilities.

In this chapter we examine why working capital is important to a firm. We identify some of the factors that affect the firm's working capital decisions by answering the following questions:

- Why is working capital important?

- How do working capital decisions affect stockholders' wealth?

- Why are current assets and current liabilities required?

- How do firms develop a working capital policy?

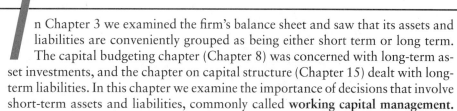

21-1
THE IMPORTANCE OF WORKING CAPITAL

umerous surveys have indicated that managers spend considerable time on day-to-day decisions that involve working capital. One reason is that current assets are short-lived investments that are continually being converted to other asset types. For example, cash is used to purchase inventory items; these inventory items eventually become accounts receivable when they are sold on credit; and finally, the receivables are transformed into cash when they are collected. The firm is responsible for paying current liabilities on a timely basis. Taken together, decisions regarding different working capital components are frequent, repetitive, and time consuming.

A firm's net working capital is also often used as a measure of its liquidity position. It represents the probability that a firm will be able to meet its financial obligations as they come due with minimum cost.[2] Therefore the more net working capital a firm has, the greater is its ability to satisfy its creditors' demands at low cost. Moreover, because net working capital serves as an illiquidity measure, the firm's net working capital position affects its ability to acquire debt financing. For example, commercial banks often impose minimum working capital constraints

---

[2] A firm with positive-NPV investments can, in principle, raise new capital to satisfy its obligations. However, there may be many practical problems associated with raising new capital for a firm in distress. In addition to explicit constraints on the firm's ability to raise new funds, there can be severe contracting problems among the firm's claimants. Thus the ability to meet its obligations quickly by maintaining working capital can increase value for the firm.

■

TABLE 21-1

Working Capital Components As a Percentage of Total Assets

	Fourth Quarter 1991	Fourth Quarter 1992
Assets		
Current assets		
Cash	2.6	2.5
Marketable securities	2.3	2.5
Accounts receivable	13.2	13.0
Inventories	13.7	13.2
Other current assets	3.3	3.7
Total	35.1	34.9
Fixed assets	64.9	65.1
Total assets	100.0	100.0
Claims on assets		
Current liabilities		
Accounts payable	7.6	7.7
Notes payable	3.9	4.2
Accrued taxes	0.8	0.9
Other current liabilities[a]	12.8	12.3
Total	25.1	25.1
Long-term liabilities	34.8	37.6
Stockholders' equity	40.1	37.3
Total claims on assets	100.0	100.0

[a]Includes current installments on long-term debt, excise and sales taxes, accrued expenses, and so forth.
SOURCE: *Quarterly Financial Report for Manufacturing and Mining Industries* (Washington, D.C.: Department of Commerce, July 1993).

on their loan agreements with firms. Similarly, bond indentures may contain such restrictions.

One measure of working capital's importance is the extent to which corporations use it. Table 21-1 contains composite common-size balance sheets for the manufacturing and mining industries. For these firms, current assets and liabilities represent sizable commitments. For example, about 35% of their total assets are devoted to current assets, and about 25% of their financing comes from current liabilities.

These aggregate figures disguise, however, the relative importance of working capital to firms with different product lines and different asset bases. Table 21-2, part a demonstrates the marked variations in the mix and level of working capital components even in the same industry. About the only generalization that can be made is that as the percentage of current assets rises, the percentage of current liabilities also rises. Table 21-2, part b shows that working capital requirements are especially important to smaller firms even in the same industry. Small firms tend to use a higher percentage of both current assets and current liabilities. This means that efficient working capital management is even more critical to them than to larger firms.

21-2

SHORT-TERM FINANCIAL DECISIONS AND VALUE MAXIMIZATION

Short-term decisions about current assets and current liabilities should be made in a manner similar to those about long-term investment and financing. A current asset is simply another type of investment that ties up cash. It should provide a return commensurate with its risk. Therefore the capital budgeting rules developed in Chapters 8 and 9 apply here; an asset's initial investment is balanced against its discounted benefits and costs. Similarly, current liabilities are just another source of financing that has costs and risks much like those of long-term sources of financing.

■

TABLE 21-2
Working Capital Components as a Percentage of Total Assets by Industry and by Firm Size

a. By industry

All Sizes	Manufacturers			Retail			Service		
	Soft Drinks	Steel Foundries	Toys	Restaurants	Groceries	Furniture	Motel–Hotel	Air Transport	Computer Programming
Current assets									
Cash and marketable securities	7.4	7.7	7.6	11.5	9.5	7.0	6.7	9.6	13.3
Accounts receivable	17.2	28.1	30.2	4.8	4.3	19.8	3.7	21.0	39.7
Inventory	11.7	18.7	34.5	7.3	32.5	50.3	1.8	8.4	8.7
All other current	2.3	2.2	1.8	2.8	1.9	1.3	1.9	1.2	3.9
Total	38.6	56.7	74.1	26.4	48.2	78.4	14.1	40.2	65.6
Current liabilities									
Accounts payable	11.2	13.9	14.6	11.3	18.8	17.7	4.4	10.7	12.9
Notes payable	4.0	9.4	17.9	6.0	4.5	12.2	4.3	7.8	11.7
Current Maturities LTD	5.1	4.2	3.4	6.0	4.8	3.2	5.0	6.8	4.2
All other current	7.4	7.7	7.2	12.6	8.2	13.7	6.6	10.6	14.4
Total	27.7	35.2	43.1	35.9	36.3	46.8	20.3	36.0	43.2

b. By asset size

	Manufacturers: Soft Drinks		Retail: Restaurants		Service: Motel–Hotel	
	<$1 million	All	<$1 million	All	<$1 million	All
Current assets						
Cash and marketable securities	5.2	7.4	12.6	11.5	10.4	6.7
Accounts receivable	20.3	17.2	4.6	4.8	4.2	3.7
Inventory	10.7	11.7	8.3	7.3	2.3	1.8
All other current	2.6	2.3	3.2	2.8	2.5	1.9
Total	38.8	38.6	28.7	26.4	19.4	14.1
Current liabilities						
Accounts payable	13.3	11.2	11.7	11.3	6.6	4.4
Notes payable	5.1	4.0	7.2	6.0	4.9	4.3
Current Maturities LTD	7.9	5.1	6.3	6.0	5.7	5.0
All other current	12.9	7.4	13.9	12.6	9.7	6.6
Total	39.2	27.7	39.1	35.9	26.9	20.3

SOURCE: Robert Morris Associates. Derived from *Annual Statement Studies,* copyright 1988. RMA cautions that the studies be regarded only as a general guideline and not as an absolute industry norm, owing to limited samples within categories, the categorization of companies by their primary Standard Industrial Classification (SIC) number only, and different methods of operations by companies within the same industry. For these reasons, RMA recommends that the figures be used only as general guidelines in addition to other methods of financial analysis.

Why Current Assets and Liabilities Are Often Separated from the Firm's Long-Term Decisions

Historically, financial theory has separated decisions concerning current assets and current liabilities from decisions concerning the long term. The basic justification for this separation is that current assets are fundamentally different types of investments. For example, current assets are a continuously fluctuating level of liquid assets that is rapidly transformed from one form into another. Long-term investments, on the other hand, occur irregularly over time, involve readily identifiable or specific assets (e.g., a fully automatic lathe), and are highly illiquid. In simple terms, current assets represent reversible investments, whereas fixed assets are irreversible investments.

Although this argument has some truth, separate treatment has the unfortunate consequence of not necessarily being consistent with a firm's objective of value maximization. More important, the link between working capital decisions and value maximization becomes obscured when such decisions are viewed in isolation. What is required is a conceptual framework or understanding of how working capital decisions affect firm value. Such decisions, unfortunately, are more difficult to link clearly to maximizing shareholder wealth.

*Working Capital
Management and
Shareholder Wealth
Maximization*

Financial theory generally operates under the simplifying assumption of perfect capital markets in order to gain insights into financial decisions and valuation. As seen in Chapters 15 and 17, this assumption produces the somewhat dissatisfying conclusion that decisions regarding a firm's capital structure or dividend policy do not affect its value. This "indifference" or "irrelevance" result carries over to working capital decisions.[3]

To illustrate, consider the role of liquidity in a firm's operations. Under the assumption of perfect capital markets, a firm's degree of liquidity should not affect the shareholders' wealth. The familiar reason is that shareholders manage their portfolios of financial assets so as to satisfy their preference for liquidity. This means that the firm should not try to do something for its shareholders that they can do more easily for themselves. On reflection, though, it would seem that a firm must maintain sufficient liquidity to make timely cash payments on its operating and financial obligations. Failure to do so could result in insolvency or forced bankruptcy by the firm's creditors, and this would adversely affect shareholder wealth. After all, bankruptcy is not without cost. Liquidation costs and other administrative fees can negatively affect a firm's value because such costs represent a cash outflow that is not necessarily offset by an associated cash inflow (as with the typical investment).

Are we facing, then, a contradiction between theory and practice? First, we need to recall that bankruptcy is a market imperfection *if* it is costly. Therefore increased liquidity should reduce the chances of insolvency or bankruptcy and its costs. In financial theory, bankruptcy is usually treated as a costless event, or at least any costs are assumed to be insignificant.[4] Therein lies the major problem in linking a firm's liquidity decisions to firm valuation: Is bankruptcy costless or costly? The answer is yet to be resolved satisfactorily.

The reader may be feeling justifiably uneasy about how working capital decisions should be made. It is generally agreed that such decisions (especially with regard to current assets) occupy the bulk of a financial manager's day-to-day activities; therefore their importance cannot be questioned. How, then, should one proceed? The fact that the basic principles of long-term asset investment decisions should apply equally well to short-term asset decisions should not be ignored. This means that an asset investment should be made whenever its benefits exceed its costs. Although quantifying this trade-off is more difficult for short-term assets, the decision criterion is still to invest in an asset if its net present value is positive.

It is useful to examine this criterion more closely, but in terms of current-asset decisions. Recall the general equation for determining present values:

$$NPV = \sum_{t=1}^{n} \frac{\Delta CFAT_t}{(1 + RRR)^t} - \Delta CFAT_0 \tag{21-1}$$

where

$\Delta CFAT_t$ is the investment's incremental cash flow after taxes at the end of period t

RRR is the after-tax required rate of return or opportunity cost

---

[3] This is analogous to the argument that a firm should not consider diversification as one of its goals because shareholders can more efficiently diversify their own portfolios.

[4] Under perfect capital markets, if a firm is unable to pay its obligations, a firm's value is assumed to be unimpaired because creditors can receive what they are due by instantaneously liquidating assets or reorganizing the firm without cost. With no time delays or costs, the firm's value should not be affected. But if bankruptcy entails costs, liquidating may affect value.

$\Delta CFAT_0$ is the initial investment (cash outflow) at time $t = 0$

n is the useful life of the investment

The first problem in applying this equation arises in establishing the "useful life" of a current asset. If the investment is being considered as part of a capital budgeting project, its useful life is the same as the useful life of the project. But what if a current-asset decision is being made separately, without relating it to a fixed-asset investment in terms of time? A practical solution is to treat the current asset as an ongoing or permanent investment with benefits that will continue for the foreseeable future. This assumption implies that n will approach infinity and $\Delta CFAT_t$ will become an *annuity in perpetuity*. Realizing this, we can simplify equation (21-1) to

$$NPV = \frac{\Delta CFAT_t}{RRR} - \Delta CFAT_0 \qquad (21\text{-}2)$$

The remaining, and stickier, problem is determining the risk and thus the appropriate discount rate to apply to the incremental cash flows, $\Delta CFAT$. This is not easy because such flows do not "trade" and are not valued separately like a security in the market.

For now, remember that equation (21-2) is the approach that we use to analyze current asset investment decisions. The emphasis is on the practical considerations in formulating the risks and returns associated with working capital decisions. Furthermore, the discussion focuses on the appropriate levels of each current asset rather than on specific assets. Fortunately, decisions about the mix between current and long-term financing are far less troublesome because the distinction between the two is largely one of maturity and management's attitude toward the risks associated with each source.

21-3
WHY CURRENT ASSETS AND CURRENT LIABILITIES ARE REQUIRED

Table 21-2 shows that business firms invest in varying degrees in current assets. The level and nature of these investments depend on the firm's product types, its operating cycle, the levels of sales and operating expenses, and management policy. As sales increase over time, more cash, receivables, and inventories usually are needed. Even within a firm's normal operating cycle, seasonal sales patterns cause the level of current assets to be relatively high or low at any particular point. Moreover, the firm's credit and inventory policies and how efficiently it manages its current assets can drastically affect a firm's working capital needs. For example, a conservative toy manufacturer may maintain a high level of inventory to satisfy unexpected demands or to hedge against delays in acquiring new inventory. A more aggressive or more efficient toy maker, on the other hand, may function with a much lower investment in inventories.

But why are current-asset investments required? The answer is that they provide the liquidity necessary to realize the expected returns from a firm's long-term investments. In fact, careful management of such assets can increase returns by stimulating sales. For example, relaxing the credit terms of the accounts receivable policy may lead to higher revenues than originally expected. The cash flows associated with long-term investments are uncertain and irregular, and it is the nonsynchronous nature of the cash flows that makes working capital necessary. Otherwise, a mismatch between cash inflows and outflows could cause a liquidity crisis. This, in turn, could disrupt or reduce the longer-term returns expected from a firm's fixed-asset investments.

If cash flows are certain, less working capital is required. Or to carry it to an extreme, if a firm could process an incoming order instantaneously by purchasing raw materials, converting them to a final product, and immediately selling them for cash, then investments in inventory and accounts receivable would not be needed. Current assets therefore act as a buffer to correct the mismatch between the cash outflows for goods and services and the cash receipts generated by sales revenues.

Cash outflows are fairly predictable. For example, goods purchased on credit require payment by a known date. The same holds for accruals (e.g., wages and taxes) and short-term loans. The problem stems from the difficulty in forecasting cash inflows because sales demand is uncertain. The result is that more current assets, representing future cash receipts, must be held to meet the more predictable (scheduled) payments for maturing liabilities.

The Operating Cash Conversion Cycle

A helpful way to illustrate a firm's operating cash flow problem is to use the concept of the operating cash conversion cycle. The **operating cash conversion cycle** measures the time it takes for the initial cash outflows for goods and services to be realized as cash inflows from sales.

The conversion cycle captures the fact that different working capital components have different life expectancies and are transformed into liquidity flows at different rates. In Figure 21-1, we assume that an investment in new equipment is used to expand production and sales. Before any benefits (cash inflows) from this capital expenditure are received, cash outflows for labor and materials must be incurred to produce a finished product. This product may then sit in inventory for weeks or months before it is sold. Moreover, if it is sold on credit, the original cash expenditures will still be tied up (invested) in accounts receivable.[5] Only when the credit customer pays the bill does the firm finally receive a cash inflow from its fixed investment. This is the imbalance in cash outflows and inflows that necessitates current-asset investments.

Assume that a firm has annual credit sales of $1,825,000. If sales are not seasonal, a sales rate of $5,000 per day is implied (with a 365-day year). Furthermore, assume that the firm's working capital position, less cash balances, is as follows:[6]

Accounts receivable	$160,000	Accounts payable	
Inventory	220,000	and accruals	$180,000
	$380,000		$180,000

To see how quickly the operating cash flows through this firm, we need to determine how fast each account turns over. In Figure 21-1, the accounts receivable conversion period is 32 sales days ($160,000/$5,000), and the inventory conversion period is 44 sales days ($220,000/$5,000).[7] These conversion periods are expressed in sales days to give an idea of how long it takes a current asset to move from one form into another. In this example, it takes 32 + 44 = 76 days in sales for cash to flow through the current-asset conversion cycle; that is, it takes 76 days from the commitment of cash for materials to the receipt of cash collected from sales.

[5] We assume here that factoring of accounts receivables is not an option.

[6] Inventory and accounts payable numbers have been adjusted upward to recognize that we are working with "sales dollars" rather than "cost dollars." This "grossing up" is done easily: inventory in sales dollars = (inventory in cost dollars)/(contribution margin). Contribution margin was defined in Chapter 19.

[7] The accounts receivable conversion period is the average collection period, and the inventory conversion period is the inventory turnover ratio divided into 365 days.

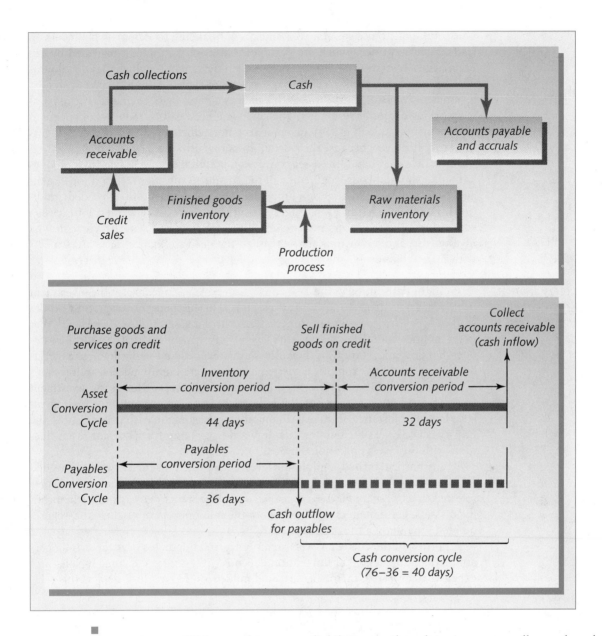

FIGURE 21-1

Operating cash conversion cycle

With regard to current liabilities, goods and services are usually purchased on credit, and it must be determined how long the firm defers these payments. The payables conversion periods for accounts payable and accruals average 36 sales days ($180,000/$5,000). The combined result is a net cash conversion cycle of 40 days:

Accounts receivable	32 days
Inventory	44 days
Asset conversion period	76 days
Payables conversion period	−36 days
Net cash conversion period	40 days

Implications of the Net Cash Conversion Cycle

This residual time indicates that a shortfall in cash flow equal to 40 sales days must be financed in some way or else there will be a liquidity crisis after 36 days.

One solution is to use spontaneous sources of financing by deferring payments on trade credit payables, which are payables that arise from credit provided by another firm. Most firms, however, are limited in the extent to which they can do this without impairing their credit rating. The more typical solution is to arrange a negotiated source of short-term credit, such as a bank loan, to finance the remaining working capital investments. This financing need can be reduced, of course, if management is able to use its current assets more efficiently (e.g., by increasing its inventory turnover) because the asset conversion period will be shorter.

If, on the other hand, the asset conversion period becomes longer than 76 days without a simultaneous lengthening of the payables conversion period (or if management decides that a larger minimum cash balance of $40,000 is needed), additional financing over an even longer period is required. Therefore a longer cash conversion cycle reflects a greater commitment to cash and noncash current-asset investments, and a concomitant increase in the need to finance these investments with current liabilities.

Temporary Current Assets and Permanent Current Assets

From the description of the cash conversion cycle, it appears as if the investment in current assets drops to $0 as the cycle ends. This happens, however, only if sales stop and the firm goes out of business. Each current asset is like a "reservoir" that never empties completely because its level of investment fluctuates with the rates of cash inflow and outflow. If the inflows are greater than the outflows, the investment level rises. For example, if there is an unexpected jump in sales, inflows into accounts receivable are temporarily greater than outflows, and hence the investment level is higher. On the other hand, if inflows are less than outflows, the investment level falls. For instance, if there is an unanticipated surge in cash expenditures, the firm's cash balances are temporarily drawn down. **Temporary current assets** fluctuate with the firm's operational needs.

At any particular time, a minimum level of investment in current assets is needed if the firm is to continue its operations. This continuous level of current assets is referred to as *permanent current assets,* and they are as permanent as the firm's fixed assets. **Permanent current assets** are the minimum level of current assets required to maintain a firm's daily operations.

A portion of the current assets is temporary and fluctuates over the firm's operating cycle. The degree of fluctuation depends on the rate of change in sales and expenses due to such factors as seasonal influences. Figure 21-2 depicts this rela-

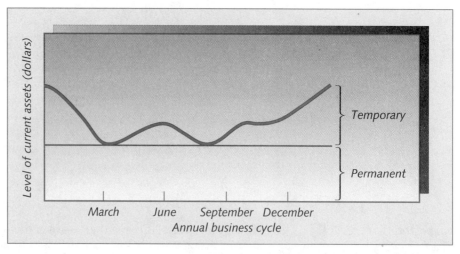

FIGURE 21-2

Temporary and permanent current assets over a retail firm's annual business cycle

tionship for a retail merchandise firm. Notice that around the Easter, beginning of school, and Christmas selling seasons, current assets temporarily rise to accommodate the seasonal increases in inventories and accounts receivable. After the selling seasons, inventory levels are low and accounts receivables decline as sales decline during the interim periods. This distinction between temporary and permanent current assets has important implications as a firm decides on its working capital policy for managing its current assets and liabilities.

21-4

DECIDING ON AN APPROPRIATE WORKING CAPITAL POLICY

*T*he greater the uncertainty associated with a firm's cash inflows, the greater margin of safety is required. A firm can ensure this margin of safety by increasing its proportion of liquid assets and/or lengthening the maturity pattern of its financing sources. Both strategies affect the firm's risk and returns. More current assets lead to greater liquidity but represent lower-yielding investments. Long-term debt usually has a higher explicit cost but a lower risk than does short-term debt. Note that *risk* here refers to the risk of illiquidity or default rather than to the systematic risk discussed in earlier chapters.

The primary consideration in developing an overall working capital policy is the risk–return trade-off associated with (1) the appropriate mix between current and fixed assets and (2) the appropriate mix between short- and long-term financing required to fund the current-asset investments.

Risk–Return Trade-off in the Asset Mix Decision

Fixed-asset investments are undertaken to generate future returns that will enhance firm value. As stated before, such undertakings often require investments in current assets to control for adverse short-term developments that arise from an imbalance in cash flows. Otherwise, the favorable long-run benefits from fixed assets may never be realized. But what is the appropriate mix between short- and long-term investments? Generally, the greater the firm's commitment is to current assets, the greater is its liquidity. But the return on current assets is usually less than the return on fixed (earning) assets. Thus, although the firm can reduce its risk of illiquidity with a relatively higher current-asset investment, it does so only by reducing its return on invested capital.

Assume that a firm is considering two different working capital plans, as depicted in Table 21-3. The two policies differ only with regard to their level of current assets.[8] Furthermore, to focus only on the asset mix decision, we assume that a higher investment in current assets is financed by equity. (This allows reported income to be unaffected by how the investment is financed.) In the bottom half of Table 21-3, notice that as the percentage of total assets invested in current assets decreases from 33.3% to 20%, the other measures of liquidity indicate that the firm becomes less liquid. The net working capital position falls from $30,000 to $10,000, and the current ratio drops from 4:1 to 2:1. In other words, a conservative policy provides less risk of illiquidity because net working capital and the current ratio are relatively higher.

In contrast, the profitability measure indicates that the risk of illiquidity is lowered only by penalizing return performance. A conservative policy provides a 37.5% return on equity, whereas a more aggressive stance gives a 50% return on equity.

---

[8] To simplify matters, assume that the additional investment in current assets (under the conservative asset policy) is placed in cash. This neutralizes any increased returns that might be forthcoming from higher sales stimulated by higher inventory or accounts receivable. Thus the asset structures for the two firms in Table 21-3 are equivalent except for the amount invested in current assets.

■
TABLE 21-3
Risk–Return Trade-off for Different Mixes of Current and Fixed Assets

	Conservative Asset Policy (lower risk, lower return)	Aggressive Asset Policy (higher risk, higher return)
	Balance Sheet Effects	
Current assets	$ 40,000	$ 20,000
Fixed assets	80,000	80,000
Total assets	$120,000	$100,000
Current liabilities	$ 10,000	$ 10,000
Long-term debt	30,000	30,000
Equity	80,000[a]	60,000[b]
Total claims	$120,000	$100,000
	Income Statement Effects	
Net income	$30,000	$30,000
Measures of liquidity	*Decreasing Liquidity*	
1. Percent current assets[c]	33.3	20.0
2. Net working capital[d]	$30,000	$10,000
3. Current ratio[e]	4:1	2:1
Measures of profitability	*Increasing Profitability*	
1. Earnings per share[f]	$7.50	$10.00
2. Rate of return on equity[g] (book value)	37.5%	50.0%

[a] 4,000 shares at $20.
[b] 3,000 shares at $20.
[c] Current assets ÷ total assets.
[d] Current assets − current liabilities.
[e] Current assets ÷ current liabilities.
[f] Net income after taxes ÷ shares outstanding.
[g] Net income after taxes ÷ book value of equity.

Therefore a relatively higher level of current assets produces a favorable effect on liquidity, but at the expense of reducing the rate of return on equity.[9] This exemplifies once again the familiar trade-off between risk and return; risk-reduction techniques invariably result in lower potential returns.

Risk–Return Trade-off in the Financing Mix Decision

A second determinant of a firm's overall working capital policy is the mix of short- and long-term financing used to fund current assets. Generally, the cost of short-term credit is lower than the cost of long-term debt. One reason is that trade credit normally has no explicit cost. Another reason is that the interest rate on short-term debt such as bank loans is typically lower than the interest rate on long-term debt.

Nevertheless, greater reliance on short-term debt relative to long-term debt has a greater risk of illiquidity for two reasons. First, a firm may not be able to refinance its short-term debt when it matures. When the debt needs to be repaid, the firm could be having financial problems, such as an extended labor strike or an economic recession that causes sales, and hence cash inflows, to decrease. Such difficulties may prevent the firm from having on hand the required funds. In fact, reduced cash inflows may have forced the firm to borrow more from banks to maintain its liquidity. Thus the more frequently a firm refinances its debt, the greater is its risk of illiquidity. Second, short-term rates vary more than long-term rates do. This means that cash outflows for interest expenses are less certain because they vary from period to period. In contrast, payments on long-term debt are certain over the entire period during which the debt is outstanding and thus can be more carefully planned for in advance. The firm has greater flexibility in repaying and refunding long-term liabilities than it does short-term debt.

[9] Because there is no theoretical consensus on the potential benefits of liquidity in enhancing firm value, we focus on the effect of liquidity on accounting rather than market-based returns.

	Conservative Financing Policy (lower risk, lower return)	Aggressive Financing Policy (higher risk, higher return)
T A B L E 2 1 - 4 *Risk–Return Trade-off for Different Mixes of Short- and Long-Term Financing*	*Balance Sheet Effects*	
Current assets	$ 40,000	$ 40,000
Fixed assets	80,000	80,000
Total assets	$120,000	$120,000
Accounts payable	$ 10,000	$ 10,000
Notes payable—bank (10%)	0	30,000
Current liabilities	$ 10,000	$ 40,000
Long-term debt (16%)	30,000	0
Equity (4,000 shares)	80,000	80,000
Total claims	$120,000	$120,000
	Income Statement Effects	
Net operating income (*NOI*)	$ 64,800	$ 64,800
Less: Interest expenses[a]	4,800	3,000
Taxable income	$ 60,000	$ 61,800
Less: Taxes (50%)	30,000	30,900
Net income	$ 30,000	$ 30,900
Measures of liquidity	*Decreasing Liquidity*	
1. Percent current assets[b]	33.3	33.3
2. Net working capital[c]	$30,000	0
3. Current ratio[d]	4:1	1:1
Measures of profitability	*Increasing Profitability*	
1. Earnings per share[e]	$7.50	$7.73
2. Rate of return on equity[f]	37.5%	38.6%

[a] Interest expense on the long-term debt is 0.16 × $30,000 = $4,800, and interest expense on the short-term bank loan is 0.10 × $30,000 = $3,000.
[b] Current assets ÷ total assets.
[c] Current assets − current liabilities.
[d] Current assets ÷ current liabilities.
[e] Net income after taxes ÷ shares outstanding.
[f] Net income after taxes ÷ book value of equity.

To show the effect of the firm's financing mix on its risk and return, we consider the conservative asset policy in Table 21-3 but now hold constant the investment decision (i.e., the percentage of current assets to total assets is fixed). As Table 21-4 shows, the conservative financing policy uses 16% long-term debt to support the current-asset investment, and the aggressive policy calls for a 10% bank loan. The bottom half of this table indicates that the more conservative policy has a lower degree of illiquidity, as evidenced by a higher net working capital position ($30,000) and current ratio (4:1). However, because this policy uses more costly long-term debt, net income is less, and hence the return on equity is lower than under the aggressive policy. Thus the risk of illiquidity can be reduced by resorting to the use of long-term debt, but only by also reducing the firm's profitability.

Risk-Return Trade-offs in the Decision on the Current Asset–Current Liability Mix

The preceding discussion treated current-asset and financing decisions separately in a static framework. These decisions, however, are related and often simultaneous. As Figure 21-2 shows, a firm's level of current assets fluctuates over its operating cycle because of the seasonal demand for its products. This implies that its short-term financing also needs to vary. Given these additional considerations, how does one determine the best overall working capital policy? Alternatively stated, what is the appropriate level of net working capital? The answer to this question requires us to consider simultaneously the current-asset and current-liability decisions.

Once the firm's management has decided on its mix of current and long-term assets, it must decide how to finance its current assets. There are several financing plans that management could adopt. We cover four of the most common types: a matching policy, a conservative policy, an aggressive policy, and a balanced policy.

A MATCHING POLICY [10]

A **matching policy** follows the guideline of matching the maturity of a financing source with an asset's useful life. Current assets, being more liquid than fixed assets, generate cash inflows that are more closely aligned with the current liabilities' payment or conversion cycle. Similarly, fixed assets' cash inflows are long term and therefore should be matched against the cash outflows of longer-term obligations. In other words, short-term assets should be financed with short-term liabilities, and long-term assets should be funded by long-term financing sources. Most financial managers would consider this policy imprudent because a larger amount of current assets relative to current liabilities is needed to serve as a buffer against the less predictable cash inflows from sales. Another reason, discussed earlier, is that a portion of current assets is permanent and therefore should be financed for the long term.

Figure 21-3 depicts the logic of the matching policy. Temporary current assets should be funded by spontaneous sources of financing (such as payables and accruals) and short-term borrowings if need be; permanent current assets and fixed assets should be financed by long-term debt and equity. We now return to the merchandise retailer example and observe what happens as the holiday season approaches. Inventory increases dramatically, which is financed in part by trade credit and in part by a short-term bank loan. As inventory is liquidated during the selling season, accounts receivable expand because of increased credit sales. Then, after December, collections on receivables are used to repay the bank loan. This suggests that a firm has no short-term borrowings at seasonal troughs because they are paid off with surplus cash.

The matching policy assumes, somewhat unrealistically, that the cash flow pattern is known with certainty. It also assumes that management can readily determine at any time which portion of current assets is a temporary investment and

[10] This is often called a *self-liquidating policy.*

FIGURE 21-3

Matching working capital policy

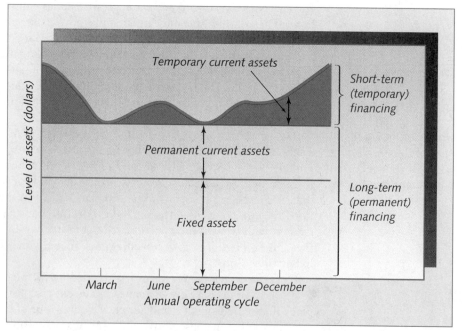

FIGURE 21-4
Conservative working capital policy

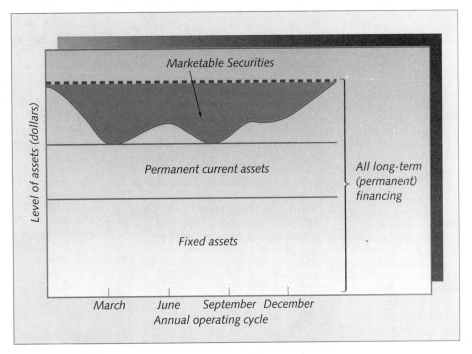

which is permanent. In practice, however, the temporary expansion and contraction of these assets may vary, so that a smaller or larger permanent current-asset requirement results. Added to this are the uncertain borrowing costs and the possibility that adequate credit may not be available when needed.

A CONSERVATIVE POLICY

A **conservative policy** ignores the distinction between temporary and permanent current assets by financing almost all asset investments with long-term capital (Figure 21-4). Under this policy, temporary swellings in current assets that cannot be covered by spontaneous financing sources are supported by long-term financing. When the level of current assets contracts, any surplus funds are invested in short-term marketable securities.

The conservative policy described in Table 21-4 greatly reduces the risk of illiquidity and eliminates the firm's exposure to fluctuating loan rates and the potential unavailability of short-term credit. On the other hand, a conservative policy is less profitable because it has a higher financing cost. First, long-term funds have a higher explicit (or implicit) cost, whether they consist of long-term debt or equity. Second, this cost differential is not normally offset by the returns earned on marketable securities because short-term financial assets earn less than it costs to finance them with long-term securities.

AN AGGRESSIVE POLICY

An **aggressive policy** takes the other extreme position of using short-term liabilities to finance not only temporary but also part or all of the permanent current-asset requirement (Figure 21-5). Table 21-4 shows that this aggressive policy is an attempt to increase the return on equity by taking advantage of the cost differential between short-term and long-term debt. Of course, such a strategy increases the risk of illiquidity because the firm must continuously refinance its short-term loans

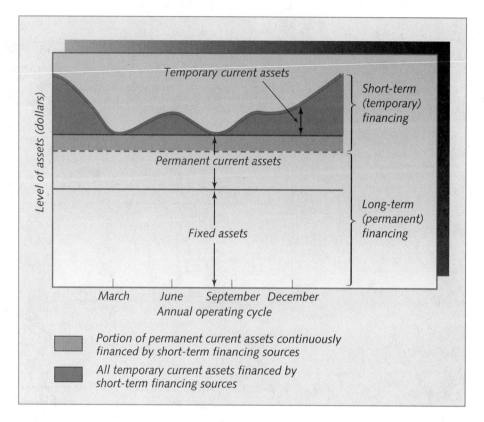

at an unpredictable interest rate. An imbalance in cash flows generated from operations, whether due to an internal reason (overinvestment in accounts receivable) or an external factor (economic slowdown), could produce a liquidity crisis. Moreover, a temporary period during which short-term interest rates are higher than long-term rates, as in the early 1980s, would eliminate the attractiveness of this policy's higher profitability and further enhance its risk of illiquidity.

A BALANCED POLICY

Because of the impracticalities of implementing the matching policy and the extreme nature of the other two policies, most financial managers opt for a compromise position, or a **balanced policy.** As its name implies, this policy balances the trade-off between risk and profitability in a manner consistent with its attitude toward bearing risk.

As illustrated in Figure 21-6, long-term financing is used to support fixed assets, permanent current assets, and part of the temporary current assets. Short-term credit is used to cover the remaining working capital needs during seasonal peaks. This implies that as any seasonal borrowings are repaid, surplus funds are invested in marketable securities. The portion above the dashed line represents short-term financing, and the troughs below it represent short-term holdings of securities.

This policy has the desirable attribute of providing a margin of safety not found in the other policies. If temporary needs for current assets exceed management's expectations, the firm still has unused short-term lines of credit to fund them. Similarly, if the contraction of current assets is less than expected, short-term loan

FIGURE 21-6
Balanced working capital policy

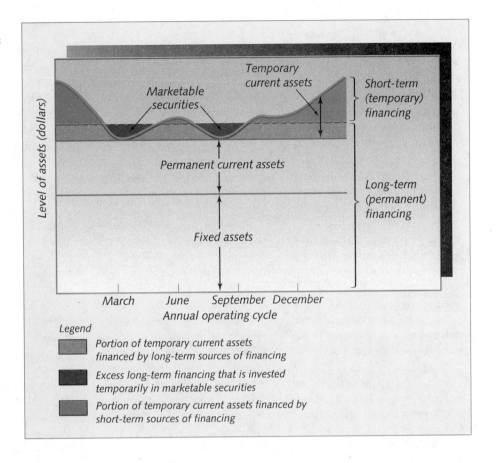

payments can still be met, but less surplus cash is available for investment in marketable securities. In contrast with the other working capital policies, a balanced policy demands more management time and effort. When using this policy, the financial manager not only must arrange and maintain short-term sources of financing but also must be prepared to oversee the investment of excess funds.

The Appropriate Working Capital Policy   Our analysis so far has offered insights into the risk profitability trade-off inherent in a variety of different policies. Just as there is no optimal capital structure that all firms should adopt, there is no one optimal working capital policy for all firms. Which policy a firm chooses should depend on the uncertainty regarding the magnitude and timing of cash flows associated with sales; the greater this uncertainty is, the higher is the level of working capital necessary. In addition, the cash conversion cycle influences a firm's working policy; the longer the time required to convert current assets to cash, the greater is the risk of illiquidity. Finally, in practice, the more risk averse the management is, the greater is its net working capital position. The management of working capital is an ongoing responsibility that requires many interrelated and simultaneous decisions about the level and financing of current assets.

Working capital management decisions for multinational firms are, in theory, the same as those for domestic firms. However, certain aspects of working capital management are unique to multinationals, as seen in the reinvoicing highlight.

*M*ultinational companies typically have several subsidiaries in different countries. These subsidiaries often buy and sell goods and services among themselves. A **reinvoicing center** is a subsidiary of a multinational corporation set up for the sole purpose of consolidating the intersubsidiary payments. Although the physical shipment of the good is directly between the multinational's various subsidiaries, the legal title to the good first passes to the reinvoicing center, which then transfers ownership to the recipient subsidiary. This means that the subsidiaries do not deal directly with one another, but rather buy from and sell to the reinvoicing center.

We can see how reinvoicing centers benefit multinational firms by examining North American Power, Inc. (NAP), an American multinational based in Tucson, Arizona. NAP has two subsidiaries. NAP-Mexico manufactures motors for sale in the United States by NAP. NAP-Brazil manufactures the housings for these motors and sells them to NAP-Mexico.

NAP has a reinvoicing center in Jamaica to facilitate the management of its intrafirm payments. Therefore, although NAP-Brazil ships its components directly to NAP-Mexico, the components are legally sold to the reinvoicing center. A similar transaction takes place when the motors are sold to NAP. These transactions are summarized in the diagram below:

The reinvoicing center benefits NAP in several ways. First, the flow of funds within the multinational is centralized in the reinvoicing center, which improves the management of cash, receivables, and inventory. Second, the reinvoicing center facilitates the management of exchange rate risk (discussed in Chapter 1). The reinvoicing center establishes intracompany exchange rates, which determine the amount of cruzeiros, pesos, and dollars that each element of NAP gets. It is often the practice, as in our example, that each subsidiary deals in its own currency when trading with the reinvoicing center. The risks that result from unanticipated changes in the exchange rate are thus shifted from the different parts of NAP to its reinvoicing center, which can more efficiently manage exchange rate risk. Finally, the reinvoicing center, by determining the relevant transfer prices among the subsidiaries, can minimize NAP's tax liabilities worldwide. (Transfer prices were discussed in the highlight in Chapter 8.)

Reinvoicing centers are not without costs. First, the reinvoicing center is a separate subsidiary of the company, and establishing one can be expensive. Second, substantial communication and co-ordination costs are involved with operating a reinvoicing center. Therefore a reinvoicing center makes sense only when the company has a sufficient volume of transactions among its subsidiaries to justify these costs. Finally, reinvoicing centers are usually looked upon by governments as a device for avoiding taxes. Their operations are thus closely monitored by government tax authorities, and the tax benefits from transfer prices are limited by government regulations.

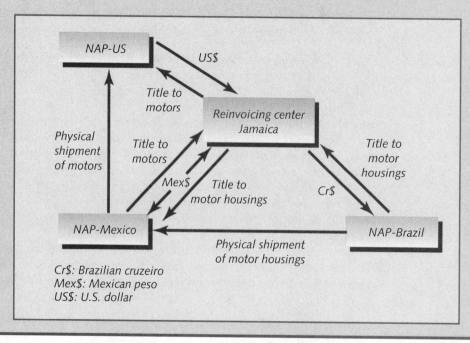

Cr$: Brazilian cruzeiro
Mex$: Mexican peso
US$: U.S. dollar

SUMMARY

Section 21-1: The Importance of Working Capital

Why is working capital important?

- Working capital refers to current assets and current liabilities. Net working capital is the difference between current assets and current liabilities.

- Working capital is important because it plays a major role in the firm's operations, and current assets make up a substantial proportion of the firm's total assets.

- Net working capital is used by both managers and those outside the firm as a major measure of the firm's liquidity.

- Because of the high turnover of current assets, managers spend a substantial amount of time making working capital decisions.

Section 21-2: Short-Term Financial Decisions and Value Maximization

How do working capital decisions affect stockholders' wealth?

- Investments in current assets theoretically must be made in a manner similar to the *NPV* approach to deciding on long-term assets. Practically, short-term and long-term asset decisions are separated because it is difficult to identify the cash flows and risks associated with a specific investment in a current asset.

- The goal of managers is still to increase stockholder wealth; however, working capital decisions are made by ensuring that the level of various working capital accounts are adequately maintained. "Adequate" in this sense means that the accounts are sufficient to allow the firm to obtain the expected cash flows from its long-term investments in assets.

- To simplify this analysis, an investment in current assets is often treated as an ongoing or permanent investment.

Section 21-3: Why Current Assets and Current Liabilities Are Required

Why are current assets and current liabilities required?

- The firm usually experiences a mismatch in the cash inflows and cash outflows from its investments. Working capital acts as a buffer to absorb this mismatch.

- The operating cash conversion cycle is a useful tool for measuring the time it takes for the initial cash outflows for goods and services to be realized as cash inflows from sales. The net cash conversion period identified using this approach indicates the shortfall in cash flow, which must be financed in some way.

- Current assets can be placed into two classes. Permanent current assets are the minimal level of current assets required to maintain the firm's daily operations. Temporary current assets rise and fall with the level of the firm's economic activity.

Section 21-4: Deciding on an Appropriate Working Capital Policy

How do firms develop a working capital policy?

- The amount of net working capital that a firm should have depends on the amount of risk it is willing to take. The greater the risk, the greater is the potential for larger returns.

- The risk–return trade-off is determined by the firm's asset mix decision—the firm's mix of short- and long-term assets—and the financing mix decision—the mix of short- and long-term liabilities to finance the firm's short-term assets.

■ One of four different policies can be followed: a matching policy, a conservative policy, an aggressive policy, and a balanced policy.

■ Working capital decisions must be made after the advantages and disadvantages of each policy individually are carefully evaluated in light of other qualitative considerations.

QUESTIONS

1. Why is working capital important to the firm?

2. Why do managers often separate short-term and long-term decisions? Is this separation desirable?

3. Integrating working capital management into a value-maximizing framework is not easy. Why not?

4. What simplification(s) is (are) required to evaluate working capital decisions in a value-maximizing framework?

5. What factors make it necessary to maintain current assets?

6. What is the operating cash conversion cycle? What does it measure? How can it be used?

7. Distinguish between temporary current assets and permanent current assets.

8. A firm can reduce its risk of illiquidity with more current-asset investments, but the return on capital goes down. What does this statement mean?

9. What are the risk–return trade-offs in choosing a mix of short- and long-term financing?

10. There are four possibilities that managers must consider when designing their working capital policy. Describe their features. What are the advantages and disadvantages of each policy?

PROBLEMS

1. The Kaler Appliance Store is considering the acquisition of a personal computer and associated software to improve the efficiency of its inventory and accounts receivable management. Andrea Kaler estimates that the initial cash outflow for the computer and software will be $15,000, and the associated net cash savings will be $3,000 annually.

    (a) If Kaler's discount rate for the cash flows associated with this project is 12% and the $3,000 savings will occur for only ten years (at which time the computer and software will be valueless), should she buy the computer?

    (b) What if the project lasts ten years but the discount rate is 16%?

    (c) What if the project lasts forever and the discount rate is 12%?

    (d) What if the project lasts forever and the discount rate is 16%?

2. Frank Ianelli is considering expanding his baseball card inventory to include hockey cards. The expansion will require an outlay of $30,000 and will generate a permanent net increase of $3,500 in Frank's annual cash flow.

(a) Should Frank expand his inventory if his required rate of return is 10%?

(b) What if Frank's annual $RRR = 14\%$?

(c) At what RRR would Frank be indifferent to expansion?

3. Jimmy Hilliard, manager of the Hilliard Racquetball Club, is considering lowering the usage fee for the courts. He estimates that this will result in an immediate (one-time) cash flow of $18,000 from new membership fees. On the other hand, the annual net cash flow from usage fees is expected to fall by $3,000 indefinitely (because of the lower fees).

(a) Should Jimmy lower the usage fee if his discount rate for this project is 15%?

(b) Should he lower the usage fee if his discount rate for this project is 20%?

(c) At what discount rate would he be indifferent to lowering the usage fee?

4. David Cordell, manager of the Berylium Records Store, currently has the following balance sheet:

Cash	$ 10,000
Marketable securities	5,000
Accounts receivable	20,000
Inventory	40,000
Current assets	$ 75,000
Fixed assets	125,000
Total assets	$200,000
Accounts payable	$ 10,000
Notes payable	20,000
Current liabilities	$ 30,000
Long-term debt	60,000
Common stock	60,000
Retained earnings	50,000
Total claims on assets	$200,000

David plans an expansion that will increase cash by $3,000, accounts receivable by $7,000, and inventory by $15,000. The financing for this expansion will come from some combination of notes payable and long-term debt.

(a) What is Berylium's level of net working capital now (i.e., before the expansion)? What is the current ratio now? What is the quick ratio now?

(b) Suppose David finances the entire expansion with notes payable. What will be the new level of working capital? The new current ratio? The new quick ratio?

(c) Suppose David finances the entire expansion with long-term debt. What will be the new level of working capital? The new current ratio? The new quick ratio?

(d) What will be the new amount of current liabilities if David chooses to keep the current ratio the same as it is now?

(e) What will be the new amount of current liabilities if David chooses to keep the quick ratio the same as it is now?

5. The Crary Seafood Company has annual sales of $1.44 million. Its average levels of accounts receivable, inventory, and accounts payable are as follows (in sales dollars):

Accounts receivable	$52,000
Inventory	14,000
Accounts payable	28,000

(a) Assuming a 360-day year, what are average daily sales?

(b) How many days of sales are represented by accounts receivable?

(c) How many days of sales are represented by inventory?

(d) How many days of sales are represented by accounts payable?

(e) What is Crary's net cash conversion cycle?

(f) Suppose that both sales and the current accounts shown are to increase by 25%. What will be the new net cash conversion cycle?

6. Ratliff McNubb, general manager of television station IBEM, is about to undertake an aggressive advertising campaign that will require increasing the level of accounts receivable by $30,000. Ratliff has to decide whether to finance this increase by borrowing the $30,000 with a one-year 12.5% bank note or by issuing long-term bonds with a 14% coupon rate. The following is a summary of IBEM's projected financial statements under each of the two plans:

	12.5% Bank Note Plan	14% Long-Term Bond Plan
Cash	$ 5,000	$ 5,000
Accounts receivable	50,000	50,000
Net fixed assets	45,000	45,000
Total assets	$100,000	$100,000
Accounts payable	$ 10,000	$ 10,000
Notes payable (12.5%)	40,000	10,000
Current liabilities	$ 50,000	$ 20,000
Long-term debt (14%)	20,000	50,000
Equity (10,000 shares)	30,000	30,000
Total claims on assets	$100,000	$100,000
Net operating income (NOI)	$ 9,000	$ 9,000
Interest	7,800	8,250
Taxes (40%)	480	300
Net income	$ 720	$ 450

(a) Calculate the level of net working capital and the current ratios of the two plans. Which plan do you think is more risky?

(b) Calculate the EPS and the return on (book value of) equity for both plans. Which plan do you think is more profitable?

(c) Suppose that IBEM pays out all its earnings as dividends and that its balance sheet and NOI at the end of the year are the same as they are today. What will be the level of the net working capital, current ratio, EPS, and return on (book value of) equity under the bank note plan if one year from today the interest rate on one-year bank notes is 16%?

7. The Corporeal Foods Company is considering certain changes that will increase the automation of its food processing and canning. This change will require an additional investment of $40,000 in fixed assets, but it will allow the level of current assets to decrease by $40,000 because of an increase in operating efficiency. Corporeal has current assets of $160,000, fixed assets of $240,000, and current liabilities of $100,000. Furthermore, Corporeal's board of directors has estimated that investment in fixed assets yields 18% on average and investment in current assets yields 8% on average. Hence, Corporeal's return on total assets is now:

$$\frac{\$160,000}{\$160,000 + \$240,000}(0.08) + \frac{\$240,000}{\$160,000 + \$240,000}(0.18) = 14\%$$

(a) Calculate Corporeal's current ratio and level of working capital.

(b) What will be Corporeal's current ratio, level of working capital, and return on total assets if the change to increased automation is made? Will the change increase or reduce the liquidity risk? Will it increase or reduce profitability?

8. The MacMinn Crane Company has a wide variation in its current asset components during the four seasons, as shown here:

	Spring	Summer	Fall	Winter
Cash	$10,000	$10,000	$ 10,000	$ 30,000
Accounts receivable	50,000	20,000	60,000	100,000
Inventory	20,000	40,000	60,000	10,000
Total current assets	$80,000	$70,000	$130,000	$140,000

MacMinn has fixed assets of $120,000.

(a) What is MacMinn's level of permanent current assets?

(b) Suppose that MacMinn adopts a conservative working capital policy, financing all net working capital requirements with long-term debt. What will be MacMinn's level of long-term financing during each of the four seasons? What will be MacMinn's current ratio during each of the four seasons?

(c) Suppose that MacMinn has decided on an aggressive working capital policy, financing all fixed assets and half of permanent current assets with long-term financing and the rest of its assets with short-term financing. What will be MacMinn's level of long-term financing during each of the four seasons? What will be MacMinn's level of short-term financing during each of the four seasons? What will be MacMinn's current ratio during each of the four seasons?

(d) Suppose that MacMinn adopts a matching working capital policy, financing all fixed assets and permanent current assets with long-term financing and the rest of its assets with short-term financing. What will be MacMinn's level of long-term financing during each of the four seasons? What will be MacMinn's level of short-term financing during each of the four seasons? What will be MacMinn's current ratio during each of the four seasons?

(e) Suppose that MacMinn adopts a balanced working capital policy, using long-term financing in the amount of 1.75 times fixed assets, and financing any assets in excess of this amount with short-term financing. If 1.75 times fixed assets exceeds the level of total assets, the excess will be invested in marketable securities. What will be MacMinn's level of long-term financing during each of the four seasons? What will be MacMinn's level of short-term financing, level of marketable securities, and current ratio during each of the four seasons?

9. Allen Motors last year had sales of $7,200,000 and current assets and liabilities as follows:

Accounts payable	$ 80,000
Notes payable	120,000
	$200,000
Cash	$ 20,000
Marketable securities	10,000
Accounts receivable	60,000
Inventory	450,000
	$540,000

Assume that the levels of cash, accounts receivable, inventory, and accounts payable change in the same proportion that sales do. For example, if sales are 10% higher next year, each of these four accounts will also be 10% higher.

(a) What is the current ratio now?

(b) If sales increase by 10%, what will be the new current ratio?

(c) To what value must sales fall for the current ratio to fall to 2.0?

(d) To what value must sales fall for the current ratio to fall to 1.0?

SUGGESTED ADDITIONAL READINGS

Kallberg, J. G., and K. Parkinson. *Current Asset Management*. New York: Wiley-Interscience, 1984.

Mehta, D. R. *Working Capital Management*. Englewood Cliffs, NJ: Prentice-Hall, 1974.

Richards, V. D., and E. J. Laughlin. "A Cash Conversion Cycle Approach to Liquidity Analysis." *Financial Management,* Spring 1980, pp. 32–38.

Vander Weide, James H., and Steven F. Maier. *Managing Corporate Liquidity: An Introduction to Working Capital Management*. New York: Wiley, 1985.

TWENTY-TWO

MANAGING CURRENT ASSETS

Cash payment is the only nexus between man and man.

—*Thomas Carlyle, 1843*

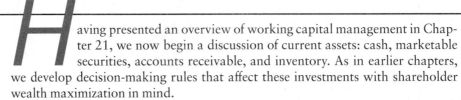

Having presented an overview of working capital management in Chapter 21, we now begin a discussion of current assets: cash, marketable securities, accounts receivable, and inventory. As in earlier chapters, we develop decision-making rules that affect these investments with shareholder wealth maximization in mind.

We examine these issues by answering the following questions:

- What role do cash balances play in the firm's operations?

- How do managers manage cash?

- How much cash should the firm hold?

- What are marketable securities? How are they used by the firm?

- How does the firm manage its accounts receivable?

The appendix to this chapter examines inventory management.

22-1

THE EFFICIENT COLLECTION AND DISBURSEMENT OF OPERATING CASH

Reasons for Holding Cash Balances

Business firms usually hold cash balances for five reasons: (1) transaction purposes, (2) compensating balance requirements, (3) precautionary reserves, (4) potential investment opportunities, and (5) speculation.

TRANSACTION PURPOSES

Firms need daily cash balances (checking accounts) to conduct their ordinary business transactions. These balances are used to meet cash outflow requirements for operational or financial obligations and to serve as temporary depositories for cash inflows from sales customers.

COMPENSATING BALANCE REQUIREMENTS

Commercial banks hold firms' cash balances and provide the conduit for collecting and disbursing cash. In addition, banks are a source of short-term financing. Not only do they charge for these services, but they may also receive an indirect fee through compensating balances. A compensating balance is a set amount of cash that a firm must leave in its checking account at all times as part of a loan agreement. These balances give banks additional compensation because they can be relent or used to satisfy reserve requirements.

PRECAUTIONARY RESERVES

Most firms hold extra cash in order to handle unexpected problems or contingencies due to the uncertain pattern of cash inflows and outflows. The extent of such buffer reserves depends on the predictability of cash flows; that is, the less predictable the cash flows are, the more cash is held. Precautionary balances also determine how quickly a firm can borrow additional cash. (Financially strong firms normally rely on prearranged lines of bank credit to satisfy most of this requirement.) Any cash balances maintained for precautionary reasons are usually invested in near-cash assets such as marketable securities because precautionary reserves are not part of normal operations.

POTENTIAL INVESTMENT OPPORTUNITIES

A firm may allow excess cash reserves to build up in anticipation of a future investment opportunity, such as the acquisition of another firm or a major capital expenditure program. In addition, the proceeds from a new debt or equity offering may temporarily swell cash reserves while being allocated to planned investment projects.

SPECULATION

A firm's managers may feel that some prices may soon change. These could be raw material prices, equipment prices, or even currency exchange rates. Managers who hope to profit from these expected price changes may delay purchases and store up cash for use later when they expect prices to be lower.

Cash Management Decisions

Cash management decisions are based on forecasts of future cash inflows and outflows. By analyzing the expected operating and financial cash receipts and disbursements, the financial manager can arrange short-term financing to cover projected cash deficits or to fund short-term investments if excess cash is expected. Financial cash outflows such as fixed-rate interest payments and tax payments are very predictable; sales and expense forecasts are much more uncertain. It is this uncertainty that necessitates the development of a cash management program. Such a program must include a control system to gather and monitor continually information about the firm's daily cash balances, cash receipts, and disbursements. In addition, the firm's portfolio of marketable securities must be evaluated continually. Figure 22-1 presents an expanded version of the cash cycle presented in Chapter 21 to illustrate the various cash flows that must be managed.

Cash management decisions deal with (1) the efficient collection and disbursement of operating cash, (2) the appropriate level of operating cash balances, and (3) the investment of temporary excess cash in near-cash assets such as marketable securities. These decisions must consider the trade-off between potential insolvency and the opportunity cost of forgone income from overinvesting in cash and near-cash assets. Large cash balances minimize the risk of illiquidity but reduce profitability and possibly firm value. Ideally, a firm prefers to collect cash as soon as possible on its credit sales. In contrast, a firm prefers to delay payment on its purchases as long as possible without hurting its credit rating. This phase of cash management focuses on accelerating cash receipts and slowing cash disbursements when possible. Because time is money, sophisticated money management strategies have been devised to meet this objective.

The Concept of Float in Cash Management

As a firm deposits customers' checks in its bank account and issues its own checks, its book balance keeps changing. The bank also records these transactions, but its balance may differ systematically from the company's book balance. This difference between the bank and book balances is called **float.**

Several types of float must be managed. A closer examination of them is useful because it explains why float exists in the first place.

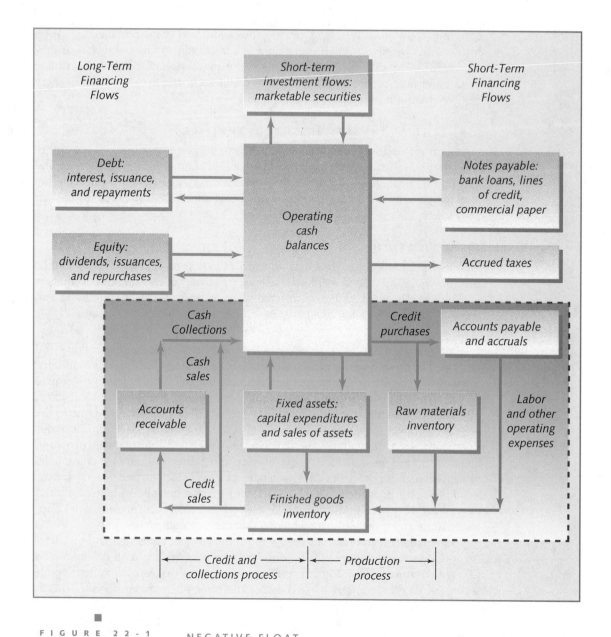

■
FIGURE 22-1

A firm's cash flow cycle, including operating, investment, and financial flows. The material inside the dashed box is part of the operating cash flow cycle.

NEGATIVE FLOAT

Negative float, which exists when the firm's book balance exceeds the bank balance, means there is more cash tied up in the collection cycle, and it earns a 0% rate of return. Negative float, which is related to customers' payments, is undesirable and should be minimized as much as possible. It consists of mail float, processing float, and clearing float.

Mail float is the dollar amount of customer payments that have been mailed by the customer but not yet received by the seller. As long as the check is in the mail, funds are not available for use.

Processing float is the dollar amount of customer payments that have been received by the seller but not yet deposited. An efficient firm does not let customers' checks sit in storage but attempts to present them for payment as soon as possible.

Clearing float is the dollar amount of customers' checks that have been depos-

TABLE 22-1
Illustration of Steady-State Float for Teeple, Inc.'s Books

Day	Disbursements	Deposits	Book Balance	Bank Balance	Float
0	$ −100	$ +100	$ 0	$ 0	$ 0
1	−100	100	0	0	0
2	−100	100	0	100	100
3	−100	100	0	200	200
4	−100	100	0	200	200
If Teeple withdraws $200 on day 5:					
5	−100	100	−200	0	200

Deposit clearing time, $CT^{dep} = 2$ days.
Disbursement clearing time, $CT^{dis} = 4$ days.

ited but not yet cleared.[1] A firm has no direct control over clearing float; however, a firm that has excessive clearing float may need to change to a more efficient bank.

POSITIVE FLOAT

Positive float is associated with the firm's payments and exists when the firm's bank balance exceeds its book balance. This type of float allows the firm to maintain control of its cash for a longer period of time, thus earning a larger return. The major positive float that we examine is disbursement float, which is the dollar amount of checks written by the firm that have not yet cleared. **Disbursement float** reduces the firm's idle cash. Thus management should try to increase this type of float.

Consider the case of Teeple, Inc. Table 22-1 shows Teeple's float situation. Teeple starts its operations on day 0 with a $0 cash balance. It takes Teeple's bank two days to clear a deposited check; that is, the deposit clearing time, CT^{dep}, is 2 days. To clear Teeple's disbursements, the bank takes four days, or the disbursement clearing time, CT^{dis}, is 4 days.

On day 0, Teeple deposits a check for $100 and simultaneously issues a check for $100. Its book balance is thus $0. However, the bank does not record the deposit or the payment because of the processing float ($CT^{dep} = 2$ days) and the disbursement float ($CT^{dis} = 4$ days). The total float is thus still $0.

On day 1, the same situation is repeated. No new entries are made in the bank's books, and the total float is still $0.

On day 2, the previous situation is repeated again. The check deposited on day 0 is credited to the firm's account, and so the bank balance rises to $100. The total float is thus $100.

On day 3, the check deposited on day 1 is credited to the firm, and the bank balance rises to $200. The disbursement check has not yet cleared. The total float is thus $200.

On day 4, two things happen. The check deposited on day 2 is credited to the firm, and the check issued on day 0 is paid by the bank. The net change in cash in the bank's books is $0, and so the total float is still $200. In fact, the total float does not change after day 4 and remains at $200. Thus Teeple has a **steady-state float** of $200.

The steady-state float of $200 allows Teeple to withdraw $200 from the bank and invest it in, say, marketable securities that earn interest. If Teeple does this on day 5, the book cash balance shows −$200 and the bank's balance is $0. This illustrates the advantage of *playing float*, or profiting from managing the steady-

---

[1] Banks use either the Federal Reserve System or another clearinghouse to clear interbank checks. The clearing float created by this process has been considerably reduced because of requirements contained in the 1980 Depository Institutions Deregulation and Monetary Control Act.

state float. The firm has, in effect, "created" $200, which can be put to productive use.

The steady-state float can easily be estimated with the following equation:

$$\text{Steady-state float} = (\text{average daily disbursements}) \times (CT^{\text{dis}} - CT^{\text{dep}}) \quad (22\text{-}1)$$

For Teeple,

$$\text{Steady-state float} = (\$100)(4 - 2) = \$200$$

thereby verifying the calculation in Table 22-1.

Strategies for Accelerating Cash Collections

Accelerating cash collections is an attempt to reduce the negative float associated with the time it takes from mailing a customer's check until it becomes usable funds to the firm. Most firms serve geographically dispersed customers. To reduce mail and processing float, many firms decentralize their collections operation by using a lockbox system, a local collection office, and/or preauthorized check payments. Each strategy must be evaluated carefully in terms of its incremental costs relative to its incremental benefits.

LOCKBOX SYSTEM

With a **lockbox system,** the firm has its customers mail their payments to a post office box in a specific city (often located in a Federal Reserve Bank city to cut the clearing time). A local bank collects the checks from this box and deposits them in the firm's checking account. The advantage of a lockbox is that checks are deposited sooner (less mail float) and become usable funds more quickly than if a centralized collection operation is used (less clearing float, especially if checks are drawn on local banks). The main disadvantage is cost. Because bank fees for this service are related to the volume of checks deposited, lockboxes are too expensive if many small checks are involved. A numerical example involving lockbox arrangements appears later in the chapter.

LOCAL COLLECTION OFFICE

If it uses a **local collection office,** a firm sets up its own collection center to handle its customers' remittances. This center can be an existing branch office or an entirely separate operation. Employees receive, record, and place all payments in a local depository bank. The billing process may be speeded up if the local office also bills its regional customers. Like a lockbox, this system reduces mail and processing float by strategically locating these systems where customers tend to cluster. The main distinctions between the two systems are cost and who processes the checks. With a lockbox system, a bank conducts all the processing for a monthly activity fee or a minimum required compensatory balance. With a local collection office, the firm must invest in personnel, equipment, and office space.

PREAUTHORIZED CHECK PAYMENTS

A low-cost alternative for speeding collections when a firm receives a large volume of fixed payments from the same customers is to use **preauthorized checks.** Under a prearranged agreement, a firm is permitted to draw a specific amount from a customer's checking account at specified intervals. Remittances for periodic insurance premiums, lease payments, and mortgage payments are often made in this way. This method allows a collecting firm to reduce greatly all three types of negative float, and it has the added feature of increasing the certainty of a firm's cash inflows.

Mechanisms for Transferring Funds

Modern telecommunications have revolutionized the transfer of funds through the use of electronic funds transfer systems (EFTS). Once deposits are made, EFTSs offer a number of options to move funds rapidly between accounts.

SWEEP ACCOUNTS

Within a particular bank, **sweep accounts** allow a firm to reduce its checking account balance to a minimum level at the end of each day. Any funds released by "sweeping" the account can then be invested overnight to earn interest income or be transferred to a centralized disbursement bank.

WIRE TRANSFERS

Interbank transfers of usable funds can be made in less than an hour through wire (telegram) transfers via a bank's or the Federal Reserve's wire system. Although wire transfers reduce mail float, they are expensive and are usually restricted to infrequent, large-dollar transfers.

ELECTRONIC DEPOSITORY TRANSFER CHECKS (DTC)

To reduce clearing float, a DTC can be made through any number of EFTS networks. With a DTC, a local collection center can place customers' checks in a local depository bank and notify the firm's central bank (located near its headquarters) of the amount. The central bank then prepares a DTC for this amount, credits the amount to the firm's account, and transmits the DTC to the local depository bank for payment. The DTC's main advantage is that a one-day clearing time is possible rather than the normal two days through the Federal Reserve.

Strategies for Controlling Disbursements

Just as speeding collections helps to convert accounts receivable to cash and reduces cash balances, slowing disbursements attempts to do the same thing. Within limits, a number of strategies can be used to control and slow down cash outflows. Abusing these strategies, however, may irritate a firm's creditors to the point that its credit rating is jeopardized or its trade credit may be withdrawn.

STRETCHING PAYABLES

A firm stretches payables when it pays accounts payable or accruals only when they are due. There is no benefit to paying sooner, which reduces the availability of cash for other investment purposes. Stretching should not be interpreted to mean paying after the credit period. The term as used here refers to paying as late as possible within the credit period. Occasionally, paying bills late may be overlooked by creditors, but a regular habit of delinquency can only lead to problems.

ZERO-BALANCE ACCOUNTS

Large corporations that have multiple branches or divisions often have many checking accounts in different banks. This may seem to justify conducting local operations, but they tend to lead to excess cash balances and a loss of disbursement control. One way to eliminate these problems is to allow each operating entity to write checks on a special checking account that contains no funds. All these accounts are located at a central bank, so that at the end of each day, the negative balances created by the divisions' checks can be restored to $0 by debiting a master account. Moreover, if the master account has a surplus of cash, it can be swept into an overnight investment. Better control over disbursements and excess balances results without usurping the payment authority of local operations. Figure 22-2 shows how a typical zero-balance arrangement might work.

■
F I G U R E 2 2 - 2
How a zero-balance arrangement (ZBA) works

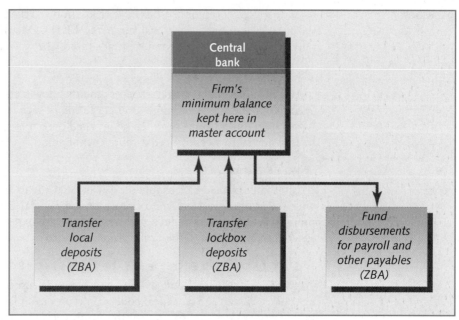

REMOTE OR CONTROLLED DISBURSING[2]

Originally, **remote,** or controlled, **disbursement** was available only at banks with remote branches, at correspondent banks (banks that have an ongoing relationship in which one bank performs a service for another), or at banks located in a remote section of the country—hence the name. Under remote disbursing, the firm does not give local operating units payment authority. Instead, all payments are made from one disbursement bank. Not only are mail and clearing floats lengthened, but this float also can be better controlled. As can be seen from Figure 22-3, the basic idea is simple. The firm does not fund disbursements until the day that its checks are presented for clearance. The checks are covered by a same-day transfer of funds by the firm. In fact, most controlled disbursement points can provide the required information by late morning, so that the firm can still tap short-term credit sources if necessary. Furthermore, this disbursement method can be applied to many accounts, all of which can be funded with a single funds transfer.

Concentration Banking: An Integrated Cash Management System

To attract large corporate customers, banks have begun to offer an integrated systems approach that uses the cash management strategies we discussed. This systems approach is called **concentration banking.** Figure 22-4 illustrates how the various strategies can be tied together for efficient cash management. A firm may use a mixture of local office and lockbox systems for local or regional cash collections. Each day, the local depository or lockbox bank transfers cash above a minimum or target balance to the firm's central concentration bank. These daily funds transfers can be made by either a wire transfer or a DTC. The transferred funds are then placed in a master account for disbursement to cover deficits in its zero-balance accounts or to cover checks drawn against its remote branch bank account. By accelerating cash collections for rapid transfer to a central concentration

[2]For more details, see S. F. Maier and D. M. Ferguson, "Disbursement System Design for the 1980s," *Journal of Cash Management,* November 1982, pp. 56–69.

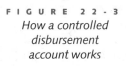

FIGURE 22-3
How a controlled disbursement account works

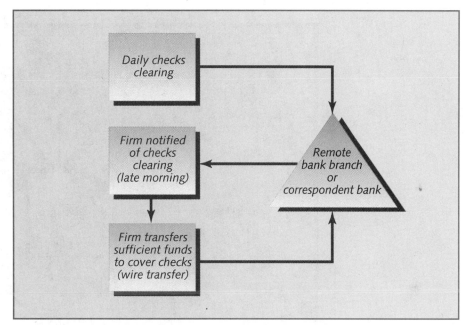

bank and by pooling these funds for controlled disbursement, a firm can achieve optimal float advantages and thus reduce its operating cash balances to a minimum. Moreover, extensive reports are generated to provide data for better control purposes. Such a system is costly, so all aspects of a concentration banking system are normally used only by the largest corporations. Nevertheless, every firm needs to evaluate these strategies to find the one(s) that justify their cost.

Evaluating Cash Management Strategies   Determining whether to adopt a specific cash management technique is analogous to evaluating a replacement decision in capital budgeting. A new technique or system is compared with an existing one in an incremental benefit–cost analysis. Typical costs are usually bank fees, employee salaries, and perhaps an investment in specialized equipment.[3] The primary benefit is the potential cash freed up by improving the float time. This released cash can be used to increase income or reduce costs. For example, released funds can be invested in short-term earning assets or used to repay short-term debt.

To assess a technique's feasibility, the net present value (*NPV*) for the current-asset investment decision must be determined using the capital budgeting methods discussed in earlier chapters:

$$NPV = \frac{\Delta CFAT_t}{RRR} - CFAT_0$$

To clarify the issues in evaluating a cash management technique, note first that many cash savings methods involve no fixed-asset investment; therefore $CFAT_0 = 0$ and this equation can be simplified as follows:

$$NPV = \frac{(\Delta \text{revenues} - \Delta \text{expenses})(1 - T)}{RRR} \tag{22-2}$$

[3] Some high-volume retailers have established their own check-processing facilities that operate the same check-sorting and encoding equipment as bank lockboxes do. When checks are high-volume, low-dollar payments, an in-house collection center can be a feasible alternative to a bank-operated facility.

FIGURE 22-4
Integrated cash management system with concentration banking collection float

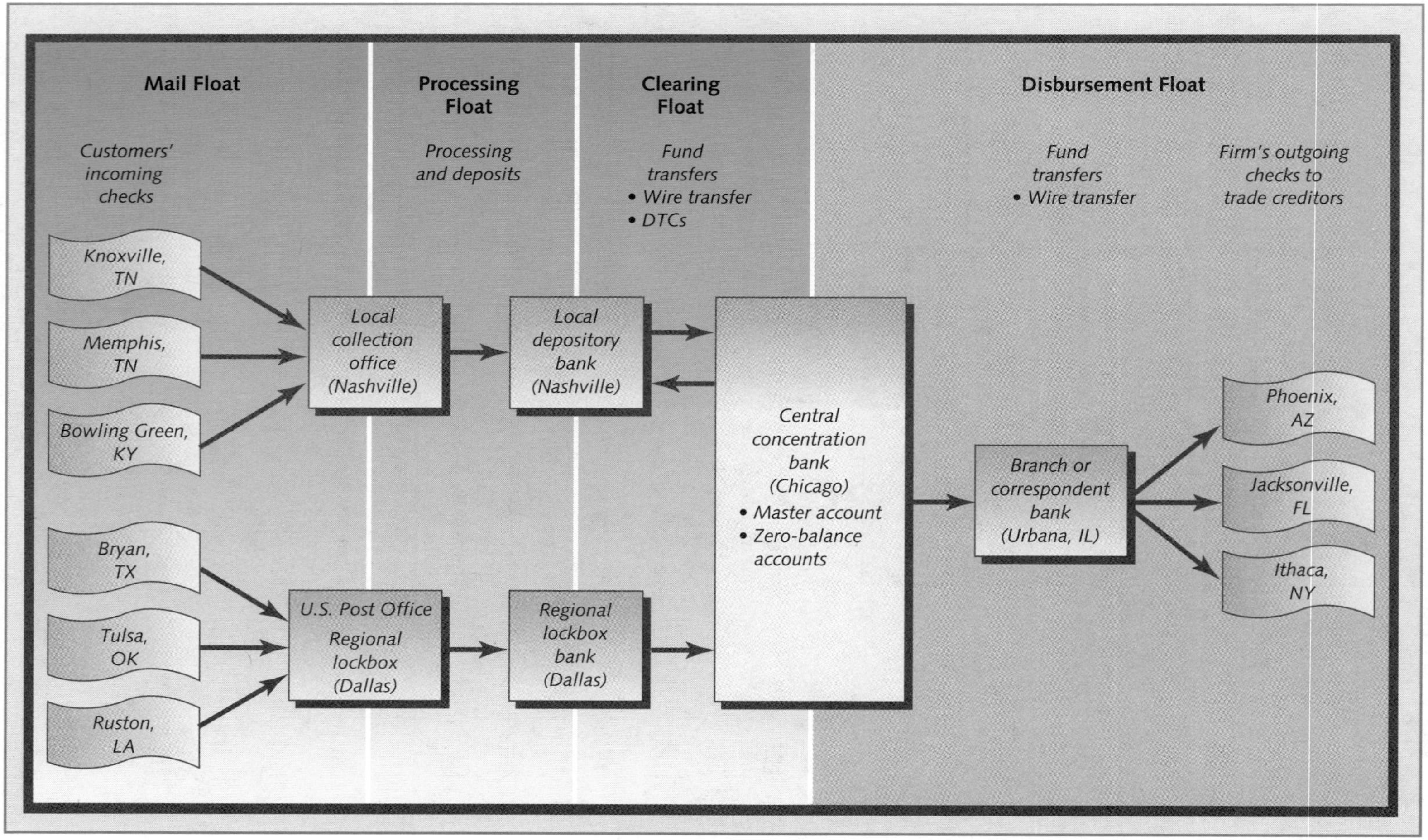

Mail Float

Customers' incoming checks

Knoxville, TN
Memphis, TN
Bowling Green, KY

Bryan, TX
Tulsa, OK
Ruston, LA

Processing Float

Processing and deposits

Local collection office (Nashville)

U.S. Post Office Regional lockbox (Dallas)

Clearing Float

Fund transfers
• Wire transfer
• DTCs

Local depository bank (Nashville)

Regional lockbox bank (Dallas)

Central concentration bank (Chicago)
• Master account
• Zero-balance accounts

Disbursement Float

Fund transfers
• Wire transfer

Branch or correspondent bank (Urbana, IL)

Firm's outgoing checks to trade creditors

Phoenix, AZ
Jacksonville, FL
Ithaca, NY

where

> Δrevenues is the change in annual before-tax cash inflows (income)

> Δexpenses is the change in annual before-tax cash outflows (costs)

> T is the marginal tax rate

> RRR is the required rate of return, or the opportunity cost of capital

The reader may ask why it is necessary to compute the NPV if, as argued, $CFAT_0 = 0$ in most cases. Notice from equation (22-2) that as long as the incremental revenues exceed the incremental expenses, NPV is positive. Why not simply go with the new project as long as revenues exceed expenses? It is certainly true that the new system is to the firm's advantage as long as revenues are greater than expenses. Calculating the NPV, however, tells us how much of an advantage (in dollars) this really is. This is important if the firm is considering alternative cash management strategies.

Uncollected Float Analysis

The fundamental tool for determining the net benefits of any cash management technique is an **uncollected float analysis.** A collection float analysis measures the expected reduction in negative float. Similarly, a disbursement float analysis measures the expected increase in positive float. More specifically,

$$\Delta F = C \times \Delta t \tag{22-3}$$

where

> ΔF is the change in the average uncollected or available cash balances (released cash)

> C is the average daily check receipts or disbursements

> Δt is the change in the average float time, in days

For example, if a firm collects $146 million annually in sales, its average daily check receipts are $C = \$146,000,000/365$ days $= \$400,000$ per day. If mail, processing, and clearing times average five days, the daily total uncollected balance associated with this float is $2 million ($\$400,000 \times 5$). If float time can be reduced by two days, the float (or average uncollected balances freed up) is reduced by

$$\Delta F = \$400,000 \times 2 \text{ days} = \$800,000$$

The before-tax change in annual cash income is the incremental income received by improving the float time. This is given by

$$\Delta\text{Revenues} = \Delta F \times RRR \tag{22-4}$$

or, substituting equation (22-3) into equation (22-4):

$$\Delta\text{Revenues} = (C \times \Delta t) \times RRR \tag{22-5}$$

In this case, the opportunity cost of capital can be viewed as the forgone interest income that could be earned by investing ΔF, or the interest expenses that could be saved by using ΔF to reduce short-term debt.

As an example, we estimate the advantages of a lockbox arrangement. Recall that adopting a lockbox system is an attempt to benefit from an improved collection system to reduce the mail, processing, and clearing floats associated with converting receipts (checks) to available or usable funds.

Assume that Herculean Corporation's annual credit sales are $136,875,000, which are billed and collected through a centralized location. A collections study indicates that 700 checks per day are processed and deposited, on average, and that a regional lockbox network could reduce Herculean's float time by two days. The lockbox banks charge $0.20 per check to operate the lockbox system. If the released cash can be used to reduce short-term debt that costs 10%, should the system be adopted (the marginal tax rate is 34%)?

In this example, according to equation (22-5),

$$\Delta \text{Revenues} = \left(\frac{136,875,000}{365}\right)(2 \text{ days}) \times 0.10$$

$$= \$750,000 \times 0.10 = \$75,000$$

Note that "revenues" in this case come from a $75,000 decrease in interest expenses. Also note that this benefit extends forever. To determine the change in cash expenses due to the banks' fees, we use:[4]

$$\Delta \text{Expenses} = 700 \text{ checks} \times 365 \text{ days} \times \$0.20/\text{check} = \$51,100$$

Therefore, the *NPV* from equation (22-2) is:

$$NPV = \frac{(\$75,000 - \$51,100)(1 - 0.34)}{0.10} = \$157,740$$

The lockbox system should be adopted. But what if the lockbox banks also require $300,000 in compensating balances? Because these funds are placed all year in a nonearning checking account, the compensating balances reduce the $75,000 in released cash. Then the net benefit becomes:

$$NPV = \frac{[\$75,000 - \$300,000(0.10) - \$51,100](1 - 0.34)}{0.10} = -\$40,260$$

The lockbox system should not be implemented.

Now we consider another example. Stretching payables is an attempt to benefit from an increase in disbursement float. Assume that a cash manager discovers that her firm is paying off its accounts payable an average of two days early. If the firm changes this practice and pays the accounts on their due date, what is the effect on the disbursement float if credit purchases are $91,250,000 annually? If the available cash released can be invested in short-term securities at 10% and the firm's tax rate is 30%, what is the net benefit to the firm?

The average increase in disbursement float is:

$$\Delta F = C \times \Delta t$$

$$= \left(\frac{\$91,250,000}{365 \text{ days}}\right) \times 2 \text{ days} = \$500,000$$

and the *NPV* is:

$$NPV = \frac{\Delta \text{revenues}(1 - T)}{RRR} = \frac{(\Delta F \times RRR)(1 - T)}{RRR}$$

$$= \frac{(\$500,000)(0.10)(0.70)}{0.10}$$

$$= \$350,000$$

---

[4]If adopting the lockbox system reduces any of the operating expenses associated with the centralized billing collection center, those benefits should be included here.

Cash Management for a Multinational Company

To many financial officers of multinational companies, international cash management presents both a rewarding challenge and a major frustration. The efficient handling of large sums of cash can result in significant cost savings to the firm; yet the methods of handling cash—in particular, cash transfers—vary from country to country. Managers are faced with a perplexing array of choices regarding cash transfers. For example, American managers in Latin America often complain that there are no standardized check-clearing times, balance verification by phone is undependable, mail systems are poor, many banks share a common computer terminal, and so on. Nevertheless, much progress is being made in increasing the quality of cash-handling procedures, with American banks such as Citibank, Chase, Bank of America, and Manufacturers Hanover Trust taking the lead.

The principles of cash management as discussed thus far also apply to firms with overseas operations. However, as in other areas, the multinational dimension adds new complications. A major problem faced by a company with subsidiaries in different countries is to coordinate the efficient flow of funds among its various offices. Idle cash at any location should be minimized, and all surplus funds should be channeled to a cash center. (Lockbox arrangements are not widely available in many countries.) In Europe, Switzerland is a popular cash center, and for Asian operations, Hong Kong is popular, although the uncertainties associated with Hong Kong reverting to China have been a major concern. An overseas cash center must be chosen very carefully. Ideally, the cash center should be in a country with a stable government that does not impede the flow of funds into and out of the country. The local currency in the cash center should also be strong and readily convertible into other currencies. This helps firms minimize the exchange risk. In addition, this country should have an active money market so that excess funds can readily be invested to earn interest. Another important feature is that the local government tax income only at the source, not every time funds are brought into the country.

Multinational managers also play the float, but transfer times for international funds are much longer. This is often a very serious concern to managers because the longer transfer times not only tie up the funds that could otherwise be put to use but also increase the exchange risk. For many years, international funds transfer messages were sent by cable. In 1977 the Society for Worldwide Interbank Financial Telecommunication (**SWIFT**) was formed. SWIFT is a computerized arrangement for speedy (within minutes) funds transfers among 800 European, North American, and Latin American banks. In addition, SWIFT is used extensively to transfer debit and credit information between bank accounts. The Clearing House Interbank Payments System (**CHIPS**) is another arrangement widely used for international funds transfers. Any credit manager can instruct her bank to initiate a CHIPS payment on her behalf, and the transaction is completed the same day. Also, an increasing number of international banks can actively work with the company in designing its working capital policies. In particular, transfer times can, for a fee, be dramatically reduced. The bank must decide whether this fee is justifiable in light of the benefits of speeded cash transfers.

For example, we assume that Implovision International's monthly overseas cash transfers amount to $6 million. The National Bank agrees to guarantee a reduction in its cash transfer time from the current 15 days to only five days. As a fee, the bank will charge 0.5% of the volume of funds transferred. Should Implovision use the services of the bank if its opportunity cost of capital is 10%?

A monthly cash transfer of $6 million amounts to an annual transfer of $72 million. If it accepts the new service, the company will be able to invest the $72 million for ten days $(15 - 5)$ to earn $(\$72,000,000 \times 0.10)(10/360) = \$200,000$. In terms of an annual yield, this works out to be $\$200,000/\$72,000,000 = 0.0028$, or 0.28%. Because the company saves only 0.28% (well below the 0.5% fee for the service), it appears that this is a bad deal for Implovision. But this conclusion may not be correct. The company must also weigh the advantages of exchange risk reduction against the incremental cost of this service of $0.5\% - 0.28\% = 0.22\%$. If the exchange risk is lowered dramatically, this arrangement may, in fact, be to the company's advantage.

22-2
THE OPTIMAL LEVEL OF OPERATING CASH BALANCES

It should be clear by now that a firm should retain as little cash as possible because cash is a nonproductive asset. Yet a firm cannot do without cash balances. A company needs cash to satisfy one or more of the requirements for holding cash discussed earlier. How does a manager decide on the optimal level of cash that the firm must maintain?

Optimal Cash Balance

The **optimal cash balance** is the larger of (1) the sum of transactions balances and precautionary reserves or (2) compensating balance requirements. If a firm estimates its transactions balance and precautionary reserve requirements to be $40,000 and $60,000, respectively, and if the bank's compensating balance requirement is $80,000, the firm should hold an optimal cash balance of $100,000. Of course, the interesting questions pertain to determining the transactions and precautionary balance requirements for the firm. Management must estimate these figures based on a variety of subjective factors. It is not easy to suggest meaningful rules to arrive at dollar amounts for these cash balances. A company's transaction–precautionary balance depends on its sales volume, the predictability of its cash flow forecasts, and the ease with which cash shortages can be covered by short-term borrowings. The higher the sales volume is and the larger the number of transactions conducted, the larger the required cash balances are. The greater the uncertainty associated with cash inflows and outflows is, the larger the required transactions and precautionary balances are. Predictable differences between daily inflows and outflows can be gauged by analyzing the past pattern of daily deposits and written checks. Variations in checking deposits may also provide guidance in deciding the average balances required. The ability to generate short-term credit by means of, say, overdraft privileges, in which banks automatically extend loans to cover checks written in excess of available balances, also affects the optimal cash balances.

Mathematical Models

INVENTORY MODEL

One way to quantify these subjective considerations in determining the optimal cash balance is to formulate the question as an inventory decision problem, familiar to students of operations research.

Assume, for example, that the Zeta Corporation has a pool of funds, $\$B$ (cash) that it uses to pay its bills. When the cash is exhausted (i.e., $B = 0$), Zeta replenishes its cash by selling T-bills, which are short-term investments that earn interest and are easily sold. In deciding how much to hold in its pool of cash, Zeta must balance costs and benefits. Every dollar held by Zeta as cash is a forgone opportunity to earn interest (at a rate i) by being invested in marketable securities. Although the initial decision would therefore be to hold very little cash, there are disadvantages to this course of action. If Zeta runs out of cash, it will have to sell some marketable securities to restore its cash position. Selling these securities is not a costless exercise. The transactions cost associated with each issue of T-bills (T) may be significant, and the more often Zeta runs out of cash, the more often it will incur this cost.

Therefore Zeta must attempt to have enough cash on hand to avoid excessive transactions costs from selling marketable securities, while at the same time not losing an excessive amount of interest by not investing in marketable securities. The optimal cash balance is therefore determined by minimizing the net cost of carrying cash balances. These costs and benefits may be quantified, and the optimal amount of cash may be computed.

If Zeta starts with a pool of B and ends up with $0 (before it has to sell new T-bills to raise cash), the average cash balance over the period is (beginning cash + ending cash)/2, and the cost of carrying the cash annually is this amount multiplied by the annual interest rate. Thus:

$$\begin{aligned} \text{Marginal cost} \atop \text{of carrying cash} &= \frac{\text{(beginning cash + ending cash)}}{2}\text{(interest rate)} \\ \end{aligned} \tag{22-6}$$

$$= \frac{\$B + \$0}{2}(i)$$

If Zeta's annual cash disbursements are D and its beginning cash balance is B, then it has to issue T-bills (D/B) times to restore its $0 cash balance to B. Each issue costs T in transactions costs, so the reduction in transactions costs from holding larger cash balances is (D/B)T:

$$\begin{aligned} \text{Marginal benefits} \atop {\text{from lower} \atop \text{transactions costs}} &= \frac{\dfrac{\text{annual cash}}{\text{disbursements}} \times \dfrac{\text{transactions costs}}{\text{per sale}}}{\text{beginning cash balance}} \\ \end{aligned} \tag{22-7}$$

$$= \frac{DT}{B}$$

Thus larger initial cash balances reduce Zeta's potential transactions costs. The total cost of carrying cash balances is therefore

$$\frac{Bi}{2} + \frac{DT}{B}$$

To find the optimal beginning cash balance, B^*, we differentiate the total cost with respect to B and solve for the optimal balance B^*, as:

$$\text{Optimal cash balance } (B^*) = \sqrt{\frac{2 \times \dfrac{\text{annual cash}}{\text{disbursements}} \times \dfrac{\text{transactions costs}}{\text{per sale}}}{\text{interest rate}}} \tag{22-8}$$

$$= \sqrt{\frac{2DT}{i}}$$

We assume that Zeta disburses $2 million in cash every year and that every sale of T-bills costs $50. If the current risk-free interest rate is 10%, Zeta's optimal cash balance is:

$$\text{Optimal cash balance} = \sqrt{\frac{2 \times \$2,000,000 \times \$50}{0.10}}$$

$$= \$44,721$$

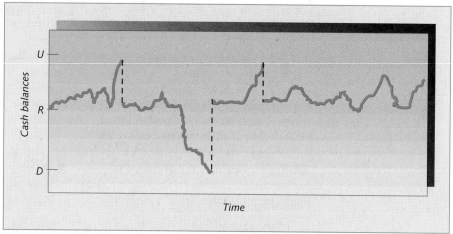

The reader can verify that Zeta's optimal cash balances will be larger if the transactions costs are higher or if the interest rate is lower. The reasoning in this situation should be clear.

MILLER–ORR MODEL

The Miller–Orr model assumes that cash balances fluctuate randomly, both up and down. It also assumes that the manager has two "control points": U, the upper control point, and D, the lower control point, and also a "return point," R. When the cash balances reach the upper control point U, the manager is supposed to transfer enough cash into, say, marketable securities so that the cash position is brought down to the return point R. Similarly, when the cash position falls to the lower control point D, the manager is supposed to sell marketable securities to bring the cash level up to R. If the firm follows this policy, then its daily cash position can be represented as in Figure 22-5.

Assume for simplicity that the lower control point D is 0. The financial manager chooses the upper control point U and the return point R to minimize the total expected transactions costs. These costs include not only the costs of switching into and out of marketable securities but also the holding costs associated with this cash management policy. The optimal value of the return point can be shown to be:[5]

$$R^* = \sqrt[3]{\frac{3f\sigma^2}{4r}}$$

(22-9)

where

    f is the fixed cost of security transactions

    σ^2 is the variance of daily net cash flows

    r is the the interest rate per day

The optimal value of U is $U^* = 3R^*$.

A weakness of the Miller–Orr model is that it assumes that cash flows are completely uncertain. Usually the financial manager knows that some cash flows are

[5] See Merton H. Miller and Daniel Orr, "A Model of the Demand for Money by Firms," *Quarterly Journal of Economics*, August 1966, pp. 413–435.

certain. Even for those cash flows that are uncertain, he or she often knows something about the cash flow magnitude, variability, and trend over time. Unfortunately, these details cannot be incorporated into the model, which assumes that the cash flows are independent of such factors.

22-3

INVESTING EXCESS CASH IN MARKETABLE SECURITIES

Typically, cash in excess of requirements for transactions, precautionary balances, and/or compensating balance purposes is temporarily invested in marketable securities.[6] Excess funds may build up during seasonal lows but are eventually needed for expanding inventory and accounts receivable during seasonally high sales periods (excess transactions balances). On the other hand, excess cash may be held to cover uncertain financing requirements or to take advantage of an investment opportunity.

An alternative to holding excess cash for these purposes is to borrow for the short term to finance uncertain cash requirements. Which approach is taken depends on management's overall working capital policy, as seen in Chapter 21. In this section, we take as given the working capital policy and the funds available for temporary investments.

Decision Criteria

Many types of temporary near-cash investments are available and are discussed later in this section. The financial manager needs criteria for determining which ones best fit his or her needs. Because these investments are temporary stores of transactions and precautionary balances, the primary consideration is how quickly they can be converted to cash without loss of value (principal). This eliminates most long-term securities from consideration because their prices tend to vary widely. Short-term debt securities, such as money market instruments, are therefore the best choice. The three most important characteristics to consider are risk, marketability, and term to maturity.

RISK

For a debt instrument issued by a business entity, two types of risk affect its value over time: default risk and interest rate risk. **Default risk** refers to the chances that the issuer may not be able to pay the interest or principal on time or at all. (U.S. government issues have no default risk.) Given the reasons for investing excess cash, a firm usually buys marketable securities that have little or no default risk. **Interest rate risk** refers to fluctuations in a security's price caused by changes in market interest rates. As rates change, the value of a debt security changes in the opposite direction. If a firm is forced to sell a security after interest rates rise, it probably loses principal. Only if a security is held to maturity and redeemed at par can the interest rate risk be avoided.

MARKETABILITY

Marketability refers to how quickly a security can be sold before maturity without a significant price concession. Some securities are very marketable, meaning that they may be sold quickly at or close to their full value. Other securities are not very marketable, meaning that they may be difficult to sell quickly or that they may be sold only by offering a deep price cut. The major determinant of a security's

---

[6]This implies that the amount of funds invested becomes a "residual" decision.

marketability is the existence of an active secondary market for that security.[7] A firm that invests in marketable securities wants to be able to obtain cash from the sale of these securities quickly and without losing value in the process. Firms therefore prefer to purchase highly marketable securities as temporary investments for cash.

TERM TO MATURITY

Firms normally limit their marketable securities purchases to issues that have relatively short maturities (less than one year). The variability in the prices of fixed-income securities tends to increase with an increase in the term to maturity because of interest rate risk. Maturity dates of marketable securities held should coincide, when possible, with the date at which the firm will no longer have excess cash to invest. Maturities of one day, ten days, or any number of days can easily be found.

Notice that yield or return is not mentioned as an important decision criterion. Highly marketable, low-risk securities have relatively low yields, but the safety of the principal is the main criterion for excess cash investments. Only after risk, maturity, and marketability have been considered should return be allowed to influence the final choice.

Types of Marketable Securities

Money market instruments are usually the securities that best satisfy the three criteria. Money market instruments are short-term securities, usually with maturities of up to one year, although some money market instruments have maturities up to five years (e.g., U.S. Treasury notes). We describe eight types of marketable securities, and Table 22-2 summarizes their characteristics and historical yields. As shown in the last three columns, the yields on these instruments vary considerably over time. The reason is that yields depend on the state of the economy, business credit demands, inflation expectations, and monetary and fiscal policies.

TREASURY BILLS

T-bills are debt obligations of the U.S. government used to finance fiscal deficits. They are issued with maturities of one year or less and are considered to be default free because they receive the full financial backing of the U.S. government. T-bills are sold as a discount instrument; that is, they trade at less than their redemption value, with the difference between the redemption and market values representing the interest received. The market for these securities is the largest, most liquid sector of the money markets. Because they are the safest and most marketable security, they have the lowest yield but are the most widely held.

FEDERAL AGENCY OBLIGATIONS

Certain U.S. government agencies raise funds by issuing short-term instruments, or federal agency obligations. These securities are relatively safe and have good marketability, though not as good as Treasury securities because they are guaranteed by the agencies themselves. (The U.S. government does have a moral obligation to back them.) Their slightly lower marketability and safety in comparison with Treasury securities causes them to have slightly higher yields. Examples of agencies that issue obligations are the Government National Mortgage Association (**Ginnie Mae**) (GNMA), Federal Farm Credit Banks (FFCBs), and Federal Home Loan Banks (FHLBs).[8]

---

[7] Chapter 1 discussed secondary markets.

[8] Of these agencies, only the FFCB issues coupon securities; all others are discount securities. In addition, unlike the other agencies, the GNMA is an arm of the Department of Housing and Urban Development (HUD), and its obligations are guaranteed directly by the Treasury Department.

■

TABLE 22-2
Summary of the Characteristics and Historical Yields of Various Money Market Instruments

Money Market Instrument	Issued Maturities	Minimum Denominations	Special Features	Historical Yields[a](%)		
				1990	1991	1992
Treasury bills[b]	91 and 182 days and 52 weeks	$10,000	No default risk; excellent marketability; discount instrument	7.50	5.38	3.43
Federal agency issues	Varies	$5,000	Low default risk; good marketability; coupon-bearing instrument	—	—	—
Banker's acceptances[c]	30 to 180 days	$25,000	Default risk relatively small but varies with the issuing bank; good marketability for acceptances issued by larger banks	7.80	5.67	3.67
Large negotiable certificates of deposit[c]	30 to 180 days	$100,000	Default risk varies with issuing bank; up to $100,000 insured by Federal Deposit Insurance Corporation (FDIC); fair marketability; deposit plus accrued interest	8.15	5.82	3.64
Commercial paper[b]	30 to 270 days	$25,000	Default risk highest of the money market instruments but normally low; poor marketability; discount instrument	8.15	5.89	3.71
Repurchase agreements	1 to 30 days	$500,000	Low default risk because lender holds the underlying securities and collateral; poor marketability because it is a two-party agreement but is self-liquidating within a few days	[d]		
Eurodollar loan deposits[b]	Overnight to 360 days	$1 million	Low default risk but depends on issuing foreign bank (deposits uninsured); poor marketability; deposit plus accrued interest	8.16	5.86	3.70
Money market mutual funds	None	$1,000	Low default risk but depends on the instruments held by the mutual fund's portfolio; good marketability; interest earned daily on shares issued	7.6	5.8	3.5

[a] Annual averages of monthly data, except as indicated.
[b] Three-month.
[c] Three-month averages of the most representative daily offering rates of dealers. Rates of top-rated banks only.
[d] Yields are negotiable but usually less than the T-bill yield.
SOURCE: *Federal Reserve Bulletin* (Washington, D.C.: Federal Reserve Board, December 1993).

BANKER'S ACCEPTANCES

Banker's acceptances are time drafts drawn on and accepted by a bank. They were designed to facilitate the import–export trade business. Because acceptances are guaranteed by the issuing bank, their safety depends on that bank's financial strength. The secondary market for them is well organized, very active, and hence very liquid. Yields are usually higher than those on Treasury securities of comparable maturity.

NEGOTIABLE CERTIFICATES OF DEPOSIT

Commercial banks issue large-denomination time deposits called **certificates of deposit (CDs)**, which entitle the holder to receive the amount deposited plus the accrued interest upon maturity. They are negotiable because once they are issued, they can be traded in the secondary market. Maturities are set to fit the investors' needs. The CDs of the largest banks are handled by government securities dealers and are therefore highly marketable. Yields on CDs are generally higher than the rates on T-bills and federal agency issues.

COMMERCIAL PAPER

Commercial paper is short-term unsecured promissory notes issued by large corporations and finance companies with high credit ratings, such as the General Motors Acceptance Corporation (GMAC). Commercial paper is sold directly to investors by the issuer and through commercial paper dealers. The secondary market for commercial paper is weak. This low marketability plus a higher default risk results in higher yields than most other money market instruments have.

REPURCHASE AGREEMENTS

A **repurchase agreement,** or *repo,* is a negotiable arrangement (not a security) between a bank or securities dealer and an investor. The investor acquires certain short-term securities (usually T-bills) with the understanding that the bank or dealer will repurchase these securities at a slightly higher price in a specified number of days. Their maturities are very short and are tailored to meet the investor's needs. A repo yield is slightly less than the rate (less a "haircut") that can be obtained from outright purchase of the underlying security. Repurchase agreements are relatively safe investments because the banker or dealer as well as the issuer of the security have to default before a loss is incurred.

EURODOLLAR LOAN DEPOSITS

Eurodollar deposits are interest-bearing (time) deposits in European banks or foreign branches of U.S. commercial banks. These deposits are denominated in dollars rather than in the local currency—hence the name **Eurodollar.** They generally carry higher interest rates than those on U.S. time deposits. Like negotiable CDs, maturities and interest rates are negotiable. Marketability is limited, although an organized secondary market is developing. The default risk varies with the issuing bank.

MONEY MARKET MUTUAL FUNDS

As Table 22-2 indicates, most of the higher-yielding marketable securities are available in only relatively large denominations. Smaller firms with only limited funds to invest are unable to purchase these securities directly. An alternative is to purchase the securities indirectly through a money market mutual fund. These mutual funds pool the investments of many small investors and buy large-denominated money market instruments. Shares, much like common stock, are issued against this portfolio of securities. By purchasing these shares, a smaller firm can attain the higher yields offered on large-denominated securities for even very short periods of time. In addition, interest is earned daily, and many mutual funds offer draft-writing privileges that allow the firm to earn interest on invested funds until the check clears. The default risk is slight and depends on the types of securities purchased by the mutual fund.

22-4
MANAGING ACCOUNTS RECEIVABLE

The investment in accounts receivable results from a firm's credit sales, and its level indicates the extent to which its credit and collections policies are used to stimulate sales. For example, if a firm charges the same price for both cash and credit sales, then offering credit is in effect a price reduction. This reduction can occur in two ways. It is a direct reduction if the firm offers a discount when the account receivable is paid off before a certain date. It is an indirect reduction if no finance charge is assessed. In effect, a firm that grants credit, say for one month, is giving its customer an interest-free loan because the customer continues for a month to have the use of this money, which can be invested to earn interest income.

Although less liquid than either cash or marketable securities, receivables are a major investment for many firms (see Table 21-1 in Chapter 21) that also involves a trade-off between risk and profitability. The issue is how much to invest in receivables in order to maximize shareholder wealth. Too little investment may deprive the firm of the marginal benefits from a higher sales level (reduced profitability). But too much investment may expose the firm to excessive costs by tying up valuable cash (increased liquidity risk).

Managers of accounts receivable (1) establish a credit extension policy, (2) establish a collection policy, and (3) monitor the receivables investment. Credit extension policies provide guidelines for granting credit, the terms of payment, and the amount of credit to extend to a customer. Collection policies provide guidelines for ensuring that customers pay their bills according to the credit terms. Monitoring the receivables investment means evaluating and controlling the quality of the total receivables investment in order to detect any problems and to suggest corrective actions.

Analyzing a Credit Extension Policy

Credit may be extended to either an individual or another firm. Credit granted to an individual is referred to as **consumer credit**. Credit extended to another firm is known as **trade credit**. Unlike a consumer, a firm has limited liability, and its life span is longer than the lives of its management and owners. Trade credit is fairly sensitive to interest rate changes, whereas consumer credit is largely affected by changes in income and unemployment. These and other distinctions affect the credit-granting (and collections) decision in different ways, making a complete discussion of both rather cumbersome. Since our focus in this book is on the firm, we confine our discussion to trade credit. Table 22-3 summarizes the more common types of credit accounts.

CREDIT STANDARDS

Credit standards are the criteria that determine which customers will be granted credit and how much. A customer must meet or exceed the minimum credit standards. Ideally, a firm's credit standards reject only those customers who would not pay their bills promptly or at all (become *bad debtors*). However, no qualitative or quantitative method can predict a customer's future bill-paying ability.[9] Also, attempting to implement "ideal" credit standards may result in a policy that is too stringent or too tight and may eliminate the risk of nonpayment (lower collection expenses and bad-debt losses) but also eliminate potential sales to those rejected

---

[9] Some credit-scoring models have shown some promise in predicting default, although their predictions are not very accurate.

■
T A B L E   2 2 - 3
Three Types of Credit Accounts Found in Credit Agreements

1. *Open book credit.* The most common type of credit is open book or open account credit. Goods and services are sold without a contract evidencing the transaction. An invoice provides an informal statement of the transaction.

2. *Installment credit.* Repayment is made by a series of regular (monthly) payments. Most of these arrangements are for a one-time purchase of an expensive item (e.g., a computer).

3. *Revolving credit.* Revolving credit is a combination of the first two types, in which the indebtedness is classified as current as long as a minimum payment (a fraction of the outstanding balance) is made each month.

1. *Financial statements.* A credit applicant is often asked to supply various types of financial information, such as audited balance sheets, income statements, and pro forma statements. Applying the financial analysis techniques studied in Chapter 20, the firm assesses the applicant's financial strength and ability to pay its obligations.

2. *Credit agencies.* An important source of credit information is credit agencies such as Dun & Bradstreet (D&B) that specialize in providing credit ratings and credit reports on individual firms. Figure 22-6 contains an example of D&B's credit *rating* system, which provides a measure of an applicant's "financial strength" (net worth) and a composite credit appraisal (from "high" to "limited"). For an extra fee, an individual credit *report* can be obtained, such as that shown in Figure 22.7.

3. *Banks.* Banks often provide credit checks for their customers. Larger banks maintain sizable credit departments that share information with one another. Limited credit information, such as loan repayment experience, can be obtained in this way.

4. *Trade associations.* Various trade associations keep records of member firms' credit experience with different suppliers. Information such as credit amount extended, payment experience (slow or prompt), and so on can easily be obtained through such sources.

customers who would have paid their bills. At the other extreme, an excessively liberal policy may lead to higher sales but also higher bad-debt losses and collection costs. Therefore the trade-off between marginal benefits and costs dictates a balance between these two extremes.

A discussion of how a firm should establish its credit standards is difficult because such standards depend on subjective and objective information. Nevertheless, credit standards often revolve around the "four C's of credit": (1) character—a customer's willingness to pay, (2) capacity—a customer's ability to generate cash flow, (3) capital—a customer's financial resources, such as collateral, and (4) conditions—current economic or business conditions. These four general characteristics are normally assessed by investigating different sources of credit information, subject to time and cost considerations. Table 22-4 describes the more common sources of credit information.

Some credit sources provide an overall credit rating. A key to the Dun & Bradstreet credit rating system is given in Figure 22-6, and an example of a Dun & Bradstreet credit report on a firm appears in Figure 22-7. If such a credit report is not available for a customer, the firm's credit standards are applied to the existing credit information about that customer, and the probability of delinquent payment or a bad-debt loss is assessed. Based on this subjective analysis, a customer may, for example, be placed into a credit risk category that in turn determines the credit amount or line of credit to be extended. Table 22-5 is one credit classification scheme. Many firms quantify this process by using a credit scoring system. Such a system assigns point values to different attributes that historically have been indicative of customers' payment behavior. Based on the total value of these points, a customer's credit application is accepted or rejected and, in some cases, placed in a classification scheme such as the one in Table 22-5.

CREDIT TERMS

After a firm determines its credit standards, the second part of a credit extension policy establishes the terms on which credit is granted. Competitive conditions or industry standards often dictate such terms. In other instances, they may be related to the perishability or turnover of the products. Credit terms define the credit period and any discount offered for early payment. They are usually stated as "net t" or "d/t_1, n/t." The first example states that payment is due within t days from a specified date, usually the date of the good's receipt. The second allows a discount of $d\%$ if payment is made within t_1 days; otherwise, the full amount is due within t days. For example, "3/10, $n/30$" means that a 3% discount from the invoice amount can be taken if payment is made within 10 days; otherwise, full payment

D&B Ratings and Symbols

D&B Rating System

The D&B Rating System is a widely used tool that uses a two-part code to represent a firm's estimated financial strength and composite credit approval. A Rating may be based on a book financial statement or on an estimated financial statement submitted by the company.

	Estimated Financial Strength		Composite Credit Appraisal			
			High	Good	Good	Limited
Estimated financial strength, based on an actual book financial statement. *For example, if a company has a Rating of "3A3," this means its financial strength is between $1,000,000 and $9,999,999 and its composite credit appraisal is "fair."*	$50,000,000 and over	**5A**	1	2	3	4
	$10,000,000 to $49,999,999	**4A**	1	2	3	4
	$1,000,000 to $9,999,999	**3A**	1	2	3	4
	$750,000 to $999,999	**2A**	1	2	3	4
	$500,000 to $749,999	**1A**	1	2	3	4
	$300,000 to $499,999	**BA**	1	2	3	4
	$200,000 to $299,999	**BB**	1	2	3	4
	$125,000 to $199,999	**CB**	1	2	3	4
	$75,000 to $124,999	**CC**	1	2	3	4
	$50,000 to $74,999	**DC**	1	2	3	4
Estimated financial strength, based on either an actual book financial statement or an estimated financial statement.	**$35,000 to $49,999**	**ED**	1	2	3	4
	$20,000 to $34,999	**EE**	1	2	3	4
	$10,000 to $19,999	**FF**	1	2	3	4
	$5,000 to $9,999	**GG**	1	2	3	4
	up to $4,999	**HH**	1	2	3	4
Estimated financial strength, based on an estimated financial statement (when an actual book financial statement is not available to us).	$125.00 and over	**1R**		2	3	4
	$50.00 to $124.999	**2R**		2	3	4

Symbols in the Rating column — what do they mean?

•• (Absence of a Rating)

A Business Information Report is available on this business, and other information products may be available as well. However, a D&B Rating has not been assigned. A "••" symbol should not be interpreted as indicating that credit should be denied. It simply means that the information available to Dun & Bradstreet does not permit us to classify the Company within our Rating key and that further inquiry should be made before reaching a credit decision.

In many cases, a "••" symbol is used because a current financial statement on the business is not available to us. Some other reasons for using a "••" symbol include:

☐ Unavailability of the source and amount of starting capital — in the case of a new business
☐ A deficit net worth ☐ Bankruptcy proceedings ☐ A critical financial condition

ER (Employee Range)

Certain lines of business, primarily banks, insurance companies and other service-type businesses, do not lend themselves to classification under the D&B Rating System. Instead, we assign these types of businesses an Employee Range symbol based on the number of people employed. No other significance should be attached to this symbol.

For example, a Rating of "ER7" means there are between 5 and 9 employees in the company.

"ERN" should not be interpreted negatively. It simply means that we don't have information indicating how many people are employed at this firm.

Key to Employee Range	
1000 or more employees	ER1
500 to 999	ER2
100 to 499	ER3
50 to 99	ER4
20 to 49	ER5
10 to 19	ER6
5 to 9	ER7
1 to 4	ER8
Not available	ERN

INV (Investigation being conducted)

"INV" means that at the time the listings were extracted for this Reference Book, we were conducting an investigation on this business to get the most current details.

Questions? Please call your D&B Customer Service Center at 1-800-234-DUNS (1-800-234-3867). Our Customer Service Representatives will be happy to help you interpret the D&B Rating System and other symbols.

**Dun & Bradstreet
Information Services**
a company of
The Dun & Bradstreet Corporation

1 Diamond Hill Road
Murray Hill, N.J. 07974-0027

18B7 (9106)

1992

BE SURE NAME, BUSINESS AND ADDRESS MATCH YOUR FILE.

ANSWERING INQUIRY

DUNS: 00 007 7743
GORMAN MFG CO INC
(Subsidiary of Gorman Holding Companies Inc.)
492 KOLLER ST
AND BRANCH(ES) OR DIVISION(S)
SAN FRANCISCO CA 94110
    TEL: 415-555-0000

DATE PRINTED:
OCT 30 199-

COMMERCIAL PRINTING
SIC NO.
27 52

	SUMMARY
RATING	3A3
STARTED	1965
PAYMENTS	SEE BELOW
SALES F	$13,007,229
WORTH F	$2,125,499
EMPLOYS	105 (100 HERE)
HISTORY	CLEAR
FINANCING	SECURED
FINANCIAL CONDITION	FAIR

CHIEF EXECUTIVE: LESLIE SMITH, PRES

SPECIAL EVENTS 09/11/9-   On Oct. 13, 199-, the subject experienced a fire due to an earthquake. Damages amounted to $35,000, which was fully covered by their insurance company. The business was closed for two days while employees settled personal matters due to the earthqauke.

PAYMENTS REPORTED (Amounts my be rounded to nearest figure within prescribed ranges)

	PAYING RECORD	HIGH CREDIT	NOW OWES	PAST DUE	SELLING TERMS	LAST SALE WITHIN
10/9-	Ppt-Slow 90	1000	500	-0-	N30	1 Mo
09/9-	Ppt	250	100			4-5 Mos
	Ppt-Slow 30	2500	2500	100		1 Mo
	Slow 30	500	500			2-3 Mos
	Slow 30 60	70000	70000	65000		1 Mo
08/9-	Disc	2500	1000			1 Mo
	Disc-Ppt	25000	25000	-0-	2 10 Prox	1 Mo
	Ppt-Slow 15	1000	500	250		1 Mo
	Ppt-Slow 30	15000	10000	500		1 Mo
	Ppt-Slow 30	1000	-0-	-0-	N30	4-5 Mos
07/9-	Ppt	250000	250000	-0-		1 Mo
	Ppt	7500	250	-0-	N15	1 Mo
	Ppt	500	-0-	-0-	N30	6-12 Mos
	Ppt	100	50	-0-	Regular terms	1 Mo
	Ppt-Slow 30	100000	100000	40000		1 Mo
	Ppt-Slow 30	70000	70000	50000	2 15 Prox	1 Mo
	Slow 30	7500	-0-	-0-		1 Mo
	Slow 30		-0-	-0-	N30	6-12 Mos
06/9-	Disc-Slow 30	30000	30000	7500		1 Mo
05/9-	Ppt	250	-0-	-0-		6-12 Mos
	Ppt-Slow 60	200000	200000	90000		1 Mo
04/9-	(022)	100	100		N30	

    * Payment experiences reflect how bills are met in relation to the terms granted. In some instances payment beyond terms can be the result of disputes over merchandise, skipped invoices, etc.
    * Each experience shown represents a separate account reported by a supplier. Updated trade experiences replace those previously reported.

FIGURE 22-7
A Dun & Bradstreet credit report

TABLE 22-5
Example of a Classification Scheme by Credit Risk Category, Line of Credit, and Historical Payment Behavior

Credit Risk Category	Line of Credit to Grant	Historical Payment Behavior	
		Average Collection Period[a] (Days)	Bad-Debt Loss Ratio[b] (%)
Lowest 1	>$500,000	20	0.5
2	<$500,000	30	1.5
3	<$250,000	45	3.0
4	<$100,000	60	6.5
5	<$ 50,000	90	10.0
Highest 6	Reject		

[a] *Average collection period* measures the average number of days that a current account is outstanding before it is paid off.
[b] *Bad-debt loss ratio* measures the percentage of outstanding credit sales that prove to be uncollectible and are written off as a charge against sales.

is due within 30 days.[10] Cash discounts are offered to reward early payments and thereby to reduce the collection period and the amount invested in accounts receivable.

COSTS AND BENEFITS OF A CREDIT EXTENSION POLICY

There are four major costs of a credit extension policy:

1. *Cash discounts*—a percentage of sales deducted as an incentive to encourage early payment

2. *Credit and collection expenses*—administrative costs for conducting an in-house credit operation

3. *Bad-debt losses*—accounts that are not collectible and are written off as a charge against sales

4. *Financing costs*—the *RRR,* or opportunity cost, of capital of funds tied up in a receivables investment

Extending credit can be a sales tool for stimulating revenues and thereby increasing the cash flows (returns) to fixed-asset investments. Moreover, a credit policy may be needed to prevent an erosion in market share. If competitors offer credit on better terms, for example, a firm is forced to follow suit simply to maintain its sales level. In contrast, restricting credit through more stringent standards or terms may produce net benefits if any reduced sales are more than offset by lower credit costs.

Exporters face unique problems when extending credit to a foreign buyer. Certain documents created to provide exporters with assurances that unknown foreign customers will pay for goods purchased on credit are described in the highlight on page 694.

Evaluating a Change in the Credit Extension Policy

Deciding whether to adopt a credit policy normally requires comparing a new policy with an existing policy. Once again, it is the incremental benefits and costs that are relevant to this decision. Assume that the Herculean Corporation currently extends credit to those customers that fall in the four lowest credit risk categories in Table 22-5 (categories 1 to 4). Management wants to know whether it is more profitable to eliminate the marginal accounts by tightening its credit standards and restricting credit to the three lowest-risk categories. Table 22-6 summarizes Herculean's current and proposed credit policy details.

The change would reduce sales because the sales to customers in the highest risk category (4) would be lost, but the amount of investment in receivables would decline. In addition, the operating and credit costs should decrease. Collection and bad-debt expenses, in particular, are normally due disproportionately to servicing the lower quality or marginal accounts. Therefore the question is: Will the lost sales be more than offset by the decrease in expenses and receivables investment?

To answer the question, the total cash flows that result from each policy are estimated first. Next, the cash flows from the current credit policy are subtracted from those of the proposed policy to determine the incremental cash flows associated with the proposed policy. Finally, the *NPV* of these incremental cash flows is estimated, and an accept/reject decision is made.

[10] Occasionally, the credit terms may specify an interest cost if payment is not received within the credit period. For example, "3/10, *n*/30, 15% over 30" indicates that an annual interest cost of 15% is assessed on any amount outstanding after 30 days.

TRADE DOCUMENTS FACILITATE FOREIGN TRADE

Extending credit to foreign purchasers of goods or services entails different types of risks than does domestic trade. In domestic transactions, sales are usually made on a cash basis or through an open-account trade credit. But these terms are often unacceptable to importers and exporters because of the time lag between the contract and the delivery of goods and the lack of adequate information to make responsible credit decisions. In addition, in the event of default, settlement through international courts may be cumbersome and costly. For these reasons, importers and exporters use three kinds of documents that facilitate international trade by giving third-party credit guarantees. These are trade drafts, bills of lading, and letters of credit.

Trade drafts are written orders initiated by the exporter informing the importer of the exact amount and time at which the importer or its agent must pay. If the trade draft is signed by the importer, the importer acknowledges his obligation to pay, and the draft is called a **trade acceptance.** If the importer's bank accepts the draft, the bank agrees to pay the exporter, thereby substituting its creditworthiness for that of the importer, and the draft is referred to as a **banker's acceptance.**

A banker's acceptance represents an unconditional promise of the bank to make payment on the draft at maturity. As an example, suppose that a company in New Jersey plans to import shoes from Italy. Because the importer in Hoboken does not know the Italian shoemaker, he goes to his bank and arranges for the bank to guarantee payment to the Italian firm, which is then authorized to draw a draft on the bank. Upon presentation of proper documents showing that the shoes have been shipped, the U.S. bank agrees, for a fee, to accept the draft for payment. The draft can also be sold by the exporter to his local bank at a discount and the funds obtained immediately. In this way he can obtain payment for the shoes even before the U.S. importer has paid for them. Banker's acceptances have an active secondary market in New York, where the main dealers are First Boston Corporation, Briggs Schaedle & Co., Discount Corporation of New York, Merrill Lynch, and Salomon Brothers.

A **bill of lading,** the next major international trade document, serves three purposes: (1) it provides a receipt of goods from the exporter to the shipper; (2) it acts as a contract between the carrier and exporter indicating that the carrier will transport the goods for a fee; and (3) it may convey legal title to the goods. Bills of lading may be either "straight" or "to order." A straight bill of lading does not convey legal title of the goods and is generally used in shipping to affiliates when the merchandise has been paid for in advance. An order bill of lading, on the other hand, conveys title to the merchandise only to the party to whom the document is addressed. When a firm deals with an unknown importer, the bill is usually addressed to the exporting firm. Therefore the exporter retains title to the merchandise until payment is made, at which time the bill of lading is signed over to the party that made the payment. This arrangement allows the exporter to sell goods to the importer without releasing title until the payment is made.

Letters of credit are the third way to reduce the risk of noncompletion of contract. Basically, letters of credit are issued by a bank on behalf of an importer. Once the bank has received the bill of lading and other proper documents, it substitutes its promise to pay for that of the importer. The exporter then has a financial arrangement only with the importer's bank, not with the importer. The letter of credit does not guarantee the underlying commercial transaction; it is simply a promise to pay upon the presentation of certain documents. The banks involved have a responsibility to examine the documents with reasonable care, but they are not responsible in any way for the goods being shipped.

These three documents—the trade draft, the bill of lading, and the letter of credit—all have greatly facilitated international trade by reducing the risks of dealing with unknown parties.

TABLE 22-6

Herculean Corporation's Proposed Change in Credit Policy

	Existing Policy	Proposed Policy
Credit standards	Categories 1–4	Categories 1–3
Average collection period	40 days	35 days
Bad-debt losses	4% of sales	2% of sales
Percent of sales taking discounts[a]	30	32

[a] The percentage of sales paid back in ten days or less.

As shown in Table 22-7, Herculean's current revenues of $136,875,000 will drop to $116,800,000 under the new credit policy, an incremental decrease in before-tax revenues of $20,075,000. On the other hand, operating and credit expenses will also decline. The net change in cash flow will be a decrease in cash flow after taxes of $884,000. But a smaller level of receivables will be required for two reasons: (1) a lower sales level and (2) a shorter credit period (average collection period). As the table indicates, these two factors cause the investment in receivables to fall by $3,800,000.

As discussed previously, incremental cash flows can be treated as a perpetuity. If the firm's opportunity cost of capital is 10%, its *NPV* can be calculated as:

$$NPV = \frac{\Delta CFAT_t}{RRR} - \Delta CFAT_0$$

$$= \frac{-\$884,000}{0.10} - (-\$3,800,000) = -\$5,040,000$$

Therefore, by restricting credit to higher-quality credit risks, Herculean will end up reducing its firm value by more than $5 million. It should keep the higher-risk customers and reject the proposed credit policy.

Finally, if relaxing a credit policy was being considered instead, the same evaluation scheme would apply, but the cash flow effects would be the opposite. For example, if Herculean's credit terms were changed from 2/10, *n*/30 to 2/10, *n*/40, sales would be stimulated, but operating costs, credit expenses, and the cost of financing the higher level of sales (higher receivables investment) would also be greater.

TABLE 22-7

Worksheet for Evaluating Herculean's Proposed Changes (in thousands)

	(1) Proposed Policy	(2) Current Policy	(3) Incremental (Δ) Cash Flows (1) − (2)
Operating cash flows			
Revenues	$116,800	$136,875	$(20,075)
Operating costs (70% of sales)	(81,760)	(95,812)	14,052
Credit expenses			
Discounts taken[a]	(1,121)	(1,232)	111
Credit and collection	(2,100)	(3,400)	1,300
Bad debts[b]	(2,336)	(5,475)	3,139
CFBT	29,483	30,956	(1,473)
Taxes (40%)	(11,793)	(12,382)	(589)
CFAT	17,690	18,574	(884)
The initial investment level of accounts receivables[c]	11,200	15,000	(3,800)

[a] Proposed policy: $116,800 × 0.32 × 0.03 = $1,121
Current policy: $136,875 × 0.30 × 0.03 = $1,232
[b] Proposed policy: $116,800 × 0.02 = $2,336
Current policy: $136,875 × 0.04 = $5,475
[c] Proposed policy: ($116,800/365 days) × 35 days = $11,200
Current policy: ($136,875/365 days) × 40 days = $15,000

Further Refinements in Analyzing Credit Policy Changes

A number of other considerations not formally recognized in the Herculean example need to be mentioned.

CHANGES IN NET WORKING CAPITAL

Whenever a credit policy change affects sales, working capital components other than accounts receivable may be affected. For example, if a policy change increases sales, then the investments in operating cash balances and inventory may need to be increased to support the higher sales level. Moreover, spontaneous financing such as current liabilities may also increase and may offset the higher current-asset investment. Therefore a proper evaluation of a policy change should account for any change in net working capital requirements.

RISK AND THE *RRR*

The primary risk associated with a credit decision is the chance that customers will not pay their bills. Because bad-debt losses are fairly predictable, the risk inherent in accounts receivable is relatively low. Presumably, restricting credit to higher-quality customers should reduce the variability in bad-debt losses and collection expenses. Nevertheless, we have ignored any differences in the variability of the cash flows under the two policies. Is this a correct procedure? No, but estimating the change in the *RRR* due to a credit policy change alone is very difficult.[11] In practice, risk differences are normally recognized by adjusting the *RRR* up or down according to a set of risk class designations.

FIXED VERSUS VARIABLE COSTS

Estimating the incremental cash flows usually involves only variable costs (those that increase directly with increased sales). Earlier, we assumed implicitly that fixed costs would remain unchanged because there was a decrease in sales. If sales increased, say because of a relaxed credit policy, fixed costs might increase also if the firm is operating near its capacity. If additional fixed costs are the result, they should also be included in the incremental cash flow analysis.

THE OPTIMAL POLICY

The best or optimal credit policy for maximizing shareholder wealth cannot be determined directly. Rather, the financial manager must evaluate alternative policies and move toward the optimal credit extension policy. For example, Herculean might next see whether relaxing its credit standards by extending credit to the highest-risk category (5) would improve its position. Altering the present credit terms might be more profitable, but should they be relaxed or tightened? Only an incremental benefit–cost analysis can tell—along with actual experience. Over time, the dynamics of a changing group of customers and a changing business environment may make a formerly optimal policy undesirable. This is why evaluation and monitoring of the investment in receivables are continually required—a topic we examine shortly.

Establishing a Collections Policy

Collecting accounts receivable is usually a routine task because most firms do pay their bills on time. But when accounts are overdue, collection procedures for these delinquent payments must be established, especially because this affects the investment in receivables and hence the return. Collection procedures usually start

---

[11] It is necessary to estimate the beta of the credit decision "project"—a difficult task.

with a second mailing indicating that the account is overdue, followed by a personal phone call or visit. If these efforts go unrewarded, the account may be turned over to a collection agency, or legal action may be initiated.

Key decisions for management include how long to wait before labeling an account overdue and initiating the collection procedures and how aggressively to pursue these accounts. Beginning too soon may antagonize customers. Aggressive collection efforts may reduce future sales and profits if customers are chased off to competitors. Changing business conditions may alter payment patterns (e.g., payments tend to slow down during an economic downturn), and often an otherwise creditworthy customer may allow a bill to become overdue for a good reason, perhaps through oversight or misplacement of the bill.

The collection agency or methods adopted should be determined by the same incremental benefit–cost analysis used to evaluate the credit extension policy. The time and effort spent on collecting an individual account must be traded off against the expected benefits. Collection efforts can be expensive. Although second or third letters or telephone calls are relatively inexpensive, collection agency and legal fees are substantial. Remember that the objective of a collection is not to minimize bad-debt losses; it is to maximize the firm's value.

Monitoring the Receivables Investment

As mentioned earlier, customers' payment patterns determine the level of investment in receivables and its return. For instance, a slow payment pattern leads to an excessive investment in receivables and a lower rate of return. To manage its receivables efficiently, a firm must monitor and evaluate its receivable collections to detect any changes in their status and composition and to take corrective actions when appropriate. One or more of several techniques involving the average collection period ratio, the aging schedule, or a collections schedule are typically used. These techniques for monitoring investments in accounts receivable are not discussed here in the interest of space.

SUMMARY

Section 22-1: The Efficient Collection and Disbursement of Operating Cash

What role do cash balances play in the firm's operations?

■ Companies need to hold cash for a variety of reasons, including handling the firm's transactions, maintaining compensating balances, serving as a contingency reserve, and being available for potential investment or speculative opportunities.

How do managers manage cash?

■ Financial managers must manage the firm's cash efficiently. Efficient cash management, which involves speeding up cash receipts and slowing down cash disbursements, can actually increase the firm's cash flows.

■ Cash receipts can be speeded up by reducing negative float and by using lockboxes, local collection offices, preauthorized checks, and other modern electronic funds transfer procedures.

■ Cash payments can be delayed by stretching payables and using zero-balance accounts and controlled disbursing. An integrated systems approach to cash management is concentration banking.

Section 22-2: The Optimal Level of Operating Cash Balances

How much cash should the firm hold?

■ Because cash is a nonproductive asset (it earns no return), the firm should hold as little cash as possible. On the other hand, the firm must have a certain amount of cash to function. Firms seek out an optimal cash balance that reconciles these two opposing facets of holding cash.

■ The optimal level of cash balances is determined as the larger of (1) the sum of transactions and precautionary balances or (2) compensating balance requirements. Mathematical models, such as the inventory model and the Miller–Orr model, can also be used to determine the optimal cash balance.

Section 22-3: Investing Excess Cash in Marketable Securities

What are marketable securities? How are they used by the firm?

■ Marketable securities are very liquid, short-term investments that can be taken on and liquidated quickly.

■ Cash in excess of the firm's requirements should be temporarily invested in marketable securities. In making this short-term investment, the firm should consider the risk of the security, its marketability, and its term to maturity.

■ There are numerous types of marketable securities with characteristics that vary widely.

Section 22-4: Managing Accounts Receivable

How does the firm manage its accounts receivable?

■ Accounts receivable involve sales on credit. Firms that use accounts receivable must thus be concerned with the creditworthiness of their customers.

■ A credit extension policy requires an analysis of credit standards, credit terms, and the costs and benefits of extending credit. Management must establish an appropriate collections policy and, in addition, monitor its investments in accounts receivable by using one or more of the following techniques: the average collection period ratio, an aging schedule, or a collections schedule.

QUESTIONS

1. Why do firms hold cash? What are the three cash management decisions that the financial manager must make?

2. What is float? Distinguish between negative and positive float. How is the steady-state float calculated?

3. Explain the various options available to firms to speed up the collection of cash.

4. What is concentration banking?

5. How are cash management strategies evaluated? How is this procedure similar to capital budgeting?

6. What is uncollected float analysis? What does it measure? Why is this information useful to a firm?

7. How does a manager determine the optimal level of cash balances?

8. What popular marketable securities are available in the marketplace? What are their distinguishing features?

9. Compare the marketable securities from Question 8 on the basis of three criteria: risk, marketability, and term to maturity.

10. What are the three decisions that an accounts receivable manager must make?

11. How would you evaluate a proposed credit extension policy in an *NPV* framework? What are some other important issues not considered in your *NPV* analysis?

PROBLEMS

1. The Jameson Building Supplies Company has annual sales of $9 million (all credit). On average, it takes five days for a customer's mailed check to be deposited. Mel Jameson believes that he can reduce this float time by two days by using a lockbox. The bank charges a flat fee of $4,000 per year to perform this service.

   (a) What are average daily sales for January? (Assume a 360-day year.)

   (b) All of January's receipts from sales go into a money market mutual fund. By how much will the average balance in this fund increase if Mel uses a lockbox?

   (c) Suppose that the money market fund earns 10% per year. Should Mel enter into a lockbox agreement?

   (d) Should Mel enter into a lockbox agreement if the money market fund earns 10% but the lockbox reduces float by only one day?

2. Newman-Markups Department Store has annual credit sales of $27 million. John Harris, the collections manager, has estimated that it takes six days for a mailed payment to be credited to Newman's account and that this time can be cut to three days if Newman opens a lockbox account with a local bank. The account in which the checks are placed earns 8% annually. The lockbox agreement calls for a monthly payment of $500 and, in addition, a charge of $0.03 per check. Newman currently processes 45,000 checks monthly. (Treat these expenses as if they occur at the beginning of the year.)

   (a) What are Newman's daily sales? (Assume a 360-day year.)

   (b) By how much will Newman's average bank balance increase if it uses a lockbox?

   (c) Should Mr. Harris use a lockbox?

   (d) Suppose that Newman's has found that a regular 20% of its customers account for 80% of its credit sales. Should Mr. Harris use a lockbox for only this 20% of the customers?

3. Tietjen Oil Co. is considering the use of a lockbox system to handle its daily collections. Tietjen's credit sales are $14.8 million per year, and it currently processes 1,300 checks per day. The cost of the lockbox system is $9,500 per year. The system allows for up to 1,000 checks per day. Any additional checks are processed at an additional charge of $0.015 per check. Tietjen estimates that the system will reduce its float by three days. The firm's discount rate for equally risky projects is 13%, its tax rate is 34%, and its cost of short-term capital is 9%. (Assume a 360-day year.)

(a) How much cash will be released for other uses if the lockbox system is used?

(b) What net benefit will Tietjen gain from using a lockbox system?

(c) Should Tietjen adopt the proposed lockbox system?

(d) Assume now that the institution that offers the lockbox system requires a $700,000 compensating balance to be held for the complete year in a non-interest-bearing account. Should Tietjen adopt the system?

4. Schuyler Industries is considering the establishment of a zero-balance account with its bank. Schuyler presently maintains $530,000 in its disbursing account. The bank requires a $400,000 non-interest-earning deposit to open the account and will charge Schuyler $1,000 per month for the service. Evaluate the proposed zero-balance account and make a recommendation to Schuyler if its opportunity cost is 14%.

5. The Texron Oil Company is headquartered in Houston but has customers in Dallas, Fort Worth, El Paso, San Antonio, and Austin as well. Mark Hannah, the collections manager, is planning to open collection offices in these cities to speed up the collection process. The dollar volume of collections, the annual cost of running the collections center, and the reduction in float time for each city are as follows:

City	Annual Collections	Annual Cost of Center	Reduction in Float Time (days)
Dallas	$300 million	$80,000	1
Fort Worth	160 million	76,000	2
El Paso	120 million	75,000	3
San Antonio	220 million	78,000	2
Austin	150 million	80,000	2

(a) Using a 360-day year, find the daily collections from each of the five cities.

(b) What marginal increase in deposits (because of reduced float) will each city's collection center contribute to Texron's deposits?

(c) Suppose that the rate earned on these accounts is 8%. In which cities (if any) should Mr. Hannah open collection centers?

6. Ommi Corporation is considering a lockbox system. Its annual credit sales are $61.5 million. A study by the corporation estimates that 31,500 checks are processed, on average, per day and that a regional lockbox system could reduce Ommi's float by three days. Lockbox banks charge $0.025 per check to operate the lockbox system. If the cash freed by the lockbox system could be used to reduce short-term debt on which Ommi pays 10% interest, should the lockbox system be implemented?

7. Your boss, the owner of a sports equipment manufacturing firm, has asked you to see whether you can improve his cash management. You easily determine that the firm makes $32.5 million in credit purchases. You then find out that the owner has always believed in paying his bills as soon as they are received. This practice results in the firm's paying its payables 18 days before they are due. If the firm paid its payables only when due and the available cash released

was invested in marketable securities earning 9%, what would be the net benefit to the firm?

8. The National Record Club (based in New York) has many mail-order customers in California and is losing substantial revenue as a result of the average of seven days between the time the customers deposit their payments and the time the deposits are credited to National's account in a New York bank. Accordingly, Socorro Quintero, the collections manager for National, is trying to find a way to reduce this float time. He has narrowed the solutions to operating a collection center in Los Angeles or opening lockbox accounts in the major California cities. Socorro estimates that a collection center in Los Angeles will require an annual expenditure of $70,000. Lockbox expenditures and the new float times for each city are shown in the following table:

City	Float Time for Los Angeles Collection Center (days)	Lockbox Expense	Float Time for Lockbox (days)	Annual Receipts
Los Angeles	1	$25,500	1	$18 million
San Francisco–Oakland	2	15,000	1	10 million
San Diego	2	18,000	1	12 million
Santa Barbara	2	14,000	1	8 million
Pasadena	3	9,000	1	6 million

Any receipts are placed in a money market fund yielding 10%.

(a) Find the net marginal benefit of opening the Los Angeles collection center.

(b) Find the net marginal benefit of opening each lockbox.

(c) What should Socorro do?

9. Corky Cage is the cash manager for the Claire Group. Claire's cash budget indicates that it will have $32,000 in excess cash for the next 90 days. Corky is considering investing the full sum in one of the following investments. Ignoring taxes, calculate the rate of return for the period for each. Which investment should Corky select?

(a) Common stock selling for $38 per share, paying a $2.70 dividend; Corky expects the stock to appreciate in price by 14% per year.

(b) A 90-day CD paying 8.80% interest compounded quarterly.

(c) A money market mutual fund, yielding 9.2% annually.

(d) Boca Raton municipal revenue bonds, maturing in four years, paying a 10% annual coupon (currently selling at par and expected to do so in the near future).

(e) Ninety-day commercial paper selling at 96.8% of face value.

(f) Preferred stock selling for $48 per share, paying an annual dividend of $5.20 (no price appreciation anticipated).

10. George Morgan is currently comptroller of Ducor, Inc. Ducor has two accounts with its bank: a demand deposit account, the balance of which earns no interest, and a money market fund, the balance of which pays 8% interest. There is a $10 fee for transferring any funds from the money market fund

to the demand deposit account. Ducor's cash disbursements total $1 million annually.

(a) When George makes a transfer from the money market fund to the demand deposit account, what should the amount of the transfer be? How often should he make a transfer?

(b) What should be the amount of the transfer if the transfer fee is raised to $15? How often should George make a transfer?

(c) What should be the amount of the transfer if the transfer fee stays at $10 while the interest rate is raised to 10%? How often should George make a transfer?

(d) What should be the amount of the transfer if the transfer fee is raised to $15 and the interest rate is raised to 10%? How often should George make a transfer?

11. Andrew Senchack, financial manager of the Phoenix Renovation Service, has been keeping the firm's funds in the Sparrow Fund, a money market fund that pays 8% on deposits and has no charge for withdrawals. Andrew has found another fund, the Hawkeye Fund, that pays 10.5% on deposits but has a $20 fee for a withdrawal of any size. Phoenix has annual cash disbursements of $4 million. Andrew is considering establishing an account with Hawkeye, transferring funds to Sparrow only occasionally, and using the Sparrow account to handle daily transactions.

(a) Using a 360-day year, find the daily disbursement of funds.

(b) When Andrew makes a transfer, what should the size of the transfer be?

(c) How often should Andrew make transfers?

(d) If Andrew does not change to the Hawkeye Fund, what will be his average balance in the Sparrow Fund (assuming the $4 million for disbursements is available at the beginning of the year)? What annual interest will this account earn?

(e) If Andrew establishes the Hawkeye account, what will be his average balance in Sparrow? His annual interest from Sparrow?

(f) What will be the average balance in Hawkeye? The annual interest from Hawkeye?

(g) What is the marginal dollar value of establishing the Hawkeye account?

12. Bob Dince, controller of the Carter Farming Group, currently keeps Carter's funds in a demand deposit account yielding 6% compounded annually. Carter's annual disbursements total $360,000. This sum is deposited in the account at the beginning of the year and is used to pay bills as they come due. Bob is considering investing the money in T-bills with an annual yield of 8.5%, selling them as necessary to replenish the demand deposit account. Suppose that it costs $45 to sell any dollar amount of T-bills.

(a) What is the current average balance in the demand deposit account? What is the amount of annual interest that this account earns?

(b) If Bob decides to buy the T-bills, what dollar amount of T-bills should he sell whenever he replenishes the demand deposit account? What are the average balance and annual interest in the demand deposit account?

(c) What is the average balance in the T-bill account? What is the annual interest earned from the T-bills?

(d) Should Bob make this switch? What is the marginal dollar value of this decision?

13. Steve Smith is the credit manager for the southeast branch of the Earnest, Pearce, and Brown Clothing Stores. The stores currently under Steve's responsibility have annual credit sales of $60 million. Operating costs total 90% of sales. The average collection period is 40 days, and bad-debt losses total 2% of sales. The Mueller Credit Corporation has guaranteed that it can reduce the average collection period to 30 days and the bad-debt loss to 0.5% of sales. However, Steve estimates that the changes necessary to implement the Mueller proposal will reduce annual credit sales to $50 million. Any reduction in current assets will allow Steve to lower current liabilities by the same amount. The estimated cost of short-term credit is 10%. Mueller Credit will charge an annual fee of $75,000 for its service. Steve will figure the marginal benefits and costs of hiring Mueller before making a final decision. Assume Mueller is hired.

(a) What will be the marginal savings from the reduced bad-debt loss?

(b) What will be the marginal savings from the reduced investment in accounts receivable?

(c) What will be the marginal expense of lost sales?

(d) What should Steve do?

14. The Sipra Audio & Video Equipment Store is considering a change in its credit policy to stimulate sales. Annual sales are currently $5 million, and 85% of this amount is operating costs. The average collection period is currently 20 days, and the bad-debt losses currently total 1%. Naim Sipra, the store's owner and manager, is considering relaxing the credit standards with one of three plans:

Plan	Sales	Average Collection Period (days)	Bad-Debt Loss
A	$6 million	25	1.5%
B	6.75 million	30	2.2
C	7.25 million	36	3.0

Any money saved from a reduction in accounts receivable will be invested in marketable securities yielding 8%. Find the net marginal cash flow for each of the three plans (compared with the current operations). Which plan should Naim choose?

15. Bobby Wolff, manager of Ace Groceries, has some extra space in one store and is trying to decide between opening a pharmacy or a record and tape department. The relevant data are as follows:

	Pharmacy	Record and Tape Department
Average age of inventory	30 days	90 days
Average collection period	30 days	60 days
Bad-debt loss	1%	2%
Annual sales	$540,000	$450,000
Operating cost as percentage of sales	0.60	0.50

Bobby estimates that any investment in current assets has an opportunity cost of 12%.

(a) What is the average level of inventory for each plan measured in sales dollars? Measured in terms of cost-of-goods-sold dollars?

(b) What is the average level of accounts receivable for each plan?

(c) What is the cost of the required increase in current assets for each plan?

(d) What is the bad-debt expense for each plan?

(e) What is the gross profit (sales − cost of goods sold) for each plan?

(f) Which plan should Bobby choose?

(g) Which plan should Bobby choose if the opportunity cost of investing in current assets is only 6%?

16. Westmark Jewelers plans to liberalize its credit policy by extending its current 30-day credit period to 60 days. The company expects that this will increase its current sales (all credit) of $348,000 by 30%. Unfortunately, however, bad debts are also expected to rise to 5%, up from the current level of 2% of total sales. The company's operating cost of 35% of sales and its credit collection costs of $4,500 are expected to remain the same. The company is in the 30% tax bracket, and it requires all investments to return 10%. Would you advise the company to go ahead with the liberalization plan? Why? Exactly how much richer or poorer will the company be if it relaxes its credit policy?

22A
MANAGING INVENTORY

Why Do Firms Hold Inventories?

Just like accounts receivable, the investment in inventory represents a sizable portion of many firms' total asset investment (see Table 21-1 in Chapter 21).

Ideally, as with cash, firms should maintain zero inventory. In practice, however, this goal is not feasible. Inventories must be held. Irrespective of the item that a company produces, a significant amount of inventory can be tied up in the production process in the form of unfinished goods. Even finished goods that are in the process of shipment are inventory, and these inventories can be significant.

Firms often hold inventory with the expectation of lowering the substantial fixed costs that accrue when ordering and/or producing additional inventories in the event of an unanticipated shortfall. These additional inventory costs can arise for a variety of reasons. *Acquisition costs* are the costs incurred to acquire the item(s) to be held in inventory. Examples of acquisition costs are the purchase price of the inventory, transportation costs, production costs, and the costs of placing purchase orders (management time, telephone calls, paperwork). *Holding costs* are all the costs associated with holding the item in inventory until it is sold. Examples are the costs of storage, security costs, and insurance. *Shortage costs* are the costs incurred when the firm cannot honor a customer's order because the item is out of stock. Shortage costs can be direct (lost revenues, higher production and transportation costs) or indirect (customer dissatisfaction). These costs can be substantial and must be included in any analysis of inventory policy.

Management costs can be high for companies that have on hand hundreds of inventory items. To facilitate inventory handling and control, therefore, many firms use sophisticated computerized inventory management systems. Of course, implementing such a system can itself be costly.

The Role of the Financial Manager in Inventory Decisions

Day-to-day inventory management rarely includes the financial manager. Rather, the financial manager's responsibility is to evaluate the overall investment in inventory. Intuitively, excessive inventories should reduce the risk of production delays or stockouts and hence should increase the firm's value. The additional carrying costs, however, may wipe out any gains. Similarly, inadequate inventories increase risk and may negatively affect the firm's value. But the offsetting benefit of lower carrying costs needs to be considered. Managers must constantly strive to balance these benefits and costs. They should allow inventory to increase as long as reduced costs and risks are more important than the cost of carrying that level of investment.

Although managing inventory appears to fall within the realm of financial management—especially because it requires an investment of costly funds—this is not how it is normally treated in practice. In contrast with other current assets, inventory is considered the direct responsibility of other functional areas, such as purchasing, production, or marketing. In fact, inventory decisions in large firms are often made jointly among the different functional managers, with the financial manager playing a somewhat passive role (if any).

Value Maximization Considerations

One could argue that the financial manager should be more involved because an opportunity cost of funds is tied up in inventory. Therefore the inventory decision should be treated like other asset decisions, with its risks and returns considered in a capital budgeting framework. If this is done, what is the link between inventory decisions and maximizing shareholder wealth?

The link between decisions concerning the optimal level of inventory or inventory policy and value maximization is unclear. Most textbooks focus on models that minimize total costs by determining the optimal inventory level or the optimal time or amount to order. But *optimal* here has no reference to the effect on firm value. Instead of going through these (sometimes elaborate) models, we merely indicate the general role of the financial manager in managing inventories.

The Goal of Inventory Management

Because of the problems of integrating inventory decisions into our standard value maximization framework, we use a modified goal of inventory management in the remainder of this chapter. The goal of **inventory management** is to minimize the total cost of investment in inventory. Because inventory is a reversible investment that continually fluctuates in size, inventory decisions usually concentrate on determining its optimal level. Therefore the incremental benefits of carrying inventory, such as more flexible production scheduling or marketing efforts, must be balanced against the incremental costs (and risks) of holding inventory, such as storage, handling, and reordering costs, as well as obsolescence and spoilage.

When holding very large inventories, a firm loses the opportunity to use the funds in other productive investments. A fundamental question in inventory man-

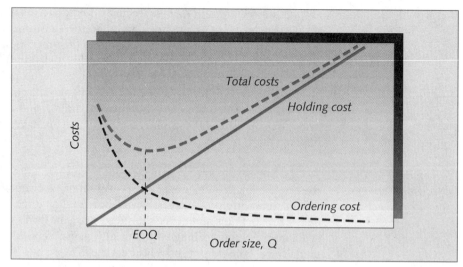

agement is how many units to order at a time. If large amounts of inventory are ordered each time, the dollar amount in inventories rises and the firm's total holding costs increase as well. On the other hand, if it orders too few units, the firm incurs excessive acquisition costs. An optimal order quantity (also called the **economic order quantity,** EOQ) balances the excessive acquisition costs associated with small order quantities and the excessive holding costs that arise with large order quantities. Figure 22A-1 shows how these costs react to the size of the inventory order placed. The total costs of inventory, which are the sum of ordering costs and holding costs, at first decline. Above a certain order size, however, the total costs rise. The economic order quantity (EOQ) is the point at which the total costs are minimized, as shown in Figure 22A-1. To find the EOQ, several models have been developed.

The EOQ *Model*   The EOQ model is a simple model commonly used to find the optimal ordering quantity. The idea underlying this model is fairly simple: First the total cost is expressed in terms of the quantity ordered, and then the quantity that yields the lowest total cost is identified as the EOQ. The EOQ can be determined by either finding the total costs associated with each order quantity or using an EOQ equation: [12]

$$EOQ = \sqrt{\frac{2DC_A}{C_H}} \qquad\qquad (22A\text{-}1)$$

where

D is the total demand per period

C_A is the acquisition cost per order

C_H is the holding cost per unit

We give an example of this method. Johnston Soft Drinks distributes about 150,000 cases of its cola drink to its 100 retail outlets in the Midwest. Johnston

---

[12] Because the derivation of this equation is similar to the derivation of equation (22-8), it is left as an exercise to the interested reader.

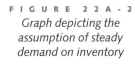

FIGURE 22A-2

Graph depicting the assumption of steady demand on inventory

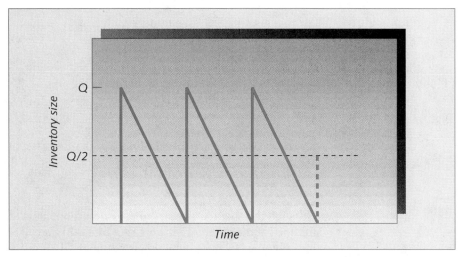

purchases its cola drink from a major bottling company at a cost of $5.25 per case (including transportation). Management has estimated that the cost of warehousing, insurance, theft, taxes, and damage (holding costs) amounts to 20% of the firm's average investment in inventories over the year. It has also calculated that the company incurs an acquisition cost of $30 per order. How many cases should Johnston order each time?

STEP 1: FIND THE FIRM'S AVERAGE INVESTMENT IN INVENTORIES

As can be seen in Figure 22A-2, if Johnston starts with Q cases and depletes the inventory gradually to 0 before reordering, the average inventory over any period is equal to (beginning inventory + ending inventory)/2, or $(Q + 0)/2 = Q/2$.

STEP 2: FIND THE AVERAGE HOLDING COST

Because the average inventory is $Q/2$, the average holding cost is $(Q/2) \times C_H$, where C_H is the holding cost per unit. For Johnston, the average holding cost per unit is 20% of $5.25 = $1.05, and the average cost therefore amounts to $(Q/2) \times$ $1.05 = $0.53Q$.

STEP 3: FIND THE ANNUAL ACQUISITION COST

If D denotes Johnston's annual demand (150,000 cases) and Q is the quantity ordered each time, the number of orders Johnston has to place is D/Q. The annual acquisition costs are therefore $(D/Q) \times C_A$, where C_A is the acquisition cost per order. For Johnston, the annual acquisition cost thus amounts to $(150,000/Q)($30) = $4,500,000/Q$.

STEP 4: CALCULATE THE TOTAL COST

Total cost = average holding cost + annual acquisition cost

$$TC = \$0.53Q + \$4,500,000/Q$$

Table 22A-1 shows the total costs for different values of Q. As can readily be seen, the *EOQ* for Johnston is 2,900 cases of cola. The total costs to Johnston are minimized when it orders 2,900 cases per order.

■

T A B L E   2 2 A - 1

Total Costs for Different Order Quantities

Order Quantity, Q	Holding Cost, $0.53Q	Acquisition Cost, $4,500,000/Q	Total Cost
500	$ 265	$9,000	$9,265
1,000	530	4,500	5,030
1,500	795	3,000	3,795
2,000	1,060	2,250	3,310
2,500	1,325	1,800	3,125
2,900	1,537	1,552	3,089
3,000	1,590	1,500	3,090
3,200	1,696	1,406	3,102

A more precise EOQ number can be obtained directly using equation (22A-1):

$$EOQ = \sqrt{\frac{2 \times 150,000 \times 30}{1.05}} = 2,928$$

Although this method appears to provide a more accurate EOQ, the practical significance of the difference in an EOQ of 2,900 units (see Table 22A-1) and 2,928 units obtained from the equation is negligible. This difference may conveniently be ignored in many instances, especially because the EOQ was calculated under two simplifying assumptions: that demand is distributed uniformly over the year and that there is no uncertainty regarding cost and demand numbers.

Refining the EOQ Model

Several subtleties in the preceding illustration were ignored. For example, a more comprehensive analysis takes into account the lead time—the delay between the order and the receipt of the cases of cola. If it takes an average of three days for an order to be processed and delivered, it is obvious that Johnston should place an order before its inventory levels reach 0. Johnston should place an order three days before the date of the new shipment's receipt. Another consideration that may be factored into an EOQ analysis is the impact of quantity discounts that suppliers sometimes offer for larger orders. With such discounts, Johnston's EOQ may be greater than 2,928 cases if discounts effectively lower the acquisition costs. In addition, safety-stock requirements can further complicate the analysis. Recall that the EOQ model discussed earlier did not explicitly consider the existence of demand uncertainty. Uncertainty can be recognized in an EOQ model by allowing the company reserve to accommodate unexpected increases in demand. Of course, the use of safety stocks increases the firm's average investment in inventories. The procedures used to recognize these additional complexities in EOQ analysis are not examined here.

QUESTIONS

1. Why do firms hold inventories? What are the costs of holding inventory?

2. What is the goal of inventory management? Why does it depart from the goal of maximizing shareholder wealth?

3. Describe the EOQ model. What are the assumptions underlying this method for calculating optimal inventory?

PROBLEMS

1. Tom Buffington, the new inventory manager for NordicDesigns, a paint company, has decided that the company's EOQ is 200 ten-gallon cans per order. He arrived at this number by taking into account the company's ordering cost of $200 per order and its annual holding cost of $4 per can. How many cans

does NordicDesigns sell? How many orders does the company have to place to meet its requirements?

2. Audio Mart, a discount electronics chain based in Tacoma, Washington, sells only one brand of stereo amplifier, which it buys in large quantities from its manufacturer at a total cost (including transportation) of $125 each. Audio Mart sells around 4,000 amplifiers annually. Warehousing, security, and the cost of maintaining a warranty service department make up 20% of the firm's average investment in inventories over the year. In addition, the company incurs a "handling fee" of $800 for every order placed with the manufacturer.

(a) How many amplifiers should Audio Mart buy with each order?

(b) How many such orders should it place during the year?

(c) What is Audio Mart's total "handling fee" expense for the year?

(d) What would Audio Mart's total expense be if it placed orders for 100 amplifiers each time?

SUGGESTED ADDITIONAL READINGS

Batlin, C. A., and Susan Hinko. "Lockbox Management and Value Maximization." *Financial Management*, Winter 1981, pp. 39–44.

Baumol, W. J. "The Transactions Demand for Cash: An Inventory Theoretic Approach." *Quarterly Journal of Economics*, November 1952, pp. 545–556.

Hill, Ned C., and Kenneth D. Riener. "Determining the Cash Discount in the Firm's Credit Policy." *Financial Management*, Spring 1979, pp. 68–73.

Kallberg, J. G., and K. Parkinson. *Current Asset Management*. New York: Wiley-Interscience, 1984.

Kim, Yong H., and Joseph C. Atkins. "Evaluating Investments in Accounts Receivable: A Wealth Maximizing Framework." *Journal of Finance*, May 1978, pp. 403–412.

Mian, Shehzad L., and Clifford W. Smith, Jr. "Accounts Receivable Management Policy: Theory and Evidence." *The Journal of Finance* 47, no. 1 (March 1992): 169–200.

Miller, M. H., and D. Orr. "A Model of the Demand for Money by Firms." *Quarterly Journal of Economics*, August 1966, pp. 413–435.

Mullins, David Wiley, Jr., and Richard B. Homonoff. "Applications of Inventory Cash Management Models." In *Modern Developments in Financial Management*, edited by S. C. Meyers. New York: Praeger, 1976.

Nauss, Robert M., and Robert E. Markland. "Solving Lockbox Location Problems." *Financial Management*, Spring 1979, pp. 21–31.

Pogue, G. A., R. B. Faucett, and R. N. Bussard. "Cash Management: A Systems Approach." *Industrial Management Review*, Winter 1970, pp. 55–76.

Sachdeva, Kanwal S., and Lawrence J. Gitman. "Accounts Receivable Decisions in a Capital Budgeting Framework." *Financial Management*, Winter 1981, pp. 45–49.

Stone, Bernell K. "The Use of Forecasts for Smoothing in Control-Limit Models for Cash Management." *Financial Management*, Spring 1972, pp. 72–84.

Stone, Bernell K., and Ned C. Hill. "The Design of a Cash Concentration System." *Journal of Financial and Quantitative Analysis*, September 1981, pp. 301–322.

Vander Weide, J., and S. F. Maier. *Managing Corporate Liquidity*. New York: Wiley, 1985.

TWENTY-THREE MANAGING CURRENT LIABILITIES

This is Sometimes of great Use: Therefore never keep borrow'd Money an Hour beyond the Time you promis'd, lest a Disappointment Shut up your Friend's Purse forever.

—Benjamin Franklin

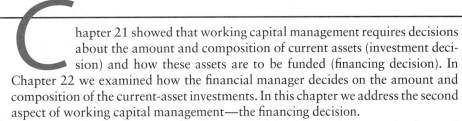

hapter 21 showed that working capital management requires decisions about the amount and composition of current assets (investment decision) and how these assets are to be funded (financing decision). In Chapter 22 we examined how the financial manager decides on the amount and composition of the current-asset investments. In this chapter we address the second aspect of working capital management—the financing decision.

Because current assets can be financed by any number of sources, the financial manager must make two financing determinations: (1) the desired proportions of short- and long-term financing sources and (2) the composition of short-term sources. We address the "desired proportions" decision first. Once this is made, two other issues relating to the composition of short-term sources of credit can be examined: (1) what types of short-term credit to use and (2) what mix of these alternative financing sources is appropriate.

The chapter answers these questions:

- What factors should managers consider when determining the mix of short-term and long-term liabilities?

- What are the characteristics of short-term credit?

- What sources of short-term credit are available to the firm?

<table>
<tr><td>

23-1

GENERAL CONSIDERATIONS IN CURRENT LIABILITY MANAGEMENT

Factors Considered When Determining the Proportions of Short-Term and Long-Term Debt

</td><td>

he first financing decision in working capital management is determining the desired proportions of short- and long-term debt to fund current assets. Associated with this decision is the evaluation of the relative flexibility, costs, and risks of these two sources. This section examines some of the qualitative considerations used in arriving at this decision. Because some considerations are subjective, it is not easy to arrive at a simple formula to enable the manager to make this decision.

FLEXIBILITY

Short-term credit is usually more flexible than long-term credit. For example, a short-term bank loan can be arranged much more quickly than can a long-term loan such as a bond issue. Lenders need more time to make a thorough examination of the firm's financial position before granting long-term credit. Lawyers need to write out, carefully and in detail, the loan agreement and any restrictions that may apply because long-term lenders are making a commitment of funds for, say, 10 to 20 years, and usually more funds are raised through long-term financing than from short-term borrowings. This process is very time consuming. Therefore, if funds are needed quickly, the financial manager should consider short-term sources of funds.

Another consideration is the purpose of the funding. Long-term funds are usually not appropriate if the manager needs only to satisfy seasonal or cyclical re-

</td></tr>
</table>

quirements. Idle (costly) cash may then build up when the need for the funds diminishes. The firm could, of course, pay off the long-term liability early, but as Section 23-2 indicates, this can be costly. Finally, long-term financing arrangements always contain provisions that may reduce management's future flexibility. Short-term credit, in contrast, rarely constrains management to the same degree.

COST

Appendix 14A discussed the term structure of interest rates: the relationship between short-term and long-term rates. As the appendix showed, short-term rates historically have been lower than long-term rates. This relationship means that short-term debt usually costs less than long-term debt does. Firms therefore often choose short-term financing because they pay less interest for it than they do for similar long-term debt.

Long-term debt involves flotation or placement costs that are not normally associated with short-term debt. Also, with long-term debt, even if the firm finds itself in a position in which it no longer needs long-term funds, it still incurs the interest expense. If it decides to repay the debt early (if possible), it may incur additional costs in the form of expensive prepayment penalties. With short-term credit, needless interest costs on idle funds can be avoided by paying off the debt immediately and without penalty.

RISK

Even though short-term credit is more flexible and often less expensive, firms typically view short-term debt as riskier. This perception stems from interest rate and refunding considerations.

FLUCTUATING INTEREST RATES Although short-term interest rates are typically lower than long-term rates, short-term rates tend to fluctuate more over time. This causes the firm's interest expenses and hence its earnings to be subject to more variation (risk) over time with short-term debt. When a firm borrows for the long term, its interest costs are relatively stable because it "locks in" a certain interest rate.[1] This also avoids the chances of higher borrowing costs in the future.

REFUNDING THE DEBT Short-term debt exposes the firm to the risk of not being able to refund (refinance) it. When the debt matures, the firm has the option of paying it off, rolling it over, or arranging new financing. Heavy use of short-term debt can lead to a number of problems. More frequent debt servicing is required. Repaying maturing debt places greater demands on the firm's cash flows. If a firm finds itself facing a labor strike, a recession, or another financial problem, sales and hence cash inflows may be insufficient to fulfill its debt obligations. On the other hand, tight credit conditions in the banking system can restrict the supply of lendable funds. This means that it may be very difficult or impossible to refinance the debt from either the same or a different source. The result is operating and financial difficulties that may lead to insolvency or even bankruptcy. The more frequently debt must be refinanced, therefore, the greater is the risk that the necessary funding will be unavailable.

Short-Term Credit: Types, Sources, and General Characteristics   The importance of short-term financing was indicated in Table 21-2 in Chapter 21, which showed that the typical firm (especially smaller firms and those in the wholesale–retail business) relies extensively on this form of financing to fund its

---

[1] Of course, it may be a high rate that is locked in.

■

TABLE 23-1

Types and Sources of Short-Term Credit

Type of Credit	*Source of Credit (Creditor)*	*Cost*	*Degree of Management Discretion*	*Security Required*
1. Accounts payable	Suppliers	Implicit	Spontaneous	Unsecured[a]
2. Accrued wages	Employees	Zero	Spontaneous	Unsecured
3. Accrued taxes	Governments: federal, state, local	Zero	Spontaneous	Unsecured
4. Deferred income	Customers	Zero	Negotiated	Unsecured
5. Notes payable	Commercial banks and other financial institutions	Explicit	Negotiated	Unsecured or secured
a. Bank loans				
b. Accounts receivable loans				
c. Inventory loans				
6. Commercial paper	Investors	Explicit	Negotiated	Unsecured

[a] Suppliers normally provide unsecured trade credit without a formal arrangement to indicate this indebtedness. Occasionally they require a promissory note to be signed to acknowledge the liability. In this case, this obligation appears as "Notes payable—trade" on the balance sheet.

operations. Short-term credit is obligations expected to be paid off within one year. These obligations appear as current liabilities on a firm's balance sheet, usually as accounts payable, accruals, and notes payable.

As shown in Table 23-1, there are several types and sources of short-term funds. A useful way to distinguish among them is to think in terms of (1) their availability, (2) their cost, (3) the degree of management discretion in utilizing them, and (4) whether or not some form of security is required by the creditor (i.e., secured or unsecured credit).

AVAILABILITY

Certain sources of short-term funds, such as accounts payable, are more readily accessible to firms that have good credit records than other sources are, and hence they are more likely to be available when needed. One source, accruals, is automatically available to all firms, whereas another, deferred income, is available to only those firms whose normal industry practices require customers to make advances or deposits against the future delivery of goods or services. Some sources, such as bank loans, are guaranteed to be available once an agreement has been signed, and the dollar amount can usually be increased or decreased easily, as needed. Receivable and inventory loans normally are viewed as a "source of last resort." They tend to be used by firms with poor credit ratings. Finally, one source, commercial paper, is available only to the largest firms with excellent credit ratings.

COST

Financial managers attempt to minimize the cost of financing, which is usually expressed as an annual interest rate. It is rare for the cost of short-term credit to be 0; usually, such credit involves costs, either implicit or explicit. This means that the financing source that has the lowest interest rate should be chosen. Accruals have no cost associated with them as long as timely payments are made. Accounts payable (trade credit) have an implicit cost if a cash discount is offered but not taken. Even a financing source such as a bank loan, which has an explicit cost in the form of an interest rate, may have additional terms such as discount interest or compensating balances, which cause the effective interest rate to be higher than the stated interest rate. This means that applying decision criteria to minimize the financing cost or annual interest rate is a bit more complex than it appears. Because different methods of stating interest charges and fees are used with short-term financing, it becomes difficult to compare the cost of alternative sources of credit.

This raises two important questions: (1) What is meant by the cost of financing? and (2) How is the annual interest rate determined?

Drawing on the concepts developed in Chapter 4 regarding the determination of interest rates, especially simple (rather than compound) interest rates, we next outline a general procedure that can be used to convert the different terms for various types of short-term credit to comparable annual effective interest rates.

The **annual interest** (effective) **rate** (AIR) is calculated as follows:

$$AIR = \left(1 + \frac{i}{m}\right)^m - 1 \tag{23-1}$$

where

> AIR is the annual compounded (effective) rate of interest
>
> i is the stated annual simple interest rate
>
> m is the number of compounding periods in one year
>
> i/m is the simple interest rate per compounding period

For example, if the annual simple interest rate i is 12% and the interest is compounded semiannually, $m = 2$ and

$$AIR = \left(1 + \frac{0.12}{2}\right)^2 - 1 = 12.36\%$$

Because most short-term credit is outstanding for only a short period of time (usually less than two to three months), the AIR on any short-term source of credit can be approximated as follows:

$$AIR = \frac{\text{interest costs per period (\$)}}{\text{usable loan amount}} \times \frac{360 \text{ days}}{\text{number of days funds borrowed}}$$

$$= \left(\begin{array}{c}\text{effective interest rate} \\ \text{per period}\end{array}\right) \times (\text{number of periods per year}) \tag{23-2}$$

Although this equation appears to be straightforward, the key to its application is carefully defining the interest costs per period and the usable loan amount. For instance, the interest costs on a bank loan may include costs other than explicit interest expenses, such as processing fees or other prepaid costs. Moreover, if this loan is for $1 million, for example, and the bank requires a $200,000 compensating balance, the usable loan amount is only $1,000,000 − $200,000 = $800,000.[2] This "adapted" way of calculating simple interest is used in the remaining sections of this chapter.

DEGREE OF MANAGEMENT DISCRETION

The third factor that distinguishes the sources of short-term credit is the degree of management discretion that can be exercised when using them. Short-term credit sources available to the firm can be described as either spontaneous or ne-

---

[2] Let P be the principal amount borrowed and let U be the usable loan amount. Then the dollar interest cost per period is $(i/m)P$. Equation (23-2) then becomes

$$AIR = \left(\frac{Pi/m}{U}\right)m = \frac{Pi}{U}$$

When all of the principal is usable, $P = U$ and $AIR = i$.

gotiated. **Spontaneous sources,** such as trade credit or accruals, arise in the normal course of business, without any action required by management. These funds become available automatically, simply as business operations are conducted. For example, as a firm expands its sales, it normally obtains more materials from its suppliers. These increased inventory purchases increase accounts payable. The firm's managers do not specifically decide to borrow short-term funds; rather, they do so informally, as a natural effect of their decision to increase sales. Therefore the amount of these funds tends to rise as the volume of business increases and to decline when the volume of business falls off. By contrast, obtaining **negotiated sources**—for example, bank credit, commercial paper, and receivables or inventory loans—requires management effort.

SECURITY REQUIRED

UNSECURED CREDIT Short-term credit may be either unsecured or secured. **Unsecured credit** includes all debt that has as security only the firm's cash-generating ability—for example, trade credit, accruals, unsecured bank loans, and commercial paper. The lender simply places faith in the firm's ability to repay the funds in a timely fashion. If the firm becomes insolvent and is forced to declare bankruptcy, the unsecured lender usually has only a small chance of recovering the amount owed.[3]

SECURED CREDIT **Secured credit** involves pledging, as collateral, specific assets such as accounts receivable, inventory, or fixed assets. If the borrower defaults on the obligation, the secured lender can seize and sell the collateral to fulfill the borrower's obligation. In a sense, then, lenders in a secured debt arrangement have two layers of security: the firm's cash-generating ability and the pledged assets' collateral value.

23-2

SOURCES OF SHORT-TERM CREDIT

Spontaneous Sources of Short-Term Credit

ACCOUNTS PAYABLE (TRADE CREDIT)

AVAILABILITY Trade credit is obtained when a firm purchases goods or services on credit from another firm (supplier).[4] It is analogous to a charge account for a consumer. By accepting cash payment at some future date (i.e., with a time lag) rather than immediately, the supplier assumes the role of a lender. This indebtedness appears as an account payable on the purchaser's balance sheet and as an account receivable on the supplier's balance sheet.

Almost all firms use trade credit as a method of financing. Although the extent of its use varies by industry, trade credit accounts for approximately 40% of the total current liabilities of business corporations. It is used extensively for two reasons. First, it is a continuous source of financing. Although the amount varies with fluctuations in purchases, the firm always has some accounts payable; as some ac-

---

[3] Exceptions include accruals such as accrued wages and taxes. In these cases, if any debts of a bankrupt firm are repaid, employees and the government must be paid what is owed them before any other creditor's claim can be satisfied.

[4] Trade credit is extended in connection with goods purchased for resale, which distinguishes it from related forms of credit. For example, a firm may purchase on credit equipment to be used in its production process rather than to be resold to others. This type of credit normally requires an installment loan contract with periodic payments of interest and principal. This is not trade credit. Similarly, consumer credit is excluded from the definition of trade credit.

counts are paid, new purchases create new payables. On the other hand, bank credit used to meet peak seasonal needs is paid off when these needs have diminished.

A second reason for the extensive use of trade credit is that it is more readily available than are negotiated sources of short-term credit. As purchases of goods and services increase in anticipation of increased production and sales, accounts payable increase automatically.

For example, suppose a firm purchases an average of $3,000 a day on terms of "net 30"; that is, the items must be paid for in 30 days after the invoice date. This means that its suppliers provide $3,000 × 30 days = $90,000 in short-term financing. Now assume that the firm's sales and hence purchases double. In this case, its accounts payable or trade credit also doubles to $180,000, thereby providing additional financing of $90,000.[5]

COST Most trade credit is in the form of an open account in which goods are shipped to the purchaser with only an invoice indicating the amount of indebtedness (i.e., the obligation is not acknowledged in writing).[6] Even though it bears no interest, trade credit on an open account is not formally costless; rather, it is implicit in the terms of credit agreed to by the borrower and suppliers. Let us now consider the effect of two credit terms—the discount policy and the credit period—on the implicit cost of trade credit.

1. *No trade discount offered.* If the credit terms are "net 30," the cost is implicit in the price paid for the goods or services. As shown in Chapter 22, a firm that extends credit to its customers incurs the expense of operating a credit department and financing its accounts receivable. Just as with any other cost of doing business, the buyers of the supplier's products ultimately bear this cost in the form of higher prices. Nothing is free. However, if the firm has the alternative of buying the same goods at a lower price for cash, it can calculate the implicit credit cost and then decide to buy the goods on either cash or credit terms, depending on which alternative is more reasonable. Moreover, if there is no difference between the cash and credit prices, the purchaser bears the credit cost whether or not credit is extended by the supplier.

2. *Trade discount offered.* More commonly, the credit terms provide for a net period with a trade discount. If the supplier allows a discount for prompt payment, an implicit cost is incurred if the discount is not taken.

   As another example, consider a firm that buys its supplies on credit terms of "2/10, *n*/30." For every $100 owed, the firm can "save" $2 if it pays its account within ten days. On the other hand, if the discount is not taken, the firm has another 30 − 10 = 20 days to pay the account in full. This means that the firm receives 20 days in financing, but the cost of this financing is the discount lost. This forgone discount is, in effect, a penalty or interest cost. To illustrate what this implies in terms of an annual interest rate, we modify equation (23-2) in terms of percentages:

---

[5] Another way that this source of financing can increase is if the credit period is extended from 30 to 45 days. Note that by lengthening the credit period, additional financing of $3,000 × (45 − 30) days = $45,000 is generated.

[6] Another form of trade credit is the promissory note, which the purchaser formally signs, indicating the amount due. These notes usually have an explicit interest cost and a specific maturity date. This type of credit is not used very frequently because of the added cost it entails. Usually only firms with a poor credit rating are forced to use this form of trade credit. It appears on the balance sheet as "Notes payable—trade."

$$AIR = \frac{\text{interest costs per period}}{\text{usable loan amount}} \times \frac{360 \text{ days}}{\text{number of days funds borrowed}}$$

$$= \frac{\text{discount (\%)}}{100\% - \text{discount (\%)}} \times \frac{360 \text{ days}}{\text{net period} - \text{discount period}} \qquad (23\text{-}3)$$

$$= \frac{2}{100 - 2} \times \frac{360 \text{ days}}{30 - 10} = 36.73\% \text{ per year}$$

Thus the interest rate being charged on the 20 days' worth of credit is about 37% on an annualized basis.

What if the trade discount was 3% instead of 2%? Using equation (23-3), we find that

$$AIR = \frac{3}{100 - 3} \times \frac{360 \text{ days}}{30 - 10} = 55.67\%$$

Clearly, both trade discount policies are an expensive source of financing. Whenever sufficient cash flow is available or a bank loan can be arranged at a lower interest rate, that is a good reason not to take a trade discount.

3. *Change in the credit period.* It is instructive to stay with the last example and examine what happens if the credit terms are changed by making the credit period "net 60" (i.e., 3/10, *n*60). According to equation (23-3),

$$AIR = \frac{3}{100 - 3} \times \frac{360 \text{ days}}{60 - 10} = 22.27\%$$

Notice that by doubling the net credit period from 30 to 60 days, the annual interest rate is cut by more than half. The reason is that the same interest cost is incurred, but now the firm has 50 days rather than 20 days over which to spread the cost.

To summarize, the cost of trade credit varies (1) directly with the size of the discount and (2) inversely with the length of time between the net credit period and the discount period.

ACCRUALS

AVAILABILITY A second source of spontaneous financing is accruals (accrued expenses), which represent liabilities for services that have been provided to the firm but have not yet been paid for by the firm. The most common expenses accrued are wages and taxes.[7]

Accrued wages are the money that a firm owes its employees. In effect, employees provide part of a firm's short-term financing by waiting two weeks or a month to be paid rather than being paid every day. Although the amount of financing available from this source can be increased by lengthening the pay period, legal and practical considerations limit the extent to which this can be done.

Similarly, the level of financing available from accrued taxes is determined by the amount of the firm's tax liability and the frequency with which these expenses are paid. For example, federal income taxes must be paid quarterly (on January 15, April 15, etc.), but the firm can use accrued taxes as a source of funds between

---

[7]Other expenses also accrue during the normal course of business, such as periodic interest payments on long-term debt, utility bills, and rental or lease payments paid at the end of the period rather than on a prepaid basis. For the average firm, these accrued expenses are relatively small compared with accrued wages and taxes.

these payment dates. The payment of property and sales taxes varies from state to state. For example, corporations that operate in Texas pay property taxes annually and sales taxes monthly.

COST Accruals have no associated explicit or implicit cost. In effect, they are valuable to the firm because they are costless substitutes for otherwise costly short-term credit. This is especially true during periods of tight credit or high interest rates. For example, if bank credit costs 14%, then $5 million in accruals can save the firm $5,000,000 × 0.14 = $700,000 per year in interest expenses. Therefore there is an incentive to accrue as many expenses as possible.

DEFERRED INCOME

AVAILABILITY In some industries, it is accepted practice to require customers to make advance payments or deposits for goods and services that a firm will deliver at a future date. Such payments are common with big-ticket items, such as jet aircraft, or with services. Because these funds increase the firm's liquidity (i.e., cash), they are a source of short-term financing. Such liabilities appear on the balance sheet as "deferred income" (i.e., income to be earned when delivery to the customer is made) or "customers' advances (or deposits)."

COST Like accruals, deferred income usually has no explicit or implicit cost. Occasionally, interest may be paid at an agreed-upon rate. In this case, the liability is considered a negotiated source of financing.

Negotiated Sources of Unsecured Short-Term Credit

UNSECURED BANK CREDIT

AVAILABILITY After trade credit, the next largest source of short-term financing for corporations is commercial bank loans. Yet, whereas nearly all firms use trade credit, not all firms necessarily use bank credit. Short-term unsecured bank loans are typically used to fund seasonal buildups in the firm's investments in accounts receivable and inventories. After these assets generate sufficient cash flow, the bank loans are paid off.

Commercial banks provide short-term business credit in essentially two forms: lines of credit and transaction (single-payment) loans. Both forms require a borrower to sign a promissory note that formally acknowledges the debt's amount and maturity, as well as the interest to be paid.

1. *Line of credit.* A **line of credit** is usually an informal agreement by a bank to lend up to a maximum amount of credit to a firm. It is usually established for a one-year period. Though not legally binding on the bank, a line of credit is almost always honored. For example, on January 2, a financial manager negotiates with the bank to provide up to $5 million in the coming year. On February 1, the manager signs a promissory note for $500,000 for 120 days. This amount is then deposited in the firm's checking account and is referred to as a **takedown** against the total credit line. Before the $500,000 is repaid, the firm may borrow additional amounts at any time as long as the total borrowed does not exceed the $5 million limit.

    A special type of line of credit is a **revolving credit agreement.** Its main distinction is that the bank makes a formal, contractual commitment to provide a maximum amount of funds to the firm. To secure this type of financing, the firm usually pays a commitment fee of 0.25%–0.50% per year on the average unused portion of the commitment. The size of the fee is dictated by credit conditions (availability of funds) and the relative bargaining power of the two parties.

The line of credit and the revolving credit agreement usually require a firm to "clean up" or pay off any loan amount at least once a year, usually for 30 to 45 days. This is done to assure the bank that the loan is for only seasonal needs. These forms of bank credit are renegotiated annually. At that time, the bank reviews the firm's future financing needs, usually by analyzing its cash budget projections, before granting a new credit line.

2. *Transaction (single-payment) loan.* The line of credit and the revolving credit agreement are best suited to firms that have multiple financing requirements that need frequent funding in varying amounts. When a firm needs short-term funds for a specific purpose (e.g., interim financing to develop raw land), a **transaction loan** is usually more appropriate. Unsecured transaction loans are similar to the other two forms of bank credit in terms of cost and maturity.

COST Most bank loans carry an explicit interest rate, which historically has been based on the **prime rate**—a benchmark rate against which other rates are set. The prime rate fluctuates over the life of the loan as interest rates change. Bank loans may also include implicit interest charges such as discount interest, compensating balances, and commitment fees. The effective cost of interest is higher in these cases than the stated interest rate.[8]

1. *Discount interest.* Banks sometimes charge interest on the basis of **discount interest.** In this case, the amount of interest charged is determined in the same way as simple interest is, but interest is deducted from the initial loan amount rather than being paid at the end of the loan. This method increases the effective rate of interest.

For example, assume that a bank has lent a firm $100,000 for 90 days at an annual interest rate of 12%. The interest cost per period is $100,000 \times 0.12 \times 90/360 = \$3,000$, or 3% per 90 days.[9] If the loan is discounted, the annual interest rate is determined from equation (23-2) as follows:

$$AIR = \frac{\text{interest costs per period}}{\text{usable loan amount}} \times \frac{360 \text{ days}}{\text{number of days funds borrowed}}$$

$$= \frac{\text{discount interest paid}}{\text{initial loan amount} - \text{discount interest paid}} \times \frac{360 \text{ days}}{\text{number of days funds borrowed}}$$

$$= \frac{\$3,000}{\$100,000 - \$3,000} \times \frac{360}{90} = 12.37\%$$

The borrower receives $97,000 at the time of the loan but is expected to repay the full $100,000. The borrowing firm is thus charged a rate of interest based on the full face amount of the loan but receives only a portion of that amount for actual use. This means that the effective interest rate is higher—12.37% versus the stated 12% rate.

---

[8] The cost of bank credit tends to vary by the size of the firm, the industry, and the geographical location. For example, the cost to a small firm is typically higher than the cost to a large firm because of the fixed costs of processing a loan. The fixed cost per loan dollar is higher for smaller dollar amounts. The other reason is that the business risk of smaller firms is greater than that of larger firms.

[9] It is common practice in the banking industry to charge interest on the basis of a 360-day calendar year.

2. *Compensating balances.* When providing loans (as well as other services), banks often require firms to maintain a minimum average account balance called a **compensating balance** (refer to Chapter 22 for more discussion). The required amount is usually computed as a percentage of the customer's loan outstanding or as a percentage of the bank's commitment to future loans, as in a line of credit arrangement. A common rate is 20% against outstanding loans or 10% against a future commitment.

We return to our calculation of the *AIR* to see what effect a 20% compensating balance requirement has on the annual interest rate. Because a compensating balance reduces the usable amount, just as the discount interest method does, the usable loan amount is:

$$\text{Usable loan amount} = \text{loan amount} - \text{discount interest} - \text{compensating balance}$$
$$= \$100,000 - \$3,000 - 0.20(\$100,000)$$
$$= \$77,000$$

The *AIR* then becomes

$$AIR = \frac{\text{interest costs per period (\$)}}{\text{usable loan amount}} \times \frac{360 \text{ days}}{\text{number of days funds borrowed}}$$

$$= \frac{\$3,000}{\$77,000} \times \frac{360}{90} = 15.58\%$$

This clearly demonstrates that the stated interest rate of 12% can be misleading if the financial manager is not careful to determine all of a loan's interest charges.

COMMERCIAL PAPER

AVAILABILITY Commercial paper consists of short-term, unsecured promissory notes (IOUs) issued by firms that have a high credit rating. Generally, only the largest firms with the greatest financial strength qualify to issue commercial paper. Maturities can range from a few days up to nine months. Although commercial paper has no set denomination, it is usually issued in minimum amounts of $100,000.

In recent years, commercial paper has become an increasingly important source of short-term credit for many types of firms, such as finance, utility, and bank holding companies. In March 1991 over $150 billion in commercial paper was outstanding. Most commercial paper (more than 75%) is issued by financial institutions and in bearer form; that is, the holder is the owner, and the issuer keeps no record of ownership. It can be issued so that it is payable to a specific investor. Commercial paper can be issued to lenders either directly by the borrower (direct placement) or indirectly through commercial paper dealers (dealer market).

The chief attraction of commercial paper to borrowers is its lower cost relative to bank financing. The interest rate on commercial paper is normally less than the prime rate. Its main disadvantage is the limited access. Even under ideal money market conditions, only the largest firms can sell commercial paper because of its unsecured nature.

COST Commercial paper is occasionally issued as a discount note, but typically it is issued as an interest-bearing security that has a stated coupon rate. At maturity, the amount owed by the borrower is the principal amount of the note plus the accrued interest. The stated interest rate is closely tied to that of other money market instruments, such as T-bills and negotiable CDs. A rule of thumb is that commercial paper is usually 1%–3% below the prime rate. Moreover, it is even less expensive than a bank loan because the costs of preparing financial statements and negotiating with a bank are avoided. On the other hand, the issuer of commercial paper must prepay certain placement fees and flotation costs. These additional expenses increase the implicit cost of commercial paper.

As an example, assume that the Espey Corporation plans to issue $100 million in commercial paper for 182 days at a stated (discounted) interest rate of 14%. If dealers charge $100,000 in placement fees and flotation costs, the annual interest rate can be calculated as follows.

Step 1:

$$\text{Interest cost per period} = \frac{\$100 \text{ million} \times 0.14 \times 182}{360}$$

$$= \$7,077,777$$

Step 2:

$$\begin{aligned}\text{Usable loan amount} &= \text{loan amount} - \text{discount interest} - \text{prepaid expenses} \\ &= \$100,000,000 - \$7,077,777 - \$100,000 \\ &= \$92,822,223\end{aligned}$$

Step 3:

$$AIR = \frac{\text{interest costs per period (\$)}}{\text{usable loan amount}} \times \frac{360 \text{ days}}{\text{number of days funds borrowed}}$$

$$= \frac{\$7,077,777}{\$92,822,223} \times \frac{360}{182} = 15.1$$

Thus the effective cost of this credit source to Espey is 15.1%.

Negotiated Sources of Secured Short-Term Credit

Ideally, both the lender and the borrower want a short-term loan to remain unsecured if the creditworthiness of the borrower can justify it. For the lender, things are kept simple. For the borrower, an unsecured loan does not encumber its assets or restrict its future borrowing flexibility. Nevertheless, in some cases specific assets must be pledged as collateral before a short-term loan is extended. For example, a firm may have reached the limit of its unsecured borrowing capacity. If additional unsecured credit cannot be justified, a bank may seek the pledge of specific assets before granting a larger loan. The two most common assets pledged as collateral are accounts receivable and inventory.

ACCOUNTS RECEIVABLE LOANS

AVAILABILITY A firm's receivables are among its most liquid assets because they can easily be converted to cash. For this reason, lenders consider receivables as prime collateral for a secured loan. Two procedures are used in arranging for short-term financing that is backed by accounts receivable: pledging and factoring.

1. *Pledging receivables.* A **pledging receivable** is the simplest and least costly procedure to administer. The borrower merely provides a given dollar amount of receivables as collateral. If the lender offers a general line on a firm's receivables, all accounts are pledged as security for the loan. Because the lender has no control over the quality of the pledged receivables, the loan amount is a relatively small percentage of the receivables' face value (e.g., less than 50%).

   A general line is the least complicated method of pledging receivables. A more complicated method is to require the borrower to submit invoices for the lender's approval before granting a loan. Only those invoices that receive the lender's approval can be pledged as collateral. Because the lender has some control over the collateral's quality, the loan amount is a large proportion of the receivables' value (e.g., 80%–90%).

2. *Factoring receivables.* A **factoring receivable** is sold to a financial institution called a **factor.** Commercial finance companies and sometimes subsidiaries of commercial banks are the main sources of this type of short-term credit. Though not strictly a secured loan because the receivables are sold rather than pledged as collateral, factoring has a comparable effect on the selling firm's cash flows. Consequently, firms tend to view factoring as an alternative to pledging accounts receivable.

Assume the general manager of Harris Graphics needs to raise $60,000 in short-term borrowing from his accounts receivable. He currently has $120,000 in accounts receivable due in 90 days, and he expects 2% of these accounts receivable to be uncollectible. If he factors $60,000 of these receivables, he will receive $54,000. What interest rate is he paying for this arrangement?

Step 1: The net amount of the accounts receivable factored is:

$$(1 - \text{percentage amount uncollectible})(\text{amount of desired loan}) = (1 - 0.02)(\$60,000)$$
$$= \$58,800$$

Step 2: The dollar amount of interest that Harris pays to the factor is

$$\$58,800 - \$54,000 = \$4,800$$

Step 3: The *AIR* is:

$$AIR = \frac{\text{interest costs per period}}{\text{usable loan amount}} \times \frac{360 \text{ days}}{\text{number of days funds borrowed}}$$

$$= \frac{\$4,800}{\$54,000} \times \frac{360}{90} = 35.56\%$$

The *AIR* for factoring the accounts receivable is 35.56%.

COST Accounts receivable loans generally carry an explicit interest rate that is 2%–5% higher than the bank prime rate. Commercial finance companies may charge an even higher rate. Furthermore, the lender usually charges a handling fee, stated as a percentage of the face value of the receivables processed. This fee is typically about 1%–2% of the face value.

Because factoring involves the outright sale of a firm's receivables to a factor, the factor bears the risk of collection and, for a fee, services the accounts. This fee is stated as a percentage of the receivables' face value and is usually 1%–3%. Offsetting this cost, though, is the fact that the lender provides credit services that eliminate or at least reduce the need for similar services by the borrower.

INVENTORY LOANS

AVAILABILITY Inventory loans are another source of short-term secured credit from financial institutions. In this case, a firm pledges part or all of its inventories as collateral. When accepting inventory as collateral, the lender is concerned with its resale value and the ability of the borrower to control its use because these two factors determine the risk of loss to the lender if the borrower defaults on the loan.

TABLE 23-2
Characteristics of Different Types of Inventory Loans

1. **Floating lien.** The lender has a general claim on all the borrower's inventory. There is no administrative expense because the lender need not monitor specific units of inventory. But it offers little security because the lender does not hold title to the inventory and cannot control its size or disposition by the borrower.

2. **Trust receipt.** The lender's control is increased because (a) the lender retains legal title to the pledged inventory and (b) specific units of the inventory are identified in writing on documents called *trust receipts*.

3. **Warehouse receipt.** The lender has even stronger control because the inventory is placed under the lender's physical as well as legal possession. The inventory being financed is shipped to a terminal or public warehouse that is controlled by the employees of the warehousing company. The inventory is released to the borrower only with the lender's authorization.

The greater the resale value is and the greater the lender's control is, the larger the percentage of the cost of the inventory that the loan can safely represent. Resale value is affected by the inventory's perishability, risk of obsolescence, and marketability. For example, the absence of a ready resale market for a certain type of inventory subjects the lender to a high risk of loss from a forced sale. Therefore such inventory does not have much (if any) loan value.

Control is affected by the type of financing arrangement. The three methods of achieving lender control are floating liens, trust receipts, and warehouse receipts. Table 23-2 describes these methods. They tend to differ principally in the way the lien or title to the inventory is established.

C O S T The cost of securing borrowing by pledging inventories is quite high and varies greatly, depending on the legal and physical means by which the lien is placed, as well as the nature or quality of the inventory collateral. Borrowing against trust or warehouse receipts usually provides the least costly inventory loans. Interest rates tend to be 2%–3% higher than the bank prime rate. Moreover, if warehousing fees are assessed, they tend to be 1%–3% of the value of the inventory stored. Because a floating lien provides relative security, the cost of such loans is rather difficult to specify. An interest rate of 3%–6% above the prime is a reasonable estimate, but it may be lower if the financial integrity of the borrower is judged to be high.

SUMMARY

Section 23-1: General Considerations in Current Liability Management

What factors should managers consider when determining the mix of short-term and long-term liabilities?

■ All firms must use current assets, which must be financed in one of several ways. The manager of a company has to decide on the proportions of long-term and short-term liabilities that will be used to finance these current assets. When making this decision, flexibility, cost, and risk considerations must be taken into account.

What are the characteristics of short-term credit?

■ It is convenient to characterize short-term credit sources by their availability, cost, the degree of management discretion they allow, and the security required.

Section 23-2: Sources of Short-Term Credit

What sources of short-term credit are available to the firm?

■ Trade credit is the largest source of spontaneous credit to a firm. By analyzing the terms of this short-term credit, the financial manager finds the opportunity cost of not taking any discounts. Accrued wages and accrued taxes are spontaneous sources that have no cost. Deferred income is another spontaneous costless source of short-term funds.

■ Bank credit is negotiated unsecured credit, and lines of credit give firms access to this source of short-term funds. It is important to calculate the annual interest rate (*AIR*) of each type of bank loan before deciding on the type of bank credit to be used. If the bank uses discounted interest or requires compensating balances, the cost of the loan is higher.

■ Commercial paper is a promissory note that can be issued by large companies. The implicit cost of commercial paper can be determined by following a four-step procedure.

■ A company can also raise short-term funds from secured credit sources. Accounts receivable loans and inventory loans are the most common forms of secured credit.

■ Regardless of the source of short-term funds, the manager must base his or her decision on the cost of the funds and weigh this against several qualitative factors (e.g., flexibility) before deciding on the composition of the firm's short-term liabilities.

QUESTIONS

1. What are some of the factors that complicate a manager's decision regarding the desired mix of short- and long-term debt?

2. What are some of the factors that make short-term debt riskier than long-term debt?

3. List the various types of credit. For each type of credit, identify (a) the source, (b) the cost, (c) the security required, and (d) the degree to which each is spontaneous.

4. Would you expect to observe a relationship between the returns on secured and unsecured credit? Explain your reasoning.

5. What is the cost of forgoing a trade discount?

6. How is the cost of not taking a discount calculated?

7. Accruals and deferrals should be used to the maximum. Do you agree? Why?

8. How do you calculate the annual interest rate for (a) discounted loans, (b) loans with compensating balances, and (c) commercial paper?

9. Accounts receivable can be a credit source in two different ways. Explain.

PROBLEMS

1. Your credit card has an interest rate of 1.5% per month.

   (a) What is the approximate annual rate (or simple annual rate)?

   (b) What is the effective annual rate (compounded annual rate)?

2. The Dylan Tambourine Company has taken out a 60-day $2,000 note from its bank. The note calls for payment of $2,050 when due.

(a) What is the approximate annual rate (or simple annual rate)?

(b) What is the effective annual rate (compounded annual rate)?

3. On August 1, you purchase some materials on terms of 1/10, *n*/40.

(a) What is the last day on which you can pay and still take a discount?

(b) What is the amount of the discount?

(c) When will payment be due if you do not take the discount?

(d) What is the approximate annual rate of interest that you are paying by failing to take the discount?

4. Your firm, the Washington Appliance Store, has virtually unlimited access to short-term loans from the First National Bank of Commerce at a cost of 16%. Your two major suppliers offer the same prices, but at different terms of payment: the Heed Distributing Company offers terms of 2/10, *n*/30, and Sitzes Wholesaling offers terms of 1.5/10, *n*/60.

(a) What is the cost of forgoing the discount if you buy your appliances through Heed?

(b) What is the cost of forgoing the discount if you buy your appliances through Sitzes?

(c) From which supplier should you purchase, and how should you pay?

5. The Traynm Distributing Company offers a 2% discount on cash purchases and a 1% discount for payment within 20 days. If you take neither discount, payment must be made in 60 days.

(a) What is the cost of forgoing the cash discount and paying in 60 days instead?

(b) What is the cost of forgoing the 20-day discount and paying in 60 days instead?

(c) What is the cost of forgoing the cash discount and paying in 20 days instead?

(d) If the interest rate on short-term notes is 18%, what should you do?

6. The Waller Corporation purchases its raw materials with terms of 1/10, *n*/40. What is the cost of forgoing the discount if it pays on the 15th day? The 20th day?

7. What is the cost of forgoing a cash discount if the terms are 1/10, *n*/20? 2/10, *n*/30?

8. The Martin Mfg. Co. has identified four possible suppliers, each offering different credit terms. The products offered by the suppliers are virtually identical in quality and price.

Supplier	Credit Terms
W	1/10, *n*/30
X	2/20, *n*/70
Y	1/20, *n*/50
Z	3/15, *n*/65

(a) What is the approximate cost of forgoing the cash discount from each supplier?

(b) Martin can now borrow short-term funds from its bank at 15%. If Martin needs short-term funds and each of the suppliers is viewed separately, which, if any, of the suppliers' cash discounts should be forgone? Why?

(c) If the company knows that it must forgo cash discounts because it needs short-term funds and has no alternative source of financing, from which of the four suppliers should it make purchases? Why?

9. Your bank lends you $16,000 for one year at 11% interest on a discounted basis. The bank requires a compensating balance of 15% of the loan's face value over the life of the loan. What is your effective annual interest rate?

10. The Eng Manufacturing Company will need funds this fall to finance an increase in inventory. Kuo Eng anticipates a need of $160,000 for 90 days but wants to have available $250,000 in case more funds are needed. The Mercantile Bank is willing to extend this line of credit provided that Kuo leaves a compensating balance of 20% of the amount actually borrowed. The account that holds the compensating balance earns no interest. The simple interest rate on the loan is 14%. Assume a 360-day year.

(a) If Kuo borrows $160,000, how much of this amount is usable?

(b) How much would Kuo have to borrow to obtain $160,000 of usable funds?

(c) What line of credit must Kuo establish to have available $250,000 in usable funds?

(d) What annual interest rate is Kuo paying if he borrows an amount sufficient to generate $160,000 in usable funds?

11. Hoffman's Bait Shop needs to refinance an increase in working capital in preparation for the fishing season. Owner Rodney Hoffman is seeking a revolving credit agreement with the Groos National Bank. He can establish a $200,000 line of credit with a commitment fee of 1.5% per year on the unused balance. The cost of borrowed funds is 15% per year. Rodney needs to borrow funds for only 90 days. The commitment fee is paid when the loan is taken out. Assume a 360-day year. What is Rodney's effective annual interest rate if he secures the $200,000 line of credit and actually borrows $100,000?

12. Alfred Stone of the Brady Produce Company wishes to secure a $500,000 loan for a 60-day period. Gilbert Bernal of the Pumice National Bank has offered to make the loan as either a regular 15.5%, 60-day note or as a prepaid-interest, 15%, 60-day note. Which should he accept? What if the rate on the prepaid-interest loan is 15.25%?

13. The Milner-Barry Vending Company needs to raise $60 million for a period of 120 days. Irv Davidson, financial manager of Milner-Barry, is choosing between two plans for issuing commercial paper. The first calls for 16% annual interest with a dealer's commission of $150,000. The second calls for 15.2% discounted interest with a dealer's commission of $300,000. Which plan should Irv choose? What if the commission on the 15.2% commercial paper was only $200,000?

14. Don Grefe, financial manager of the Minihan Publishing Company, needs to raise $800,000. Fortunately, Minihan has $1.5 million of receivables due in the next 120 days. Don is considering pledging these receivables and obtaining a 15% loan or factoring $800,000 of the receivables. If he does the latter,

he will receive only $750,000. Based on past experience, Don judges that 1.5% of the receivables will eventually be written off as bad-debt losses. What is the implicit interest rate of factoring the accounts receivable? Should Don factor or pledge the accounts?

15. The Campbell Sporting Goods Store currently pays its employees on the first and the fifteenth of every month and is considering paying wages monthly instead. (Assume that there are 30 days in every month.) Campbell has 340 employees who are paid an average of $2,000 monthly. If Campbell's other sources of short-term credit have a cost of 12%, how much will Campbell save annually by switching to monthly wages?

16. Steve Stern of the Baird Boat Company is about to take out a 15% prepaid-interest loan for $600,000. What is the annual interest rate if the period of the loan is 30 days? 40 days?

17. Anita Ewing's electricity bill is for $120 and is due May 5. There is a 5% discount if the bill is paid by April 5. What is the implicit simple annual interest rate being paid by not taking the discount? The implicit compound annual interest rate?

18. Leonard's Sporting Goods, Inc., wants to receive an advance from its factor on a $140,000 account, due in 60 days. The factor charges a 1.8% factor commission, holds a 10% factor's reserve, and charges 13% annual interest (paid in advance) on advances.

    (a) What is the amount of interest to be paid?

    (b) What amount will Leonard's actually receive?

    (c) What is Leonard's effective interest rate?

SUGGESTED ADDITIONAL READINGS

Hayes, D. A. *Bank Lending Policies, Domestic and International*. Ann Arbor: University of Michigan, Bureau of Business Research, 1971.

Maier, Steven F., and James H. Vander Weide. "A Practical Approach to Short-Run Financial Planning." *Financial Management*, Winter 1978, pp. 10–16.

Mehta, Dileep R. *Working Capital Management*. Englewood Cliffs, NJ: Prentice-Hall, 1974.

Merville, Larry J., and Lee A. Tavis. "Optimal Working Capital Policies: A Chance-Constrained Programming Approach." *Journal of Financial and Quantitative Analysis*, January 1973, pp. 47–60.

Moskowitz, L. A. *Modern Factoring and Commercial Finance*. New York: Crowell, 1977.

Smith, Keith Y. *Guide to Working Capital Management*. New York: McGraw-Hill, 1979.

Yardini, Edward E. "A Portfolio-Balance Model of Corporate Working Capital." *Journal of Finance*, May 1979, pp. 535–552.

PART SEVEN AGENCY CONSIDERATIONS IN FINANCIAL MANAGEMENT

TWENTY-FOUR CONTROLLING AGENCY COSTS

*He who is a hireling,
and not a shepherd,
who is not the owner of
the sheep, beholds the
wolf coming, and leaves
the sheep, and flees,
and the wolf snatches
them, and scatters them.
He flees because he is
a hireling and is not
concerned about the
sheep.*

—John 10:12, 13

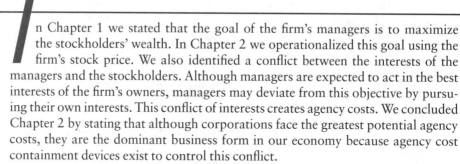

In Chapter 1 we stated that the goal of the firm's managers is to maximize the stockholders' wealth. In Chapter 2 we operationalized this goal using the firm's stock price. We also identified a conflict between the interests of the managers and the stockholders. Although managers are expected to act in the best interests of the firm's owners, managers may deviate from this objective by pursuing their own interests. This conflict of interests creates agency costs. We concluded Chapter 2 by stating that although corporations face the greatest potential agency costs, they are the dominant business form in our economy because agency cost containment devices exist to control this conflict.

In this chapter we examine these devices by answering the following questions:

- How useful is accounting information in controlling agency costs?

- How can compensation contracts reduce agency costs?

- Is the board of directors effective in controlling agency costs?

- What is corporate mismanagement? How can stockholders deal with it?

- How can organizational form affect agency costs?

- What are some other agency cost containment devices?

24-1

CONTROLLING AGENCY COSTS WITH ACCOUNTING INFORMATION

Accounting Information and Contracts

There are two positive roles for accounting information in managing agency costs. The first is in establishing contracts among the various parties in the firm. *Accounting variables* can be used to structure these contractual relationships and thus limit the discretion available to the parties to the contract. The second role of accounting is in establishing a monitoring system to ensure compliance with the contract. *Accounting information,* the realized values of these accounting variables, can show the extent to which there is compliance with the contractual provisions.

ACCOUNTING VARIABLES AS A BASIS FOR CONTRACT DESIGN

When the firm is viewed as a nexus of contracts, there must be implicit and/or explicit specifications that define the contracts. Without such specifications, the contracts are useless. Many contracts stipulate what one party can or cannot do, depending on the outcome of some accounting-based numbers. A wide array of contracts rely on accounting numbers, such as corporate charters, bylaws, management compensation contracts, debt covenants, dividend covenants, tax rules, and pension fund plans. Thus accounting information is at the core of contractual agreements and is often the primary means by which managerial actions can be controlled.

Chapter 2 explained why managerial compensation schemes can be viewed as internal control mechanisms designed to keep agency costs in check. Because many compensation plans, such as bonus plans, are defined in terms of accounting numbers (profits), a firm's accounting procedures and actual performance can affect the firm's managerial incentives. Managers who are rewarded on the basis of earnings performance have an incentive to favor projects that yield high accounting earnings over projects that increase shareholder wealth. Clearly, in this case, the reliance on accounting information leads to suboptimal managerial behavior that lowers the firm's value (the market value of debt plus equity).

If this is the case, then why do managers continue to be rewarded on the basis of accounting numbers? Why don't companies reward managers purely on the basis of market-determined performance measures, such as the firm's value? This is easier said than done. Part of the problem is that, first, much corporate debt is not traded actively, and so it is extremely difficult to evaluate the impact of managerial performance on the firm's value. A firm's value cannot be easily determined. Second, even if a firm's value could be ascertained easily, how would one go about disaggregating performance? Should the increase in market value be attributed just to the firm's CEO or to all or a few of the several division managers? And how would one identify the managers who give a superior performance? These questions are not easily answered. It is not surprising that most corporate bonus plans use accounting measures of performance, and they even develop accounting-based measures for an individual division's performance.

The fundamental issue that must be borne in mind when designing managerial compensation plans is that because reliance on accounting numbers can alter managerial behavior, it can also affect the firm's market value.

When they lend money to a firm, bondholders are aware of the problems caused by the manager's incentive to make decisions in his or her and the stockholders' best interests. Although bondholders cannot fully protect themselves against such decisions, they typically do impose some restrictions on firm behavior that can afford them some measure of protection. Many of these *restrictive covenants* or *indenture restrictions* are specified in terms of book values (accounting numbers).[1] For example, to prevent managers from paying out the firm's assets as dividends to the residual risk bearers, bondholders often impose a dividend covenant. The debt agreement defines an *inventory of payable funds* (IPF) in terms of accounting numbers such as reported earnings, total number of shares outstanding, and the total amount of dividends paid thus far. Without getting into the specifics of IPF formulas, we merely note that these accounting-based rules constrain managers' investment choices.[2] Similar restrictions, couched in terms of book values, influence a firm's ability to incur additional debt, to merge with another firm, to sell its assets, and to maintain working capital. Thus accounting numbers can influence the firm's investment policy and hence its market value.

ACCOUNTING INFORMATION AS A BASIS FOR MONITORING

Setting up contractual arrangements using accounting variables is only the first step in controlling agency problems. The next step requires that the contractors' behavior be monitored. The realized values of the accounting variables in the (explicit or implicit) contract can be used to gauge the extent to which there is contractual compliance. This monitoring role of accounting information can lower agency costs.

[1] The American Bar Association's *Commentaries on Indentures* provides a comprehensive list of such covenants as well as samples of them.

[2] A discussion of typical IPF formulas and their influence on the firm's decisions is contained in A. Kalay, "Stockholder–Bondholder Conflict and Dividend Constraints," *Journal of Financial Economics* 10 (1982): 855–869.

A significant portion of the contracts that define a firm involve its managers and employees. These contracts are often specified in terms of accounting variables, and compliance with them is measured by accounting information. Strategic objectives are set by the board of directors. As these objectives are transmitted down the hierarchy to lower-level managers, they are translated into more and more specific operational directives. A monitoring system must be set up to ensure that these operational directives do, in fact, result in achievement of the firm's goals.

Accounting information can give valuable insights into the firm's actual operations. For example, internal cash budgets can help management get a good idea of how and where expenditures are being incurred, where there is excessive reliance on credit, where there is a need to monitor declining sales, and where there are losses from waste, spillage, or obsolete inventory. Moreover, accounting information is useful for allocating capital within the firm to the different divisions. In many large multidivisional organizations, standard operating procedure requires division heads to submit proposals along with detailed accounting information (budgets, cash flow projections, profit/loss for proposed operation) before any funds are allocated to that division. Accounting data also are used to evaluate the performance of these divisions at the end of the review period. In sum, accounting information gives management a means for monitoring the contractual performance of individuals and divisions in the firm.

Monitoring is required not only inside but also outside the firm. To see how accounting information facilitates monitoring by outside stakeholders, we digress briefly into a discussion of bond ratings. Although this may appear to be relevant to only one class of stakeholder, it serves our purposes by demonstrating that virtually all stakeholders can monitor the firm better with reliable accounting information.

The risk of corporate bonds is routinely ranked by rating agencies such as Moody's and Standard & Poor's, and there is strong evidence that these rating agencies use accounting data in determining bond ratings.[3] It appears reasonable that investors use these ratings to determine bond prices. Wakeman shows that rating change announcements provide no new information to financial markets. Bond prices do not react to rating changes; rather, the rating change merely reflects the market's sentiments about the company. Rating changes thus do not affect, but simply reflect, the market's revised estimation of bond values. The fact that price changes precede rating changes suggests that investors are not the main beneficiaries of rating change announcements.

Then why do rating agencies exist? Who benefits from them? It is the firm's stakeholders—suppliers of raw materials, managers, workers, regulatory authorities, and even the courts—that are the prime beneficiaries. This is best appreciated in the context of our discussion in Chapter 2 about bonding costs. Because bondholders' and other stakeholders' relationships with the company are determined by the company's riskiness, they factor these agency costs into their contractual relationship with the firm. As we saw earlier, if these agency costs can be reduced, the value of the firm (the value of the nexus of contracts) increases. It is for this

[3] Wakeman argues that there are three sets of evidence in this instance. First, the rating agencies have historically given accounting-based explanations (e.g., changes in coverage and book-value leverage ratios) for most rating changes that are not caused by major events such as mergers or new financing. Second, the distribution of rating changes is not uniform across the year; rather, most changes occur in May and June, shortly after the publication of companies' annual reports. Third, empirical studies that attempt to predict rating changes correctly classify 80% of the rating changes in their sample using publicly available accounting data. See L. M. Wakeman, "The Function of Bond Rating Agencies: Theory and Evidence," working paper, University of Rochester, Rochester, New York, 1981.

reason that companies actually pay rating agencies to rate their bonds (i.e., they post a bond). These rating agencies have a comparative advantage in processing large amounts of information, and they issue an independent opinion regarding the firm's risk (they value their reputation and record of reliability) and monitor the firm after issuing it. The cost of doing all this is much lower for these agencies than for individual stakeholders. In sum, the company's bonding cost (payment to the rating agencies) lowers the monitoring costs to the stakeholders, reduces agency costs, and thus increases the firm's value.

Investors also use ratings to check the performance of fund managers and trustees. Trustees of investment funds are often required to sell bonds that have been downgraded, and they are not allowed to invest in bonds that have a low rating. Regulatory agencies that supervise bank behavior also use ratings as a criterion, and most recently, even the courts have been influenced by ratings because they perceive the rating agencies to be "disinterested parties."

The point of this entire discussion is fairly straightforward: Stakeholders as a whole can benefit from the use of accounting information. Accounting numbers can, and often do, affect market values in the contracting view of the firm by influencing agency costs.

The Veracity of Accounting Information

Companies voluntarily supplied accounting information to the public long before they were required to do so by law.[4] The bonding aspect of agency theory, which holds that a firm's stakeholders can benefit from the disclosure of accounting information, explains this phenomenon. Yet these bonding benefits would disappear if there was not sufficient reason to believe these numbers. To facilitate the acceptance of accounting information, rules have been established to provide standardized financial statements. Companies are expected to follow certain generally accepted accounting principles (GAAP) when generating these statements. Rules have also been passed to require an independent verification (audits) of these documents.

There are very clear guidelines on the kind of accounting information that must be presented to tax authorities, to the Securities and Exchange Commission, and the like, which is why auditing and the reputation of the auditing firm are important.

The Political Process and Accounting Data

There is a large and growing body of literature that extends the nexus of contracts view of the firm to include the role of politicians and the political process. According to this view, politicians are assumed to act in their own self-interest, and the political process is seen as a competition for wealth transfers. As Watts and Zimmerman point out, taxes and regulations transfer wealth to individuals via government services (such as education, roads, and parks), subsidies, protective tariffs, and government-created monopolies.[5] Individuals must bear the costs of collecting information on how prospective government actions can affect them. In addition, they must bear the costs of collectively voting and lobbying, and the magnitude of these costs can determine the outcome of the political process. Managers of firms, according to this view, take actions that minimize wealth transfers away

---

[4] General Electric, National Biscuit Company, American Tobacco Company, American Hide and Leather Company, Federated Steel Company, and Continental Tobacco Company voluntarily issued accounting reports as far back as 1899. See D. F. Hawkins, "The Development of Modern Financial Reporting Practices Among American Manufacturing Corporations," *Business History Review,* Autumn 1963, reprinted in *Contemporary Studies in the Evolution of Accounting Thought,* edited by M. Chatfield, pp. 247–279 (Belmont, CA: Dickerson, 1968).

[5] R. L. Watts and J. L. Zimmerman, *Positive Accounting Theory* (Englewood Cliffs, NJ: Prentice-Hall, 1986).

from the firm to the government. To the extent that accounting policies and practices affect these wealth transfers, managers' choices of accounting procedures can affect a firm's value.

Exactly how do accounting numbers affect these wealth transfers, and how do managers' decisions reduce these transfers? It is commonly recognized that politicians rely on earnings numbers to identify a firm that has "obscene" profits and to take a public position that they will address this "crisis" if elected. Little consideration is given to whether this profit is fair, considering the firm's invested capital and risk, or to the rate of return earned by the residual risk bearers. These excessive profits could have resulted from a variety of external factors—say, changes in exchange rates, inflation-induced inventory profits, or simply changes in accounting procedures. If they anticipate that this politician will be elected, managers may therefore find it expedient to change accounting policies to show smaller profits.

That the political process can affect a firm's economic well-being is easily appreciated through an example. The major American oil companies experienced substantial increases in profits because of the actions of the OPEC oil cartel in the late 1970s. The widespread publicity given these profits led to a public outcry that ultimately pressured Congress to pass the "windfall profits tax."

Accounting information can influence political decisions not only through taxes but also through regulatory policies. Many public utility companies are allowed to earn only a specified "fair" rate of return that is often calculated using accounting information. Thus a firm's economic health can depend to a great extent on accounting numbers.

24-2

CONTROLLING AGENCY COSTS WITH COMPENSATION CONTRACTS

Because agency problems arise from the wedge of incentive misalignments between owners and managers, a highly effective approach to minimizing this wedge is through compensation contracts. The idea is to design managerial reward and pay contracts that benefit managers when they pursue a course of action that is in the best interest of the owners. This can, at least to some extent, induce managers to worry about the stockholders' interests because, in doing so, they too benefit. Managerial compensation contracts can be divided into two categories: short term and long term. Another classification of compensation contracts distinguishes among the criteria used in evaluating the managers' rewards, profits, earnings, stock price, dividends, and the like. Depending on the particular agency problems being addressed, different compensation plans are effective. Indeed, there is a long list of alternative arrangements, such as stock options, bonus plans, phantom stock, shared appreciation rights, and letter stock. These arrangements are described later in this chapter.

Here we focus on how compensation contracts can be used to mitigate suboptimal managerial behavior.[6] The fundamental characteristic of compensation contracts is that they tie managerial rewards to some measure of performance. As Table 24-1 shows, depending on the compensation scheme, the relevant measure of performance can be profits, stock price, or dividends.

[6] We take the view here that compensation contracts are designed solely to address certain agency problems. This view may be restrictive, however, because compensation contracts may also be explained by tax considerations. These issues are addressed in detail in M. Miller and M. Scholes, "Executive Compensation, Taxes and Incentives," in *Financial Economics: Essays in Honor of Paul Cootner*, edited by W. F. Sharpe and C. M. Cootner (Englewood Cliffs, NJ: Prentice-Hall, 1982) and in C. W. Smith and R. L. Watts, "Incentive and Tax Effects in Executive Compensation Plans," *Australian Journal of Management* 7(1982): 139–157.

■
TABLE 24-1
Compensation Contracts and Associated Performance Measures

Compensation Contract	Compensation Depends On
Bonus plan Performance plans	Reported profits
Stock options Stock appreciation rights (SARs) Phantom stock Restricted stock (letter stock)	Stock price
Dividend units	Dividends

■
TABLE 24-2
Popularity of Bonus Plans

Industry Category	Percentage of Firms in Industry with Plans (1990 data)	Median CEO Bonus Awards As Percentage of Salary (1989 data)
Diversified services	97%	55%
Manufacturing	95	60
Energy	97	60
Commercial banking	92	40
Insurance	92	49
Communications	100	50
Trade	97	47
Utilities	87	35

SOURCE: The Conference Board, *Top Executive Compensation* (New York: 1990 edition).

Short-Term Compensation Contracts

Compensation contracts for which the managers' performances are evaluated for no more than a year are considered to be short-term contracts.

ANNUAL SALARY CONTRACTS

The annual salary contract is an obvious short-term compensation plan. A manager's salary is adjusted annually according to his or her performance during the previous year. Although this recurring evaluation can control agency problems to some extent, it is not very effective in controlling the **horizon problem,** where a manager's planning horizon does not match that of the firm. A manager who is just one year away from retirement is not much concerned about changes in his future salary and so may continue to make decisions that may benefit him more than would a loss in salary increases. Likewise, a manager who has a fixed salary may avoid risky projects because if the firm becomes bankrupt, she will probably lose her job, whereas if the risky project pays off handsomely, she will share nothing on the "upside." Fixed salaries do little to mitigate the implications of managers' risk aversion.

BONUS PLANS

A common way to overcome at least partially the problem posed by managers' reluctance to make good but risky investments is the use of bonus plans. In 1980, 90% of the 1,000 largest firms in the United States used bonus plans, and the managers for half of these firms received at least 52 cents in bonuses for every dollar of straight salary.[7] The increasing popularity of these plans is evidenced by the statistics summarized in Table 24-2.

Bonus plans award managers cash or stock if they achieve their short-term earnings targets. The targets are typically defined in terms of earnings per share, return on assets, or return on equity. Although the precise wording of bonus plans varies from company to company, most plans have several features in common: They define some measure of earnings (E) and an earnings target (T). If the reported earnings exceed the target T, the contract indicates the bonus percentage (b) of the

[7]See Harland Fox, *Top Executive Bonus Plans* (New York: The Conference Board, 1980).

difference between E and T that can be allocated to a "bonus pool." If $E - T <$ 0, no bonus is payable. Thus the maximum transfer to the bonus pool (B) is given by the formula

$$B = b[\max(E - T, 0)] \qquad (24\text{-}1)$$

Consider the bonus plan for Standard Oil Company of California: "The annual fund from which awards may be made is 2% of the amount by which the company's annual income for the award year exceeds 6% of its annual capital investment for such year." Thus, for Standard Oil, $b = 0.02$. Standard Oil defines annual income (E) as audited net income before expense and interest, and capital investment as the average of the opening and closing values of long-term liabilities plus equity.

The bonus pool is used to award executives. The exact amount of the bonus to be awarded and the actual allocation to the various employees are decided by the compensation committee of the board of directors. Awards are made in cash, stock, stock options, or dividend equivalents. Unallocated funds in the pool can be used for future years, and at the discretion of this committee, awards can be deferred to future bonuses.[8]

A major weakness of bonus plans is that they encourage managers to focus on the short term, and in this way they can distort the firm's investment and financing decisions. For example, managers have an incentive to begin projects that "look good" in the near term. A project for which most of the expenses will be incurred in the future tends to increase profits in the first few years of its implementation. Excellent projects that look unattractive during the first few years but can produce large payoffs in later years thus may not appeal to management. If the bonus plan is calculated in terms of debt or equity, other problems can arise. Managers have an incentive to alter the firm's debt–equity ratio more for personal considerations than for what is best for the firm.

A common way to control the horizon problem is to defer bonuses to the retirement period. This coupled with a forfeiture clause can provide strong incentives for a manager to stay with the company. This practice is particularly common in the publishing industry, which has recently seen a dramatic turnover in personnel. Managers who have "signed on" an author receive handsome bonuses with a successful publication, but they forfeit almost all of their bonuses if they choose to work for another firm before the book is printed.

Long-Term Compensation Contracts

PERFORMANCE PLANS

Performance plans evaluate and reward managers according to company goals based on accounting numbers (e.g., earnings per share and growth in earnings). These plans typically evaluate performance over four or five years. American companies commonly use one of two performance plans: performance units or performance shares. With **performance units,** at the start of the award period, each member of the performance unit plan is awarded a certain number of units, each with a dollar value. They do not have access to the units until they have been "earned out." At the end of the performance period, the manager's "earned out" units are calculated by evaluating the extent to which the company reached its, say, target earnings per share. The last decade has seen an increasing use of perfor-

---

[8] If their bonuses are tied to measures of accounting performance, managers make accounting decisions and adopt accounting policies that are in their best interests. These issues are examined in P. M. Healey, "Effects of Bonus Schemes on Accounting Decisions," *Journal of Accounting and Economics,* April 1985, pp. 85–107.

mance units. **Performance shares** are similar in spirit to performance units, except that managers receive shares of the company's stock instead of units. Thus, unlike performance units that fix the value of a unit, the value of these performance shares changes as the firm's stock price changes. As before, managers have to "earn out" these shares, and the extent to which they are rewarded depends on how close the firm is to its prespecified goals.

EQUITY-BASED COMPENSATION PLANS

In a **stock option plan,** a stock option is awarded to managers that allows them to buy a certain number of the firm's shares within a certain time and at a specified price, known as the *exercise price*.[9] Assume, for example, that a firm's stock is currently priced at $55. If managers are awarded an option to buy 100 shares of the firm's stock at $75 within ten years, this reward will become meaningful only if the stock price exceeds the exercise price of $75. By exercising this option, the manager can pocket the difference between the market price of the share and the exercise price: the profit per share. Thus the risk aversion problem that encourages managers to adopt low-risk projects with limited upside potential is to some extent mitigated. Managers may be more likely to take on good but risky projects. If their projects turn out to be successful, the company's stock price can be expected to rise, and managers can reap the benefits of their decisions by exercising their options.

Stock appreciation rights (**SARs**), which generally go hand in hand with stock options, are becoming increasingly popular among large corporations. Managers awarded a SAR can exercise the option to buy the company's stock or cash in and receive the stock appreciation. Continuing the earlier example of stock options, we assume that a firm's current stock price is $80. Managers can exercise the option by buying 100 shares of the stock at $75 (the exercise price), yielding an immediate profit of $500 ($100 \times $5 per share), or they can trade in the option to the company for a cash payment of $500 (the appreciation). The SAR thus allows managers to get the same benefit as that of the stock options without having to buy 100 shares of the firm's stock. They can receive the $500 appreciation without incurring the transactions costs and the risk associated with buying the 100 shares. From the manager's perspective, the SAR can be a more cost-efficient compensation contract.

To preclude the horizon problem, companies often reward their executives with **restricted stock.** The sale of the stock is restricted until certain conditions are met—for example, until the employee has worked for the company for six years. This gives the company some measure of protection. The chances of its benefiting from its expenditures on personnel are increased.

Restricted stock plans are gaining in popularity. Gulf Oil, for example, uses restricted stock as part of its bonus plan. And in this way, many new high-tech, developmental-stage companies lure managerial and technical talent away from major established companies (the human capital expropriation problem). The new firms offer these managers much higher wages and restricted stock, which in this context is called **letter stock.** A familiar stipulation concerning letter stock is that it can be sold by the owner only when the company's sales reach a certain level. Thus the firm hopes to succeed by keeping managers on board with a combination of a higher salary and the potential future value of the letter stock.

Phantom stock plans are restricted stock plans with one major difference. As the restrictions lapse, the recipient of the phantom stock is given cash equal to the

---

[9] Although they are commonly referred to as *stock options*, this usage is not precise. When a firm issues options, they are called *warrants*.

market value of the firm's shares. In 1979 approximately 15% of manufacturing companies used some form of phantom stock plans in conjunction with bonus plans.

Dividend units may just as well be called phantom dividends. Just as phantom stock plans offer executives phantom stock shares, dividend units give managers dividends, with the number awarded determining the dollar amount paid as **dividend equivalents**. The managers' benefits from this compensation plan increase as the firm raises its dividends. The rationale for using dividend units is that risk-averse managers who have an incentive to retain as much cash as possible within the firm (to lower the firm's default probability) will be more likely to pay out more dividends.

24-3
CORPORATE GOVERNANCE WITH MANAGERS AND DIRECTORS

Because of the possible problems caused by the separation between corporations' owners and managers, corporate structures include a mechanism for monitoring their officers' behavior. This monitoring device, which is the fundamental component of the firm's governance structure, is the board of directors. The directors are elected by the shareholders to supervise the actions of the managers, provide advice, and veto poor management decisions. These issues were introduced in Chapter 2; in this section, we look at some of the factors that can reduce boards' efficacy.

Why the Separation of Management and Control Can Be Ineffective

From the comparisons drawn between board-level and manager-level rights, we can see that board-level rights are those that control the corporation. The term **corporate control** refers to these rights. Thus corporate control is the bundle of rights used to determine the management of corporate resources. Because the value of the company is directly controlled by the usage of the firm's resources, it follows that control has economic value.

Although the separation of management and control can reduce agency problems, its effectiveness depends on the extent to which the directors fulfill their duties. The potential benefits from this separation may evaporate if directors neglect their duties.

Although the directors serve a critical function in the governance of corporations, they have traditionally been characterized as figureheads with little real control over management's actions. The ultimate responsibility for the firm's performance lies with its board of directors, but many boards fail to assume this responsibility or take the actions necessary to ensure the efficient management of the company's resources. In the past, boards of directors have been reluctant to interfere in the firm's routine activities. This realm has been left primarily to the firm's top managers, with the boards more or less rubber-stamping the managers' decisions. As a result, the firm's valuable resources are not used efficiently.

A strong case can be made that more board intervention into corporate affairs is required to improve overall corporate performance. Such views are not confined to the United States. In 1962, Lord Boothby, an important Tory politician, addressing a group of Yorkshire clubwomen, described a director's job thus:

No effort of any kind is called for. You go to a meeting once a month in a car supplied by the company. You look both grave and sage, and on two occasions say "I agree," say "I don't think so" once, and if all goes well, you get

TABLE 24-3
Frequency of Outsider Representation of NYSE Boards

Percentage of Outside Directors	Number of Firms	Percentage of Outside Directors	Number of Firms
0–10%	3	50–60%	58
10–20	13	60–70	58
20–30	20	70–80	48
30–40	57	80–90	12
40–50	98	90–100	0

SOURCE: Adapted from M. S. Weisbach, "Outside Directors and CEO Turnover," *Journal of Financial Economics*, January–March 1988, pp. 431–460.

£500 a year. If you have five of them, it is total heaven, like having a permanent hot bath.[10]

In recent years, this image of the board as a veritable rubber stamp for any and all management suggestions is fading with developments such as board activism and the market for corporate control—issues we examine later in this and the next chapter.

Inside Versus Outside Directors

If the board members elected by the shareholders are also officers or senior managers of the corporation, they are referred to as **inside directors**. If they have no affiliation with the corporation other than their seat on the board, they are called **outside directors**. The proportion of outsiders on the board varies by corporation and can be the source of controversy. Table 24-3 lists the percentages of outsiders on the boards of 377 firms listed on the New York Stock Exchange (NYSE). Outside directors are widely believed to play a more significant role in monitoring and disciplining the managers' behavior than inside directors do.

PROBLEMS WITH INSIDER REPRESENTATION ON THE BOARD

A board's effectiveness is contingent on its independence of the company's management, and this independence is derived from the number of insiders who serve on the board. The first loyalty of the inside directors, who are typically selected from the chief executive officer's (CEO) senior management team, is often—not surprisingly—to the CEO and not to the shareholders. Because their careers are tied to the CEO's, it is difficult for them to be objective when evaluating the CEO's performance. In this regard, Courtney Brown, former dean of Columbia University's Business School and a director of numerous corporations, pointed out that he cannot remember a "single instance in which a subordinate officer has dissented with his CEO in formal meetings."[11] Such conflicts of interest can arise in innumerable situations when a firm is dominated by insiders. The outside directors are forced to rely on these insiders and the CEO for accurate and complete information in order to make decisions that will best serve the stockholders. Because of their superior knowledge of the firm's activities, managers are in a position to distort, screen, or manipulate this information in a way that favors their own interests. Giving them representation on the board only increases their ability to pursue these personal agendas by giving them influence over the structure that is supposed to keep these activities in check.[12]

WHY DO BOARDS HAVE INSIDE DIRECTORS? The potential for abuses by inside directors might suggest that the ideal board should include no inside

---

[10] Quoted in Leo Herzel, R. W. Shepero, and L. Katz, "From the Boardroom," *Harvard Business Review,* January–February 1987, p. 38.

[11] AMA Forum, August 1978.

[12] O. E. Williamson, *The Economic Institutions of Capitalism* (New York: Free Press, 1985).

directors. There are, however, important advantages to having management participate on the board. Such members can improve both the amount and the quality of information given to the board, thereby leading to better decisions and enhanced firm value. Allowing insiders to serve on the board also gives the other directors an opportunity to evaluate them as potential replacements for the CEO and even prepares the insiders themselves for the CEO position.

WHY DO FIRMS HAVE OUTSIDE DIRECTORS? Outside directors are not dependent on the company for their livelihood and are thus free to examine its programs objectively. Because they are not company managers already committed to certain courses of action, they are more likely to propose course changes. Their detachment furthermore enables them to spot long-range problems hidden from insiders who are preoccupied with short-range details. Finally, because of their diversified experience, outsiders usually offer a more comprehensive view of how external considerations will affect the firm's operations.

It has been suggested that outside directors are less reluctant than insiders to fire or discipline inefficient officers with whom they do not have to deal every day. But others believe that outside directors have no reason to alienate the existing managers because they (the outside directors) do not have a significant stake in the firm. This view, however, ignores the fact that these directors sit on the board with good reason. Apart from the obvious intangible and monetary benefits, they are motivated by the market to serve as directors. They want to build reputations as decision experts, and their value in the marketplace is determined by their performance as directors of other organizations. Outside directors thus are indeed motivated to remove incompetent managers because if they fail to do so and the firm's performance wavers, this signals to the marketplace the directors' incompetence as effective decision makers.[13] Furthermore, studies have shown that boards that are dominated by outsiders are significantly more likely than are those dominated by insiders to remove the CEO based on performance assessments. Thus outside directors are considered to play a larger role than insiders do in monitoring managerial behavior.

TECHNIQUES FOR REDUCING THE PROBLEMS CREATED BY INSIDERS ON THE BOARD

Some firms have devised innovative methods for dealing with the conflicts and benefits that arise from insider representation on the board. We describe the three most commonly used ones.

OUTSIDE DIRECTORS' EXCLUSIVE JURISDICTION OVER CERTAIN FUNCTIONS Recognizing that it is difficult, if not impossible, for inside directors to be able to evaluate the CEO's performance impartially and select a successor objectively when required, some corporations simply assign those responsibilities to outside directors. Allegis Corporation, for example, holds a board meeting each March to which only the outside directors are invited. At these meetings, the directors review the CEO's performance and discuss plans for his or her succession. Indeed, they have reported that they feel able to comment more candidly on the CEO's effectiveness when not in the company of his or her subordinates.[14]

[13] E. F. Fama and M. C. Jensen, "Organizational Forms and Investment Decisions," *Journal of Financial Economics* 14 (1985): 101–118.
[14] "A Seat on the Board Is Getting Hotter," *Business Week,* July 3, 1989, pp. 72–73.

COMMITTEES OF EXPERTS AND OUTSIDE PROFESSIONALS THAT EVALUATE INSIDER INPUT Many corporations have special committees to review information provided to the board by management in an effort to reduce the likelihood of the information being distorted and manipulated. Such special committees, consisting of directors who have no financial or other interest in the specific transaction, are increasingly being used when the board must make decisions involving mergers, acquisitions, or hostile takeovers. These transactions are particularly likely to create conflicts between the stockholders' and the managers' interests. Special audit committees, standing committees made up of outside directors and independent audit professionals, are commonly used to review financial information submitted to the board by management.

INCLUDING INSIDERS IN A NONVOTING CAPACITY Another alternative is to include insiders only in a nonvoting capacity. By allowing key managers to sit in on board meetings and give frequent presentations to the board, the board can improve the transmission of information, evaluate the managers for the CEO's position, and train the managers yet still remain independent in regard to the final vote.

Problems Associated with the CEO As Chairman of the Board

Just as having insiders review managers' performance can create conflicts, allowing the corporation's CEO to serve also as the leader of the board can lead to problems. Although it is the board that ultimately evaluates the CEO's performance, because the choice of directors is heavily influenced by the CEO, this monitoring/evaluation function may be compromised. The chairman controls the board's agenda and makes committee assignments. If the chairman is also the CEO, he or she can fill with sympathetic members committees that decide on such issues as compensation, board nominations, and audits. As the chairman of the board of Campbell's Soup noted, "There's an inherent conflict of interest when the CEO, the man who works for the board, is also the chairman of that group. It's a little like working for yourself."[15] Campbell has always separated the duties of chairman and CEO.

With the CEO serving as chairman, the likelihood of management entrenchment increases, when managers garner so much power that they are able to use the firm's assets to pursue their own interests rather than those of the shareholders. For example, if the CEO controls the board, the firm may be able to take on projects that are not in the shareholders' best interests but that benefit the managers' own personal goals. Despite this possibility, combining the positions of CEO and chairman of the board continues to be a common practice, as evidenced by the list in Table 24-4 of the top 20 *Fortune* 100 firms.

[15] J. H. Dobrzynski, "Corporate Boards Taking Charge," *Business Week,* July 3, 1989, p. 71.

■

TABLE 24-4

Positions of CEO and Chairman of the Board at Top 20 Fortune 100 Firms

U.S. Company	Positions of Chairman of the Board and CEO Combined?	U.S. Company	Positions of Chairman of the Board and CEO Combined?
General Motors	Yes	Chevron	No
Exxon	No	Philip Morris	Yes
Ford	Yes	Shell	No
IBM	Yes	Amoco	Yes
Mobil Oil	Yes	United Technologies	Yes
General Electric	Yes	Occidental Petroleum	Yes
Texaco	No	Procter & Gamble	Yes
AT&T	Yes	Atlantic Richfield	Yes
Dupont	Yes	RJR Nabisco	No
Chrysler	Yes	Boeing	Yes

24-4

CORPORATE MISMANAGEMENT

The board serves as the stockholders' first line of defense against corporate mismanagement. But what happens when the board, the bylaws, and the disclosure rules fail to control management's behavior? What are the consequences when the corporate governance structure breaks down, when managers cease to pursue a course of action that maximizes the shareholders' wealth? Any strategy that fails to maximize the shareholders' wealth may be labeled mismanagement. Unfortunately, however, mismanagement is much easier to define than it is to identify because many of the behaviors that constitute mismanagement cannot be observed.

Acts of Commission and Acts of Omission

It is convenient to divide mismanagement into observable and unobservable behaviors. Those behaviors that can be readily observed, which managers plan and/or actively participate in, are "acts of commission," and those behaviors that cannot be observed, or the failure of managers to act at all, are "acts of omission." The most common forms of both categories of mismanagement are listed in Table 24-5.

Precisely because they can be observed, acts of commission are the easiest to identify and thus combat. Acts of omission are more insidious. For instance, it is much more difficult to identify—much less quantify—losses from a forgone opportunity than it is to detect and quantify losses from embezzled corporate funds, although the former may actually have a more deleterious effect on shareholder wealth than the latter does.

Whenever a manager engages in behavior, observable or otherwise, that does not further the interests of the stockholders, it is the board's responsibility to discipline or dismiss him or her. Even board directors may be guilty of mismanaging their corporation. Directors that do not discipline the behavior of an errant manager, for instance, are guilty of an act of omission.

Just such a failure to act is exemplified by the behavior of the directors of Allegheny International. The former CEO of the company, Robert J. Buckley, lavished extravagant perks on himself and members of his management team, burdened the company with debt from excessive acquisitions, and risked corporate funds in highly speculative real estate and energy ventures. Buckley became increasingly erratic, often firing and then rehiring employees for no apparent cause. The board did eventually fire Buckley, but not until August 8, 1986, although one director testified that they had considered removing him as early as January 1985. After Buckley's dismissal, Allegheny declared bankruptcy.

Stockholders' Response to Corporate Mismanagement

If the board loses control to management, engages in mismanagement itself, or fails to deal effectively with inappropriate behavior, the stockholders themselves must take action.

TABLE 24-5
Corporate Mismanagement

Acts of Commission	Acts of Omission
Excessive consumption of perquisites	Failure to pursue projects that increase the stockholders' wealth[b]
Embezzlement[a]	
Manipulation of stock prices[a]	Failure to remain adequately informed[b]
Fraud[a]	Failure to report known acts of mismanagement[b]
Insider trading[a]	
Antitakeover maneuvers that do not ultimately benefit the stockholders[b]	
Negligence, not acting as a fiduciary[b]	

[a] Controlled by the Securities and Exchange Commission and stock exchange governance rules.
[b] Controlled by threat of lawsuits and personal liability.

RELINQUISHING OWNERSHIP

The simplest and certainly the swiftest way for stockholders to react to self-serving managers is to sell their shares in the secondary market. In this way they "vote with their feet." By relinquishing their ownership in the corporation, they are protecting their wealth from being expropriated by the managers while at the same time indicating their dissatisfaction with the managers' performance. For all but the largest block holders of stock, however, selling the stock of an improperly managed firm serves only to protect the selling shareholder from further losses; it does not affect management's behavior. For stockholders to catch the attention of managers who are engaging in mismanagement, the sale of their shares must effectively lower the price of the stock in the marketplace. Thus it is unlikely that small investors with only a few shares to trade will have a significant effect on the stock's price. For small investors, therefore, selling their stock in response to mismanagement is often ineffective in altering management's behavior, and it does not allow them to recover any losses already incurred as a result of managerial self-dealing. Furthermore, although selling stock is an option for small investors, they usually are not aware of the managers' day-to-day activities and therefore are the last to recognize the symptoms of mismanagement.

REMOVING MANAGERS OR DIRECTORS

Rather than voice their displeasure by selling their stock, stockholders can "vote with their hands." That is, they can use their control rights as owners to vote for directors or managers of their choosing and thus replace those who are not performing satisfactorily. The advantage of this recourse is that unlike selling their stock, it gives stockholders an opportunity to recover any losses incurred as a result of mismanagement. Presumably, the new managers and directors will restore the original value of the stock by resuming the pursuit of stockholder wealth maximization rather than their own self-interests.

Again, this option is best exercised by the larger shareholders who control enough shares to oust the offending managers and directors and replace them with their own people. Replacing managers entails a proxy contest, and smaller investors often lack the organization and the resources required to stage and win such a contest. Even if they can do this, it is unlikely that they can win against an entrenched management that can use corporate resources to defend against a proxy fight. The unlikelihood of staging a successful proxy contest explains why the number of proxy contests has dropped since the 1950s. Today, disgruntled stockholders are much more likely to use tender offers, which are more effective and accomplish the same objective—to recover control from the errant managers and directors and give it back to the stockholders.

BOARD ACTIVISM Board members are facing increasing pressure from stockholders, especially institutional investors that often hold large blocks of stock and actively vote their shares at annual meetings. Even small shareholders are prodding directors into action through director liability suits, which are being served more frequently and for escalating damage amounts.

There are numerous recent examples of such board activism. In 1987 Mellon Bank, faced with the first quarterly loss in the bank's 118-year history as a result of bad-loan losses, requested the resignation of CEO J. David Barnes. In 1989 Oak Industries director Roderick M. Hills, who was unsuccessful in his attempts to pass managerial reforms, staged a successful proxy fight to unseat the CEO and four other directors. And in 1989 Tambrands, Inc.'s CEO, Edwin H. Shutt, Jr., was ousted by the board when he was unable to halt slipping market share or bolster stagnant stock performance in his seven years in office.

RELATIONSHIP INVESTING Board activism has taken on new importance in the 1990s in the form of **relationship investing,** a control device based on a special relationship between large investors and a corporation. This relationship allows the large investor access to more detailed information than other investors who have relatively minor stakes in the firm, and it provides the investor with more influence over the direction of the firm.

Relationship investing was prevalent in the early part of this century, when major investors had substantial influence on corporations. For example, J. P. Morgan had substantial ownership in the International Mercantile Marine, a shipping combine that controlled many firms operating in the North Atlantic (including the White Star Line, owner of the *Titanic*). As a large investor, he was assured of detailed information concerning the running of these companies, and he also had a substantial say in how the firms were run. Such substantial influence was thought to be damaging to society as a whole because it could lead to oligopolistic control of industries and abuse of the public good. This distrust of relationship investing, reinforced by the Great Depression, led to government action to reduce the influence of large investors. Corporations were prohibited from giving special information or consideration to any small group of investors. This reduced some of the abuses of the past but also removed a control on managerial actions.

The ability of forces external to the firm, such as hostile takeovers, to discipline managers was reduced in the late 1980s. Regulators felt that some of these takeovers were based on short-term speculative strategies and did not contribute to society. A number of observers also felt that the threat of a hostile and traumatic takeover was an extreme and destructive means of keeping the agency problem in check. More and more observers felt that managers were seeking short-term results at the cost of long-run economic health.

To remedy these concerns, large investors have recently been allowed to meet with each other and with managers. For example, Warren Buffet, chairman of Berkshire Hathaway Inc., is noted for taking a long-run view of his investments. When Salomon Brothers experienced difficulties during the government bond scandal (see the highlight in Chapter 1), Buffet did not sell his shares. Rather, he worked with the firm, not only advising it on actions to take but also actually running it for a short time in order to guide it back to health.

With relationship investing, large investors purchase shares in a corporation with the intention of holding these shares for a number of years. They then develop a more in-depth understanding of how the corporation is functioning and guide managers toward making good long-term plans. If the firm experiences difficulties, the investors do not sell their stock but rather work toward necessary changes to restore the firm to profitability. An example of a major investor who takes a close (and for some managers a too close) interest in its investments is contained in the following highlight.

SUING DIRECTORS OR MANAGERS FOR INADEQUATE PERFORMANCE

Suing the offending managers or directors is an option for any investor, regardless of the number of shares he or she owns. Holding the directors or managers

THE BOSS IS WATCHING

On September 15, 1992, a major U.S. corporation's CEO received a letter from one of its large shareholders. The letter pointed out that the firm had offered its shareholders a −40.1% return over the past five years and that the CEO had received $1.5 million in compensation just a month before "the company took a major charge against 1990 results." The letter also stated that "because of our growing concern regarding the economic performance of this investment, we recently commissioned an outside evaluation of this company, and the conclusions presented do not in any way diminish our alarm. This report describes consistent declines in numerous performance indicators." Concerned with this poor performance, the stockholder wanted a meeting with the board's outside directors to discuss improving the corporation's performance.

The investor was the California Public Employees' Retirement System (Calpers) pension fund, which held 2 million shares in the corporation, Westinghouse Electric Inc. As a result of the meeting Westinghouse Electric:

1. Eliminated several nonperforming subsidiaries

2. Established a new nominating and governance committee composed only of independent directors

3. Rescinded some antitakeover defenses

4. Ended staggered terms for directors

5. Began a confidential voting system within the board

6. Replaced the CEO

Calpers and other relationship investors stress that their objective is to improve the performance of their investments, not to micromanage the firms they have an interest in. However, many executives and analysts believe that institutional investors should concentrate on managing their own assets and not those of the corporations they invest in.

Is relationship investing successful? Several observers feel that the changes in Westinghouse Electric and other targeted firms would have occurred even without intervention by large investors. However, a study by Wilshire Associates examining 27 firms showed that they averaged 9.3% below the S&P 500 Index in the six months prior to being targeted by Calpers, but were 5.7% above the index in the six months after being involved with Calpers.

SOURCE: "How Calpers Can Ruin a CEO's Day," Fortune, February 1993, pp. 34–39.

personally responsible for their actions or inactions as fiduciaries of the stockholders may be just as effective for the individual investor with a single share of stock as it is for the largest institutional investor that holds a major share of the company's equity. Like a proxy fight, however, a court battle is often expensive, with no guarantees for success.

If the stockholders are successful in proving mismanagement, this recourse, like a proxy fight, offers them the opportunity to recover any losses sustained as a result. Director and officer liability laws, which allow stockholders to hold their fiduciaries personally liable for mismanagement, are a recognition of the deficiencies of the other options. Indeed, the recent explosion in the number of director and officer liability suits brought by frustrated stockholders attest to its rise as the option of choice when mismanagement is suspected. But personal liability is very difficult to prove.

ORGANIZATIONAL FORM AS AN AGENCY COST CONTROL DEVICE

The Chapter 2 analysis of agency theory focused on the standard corporation. However, the other forms of business organizations introduced in Chapter 1 can also be distinguished by the extent to which ownership and control are separated and by the restrictions placed on the residual claims.[16] This perspective is useful in explaining the existence of other types of business arrangements. It helps us see why restrictions on residual claims affect incentive problems in specific types of business transactions. Finally, we look at a special type of organizational form, the franchise, to see why this arrangement is popular in certain business transactions.

Organizational Forms As Alternative Restrictions on Residual Claims

PROPRIETORSHIPS

We defined the fundamental characteristics of proprietorships in Chapter 1. In this arrangement, the holder of the residual claims is the decision maker, and so there is no separation between the owner and the manager and no agency problems arising from the owner–manager conflict.

CLOSED CORPORATIONS

Many partnerships are classified as closed corporations—organizations that involve a few partners but assume the legal status of a corporation. The investment firm Goldman Sachs, the accounting firm Ernst & Young, and the national law firm Baker and Botts are examples. For these closed partnerships, residual claims are restricted to the major internal decision makers. Agency problems among the partners may exist, but they are minimized because all the partners are affected by the agency problems. Moreover, the partners monitor one another carefully and keep agency costs down.

MUTUALS

Mutuals are organizations such as Farmers Bureau International (a producers' cooperative) and the hundreds of mutual funds (e.g., Fidelity Magellan fund, Windsor fund) that make various investments on behalf of their owner-customers. As another example, the customers (policyholders) of many mutual insurance companies are also their owners. In this form of organization, residual claims are restricted to those customers who can redeem or withdraw from the organization at any time and receive the market value of their investment. For example, investors in a stock mutual fund can withdraw their investment at any time and thereby deprive management of control over some assets (investment). This ability of the risk bearers in the mutual form of business to terminate their owner-manager relationship with the firm at low cost is a cost-effective way of keeping the agency problem in check.

NONPROFITS

Examples of nonprofit organizations are the American Cancer Society, CARE, and Mothers Against Drunk Driving (MADD). In contrast with the other organizational forms, these institutions have no residual claims, and so the ownership–management separation issue is irrelevant.

[16] These arguments were first advanced in E. F. Fama and M. C. Jensen, "Organizational Forms and Investment Decisions," *Journal of Financial Economics* 14 (1985): 101–118; and in their other writings (see the readings at the end of this chapter).

OPEN CORPORATIONS

Open corporations are the large corporations such as General Electric, Teledyne, Toys 'R' Us, and Xerox, firms in which anyone can hold a residual claim. The ownership claims are entirely unrestricted.[17] Ownership and management of the firm are separate, as we have seen. Agency problems can be severe in this organizational form.

It is beyond the intended scope of this chapter to analyze in detail the various organizational forms from an agency cost perspective. Note, however, that the best organizational structure for a particular activity is dictated by the nature of the business, the characteristics of the firm's assets, the extent to which monitoring is cost effective, and the extent to which explicit control mechanisms and restrictions on residual risk bearers can be imposed. Thus an organizational form that is "best" for one business may not be suitable for another. A case-by-case analysis of the specific circumstances surrounding the business is necessary. This interdependence among these various factors not only determines the firm's organizational form but also explains the contractual relationship in specific transactions.

The Franchising Arrangement[18]

In some businesses, monitoring costs are low, and it may be easy to hold agency problems in check through monitoring, but in others, in which monitoring is difficult, the residual claims might be restricted. Of course, one method need not exclude the other. The franchising business arrangement is an interesting hybrid that incorporates both types of agency cost containment devices.

To illustrate how specific contractual arrangements respond to specific agency problems, we now examine the case of franchising from the agency perspective. The popular franchising arrangement is a special set of restrictions on residual claims.

WHAT IS A FRANCHISE ARRANGEMENT?

Franchising is generally associated with companies that own valuable brand names (McDonald's, Kentucky Fried Chicken, Chemlawn, Petland). A franchise ensures customers of uniform product quality. The **franchiser** who owns the brand name (say, McDonald's Corporation) enters into a business arrangement with the **franchisee** (say, the neighborhood McDonald's outlet). The franchisee purchases the residual claim (equity) for his unit, but his discretionary decision making (e.g., menu selection, decor, advertising) is severely restricted by the franchise agreement. Moreover, the franchiser monitors the unit for product quality and can terminate the franchise if its quality is not up to specifications. The franchiser receives a fixed percentage (typically 5%–10%) of sales revenues as a fee.

WHY FRANCHISE?

Why can't McDonald's own and run all its local outlets itself? Why does it franchise? What are the advantages and the disadvantages to the franchiser? Let us consider these issues, focusing on agency problems from the franchiser's perspective.

It would be extremely difficult and expensive for McDonald's to operate directly the thousands of its outlets. Considering the outlets' wide geographical dispersion,

---

[17] Open corporations must be distinguished from public corporations (e.g., Tennesse Valley Authority), which are quasi-governmental units, and closed corporations, which are privately held corporations.

[18] See J. A. Brickley and F. H. Dark, "The Choice of Organizational Form: The Case of Franchising," *Journal of Financial Economics* 18 (1987): 401–420.

administrative costs would be high, and instituting monitoring systems to control employees' behavior would be expensive. The managers of these units would be susceptible to shirking and excessive perk consumption. Although McDonald's cannot force managers to maintain its brand reputation, excessive perk consumption can be eliminated by selling units outright to the managers.

On the other hand, allowing local businesspersons to buy an outlet outright can cause serious agency problems. Consider an outlet on a remote highway. What if the owner lowers the quality of the food, confident that the McDonald's brand name alone will lure passing motorists, who are nonrepeat customers anyway? Why should she worry about maintaining the value of the trademark? As long as the other McDonald's units strive to keep up the quality, she can take a "free ride" on the reputation of the brand name.

Franchising holds perk consumption and shirking to a minimum and at the same time ensures that the outlet will not tarnish the reputation of the brand name. Because the franchisee is the residual owner, she suffers the consequences of inefficiencies and shirking. Through quality control inspections by the franchiser and stipulated advertising and promotional campaigns, the reputation of the product's quality is held intact. The franchisee has yet another major incentive to avoid the termination of the agreement. Suppose that she has invested in building the local outlet. Because the assets (building, equipment, golden arches) are specific to the franchise, the market value of these assets will be much lower for alternative uses. So if the franchise is terminated, these assets may have to be sold at a fraction of the original investment. Thus the franchise arrangement may be the most cost-effective way for McDonald's to contain agency problems.

24-6
OTHER AGENCY COST CONTROL DEVICES

Internal Monitoring Within the Firm

Competition and monitoring between managers can reduce agency problems, and in most companies there is a clear chain of command. Employees are accountable to their immediate supervisors, who in turn report to their managers. Lower-level managers are made aware of who their bosses are, and subordinate–superior roles are generally obvious. Vice-presidents typically oversee the performance of managers, and the president reports to the board of directors. Employees at lower levels may initiate certain actions, but they must go to higher-level managers for their approval and ratification. Even after an individual is authorized to proceed with a particular course of action, he or she can expect to be monitored by one or more persons at a higher level in the management hierarchy. Lower-level managerial actions are thus controlled by higher authorities in the firm. This monitoring feature implied by the hierarchical organizational structure has the effect of lowering agency costs within the firm.

The Market for Corporate Control

Recent years have witnessed the development of a "market" in which groups or individuals from both inside and outside the firm bid for the control of desired target corporations. Through this process, the control of poorly managed firms is transferred to managers who can more efficiently allocate the firms' resources. Thus a board's rights bundles are valuable to groups or individual persons interested in taking over a company. This market, called the **market for corporate control,** also known as the **takeover market,** is an active market in which the control rights of public corporations are traded.[19]

---

[19] A *takeover* is simply an action that results in the transfer of corporate control from one group or individual to another. Takeovers can be supported by the target management, in which case they are referred to as *friendly,* or they can be opposed by the target management, in which case they are called *hostile.* Friendly and hostile takeovers are discussed further in Chapter 25.

The market for corporate control (discussed in greater detail in the next chapter) can be viewed as an arena in which competing management teams vie for the rights bundles that enable them to manage the corporate resources of desired target firms. The existence of an active, observable "market" for corporate control confirms the conclusion that the control of a corporation itself has a value that is not represented in a firm's stock price. The value of a firm's control rights bundle is often reflected in the amount that acquiring firms offer target firms that is over and above the market value of their stock. This value is an important element of the corporate control market and a key to understanding the complex inner workings of the takeover game.

The management teams that compete in the market for corporate control can assume any of several forms. For example, in small takeovers, management teams are often composed of either a sole proprietor with staff or a partnership of managers. In contrast, management teams in large takeovers are frequently organized in a corporate form, consisting of a board of directors and top-level managers.

These competing management teams engage in takeovers in an attempt to capture the gains they expect from the various corporate synergies generated by a combination of two or more firms. These synergistic effects can arise from any combination of operating economies, financial economies, differential managerial efficiencies, increased market power, or technological advances that result from the takeover, but in any event, the threat of a takeover that can destroy their jobs and perhaps their careers puts considerable pressure on board members and managers alike to put the company's interests before their own immediate objectives and thus minimize the agency costs.

The Managerial Labor Market

The market for professional managers can restrain them and thus hold agency problems in check. Managers are not permanently affiliated with a particular company and, in their quest for upward mobility, may visit the **managerial labor market,** an informal market in which managerial labor is traded. Many professional firms that are in this business match a company's managerial requirements with prospective managers. These "headhunters" and potential employers rely heavily on managers' historical performance records, professional reputations, and colleagues' perceptions of them in making their decisions. The future prospects of managers with reputations (good or bad) are affected by outside perceptions of them. A manager who is known as an excessive spender, for example, can expect others to recognize this and thereby lower the demand for his services. Thus, the managerial labor market can theoretically make a manager "pay" for self-serving behavior.

Many people argue, however, that the labor market is not a very effective device for disciplining managers because it is difficult to pinpoint the effects of a manager's self-serving behavior and the performance of the firm as a whole. If a manager leaves a failing firm, how should this be interpreted? Is the firm failing because of managerial incompetence, or is the manager quitting because the firm's business has dried up?

Governance to Protect Stakeholders' Interests

Although the stockholders are the owners of the corporation, they are not the only ones who have a stake in the board's success or failure. These "stakeholders," to use the terminology of Chapter 2, include bondholders, employees, major buyers and suppliers, and even the communities in which the corporation operates. All can be adversely affected when managers engage in self-serving behavior.

For example, suppose that a board of directors ratifies a decision by the managers to shut down an ailing production facility. Closing such a facility may be a wise move for the stockholders because it eliminates an unprofitable operation, but what about the employees who staff the plant or the community in which those employees live and shop? From their point of view, the decision is not a good one. Recognition of the need for recourses for other stakeholders in the face of corporate mismanagement has been heightened by recent industrial accidents and their devastating effects on the population and environment. Clearly, the residents of Bhopal, India, and of Prince William Sound, Alaska, had a stake in the operations of Union Carbide and Exxon in their respective communities.

The stakeholders' interests are protected by various state and federal laws, regulatory agencies such as the Federal Trade Commission, the federal government's antitrust enforcement division, the Better Business Bureaus in local communities, consumer advocacy groups, offices of the state attorney general, the Department of Labor, and so on. The various checks and balances that govern the myriad aspects of corporate behavior are clearly beyond the scope of this chapter (and this text), and so we do not pursue them. But we look at a few governance structures: state laws that have broadened directors' considerations and the information disclosure requirements and rules of the Securities Exchange Commission and the stock exchanges.

STAKEHOLDERS' RESPONSES TO OPERATIONAL MANAGEMENT

Sympathy for other stakeholders' interests is on the rise in political and legislative circles. Many of the new director liability laws include expanded constituency provisions that permit directors to consider the interests of other stakeholders when making decisions. Although these new laws allow stockholders to limit directors' liability to stockholders' suits, they do not permit stockholders to limit directors' liability to third-party suits. A director who is under the protection of a liability limitation statute is still liable for faulty products produced by the firm that cause injury to consumers.

Other recourses from mismanagement regarding general firm operations are remedies available under state laws and through the governance of the corporation itself (i.e., employee grievance committees) or through pressure applied by organized special-interest groups in the form of consumer boycotts and other measures.

NONSTOCKHOLDER CONSTITUENCY STATUTES

Following the adoption by some companies of nonstockholder constituency statutes (Control Data is considered to be the first), 14 states expanded the criteria that directors may consider when making decisions on behalf of their corporations.[20] In all of these states (except Missouri), directors can consider nonstockholder constituencies when making decisions.[21] The Minnesota statute, which was passed in June 1987, is typical:

> *In discharging the duties of the position of director, a director may, in considering the best interests of the corporation, consider the interests of the corporation's employees, customers, suppliers, and creditors, the economy of the state and nation, community and societal considerations, and the long-term as well as the short-term interests of the corporation and its shareholders including the possibility that these interests may be best served by the continued independence of the corporation.*[22]

---

[20] These states are Arizona, Idaho, Illinois, Indiana, Kentucky, Maine, Minnesota, Missouri, Nebraska, New Mexico, New York, Ohio, Pennsylvania, and Wisconsin.

[21] Missouri allows this only in acquisition decisions.

[22] Minnesota Stat. 302A251(5) (Supp. 1988). Quoted in J. J. Hanks, Jr., "Evaluating Recent State

This and similar laws that purport to take into account stakeholder interests may actually be adding little. First, the laws say only that managers may, but are not required to, take into account these additional factors. This adds nothing to the existing laws because managers can consider anything they want to when making a decision. Second, these additional considerations appear to be relevant only to the extent that they serve the corporation and its existing shareholders.

Legal Responses
to Financial
Mismanagement

Mismanagement involving the securities markets (fraud, manipulation, insider trading, etc.) may be addressed by additional methods of recourse through regulatory bodies such as the Securities and Exchange Commission (SEC) and the organized security exchange markets such as the New York Stock Exchange (NYSE). Disclosure requirements and restrictions on insiders' short-term profit taking prevent managers and directors from profiting at the expense of stakeholders and the investment community at large. Disclosure requirements and trading restrictions also attempt to prevent managers and officers from distorting, delaying, or screening information pertinent to investment or employment decisions.

SECURITIES AND EXCHANGE COMMISSION

The Securities Act of 1933, sometimes called the "truth in securities law," requires the issuers of securities to disclose material financial information of publicly offered stock and bond issues. The 1933 act had two main purposes: first, to give investors meaningful information to enable them to make informed investment decisions, and second, to prohibit fraud in the sale of securities. The SEC was actually established by a 1934 act whose major requirements are the registration of securities traded on exchanges, certain periodic reporting, and standards for transactions among managers, board members, and insiders.

The SEC disclosure system requires certain periodic reports from registered corporations (Forms 10-K, 10-Q, and 8-K) and certain reports registering new issues offered (Forms S-1, S-7, S-14, and S-16). In addition, the SEC requires detailed reports from investment managers and advisers and from brokers and dealers.

The 1933 and 1934 acts were passed in order to prevent conflicts of interest that arise from insiders' knowledge of firm operations. Trading on knowledge that is not available to the public has the effect of expropriating wealth from other less well-informed stockholders, potential investors, or other stakeholders.

MANAGERIAL FRAUD AND THE SEC: THE CASE OF TEXAS GULF SULPHUR COMPANY The best way to ensure that a company serves its stakeholder constituency is to see that valuable information is readily and freely available. To appreciate this, consider the following well-known example.

In November 1963, Texas Gulf Sulphur Company drilled a hole near Timmins, Ontario, that appeared to yield a core with an exceedingly high mineral content. Texas Gulf Sulphur, however, did not own the land on which the discovery was made. Realizing the implications, the company camouflaged the drill site and mounted an extensive land acquisition program in the area. But rumors of a staking rush spread, and the report of an extraordinary mineral discovery made its way into the papers on April 12, 1964.

The following day, Texas Gulf Sulphur issued a press release that played down the significance of the find and indicated that it was too early to tell whether

---

Legislation on Director and Officer Liability Limitation and Indemnification," *The Business Lawyer,* August 1988, p. 1227.

the strike was substantial. Before this press release, however, the executive vice-president and numerous employees of the company had purchased large amounts of corporate stock and options. The SEC and the courts ruled that the information in the press release was misleading and deceptive. Following that decision, numerous civil suits for damages were brought against the company by Texas Gulf Sulphur investors who had sold their stock as a result of the deceptively gloomy press release.

It was argued that this deceptive move effectively expropriated wealth from (1) the landowners who sold the land without full knowledge of its value,[23] (2) potential investors who decided not to invest because of the false press release, (3) current investors who sold their stock because of the release, and (4) stockholders who did not sell. Those investors who did not sell were not able to recover the full value of the mineral discovery because they were forced to give up portions of what should have been theirs in the form of damages awarded to third parties who brought successful civil suits against the company.

Although the Texas Gulf Sulphur fraud affected those securities currently outstanding, similar deceptive moves can also be used to manipulate the price of new security offerings. The SEC therefore attempts to prevent fraud in new security issues by requiring a separate registration for each new offering by a corporation. The registration statement requires the submission of all material information that can reasonably be assumed by the "average prudent investor" to have a bearing on the decision to invest in the security. These statements often contain certifications from accountants, engineers, or appraisers that attest to the legitimacy of this information. When these professionals sign their names to the statement, they, as well as the officers and directors involved, can be held liable for engaging in fraud.

Both this liability and the market for professional services help constrain accountants and other professionals from certifying false, misleading, or incomplete statements. In turn, this certification increases the value of the security offering by reducing the risk of fraud and thus effectively bonding the officers and directors of the issuing corporation against the agency costs implied by their superior access to information. Recently there have been many successful lawsuits against accounting firms for not adequately meeting their professional duties.

THE SECURITIES ACT OF 1934 AND MANAGER LIABILITY Section 9 of the Securities Act of 1934 pertains to antimanipulation provisions because it prohibits transactions that may create a false or misleading impression of active trading in a security. This section of the act is intended to discourage manipulative trades such as wash sales (transactions that involve no real change in ownership) and matched orders (orders for the purchase or sale of a security knowing that similar orders will be placed by the same or different persons) from influencing market perceptions.

Easier access to information enables managers and other insiders to pursue personal profits not available to those without similar access. Rule 10b-5 of the Securities Exchange Act of 1934 seeks to prevent a broad array of mismanagement activities made possible by this access. It prohibits the issuance of shares to

---

[23] A fundamental question is whether a manager is obligated to tell the potential seller of an asset that he or she (the seller) is not getting the best price. If the manager is trying to minimize the cost of operations, it simply makes no sense to suggest that he or she should alert potential sellers to the possibility that they could have charged more. Nevertheless, many government and regulatory agencies evaluate these issues not just from the stockholders' but also from the broader stakeholders' perspective.

perpetuate control, unduly low payments to stockholders in connection with a merger, the purchase of shares from insiders for too high a price, the issuance of shares to insiders for too low a price, and the sale of control under circumstances detrimental to the corporation's future prospects.

Rule 10b-5 also prohibits insider trading based on material, private information. According to this rule, insiders are required to refrain from trading or encouraging others to trade for a "reasonable waiting period" once the information is made public. As a further measure against profiting from inside information by directors and officers, Section 16b of the act offers means for recovering such ill-gained profits. Any owner of more than 10% of a registered equity security must surrender to the issuing corporation all profits realized on either the sale and purchase or the purchase and sale of the security when both transactions occur within six months. This prevents insiders and major stockholders who have a potential advantage over smaller equityholders from profiting from short-swing profits and helps damper volatility in the stock price from such trades.

Proxy statements are covered by Section 14a, which makes it unlawful for any person to solicit or to permit the use of his or her name to solicit any proxy that is inconsistent with the SEC's rules. This rule is intended to encourage stockholders' free exercise of their voting rights. In addition, the proxies cannot contain any misleading information. Tender offers are covered by Section 14e, which requires any individual or institution that engages in private placements and tenders to disclose any large stock acquisitions.

In response to recent insider trading scandals involving billions of dollars in profit to the offending insiders, the Insider Trading Sanctions Act of 1984 was passed to increase the penalties that the SEC can impose, to a level commensurate with the huge profits being generated. This act allows the SEC to bring a federal suit against the insider and also allows the court to assess penalties as high as triple the profits gained or the loss avoided by the guilty party. The act also increases the criminal penalty from $10,000 to $100,000.

CORPORATE RESTRICTIONS IMPOSED BY THE NYSE

In addition to the various reporting requirements imposed by the SEC, stock exchanges such as the American and New York have their own reporting requirements. We concentrate here on the New York Stock Exchange (NYSE).

Corporations listed on the NYSE are required to release to the public any new or other information that might be reasonably expected to materially affect the market price of its securities. Moreover, they are required to disclose this information quickly and to all parties, public and private. If a firm fails to meet this disclosure requirement, the NYSE interprets this to be a breach of the listing agreement with the exchange. To summarize, the NYSE expects the company to release all information as soon as possible except in circumstances in which the information can disorient the market. In these extreme instances, the NYSE can temporarily halt trading of that stock.

The NYSE monitors the activities of all firms listed on it. A separate division, the Division of Regulation and Surveillance, attempts to identify any unusual activity in the volume or price of a company's shares. In extreme cases, the exchange can demand that a firm provide it with all the information it reasonably requires.

The NYSE can also govern firm disclosure behavior as it pertains to the internal handling of private corporate matters, corporate liaisons, relationships between the company and security analysts, and the relationship between company officials and NYSE personnel who serve on the company's board.

SUMMARY

Section 24-1:
Controlling Agency
Costs with Accounting
Information

How useful is accounting information in controlling agency costs?

- Accounting variables can be used to structure the contractual relationships among the firm's many stakeholders and thus limit the discretion available to the parties to the contract.

- Accounting information, the realized values of these accounting variables, shows the extent of compliance with these contracts.

- To facilitate the acceptance of accounting information, companies are expected to follow certain standardized procedures in developing these statements. Rules also stipulate that these documents must be audited.

- The government, because of taxes, is a major claimant on the firm. Managerial choices of accounting procedures can minimize wealth transfers from the firm to the government and thus increase firm value.

Section 24-2:
Controlling Agency
Costs with
Compensation
Contracts

How can compensation contracts reduce agency costs?

- Managerial compensation contracts can be designed to align managers' incentives with those of the owners.

- Short-term compensation plans include annual salary contracts and bonus plans. Both encourage management to focus on the short term. Deferring the bonus to the retirement period can correct this problem.

- Long-term compensation contracts include performance plans (performance units and performance shares) and equity-based compensation plans (stock option plans, shared appreciation rights, and restricted stock, phantom stock, and dividend units). Each of these can reduce agency problems by aligning managers' interests with those of the stockholders.

Section 24-3:
Corporate Governance
with Managers and
Directors

Is the board of directors effective in controlling agency costs?

- Separating management from control through the board of directors can lower agency costs. Although inside directors' extensive knowledge of the firm's operations can benefit the board's decision-making process, it can also reduce the benefits of separating management from control.

- The board's effectiveness can be improved by appointing independent, or outside, directors and by giving them control of key functions such as managerial compensation or budgeting.

- The problems associated with insiders on the board are compounded when the chairman of the board is also the chief executive officer.

Section 24-4:
Corporate
Mismanagement

What is corporate mismanagement? How can stockholders deal with it?

- Corporate mismanagement is generally defined as either an "act of commission," in which managers take overt actions that are detrimental to stockholders, or an "act of omission," in which managers fail to take appropriate actions to protect stockholder interests.

- Stockholders faced with corporate mismanagement can sell their shares in the firm, remove managers and/or directors, or sue directors for inadequate performance.

■ Board activism, in which stockholders pressure board members to provide stronger oversight of the corporation's operations, is becoming more prevalent through relationship investing.

Section 24-5:
Organizational Form
As an Agency Cost
Control Device

How can organizational form affect agency costs?

■ In addition to the public corporation, other organizational forms are proprietorships, closed corporations, franchises, mutuals, and nonprofit organizations. These different organizational forms, by imposing different restrictions on the nature of the residual claims, can control agency problems.

■ The franchise arrangement combines features of the proprietorship and the corporate forms of organization. By imposing restrictions on the franchisee's residual claims, the franchiser can reduce monitoring costs, the "free rider" problem, and the problem of excessive perquisite consumption.

Section 24-6:
Other Agency Cost
Control Devices

What are some other agency cost containment devices?

■ Mutual monitoring among the various managers can reduce agency problems.

■ In the market for corporate control, groups or individuals bid for control of a corporation. This takeover market pressures managers to make decisions consistent with maximizing shareholder wealth.

■ Managers may at various times in their careers seek out or be forced into the managerial labor market. The reputation that they develop through the performance of their duties affects their success in this market. Managers thus have an incentive to maximize stockholder wealth in order to improve their value in this market.

■ Legal and regulatory remedies are available to both the stockholders and other stakeholders who may be damaged by managerial actions.

QUESTIONS

1. In designing compensation contracts to lower agency costs, firms may, in some instances, have to rely on accounting information rather than on market-determined performance measures. Explain.

2. How is accounting information made more dependable as a measure of actual firm performance?

3. List the types of compensation contracts, along with the information that each one is based on. What are the specific agency problems each can potentially reduce?

4. What are the similarities and differences between stock options and stock appreciation rights?

5. Why do firms have both inside and outside directors? What are the advantages and disadvantages of this arrangement? What are some of the ways that the problems posed by this practice can be resolved?

6. Review the roles and responsibilities of the directors of the modern corporation from Chapter 2. How can the current practices regarding board appointments and structures compromise some of these responsibilities?

7. Managers should be held accountable only for "acts of commission" that represent mismanagement. Do you agree? If not, how should acts of omission be addressed?

8. What are the different ways in which stockholders can respond to corporate mismanagement?

9. How does the development of "relationship investing" affect the management of corporations?

10. Distinguish among the residual claims for proprietorships, partnerships, open corporations, nonprofits, and mutuals. Comment on the extent to which agency problems are mitigated by these different residual claims.

11. The franchise arrangement is a "hybrid" control device. What does this mean?

12. What is the market for corporate control? How effective is this market in controlling agency costs?

13. How can the managerial labor market control agency costs?

14. What recourse do the firm's other stakeholders have when faced with corporate mismanagement?

15. How does the Securities and Exchange Commission (SEC) hold managerial mismanagement in check? Exactly what kinds of mismanagement does the SEC control?

SUGGESTED ADDITIONAL READINGS

Barnea, A., R. A. Haugen, and L. W. Senbet. *Agency Problems and Financial Contracting.* Englewood Cliffs, NJ: Prentice-Hall, 1985.

Barnea, A., R. A. Haugen, and L. W. Senbet. "Market Imperfections, Agency Problems and Capital Structure: A Review." *Financial Management,* Summer 1981, pp. 7–22.

Brickley, J. A., S. Bhagat, and R. C. Lease. "The Impact of Long-Range Managerial Compensation Plans on Shareholder Wealth." *Journal of Accounting and Economics,* 1985, pp. 115–129.

Coase, R. H. "The Nature of the Firm." *Economica,* November 1937, pp. 386–405.

Cornell, B., and A. C. Shapiro. "Corporate Stakeholders and Corporate Finance." *Financial Management,* Spring 1987, pp. 5–14.

Fama, E. F. "Agency Problems and the Theory of the Firm." *Journal of Political Economy* 88 (April 1980): 288–307.

Fama, E. F., and M. C. Jensen. "Agency Problems and Residual Claims." *Journal of Law and Economics* 26 (June 1983): 327–350.

Fama, E. F., and M. C. Jensen. "Organizational Forms and Investment Decisions." *Journal of Financial Economics* 14 (1985): 101–118.

Fama, E. F., and M. C. Jensen. "Separation of Ownership and Control." *Journal of Law and Economics* 26 (June 1983): 301–326.

Jensen, M. C., and W. H. Meckling. "Theory of the Firm, Managerial Behavior, Agency Costs and Ownership Structure." *Journal of Financial Economics* 3 (1976): 305–360.

Williamson, O. E. *The Economic Institutions of Capitalism.* New York: Free Press, 1985.

Williamson, O. E. *Markets and Hierarchies.* New York: Free Press, 1975.

TWENTY-FIVE — THE MARKET FOR CORPORATE CONTROL

*But there is one thing
all boards have in
common. . . . They
do not function.*

—Peter F. Drucker[1]

[1] In *Management: Tasks, Responsibilities, Practices* (New York: Harper & Row, 1974).

Many critics of American corporate management believe that inefficient management has a lot to do with the declining competitive position of the United States in the global marketplace. They feel that somewhere in the shuffle between assuming fiduciary responsibility for running their firms and actually getting the job done, managers have repeatedly adopted courses of action that are inefficient and inept. These critics are also convinced that in many cases, managers' decisions have even created serious conflicts of interest between themselves and their shareholders. As we saw in Chapters 2 and 24, conflicts of interest can cause managers to make decisions that benefit themselves more than their shareholders. In these instances, management's ability to perform its major function—maximize the shareholders' wealth—is compromised. Chapter 24 also presented several means by which agency costs can be contained. This chapter continues the discussion by examining another control device, the market for corporate control, that may serve to increase stockholders' wealth by reducing agency costs.

The lore and terminology that accompany the subject of corporate control conjure up fantastic images in even the most unimaginative among us. Terms like *raider, shark repellent, greenmail,* and *white knight* certainly do attract attention and invite scrutiny. Looking beyond this colorful lexicon, however, we find the depth and complexity of the issues in the takeover market.

Are takeovers good or bad? At first glance, this may appear to be a rather innocuous question with an unambiguous answer. Based on the many stories about the takeover activities of raiders and sharks, an immediate "bad" may spring to the minds of many. Others, however, may remember the stories of huge overnight premiums above current market values that the shareholders of takeover targets received and so just as readily answer "good." In short, the question is complicated, and people in different circumstances often have opposing viewpoints on the subject.

In any discussion of corporate control issues, few questions can be answered confidently. Part of the reason for this is the difficulty of quantifying all of the information necessary to analyze the topic completely and accurately. Nevertheless, corporate control has recently become a major area of research, and there is a large body of theoretical and empirical work from which to draw inferences and derive starting points. This chapter addresses the following issues:

- What is corporate control? Why does it have value?

- How do friendly and hostile takeovers differ?

- How are takeovers accomplished?

- How are takeovers financed?

- How can takeover attempts be blocked?

- How do takeovers affect shareholders' wealth?

25-1

THE MARKET FOR CORPORATE CONTROL

Corporate control is the bundle of rights used to determine how corporate resources are managed. These include the rights to hire and to fire personnel, to influence investment and financing decisions, and to design compensation contracts for top-level managers.[2] Corporate boards always retain the highest control rights, but they usually delegate other rights to lower-level managers. These board-level rights have a value in the market and are sought by competing management teams that are eager to capture the gains from various perceived synergies or undervaluations. By taking over control of the firm, the top management of an acquiring firm can control the resources of the target firm.

The corporate control market is an intangible entity. Unlike securities exchanges, which have physical locations for trading securities, the market for trading corporate control exists only conceptually. Rather than a single place, the market for corporate control is an informal, diffuse market where perceived opportunities are traded by those involved. Although the transactions themselves can be traced only through electronic documentation or audit trails, it is impossible to ignore their impact on the American economy.

As Figure 25-1 shows, the market for corporate control, as measured by merger and acquisition activity in the United States, increased steadily and dramatically in both the number of transactions and the total value of the transactions between 1983 and 1992. The number of transactions during this period rose from 2,087 to 3,502 (an increase of 67.8%), and the value of the transactions jumped from $72.9 billion to $125.3 billion (an increase of 71%). To appreciate the magnitude and the importance that the corporate control market attained, we must first ask why a management team would attempt a takeover.

Why Are Takeovers Initiated?

The main reason for mounting a takeover must be to increase the shareholders' wealth because that is the major goal of a firm's management. But when is an acquisition the most efficient way to increase the shareholders' wealth? Among the most commonly cited reasons for launching a takeover are satisfaction of growth goals, diversification, the realization of various synergies resulting from operating and financial economies, correction of managerial inefficiencies, and greater market power. A recent addition is to advance technological innovation.

In many instances, the merger is "friendly"; that is, both firms believe they can gain from a takeover for one or more of the reasons just cited. Such takeovers are negotiated between the parties involved and usually result in terms that are satisfactory to both sides. Both sides generally are winners in the resulting combination. Any ill will that results from a friendly takeover is usually minimal, and the acquired firm's managers usually keep their jobs and some portion of their premerger authority in the new firm. Electrolux's takeover of Regina Corporation, in the vacuum cleaner industry, and Leisure Investments U.S.A., Inc.'s acquisition of Intermark Gaming International, Inc., in the video game industry, during 1989 are examples of friendly takeovers.

"Hostile" takeovers, on the other hand, are not welcomed by the target firm's management, and they usually produce substantial ill will between the target and the bidder. This chapter focuses on takeovers that are done to reduce or eliminate existing management inefficiencies. Of course, the bidding firm does not state explicitly that this is its motive. If it believes that by taking over the target firm it can,

[2] This definition was proposed by E. F. Fama and M. C. Jensen in "Separation of Ownership and Control," *Journal of Law and Economics* 26 (June 1983): 301–323; and in "Agency Problems and Residual Claims," *Journal of Law and Economics* 26 (June 1983): 327–349.

■
FIGURE 25-1
U.S. mergers and acquisitions record, 1983–1992

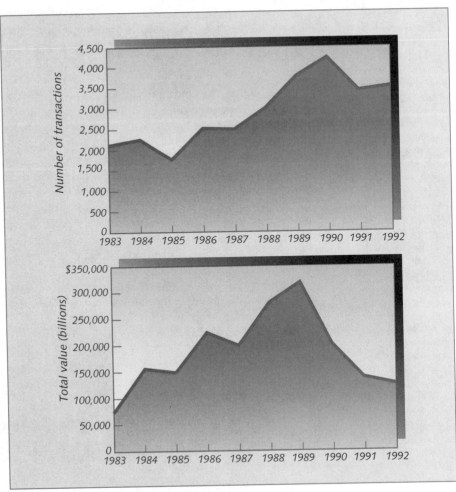

Graphs generated from information from *Mergers & Acquisitions*, May–June 1993.

for example, eliminate certain costs caused by operating inefficiencies or gain new advantages from pooling the two companies' talent, then it is, in effect, saying that the target firm's management failed to recognize these possibilities. But whether a firm is taken over to reduce existing management inefficiencies or to gain in other ways is often difficult to determine.

In this chapter we examine the takeover market from the perspective of agency theory. Firms are taken over to reduce managerial inefficiencies, whatever their origins. The bidding firm seeks to control the assets of the target firm by means of a takeover in order to increase the firm's value by reducing existing inefficiencies.

Why Are Takeovers Resisted?

Understanding why takeovers are resisted requires understanding who is resisting them. As might be expected, most of the resistance comes from the target firm's management. This is not really surprising because the target firm's managers have the most to lose following a takeover. Almost 50% of the top-level managers of target firms lose their jobs within three years after a takeover, whether friendly or hostile.[3] Other negative outcomes include loss of authority and valuable benefits and reductions in compensation.

[3] M. C. Jensen, "Takeovers: Their Causes and Consequences," *Journal of Economic Perspectives*, Winter 1988, pp. 21–48.

In response to these threats, managers may recommend that shareholders reject takeover proposals, even when a takeover is clearly in their best interests. This is one example of a conflict of interest between management and shareholders because managers are responsible for taking actions that maximize the shareholders' wealth. Many managers use **antitakeover measures** to try to prevent takeovers.

Managers do not always act in their own interests when confronted with takeover attempts, however. A management team may reject an offer based on the sincere belief that the offer does not accurately reflect the firm's underlying value. This belief can be based on management's assessment of the firm's present value and/or on inside information it has concerning the firm's future prospects. Under these circumstances, the firm's managers are fulfilling their fiduciary responsibility to maximize the shareholders' wealth by recommending rejection of the offer, with no evidence of a conflict of interests. In fact, actions of this type are often followed by a "sweetened" offer from the bidding firm.

25-2

METHODS FOR EFFECTING TAKEOVERS

The mechanisms for transferring corporate control alter the composition of the target firm's board of directors. Because a firm's directors are elected by its shareholders, the party that holds a majority of a firm's shares also has the power to elect a majority of its directors and thus to control the company. The three basic transactions that transfer control of the board to the acquiring party are mergers, tender offers, and proxy contests.

Mergers

The merger has long been, and remains today, the most common method of changing corporate control. The term **merger** refers to any business combination in which one or more of the firms involved does not survive in name. In a more formal definition, a merger is a combination of two or more corporations that results in only one legally surviving corporation. The other(s) is dissolved in accordance with the laws of its state of incorporation. The surviving (acquiring) firm secures title to the stock or assets of the dissolved (target) firm. For example, A (acquiring) + B (target) = A^* (surviving). B is said to have been merged into A, and its shareholders receive either shares of stock in the acquiring firm or some other form of compensation, such as cash. Table 25-1 lists the largest merger and

TABLE 25-1

Largest M&A Transactions in 1992

Acquiring Company *Financial Advisers (Where Known)*	Acquired/Merged Company *Financial Advisers (Where Known)*	Price *(millions)*
BankAmerica Corp. Morgan Stanley; Hellman & Friedman	**Security Pacific Corp.** First Boston	$4,212.7
Bell Atlantic Corp. Salomon Brothers	**Metro Mobile CTS Inc.** Lipper & Co. Inc.; Smith Barney	2,464.0
Northeast Utilities Morgan Stanley	**Public Service Co. of New Hampshire** Salomon Brothers; Rothschild Inc.; First Boston	2,300.0
Time Warner Inc. Lazard Frères; Alpine Securities	**Remaining 18% of American Television & Communications Corp.** First Boston	1,699.5
Philip Morris Cos. Inc. Rothschild Bank AG; Rothschild et Compagnie	**Jacobs Suchard AG** Bank J. Vontobel AG; N. M. Rothschild & Sons	1,586.1
American Re Corp. Merrill Lynch	**American Re-Insurance Co.** Goldman, Sachs	1,430.0
Bacardi Corp. Morgan Guaranty Trust	**General Beverage Corp.** Colker, Gelardin	1,404.3
Emerson Electric Co. Goldman, Sachs	**Fisher Controls International Inc.** Not available	1,275.0
Society Corp. First Boston	**AmeriTrust Corp.** Goldman, Sachs	1,186.0
Pennzoil Co. Lehman Brothers	**Chevron PBC Inc.** Goldman, Sachs	1,170.0

SOURCE: *Mergers & Acquisitions,* May–June 1993.

	New Name	Former Name
■ **TABLE 25-2** *Name Changes Resulting from 1992 U.S. Merger and Acquisition and Restructuring Activity*	Advanced Technology Laboratories Inc.	Westmark International Inc.
	Bolsa Chica	Henley Properties Inc.
	Ceridian Corp.	Control Data Corp.
	Computervision Inc.	Prime Computer Inc.
	Continental Can Co.	Viatech Inc.
	Fleet Financial Group Inc.	Fleet Norstar International Inc.
	Snapple Beverage Corp.	Unadulterated Food Products Co.
	Sprint Corp.	United Telecommunications Inc.
	SuperValue Inc.	Super Value Stores Inc.
	Western Resources Inc.	Kansas Power & Light Co.

SOURCE: *Mergers & Acquisitions*, May–June 1993.

acquisition (M&A) transactions in 1992, and Table 25-2 gives the new and old names for some of the companies that merged.

Figure 25-2 shows the steps in a typical merger transaction. Firm *A* (acquiring) decides that a merger with firm *B* (target) is in the best interests of its shareholders. Firm *A* then enters into negotiations with firm *B*'s management and draws up a merger proposal. Because mergers require the approval of the target firm's board, *B*'s managers present *A*'s proposal to *B*'s board. If *B*'s board approves the proposal, the merger is then put to a vote by the stockholders. The merger is then either accepted or rejected, depending on the percentage of favorable votes required for approval by the corporate code of *B*'s state of incorporation. Upon approval by *B*'s stockholders, the merger is consummated.

Stockholders accept most board-approved merger proposals. If, however, *B*'s stockholders reject *A*'s initial proposal, *A* is then free to "sweeten" its offer and resubmit it to *B*'s board. This process can continue indefinitely until either *B*'s stockholders accept the offer or *A* loses interest in the transaction. Without the approval of *B*'s stockholders, *A* has no further recourse in its attempt to merge with *B*. If *A*'s proposal is rejected by *B*'s board and *A* believes *B*'s stockholders would accept its offer if given the opportunity, *A* may decide to undertake a tender offer to gain control of *B* (this is an attempt at a hostile takeover). Chapter 26 examines mergers in more detail.

Tender Offers

A **tender offer** is a public offer made by a management team (bidder) to purchase a designated percentage of the target firm's outstanding common stock. In contrast with merger proposals, tender offers do not require the approval of the target firm's board of directors. Rather, tender offers are made directly to the target firm's shareholders through public announcements in newspapers and other media. Figure 25-3 shows a typical tender offer announcement in *The Wall Street Journal*. Following the announcement of the offer, the individual shareholders decide for themselves whether to tender their shares for sale to the bidder. If enough shares are tendered by the target firm's shareholders, control of the corporation passes to the bidding firm.

When compared with mergers and proxy contests (discussed later), tender offers are the "new kid on the block." The first tender offer recorded by the Securities and Exchange Commission (SEC) was made in 1956. Now, however, tender offers are much more commonly used than proxy contests in obtaining corporate control. Although in numerical terms they usually represent only a small fraction of the total number of M&A transactions, they have become the primary method of completing large deals that involve public companies. For example, in 1988 tender offers accounted for only 5.7% of the total number of M&A transactions, yet they were responsible for 67.9% of the total value of all M&A transactions in that year.

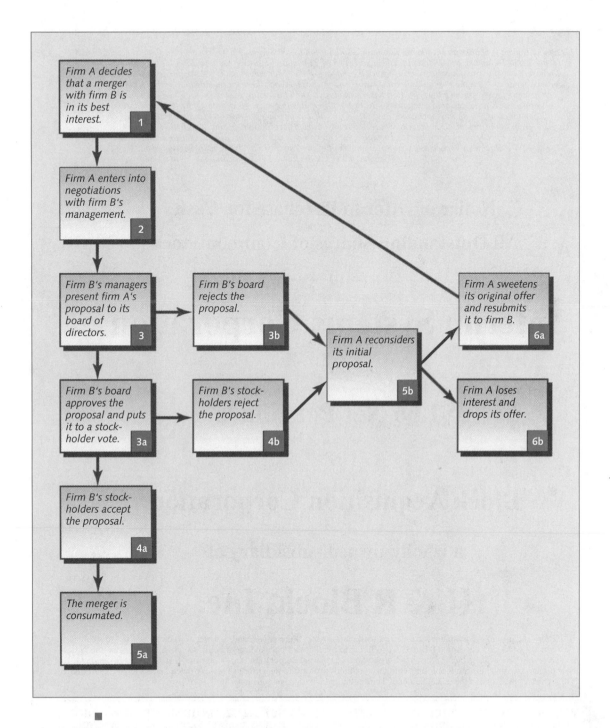

FIGURE 25-2
Typical merger transaction

Two events are often cited as reasons for the emergence of tender offers. First, in 1956 the SEC's rules requiring full disclosure in proxy materials made proxy contests much more costly. Second, a court ruling in 1955 declared that the proceeds from the sale of a controlling interest in a corporation must be shared equally among all shareholders. It can therefore be argued that tender offers began to dominate proxy contests as takeover mechanisms when the actual and potential costs of proxy fights increased because of regulatory and legal events in the mid-1950s.

This announcement is neither an offer to purchase nor a solicitation to sell Shares. The Offer is made solely by the Offer to Purchase dated December 19, 1990 and the related Letter of Transmittal is being made to all holders of Shares. The Purchaser is not aware of any jurisdiction where the making of the Offer would not be in compliance with the laws of such jurisdiction. If the Purchaser becomes aware of any jurisdiction where the making of the Offer would not be in compliance with such laws, the Purchaser will make a good faith effort to comply with such laws or seek to have such laws declared inapplicable to to the Offer. If, after such good faith effort, the Purchaser cannot comply with any applicable law, the Offer will not be made to, nor will tenders be accepted from or on behalf of, holders of Shares residing in such jurisdiction. In any jurisdiction whose securities, blue sky or other laws rewuire the Offer to be made by a licensed broker or dealer, the Offer shall be deemed to be made on behalf of the Purchaser by one or more registered brokers or dealers licensed under the the laws of such jurisdiction.

Notice of Offer to Purchase for Cash

All Outstanding Shares of Common Stock

of

Interim Systems Corporation

at

$1.66 Net Per Share

by

Block Acquisition Corporation

a wholly-owned subsidiary of

H & R Block, Inc.

Block Acquisition Corporation, a Delaware corporation (the "Purchaser") and a wholly-owned subsidiary of H & R Block. Inc., a Missouri corporation ("Block"), is offering to purchase all outstanding shares of Common Stock, par value $.01 per share (the "Shares"), of Interim Systems Corporation, a Delaware corporation (the "Company"), at $1.66 per Share, net to the seller in cash, upon the terms and subject to the conditions set forth in the Offer to Purchase dated December 19, 1990 (the "Offer to Purchase") and in the related Letter of Transmittal (which together constitute the "Offer").

THE OFFER AND WITHDRAWAL RIGHTS WILL EXPIRE AT 12:00 MIDNIGHT, NEW YORK CITY TIME, ON THURSDAY, JANUARY 17, 1991, UNLESS THE OFFER IS EXTENDED.

■

FIGURE 25-3
Typical tender offer announcement

TABLE 25-3
Ten Largest Completed Tender Offers in 1992

Acquirer	Target	Price (millions)
Philip Morris Cos. Inc.	Jacobs Suchard AG	$1,586.1
Homestake Mining Co.	International Corona Corp.	559.8
Bergen Brunswig Corp.	Durr-Fillauer Medical Inc.	448.6
Chris-Craft Industries Inc.	Pinelands Inc.	295.6
Marvel Entertainment Group Inc.	Fleer Corp.	264.2
Brambles Industries Ltd.	Environmental Systems Co.	240.6
American Financial Corp.	STI Group Inc.	193.1
Thermo Electron Corp.	Nicolet Instrument Corp.	180.6
Conner Peripherals Inc.	Archive Corp.	164.0
Blockbuster Entertainment Corp.	Cityvision PLC	134.7

SOURCE: SDC Merger & Corporate Transactions Database.

Table 25-3 lists the ten largest tender offers in 1992. Figure 25-4 shows the breakdown of the methods of payment used in these tender offers. As can be seen, all-cash tender offers in 1992 accounted for 76% of the total number of tenders.

Proxy Contests

Recall that a corporation's control rights rest with its board of directors. The board is required to supervise the firm's ongoing business operations and to exercise its powers in the corporation's best interests. Recall also that the board normally delegates responsibility for day-to-day operations to appointed officers but reserves the right to replace them if it so desires.

A **proxy contest** is a direct attempt by dissident shareholders to gain a controlling number of seats on a firm's board of directors through a formal vote. The shareholders' goal is to remove incumbent directors who, they believe, are inefficient and to replace them with their own slate of directors. Shareholders can also use a proxy contest to change the firm's entire board. Because the board controls the company, changes in the board effected by a proxy contest represent a transfer of corporate control.

We now describe the mechanics of a proxy contest. A firm's directors are elected by its shareholders at the firm's annual meeting. Proxy contests typically begin in the months before the annual meeting, with the stockholders being asked to choose between two opposing slates of nominees for board positions. Dissident shareholders solicit votes from other stockholders to elect directors other than those nominated by management. Both dissidents and incumbents wage battles much like political campaigns, replete with promises to voters and charges against the opposition.

FIGURE 25-4
Methods of payment in 1992 tender offers

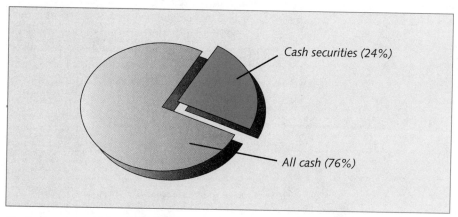

Pie chart prepared from information from *Mergers & Acquisitions*, May–June 1993.

Proxy solicitation materials are sent to the stockholders, who in turn sign and return the proxy forms for their preferred slate, authorizing its sponsors to vote their shares in the election. Each group accumulates votes by means of these proxies and casts the total number of accumulated votes at the annual meeting. As a general rule, the group that secures a majority of the votes elects a majority of the board members.

As discussed in Chapter 13, there are two types of voting in the United States: noncumulative and cumulative. The voting method to be used is determined by the corporation's bylaws and the corporation laws of the state of incorporation. Noncumulative voting treats each director's position as a separate election. Proxy holders cast the same number of votes as shares for which they hold proxies for each slot on the board. Successful nominees are those that win the majority of the votes cast. Under this method, minority interests are usually prevented from electing any directors.

Cumulative voting, however, entitles proxy holders to cast the same number of votes as shares for which they hold proxies times the number of directors. They can cast all their votes for one director or distribute them among the nominees. Each nominee is ranked in descending order according to the number of votes he or she receives. The required number of directors is then elected from this ranking.[4]

As a result of the proxy fight, if the dissident group obtains a majority of the board's seats, it has effected a change in corporate control. These contests are often undertaken by former managers or large stockholders who are unhappy with the current board's strategic plan for the firm. The outcome of the election, however, has no effect on the distribution of the firm's ownership because in proxy contests there is no transfer of ownership of the corporation; there is only a transfer of its control.

25-3

TAKEOVER FINANCING TECHNIQUES

Because takeovers can be considered corporate investment projects, they are financed in the same manner as is any other corporate undertaking— that is, with cash, securities, or a combination of the two. A variety of securities are available, such as common and preferred stock, notes, and bonds (straight, convertible, or "junk"). Other instruments like options and warrants are sometimes offered to "sweeten" the deal for the target firm's shareholders.

Financing with Cash

In a **cash-for-stock exchange,** the target shareholders receive a 100% cash payment for their stock. Some believe that is a desirable method for the acquiring firm because it is able to acquire the earnings of the target company without diluting its own earnings by issuing new common stock. However, this view is difficult to justify in an efficient market. The target firm's shareholders may not prefer an all-cash exchange. They may have to pay a capital gains tax on the proceeds, which makes it a less desirable form of payment. In general, the acquiring firm prefers cash, but the target firm's shareholders do not.

According to Figure 25-5, 56.4% of all U.S. merger activity in 1992 was financed by all-cash transactions, making it by far the most common method of financing takeovers in that year.

---

[4]The importance of voting schemes is illustrated by the case of T. Boone Pickens (and his investors), who acquired 13% of Gulf Oil in 1983. Gulf changed its state of incorporation from Pennsylvania to Delaware. The reason given was that the former had cumulative, the latter noncumulative voting. This kept Pickens off the board.

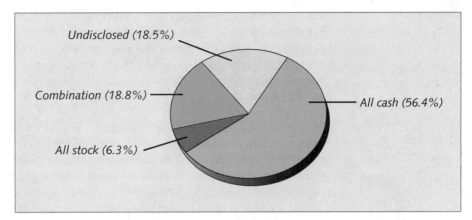

SOURCE: *Mergers & Acquisitions,* May–June 1993.

Financing with Stock

In a **stock swap,** the acquiring firm issues additional shares of common stock in exchange for the target firm's outstanding common stock. The target firm's shareholders generally like this method because it is a tax-deferred exchange for them. Any capital gains they may realize from the transaction cannot be taxed until they sell the shares. All-stock transactions accounted for 6.3% of all U.S. merger financing in 1992 (see Figure 25-5).

Financing with Debt

The use of various forms of debt in financing takeovers is also common. Combinations of notes and bonds alone or with cash or stock are often part of a financing package used to make the exchange with the target firm's shareholders. Figure 25-5 shows that 18.8% of all U.S. mergers in 1992 were financed by combinations of cash and securities.

JUNK BONDS

In the 1980s, there was a great deal of controversy over and attention to an area of the debt market called the *junk bond* or *high-yield debt* market. The use of junk bonds to finance takeover deals was hotly debated. Junk bonds, or high-yield bonds, as they are labeled by their proponents, are simply corporate bonds that are either unrated or rated below an investment-grade level. Before 1977, the junk bond market was composed of bonds whose initial ratings had fallen below an investment-grade level. (Bond ratings were discussed in Chapter 14.) These bonds were known as *fallen angels*. Between 1970 and 1976, they accounted for about 5%, on average, of the United States' total outstanding public straight debt.

In 1977, however, the junk bond market began to change as bonds were issued with ratings below investment grade. Lehman Brothers (now Shearson Lehman Hutton) underwrote the first such issue, but Drexel Burnham Lambert was the firm that nurtured and developed the market, and it quickly became the individual leader in junk bond underwriting. Much of the attractiveness of junk bond financing is the liquidity of the secondary market, which Drexel had a major hand in creating. A 1987 Drexel Burnham report estimated that junk bonds made up 23% of total corporate bonds at year-end 1986. Appendix 27A contains a more in-depth discussion of junk bonds.

JUNK BONDS IN TAKEOVER ACTIVITY

One of the most controversial roles of junk bonds is their use as takeover financing mechanisms. The transaction that has attracted the most attention is when the acquirer receives financing commitments from a group of investors and then launches a tender offer for a specified fraction of the target company's outstanding common stock. The investors agree to purchase a certain amount of junk bonds from the acquirer upon the tender of the desired percentage of shares. The shares are not collateral for the junk bonds, but if the tender offer is successful, the assets of the target can be used as collateral for any loans needed to complete the takeover.

One of the most attractive features of the junk bond market is its ability to obtain sizable amounts of financing commitments in a very short time. Speed is important to the acquirer because delays in the takeover process favor the target company, and raising large amounts of capital on very short notice is difficult. This capability of raising huge amounts of capital very quickly thus enables sharks or raiders to attempt to take over companies even much larger than themselves. The result is much distrust in both business and government.

Although the use of junk bonds has generated much controversy, the importance of their actual role in takeover activity is much less certain. According to Drexel Burnham, 11% of the total number of 1984 junk bond issues were related to merger and acquisition activity, which accounts for only about 1.4% of the total value of takeover activity for this period. The Federal Reserve Board, however, estimates that 41% of total 1984 junk bond issues, or 9% of the total value of acquisitions, for the same period were related to takeover activity. In contrast, Morgan Stanley estimates that acquisition financing accounted for 21% of 1984's total junk bond market and 31% of the total junk bond market in 1985. These amounts represented 2.6% and 45%, respectively, of the total value of takeover transactions for this period.

Another common charge levied against junk bond financing is that their use in corporate control changes contributed heavily to the huge increases in the United States' total debt. Recent studies argue, however, that there is no statistical linkage between the two. But even if one does not accept this premise, the total amount of the merger and acquisition market accounted for by junk bonds is so small that it is difficult to believe it could have had much impact on the total amount of domestic debt.

25-4

STRATEGIES TO FOIL TAKEOVERS

*I*n an effort to keep their jobs, more and more corporate managers have adopted antitakeover measures, including *porcupine amendments, shark repellents, poison pills,* and *golden parachutes.* Regardless of their names, these methods are designed to discourage change and to preserve managers' jobs. Takeover defense mechanisms can be classified as either proactive (preoffer) measures or reactive (postoffer) measures. This section examines the most widely used antitakeover measures within these two categories and analyzes their effect on the target firm and its shareholders.

Proactive (Preoffer) Measures

Proactive measures are antitakeover mechanisms that can be activated before a raider attempts to take over a firm. The target firm's shareholders may object to these tactics for the following reasons: (1) they may be dissatisfied with some or all of top management's business decisions; (2) they may believe that the managers are simply trying to protect their jobs; and (3) they may believe that these antitakeover measures, sometimes called **shark repellents,** actually reduce the value of their stock. Therefore managers should undertake these measures only after thoroughly investigating their stockholders' sentiments.

One of the most popular takeover defense mechanisms is the adoption of bylaw and charter amendments designed to make the transfer of corporate control very difficult. Between 1974 and 1979, approximately 200 of the companies listed on the New York Stock Exchange adopted amendments of this type. These strategies, commonly known as **porcupine amendments,** are usually the mainstay of comprehensive takeover defense packages designed and marketed for client firms by investment bankers.

STAGGERED BOARD PROVISIONS

Staggered board provisions divide a firm's board of directors into sections so that only one section stands for election each year. A typical provision divides the board into three sections, with each member serving a three-year term. By comparison, all the members of nonstaggered boards stand for election each year.

Staggered board provisions hinder takeover actions because a majority stockholder must wait two years before being able to obtain a majority representation on the firm's board and thus to present the merger proposal for the stockholders' vote. In most instances, two years is much too long for the acquirer to wait, and so the takeover proposal is usually abandoned. Dayton Hudson, General Public Utilities, and Harley-Davidson are examples of the many firms that have adopted staggered board provisions.

SUPERMAJORITY MERGER APPROVAL

Supermajority merger approval provisions require approval by an abnormally large number of shareholder votes to enable mergers or other transactions that involve "interested parties" or "substantial stockholders." A substantial stockholder is usually defined as any entity that has an equity holding equal to or greater than 5% of a firm's outstanding common stock.

Most supermajority provisions require stockholder approval percentages between $66\frac{2}{3}\%$ and 80%. For example, Showboat, Inc., adopted a provision requiring a $66\frac{2}{3}\%$ vote to approve any merger. Some supermajority provisions, however, require supermajority approval of those shares not held by the acquirer.

Supermajority provisions usually contain escape clauses that suspend supermajority approval for mergers with subsidiaries or mergers approved by the **continuing board members**—that is, those not elected by an "interested party."

FAIR MERGER PRICE PROVISIONS

Fair merger price provisions specify the minimum share prices in mergers that involve major stockholders, typically someone holding a 20%–30% or larger equity position. This means that all stockholders who tender their shares in the proposed merger must receive at least the maximum share price paid to acquire a majority stake in the company. Stipulations of this type protect minority shareholders from being forced to accept prices lower than those offered to the majority stockholders by the bidding firm after it has obtained a majority share of the target firm's outstanding stock. Both Newhall Land & Farming and Wisconsin Public Service adopted fair price provisions in 1988, with their shareholders' approval.

LOCKUP PROVISIONS

Lockup provisions are designed to prevent the circumvention of the firm's antitakeover provisions. One of the most popular types requires supermajority approval to repeal other antitakeover amendments. In 1988, for example, Omnicom Group approved a provision that requires a two-thirds vote to change or repeal its bylaws. Another example is a provision limiting the number of directors, which prevents a new majority shareholder from enlarging the size of the board and diluting the incumbent directors' voting power by filling the board with directors of his or her own choosing.

INCREASING THE NUMBER OF AUTHORIZED SHARES OF COMMON STOCK

Increasing the number of authorized shares of common stock is a common antitakeover device justified by many corporate boards as necessary to use in connection with stock splits and dividends as well as to raise cash. Sale of the corporation's stock for cash results in increasing the number of shares necessary to acquire a controlling interest in the firm. This in turn deters a firm that is seeking control of the target firm by raising the necessary costs of the takeover. For example, in a move acknowledged by the firm as defensive, Outboard Marine Corporation's shareholders in 1988 approved tripling the number of the firm's outstanding common shares.

A firm can also use the newly issued shares to make acquisitions of its own. The assets and obligations of the target firm's acquisition(s) may affect its balance sheet so as to make it unattractive to the acquirer as a takeover candidate. In this instance, issuing new shares is an effective antitakeover measure.

GOLDEN PARACHUTES

Golden parachutes are contractual agreements between top managers and the corporation that guarantee the managers a minimum salary and bonus in the event of a takeover. Using these parachutes, managers can "bail out" of the firm if it is taken over and still benefit substantially. Many business leaders today believe that golden parachutes are necessary to attract quality personnel into the currently unstable corporate climate. Their reasoning is that managers will think of the stockholders' interests, and not the security of their own positions, in the event of a possible merger.

Although these arrangements can add substantially to the acquiring firm's cost of a takeover, the total amount of these agreements is generally insufficient to be regarded as a serious preventive measure. Recent studies have found no evidence of negative effects on the shareholders' wealth as a result of golden parachutes. In those cases in which they have helped prevent a takeover, it is more likely that overly compensating top managers with golden parachutes without any perceived benefits to the firm made the firm unattractive. For an example of conflicts in the use of golden parachutes, see the highlight.

BUY-OPS

A **buy-op** is a scheduled repurchase of a firm's own shares in the open market over a specified period of time. These shares are then placed in an employee stock ownership plan (ESOP) for later distribution to the firm's directors and employees. This policy reduces the threat of a hostile takeover because it removes the shares from the grasp of potentially unfriendly hands and places them in friendly hands. The management's current position is also strengthened by giving it control of more shares and thus more votes at shareholders' meetings.

An example of the use of this strategy is Polaroid Corporation's 1988 establishment of an ESOP in its successful defeat of a hostile bid from Shamrock Holdings, Inc. Other firms that have established or modified ESOP plans are Texaco, Inc., Lockheed Corporation, and Anheuser Busch.

ALLIED-SIGNAL'S GOLDEN PARACHUTES

When Signal Companies merged with Allied Corporation in 1985, there was $100 million worth of "golden parachutes" waiting to ease the descent of Signal's top executives. Signal's shareholders consequently took exception to what they saw as an obvious waste of corporate assets and subsequently filed a lawsuit against the company.

The case was settled in early 1986. The original compensation agreements were substantially changed, with the overall package reduced by $23 million. Even though Signal's shareholders did not win the case outright, they did gain support for a reassessment of the business judgment rule, the rule that courts apply to any suit brought by a firm's shareholders. The rule presumes that a firm's management is acting in good faith for the corporation's benefit. The law does not dictate that a firm's management be right, only that it take actions that it deems to be in the best interests of the firm's shareholders. To overcome that presumption, the shareholders must show evidence of some type of bad faith by the firm's management, such as fraud or a conflict of interest. Such charges are very difficult to prove, and as a result, lawsuits brought by shareholders are very difficult for them to win. Nonetheless, the success of Signal's shareholders in achieving a reduction in the original parachute amounts is regarded as an important step forward for shareholders' rights.

POISON PILLS

Poison pills are relative newcomers to the list of takeover defenses available to target firms. Only three pills were used before 1985; now hundreds of firms have adopted them, including General Dynamics, Bell Atlantic, James River, and Southmark Corporation. The poison pill is a very severe antitakeover measure—it cannot be circumvented—and it completely protects incumbent managers from unwanted takeover attempts by greatly inflating the ultimate cost of the takeover to the acquiring firm.

Poison pills are stock rights plans adopted by a firm's board of directors; they usually do not require the shareholders' approval. These rights are issued to stockholders and remain inactive until triggered. A triggering event is typically either a tender offer for a large fraction of the firm (usually about 30%) or a single shareholder's accumulation of a large block of the firm's common stock (generally around 15%). Therein lies the logic behind the name: Upon reaching either plateau just mentioned, the pill is put into effect, and the potential acquirer subsequently is "poisoned."

The firm's board can redeem these rights for a specified period after a triggering event. If they do not redeem these rights during this period, the rights can be exercised. Exercised rights are used in one of two different plans: flip-over plans or flip-in plans.

Flip-over plans use the exercised rights to purchase stock that can be converted to the common stock of the bidding firm in the event of a takeover. A typical transaction sets the price of the preferred stock at $50 and makes it convertible to $100 of equity. The purpose is to raise substantially the minimum offer price that shareholders would accept in a tender offer. The offer price is the price per share offered by the acquiring firm to the target firm's shareholders for their stock. This was West Point–Pepperell's intention when it adopted the flip-over portion of its poison pill plan. The target firm's managers hope that this higher cost is enough to dissuade the bidding firm from pursuing a takeover attempt.

Flip-in plans enable the issuing firm to repurchase stock rights from its shareholders at a large premium, usually 100%. In our example, the $50 of stock is

PHILLIPS PETROLEUM'S POISON PILL

One of the most publicized poison pills in recent takeover history was the one designed by Phillips Petroleum in 1985 to fend off a well-known corporate raider, Carl Icahn. Mr. Icahn emerged as a bidder for Phillips after a failed attempt by T. Boone Pickens, Jr., to acquire Phillips through his company, Mesa Partners. Following Pickens's attempt to acquire the company, Phillips proposed a capital restructuring plan that would permit its shareholders to exchange their existing stock for a combination of new common stock and debentures. In addition, Phillips adopted a poison pill in the form of a distribution of rights to Phillips's shareholders, granting them the right to exchange each of their shares for a one-year 15% senior note worth $62.

These rights could be exercised only upon the acquisition by an outsider of 30% or more of Phillips's outstanding shares. If the potential acquirer agreed to pay $62 for the remainder of the outstanding shares, then the pill would be dissolved. If not, then the acquirer would inherit about $6.7 billion in new debt, over and above the purchase price of the firm.

Icahn subsequently attempted to call Phillips's bluff by acquiring just over 30% of its shares, but the pill was never activated because Phillips's shareholders adopted the proposed restructuring plan and the pill was dissolved. Icahn then abandoned his takeover attempt and sold his shares in Phillips.

repurchased for $100. The firm that triggers the offer is excluded from the repurchase. The effect of this device is two-pronged: First, a lowest limit is set on the minimum offer price that the target firm's shareholders will accept, and second, the value of the bidding firm's equity position in the target is reduced. The stock often is repurchased using newly issued debt securities instead of cash. Thus the acquirer is now pursuing a target that is heavily laden with debt and so is probably much less attractive. To make matters worse, flip-ins also often contain flip-over provisions, making the target even less attractive to the bidder.

The empirical evidence regarding poison pills so far shows mixed and inconclusive effects on shareholder wealth. Some researchers have found negative abnormal returns (also called excess returns, first defined in Chapter 7) associated with the adoption of poison pills, but others have found no abnormal returns. Therefore, although poison pills are expected to be harmful, their impact is currently unclear. For an example of how poison pills can be used, see the Phillips highlight.

Reactive (Postoffer) Measures

In addition to the proactive strategies, several reactive measures are available to target management to use in preventing takeover attempts. Reactive measures are usually initiated after a bidding firm has begun its takeover attempt. They are usually installed in chaos and crisis and generally have a short-term focus.

STANDSTILL AGREEMENTS

A **standstill agreement** is a voluntary contract between a corporation and a substantial stockholder that limits the ownership of voting shares in the company to a maximum percentage for a specified period of time. This percentage is less than a controlling interest in the firm. In exchange for their cooperation with the target, the potential acquirers are generally granted access to confidential information about the target firm's operations. These agreements also are confidential and do not require the target firm's shareholders' approval. Standstills often contain clauses that prohibit stockholders from selling a block of shares without the firm's approval. Such an agreement was reached in 1988 between Gillette and six potential acquirers, including Coniston Partners, a merchant bank that owned 6% of Gillette at the time of the agreement.

Another element contained in many of these agreements is the allocation of a number of board seats to a large stockholder. This provision usually carries with it a promise by the shareholder to vote with management on issues that face the board during the period of the agreement.

The key word in the description of standstill agreements is *voluntary*. Standstills act as takeover defenses against unwanted suitors, but they usually grant some control over corporate assets through the allocation of board seats to the large stockholder. Because of these features and because they are voluntary, standstill agreements are more like treaties than defenses.

Recent studies show that the adoption of standstill agreements is associated with an average 4% reduction in share prices. Thus reduced stockholder wealth is a by-product of standstill agreements and raises the question of whether target firm managers who undertake these actions are acting in the best interests of their firm's shareholders.

TARGETED SHARE REPURCHASES

Standstills are frequently followed by **targeted share repurchases.** At the end of the time period specified in a standstill agreement, the firm often buys the large block of shares held by the major stockholder in the agreement, at a substantial premium over the open-market price. This premium is commonly known as **greenmail** and is viewed as an inducement to prevent the major stockholder from initiating a takeover bid for the firm.

Targeted share repurchases are not always connected with standstill agreements, however. For example, an investor can buy a large block of stock in a company and then threaten a takeover. The firm's management often becomes anxious and, in response, offers to buy the stock back from the investor at a substantial premium above the original share price. In this way, they are able to get rid of both the raider and the threat of a takeover.

A case in point is that of Saul Steinberg and Walt Disney Productions. In 1984 Steinberg bought an 11.1% stake in Disney and indicated that he was interested in acquiring the company. Disney's management became very upset at the prospect and, after a long battle with Steinberg, agreed to buy his stock back at a price that would give him a $60 million profit. (Just before his attempt to take over Disney, Steinberg had successfully greenmailed Quaker State Oil Refining for a $10.5 million profit.)

This negotiated price above market value that greenmailers receive for their shares is not offered to other stockholders. Greenmail has recently drawn the ire of the many investors who are not afforded the opportunities of large block shareholders. Though generally not well received, greenmail is perfectly legal if the firm can prove that it made differential payments to large block shareholders for valid business purposes. The courts have adopted two very broad interpretations of "valid business purposes": (1) a difference in philosophy between management and the selling stockholder and (2) the elimination of future threats to business and the preservation of management's "business policy."

Empirical studies indicate a -3% return on stock prices upon the announcement of a targeted share repurchase, although there follows a positive overall total return of about 7% during the interval between the announcement and the actual repurchase. Thus targeted share repurchase plans initially lower the shareholders' wealth but are usually followed by price increases based on the speculation that there will be other takeover attempts in the future.

PAC-MAN DEFENSE

A less common reactive strategy is known as the **Pac-Man defense,** in which the target company in a hostile tender offer initiates a hostile tender offer of its own for the acquiring company. Such was the case in American Brands, Inc.'s 1988 acquisition of E-II Holdings, Inc. E-II's attempt to acquire American was thwarted when American made a successful counteroffer to E-II's shareholders. Thus the target became the acquirer.

The psychological effect of the target's becoming the aggressor is significant in this scenario because it places the managers of the original acquiring company in a defensive posture in order to save their own company from their original target. Even if the reactive tender offer by the original target firm is not successful, it can jeopardize the success of the original acquirer's takeover attempt. In the few instances in which it has been used, the Pac-Man defense has proved very costly to the target firm and thus reduces the shareholders' wealth. In American's case, only a very few parts of E-II proved strategically appealing, and the bulk of E-II's units were subsequently sold in a package deal to the Riklis Family Corporation.

WHITE KNIGHT TO THE RESCUE

Enlisting the aid of a **white knight** is an act of outright desperation. By searching for a white knight to bid for the firm against the original hostile tender offer, the target firm admits its defeat but still tries to negotiate its terms of surrender. These terms usually include a higher price than the original tender offer and more agreeable options for the target firm's current managers.

An example of a firm courting a white knight to avoid an unfriendly bid is the 1981 case of St. Joe Minerals Corporation. Having received a hostile offer from Seagram Co. in March 1981, St. Joe called on Fluor Corporation, an engineering and construction business, and suggested that Fluor play the white knight to St. Joe. The strategy was successful, and St. Joe was later acquired by Fluor in a $2.2 billion deal.

ASSET SPIN-OFFS

If a target company can identify a specific asset(s) that makes it attractive to a bidding firm, it may be possible to discourage the bidder by spinning off that asset(s) to its stockholders. A **spin-off** involves separating the operations of a subsidiary from those of the parent by distributing to all existing shareholders of the parent, on a pro rata basis, those shares that the parent owns in the subsidiary. Spin-offs are examined in greater detail in Chapter 27. The desired asset is typically a subsidiary of the target in which the acquirer has a particular interest. If the target is perceptive enough to spin off the exact asset(s) in which the acquirer is interested, there is a good possibility that the raider will go after the spin-off and leave the parent company alone. This antitakeover device is often called the **crown jewel strategy.** An example is MCA, Inc.'s 1988 announcement that if it became the target of a hostile bid, it would spin off its interest in the coveted Cineplex Odeon Corporation, a Canadian theater chain.

25-5

WINNERS AND LOSERS IN THE BATTLE FOR CORPORATE CONTROL

In this final section we explore evidence concerning the effects on shareholder wealth of both the acquiring and the target firms in successful and unsuccessful takeover attempts. Success in this sense is when the bidder acquires a substantial fraction of the shares initially desired. We also discuss the merits and drawbacks of an active market for corporate control for the economy as a whole.

Successful Takeovers   Evidence indicates that the shareholders of target firms in successful tender offers and mergers earn significant positive abnormal returns at the announcement and through the completion of the offers. An **abnormal return** is the return earned above or below the expected return on a security. In the case of tender offers, studies have found these abnormal returns to range from 16.9% to 34.1%, with an average abnormal return of 29.1%. For mergers, the abnormal returns range from 15.5% to 34%, with an average of 20.2%.

Abnormal returns for the shareholders of bidding firms engaged in successful tender offers are also significantly positive from the time of the announcement through the completion of the takeover. The abnormal returns to successful bidding firms range from 2.4% to 6.7%, with a weighted average abnormal return of 3.8%. Evidence on the returns to shareholders of bidding firms involved in successful mergers, on the other hand, is mixed and difficult to interpret. On the whole, however, indications are that the returns to bidders in mergers are about 0%.

In summary, the evidence indicates that no one loses in a successful takeover. Both the target firm's and the bidding firm's shareholders earn significant positive abnormal returns during and upon completion of successful tender offers. Successful mergers produce positive abnormal returns for the target firm's shareholders but mixed returns approaching 0% for the bidding firm's shareholders.

Unsuccessful Takeovers   The abnormal returns for the targets of unsuccessful tender offers range from 16.3% to 47.3%, with an average abnormal return of 35.2% at the time of the offer announcement. Unfortunately, no study has determined the abnormal return for the period up through the failure announcement. The existing evidence indicates, however, that targets of unsuccessful tender offers that receive no additional offers within two years after the failure announcement lose all their previous gains, whereas those that do receive new offers earn even higher positive returns.

The abnormal returns for the targets of unsuccessful mergers range from 3.7% to −9%, with an average abnormal return of −2.9%. Thus, by the time of the failure announcement, the targets of unsuccessful mergers lose all of the gains realized at the time of the offer announcement.

Research on wealth effects of the bidding firm's shareholders in unsuccessful tender offers and mergers is difficult to interpret because there are mixed results. On the whole, the abnormal returns produced are negative.

In summary, the targets of unsuccessful tender offers generally earn significant positive abnormal returns at the time of the offer announcement and through the failure announcement. But if they receive no additional offers in the following two years, they lose all their gains. Targets of unsuccessful mergers appear to lose all gains earned at the offer announcement by the time of the failure announcement. Bidding firms involved in either unsuccessful tender offers or unsuccessful mergers generally earn negative abnormal returns.

Proxy Contests   The evidence concerning proxy contests suggests that shareholders earn positive average abnormal returns of approximately 10.5% for 10 to 20 days before and including the day of the contest announcement. There is also evidence that a portion of the positive share price movement is not permanent, which leads to the conclusion that the negative excess returns observed in the later stages of proxy contests can be attributed to a decline in the value of the shareholders' vote.

In summary, proxy contests produce positive abnormal returns to shareholders in the early stages but produce negative excess returns, owing to a decline in the market value of the shareholders' vote, in the later stages of the proxy contest.

Implications for the Economy As a Whole

Opinions are mixed regarding the value of the market for corporate control to the economy as a whole. Although the evidence seems to show that an active market for corporate control generally benefits stockholders, there still is considerable debate about the consequences to U.S. competitiveness in the global arena.

Arguments against permitting a free market for corporate control revolve around the efficiency of the economy. Opponents of the market for corporate control feel that managers who are constantly worried about avoiding takeovers are less able to concentrate on running their companies properly. Decisions that ensure long-term competitiveness often entail near-term setbacks for a firm. Knowing that an active market for the transfer of corporate control exists often pressures managers to adopt very short-term perspectives in their decision making. Another argument against the market for corporate control is that hostile takeovers involve excessive debt, which benefits only the takeover "artists." This excessive debt prevents the target firm from pursuing growth opportunities and requires it essentially to eliminate research and development.

Supporting a free market for corporate control is a growing body of research that demonstrates the beneficial effects of this market for both the firms involved and the economy as a whole.[5] Recent research shows that most hostile takeovers accomplished through the market for corporate control are motivated by anticipated profits from restructuring the assets of the target firm. In many cases, these target firms are poor performers composed of widely diversified lines of operations. Hostile takeovers do not result in substantial reductions in investment, employment, or research and development. Reductions in these areas occur through cuts in corporate overhead or excess, underutilized capacity.

An additional finding is that many firms taken over by means of leveraged buyouts set a high priority on reducing the level of debt soon after the takeover by selling off unneeded or ill-fitting assets. The surviving firm is not only more profitable but also free of the temporary leverage used to achieve the takeover. Finally, although many restructured companies are smaller, they actually devote a larger percentage of their sales revenues to research and development.

Certainly, disagreements concerning the benefits of the market for corporate control will continue for some time. Although the arguments against this market should be carefully examined, the growing body of evidence supporting it cautions against any severe government action to restrict management's ability to bid for the control of assets in the economy.

SUMMARY

Section 25-1: The Market for Corporate Control

What is corporate control? Why does it have value?

- Corporate control is the rights bundle used to determine how corporate resources are managed.

- These bundles of rights have a value in the market because they allow competing management teams to capture the gains from various perceived benefits of control: satisfaction of growth goals, diversification, synergies from operating

---

[5] For example, see Amar Bhide, "The Causes and Consequences of Hostile Takeovers," *Journal of Applied Corporate Finance* 2 (Summer 1989): 35–59; and a review in *Forbes*, November 13, 1989, of the results of a seminar of the National Academies of Science and Engineering concerning corporate restructuring.

and financial economies, correction of managerial inefficiencies, and greater market power.

How do friendly and hostile takeovers differ?

- Friendly takeovers are accepted by the target firm's management. Hostile takeovers are resisted by the target firm's managers, who may fear losing their jobs or authority or may feel that the takeover is not in the interest of their stockholders. Hostile takeover attempts result in a fight between competing parties for control of the firm.

Section 25-2: Methods for Effecting Takeovers

How are takeovers accomplished?

- Mergers, in which one of the combined firms does not survive in name, are the most common method of changing corporate control.

- A tender offer is a public offer made by a management team to purchase a designated percentage of a target firm's outstanding common stock. This offer is made to the target firm's stockholders and does not require the approval of the board of directors.

- A proxy contest is a direct attempt by dissident stockholders to gain a controlling number of seats on a firm's board of directors. Voting can be cumulative or noncumulative.

Section 25-3: Takeover Financing Techniques

How are takeovers financed?

- Various methods of financing a takeover are available, such as cash, equity, and debt, as well as the controversial junk bond market.

Section 25-4: Strategies to Foil Takeovers

How can takeover attempts be blocked?

- Several antitakeover strategies are available to a target firm's incumbent managers, who usually resist takeovers in order to prevent change or to preserve their jobs.

- Takeover defenses are either proactive (preoffer) or reactive (postoffer). Examples are antitakeover amendments, golden parachutes, and asset spin-offs.

Section 25-5: Winners and Losers in the Battle for Corporate Control

How do takeovers affect shareholders' wealth?

- In the case of successful tender offers and mergers, both the target and the bidding firms receive positive abnormal returns and so are winners (with the exception of 0% returns for bidders in successful mergers).

- In the case of unsuccessful tender offers, the target firm receives positive abnormal returns, and the bidding firm earns negative abnormal returns. Both the targets and the bidders suffer negative abnormal returns when associated with unsuccessful mergers.

- To date, the market for corporate control appears to have a positive effect on firm performance and asset utilization, which benefit the economy as a whole.

QUESTIONS

1. Why does control have value? What are the control rights for which there is an active market? Why is there a market for corporate control?

2. How does a proxy contest differ from a friendly merger?

3. What are the differences between the procedures for a merger and those for a tender offer?

4. What factors have led to the increased popularity of tender offers? Is this trend likely to continue?

5. Is there a valid role for junk bonds in corporate acquisitions?

6. What are some takeover defenses? What are the effects of these defenses on the value of the target firm?

7. Who wins and who loses in successful takeovers? Unsuccessful takeovers?

8. What are the implications of the takeover market for the economy as a whole?

SUGGESTED
ADDITIONAL
READINGS

Asquith, Paul. "Merger Bids, Uncertainty, and Stockholder Returns." *Journal of Financial Economics*, April 1983, pp. 51–83.

Bhide, Amar. "The Causes and Consequences of Hostile Takeovers." *Journal of Applied Corporate Finance*, Summer 1989, pp. 36–59.

Bradley, Michael. "Interfirm Tender Offers and the Market for Corporate Control." *Journal of Business* 53 (1980): 345–376.

Bradley, Michael, and L. MacDonald Wakeman. "The Wealth Effects of Targeted Share Repurchases." *Journal of Financial Economics*, April 1983, pp. 301–328.

Dann, Larry Y., and Harry DeAngelo. "Standstill Agreements, Privately Negotiated Stock Repurchases, and the Market for Corporate Control." *Journal of Financial Economics*, April 1983, pp. 275–300.

DeAngelo, Harry, and L. MacDonald Wakeman. "The Wealth Effects of Targeted Share Repurchases." *Journal of Financial Economics*, April 1983, pp. 301–328.

Dodd, Peter. "The Market for Corporate Control: A Review of the Evidence." *Midland Corporate Finance Journal*, Summer 1983, pp. 6–20.

Dodd, Peter. "Merger Proposals, Management Discretion and Shareholder Wealth." *Journal of Financial Economics* 8 (1980): 105–138.

Dodd, Peter, and Richard Ruback. "Tender Offers and Stockholder Returns: An Empirical Analysis." *Journal of Financial Economics* 5 (1977): 351–374.

Dodd, Peter, and Jerold B. Warner. "On Corporate Governance: A Study of Proxy Contests." *Journal of Financial Economics*, April 1983, pp. 401–438.

Fama, Eugene F., and Michael C. Jensen. "Separation of Ownership and Control." *Journal of Law and Economics*, June 1983, pp. 301–323.

Jarrell, Gregg, and Michael Bradley. "The Economic Effects of Federal and State Regulation of Cash Tender Offers." *Journal of Law and Economics* 23 (1980): 371–407.

Jarrell, Gregg A., James A. Brickley, and Jeffry M. Netter. "The Market for Corporate Control: The Empirical Evidence Since 1980." *Journal of Economic Perspectives*, Winter 1988, pp. 49–68.

Jensen, Michael C. "Takeovers: Their Causes and Consequences." *Journal of Economic Perspectives*, Winter 1988, pp. 21–48.

Jensen, Michael, and Richard S. Ruback. "The Market for Corporate Control." *Journal of Financial Economics*, April 1983, pp. 1–50.

Kummer, D., and R. Hoffmeister. "Valuation Consequences of Cash Tender Offers." *Journal of Finance* 73 (1978): 505–516.

Linn, Scott C., and John J. McConnell. "An Empirical Investigation of the Impact of 'Antitakeover' Amendments on Common Stock Prices." *Journal of Financial Economics,* April 1983, pp. 361–399.

Ruback, Richard S. "An Overview of Takeover Defenses," in *Mergers—And Acquisitions,* edited by A. J. Auerbach, pp. 49–67. Chicago: University of Chicago Press, 1988.

Shleifer, Andrei, and R. W. Vishney. "Value Maximization and the Acquisition Process." *Journal of Economic Perspectives* 2, no. 1 (Winter 1988).

"Takeover Tactics on Trial." *Fortune,* June 10, 1985, pp. 11–12.

"Tender Offer Update: 1989." *Mergers & Acquisitions,* May–June 1989, pp. 25–27.

Wier, Peggy G. "The Costs of Antitakeover Lawsuits: Evidence from the Stock Market." *Journal of Financial Economics,* April 1983, pp. 207–223.

PART EIGHT CORPORATE RESTRUCTURING

TWENTY-SIX MERGERS

Let me not to the marriage of true minds admit impediments.

—*Shakespeare, Sonnet 116*

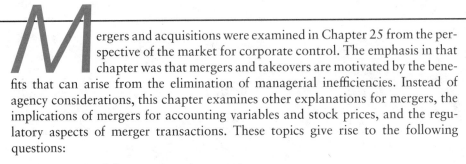

ergers and acquisitions were examined in Chapter 25 from the perspective of the market for corporate control. The emphasis in that chapter was that mergers and takeovers are motivated by the benefits that can arise from the elimination of managerial inefficiencies. Instead of agency considerations, this chapter examines other explanations for mergers, the implications of mergers for accounting variables and stock prices, and the regulatory aspects of merger transactions. These topics give rise to the following questions:

- What are the different types of mergers?

- Why do firms merge?

- Can increasing earnings per share by merging create value?

- How are the benefits of a merger shared between the acquiring and acquired firms?

- What are some of the antitrust issues surrounding merger activity?

26-1
TYPES OF MERGERS AND THEIR RATIONALE

A merger refers to the combination of two (or more) corporations in such a way that legally only one corporation survives and the other is "dissolved" according to the laws of the state in which it is incorporated.[1] The legally surviving (*acquiring*) firm ends up owning the assets of the dissolved (*target*) firm, and only the acquiring firm's name and common stock continue to exist. For example, a merger occurs when firm A purchases firm B and the surviving firm is firm A. The target firm is said to have been merged into the surviving firm. Its shareholders receive either shares of stock in the acquiring firm or some other form of compensation, such as cash.

In contrast, a **consolidation** occurs when two (or more) corporations combine to create an entirely new corporate entity. Following a consolidation, neither of the original firms exists as a separate entity. Rather, they are dissolved, and a new corporate entity is created according to the laws of the state in which it is incorporated. For example, a consolidation occurs when firm A combines with firm B in order to form firm C. Both A's and B's shareholders give up their respective shares and receive new shares in firm C, or some other form of consideration.

A **holding company** is a firm that owns sufficient voting stock in one or more other companies so as to have effective control over them. A holding company is frequently called the **parent company,** which controls the **subsidiary** companies.

---

[1] The term *acquisition* is sometimes used in reference to mergers. In the vernacular of the financial press, the word *mergers* is used quite broadly, and *acquisitions* normally refers only to the situation in which one firm acquires another firm and the latter ceases to exist in name or as a legal entity, or only part of another firm's assets are purchased.

Depending on how widely dispersed the stock of the subsidiary is, effective control may be gained with as little as 10% ownership. In fact, control of some major corporations can be had for less than 10% ownership interest in them. Seldom does it require a full 51% ownership interest to maintain control in a publicly held corporation.

Specific Types of Mergers

During different periods in American corporate history, several types of mergers and acquisitions have enjoyed prominence. **Congeneric mergers** occur between firms that have related business interests. They can be classified as either horizontal or vertical. **Horizontal mergers** were prevalent around the turn of this century. They involve the combination of two firms that are engaged in the same business. The surviving firm continues in the same business but is simply larger. These horizontal mergers are most notably associated with the "robber baron" era in the late 19th century. Large corporations such as U.S. Steel and Standard Oil joined their smaller competitors by way of mergers. This created monolithic concerns that ultimately gave rise to antitrust legislation.

Vertical mergers, in vogue during the 1920s, occur when a firm acquires firms "upstream" from it, such as its suppliers, and/or firms "downstream" from it, such as its product distributors. This process may go all the way upstream to the suppliers of raw materials and downstream to those firms that sell to the ultimate consumer. Therefore these mergers are a vertical integration (combination) of two or more stages of production or distribution that are usually separate. The advantages are lower transactions costs, assured supplies, improved coordination, and higher barriers to entry (for potential competitors). The disadvantages are larger capital requirements, reduced flexibility, and loss of specialization.

Conglomerate mergers occur when unrelated businesses combine. The business world saw an explosion of conglomerate mergers in the 1960s. A prime example of a successful series of conglomerate mergers is the Teledyne Corporation, which became one of America's largest firms by acquiring many unrelated businesses. Today this type of merger continues to be an important part of the total merger picture.

Compared with the ebb and flow of early merger activity, the dollar magnitude of today's mergers is enormous. In the early 1980s, industrial giants such as U.S. Steel–Marathon Oil, DuPont–Conoco, Getty–Texaco, and Socal–Gulf participated in this game. For example, Texaco's acquisition of Getty cost $10.1 billion, and the Socal–Gulf deal cost $13.2 billion. Merger activity should continue to be significant in the 1990s.

Economic Reasons for Combining Businesses

The underlying objective for a potential merger should be to maximize the shareholders' wealth, and a merger should be evaluated in terms of whether or not it will contribute to this objective. As with any investment decision, the cost of merging with another firm should be in terms of the net present value of its expected future cash flows. Next we discuss some of the reasons that businesses combine their activities.[2]

OPERATING ADVANTAGES

A merger may be considered because of the economies of scale it can achieve. This is the most often cited and easiest justification for a merger. **Economies of**

---

[2] The reader should recognize that it is some form of market imperfection(s) that leads to these advantages.

scale refer to the reduction in the average cost of producing and selling a product as production volume increases. For example, overhead costs can typically be reduced because what were formerly two departments, such as accounting activities, can be collapsed into one. Although the surviving department may be larger than the department of either of the premerger firms, it usually is smaller than both of them together. Horizontal mergers often take advantage of reduced production costs by increasing the volume of production. By controlling suppliers or distributors, a vertical merger may take advantage of enhanced scheduling and inventorying opportunities.

ENHANCED GROWTH OPPORTUNITIES

Equation (13-13) in Chapter 13 showed that the price of a company's stock (S_0) depends on its earnings per share (EPS), its required rate of return (k_s), and the present value of growth opportunities ($PVGO$) per share:

$$S_0 = \frac{EPS}{k_s} + PVGO \text{ (per share)}$$

Companies may merge in order to grow faster in a manner other than by internal expansion alone. Moreover, a merger may be a quicker and cheaper way to expand into new or related products or to acquire production facilities to increase the production of already existing items. Building a new plant to produce a new product can take years and be very costly. There are also uncertainties associated with cost overruns, the quality of the plant to be built, and the acceptability of the product. When a firm acquires another firm, it can do so relatively quickly at a more certain price, thus providing a product in a more timely fashion. Pooling resources and technical talent can increase the firm's growth potential. In other instances, a firm may be able to tap into patented technology and reap benefits. If the merger can increase the combined firm's growth opportunities, then the stock price will see upward pressure.

Of course, the reverse is also a possibility; firms may be better off separating operations to gain advantages. In the 1980s, a major movement to "deconglomerate" through asset deployments began. Essentially, firms began selling off entire operating units that no longer fit into their long-term corporate strategy. Some simply wanted to "respecialize," whereas others found that historically profitable businesses were not sufficiently profitable, owing to higher opportunity costs of capital. One of the larger asset deployments occurred when BSN–Gervais, a French firm, bought the Dannon Yogurt operations from Beatrice Foods. Beatrice was able to shrug off the mounting competition in the yogurt business, and BSN–Gervais was able to gain a quick market access for its diverse dairy products. Asset restructurings of this form are discussed in greater detail in Chapter 27.

FINANCING ADVANTAGES

A postmerger firm may be able to take advantage of new opportunities in the financial markets because of its increased size or efficiencies. For instance, because of some market imperfections, two firms may be far from their optimal debt capacity: one is overextended, and the other is underextended. By merging, they may achieve greater debt capacity (if, say, the combined firm has more growth options and hence greater firm value). This, in turn, may lead to a lower cost of capital for the postmerger firm.

The postmerger firm may also be able to raise funds at a lower cost than that needed by either of the premerger firms. The increased asset size (because of new growth options) can reduce the risk of default. Moreover, a (larger) postmerger firm is able to issue new securities in larger dollar amounts and thereby at a *reduced flotation cost*. That is, the cost associated with issuing stocks and bonds normally decreases as the size of the issue increases.[3] However, it is doubtful whether these savings alone are sufficient to justify a merger.[4]

TAX ADVANTAGES

An earlier form of the federal tax code offered considerable tax advantages to mergers of certain firms. There once was a brisk activity in corporations acquiring other corporations just to use the operating losses of the acquired company to offset the acquiring company's income. The purpose was to reduce the acquiring firm's tax liability. Both the target firm, which had little prospect of earning enough to take advantage of its tax loss carryforwards, and the acquiring firm could benefit from a merger. Later, new federal tax laws severely restricted the use of this operating loss deduction. Nevertheless, in some circumstances, a corporation may still be able to use an acquired firm's tax losses to reduce its own tax liabilities. In these cases, a financial manager needs to be careful when analyzing the merger's tax consequences to be certain that the advantages will accrue to the acquiring firm.

DIVERSIFICATION

It is sometimes suggested that mergers take place so that the acquiring company can obtain the benefits of diversification by acquiring new product lines and other assets. But this explanation is dubious. In well-functioning capital markets, there is no reason for a firm to diversify on behalf of its stockholders. Instead, stockholders can create "homemade diversification." They can buy stock in both the acquiring and the acquired companies on their own and in that way achieve diversification. Moreover, investors' diversification is cheaper than firms' diversification.

26-2
EVALUATING PROSPECTIVE MERGERS

Evaluating a prospective merger is like evaluating any other proposed capital budgeting project. The financial manager must compare the present value of the expected cash flows derived from the target's operations with the cost of acquiring the target's outstanding shares of stock or its assets. He or she needs to determine the following:

1. What benefits the merger may achieve from economies of scale

2. How much it will cost to acquire the firm

3. How the financing package should be designed

4. How the expected benefits should be apportioned among the shareholders of the premerger firms

---

[3] The SEC estimated that the costs associated with issuing less than $500,000 in common stock on average exceeded 20% of the gross proceeds. For issues over $20 million, the costs were less than 5% of gross proceeds.

[4] Quite often a catchall term, *synergy*, is used to explain a prospective merger. Synergy refers to the notion that the whole is greater than the sum of its parts. It simply means that the surviving firm's future earnings will be greater than the sum of the individual firms' earnings. Synergy results from the operating and financing advantages of a merger as well as the "nonquantitative" benefits such as improved management.

Such considerations merit careful analysis to improve the chances that a merger will be successful.

Expected Benefits from Economies of Scale

Determining the benefits requires answering such questions as: Can operations be compatibly integrated? Can any duplicated functions be eliminated? Are new or different technologies available? Can the sales distribution network be improved? In other words, to what extent will the surviving firm realize economies of scale and other benefits, and to what extent will these benefits increase the surviving firm's value over the summed value of the premerger firms?

Cost of Acquiring a Firm

With regard to the second consideration, the acquiring firm must normally pay a premium in addition to the target's market price per share that is in effect before the announced merger. This is done to persuade the target's shareholders not only to sell their shares but to do so quickly. Delays in acquiring the target's shares can cause the share price to go up and make the acquisition more costly. The idea is to get the shareholders to give up their shares before another firm enters and starts a bidding war. Thus the price must be set sufficiently high at the outset to satisfy the target's shareholders and to discourage anyone else interested in bidding for the target's shares.

Although these first two considerations are critical to any merger analysis, they require knowledge of the specific firms involved and usually entail nonfinancial and nonquantitative factors dealing with long-term corporate strategies. Nevertheless, standard financial analyses are still important in evaluating a merger, especially with regard to the latter two considerations: designing the financing package and apportioning the expected benefits among the premerger firm's stockholders.

Financing Prospective Mergers

The financing packages used in mergers can be quite varied. The offer may be made with cash, a variety of securities, or a combination of cash and securities. These include securities such as notes, bonds, or preferred stock (either straight or convertible) and common stock. "Sweeteners," such as options and warrants, are occasionally included as an extra financial incentive.

The financing package puts together an exchange that encourages the target's shareholders to approve the merger. This requires understanding the target's stockholders, especially the major stockholders, their tax position, and their investment motives. On the other hand, the acquiring firm needs to trade off these factors against its own liquidity and capital needs, especially with regard to how a pending merger may affect its capital structure. For example, will a cash offer be funded internally or through bank credit? What effect will these alternatives have on the surviving firm's cash flow needs? If debt securities are issued, will this seriously affect the surviving firm's financial risk? Will the added interest expenses have a negative effect on earnings growth?

In a **cash-for-stock exchange,** the target's shareholders receive cash for their stock. However, the target's shareholders may have to pay a capital gains tax on their proceeds, which makes it a less desirable method of payment to them. In a **stock swap,** the acquiring firm issues new common shares for the target firm's common stock. The target's shareholders may prefer this financing arrangement because it is a tax-deferred exchange.

The Effect of a Merger on Earnings per Share

During the early years of the merger boom, managers justified mergers because they helped in the "bootstrapping" of earnings per share (*EPS*). Simply by merging, an acquiring firm can, for example, increase its earnings per share in the short run. This apparent "benefit" is spurious, however, because the earnings of the

TABLE 26-1
Effect of a Merger on the Surviving Firm's Earnings per Share

a. *Premerger firms*

	Firm A	Firm T
Net income (NI)	$10 million	$5 million
Number of shares outstanding	2 million	1 million
Earnings per share (EPS)	$5.00	$5.00
Market price per share	$50	$20
P-E ratio[a]	10×	4×
Market value	$100 million	$20 million

b. *Postmerger (surviving) firm*

	Exchange Ratio		
	2.5:1	2:1	1:1
Net income (NI_M)	$15 million	$15 million	$15 million
Number of shares outstanding	2.4 million	2.5 million	3 million
Earnings per share (EPS)	$6.25	$6.00	$5.00
Implied P-E ratio in the exchange[b]	4×	5×	10×
Market value[c]	$150 million	$150 million	$150 million

[a] $P\text{-}E\ ratio = \dfrac{price/share}{earnings/share}.$

[b] $Implied\ P\text{-}E\ ratio = \dfrac{share\ price\ (acquiring\ firm)}{exchange\ ratio \times EPS\ of\ target\ firm}.$

[c] Assumes P-E ratio is 10.

combined firms are not increased but are simply summed. If fewer shares are issued by acquiring firm *B* to purchase target firm *T*'s stock than were outstanding before the merger, then the same level of total earnings is owned by fewer shares, which gives rise to a higher *EPS*. This "bootstrap" financing has historically been viewed as an important consideration in many mergers, and this view merits further attention. After our earlier discussion about the determinants of economic value and of efficient markets, this idea should be obvious. Nevertheless, given the widespread historical belief that bootstrapping can create value, we reexamine why this line of reasoning is fallacious.

Assume that two firms with identical earnings per share plan to merge (refer to Table 26-1). Although they both have an *EPS* of $5, notice that the market places a higher relative value on firm *A*; that is, its price–earnings (*P-E*) ratio is higher (10× versus 4×). This may be so for a number of reasons; firm *A* may be growing faster or may be less risky than firm *T*.[5] Furthermore, assume initially that their combination will have no synergistic or other benefits (i.e., the only "benefit" is a change in *EPS*) and that *A* can purchase all of *T*'s stock for the current $20 per share. To determine the required number of new shares that *A* must issue, the merger's exchange ratio can be calculated as follows:

$$Exchange\ ratio = \frac{price\ of\ acquiring\ firm's\ stock}{offer\ price\ for\ target\ firm's\ stock} \tag{26-1}$$

$$= \frac{\$50}{\$20} = 2.5:1$$

That is, in a stock swap such as this, *A* offers 1 new share of its stock for every 2.5 shares of *T*, or 400,000 new shares (1,000,000/2.5).

[5] Equation (13-14) states that

$$P\text{-}E = \frac{1}{k_s} + \frac{PVGO\ (per\ share)}{EPS}$$

Thus the P-E ratio can be different because of the present value of the growth options per share.

We determine the postmerger earnings per share, EPS_M:

$$EPS_M = \frac{NI_A + NI_T}{N_A + \Delta N_A}$$

$$= \frac{\$10,000,000 + \$5,000,000}{2,000,000 + 400,000} = \frac{\$15,000,000}{2,400,000} \qquad (26\text{-}2)$$

$$= \$6.25 \text{ per share}$$

where

NI_A and NI_T are the premerger net incomes of the acquiring and target firms, respectively

N_A is the premerger number of A's shares outstanding

ΔN_A is the number of new A shares issued for T's stock

Therefore the surviving firm's EPS will increase from $5 to $6.25, an apparent 25% increase in EPS. The word *apparent* is used because this "growth" in earnings arises from an accounting or "paper" transaction in which fewer shares are outstanding after the merger. Whereas the total earnings of the merged firms sum to $15 million, the original number of shares outstanding declines from 3.0 million to 2.4 million.

If investors erroneously perceive this earnings increase as real growth and apply the same *P-E* ratio of $10\times$ to the new earnings, the surviving firm's price per share, P_M, is

$$P_M = EPS_M \times \left(\frac{P}{E}\right)_M \qquad (26\text{-}3)$$

$$= \$6.25 \times 10 = \$62.50 \text{ per share}$$

where $(P/E)_M$ is the postmerger price–earning ratio. If stockholders correctly perceive this merger to have no real benefits, the postmerger firm's price remains constant at $50. Thus, although the EPS still increases to $6.25, its relative value is less, as indicated by a decrease in the *P-E* ratio from $10\times$ to $8\times$ ($50/$6.25).[6] In an efficient market you cannot "fool" investors simply by increasing the EPS.

---

[6] To determine whether the EPS will increase, one need only observe the *P-E* ratio implied by the exchange ratio, which is:

$$\frac{\text{Price of acquiring company's stock}}{\text{Exchange ratio} \times EPS \text{ of target firm}}$$

As long as the acquiring firm's *P-E* ratio is greater than the exchange ratio's implied *P-E* ratio, the acquiring firm will have to exchange fewer shares for T's stock, and an increase in EPS will result. To illustrate, assume that T's shareholders demand a premium over the current $20 market price to induce them to accept the merger. If this price is $25, the exchange ratio from equation (26-1) becomes 2 to 1 ($50/$25) and the implied *P-E* ratio is $50/(2 $\times$ $5) = 5. Although the total earnings are still $15 million, notice that the increase in EPS is only 20%, to $6 per share, because 2.5 million rather than 2.4 million shares are outstanding. According to equation (26-2),

$$EPS_M = \frac{\$10,000,000 + \$5,000,000}{2,000,000 + 500,000} = \$6 \text{ per share}$$

At the extreme, if A offers $50 per share for T's stock, the exchange ratio is 1 to 1 and the EPS stays the same. In other words, such a business combination leaves the number of shares outstanding unchanged because the exchange ratio's implied *P-E* ratio is the same as A's *P-E* ratio.

According to one hypothesis, mistaking the increased *EPS* as real growth is what made bootstrapping so successful during the wave of conglomerate mergers in the 1960s. To maintain their image of growth, conglomerates had to continue merging with more and more firms. Finally investors realized that this growth was spurious, and the conglomerate bubble burst and prices (*P-E* ratios) came tumbling down. For example, one of the more celebrated conglomerates, LTV, saw its market value plunge by over 80% in less than a year.

KEY   CONCEPT

"Bootstrapping" earnings per share by merging firms cannot, by itself, add economic value in an efficient market.

26-3

TERMS OF EXCHANGE AND MERGER VALUE

To effect a merger, the acquiring firm must offer a premium to the acquired firm's shareholders in recognition of the potential economic value added by the merger. Two questions that come up are: How should this premium be calculated? How should the expected benefits be apportioned among the shareholders of the premerger firms?

The premium depends on the market's assessment of the postmerger firm value and on the relative bargaining positions of the two firms. Determining the actual premium is a complex issue, and we do not address it here. Instead, we take the market's assessment of the merged firm's *P-E* ratio as a given and then examine how the exchange ratio determines how the economic benefits of the merger are shared between the acquiring and acquired firms.

Referring again to Table 26-1, note that the market values of firms *A* and *T* are $100 million and $20 million, respectively. Now assume that their merger will lead to real economic gains (in contrast with the "bootstrap" case, in which there are no economic gains). The question is: How will the gains from the merger be shared between *A*'s and *T*'s stockholders?

First, it is necessary to determine the expected gain from the merger. Suppose that the benefits derived from this merger are such that the *P-E* ratio stays at $10\times$ after the merger. In a 2.5:1 stock exchange, *A* issues 400,000 new shares for *T*'s 1 million shares outstanding, and the postmerger stock price from equation (26-2) is $62.50. The surviving firm's total market value, *V*, becomes

$$V_M = P_M(N_A + \Delta N_A)$$
$$= \$62.50(2,000,000 + 400,000) = \$150,000,000$$

From this, the expected gain in market value, ΔV, from the merger is simply

$$\Delta V = V_M - (V_A + V_T)$$
$$= \$150,000,000 - (\$100,000,000 + \$20,000,000) \tag{26-4}$$
$$= \$30,000,000$$

or the difference between the post- and premerger values of the two firms.

Next, to determine the extent to which the respective stockholders share in this merger gain, we use equation (26-4), substitute for V_M, and rewrite the result as a merger sharing rule:

$$\Delta V = P_M(N_A + \Delta N_A) - (V_A + V_T) \tag{26-5}$$
$$= (P_M N_A - V_A) + (P_M \Delta N_A - V_T)$$

where the first parenthetical expression represents the merger gains that go to the original shareholders of *A* and the second expression is the merger gains received by T's shareholders. Returning to the earlier example, we find the $30 million gain is split as follows:

$$\Delta V = [\$62.50(2{,}000{,}000) - \$100{,}000{,}000] - [\$62.50(400{,}000) - \$20{,}000{,}000]$$
$$= \$25{,}000{,}000 + \$5{,}000{,}000$$

or A's shareholders receive $25 million and T's shareholders receive $5 million.

Suppose, however, that T's management is a hard bargainer, or that T's shareholders are unwilling to part with their shares for $20 per share. Then A must offer a premium price—say, $25 or a 2:1 exchange ratio. This implies that 500,000 new shares need to be offered (1,000,000/2). From equation (26-3), the postmerger stock price is

$$P_M = \$6 \times 10 = \$60$$

Therefore, according to equation (26-5), the split in the potential merger gains is

$$\Delta V = [\$60(2{,}000{,}000) - \$100{,}000{,}000] + [\$60(500{,}000) - \$20{,}000{,}000]$$
$$= \$20{,}000{,}000 + \$10{,}000{,}000$$

or A's and T's stockholders receive two-thirds and one-third of the expected gain, respectively. By solving the **merger sharing rule** repeatedly for different exchange ratios, we can place reasonable bounds on the price that A should be willing to pay for T.

As seen in Table 26-2 and Figure 26-1, a share price of $50 (a 1:1 exchange ratio) results in all of the merger benefits accruing to T's stockholders. At the other extreme, a $16.67 price (a 3:1 ratio) leads to all merger benefits going to A's stockholders. But T's stockholders will not accept the latter price because it is less than their current $20 per share. Therefore the range of prices (exchange ratios) within which both sides can negotiate without either side realizing a loss is $20 (2.5:1) to $50 (1:1). The ultimate exchange ratio depends on the relative bargaining positions of the two firms and the market's reaction to the merger announcement.

The market's reaction to the merger (or their perceived value of the merger) is critical because it determines the relative value placed on the postmerger *EPS*. We assumed that the postmerger *P-E* ratio stayed at $10\times$. If the *P-E* ratio becomes less than $10\times$, A's former shareholders will suffer a loss in value. To see this, assume that $25 per share is paid for T's stock and that the postmerger *P-E* ratio falls to $8\times$. From Table 26-1, the surviving firm's *EPS* is $6 and hence its share value is $48 ($6 \times 8$), a loss of $2 per share.

In our example, A should be willing to pay up to a premium of $30 per share for T's stock ($50 - $20). A low premium (high exchange ratio) is not very realistic. When synergistic benefits are expected, T's shareholders will not give up their shares so cheaply. Firm A will thus have to sweeten the deal by offering a higher premium. Firm T's management will argue for an exchange ratio as low as possible, realizing that at less than a 1:1 rate, A's management will lose interest. Firm

TABLE 26-2 Exchange Ratios and the Sharing of Merger Benefits	Price per Share Offered	Exchange Ratio	Number of Shares Issued	Merger Benefits Accruing to A's Stockholders	Merger Benefits Accruing to T's Stockholders
	$16.67	3:1	333,333	$30 million	$0
	20.00	2.5:1	400,000	25 million	5 million
	25.00	2:1	500,000	20 million	10 million
	50.00	1:1	1,000,000	0	30 million

F I G U R E   2 6 - 1
*Merger sharing rules for
different exchange ratios*

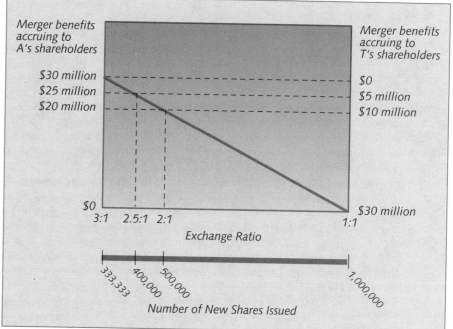

F I G U R E   2 6 - 1
*Merger sharing rules for
different exchange ratios*

A's management will argue for as high an exchange ratio as possible, realizing that at a 2.5 : 1 or higher rate, *T*'s management certainly will have no interest.[7]

KEY CONCEPT The value created by the merger is determined by the marketplace, but the sharing of the merger gains depends on the exchange ratio determined by the relative bargaining positions of the two firms.

Figure 26-1 shows how the gains from merging are distributed between the acquiring and the target firms' shareholders, depending on the exchange ratio.

**A Word on
Merger Prices**

In mergers and acquisitions, the acquiring firm normally pays a price higher than the current market price in order to induce the target's shareholders to tender their shares. But once word of the proposed merger gets out (sometimes based only on rumors), the share price of a prospective merger jumps. Thus, if the market price reflects a premium above the intrinsic worth of the target firm, the financial manager should be aware of this and count it as part of the cost of the merger. This rise in the market price constitutes part of the merger value being conferred to *T*'s stockholders, and there is little that *A* can do about the allocation of this benefit. This is why most merger talks are conducted in secrecy.

**A Word on Book Value
per Share**

The book value of the target firm should be of little interest in most situations. Seldom does it reflect the value of the firm in a manner that is useful to the acquiring firm. (The basis for this statement was developed in Chapter 2.) An exception is when the book value of the target's shares is significantly above the market value or when the target's balance sheet contains excess cash or "hidden assets," such as real estate, with appreciably higher market or replacement values. In these cases,

[7]Recent surveys show that the lion's share of the immediate merger benefits tend to go to the target firm's shareholders. Empirical studies have shown that the target company's returns often improve dramatically immediately before a merger when compared with the acquiring firm's returns.

MERGERS CAN CAUSE GROWING PAINS

In December 1983, American Express Company shocked investors when it announced that its 35-year string of annual earnings gains had been broken by a 10% drop in 1983 profits. The reason given was problems at its Fireman's Fund Insurance Company unit. But this turned out to be only the tip of the iceberg. American Express had often been cited as a prototype of the conglomerates that someday could dominate financial services. Its businesses included charge cards and traveler's checks, securities brokerage, insurance, and international banking. Most of its recent growth had come through acquisitions, but the acquisitions apparently continued despite signs of indigestion. Interviews with company insiders and outside observers revealed that American Express had acquired so many companies so quickly that it had lost management control over some of them. An overextended management allegedly had difficulty integrating the various subsidiaries, and internal rivalries undermined efforts to coordinate the various units.

One investment banker questioned whether there were any synergy possibilities among its various operations because they were very different businesses with very different markets and customer bases. A more serious impediment to a successful integration was the fact that American Express acquired companies with "different cultures." One example cited was the contrast of the aggressive Wall Street style of Shearson; the quiet, paternalistic nature of Lehman Brothers; and the more conservative "square-headed Minnesota types" at IDS/American Express. A final nagging problem was the tension among American Express executives. The company had long had a reputation for internal politics, and the recent acquisitions seemed to have intensified the political maneuverings by creating more factions. As one consultant remarked, "On a scale of 1 to 10, with 10 a Machiavellian jungle, they're at 9 and change."

The consensus is that three to five years will be needed to iron out all the wrinkles. American Express is a classic example of what can happen to a merger(s) if a postmerger plan for integrating operations is not well developed beforehand.

SOURCE: D. B. Hilder and T. Metz, "A Spate of Acquisitions Puts American Express in a Management Bind," The Wall Street Journal, August 15, 1984, pp. 1. Reprinted by permission of The Wall Street Journal, © 1984 Dow Jones & Company, Inc. All rights reserved worldwide.

the acquiring firm seeks the target for its liquidity or assets rather than for its future earning power.

Postmerger Integration

Numerous difficulties can arise when two firms are merged. One is the various misjudgments about the value of the target firm. Perhaps its assets are not what they seemed—inventory is obsolete or accounts receivable are uncollectible—or worse, there are hidden or contingent liabilities. These liabilities can crop up at any time in many ways. For example, no one anticipated that Johns-Manville would find itself defending against billions of dollars in hazardous asbestos claims 20 years after the products had been made. A firm that had acquired Johns-Manville before those claims were filed could have found itself in bankruptcy proceedings (as happened to Johns-Manville) because of the magnitude of these claims.

A more common and vexing problem is integrating the two firms' operations. Integration of different departments must take into account different policies, practices, and standards concerning production processes, accounting, marketing, and finance. Careful planning must be done to ensure the best chance for success.

Finally, the most difficult problems often arise with people. In the best of circumstances, the introduction of new policies and procedures as well as new people requires a sometimes lengthy adjustment period. All of these postmerger integration issues should concern the financial manager at the earliest stages in the merger proceedings. See the accompanying highlight.

26-4

MERGERS AND ANTITRUST PROSECUTIONS[8]

Although the market for corporate control can increase stockholders' wealth, certain mergers can affect the economy adversely. For example, when a firm merges with a competing company, this can reduce the competition in the market for goods and services. Indeed, such mergers can reduce competition to the detriment of customers, and the government may have to step in and return the market to its former, more competitive state. Through its antitrust division, the government can act as a check on mergers that are deemed anticompetitive.

When does a business become anticompetitive? There is no agreement on how much concentration in an industry is acceptable. As a firm increases in size, it can become more efficient and benefit the consumer through lower prices. But at what point can a large firm use its size to set prices for its goods higher than their market value? The government regulates business practices with antitrust laws designed to protect consumers from the abuses of monopoly power.

Antitrust History

The U.S. government first became concerned about business monopolies just after the Civil War, primarily because of abuses during and after this event. Giant companies, particularly the railroads, that were expanding with large amounts of capital invested during the war became monopolies that governed large segments of the economy, often secretly and fraudulently.

The **Sherman Act** became law in 1890. It forbids contracts, combinations, or conspiracies that result in a restraint of trade. At first the law was largely ignored by an understaffed Justice Department; in fact, it initially was used against labor unions and not corporations. Under President Theodore Roosevelt, the Justice Department used the act to try to break up the great "trusts" or monopolies that fixed consumer prices at high levels, but it became more effective after passage of the Clayton Act in 1914, which was designed to plug loopholes in the Sherman Act.

Section 7 of the Clayton Act concerns mergers and forbids the acquisition of the stock of one company by another when the effect is to substantially lessen competition in that industry. Mergers that restrain commerce or create a monopoly are also forbidden. The law is not concerned with reduced competition between the two merging corporations, but rather with whether competition in the industry as a whole is discouraged.

The **Federal Trade Commission (FTC) Act,** also passed in 1914, has the power to enforce the antitrust laws, along with the Justice Department. The act forbids unfair methods of competition and unfair or deceptive acts or practices in commerce. The FTC can also use the Clayton Act as a basis for its case; in fact, it frequently alleges violations of both acts when challenging a merger.

Loopholes still remained, however, and in 1950 the **Cellar–Kefauver Amendment** to the Clayton Act made the acquisition of assets as well as an entire company subject to antitrust scrutiny. Congress stated that there is a relationship between decentralized economic power and the preservation of democracy. Small businesses and the dispersion of economic power are encouraged. The emphasis is on probability; a merger does not actually have to lessen competition to be illegal—the government only has to show that the merger might lessen competition. In addition, the violation can occur in any of the firm's lines of commerce, not just in its major business. The relevant market is not the entire country but the section of the country in which either the bidder or the target firm does its business. A 1957 amendment requires criminally convicted business executives to serve jail time.

---

[8]I am grateful to Susan White for her help in the development of this section.

In the 1960s the Supreme Court supported almost all of the government's challenges. Horizontal mergers, those between two firms in the same line of business, were attacked for increasing industrial concentration and keeping small businesses from becoming successful competitors. Vertical mergers, those between a firm that buys in a certain market and a firm that sells in that market—for example, a merger of a shoe manufacturing firm and a shoe retail sales firm—were attacked because they were seen as monopolizing a share of the market that would otherwise be open to competitors. And conglomerate mergers, those between unrelated firms, were attacked because they were said to raise entry barriers and eliminate potential competition. The important question at the time was not whether the court would declare a merger illegal but whether the government would challenge the mergers because, once attacked, the merger had little chance of standing.

The court's stance relaxed in the 1970s. The government still won a majority of its cases, but by no means all. The Justice Department was concerned mainly with horizontal mergers, which are thought to be more anticompetitive than the other kinds of mergers. The 1976 **Hart–Scott–Rodino Antitrust Improvements Act** requires premerger notification to the government for all mergers above a minimum size. (The bidder's minimum size is $100 million in assets or annual net sales, and the target's minimum size is $10 million in sales or assets.) There is a waiting period before the merger can be completed. The government has the option of asking for more information, extending the waiting period, or allowing the merger to proceed.

Enforcement of Antitrust Policies

The role of enforcing the Sherman and Clayton Acts falls on the Antitrust Division of the Justice Department and the Federal Trade Commission. The Antitrust Division is headed by an assistant attorney general, appointed by the president, and several deputy assistant attorney generals. Justice Department lawyers investigate possible violations of the law, recommend whether the cases should be prosecuted, and try those cases that are not settled out of court. The division institutes an average of 40 cases a year, most of which are settled by consent decree without coming to trial. A **consent decree,** which can be used in noncriminal cases, is an agreement between the government and the firm. If the court approves the decree, the case is finished, and the decree is as binding as is a court order resulting from a trial.

The Federal Trade Commission (FTC) acts simultaneously as prosecutor, trial judge, and appellate judge. It is headed by five commissioners appointed by the president for seven-year terms. The FTC complaint counsel investigates and prosecutes cases before the FTC's administrative judge. The FTC and Justice Department also coordinate their efforts; each agency notifies the other when a complaint is filed or an investigation is begun. If both agencies are working on the same case, they meet and negotiate which agency will have jurisdiction over that particular case. Each agency has developed its own economic specialties and tends to defer to the other in its area of expertise. For example, the FTC handles most merger cases pertaining to the cement, food distribution, and textile industries. When an industry is actively involved in mergers, the FTC may require such firms to file reports about their future plans. It has set standards for mergers in a number of industries, including cement, food distribution, grocery product manufacturing, and textiles.

Some of the tests used by the FTC in reviewing mergers are:

How many competitors there are in the market

Whether substantial competition has been eliminated by the merger

The market shares of the acquiring and the acquired firms

The threat of defensive mergers from the merged firm's competitors

The increased competitiveness of the merged firm

Ease of entry into the market

Enforcing the laws is not clear cut. The existing antitrust legislation does not specifically define terms like *restraint of trade, tend to create a monopoly, line of commerce,* and *substantially lessen competition.* Prosecutors must thus rely on previous cases to decide whether the law has been broken.

Merger Challenges   How does the Justice Department decide which mergers to challenge? One source of information about possible antitrust violations is complaints from businesspersons, congresspersons, or other government agencies. Another source is the reports that firms must file with agencies such as the SEC when there is a major stock transfer. Other information sources are the general and business press, personal contacts of the antitrust lawyers, and studies of specific industries or practices. Once an antitrust lawyer receives information about an alleged violation, he or she must decide whether to begin a preliminary investigation, whether to ask for a full investigation, and whether to recommend prosecution.

The Justice Department follows general guidelines in deciding whether to challenge a merger. A horizontal merger should be challenged if it creates market power, the ability to set prices above the level that supply and demand dictate. Market power is effective only in those industries in which there are significant barriers to new entry and in which the industry is sufficiently concentrated. A merger is more likely to be challenged if the firms produce a homogeneous product because it is easier to set and monitor such prices than those of differentiated or customized products. The department uses the **Herfindahl–Herschman Index** (*HHI*) to measure market concentration. This index is calculated by summing the squares of the market shares of each of the firms in that particular market. For example, if there are three firms in a market, one with a 50% share and the others with 25% each, the *HHI* for that market is 3,750, or $50^2 + 25^2 + 25^2$. The index ranges from near 0 for a highly diverse market to 10,000 for a market monopolized by a single firm. The department looks at the index before and after a merger. A merger in a market with a score below 1,000 is unlikely to be challenged. An index between 1,000 and 1,800 is moderately concentrated, and a merger is most likely to be challenged if it causes the index to increase by 100 or more points. A market with an index above 1,800 is highly concentrated, and mergers that increase the index 50 to 100 points may be challenged.

The department also looks at whether there has been a trend toward concentration in the past in this industry. The merger will not be challenged if one of the firms is a failing company—that is, one with no reasonable prospect of staying in business without the merger.

Often the first step that the department takes in initiating an investigation is to send a letter of inquiry to the acquiring firm requesting more information about its proposed merger. Often just the hint of a challenge is enough to make some firms abandon their merger plans. After a merger has been investigated and the department believes there are grounds for prosecution, a complaint is filed in the appropriate district court. A statement of evidence that will be used at the trial to support the charge, including the relief requested, is also prepared. This filing should not be a surprise to the merging companies because by this time they have been consulted by government lawyers seeking documents concerning the merger and related economic information. If the target company does not wish to be acquired, it can be a prime supplier of information that competition would be substantially lessened if the merger was allowed. In cases in which the merger has not yet been completed, the government may request an injunction to stop the merger proceedings until the case is resolved. After the complaint is filed, there is a period of discovery during which witnesses make depositions concerning, for example, business volume and market structure.

Antitrust Remedies

Most cases never go to trial. A majority of the government's suits are settled by consent decree, when both parties agree on what action will be taken concerning the merger. Negotiations for a settlement may begin before the complaint is formally filed, which results in the complaint and consent decrees' being announced at the same time.

Relief imposed by the court or a consent decree may include abandonment of the merger or partial or total divestiture if the merger has already taken place. Divestiture can include recision, returning the acquired business to its former owners; spin-off, which allows the acquired business to become a freestanding company; or sale of the acquired firm to a third party. Partial divestiture is the most common settlement, which can be accomplished by selling a subsidiary or division, or the divestiture may be limited to certain assets. The relief may forbid the acquiring company to purchase any other company for a specified period of time. This is generally seen as unusually restrictive because industry conditions may change rapidly and are unpredictable. More common is an order requiring the government's approval before making acquisitions in the future. Remedies may include provisions to create or strengthen competitors of the merged firm, such as providing royalty-free patents to competitors. There may be conduct restrictions, such as forbidding common management of the merged firm, setting limits on information exchanges, and making rules about sales to each other.

Antitrust cases are time consuming. About a quarter of the cases are settled within six months, but the average length of time for the remaining contested cases is three years. Cases that go to the Supreme Court take even longer—an average of six to seven years until settlement.

The banking industry was not subject to antitrust scrutiny until after the 1950 Clayton Act amendment made asset, as well as stock, acquisitions illegal whenever they restrained trade. Banks are merged when the acquiring bank absorbs the assets of the target bank. The Bank Merger Act of 1960 gives the Federal Reserve Board, the Federal Deposit Insurance Corporation (FDIC), and the comptroller of the currency the right to approve or disprove mergers. The Justice Department still has the right to challenge mergers it believes are anticompetitive. It can easily obtain information about proposed mergers because they are required to have federal agency approval before they can be completed.

Other Antitrust Enforcement Measures

The Clayton Act also allows private parties to challenge mergers, in addition to or in place of a government case. If successful, the injured party can receive treble damages—three times the actual dollar amount of damages that result from the merger. A successful FTC or antitrust division conviction of a violation of the Clayton Act can be used as evidence in a private suit.

A few industries fall outside the Justice Department's and the FTC's jurisdiction. The Interstate Commerce Commission regulates railroad and truck line mergers; the Civil Aeronautics Board rules on mergers of air carriers; the Federal Communications Commission regulates mergers within the broadcasting industry; the

Federal Maritime Commission oversees the shipping industry; and the Federal Power Commission governs utility mergers. The agency that reviews the mergers is expected to balance the potential anticompetitive effects of the merger against the needs of the community.

SUMMARY

Section 26-1: Types of Mergers and Their Rationale

What are the different types of mergers?

- Mergers attempt to foster company growth through external expansion. The term *mergers* is often used loosely to refer to the various business combinations into which a firm can enter. More specifically, a merger refers to the combination of two or more corporations in such a way that legally just one corporation survives. A consolidation occurs when two or more corporations combine to create an entirely new corporation. A holding company is the firm that owns sufficient voting stock in one or more other companies so as to have effective control over them.

- Mergers can be congeneric—between companies that have related business interests. Congeneric mergers may be horizontal mergers, which are combinations of firms engaged in the same business, or vertical mergers, which are combinations of firms in different stages of the production process.

- Conglomerate mergers are those among unrelated businesses.

Why do firms merge?

- Merger activity should be undertaken to maximize stockholder wealth. Mergers may produce operating advantages through economies of scale or financing advantages through improved debt capacity or lower cost of funds.

- Mergers may also produce enhanced growth opportunities, provide tax advantages, or facilitate diversification.

Section 26-2: Evaluating Prospective Mergers

Can increasing earnings per share by merging create value?

- It is often said that mergers are good because they can increase the firm's earnings per share.

- An increase in *EPS* alone, without a real increase in the firm's operating income, has no effect on firm value.

- In evaluating the benefits of a merger, managers must also consider the potential problems of administering and controlling the larger firm after the merger is effected. Without a well-laid plan for "postmerger integration," the anticipated benefits of the merger may not be realized.

Section 26-3: Terms of Exchange and Merger Value

How are the benefits of a merger shared between the acquiring and acquired firms?

- The net gains from merger activity are determined by the marketplace based on an assessment of the postmerger expected cash flows and risks.

- The merger gains are shared between the acquiring firm and the acquired firm according to the exchange ratio.

■ The exchange ratio in a merger is a function of the relative bargaining positions of the two firms.

Section 26-4: Mergers and Antitrust Prosecutions

What are some of the antitrust issues surrounding merger activity?

■ Mergers may increase a firm's economic efficiency and thus benefit society as a whole. But some mergers may have an adverse effect on competition and thus not serve the best interests of society.

■ To counter what it feels are anticompetitive mergers, the government has established laws and regulations that limit the ability of firms to merge. These limits, commonly called antitrust laws, are enforced by the U.S. Justice Department and the Federal Trade Commission. The agencies evaluate proposed mergers for their effect on competitiveness, and they may prohibit or modify a proposed merger.

QUESTIONS

1. What is a merger? What are the different types of mergers?

2. What are the potential economic advantages of mergers?

3. What is a holding company? Holding companies are said to have an extra layer of taxation. What does this mean?

4. What are some of the relevant issues to be addressed when evaluating a proposed merger?

5. How are mergers financed?

6. How is the expected gain from a merger determined?

7. How are these merger gains shared between the acquiring and the acquired firms?

8. When evaluating a potential merger for its effect on competition, how does the FTC define the market under consideration?

9. Are the laws that prohibit anticompetitive mergers clearly stated? How might this degree of clarity affect the approval of the merger?

10. What criteria does the Justice Department use to challenge a proposed merger?

PROBLEMS

1. The Kodoid Co. wishes to acquire a controlling interest in the Polar Co. and in the Nidak Corp. The companies' outstanding shares and share prices are as follows:

Corporation	Outstanding Shares	Share Price
Polar	10 million	$5
Nidak	6 million	8

Kodoid estimates that whereas ownership of 20% of Nidak's shares should be sufficient to acquire a controlling interest, 40% of Polar's shares will be necessary because there are already several large shareholders.

(a) How much capital will Kodoid's current shareholders have to provide if it acquires a controlling interest in Polar and then gets Polar to acquire a controlling interest in Nidak?

(b) How much capital will Kodoid's current shareholders have to provide if it acquires a controlling interest in Nidak and then gets Nidak to acquire a controlling interest in Polar?

(c) Are the answers to parts (a) and (b) different? Can you formulate a general rule about the order in which the pyramid should be constructed (i.e., which company should be acquired first)?

2. The Prometheus Iron Co. wishes to acquire the Pioneer Lumber Co. Relevant information for both companies is as follows:

Company	Outstanding Shares	Share Price	Earnings
Prometheus	2,000,000	$50	$4,000,000
Pioneer	200,000	20	400,000

Prometheus is considering three different acquisition plans:

1. Pay $25 per share for each Pioneer share.
2. Trade $50 cash and one new Prometheus share for every four Pioneer shares.
3. Trade one new Prometheus share for every two Pioneer shares.

(a) What are the two companies' *EPS* and *P-E* ratios today?

(b) What will Prometheus's *EPS* be under each of the three plans?

(c) If Prometheus's *P-E* ratio remains what it is today, what will the share price be under each of the three plans?

3. Sherman Recreation Equipment, Inc., is considering merging with the Grant Tank Co., makers of scuba-diving accessories. Sherman's shares are trading at $20, and Sherman has 4 million shares outstanding and earnings of $8 million. Grant has 2 million shares outstanding and earnings of $2 million. The merger will occur by means of a stock swap. Grant has agreed to a plan under which Sherman will offer current market value for Grant shares (i.e., if Grant shares are trading at $10, the exchange ratio will be 20/10 = 2).

(a) What is Sherman's *EPS* before the merger?

(b) If Grant's *P-E* ratio is 4, what is Grant's current share price? What is the exchange ratio? What will Sherman's postexchange *EPS* be?

(c) If Grant's *P-E* ratio is 8, what is Grant's current share price? What is the exchange ratio? What will Sherman's postexchange *EPS* be?

(d) If Grant's *P-E* ratio is 12, what is Grant's current share price? What is the exchange ratio? What will Sherman's postexchange *EPS* be?

(e) What must the exchange ratio be for Sherman's postexchange *EPS* to be the same as its *EPS* before the exchange?

4. The Joule Electric Co. has agreed to a merger with Tesla Power Co. The takeover is to be by means of a swap exchange. The plan to which Tesla has agreed specifies an offer price equal to the share price in the market. Joule's earnings

are $5 million, and its *P-E* ratio is 12; Tesla's earnings are $1 million, and its *P-E* ratio is 30.

(a) What are the total market values for all shares of Joule and Tesla, respectively?

(b) What is the *E-P* ratio for Joule and Tesla, respectively?

(c) What will Joule's postexchange *E-P* ratio be if there are no synergy effects? (*Hint:* Find Joule's postexchange *E-P* ratio and take its reciprocal.)

(d) Repeat parts (a)–(c) with Tesla's earnings equal to $2 million.

(e) If there are no synergy effects, find a general expression for Joule's postexchange *E-P* ratio in terms of the preexchange *E-P* ratios (call them EP_J and EP_T) and market values (call them M_J and M_T).

5. Phil Slackmeyer of Walden Corp. has been instructed to analyze the possibility of a takeover of Trendex, Inc. The earnings, shares outstanding, and *P-E* ratios of the two firms are as follows:

	Walden	Trendex
Earnings	$37.5 million	$12.5 million
Shares outstanding	12.5 million	2.5 million
P-E ratio	15	6

(a) What are the *EPS* and the share price for Walden and Trendex, respectively? What is the *ROE* for each firm?

(b) What is the market value of each firm?

(c) Phil believes that an offer of four Walden shares for every five Trendex shares tendered will be sufficient to ensure a successful merger. If the postmerger *P-E* ratio is 12, what will be Walden's postmerger share price? Should the merger attempt be undertaken? What if the postmerger *P-E* ratio is 14?

6. The Longhorn Brick Co. is attempting a merger with the Bevo Construction Co. by offering four shares for every three shares of Bevo. The current share price of Longhorn is $40, and the current share price of Bevo is $45. Longhorn's *EPS* is $2.00, and that of Bevo is $3.00. Finally, Longhorn currently has outstanding 50,000 common shares, and Bevo has 30,000 outstanding.

(a) What are the *P-E* ratio and the total market value for each company before the merger?

(b) What will be the total market value of the shares of the Longhorn Brick Co. if the merger is successful and the postmerger *P-E* ratio is 16? What will be the breakdown of the merger benefits between the current shareholders of each company? What immediate rate of return will the current shareholders of each company get?

(c) What will be Longhorn's total market value if the postmerger *P-E* ratio is 17? What will be the breakdown of these benefits between the current shareholders of each company? What immediate rate of return will the current shareholders of each company get?

(d) What will be Longhorn's total market value if the postmerger *P-E* ratio is

18? What will be the breakdown of these benefits between the current share-holders of each company? What immediate rate of return will the current shareholders of each company get?

(e) If the *P-E* ratios of parts (b)–(d) are typical, what can you say about the terms of the merger?

7. Dowling Bryan of Universal Petroleum is evaluating a merger with Spanco Corp. The shares outstanding, earnings, and *P-E* ratios of both firms are as follows:

	Universal Petroleum	Spanco
Shares outstanding	1,500,000	500,000
Earnings	$6 million	$1.5 million
P-E ratio	12	18

Dowling believes that Universal Petroleum's *P-E* ratio after the merger will be 14.

(a) What will be the value of the postmerger firm? By how much does this exceed the sum of the values of the two firms individually?

(b) How will the merger benefits be divided if the terms of the merger are that Universal will give four shares to acquire five shares of Spanco? What will be the immediate rate of return to the shareholders of each company?

(c) How will the merger benefits be divided if the terms of the merger are that Universal will give six shares to acquire five shares of Spanco? What will be the immediate rate of return to the shareholders of each company?

(d) How will the merger benefits be divided if the terms of the merger are that Universal will give eight shares to acquire five shares of Spanco? What will be the immediate rate of return to the shareholders of each company?

(e) What must be the number of Universal shares given for one Spanco share in order to leave no net benefit for Universal shareholders? For Spanco shareholders?

SUGGESTED ADDITIONAL READINGS

Dodd, Peter, and Richard Ruback. "Tender Offers and Stockholder Returns." *Journal of Financial Economics*, November 1977, pp. 351–373.

Fishman, Michael J. "Preemptive Bidding and the Role of the Medium of Exchange in Acquisitions." *Journal of Finance* 44, no. 1 (1989).

Haugen, Robert A., and Terence C. Langetieg. "An Empirical Test for Synergism in Merger." *Journal of Finance*, September 1975, pp. 1003–1014.

Jensen, M. C., and R. S. Ruback. "The Market for Corporate Control: The Scientific Evidence." *Journal of Financial Economics*, April 1983, pp. 5–50.

Mandelker, Gershon. "Risk and Return: The Case of Merging Firms." *Journal of Financial Economics*, December 1974, pp. 303–335.

Mitchell, Mark, and Kenneth Lehn. "Do Bad Bidders Become Good Targets?" *Journal of Political Economy* 98, no. 2 (1990).

Mueller, Dennis C. "The Effects of Conglomerate Mergers." *Journal of Banking and Finance*, December 1977, pp. 315–347.

Myers, S. C. "A Framework for Evaluating Mergers." In *Modern Developments in Financial Management,* edited by S. C. Myers. New York: Praeger, 1976.

Schipper, K., and R. Thompson. "Evidence on the Capitalized Value of Merger Activity for Acquiring Firms." *Journal of Financial Economics,* April 1983, pp. 85–119.

Shad, S. R. "The Financial Realities of Mergers." *Harvard Business Review,* November–December 1969, pp. 133–146.

TWENTY-SEVEN

CORPORATE RESTRUCTURING

*Reorganization is the
permanent condition of
a vigorous organization.*

—Roy L. Ash, 1971

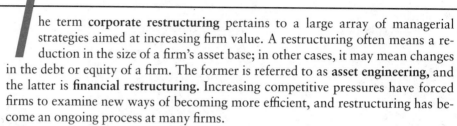

The term **corporate restructuring** pertains to a large array of managerial strategies aimed at increasing firm value. A restructuring often means a reduction in the size of a firm's asset base; in other cases, it may mean changes in the debt or equity of a firm. The former is referred to as **asset engineering,** and the latter is **financial restructuring.** Increasing competitive pressures have forced firms to examine new ways of becoming more efficient, and restructuring has become an ongoing process at many firms.

We examine several of these restructuring methods by answering the following questions:

- What are some of the different forms of corporate restructuring?

- What are spin-offs, equity carve-outs, and sell-offs?

- Why would a firm want to liquidate?

- Why do firms "go private"?

An appendix on the buyout market explains the mechanics of a typical buyout transaction and examines some of the reasons for the immense popularity of buyouts. It also examines the criticism of this form of financial restructuring.

27-1

A TAXONOMY OF CORPORATE RESTRUCTURING ACTIVITIES

Corporate restructuring encompasses several different types of transactions, including spin-offs, sell-offs, liquidations, share repurchases, and buyouts. The 1980s witnessed a wave of restructuring activity, and managers have provided various explanations for this massive "restructuring of corporate America." Some argue that the firm can achieve superior rates of return on assets by eliminating those assets that are less productive and using the proceeds elsewhere; others believe that the large conglomerates of the 1960s were inefficient users of resources. For example, a belief that a unit is achieving lower than average returns may suggest that a divestiture or spin-off is needed. Some restructuring activity involving changes in the relationship between the incumbent management and the shareholders is aimed at reducing agency costs. Examples of such transactions are buyouts such as those by Safeway in 1986 and RJR Nabisco in 1988. The factors mentioned here—namely, efficient asset allocation, a move away from conglomerates, and lower agency costs—are responsible for creating an environment conducive to the rapid increase in corporate restructuring.

A convenient framework for examining corporate restructuring is the balance sheet. Asset engineering refers to changes on the left (assets) side of the balance sheet, and financial restructuring concentrates on the right (claims) side. Table 27-1 depicts this classification of corporate restructuring. Asset engineering includes asset sales and liquidations, and asset sales can be divided into various forms of spin-offs, sell-offs, and equity carve-outs. Financial restructuring methods include exchange offers, share repurchases, and "going-private transactions" (leveraged buyouts, or LBOs, and management buyouts, or MBOs).

	Asset Engineering	Financial Restructuring

TABLE 27-1
Corporate Restructuring
Methodologies
	Asset sales
	  Spin-offs, split-offs, and split-ups
	  Equity carve-outs
	  Sell-offs
	Liquidations
		Exchange offers[a]
		Share repurchases[a]
		Going-private transactions
		  Leveraged buyouts (LBOs)
		  Management buyouts (MBOs)

[a] Exchange offers and share repurchases were covered in Appendix 15C.

27-2

ASSET SALES

Asset sales are the sales of a subsidiary, division, or product line by one company to another. There are three variations of this basic transaction: spin-offs, equity carve-outs, and sell-offs. Although all three involve a change in the parent–subsidiary relationship, the mechanics and motives underlying each differ.

Spin-offs

FORMS OF SPIN-OFFS

In the 1980s, many firms with diverse business activities sought to reduce their ownership of some of their businesses while still retaining control of them. Many thus opted for spin-offs. In a pure **spin-off,** a firm separates the operations of a subsidiary from that of the parent by distributing to all existing shareholders of the parent, on a pro rata basis, those shares that the parent owns in the subsidiary. This creates a new company with, initially, the same shareholders as the parent has. In this transaction, there is no transfer of equity control to a third party because the existing shareholders maintain their claims on both the parent and the spun-off subsidiary. Most spin-offs are treated as stock dividends and are therefore considered, from the shareholders' viewpoint, a tax-free exchange.

A popular example of such a spin-off is the 1984 breakup of AT&T. AT&T, which until then had been viewed by some as a monopolist in the American telephone company business, was split into seven regional companies. Each of these companies began operating as an independent firm in order to increase competition in the market. This reorganization took the form of a spin-off, with the parent shareholders receiving shares in the new entities on a pro rata basis.

In spin-offs, investors gain more control over a specific bundle of the original firm's activities because they now hold stock in a new firm (what used to be the subsidiary) that conducts some of the old firm's activities, but in a different setting. The new firm has the status of an independent public corporation and has its own management team. Thus investors can choose the managers who control these specific activities. It is important to recognize that in a spin-off there is no sale involving the exchange of cash or securities between parties. Rather, a spin-off transfers the management of certain of the parent's activities to a new group.

The most frequently cited motive for spin-offs is the parent firm's desire to specialize in a limited number of activities. Occasionally, however, a firm may be forced by the government to eliminate assets for antitrust reasons.[1] The AT&T transaction was an involuntary spin-off because AT&T was forced to spin off its subsidiaries in order to avoid antitrust challenges from the government.

Split-offs occur when a firm offers to its shareholders some, but not all, of its shares in a subsidiary in exchange for their shares in the parent. Unlike in a spin-off, the proportionate ownership of the two firms changes, with the parent firm's remaining shareholders no longer exercising even indirect control over the subsidiary. Split-offs tend to be much less common than pure spin-offs because they

---

[1] Antitrust issues were discussed in Chapter 26.

require that there be a group of shareholders willing to give up their interest in the parent in order to invest in the subsidiary.

As an example of a split-off transaction, James River Corporation decided in 1986 to acquire Crown Zellerbach Corporation but did not want all of Crown Zellerbach's assets. Three "unwanted" companies—Cavenham Forest Industries, ECZEL Corporation, and Gaylord Holdings Limited—were therefore split off from Crown Zellerbach. Some of Crown Zellerbach's shareholders exchanged their shares for shares in these three companies and some cash payments. These shareholders no longer had any interest in Crown Zellerbach or in the entity that resulted from the merger but, instead, now owned shares in three independent firms.

A **split-up** is similar to a pure spin-off in that the parent hands over control of its subsidiaries to its shareholders. In a split-up, however, the parent spins off all of its subsidiaries and thus ceases to exist. In addition to the change in management, the proportional ownership may change, depending on how the firm chooses to offer the subsidiaries' shares to its stockholders. In mid-1990, for example, Henley Group, Inc., chose to spin off its subsidiaries one after the other so that it would, by the end of the reorganization, cease to exist. It planned to do this through the split-up of units to its shareholders and then through the disposal of its remaining assets in 1991.

Table 27-2 summarizes the salient differences regarding ownership and the distribution of shares in each of the three types of spin-offs.

THE RATIONALE FOR SPIN-OFFS

A spin-off is often motivated by management's desire to narrow the range of a firm's activities. For example, in 1986 Singer spun off its sewing machine unit in order to focus on its aerospace and electronics industries. In addition to concentrating on specific activities, some companies spin off in order to take advantage of changing technologies, regulatory and tax requirements, and shifts in economic opportunities. With changing technologies and tax structures, the existing arrangement between the parent and the subsidiary may become inefficient, thereby making it more sensible for the parent to spin off the unit. These forces are often mentioned as contributing factors but are rarely considered the only cause for the change.

A spin-off may create value by eliminating "negative synergies"; that is, the firm as a whole may be worth less than the parts. For example, a very large firm may have operating inefficiencies that can be eliminated or reduced if it is divided into two separate entities with different managements. Some economists argue that a spin-off gives the subsidiary a new corporate identity, which may sharpen the focus of both the parent and the spun-off subsidiary by identifying their individual com-

■

TABLE 27-2

Features of Different Forms of Spin-offs

Type of Transaction	Ownership	Management	Firms
Spin-offs	Existing shareholders have pro rata ownership in both parent and subsidiary.	Management changes because subsidiary's management is now at new firm.	Subsidiary becomes a new public firm.
Split-offs	Some of the existing shareholders exchange stock in parent for stock in subsidiary. Proportionate ownership changes.	Management changes because it joins split-off firm.	Subsidiary becomes a new public firm.
Split-ups	Existing shareholders obtain ownership in the different subsidiaries. Proportionate ownership may change.	Management is now part of subsidiary firms.	Subsidiaries become independent public firms.

parative advantages, in turn creating greater shareholder value. A spin-off can often create a streamlined, decentralized, and more entrepreneurial organization that can respond more quickly to changes in the environment.

A spin-off can better align the interests of management and shareholders, thereby reducing agency costs because managers now can concentrate better on the firm's fewer activities. In addition, a spin-off has effects on managerial compensation that also reduce agency costs. In terms of direct rewards, the managers of the spun-off company are motivated by contracts that tie their compensation directly to the stock price of that unit, rather than to that of the parent. The managers of both the parent and the subsidiary may also now believe that they can affect the company's performance more directly, and compensation contracts such as stock options and other direct payments can spur them further. In terms of indirect rewards, managers may have greater autonomy and responsibility and hence greater financial rewards than they could in a unit of a larger firm.

Spin-offs also have implications in the market for corporate control, as indicated in Chapter 25. There are two major reasons for asset spin-offs associated with corporate control situations. First, a subsidiary may be sold off because it no longer "fits" the rest of the parent company's activities. In this case, the objective is to create a better fit for the parent so that it can simplify the merger or the friendly takeover of either the parent or the subsidiary. Second, the spin-off may be the key in a "crown jewel" defense (again, see Chapter 25). If a hostile raider would like to acquire the parent solely for assets associated with the subsidiary, the parent can spin off the subsidiary. This may satisfy the raider's desire to acquire the parent and still preserve the firm's corporate independence.

Taxes and regulation are sometimes mentioned as reasons for spin-offs, but only a few firms can realize these benefits. These include firms that create real estate investment trusts (REITs) and royalty trusts through their spin-offs, in order to shelter income from taxes, and U.S. firms performing spin-offs in other countries that provide preferential tax treatment for spin-offs.[2] Some spin-offs may also be inspired by the parent's need to avoid prosecution under antitrust laws. In other cases, some non-rate-regulated parents might choose to spin off a regulated subsidy that is proving to be a "cross-subsidization burden." Such was the case with Southern Union Corporation's spin-off of the Gas Company of New Mexico. Southern Union found that the Gas Company, a regulated business, was proving to be a burden to the firm as whole because regulation did not allow the Gas Company to achieve returns similar to those attained by the other units of Southern Union. This caused the other units to subsidize the Gas Company's profits. In order to avoid this problem, Southern Union spun off the Gas Company.

MARKET REACTION TO SPIN-OFFS

Several studies have examined the impact of spin-offs on shareholder wealth. Most use the event study methodology detailed in the appendix to Chapter 7 to examine the abnormal or excess returns to the equityholders created by the spin-off. Two studies in 1983 by Schipper and Smith and by Hite and Owers found positive abnormal returns of 3% on average on the announcement date.[3] In addi-

---

[2] Real estate investment trusts are restricted to investments in real estate-related assets, and royalty trusts are restricted to investments in natural resource-related assets. As long as these pay out 90% of their income to shareholders, they pay no taxes.

[3] Katherine Schipper and Abbie Smith, "Effects of Recontracting on Shareholder Wealth: The Case of Voluntary Spin-Offs," *Journal of Financial Economics* 12 (1983): 437–467; and Gailen L. Hite and James E. Owers, "Security Price Reactions Around Corporate Spin-off Announcements," *Journal of Financial Economics* 12 (1983): 409–436.

tion, Hite and Owers found that large spin-offs—defined as those involving more than 10% of the firm's equity—generate excess returns over six times as large as those of small spin-offs (5.2% compared with 0.8% for small spin-offs). They also found that when highly diverse units were spun off from otherwise homogeneous firms, there was a significant positive reaction, in contrast with the spin-off of a closely related subsidiary.

It is sometimes suggested that such gains to the equityholders come at the expense of other stakeholders, specifically the firm's bondholders, because their collateral is reduced (the bondholder expropriation hypothesis). Support for this hypothesis, however, has been weak. Furthermore, Schipper and Smith found convertible bondholders' gains to be in line with those for common stockholders. They contend that the expropriation hypothesis does not hold here because most debt issues have covenants that cover asset dispositions and dividends. Their study also found that the average rating of the debt did not drop significantly, which indicates that the spin-off was not perceived as having a direct impact on the bonds' risk.

A recent study by Copeland, Lemgruber, and Mayers found that in a spin-off, the parent's value is virtually unchanged but the subsidiary acquires a new independent value.[4] Assume that the pre-spin-off value of a firm is 7. If the subsidiary's market value after it is spun off is 1 and the parent's value remains at 7, the total value rises to 8.

In summary, spin-offs do create shareholder wealth, although the magnitude of the gain depends on the nature of the transaction.

Equity Carve-outs   **Equity carve-outs** are transactions in which some of a subsidiary's shares are sold to the general public. Thus an equity carve-out is an initial public offering (IPO) of some portion of the subsidiary's equity. Examples are Borden, Inc.'s carve-out of Borden Chemicals and Plastics in late 1987, and USX Corporation's offering of Aristech Chemical Corporation in late 1986.

Carve-outs are different from pure spin-offs in two ways. First, because equity carve-outs usually involve only part of the subsidiary's equity, the parent continues to retain control of the subsidiary's assets and operations. Second, shares are offered to the general public in return for cash, which contrasts with pure spin-offs, in which shares are offered to existing shareholders without any cash exchange.

MARKET REACTION TO EQUITY CARVE-OUTS

A parent firm can raise capital by issuing new shares directly or by selling shares of the subsidiary through a carve-out. The empirical evidence indicates that the former strategy is not welcomed by the markets. Smith found that when a firm issues shares of its own through a public offering, as opposed to issuing shares in a subsidiary, there are significant negative returns of about 2%–3%.[5] Schipper and Smith found that equity carve-outs are associated with positive abnormal returns of almost 2% over a similar five-day announcement period.[6] These studies suggest that an equity carve-out is seen by the market as benefiting the parent firm.

[4] Thomas E. Copeland, E. F. Lemgruber, and D. Mayers, "Corporate Spinoffs: Multiple Announcement and Ex-Date Abnormal Performance," in *Modern Finance and Industrial Economics,* edited by T. E. Copeland, chap. 7 (New York: Basil Blackwell, 1987).

[5] Clifford W. Smith, Jr., "Investment Banking and the Capital Acquisition Process," *Journal of Financial Economics* 15 (1986): 3–29, and "Raising Capital: Theory and Evidence," *Midland Corporation Finance Journal,* Spring 1986, pp. 6–22.

[6] Katherine Schipper and Abbie Smith, "A Comparison of Equity Carve-outs and Equity Offerings: Share Price Effects and Corporate Restructuring," *Journal of Financial Economics* 15 (1986): 153–186.

Schipper and Smith examined the returns on the new issues and found that the average abnormal returns on equity carve-out IPOs are 1.7% after the first day of trading. Schipper and Smith's results tend to apply to most equity carve-outs. Ibbotson, however, who examined all IPOs, found average initial returns of 11.4%,[7] and a small sample reported in *Corporate Restructuring*, which included the USX and Borden transactions mentioned earlier, documented much larger returns.[8] Although the details are too extensive to be repeated here, the study found that the postoffering performance of these carve-outs was closely related to the performance trends in the firms' industries.

SOME EXPLANATIONS FOR THE MARKET REACTION

A number of reasons and hypotheses have been presented to explain the positive returns associated with the parent firm in an equity carve-out. Some of these reasons are similar to those given for the spin-offs. A carve-out serves to reduce agency costs because it creates an independent entity with financial statements and stock of its own, thus making it easier to evaluate managers and determine their compensation based on the performance of the new stock. Furthermore, a carve-out has implications in the market for corporate control because creating a level of independence for the subsidiary might make the parent more attractive to a potential bidder. If the parent firm—in this case the target—does not want to sell all of the subsidiary until after the merger (for whatever reason), it may choose to perform a carve-out in order to initiate the subsequent outright postmerger sale. Finally, tax and regulatory factors may be a consideration in some carve-outs.

Sell-offs

Sell-offs, also known as **divestitures,** are common in the United States. A **sell-off** is a relatively straightforward transaction in which a segment of a firm is sold to a third party for cash, securities, or a combination of the two. For example, in April 1990, American Home Products Corporation announced that it would sell its household-products and depilatory businesses to Reckitt and Colman, a British firm, for $1.25 billion. The recent wave of such sell-offs was closely related to the wave of mergers and acquisition (M&A) transactions that took place in the middle and late 1980s. A well-known example of such a transaction is the sale by Kohlberg, Kravis, Roberts & Co. (KKR) of certain units of RJR Nabisco's European food operations to BSN S.A. for $2.5 billion, following its buyout of RJR Nabisco.

Sell-offs are often classified as *voluntary* or *involuntary,* depending on the reason for the decision to divest. Voluntary sell-offs occur when a firm's management sees that the transaction has a positive net present value and therefore voluntarily sells off the asset in order to enhance its shareholders' wealth. The sale by RJR Nabisco of some of its units to BSN was a voluntary divestiture.

Involuntary or forced sell-offs occur when a firm is forced by the Federal Trade Commission (FTC) or the U.S. Department of Justice to divest some assets to avoid antitrust problems. In many M&A transactions, either of these bodies may indicate that the posttransaction firm will have too much control over a certain segment of the market and so may ask it to divest some of its units. The government may believe that if the merger is completed, the resulting firm will control a market share that is too large for the market to be truly competitive. For example, when

---

[7] R. Ibbotson, "Price Performance of Common Stock Issues," *Journal of Financial Economics,* September 1975, pp. 235–272.

[8] *Corporate Restructuring, Mergers and Acquisitions Magazine,* August 1988.

KKR bought RJR Nabisco in 1989, it was forced to sell its Del Monte foods unit to Polly Peck International in order to obtain both the FTC's and the Justice Department's approval for the merger because KKR already had interests in the same business.

MOTIVATIONS FOR VOLUNTARY SELL-OFFS

Several of the commonly advanced reasons for sell-offs are unsatisfactory. For example, a sell-off is often viewed as a means of raising capital. But this is incorrect because a sell-off does not generate capital; it merely transforms assets from one form into another. Of course, to the extent that a long-term asset is converted to cash, the firm's working capital may increase. To sell off assets in order to raise cash ignores the fact that raising capital through debt or equity issues is usually less expensive than a sell-off. Another explanation for a sell-off, that it is done to repay debt, confuses the result of a sell-off with its cause. The debt repayment should not be the motivation for selling because it is an expensive method of repaying debt. It is sometimes suggested that firms sell off assets in order to get out of capital-intensive businesses. Implicit in this argument is the view that these capital-intensive investments are uneconomic. Many industries do require capital-intensive investments to be profitable, and clearly, to the extent that the buyer is willing to undertake these investments, such assets must have economic benefits. If these assets are uneconomic, why is the buyer interested in them? Finally, there is the view that firms sell units because they are losing money. This again is not a sufficient reason to divest because an underperforming unit can often be turned around (with perhaps a different group of managers). The stated aim of a divestiture may be to increase shareholder value. If a unit is underperforming, the market recognizes this, and it is reflected in the firm's share price. The firm can therefore benefit from the sale of a unit only if it can sell the unit for more than its market value. Selling off assets can make economic sense only when the assets are creating diseconomies for the firm or when the assets can be put to better use by more efficient users.

Several more satisfactory motivations for sell-offs have been suggested. One is that many of the conglomerates assembled in the 1960s were inefficient users of their resources and that dismantling these conglomerates through sell-offs enabled managers to narrow their focus and improve efficiency. Changes in technology and the economy in general may cause firms to abandon businesses, and changes in strategy may have the same effects on some product lines. Often firms find that even though a business unit has been very profitable in the past, the firm as a whole can benefit more if it can harvest the past success through a sell-off and invest the proceeds in a more profitable line. Thus there are basically two reasons for sell-offs:[9] (1) the assets are worth more as part of the buyer's organization than as part of the seller's, and (2) the assets are actively interfering with the seller's other profitable operations. These are the reason of fit and the reason of negative synergy discussed earlier, considered to be the two valid motivations for sell-offs. This view is strengthened by the observation that most of the other explanations of sell-offs tend to be financing decisions that can be accomplished through actions other than divestitures. It is unlikely that such financing decisions alone can increase shareholder value.

In some mergers or acquisitions, it may be necessary to discard a unit to match

---

[9] Scott C. Linn and Michael S. Rozeff, "The Corporate Sell-off," *Midland Corporate Finance Journal,* Summer 1984, pp. 17–26.

the company's "fit" better. This, unlike a forced sell-off, is often planned in advance and is done once the triggering transaction has been consummated. Often firms resort to sell-offs to avoid takeovers through the crown jewel defense. Firms may also choose to divest when they attempt to correct a past mistake, say an attempt at diversification, as was the case with Mobil's takeover and subsequent divestiture of Montgomery Ward.

MARKET REACTIONS TO VOLUNTARY SELL-OFFS

There is extensive evidence regarding the effects of sell-offs on shareholder value. Alexander, Benson, and Kampmeyer found in 1984 that the announcement of a voluntary sell-off has a slight positive abnormal impact on the divesting firm's share price, although it is not significant.[10] But their conclusion is not consistent with several other studies that found significant positive abnormal gains. Zaima and Hearth found that the sell-offs tended to come after a period of generally negative abnormal returns, which suggests that the transaction occurs after negative information about the firm has been released.[11] This may mean that the motives behind the sell-offs themselves are negative, such as attempting to sell unprofitable units or trying to raise capital for other parts of the firm.

Another study, by Hite, Owers, and Rogers, divided firms on the basis of buyers and sellers and whether or not they were successful, to see whether the market was able to anticipate success.[12] Although successful sellers had significant abnormal gains of 2.28% for the period from announcement to outcome, successful bidders' gains were significant but were only 1.39% on average. On the other hand, unsuccessful sellers saw gains of 1.41% at the time of announcement and the gains had totally dissipated by the time of the cancellation. Unsuccessful bidders' share prices registered no significant abnormal gains over the duration of the process.

Although sell-offs appear to generate smaller abnormal gains for stockholders, when these gains are aggregated over time, they still represent a substantial amount. Black and Grundfest estimated that the abnormal increases in shareholder value for sellers in divestitures from 1981 to 1986 were at least $27.6 billion.[13] The magnitude of these gains shows the enormity of the market for such transactions and their economic value to the stockholders.

MARKET REACTIONS TO INVOLUNTARY SELL-OFFS

The majority of research studies find that involuntary sell-offs tend to reduce the value of the divesting firm's stock. For example, one study, by Ellert, that examined sell-offs associated with antitrust merger cases, found a significant -1.86% average abnormal percentage drop in the month that the FTC or Justice Department filed an antitrust complaint about a merger.[14] Kummer examined the stock prices from one month before to one month after the merger and found a significant drop

---

[10] Gordon J. Alexander, P. George Benson, and Joan M. Kampmeyer, "Investigating the Value Effects of Announcements of Voluntary Corporate Sell-offs," *Journal of Finance*, June 1984, pp. 503–517.

[11] Janis K. Zaima and Douglas Hearth, "The Wealth Effects of Voluntary Sell-offs: Implications for Divesting and Acquiring Firms," *Journal of Financial Research*, Fall 1985, pp. 227–236.

[12] Gailen L. Hite, James E. Owers, and Ronald C. Rogers, "The Market for Interfirm Asset Sales: Partial Sell-offs and Total Liquidations," *Journal of Financial Economics* 18 (1987): 229–252.

[13] Bernard S. Black and Joseph A. Grundfest, "Shareholder Gains from Takeovers and Restructurings Between 1981 and 1986: $162 Billion Is a Lot of Money," *Journal of Applied Corporate Finance*, Spring 1988, pp. 5–15.

[14] James Ellert, "Mergers, Antitrust Law Enforcement and Stockholders Returns," *Journal of Finance*, May 1976, pp. 715–732.

of -1.63% for horizontal mergers and an abnormal return not significantly different from 0% for vertical and conglomerate mergers.[15]

There have been various explanations for these results. The "fair price hypothesis" maintains that in a forced divestiture the market may expect that a firm will not receive a fair price and in effect has to settle for a "fire sale." But if the market for asset acquisitions is competitive, this cannot be a plausible explanation. Another explanation is the "monopoly limitation hypothesis." When the government requires a firm to divest, it limits its monopolistic power, causing the firm's revenues and hence its share price to drop. If this was indeed the case, then one should expect a similar drop in share prices for all firms in the industry because the breakup of a monopoly should increase competition, thereby creating lower prices for their services and also lower profits. According to the data, however, there is no such widespread drop in share prices, and there is little support for this theory. The "structure destruction hypothesis" holds that the drop in share prices arises from the belief that divestiture generally destroys efficient asset structures. Over time, firms may build up efficient infrastructures that provide benefits through economies of scale or better asset utilization. A divestiture is seen as destroying these synergies, raising costs, and lowering profits, and therefore the share price, which led to the abnormal drop detected in the empirical studies.

An examination of the difference in returns depending on the type of merger with which the divestiture is connected has yielded some definitive conclusions. Kummer's study, mentioned earlier, also looked at the possible sources of and reasons for the loss to shareholders. He found that the losses were related to lost cash flows and the regulator's specific requirements. He then examined two subsets of the data to see whether the type of merger affected the level of returns. The two subsets were divestitures related to horizontal mergers and those connected with vertical or conglomerate mergers. He discovered that sell-offs connected with horizontal mergers were seen to reduce monopoly power and that there could be a real loss in synergy, giving rise to the significant negative average abnormal return. On the other hand, divestitures associated with vertical or conglomerate mergers also had no abnormal returns, either because the market assumed that the regulatory bodies would take no action or because the market anticipated no real efficiencies generated by such mergers.

27-3
LIQUIDATIONS

A liquidation is a transaction in which a firm sells its entire portfolio of assets to one or more firms for cash, which is then distributed to its shareholders. The liquidating firm then ceases to exist as a corporate entity. Henley Group, Inc., for example, was spun off from Allied Signal in 1986 because it was felt that the 35 business units of Allied Signal did not match its long-term fit. These units were then consolidated into Henley. Henley, in turn, has been reorganizing and spinning off its own units to enhance its shareholder value. Henley chose to liquidate all its assets by 1991 because it felt that this would be the best way to increase value. Then it no longer exists as a firm because it has disposed of all its assets and passed on the proceeds to its shareholders. A voluntary liquidation aims to increase shareholder value, unlike a liquidation associated with bankruptcy proceedings, which is more common and is often forced on the firm

---

[15] Donald R. Kummer, "Valuation Consequences of Forced Divestiture Announcements," *Journal of Economics and Business* 30, no. 2 (1978): 130–136.

by its creditors or by legal forces. We do not cover involuntary liquidations here because they are not motivated by a desire to enhance firm value.

Reasons for Liquidations

When a firm can be sold for an amount that exceeds the market value of the sum of its outstanding securities, liquidation is in the best interests of the security-holders. In that case, managers have an incentive to liquidate because outsiders can mount a proxy contest (see Chapter 25) and then conduct the liquidation themselves. There are other reasons that a firm may choose to liquidate. The market may be misinformed about the true value of the firm's assets because its managers may not be able to reveal all of the information that they have (the asymmetric information problem), or the firm's management may be following a suboptimal operating policy. Either of these can lead to an undervaluing of the firm's assets, making liquidation more rewarding for the shareholders. Liquidations are also seen as means of eliminating diseconomies. Diseconomies from overdiversification can be remedied through the piecemeal sale of assets to firms that have characteristics similar to those of the division being sold. This argument finds additional support in the evidence that in liquidations, the existing management takes certain portions of the firm private. This indicates that the managers believe that the divisions can operate efficiently if they are independent, thereby avoiding existing diseconomies.

Although agency explanations for liquidations are sometimes proposed, they are weak. Typically, liquidating firms have profitability measures consistent with those of the industry. Furthermore, the liquidations are proposed by the management and accepted by the shareholders, which indicates that both groups have similar objectives for the firm, especially because managers often own significant portions of the firm's common stock. Agency problems, therefore, do not appear to drive liquidations.

Liquidations are sometimes motivated by tax considerations. A liquidation can yield tax benefits for shareholders and buyers because the firm avoids taxes on any accounting gains, and the buyer is able to step up the tax basis of the assets acquired (except for depreciation recapture). In their study, however, Kim and Schatzberg indicate that in terms of tax benefits, a liquidation may not be as favorable as a nontaxable merger.[16] The main reasons for a liquidation, therefore, appear to be to sell undervalued assets and to eliminate diseconomies.

Market Reaction to Voluntary Liquidations

Three studies provide empirical evidence regarding the effect of liquidations on shareholder wealth. In 1986 Hite, Owers, and Rogers found that there is an average abnormal gain of 12.24% over the two-day announcement period.[17] They also found that participants in the market agree with management's contention that the firm's assets have been undervalued. But they were unable to determine whether this undervaluing occurred because of market inefficiency or managerial inefficiency.

Another study by Skantz and Marchesini found average abnormal gains of 21.4% during the month of the announcement, with a cumulative average excess return of 41.3%.[18] They also found that the firms were not performing below the industry averages, thus contradicting the previous study. Skantz and Marchesini

---

[16]E. Han Kim and John D. Schatzberg, "Voluntary Corporate Liquidations," *Midland Corporate Finance Journal*, Spring 1987, pp. 311–328.

[17]Gailen Hite, James C. Owers, and Ronald C. Rogers, "The Market for Interfirm Asset Sales: Partial Sell-offs and Total Liquidations," *Journal of Financial Economics* 18 (1987): 229–252.

[18]Terrance R. Skantz and Roberto Marchesini, "The Effect of Voluntary Corporate Liquidation on Shareholder Wealth," *Journal of Financial Research*, Spring 1987, pp. 65–75.

attribute the large gains to the tax benefits available through liquidations, although this does not appear to be enough to account for such large abnormal gains.

Kim and Schatzberg's study turned up average abnormal gains of 14% over a three-day announcement period for liquidating firms, and an additional 3% if the shareholders approved the liquidation. Abnormal returns rose a further 9% if there had been earlier announcements regarding mergers, tender offers, or partial sell-offs. They also found that the stockholders of the acquiring firms neither gained nor lost in these transactions. They believe that whereas in liquidations there may be several purchasers, creating a competitive environment, in mergers there is often only one. This allows liquidating firms to transfer their assets to those firms that they believe can give them the greatest value. On the other hand, the stockholders of the acquiring firms neither gain nor lose because they are bidding in a competitive market. They neither underpay nor overpay for the liquidating firm's assets.

27-4

GOING-PRIVATE TRANSACTIONS

A going-private transaction or a **buyout** is the transformation of a public corporation into a privately held firm. Such transactions include pure going-private transactions, management buyouts (MBOs), and leveraged buyouts (LBOs). These different forms of going private have similar motivations; only their mechanics vary.

Going-private transactions have become a common form of corporate restructuring, especially through leveraged buyouts. The activity in these markets has been intense. Table 27-3 lists some of the bigger recent going-private transactions. Poor economic conditions since 1988 have caused decreases in the number of going-private transactions.

Forms of Going-Private Transactions

The simplest going-private transaction is a **pure going-private transaction,** in which the only group that takes an equity stake in the firm is the firm's management. There is no third-party equity participation (i.e., no outside equityholders) in the transaction. Usually such a transaction is used for a relatively small entity because management does not solicit outside sources of funding.

Management buyouts (MBOs) are transactions in which a unit's management acquires the unit from its parent firm. An MBO is similar to a sell-off in that part of the firm is sold to a party that theoretically can put the assets to better use. A recent large MBO, for example, was the 1989 sale for $570 million by Marriott Corporation of its Marriott Inflight Services unit to its management. Although this

■

T A B L E   2 7 - 3

Largest Going-Private Transactions, 1983–1992

Company Name	Year	Purchase Price (millions)
RJR Nabisco	1988	$25,561.6
Beatrice	1985	$5,361.6
Safeway Stores	1986	$4,198.4
Borg-Warner	1987	$3,798.6
Southland	1987	$3,723.3
Owens-Illinois	1986	$3,631.9
Hospital Corporation of America	1988	$3,602.1
Fort Howard Paper	1988	$3,574.2
NWA	1989	$3,524.5
R. H. Macy	1985	$3,484.7
Burlington Industries	1987	$2,128.6
National Gypsum	1985	$2,059.1

SOURCE: *Mergerstat Review* (annual), 1992.

TABLE 27-4

Largest Management Buyouts

Company Name	Year	Purchase Price (millions)
Union Texas Petroleum, 50% sold by Allied	1985	$1,700
Montgomery Ward, sold by Mobil	1988	$1,500
Reliance Electric, sold by Exxon	1986	$1,350
Hertz, sold by Allegis	1987	$1,300
Rheem Manufacturing and associated units, sold by City Investing	1984	$1,251

SOURCE: *Mergerstat Review* (annual), 1992.

was the largest transaction in 1989, transactions in earlier years have been larger, and Table 27-4 lists some of them.

Leveraged buyouts occur when a small group of investors acquires—primarily through borrowing—the stock or the assets of a formerly public company. The group of investors may be sponsored by buyout specialists such as Kohlberg, Kravis, Roberts (KKR), or investment bankers that arrange such deals in cooperation with incumbent management. The phenomenal activity in the LBO market during the last decade is documented in Figure 27-1. Note that the popularity of LBOs declined dramatically in 1989.

Most MBOs are also LBOs, although MBOs are led by the incumbent management team and tend to involve smaller firms. The average price paid for MBOs is much less than that for LBOs. Until 1987, the numbers of MBO transactions was about twice as large as the number of public-company LBOs. Since that time, the numbers of LBOs and MBOs have been approximately similar. The large volume of LBO transactions in 1988 was to a large extent the result of the largest LBO ever, the LBO by KKR of RJR Nabisco. Because the mechanics of this buyout were essentially the same as those of most other LBOs, we describe this transaction in the Nabisco highlight.

FIGURE 27-1

Value of leveraged buyouts, 1983–1992

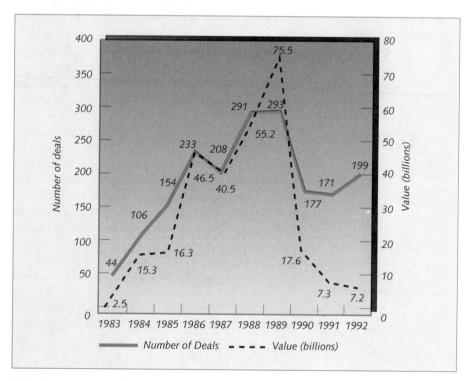

SOURCE: *M & A Almanac*, May/June 1993.

THE RJR NABISCO BUYOUT

The biggest leveraged buyout to date was the 1989 purchase of RJR Nabisco (hereafter RJR) for more than $25 billion by Kohlberg, Kravis, Roberts (KKR).* RJR was a large tobacco and food company, with over $17 billion in assets, based in the United States and with operations in 40 countries and sales in 160 countries. In October 1988, Ross Johnson, RJR's CEO, indicated that he, along with a management team and the support of Shearson as a buyout specialist, planned to take RJR private at $75 per share. When this was announced, the board of directors set up a committee of outside directors to invite other bids and evaluate them. The final competitors were the Johnson group and an offer by KKR. The board insisted that the final bid include an equity option in the private company for existing shareholders and that assets be sold off more slowly to reduce the impact on the bondholders and employees. Because of intense competition, the share price was bid up to a premium of almost 100% over the preoffer price of $55⅞. The winning bid was submitted by KKR on November 30, 1988—$109 per share, with $81 million in cash, $10 million in convertible debentures, and $18 million of preferred stock.

By 1990, after a year as a private firm, RJR Nabisco continued to show growth in sales and operating income, although it reported a loss of over $1 billion owing to interest expenses, accounting costs, and the reduction of excess inventories. This transaction and its subsequent stages illustrate several aspects of corporate restructuring.

After the original buyout, RJR divested two of its units. First, in a voluntary move, RJR sold some of its European units to BSN S.A. It also sold its Del Monte units through two separate transactions; the Del Monte foods unit to Polly Peck International through an involuntary divestiture, and the Del Monte canned foods unit to a group consisting of its management, along with Merrill Lynch, in a $1.48 billion management buyout.

In the final analysis, RJR says that the buyout benefited productivity, helped lower inventories, and improved the firm's focus.

* Although the initial offer occurred in October 1988, the mechanics were not completed until May 1989.

Following a going-private transaction, many firms opt to go public again. This transaction, a **secondary initial public offering** (SIPO) or a **reverse LBO,** is one of the most interesting steps in a firm's life cycle, and it has been the subject of extensive analysis.

The Rationale for Going Private

The most commonly cited reason for a going-private transaction is greater managerial efficiency. In a large public firm, management's ownership is typically small. A 1988 study found that the managers of the average publicly held firm hold little stock and are inadequately compensated. With compensation contracts not strongly influencing management's behavior, agency costs are not reduced.[19] But if the firm goes private, management's stake in the firm increases, and so managers have an incentive to make the firm more efficient and productive. Compensation schemes can be more closely tied to performance, which leads to more profitable investments. In a public corporation, this may be infeasible because the stockholders may object to these compensation plans on grounds that they are too good for management.[20]

Because information about management's performance is difficult to obtain in a large public company, managers may attempt to strengthen their reputations by

[19] Michael C. Jensen and Kevin J. Murphy, "Performance Pay and Top Management Incentives," *Journal of Political Economy,* April 1990, pp. 225–264.

[20] H. DeAngelo, L. DeAngelo, and E. Rice, "Going Private: Minority Freezeouts and Stockholder Wealth," *Journal of Law and Economics,* October 1984, pp. 367–401.

taking on projects that are less rewarding for the firm but whose results are clear to outsiders. Going private eliminates these costs to the firm. Buyout specialists and other promoters hold large equity stakes in the firm, and this gives them an incentive to monitor the managers' performance, thus reducing information asymmetry between management and shareholders and lowering agency costs.

The reduction of the firm's "free cash flow," often cited as a reason for going-private transactions, may increase the firm's value. Free cash flow is the cash flow in excess of that required to make positive net present value investments. It is reduced in a going-private transaction financed with debt. Increasing debt through a buyout commits cash to repaying debt, which effectively reduces management's ability to choose what it would like to do with the cash. Thus the large debt acts as a bonding device (see Chapter 24) that pressures managers into running the firm more efficiently. There is a concomitant reduction in the agency costs associated with free cash flow.[21] In fact, this explanation is consistent with the empirical finding that the likelihood of going private is directly related to undistributed cash flows to equity.[22]

Another incentive created by the added debt is the threat of bankruptcy.[23] If management believes that this danger has increased, their incentive to perform is greater because bankruptcy will hurt them personally (loss of power, prestige, reputation, benefits, etc.). The LBO is therefore a debt-bonding activity; it commits management to meet more demanding targets.

There also are tax arguments for going private. First, the large debt associated with privatization can offer the firm large tax shields (see Chapter 15), thereby increasing its value. Second, the depreciable base for many purchased assets can be stepped up, providing yet another level of tax shields. A study by Kaplan found that to a certain extent, prebuyout shareholders can expect some of these tax benefits, but many of these benefits are the result of the buyout itself and cannot be predicted unless the buyout structure is in place.[24]

Finally, by going private, a firm may lower some of its costs. A private firm does not have to incur the costs associated with exchange registration, listing requirements, and shareholder servicing. These costs can be trivial for large firms, but for small companies, they can be significant.

Market Reactions to Buyouts

The first comprehensive study of the effect on wealth of going-private transactions was conducted in 1984 by DeAngelo, DeAngelo, and Rice, using a sample of 72 firms involved in pure going-private or LBO transactions.[25] They discovered that the average change in stockholder wealth over a two-day announcement period was 22%. But they also found that there were abnormal gains of over 30% in the stock price over the two-month period leading up to and including the announcement date. This appears to indicate that the market anticipates the announcement and tries to compensate for it. The authors also examined the effect on the stock price of canceling an announcement. Although the price fell at the

[21] Michael Jensen, "Agency Cost of Free Cash Flows, Corporate Finance and Takeovers," *American Economic Review* 76 (1986): 323–329.

[22] K. Lehn and Annette Poulson, "Free Cash Flows and Stockholder Gains in Going-Private Transactions," *Journal of Finance* 45 (1989): 771–787.

[23] This is why LBOs are often called, only half-jokingly, Large Bankruptcy Opportunities.

[24] S. Kaplan, "A Summary of Sources of Value in Management Buyouts," unpublished manuscript, Harvard Business School, May 1988.

[25] Harry DeAngelo, Linda DeAngelo, and Edward M. Rice, "Going Private: The Effects of a Change in Corporate Ownership," in *The Revolution in Corporate Finance,* edited by J. M. Stern and D. H. Chew, Jr., pp. 444–452 (New York: Basil Blackwell, 1988).

time of the announcement, when the authors looked at a similar period leading up to the withdrawal, the stock price had risen, leading to a cumulative net abnormal gain of 4%, which doubled in the next 40-day period if the offer was withdrawn. The authors suggested three explanations for this net upward shift, irrespective of the nature of the news. First, the offer may have released some information that caused a permanent upward revaluation of the firm's prospects. Second, there may still have been a possibility that managers would revive the going-private proposal. Because the average premiums in their study were over 56% in the all-cash proposals, this would still be a very attractive offer. Third, the positive returns may indicate a continued probability that another firm will offer to purchase this firm.

Lehn and Poulsen's study (discussed earlier) looked at the share prices of 92 LBOs from 20 days before the announcement of the going-private offer to 20 days after the announcement. They found abnormal returns of 20%, with an average premium of 41%. These results were somewhat lower than the figures obtained in the previous study, probably because the studies looked at LBOs in different time periods and examined share price movements across different times. They also found that debt–equity ratios rose from a pre-LBO level of 0.46 to a post-LBO average of 5.52.

LBOs are often criticized as not actually creating wealth for the stockholders but merely transferring wealth to shareholders from other stakeholders such as bondholders, employees, and the government. LBOs benefit equityholders at the expense of others in the firm. Empirical evidence on this issue is mixed. Although some studies find that bondholders and preferred stockholders do not lose value, other studies indicate that there might be losses for these stakeholders at the time of the announcement, although these are less than the gains to prebuyout shareholders, which indicates that this wealth transfer by itself cannot be the source of gains. Therefore, although not all of the increase in wealth may be attributed to pure wealth gains, it is clear that any wealth transfer is small when compared with the substantial gains seen in LBOs.

Finally, a 1988 study by Hite and Vetsuypens examined MBOs and found small but significant gains in shareholder wealth for the parent company's stockholders.[26] Even if the returns were extrapolated to correspond to those of a full LBO, the gains would still be much smaller than expected. The authors suggest the reason is that an MBO moves the ownership of assets to more highly valued uses and the parent company's shareholders share in the benefits expected from the MBO.

Most of the gains seen in LBOs appear to come from greater management incentives, reduced agency costs, and tax benefits. The evidence regarding the effect of wealth transfers, as opposed to wealth creation, is mixed, and it is insufficient to determine the exact role played by efficiency considerations in generating the substantial gains.

The future for restructuring activity appears to be promising. Changes in the external environment (e.g., legal and tax changes) will be the major force behind such changes, although the choice of one form over the other will depend on the interdependencies between managerial and corporate activity and the external environment. Some of the reasons for such transactions are attempts by firms to reach an optimal size, their recognition of agency costs, and a corresponding need to narrow their focus. Other factors are the need for "strategic alliances," the rate of general economic growth, federal legislation, and the way these transactions are perceived by society. Although the market for such transactions will continue to

---

[26] Gailen I. Hite and Michael R. Vetsuypens, "Management Buyouts of Divisions and Shareholder Wealth," *Journal of Finance*, September 1989, pp. 953–970.

expand, generalizations are difficult. The motivations and expectations behind such restructurings will continue to differ from firm to firm, and they will determine a firm's choice of one type of transaction over the others.

SUMMARY

Section 27-1:
A Taxonomy
of Corporate
Restructuring Activities

What are some of the different forms of corporate restructuring?

- Corporate restructuring activities on the left-hand side of the balance sheet are referred to as asset engineering and activities on the right-hand side as financial restructuring.

- Asset engineering includes various forms of asset sales (spin-offs, sell-offs, equity carve-outs) and asset liquidations. Financial restructuring includes exchange offers, share repurchases, and various forms of "going-private" transactions (LBOs and MBOs).

Section 27-2:
Asset Sales

What are spin-offs, equity carve-outs, and sell-offs?

- In a spin-off, the operations of a subsidiary are separated from those of the parent, with existing shareholders holding shares in both. Firms may spin off to specialize, to avoid antitrust challenges, to reduce incentive misalignments, to thwart takeovers, or for tax reasons.

- In an equity carve-out, some of the subsidiary's shares are sold to the public for cash, with the parent retaining control of the subsidiary's assets.

- A sell-off is a transaction in which some segment of the firm is sold, either voluntarily or involuntarily. Voluntary sell-offs can make sense when the assets can be better used by the buyer or when the assets are lowering the efficiency of current operations. Involuntary sell-offs can occur because of antitrust considerations.

Section 27-3:
Liquidations

Why would a firm want to liquidate?

- Liquidations make economic sense if the firm is worth more to the stockholders in separate parts than as a whole. This might be the case if the markets are misinformed about the true value of the firm, if managers are not able to reveal all information about the future prospects of the firm, or if there are diseconomies inherent in the current structure of the firm.

Section 27-4:
Going-Private
Transactions

Why do firms "go private"?

- Going private can reduce agency costs because it usually increases managers' ownership in the firm and reduces the information asymmetry between owners and managers. The increased debt associated with these transactions reduces free cash flow, which serves to reduce agency costs.

- Going-private transactions constitute the large majority of recent restructurings. Management buyouts (MBOs) and leveraged buyouts (LBOs) are the other forms of going-private transactions. A private firm may choose to go public after a certain period; this is called a secondary initial public offering (SIPO).

QUESTIONS

1. Distinguish among spin-offs, split-offs, and split-ups.

2. Under what circumstances would a firm's management choose one of the following transactions over another: spin-offs, sell-offs, equity carve-outs?

3. What is the economic rationale for voluntary sell-offs? For involuntary sell-offs? How does the market react to these transactions?

4. Why would a firm choose to liquidate?

5. What is the explanation for the recent activity in the buyout markets? What is the empirical evidence in regard to these transactions?

27-A

CORPORATE BUYOUTS: THE MECHANICS, THEIR POPULARITY, AND CRITICISMS

The Life Cycle of a Leveraged Buyout

There are four stages in the life cycle of an LBO. The first is the decision to make a buyout. This means determining how to raise the necessary capital and devising an incentive scheme to motivate the new management. Standard transactions usually require the investor group—made up of the firm's management and/or buyout specialists—to put up only 10% of the purchase price as its equity contribution. But by awarding to management compensation in the form of stock options or warrants, management's share of the capital base may increase to as much as 30% of the total. The remainder of the equity is raised through other third-party investors, such as pension funds, insurance companies, or the new "equity pools" formed recently by buyout specialists. The remainder of the capital consists of debt, some of which is secured loans from banks or insurance companies and venture-capital firms. The remaining cash is obtained through the use of subordinated, and often unsecured, debt.

In the second stage, the firm's outstanding stock is purchased by the buying group, which is organized as a shell corporation, through either the stock-purchase or the asset-purchase format. A shell corporation is set up by the acquirer for the purpose of a M&A transaction in order to complete the transaction without involving its own assets. In a stock-purchase format, the shell corporation buys the shares of the target company, and the two firms are subsequently merged. In an asset-purchase format, the target company sells its assets to the shell, and the target then issues a liquidating dividend, obtained through the sale of its assets, to its shareholders.

Most buyouts are evaluated on the basis of two measures. The first is the purchase price as a multiple of its cash flows. The other is the price paid as a modified multiple of the assets' book value.[27] As is clear, both of these measures' primary concern is the firm's ability to service its debt, either through its operations, as measured by cash flows, or through liquidation values, as determined by the assets' liquidation value. At this point, the new firm may hold some preplanned asset sales to reduce debt or streamline its operations.

In the third stage of an LBO, the firm tries to improve its profits and cash flows by cutting costs and shifting strategies. This typically includes laying off employees, reorganizing production, improving inventory control and accounts receivable management, and selling divisions that do not match the firm's fit.

In the fourth stage, if its aim of a leaner and tougher firm has been realized, the investor group may choose to take the firm public again through an SIPO. The

---

[27] This is not a direct book-value figure but is often adjusted to eliminate those assets that are "soft," such as goodwill, trademarks, and other assets. The figure therefore concentrates on the hard assets of the firm—those that can readily be sold.

reverse LBO is often used to create liquidity for the investor group, to allow them to realize some of their gains. In addition to this, a reverse LBO is often used to raise funds to repay corporate debt. Muscarella and Vetsuypens found that this was indeed the case for 86% of the firms studied; the other 14% planned to use the proceeds to increase capital expenditure.[28] They also discovered that the median time period between LBO and SIPO was 23 months, the median return on the firms' investment during that period was 1,965.6%, and the median annualized rate of return was 268.4%—an impressive appreciation of the original investment. Some recent SIPOs have proved extremely beneficial to the original group of LBO investors. Take, for example, the 1986 LBO of Safeway Stores by KKR and the subsequent SIPO in 1990. In 1986, KKR took Safeway private after purchasing it for $4.3 billion. KKR's equity contribution, along with that of its affiliated investors, had totaled only $175 million. In the 1990 SIPO, 10% of the fully diluted shares of the firm were floated at a price of $11.25 per share. This gives the company as a whole a market value of $1.125 billion, and KKR an annualized return of almost 60%.

Within the market, LBO specialists such as KKR perform two key functions. First, these firms arrange the debt and equity financing necessary to purchase the outstanding stock. Second, they serve as the financial adviser and director of the buyout firm, using their experience to help the firm through the initial period of existing as a private entity. Because the specialists usually own a large percentage of the firm's stock, they have a motive to monitor management and to ensure that it acts in the best interests of the shareholders. Furthermore, because these firms are repeat players in the LBO market, they have a reason to protect their reputations by safeguarding the interests of the bondholders. Buyout specialists usually have interests in several privately held firms at any one time. Because the role of buyout specialists is to raise capital and advise the firm through the early stages, they tend to have investment horizons of no longer than five to ten years and sometimes less. As soon as possible, they want to sell their interests in order to use the capital in new buyouts with greater returns. Despite this possible disadvantage, such firms perform a useful role in the market because, as some argue, they ensure that firms go private with the best advice and financial guidance available.

Factors That Sustain the Buyout Market

The explosive growth of the buyout market was the result of several factors coming together at the same time. The late 1960s witnessed an acceleration in the inflation rate, which continued until 1982. This persistent inflation lowered firms' **q-ratios**. Also known as **Tobin's q**, this is the ratio of the market value of a firm's securities to the replacement value of its physical assets. Profitable firms have q-ratios in excess of 1. With low q-ratios in the 1980s (a low of 0.52 in 1981), firms could be purchased as going concerns for a fraction of what it would have cost to purchase their plant, equipment, and inventories. This was clearly the reason for many takeovers. Another influence on the growth in buyouts was the period of sustained economic growth that started in 1982. This started a wave of buyout activity because the use of leverage in such an environment could magnify a firm's earnings. When this growth began to slow in the late 1980s, the market for buyouts peaked.

Legislative factors played a major role in the increase in buyout activity in the 1980s. The Economic Recovery Tax Act (ERTA) of 1981 allowed the old assets' basis to be stepped up when they were purchased. These higher values could then

---

[28] C. J. Muscarella and M. R. Vetsuypens, "Efficiency and Organizational Structure: A Study of Reverse LBO's," *Journal of Finance*, December 1990, pp. 1389–1414.

be depreciated on an accelerated basis. In periods of high inflation, this high value was also greater than the assets' historical cost, allowing a large step-up. This in turn provided tax savings through higher depreciation. Thus firms often chose buyouts to create such tax savings for themselves. The 1981 ERTA also encouraged MBOs by making employee stock ownership plans (ESOPs) more attractive and by allowing ESOPs to borrow from a bank to invest in the firm's shares. Firms were allowed to deduct from their taxes all contributions to the ESOP that were used to cover interest and principal payments on the bank loan.

Finally, in 1980, there was a change in the antitrust climate, with clear indications that the stringent restrictions regarding certain types of mergers were being loosened. It has been suggested that this loosening in regulation was in part responsible for the rise in buyout activity because buyouts were sometimes considered to be responses to the increased threat of takeovers.

A study by Kitching Associates looked at managers' motivations for taking their firms private.[29] In decreasing order of importance, managers provided the following reasons for buying their firms:

- To avoid a sale to another firm

- To make their own fortune

- To make their own decisions

- To enjoy the hard work and dangerous living

- To develop unexploited strategic opportunities

- To save a unit starved of capital by the parent

Furthermore, on a scale of 1 (disaster) to 10 (highest expectations fulfilled), more than 40% of the managers rated their firm's postbuyout performance 10, and over two-thirds ranked it 8 or higher. This indicates that management generally tends to be satisfied with the results of an LBO.

Typical targets for a buyout tend to be manufacturing firms in stable, nonregulated industries. Such industries as retailing, textiles, food processing, apparel, and soft drinks are mature and have limited growth opportunities. The firms tend to have stable and predictable earnings and cash flows, which are essential to postbuyout debt servicing. Target firms also usually have strong positions within the industry to help them weather economic fluctuations. They have liquid balance sheets, with large borrowing capacities. Borrowing capacity is often a function of a firm's cash and undervalued assets ("hidden equity"). Finally, target firms tend to have management teams with proven records of above-average performance.

A recent LBO consummated by the takeover specialists Clayton & Dubilier, Inc., is consistent with these generalizations. In August 1990 the firm decided to buy out IBM's "low-tech" businesses, consisting of its typewriter, computer printers, and equipment parts lines, for $2 billion to $2.5 billion. This is an example of a buyout of a mature business with relatively stable earnings and a strong brand name and position in the industry. (See also the empirical evidence examined by Lehn and Poulsen in a study of LBOs.[30])

MBO targets, on the other hand, tend to be divestitures of unwanted units by

[29] John Kitching, "Early Returns on LBOs," *Harvard Business Review,* November–December 1989, pp. 74–81.

[30] Kenneth Lehn and Annette B. Poulsen, "Leveraged Buyouts: Wealth Created or Wealth Redistributed?" in *Public Policy Towards Corporate Takeovers,* edited by M. Weidenbaum and K. Chilton, pp. 46–62 (New Brunswick, NJ: Transaction Publishers, 1988).

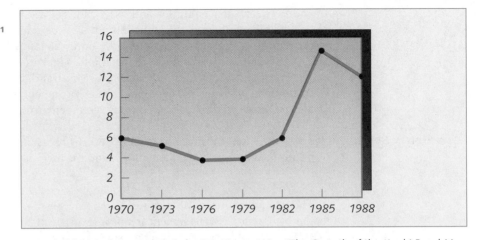
Compiled from information in Robert A. Taggart, Jr., "The Growth of the 'Junk' Bond Market and Its Role in Financing Takeovers," in *Mergers and Acquisitions,* edited by Alan Auerbach (Chicago: University of Chicago Press, 1988), and Robert A. Taggart, Jr., and Eric S. Rosengren, "The Case for Junk Bonds," *New England Economic Review,* May–June 1990, p. 42.

public firms, underperforming privately owned businesses, and smaller public firms whose shares might be selling at earnings multiples that represent a discount from book value.

In the early 1980s, a new form of debt financing appeared on the market. This was high-yield, non-investment-grade debt, formally known as high-yield bonds. Earlier, these issues, known as "fallen angels," had been investment-grade issues whose ratings had fallen. The market of the early 1980s now saw firms issuing such non-investment-grade debt. Although such issues constituted about 4%–5% of the outstanding total straight debt in the United States between 1970 and 1979, this percentage rose to 14.4% by 1985, as seen in Figure 27A-1, but fell to 12% by 1988.

The success of high-yield bonds can be attributed to one key factor. For the first time, the market for debt securities was no longer restricted to only those firms whose credit ratings were good enough to qualify them as investment-grade debt issuers. In compensation for not having investment-grade quality, the bonds gave the investor relatively high annual returns, often as much as 115%–125% of those offered by investment-grade corporate issues.[31] This type of security, soon called "junk" for its lack of credit quality, allowed many firms that had been restricted to raising capital through equity or collateralized bank loans the freedom to issue debt securities. These securities were first applied to buyouts and other corporate restructurings by Drexel Burnham Lambert and its senior executive, Michael Milken. By 1989, about 25% of the market consisted of "fallen angels," another quarter was made up of below-investment-grade bonds, and the remaining 50% consisted of high-yield bonds issued to finance large corporate restructurings between 1986 and 1989.

Although many financial firms would not buy these issues, they nonetheless were eagerly snapped up by high-yield mutual funds, savings and loans, and insurance firms, which were hungry for high-yield issues to maintain the interest rate

[31] That is, 20.3% as opposed to 15.0% for AAA-rated bonds (January 1982 to May 1984), as found by M. E. Blume and D. B. Keim, "Risk and Return Characteristics of Lower-Grade Bonds," working paper, Rodney White Center for Financial Research, Wharton School, December 1984.

spread between their liabilities and assets. To get around the requirements that some of these purchasers buy only debt above a certain grade, many issues were sold as unrated. The market rose rapidly until the late 1980s when it peaked at about $200 billion. Junk bonds then fell into a steep decline, brought on by the earlier arrest and conviction of Milken on stock fraud charges, the bankruptcy of Drexel in late 1989, the changed financial environment with the S & L and insurance firms' crisis, and the more restrictive credit environment.

Criticisms of Buyouts   There are several implications and concerns regarding buyouts and their relationships to shareholders, management, and the market.

ASYMMETRIC INFORMATION

The strongest concern of existing shareholders is that a buyout is not an arm's-length transaction. Management is not just an agent for the sellers—that is, the existing shareholders; it also is, in most cases, the purchaser of the stock. There is no evidence, however, that this potential conflict of interest has jeopardized stockholders' wealth gains. Although stockholders gain less in going-private transactions than they do in interfirm tender offers, these gains are larger than the expected gains from mergers. Furthermore, the premium paid for prebuyout stock is comparable to that paid in interfirm tender offers. Despite this evidence, stockholders continue to question whether management's unique position gives it the opportunity to suboptimize shareholder premiums, compared with what they might have received in a nonbuyout transaction. Critics of buyouts claim that management might use the informational advantages that they have over shareholders to the shareholders' detriment.

MBO negotiations have the potential for such an asymmetric information scenario. The purchasing unit's managers may be able to negotiate a favorable price, which adversely affects the parent and therefore its stockholders, through their relationship with the parent's managers. Also, if the unit's managers have an informational advantage over the parent's executives or if they are able to manipulate the unit's financial results, they may purchase the unit at a price that does not fully reflect its intrinsic value. Finally, because the unit does not have a prebuyout market value, it might be difficult to determine this without a market appraisal mechanism.

All the evidence to date indicates that managers do not attempt to understate earnings in order to depress stock prices. The possibility that the purchase price of the stock represents a discount of the true value cannot, however, be ruled out.

OTHER STAKEHOLDERS' LOSSES

If buyout premiums are more than 30% of the market value, at whose expense does this gain occur? This issue was covered in our discussion of empirical evidence and the hypotheses used to explain the gains, but we expand on it here. If there are wealth effects for the shareholders, it is clear that there must be real gains in productivity associated with the buyout and any subsequent restructuring. Otherwise, the gains are associated with wealth transfers from other stakeholders, rather than with wealth creation. The evidence is mixed and indicates that at least a portion of the gains may come at the expense of other stakeholders. The extent to which the shareholders and other stakeholders participate in the productive gains is determined by the bargaining process, which determines the buyout price. The buyout price depends on, among other factors, the current market price, expected returns on the market price, expected present value of the existing firm's future cash flows, whether a hostile bid appears, the cost of capital, management's sense of fairness, the SEC's disclosure rules, and management's risk profile.

A going-private announcement may implicitly reveal information about the firm, which is then reflected in the share price. These announcements also tend to reveal only good news because management wants to accept risks only if there is a possibility of positive cash flows and hence success. Bad news revealed at such a time would make shareholders view the proposal more favorably, and so it is unlikely that management would suppress bad news.

On the other hand, going private has several implications for the bondholders' "event risk" (default risk). Any change in this risk is reflected in the buyout price because the bondholders are one group of the firm's stakeholders. The bondholders may claim detrimental treatment because of the added default risk associated with going private, and the SEC has found that target firms' bond prices fall 3% from one month before the announcement through the completion of the transaction. However, the research also sees these declines as being insignificantly correlated with the shareholders' gains. This indicates that the shareholders' gains do not occur primarily at the expense of the bondholders. Going private may also create operating efficiencies, which increase cash flows to service the debt and thereby affect the bondholders favorably. In some cases, though, the increased cash flows may be offset by the greater debt. Furthermore, in the event of a buyout offer, many issues are convertible into common stock at a premium or may be exchanged for cash or other securities under potentially favorable terms. If this is indeed the case, a privatization offer should be seen as a favorable event and should provide gains to the bondholders. The threat of a shareholder backlash, through either a veto of the offer or protracted litigation, causes management to ensure that the shareholders participate in these gains, and this therefore affects the buyout price.

In the final analysis, the decision to pursue or abandon a buyout is a capital budgeting issue. After all factors are considered, if a firm and the investors believe that the net present value of the LBO project is positive, then it is in their best interest to go ahead with the offer. The net present value of the LBO is the difference between the present value of the private firm's future cash flows and the sum of present values of the purchase of the shares at a premium, the cost of servicing the debt, and the cost of implementing the buyout. If this difference is positive, it is financially viable for the team to make an LBO. It is in the present value of the future cash flows that the management team and investors see the possibility of obtaining their required returns if they are to take on the risk of investing in the LBO.

Essential to a successful LBO is the ability of the firm's management to gain efficiency in operating the company because such gains lead to increased cash flows for the firm. However, there is a concern that management will make the changes in a way that adversely affects the firm's future, although this is not supported by the evidence. Failure to trim the firm could result in the LBO's failure, and so it is essential that management exercise the added control obtained through the privatization. Management often makes significant strategic changes in operating philosophy. Although these may not result in greater sales growth than the industry average, gains are seen in operating margins and productivity both on an absolute level and relative to the industry.

Another concern is that such efficiencies, and therefore the shareholders' gains, occur at a cost to the firm's employees through lower employment levels, fewer benefits, and adverse employee relationships. These worries do not appear to be borne out by the evidence. The evidence does indicate, however, that these firms operate differently from nonbuyout firms. After the buyout, although they do not reduce employment, firms tend to increase their employment at rates slower than average. Privatized firms tend to consolidate overfunded pension plans; however, because pension plans have been large beneficiaries of premiums paid in corporate restructurings, the phenomenon has led to an increase in their assets, and therefore they can pay more to employees at termination.

SACRIFICE OF LONG-TERM INVESTMENTS

Still another concern is that in attempting to maximize cash flows, management will forsake long-term investment in order to maximize short-term gains, thereby weakening the firm's long-run competitive position. The evidence, however, does not support this view. To the extent that the managers are also shareholders, management does have a long-term commitment to the firm. The emphasis on increased cash flows can generate more funds that can be used for long-term investments. Lower levels of spending do not automatically imply reduced commitment, perhaps because of the more efficient use of the funds. The firm may be able to create additional efficiencies, which help it reduce the long-term spending required to allow it to perform effectively. With management owning the firm, the firm no longer has to defend against attempts at a transfer of control, as it might in a public firm. Furthermore, privatization reduces the number and complexity of decisions, thereby possibly eliminating some diseconomies of scope. The cost of disclosing potentially sensitive information is also avoided because the required information disclosure for a private firm is far less than for a public one. Finally, the real costs of disseminating information to shareholders are eliminated because the number of shareholders is sharply reduced, and it is now in their best interest to be aware of the firm's functioning. Although these costs are real, it must be remembered that they alone are not enough to cause a firm to go private.

Management is willing to make such changes in its operating strategy for a number of reasons. The sheer magnitude of the firm's debt is often overwhelming, and management may realize the need for radical changes in order to resolve this problem. As the firm's owners, managers are aware that a large fraction of their life savings is invested in the firm's success, and as owners, they now also have the authority to enact and enforce such changes in strategy. The more attractive compensation packages often ensure that managers are rewarded adequately for their performance. The buyout specialists play a monitoring role to avoid undisciplined spending by management and to ensure that the firm is run efficiently. Furthermore, management recognizes that the buyout specialists are as interested in the firm's success as they are, so it often follows their advice in developing an operating strategy.

Firms that are considering buyouts are also looking to newer methods of debt financing. Because of the high levels of debt, LBO firms are likely to encounter financial difficulties sooner when cash flows decline than are comparable conventionally financed firms. On the other hand, if an LBO firm realizes the potential danger sooner than conventional firms do, it is in a better position to restructure than are the other firms. The evidence appears to indicate that firms are not taking gambles but, rather, calculated risks.

The changed capital structure reduces the firm's ability to tap the public equity markets, and this also reduces the marketability of the firm's stock. The reduced marketability may also impose direct costs on the managers because they are forced to hold personal portfolios that are underdiversified. The absence of a ready market makes it difficult to resolve disagreements among shareholders regarding corporate policy. In a public firm, those who object to a firm's policy can simply sell their shares and find an investment that better suits them.

Abnormal returns from LBOs are seen to originate from certain specific sources. Prebuyout shareholders earn abnormal returns in the buyout price from the known tax and depreciation effects that will occur after the buyout. On the other hand, managers obtain returns from other sources. They do not obtain their abnormal returns from wealth transfers from other stakeholders or from the debt structure. Their gains arise from their ability to create operating gains, from the changed ownership structure, from the realignment of management and ownership incentives, and from the reduction of agency costs.

SUGGESTED ADDITIONAL READINGS

Burrough, Bryan, and John Helyar. *Barbarians at the Gate.* New York: Harper & Row, 1990.

Continental Bank. *Journal of Applied Corporate Finance,* Spring 1989 and Summer 1990.

Coyne, John, and Mike Wright, eds. *Divestment and Strategic Change.* Totowa, NJ: Barnes & Noble, 1988.

Stern, Joel M., and Donald H. Chew, Jr., eds. *The Revolution in Corporate Finance.* New York: Basil Blackwell, 1988.

Taylor, Marilyn L. *Divesting Business Units.* Lexington, MA: Lexington Books, 1988.

Weston, J. Fred, Kwang S. Chung, and Susan E. Hoag. *Mergers, Restructuring, and Corporate Control.* Englewood Cliffs, NJ: Prentice-Hall, 1990.

W. T. Grimm and Co. *Mergerstat Review 1990.* Chicago: W. T. Grimm and Co.

APPENDIX:
TIME VALUE TABLES

Future Value Factor for a $1 Single Sum: FVF$_{i,n}$

Number of Periods	1%	2%	3%	4%	5%	6%	7%	8%	9%	10%	12%	14%	15%	16%	18%	20%	24%
1	1.0100	1.0200	1.0300	1.0400	1.0500	1.0600	1.0700	1.0800	1.0900	1.1000	1.1200	1.1400	1.1500	1.1600	1.1800	1.2000	1.2400
2	1.0201	1.0404	1.0609	1.0816	1.1025	1.1236	1.1449	1.1664	1.1881	1.2100	1.2544	1.2996	1.3225	1.3456	1.3924	1.4400	1.5376
3	1.0303	1.0612	1.0927	1.1249	1.1576	1.1910	1.2250	1.2597	1.2950	1.3310	1.4049	1.4815	1.5209	1.5609	1.6430	1.7280	1.9066
4	1.0406	1.0824	1.1255	1.1699	1.2155	1.2625	1.3108	1.3605	1.4116	1.4641	1.5735	1.6890	1.7490	1.8106	1.9388	2.0736	2.3642
5	1.0510	1.1041	1.1593	1.2167	1.2763	1.3382	1.4026	1.4693	1.5386	1.6105	1.7623	1.9254	2.0114	2.1003	2.2878	2.4883	2.9316
6	1.0615	1.1262	1.1941	1.2653	1.3401	1.4185	1.5007	1.5869	1.6771	1.7716	1.9738	2.1950	2.3131	2.4364	2.6996	2.9860	3.6352
7	1.0721	1.1487	1.2299	1.3159	1.4071	1.5036	1.6058	1.7138	1.8280	1.9487	2.2107	2.5023	2.6600	2.8262	3.1855	3.5832	4.5077
8	1.0829	1.1717	1.2668	1.3686	1.4775	1.5938	1.7182	1.8509	1.9926	2.1436	2.4760	2.8526	3.0590	3.2784	3.7589	4.2998	5.5895
9	1.0937	1.1951	1.3048	1.4233	1.5513	1.6895	1.8385	1.9990	2.1719	2.3579	2.7731	3.2519	3.5179	3.8030	4.4355	5.1598	6.9310
10	1.1046	1.2190	1.3439	1.4802	1.6289	1.7908	1.9672	2.1589	2.3674	2.5937	3.1058	3.7072	4.0456	4.4114	5.2338	6.1917	8.5944
11	1.1157	1.2434	1.3842	1.5395	1.7103	1.8983	2.1049	2.3316	2.5804	2.8531	3.4785	4.2262	4.6524	5.1173	6.1759	7.4301	10.657
12	1.1268	1.2682	1.4258	1.6010	1.7959	2.0122	2.2522	2.5182	2.8127	3.1384	3.8960	4.8179	5.3502	5.9360	7.2876	8.9161	13.214
13	1.1381	1.2936	1.4685	1.6651	1.8856	2.1329	2.4098	2.7196	3.0658	3.4523	4.3635	5.4924	6.1528	6.8858	8.5994	10.699	16.386
14	1.1495	1.3195	1.5126	1.7317	1.9799	2.2609	2.5785	2.9372	3.3417	3.7975	4.8871	6.2613	7.0757	7.9875	10.147	12.839	20.319
15	1.1610	1.3459	1.5580	1.8009	2.0789	2.3966	2.7590	3.1722	3.6425	4.1772	5.4736	7.1379	8.1371	9.2655	11.973	15.407	25.195
16	1.1726	1.3728	1.6047	1.8730	2.1829	2.5404	2.9522	3.4259	3.9703	4.5950	6.1304	8.1372	9.3576	10.748	14.129	18.488	31.242
17	1.1843	1.4002	1.6528	1.9479	2.2920	2.6928	3.1588	3.7000	4.3276	5.0545	6.8660	9.2765	10.761	12.467	16.672	22.186	38.740
18	1.1961	1.4282	1.7024	2.0258	2.4066	2.8543	3.3799	3.9960	4.7171	5.5599	7.6900	10.575	12.375	14.463	19.673	26.623	48.038
19	1.2081	1.4568	1.7535	2.1068	2.5270	3.0256	3.6165	4.3157	5.1417	6.1159	8.6128	12.055	14.232	16.776	23.214	31.948	59.568
20	1.2202	1.4859	1.8061	2.1911	2.6533	3.2071	3.8697	4.6610	5.6044	6.7275	9.6463	13.743	16.367	19.460	27.393	38.338	73.864
21	1.2324	1.5157	1.8603	2.2788	2.7860	3.3996	4.1406	5.0338	6.1088	7.4002	10.804	15.667	18.822	22.574	32.323	46.005	91.591
22	1.2447	1.5460	1.9161	2.3699	2.9253	3.6035	4.4304	5.4365	6.6586	8.1403	12.100	17.861	21.645	26.186	38.142	55.206	113.57
23	1.2572	1.5769	1.9736	2.4647	3.0715	3.8197	4.7405	5.8715	7.2579	8.9543	13.552	20.361	24.891	30.376	45.007	66.247	140.83
24	1.2697	1.6084	2.0328	2.5633	3.2251	4.0489	5.0724	6.3412	7.9111	9.8497	15.178	23.212	28.625	35.236	53.108	79.496	174.63
25	1.2824	1.6406	2.0938	2.6658	3.3864	4.2919	5.4274	6.8485	8.6231	10.834	17.000	26.461	32.918	40.874	62.668	95.396	216.54
26	1.2953	1.6734	2.1566	2.7725	3.5557	4.5494	5.8074	7.3964	9.3992	11.918	19.040	30.166	37.856	47.414	73.948	114.47	268.51
27	1.3082	1.7069	2.2213	2.8834	3.7335	4.8223	6.2139	7.9881	10.245	13.110	21.324	34.389	43.535	55.000	87.259	137.37	332.95
28	1.3213	1.7410	2.2879	2.9987	3.9201	5.1117	6.6488	8.6271	11.167	14.421	23.883	39.204	50.065	63.800	102.96	164.84	412.86
29	1.3345	1.7758	2.3566	3.1187	4.1161	5.4184	7.1143	9.3173	12.172	15.863	26.749	44.693	57.575	74.008	121.50	197.81	511.95
30	1.3478	1.8114	2.4273	3.2434	4.3219	5.7435	7.6123	10.062	13.267	17.449	29.959	50.950	66.211	85.849	143.37	237.37	634.81
40	1.4889	2.2080	3.2620	4.8010	7.0400	10.285	14.974	21.724	31.409	45.259	93.050	188.88	267.86	378.72	750.37	1469.8	5455.9
50	1.6446	2.6916	4.3839	7.1067	11.467	18.420	29.457	46.901	74.357	117.39	289.00	700.23	1083.6	1670.7	3927.3	9100.4	46890.
60	1.8167	3.2810	5.8916	10.519	18.679	32.987	57.946	101.25	176.03	304.48	897.59	2595.9	4383.9	7370.1	20555.	56347.	—

Present Value Factor for a $1 Annuity, PVFA$_{i,n}$

Number of Periods	1%	2%	3%	4%	5%	6%	7%	8%	9%	10%	12%	14%	15%	16%	18%	20%	24%
1	0.9901	0.9804	0.9709	0.9615	0.9524	0.9434	0.9346	0.9259	0.9174	0.9091	0.8929	0.8772	0.8696	0.8621	0.8475	0.8333	0.8065
2	1.9704	1.9416	1.9135	1.8861	1.8594	1.8334	1.8080	1.7833	1.7591	1.7355	1.6901	1.6467	1.6257	1.6052	1.5656	1.5278	1.4568
3	2.9410	2.8839	2.8286	2.7751	2.7232	2.6730	2.6243	2.5771	2.5313	2.4869	2.4018	2.3216	2.2832	2.2459	2.1743	2.1065	1.9813
4	3.9020	3.8077	3.7171	3.6299	3.5460	3.4651	3.3872	3.3121	3.2397	3.1699	3.0373	2.9137	2.8550	2.7982	2.6901	2.5887	2.4043
5	4.8534	4.7135	4.5797	4.4518	4.3295	4.2124	4.1002	3.9927	3.8897	3.7908	3.6048	3.4331	3.3522	3.2743	3.1272	2.9906	2.7454
6	5.7955	5.6014	5.4172	5.2421	5.0757	4.9173	4.7665	4.6229	4.4859	4.3553	4.1114	3.8887	3.7845	3.6847	3.4976	3.3255	3.0205
7	6.7282	6.4720	6.2303	6.0021	5.7864	5.5824	5.3893	5.2064	5.0330	4.8684	4.5638	4.2883	4.1604	4.0386	3.8115	3.6046	3.2423
8	7.6517	7.3255	7.0197	6.7327	6.4632	6.2098	5.9713	5.7466	5.5348	5.3349	4.9676	4.6389	4.4873	4.3436	4.0776	3.8372	3.4212
9	8.5660	8.1622	7.7861	7.4353	7.1078	6.8017	6.5152	6.2469	5.9952	5.7590	5.3282	4.9464	4.7716	4.6065	4.3030	4.0310	3.5655
10	9.4713	8.9826	8.5302	8.1109	7.7217	7.3601	7.0236	6.7101	6.4177	6.1446	5.6502	5.2161	5.0188	4.8332	4.4941	4.1925	3.6819
11	10.3676	9.7868	9.2526	8.7605	8.3064	7.8869	7.4987	7.1390	6.8052	6.4951	5.9377	5.4527	5.2337	5.0286	4.6560	4.3271	3.7757
12	11.2551	10.5753	9.9540	9.3851	8.8633	8.3838	7.9427	7.5361	7.1607	6.8137	6.1944	5.6603	5.4206	5.1971	4.7932	4.4392	3.8514
13	12.1337	11.3484	10.6350	9.9856	9.3936	8.8527	8.3577	7.9038	7.4869	7.1034	6.4235	5.8424	5.5831	5.3423	4.9095	4.5327	3.9124
14	13.0037	12.1062	11.2961	10.5631	9.8986	9.2950	8.7455	8.2442	7.7862	7.3667	6.6282	6.0021	5.7245	5.4675	5.0081	4.6106	3.9616
15	13.8651	12.8493	11.9379	11.1184	10.3797	9.7122	9.1079	8.5595	8.0607	7.6061	6.8109	6.1422	5.8474	5.5755	5.0916	4.6755	4.0013
16	14.7179	13.5777	12.5611	11.6523	10.8378	10.1059	9.4466	8.8514	8.3126	7.8237	6.9740	6.2651	5.9542	5.6685	5.1624	4.7296	4.0333
17	15.5623	14.2919	13.1661	12.1657	11.2741	10.4773	9.7632	9.1216	8.5436	8.0216	7.1196	6.3729	6.0472	5.7487	5.2223	4.7746	4.0591
18	16.3983	14.9920	13.7535	12.6593	11.6896	10.8276	10.0591	9.3719	8.7556	8.2014	7.2497	6.4674	6.1280	5.8178	5.2732	4.8122	4.0799
19	17.2260	15.6785	14.3238	13.1339	12.0853	11.1581	10.3356	9.6036	8.9501	8.3649	7.3658	6.5504	6.1982	5.8775	5.3162	4.8435	4.0967
20	18.0456	16.3514	14.8775	13.5903	12.4622	11.4699	10.5940	9.8181	9.1285	8.5136	7.4694	6.6231	6.2593	5.9288	5.3527	4.8696	4.1103
25	22.0232	19.5235	17.4131	15.6221	14.0939	12.7834	11.6536	10.6748	9.8226	9.0770	7.8431	6.8729	6.4641	6.0971	5.4669	4.9476	4.1474
30	25.8077	22.3965	19.6004	17.2920	15.3725	13.7648	12.4090	11.2578	10.2737	9.4269	8.0552	7.0027	6.5660	6.1772	5.5168	4.9789	4.1601
40	32.8347	27.3555	23.1148	19.7928	17.1591	15.0463	13.3317	11.9246	10.7574	9.7791	8.2438	7.1050	6.6418	6.2335	5.5482	4.9966	4.1659
50	39.1961	31.4236	25.7298	21.4822	18.2559	15.7619	13.8007	12.2335	10.9617	9.9148	8.3045	7.1327	6.6605	6.2463	5.5541	4.9995	4.1666
60	44.9550	34.7609	27.6756	22.6235	18.9293	16.1614	14.0392	12.3766	11.0480	9.9672	8.3240	7.1401	6.6651	6.2492	5.5553	4.9999	4.1667

Present Value Factor for a $1 Single Sum: PVF$_{i,n}$

Number of Periods	1%	2%	3%	4%	5%	6%	7%	8%	9%	10%	12%	14%	15%	16%	18%	20%	24%
1	.9901	.9804	.9709	.9615	.9524	.9434	.9346	.9259	.9174	.9091	.8929	.8772	.8696	.8621	.8475	.8333	.8065
2	.9803	.9612	.9426	.9246	.9070	.8900	.8734	.8573	.8417	.8264	.7972	.7695	.7561	.7432	.7182	.6944	.6504
3	.9706	.9423	.9151	.8890	.8638	.8396	.8163	.7938	.7722	.7513	.7118	.6750	.6575	.6407	.6086	.5787	.5245
4	.9610	.9238	.8885	.8548	.8227	.7921	.7629	.7350	.7084	.6830	.6355	.5921	.5718	.5523	.5158	.4823	.4230
5	.9515	.9057	.8626	.8219	.7835	.7473	.7130	.6806	.6499	.6209	.5674	.5194	.4972	.4761	.4371	.4019	.3411
6	.9420	.8880	.8375	.7903	.7462	.7050	.6663	.6302	.5963	.5645	.5066	.4556	.4323	.4104	.3704	.3349	.2751
7	.9327	.8706	.8131	.7599	.7107	.6651	.6227	.5835	.5470	.5132	.4523	.3996	.3759	.3538	.3139	.2791	.2218
8	.9235	.8535	.7894	.7307	.6768	.6274	.5820	.5403	.5019	.4665	.4039	.3506	.3269	.3050	.2660	.2326	.1789
9	.9143	.8368	.7664	.7026	.6446	.5919	.5439	.5002	.4604	.4241	.3606	.3075	.2843	.2630	.2255	.1938	.1443
10	.9053	.8203	.7441	.6756	.6139	.5584	.5083	.4632	.4224	.3855	.3220	.2697	.2472	.2267	.1911	.1615	.1164
11	.8963	.8043	.7224	.6496	.5847	.5268	.4751	.4289	.3875	.3505	.2875	.2366	.2149	.1954	.1619	.1346	.0938
12	.8874	.7885	.7014	.6246	.5568	.4970	.4440	.3971	.3555	.3186	.2567	.2076	.1869	.1685	.1372	.1122	.0757
13	.8787	.7730	.6810	.6006	.5303	.4688	.4150	.3677	.3262	.2897	.2292	.1821	.1625	.1452	.1163	.0935	.0610
14	.8700	.7579	.6611	.5775	.5051	.4423	.3878	.3405	.2992	.2633	.2046	.1597	.1413	.1252	.0985	.0779	.0492
15	.8613	.7430	.6419	.5553	.4810	.4173	.3624	.3152	.2745	.2394	.1827	.1401	.1229	.1079	.0835	.0649	.0397
16	.8528	.7284	.6232	.5339	.4581	.3936	.3387	.2919	.2519	.2176	.1631	.1229	.1069	.0930	.0708	.0541	.0320
17	.8444	.7142	.6050	.5134	.4363	.3714	.3166	.2703	.2311	.1978	.1456	.1078	.0929	.0802	.0600	.0451	.0258
18	.8360	.7002	.5874	.4936	.4155	.3503	.2959	.2502	.2120	.1799	.1300	.0946	.0808	.0691	.0508	.0376	.0208
19	.8277	.6864	.5703	.4746	.3957	.3305	.2765	.2317	.1945	.1635	.1161	.0829	.0703	.0596	.0431	.0313	.0168
20	.8195	.6730	.5537	.4564	.3769	.3118	.2584	.2145	.1784	.1486	.1037	.0728	.0611	.0514	.0365	.0261	.0135
25	.7798	.6095	.4776	.3751	.2953	.2330	.1842	.1460	.1160	.0923	.0588	.0378	.0304	.0245	.0160	.0105	.0046
30	.7419	.5521	.4120	.3083	.2314	.1741	.1314	.0994	.0754	.0573	.0334	.0196	.0151	.0116	.0070	.0042	.0016
40	.6717	.4529	.3066	.2083	.1420	.0972	.0668	.0460	.0318	.0221	.0107	.0053	.0037	.0026	.0013	.0007	.0002
50	.6080	.3715	.2281	.1407	.0872	.0543	.0339	.0213	.0134	.0085	.0035	.0014	.0009	.0006	.0003	.0001	—
60	.5504	.3048	.1697	.0951	.0535	.0303	.0173	.0099	.0057	.0033	.0011	.0004	.0002	.0001	—	—	—

Future Value Factor for a $1 Annuity: FVFA$_{i,n}$

Number of Periods	1%	2%	3%	4%	5%	6%	7%	8%	9%	10%	12%	14%	15%	16%	18%	20%	24%
1	1.0000	1.0000	1.0000	1.0000	1.0000	1.0000	1.0000	1.0000	1.0000	1.0000	1.0000	1.0000	1.0000	1.0000	1.0000	1.0000	1.0000
2	2.0100	2.0200	2.0300	2.0400	2.0500	2.0600	2.0700	2.0800	2.0900	2.1000	2.1200	2.1400	2.1500	2.1600	2.1800	2.2000	2.2400
3	3.0301	3.0604	3.0909	3.1216	3.1525	3.1836	3.2149	3.2464	3.2781	3.3100	3.3744	3.4396	3.4725	3.5056	3.5724	3.6400	3.7776
4	4.0604	4.1216	4.1836	4.2465	4.3101	4.3746	4.4399	4.5061	4.5731	4.6410	4.7793	4.9211	4.9934	5.0665	5.2154	5.3680	5.6842
5	5.1010	5.2040	5.3091	5.4163	5.5256	5.6371	5.7507	5.8666	5.9847	6.1051	6.3528	6.6101	6.7424	6.8771	7.1542	7.4416	8.0484
6	6.1520	6.3081	6.4684	6.6330	6.8019	6.9753	7.1533	7.3359	7.5233	7.7156	8.1152	8.5355	8.7537	8.9775	9.4420	9.9299	10.980
7	7.2135	7.4343	7.6625	7.8983	8.1420	8.3938	8.6540	8.9228	9.2004	9.4872	10.089	10.730	11.066	11.413	12.141	12.915	14.615
8	8.2857	8.5830	8.8923	9.2142	9.5491	9.8975	10.259	10.636	11.028	11.435	12.299	13.232	13.726	14.240	15.327	16.499	19.122
9	9.3685	9.7546	10.159	10.582	11.026	11.491	11.978	12.487	13.021	13.579	14.775	16.085	16.785	17.518	19.085	20.798	24.712
10	10.462	10.949	11.463	12.006	12.577	13.180	13.816	14.486	15.192	15.937	17.548	19.337	20.303	21.321	23.521	25.958	31.643
11	11.566	12.168	12.807	13.486	14.206	14.971	15.783	16.645	17.560	18.531	20.654	23.044	24.349	25.732	28.755	32.150	40.237
12	12.682	13.412	14.192	15.025	15.917	16.869	17.888	18.977	20.140	21.384	24.133	27.270	29.001	30.850	34.931	39.580	50.894
13	13.809	14.680	15.617	16.626	17.713	18.882	20.140	21.495	22.953	24.522	28.029	32.088	34.351	36.786	42.218	48.496	64.109
14	14.947	15.973	17.086	18.291	19.598	21.015	22.550	24.214	26.019	27.975	32.392	37.581	40.504	43.672	50.818	59.195	80.496
15	16.096	17.293	18.598	20.023	21.578	23.276	25.129	27.152	29.360	31.772	37.279	43.842	47.580	51.659	60.965	72.035	100.81
16	17.257	18.639	20.156	21.824	23.657	25.672	27.888	30.324	33.003	35.949	42.753	50.980	55.717	90.825	72.939	87.442	126.01
17	18.430	20.012	21.761	23.697	25.840	28.212	30.840	33.750	36.973	40.544	48.883	59.117	65.075	71.673	87.068	105.93	157.25
18	19.614	21.412	23.414	25.645	28.132	30.905	33.999	37.450	41.301	45.599	55.749	68.394	75.836	84.140	103.74	128.11	195.99
19	20.810	22.840	25.116	27.671	30.539	33.760	37.379	41.446	48.018	51.159	63.439	78.969	88.211	96.603	123.41	154.74	244.03
20	22.019	24.297	26.870	29.778	33.066	36.785	40.995	45.762	51.160	57.275	72.052	91.024	102.44	115.37	146.62	186.68	303.60
21	23.239	25.783	28.676	31.969	35.719	39.992	44.865	50.422	56.764	64.002	81.698	104.76	118.81	134.84	174.02	225.02	377.46
22	24.471	27.299	30.536	34.248	38.505	43.392	49.005	55.456	62.873	71.402	92.502	120.43	137.63	157.41	206.34	271.03	469.05
23	25.716	28.845	32.452	36.617	41.430	46.995	53.436	60.893	69.531	79.543	104.60	138.29	159.27	183.60	244.48	326.23	582.62
24	26.973	30.421	34.426	39.082	44.502	50.815	58.176	66.764	76.789	88.497	118.15	158.65	184.16	213.97	289.49	392.48	723.46
25	28.243	32.030	36.459	41.645	47.727	54.864	63.249	73.105	84.700	98.347	133.33	181.87	212.79	249.21	342.60	471.98	898.09
26	29.525	33.670	38.553	44.311	51.113	59.156	68.676	79.954	93.323	109.18	150.33	208.33	245.71	290.08	405.27	567.37	1114.6
27	30.820	35.344	40.709	47.084	54.669	63.705	74.483	87.350	102.72	121.09	169.37	238.49	283.56	337.50	479.22	681.85	1383.1
28	32.129	37.051	42.930	49.967	58.402	68.528	80.697	95.338	112.96	134.20	190.69	272.88	327.10	392.50	566.48	819.22	1716.0
29	33.450	38.792	45.218	52.966	62.322	73.639	87.346	103.96	124.13	148.63	214.58	312.09	377.16	456.30	669.44	984.06	2128.9
30	34.784	40.568	47.575	56.084	66.438	79.058	94.460	113.28	136.30	164.49	241.33	356.78	434.74	530.31	790.94	1181.8	2640.9
40	48.886	60.402	75.401	95.025	120.79	154.76	199.63	259.05	337.88	442.59	767.09	1342.0	1779.0	2360.7	4163.2	7343.8	22728.
50	64.463	84.579	112.79	152.66	239.34	290.33	406.52	573.76	815.08	1163.9	2400.0	4994.5	7217.7	10435.	21813.	45497.	—
60	81.669	114.05	163.05	237.99	353.58	533.12	813.52	1253.2	1944.7	3034.8	7471.6	18535.	29219.	46057.	—	—	—

CHAPTER 1

1. (a) $165,110.40.
   (b) Between $158,476 and $169,638

CHAPTER 3

5. (a) $NOI = \$100,000$
   (b) $NPBT = \$32,000$
   (c) $NI = \$19,200$
   (d) $RE_{95} = \$179,200$
7. (a) Net cash flow for fourth quarter = $23,000
   (b) Cash balance at 9/30/95 = $32,000
9. Net cash flow from operations = $104,000
   Net financial cash flow = $-\$25,000$
   Net investment cash flow = $-\$27,000$
17. (a) Annual depreciation = $11,500
    (b) Accumulated depreciation after four years = $46,000

CHAPTER 4

1. $FV_{50} = \$4,690.10$
3. $FV_{100} = \$19,024$
   $FV_{200} = \$19,293$
5. (a) growth rate = 3 percent
   (b) $FV_{30} = 8,279,520,300$ people
   (c) the population will reach 500,000 in 13 years
7. $PV = \$4,290.92$
9. 14.21 yr
11. (a) prefer the $2,000 invested 5 years ago
    (b) prefer the $1,000 invested 10 years ago
    (c) prefer the $3,000 invested today
13. (a) $FVA = \$477.93$
    (b) $FVA = \$477.93$
    (c) $FV_4 = \$477.93$
15. $PVA = \$1,046.10$
17. $PVA = \$2,735.60$
19. $PVA = \$10,603.60$
21. (a) $139,904
    (b) $414.06
    (c) $2,734.64

23. Since Jackne can sell either bond in the market for $1,000, they would prefer option 1, since they are receiving $1,000 today in exchange for promised payments worth only $750.
25. (a) $108
    (b) $108.24
    (c) $108.33
27. The value of each contract is established by using the growth annuity expression. The solution here is shown in millions of dollars.
    (a) Bonds: Value of contract = $16 million
        Clark: Value of contract = $15.6 million
    (b) The present value of both deals is equal when Bonds earns $3.9 million in the first year.
29. Value of annuity = $2,537.50
31. $IRR = 12\%$ (using calculator)
33. $11,103.71
35. $UAS = \$8,038$

CHAPTER 5

1. Expected return = .12
3. Expected dividend yield = 3.79%
5. (a) $Range_A = 30\%$
       $Range_B = 20\%$
   (b) $E(R_A) = .15$
       $E(R_B) = .15$
   (c) $\sigma_A = .0671$
       $\sigma_B = .0775$
9. (a) $E(R_X) = .13$
       $E(R_Y) = .144$
   (b) $\sigma_X = (.00066)^{.5} = .0257$
       $\sigma_Y = (.00218)^{.5} = .0467$
   (c) $\sigma_{XY} = .00048$
       $corr_{XY} = .40$
   (d) $E(R_p) = .1346$
       $\sigma_p = .0273$
11. (a) $E(R_A) = E(R_B) = E(R_C) = .16$
    (b) $\sigma_A = (.00027)^{.5} = .0164$
        $\sigma_B = (.00027)^{.5} = .0164$
        $\sigma_C = (.00027)^{.5} = .0164$

(c) $E(R_{AB}) = E(R_{AC}) = E(R_{BC}) = .16$

(d) A and B are perfectly negatively correlated; A and C are perfectly positively correlated; B and C are perfectly negatively correlated.

(e) $\sigma_{AB} = 0$

$\sigma_{AC} = .0164$

Since A and C are identical, $\sigma_{BC}{}^2 = 0$;

$\sigma_{BC} = 0$

(f) Choose either AB or BC. All three portfolios have $E(R_p) = .16$, but AB and BC have no risk, while AC has $\sigma = .0164$. Therefore, AB and BC provide the most reward for the least amount of risk.

17. (a) The gain from diversification is

$$\frac{.075 - .0716}{.075} = 4.53\%$$

(b) To obtain a diversification gain of 3%, the weighting of the portfolio would be 30% to 70%.

CHAPTER 6

1. $V[\tilde{R}_p] = .011$

3. $\beta_{bud} = 1.067$

4. $\beta_i = \sigma_{i,m}/\sigma^2{}_m$

5. (a) $E(R_i) = .16$

(b) $E(R_i) = .19$

(c) $E(R_i) = .22$

7. $R_f = .09$

9. (a) $E(R_x) = .14$

(b) $E(R_y) = .18$

(c) $E(R_z) = .20$

(d) $E(R_P) = .172$

(e) $\beta_p = .9$

(f) $E(R_P) = .172$

11. (a) $E(R_{GM}) = .18$

(b) $E(R_{FORD}) = .22$

(c) $E(R_{GM}) = .22$

$E(R_{FORD}) = .26$

(d) $\beta_p = 1.15$

$E[\tilde{R}_p] = .252$

13. $P_0 = \$40.82$

15. (a) $\beta_P = 1.3$

$E(R_P) = .178$

(b) $\$45,000$

(c) $\$9,000$

(d) $\$6,000$

CHAPTER 7

1. $\$7,722$

3. Dempsey plan: $\$237$/month payment, $-\$9,999.84$ NPV

Tunney plan: $\$233.98$/month payment, $-\$9,885.16$ NPV

5. (a) The book profit is $\$1,000$.

(b) The economic profit is $-\$221$.

7. (a) $\$55,343.57$

(b) $PV = \$209,796.41$

(c) In order for you to be indifferent, Wolff's price would have to be $\$181,127.99$.

9. PV of Computer World payments = $\$3,000$

PV of Computervision payments = $\$2,961.66$

PV of Discount Computers payments = $\$3,331.46$

11. The $\$100$ NPV is the present value of the cash flows above what is required to produce a 12% return. Hence, the return on the project is well over 12%. Even if $\$2,000$ is available, you should accept the project and reject the CD, since the CD (yielding 11%) doesn't cover your opportunity cost of 12%.

13. Cloisters: $NPV = -\$5,796.40$

Woodward: $NPV = -\$5797.48$

15. $\$18.69$

CHAPTER 8

1. (a) $BV = \$130,000$

(b) $CFAT = \$107,500$

(c) $CFAT = \$145,000$

3. Net initial CF from replacement $= -\$31,000 + \$11,250 = -\$19,750$

5. $\Delta CFAT = \$11,125$

7. (a) $\Delta CFAT = \$24,500$

(b) Payback period $= 8.16$ years

(c) $AROR = 10.31\%$

(d) $NPV = -\$22,930$

(e) Profitability index $= .8854$

(f) $IRR = 9.7\%$

9. (a) Initial outlay $= \$340,000$

(b) $CFAT = \$75,313$

(c) $\$90,000$

(d) 4.51 years

(e) $AROR = 20.49\%$

(f) $NPV = \$14,580$

Profitability index $= 1.04$

(g) $IRR = 17.21\%$

11. (a) $BV = \$90,000$

(b) Total initial $CF = -\$300,000 + \$82,500 = -\$217,500$

(c) $\Delta CFAT = \$15,000$

(d) Payback period $= 14.5$ years

(e) $NPV = -\$113,427$

Profitability index $= .4785$

(f) $NPV = -\$131,400$
   Profitability index = .3171
(g) $IRR = .51\%$
13. (a) $NPV_{New} = \$160,400$
      $NPV_{Old} = \$379,078$
   (b) $NPV_{New} = \$560,400$
      $NPV_{Old} = \$379,078$

APPENDIX 9A

1. (a) $NPV_H = \$10,614.90$
      $IRR \approx 12.5\%$ (This is the rate that sets $NPV = 0$.)
   (b) $NPV_D = \$6,951.47$
      $IRR \approx 12.7\%$
   (c) The NPV of the difference between the projects is $3,663.43.

APPENDIX 9B

1. (a) $NPV = -\$181,237$; $IRR = 8.64\%$.
   (b) Yes. $k^* = [(1.12)(1.06)] - 1 = .1872 = 18.72\%$.

CHAPTER 10

1. (a) 16.2%
   (b) 14%
3. (a) APV. The WACC method only provides an approximation of the project value.
   (b) $APV = -\$240,900$
   (c) $APV = \$627,000$
5. (a) 14.32%
   (b) $APV = -\$43,358,540$
7. (a) The equity beta of the chain is 0.56.
   (b) $k_E = 14.48\%$
   (c) $\beta_E = .9333$
   (d) $k_E = 17.47\%$
9. $\beta_{Proj} = .654$
11. (a) .1906
   (b) .1420
   (c) .2320
   (d) .1024
   (e) .1798
13. (a) 1.92
   (b) 1.848
   (c) 1.776
   (d) 1.668
   (e) 1.56
15. Let D = amount of debt, and let E = amount of equity. Then $E = \$800,000 - D$. Since $\beta_E/\beta_A = 1 + (D/E)$, we can solve for debt and equity in each case:
   (a) $D = \$0$; $E = \$800,000$
   (b) $D = \$120,000$; $E = \$680,000$

(c) $D = \$442,106$; $E = \$357,894$
(d) $D = \$538,461$; $E = \$261,539$
17. (a) $D = \$0$; $E = \$200,000$
   (b) $D = \$40,000$; $E = \$160,000$
   (c) $D = \$72,000$; $E = \$128,000$
   (d) $D = \$93,333$; $E = \$106,667$
   (e) $D = \$146,667$; $E = \$53,333$

CHAPTER 11

1. (b) The expected cost of wheat in September is $60,000(4.50) = \$270,000$.
   (c) If the cash price of wheat is $4.25 per bushel, the cost of wheat without the hedge would be $60,000(4.25) = \$255,000$.
3. (a) Jackne faces the risk that the Peso might appreciate against the U.S. dollar.
   (b) Since the 120-day forward rate is higher than the current spot rate, Jackne is better advised to pay for the limestone immediately.
7. Since I expect the spot exchange rate to be $0.5045/DM, which is less than the exercise price of $0.505/DM on the call option, I would NOT buy the call. However, since $0.5045 < \$0.5060$, the exercise price of the *put*, I would buy the put option.
9. (a) The per period loss therefore is $100,000,000((.08 - 0.072)/2) = 400,000$.
   (b) The economic value of the swap is $1,465,750.51.
   (c) The economic value of the swap is $722,570.16.

APPENDIX 11B

1. (a) $C = \$3.41$
   (b) $C > \$2.75$ (the option's current intrinsic value) due to the time premium contained in the option's price.
   (c) $C = \$3.43$
3. (b) $C = \$6.59$
      $P = \$5.35$

APPENDIX 12A

1. (a) 1,200,000 (one for each share!)
   (b) Four rights will be required for each new share.
   (c) $2
   (d) $58
3. (a) 400,000 (one for each share)
   (b) Five rights will be required to buy a new share.
   (c) $.83

(d) $5,000
(e) $5,000
(f) $4,917
5. (a) Four rights
(b) $5
(c) $30
(d) $3,000,000

CHAPTER 13

1. (a) 8.75%
(b) 16.25%
3. $17.50
5. 14.36%
7. $12.00
9. (a) $33.60
(b) $24.00
(c) $18.67
(d) $15.27
11. (a) $166.67 is the maximum price that you would be willing to pay for a telephone.
(b) 5.5% monthly; 90.12% annually
13. $24.35
15. (a) $43.33
(b) $65.00
17. (a) The price-earnings ratio without the new project is 14.3.
(b) $4,285,714 is the maximum initial investment; if General pays more, the NPV will be negative.
(c) 14.7 times

CHAPTER 14

1. Assuming that the coupon rate is equal to the required yield-to-maturity, the bond is priced at par value.
3. (a) $1,095.29
(b) $956.48
(c) $876.63
5. (a) 9.01%
(b) 9.07%
7. $i = 13.32\%$
9. The coupon rate is 7.99%.
11. (a) If $k_d = .12$, $D_0 = \$1,000$
If $k_d = .15$, $D_0 = \$842.94$
If $k_d = .08$, $D_0 = \$1,285.58$
13. $P_0 = \$41.67$

APPENDIX 14A

1. $r_0(1) = .08$
$r_0(2) = .085$
$r_0(3) = .09$
$r_0(4) = .115$

3. $r_1(2) = .0925$
$r_1(3) = .095$
5. $r_0(1) = .10$
$r_0(2) = .105$
$r_0(3) = .1067$

APPENDIX 14B

1. $25,033,089 and $28,766,284
3. (a) The value of equity is $83,982,268; the value of debt is $91,017,732. If the return variance increases and the bond maturity is shortened, the expected decrease in debt value from the increase in variance is more than offset by the reduction in time to maturity, resulting in a $1,594,690 increase in the market value of the debt. The bondholders would accept!
(b) Raising the payoff increases the market value of the debt by $2,308,312 and $4,446,021, respectively.
(c) As the volatility of a firm's assets increases, the market value of its debt decreases. Consequently, bondholders are normally opposed to actions undertaken by a firm that would increase asset variance. Shortening debt maturities and increasing debt payoffs are actions that firms can undertake to increase the market value of their debt, thus gaining bondholder support.

CHAPTER 15

1. You would expect to earn 16% with no financial leverage.
3. (a) .15
(b) .1575
(c) .165
(d) .18
(e) .21
(f) .30
(g) .90
5. $\beta_E = \beta_A (1 + D/E) - \beta_D(D/A)$
7. The firm's capital structure is 60% equity and 40% debt.
9. (a) The 50%E-50%D capital structure provides the greatest total income to securityholders.
(b) With 50% debt in the capital structure, the value of the tax shield is $3,415.
(c) The 50% equity/50% debt capital structure provides the greatest total equity value.
11. (a) $30,580,543
(b) $31,120,000

13. (a) @ 0% $D*/E* = \rightarrow D*/A* = 0\%$
$V_L = \$2,000,000 + \$2,000,000(0)(.34) =$
$\$2,000,000$
@ 60% $D*/E* = \rightarrow D*/A* = .375$
$V_L = \$2,000,000 + (\$750,000)(.34) =$
$\$2,255,000$

(b) @ 0% $D*/E*$
$V_L = V_U + PV(TD) - PV(c)$
$= \$2,000,000 + 0$
$- \$500,000(.01) = \$1,995,000$
@ 60% $D*/E*$
$VL = \$2,255,000 - \$500,000(.60)$
$= \$1,955,000$

CHAPTER 16

1. (a) Expected cash flow next period = $2,400.
The present value of the expected cash flow
is $2,182.
(b) The expected payoff to the bondholders is
$1,920. The present value of the expected
payoff is $1,745.
(c) Yes
(d) No
3. The present value of the expected cash flow to
equity is $144; that is the minimum value that
the stockholders would require to liquidate.

CHAPTER 17

1. Mr. Biggy is entitled to the dividend because
he was the shareholder of record on May 14.
5. The new stock price will be $60. Conrad does
not lose money.

CHAPTER 18

1. (a) Annual $TD = \$3,400$
(b) $CFAT$ from leasing = $7,260
(c) Financing provided by lease = $50,000 −
$7,260 = $42,740
(d) Sally should lease the crane since the PV of
the decremental cost is positive under both
after-tax interest rates.
3. (a) Annual $TD = \$6,120$
(b) $CFAT$ from leasing = $9,900
(c) Financing provided by lease = $90,000 −
$9,900 = $80,100
(d) $i_{at} = .16(1 - .34) = .1056$; PV of decremental CF = $9,907.05. William should
lease the margarita machine.
(e) $PV(DCF) = \$1,461.48$
5. (a) Annual $TD = \$2,720$
(b) $CFAT$ from leasing = $6,699

(d) $i_{at} = .15(1 - .34) = .099$; PV of decremental CF = $1,682.93
(e) Annual $TD = \$2,000$
(f) $CFAT$ from leasing = $7,613
(g) Financing provided by lease = $32,387
After tax cost of debt = $.15(1 - .25) =$
$.1125$
PV decremental CF = $1,550.10
7. (a) $PV(DCF) = \$62,700.50$
(b) $PV(DCF) = -\$8,685.90$
9. (a) Net financing provided by the lease =
$18,000 − $3,750 = $14,250
(b) Annual $TD = \$1,500$
(c) The equivalent loan is $10,050.88. Don
should lease the tractor since the equivalent
loan is less than the net financing from
leasing.

CHAPTER 19

1. (a) $BE = 230,000$
(b) $BE = 170,000$
(c) $NOI = \$1,200$
(d) $BE = 200,000$
$NOI = \$1,750$
3. $Q*(\$) = F/[1 - (V/P)] = \$8,000 / [1 - (V/1.2V)] = \$48,000$
5. (a) $BE = F/(P - V) = \$4,000/(\$20 - \$4) =$
250 units
$NOI = Q(P - V) - F = [300(\$20 - \$4) - \$4,000] = \$800$
$DOL = [300(\$20 - \$4)] / [300(\$20 - \$4) - \$4,000] = 6$
(b) $BE = F/(P - V) = \$4,000 / (\$20 - \$6) =$
285.71 units
$NOI = Q(P - V) - F = [300(\$20 - \$6) - \$4,000] = \$200$
$DOL = [300(\$20 - \$6)] / [300(\$20 - \$6) - \$4,000] = 21$
(c) $BE = F/(P - V) = \$4,000 / (\$22 - \$6) =$
250 units
$NOI = Q(P - V) - F = [300(\$22 - \$6) - \$4,000] = \$800$
$DOL = [300(\$22 - \$6)] / [300(\$22 - \$6) - \$4,000] = 6$
(d) $BE = F/(P - V) = \$4,500 / (\$22 - \$6) =$
281.25 units
$NOI = Q(P - V) - F = [300(\$22 - \$6) - \$4,500] = \$300$
$DOL = [300(\$22 - \$6)] / [300(\$22 - \$6) - \$4,500] = 16$
7. (a) 2,000,000 kw hours
(b) $DOL = 3.67$

9. (a) New $NOI = -\$60,000 + (1)(-\$60,000)$
   $= -\$120,000$
   (b) New $NOI = -\$60,000 +$
   $(-2)(-\$60,000) = \$60,000$
   (c) New $S = \$1,200,000 + (.0833) \times$
   $\$1,200,000 = \$1,299,960$
   (d) Fixed costs $= \$780,000$

11. (a) $NOI = \$10,000$; earnings $= \$3,600$
    (b) $DOL = 4$
    (c) $DFL = 2$
    (d) $DCL = 8$
    (e) If S falls to $\$57,000$, it will have changed
       by $(\$57,000 - \$60,000)/\$60,000 =$
       -5%. Since $DOL = 4$, NOI will have
       changed by $4(-5\%) = -20\%$, and new
       NOI will be $\$10,000(1 - .20) = \$8,000$.
       Finally, next year's earnings must have
       changed by $8(-5\%) = -40\%$, so they
       will be $\$3,600(1 - .40) = \$2,160$.

13. (a) **100% Equity**
    EPS: $\$337,500 / 600,000 = \$.56$
    DFL: $NOI/(NOI - I) = 1$
    50% Debt
    EPS: $\$157,500 / 500,000 = \$.315$
    DFL: $NOI/(NOI - I) = \$450,000$
    $\div \$210,000 = 2.14$
    (b) $Q = 98,353$

15. (a) $\$40(1 - .20) = \$32$
    (b) $\$30$
    (c) $\$6$
    (d) $\$24$

17. (a) $\$10/\$100 = .10 = 10\%$
    (b) $i_{at} = .10(1 - .20) = .08 = 8\%$
    (c) $ROE = .16 + (\$100/\$100)(.16 - .08) = .24$
    (d) Yes, they are the same.

19. $ROA = 5\%$
    $ROE = 2\%$

21. (a) $BE = F/(P - V) = \$4,800,000 \div$
    $(\$40 - \$30) = 480,000$
    $BE_{CF} = 230,000$
    (b) $NOI = \$1,200,000$
    $OCF = \$2,664,000$
    (c) $DOL = 5$
    $DOL_{CF} = 1.622$
    (d) New $CF = \$3,744,252$

23. $T = 33\%$

25. (a) $NOI = \$20,000$
    $EPS = \$144$
    $OCF = \$34,400$
    CF per share $= \$544$
    (b) $DOL = 2.5$

$DFL = 2$
$DCL = 5$
(c) $DOL_{CF} = 1.047$
$DFL_{CF} = 1.265$
$DCL_{CF} = 1.324$

27. (a) New OCF will be $1.8(\$293,750) =$
    $\$528,750$.
    New NCF per share will be $2.25(\$2.625)$
    $= \$5.91$.
    (b) New OCF will be $.60(\$293,750) =$
    $\$176,250$.
    New NCF per share will be $(1 - .625)$
    $\times (\$2.625) = \$.98$.
    (c) If S increases to 27,500 signs, it has in-
    creased by 37.5%.
    NCF per share is $(\$2.625)(1.9375) =$
    $\$5.09$.
    If x new shares are issued, NCF per share
    $= (\$5.09)(10,000) / (10,000 + x)$.
    If NCF per share $= \$2.50$, then $x =$
    $10,360$ new shares.

APPENDIX 20

1. Current | $47/15 = 3.13$

Current	$47/15 = 3.13$
Quick	$(47 - 16 - 6)/15 = 1.67$
Debt/equity	$(15 + 35)/66 = .76$
Times interest earned	$(29 + 4)/4 = 8.25$
Average collection period	$3/(1072 \div 365) = 1.02$
Inventory turnover	$921/16 = 57.56$
Fixed asset turnover	$1072/69 = 15.54$
Operating profit margin	$33/1072 = .031$
Net profit margin	$17/1072 = .016$
Book ROA	$33[1 - (12/29)] \div$ $116 = .167$
Book ROE	$17/66 = .258$

3. Inventory $= \$100,000$
   Accounts receivable $= \$150,000$
   Net plant & equipment $= \$600,000$
   Long-term debt $=$ common stock $= \$300,000$
   Cost of goods sold $= \$840,000$
   Net income $= \$10,000$
   Interest $= \$10,000$
   Operating income $= \$60,000$
   Fixed costs $= \$300,000$

5. Genco already has a great deal more debt than
   Barzini and is also having a harder time meeting their interest expense. You should recommend that the loan not be made.

CHAPTER 21

1. (a) $NPV = \$3,000(PVFA_{.12,10}) - \$15,000 = \$1,951 > \$0$

   (b) $NPV = \$3,000(PVFA_{.16,10}) - \$15,000 = -\$500 < \$0$

   (c) $NPV = (\$3,000/.12) - \$15,000 = \$10,000 > \$0$

   (d) $NPV = (\$3,000/.16) - \$15,000 = \$3,750 > \$0$

3. (a) $NPV = (-\$3,000/.15) + \$18,000 = -\$2,000 < \$0$

   (b) $NPV = (-\$3,000/.20) + \$18,000 = \$3,000 > \$0$

   (c) $(-\$3,000/i) + \$18,000 = \$0$ when $i = 16.67\%$

5. (a) $\$1,440,000/360 = \$4,000$

   (b) $\$52,000/\$4,000 = 13$

   (c) $\$14,000/\$4,000 = 3.5$

   (d) $\$28,000/\$4,000 = 7$

   (e) $13 + 3.5 - 7 = 9.5$

   (f) 9.5

7. (a) $CR = \$160,000/\$100,000 = 1.6$
   $WC = \$160,000 - \$100,000 = \$60,000$

   (b) $CR = \$120,000/\$100,000 = 1.2$
   $WC = \$120,000 - \$100,000 = \$20,000$
   $ROA = (\$120,000/\$400,000)(.08) + (\$280,000/\$400,000)(.18) = 15\%$

9. (a) $CR = \$540,000/\$200,000 = 2.7$

   (b) $CR = [1.1(\$530,000) + \$10,000] \div [1.1(\$80,000) + \$120,000] = 2.851$

   (c) $\$4,475,520$

   (d) $\$1,759,680$

CHAPTER 22

1. (a) $\$9,000,000/360 = \$25,000$

   (b) The funds made available are $\Delta F = 2(\$25,000) = \$50,000$

   (c) Marginal revenue $= .10(\$50,000) = \$5,000$: marginal cost $= \$4,000$; use the lockbox, since $MR > MC$.

   (d) The funds made available are $\Delta F = 1(\$25,000) = \$25,000$; $MR = .10(\$25,000) = \$2,500$; $MC = \$4,000$; decline the lockbox, since $(MR < MC)$

3. (a) Cash released $= (\$14,800,000/360)(3) = \$123,333$

   (b) $MR = (\$14,800,000/360)(3)(.09) = \$11,100$; $MC = \$9,500 + (1,300 - 1,000)(\$.015)(360) = \$11,120$
   $NPV = [(\$11,100 - \$11,120)(1 - .34)] \div .13 = -\$101.54$

(c) Do not adopt the lockbox system. ($NPV < \$0$)

(d) $NPV = [\$11,100 - (\$700,000)(.09) - \$11,120](1 - .34)/.13 = -\$319,948$
You would still not adopt the system. ($NPV < \$0$)

5. (c)

City	Net Present Value
Dallas:	$\$833,333(.08) - \$80,000$ $= -\$13,333$
Fort Worth:	$\$888,888(.08) - \$76,000$ $= -\$\ 4,889$
El Paso:	$\$999,999(.08) - \$75,000$ $= \$\ 5,000$
San Antonio:	$\$1,222,222(.08) - \$78,000$ $= \$19,778$
Austin:	$\$833,334(.08) - \$80,000$ $= -\$13,333$

7. $\Delta F = (\$32,500,000/360)(18) = \$1,625,000$
$NPV = (\$1,625,000)(.09)/.09 = \$1,625,000$

9. (a) $E(R_{CS}) = [[\$38 + (\$2.70/4) + [(.14)(\$38)/4] - \$38]/\$38 = 5.3\%$
$E(R_{CD}) = .088/4 = 2.2\%$
$E(R_{MM}) = .092/4 = 2.3\%$
$E(R_{MB}) = .10/4 = 2.5\%$
$E(R_{CP}) = (100 - 96.8)/100 = 3.2\%$
$E(R_{PS}) = (\$5.20/4)/\$48 = 2.7\%$

11. (a) $\$4,000,000/360 = \$11,111$

   (b) $\sqrt{(2)(\$20)(\$4,000,000)/(.105 - .08)} = \$80,000$

   (c) $\$4,000,000/\$80,000 = 50$ times per year or every 7 days

   (d) Average balance $= (\$4,000,000 + \$0)/2 = \$2,000,000$; interest $= .08(\$2,000,000) = \$160,000$

   (e) Average balance $= (\$80,000 + \$0)/2 = \$40,000$; interest $= .08(\$40,000) = \$3,200$

   (f) Average balance $= [(\$4,000,000 - \$80,000) + \$0]/2 = \$1,960,000$; interest $= (.105)(\$1,960,000) = \$205,800$

   (g) $M\$V = [\$205,800 + \$3,200 - 49(\$20)] - \$160,000 = \$48,020$

13. (a) $.02(\$60,000,000) - .005(\$50,000,000) = \$950,000$

   (b) $\Delta A/R = [\$60,000,000/(360/40)] - [\$50,000,000/(360/30)] = \$2,500,000$; annual marginal savings $= .10(\$2,500,000) = \$250,000$

   (c) $(1 - .90)(\$60,000,000 - \$50,000,000) = \$1,000,000$

   (d) $NPV = \$1,250,000$

CHAPTER 23

1. (a) $(.015)(12) = 18\%$
   (b) $(1.015)^{12} - 1 = 19.56\%$
3. (a) August 11
   (b) 1%
   (c) September 10
   (d) $[1/(100 - 1)][360/(40 - 10)] = 12.12\%$
5. (a) 12.24%
   (b) 9.09%
   (c) 18.18%
   (d) Take the 1% discount and pay in 60 days.
7. (a) $AIR = (1/99)[360/(20 - 10)] = 36.36\%$
   (b) $AIR = (2/98)[360/(30 - 10)] = 36.73\%$
9. $AIR = [(.11)(\$16,000)/\$11,840](1) = 14.87\%$
11. $AIR = [\$3,750/(\$100,000 - \$375)](360/90) = 15.06\%$
15. Savings $= (.12)(\$340,000 - \$170,000) = \$20,400$
17. Simple interest rate $= [\$6/(\$120 - \$6)](360/30) = 63.16\%$; compound interest rate $= [1 + (\$6/\$114)]^{12} - 1 = 85.06\%$

CHAPTER 26

1. (a) $.40(10,000,000)(\$5) + .20(.40) \times (6,000,000)(\$8) = \$23,840,000$
   (b) $.20(6,000,000)(\$8) + .20(.40) \times (10,000,000)(\$5) = \$13,600,000$
   (c) Yes. First, acquire the company requiring the smallest proportion of ownership for control. This provides maximum leverage for the next acquisition.
3. (a) $EPS_S = \$2$
   (b) $EPS_{PX} = \$2.27$
   (c) $EPS_{PX} = \$2.08$
   (d) $EPS_{PX} = \$1.92$
   (e) Exchange ratio $= 2$
5. (a) $ROE_W = .0667$
   $ROE_T = \$5 / \$30 = .1667$
   (b) $V_W = \$562,500,000$
   $V_T = \$75,000,000$
   (c) The merger under these proposed terms should not be undertaken since it will result in an 8% reduction in Walden's share price, from \$45 to \$41.40. If the post-merger P/E ratio is 14, Walden's new share price will be $14(\$3.45) = \$48.30$. Thus, the merger should be undertaken since it will result in a 7.33% increase in Walden's share price, from \$45 to \$48.30.

GLOSSARY

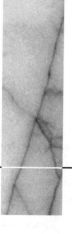

Abnormal return The realized return less the expected return on a security; also referred to as excess returns in the context of event studies.

Absolute priority rule Establishes priority of claims in bankruptcy and requires that these claims be paid in order of priority.

Accounting balance sheet Financial statement that lists the book values of a firm's assets and the claims against those assets (liabilities and owner's equity) at a particular point in time.

Accrued interest The interest earned from the date of the last coupon payment to the date when the bond is purchased.

Accumulated depreciation The sum total of all the depreciation accrued on a physical asset from the time of its purchase.

Accumulated earnings tax A penalty tax designed to prevent companies from "unreasonably" retaining earnings.

Accumulated profits test According to this, only profit-derived assets may legally be used for dividend distribution.

Aftermarket The period immediately following the initial offering of a security to the public.

Agency costs The loss in owners' welfare from inefficient allocation of resources because of conflicts of interest among stockholders, bondholders, and managers.

Agency problem The problems that arise because of separation of ownership and control, since managerial decisions are influenced by factors other than just the welfare of the owner.

Agency relationship The relationship between the principal (equityholder) and the agent (manager of the firm).

Agent A manager who acts on behalf of the equityholders of the firm.

Aggressive policy A matching policy that uses short-term liabilities to finance not only temporary but also part or all of the permanent current-asset requirement.

All-equity NPV The net present value of a project that is financed with only equity.

American option An option contract that may be exercised at any time up to its expiration date.

Amortizing swap A swap whose notional principal declines over the life of the agreement.

Annual depreciation The amount of depreciation taken each year.

Annual percentage rate The interest rate that recognizes the nominal (or annual) interest rate plus the extra interest earned from compounding; also called the effective interest rate.

Annuity A series of uninterrupted, equal cash flows occurring at regular intervals.

Annuity due A series of uninterrupted, equal cash flows at regular intervals, with the payments (receipts) occurring at the beginning of each period.

Antitakeover measures Tactics managers use to prevent takeovers.

Appreciating currency A currency that gains in value relative to another currency.

Arbitrage The act of buying an underpriced asset in one market and simultaneously selling an identical overpriced asset in another market, thereby generating a riskless profit at zero cost.

Arbitrage pricing theory An equilibrium asset pricing theory that shows the expected return on any asset as a linear combination of various factors that affect the economy.

Arrearages Preferred dividends that a company has been unable to pay out.

Articles of incorporation A document that is filed in order to form a corporation.

Articles of partnership A written contract among partners, establishing the partnership.

Asset engineering Corporate restructuring that reduces the size of a firm's asset base.

Assets definition Says that the firm's value is the value of the left-hand side of its economic balance sheet—that is, the value of the firm's total assets.

Asymmetric information hypotheses Offered in this book to explain the underpricing of initial public offerings. These hypotheses assume either that investment bankers possess more knowledge than issuers about investors' demand for securities, or that there is disparity in the quality of information among various investor groups.

Automatic stay Suspends virtually all litigation and other actions by creditors against the debtor.

Average abnormal return Difference between estimated and actual return, averaged across all companies for any given month.

Average collection period ratio A measure of a firm's efficiency in collecting on its credit sales; calculated as accounts receivable divided by net sales per day.

Average tax rate The average tax paid per dollar of taxable income; calculated as total taxes paid divided by the total taxable income.

Balance sheet A summary of a firm's financial position, its assets and the claims on those assets, at a particular time, typically the last day of the year.

Balanced policy A matching policy that balances the trade-off between risk and profitability by using long-term financing to support permanent current assets and part of the temporary current assets.

Banker's acceptance Short-term instrument set up by international buyers with large banks to guarantee payment to international sellers.

Bankruptcy The situation where the firm pursues legal avenues to resolve its financial problems.

Bankruptcy costs Direct and indirect costs associated with bankruptcy, such as legal and administrative fees and lost business opportunities.

Bankruptcy filing To file bankruptcy papers in the federal district court.

Basic financial statements Balance sheet, income statement, and statement of retained earnings.

Basis swap A swap in which both rates are floating—for example, LIBOR versus a commercial paper index rate.

Benefit stream Cash benefits that occur over several periods; also called cash flow stream or income stream.

Best efforts An offering in which an underwriter agrees to sell as much of the offering as possible and to return any unsold shares to the issuer.

Beta A statistical concept that measures the sensitivity of a security's returns to changes in the returns on the market.

Beta coefficient Measure of the sensitivity of an asset to market conditions; it is the relevant risk measure for calculating an asset's required rate of return.

Bill of lading An international trade document that serves three purposes: (1) provides a receipt of goods from the exporter to the shipper; (2) acts as a contract between the carrier and exporter, indicating that the carrier will transport the goods for a fee; and (3) may convey legal title to the goods.

Black-Scholes option pricing model A model (equation)

for calculating the value of a European call option on a non-dividend-paying stock.

Blue-sky laws Laws intended to protect state residents from being misled by untrustworthy securities marketers.

Bond A long-term debt instrument representing money borrowed from a firm.

Bond markets Market where bondholders can sell their debt securities.

Bond-refunding explanation Tries to explain the existence of callable debt by maintaining that the only reason for a call feature is to reduce future interest costs.

Bondholder A person or group that lends debt capital to a firm; a bond or debenture evidences this arrangement.

Bondholder expropriation hypothesis Suggests that a firm takes actions in order to increase its value at the expense of its bondholders.

Bondholding costs The costs incurred by the manager to reassure the stockholders and bondholders that he or she will do only what is specified in the contract.

Bonding mechanism The phenomenon of managers trying to endear themselves to the marketplace.

Book value The value of a firm's assets as stated in the accounting financial statements.

Break-even analysis A tool for assessing how profits will vary when production costs, sales volume, and selling price vary.

Break-even point The point at which revenues exactly offset all operating costs, leading to zero net operating income.

Break-even quantity The level of production and sales at which total revenues (dollar sales) are exactly equal to total operating costs.

Business judgment rule A court defense that protects directors and officers from liability when their honest mistakes in judgment result in poor business decisions.

Business plan A proposal prepared by a company that includes projected financial statements.

Buy-op A scheduled repurchase of a firm's own shares in the open market over a specified period of time.

Buyout The transformation of a public corporation into a privately held firm; also called a going-private transaction.

Bylaws The document in which the number of officers, their titles, and their functions are spelled out.

Call buyer An investor who buys a call option in the hope of realizing a profit from an increase in the stock price.

Call option A financial instrument that allows the holder to buy (or "call") a fixed quantity of the underlying asset at a prespecified price within a certain time period.

Call premium The price of a call option on common stock. The amount above the face value of a bond that the issuing firm needs to pay in order to call it before maturity.

Call price of a bond The price at which the firm has the right to repurchase its bonds or debentures before the stated maturity date; always set equal to or greater than the par value.

Call provision A feature of a bond issue that gives the corporation the right but not the obligation to redeem the bond at a specified price before the maturity date.

Call seller An investor who sells a call option in the hope of realizing a profit from a decrease in the stock price.

Capital Productive resources that a firm uses to produce goods or services.

Capital asset pricing model (CAPM) An equilibrium asset pricing theory that says the equilibrium rates of return on all assets are a linear function of their covariance with the market portfolio.

Capital assets Productive resources that a firm uses to produce goods or services.

Capital budget Summary of the plans for capital expenditures.

Capital budgeting The process of selecting projects that can increase firm value.

Capital budgeting analysis *See* Capital budgeting.

Capital budgeting project A project that is being subjected to capital budgeting analysis.

Capital expenditure budget Forecast of cash outflows associated with a long-term investment or capital budgeting project.

Capital expenditures Cash outlays associated with a long-term investment or capital budgeting projects.

Capital gains The appreciation, over time, in the value of an asset.

Capital gains yield The rate of return to the investor that arises solely from capital gains.

Capital lease A noncancelable, longer-term lease that fully amortizes the lease's cost for equipment.

Capital market Financial markets for equity shares and long-term debt.

Capital rationing The case when funds available to a firm or division are limited and a decision needs to be made on their efficient allocation to various competing projects.

Capital structure The proportion of debt and equity in a firm's total capital.

Capitalism An economic system characterized by individual and corporate ownership of capital.

Capitalization Finding the present value of a stream of cash flows.

Cash dividend Periodic payment of a firm's earnings in the form of cash to stockholders.

Cash fixed costs Fixed costs other than depreciation.

Cash flow The funds available to a company for productive uses; approximated as net income plus depreciation.

Cash flow break-even point The level of production at which the operating cash flows equal zero.

Cash flow budget Forecast of cash receipts and cash expenditures over specific intervals (usually a weekly or monthly basis).

Cash flow stream *See* Benefit stream.

Cash-for-stock exchange A takeover financing technique, whereby the target shareholders receive a 100% cash payment for their stock.

Cash markets Markets that require the immediate delivery of assets being bought or sold.

Cellar-Kefauver amendment Amendment to the Clayton Act that made the acquisition of assets as well as an entire company subject to antitrust scrutiny.

Certificates of deposit (CDs) Large-denomination time deposits that entitle the holder to receive the amount deposited plus the accrued interest upon maturity.

Chapter 7 Section of the Bankruptcy Code that covers liquidation.

Chapter 11 Section of the Bankruptcy Code that covers reorganization.

Charter The document in which the rights and duties of management are spelled out.

CHIPS—The Clearing House Interbank Payments System An arrangement widely used for international fund transfers.

Claims on assets Liabilities and stockholders' equity.

Class voting Each class of shares votes as a separate unit; also called series voting.

Clearing float The time taken by a deposited check to clear the banking system and become usable funds.

Clearinghouse A corporation established by an exchange to facilitate transactions.

Closed corporation A group of partners who operate under the legal status of a corporation.

Closely held company A company controlled by a small group of people.

Collateral trust bonds Bonds that are secured by the company's holdings of stocks, notes, or bonds.

Combined cash flow leverage factor A factor that measures the effect of changes in sales on net cash flows.

Combined leverage A factor that measures the effect of a change in sales on net income.

Common-size balance sheet *See* Common-size statement.

Common-size income statement *See* Common-size statement.

Common-size statement A balance sheet or income statement in which items are expressed in percentages rather than in dollars.

Common stock certificate A document or financial security that a stockholder keeps as proof of ownership in a corporation.

Compensating balance The minimum average daily balance that a firm is required to maintain when taking a loan from a bank.

Compensation contract Employee compensation packages that are often designed to reduce the agency costs of a firm.

Competitive bid A method of selecting an investment banker for a new issue by offering the securities to the underwriter that bids highest.

Complementary proposals Two proposals that would generate higher cash flows together than the sum of the

cash flows generated individually by them.

Concentration banking An integrated systems approach that uses different types of cash management strategies and is offered by banks to attract large corporate customers.

Conditional sale lease An arrangement in which the lessee is viewed as having purchased the asset rather than having leased it, and the lessor is viewed as having financed this purchase by a loan.

Confirmed A Chapter 11 plan that is accepted by all classes of creditors.

Congeneric mergers Mergers that occur between firms that have related business interests.

Conglomerate mergers Mergers that occur between unrelated businesses.

Consent decree An agreement between the government and the firm that can be used in noncriminal cases.

Conservative policy A matching policy that ignores the distinction between temporary and permanent current assets by financing almost all asset investments with long-term capital.

Consolidation When two or more corporations combine to create an entirely new corporate entity.

Consumer credit Credit granted by a firm to an individual.

Contingent claims *See* Derivative securities.

Contingent voting Certain classes of stock earn the right to vote upon the occurrence of certain contingencies.

Continuing board members Board members not elected by an interested party.

Continuous compounding When interest is compounded continuously at every instant of time, rather than at discrete intervals.

Continuous distribution A probability distribution that represents the uncertainty in returns when there are infinitely many values.

Contract An agreement that defines (implicitly or explicitly) each party's role in the agreement, with the added feature of a cost (penalty) associated with breaking the agreement.

Contribution margin per unit The dollar amount that each unit sold contributes to meeting the fixed costs.

Control hypothesis for debt A hypothesis that maintains that the use of debt, without managers' retention of the proceeds, can lower agency costs.

Conventional project A project with an initial net cash outflow followed by a series of net cash inflows.

Conversion price The effective price at which the convertible bondholders obtain common stock upon exercising their option to convert.

Conversion ratio The number of shares of stock into which a convertible bond or preferred stock may be converted.

Corporate bylaws A document that spells out the number of officers, their titles, and their functions in a corporation.

Corporate control The bundle of rights used to determine the management of corporate resources.

Corporate restructuring A large array of managerial strategies aimed at increasing firm value.

Corporation A legal entity that is totally separate from its owners and is created by a state charter.

Correlation Statistical relationship between two random variables.

Correlation coefficient A statistic that measures the relationship between two random variables; defined as the covariance divided by the standard deviation of the two random variables.

Cost of financing The annual rate of interest a firm pays the financing source.

Cost-reduction proposal A project or investment whose primary benefit is that it will lower the firm's operating costs.

Coupon amount The annual interest on a bond or debenture stated in dollar terms.

Coupon interest rate The stated annual rate of interest on a bond.

Covariance Measure of the relationship between assets; calculated as the product of the correlation between the assets and the respective standard deviations.

Covered interest rate parity The link between forward and spot exchange rates under the assumption that investors hedge their foreign cash flows through forward markets.

Cram down When a reorganization plan is forced upon dissenting creditors or equityholders.

Credit standards The criteria that determine which customers will be granted credit and how much.

Crown jewel strategy A strategy whereby the target company in a takeover attempt spins off the asset that the acquirer is interested in. The acquirer then goes after the spun-off asset and leaves the parent company alone.

Cumulative abnormal return The sum of the average abnormal returns over all months from the beginning of the study period. This is one of the measures used to see if an event had any impact on the wealth of the equityholders.

Cumulative adjustment account An account that recognizes the gains or losses generated from changes in foreign exchange rates.

Cumulative provision A provision that stipulates that the company must pay all the preferred dividends that it has skipped.

Cumulative voting A method for electing a corporate director in which the stockholder may cast any or all of his or her votes for a single director.

Currency swap A swap in which rates are denominated in different currencies—for example, a fixed rate in Japanese yen versus U.S. dollar LIBOR.

Current assets Cash or other assets that will be used or converted into cash within one year or within the firm's normal operating cycle.

Current liabilities Obligations that must be paid within one year or within the firm's normal operating cycle.

Current ratio Current assets divided by current liabilities; measures the extent to which assets cover the firm's liabilities.

Debentures Bonds that are not secured by the assets of the firm.

Debt-equity ratio The value of total debt divided by the book value of equity.

Debt-to-assets ratio The value

of total debt divided by the book value of assets.

Debtor in possession (DIP) When a debtor firm's management is left in position to continue operating the firm after it (the firm) has filed for Chapter 11 bankruptcy protection.

Debtor in possession (DIP) financing Financing provided by new creditors to a firm that has filed for Chapter 11 bankruptcy protection.

Default When a firm is unable to make required payments, either interest or principal.

Default risk The risk borne by bondholders that the bond issuer may not be able to pay the interest or principal on time or at all.

Deferred call provision A provision that prohibits the issuer company from calling the callable bond before a certain date.

Deficiency memorandum A list of changes in a prospectus that the SEC desires, sent by the SEC to the company making the public offering.

Degree of combined cash flow leverage Measures the overall sensitivity of net cash flows to changes in sales; calculated as the percentage change in net cash flows divided by the percentage change in sales.

Degree of combined leverage Measures the overall sensitivity of net income to changes in sales; calculated as the percentage change in net income divided by the percentage change in sales.

Degree of financial cash flow leverage Measures the sensitivity of net cash flows to changes in operating cash flows; calculated as the percentage change in net cash flows divided by the percentage change in operating cash flows.

Degree of financial leverage Measures the sensitivity of net income to changes in net operating income; calculated as the percentage change in net income divided by the percentage change in net operating income.

Degree of operating cash flow leverage Measures the sensitivity of a firm's operating cash flows to changes in sales; calculated as the percentage change in operating cash flows divided by the percentage change in sales.

Degree of operating leverage Measures the sensitivity of net operating income to changes in sales; calculated as the percentage change in net operating income divided by the percentage change in sales.

Delivery date The future date in a futures contract at which a purchaser is obligated to buy a given amount of a specific asset at a given price.

Depreciating currency A currency that is losing value at a faster rate than another currency.

Depreciation Allocation of the historical cost of an asset over its economic life, the period over which it is expected to provide benefits to its owner.

Derivative assets Assets whose values depend on the performance of some primary assets; also called derivative securities.

Derivative financial statements Statements derived from the basic financial statements and offering additional information for interpreting the accounting data and establishing basic financial relationships; examples are the cash flow statement and the common-size balance sheet.

Derivative securities Securities like call options, usually not issued by the firm but whose values nevertheless are determined by the performance of the primary securities.

Differential information The difference in information between the agent and the principal about the details of the firm's current operations and future plans.

Dilution A reduction in the earnings per share due to an increase in the number of shares outstanding without a corresponding increase in net income.

Direct foreign investment Investments in foreign physical assets.

Direct lease A lease arrangement in which the lessee does not necessarily own the leased asset.

Disbursement float The time taken by checks written by a firm to clear the banking system.

Discount interest Interest amount deducted by the bank from the initial loan amount rather than being paid at the end of the loan.

Discount rate Rate used to convert future cash flows to present values (i.e., opportunity cost).

Discounted dividend-valuation model A general formulation of common stock valuation that treats the firm and its stock as if they will exist forever, with the stock's value being derived from a stream of expected dividends in perpetuity.

Discrete distributions Probability distribution where the variables of interest (returns or stock prices) can take on only discrete values, with a probability assigned to each value.

Disproportionate voting Voting when different classes of shares have different voting rights.

Distressed on a flow basis When a firm does not have enough cash flow to honor its obligations in a particular time period.

Distressed on a stock basis When the market value of a firm's assets is less than its liabilities.

Distribution networks The systems used to transport products to the marketplace.

Diversifiable risk Risks that are unique to a company and can be diversified away.

Diversification Process of reducing risk by forming portfolios of imperfectly correlated assets.

Divestitures Transaction in which a segment of a firm is sold to a third party for cash, securities, or a combination of the two; also called sell-offs.

Dividend equivalents The dollar amount paid for dividend units.

Dividend hypothesis Maintains that share repurchases are substitutes for dividends.

Dividend payout ratio Ratio of dividends paid out to total earnings (net income).

Dividend units Compensation to managers tied to the cash dividends paid by the firm.

Dividend yield Annual dividend paid out per share of common stock as a percentage of the market price of the stock.

Divisible Something that can be accepted in part as well as in its entirety.

Due diligence Practice by investment bankers of fully investigating all aspects of a firm before raising any capital for it.

Economic balance sheet A balance sheet that considers the market values of the assets and claims rather than their accounting values; also called a market value balance sheet.

Economic dependence Exists when the acceptance of a particular proposal alters the cash flows of another proposal.

Economic life The period over which an asset is expected to provide benefits to its owner.

Economic order quantity The optimal order quantity that balances the excessive acquisition costs associated with small order quantities and the excessive holding costs that arise with large order quantities.

Economic profit The excess profit that is gained from an investment over and above the profit that could be obtained from the best alternative forgone.

Economic rents The economic profit or wealth created by the use of an asset.

Economies of scale Decreased average costs resulting from increased production levels.

Effective interest rate *See* Annual percentage rate.

Efficient capital market Efficient market for capital. *See* Efficient market.

Efficient market A market in which the value of an asset reflects all available information about the asset. In such a market, it is impossible to generate excess returns consistently.

Efficient market hypothesis The theory that U.S. capital markets are efficient.

Enforcement costs The costs of enforcing an agreement or contract (usually the agreement between the agent and principal).

Equity Ownership in a company.

Equity carve-outs Transactions in which some of a subsidiary's shares are sold to the general public.

Equityholder Person or group holding ownership in a firm.

Equivalent loan Loan for property or equipment whose net after-tax cost is equivalent to the cost of leasing the same property or equipment.

Eurobond A bond denominated in a currency different from that of the country or countries in which it is issued.

Eurobond offering A bond offering made overseas in foreign currency.

Eurodollar deposits Interest-bearing deposits in European banks or foreign branches of U.S. commercial banks, denominated in dollars.

Eurodollars Unsecured debt offerings in Europe.

European option An option that can be exercised only at maturity.

Event Any news that is made public and that can affect a firm.

Event date The date on which the event occurred.

Event study methodology A technique that enables one to study and then draw conclusions about whether an event has increased or decreased equityholders' wealth.

Ex ante return The uncertain return that one expects to receive from an investment.

Ex post return The certain return that one has actually received from an investment; also known as realized return.

Ex-rights shares Shares bought after the record date and sold without the rights.

Excess returns *See* Abnormal return.

Excessive perquisite consumption problem The problem associated with the leakage of resources from the company to the agent, when the manager gives himself or herself excessive nonpecuniary benefits.

Exchange offer An offer that gives one or more classes of securities the right or option to exchange part or all of their holdings for a different class of the firm's securities.

Exchange rate The rate of currency conversion.

Exchange rate risk The risk that arises from fluctuations in exchange rates.

Exclusivity period The 120-day period after the date of the order for relief, during which only the debtor may file a plan of reorganization.

Executory contract A contract that has not yet been fully performed by both parties.

Exercise price The prespecified price at which an option can be exercised; also called the striking price.

Expected return The average return from an investment, calculated as the probability-weighted sum of all possible returns.

Expert systems Computerized systems used by financial managers.

Expropriation The strongest form of blocked funds—for example, a country nationalizes the assets of the investing firm.

Face value The actual stated value of a bond, typically $1,000.

Factor A financial institution that buys the receivables of a firm.

Factor beta The sensitivity of an asset's returns to a factor.

Factoring receivable A procedure used in arranging for short-term financing backed by accounts receivables, whereby the receivables of the borrower are sold to a factor.

Failure Status of a corporation when the realized rate of return on a business is consistently less than investors' opportunity costs.

Fair merger price provisions Specify the minimum share prices in mergers that involve major stockholders, typically someone holding a 20%–30% larger equity position.

Federal Trade Commission (FTC) Act Forbids unfair methods of competition and unfair or deceptive acts or practices in commerce. Through this act, the FTC was given the power to enforce antitrust laws.

Fiduciary responsibility Manager's responsibility to act in the shareholders' best interests.

Financial assets Resources, such as cash or loans, that are needed to acquire real assets.

Financial decision A company manager's decision about the type of security to be issued in order to acquire cash from the financial markets. Also included is the decision regarding the appropriate mix of short-term credit, long-term debt, and equity.

Financial distress The situation when a firm is not able to make good on its obligations and faces the risk of insolvency.

Financial expenses Any borrowing costs incurred by a firm: interest payments on loans or bonds, the cost of issuing stocks and bonds, and so on.

Financial lease *See* Capital lease.

Financial leverage A firm's ability to magnify the sensitivity of its net income to changes in its net operating income by the use of financing that carries a fixed obligation in the form of interest.

Financial management The art and science of making the right financial decisions for the firm.

Financial planning Involves anticipating the impact of operating and financial policies on the firm's future financial position and instituting remedial measures as needed.

Financial ratio analysis Use of ratios derived from financial statements to analyze a firm over time or to compare the firm to other firms in the industry.

Financial restructuring Changes in the debt or equity of a firm.

Financial security A document given to persons who provide financing for the company as evidence of their contribution.

Financing and dividend covenants Covenants aimed at restricting a company from engaging in activities that can hurt the safety of the bondholders' position, or that can benefit stockholders at the expense of bondholders.

Firm commitment offering A security offering where the underwriter guarantees that if investors fail to buy the entire offering, he (the underwriter) will buy the remaining unsold lots at a previously specified price.

Firm-specific human capital The value of investments (in terms of time and effort) made by managers in gathering firm-specific skills.

Firm value The market value of a firm's debt and equity.

Fixed-asset turnover ratio Measures how efficiently a firm is using its assets to generate sales; calculated as the ratio of sales to fixed assets.

Fixed assets Long-term assets, or assets that will be around for longer than one year—for example, property, plant, and equipment.

Fixed-charge coverage ratio A ratio that measures the extent to which all fixed financial charges (long-term leases, rental expenses, etc.) are covered by net profits before taxes.

Fixed operating costs Costs that do not vary with production levels for a given range of production.

Flip-in plans Plans that enable the issuing firm to repurchase stock rights from the shareholders at a large premium, usually 100%.

Flip-over plans Plans that use exercised rights to purchase stock that can be converted to the common stock of the bidding firm in the event of a takeover.

Float Difference between the bank's balance for a firm's account and the balance that the firm shows on its own books.

Flotation costs Fees charged by an investment bank that is acting as a financial intermediary for a company issuing securities in the marketplace.

Flow variables A stream of cash flows per unit time, such as rental income per month or salary per year.

Foreign bond A bond issued in the currency of the country in which it is sold or traded.

Formal default The situation when a firm is unable to meet its interest obligations toward the creditors.

Forward contract An arrangement that requires the delivery, at some point in the future, of an asset at a price agreed upon today.

Forward exchange rate An exchange rate for currencies traded today for delivery at a future date.

Forward market A market that allows investors to fix the price today at which they will buy or sell assets at a future date.

Forward price The price set in a forward contract that is agreed upon today.

Forward rate The rate set in a forward contract that is agreed upon today.

Forward swap A swap that has a start date sometime in the future.

Franchisee The person or company that enters into a business agreement with a fran-

chiser by the purchase of equity, but whose decision making is severely restricted by the franchise agreement.

Franchiser The person or company that owns a particular brand name that a franchisee uses for a fee.

Fraudulent conveyance A legal concept that permits courts to go back and undo a leveraged buyout (LBO) by ordering all shareholders who sold stock to return the proceeds to the bankruptcy estate.

Free cash flow The cash flow in excess of that required to finance all positive-NPV projects.

Free-enterprise system Economic system wherein people are allowed to organize and operate (invest) at a profit without excessive government intervention.

Freely callable Describes a security issue that can be called any time.

Fundamental analysis Process of using historical stock price data and any other publicly available data on a firm in order to predict stock price behavior.

Funded debt Any type of borrowing with a maturity of more than one year.

Funds Net working capital; the difference between current assets and current liabilities.

Futures contracts Contracts to buy or sell certain assets on a certain date in the future at a

price set today in the marketplace.

Futures exchanges Organized markets on which futures contracts are traded.

Futures price The price in the futures market of any asset.

General cash offer When a firm sells its equity securities to the public for cash, typically through the services of an investment banker.

General partner The partner in a partnership who has unlimited liability.

Going-concern value The value of a firm that is in operation.

Going-private transaction The transformation of a public corporation into a privately held firm.

Gordon valuation model A straightforward dividend valuation model that assumes that dividends increase steadily at a constant growth rate forever.

Government regulations Laws and rules enacted by the government.

Green shoe A provision in many underwriting contracts that grants to the syndicate the option to purchase a predetermined number of additional shares at the offering price within a certain time period.

Greenmail The premium a firm has to pay over the open market price when it buys the large block of shares held by a major stockholder in a standstill agreement.

Gross profit Sales minus the cost of producing the goods sold.

Hart-Scott-Rodino Antitrust Improvements Act Requires premerger notification to the government for all mergers above a minimum size.

Hedging When a firm takes a position in an asset to offset its position in another investment in the hope of reducing risk.

Herfindahl-Herschman Index (HHI) An index used by the Justice Department to measure market concentration.

Holding company A firm that owns sufficient voting stock in one or more other companies so as to have effective control over them; also called parent company.

Holdout problem The problem arising from the incentives of claimants who refuse to cooperate with the firm's management because they expect more from a court-ordered restructuring plan.

Homemade leverage The replication of the firm's leverage effects on personal account.

Homogeneous expectations The notion that all individuals have the same beliefs concerning future investments, profits, and dividends.

Horizon problem The agency problem that arises when a manager's planning horizon does not match that of the firm.

Horizontal mergers Merger involving the combination of two firms that are engaged in the same business.

Horizontal revenue expansion proposal Involves proposals that are unrelated to a company's existing activities.

Human capital Intangible assets of the firm such as dedicated workers and management skills.

Human capital expropriation problem The problem associated with the loss in value to the company when managers and other professionals trained with the firm's resources leave to work for a competing firm.

Idiosyncratic factors Factors unique to a firm that affect its asset returns.

Imperfect correlation Projects that have a correlation coefficient of less than 1, meaning that their returns do not move exactly together.

Imperfect hedge When a hedge does not fully offset the risk of the underlying investment

Imperfect markets theory A theory that recognizes market imperfections.

Implicit dividend Even if a company pays no dividend, some day it will liquidate and pay a liquidating dividend. Thus, an implicit dividend is built into the stock price.

Implied cash flow change hypothesis Postulates that stock price reactions offer information about a firm's future net operating cash flows.

Income statement Reports a firm's performance by measuring the profits (losses) generated over a period of time, typically a quarter or a fiscal year.

Income stream *See* Benefit stream.

Increasing the number of authorized shares of common stock A common antitakeover device justified by many corporate boards as necessary to use in connection with stock splits and dividends as well as to raise cash.

Incremental cash flows after taxes The periodic cash outflows and inflows that would occur if, and only if, an investment project is accepted.

Indenture A legal document that specifies all the requirements and conditions that must be met by bondholders and the corporation in order to protect both parties.

Independent proposals Proposals whose acceptance or rejection is independent of the acceptance or rejection of other proposals.

Indivisible Something that must be accepted or rejected in its entirety.

Inflation The reduction in money's ability to purchase goods and services over time.

Information asymmetry hypothesis Holds that corporate managers have more information than securities purchasers do and so are more likely to issue new securities when they are overpriced in the market.

Information or signaling hypothesis States that the announcement of a repurchase is a signal to investors that management thinks the stock is undervalued.

Informational asymmetry The difference in the amount and kind of information available between the agent and the principal.

Inside directors Board members, elected by the shareholders, who are also officers or senior managers of the corporation.

Insider dealings Trading of a company's stock by company insiders, based on company information that has not yet been made public.

Insider information Company information that has not yet been made public and is possessed by people in special positions inside the firm.

Insolvency Inability to make good on one's obligations.

Insolvency test Forbids a company to pay dividends when it is insolvent.

Insurance hypothesis States that underpricing of initial public offerings (IPOs) serves as a type of insurance that insulates issuers and their in-

vestment bankers from any legal liability and/or damage to reputation that may result from floating the IPO.

Interbank market An informal market composed of electronic links among banks that deal with foreign exchange and their corporate and government customers.

Interest coverage ratio Measures the extent to which interest expenses are "covered" by profits. Calculated as net profit before taxes divided by interest expenses plus one; also called times interest earned ratio.

Interest rate The price paid for borrowing money.

Interest rate risk Fluctuations in a security's price caused by changes in market interest rates.

Interest rate swap An agreement between two parties—usually a corporation and a financial institution such as a commercial bank—to exchange cash flows on a periodic basis for a specified length of time.

Interfirm analysis Use of ratios to make comparisons between firms in the same industry at a particular time.

Interim trustee A temporary trustee appointed until the first meeting of creditors, after an order of relief is filed in a bankruptcy court.

Internal rate of return Discount rate that makes the net present value equal to zero.

Intrafirm analysis Use of ratios to examine the performance of a specific company over an extended period of time; also known as trend analysis.

Inventory management Balancing the benefits of carrying inventory, such as flexible production scheduling, against the incremental costs (and risks) of holding inventory, such as storage, handling and reordering costs, obsolescence, and spoilage.

Inventory turnover ratio Measures how many times inventory is sold, or turned over; calculated as cost of goods sold divided by inventory.

Investing Accepting reasonable risks in the expectation of gaining a reasonable return on the investment.

Investment banker A banker that is employed by a firm to sell the firm's securities to the public for cash; performs origination, underwriting, and distribution functions in the capital acquisition process; also called an underwriter.

Investment decision The decision of the manager about what real assets the company must own in order to produce goods and services.

Investment flexibility The ability to delay an irreversible investment until additional information becomes available.

Investment tax credits Tax credits granted to a firm making investments that encourage economic growth. These credits allow the firm to deduct a portion of its new investment from its tax liability.

IRR Internal rate of return.

IRR rule Accept a project if the internal rate of return (IRR) is greater than the required rate of return; otherwise reject the project.

Junk bonds Bonds rated BB and below by a rating service such as Standard & Poor's Corporation.

Lease A legal agreement under which the owner of property allows another party to use the property for a specified period and previously arranged payments.

Legal and administrative costs A component of agency cost incurred in the writing of detailed contracts between shareholders and managers.

Lessee The party to whom the property is being leased.

Lessor The party who owns the property being leased.

Letter stock Restricted stock used by new firms to lure managerial and technical talent away from major established companies.

Letters of credit A promise to pay upon the presentation of certain documents; issued by a bank on behalf of an importer.

Leverage hypothesis A hypothesis that suggests that when a firm makes a share repurchase, its debt-equity ratio increases because of the lower equity level and often additional debt on which interest is tax deductible. This leads to an increase in earnings, thereby increasing the price of the stock.

Leveraged buyout Takeover of a company using borrowed funds, usually by a group including some member(s) of existing management.

Leveraged lease A special lease arrangement under which the lessor borrows a substantial portion of the acquisition cost of the leased asset from a third party.

Levered firm A firm that has debt in its capital structure.

Liabilities Obligations of a firm to provide services or transfer assets to outsiders.

Limited liability An owner's liability is limited to his or her investment in the firm; the corporation can go bankrupt without exposing owners to the risk of having their personal assets confiscated.

Limited partners The partner(s) in a partnership whose liability is limited to the amount of their contributions to the partnership.

Limited partnership A partnership in which one or more of the partners' liability is limited to the amount of their contributions to the partnership.

Line of credit An informal agreement, usually established for a one-year period, by a bank to lend up to a maximum amount of credit to a firm.

Liquidating dividend A final dividend that is paid out upon a firm's liquidation.

Liquidation A shutdown of a firm's operations by a complete sale of its assets.

Liquidity Ability of an asset to be converted rapidly to cash.

Liquidity preference Preferring short-term investments to long-term ones.

Liquidity premium Additional compensation required by investors to invest in long-term investments over short-term ones.

Loan guarantee The insurance that protects against default on a loan contract.

Lockup provisions Provisions designed to prevent the circumvention of the firm's anti-takeover provisions.

London Interbank Offered Rate (LIBOR) Interest rate that the most creditworthy banks charge one another for large loans of Eurodollars overnight in the London market; the most commonly used index in the swap market.

Long position The position of a firm when it currently holds an asset or is obligated to own the asset in the future; also called long exposure.

Long-term financial planning The financial planning function as it applies to a three-, four-, or even five-year period.

Loss carryback A net operating loss that is offset against taxable income in the prior three years.

Loss carryforward A net operating loss that is offset against taxable income as far as 15 years into the future.

LTV ruling A court ruling that bondholders who agree to an exchange offer before a Chapter 11 filing are entitled to only the market value of the new bonds, and not their face value.

M&M hypothesis Advanced by Modigliani and Miller, this hypothesis asserts that, in a world with riskless debt and without taxes, a firm cannot change the total value of its outstanding securities by changing its capital structure.

Mail float The time during which a customer's check is in the postal system and the funds are not available for use.

Maintenance margin The minimum dollar amount to be maintained in a margin account.

Majority voting A method for electing a corporate director in which the shareholder votes on each director independently.

Management The initiation and implementation of a firm's decision process.

Management function Composed of the development of ideas and the day-to-day running of the company.

Managerial labor market An informal market in which managerial labor is traded.

Margin A portion of the full purchase price of a commodity or security that investors and speculators are required to post.

Margin call When a broker notifies the investor or speculator that the margin account has dropped below the maintenance margin and requests that additional funds be deposited in the margin account.

Marginal investor The "last" investor who equilibrates the demand and supply and determines the equilibrium price of the stock.

Marginal tax rates The IRS policy of applying successively higher tax rates to incremental income.

Market for corporate control An active market in which the control rights of public corporations are traded; also called the takeover market.

Market portfolio A portfolio that contains every asset in the economy.

Market power The ability of a firm to extract higher prices for its products.

Market risk Risk that cannot be eliminated by diversifica-

tion; risk that is systematically related to the economy as a whole; also known as systematic risk or undiversifiable risk.

Matching policy The policy of matching the maturity of a financing source with an asset's useful life.

Maturity date The date that bonds become due. The amount of principal borrowed is repaid on this date.

Maturity value The par value or face value of a bond; $1,000 unless specified otherwise.

Merger The combination of two (or more) corporations in such a way that legally only one corporation survives and the other is dissolved according to the laws of the state in which it is incorporated.

Merger sharing rule The rule for dividing the gains from a merger between bidding and target firms.

Modified NPV The net present value that includes the value of a flexibility option.

Money market mutual fund A firm that pools the investments of many small investors and buys large-denomination money market instruments.

Monitoring costs Expenditures that arise from monitoring the manager's activities.

Monopsony power hypothesis According to this hypothesis, the gross underpricing of initial public offerings may be the result of monopsony power of the investment bankers that underwrite the common stocks of small, speculative firms.

Monte Carlo simulation method A computer simulation that permits one to evaluate the impact of changes in several variables simultaneously.

Mortgage bonds Bonds secured by a mortgage on the real property of the owner.

Mutually exclusive proposals Proposals in which the acceptance of one project automatically implies the rejection of another.

Negative float Increases the amount of cash tied up in the collection cycle and earns a zero rate of return.

Negotiated sources Short-term loans, such as bank credit or commercial paper, that require management effort.

Net income Net profit before taxes minus taxes.

Net present value The difference between the present value of the inflows and the present value of the outflows; represents the economic profit adjusted for risk and timing.

Net profit after taxes Net profits before taxes less taxes; also called net income.

Net profit before taxes Also known as taxable income, it is all revenues (operating and nonoperating) minus all expenses (operating and financial).

Net profits text Generally means that dividends may be paid out of current net profits, defined as earnings minus costs and taxes, or they may be paid out of accumulated earnings.

Net translation exposure The difference between exposed assets and exposed liabilities.

Net working capital The difference between a firm's current assets and current liabilities.

Nexus of contracts The contractual relationship that exists between all parties in the firm, such as suppliers, creditors, and customers.

Nimble dividends Although dividends that reduce capital are not permitted, some states allow dividends in a year when the corporation had no earnings as long as it had earnings in the preceding year. Such dividends are called nimble dividends.

Noise Non-information-based factors that affect security prices.

Nominal interest rate The stated interest rate, not taking into account compounding or inflation.

Noncallable A security that cannot be called.

Nonconventional project A project that is not a conventional project. *See also* Conventional project.

Noncurrent assets Long-term assets, or assets that will be around for longer than one year—for example, property, plant, and equipment.

Noncurrent liabilities Liabilities that are not due within one year, such as mortgages, bonds, or other forms of long-term debt.

Nonimpairment of capital test Does not permit dividends to be paid out of the firm's capital.

Non-par-value swap A swap in which one party makes an initial payment to the other; also called an off-market swap.

Nonpecuniary benefits Nonmonetary benefits.

Normal distribution Symmetric bell-shaped frequency distribution that can be defined fully by its mean and standard deviation.

Notional principal A dollar amount implicitly used to determine the scale of a swap transaction.

NPV profile Graph that displays the net present values for a project at different discount rates.

NPV rule Rule that accepts projects with net present values greater than zero and rejects all others.

Off-market swap *See* Non-par-value swap.

Offering circular A document to be filed with the SEC before a security offering, consisting of the company's financial statements, management, history, projections, and intended use of the proceeds of the offering; also called the prospectus.

Open corporation A firm in which anyone can hold a residual claim, that is, ownership claims are entirely unrestricted.

Open-market purchases The action of a firm when it buys back its stock directly from the stock market.

Operating cash conversion cycle The time it takes for the initial cash outflows for goods and services to be realized as cash inflows from sales.

Operating expenditures Those cash outlays that provide no benefits beyond the current period.

Operating expenses Costs to a firm that are not part of the costs of goods sold; these include administrative, rent, and depreciation expenses.

Operating flexibilities The ability of managers to use the capital assets in different ways to respond to changing economic conditions.

Operating lease A type of lease under which the maintenance and service of the leased equipment are provided by the lessor.

Operating leverage Magnification in net operating income resulting from changes in

sales; exists because of fixed costs.

Opportunism Unethical conduct such as misleading, distorting, disguising, obfuscating, or otherwise confusing someone.

Opportunity cost Rate of return forgone on the next best comparable alternative; it is the required rate of return or discount rate for an investment.

Opportunity cost of capital Relevant discount rate to be used for financial decision making; it is the rate of return forgone from the next best alternative, equal to the required rate of return (RRR).

Optimal capital structure That debt-to-equity or debt-to-value ratio at which the value of a firm is maximized.

Optimal capital structure hypothesis Holds that a firm has an optimal capital structure—a mix of debt and equity—that maximizes the value of the firm.

Optimal cash balance The optimal level of cash to be maintained by the firm, it is equal to the larger of (1) the sum of transactions balances and precautionary reserves and (2) compensating balance requirements.

Option A derivative security that gives the holder the right, but not the obligation, to buy or sell a specified quantity of a specified asset within a specified time period.

Option premium The price at which an option is sold by the option writer.

Order for relief Protection from creditors provided by the courts to a firm that files for bankruptcy.

Ordinary annuity A series of uninterrupted equal cash flows at regular intervals, with the payments (receipts) occurring at the end of each period.

Outside directors Board members, elected by the shareholders, who have no affiliation with the corporation other than their seats on the board.

Outstanding issues Bonds that have been on the market for more than a couple of weeks; also called seasoned issues.

Over-the-counter contracts Another name for contracts not traded on organized exchanges.

Over-the-counter market A financial market that is not physically located in a specific place, with trades being made by communications, usually by telephone or computers, among brokers across the country.

Overreaction hypothesis Holds that investors in the marketplace respond irrationally by overreacting to new and unexpected information, both good and bad.

Overretention problem Problem that arises when managers are hesitant to increase dividends—that is, when they prefer to keep these resources in the firm in order to increase the firm's liquidity and thereby lower the probability of bankruptcy.

Ownership changes hypothesis Holds that transactions affecting the distribution of control rights in a firm affect its share prices.

Pac-Man defense A reactive strategy to foil a takeover attempt. The target company in a hostile tender offer initiates a hostile tender offer of its own for the acquiring company.

Paid-in capital Additional funds received upon selling equity shares at a price above the par value of the shares.

Par debt When a debt instrument's market value equals its par or face value.

Par value A technical value placed on equity shares to comply with state law that has little to do with the stock's market value. For a bond, it is the face value or maturity value and is equal to $1,000, unless otherwise stated.

Parent company *See* Holding company.

Partnership Similar to a proprietorship except that it has several owners.

Patent A government-awarded right that allows a firm to manufacture and sell a prod-

uct while limiting the competition from doing so for a prespecified period of time.

Pecuniary benefits Benefits stipulated in managers' employment contracts, such as salary, retirement benefits, and bonuses.

Penny stocks Any stock issue whose shares are offered for less than $5 a share.

Percent of sales forecasting method Constructs pro forma financial statements by assuming that the relevant items maintain a constant percentage relationship to sales.

Perfectly positively correlated When the correlation coefficient between returns on two securities is +1.

Performance period The period between the time a contract is agreed upon and the time it is exercised and the profits or losses recognized.

Performance shares An incentive plan that awards managers a certain number of restricted shares of company stock on the basis of firm performance.

Performance units An incentive plan that awards managers a certain number of restricted units.

Permanent current assets The portion of a firm's current assets required to maintain the firm's daily operations.

Perpetuity A series of equal cash flows at regular inter-

vals of time that continues forever (to infinity).

Phantom stock plans Restricted stock plans that, as restrictions lapse, entitle the recipient to cash equal to the market value of the firm's shares.

Physical capital Financial assets and real assets.

PI rule Accept a project if the index is greater than 1. Otherwise, reject the project.

Plain vanilla swap A swap that requires one of the participants (commonly referred to as a counterparty) to make its payments based on a fixed rate of interest that does not change throughout the life of the agreement. The level of the other counterparty's required payments is then structured to vary with the movements of an interest rate index that changes over time.

Plan of reorganization A fair and equitable plan filed under Chapter 11 of the Bankruptcy Code that includes the debtor's commitment to pay creditors and the proposed modification of the firm's financial affairs and operations.

Pledging receivable The act (by a borrower) of providing a given dollar amount of receivables as collateral.

Poison pill A very severe antitakeover measure that cannot be circumvented and completely protects incumbent managers from unwanted takeover attempts by greatly inflating the ultimate cost of the takeover to the acquiring firm.

Political risk The risk facing multinationals and arising from changes in foreign government policies on multinational's business operations within the foreign country.

Porcupine amendments Amendments designed to make the transfer of corporate control very difficult; a popular takeover defense mechanism.

Portfolio A group of assets.

Positive float *See* Float.

Preemptive rights Allow stockholders to buy any additional shares offered by the company, thereby protecting them from dilution of the value of their shares.

Prepackaged bankruptcy A combination of private workout and legal bankruptcy where the firm and most of its creditors agree to a private reorganization outside formal bankruptcy. Thus, the bankruptcy petition and the reorganization plan are filed together.

Prepaid expenses Cash expenditures made in advance of the use of goods or services for which they were made.

Primary assets Assets bought and sold in the primary markets—for example, stocks, bonds, metals, or foreign exchange.

Primary market Financial market where original issues of financial securities are sold.

Primary securities The claims, like stocks and bonds, issued by the firm to finance its operations.

Prime rate. The interest rate that banks typically charge on loans to their most favored customers. It is a benchmark rate against which other rates are set.

Principal Equityholder of the firm; also, the face value of a bond.

Principle of comparative advantage A traditional justification for international trade, this principle suggests that countries should specialize in what they do best and then trade these goods among themselves.

Priority A ranking or position given to each class of claims in a bankruptcy proceeding.

Private negotiation Negotiation by a firm with one or more parties, through a private transaction, to buy back its shares.

Private placement The sale of a bond or other security directly to a limited number of investors.

Privileged subscription Shareholders as of a certain future date may purchase additional shares in the company by relinquishing a certain number of rights plus a specified amount of cash; also called a rights offering.

Pro forma balance sheet A projected balance sheet as of a future date.

Pro forma income statement A projected income statement for a future period.

Pro forma statements Projected financial statements, such as a balance sheet or income statement, for future periods.

Probability distribution A collection of the different possible outcomes for an uncertain variable together with the probability of each possible outcome.

Processing float The time it takes a firm to deposit a customer's check in the bank.

Product differentiation The degree to which a product or service is perceived as unique or distinct from the competition.

Production and investment covenants These covenants can prohibit certain actions by a company, such as limiting the company's stake in other enterprises, or require certain actions, such as investing in particular projects or holding specified assets.

Productivity of capital The ability of capital to create wealth.

Profit maximization Objective of a firm to maximize accounting profits. This is not necessarily the same as maximizing shareholder wealth.

Profitability index The benefit-to-cost ratio of a project; calculated as the present value of cash inflows divided by the present value of cash outflows.

Program trading The use of high-speed computers to execute buy and sell transactions in order to make arbitrage profits.

Progressive tax system The existing tax system for corporate taxes in which firms that make greater profits pay a higher proportion of taxes.

Project A single proposal or a collection of economically dependent proposals.

Project beta Systematic risk of a project; measures the sensitivity of a project's returns to changes in the market's returns.

Project ranking Attempts to identify (rank) various projects in order of decreasing attractiveness.

Project selection The analysis of whether or not a project is acceptable.

Promised interest rate The interest rate that the issuer has promised to pay; the coupon rate.

Property right A right that guarantees the owner a fractional ownership in the firm upon liquidation.

Proposal Any alternative that is under consideration.

Proprietorship The oldest, simplest, and most common legal form of business in which a single person has the controlling interest in the business.

Prospectus *See* Offering circular.

Proxy A grant of authority by the shareholder to transfer his or her voting rights to another party.

Proxy contest A direct attempt by dissident shareholders to gain a controlling number of seats on a firm's board of directors through a formal vote.

Proxy fight An attempt to gain control of a firm by soliciting the proxies, or votes, of existing shareholders.

Public issue. An issue of securities to the public.

Purchasing power parity A theory that implies that goods of equal value in differing countries may be equated through the exchange rate.

Pure-play company A publicly traded firm whose business is as similar as possible to the project under consideration.

Put bond Conventional bonds that the holder may redeem at par value at a specified time before maturity.

Put buyer An investor who buys a put option in the hope of realizing a profit from a decrease in the stock price.

Put-call parity The relationship between put and call option prices.

Put option A financial instrument that allows the holder to sell (or "put") a fixed quantity of the underlying asset at a prespecified price within a certain time period.

Put seller An investor who sells a put option in the hope of realizing a profit from an increase in the stock price.

Quasi-rents Short-term advantages arising from factors such as specialization, favorable locations, and excess capacity.

Quick ratio A ratio that is used as a test for liquidity; calculated as those current assets that can be readily converted to cash divided by current liabilities.

Rate of return The percentage rate at which invested money is growing.

Real assets Physical assets (plant and equipment), in contrast to financial assets.

Realized return The actual return received from an investment; also known as ex post return.

Record date A date set when a company announces a rights offering. Before this date, shares are sold with the rights; after this date, shares are sold without the rights.

Red herring Preliminary prospectus that carries a warning in red ink that it is not an offer to sell at that time.

Refunding operation An action by a company to replace an entire old bond issue with a new one.

Registration statement Consists of the prospectus and other legal documents required by the SEC to be filed before the sale of public interstate offerings valued for more than $1.5 million.

Reinvoicing center A subsidiary of a multinational corporation set up for the sole purpose of consolidating the intersubsidiary payments.

Relationship investing Investing long term in a company to develop a relationship with management.

Relevant risk The portion of an asset's total risk that affects the asset's market price; the asset's nondiversifiable risk.

Reorganization Financial restructuring of a firm in financial distress. Both the firm's asset structure and its financial structure are changed to reflect their true value. Reorganization is one of the outcomes of bankruptcy filing, covered under Chapter 11 of the Bankruptcy Code.

Replacement chain A capital budgeting method that assumes replacement of an asset at the end of its useful life with an identical asset that has the same operating costs and benefits.

Required rate of return (RRR) The minimum expected rate of return that the project must yield to justify its acceptance; the firm's opportunity cost of capital.

Residual claim The claim on the portion of the output that remains after other claimants have been fully compensated; generally refers to the firm's equity shares.

Residual loss The loss in firm value because of poor decisions induced by agency problems; an agency cost.

Residual return *See* Abnormal return.

Residual risk bearers Investors who take on most of the risk associated with the business; they receive rewards only from what is left after all other claims have been satisfied. Usually refers to the equityholders.

Residual theory of dividends A theory that dividend policy is a residual from investment policy; whether or not a company pays dividends depends on its investment policy.

Restricted stock Stock whose sale is restricted until certain conditions are met.

Restrictive covenant explanation Rationalizes the call feature in bonds as a way of overcoming restrictive covenants.

Restrictive covenants Restrictions placed by bondholders on the investments and financing decisions of a firm in order to protect themselves against agency problems.

Retained earnings All of the net income that has been reinvested in the company rather than distributed to stockholders as dividends since the company's inception.

Retention ratio The proportion of earnings retained by the firm; calculated as 1 minus the payout ratio.

Revenues The total dollar amount that a firm derives from selling its goods and services.

Reverse LBO A repetition of the steps that were taken when the firm went public; it provides a basis for examining how the firm fared as a public company.

Reverse splits A form of stock splits, the objective of which is to reduce the number of shares outstanding and increase the price per share.

Revolving credit agreement A formal contractual commitment made to a firm by a bank to provide a maximum amount of funds to the firm.

Rights offerings *See* Privileged subscription.

Rights-on shares Shares with rights, bought before the record date.

Risk Quantifiable uncertainty.

Risk-averse underwriter hypothesis States that investment bankers purposely underprice initial public offerings in order to reduce the risk of being stuck with an unsuccessful offering and its associated losses.

Risk-aversion problem The problem that arises when managers with a fixed salary are hesitant to take on good but risky projects because of the fear of losing their jobs if the project were to fail.

Royalties Contractually arranged periodic remissions of funds by the subsidiary to the parent company, with the remissions representing a "fee"; also called supervisory fees.

S corporation An entity taxed not at the corporate tax rate but at the shareholders' individual tax rate, with 35 or fewer stockholders.

Sale-leaseback arrangement An arrangement whereby assets already owned by a firm are purchased by a lessor and leased back to the firm.

Scale-enhancing Projects that have cash flows perfectly correlated with the firm's existing cash flows.

Seasoned issues *See* Outstanding issues.

Secondary initial offering *See* Reverse LBO.

Secondary market Financial market in which existing securities are resold; considerably more active than the primary market.

Section 7 of the Clayton Act Forbids the acquisition of the stock of one company by another when the effect of the merger would substantially lessen competition in that industry.

Secured credit Short-term credit backed by an asset, such as accounts receivable or inventory.

Securities and Exchange Commission A regulatory agency of the federal government.

Security Refers to the recourse of the debt holder in the event of default.

Security market line The straight line in the beta-return space on which all assets should exactly plot; the graphical representation of the capital asset pricing model.

Securityholders Investors who have contributed capital to a firm in the form of either debt or equity.

Seed capital Start-up funds for a new business.

Segmented markets Markets that offer different risk-return trade-offs and thus different prices for newly issued securities.

Semifixed cost A cost, one portion of which is fixed and another portion variable; also known as semivariable.

Semistrong efficient market A market is said to be semi-strong form efficient if stock prices already reflect all historical and publicly available information.

Semivariable cost *See* Semifixed cost.

Senior A term used to indicate a preference in position over other debt issues.

Separation of ownership and control Refers to firms in which the persons who are managing the firm are not the same persons who are controlling the firm.

Series voting Each class of shares votes as a separate unit; also called class voting.

Share A document of financial security that a stockholder keeps as proof of ownership; also called a common stock certificate.

Share repurchases. Cash offers made by the firm for its own outstanding shares.

Shark repellents Proactive anti-takeover measures that can be activated before a raider attempts to take over a firm.

Shelf registration The firm files a master registration statement to sell securities and has up to two years to sell them, leaving the offering documents "on the shelf" until needed.

Sherman Act Forbids contracts, combinations, or conspiracies that result in a restraint of trade.

Short exposure Exposure of a firm that is obligated to give up an asset in the future.

Short-term financial planning The planning function as it applies to a limited term, such as one year.

Signaling explanation Managers can signal the firm's better prospects through a call provision on the debt.

Sinking fund Originally referred to an actual money fund that was set aside, invested, and then used to retire bonds at maturity; currently, bonds are retired before their maturity.

Socialism An economic policy that attempts to balance both individuals' and the state's interests.

Speculation Taking above-average risks with the expectation of receiving substantial returns.

Speculative bubble hypothesis States that excess returns on initial public offerings (IPOs) result from the speculative demand of investors who are unable to obtain shares of oversubscribed IPOs at the offering prices from their underwriters.

Spin-off The action of a firm that separates the operations of a subsidiary from those of the parent by distributing to all existing shareholders of the parent, on a pro rata basis, those shares that the parent owns in the subsidiary.

Split-up Similar to a spin-off, except that the parent hands over control of all its subsidiaries to its shareholders and thus ceases to exist.

Spontaneous sources Credits, like trade credits or accruals, that arise in the normal course of business without any action required by management.

Spot exchange rate Currency exchange rate at any instant of time for immediate delivery.

Spot price The cash market price of commodities, currencies, and interest-bearing instruments.

Staggered board provisions A provision that divides a firm's board of directors into sections so that only one section stands for election each year.

Stakeholders All participants who have a stake in the firm; those who benefit from or are hurt by the fate of the business.

Standard deviation Square root of the variance of a probability distribution.

Standby commitment Agreement by the underwriter that he or she will buy shares offered through a rights issue at a specified price below the subscription if the company cannot sell them on the market.

Standby commitment fees Fees charged by an underwriter to make a standby commitment.

Standstill agreement A voluntary contract between a corporation and a substantial stockholder that limits the ownership of voting shares in the company to a maximum percentage for a specified period of time.

Stated interest rate *See* Nominal interest rate.

Statement of retained earnings A financial statement that reconciles the balance in the retained earnings account at the beginning of the income

statement period to the balance at the end of the period.

Steady-state float The dollar amount of float that does not change from day to day.

Stock appreciation rights (SARs) Allow managers to exercise their option and buy the company's stock or receive the stock appreciation directly.

Stock dividend A dividend payment of additional shares of stock to the firm's existing shareholders; the stock's par value is unaffected, but the number of shares outstanding increases.

Stock market A financial market where investors buy and sell shares of stock.

Stock split A large stock dividend that lowers the stock's par value and increases the number of shares outstanding.

Stock swap Financing an acquisition by issuing additional shares of common stock in exchange for the target firm's outstanding common stock.

Stock variable A number at a particular time that has no time dimension.

Stockholder An investor who holds an equity stake in a firm and has a residual claim on the output.

Stockholders' equity The residual difference between assets and liabilities.

Straight-line depreciation A depreciation technique that spreads the historic cost of an asset evenly over its economic life.

Strategic investment proposal A proposal that involves investments that can change the very character of a firm, such as entering a new product market or acquiring another company.

Striking price *See* Exercise price.

Strong form efficient A market is said to be strong form efficient if stock prices reflect both private and publicly available information.

Subordinated Debt whose claims can be entertained only after claims of senior debt holders have been satisfied.

Subscription agent An agent who handles the paperwork for the rights sale.

Subscription price The price at which each share may be purchased by existing shareholders in a rights offering.

Subsidiary A company controlled by another company, called a parent or holding company.

Substitute proposals A set of proposals in which the acceptance of one reduces the cash flows of another.

Sunk costs Money that has already been spent on a project; it cannot be affected by the manager's decision.

Supermajority merger approval provisions Proactive anti-takeover provisions that require approval by an abnormally large number of shareholder votes to enable mergers or other transactions involving "interested parties" or "substantial stockholders."

Superpriority status Status for new lenders of a bankrupt firm when their debt is made senior to that of the existing creditors.

Supervisory fees *See* Royalties.

Surplus test Dividends may be paid out of earned surplus, which includes the undistributed net profits of the corporation since its creation, including gains from the sale of fixed assets.

SWIFT—The Society for Worldwide Interbank Financial Telecommunication A computerized arrangement for speedy (within minutes) funds transfers among 800 European, North American, and Latin American banks.

Syndicate A group of investment bankers formed to increase marketing outlets and reduce risks associated with underwriting a security offering.

Systematic risk Portion of an asset's total risk that cannot be diversified away; *see* Market risk.

Tactical investment proposal A proposal that involves investments that can affect a firm's cash flows and economic wealth but does not necessarily change the character of the firm.

Takedown The amount of money that has been borrowed by a firm within the limits of its line of credit.

Takeover defense hypothesis Holds that share repurchases set up a defense against takeovers.

Takeover market *See* Market for corporate control.

Target payout ratio The ratio of residual funds to total earnings.

Targeted share repurchases The action of a firm that, at the end of the time period specified in a standstill agreement, buys back the large block of shares held by the major stockholder in the agreement at a substantial premium over the open market price.

Tariffs Taxes on imported goods.

Tax shield That which reduces taxable income and thus taxes.

Technical analysis Process of analyzing historical stock price data to predict stock price behavior.

Technical default Arises when a firm violates a legally binding agreement with a creditor.

Temporary current assets Assets, such as cash, that fluctuate with the firm's operational needs.

Tender offer A public offer made by another firm or investor to purchase shares of a firm's stock for a specified price, usually above the current market price.

Term loans Unsecured loans with various repayment schedules.

Term structure of interest rates The relationship between a bond's yield to maturity and its time to maturity.

Theory of agency The theory that identifies and tries to mitigate the potential conflicts among the various participants in a business—for example, conflicts among stockholders, bondholders, suppliers, and managers.

Tie-in sale Arrangement between a parent firm and its subsidiary that requires the subsidiary to, say, buy certain materials from the parent.

Time preference Preference of current consumption over future consumption.

Time value of money The potential to earn interest on money affects its relative value; a dollar today is worth more than a dollar next year because a dollar invested today will earn interest and be worth more than a dollar by the end of the year. This productivity of money is known as its time value.

Times common covered ratio Measures the extent to which net operating income "covers" interest payments on debt, dividends for common and preferred stocks, and payments to the sinking fund.

Times interest earned ratio *See* Interest coverage ratio.

Times preferred coverage ratio Measures the extent to which net operating income covers interest payments, preferred dividends, and sinking fund contributions.

Tombstone advertisements An advertisement announcing a public offering of securities and identifying the issuer, the type of security, and the underwriters.

Total asset turnover ratio Signifies how efficiently total resources are being used; calculated as sales divided by total assets.

Total operating costs Sum of the fixed operating costs and the total variable operating costs.

Total variable operating costs Expenses that increase or decrease as the quantity produced increases or decreases.

Trade acceptance A trade draft signed by an importer who acknowledges his obligation to pay a given sum of money at a future date.

Trade credit Credit extended by one firm to another.

Trade drafts Written orders initiated by an exporter informing the importer of the exact amount and time at which the importer or its agent must pay.

Transaction loan Loans that do not have multiple financing requirements.

Transfer prices The prices charged by one affiliate of a multinational firm to another affiliate.

True lease A lease that allows the lessee to fully deduct the lease payments for tax purposes.

Trustee One that assumes a fiduciary responsibility for another party; often refers to a bank official who oversees the bondholders' interests.

Unanticipated announcement hypothesis States that stock price changes reflect only the unanticipated part of the announcement of a security sale.

Uncertain information hypothesis Maintains that because investors are risk averse, they respond to both good and bad news by setting prices below what they would if all of the information were readily available.

Uncertainty Exists when a decision maker knows all the possible outcomes of a certain act but, for one reason or another, cannot assign probability to the various outcomes.

Uncollected float analysis The fundamental tool in determining the net benefits of any cash management technique.

Uncovered interest rate parity A modified version of IRP that assumes that forward hedging is not possible.

Underinvestment problem explanation Tries to explain the popularity of callable debt by holding that the call feature can lower agency costs by reducing the firm's incentive to pass up certain wealth-increasing projects.

Underwriter An investment firm that buys a security issue from the issuing firm and resells it to investors.

Undiversifiable risks *See* Market risk.

Uniform annual series An annuity that has the same present value as another series of cash flows and occurs over the same time period.

Uniform Partnership Act Lays out the legal rules pertaining to partnerships.

Unique risks Risks that are specific to a company and are diversifiable.

Unlevered firm A firm that has no debt in its capital structure.

Unseasoned issues Bonds issued for the first time.

Unsecured credit All debt, such as trade credit, accruals, unsecured bank loans, and commercial paper, that has as security only the firm's cash-generating ability.

Unsystematic risk That portion of an asset's total risk that can be eliminated by diversification; same as unique risk.

Valuation Process of capitalizing the cash flows provided by an asset.

Value Maximum dollar amount that one is willing to pay for an asset.

Value additivity The property that the market value of two assets combined, $(x + y)$, is equal to the sum of the individual market values of x and y.

Value in exchange The price at which an asset can be transferred from one owner to another; loosely known as the asset's replacement value.

Value in use The benefit that a firm obtains from the use of the asset.

Value of the futures contract The number of units of the underlying asset multiplied by the futures price per unit.

Variable cost per unit Total variable cost divided by the number of units produced.

Variable operating costs Costs that vary directly with the level of production and sales.

Variance The sum of the probability-weighted squared deviations of returns from the mean. It measures the variability inherent in a probability distribution and is a measure of risk.

Venture capitalists Individuals or corporations that have raised funds to invest in portfolios of promising, young companies.

Vertical mergers When firms acquire other firms "upstream" from them, such as their suppliers, and/or firms "downstream" from them, such as their product distributors.

Vertical revenue-expansion proposal A proposal to increase a company's revenues by increasing the production of an existing product.

Waiting period The 20-day period before an offer to sell securities is actually made.

Weak form efficient A market is said to be weak form efficient if stock prices reflect all historical price information.

Wealth transfer explanation Holds that bondholders favor call provisions in bonds because they can transfer wealth away from stockholders in certain situations.

Wealth transfer hypothesis Maintains that wealth is transferred between those shareholders who offer to repurchase shares and those who choose not to do so.

Wealth transfer problem Problems caused by managerial decisions that benefit either the bondholder or the stockholder at the cost of the other.

Wealth transfers When wealth is transferred away from one stakeholder to another—say from bondholders to stockholders.

White knight A firm that is asked by the target firm to bid for it (the target firm) against the original hostile tender offer.

Working capital Collectively, current assets and current liabilities.

Working capital management Decisions that involve short-term assets and liabilities.

Workout A firm's private negotiation with creditors.

Yield curves Graphical representations of the term structure of interest rates.

Yield to maturity The discount rate that equates the present value of the bond's cash flows to the current market price; the internal rate of return of the cash flows provided by the bond.

Zero-coupon bonds Bonds that pay no coupon interest and are sold at deep, or very big, discounts.

Zero growth When a firm is expected to pay a stable dividend, a constant or zero growth dividend pattern is implied.

Zero payout ratio When the firm pays no dividends, the payout ratio will be zero.

INDEX

COMPANY INDEX